THE
CELTIC
WORLD

BARRY CUNLIFFE

PROFESSOR OF EUROPEAN ARCHAEOLOGY, UNIVERSITY OF OXFORD

THE CELTIC WORLD

DESIGNED BY
EMIL M. BÜHRER

St. Martin's Press
New York

A production of EMB-Service for Publishers
Lucerne, Switzerland
© EMB-Service for Publishers, 1990
All rights reserved. For information, write:
St. Martin's Press, Inc.
175 Fifth Avenue
New York, N.Y. 10010
First published in the
United States of America in 1993
Printed in Singapore
ISBN 0-312-09700-X

Library of Congress
Cataloging-in-Publication Data applied for

CONTENTS

Physically the Celts are terrifying in appearance, with deep-sounding and very harsh voices. In conversation they use few words and speak in riddles, for the most part hinting at things and leaving a great deal to be understood. They frequently exaggerate with the aim of extolling themselves and diminishing the status of others. They are boasters and threateners and given to bombastic self-dramatization, and yet they are quick of mind and with good natural ability for learning. They have also lyric poets whom they call Bards. They sing to the accompaniment of instruments resembling lyres, sometimes a eulogy and sometimes a satire.

Diodorus Siculus, first century B.C.

At any time or place, you will find them

The Celts seen through Roman eyes were ferocious, flamboyant, and tensed with energy. This small bronze figure found near Rome and probably dating to the third century B.C. gives a brilliant impression of a Celt in battle wearing only his helmet, neck torque, and belt. Polybius describes how the *Gaesatae* fought in this manner, naked but for their torques.

A rather calmer impression is given by the warrior shown on the Gundestrup caldron *(right),* a large silver vessel of the second or first century B.C. found in a bog in Denmark. He marches to battle clothed in tight-fitting trousers, armed with shield, spear, and possibly a sword.

6

THE PORTRAIT
OF A CIVILIZATION

ready to face danger, even if they have nothing on their side but their own strength and courage. —Strabo

The Celts were the inhabitants of Europe in the pre-Roman period, occupying a vast territory stretching from the Pyrenees to the Rhine and from Ireland to Romania. They were barbarian in the classical sense of the word, energetic, quick-tempered, and "war-mad"; but their craftsmen created a brilliant art style and by the first century B.C. a truly urban society had begun to develop in many areas. It was against these people that the Roman armies moved in the first centuries B.C. and A.D., leaving only a Celtic fringe in Scotland, Ireland, Wales, and Brittany to survive unconquered. When the Roman world collapsed in the fifth century A.D., the Celts once more emerged from the obscurity of their windswept Atlantic regions. Populations moved from Ireland to Britain and from Cornwall to Brittany, while individuals—chiefly monks—carried the ideals of Irish monasticism deep into Europe. Politically and culturally the western Celts have been persecuted and subjugated; today their cry for the recognition of their separate identity is becoming louder... Our aim in this work is to follow the Celts throughout their entire history, beginning in the vague realms of European pre-history. But far more than a chronological account, the study of Celtic achievement in all its diversity acquaints us with a people too often dismissed as barbaric, too long neglected and misunderstood—a whole civilization, many-faceted but with an underlying unity.

7

Until just before 6000 B.C. most of Europe was still peopled with communities who subsisted by hunting wild animals and by collecting uncultivated fruits and plants. Yet a mere four thousand years later the first true European civilization had begun to emerge among the Mycenaean-Minoan cultures of the east Mediterranean. Thereafter, with minor setbacks, the Mediterranean became the forcing ground for the great civilizations of Greece and Rome while from the depths of temperate Europe the barbarian communities looked on, sometimes benefiting from lively trade and reciprocal exchange with their southern neighbors, sometimes moving against them

A PEOPLE WHOSE ROOTS LIE BURIED IN THE PAST

in violent onslaughts. Finally these barbarian communities were overcome and largely absorbed, as Rome perfected its military machine and employed it for colonialist expansion.

THE GREEK VIEW OF THE CELTS

One of the many cultural and intellectual advances which sprang from the civilization of Greece was the development of the scientific study of history and of geography. Curious about the barbarian peoples with whom they came into contact, and about whom they heard from travelers in distant lands, Greek writers became concerned to describe, in systematic fashion, the wider world and its populations. In the fourth century B.C. Ephorus claimed that there were four great barbarian peoples in the known world: the Libyans in Africa, the

Persians in the east, and in Europe the Scythians and the Celts.

The Celts (*Keltoi* in Greek) were, by then, well known to classical writers. The earliest reference to them was in an early sixth-century B.C. account of coastal travel from Cadiz and Marseilles. The original document has long since disappeared, but by a remarkable chance it is quoted in a Coastal Survey *(Ora Maritima)* compiled by Festus Rufus Avienus, Roman proconsul of Africa in A.D. 566. Though obscure in detail, it gives the clear impression that peoples, who could be classed together as Celts, lived close to the North Sea, in France, and in the southwest of Spain. This geographical spread is to some extent confirmed by Hecataeus of Miletus, who was writing about 500 B.C. He mentions two Celtic towns, Narbonne in southern France and Nyrax, probably in Carinthia, and in describing the Greek colony at Marseilles he notes that it lies close to the land of the Celts. Half a century or so later the great Greek historian Herodotus tells us that the Celts were living in the upper Danube valley, near the Pyrenees, and in Spain. Tantalizing and imprecise though these scraps of evidence are, the general impression to be gained is that by about 600 B.C. most of western Europe from Austria to the Atlantic was occupied by tribes who were sufficiently similar to be thought of as culturally one people and who probably referred to themselves by a name which when translated into Greek sounded like *Keltoi*.

THE BEGINNINGS OF SETTLED LIFE IN EUROPE

How and when this cultural unity emerged can only be assessed by considering the archaeological evidence for man's development in Europe from the sixth to the first millennium B.C. Sometime within this span, so crucial to the history of the world, must lie the ethnogenesis of the Celts.

The spread of food production as a mode of subsistence, as opposed to food collection, was of vital significance in the development of European society. It freed man from the necessity to travel vast distances in seasonal pursuit of his food supply and allowed him, indeed forced him, to settle in hamlets and villages close

Opposite: The Neolithic way of life provided the community with a degree of leisure which allowed the development of various kinds of artistic expression. Inevitably much time would have been lavished on the gods and goddesses, who by the late Neolithic and Bronze Age were being depicted in a variety of guises. This small ceramic statuette of a goddess from this period was found at Cirna in Romania.

Overleaf (pp. 10–11): The Danube valley, as early as the sixth millennium B.C., was one of the two major pathways for important westward-bound migrations. Populations from southeastern Europe followed this route and also spread out along the northern shores of the Mediterranean.

As time went by,
men began to build huts
and to use skins and fire.
Male and female
learnt to live together
in a stable union and
to watch over
their joint progeny.

Then it was
that humanity first
began to mellow.
Then neighbors began
to form mutual alliances,
wishing neither to do
nor to suffer violence
among themselves.

Lucretius, Book V

to his growing crops. A more sedentary way of life led to the creation of larger communities, to a growth in population, and to craft specialization, thus paving the way for the eventual emergence of civilization.

It was in the latter part of the seventh millennium B.C. that food-producing economies first appeared in southeastern Europe, in Crete, Greece, and Bulgaria, encouraged and no doubt directly inspired by the farming communities already established in nearby Anatolia.

Once established on the European mainland, food-producing economies spread rapidly. Within fifteen hundred years (by 4500 B.C.) there were farmers as far west as Holland; soon after 4000 B.C. southern and western France were colonized; by 3000 B.C. farming communities had sprung up over most of the British Isles; and within a few centuries food was being produced in Denmark. Thus it took only three and a half thousand years for communities extending over the whole of Mediterranean and temperate Europe to acquire the skills necessary to ensure a constant supply of food, controlled, albeit sometimes precariously, by their own skills and efforts.

In the initial zone of settlement, in Greece and the southern Balkans, permanent villages soon sprang up. Rectangular houses, built of packed mud or sun-dried bricks and roofed with steeply sloping gabled roofs of timber, were renewed many times on the same site, each one being erected on the debris of its predecessor. So intense was the activity that many of the villages created great mounds (or tells). At Karanovo in Bulgaria the Neolithic occupation gave rise to a mound twelve meters in height, while at Knossos, on Crete, below the latest palace, trial excavations have shown there to be seven meters of accumulated Neolithic debris.

As time went on, the Neolithic villages grew. At Knossos the earliest settlement covered half a hectare (nearly an acre), by the end of the Neolithic period it was nine times the size, while on the Greek mainland at Sesklo the settlement eventually reached ten hectares in extent.

This dramatic growth in the size of the population in southeastern Europe was matched by the speed with which farming communities spread across the rest of the continent. There were two main lines of

9

And this race of men from the plains
were all the harder, for hard land
had borne them; built on stronger
and firmer bones, and endowed with mighty
sinew, they were a race
undaunted by heat or cold, plague,
strange new foodstuffs. For many years,
among the beasts of the earth
they led their life. And none was yet
a driver of the curved plow,
none yet could turn the soil with iron blade,
nor bury a new shoot in the ground
nor prune the ripened branch from the tree.

Lucretius

advance: through temperate Europe along the easily worked loess soils which fringed the Danube and the Rhine, and around the northern shores of the Mediterranean.

The peasant communities who spread westward along the Danube soon adapted their way of life to suit their new environment. The most important difference was that since the area into which they moved was heavily forested, the most efficient agricultural regime involved a slash-and-burn economy. A community moving into an area of virgin forest would cut all easily

Until man could begin to control his principal food sources, he was dependent on the seasonal movement of the herds, on which he preyed, and on the collection of plant foodstuffs. But once animals had been domesticated and plants cultivated, the way was prepared for a more sedentary mode of life. The "Neolithic Revolution," as this complex of developments was once called, took

place in Anatolia and the Fertile Crescent (a wide zone of hilly land stretching from the Persian Gulf north to Syria and south again through the Lebanon) in the eighth and seventh millennia B.C. But as early as the ninth millennium, in a cave and village site at Zawi Chemi Shanidar, in modern Iraq, the first signs of the incipient domestication of sheep have been recognized.

Among the early Neolithic communities sheep and goats were herded while two-rowed barley, emmer, spelt, and peas were cultivated. As the art of food production spread southward into the valleys of the Tigris and Euphrates, modes of production changed to suit the different environmental conditions and cattle became a significant element in the economy—as this seal stamp from Mesopotamia, dating to the end of the fifth millennium B.C., vividly demonstrates.

manageable undergrowth, reserving the best timber for building the great long houses in which they lived, and would burn the rest, the ash adding to the fertility of the soil. Amid the charred stumps the crops would be sown. After several seasons of cropping, soil fertility would begin to fail and the group would have to move on to a new territory. Some part of the population would perhaps return to old sites to begin again after the forest had regenerated, while other families would move off farther west to break new ground. In this way a vast territory from Romania to Holland was colonized in little more than seven hundred years.

By the third millennium it is possible to recognize significant changes. The cultural unity of the period of colonization was beginning to break down into distinct regional groups, while many of the settlements now show signs of defensive works. No doubt the phase of rapid movement

was over and people were beginning to settle down in defined territories as growth in population and the pressure on land forced them to protect their homes and their flocks.

While temperate Europe was in this way being opened up, other groups of farmers were working their way around the northern shores of the Mediterranean establishing coastal settlements in Italy, Sicily, southern France, and parts of Spain and Portugal. Once more the movement was rapid. Neolithic communities were established in Italy by 5600 and southern France by about 4000 B.C. The essentially coastal distribution of these early settlements strongly suggests that the colonists were sailors, probably fishermen as well as farmers, working their way from place to place and setting up new settlements wherever a suitable landfall was made.

In France the two streams of colonists met and merged and it was from here, sometime towards the middle of the fourth millennium, that boatloads of settlers, together with their seed, corn, and animals, began to cross the Channel to Britain and to brave the Celtic Sea to reach Ireland.

It is in these western regions, Iberia, France, and Britain, that the religious life of the Neolithic farmers reached its highest peak of elaboration, or more correctly, it is here that the most remarkable of their religious monuments survive. The dead were buried in collective tombs frequently built of large stone slabs set within mounds of soil and rubble. These megalithic tombs extend along the Atlantic seaboard from Spain to Denmark, and all seem to have been built in the comparatively short period between ca. 3500 and 2500 B.C.

Even more impressive are the sacred sites not apparently associated with burial: the finely built stone temples of Malta, the stone alignments of Brittany and Britain, and the circular henge monuments built of upright stones or timbers and often enclosed with banks and ditches which occur in some numbers in Britain and are most dramatically represented today by Avebury on Salisbury Plain in southern England. There is now little doubt that those responsible for their construction had a detailed knowledge of the movement of the sun and moon and were able to incorporate observations, made over many generations, into their planning and construction.

While these remarkable developments were taking place in the west, other parts of Europe, favored by their mineral wealth, were developing special skills in the mining of copper ores and the extraction of copper to make ornaments and weapons. The earliest exploitation of metal in Europe took place in the eastern Balkans as early as the fourth millennium, probably under influences from the east where copper working was by this time under way. Not long after, the east Alpine ores began to be worked as did those in Thuringia, and by 2400 B.C. the communities of Almeria, Algarve, and Alemtejo in Iberia were skillfully involved in extracting, alloying, and casting copper. Rich though these areas were in raw materials, they did not achieve the heights of civilization to which their more poorly endowed neighbors in Greece and the Aegean were soon to aspire.

MINOAN-MYCENAEAN CIVILIZATION

The rise of Minoan-Mycenaean civilization is one of the most dramatic events in European history, but to understand its basis it is necessary to look briefly at the situation in the area in the third millennium. During this period there developed in the Troad (in what is now western Turkey) a warlike society whose chieftains and their retainers lived in small defended settlements like the early "cities" on the site of Troy. There were a number of them, each commanding distinct territories and each supporting specialist smiths whose skills extended to alloying copper with tin to give greater strength to the weapons which they made. Tin was a rare commodity which had to be obtained by exchange via neighboring tribes. Thus there soon developed a complex network of reciprocal exchange involving the movement of tin and of other raw materials such as gold, silver, and lapis lazuli. As the Greek islands were drawn into the network, so the range of commodities was extended: silver from Siphnos, marble from Paros, and obsidian from Melos soon began to be exploited in the ever expanding system of exchange which linked Greece, Anatolia, and Crete. By the end of the third millennium one center, Crete, began to emerge above the rest. Its comparative fertility, long tradition

of settled economy, and large population, as well as its central position, were all factors favoring a quickening pace of development. By 2000–1900 B.C. there emerged on the island a palace-centered sociopolitical organization which can fairly be classed as a civilization. The island was divided into a number of distinct territories each dominated by a palace which would have served as the administrative and economic center of its region. The palaces were above all centers of redistribution where commodities were collected and stored prior to exchange and where manufactur-

The importance of cattle to the primitive Neolithic economy was considerable. Even a small cow would provide at least three times more meat than a sheep, but it was also the source of a wide range of other products: milk, leather, horn, bone, and blood. (Blood was an important source of salt among primitive agriculturists.) Moreover, the cow was a beast of burden.

This magnificent frieze, in bronze, stone, and bitumen, from the façade of a temple at Tell al'Ubaid in Mesopotamia, dating to the early third millennium, shows dairying activities in progress.
Although the forests of Europe supported wild oxen, domesticated cattle, together with sheep and goats, were introduced into southeast Europe from Anatolia by the earliest farmers.

ing industries were centered. Minoan culture flourished in a time of peace and stability, but two natural disasters, apparently earthquakes of some magnitude, intervened in about 1750 and 1500 B.C. It was after the latter, which must have shaken the strength of the community, that there is some evidence to suggest a takeover by a new hierarchy dominated by Greek speakers from the mainland Mycenaean culture.

The Mycenaean communities of mainland Greece were organized in small chiefdoms ruled by a prince or king called a *wanax* who, together with his retainers, lived in a fortified palace of the kind found at Mycenae, Tiryns, and Gla. Enormous energy was lavished on the tombs of the aristocracy, not only in the building of colossal structures like the so-called Treasury of Atreus at Mycenae (with its fine corbeled vault fifteen meters in height and diameter and its imposing entrance passage) but also

One of the greatest of Europe's religious monuments is Stonehenge on Salisbury Plain in southern England—a complex ritual site used and modified over many centuries. The earliest phase consisted of the outer bank and ditch with a circle of holes on the inside of the bank. Later a circle of blue stones, brought from Wales, was erected; and in its final stage (first half of second millennium B.C.) the great trilithons which now dominate the site were put up.

Pottery is a very important indicator of cultural differences and is much used by archaeologists to plot regional and chronological changes. Vessels like these two cremation urns of the Urnfield culture of southern Germany can readily be distinguished in form and decoration from this "bell beaker" from Britain, which is almost a thousand years older.

in providing the dead, buried in the somewhat earlier shaft graves at Mycenae, with quantities of gold, silver, ivory, and jewelry of a quality and variety never before seen in Europe.

It has been necessary to digress briefly to consider the Minoan-Mycenaean culture of the Aegean in the second millennium in order to understand something of the cultural influences which impinged upon central and western Europe at this time. Aegean civilization, with its complex network of exchange systems and its conspicuous consumption in beautifying the life and death of its leaders, made enormous demands on the raw material resources of Europe. Tin was acquired from northern Germany, Armorica, and Britain, gold from Ireland and Spain, amber from the Baltic,

and no doubt there was much more besides: rare woods, herbs, furs, and a host of other commodities no longer recognizable in the archaeological record.

The stimulus to production and exchange, which the Minoan-Mycenaean culture created, impinged upon much of Europe. In Armorica, Wessex, Germany, northern Italy, and Denmark flourishing cultures developed. All the while that the Minoan-Mycenaean world served as the pulse, the circulatory network of reciprocal exchange could invigorate far-flung parts of Europe.

The end came soon after 1200 B.C. The Hittite empire in Asia collapsed as the result of attacks by enemies from without, and rebellion within, while at the same time the Egyptian records talk of marauders

These six maps show, in very simplified diagrammatic form, significant successive stages in the development of European prehistoric culture. Although movements of people were involved, it is now clear that local inventiveness also played a role.

NEOLITHIC CULTURES

From the sixth to the third millennium, food-producing economies spread across Europe with astonishing speed, overland by way of the Danube, and by sea.

MEGALITHIC STRUCTURES

The third millennium saw the development, in western Europe, of a religious architecture which used large stone blocks to build tombs and temples.

BRONZE TECHNOLOGY

Knowledge of copper and bronze working developed in southeast Europe about 4000 B.C. and spread rapidly by the second millennium.

coming from the sea causing panic further heightened by invasions from Palestine. In this time of unrest the cultural and economic system of Aegean civilization broke down. Its structure had been complex and refined. Once the delicate balance had been upset by external troubles disturbing its essential systems of exchange and redistribution, the entire edifice tumbled and the Aegean plunged into a Dark Age from which, four centuries later, a greater civilization—that of Greece—was to emerge, rooted in the old.

URNFIELD CULTURE

With the loss of the stimulus provided by the Minoan-Mycenaean world, the pace of development in central and western Europe slackened: new centers of innovation and new axes of power emerged. This period, generally referred to in archaeological shorthand as the Urnfield period, is typified by the appearance of large cremation cemeteries, the ashes of the dead interred in urns. The tradition took form in Hungary sometime in the thirteenth century B.C. and was rapidly adopted farther west, in the area between the Elbe and Vistula, in southern Germany and the Alpine area, and in the Po Valley and the Italian peninsula. By the tenth century this entire region shared a similar culture, though regional differences in pottery styles and decorative techniques used on the now copious bronze work emphasize local differences. It is

difficult to resist the conclusion that, freed from their links with Aegean civilization, the communities of barbarian Europe established new and closer links of their own leading to a remarkable degree of convergent development.

Soon elements of the Urnfield culture penetrated the west, appearing in the Low Countries, France, Spain, and Britain. Whether to interpret this phenomenon in terms of a westward folk movement of Urnfield invaders, or to see it in terms of a gradual expansion of the exchange and redistribution system embracing the western communities, is a matter of debate. Probably we will never know the answer, but what is abundantly clear is that it was within this Late Bronze Age cultural complex of barbarian Europe that the Celts had their origins. The word *Celts* may have been the name of a particularly powerful tribe or even of a ruling household, or it may have been a generic term by which the disparate groups of central and western Europe distinguished themselves from their more distant neighbors. Once more we will never know. What is significant is that the whole region was bound by a common culture and that they spoke dialects of a branch of the Indo-European language group which linguists now recognize as sufficiently similar to be classed together and called Celtic. It was a realization of these things that allowed the early Greek geographers to generalize about the *Keltoi* of Europe—one of the four great peoples of the barbarian world.

Metal types also show marked regional and chronological variations. One region to support a highly developed bronze industry was Denmark (in spite of the fact that all the metal had to be imported). This elaborately decorated belt fitting of bronze, dating to about the fifteenth century B.C., from Langstrup, Zealand, indicates the skill of the Danish craftsmen. Belt plates of this kind have been found in a number of graves of females.

Throughout the Neolithic period and much of the Bronze Age, stone formed the principal material from which heavy-duty tools and weapons were made. Greater efficiency in making cutting edges was achieved by polishing the stone. Stone implements continued to be used throughout the Early Bronze Age, but it is frequently possible to see that they were being made in imitation of the more expensive bronze types. These stone axes of Neolithic date come from Switzerland.

THE BEAKER CULTURE

A mobile group, recognized largely from their distinctive pottery, can be traced in various parts of Europe in the early second millennium.

URNFIELD CULTURES

Following the breakdown of Aegean civilization, ca. 1200 B.C., central Europe developed a distinctive Late Bronze Age culture from which the Celts emerged.

HALLSTATT CULTURE

By about 700 B.C. the Hallstatt culture—the culture of the Celts—covered much of western Europe. It lasted into the fifth century B.C.

The expansion of the various cultures in Europe occurred in stages. Red shows the first phase; brown, the second; and yellow, the final stage.

HALLSTATT AND LA TÈNE CULTURES

Hallstatt culture (eighth–fifth century B.C.): The earliest phase of the European Iron Age—and the first phase of Celtic culture—is named after the site of Hallstatt in Austria. Hallstatt became important in the eighth to sixth centuries B.C. because of the salt deposits which were mined nearby. The community grew

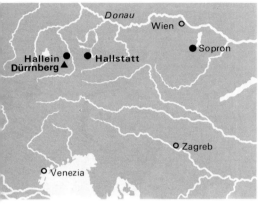

rich by exchanging its salt for other commodities. It also occupied a significant position on the route along which Baltic amber passed to the Mediterranean.

Shown on these pages are typical objects of Hallstatt and La Tène culture. *From left to right:*

Horse rider used as decoration on a sixth-century bronze axe from Hallstatt.

Bronze pail, elaborately decorated in repoussé style. Sixth century, from Hallstatt.

When, in the early years of the nineteenth century, the great Danish archaeologist C. J. Thomsen was attempting to bring some order into the national archaeological collection in Copenhagen, he hit upon the scheme of dividing the prehistoric period in Europe into three ages—an age of Stone, an age of Bronze, and an age of Iron. This simple classification has remained a convenient shorthand ever since. But as the pace of discovery quickened during the nineteenth century, finer subdivisions were called for to contain the bewildering mass of new data that flooded into our museums and into private collections.

In 1846, on the shores of Lake Hallstatt in Austria, amid the magnificent mountain country of the Salzkammergut, Georg Ramsauer, director of the Hallstatt state mine, began to excavate the graves of a prehistoric cemetery where a flourishing community had buried their dead in the first half of the first millennium B.C. Between 1846 and 1862 he uncovered no less than 980 bodies. In 1876 the Vienna Academy of Sciences began to excavate

Small bronze figure, Hallstatt period, showing the dress of the period.

Human head detail from a fifth-century gold bracelet from a grave at Reinheim, Germany.

Iron spearhead of the third to second century B.C. from the site of La Tène, Switzerland.

Insular Celtic art on a cart handle found in the River Thames.

A brooch terminal of the fourth century from Oberwittighausen, Germany.

the nearby prehistoric salt mine. The finds were spectacular, not for their wealth but for the remarkable degree to which the salt-laden soil had preserved common things like the protective clothing of the prehistoric miners, the framed leather sacks which they had used to carry the rock salt, and their wooden implements.

Meanwhile in Switzerland other important discoveries were being made at La Tène, on the banks of Lake Neuchâtel. At the northeastern end, where the River Thielle flowed into the lake, a lowering of the water level in 1858 revealed lines of blackened timbers projecting from the mud. The discovery was immediately investigated by archaeologists sent from Zurich. The museum authorities were well prepared for such eventualities, for a few years before, when the waters of the Lake of Zurich were low, they had discovered the remains of several prehistoric settlements along the shore. At La Tène they were not disappointed; vast quantities of Iron Age metalwork were found: swords in their decorated sheaths, spears, shield bosses, horse gear, tools of all kinds to-

16

The discoveries at La Tène had provided a range of artifacts which could be compared with the finds from Hallstatt. They were clearly different and later. Thus when the Swedish archaeologist B.E. Hildebrand came to write of the Iron Age in 1872, he divided it into an earlier and a later phase named after the two great type sites of Hallstatt and La Tène. But archaeologists were not content with such a simple scheme: soon elaborations and subdivisions were introduced. The Hallstatt culture was divided into four phases called A, B, C, D, while the La Tène period was subdivided into three, I, II, and III. Although these terminologies are still in use, work in this century has focused on further refinements of phasing and of dating, each regional sequence producing idiosyncrasies of its own. As a working generalization, however, we can say that Hallstatt A and B phases belong to the Late Bronze Age and date roughly to the period 1100–700 B.C.; Hallstatt C (the first iron-using phase) falls within the seventh century; Hallstatt D spans the sixth and extends into the fifth. The La Tène phase begins in the second half of the fifth century and continues until the spread of Roman power swamps native culture, for which the dates differ across Europe.

Above all we must remember that the Hallstatt–La Tène terminology is simply a classificatory convenience imposed by archaeologists upon the changing cultures of late prehistoric Europe. The names do not imply different ethnic groups. Quite the contrary, it is highly probable that all communities which fall within this classification were Celts.

gether with ornaments, coins, and a host of other objects. For years it was conventional to regard the wealth of material recovered from La Tène as a votive deposit thrown into the lake to placate the gods. Recent scientific research has suggested, however, that it is more likely to have been a domestic and industrial settlement on dry land which was suddenly overwhelmed by a flood.

Above: Hallstatt occupies a spectacular location in the Austrian mountains on the side of a lake. The late nineteenth-century excavations of the salt mines and cemetery have made it one of the most famous prehistoric sites in Europe. Painting by Isidor Engl.

La Tène culture (fifth century onward): The type-site for the second stage of the European Iron Age is La Tène on the ancient course of the River Thielle, which flows into Lake Neuchâtel. Although producing a

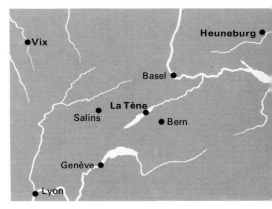

wide range of material, La Tène did not occupy the central position in the later Iron Age that Hallstatt did in the earlier.

THE EMERGENCE OF
THE CELTS

CORNOVII

CALEDONES

Abernethy

DAM
NONII VOTADINI

Cruachan

Emain Macha

Dun Aengus

Tara

BRIGANTES

Gundestrup

PARISII

ORDOVICES CORITANI

CORNOVII

ICENI

SILURES

Uffington

Celtic Europe in the Hallstatt period,
sixth and seventh centuries B.C., is
shown in brown shading on the map.
By the second century B.C. the Celts
reached their fullest expansion
(lighter shade).

DUMNONII ATREBATES Battersea

REGNI

White: Celtic agglomerations

Green: Celtic archaeological sites

Red: Important non-Celtic cities

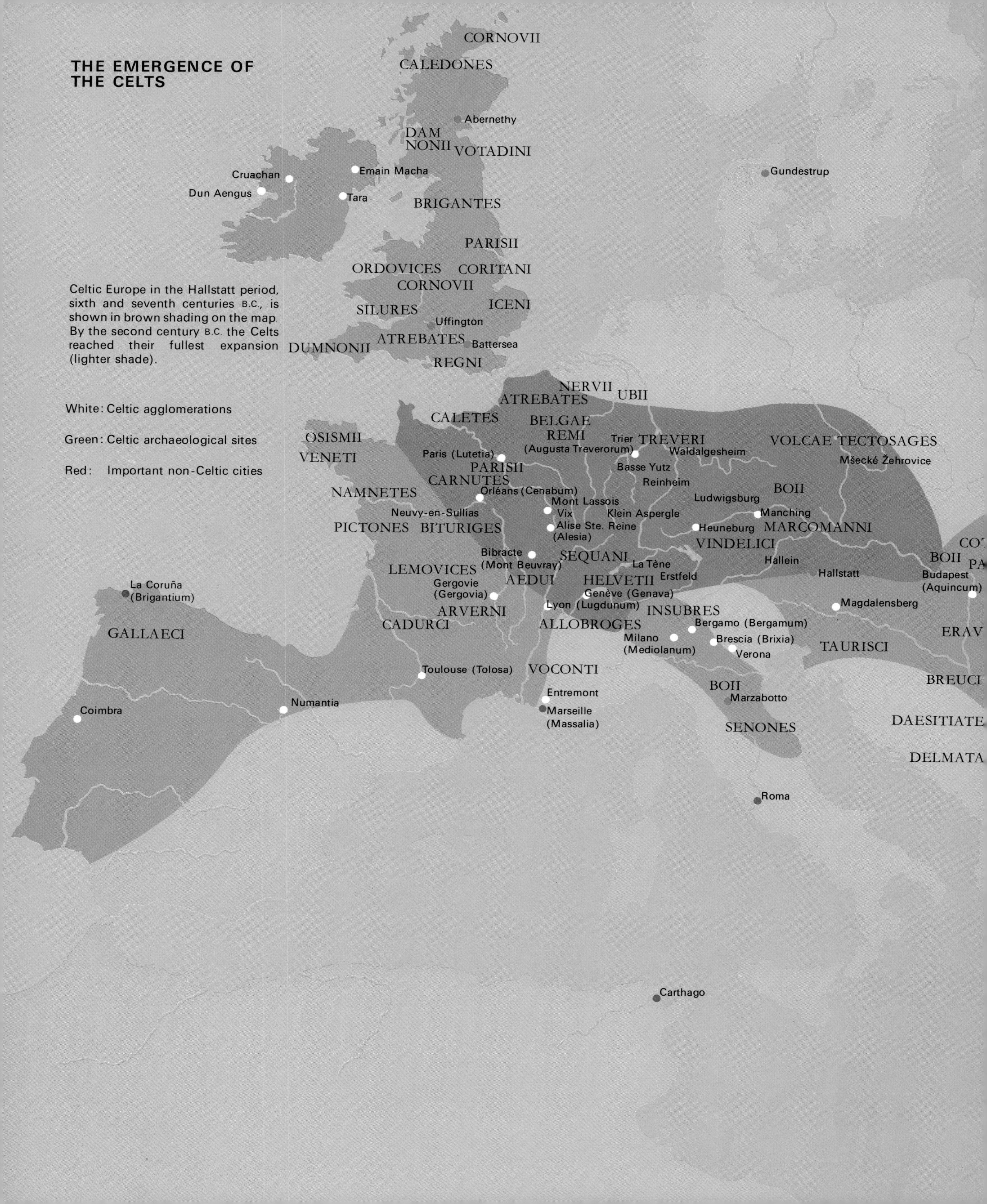

NERVII UBII

ATREBATES

CALETES

BELGAE

OSISMII

REMI TREVERI VOLCAE TECTOSAGES

VENETI

Trier
(Augusta Treverorum) Waldalgesheim

Mšecké Žehrovice

Paris (Lutetia)

PARISII

Basse Yutz

CARNUTES

Reinheim

NAMNETES

Orléans (Cenabum)

Mont Lassois

BOII

Ludwigsburg

Neuvy-en-Sullias

Vix Klein Aspergle

Manching

PICTONES BITURIGES

Alise Ste. Reine
(Alesia)

Heuneburg MARCOMANNI

VINDELICI

Bibracte

La Tène

CO

LEMOVICES

(Mont Beuvray)

SEQUANI

Erstfeld

BOII PA

Gergovie

AEDUI HELVETII

Hallein

Hallstatt

Budapest
(Aquincum)

Gergovie
(Gergovia)

Genève (Genava)

Magdalensberg

La Coruña
(Brigantium)

ARVERNI

Lyon (Lugdunum)

INSUBRES

ERAV

GALLAECI

CADURCI

ALLOBROGES

Bergamo (Bergamum)

Milano
(Mediolanum)

Brescia (Brixia)

TAURISCI

Verona

Toulouse (Tolosa) VOCONTI

BOII BREUCI

Entremont

Marzabotto

Coimbra

Numantia

Marseille
(Massalia)

SENONES

DAESITIATE

DELMATA

Roma

Carthago

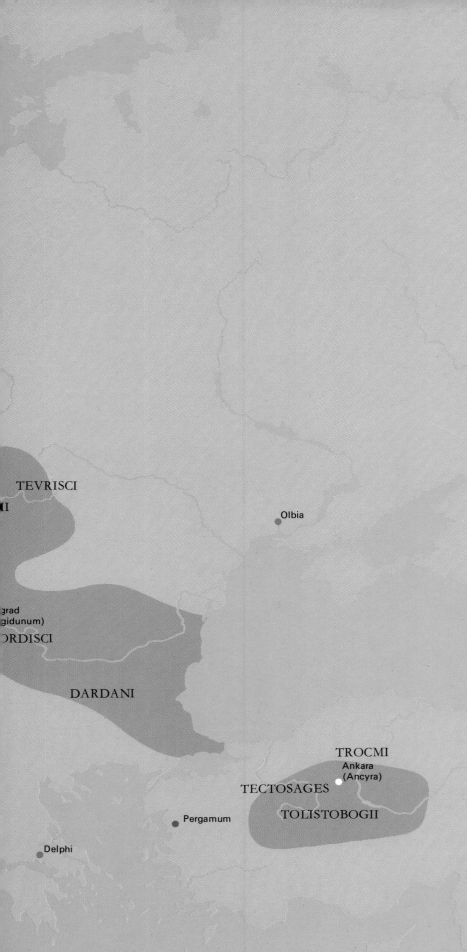

TEVRISCI

Olbia

grad
gidunum)

ORDISCI

DARDANI

TROCMI

Ankara
(Ancyra)

TECTOSAGES

Pergamum

TOLISTOBOGII

Delphi

The eighth century B.C. was a crucial time for the emergence of the Celtic peoples, a time of change and readjustment.

The Urnfield communities of central and western Europe—from about 1300 to 700—have left little evidence to suggest that there was any great disparity in wealth between the leaders and their subjects. Some burials have, admittedly, produced elaborate weapons or personal ornaments suggesting a certain level of wealth appropriate to a chieftain or warrior, but the stark differences of the preceding periods are unknown at this time—until the eighth century, when we begin to find hints of the emergence of a wealthy class. At Hart-an-der-Alz in Bavaria, for example, a cremation was found accompanied by a range of fine pottery together with three bronze vessels, representing the dead man's feast, his sword, and the bronze fittings from the wooden cart which would have conveyed him to the funeral pyre: here is a man above other men. It was at about this time too that evidence for horses, in the form of bridle fittings, increases; we are on the threshold of significant changes in the socio-political system.

Factors which may well have been instrumental in these social changes were the events now being played out in eastern Europe, the Pontic steppes, and beyond. We know that in this period the nomadic and semi-nomadic tribes whose traditional homeland lay in the steppe lands fringing the north shores of the Black Sea—peoples known to Greek writers as Cimmerians—were coming under increasing pressures from their easterly neighbors, Scythians. Eventually they decided to yield and move off. One branch penetrated Anatolia and throughout the seventh century served as a mercenary army in the battles between the kingdom of Uratu and the Assyrians, their name appearing many times in Assyrian documents of the period. Another group seems to have moved off westward into Europe, spreading along the Danube into Bulgaria and reaching as far west as the Great Hungarian Plain, where their burials, with echoes of their Pontic origins, have recently been recognized. It is possible that the appearance of these foreigners, bringing with them finely bred horses, may in some way have influenced the emerging aristocracy of the west.

Traces of the Celts can be found almost anywhere in temperate Europe. Their fortifications—hillforts and oppida—are to be seen spreading in a broad arc from Yugoslavia to the north of Scotland; the museums of Europe store thousands of objects recovered from the excavation of graves and of settlement sites or dredged from rivers and bogs; while many of our great cities, including Budapest, Paris, Belgrade, stand on Celtic foundations. But the influence of the Celts is even more pervading: elements of the Celtic language survive in modern place names in many parts of Europe. The *dun* element in names

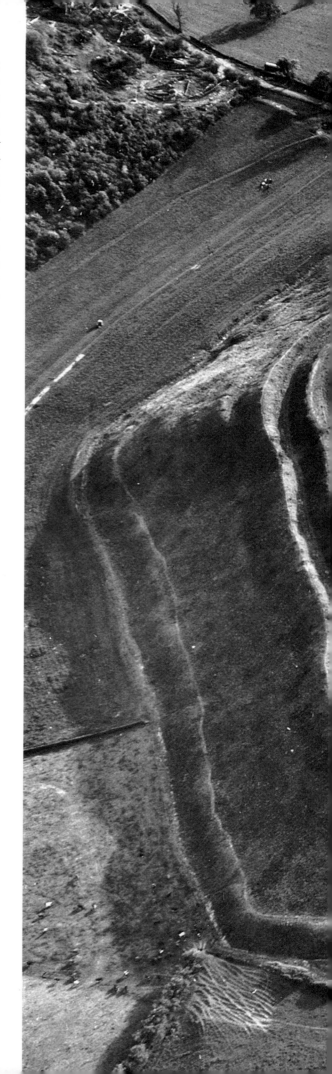

DISCOVERY OF THE CELTS

The most dramatic surviving monuments left by the Celts are their hillforts—massively defended settlements which dominate the landscape. Old Oswestry, in the Welsh borderland, was used throughout the second half of the first millennium B.C. Its defenses, seen here from the air, incorporate many phases of rebuilding.

like London probably derives from the Celtic *dúnon* meaning a "fort" or "strong," while *vindos*, "white," and *maros*, "big," are name elements still recurring from place to place. Descriptive words like these, referring to natural landscape features, passed easily into everyday usage even though the area might be overrun by an alien culture with a language of its own. What makes the Celts live is that our knowledge of them does not depend solely upon dead scattered relics—archaeological and linguistic—but is greatly enlivened by descriptions of them as a people which come down to us from many classical authors. But even more remarkable is the survival of a considerable body of Celtic literature in the form of an oral tradition of heroic folktales which were eventually written down in Ireland in the latter part of the first millennium A.D. To read them today is to place oneself immediately in direct and startling communication with the world of the Celts, while to hear Gaelic, Welsh, or Irish spoken in the western fringes of Britain is to experience an eerie echo from the past.

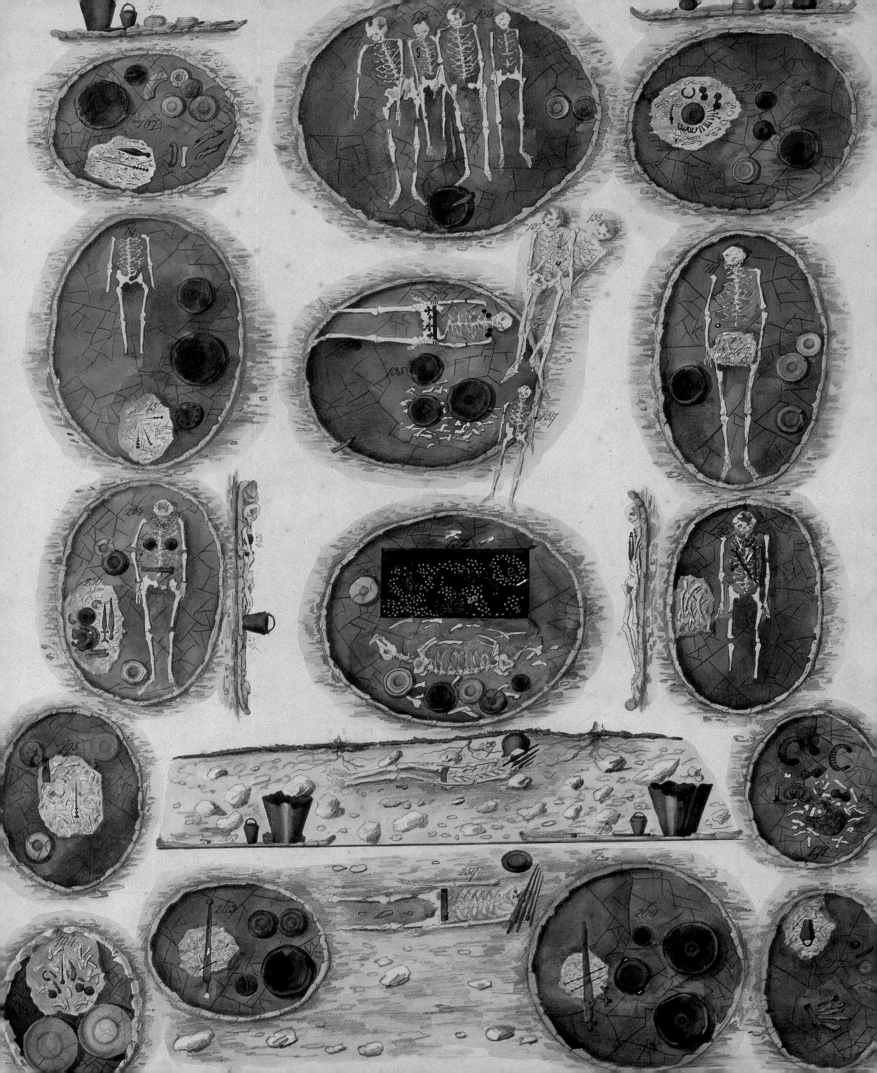

GRAVES

The most prolific source of archaeological material relevant to the Celts comes from the excavation of their cemeteries. Across the length and breadth of Europe tens of thousands of Hallstatt and La Tène graves have been excavated. Many, found in the last century, were grubbed out unceremoniously to satisfy the contemporary lust for collectable objects. Today cemeteries are excavated with minute care using a battery of scientific aids in an attempt to recover every last scrap of evidence.

The Celts, like most primitive peoples, believed in an afterlife; indeed one ancient writer tells us that so firm was their belief that they would even put off the settling of debts until they met again in the next world! Their attitude to the world to come is shown with great clarity by the way their graves were furnished with the equipment they would need—each according to his status. A wealthy female like the so-called princess buried at Vix in Burgundy was accompanied by all the equipment appropriate to the feast: a great krater or wine storage vessel, jugs, bowls, and cups, all imported from different parts of the classical world in the last decade of the sixth century. She also took with her her jewelry, including an enormous gold diadem, her amber necklace, and brooches. At the other end of the social scale, a poor woman

B.C. sees a leveling down with the development of large inhumation cemeteries, the individual graves showing little sign of widely differing status.

Although most of the objects buried with the dead were their personal ornaments and domestic equipment (like that accompanying the men and women from the Hallstatt cemetery shown opposite), occasionally one finds specialist equipment as well, like the collection from a second-century grave at Obermenzingen in southern Germany. Here, in addition to the usual sword, spear, and shield boss, were found three tools appropriate to a surgeon: a probe, retractor, and trephining saw.

The value of cemetery evidence to an archaeologist is considerable. Not only does it provide a wealth of domestic material reflecting on the life-styles of the

This page illustrates a selection of objects from Celtic graves. Shown above are four pottery vessels made by the La Tène communities living in the Marne region of France. The articles below are bronze personal ornaments from cremation graves of the Urnfield period in southern Germany.

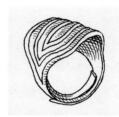

might be lucky enough to possess a brooch or a cloak pin.

There was also a disparity in ritual, particularly evident in the early Hallstatt cemeteries. The poorer people tended still to cling to the old Urnfield cremation ritual, while the chieftains were usually inhumed in wooden chambers set within large barrows and were often accompanied by the funeral carts which took them to their graves and perhaps a joint of pork to sustain them on their journey. Later, in the La Tène period, although wealth differences are still evident at first, the third century

different communities but it enables the composition of populations to be assessed —physical types, nutrition, diseases, and death rates. Moreover, by observing their attitudes to death we can begin to come closer to the people themselves, to their fears, hopes, and aspirations. Writing of funerals in Gaul, Caesar says that everything the dead man was fond of, including his animals, was placed on his pyre and "slaves and retainers known to have been beloved by their masters were burned with them at the conclusion of the funeral rites." Celtic funerals were spectacular.

Opposite: Our knowledge of the famous cemetery of Hallstatt depends entirely on the meticulous records kept at the time, of which this painting by Austrian artist Isidor Engl is a superb example. It illustrates a wide range of burial practices.

23

The Celts were technically highly skilled. By the seventh century B.C. they had mastered all the techniques necessary to work bronze: It could be cast into elaborate forms for ornaments and tools or worked into sheets to make vessels which could be decorated in repoussé style by beating out designs from the back or enlivened with inscribed or chased decoration.

The extraction and forging of iron soon became widespread, iron by virtue of its strength being much favored for weapons and for tools. Raw materials were abun-

can offer fascinating insights into aspects of life undiscoverable by any other means. The three decorated items shown on this page give an incomparable impression of warriors, infantry and cavalry alike, progressing in orderly fashion to battle; but even more important they give precise details of clothing, a subject upon which classical writers are not particularly forthcoming, and since fabrics are seldom preserved in archaeological contexts, contemporary illustrations of this kind are our only source.

To an archaeologist, objects have an added interest. Man has always been prone to the dictates of fashion. Styles and forms change, sometimes rapidly, sometimes imperceptibly. A wealthy man would want the most up-to-date type of sword, while his wife would demand a fashionable brooch. Human pressures of this kind would ensure change, but change was not consistent. Once a satisfactory type of iron spearhead had evolved, there was little one could do to improve it and since spears were seldom decorated, all that the craftsman could do was to vary shape and weight slightly to better suit the object to its specific function as, for example, a lance for cavalry, or a throwing spear for infantry. Thus, although there was variation, there was little

In the valley of the River Po there developed a school of craftsmen whose particular skill lay in decorating bronze *situlae* (buckets probably for wine) in repoussé style. Ornamentation usually consisted of horizontal panels containing scenes from everyday life, or views of animals as in this detail from a fourth-century B.C. *situla* from the region of Este, northern Italy.

dant: iron was everywhere to be found; efficient copper and tin extraction had been organized for a thousand years; graphite and hematite to decorate pottery were being widely distributed; while materials like gold, silver, coral, amber, and glass, used to make luxury objects, were readily available for those who could afford them. In short, the surviving material remains of Celtic culture show that society was endowed with technology and the craft skills unsurpassed in Europe until the eighteenth century A.D.

Apart from providing evidence of a purely technological and functional kind, objects

significant evolution. Much the same could be said of swords. Once iron had replaced bronze for sword blades, the only significant factor affecting form was the nature of the warfare: a long slashing sword was ideal for cavalry tactics, but a short stabbing sword was much more efficient in close hand-to-hand fighting. While, therefore, the sword itself changed only within closely prescribed limits, its sheath, which was often decorated, could be subjected to the whims of fashion.

The study of changing styles, known to archaeologists as typology, is of considerable value in dating the graves or settle-

ments of the Celts. Typology works on the simple assumption that changes in style and form have a momentum and that the direction of change can be recognized, allowing objects to be arranged in a sequence which reflects their age. This is much the same kind of reasoning which would allow us, confronted with motor cars of different dates, to put them in a rough chronological order.

Brooches *(fibulae)* are particularly susceptible to change, not least because they are fashion objects, and thus provide a particularly valuable field for typological studies.

bows could be inscribed or inlaid, while their plates provided settings for coral or were worked into elaborate forms. Variations such as these allow regional styles to be defined and their distributions to be plotted.

The final stage in the typological study of objects is to assign absolute dates to the relative chronology of the sequence. For the Iron Age there are three principal methods: (1) by dating timbers through the study of tree rings (dendrochronology); (2) by association with datable imports from the classical world; and (3) by correlation with historical events.

The first of these methods has only recently been applied to Iron Age studies but is well developed in other fields of research. By establishing long sequences of tree ring variation for prehistoric Europe and linking them to sequences for the historic period, it will eventually be possible to date the cutting of any suitably preserved timber, for example in a burial chamber, to within a few years. More widely used at present is the second method. If in a

Far left: The famous silver caldron from Gundestrup in Denmark provides a marvelous range of detail about warrior equipment. Here we see a mounted warrior wearing a helmet with an animal crest.

Celtic weapons are frequently recovered not only from warrior graves but also from ritual deposits representing the spoils of war offered to the gods. The spears below, from La Tène (mid-third to second century B.C.), give some idea of the variation in type used. The bronze sword (third from top) is earlier; it also comes from Switzerland but dates to the eighth century B.C.

Below, center: The decorated bronze sheath for an iron sword found at Hallstatt (seen here in a redrawing) shows how much we can learn about a people who illustrate their own daily life. These military scenes depict wrestling (far left), foot soldiers and

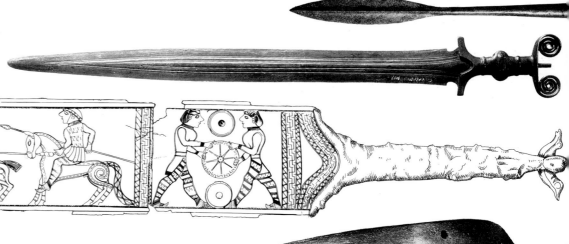

Technically these brooches are of safety pin type, the end of the spring pin being secured in a catch plate. Long unsupported catch plates of the type common in the Hallstatt period were "improved" in the early La Tène period by bending the end of the catch plate back towards the bow of the brooch to give added strength. In the middle La Tène period the ends of the plates were actually wrapped around the bow, and by the end of the period the resulting triangular-shaped plate was cast in one with the bow. This simple technological improvement was accompanied by a wide range of decorative variations—the

Celtic burial one finds Greek pottery vessels which are known to have been manufactured at a particular date, then the burial is likely to have taken place soon after that date (see pp. 36–37). Finally if objects can be shown to have been associated with an historical event, as for example the mass of coins and weapons buried at Mont Réa during the siege of Alesia in 52 B.C. (pp. 152–153), then one can assume that most of them were in current use at the time of the siege.

cavalrymen with typical weapons and gear, flanked by pairs of men who hold the circular symbol of warfare. The fourth-century B.C. sheath is about 70 centimeters (28 inches) long.

SCULPTURE AND COINS

The Celts of the Hallstatt period did not provide a great deal of visual evidence of their world and of themselves. Later, however, with growing contacts with the classical world and the introduction of coinage, representations become increasingly common and under Roman rule the Celtic population of countries like Gaul developed a vigorous style of representational art, in stone, bronze, and wood, largely ignoring the heavy hand of Roman classicism and allowing their inbred love of sinuous form to excel.

Celtic sculpture is generally very simple, the characteristics of the material used determining the form of the resulting creation. For example, the large pillar-like sculptures from Germany required the minimum of stone to be removed to produce the desired effect. It is, however, possible that these early works are rare copies, in stone, of subjects that were normally carved from tree trunks.

Metal, particularly bronze and gold, gave Celtic craftsmen greater scope, but throughout most of the La Tène period human and animal forms were subservient to the overall design. A human face might be incorporated, but it was simplified and broken down into its component parts according to the demands of the pattern. Only with the extension of Roman influence did the free human figure come into its own.

The classical cultures with which the Celts came into contact were by no means unprepared to depict these strange barbarians. King Attalus I of Pergamum was responsible for creating perhaps the most famous of all representations of a Celt in the bronze statue *The Dying Gaul* erected at Pergamum in the second century B.C. and widely copied elsewhere (for example, in marble in the Museo Capitolino, Rome). Pergamum also provides a vivid impression of Celtic armor in the famous reliefs, depicting spoils of war, which once decorated the Temple of Athene Nikepharos. Sculptures of this kind are an invaluable source of information for their realism and the accuracy of their representation.

In the late third century B.C. the Celts of central and western Europe began to adopt coinage inspired by the gold staters of the Macedonian kings and the silver of the western Greek colonies which had began to find their way into Celtic lands, possibly as pay or loot brought back by returning mercenaries. Once introduced, the art of coinage was widely adopted and spread rapidly, reaching the southeast of Britain by the beginning of the first century B.C. Coins soon became a medium for both artistic and political display. Celtic die engravers presented their motifs with great skill, interpreting conventional subjects like heads, horses, and chariots with typical Celtic vitality and love of flowing form, each tribe producing its own distinctive series which in later periods were frequently inscribed with the name of the ruler and sometimes his pedigree.

Celtic spirit pervaded the art of Roman Gaul. Some of the most beautiful representations of Gallo-Roman dress and manners come from this hybrid culture, by far the most outstanding being the three bronze figurines found at Neuvy-en-Sullias, and dating to the second or third century A.D.: a musician *(below)*; a figure believed to be a priest *(center)*; and a dancing girl *(far right)*.

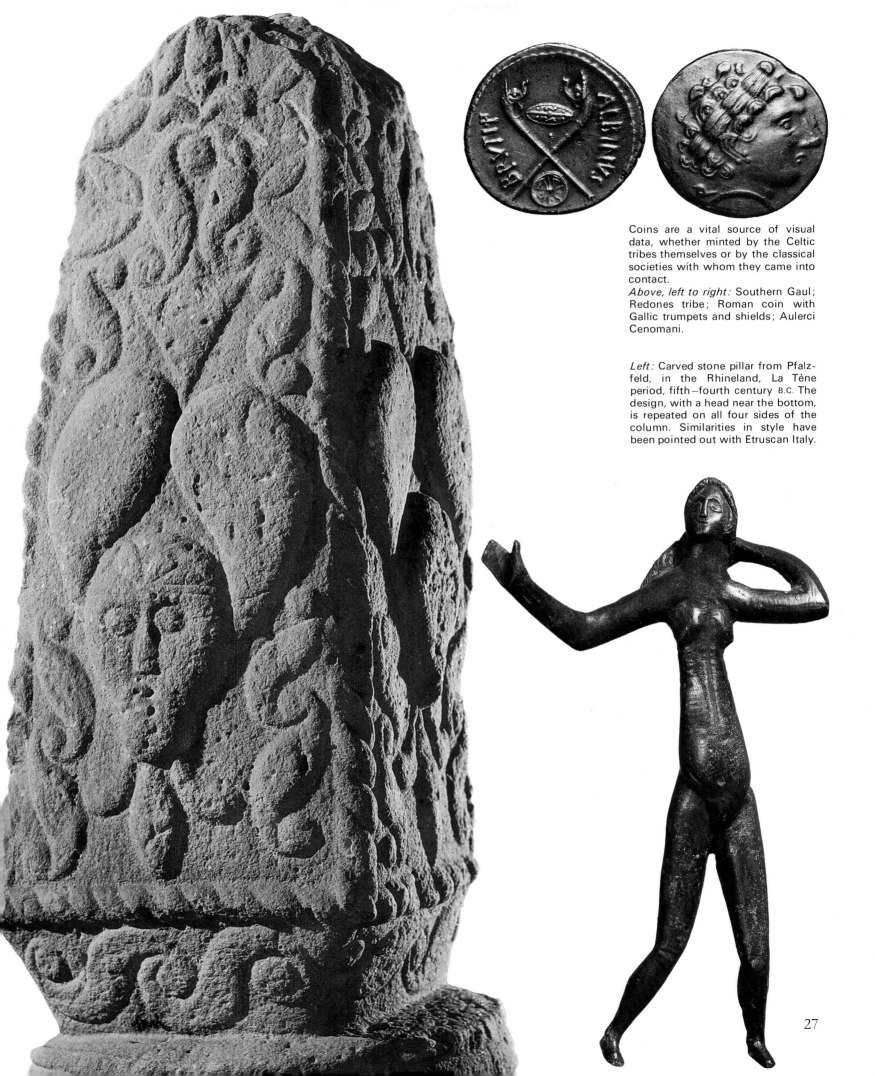

Coins are a vital source of visual data, whether minted by the Celtic tribes themselves or by the classical societies with whom they came into contact.

Above, left to right: Southern Gaul; Redones tribe; Roman coin with Gallic trumpets and shields; Aulerci Cenomani.

Left: Carved stone pillar from Pfalzfeld, in the Rhineland, La Tène period, fifth—fourth century B.C. The design, with a head near the bottom, is repeated on all four sides of the column. Similarities in style have been pointed out with Etruscan Italy.

27

WRITTEN EVIDENCE

From ancient travelers' tales and traditions, or from their own experiences, Greek and Roman historians compiled descriptions of the Celts that we continue to rely on for information. Fifth-century B.C. historians like Herodotus (seen below right in a Roman bust of the second

century A.D. from Egypt) was heavily dependent on his informants, but his works stand at the head of the Greek historical tradition.

Most of the later accounts of the Celts depend directly or indirectly upon the lost works of Posidonius or on Caesar. This is particularly true of poets such as Lucan or Virgil, who refer romantically to Celts in much the same way as did the nineteenth-century poets.

Above: Virgil, seated between the Muses of Epic and Tragedy, in a mosaic from Tunisia.

Above right: Without the medieval scribes, who preserved and often re-copied ancient manuscripts, many Greek and Roman texts would never have survived. Monks also transcribed many Celtic folktales that had been passed down orally for centuries, particularly in Ireland. In this miniature painting from a medieval manuscript, a monastic copyist is shown at work.

The whole race, which is now called
Gallic or Galatic,
is madly fond of war, high-spirited
and quick to battle,
but otherwise straightforward
and not of evil character.
And so when they are stirred up
they assemble in their bands for battle,
quite openly and without forethought,
so that they are easily handled
by those who desire to outwit them;
for at any time or place
and on whatever pretext
you stir them up, you will have them
ready to face danger,
even if they have nothing on their side
but their own strength and courage.

Strabo

These are the researches of
Herodotus of Halicanarssus
which he publishes in the hope of
thereby preserving from decay
the remembrance of
what men have done,
and of preventing the great and
wonderful actions of the Greeks
and the Barbarians,
from losing their due meed
of glory.

Herodotus

Seen through the eyes of Greek and Roman writers, the Celts were barbarians—people who spoke no civilized language. Hecataeus, Herodotus, Xenophon, Aristotle, Hieronymus, Polybius, and Livy all have something to tell us of Celtic manners and of historical events involving Celtic invasions against the civilized world, but the amount of reliable ethnographic detail which they present is slight. The notable exception is Polybius, who, in describing the Celtic invasion of Italy, enlivens his story with fascinating asides on Celtic clothing, living conditions, and the selfless courage of the warriors.

It is, however, Posidonius, a Stoic philosopher who lived in the first century B.C., who provides the deepest insight into Celtic society. In Book 23 of his *History* he presented a detailed ethnographic account of the Celts as a prelude to discussing the first transalpine war, which took place in 125–131 B.C. Since it is known that he lived in southern Gaul for some while, we may reasonably suppose that he collected his material by firsthand observation. Unfortunately his "Celtic ethnography" no longer survives intact but comes down to us in extensive summaries provided by later Greek writers, Diodorus Siculus, Strabo, and Athenaeus. Although they naturally make modifications and additions of their own, their basic source is clearly Posidonius.

In addition we have the writings of Julius Caesar, general, politican, and polymath, who between 58 and 51 B.C. fought a series of bitter campaigns against the Celts of Gaul and Britain. Though not entirely unbiased, his accounts of Celtic society provide the last sight of the free Celts on the European mainland before their culture was subsumed by Rome, leaving only the Britons to carry on the Celtic traditions.

ARISTOTLE
The great Greek philosopher, writing about 330 B.C., uses the example of the Celts to discuss the nature of bravery.

POLYBIUS
Writing in the second century B.C., he gives a brilliant evocation of the relentless force of the Celts in his history of the third century B.C.—a time when the Celts were still a power to be reckoned with in Italy and when they were actually advancing into Greece and Asia Minor.

LIVY
In his great *History of Rome*, composed in the late first century B.C., Livy describes the Celtic attack on Rome in the early fourth century and its aftermath. He relied heavily on earlier sources including the writings of Posidonius.

STRABO
A Greek geographer who lived in Rome and Alexandria and traveled widely in the late first century B.C. and early first century A.D. His seventeen books on *Geography*, most of which survive, contain a valuable compilation of data from the Roman world and beyond. For his information on the Celts he used Posidonius as a primary source.

PLINY THE ELDER
Pliny (d. A.D. 79) composed a considerable work on *Natural History* in which he gives details of Druids and of Celtic medicine. His information comes from an unknown source.

JULIUS CAESAR
Caesar (d. 44 B.C.) came into close contact with the Celts when he conquered Gaul between the years 58 and 51 and led two expeditions to Britain. He had a unique opportunity to observe Celtic society firsthand, as recorded in his *Gallic Wars*.

CORNELIUS TACITUS
Tacitus (A.D. 56–ca. 120) was a famous historian whose *Annals* and *Histories* cover the period from the death of Augustus in A.D. 14 to the year 96. His earliest works, the *Agricola* and *Germania*, completed in 98, provide brilliantly observed accounts of the Britons and the Germans. The details of the Britons were probably obtained firsthand from his father-in-law, Julius Agricola, governor in Britain from A.D. 78 to 84.

We have no word for the man who is excessively fearless; perhaps one may call such a man mad or bereft of feeling, who fears nothing, neither earthquakes nor waves, as they say of the Celts. ...It is not bravery to withstand fearful things through ignorance, for example, if through madness one were to withstand the onset of thunderbolts, and again, even if one understands how great the danger is, it is not bravery to withstand it through high-spiritedness, as when the Celts take up arms to attack the waves; and in general the courage of barbarians is compounded with high-spiritedness.

Aristotle

Next in order is the Celtic country beyond the Alps. Its general shape and size have been previously described but now we must describe it in detail. Some authorities have divided the country into three parts, calling their inhabitants Aquitani, Belgae and Celtae, respectively. Of these they describe the Aquitani as completely different from the others, not alone in language but also in physical characteristics, being closer to the Iberians than to the Gauls. The rest of the population is Gaulish in physical appearance, but they do not all share the same language and furthermore, there exist slight differences in their respective ways of life and methods of government.

Strabo

Gaul comprises three areas, inhabited respectively by the Belgae, the Aquitani, and a people who call themselves Celts, though we call them Gauls. All of these have different languages, customs, and laws. The Celts are separated from the Aquitani by the river Garonne, from the Belgae by the Marne and Seine. The Belgae are the bravest of the three peoples, being farthest removed from the highly developed civilization of the Roman Province, least often visited by merchants with enervating luxuries for sale, and nearest to the Germans across the Rhine, with whom they are continually at war.

Caesar, *Gallic Wars*

The occupation of the Gauls by Roman generals and emperors was not prompted by self-interest, but happened at the invitation of the forefathers, whose quarrels had exhausted them to the point of collapse, while the Germans summoned to the rescue had imposed their yoke on friend and foe alike.

Tacitus, *Histories*

STRABO

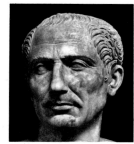

JULIUS CAESAR

PLINY THE ELDER

POSIDONIUS

ANCIENT STORIES RETOLD

The Irish sagas, the heroic tales of the Celts, were first written down by Christian scribes in monasteries in the early eighth century. The monasteries were the foremost, and for some while the only, oases of literacy in an otherwise illiterate world. Here scribes had the leisure to produce masterpieces of calligraphy like the colophon to St. Matthew's Gospel from Durham, England, a detail of which is shown below.

Top: The Celts had transmitted their sagas in oral tradition from one generation to another. References to these stories turn up very occasionally in decorative form, as for example on the Gundestrup caldron, which was found in a bog in Denmark. It evidently illustrates a narrative involving supernatural beings: the grotesque female shown here may be Queen Medb, a character who appears in the Ulster Cycle.

Opposite: Typical of the monastic art of medieval Ireland, this brilliant illuminated manuscript painting from the seventh-century Book of Durrow shows Celtic influence. This small volume of the Gospels was once owned by the Columban monastery of Barrow, near Tullamore, County Offaly, Ireland.

The Roman invasion of Britain, in the years between A.D. 43 and 84, imposed upon much of the country a veneer of classical civilization which was abruptly dispelled in the fifth century A.D. by Germanic invasions. The result of these two cultural incursions was that Celtic tradition was all but destroyed in the area soon to become England. In the remoter parts of the west, however—in Cornwall, Wales, and Scotland—the Celtic language and elements of Celtic culture survived. But it was in Ireland, protected by the wild Irish Sea from the destructive effects of close contact with the European mainland, that the spirit of the Celts flourished and developed. While the rest of Britain was governed by Rome, Ireland was experiencing the rule of a flamboyant aristocracy whose exploits were extolled in a series of ballads and poems which together form one of the great heroic traditions of European literature.

For centuries these tales would have been retold at communal gatherings. They became an essential element of the folk memory of the people and were learned by rote until sometime in the eighth century A.D., when they began to be written down by scribes in the early Irish monasteries. In later medieval copies of these first transcriptions they come down to us today. Amid the mass of miscellaneous literary fragments recorded in these medieval manuscripts there are four cycles of stories. The first are mythological stories about the "Tribes of the Goddess Danann" *(Tuatha*

Dé Danann), an ancient race of gods who inhabited Ireland in pre-Celtic times. Then comes the Ulster cycle, which describes the exploits of King Conchobar and his followers including the famous Cú Chulainn, the Hound of Ulster. Third is the Fenian cycle concerning the dealings of Finn mac Cumaill and his son Oisín. Fourth and finally, several stories are concerned with the kings who traditionally reigned in the period from the third century B.C. until the eighth century A.D.

Of these the most informative is the Ulster cycle, which contains one of the greatest prose sagas of the ancient world, "The Cattle-Raid of Cooley" *(Táin Bó Cualnge)*. Although it did not take its final form until early in the eighth century, it is clear that it refers to a much earlier period and the storyteller has been at pains to retain the original flavor of the times. Ireland at this time was divided into four provinces *Ulaid* (Ulster), *Connachta* (Connacht), *Laigin* (Leinster), and *Mumu* (Munster). *Ulaid*, where the story is based, was ruled by a high king, Conchobar, whose court *(ráth)* was at Emain Macha near Armagh.

The society presented has remarkable similarities to Gaulish society at the time of Caesar and earlier. The methods of warfare, in particular, have an odd familiarity about them: the warriors are headstrong, courageous, and boastful. They fight in single combat or en masse, the noblemen in their chariots driven by charioteers; cattle raiding is a manly exploit, and head hunting an acceptable pursuit. There is much more besides. Noble women like Medb and Derdriu stand out as strong godlike personalities; the men are rounded individuals, fierce and brave at one moment, in fear and panic the next, while everywhere the gods are weaving a consistent skein of superstition throughout the narrative.

31

CELTIC SOCIETY

The prestige and wealth of the Celtic aristocratic class are evoked in this Gallo-Roman sculpture from the Paris area.

Opposite: Coin from the Danube region depicting a Celtic equestrian warrior. Ornate bronze sword handle from France, first century B.C.

They dine together in a circle,
with the most influential man in the center...
whether he surpass the others
in warlike skill, or nobility of family, or wealth.

Athenaeus

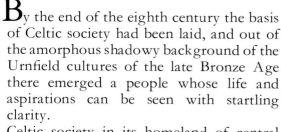

They terrified and fascinated their Greek and Roman neighbors, these "barbarian" inhabitants of the European heartland. They had no written history, not even a written language of their own, no dominant city-states to impose order and unity, no clear-cut boundaries. But as the shifting, roaming Celtic tribes began to settle, clustered here and there around a local chieftain in a natural hilltop defensive site, civilized life took shape. Their skills and resources were many: horsemanship, mastery of the wheel, mining, metalworking. This ingenuity gave them some control over a harsh environment and allowed for impressive cultural developments. They traded with the cultivated Mediterranean cities, accumulated surplus wealth, built stronger fortress-towns and ever more imposing tombs for their leaders.

Before this ancient Celtic world dispersed, to collide fatally with Rome, it enjoyed a brief flowering that has left enduring traces. Its tribes bequeathed a social structure across the centuries to the Irish Celts. Its hillforts were growing into cities and, by the time of the great collision, its craftsmen had become artists.

By the end of the eighth century the basis of Celtic society had been laid, and out of the amorphous shadowy background of the Urnfield cultures of the late Bronze Age there emerged a people whose life and aspirations can be seen with startling clarity.

Celtic society in its homeland of central and western Europe passed through three principal stages. At the beginning, ca. 700–400 B.C., its leaders were immensely rich. Into their hands passed societies' wealth gleaned from production and from the control of the networks of trade and exchange which developed in response to the demands of the classical world for raw materials. They lived in princely strongholds and were buried with their wealth in the traditional burial grounds of their dynasty. But all this was soon to pass: Towards the end of the fifth century a crisis arose as the result of which the old order collapsed and large sections of the population began to migrate southward to Italy and east to Greece and Anatolia. Soon after 200 B.C. the migrations were at an end and society gradually readjusted to a more organized and sedentary way of life, developing a thoroughly urban economy. In this section we start by looking at the flamboyant princely society of the early period known only through archaeological evidence, taking the story up to the moment when the great migrations get under way. The course of the invasions and the retrenchments and retreats which follow are the subject of another chapter (pp. 126–159). Here we must pause to look at the Celts in detail, their physical appearance, dress, their weapons and warfare, and the organization of their society. It is probably true that no barbarian people in the prehistory of the Old World has been so fully described. They were a menace to Greece and Rome—a people to be feared but also respected. In a world growing increasingly enervated by luxury, the Celts were a people to whom the classical writers could look in wistful envy. In consequence they were frequently presented as the "noble savage" contrasting with the decadence of the times. Such an approach necessarily colored objectivity, yet if we carefully skim off the polemic and reassemble the fragments, the Celts emerge resplendent in their energy, fearfully courageous, and yet doomed to failure.

The three centuries from about 700 to 400 B.C. saw the emergence and the fall of a rich aristocratic culture in the very heart of the Celtic world occupying a zone stretching from Bohemia to Burgundy. While the peasant population were, for the most part, still being buried in simple cremation graves in the old Urnfield tradition, their leaders were being carried to their tombs on beautifully carpentered funerary carts drawn by two horses, and inhumed in timber-built graves beneath great barrows, together with their luxurious possessions.

There are striking similarities between the burial of the rich Hallstatt chieftains and the old established rituals long practiced farther east in the area of the Pontic steppes: Inhumation, wooden vehicles, horses, rich grave goods, plank-built grave

but they represent only one element in a rapidly changing society. Alongside them, often in the same cemeteries but in much larger numbers, are the graves of warriors, each man buried with his long sword of bronze or iron. Some were otherwise unaccompanied or were perhaps provided with a joint of pork and a knife to eat it with; others would have in addition an array of vessels in pottery and bronze; while the richer graves would contain the harness of the dead man's horse. In other words, within the material derived from the many hundreds of graves of this period excavated in Czechoslovakia and southern Germany, it is possible to detect a closely stratified society based on the prowess of the warrior and ruled by a hierarchy whose social position provided the power which enabled them to grow rich.

THE EARLY CHIEFTAINS

chambers, and large barrows are all characteristics which can be found among the Scythians of the period. So impressive are the parallels that some archaeologists have been led to believe that the Hallstatt chieftains were actually a dynasty of Pontic horsemen who traveled westward and set themselves up as overlords. But when one looks closely at late Urnfield society, all the significant elements can already be distinguished—the increasing use of horses, burial carts, and a growing disparity between the rich and poor. The emergence of the Hallstatt chieftains is, then, the culmination of a process of socio-political change which had its roots in the past. What is new is the greatly increased differential in wealth and the desire to demonstrate, even to monumentalize, this. The rich burials of this early Hallstatt period (Hallstatt C) are concentrated in the east of the region, in Bohemia and Bavaria,

The sixth century saw a distinct shift in the focus of the rich aristocratic burials farther west to the zone between Stuttgart and Zurich, the Jura, and the Côte d'Or (Burgundy). One reason for this change in the center of wealth probably lies in the foundation of the Greek trading port of Massilia (Marseilles) close to the mouth of the Rhone. The port would have provided the principal funnel by which trade and reciprocal exchange was facilitated between the civilized Mediterranean world and the Celtic, barbarian, hinterland (see pp. 38–39). Those barbarian communities, by virtue of their positions on trade routes or because of the commodities and mineral wealth which they could command, were able to engage in this lucrative contact and to accumulate wealth which, because of their social structure, soon became concentrated in the hands of the aristocracy.

By the middle of the fifth century another shift of focus north and west can be detected: the richer aristocratic graves are now concentrated on the Middle Rhine and in the Marne area of northern France. Why this movement should have taken place is not immediately apparent, but it may in part have resulted from a reorientation of trade routes which came about in the early fifth century when the Etruscans extended their power across the Apennines into the Po valley and began to trade directly with the Celts through the Alpine passes. From the distribution of imported Etruscan wine flagons among the barbarians it would seem that the new trade routes bypassed Burgundy, Jura, and the upper Danube and dealt directly with the new power complexes on the Middle Rhine and the Marne. While a shift in power may have been affect-

ed by developing Etruscan trading patterns, there may well have been other more direct causes which we can no longer isolate—perhaps land exhaustion and increasing population led to a migration, or maybe there was a change in political power brought about by some internal struggle. We are unlikely ever to know for certain. The fact, however, remains that in these fifth-century centers of power and wealth

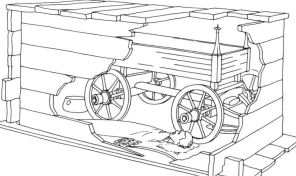

Burial chamber of a wealthy Celtic warrior, laid to rest beside his funerary cart, his archer's equipment, and other possessions. This reconstruction sketch depicts one of the many wooden graves in the great aristocratic burial mound of Hohmichele in the Heuneburg region of southern Germany, dating to the sixth century B.C.

Below left: An elaborately decorated dagger from a chieftain's grave at Magdalenberg.

The focus of the rich aristocratic burials of the seventh to fifth century changed with time: there seems to have been a consistent move to the west and north away from the original center in Bohemia and the Upper Danube. The map emphasizes how small was the territory within the total Celtic area which was dominated by the wealthy aristocracy. Elsewhere there were many hundreds, even thousands, of burials, but none with the range of luxury objects found in the central region.

on the Rhine and the Marne we see the last and most brilliant flowering of early Celtic aristocratic culture. No longer were imported luxuries—the Etruscan wine-drinking equipment and Greek red-figured vases—considered sufficient in their own right, but in addition there developed, in the courts of the rich, an entirely new lively art style.

Opposite page:
A variety of opulent goods from the Greek world found their way into the courts and the graves of the Celtic chieftains. The bronze hydria, a water or wine vessel some 60 centimeters (24 inches) high, from Grächwil, Switzerland, shows Greek-style decoration; early sixth century B.C.
The small Scythian horseman is a fourth-century gold collar ornament from Kul Oba.

35

WEALTH AND POWER

Of the centers of wealth and power in the Hallstatt and early La Tène world, two stand out above all others: Mont Lassois in the upper valley of the Seine, and the Heuneburg on the edge of the Swabian Alb overlooking the upper Danube. Both commanded important trade routes and both developed during the sixth century as the centers of wealthy aristocratic chiefdoms. About the site of Mont Lassois comparatively little is known because large-scale excavations have not yet been undertaken. Today the site stands out as an isolated hill dominating the route leading from the Rhone valley to the Seine. It is enclosed by defensive earthworks within which trial excavations have produced ample evidence of the wealth of the community: hundreds

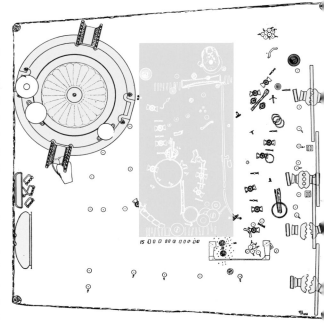

The huge bronze krater, 1.64 meters in height, found in the Vix burial chamber (see plan above). This wine vessel was so large that it had to be transported from the Mediterranean in sections and assembled on site. It is even possible that the Greek master craftsman traveled with his creation and put it together himself. Only one other vessel of this kind has been found, again in a barbarian grave, at Trebeniste in Yugoslavia. Both were probably made specifically for export. They were diplomatic gifts to satisfy barbarian taste.

Above right: Detail from the neck of the Vix krater.

of brooches, ornate locally made pottery, and a range of exotic imports including shards of Greek black-figured pottery and fragments of amphorae in which the Mediterranean wine was imported. There can be little doubt that the occupants enjoyed a level of luxury denied to the rest of the population.

Within sight of Mont Lassois, near the village of Vix, French archaeologists uncovered what must rank as one of the greatest archaeological discoveries in barbarian Europe—the tomb of a woman, quite possibly a member of the ruling hierarchy, filled with objects of outstanding value dating to the end of the sixth century. The burial was housed in a timber chamber beneath a vast barrow 42 meters in diameter and more than 6 meters high. The female, judged to have been about 35 years old, lay in the center of the chamber decked

out in her finery. The date of the burial is indicated by the objects found in it: one of the bronze basins was very similar to one found in a tomb in Tarquinia dated 520 B.C.; of the Greek cups one was made between 530 and 520, the other between 520 and 515. Thus it is probable that the woman was buried sometime within the last twenty years or so of the sixth century. The lavish care with which the "princess" of Vix was buried is a reminder of the high regard with which women could be held in Celtic society. Much the same impression is gained from the great burial mound of Hochmichele, near Hundersingen close to the stronghold of Heuneburg. Here excavations were able to show that the principal burial, though robbed in antiquity, had once housed the body of a woman wearing amber and glass beads. She had been accompanied by her funeral

36

Floor plan of the magnificent tomb uncovered at Vix, near Châtillon-sur-Seine, France, in 1953.

The sixth-century Vix burial chamber contained, in the center, the skeleton of a woman who had died at the age of thirty to thirty-five years. Her remains were surrounded by considerable quantities of jewelry, including bracelets, torques, brooches, a necklace, and a golden diadem.

At the upper left of the chamber were the large krater (see photograph opposite) and several cups.

The area at the right contained the four detached wheels of the funerary cart. The skeleton, at center, lay on the chassis of this cart.

another as the courts of the local aristocracy, but our knowledge is restricted to the former where an extensive program of large-scale excavation has recently been completed. It was to the late Hallstatt (Hallstatt D) period that the principal occupation belongs. The most remarkable aspect of the settlement was that in one phase (Heuneburg IV) the fortifications were rebuilt in a style totally alien to barbarian Europe: A stone foundation 3 meters broad was laid to support a wall of sun-dried mud bricks, some 4 meters in height, and along one side it was protected at regular intervals by forward-projecting rectangular bastions. Every detail has a foreign appearance, and we can only assume that the entire work was erected under the direction

The Heuneburg, in southern Germany overlooking the Danube, became the strongly defended seat of a noble Celtic family in the late sixth and early fifth centuries. Exotic imports such as wine and fine pottery were acquired from the Mediterranean, while the local craftsmen produced a range of jewelry and high-quality pottery of native inspiration. The site had been defended in the Bronze Age and was fortified again later in the Middle Ages.

cart and the chamber had been decked out with finely woven fabrics. Nearby and undisturbed was a smaller chamber in which a man and woman had been interred on an ox hide, the man accompanied by his bow and quiver of arrows (pp. 34–35). In an adjacent chamber was another man, this time with a spear. In all, a total of thirteen burials were discovered in the mound. The elaboration of this tomb, carrying with it the possibility that some of the bodies found were those of servants or retainers ritually slaughtered to accompany the dead leader to the grave, gives an impression of the pomp and ritual which must have attended the burials of the Celtic aristocracy.

The Hochmichele cemetery is close to two strongly defended hillforts, the Little Heuneburg and the Great Heuneburg. Both are likely to have served at one time or

of a man thoroughly conversant with Greek building techniques. That mud-brick architecture proved totally unsuitable in a north European climate is shown by the fact that the defenses were soon rebuilt as timber-laced earthworks in traditional Celtic manner.

Inside the stronghold excavations have shown the interior to have been densely built up with large timber houses and workshops replaced by new structures at frequent intervals. The occupants clearly enjoyed a standard of luxury comparable to that of the lords of Mont Lassois: Locally made jewelry was plentiful, wine and Greek painted pottery were imported, while local potters copied Etruscan black (bucchero) vessels and made elegant red, black, and white painted vessels of their own. The dynasty was short-lived, but must have been a source of wonder to the peasants.

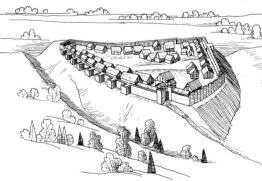

An overlay on the photograph of the Heuneburg, above, indicates the fortifications of this site in the Hallstatt period. The sketch (directly above) gives some idea of the unusual Greek-style mud brick wall, some four meters high, with projecting bastions.

THE MEETING OF TWO WORLDS

Throughout the eighth, seventh, and sixth centuries B.C. the Greek cities of mainland Greece and of western Anatolia were busy establishing colonies around the shores of the Mediterranean and the Black Sea. By 700 B.C. Sicily, southern Italy, and the Bay of Naples had been reached; by 600 B.C. colonists had extended to the western shores of the Black Sea and to the southern coast of France. By 480 B.C. the Black Sea was encircled, while in the Mediterranean colonies spread westward along the Mediterranean coast of Iberia.

The expansion and consolidation of Greek trading interests soon began to impinge upon those of their rivals, the Estruscans. For the Etruscans the situation was made worse by the growing power of the Carthaginians in the western Mediterranean and by the emerging Roman state much nearer

Wine, imported from the Mediterranean lands, was consumed in quantity in the Celtic world. "Many Italian merchants, with their usual desire for easy money, look on the Gallic love of wine as their treasure trove," said the historian Diodorus Siculus. He describes (see full quotation at right) the transport of wine by boat or wagon. This Gallo-Roman relief shows a river barge laden with wine casks. From Cabrières-d'Aygues, Vaucluse, in France.

to home. The crisis came to a head at the beginning of the fifth century, when the Strait of Messina between Sicily and Italy was closed to Etruscan shipping and, after the resounding defeats of two military expeditions, at Himera and Cumae (474), the cities of Etruria began to reorganize their trading patterns, reaching northward across the Po valley and through the Alps to the rich barbarian lands beyond.

Barbarian Europe had much to offer the cities of the Mediterranean. Of prime importance were rare metals like tin which could be got from Cornwall, Britanny, and northwest Iberia by means of a complex network of coastal and riverine routes.

And since the qualities
of the climate
are spoiled by the excess of cold,
the land bears
neither wine nor oil, and
therefore the Gauls,
being deprived of these fruits,
concoct a drink out of barley
called zythos (beer),
and they wash honeycombs
and use the washings as a drink.
They are
exeedingly fond of wine and
sate themselves
with the unmixed wine imported
by merchants;
their desire
makes them drink it greedily
and when they become drunk
they fall into a stupor or into
a maniacal disposition.
And therefore
many Italian merchants
with their usual love of lucre
look on the Gallic love of wine
as their treasure trove.
They transport the wine by boat
on the navigable rivers
and by wagon through the plains
and receive
in return for it
an incredibly large price;
for one jar of wine
they receive in return a slave,
a servant
in exchange for the drink.

Diodorus Siculus

Given the importance of tin (an essential component in bronze), it is easy to understand the prominence accorded to their western trade routes by the early Greek writers. Gold, silver, and bronze were to be had more widely. Amber from the Baltic

which the Celts made jewelry, and of course Mediterranean wine in quantity.

It would be wrong to think of the exchange of these commodities taking place according to modern methods of buying and selling. While there were undoubtedly reg-

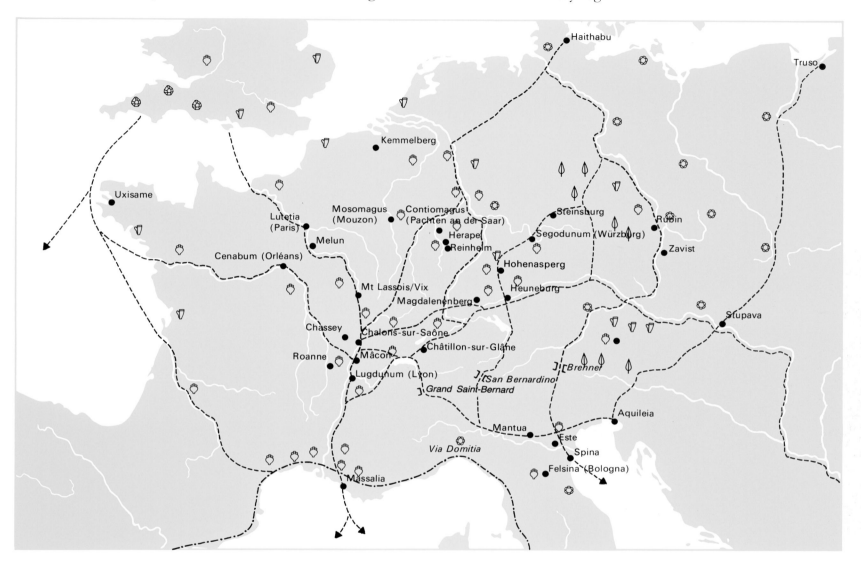

shores was a highly desirable commodity. There was also salt to be acquired from the salt deposits of Austria and Germany or from the western coastal salt works.

In addition to mineral extraction there were also items which leave less tangible remains in archeological terms: corn from the Scythian steppe lands, furs from the European forests, and no doubt a wide range of plant products. Nor should we forget that Strabo listed among the exports from Britain hunting dogs and slaves.

In return the classical world could offer manufactured goods like the bronze vessels and Attic pottery mentioned above as well as materials such as glass and coral, from

ular trading expeditions, like those which set out to acquire Cornish tin by barter from the natives, the process would generally have been more complex, involving reciprocal exchanges of various kinds between the Celtic tribesmen—exchanges determined by social mechanisms such as bride-price, gift exchange, and the payment of tithes. No doubt diplomatic gifts and payments made to secure rights of passage were another mechanism by which such exotic items as the Vix krater could enter the barbarian world.

⬥ Iron

⬥ Tin

⬥ Amphorae (proving trade with Greeks)

⬥ Amber

⬥ Salt production

Map showing the principal trade routes used by the Celts, as well as the Celtic commercial centers, in the eighth to sixth century B.C. Commodities and products are designated by symbols, as explained in the key.

REVOLUTION
AND MIGRATION

During the fifth century B.C. the political and social organization which supported the princely aristocracy of Germany and France began to break down. Wide disparities in wealth lessen considerably, many of the old strongholds go out of use (Heuneburg was burned), and there is increasing evidence of unrest and movement culminating, in the fourth and third centuries, in vast migrations which brought the Celts into conflict with the Romans, Greeks, and the Hellenistic rulers of Asia Minor.

To classical historians like Livy the migration of the Celtic peoples could be explained in simple terms (quotation at far right)—"excess of population" and "adventurous young men" were sufficient to provide both the cause and the means. But we must remember that Livy was attempting to explain to this audience a dimly remembered episode in terms which they would easily understand—not dissimilar to those used by historians to account for the Greek colonization of the Mediterranean. He was not presenting a reasoned socio-economic analysis; nor are we now in a position to do so. At best we can attempt to isolate some of the potentially relevant factors. At a simple economic level, we have seen that exchange mechanisms involving the Greeks via Massilia and later the Etruscans through the Alpine passes were responsible for providing the physical trappings of wealth. It is possible that the growing threat of Roman expansion through Etruria had a sufficiently disruptive effect on the Etruscan economy to deflect them from their northern markets. Rome, with the whole of the Mediterranean at its disposal, had little need of these markets. If this is so, it will have contributed to the changes now under way in barbarian Europe.

The society of the early chieftains was a society based on conspicuous consumption. Vast quantities of wine and no doubt food were dissipated at feasts, and each luxury object used must have represented a colossal expenditure of society's surplus consolidated in the hands of the aristocracy. If this surplus had been constantly redistributed (as it would appear to have been in, say, Minoan society), little problem would have arisen; instead it was ritually destroyed by being buried with the dead aristocrat. The amount of gold alone which was confined to the soil in two centuries or

so was staggering. It is highly unlikely that a primitive economy rooted to one location could have sustained such a level of consumption for long. But throughout the period of the early chieftains (700–400 B.C.) there was a constant shift of location which might, in part, have resulted from the overexploitation of the environment and the search for new productive land.

Another factor, clearly reflected in Livy's account, is population. Throughout the Late Bronze Age and into the Hallstatt period there is a considerable body of archaeological evidence to suggest an increase in population—the land is packed with settlement. In theory all the time that the carrying capacity of the environment can support the population there is little tension, but as soon as saturation point is reached and population approaches carrying capacity, society will begin to take preventive measures. The appearance of well-defined territories is one such measure, so clearly demonstrated in the archaeology of the chieftain settlements. Another procedure commonly adopted is for surplus population to be sent from the parent territory to colonize new areas. This is precisely what Livy believed to have happened with the Celts. His description perfectly fits the demographic model.

Inevitably, at a time of population increase, there was stress. That the Heuneburg was burned on several occasions is witness to the fact. The flagrant disparity in wealth, so evident in the archaeology of the period, cannot have failed to contribute to the tensions which built up in society. Ambitious younger sons of the aristocracy, had they wished to maintain their status, had no option but to gather a band of followers and move off to seek their fortunes, leaving the homeland in the hands of old men clinging to traditional ideals.

The picture of these times is far too complex for us ever to be able to reconstruct it in great detail.

The Celts are now on the threshold of history, but before we can follow them farther we must pause to discover, in the pages that follow, with what manner of men we are dealing.

Hemmed in by the great forests of the European plain to the north, the Atlantic to the west, and the Scythian settlement to the east, the Celts could migrate in only one direction: south through the Alpine passes into Italy and southeast through the territory of the Illyrians (Yugoslavia) to Greece and Anatolia. The Alpine passes like the St. Gotthard, Switzerland (shown here), were well known to them: Luxury goods of Mediterranean manufacture had long been imported over these mountain routes.

Contemporary descriptions supplemented by archaeological detail provide us with an intimate and fascinating picture of the Celts. We know not only what they produced, but how they lived.

Central to Celtic life was the feast. It was above all a time when the community could come together to reaffirm its oneness. The people could relive the glories of the past, display their hierarchies and loyalties, and communally enjoy the largess redistributed by their chieftains.

PROFILE OF THE CELTS

The caldron and the hearth formed the focal point of the feast. Bronze caldrons and iron caldron chains, together with flesh hooks for lifting the joint out of the stew, have been found on a number of archaeological sites. The reconstruction shown here from the museum of Asparn, near Vienna, is based on precise archaeological detail.

The classical writers are quite specific about Celtic feasts. It was the responsibility of kings to provide lavishly for their people. Posidonius (quoted by Athenaeus) tells us of the Gaulish king Louernius, who built a vast square enclosure within which "he filled vats with expensive liquor and prepared so great a quantity of food that for many days all who wished could enter and enjoy the feast prepared, being served without break by the attendants." How common such a display was in the Celtic world it is difficult to say, but for the most part feasts appear to have been more intimate and held indoors.

Drink was all important. "The drink of the wealthy class is wine imported from Italy or from the territory of Massilia. This is unadulterated, but sometimes a little water is added. The lower classes drink wheaten beer prepared with honey, but most people drink it without: it is called *cornia*" (Posidonius/Athenaeus). The communal nature of the gathering was further emphasized by drinking from a common cup carried from one person to another by a slave. "The slave serves the cup towards the right not towards the left"; they drink "a little at a time, not more than a mouthful—but they do it rather frequently!" Polybius too was impressed by Celtic capacity for alcohol.

Various foods would have been served. Strabo, writing of the Belgae, says, "They have large quantities of food together with all kinds of meat especially fresh and salt pork." The importance of pork to the diet is amply demonstrated by the evidence from graves, in many of which the dead man was provided with a joint of pork or even a whole pig for his first feast in the afterworld.

The scene inside the house is brilliantly set by Diodorus Siculus. Describing the participants, he goes on to say that "beside them are hearths blazing with fire, with caldrons and spits containing large pieces of meat. Brave warriors they honor with the finest portions of meat." This last point is amplified by Athenaeus, who says, "And in former times when the hindquarters were served up, the bravest hero took the thigh piece, and if another man claimed it they stood up and fought in single combat to death." Expanding upon the matter of single combat at feasts, he adds, "Assembling in arms they engage in mock battle-drill and mutual thrust and parry. But sometimes wounds are inflicted and the irritation caused by this may lead even to the slaying of the opponent unless bystanders hold them back."

Now this is a particularly fascinating series of observations. Athenaeus, or more correctly Posidonius from whom he was quoting, was interested only to record curiosities of behavior, but behind these comments it is possible to see something of the mechanisms of social order at work. First of all the person who considered himself the bravest hero took, or expected to be given, a particular cut of meat which demonstrated his assumed status to the assembled company. If the action passed without comment, his status was thus confirmed in the eyes of all, but if another man aspired to this position he could dispute the apportionment. Simulated combat might decide the issue, but the dispute could easily escalate and bloodshed ensue. In this simple ritual, then, we can recognize one of the procedures by which social status was acquired and confirmed.

The later Irish literature adds striking confirmation. In the story of *Bricriu's Feast (Fled Bricrenn)* the chief character Cú Chulainn has to contend with two other warriors for the "hero's portion." The same theme is reiterated in *The Story of Mac-*

Dathó's Pig (Scéla Mucce Meic Dathó). Here, amid showers of abuse and boasting one warrior after another claimed his right to carve the pig until Conall, having speared his rival in the chest "so that blood flowed from his mouth," took up his position with the carving knife. By keeping the best part for himself and giving only the forelegs to the Connacht men present, he insulted them sufficiently to provoke a fight. The result of the evening's entertainment was a pile of corpses on the floor and blood flowing through the doorway. In this particular tale the feast provides the vehicle for the aggression between the two groups (the men of Connacht and the Ulster-men) to be played out ritually. Although there is violence, it is at least contained.

> They also invite strangers
>   to their banquets,
> and only after the meal
>   do they ask who they are
> and of what they stand in need.
> At dinner they are wont to be moved
> by chance remarks to wordy disputes,
>   and to fight in single combat,
>   regarding their lives as naught.
>
> Diodorus Siculus

An important social event like a feast was circumscribed by formality. Athenaeus (quoting Posidonius) provides the details: "When a large number dine together they sit around in a circle with the most influential man in the center, like the leader of a chorus.... Beside him sits the host and next, on either side, the others in order of distinction. Their shieldsmen stand behind them while their spearmen are seated in a circle on the opposite side and feast in common like their lords." Clearly the seating plan was of great import if delicate susceptibilities were not to be upset.

The feast was also an occasion when the community could reminisce about the past —about its history and the exploits of its heroes—and could plan its future. It was no doubt on an occasion such as this that the professional bards would sing or recite the oral traditions of the tribe contained in the great sagas of the kind which survive in the Irish literature—partisan works lavishing praise upon the ancestors of the

audience. Diodorus Siculus tells us of these men. "They have lyric poets," he says, "whom they call Bards. They sing to the accompaniment of instruments resembling lyres, sometimes an eulogy and sometimes a satire." But the bards are not to be confused with men whose task it was to proclaim the praise of those present: "The Celts have in their company... companions whom they call parasites. These men pronounce their praises before the whole

assembly and before each of the chieftains in turn" (Athenaeus).

So something of the flavor of the Celtic feast emerges: noisy, drunken, bombastic, resounding with exaggerated boasting, redolent with threats, and often very dangerous. Yet it was an essential mechanism to hold society in check, an institution vital to the ordered functioning of the community.

The Celtic feast was a raucous, boastful affair. From the classical writers we learn that the Celts sat on the floor on skins or dried grass but had their food served on low wooden tables. A great deal of wine was consumed. The reconstruction above is by the Swiss painter, Mark Adrian.

PHYSICAL APPEARANCE

Above right: Celtic heads forming a decorative motif: their ferocious look, consistent with Greek and Roman descriptions of the Celts, is mitigated by the rather abstract treatment. Silver disk from Manerbio, northern Italy, third—second century B.C., probably a horse harness fitting.

Physical likenesses of the Celts, in various degrees of stylization, are found frequently throughout the Celtic world. This stone sculpture of a woman, a work of the first century B.C. or A.D. found in France, is sufficiently realistic and individualized to be a portrait study.

Opposite: Altogether different from the works shown above, this magnificent bronze of a young man is the work of an artist thoroughly schooled in Roman techniques. Yet his treatment of the hair, and the way the sideburns form flowing scrolls, show the Celtic spirit. This first-century A.D. work, found at Prilly, Switzerland, no doubt gives a faithful likeness.

The classical writers were all agreed that the Celts were a dramatic looking people, quite distinctive in their appearance. A miscellany of contemporary opinions will serve to set the scene:

"Almost all the Gauls are of tall stature, fair and ruddy, terrible for the fierceness of their eyes, fond of quarreling and of overbearing insolence" (Ammianus Marcellinus).

"Physically the Gauls are terrifying in appearance, with deep sounding and very harsh voices. The Gallic women are not only equal to their husbands in stature but rival them in strength as well" (Diodorus Siculus).

Queen Boudicca "was huge of frame and terrifying of aspect with a harsh voice. A great mass of bright red hair fell to her knees" (Dio Cassius).

To a dweller in the Mediterranean, then, these northern barbarians were tall, fair, well built, and with raucous sounding voices, but like all ethnic descriptions these generalizations must obscure the great underlying variety. Tacitus, a more perceptive observer, distinguished several types among the Britons: the inhabitants of Scotland with reddish hair and large limbs, the southern Welsh with swarthy faces and curly hair, and those occupying the southeast of the country who most resembled the Gauls. Here is a firm reminder that, while the Celts as a whole may have differed from the Mediterranean races in the lightness of their pigmentation and their greater bulk, there were many outlying groups who had developed distinctive characteristics sufficient to distinguish them from the generalized norm.

The classical observers were particularly interested in the Celts' treatment of their hair. There was evidently some variation. Diodorus Siculus says that some Celtic men wore short beards while others did not. He adds "the nobles shave the cheeks but let the moustache grow freely so that it covers the mouth." Writing of the Britons, however, Caesar tells us that "they wear their hair long and shave the whole of their bodies except the head and the upper lip." Strabo provides a particularly interesting detail: "Their hair is not only naturally blond, but they also use artificial means to increase this natural quality of color. For they continually wash their hair with limewash and draw it back from the forehead to the crown and to the nape of the neck, with the result that their appearance resembles that of Satyrs or of Pans, for their hair is so thickened by this treatment that it differs in no way from a horse's mane." To confront in battle a tall, heavy-limbed Celt with his hair standing out in a spiky mass must have been, to say the least, intimidating. (The Roman name for Gaul, Gallia Comata, meant the shaggy-haired Gauls!)

Personal appearance was clearly a matter of some concern to the Celt. Strabo mentions that to be fat was socially unacceptable, while the archaeological evidence shows that women used mirrors as well as tweezers, presumably for plucking hair. That they also used makeup is mentioned indirectly by the Roman poet Propertius who chides his mistress for painting herself like a Celt. The decoration of the body, though for more warlike pursuits, is also mentioned by Caesar in his famous account of the Britons, who dyed their bodies with woad which produced a blue color and made them appear more terrifying in battle. These varied accounts, borne out many times over by representations of the Celts in bronze and stone, endow the bones of the archaeological evidence with flesh and blood.

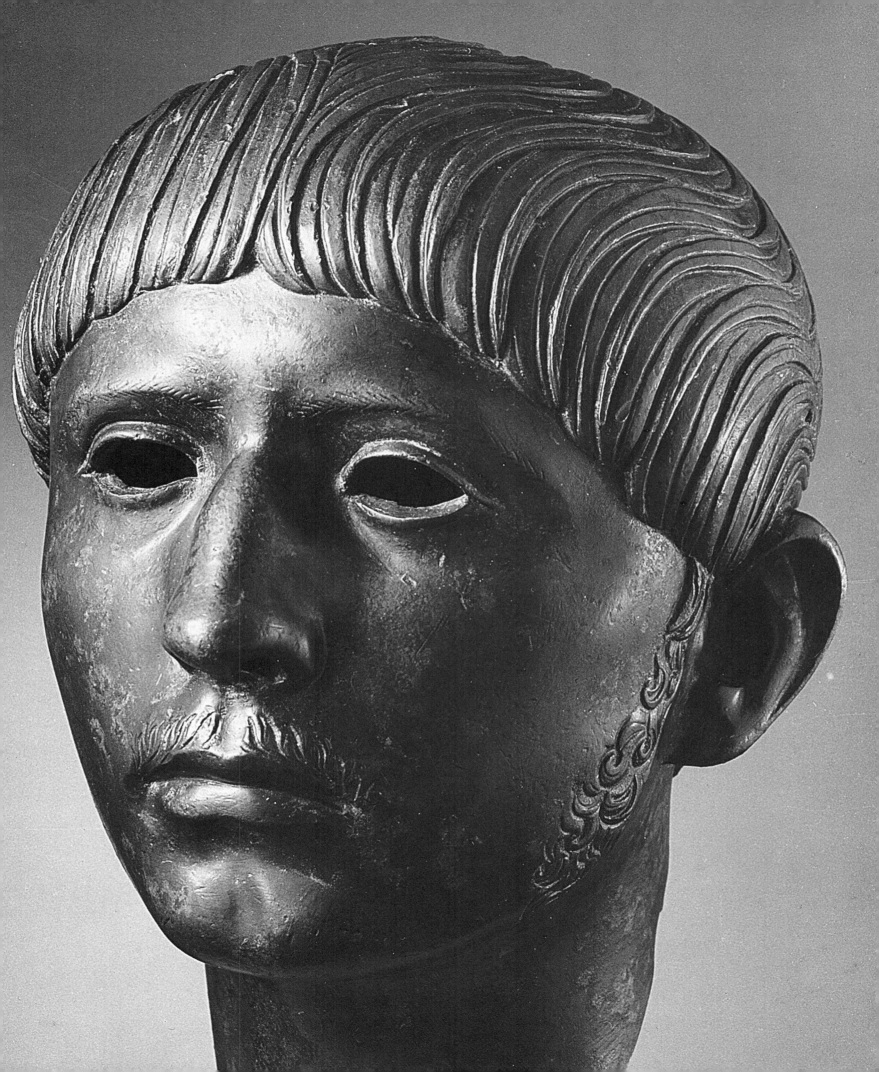

DRESS AND ARMS

The Celtic chieftain who dominates this page has been pieced together from a wide range of archaeological and literary evidence. Every significant detail in the reconstruction can be supported. Most of the evidence for ornaments and weapons comes from the excavation of graves and settlement sites. For details of clothing we have to rely largely on the accounts of the ancient historians, supported by the occasional sculptural representation.

Few pieces of Celtic art portray the people as vividly as this small bronze face mask *(above right),* with its swept-back hair and drooping mustache, from a late first-century B.C. grave at Welwyn in southern Britain.

Below: An elaborately decorated bronze clasp from a leather belt, dating to the early fourth century B.C., from Hölzelsau in Austria. Belts were almost always worn by men; women sometimes wore girdle chains composed entirely of bronze links.

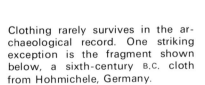

Clothing rarely survives in the archaeological record. One striking exception is the fragment shown below, a sixth-century B.C. cloth from Hohmichele, Germany.

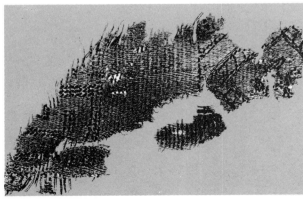

Far right: Neck torques had a magical significance. Sometimes the Celt would go into battle naked but for his neck torque, which he believed would protect him from danger. The great silver torque from Trichtingen, Germany, dating to the second century B.C., may have been made for a cult figure. It was probably too heavy to wear.

Above and at right: Gold bracelets or arm rings were popular among the aristocracy. They were usually elaborately decorated by Celtic craftsmen working in the courts of the aristocracy. The example shown above is from the rich grave of Waldalgesheim, Germany. At right, gold bracelets from a hoard discovered at Erstfeld, Switzerland. All three are from the fourth century B.C.

Above: Brooches *(fibulae)* were used to fasten cloaks at the breast or on the shoulder. They were often worn in pairs joined by a chain. The left-hand example, in silver, comes from Switzerland. The other two, in bronze, are German.

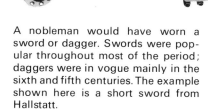
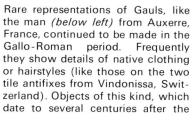

Comparatively little is known of clothing from archaeological evidence, but the classical writers refer to Celtic trousers, tunics, and cloaks and tell us that they were often brightly colored. It is possible that the tartans of the Scottish clans continue the Celtic tradition.

A nobleman would have worn a sword or dagger. Swords were popular throughout most of the period; daggers were in vogue mainly in the sixth and fifth centuries. The example shown here is a short sword from Hallstatt.

Rare representations of Gauls, like the man *(below left)* from Auxerre, France, continued to be made in the Gallo-Roman period. Frequently they show details of native clothing or hairstyles (like those on the two tile antifixes from Vindonissa, Switzerland). Objects of this kind, which date to several centuries after the

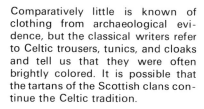

end of Gaulish independence, demonstrate the tenacity of Celtic culture.

THE ORGANIZATION OF THE TRIBE

Those tribes
which are regarded
as enjoying good government
have a solemn ordinance
that any rumor
or news of state interest
which comes
from a neighboring tribe,
must be brought
to a magistrate
and shared
with no one else.

Caesar

Caesar clearly recognized the difference between the noble class, which included the men of learning, and the rest, but he was not specific about the important distinction between the free and unfree, which must surely have existed. His reticence may be explained by the fact that neither of these classes would have been of any significance to him in his wars.

The one important point of difference between Irish and Gallic society is that among some of the more civilized Celtic tribes the institution of kingship had been abandoned by Caesar's time, the leadership of the community now being placed in the hands of an annually elected chief magistrate *(vergobret)*.

Caesar's comment quoted above makes reference to clients and dependents. This institution was of crucial importance to Celtic society. In essence, a commoner attached himself voluntarily to a nobleman,

providing armed attendance when demanded in return for protection. But the relationship also had an economic significance. The lord (who did not himself engage in food production) owned cattle which he would grant on loan to his clients in return for a fixed rent in kind and in service. In Irish law, for example, the annual rent for six cows was a calf, a salted pig, three sacks of malt, half a sack of wheat, and a handful of rush candles. In this way the food produced by the free commoners was redistributed to the nonproductive aristocrats, cattle forming the medium by which the process was carried out. As Caesar was at pains to point out, the rank of a nobleman was directly related to his following of clients. A man with many clients who all owed him allegiance could field a large force when it came to organizing a raid. And since a successful raid would bring a man more cattle, which could be invested in additional clients, society provided the mechanism by which the aristocracy could maintain its hold and increase its power.

The Irish literature provides an intimate picture of the intricacies of Celtic tribal organization in the first millennium A.D. The tribe *(túath)* was ruled by a king *(rí)* through a general assembly of the people *(óenach)* which usually met once a year in the open countryside often amid the ancestral tombs. Society was rigidly divided into three classes: the Nobles, the Freecommoners, and the Unfree; and within each class there were grades of status which were formalized by each free man having a carefully defined *honor price*. This formed the basis of any assessment for compensation which might, for example, have to be paid to him or his family in the event of insult, injury, or death.

Tribal or family life is seldom depicted in Celtic or Gallo-Roman art. The heads which appeared on coinage, like the stater of the Andecavi *(above)*, are intended to represent the kings though usually they are very stylized

Motherhood is occasionally represented in religious sculpture. The delicate relief of the "Three Mothers," a commonly recurring triad of deities, from the town of Vertillum, in Burgundy *(top, and detail at right)*, provides a Gallo-Roman version.

Opposite page: The three cloaked figures, from the Roman fort of Housteads on Hadrian's Wall in northern Britain, are probably also a triad of local deities. The recurrence of the group of three reflects Celtic belief in strength in numbers.

Within the Noble class were placed, in addition to the warriors, the specialists and master craftsmen (*oesdána*), the jurists, the doctors, the carpenters, the metal workers, and the men of learning—the bards and the priests. The Freecommoners comprised the peasant farmers and the craftsmen of lesser ability. Together they formed the productive level of society providing the surplus upon which the aristocrats, and those serving their needs, could be maintained. Finally there was the amorphous mass of the Unfree, the families who had been degraded, subjugated communities, and slaves. These groups provided the bulk of the labor.

This outline of Irish society seems to be very similar to the situation in Gaul which Caesar describes, with one notable exception which will be considered later. "Throughout Gaul," he says, "there are two classes of men of some dignity and

importance. The common people are nearly regarded as slaves; they possess no initiative and their views are never invited on any question." He goes on to discuss the two upper classes, the Druids (the learned men whom we will consider in detail later, pp. 106ff) and the Knights who "all take part in war whenever there is need and war is declared. The greater their rank and resources, the more dependents and clients do they possess. This is their only source of influence and power."

The Family

The tribe was composed of a number of kins or families, which in Irish and Welsh law were considered to extend to four generations. The basic family unit for practical purposes consisted of the man and his wife or wives, along with their children with their wives and any children (and possibly also grandchildren): the grouping known as the *gelfine* (see chart at right). The family or kin could also be defined much more broadly, to include all the members of older generations and their descendants (as in the other groupings in the chart). The most frequent grouping for legal matters was the four-generation *derbfine*: the descendants of a common great-grandfather.

Land was held in common by the kin and distributed for use among the individual families, and when there were goods to be inherited or fines to be paid, all members of the *derbfine* were expected to share.

Kingship was based on a similar social unit: any male member of the royal family was eligible to succeed. Marriages usually took place outside the *derbfine*, and in the case of the royal household they were probably contracted outside the *túath*. An institution of great importance was that of fosterage. Children (both sexes) were placed in the care of foster parents whose responsibility it was to train the children in adult skills. In Irish law a boy would return home at seventeen, a girl at fourteen. The ties made during this period, especially between foster brothers, were particularly binding.

GELFINE

Man (A) and wife

This basic family group includes a man and wife (*above*), plus the generations of their direct descendants (*below*). Thus the row of four

couples here symbolizes the son, grandson, great-grandson, and great-great-grandson (with their wives) of the man A and his wife.

Broader groups can be associated with the basic line of the *gelfine*. The *derbfine*, for example, includes the *gelfine*, but starts one generation

DERBFINE

earlier with the father of the man A, plus the brothers of A and each brother's direct descendants for two more generations.

IARFINE

Extending the family still wider, the *iarfine* begins with the grandfather of A, to include the two groups shown above, plus another direct line descending from the grandfather of A for four generations.

INDFINE

The largest grouping includes the groups shown above, plus the great-grandfather of A and three generations of his direct descendants.

For their journeys and
in battle
they use two-horse chariots,
the chariot carrying
both charioteer and chieftain.
When they meet with
cavalry in the battle
they cast their javelins
at the enemy
and then descending
from the chariot
join battle with their swords.

Diodorus Siculus

A Nation of Horsemen

Surely the most brilliant representation of the spirit of the horse: a design carved through the turf to the underlying chalk on a hillside near the fort of Uffington in southern Britain. The White Horse, some 110

The horse was essential to the Celts, both in war and in peace. The Greek and Roman historians naturally emphasized its military aspects, but this gives a very one-sided impression. When we look at other kinds of evidence, we find the horse everywhere present: in the graves and in the farmstead, on coins, and in one unique and resplendent example (shown on this page), on the British chalk hill at Uffington, carved into the landscape itself. We must weigh all the evidence if we are to understand how the horse could emerge so dramatically into the military arena, to terrify the armies of Caesar.

There is little doubt that the domesticated horse had been introduced into Europe before the emergence of the Celts (and it has been suggested that the horse may have been harnessed as far back as Upper Paleolithic times). In the Later Bronze Age of central Europe, horses would have been

700 B.C. The fact that much of the horse gear of this period bears strong similarities to that in use among the horse-riding communities occupying the Pontic steppes—the natural home of the horse—suggests that there may well have been a sudden influx of eastern horses, complete with gear, into central and western Europe at this time. There is no need to explain this phenomenon as an actual invasion. On present evidence it is more likely to result from a new pattern of reciprocal exchange, following the movement of people from the Pontic steppes into the Great Hungarian Plain. For the Celtic aristocracy the horse became a symbol of prestige and was eagerly acquired.

In many of the rich Hallstatt and early La Tène graves, as we have seen, the funeral cart which carried the dead aristocrat to the tomb was interred with him; so too were the harnesses of the horses that were yoked to the vehicle—but not the horses themselves. Either the horse was too valuable a commodity to be killed or, more likely, the ritual precluded horse burial. This is in striking contrast to the burials of the horse-riding communities who now inhabited the eastern parts of Hungary. A number of the Hallstatt graves have produced three sets of harness fittings; two

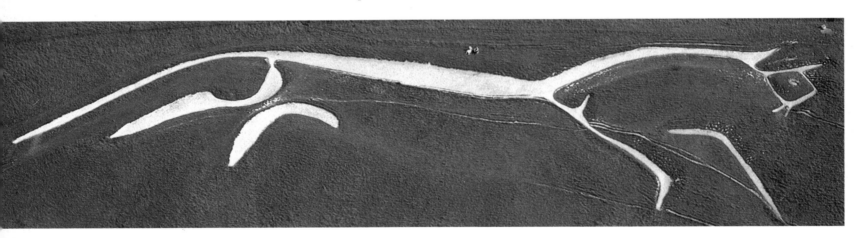

meters long, probably dates to the first century B.C. The scouring of the white horse was carried out annually by the local population until comparatively recently.

Opposite: This Gallo-Roman sculpture from Portieux, Vosges, France, though of native workmanship, attempts a realistic representation of the horse. The group symbolizes the victory of heavenly powers over the underworld.

extensively used for traction, harnessed in yokes with bridles of leather and mouthpieces probably of leather, and with side pieces of wood or occasionally bone. Towards the end of the Urnfield period bronze harness fittings start to become more common, and with the beginning of the Hallstatt C period, Europe is swamped in bronze horse gear.

All this would seem to imply that horses suddenly came more widely into use about

were for the draught animals, and the third presumably for the chieftain's riding horse. Although horse riding is sporadically attested heretofore in central and western Europe, this is the first clear evidence that it has now become widespread. The long slashing sword which at this time became popular—a type particularly suitable for fighting from horseback—is an added reminder that cavalry now played an important part in Celtic warfare. The scene of

Horses are sometimes depicted as the bearers of deities. The goddess Epona *(right)* is shown riding side-saddle, on this Gallo-Roman relief from Altbachtal (Rheinland). The unknown rider god *(far right)*, probably of Thracian origin, was found at Whitcombe in Dorset, England.

A lively trade in horses must have developed in Celtic Europe. This Gallo-Roman relief from Dijon, France, shows a cloaked horse trader at work. Many beasts were probably obtained through exchange mecha-

nisms from the steppes via eastern Europe, but horse breeding must have been carried out by most communities, so that the breaking of young horses was a common scene.

Below: Two beautiful Gallo-Roman bronzes of spirited young foals: from Châlon-sur-Marne, France, and *(at right)* from Aventicum, in Switzerland.

the four horsemen on the scabbard from Hallstatt (pp. 24–25) shows that the lance was also a favored cavalry weapon.

By the end of the seventh century, then, we can be tolerably certain that fighting from horseback was a significant element in Celtic life. The horse was also used to pull war chariots, but this, as part of the battle, will be considered in more detail below (pp. 54–55). In the works of the classical writers, charioteering greatly overshadowed fighting from horseback. While this may reflect merely the novelty of chariot warfare in classical eyes, it may well imply that in the third and second centuries B.C. cavalry played only a subservient part in warfare. An interesting Celtic institution is, however, referred to by Pausanius when he writes of the *trimarcisia*—a unit of three riders consisting of a nobleman and two attendants, much like the knight and squire of the Middle Ages. The function of these attendants was to look after their lord and provide him with a new horse if necessary. It is possible that a similar institution was in force among the Brigantes of Yorkshire in the first century A.D. We hear that Queen Cartimandua insulted her husband Venutius by running off with his armor bearer.

If this man had been a member of Venutius's *trimarcisia*, then by seducing him Cartimandua had greatly weakened her ex-husband's fighting efficiency.

By the time that Caesar was fighting his way through Gaul, chariot warfare was a thing of the past: he encountered only infrantry and cavalry. As the Celts came increasingly into contact with the classical world, so their fighting methods were modified. The importance of cavalry is many times emphasized by Caesar. Of King Dumnorix, Caesar says, "He maintained at his own expense a considerable force of cavalry which he kept in attendance upon him"—a nobleman with a personal squadron of well-trained horsemen would have been a formidable foe. Of cavalry tactics we learn a little from Caesar's battle against the Nervii in 57 B.C. Although we are told that the Nervii had practically no cavalry, the few they deployed were put to good use against the Romans. "Our cavalry [i.e., the Romans] crossed the river with the slingers and archers and engaged the enemy's horsemen. These kept retiring into the wood where their comrades were and then reappearing to charge our troops who dared not pursue them beyond the end of

the open ground." Here the horsemen were used as an irritant to distract the Romans before the battle proper ensued. They could, however, be used more aggressively to break their opponents' ranks.

As the result of a rabble-rousing speech given by the Celtic war leader Vercingetorix, as a prelude to a set piece engagement with Caesar, his horsemen cried that they would swear a solemn oath not to allow any man who had not ridden twice through the enemy's column to enter his home again or to see his relatives. In the event, the onslaught failed and the cavalry fled, afraid of being surrounded, only to be hacked down all over the field.

A motif much favored on Celtic coins: Ultimately the inspiration came from Hellenistic prototypes, but Celtic die cutters interpreted the horse in their own style, sometimes reducing it to its constituent elements in a pleasing abstract design. Shown here are coins from different tribes of the Celtic world: the Unelli *(left)*, Parisii *(above)*, and coins from the Atrebates, the Jura area, and *(bottom)* Romania.

The Celtiberians of western Spain, renowned for their horsemanship, were readily employed by the Romans as cavalry auxiliaries. This small cult wagon in bronze comes from Mérida in Spain, second—first century B.C.

The classical writers were particularly impressed by the effectiveness of the Celtic chariot in warfare. Chariots were not new to Europe at this time; examples have been found in Sweden depicted on tombs of the tenth century B.C., and were well known to the Mycenaean Greeks. In the hands of the Celts of the third and second centuries the chariot came into its own as a formidable and highly effective item of military equipment. By the middle of the first century B.C., however, when Caesar was making his way through Gaul, new methods of cavalry fighting had replaced the old and not until he set foot on the remote and backward island of Britain did he encounter chariots, apparently for the first time. His shrewd military assessment of them cannot be bettered. He starts by describing how in chariot warfare the Britons begin by driving all over the field hurling javelins and causing as much pandemonium as possible. "Then after making their way between the squadrons of their own cavalry, they jump down from

check and return them in a moment. They can run along the chariot pole, stand on the yoke, and get back into the chariot as quick as lightning." When it is remembered that Cassivellaunus, the local resistance leader, was able to command four thousand

chariots, the nature of Caesar's difficulties can more easily be appreciated.

Chariots were used in all the subsequent major battles between the Romans and the Britons and as late as A.D. 84, when Agricola was fighting in the north of Scotland, we still read of the noise of the maneuvering chariots in the field between the two armies drawn up in readiness for the battle. Agricola's cavalry squadrons easily routed the war chariots and one of the last vignettes we are given is of the runaway chariots and the riderless horses of the cavalry wheeling about in their terror and plunging head-on into the ranks of the infantry.

The literary evidence, with all its vivid detail, is supported by other types of data. Chariots driven by wild-haired Celts are a favorite motif for the reverses of Celtic coins, while pieces of chariots, invariably the bronze and iron fittings, have been recovered from a variety of contexts ranging from burial chambers to ritual deposits in bogs. From all these scraps it is possible to build up a detailed picture of the Celtic chariot. Two-wheeled, strong in structure, pared down to the minimum, it was, in trained hands, quite lethal.

Chariot warfare earned the Celts a particularly terrifying reputation, and inspired a great diversity of artistic representations. This clay model of a horse-drawn chariot is among the earliest portrayals of a horse-drawn vehicle found in Europe. From Grosseto province, central Italy, possibly as early as the ninth century B.C.

the chariots and fight on foot. In the meantime their charioteers retire a short distance from the battle and place the chariots in such a position that their masters, if hard pressed by numbers, have an easy means of retreat to their own lines." Thus, he concludes, with a soldier's admiration, "they combine the mobility of cavalry with the staying power of infantry."

The immense skill of the charioteers evidently made a deep impression on him. He describes how by daily training and practice they became so proficient that "even on a steep incline they are able to control the horses at full gallop and to

Chariot scenes abound on Gallic and Roman coins. The two Roman examples shown at left present an interesting contrast to the flamboyant Celtic interpretation *(below left)*.

The reconstruction below, in the National Museum of Wales, is based on a large hoard of chariot fittings found in a bog at Llyn Cerrig Bach in Anglesea. The hoard dates to the first century A.D.

ARMS, ARMOR AND WARFARE

Celtic warfare changed dramatically over the centuries. The violent and ill-organized onslaughts of the fourth and third centuries have little in common with the carefully planned campaigns fought by the Gauls against Caesar in the first century. Such a change was the inevitable result of the contact between the two peoples. Here we will be concerned with the more archaic form of Celtic warfare viewed through the eyes of men writing of events on the Italian peninsula from the third to the first century. Strabo, with evident fascination, describes

the armor of a typical Celt. He carries, he says, "a long sword fastened on the right side and a long shield, and spears of like dimension, and the *madaris* which is a kind of javelin. There is also a wooden weapon resembling a 'grosphus' which is thrown by hand... with a range greater than that of an arrow." He also mentions the use of bows and slings but implies that they were of only limited importance.

Swords and spears of various types are well attested in the archaeological record. We learn from Diodorus Siculus something of the subtlety of the Celtic spear. Some of the javelins, he says, were forged with a straight head while some are twisted with breaks throughout the entire length so that the blow not only cuts but also tears the flesh—the recovery of the weapon ripping open the wound.

For protection the warrior carried an oval-shaped shield in his left hand of sufficient size to cover most of the body. The majority of them were made of wickerwork or of two planks joined together. They may also have been covered with leather to give added strength or, more rarely, with bronze, but shields of this kind were designed for display rather than active fight-

ing. Helmets were also worn, the majority of them probably being of leather.

The more wealthy warriors could have afforded to adorn themselves with bronze helmets of the kind which Diodorus Siculus so vividly describes: "On their heads they wear bronze helmets which possess projecting figures lending the appearance of enormous stature to the wearer. In some cases horns form one piece with the helmet while in other cases it is the relief figures or the fore parts of birds or quadrupeds." Helmets of this kind have been found from time to time (p. 59) and are shown worn by the riders depicted on the Gunderstrup caldron (p. 25)—a very satisfying example of how literary, archaeological, and illustrative evidence come together in mutual support.

Celtic warfare was not complete without noise—noise from the yelling warriors, from the beating of the sides of their carts and wagons, and from their war trumpets. "Their trumpets," says Diodorus, "are of a peculiar barbaric kind. They blow into them and produce a harsh sound which suits the tumult of war." Trumpets of this kind, the carynx, are beautifully illustrated on the Gundestrup caldron (p. 56) as well as on coins, and actual examples have been found in Britain.

The Celt is now ready for battle—hot-headed, excitable, but totally without coordination. "The whole race is war-mad, high-spirited and quick to battle," writes Strabo.

And when they are stirred up they assemble in their bands for battle quite openly and without forethought, and so they are easily handled by those who desire to outwit them. For at any time or place, and on whatever pretext you stir them up, you will have them ready to face danger, even if they have nothing on their side but their own strength and courage.

The easily provoked Celt, however brave, was no match for a cold, calculating Roman commander.

We have already seen that the feast provided the institution by which disputes within the tribe could be settled or at least contained. At a different level the battle, in early Celtic warfare, allowed intertribal differences to be displayed and resolved, sometimes without much bloodshed. A most interesting description of Celtic battle procedure, which allows us to consider these matters more fully, is given by Diodorus Siculus and deserves to be quoted *in extensio.*

Diodorus begins by describing the general preparations, the cavalry and chariots and the overall lineup with the nobles and their supporters: "They bring into battle as their attendants free men, chosen from among the poorer class, whom they use as char-

ioteers and shield-bearers in battle." He proceeds to describe the opening movements of the battle:

When the armies are drawn up in battle array they are wont to advance before the battle-line and to challenge the bravest of their opponents to single combat, at the same time brandishing before them their arms so as to terrify their foe. And when someone accepts their challenge to battle, they loudly recite the deeds of valor of their ancestors and proclaim their own valorous quality, at the same time abusing and making little of their opponent and generally attempting to rob him beforehand of his fighting spirit.

In another passage Diodorus talks of the power of the Druids in time of battle.

The Celtic shield of wood or leather, sometimes covered in bronze, protected the whole body from the knees to the shoulders, as in the Gallo-Roman sculpture of a Celt *(left)*, from Mondragon, France. Above *(left to right)* are shields from Witham, northern England, and Horath, Germany (reconstructions), and the Battersea shield from the River Thames.

Opposite page: The harsh-sounding Celtic war trumpets with their frightening animal-head terminals are shown in operation on the Gundestrup caldron found in Denmark.

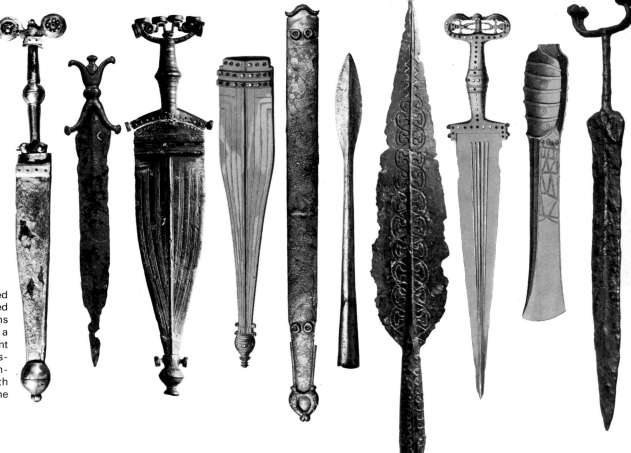

The Celt at war, so fully described by classical writers, is also illustrated by a wide range of Celtic weapons found in archaeological contexts, a selection of which, from different parts of western Europe, are illustrated here. Of the body armor mentioned in the texts little survives with the exception of a number of fine bronze helmets.

In addition to the weapons themselves, and the occasional representation of warriors on repoussé or inscribed metalwork (pp. 24–25), models of warriors have been found. The horseman above dates to the seventh century B.C. and comes with others from a cult chariot found at Strettweg in Austria.

For often as armies approach each other in line of battle with their swords drawn and their spears raised for the charge, these men come forth before them and stop the conflict, as though they had spellbound some kind of wild animals. He adds the moral rationalization, "Thus even among the most savage barbarians anger yields to wisdom."

Here is a brilliant evocation of early Celtic warfare, the very essence of which is the institution of single combat—conflicts between tribes could be, and probably usually were, resolved by a display of arms followed by individual contests between warriors. This is precisely the kind of warfare which is found in Homer and which is reflected in the biblical story of David and Goliath. Only if spirits ran high would general battle ensue, and then if such a situation threatened, the priests could intervene. In other words, we are dealing with ritualized warfare sparing of manpower. Contact with the Romans, of course, changed all this. The Roman mentality required the pitched battle with a clear-cut result. The Celts had to adapt. In one of the finest battle descriptions available to us, the historian Polybius describes the confrontation between the Romans and the Celts at Telamon, in Tuscany, in 225 B.C. To begin with, the battle was confined to

the hill and opened with a cavalry engagement, the rest of the two armies looking on, but the Romans, having caught the Celts between two forces, closed in on them.

They were terrified by the fine order of the Celtic host, and the dreadful din, for there were innumerable horn blowers and trumpeters, and the whole army was shouting their war cries at the same time: there was such a tumult of sound that it seemed that... all the country round had got a voice and caught up the cry. Very terrifying too were the appearance and gestures of the naked warriors in front, all in the prime of life and finely built men, and all in the leading companies richly adorned with gold torques and armlets.

Eventually Roman discipline prevailed and the Celts were routed.

Some of them, in their impotent rage rushed wildly on the enemy and sacrificed their lives, while others, retreating step by step on the ranks of their comrades, threw them into disorder by their display of faint-heartedness.

The Celtic mentality could not cope with the relentless Roman military machine; once the fortunes of battle had turned, their resolve crumbled and they went berserk or panicked.

More than three hundred years later in the north of Scotland a similar scene was played

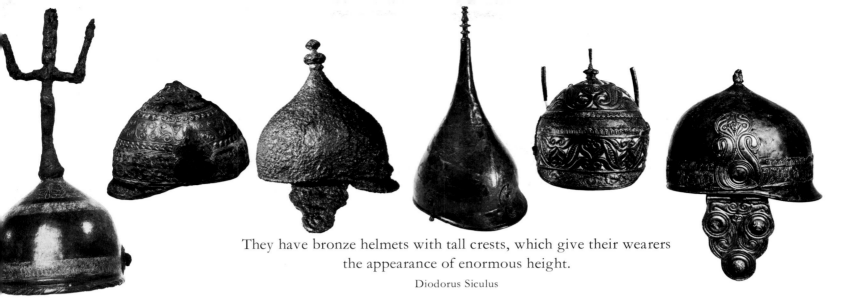

They have bronze helmets with tall crests, which give their wearers
the appearance of enormous height.

Diodorus Siculus

out following the battle of Mons Graupius (p. 154)—after a crushing defeat the Britons fled, "the men and women wailing together... many left their homes and in their rage set fire to them... they would try to concert plans, then suddenly break off. Sometimes the sight of their dead ones broke their hearts—more often it goaded them to fury—some of them laid violent hands on their wives and children in a kind of pity" (Tacitus). This terrible collapse of morale and reason was the fatal flaw in the Celtic mentality.

The selection of arms and helmets illustrated here come from northern Italy, France, and Switzerland and date from the fourth to the second century B.C.

The typical Celtic helmet had a narrow projecting neck guard (which might otherwise be mistaken for a peak) and was often provided with hinged ear flaps. Occasionally they supported the horns and other protuberances which Posidonius noted.

This magnificent helmet was found in a third-century B.C. Celtic grave at Ciumesti in Romania. The bronze bird of prey which perches on the crest had eyes of colored glass and its wings are articulated.

A stone-built house at Vaucluse, France. Of uncertain date but built in native style.

FROM HAMLETS TO CITIES

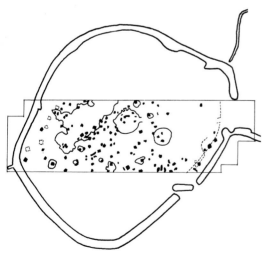

The roundhouse occurs in western Celtic regions, particularly in Britain. The plan above shows a typical Iron Age farmstead excavated at Little Woodbury in southern Britain. The two timber-built roundhouses were of different dates. The enclosure contains the storage pits, granaries, and working areas of the farm.

Celtic settlement pattern was diverse: each region had its own vernacular architecture, determined to some extent by the raw materials available, and settlements ranged in size and complexity depending upon the organization of the community represented. In the Hallstatt period the two extremes are defined by peasant farms, on the one hand, and princely strongholds, such as Heuneburg, on the other. Later, in the first century B.C., urban centers of enormous size developed to serve the increasingly complex needs of society.

Throughout the whole of the Hallstatt and La Tène periods, whatever the nature of the large nucleated settlement, the basic settlement unit was the isolated farm or small hamlet—a cluster of simple houses integrated into an agricultural landscape.

Houses were well built and usually of sufficient size to accommodate the extended family. An interesting divergence in tradition can readily be recognized between the circular houses, which are found in all parts of the British Isles, and rectangular buildings prevalent in continental Europe: the British house-type harks back to an older, Atlantic tradition of building. Among the rectangular houses there is a considerable variation in size and style, from the little one-roomed log cabins recently found at Most-na-Soci in Slovenia to the great aisled halls of the Low Countries.

Sometimes, particularly in Britain, a few houses were grouped together in an enclosure, the total complex representing the installations necessary for a single family. In mainland Europe the hamlet or the village appears to have been the more usual unit of settlement, but once more the diversity of the pattern should be emphasized.

The house (or family complex) was for the most part a self-contained unit wherein many of the basic necessities of life could be manufactured. Corn brought in from the fields was threshed and stored, either long-term in below-ground silos, or for immediate use in small granaries raised above ground to keep the corn away from damp and from rodents. Milling to make flour would have been a regular activity for the womenfolk, while most houses were provided with their own bread ovens.

Clothing would have been made in the home. There is ample evidence from settlement sites of spinning and of weaving on large upright looms, while finer weaving to make braid and a form of tablet weaving are also attested. Carpentry, not only of the basic kind necessary for house building and repairs, was highly advanced, as our discussions below (pp. 124–125) will serve to demonstrate, and knowledge of timber, coppicing, and other forms of forest management was commonplace. It is likely that, for much of the period, pottery making was carried out in the village, but later, with the development of urban centers, commercial production soon got under way.

The extent to which iron and bronze working were home industries is debatable. Most communities would have had their own blacksmith and the manufacture of small bronze trinkets is a comparatively simple task, but the knowledge and skills required to extract the metals in the first place and, in the case of bronze, to produce a suitable alloy, were most likely in the hands of specialists. We must suppose, then, that some communities, probably working full time, like the copper miners in the Tyrol (pp. 114–115), made their living producing ingots of metal which could then enter the exchange network and eventually end up in the farms and hamlets.

The house plan typical of most of Europe was rectangular, but the superstructures were built in a variety of techniques. At the open air museum of Asparn near Vienna, reconstructions of all the major types have been attempted, based on a careful consideration of the archaeological evidence.

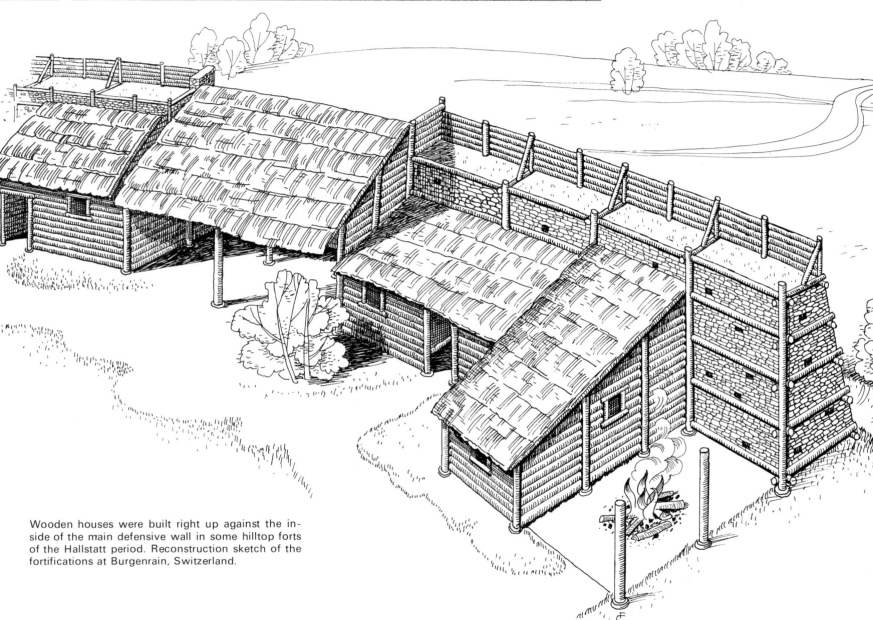

Wooden houses were built right up against the inside of the main defensive wall in some hilltop forts of the Hallstatt period. Reconstruction sketch of the fortifications at Burgenrain, Switzerland.

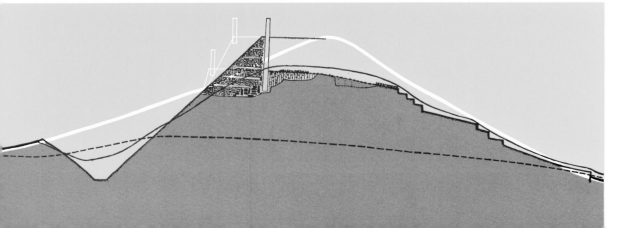

The defenses of Wittnauer Horn in Switzerland were massive. The Hallstatt period rampart, built of timbers and stone (and fronted by a ditch 3 meters deep), was set into the front of an earlier, more massive rampart of the Late Bronze Age.

61

HILLFORTS

At times of stress, Celtic communities throughout Europe built defended enclosures, usually on well-protected hilltop sites. These hillforts performed a variety of functions, but for the most part they were communal structures built by the inhabitants of the surrounding countryside for the use of the clan. Some show signs of having performed functions of an urban kind.

The tradition of defending a hilltop with an earthwork or a palisade was long established in Europe, and indeed can be traced back to Neolithic times, but it was not until the Urnfield period that hillforts became at all common in Europe. One of the most impressive of these early forts is the Wittnauer Horn in the Jura, a settlement spectacularly perched on a steep-sided ridge and defended by a single massive bank cutting off the approach. The bank, 40 meters in width, is composed of a loose framework of horizontal timbers packed with stone and soil. On one estimate the bank contains no less than 24,000 cubic meters of timber all of which would have had to be cut, trimmed, and hauled into position. Quite clearly, to build even a modest-sized fort of this kind would have involved a colossal expenditure of energy and must imply organized communal effort of a grand scale.

The explanation for the early hillforts must be sought in the increasingly aggressive

Maiden Castle, in Dorset, England, is one of Britain's largest and strongest hillforts. The central plateau, measuring some 18 hectares (about 35 acres) in area, was occupied from the fourth century to A.D. 70. The multiple

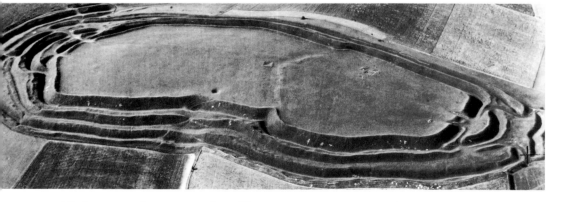

ditches, sometimes more than 20 meters deep, and the ramparts between, supplementing the natural slope, stand out as shadows in this aerial photograph. The fort was attacked by the Roman general Vespasian in A.D. 43. The cemetery of the defenders was found at the entrance.

nature of society—defenses on this scale are a sure sign that the people were in a state of sustained stress, and the fact that over much of Celtic Europe forts continued to be built throughout most of the first half of the first millennium B.C. is an indication of how long this situation lasted.

Although these early hillforts have a superficial resemblance to each other, there is no need to suppose that all performed the same functions. In Britain, where the archaeological evidence is at its best, many of the early forts were only very lightly occupied and it may be that they were inhabited only in times of stress or perhaps were used as communal storage areas for grain or animals frequented at certain times during the year. Wittnauer Horn, however, with its rows of well-constructed houses, gives the appearance of more permanent occupation, but there are no signs that any member of the community possessed exceptional wealth. In the sixth century, on the other hand, hillforts were being built, or renovated, by the aristocracy as we have seen at Mont Lassois and Heuneburg.

It seems, then, as though the technique of hilltop defense was being employed to serve a multitude of functions, the common factors being the need for defense and the

The sites chosen for hillforts usually had strong natural defenses which could be enhanced by walls or banks and ditches. The desire for protection is dramatically illustrated by the fort of Dún Aengusa on the island of Aran off the Irish coast.

The entrance was potentially the weakest point of most hillforts. Accordingly entrances were often protected by additional earthworks designed to confuse the attacker and protect the main gate. At the south-

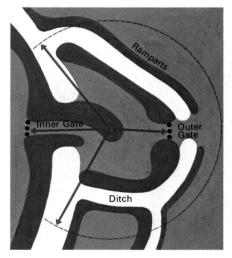

ern British hillfort of Danebury there were two gates at the main entrance with a flat topped earthwork between providing a command post from which the occupants, armed with slings, could protect the gates and command the approach.

ability of the community to work together to satisfy that need.

With the social upheaval which began in the fifth century B.C. the majority of the hillforts in Europe show signs of abandonment. One explanation for this might be that the massive folk movements which ensued relieved much of the pressure on land and thus reduced stress in the central areas, but the full story is likely to be far more complex and can only begin to be understood when we know more of the settlement type of the fourth and third centuries.

There are several exceptions to this generalization, of which Britain provides one of the best-known examples. Here, in a wide arc of land stretching from north Wales southward and eastward towards Kent, hillforts continued to be built, and were increasingly strongly defended, from the fifth to the first century. Each fort now seemed to dominate a well-defined territory within which it now played an important central function providing its hinterland with many benefits of an urban kind: facilities for trade and exchange; a religious center; defense when needed; a resident population, some of whom were engaged in manufacturing pursuits; and presumably administrative control of the community. Hillforts were still being built in the first century B.C. in France against Caesar's advance, and almost a hundred years later, a Roman general had to hack his way through more than twenty forts before he could claim to have conquered the southwest of Britain. In the Celtic fringes of Britain some forts were still occupied well into the Roman period.

THE FIRST CITIES

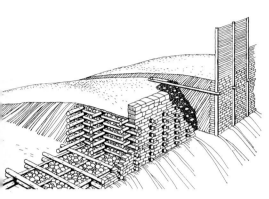

Towards the end of the second century B.C. barbarian Europe began to develop a range of new settlements, large enough and sufficiently complex in their functions to be called cities. The cause of this significant cultural advance is probably two-fold. Society had now, after centuries of unrest, stabilized and became more sedentary; moreover, transalpine Europe had been exposed to influence from the urban world of the Mediterranean for four hundred years. Trade between them was vigorous and it is easy to understand how southern ways will have been absorbed and emulated. This is not to say that the creation of cities was superficial, quite the contrary; the emergence of urban life reflects deep-rooted changes in Celtic society.

government was an important step towards civilization.

Another factor of significance was the widespread acceptance of coinage as a form of exchange. Gold and silver coins minted by the different tribes came into general use in central and western Europe from the third century B.C. onward, based on Macedonian and Greek prototypes. Mercenaries or raiders returning from expeditions in Mediterranean lands would have become conversant with such curiosities. To begin with, coins (imported and local) would have functioned largely in gift exchange, but by the end of the second century smaller denominations were in use, demonstrating the existence of a full money economy with coins being used in market

Top: The Murus Gallicus, which so impressed Caesar, was composed of timbers faced with stone and embedded in earth.

Urban centers (or oppida), as the map shows, sprang up all over Celtic Europe in the first century B.C. and spread to Britain by the early first century A.D.

In the central area from Bohemia to central France the old Celtic aristocracy was a thing of the past. Caesar tells us how in many tribes the head of state was now an annually elected magistrate and to aspire to kingship was an offense punishable by death. The emergence of an oligarchic

exchange. Such a system would have greatly facilitated trade with the classical world as well as between neighboring tribes.

To gain some idea of how these sites functioned, we must consider the urban center at Manching, close to the Danube in upper Bavaria. At its greatest extent the ramparts of Manching, 7 kilometers in length, enclosed some 375 hectares (or 700 acres). Although the built-up area was substantially less, it was still a very large settlement by any standards (compare, for example, the Iron Age town with its modern successor: this page left). Within the built-up area it is possible to recognize well-laid-out streets with orderly arrangements of timber buildings erected alongside. Iron working was carried out on a very large scale, use being made of the nearby deposits of bog iron. (It is estimated that the nails holding the timbers in the rampart together would alone have weighed 300 tons.) Other industrial activities included the working of copper and bronze to make brooches and cart fittings (stone molds for the castings were found), the minting of coins (represented by a number of fragments of clay molds for making the coin blanks before striking), the manufacture of glass beads and bracelets, and a pottery industry which was producing high-class wares for distribution over a very considerable area.

The great rampart erected to protect the community incorporated a type of construction which Julius Caesar saw and described in France, calling it a *murus Gallicus* (Gallic wall). The technique involved was to build up an open-box structure with a crisscross of timbers laid horizontally. These were nailed firmly together and a vertical stone wall was built in front with the ends of the cross timbers poking through. Behind the wall and within and behind the timber framework, soil and rubble were piled. Caesar was impressed with the solidity of construction, noting that the stonework protected it from fire while the timber structure gave a resilience which it was impossible for a battering ram to breach. The *murus Gallicus* style of building was widely adopted in Europe in the first century B.C., but it clearly develops from a tradition of rampart construction which goes back to the Urnfield period. Manching was the chief town of a tribe called the *Vindelici*, and according to the evidence of the objects found, it was in use throughout the first century B.C., ending its life in destruction some time towards the end of the century. One possibility is that it was destroyed by the Romans, who campaigned through the area in 15 B.C.

Each of the more advanced of the central

group of tribes will have had one or more towns of this type. Caesar encountered a number as he campaigned through Gaul, perhaps the most famous being Bibracte (Mont Beuvray), the capital of the pro-Roman tribe called the Aedui. The formidable hilltop is enclosed by 5 kilometers of defenses estimated to have stood 5 meters in height. Within, roads meandered from one quarter to another without evidence of rigid planning except that certain areas were set aside for different functions. The iron workers, for example, tended to occupy the slopes of the hill, while jewelers and the enamelers had their workshops close together along one of the main streets. The excavators also identified a consecrated place, a market area, and

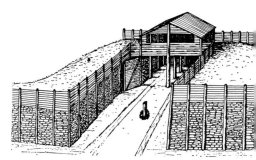

Reconstruction of one of the main entrances of the oppidum at Manching, with its gate set back between the inturned ends of the rampart to give added protection.

what they believed to be an aristocratic quarter.

Bibracte continued to thrive well after Caesar's conquest and remained in use up to about 5 B.C., by which time the urban life of the region had begun to focus on the new Roman foundation at Autun in the valley some kilometers away to the east.

The Celtic urban center (oppidum) at Manching is one of the best known in Europe as the result of meticulous excavations carried out between 1953 and 1967. The defensive circuit (in white) makes use of the River Paar, a tributary of the Danube.

THE SHIFTING TRIBES

The god of the hunt, a favorite deity among so many of the diverse Celtic tribes. Hunting was very popular with the Celts, as so much evidence attests, although they were also an agrarian people whose frequent migrations were often motivated by the exhaustion of old farmland and the quest for new. This statue is one of the few Celtic artworks that show the typical coat worn by the people.

The tribal situation was always fluid. At the height of the migrations whole tribes or parts of tribes would move across vast territories settling temporarily and then moving on again. Even as late as the first century B.C., when the main phase of migration was at an end, we learn from Caesar how the Helvetii of Switzerland, considering that they had outgrown their territory, burned their homes and moved west en masse only to be intercepted, defeated in battle, and sent back by Caesar.

Another factor affecting the tribal map was the changing fortunes, of the individual tribes—a tribe, powerful at one moment with many lesser tribes dependent upon it, might suddenly lose prestige and sink into oblivion. The situation in Gaul in the middle of the first century B.C. provides an insight into these matters. There were two principal factions headed, respectively, by the Aedui and the Sequani. Caesar sums up the situation: "As the Aedui had long enjoyed very great prestige and had many satellite tribes, the Sequani were the weaker of the two since they depended on their own resources." It would seem then that a system of clientage existed at tribal level, the principal tribes receiving tribute from their satellites, presumably in return for protection. However, as the result of battles, in which the Aeduian aristocracy was wiped out, the Sequani demonstrated their superiority, and many of the tribes previously dependent on the Aedui went over to them. To counter this the Aedui solicited, and eventually obtained, the patronage of Rome, as a result of which dependent tribes flocked back to them, leaving the Sequani isolated. Those lesser tribes who for reasons of ancient feuds and rivalries could not bring themselves to be clients of the Aedui chose instead the Remi as protector who, as Caesar says, "by taking good care of them, were able to maintain the unaccustomed power they had suddenly acquired."

The example typifies the fickle nature of tribal allegiances; it also demonstrates with great clarity how important Roman patronage had now become in upsetting and readjusting the balance of power. Yet in spite of all this the tribal pattern was sufficiently well established for tribal units to form a basis of the administrative structure under Roman rule when one by one the Celtic territories were subsumed.

BOII

The Boii were one of the more mobile of the Celtic tribes. In the fifth century a substantial number migrated from north of the Alps and settled in the Po valley, the rest staying in the traditional territories in Bohemia. The north Italian group suffered under the Roman advance, while those in Bohemia later migrated westward into France, forced out by the Cimbri and Teutones.

HELVETII

A tribe occupying much of modern Switzerland. In the first century A.D., as the result of population growth and pressure from tribes to the north, they decided to migrate westward into Gaul. In 58 B.C. Caesar halted their migration and defeated them, forcing the remnants to return home.

AEDUI

Paramount tribe in central France occupying the territory around Autun. By virtue of their position close to the Rhône trade route, they adopted elements of classical culture. By Caesar's time, because of intertribal fighting, their position of supremacy was in decline, but by aligning themselves with Rome they soon restored their former importance.

ARVERNI

Powerful tribe occupying the Massif Central in Caesar's time. They were violently opposed to Rome.

VENETII

Maritime tribe living in the southwest of the Armorican peninsula. They were traders and acted as middlemen in shipping goods from Britain to the south. In 56 B.C. they rebelled against Caesar but were soundly beaten in a sea battle at Quiberon, and as a result all the leading men were executed and the rest sold as slaves.

NERVII

One of the Belgic tribes of northern Gaul living in central Belgium, east of the Scheldt. They put up powerful resistance to Caesar and were virtually annihilated by him.

SCORDISCI

After the migration into Greece had failed, many thousands of Celts poured back into central Europe to find land to settle. One group, the Scordisci, led by Bathanatos settled between the rivers Drava and Sava with an oppidum on the site of Beograd. They were a powerful force in the subsequent settlement in the rest of Transdanubia.

DUROTRIGES

Powerful but politically backward tribe occupying Dorset in southern Britain. Vespasian, then a legionary commander, had to destroy more than twenty native hillforts, including Maiden Castle, before the tribe would submit.

ICENI

British tribe occupying Norfolk and Suffolk. They allied themselves to Rome after the invasion of Claudius and were ruled by a client king, Prasutagus. When he died, there was trouble resulting in a widespread uprising led by Queen Boudicca. The rebellion was ill-prepared and soon failed.

whom settled in southern Gaul while the other moved into Anatolia. The Gaulish group possessed a vast treasure of gold and silver which was pillaged by the Romans in 106 B.C.

ERAVISCI

Tribe occupying much of Transdanubia (in modern Hungary) with one of their principal settlements on the Danube at Budapest. It is possible that they moved into the region from the north in the first century A.D. Eraviscan culture remained strong throughout the early part of the Roman occupation: Celtic dress and jewelry continued to be worn even by the rich families as is witnessed by tombstone reliefs.

They are wont
to change their abode
on slight provocation,
migrating in bands
with all their battle-array,
or rather setting out
with their households
when displaced
by a stronger enemy.

Strabo

TRINOVANTES

Occupied part of eastern England just north of the Thames. In Caesar's time they were in conflict with their neighbors the Catuvellauni. They became allies of Rome and their chieftains grew rich on trade with the Roman world, acquiring luxury objects and wine.

VOLCAE

The Volcae were originally neighbors of the Boii in central Europe. An offshoot of the tribe probably contributed to the Volcae Tectosages, one branch of

BRIGANTES

Large confederacy stretching across northern England from the Irish Sea to the North Sea. In the first century A.D. it seems to have been allied to Rome, but jealousies broke out between Queen Cartimandua and her husband Venutius and eventually Roman troops had to intercede on the queen's behalf. Venutius was later beaten in a pitched battle.

PARISII

A tribe living in the region of modern Paris. Their chief city, Lutetia, was the predecessor of Paris.

La Tène—site of fifth to second-century Celtic settlements on the shores of Lake Neuchâtel in Switzerland. This name, associated with a site that now lies submerged, has come to designate a period in time rather than a place.

67

RELIGION AND MYSTERY

As a nation the Gauls are extremely superstitious;
and so persons suffering from
serious diseases, as well as those who are exposed
to the perils of battle, offer human sacrifices.

Caesar

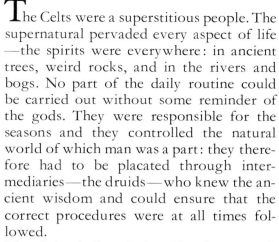

Skulls that gaze out from stone temple walls . . . statues of animals, horned figures, men-beasts . . . and everywhere triple groupings of gods, priests, heads. Such evidence leaves no doubt that the Celts carried on an active spiritual life, marked by apparitions, cults, talismans, and supernatural symbolism. Roman witnesses, some sympathetic and some contemptuous, have added their words to the record, giving us accounts of coldblooded human sacrifices and superstitious taboos, while explaining the priestly role of the druidic elite. The shadow-world of the Celtic supernatural is filled with landmarks. What our guides do not provide—for no doubt it did not exist—is a master-plan, a world-system, a hierarchy like that of the Greek and Roman pantheon. Moreover, the deeper significance of so many Celtic religious symbols eludes us as it did the Romans, since the druids imparted their teaching only by word of mouth, in woodland clearings, by sacred springs, or in temple sanctuaries closed to any outsider. And thus we find ourselves with more questions than answers concerning the religion— or religions—of the Celts.

The Celts were a superstitious people. The supernatural pervaded every aspect of life —the spirits were everywhere: in ancient trees, weird rocks, and in the rivers and bogs. No part of the daily routine could be carried out without some reminder of the gods. They were responsible for the seasons and they controlled the natural world of which man was a part: they therefore had to be placated through intermediaries—the druids—who knew the ancient wisdom and could ensure that the correct procedures were at all times followed.

The Celts believed that if a human life was at risk through serious disease or because of exposure to danger, it was because the gods were wrathful. The only way to placate their antagonisms, and to save the endangered life, was therefore to offer another life in its place. Criminals were preferred as sacrifices, but if the supply of criminals was insufficient, numbers could be made up by substituting innocent men. The method of sacrifice varied, but the most dramatic of the practices described by the ancient writers comes once more from the pen of Caesar. "Some tribes," he says, "have colossal images made of wickerwork, the limbs of which they fill with living men: they are then set on fire, and the victims are burned to death."

Caesar may well have overemphasized human sacrifice, at which he professed horror, in order to justify in the minds of his readers his brutal campaigns against the Celts in Gaul. But that it formed a part of Celtic ritual there can be no doubt.

The evidence concerning Celtic religion is particularly rich. The classical writers provide tantalizing insights into the nature of offerings, of beliefs, and, in particular, about the priestly class, the druids (pp. 106–111). It is possible to extend this picture, with data derived from archaeological excavations, to throw more light on the location and arrangement of ritual sites. To this we may add interpretations based on the enormous range of iconographic data which survives, including religious sculpture and dedications, much of it created by Celtic populations under Roman domination. Finally there is available the wealth of detail, often obscure and difficult to use, which escaped the censorship of the Christian scribes who committed the sagas of the pagan Irish to writing.

A PAGAN TRINITY

Three was a sacred or auspicious number in the ancient world. It is hardly surprising therefore that triplism recurs, to some extent, as an element in the Celtic supernatural. Less mystical than the Christian trinity, this Celtic theme simply implied an added strength or potency because it is more than one. We have already mentioned the fighting unit, the *trimarcisia*, which comprised the nobleman and his two supporters—a somewhat secular and more practical expression of the same concept. Allusions to triplism occur in the Irish literature. The three mother goddesses of war, Mórrígan, Macha, and Bodb, are known collectively as Mórrígna (the great queens).

"I swear," said Cú Chulainn, "by the gods by whom Ultonians swear, that I will bruise you against a green stone of the ford."
"I will become a gray wolf for you," said the Mórrígan, "and take the flesh from your right hand as far as to your left arm."
"I will encounter you with my spear," he said, "until your left or right eye is forced out."
"I will become a white red-eared cow," she said, "and I will go into the pond beside the ford in which you are in combat, with a hundred white red-eared cows behind me. And I and all behind me will rush into the ford, and the Fair Play of Men that day shall be brought to a test, and your head shall be cut off from you."
"Your right or your left leg," he said, "I will break with a cast of my sling, and you shall never have any help from me, if you leave me not."
Thereupon the Mórrígan departed into the Fairy Hill of Cruachan in Connacht, and Cú Chulainn returned to his bed.

The *Taín*

Because the number three represents strength, many deities were depicted in triple from. The style of representation varies considerably, from very crude engravings like the "three mothers" *(above)* from Burgundy dating to the third century A.D., to such sophisticated Gallo-Roman renderings as the three-headed god molded on the side of a terracotta vase from Bavay, France, second century B.C. *(opposite)*.

The goddess Brigit also has three aspects. The male gods show the tendency less clearly, though Lugh appears with two brothers and Dagdá is sometimes associated with two other names.

In Celtic and Romano-Celtic iconography triplism is amply represented, in particular in the reliefs of the "Three Mothers" which recur in virtually every part of the Celtic world. They are usually depicted as seated deities accompanied by attributes of fertility such as fruit, cornucopias, and occasionally infants. See, for example, the fine relief from Vertillum in the Côte d'Or (page 48). Triads of this kind, which are particularly common in this area of Burgundy, must represent the aspects of a popular local deity. A similar concentration occurs in the Cotswolds in southern England. Male triads have been found there as well, but less frequently (p. 49, above).

Another form in which triplism can manifest itself is in the tricephalos—the three-faced head. This might take the form of a simple boulder carved with three faces: a well-known example was found at Corleck, Cavan, in Ireland, and another has turned up more recently in Wiltshire. A more sophisticated representation is shown opposite.

Finally we might mention the triskele—a simple decorative motif consisting of three elements which appear to move in the same direction about a single central point. Triskeles, quite commonly used in Celtic art, must ultimately have derived from a solar symbol to which, of course, connotations of strength are attached. It is possibly significant that the triskele was the motif used to decorate the boss of a shield found at Llyn Cerrig in Anglesey. Could it be that by decorating the shield in this way, the craftsman sought to give his patron more than just physical protection?

"Dark one are you restless
do you guess they gather
to certain slaughter the wise raven
groans aloud
that enemies infest
the fair fields
ravaging in packs
learn I discern rich plains
softly wavelike
baring their necks
greenness of grass
beauty of blossoms
on the plains war
grinding heroic
hosts to dust
cattle groans the Badb
the raven ravenous
among corpses of men
affliction and outcry
and war everlasting
raging over Cuailnge death of sons
death of kinsmen
death death!"

The Mórrígan in the *Taín*

EARTH MOTHER AND TRIBAL FATHER

Beneath the confusing mass of detail about the Celtic supernatural which survives in the Irish literature and is reflected in the iconography remaining from the Roman period, a simple underlying theme emerges: The female deities are all in some way reflections of an earth mother-goddess, while the male gods, whatever their specific attributes, all have abilities appropriate to the tribal god. We can perhaps see in this apparent simplicity the foundation stone of Celtic religion.

The Irish literature helps us to endow these shadowy concepts with a certain substance. The great male god—the god on whom the tribal deities were based—was the Dagdá, a name which means "The Good God." The Irish story of the "battle of

I am she
that is the natural
mother of all things,
mistress and governess
of all the elements,
the initial progeny of worlds,
chief of the powers divine,
queen of all that are in hell,
the principal of them
that dwell in heaven,
manifested alone
and under one form
of all the gods and goddesses.

Lucius Apuleius

Moytura" explains the meaning of the epithet. In the council of war before the battle, each god declares his qualifications. When it comes to the Dagdá's turn, he simply says, "All that you promise to do I will do myself alone," to which the others reply, "It is you who are the *good god*." Clearly then, "good" in this context has no moral implication, it means the "all-competent"—"the good-at-everything." The Dagdá, thus endowed, is the basis for all other personifications of the deity.

His female counterpart, in the Irish literature, was the Mórrígan—the "great queen." She appears in many guises as Panic, the Raven of Battle, and in triple form with Macha and Bodb. She is essentially a mother-goddess—a goddess of fertility—but more than that, she is the introducer of fear and irrationality, who can undermine men in times of crisis and sometimes delights in doing so.

In the relationship between the two, the male Dagdá (the tribal personification of all skills), and the female Mórrígan (the earth, fertility, and uncertainty), everything can be explained: good and evil, rational and irrational, bravery and fear. Life results from the interplay of these opposing elements.

In the Celtic world of Ireland these two aspects were annually united for the common good at the festival of *Samhain* celebrated on the first of November. During Samhain, the limbo period between the ending of one year and the beginning of the next, the spirits were loosed and the world was in chaos. The word appears to mean a coming together; on these occasions the whole tribe presumably assembled for feasting and to ensure, through sacrifice, the continued fertility of the crops and herds. In Celtic mythology Samhain was the time of reconciliation between the tribal god and the earth-mother in her tribal guise, when they came together for intercourse—the act ensuring that the balance of the forces had been restored and that the fertility of the land and of the people was renewed.

In these pages we endeavor to reduce the plethora of Celtic myths and deities to their essentials. What emerges is clearly the survival of a very ancient pan-European belief, which the Celts in their different territories and at different times embroidered, to provide a fabric of great intricacy.

Northern Irish sculpture of a radiating god.

The belief in a goddess of creation and destruction is very deep-rooted, and in spite of a veneer of Christianity, it can be traced throughout medieval Europe. The sculpture *(right)* of a Sheela-na-gig—evidently a fertility deity—is on a corbel in the medieval church at Kilpeck in Herefordshire. It is one of the few that survived destruction in a spate of nineteenth-century puritanism.

The tribal god could take on many guises, but one of the most popular was that of a hunter. Here we see him, resplendent in his antler crown and holding a magical torque, on the first-century B.C. Gundestrup caldron, found in Denmark.

The good god, Dagda, in the Irish literature, is represented as a figure of great strength. He carries a massive club and a magic caldron which is inexhaustible and possesses the power to inspire and rejuvenate. In this Gallo-Roman bronze from Prémeaux, in France, he is depicted as the Dis Pater—a version of the Roman Jupiter.

The rich iconography of Celtic Europe presents us with a bewildering variety of deities. In all, more than four hundred names are recorded, but three-quarters of these occur only once, leaving little doubt that each locality probably supported its own versions of the pan-Celtic tribal and nature gods.

Caesar, evidently not concerned to discuss the variety of Celtic deities in any detail, merely reports the diversity and interprets it in terms which his Roman readers could understand: If a Celtic god, no matter what he was called, had the same characteristics as a Roman god, then surely they must be the same.

The other classical authors are no more helpful. However, Lucan, a Greek poet who wrote in the second century A.D. after traveling in Gaul, mentions three Celtic gods by name—Esus, Taranis, and Teutates —who clearly have their counterparts in Ireland and Wales. Taranis comes from the same word as the Welsh *taran* and Irish *torann*, meaning "thunder," while the name Teutates is the same root as *tuáth*, "tribe" in Irish. Why Lucan should have given special preference to these three is not immediately apparent; they occur but rarely in the archaeological record. In all probability he simply enlarged on some scrap of inconsequential data with a poet's license. It would be wrong to think of the Celtic gods arrayed in a *pantheon* as were the more ordered deities of the Greeks and Romans. The Celtic supernatural beings were more shadowy figures whose relationships and hierarchies are ill-defined, but there are vague hints in the Irish literature that the gods were conceived of in rather the same way as the tribe was organized. At the head was the tribal god and his consort, the earth mother (as we have already seen, p. 72–73), but above them there is the vague concept of the "mother of the gods"—an upper echelon from whom the tribal gods were descended. Thus, in this very ill-defined area, it would seem that the tribal gods related to some higher deities in the same way as the tribal chief was descended from the tribal gods. The parallel might be extended down to the next level. Just as the skilled class in the tribe was divided into craftsmen, healers, and men of learning, so there is evidence among the deities of these same specializations, although how these craftsmen-gods related to the tribal, all-

competent deity is obscure. These matters were probably equally vague even in the minds of the Celts.

The problem of whether or not there was

a defined hierarchy among the Celtic gods is further complicated by the Irish *Túatha Dé Dannan*, "the peoples of the Goddess Dann"—a confederation composed of a number of deities. While this may dimly reflect the notion of a family of gods, it could equally well be explained in terms of clientage and the dominance of one tribal god over those of subservient tribes.

When we consider the individual gods, one stands out above the myriad of minor immortals by virtue of his extensive distribution—the god Lug. In Ireland his special day, *Lugnasadh* (the first of August), was one of the four great festivals in the Irish calendar (pp. 110–111), while at Lugdunum (Lyons) in Gaul the feast of the divine emperor Augustus was celebrated on the same day—an interesting example of how the Romans adapted native religious susceptibilities to their own official uses. The god's name survives as an element in Celtic place names throughout Europe, while dedications to the deity have been found as far apart as Switzerland and Spain. In another guise, that of Find—"the Fair-haired One"—his name survives in the Roman

Right: Riding gods were popular throughout the Celtic world. They represented the tribal god as a warrior. This Romano-British example comes from Willingham Fen near Cambridge.

Taranis, Celtic god associated with thunder, was conflated in the Roman mind with Jupiter. In the Gallo-Roman period he was therefore often depicted with such attributes of Jupiter as the thunder bolt. In this bronze statuette from France he is also shown with a wheel in his left hand.

The Gauls all assert their descent
from Dis pater
and say that it is the Druidic belief.
For this reason they count periods of time
not by the number of days
but by the number of nights;
and in reckoning birthdays
and the new moon and new year
their unit of reckoning is
the night followed by the day.

Caesar

names of *Vindobona* (Vienna), and *Vindonissa* in Switzerland. So widespread, and no doubt powerful, a deity must have had a deep-seated appeal to the Celts. His association with the August festival—an important date in the agrarian calendar—suggests that he may have been a fertility god.

A recurring theme in Celtic iconography is the horned god of which two main types may be distinguished: the antler horned god, Cernunnos, and the bull- or ram-horned god, who is unnamed. Cernunnos, wearing his antler headgear, with two gold torques, one around his neck and the other in his right hand, is shown sitting among his beasts on the Gundestrup caldron (p. 73). In this guise he is seen at his most typical, accompanied by a stag and a horned serpent. Clearly a deity of some antiquity, Cernunnos may well reflect a hunting god of the pre-farming period. Pierced antler frontlets have been found at the camps of Mesolithic hunters, and the wearing of antlers by shamans (magicians and seers) is well attested among the later pastoral communities of Russia and the circumpolar zone. The torque, was widely regarded in the Celtic period as having magical properties in warding off evil, while a serpent is a frequent attribute of the Celtic version of the war god. The other, unnamed, horned god must also be associated with warfare, since he is often depicted naked but armed. The serpent may be a reminder of the god's other attribute as a healer. There is nothing inconsistent in this suggestion; the Celtic tribal god was, after all, skilled at all things. There is an interesting example of just such

The tribal gods appear in many artworks as blacksmiths or other craftsmen. *Left:* Dis Pater (father of the gods) from Visp, Switzerland. *Above:* Wood-cutter god from Trier, Germany.

75

is well attested in Irish mythology and re-appears in Wales as Govannon, but it is not certain whether we are dealing here with a separate deity or merely with an aspect of the all-competent tribal god.

Taranis sometimes appears in another form, holding a wheel. In this guise, he is intended to be a sky god, comparable to the Roman Jupiter. In Romano-Celtic iconography he may also appear as a bearded horseman, dressed in Roman style, trampling on a giant (p. 51). Representations of this kind, set on columns, have a restricted distribution from the Middle Rhine to northeastern Gaul, where the cult was evidently very popular.

The tribal goddesses were all, in one way or another, deities of fertility and of bounty. We have already discussed the triads of *matres* (mothers), which gained wide popularity in the Celtic world, where the emphasis was always on plenty (the cornucopia) or fertility (infants). Female deities also presented themselves in other styles. The Irish Flidais was evidently a woodland spirit who commanded the animals. As a huntress she was clearly the counterpart of the Roman Diana, whose other concerns were, of course, fertility (so vividly demonstrated in her appearance as the many-breasted Artemis).

Another female deity who gained great popularity in the Romano-Celtic world was Epona, whose cult seems to have been based in the region of Alesia in eastern France. Epona is usually shown riding a horse sidesaddle and may be accompanied by a bird, a dog, or a foal. In one dedication she is referred to in the plural—*Eponabus*—a hint that she, like the *matres*, may have been conceived of as triple. Although

Rider-goddess Epona, Gallo-Roman statuette from Alesia, France, one of the main centers of the cult. Other female deities popular in eastern France were the "three mothers," a triad of fertility and plenty.

a combination of skills in the Irish literature. In the *Túatha Dé Danann*, one of the gods, renowned as a warrior, heals the wounded hero Cú Chulainn with magical chants and sacred herbs.

Another aspect of the tribal deity, which is sometimes emphasized, is his ability as a smith—his identity proclaimed by association with the tools of the trade. In this guise he is presumably Taranis "the thunderer" mentioned by Lucan—and conflation with the Roman Vulcan would have been inevitable. The divine smith, Goibniu,

Irish sagas, whose sexual advances the hero Cú Chulainn ignores. Enraged and craving revenge, she attempts to distract him while he is locked in deadly single combat with Lóch:

So the Mórrígan came there in the guise of a white red-eared heifer accompanied by fifty heifers.... Cú Chulainn made a cast at the Mórrígan and shattered one of her eyes. Then the Mórrígan appeared in the form of a slippery, black eel swimming downstream and went into the pool and coiled herself around Cú Chulainn's legs.... Then the Mórrígan came in the guise of a shaggy russet-colored she-wolf. While Cú Chulainn was warding her off, Lóch wounded him. Thereupon Cú Chulainn was filled with rage and wounded him ... and pierced his heart in his breast.

A great weariness fell on Cú Chulainn. The Mórrígan appeared to him in the shape of a squint-eyed old woman milking a cow with three teats. He asked her for a drink and she gave him milk from the first teat.

"Good health to the giver!" Cú Chulainn said. "The blessing of God and man on you."

And her head was healed and made whole. She gave him milk from the second teat and her eye was made whole. She gave him milk from the third teat and her legs were made whole.

"You said you would never heal me," the Mórrígan said.

"If I had known it was you I wouldn't have done it," Cú Chulainn said.

To a Celt the shadowy world of the gods was to be avoided if possible, but if contact was inevitable the correct form of propitiation was essential—otherwise unknown catastrophe might ensue.

Epona was a Gaulish deity, later introduced into Britain, there already existed native equivalents in the British Riannon and the Irish Macha.

Female deities endowed with healing powers are frequently associated with rivers or springs. The great thermal springs at Bath in England were presided over by the native goddess Sulis, who was inevitably conflated with the Roman Minerva, while at the source of the Seine the native shrine of Sequanna has yielded a range of votive offerings (discussed below, pp. 90–91) which dramatically emphasized her powers to cure the sick.

On the other hand, the goddess could be vengeful, as was the great Mórrígan of the

Overleaf (pp. 78–79): On the bronze funerary cart from a grave mound at Strettweg in Austria, a goddess directs the procession accompanying a soul to the afterlife. The Hallstatt peoples, many of whom practiced cremation, occasionally placed such miniature carts in the grave as a symbol of the death journey. Bronze wagon, 35 cm (14 in.) long; seventh century B.C.

The poet Lucan named three Celtic gods of which one was Esus, shown on this relief from Paris as a war god. The inscription above his head identifies him.

Below: A gallery of deities from all over the Celtic world, some of them as they were represented in the Roman period: *From left to right:*

Boar-god wearing a heavy torque around his neck, from Euffigneix, France. Gallo-Roman period.

Mother goddess holding fruit and foliage, emblems of productive fertility, from Caerwent, Wales. Romano-British.

God of unknown speciality sitting cross-legged. He wears a torque giving him magical protection. From Bouray, France. First century A.D.

Hunting god of the second century A.D., from Touget, France.

Horned god from Burgh-by-Sands, northern England. It was from powerful depictions of this type that the medieval vision of the devil was derived.

A goddess of serpents, possibly a healing goddess. From Ilkley, northern England. Romano-British.

Celtic god of the pre-Roman Iron Age, from France.

SACRED ANIMALS

The Celts, unlike their contemporaries in eastern Europe, were not particularly interested in mythical animals. The beasts which they chose to represent were those they saw in their everyday lives or encountered in the hunt. Because the gods could take on animal form if they wished, all animals could be gods in disguise. For this reason animal iconography became well developed.

Sometimes the deities were associated with their related animal, like Epona and the horse (p. 78) or the bear and goddess Artio shown here *(top right)* from Muri, Switzerland. The style of this particular piece suggests a date in the second to third century A.D.
Other favorite animals were the bull (Lillebonne, France), the horse (Freisen, Germany), and the dog (Moudon, Switzerland).

The Irish myth of the Mórrígan harassing Cú Chulainn (p. 77) is a reminder that the Celtic gods had the power to transform themselves into animals at will. Thus animals were often regarded with respect, not least because they might be a god who had indulged in shape-shifting. Some animals, moreover, were believed to possess magical powers.

Of the sacred animals the most important was the boar. The symbol of strength and of power, the boar was a suitable animal with which to adorn one's armor. For this reason, crests in the shape of boars are sometimes found on Celtic helmets. A stylized rendering of a boar was also applied to the surface of a bronze shield dredged from the River Witham in England. In contexts such as these we may assume that the

beast was intended to protect the wearer from the blows of his opponent. Perhaps the most famous representation of a boar is carved on the stone sculpture of a god found at Euffigneix in France (p. 76), but the identity of this boar-god remains unknown. It may also be relevant to the animal's magical status that joints of pork and sometimes whole carcasses were buried with the dead. While this could mean merely the provision of a meal in the afterworld, the animal's presence might have been intended to offer strength and support for the journey.

Another animal of considerable cult significance was the dog. Hunting dogs were well known among the Celts, and in this capacity the dog accompanied the Celtic goddess of the forest. Dogs are also found in association with the goddess Epona and with a local god Nodens, the Irish Nuadu, who, traditionally, had an artificial hand made of silver. Nodens was worshiped at a late Roman temple found at Lydney in Gloucestershire where excavations brought to light votive offerings in the form of hands, and, significantly, a small bronze casting of a dog of a breed which closely resembles an Irish wolfhound.

Of the other animals invested with super-

frequent. The swan, in particular, is a recurring motif on bronzework of the Urnfield and Hallstatt period. The Irish literature is full of bird symbolism. The raven, a dangerous and menacing creature, was the form the Irish goddess of war might assume, while the crane was thought to be wholly evil. The variety of European folklore about birds reflects the considerable range of beliefs which once surrounded them.

The bird-god Abraxas inspired numerous portrayals of the cock, as in this relief from Nyon, near Geneva.

natural powers, we have already mentioned the stag, so often associated with Cernunnos, and the horse, from which Epona was inseparable. To these should be added the bull and the ram. The bull, usually with three horns, was popular in certain areas of Gaul, while ram-horned serpents and occasionally gods with ram's horns have been found, but they are only of subsidiary significance.

Birds too were a potent force in Celtic mythology and representations of them are

The power of the boar, its loneness and its ferocity when hunted, helped to endow it with magical properties in the Celtic mind. This fine specimen, from Neuvy-en-Sullias, France, dates from the Gallo-Roman period.

THE CULT OF THE HUMAN HEAD

They embalm in cedar-oil
the heads of
the most distinguished enemies
and preserve them carefully in a chest
and display them
with pride to strangers
saying that for this head
one of their ancestors, or his father,
or the man himself,
refused the offer of a large sum of money.
They say that some of them
boast that they refused
the weight of the head in gold.

Diodorus Siculus

The cult of the severed head is dramatically revealed in the two famous temples of southern Gaul, Entremont and Roquepertuse. In the pillars of the portico of the temple of Roquepertuse, niches were carved to hold human skulls. At Entremont *(opposite)* the same concept is transformed into stone and stylized. Both temples were destroyed when the Romans colonized the area in the late second century B.C.

82

They cut off the heads of enemies slain in battle and attach them to the necks of their horses. The blood-stained spoils they hand over to their attendants and carry off as booty, while striking up a paean and singing a song of victory; and they nail up these first fruits upon their houses.... They embalm in cedar oil the heads of the most distinguished enemies, and preserve them carefully in a chest and display them with pride to strangers saying that for this head one of their ancestors, or his father, or the man himself refused the offer of a large sum of money. They say that some of them boast that they refused the weight of the head in gold.

This explicit account by Diodorus Siculus typifies the head hunting that was so common among the Celts. The practice was not merely bloodthirstiness, however. In common with many primitive peoples, the Celts believed that the soul resided in the head. The head symbolized the very essence of being, and consequently could exist in its own right. By possessing someone's head, one controlled that person and his spirit. These beliefs are manifest in the archaeological evidence, the classical tradition, and the Irish and Welsh literature.

The same theme is echoed by Livy writing of events in the third century B.C.:

The Consuls got no report of the disaster until some Gallic horsemen came in sight, with heads hanging at their horses' breasts, or fixed on their lances, and singing their customary songs of triumph.

Elsewhere the same writer gives an account of the aftermath of an ambush in northern Italy in which the Roman consul-elect Lucius Postumius was killed. The Boii (a Celtic tribe at this time occupying part of the Po valley) "stripped his body, cut off the head, and carried their spoils in triumph to the most hallowed of their temples. There they cleaned out the head, as is their custom, and gilded the skull, which thereafter served them as a holy vessel to pour libations from and as a drinking cup for the priest and the temple attendants."

Several points of considerable interest are contained in these accounts. First there is the carrying away of the spoils in triumph accompanied by battle songs, then their subsequent deposition, as trophies placed over the gate, or as specially revered items accorded some place of honor. The conqueror now owned the power of his vanquished foe. By attaching heads of lesser enemies to the gate, he was doing more

than boasting, he was using the power of the heads for the protection of his own community. A pictorial representation of just such a scene is shown on Trajan's Column. In this instance the heads are those of Roman soldiers captured by the Dacians in Transylvania. Each is shown elevated on a stake, looking out from behind the Dacian fortifications.

The special treatment afforded to the heads of high-ranking or famous enemies sets them aside as part of the portable history of the society. Such collections were maintained either by the community as a whole (in the case of the head pressed into service in the temple of the Boii) or by the individual family, in whose care they became priceless heirlooms, giving protection and providing a constant demonstration of their owners' greatness.

Skulls are often found in excavation on quite ordinary domestic sites, such as farms and hillforts which otherwise have no special ritual association. In one instance, at Stanwick in Yorkshire, a skull, which had presumably been nailed over the gate, was found nearby in the ditch where it had fallen. At Danebury, in southern Britain, skulls were sometimes found on the bottom of storage pits, placed there presumably when the pits had ceased to be used but before they were refilled. It is difficult to know how to interpret this phenomenon unless the head was being dedicated to the gods as thanks for a successful period of storage. Fragments of skull have been found amid the domestic remains of a number of settlements, often worn smooth by handling and occasionally perforated so that they could be worn as amulets. These were perhaps treasured relics handed down from one generation to the next in a manner similar to that described by Diodorus.

But the Celts were not mere head hunters. The head represented an aspect of divinity, and as such was an appropriate offering with which to adorn a temple. The most dramatic evidence for the cult of the severed head comes from the south of France. Within the oppidum of Entremont in Provence (a defended settlement destroyed by the Romans in 124 B.C.), a shrine was uncovered on the highest part of the hill, approached by a pathway lined with statues of heroes. Within the shrine itself stood a tall pillar carved with twelve simplified human heads (opposite). The

The Celtic head cult probably has very ancient origins. The early prehistoric inhabitants of eastern France, in sites such as this cave in the "Dame Jouanne" hills (Seine-et-Marne), practiced a severed head cult long before the Celts.

The head remained a powerful motif throughout the Christian period in Ireland and indeed in the rest of Britain. The gargoyles, corbels, and other decorative heads which decorate many churches, particularly of the eleventh to twelfth centuries A.D., owe much to the Celtic interpretation

of the head. Often it is impossible to distinguish Celtic from Christian carvings. In a Christian context, heads would have encapsulated and made safe the spirits that haunted the folk memory.
Above: Doorway from Dysert O'Dea, Ireland. *Right:* From the church at Clonfert, Ireland. Both Romanesque.

same site has produced a remarkable array of severed-head sculpture, including individual representations of men, women and children as well as groups of heads (picture, p. 86).

Even more vivid evidence of the cult has been uncovered at the nearby sanctuary of Roquepertuse. Here the shrine, arranged on two terraces, was adorned with a portal of three upright columns carrying a horizontal lintel, upon which perched a huge bird, poised to fly away—a symbol perhaps of the flight of spirits to the Other World. Particular interest attaches to the columns which were each carved with a series of niches to take human heads, some of which are actually in position (shown on p. 82). The columns were originally painted with fish and foliage. In addition to these structural monuments, the shrine also produced two carvings of squatting figures, possibly priests or gods, one with a torque and armlet and the other with a belted tunic

painted in bright colors in a check pattern. From the same shrine came a fine sculpture of two heads clasped in what appears to be the beak of a bird of prey (p. 87).

Finally, from the same region comes the famous "Tarasque" at Noves, a fearsome monster covered in scales depicted in the act of devouring a human being and holding, in both paws, severed human heads (illustrated on p. 107).

Together this remarkable group brings us close to the reality of the cult of the severed head, a cult evidently well established in the hinterland of Marseilles. The richness of the surviving evidence is, in part at least, due to the influence of the classical world which taught the native Celts the art of stone building and sculpture; but what we are seeing is nevertheless a purely Celtic religious expression. The apparent uniqueness of these sites should not obscure the fact that all over the Celtic world there were probably similar sanctuaries, similarly adorned, but built of timber, leaving few traces save for a few post-holes in the bedrock.

The cult of the severed head is a recurring theme in the Irish literature. The hero Cú Chulainn, by the end of his exploits, had an enormous collection to his credit. His arrival at Emain Macha is described thus: "A single chariot warrior is here… and terribly he comes. He has in the chariot the bloody heads of his enemies." The exuberance of his approach has its counterpart in war songs of the triumphant warriors described by Livy and Diodorus. On another occasion, however, he leaves the heads of his enemies at the ford where he had slain them. The grim scene is described by a traveler who arrived after the encounter was over: "He saw only the forked pole in the middle of the ford with four heads on it dripping blood down the stem of the pole into the current of the stream, and the hoof marks of the two horses, and the track of a single charioteer and of a single warrior leading eastward out of the ford." This practice of leaving the heads where they were taken is again mentioned when, as the result of another encounter, Cú Chulainn acquired twelve heads which he proceeded to display on twelve stones. This particular behavior pattern may reflect the belief in the need to propitiate the spirits of the location who had allowed the victory to be achieved.

The head was regarded as the dwelling place of the soul and thus it had both a divine and a protective aspect. To possess the head of an enemy was to control his power. It is hardly surprising therefore that the motif of the head pervaded Celtic art.

The face was depicted in a variety of ways, a range of which are shown here. *Below:* In repoussé, female head from a caldron found at Krag-hede Denmark. The hair style compares with a mount *(center)* from a wooden flagon of ca. 400 B.C. from Dürrnberg, Austria, though the figure is male.

The cult of the severed head is also reflected in the Welsh literature. In the *Mabinogion* the severed head of the god Bran goes on actively directing events long after it has been removed from its wounded body. The story is a fascinating example of the power with which the head was believed to be endowed. Another expression of the same belief, continuing into later centuries, is amply demonstrated by the popularity of the head in medieval religious architecture in the Celtic fringes of Britain and in Ireland. The remarkable door of the church of Cloufert (picture on p. 85) is a sharp and unexpected reminder of Roquepertuse.

The Celtic iconography of the head, as the selection of illustrations on this page will demonstrate, is extremely varied. The head

Above: The cult of the severed head led to the development of a lively representational art in the region around the mouth of the Rhône, influenced by Greek styles. This group of four heads from the shrine at Entremont includes two females with tight-fitting head-dresses, and two males (below them), their hair brushed back in the Celtic manner.

is a recurring theme in most forms of artistic expression, on coins, on decorative fittings and of course in religious sculpture. There were two traditions of religious sculpture among the free Celts; that of the Mediterranean fringe, which we have briefly mentioned in discussing Roquepertuse and Entremont, and a somewhat earlier expression which appears in the Middle Rhine and is thought to owe its origins to inspiration from the Etruscans. The Rhenish carvings are far less representational than those from Provence, the head being conceived of as a series of patterns, resulting in a degree of similarity between the individual pieces: the nose is wedge-shaped, the brow is usually furrowed, and the eyes are often lentoid. Some of the heads are also shown with a turban-like head-dress, which is sometimes, rather unconvincingly, referred to as a "leaf crown." Within the same general tradition, though

Several stone carvings from Germany, however, illustrate male deities with turban-like headdresses as on the Pfalzfeld pillar *(far right)* and the Heidelberg head *(bottom right)*. The heads on coins derive ultimately from Hellenistic prototypes, but Celtic genius has usually been at work restructuring the elements according to Celtic taste. This coin of the Parisii tribe is worthy of Picasso.

showing striking innovations of its own, is the famous stone head from Mšecké-Žehrovice in Bohemia. The swept-back hair and neck torque belie its Celtic origins; while the face itself, less austere than its Rhenish contemporaries, is a masterpiece of Celtic art, with the eyes and mustaches rendered as simple scroll-like motifs. Here the face has been simplified to become an elegant symmetrical pattern—the essence of a face, interpreted by an artist who thinks abstractly.

The face, broken down into its different elements, pervades Celtic art—particularly the art of the bronzeworker. Sometimes it is perfectly clear, on other occasions obscure. The flavor of this kind of enigmatic expression was elegantly summed up by the great art historian Paul Jacobstahl. Referring to the Alice-in-Wonderland quality of Celtic art, he likened the face to the Cheshire cat who appeared and disappeared in the tree: sometimes the whole cat was visible, sometimes just its grin. The bronze disk from Ireland illustrated on this page is a perfect example—is it a face or is it not? We have advanced some way from the vision of warriors clutching their bloody trophies. The cult of the severed head was indeed widespread across the Celtic world, but its more gruesome aspects should not obscure the philosophical and artistic context; the head, because it housed the soul, was endowed with dignity and divinity.

Amongst the Celts
the human head was venerated
above all else,
since the head was to the Celt the soul,
center of the emotions
as well as of life itself,
a symbol of divinity
and of the powers
of the other-world.

Paul Jacobsthal

Variation in the treatment of a single theme is exemplified in the selection of Celtic heads illustrated here.

Left: A highly individual evocation in bronze from Tarbes, France; third century B.C. The hollow neck would have allowed the head to be mounted on a pole for display.

Middle row, left: Two heads held in the beak of a massive bird, from Roquepertuse, France. *Right:* A triple, mustached head, presumably a god, from Reims, France; Gallo-Roman.

Bottom row, left to right: Stylized stone head, with prominent, close-set eyes and scroll-like eyebrows and mustache, ca. 150 B.C., found near Prague.
Female head, rough stone sculpture from pre-Roman Gaul.
Head of a divinity, with typical Celtic treatment of the beard, from the Gundestrup caldron.

Top: An enigma of the kind frequently seen in Celtic art: this bronze disk from Ireland, first—second century A.D., could be either an entirely abstract design, or else the witty, far-fetched suggestion of a face.

Such an intense supernatural life as that of the Celts required a large number of sacred places where the gods and man could communicate. We have already discussed two elaborate sanctuaries, at Entremont and Roquepertuse, but these are likely to be atypical, influenced by the Greek community at nearby Massilia. More commonly, according to the classical writers, the Celtic sacred places were architecturally unadorned. Quite often they were sacred groves situated deep in the solitude of ancient forests, as Lucan's poem so vividly describes.

When the Roman army was campaigning through north Wales in A.D. 59, one of the last strongholds of the druids was attacked and destroyed on the island of Anglesey. Tacitus describes the Roman soldiers hack-

> And there were
> many dark springs
> running there,
> and grim-faced
> figures of gods
> uncouthly hewn by the axe
> from the untrimmed tree-trunk,
> rotted to whiteness....
>
> Lucan

THE SACRED PLACES

> They prepare
> a ritual sacrifice
> and feast
> under the tree,
> and lead up two white bulls
> whose horns are bound
> for the first time
> on this occasion.
> A priest (sacerdos) attired
> in a white vestment
> ascends the tree
> and with a golden
> pruning-hook cuts the mistletoe
> which is caught
> in a white cloth.
>
> Pliny, *Natural History*

ing down the groves, sacred to savage rites and drenched with the blood of prisoners. Some indication of the prevalence of these sacred groves is given by the distribution of the place-name element *nemeton*, which can be traced across Europe from Spain and Britain in the west, to Asia Minor in the east. Reference to a wood called Nemet in an eleventh-century cartulary in Brittany further emphasizes the strength of the tradition.

Woodland locations were but one setting for Celtic ritual. The countryside would have abounded with others: weird-shaped rocks, ancient gnarled trees, and springs and bogs—the gods could be reached almost anywhere. There is extensive archaeological evidence, particularly of offerings made at rivers and springs, and an increasing body of new material is showing us that, contrary to the impression given by the ancient writers, the Celts also constructed permanent shrines of timber and ritual enclosures where the gods could be propitiated.

SACRED SPRINGS

Fresh, limpid water catching the light as it wells up from the ground exerts an undeniable fascination. To the Celtic mind a particular sanctity was attached to springs, especially those at the source of a great river. Spring water had a special quality, usually curative, which could be enjoyed by man so long as he placated the deity who presided over the location. Since water came from the earth, it was appropriate for the deity of the source to be female, reflecting one of the powers of the earth mother. The continuing strength of this pagan tradition throughout the medieval period and indeed to the present day is shown by the way in which springs and wells were rapidly Christianized and were almost invariably associated with a female patron saint, as at Lourdes.

At Coventina's well on Hadrian's Wall, a spring, presumably of some note in the pre-Roman period, was enclosed by a roughly built wall forming a small pool into which offerings such as coins were thrown. This kind of simple treatment is likely to have been common throughout the Celtic world. But other springs, by virtue of their special sanctity or impressive physical form, might be more elaborately adorned. The thermal spring at Bath, where hot water gushed out of the ground at the rate of a quarter of a million gallons a day, was, under Roman auspices, provided with a most elaborate complex of monumental buildings. Yet beneath the grandiose façade there lurked the native goddess Sulis whose name continued to be associated with the spring throughout the Roman period.

Sacred springs were usually presided over by female deities who were sometimes shown in triple form. The sacred spring at Carrowburgh, on Hadrian's Wall, where Coventina was all-powerful, produced this triad. The goddess is shown here as three water nymphs each of whom holds a beaker in one hand, while in her other she supports an up-turned urn from which the sacred water gushes. Although the relief has many classical aspects (and indeed dates to the period of the Roman occupation), the style and the iconography are purely Celtic.

The Seine rises in a secluded valley in the wooded hills to the west of Dijon. Totally undramatic in aspect, the source was an ideal place for the development of a healing shrine, presided over by the goddess Sequanna. There the pilgrims could rest in peace after making their offering to the deity and wait for her curative powers to work.

The shrine at the source has remained a place of fascination for the French. It was romanticized by Napoleon III and is still visited by coach loads of present-day pilgrims.

VOTIVE OFFERINGS

Votive offerings from the springs are a poignant reminder of the hopes of the pilgrims. The shrine at the source of the Seine has produced many *ex votos*, some, like this blind girl, reflecting the ills of the visitors. Others are of organs or limbs *(right)* presumably to focus the god's attention on the diseased part; or complete figures such as those shown on the opposite page.

The Celtic religious sense was strongly marked by the principle of reciprocity. To save a life, another would be sacrificed. Similarly, if sacred waters were used by someone wanting a cure, a gift in exchange was expected of the user.

To a warlike people like the Celts, the rituals associated with victory were of great significance—a victory granted had to be paid for with the spoils of war. It was for this reason that great quantities of arms were thrown into lakes and rivers: indeed virtually all the fine metalwork associated with warfare found in Britain has been recovered from under water.

Two sites deserve particular attention. A remarkable collection of metalwork was found in a bog at Llyn Cerrig Bach in Anglesey in 1943. The collection—composed of swords, spears, shields, chariot and harness fittings, ironworkers' tools, trumpets, caldrons, and a slave chain—had been thrown from a projecting rock into a pool some time in the first century A.D. The exact circumstances of the deposition are unknown, but the collection may well have comprised loot collected during the intertribal fighting preceding the Roman advance, and have been consigned to the care of the gods in thanks for victory.

A somewhat similar deposit was found in a bog at Hjortspring on the Danish island of Als. Here, during peat cutting, a long boat was discovered, some 16 meters in length and large enough to carry about 20 men. It had been sunk in the bog together with a range of war gear including 150 wooden shields, 169 spears, and 8 iron swords, together with a number of other objects. Although strictly a Germanic rather than a Celtic find, the equipment—particularly the shields—is clearly Celtic in form. Once more we must suppose that the boat and its contents were dedicated to the gods.

Strabo, writing of the Celtic tribe called the Volcae Tectosages, who occupied the region of Toulouse, offers an interesting insight into ritual deposits. Quoting Posidonius, he tells us that a considerable treasure of unworked gold and silver bullion was stored in the temple enclosures and in sacred lakes—"the lakes in particular provided inviolability for their treasures, into which they let down heavy masses of silver and gold." He goes on to say that the treasure stored in these sacred

sites was quite safe because no one would dare to profane them—except, that is, the Romans, who, when they conquered the region, "sold the lakes by public auction, and many of the purchasers found there hammered millstones of silver."

It is an interesting comment on the power of superstition over the people that objects of great value dedicated to the gods were safe from theft. The same point, in a different aspect, is emphasized by Caesar when he mentions that the heaviest sanction that can be imposed on a Gaul is to be banned from taking part in sacrifice to the gods. "Those who are laid under such a ban are

regarded as impious criminals. Everyone shuns them and avoids going near or speaking to them for fear of taking some harm by contact with what is unclean." Here is the essence of Celtic religion: to be whole a man has to be in communion with the gods through the medium of sacrifice and offerings.

We have already mentioned the ritual significance of springs. One, the source of the

Seine, stands out in particular for the great fascination of the evidence which excavations over the last hundred years have brought to light. Here, in a secluded valley some thirty-five kilometers from Dijon, lay the shrine to Sequanna, a Celtic deity who continued to be revered throughout the Roman period (and whose shrine received a new lease of life when Napoleon III erected a charming if irrelevant grotto on the site to house the statue of a portly water nymph). In addition to the buildings with which the Romans monumentalized the shrine, the excavations have yielded a rich collection of votive offerings which allow us to glimpse something of the hopes and beliefs of the pilgrims.

Of particular interest are the wooden votives, found in 1963, in waterlogged deposits. Most of them were simply carved from the heart wood of oak to represent all or part of the human form. Twenty-seven complete human figurines were recovered, mostly wearing cloaks, but the collection

feet. By offering the goddess a physical representation of a diseased organ or limb, the pilgrims were hoping with the aid of the deity to transfer the ailment to the inanimate object and thus effect their cure. Judging from the range of *ex votos* represented, the goddess seems to have been thought able to cure arthritis, respiratory diseases, hernias, tumors, infertility, and blindness.

Another sacred spring has recently been examined at Chamalières, near Clermont-Ferrand. Once more, it seems to have been presided over by a goddess, unnamed but depicted as a seated matron. The shrine —little more than a pool enclosed by a surrounding wall—seems from coin evidence to have been in active use for only a century or so following Caesar's conquest. Thereafter attention was transferred to the springs at Vichy. The waters at Chamalières, unlike those at Sequanna's spring, were heavily mineralized and thus possessed real curative properties. The people's belief

Votive offerings and portrayals from various sites in the Celtic world. *Left to right:*

Relief from Wilsford, Lincolnshire.

Wooden *ex voto,* from Montboux.

Limestone pilgrim figure, holding a small dog, from the source of the Seine, France.
Wooden *ex voto,* source of the Seine.

Bronze votive of Minerva, from Ehl, near Strasbourg, second century A.D.

Female statue of wood, 1.5 meters in height, from the source of the Seine, first century A.D.

Votive statuette, also from the Seine shrine.

also included heads, limbs (usually legs but occasionally arms and hands), and trunks. Even more interest attaches to a group of twenty-two wooden plaques carved in relief to represent internal organs, one of which is an anatomically accurate depiction of the trachea and lungs. Other remarkable items include a collection of bronze and stone votives illustrating eyes, sex organs, and breasts, as well as heads, hands, and

in these powers is reflected in the magnificent and excellently preserved collection of *ex votos* discovered in the mud of the pool. The collection is similar to that found at the source of the Seine but with an emphasis on the eyes, for the cure of which, no doubt, the waters had a particular renown.

RITUAL SHAFTS AND ENCLOSURES

Among the Graeco-Roman cultures of the Mediterranean, it was believed that contact could be made with the underworld by means of ritual shafts dug into the ground. The Greeks called such an excavation a *bothros*, while in Latin it was a *mundus*. The Celts seem to have held to a similar concept. Although there is no clear reference to it in the classical or Irish literature, archaeological evidence for these ritual shafts is becoming increasingly common.

One of the best-known examples of a religious complex containing shafts was found at Holzhausen in Bavaria, where a rectangular earthwork, presumably a ritual enclosure, preceded by timber palisades of the same plan, contained three shafts of which the largest was about forty meters deep. In one of the shallower shafts, eight meters deep, the excavators found a wooden pole, set upright in the bottom of the pit, surrounded by an organic substance

While it is possible that the Celts learned the practice from the Mediterranean world, it is now becoming clear that ritual shafts have an ancient origin in barbarian Europe and, in particular, in Britain. Groups of shafts, apparently nonutilitarian in function, have now been found as far back as the Neolithic period in Hampshire and Norfolk, and other examples have been excavated belonging to the Bronze Age. At Wilsford, close to Stonehenge, a shaft some thirty-four meters in depth had been cut into the solid chalk in the fourteenth century B.C. Although it had functioned as a well, and nothing that could be regarded to be of ritual character was found in it, its size and its situation close to Stonehenge strongly suggest a religious use. Perhaps we are seeing here a combination of the superstition associated with a shaft and the belief in the special properties of spring water.

Shafts were filled with votive offerings, apparently to propitiate the gods residing underground. In the Holzhausen shaft *(above right)*, wooden scaffolding was installed for safety during excavations.

which, according to subsequent analysis, resulted from the decomposition of flesh and blood. The practice of burying a pole or a trunk is also demonstrated by a shaft at Vendée in which was found a four-meter-high Cyprus tree. The ritual nature of these shafts seems indisputable.

A more convincing example of a Bronze Age ritual shaft was found in a brickworks at Swanwick, Hampshire. Here a pit nearly eight meters in depth was excavated. As at Holzhausen, a vertical post was found in the bottom, packed in position with clay, and in the soil around were traces of dried

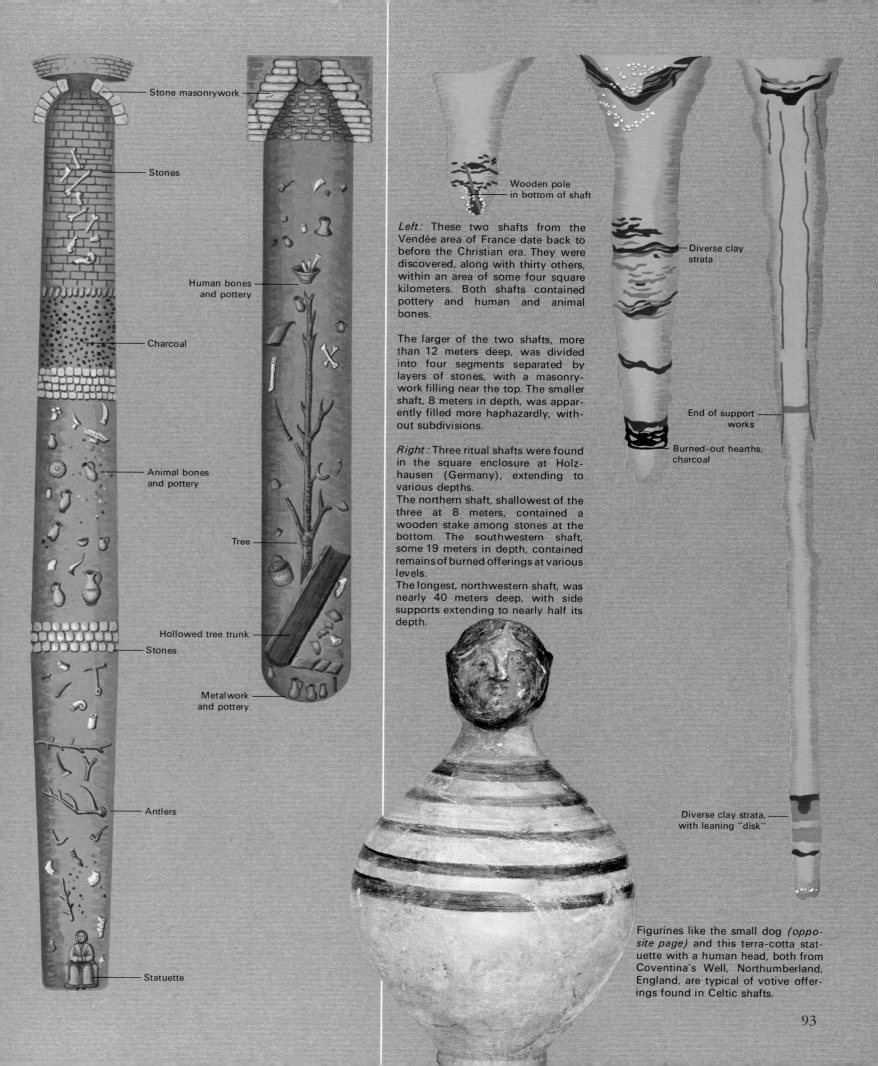

Stone masonrywork

Stones

Charcoal

Human bones
and pottery

Animal bones
and pottery

Tree

Hollowed tree trunk

Stones

Metalwork
and pottery

Antlers

Statuette

Wooden pole
in bottom of shaft

Diverse clay
strata

End of support
works

Burned-out hearths,
charcoal

Diverse clay strata,
with leaning "disk"

Left: These two shafts from the Vendée area of France date back to before the Christian era. They were discovered, along with thirty others, within an area of some four square kilometers. Both shafts contained pottery and human and animal bones.

The larger of the two shafts, more than 12 meters deep, was divided into four segments separated by layers of stones, with a masonrywork filling near the top. The smaller shaft, 8 meters in depth, was apparently filled more haphazardly, without subdivisions.

Right: Three ritual shafts were found in the square enclosure at Holzhausen (Germany), extending to various depths.
The northern shaft, shallowest of the three at 8 meters, contained a wooden stake among stones at the bottom. The southwestern shaft, some 19 meters in depth, contained remains of burned offerings at various levels.
The longest, northwestern shaft, was nearly 40 meters deep, with side supports extending to nearly half its depth.

Figurines like the small dog *(opposite page)* and this terra-cotta statuette with a human head, both from Coventina's Well, Northumberland, England, are typical of votive offerings found in Celtic shafts.

93

flesh and blood. Although precise dating evidence is not available, a date about 1000 B.C. seems probable. Thus the Swanwick shaft presents a convincing predecessor for a tradition that later became widespread in Europe: it is even possible that the belief which required the shafts to be dug originated in Britain and spread from there. The ritual site at Holzhausen was, as we have mentioned, associated with rectangular enclosures. Enclosures of this kind, generally referred to by their German name, *Viereckschanze*, are commonly found north of the Alps concentrated in the triangle between Zurich, Salzburg, and Frankfurt and extending into eastern France. For the most part, they date to the end of the free Celtic period and continued

Libenice in Bohemia provides a particularly interesting example, where, in the third century B.C., an oblong area some eighty by twenty meters was enclosed with a continuous ditch. At one end was an irregular floor created in a hollow dug down into the subsoil containing a stone stela and nearby the holes for two timbers, the charred remains of which were found together with two bronze torques. Apparently the shrines had been adorned with large wooden statues wearing torques. In the floor of the shrine were found several pits, probably dug to take libations, and in addition, there was evidence of human and animal sacrifice together with the burial of an elderly woman who might possibly have been a priestess. Another enclosure, closely com-

Typical Roman Celtic temples consisted of a central cella and a surrounding ambulatory *(reconstruction, top)*. The plan was derived from a

There are also other accounts
of their human sacrifices;
for they used to shoot men down with arrows,
and impale them in the temples,
or making a large statue
of straw and wood,
throw into it cattle
and all sorts of wild animals and
human beings,
and thus make a burnt offering.

Strabo

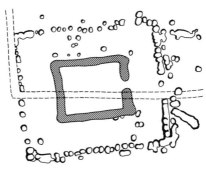

purely Celtic type of which the only example so far known was excavated at Heathrow Airport, London *(diagram above)*, some 10 meters in length. The photograph shows the hilltop shrine, or *cromlech,* of Castlerigg, Cumberland, England: an arrangement of 39 stones in a circle 30 meters in diameter—a religious site of an earlier period.

in use into Roman times. Some are devoid of features, many are associated with burials, and a few with shafts. In all probability they served a ritual function, perhaps simply defining a sacred location where open-air religious practices could be enacted. Once more, a prototype can be found in Britain among the complex of Neolithic ritual monuments excavated at Dorchester-on-Thames in southern Britain, but to suggest a direct relationship is to exceed the reasonable limits of the evidence.

The procedure of defining a ritual area with a fence, bank, or ditch is very ancient and common to many cultures. The *Viereckschanze* is but one manifestation of this practice in the Celtic world. The site of

parable in size and shape but dating to the Late Bronze Age, was found in the Marne at Aulnay-aux-Planches. Within the enclosure there were several human burials, including what is thought to have been a sacrificed infant, and two large post holes, by one of which was a complete ox skull, which had possibly once been attached to one of the posts. It is, of course, impossible to say exactly what went on at Libenice and Aulnay, but we can reasonably classify both enclosures as ritual structures. The seven-hundred year interval separating them is a reminder of the strength and continuity of religious traditions.

Reading the classical sources, one would get the distinct impression that Celtic

Artist's impression of the Romano-British temple of the Celtic god Nodons, at Lydney Park, on the banks of the Severn River. The temple was built late in the Roman period in an old Iron Age hillfort and may represent the revival of an ancient native shrine. Under Roman rule, Celtic sanctuaries became larger and more complex than before.

observances took place in the open or in clearings in woods, perhaps at places like Aulnay and Libenice. Yet sites like Roquepertuse and Entremont show that sacred locations were sometimes monumentalized. Outside the Mediterranean fringe, however, evidence for temples or shrines is still not extensive, but that they did exist is demonstrated by Strabo (quoting Posidonius) in his description of a community of priestesses who inhabited an island close to the mouth of the Loire. "It is their custom," he says, "once a year to remove the roof from their temple and to roof it again in the same day before sunset."

Other evidence of religious buildings comes from excavations, perhaps the best example being a timber-built temple found at Heathrow Airport, London, where a small rectangular cella surrounded by an ambulatory (or corridor), was discovered dating, apparently, to the third century B.C. Similar cella-like structures have recently been found in the hillforts of Danebury and South Cadbury in southern Britain. The particular interest of the Heathrow temple lies in the fact that its plan is exactly mirrored by many hundreds of masonry-built temples erected in Gaul and Britain during the Roman period. The continuity of building form is impressive; so too is the actual continuity in use, which can be demonstrated at a number of locations, where rather ill-defined Iron Age structures were replaced by distinctive Romano-Celtic temples.

While it is true that the rectangular temple is the normal type throughout most of

Europe, circular shrines are not uncommon in western France and in Britain. It may be that the two styles simply reflect the different traditions of house building prevalent in these regions.

Map of the principal Celtic religious sites, according to archaeological and literary evidence. Our knowledge of Celtic religious centers is incomplete, particularly because so many shrines were simple outdoor sites, rather than monumental buildings in the style of Greece or Rome.

The Celts favored the forest clearing, as in the reconstruction sketch (left), as a place of worship.

THE GENIUS OF THE CELTS

Celtic craftsmen perfected, and brought into wide use, the spoked wheel, as shown in this reconstruction of a La Tène original.

Opposite page (from top): Examples of brilliant Celtic art: open bronze plaque of a first-century A.D. horse harness; reconstruction drawing of the Desborough mirror; enameled ornament from a horse harness.

Their man-sized shields
are decorated, each in individual fashion.
Some include projecting bronze animals
of brilliant workmanship
which serve for defense as well as decoration.

Diodorus Siculus

The arts of war, in time of crisis, absorbed the efforts and talents of the Celts. Their opponents might thus dismiss them as backward, incapable of seasoned thought, refinement, or the development of sophisticated socio-political institutions. Indeed, their gifts lay in a different area from those of classical Mediterranean civilization. At an early stage the Celts excelled at mining and metalworking, skills that led to all-important mastery of the wheel and the plow. The Celts produced an art that might be called baroque rather than classical: In place of Greek abstraction, a whimsical profusion of detail and daring line. Rather than sober balance and harmonious proportion, a taste for stylization and grotesquery. The Celtic freedom could shock the spectator—force him to rediscover the world, see reality anew. The same creative freshness was to burst upon the European literary scene centuries and centuries later, when the fantastical Irish and Breton legends would fertilize medieval literature.

In recognizing the *Keltoi* as one of the four peoples of the barbarian world, the Greek geographers were tacitly admitting that a vast area of temperate Europe, stretching from Transdanubia to the Atlantic, shared one culture. The linguistic evidence, the documentary evidence bearing upon society and behavior, and the iconographic evidence reflecting the supernatural—all combine to demonstrate a remarkable degree of unity linking all parts of the Celtic territories.

The Celts were one of the last barbarian peoples of temperate Europe, their culture representing the culmination of six thousand years of indigenous development. It had evolved slowly but surely, aberrant developments quickly dying out while beneficial changes were retained and integrated into the communal experience. By the middle of the first millennium B.C. a technological equilibrium had been reached. Comparing Celtic technology with that of preindustrial Europe of the eighteenth century A.D., one finds surprisingly few significant differences apart from knowledge of gunpowder and its associated developments. Iron was not cast and the horse collar had not yet been introduced from China, nor had the Celts shown any aptitude for hydraulic engineering. (This is not surprising: engineering would not have appealed to the Celtic temperament.) The Celt was immediate and spontaneous in his responses, able to carry out communal projects like the building of defenses when they became necessary to protect his social institutions, but with no particular facility for abstract calculations.

From whichever direction we approach the Celts, through literature, art, or archaeology, the overriding impression one gets is of immense energy. Celtic society was coiled like a spring, tensed ready for action. This shows in the boisterous nature of social gatherings and in conduct in battle; it also pervades Celtic art—one has only to look at the mirror back (p. 99) to sense the restlessness of it all.

The quick, agile mind of the Celt, his love of riddles and of the half-stated are characteristics noted by classical observers: this sense of enigma lies behind the best of his abstract art. Free Celtic society at its most developed cannot be regarded as a mature expression of a people; it was a society in its adolescence.

To the Greeks anyone who did not speak Greek but made unintelligible sounds was called a barbarian. The word was not overtly derogatory; it implied that one was non-civilized, but it did not have its modern connotation of lacking in culture and sensitivity. No one who has looked at items of decorated Celtic metalwork or has read the Irish sagas could accuse the Celts of that. In the visual arts, Celtic craftsmen working under the patronage of the aristocracy produced a style that was both original and exciting. It was an abstract art which, from a close observation of the natural world, distilled the essence of line and form. There was no desire to depict reality, but instead to capture the spirit, the intangible, and the fleeting. Just as Celtic literature is ridden with illusions, surprise, and shape-shifting, so too is Celtic art.

THE SO-CALLED BARBARIANS

Although, in its first flowering, Celtic art was reserved to the aristocracy, it soon became the art of the people. An Iron Age potter was as concerned to produce a satisfying decoration on his cooking pot as was the bronzesmith. His medium of expression may have been less exotic and his skill less developed, but the essential love of form was shared by both. The humble domestic pottery and decorated wooden vessels from the Somerset marshes are a vivid reminder that decoration, and presumably bright color, formed a normal part of everyday experience.

Most of the Celtic world was eventually submerged beneath the tide of Roman imperial aggression, and the hand of classicism lay heavy upon Celtic creative abilities. There could be no turning back; nor was there submission. Although representation became the accepted mode of display, it was often representation on Celtic terms, with pictorial accuracy subservient to line and movement.

He saw a woman
at the edge of the spring,
with a bright silver comb
ornamented with gold,
washing her hair in a
silver bowl with four
golden birds on it, and little
flashing jewels of purple
carbuncle on the rims
of the bowl. She had a
shaggy purple cloak made
of fine fleece, and silver
brooches of filigree work
decorated with handsome
gold, in the cloak;
a long-hooded tunic on her,
stiff and smooth, of green
silk with embroidery
of red gold. Wonderful
ornaments of gold and
silver with twining animal
designs, in the tunic on her
breast and her shoulders
and her shoulder-blades
on both sides.

Irish poem, ninth century

At every level of their lives the Celts liked to be surrounded by ornaments and decoration. Even quite humble items like safety-pin-type brooches were frequently elaborated. This little brooch from Reinheim, Germany, was worked into the form of a cock, inset with pieces of imported coral. It dates from the late fifth or early fourth century B.C.

Schools of craftsmen developed local styles in many parts of Europe. In Britain, for example, in the first century B.C. and early first century A.D., decorated mirrors became popular and were made by many different hands; at least one was exported to Holland. This brilliant example is from Old Warden in Bedfordshire, England.

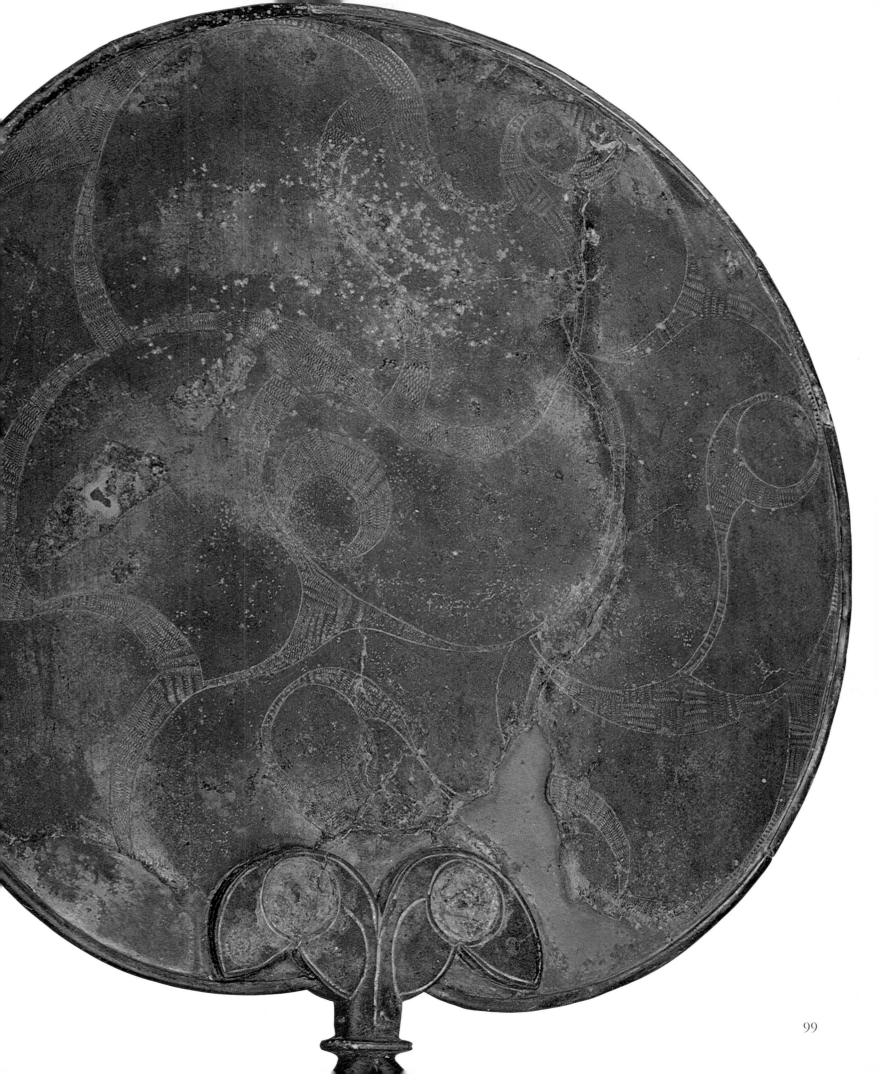

The genesis of Celtic art lay in the molding together of several disparate styles into something quite unique and distinctive. Beneath everything lay indigenous Hallstatt modes of decoration—a sense of contrasting colors and textures, but a style essentially four-square and geometric. Superimposed upon this was the art of the classical world interpreted particularly through its Graeco-Etruscan manifestations. Bronze vessels decorated with palmettes and tendrils flooded into the Celtic world and into the households of the chieftains. A third, more shadowy, element came from the east, though by what mechanism is unknown. Eastern Europe had for some while been settled by peoples closely related to the Scythians practicing their own exquisite style of animal art. Upon this was superimposed a Persian flavor. Perhaps the craftsmen serving this strange hybrid of Greek, Scythian, and Persian migrated to the west—perhaps it was little more than traded goods, saddle cloths, leatherwork, and fabric wall hangings that brought the eastern flavor to the courts of the Celtic aristocracy. At any event, in the latter part of the fifth century we can see the different elements coming together in the earliest manifestation of a truly Celtic art known as the Early Strict Style—Celtic, yet of recognizable parentage.

In the ensuing centuries Celtic art became an expression of the Celtic spirit. There developed what is called the Free Style: free graphic for its two dimensional form, free plastic when in three dimensions. It is a style which eschews bilateral symmetry and adapts design to form—elements grow and die away again and everything is in a state of tense balance. Finally, growing contact with the world of Rome, introducing new standards of formality and leading to the emergence of more stable, urban forms of government, gives rise to a more staid art style which reflects the change of the times.

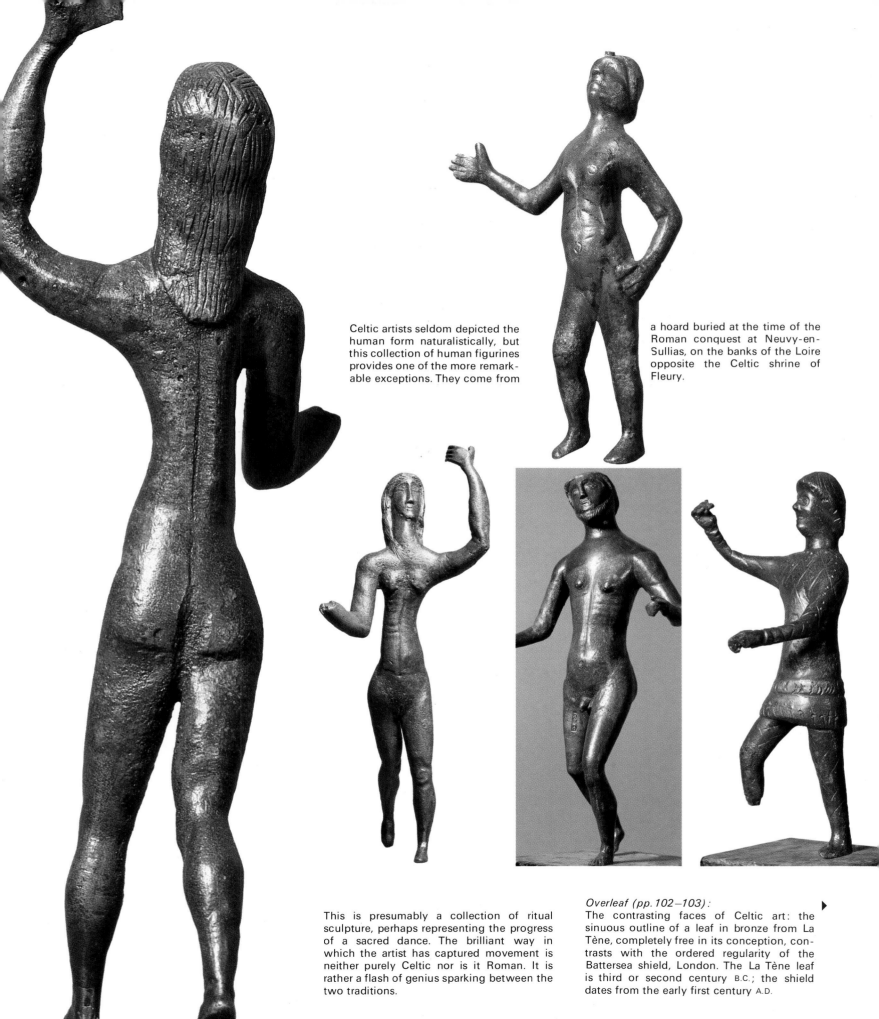

Celtic artists seldom depicted the human form naturalistically, but this collection of human figurines provides one of the more remarkable exceptions. They come from a hoard buried at the time of the Roman conquest at Neuvy-en-Sullias, on the banks of the Loire opposite the Celtic shrine of Fleury.

This is presumably a collection of ritual sculpture, perhaps representing the progress of a sacred dance. The brilliant way in which the artist has captured movement is neither purely Celtic nor is it Roman. It is rather a flash of genius sparking between the two traditions.

Overleaf (pp. 102–103): ▶
The contrasting faces of Celtic art: the sinuous outline of a leaf in bronze from La Tène, completely free in its conception, contrasts with the ordered regularity of the Battersea shield, London. The La Tène leaf is third or second century B.C.; the shield dates from the early first century A.D.

One can recognize in the earlier manifestation of Celtic art the disparate influences which led to its genesis. The palmette and lyre motifs of the Graeco-Etruscan world can readily be distinguished in two gold openwork designs illustrated here: the cup from the chieftain's grave at Schwarzenbach, Germany *(right)*, and the gold mounting from Eigenbilzen, Belgium *(bottom)*.

The flagon from Basse-Yutz in the Lorraine *(far right)* is a fine example of the fusing of the different traditions. In form, and in the decoration beneath its spout, the flagon is clearly dependent on Etruscan inspiration, but the magnificent beast which forms its handle is ultimately Scythian in style.

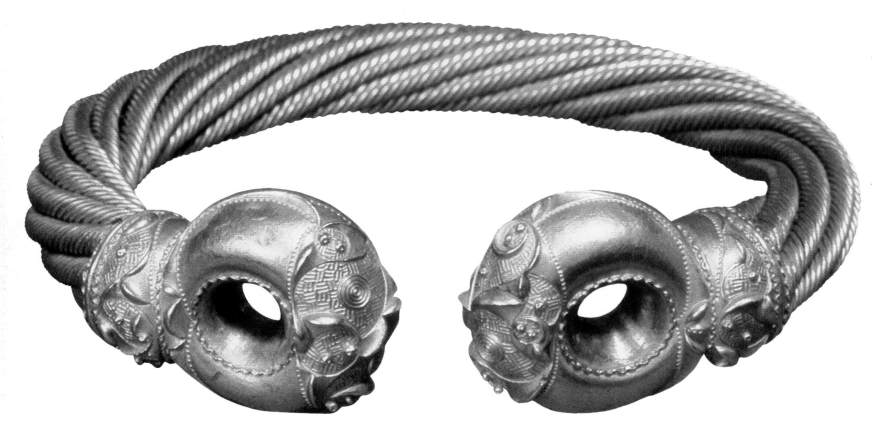

Although Celtic art in its later stages became a folk art, there were still some schools of craftsmen working in precious metals for aristocratic patrons. One of these schools, probably located somewhere in the east of England, made gold torques of enormous value, of which the example illustrated above from Snettisham in Norfolk is justly the most famous.

Opposite: Celtic artists were so adept at capturing the essence of a figure or face with an economy of detail that it is often very difficult to be sure of the dating of some pieces, like the god from Bouvray, France. His features strongly suggest the work of a Celt in the first century B.C.

THE DRUIDS: PRIESTS, SEERS, JUDGES

Within the upper echelons of Celtic society was a learned class, respected for their wisdom and for their special powers as intermediaries between the tribe and the gods. These men were known as druids—a word which probably derives from a term for "knowledge of the oak" or alternatively "profound knowledge." They were wise men: in their hands lay all the intellectual activities necessary for the satisfactory running of society. Caesar is quite specific about the duties of the druids: they "officiate at the worship of the gods, regulate public and private sacrifices, and give rulings on all religious questions. Large numbers of young men flock to them for instruction, and they are held in great honor by the people. They act as judges in practically all disputes whether between tribes or between individuals." Here then is a succinct summary of their powers; priests and magicians, teachers and judges, they command respect well beyond that of their own tribe of origin.

The order was under the control of an archdruid appointed by his fellows by virtue of his outstanding merit. Caesar mentions that election ensues if several people of equal ability present themselves, and adds that orderly voting sometimes degenerates into an outright fight between the contestants—a not unexpected eventuality in the Celtic world.

The druids formed a privileged class exempt from taxes and from military service, attractions which apparently encouraged large numbers of young men to seek admission to the order. Training, however, was rigorous. The initiates were required to memorize a great volume of oral learning; so much, says Caesar, that some of them spent twenty years at their studies. "The druids believe that their religion forbids them to commit their teachings to writing... but," he adds, "I imagine that this rule was originally established for other reasons—because they did not want their doctrine to become public property and in order to prevent their pupils from relying on the written word and neglecting to train their memories." His explanation was superfluous since the real reason was that Celtic was not a written language. What the druids committed to memory was the entire knowledge store of the community: magic formulas, ritual procedures, medical knowledge, law, folk history, and genealogies. To aid the memory a simple verse form with repeated epithets would have been adopted. It was by this means that the Irish folktales were passed from one generation to the next until they were eventually written down by Christian scribes in the eighth century.

Caesar recognized the druids as the only class of intellectuals in Gaul, but this seems to be an oversimplification. Other writers —Strabo, Diodorus, Athenaeus—supported by the Irish literature, distinguish three distinct categories: the bards, in whose poetry the history and traditions of the tribe were immortalized; the augurers, who oversaw the sacrifices and foretold the future; and the druids proper, versed in law and philosophy—the conservers of the ancient wisdoms. An occasional overlap in function may have obscured the differences and led Caesar into his somewhat inaccurate generalization.

The function of the bards was clearly defined by Athenaeus (quoting Posidonius). He refers to them as entertainers. "These are the poets who deliver eulogies in song"—it was they who were responsible for extolling the virtues of their aristocratic patrons. In Ireland the *fili* shared some of the functions of the *bard*: he learned by heart the traditions and genealogies of his people and composed his own verses, often in praise of his patron or of other aristocrats. Bardic schools, where these skills were taught, flourished in Ireland even as late as the seventeenth century.

The judicial functions of the druids were very important to the stability of society: their powers were wide ranging. Disputes

The wise men of Celtic society, who were sometimes classed together and called "druids," were healers, teachers, musicians, poets, augurers, priests, and judges. Some of the contemporary writers recognize their specialities and distinguish between them. One function of the druids was to officiate at sacrifices, often the sacrifice of human beings. The more forbidding side of Celtic supernatural belief is intimated in this sculpture from Noves in southern France, dating to the third or second century B.C. The fearsome scaly beast squats on the ground: he is in the act of devouring someone and holds severed heads in each paw.

Control of healing plants figured among the responsibilities of the druids. Healing was also a function of some of the gods. The Dagda, in Irish mythology, was usually accompanied by a caldron, the contents of which, among its other properties, had healing powers. According to one interpretation, this scene on the Gundestrup caldron shows the Great God allowing a mortal to partake of the caldron. Another suggestion, no less plausible, is that the small figure is a sacrifice being thrown into a sacred shaft!

between individuals, crimes including man-slaughter, disagreements over boundaries or inheritances, all came within their jurisdiction. According to Caesar, an annual gathering was held each year near Chartres in Gaul on an appointed day. "Those who are involved in disputes assemble here from all parts and accept the druids' judgments and awards." Their decisions were final. "They ... adjudicate the matter and appoint the compensation to be paid and received by the parties concerned. Any individual or tribe failing to accept the award is banned from taking part in sacrifice." The power of the druids, then, transcended tribal boundaries: they were even able to come between opposing forces and halt battles.

The druids were also the philosophers of society. They studied the movements of the heavenly bodies, and according to Caesar they gave instruction to young men in astronomy, the size of the universe and of the earth, and the power and abilities of the gods. Another aspect of their teaching concerned life after death. They believed that the soul did not perish, but after death passed from one body to another—a philosophical concept which the military mind of Caesar interprets somewhat mundanely: "They think that this is the best incentive to bravery, because it teaches men to disregard the terrors of death." These tantalizing references to a philosophical tradition among the Celts imply a degree of sophisticated thought which some modern writers believe to have been influenced by the stoic philosophy of Greece.

Caesar is explicit about the sacrificial duties of druids: they officiate at the worship of the gods and regulate public and private sacrifice. Other writers, however, imply that the actual augury was undertaken by special officials, though it is of course possible that a druid had to be present at these ceremonies to make sure that the correct procedures were followed.

Strabo explains:

They used to strike a man whom they had devoted to death in the back with a knife, and then divine from his death-throes, but they did not sacrifice without a druid.... We are told of still other kinds of sacrifices; for example they would shoot victims to death with their arrows, or impale them in temples....

The point to emphasize here is the essential presence, though not necessarily the participation, of the druid.

The rite of human sacrifice is emphasized, with explicit disgust, by several Roman writers (though it comes incongruously from a society that relished as entertainment mass slaughter in the amphitheater). The poet Lucan writes of a Celtic shrine near Massilia where "there were many dark springs running, and grim-faced figures of gods roughly hewn by the axe from the untrimmed tree-trunk rotted to whiteness"—these places were steeped in human blood from victims sacrificed to the gods. Exactly the same point is made by Tacitus in describing the Roman attack on the druid stronghold on Anglesey in A.D. 59, as the result of which the army hacked down the groves "sacred to the savage rites... for their religion enjoined them to drench their altars with the blood of prisoners, and to find out the will of the gods by consulting the entrails of human beings."

The self-satisfied Pliny concludes, "We can hardly realize how much is owed to the Romans, who swept away the monstrous conditions in which to kill a man was the highest religious function, and to eat him was even more highly salubrious." No doubt human sacrifice was unpalatable to some Romans. More to the point, it provided Roman propagandists with an excellent self-righteous excuse to annihilate Celtic religion, when really what they feared was the ability of the druids to unite the Celts in resistance to Rome. To the Celt human sacrifice was simply a means by which their augurers could communicate with the gods.

We know little in detail of the ritual procedures guided by the druids, but in one unique and charming passage, recorded by Pliny, we can come close to the reality of a Celtic ceremony. He tells us that mistletoe is a well-known healing plant and that if it is found growing on an oak tree it is thought to be particularly potent, if cut according to a strict ritual. First of all two white bulls have to be brought to the spot. Then the white-robed priest clutching a golden sickle climbs the tree and cuts the mistletoe, which is caught in a white robe by those standing below. The bulls are then sacrificed, while prayers to the gods ask that they allow the gift to be propitious. Mistletoe, harvested in this way and taken

The druids are wont
to be absent from war,
nor do they pay taxes
like the others;
they are dispensed
from military service
and free
of all other obligations.
Attracted by these prizes
many join the order
of their own accord
or are sent by parents
or relatives. It is said
that they commit to memory
immense amounts of poetry.
And so some of them
continue their studies
for twenty years.
They consider it improper
to entrust their studies
to writing,
although they use
the Greek alphabet
in nearly everything else,
in their public
and private accounts.

Caesar

The bronze calendar of Coligny is one of the most remarkable Celtic objects to be discovered. Dating to the late first century B.C., it is wholly Celtic in concept and is the oldest document written in the Celtic language.

It was divided into 16 columns, each of four months, representing a five-year cycle (62 lunar months plus two intercalary months). It may be that the surviving section was part of a larger 19-year calendar. Each month, of 29 or 30 days, is divided into a dark and a light half, and the days in each one are separately numbered. The months are divided between good ("MAT") and not good ("ANM"), and some of the festivals, those corresponding to Beltine and Lugnasad, are indicated. The months are also named.

The calendar uses Roman lettering, but this should not obscure its purely Celtic nature.

110

in a drink, could make barren animals fertile and was an antidote for all poisons. "Such are the religious feelings that are entertained towards trifling things by many peoples" adds Pliny. The record is fascinating not only for the immediacy which it imparts to Celtic ritual, but as a reminder that the druids were also responsible for preserving the medical knowledge of the community. It is an aspect upon which other contemporary writers are silent.

The reference to the fertility of herds is a reflection of the importance of the druids in ensuring the well-being of the community, particularly with respect to seasonal activities and the appropriate rituals which accompanied them. Everything was determined by the calendar, which it was the druids' responsibility to maintain and observe. In Celtic Ireland the year was divided into two halves, which were each once subdivided. The old year ended and the new year began at the festival of *Samain* (the first of November), which marked the beginning of the dark half of the year. The second (light) half began at *Beltine*, celebrated on May the first. Between these two major ceremonies were two other of lesser importance, *Imbolc*, held on the first of February, and *Lugnasad* on the first of August. The calendar was regulated by the druids and calculated by lunar observations, the passage of time being measured by the passing of nights.

The famous calendar found at Coligny *(opposite)* shows just how well-ordered Celtic astronomy was. The year, divided into twelve lunar months, was adapted to the solar year by adding an extra month of thirty days in every three-year cycle. Each month, of thirty or twenty-nine days, was divided into two halves, a light and a dark half, echoing the division of the year. The thirty-day month was auspicious and the twenty-nine-day month inauspicious, and within each some days were lucky while others were not. Clearly, for the good of the community, it was essential that certain acts, the beginning of the planting season, the bringing in of the herds, or the initiation of a conflict, should be undertaken on the most auspicious day possible, and only the druids could advise on this. By controlling the calendar, the druids controlled society. It is easy to understand their preeminent position in the Celtic world.

> Then by slow degrees
> the iron sword
> came to the fore,
> the bronze sickle
> fell into disrepute,
> the plowman began to cleave
> the earth with iron,
> and on the darkling
> field of battle
> the odds were made even.
>
> Lucretius

NEW TOOLS AND SKILLS

The importance of the craft of the ironworker in the Celtic world is demonstrated by the fact that the tribal god is sometimes shown in the guise of a smith, conflated, in the Roman period, with the god Vulcan. Representations of this kind (this example is Romano-British) provide evidence of the smithying tools of the period.

By about 1000 B.C. bronzeworking technology had reached its peak of achievement. The metal could be cast into a variety of complex forms: it could be beaten into thin sheets and riveted to form vessels, and alloys could be produced of varying composition with qualities suitable for a range of different uses. These skills marked the culmination of some three thousand years of practice and experiment. In the eighth century B.C., barbarian Europe was introduced to a new metal—iron. Knowledge of iron extraction can be traced back to the second millennium in the east. By 1500 B.C. the metal was being produced in significant quantities by the Hittites of the New Empire in Anatolia, but the skills involved were a closely guarded secret. In the thirteenth century B.C., King Hattusilis III wrote to the king of Assyria:

As for the iron which you wrote to me about, good iron is not available.... That it is a bad time for producing iron I have written. They will produce good iron, but as yet they will not have finished. When they have finished I shall send it to you. Today I am dispatching an iron dagger blade to you.

This fascinating insight implies that the Hittites held a monopoly over iron production, while the reference to the wrong season hints that iron extraction may well have been in the hands of peasants working in the winter when agricultural demands were slack. The rarity of iron is further emphasized at this time by a letter from the pharaoh of Egypt to the king of the Hittites asking for a supply of the metal. A little earlier, in the mid-fourteenth century, we find iron armlets and an iron dagger among the treasures buried with Tutankhamen.

In the twelfth century, partly as the result of barbarian attacks, the Hittite empire collapsed and in the chaos of folk movement which engulfed the Aegean world at this time, knowledge of iron smelting spread to Europe. The links are tenuous in the extreme. Cyprus and Palestine soon shared the new technology, and from the former, in the early eleventh century B.C., knowledge of ironworking spread to the isolated communities along the Aegean coasts of Greece. With the emergence of Greek civilization an iron industry became firmly established in Europe.

By the eighth century the Greeks had established a colony at Pithekoussai on the island of Ischia near Naples. Here, in eighth-century contexts, there is indisputable evidence that iron, imported from the island of Elba some 250 miles to the north, was being smelted in quantity. However, there is evidence of even earlier ironworking in Italy, suggesting that the Greek colonists merely intensified a production which had probably already been initiated by direct contacts between Cyprus and the east and Italy. Once established on the Italian mainland, a knowledge of ironworking could naturally have spread northward into Europe.

The new technology may, however, have reached the Celts by another route. Recent work in Hungary, in the northern part of the Great Hungarian Plain, has unearthed iron trinkets located in tombs dating to the eighth century. These graves and their contexts have similarities to the culture which extends from the north Pontic region into the valley of the lower Danube. We have seen (p. 19) that these peoples may well represent horse-riding communities who moved into Europe as the result of Scythian pressures on their Pontic homeland in the ninth and eighth centuries; if so, they could well have brought a knowledge of ironworking with them into Hungary. Trade and exchange with the communities to the west would have led inevitably to the spread of the new technology. Thus from the east and the south the Late Bronze Age communities of the Alpine fringes were introduced to the benefits of iron.

Although ironworking spread rapidly across central and western Europe, reaching the western parts of Britain by the seventh century B.C., the metal was at first by no means common. Presumably broken weapons and worn-out tools were reforged to make new implements rather than being discarded in the rubbish heaps of the farmsteads. In burials and votive deposits, on the other hand, iron weapons occur quite frequently. By the first century B.C., rejected implements are commonly found, and the extensive use of nails in the ramparts of *murus Gallicus* type (300 tons at Manching) shows that the community could afford to be lavish with its iron. Clearly, production methods had so improved, as the result of industrial intensification, that the metal was in plentiful supply.

Iron had many advantages over bronze, not the least of which was its durability. Moreover, its natural distribution was wider than that of copper and tin and it was comparatively easy to work. The ore occurred in many forms, quite close to the surface and could therefore be gathered without elaborate mining. After initial roasting, the ore was mixed with charcoal and heated in a small bowl furnace, to about 900°C. At this temperature the ore was reduced to iron and the impurities melted to form a slag which accumulated in the bottom of the furnace, leaving the

iron as a spongy mass known as a bloom, which had to be reheated and beaten to remove the remaining slag inclusions.

At an early stage, production was no doubt organized on a cottage industry basis, most communities being able to produce sufficient for their own needs. With increasing specialization, however, a few centers began to concentrate on iron extraction, forging the crude metal into ingots of various shapes for transport and exchange. Thus, by the first century B.C., the majority of iron used, whether by the small farmers

or by the specialist smiths in the towns, reached them in ingot form from well-organized production centers. Those tribes who could control the main iron deposits grew rich on the proceeds. It is hardly a coincidence that several of the newly developing urban centers of Celtic Europe grew up in close proximity to rich supplies of iron ore.

A durable testimony to the metal-working technology of the Celts is the sword sheath, a fourth-century B.C. product found at Hallstatt, Austria. In this detail view, two warriors are holding a wheel believed to be a symbol sacred to the war god. A sketch of the whole sheath is found on pages 24–25.

MINING TECHNOLOGY

A La Tène swordsmith's trademark, stamped on the blade of a sword. In a warrior society the role of the swordsmith was important and the manufacture of weapons became a highly skilled craft in the La Tène period. We may suppose from the evidence of such surviving trade marks that the work of specific armorers whose identities are otherwise lost to us was particularly valued for its excellence.

While iron ore could, for the most part, be gathered from shallow surface workings, certain mineral deposits—in particular, rock salt and copper—were only obtainable in some regions by deep mining. Mining technology in Europe had a considerable ancestry going back to the Neolithic period when extensive shafts and radiating galleries were dug through the chalk of southern Britain and the Low Countries to reach the bands of flint required to make tools. At about the same time, in parts of southeastern Europe, pits were being sunk to reach rich lodes of copper. Thus by the Late Bronze Age some two thousand years of experience had been gained in the intricacies of mining engineering.

The extraction of rock salt is best exemplified in the mines of the eastern Alps, in the region of Salzburg, Hallstatt, and Dürrnberg. At Hallstatt, using socketed bronze picks and winged axes, the miners hacked their way deep into the mountain side, their shuttered galleries extending as far as 350 meters from the surface. In the salt-laden conditions within the galleries a wide range of organic material survived, including the wooden shovels of the miners and the framed leather sacks which they used to transport the rock salt from the mine face.

While the rock salt was comparatively easy to extract, the copper lodes embedded in hard crystalline rocks in the vicinity of Salzburg presented more formidable problems to the miners of the Late Bronze Age. The best known of their workings occurs on the Mitterberg in the Mühlbach-Beschofshofen region where a vein of copper pyrites some two meters thick outcropped in the mountainside over a distance in excess of 1,600 meters. The two principal problems faced by the miners were how to break up the excessively hard rock and how to remove water from the shafts which followed the vein into the mountain sloping down at between 20 and 30 degrees below the horizontal. Although simple mining tools were available, the method used to break the rock was firesetting. A fire was lit against the working face and after the rock had been given time to heat, cold water was thrown on it inducing extensive cracking. This allowed the face to be more easily worked with picks and axes. The technique was, of course, very wasteful of wood: it was estimated that for each cubic meter of ore extracted nine cubic meters of wood were required. When it is remembered that the galleries needed extensive propping and shuttering, it is no surprise that lumbermen were estimated to constitute one-third of the total labor force.

The mining operation began by attacking the vein where it outcropped on the surface, but gradually as the tunnel deepened, an intermediate platform was introduced upon which debris could be piled to form a suitable basis for fires set against the roof of the shaft. An added advantage of this system was that the two levels provided ample means for air to circulate, and indeed the heat from the fires set up a vigorous convection current. The lower shaft also allowed surface water to be collected behind a dam, from where it could be bucketed out of the workings. In this way, and with the insertion of additional staging where necessary, the shaft bored deep into the mountain, the largest reaching a length of 160 meters and a height of 30 meters. The ore would have been dragged out of the shaft on sledges and then sorted, roasted, and smelted. To facilitate this, ancillary works like water channels for the ore washing and roasting ovens for the secondary preparation had to be built and maintained. The entire enterprise was evidently thoroughly co-ordinated and heavily manned—one estimate suggests that to service each fully developed shaft about 180 men would have been needed. How they were recruited we will never know, but in all probability they would have worked together for several months at a time, returning home to their families in spring in time to take part in the activities of the farming year. Their life in the high mountain valleys cannot have been easy. Camping out among the waste heaps of the workings, the atmosphere heavy with smoke belching from the mine shafts and sulfurous fumes from the roasting furnaces, their daily routine was rigorous. Felling and dragging timber for the shuttering and the fires, hacking rock from the work face and carting it to the furnaces—the simple life of the farmer must have seemed idyllic in comparison. Something of the immense effort involved can be gauged when it is said that the Mitterberg mines are estimated to have produced twenty thousand metric tons of crude copper during their life.

Extensive Celtic salt mining operations are known in the Eastern Alps, with tunnels running up to 350 meters into the mountain side. The actual extraction of the salt was in some cases effected by the use of water-power, as shown in the sketch, left. A nearby stream was diverted to flood into the mineshaft. The rock salt was thus washed out of the mine, and led through a conduit system into large vats, where the water was evaporated off, using heat from the sun, or wood fires under the vats.

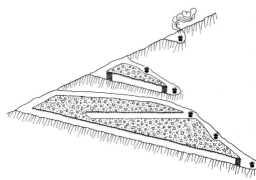

The diagram above shows the development of the deep shafts necessary to extract copper ore at Mühlbach-Bischofshafen. At the top is the first stage in the technique, known as firesetting; the building of a fire at the start of the shaft. Alternate heating and cooling with water cracked the stone and enabled the shaft to be deepened. In the second stage, as the tunnel lengthened and widened, a platform was erected, built up with debris from the excavation. On this further fires were built, to attack the roof of the shaft, and also to assist the circulation of air in the workings. This system could be extended, as in the third stage, up to 160 meters into the mountain. Damming the bottom shaft also enabled the water level in the mine to be controlled.

MASTERY OF
THE WHEEL

The Celts learned how to shrink an iron tire on a wooden wheel. This seventeenth-century French engraving by Benard shows a contemporary wheelwright at work using techniques and tools which would have been wholly familiar to a Celt. The

Wheeled vehicles were extensively used in the Celtic world to carry warriors into battle, dead chieftains to their graves, and for a whole range of more mundane purposes about the village or farm. To judge from the surviving remains, the art of the wheelwright was both widespread and highly developed: indeed the craft has shown little significant improvement since the second century B.C. It was during the first millennium B.C. that the spoked wheel as we know it today was perfected.

The early prehistory of the wheel is not our concern: suffice it to say that plank-wheeled vehicles had reached all parts of Europe long before the emergence of the Celts and

cast in bronze in a single piece. On average these bronze wheel centers were about fifty centimeters in diameter, and clearly they were meant to be fitted with a wooden tire set into a channel in the bronze wheel rim and secured by rivets. How wide these tires were cannot now be determined, but they are unlikely to have exceeded ten centimeters. Thus the completed wheel would be quite small, never more than seventy centimeters in diameter. Since the spokes were of cast bronze, they were strong and needed only to be few: normally there were four, five, or six. Finally to create a durable running surface nails with expanded heads were sometimes set in the

wheel is first constructed of its wooden parts. Then an iron tire is made fractionally too small for the wheel. The idea is that when the tire is heated, it will expand and can be forced over the wheel (left), burning itself into position. On cooling, the iron will contract and the tire will shrink on to the felly, binding all parts of the wheel tightly together.

that spoked-wheeled chariots were evidently in use among the Mycenaeans of Greece in the thirteenth century B.C. The wheels of the Mycenaean chariot, however, insofar as one can judge from contemporary representations, were of a specific type which appears to be identical to Late Bronze Age wheels from the rest of Europe. Essentially the hub, spokes, and rim were

wooden tire. This then was the prototype from which the more advanced wheel type was to develop.

The next stage is represented by a wheel found in a late seventh-century grave at Salamis in Cyprus. It was composed largely of wood with eight spokes set into a wooden felly made up of two strips of wood both bent into a circle, their overlapping ends being secured with nails. Strictly speaking, the inner felly, the spokes, and the hub together formed that part of the wheel which, in the earlier examples we have described, had been made of bronze; while the outer felly of wood was the equivalent to the wooden tire. How it was attached to the inner member is uncertain, but in all probability some kind of tongue-and-groove joint was perfected, much as the wooden tire had been set into the channel of the bronze wheel center.

Wheels of this type are depicted on Assyrian reliefs and frescoes, and it may have been from this region that the technique

spread to the eastern Mediterranean and thus to the European mainland, perhaps via the Etruscans in northern Italy. But rather like the problem of the spread of iron technology (pp. 112–113), the idea of the multiple felly wheel may have penetrated Europe by another route: that is, from the east, overland along the Danube valley since the oldest known spoked wheel

with a broad felly was found in Transcaucasia. Which route of introduction had precedence over the other it is impossible to say. It may be that the Celtic wheelwrights, already adept at wheel making, simply absorbed new ideas brought to their attention by travelers and traders from surrounding areas, and created a concept of their own.

The resulting spoked wheel found in graves of the seventh century in Germany and Bohemia, was a sophisticated device. It was composed entirely of wood with iron fittings. In general construction it resembled the wheels from Cyprus, but there were significant differences. The fellies were of double thickness, the inner one being composed of a single piece of wood bent into a circle, while the outer one was made up of several separate sections each bent

into an arc to suit the curvature of the inner felly. They were joined with iron clamps which also bound the two fellies together. The wooden parts of these wheels have rotted, but the structure can be reconstructed because the separate wooden sections have left grain impressions preserved in the rust on the iron clamps.

To give the wheel added rigidity, the ends of the spokes penetrated both inner and outer fellies and the whole was bound by an iron tire which was attached to the wood with large-headed iron nails, the nail heads forming the actual running surface.

These early Hallstatt wheels provide a fascinating glimpse of technology in a state of change: they owe much to the earlier bronze type but have adopted the double-thickness felly of the Assyrian type of wheel to which has been added the sig-

Below: Cast bronze wheels, as on this ritual model from Schlesien, Germany, were well known in central Europe in the Late Bronze Age. But the spoked wheel of wood did not make an appearance in the archaeological record until the seventh century, and then it is found only in chieftains' graves. These early wheels were cumbersome, but from the fifth century onward the technology of wheelmaking had been mastered and elegant vehicles, like the cart from Dejbjerg, Denmark *(left),* became more widely distributed. The wheel was a recurring motif in Celtic iconography, ultimately deriving perhaps from a solar symbol. *Far left:* A Romano-Celtic deity holding a wheel, from Carlisle, England.

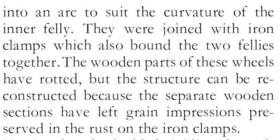

The shrinking-on of iron tires was a technique used by the barrel-maker. Celtic barrels are unknown, but Roman wine was imported in bound barrels of this type. *Above:* Detail of wine barrels on a river boat; Gallo-Roman relief from Cabrières-d'Aygues.

117

nificant innovation of the iron tire. Wheels of this kind were resilient, strong, and hard wearing, but they were still rather heavy; and although the weight did not matter much in general-purpose vehicles, the emergence of chariot warfare in the fifth century B.C. demanded a lighter structure but one of great strength. It was quite possibly this need that encouraged the final improvements to be made in the technology of the Celtic wheel.

The perfected wheel is best demonstrated by the four-wheeled ritual vehicle of the first century B.C. found in a bog near Dejbjerg in Denmark. The felly was now a single piece of wood, as little as five centimeters thick, bent and clamped at the joint,

harness pole to the chassis was a somewhat cumbersome arrangement which must have affected maneuverability. The Dejbjerg cart was, however, designed for stately ritual processions in which rapid changes of direction were likely to have been unnecessary. In war chariots we might expect this problem to have been overcome. With the Celts, as in so many cultures, it was the need to perfect war gear that forced technological improvements.

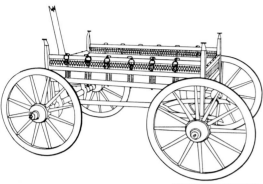

Wheelwrights of great skill were employed by the Celtic chieftains, and fine examples of their work have been found in aristocratic graves of the Hallstatt and early La Tène periods. *Above:* Reconstruction of the funerary cart from the grave at Ohnenheim, Germany. *Above right:* Bronze hub binding from one of the four wheels of the cart buried with the "princess" of Vix, Burgundy.

kept rigid with a nail-less iron tire which had been shrunk on. Wheels of this type, which became common in the La Tène period, are elegant in their simplicity — the unnecessary wood of the double felly has been pared down to a minimum, while the heavy iron nails, which originally attached the tire, have been omitted altogether. What remains is a highly efficient device which it was impossible to improve upon until the development of twentieth-century technology.

Although we have concentrated here upon the evolution of the wheel, it should be remembered that there would also have been improvements in the frame of the vehicle itself. The well-preserved Dejbjerg cart, already referred to, showed one particularly interesting innovation. In the hub-box, between the hub and the axle, several hardwood pegs of circular cross-section had been placed to ease the rotation of the wheel — much the same idea as the modern ball-bearing! Yet the attachment of the

The ritual concept behind the wheeled vehicle is difficult to untangle, but many different cultures in far-flung parts of Europe produced what are evidently ritual vehicles: Trundholm, in Denmark; Strettweg, in Austria (p. 78/79); Mérida, in Spain (p. 53); and the example from Glasinac, in Yugoslavia, illustrated here, dating to the middle of the first millennium B.C. The tradition is clearly deep-rooted. In Yugoslavia a

similar vehicle made in clay, this time carrying a god and drawn by water birds, was found at Dupljaja (Serbia) and dates to the middle of the second millennium. The rich cart burials of the Hallstatt period are therefore only one manifestation of a very ancient cart ritual.

119

THE PLOW

The plow, so vital to prehistoric society, was an invention of great antiquity. To sow crops efficiently it was necessary first to pulverize the soil, and the simplest way to do this was with a digging stick or hoe. It would not have taken a great feat of inventive genius to realize that a hoe dragged through the soil created an acceptable furrow, and it was only a matter of time before man was replaced by yoked oxen as a means of traction.

Evidence for the use of the plow in prehistoric Europe is of four kinds: plow marks preserved in ancient ground surfaces below later earthworks; field banks (lynchets) caused by the movement of soil consequent upon plowing; contemporary illustrations, usually rock carvings, showing plow teams in action; and the remains of the plows themselves. Taken together, the evidence points to an intensification of cultivation taking place some time in the middle of the second millennium.

There are two principal classes of plow—light plows, or ards, and heavy plows—the difference being that while the ard scratched a furrow in the soil, the heavy plow could turn a furrow. It was the ard that was in common use throughout the pre-Roman Celtic period.

Discoveries of ards preserved in the peat bogs of northwestern Europe show that there were two basic types of construction: The simplest, called a "crook ard," has the plow beam (for harnessing to the oxen), and the sole (i.e., the cutting edge) made from a single piece of wood. In the more complex, and presumably later, type known as the spade ard, the stilt (guiding handle) and share were inserted through a hole in the base of a separate plow beam. It is this type which appears to be illustrated on the rock engraving from Val Camonica (far left).

For the most part the simple ards were made entirely of wood, the inherent weakness in the implement being the actual point which was in contact with the soil. Under normal conditions a wooden point would have quickly worn out, but in the case of the spade ard a new wooden shear could easily have been slipped into place. In some areas, stone shears were used, but among the Celtic communities iron shears are found sufficiently frequently to suggest that they were in common use. In fact, two types of iron strengthening were employed: long

bars of iron could be wedged in position on top of the wooden shear base but projecting in front of it so that the iron tip ripped through the soil. This type had the advantage that when the tip had worn out, the bar could be hammered forward to become once more the effective cutting point. The other type entailed enclosing the tip of the wooden share with an iron shoe. The arrangement was perfectly effective but was liable to wear out.

By means of simple ards of this type, drawn by two yoked oxen and guided from behind by a plowman, vast areas of temperate Europe were opened up to agriculture. Well before the emergence of the Celts the forest clearings were beginning to coalesce into an ordered arable landscape. It was, however, the spread of iron that so accelerated

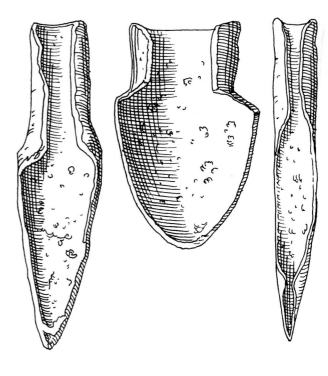

the process, for the iron axe and iron-shod plow were highly efficient implements for hacking down the forest and breaking the land. Thus equipped, the Celtic farmers could penetrate regions previously impossible to tame.

The Celtic ard, unlike the medieval plow, simply scratched a furrow in the soil; it did not turn the sod, but by careful tilting, the displaced soil could be ridged upon one side of the furrow. To break down the soil to produce an adequate seed bed, it appears to have been necessary to plow each field

Rock engravings depicting agricultural scenes occur in Scandinavia, in the Ligurian Alps, and in particular at Val Camonica, north of Milan, where this example was found. Several plowing scenes have been recorded, usually with a single ox team and a man guiding the plow. Occasionally a second man is shown leading the team. In the scene from which this example is extracted, the plow team is followed by five men (or women) with hoes, suggesting that it may have been necessary to break up the soil by hand after the plow had loosened it.

beam, which made a vertical cut through the soil at the same time as the shear sliced horizontally. Behind the coulter was a mold board so angled that the loosened soil was turned over upon itself. The problem, archaeologically, is to know how to recognize the improved implement: a number of iron blades have been found which *could* be coulters, but simple blades of this sort could have many functions. However, towards the end of the free-Celtic period heavy land was being broken for the first time—a fair indication that the improved heavy plow was coming into general use in many areas.

The regular plowing of defined areas gave rise to regular fields, the boundaries of which, fenced or otherwise, soon became distinctive landscape features as soil accu-

Not all plows were pulled by animals. On the island of Skye, off the west coast of Scotland, this crofter used a foot plow into the early decades of this century. On steep slopes and rocky ground this method of cultivation was far less cumbersome than trying to maneuver a team of horses or oxen.

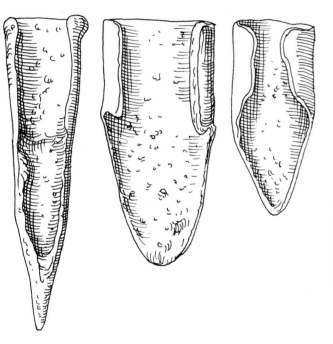

Above left: Plowshares of various types, as shown in these sketches, have been found on many Celtic sites. Strictly they are only the iron shoes which clad and strengthened the wooden shear. Although of course far cruder than the modern shears *(above)*, which cut and turn the soil in one operation, the plowing principle in both cases is the same and the shape of the blades has changed little in the intervening millennia.

twice, the second plowing being at right angles to the first. Grooves formed by this kind of cross-plowing have been recognized in ground surfaces now preserved beneath later earthworks in Holland and Denmark, and it is reasonable to assume that the technique was widely adopted elsewhere in Europe.

Whether or not the Celts had developed the heavy plow before the Roman period, is a difficult question. The essential difference was that the heavy plow was provided with a *coulter* (or knife) attached to the plow

mulated on downhill slopes and rocks were thrown off the field and piled along the boundaries where hedges grew. In this way checkerboards of little fields blanketed the landscape. They can still be seen in marginal areas of Britain, beyond the present limit of agriculture, a tribute to the skill and persistence of the Celtic farmers.

ART COMBINED WITH PRACTICALITY

Celtic art has a humor of its own: faces peer out of designs when they are least expected. The delightfully doleful horse *(right)* from Stanwick in Yorkshire is brilliantly captured by placing two simple trumpet scrolls together and adding eyes. The cleverness of the design would have amused a Celt.

Horses and chariots were enlivened with elaborate decoration wherever opportunity presented itself. Even functional objects were ornamented.

Below, left to right:
This linchpin from Kings Langley in Herefordshire served to keep the wheel from slipping off the axle, but its head provided a convenient medium for decoration.

Bridle bit from Attymon, Galway, Ireland. Here again, the craftsman could not resist the temptation to enliven a functional object with decoration.

Celtic art of the fifth and early fourth centuries B.C. was essentially the art of the aristocratic class, an art style developed by specialists to adorn the luxury objects of their masters. But during the migration period in the fourth and third centuries, Celtic art styles became widely dispersed both geographically and socially, and decorative skills are found lavished on quite mundane items. In other words, Celtic art became the folk art of the people.

A warlike people like the Celts inevitably lavished considerable skill in decorating their arms and armor. Flamboyance and display were the keynotes of the fourth and third centuries. Simple functional items were frequently chosen for decoration. Bronze scabbards for swords, for example, were enhanced with chased, tendril patterns. Indeed, so popular did decorated scabbards become that schools of craftsmen grew up specializing in these matters in Hungary and in Switzerland, each area producing its own distinctive repertoire of designs. The horse and the war chariot were

Chariot mount from a fourth-century burial at Waldalgesheim, Germany.

Harness ornament (phalera) from Horovicky, Czechoslovakia, late fifth to early fourth century.

Detail from a bronze shield, Wandsworth, third to second century.

Phalera from Manerbio sul Mella, Italy, third to second century.

Right: Reconstruction drawing showing an elaborate harness of the Hallstatt period.

also favorite items of display. After all, the warrior driving up and down in front of the enemies' lines, while hurling abuse at his adversaries, wanted to look both frightening and spectacular. The harness of his horses and the metal fittings of his chariot allowed him plenty of scope for decoration, as we can see from the items illustrated on this page. Every fitting, however simple, was a vehicle for flashy display: the bright red enamel contrasting with the glint of

polished bronze must surely have been an impressive spectacle.

Horse fittings of this kind were comparatively simple to manufacture. They required skillful handling of materials but no bulky equipment. A single craftsman with a few bars of iron, a bag of scrap bronze, some crude glass, beeswax, and a few basic tools could have made everything required to deck out a chariot and its team. Sheets of bronze could easily have been produced from scrap. Attached to some suitable yielding base—perhaps a slab of leather or soft wood covered with layers of cloth—the sheet could quite quickly have been indented, using wooden hammers and punches, to create repoussé designs. If more complex items were required, they could be cast. Inscribed or chased decoration could later be worked onto the surface, or heat-softened glass or enamels could be applied to reserved areas.

The exact social position of the craftsman who produced such work is not immediately apparent. The Irish literature recog-

So far we have been concerned with items of display made by specialists, but love of decoration went far deeper, to pervade all aspects of everyday life. A good example is seen in Celtic pottery, particularly the folk pottery made in the home or village. During manufacture the leather-hard vessel would have provided an irresistible medium for design—simple stamped pottery of elegant simplicity in Hungary, energetic curvilinear designs drawn with a shallow pointed tool in Brittany, or the combination of curvilinear and geometric patterning found in the south of Britain. Although there is great regional variation, the essential Celtic spirit shines through them all. Nor should we forget the importance of wood as a medium for decoration. Wooden vessels, handles, as well as the furniture and fittings for the house, would, for the most

Reconstructed harness based on items found at La Tène, third to second century B.C.

nizes the skilled craftsman as a man of status in society, implying that he was free of the necessity to produce his own food. In all probability each warrior of any status had one or more metalworkers among his clients. Such a man might be allowed to work for others from time to time, or more likely, the surplus to his master's needs might have been distributed as gifts, since a single craftsman working fulltime could have provided for many families.

part, have been decorated in some way—by carving, painting, or a combination of both. Brightness and visual liveliness must have characterized the Celtic environment.

The first century A.D. in Britain saw the development of the art of enameling. Both of these pieces functioned as harness mounts; they were inlaid with red enamel.

Above: From Santon, Norfolk. *Below:* from the Polden Hills, Somerset.

123

A WIDE RANGE OF IMPLEMENTS

Right: Reconstruction of various tools from the La Tène period hanging on the inside wall of a reconstructed La Tène house. From left to right: sickles, a scythe, and an adze.

The introduction of iron gave a new flexibility to the toolmaker. Bronze, because of its comparative softness, needed careful attention paid to hafting arrangements, which affected the form of the individual tool. Iron, on the other hand, was much tougher and was therefore far more flexible. Thus socketed hafting, common during the Late Bronze Age, was replaced by the shaft-hole technique, while cutting tools could be attached to their handles by means of quite simple tangs. The introduction of iron technology, therefore, paved the way for the development of the modern tool kit. Indeed, with the exception of scissors and screws, the hand tools we use today were all anticipated by types in use by the first century B.C.

Apart from the plow the most important tools were those of the wood worker: axes, adzes, saws, drills, files, and chisels. It was, after all, the axe which allowed land to be cleared for farming and provided the raw material necessary for practically every kind of construction, from houses to war chariots. The skill required in making the moving parts of a chariot or the yokes for harnessing the horses leaves little doubt that carpentry had reached a high degree of proficiency. The tools of the smith were of equal importance. They would have included a range of heavy hammers for forging the iron, the tongs to hold it, and iron anvils. The smith would also have needed heavy points and chisels with which to cut and perforate the metal. A distinction seems to have been made between the heavy tool kit of the resident smith, and a lighter range of implements which could be taken into the fields to make running repairs on agricultural implements in active use. One characteristic type is the small field anvil which could be hammered into a convenient tree stump to enable tools like sickles to be repaired.

The farming community would have needed several specialized types of tool. We have already considered the plow (pp. 120–121). In addition, there was a range of reaping tools in common use: sickles for cutting the corn; long-handled reaping knives for collecting reeds or for hacking branches from trees to provide fodder for cattle; and smaller hooks for stripping off the leaves. These little hooks were also well suited for trimming and splitting branches to make wattle work. Then, of course, there would have been knives of all sizes and a great variety of minor fittings, such as nails, bolts, rings, pivots, clamps, and bindings.

Iron was, after all, a highly flexible material that could be turned to almost any use. One activity that needed little iron was the manufacture of woolen fabrics. Many of the sheep could quite easily have been plucked of their wool, but some breeds may have needed shearing with sharp knives and less commonly with sprung two-bladed shears. Once the wool was collected, spinning could take place on a hand spindle weighted with a whorl of baked clay; then followed the weaving of the cloth on an upright timber-framed loom. Apart from the loom weights, of clay or stone, no special fittings were needed that could not be made in wood—the shuttle and the sword (for beat-

Decorated Celtic pottery was discovered at Sopron (Hungary) in 1900. The drawing, left, shows a woman spinning. The second woman plays a musical instrument. The patterns on the stylized figures are similar to cloth weaves used by the Celts.

ing the weave tight) were the only movable parts. Sometimes, however, the shuttles were made from bone, and in Britain large numbers of bone combs, thought to be for weaving, have come to light. For stitching the fabric to make clothing, bone or hard wood needles would have sufficed.

Of the wooden tools in use we know very little, but water-logged deposits have ensured the survival of a sufficient quantity of material to show just how important wood was, for making tool handles, containers, shovels, mallets, spoons, and a wide range of other items. Nor should we forget the basketry, matting, and nets which would have been made for home use as well as for fishing. Each community would have been essentially self-sufficient, capable of making everything it needed to live a comfortable and well-provided existence.

The Celts were renowned as exceptionally able horsemen. They were able to make perfectly functional snaffle bits over two thousand years ago. Below is shown a modern snaffle bit for comparison.

Highly developed tool manufacture from the La Tène period. From left to right: tweezers, shears, fishing trident, four various types of knife, file, awl, needle, cutter, pick, saw, edgetool, pointed hook, pruning-knifes and sickle, two mattocks.

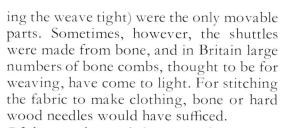

From the Pyrenees to the Alps,
the Cevennes, the Rhine,
and the Rhone—
Caesar reduced all Gaul to a province.

Suetonius

Clasp from St. Margarethen, Austria, showing a rider and two men fighting; Hallstatt period.

Opposite page: Head of a Gaul, on a first-century B.C. coin commemorating Caesar's conquests. The relief statue is a Praetorian guard, second century A.D.

THE
DESTINY
OF THE CELTS

A thanksgiving of twenty days
was celebrated
in Rome.
The whole of Gaul
was now conquered.

Caesar

A time of upheaval came in the fifth century B.C. in the Celtic world. Social unrest, population expansion, possibly also climactic deterioration, combined to force large sections of the community to migrate from their central European homelands southward into Italy and eastward to Greece and beyond. Their exploits are vividly recounted by the Mediterranean peoples with whom they clashed. Rome fell to them, and sacred Delphi was overrun. These Celtic warriors, however, were no match for the citizen armies of Greece and the might of Rome. Pushed back once again beyond the Alps, the Celts were destined to suffer a still more momentous defeat in the last century B.C. It would be their fate, ironically, to be crushed between new barbarian forces—the Germans to the north, the Dacians to the east—and the efficient, modern Roman legions under Julius Caesar. Celtic Europe came under Roman rule, forced to surrender its identity in the Imperial melting pot. Gallo-Roman art, a new hybrid, was the cultural fruit of this domination. Gauls would henceforth gain military glory only as auxiliaries serving under Rome. The conquerors of old—once the terror of Europe—had now been conquered.

The rise and fall of the Celts was spectacular. From their homeland north of the Alps, migrating bands in the fifth to third century spread in all directions. They infiltrated south through the Alpine passes, traveled east along the Danube into Hungary, and sailed across the North Sea to Yorkshire. From the Po valley warrior hordes spilled across the Apennines to strike terror into the hearts of the Etruscans and the Romans. Even Rome itself was pillaged. In the east, the combined effort of the Greek city-states failed to prevent Celtic hordes reaching Apollo's shrine at Delphi. These initial thrusts were irresistible, but they lacked long-term planning and purpose. Once the first flood of energy had subsided, the warrior bands remained at large in the countryside, always willing to sell their swords to the highest bidder. Gradually, as the Roman and Hellenistic world gained strength, the barbarians were controlled and evicted. For a while they were allowed to remain in the Po valley, but the Second Punic War showed Rome how dangerous the Celtic settlement on their northern boundary could be, and subjugation ensued. In Anatolia, however, the Celts (Galatians) were settled on marginal lands and there remained.

The beginning of the second century B.C. saw the Celts in retreat: Cisalpine Gaul was annexed by Rome after a series of decisive victories, and at about the same time the Galatians were defeated by the kings of Pergamum. It was the beginning of the end. Germanic tribes from the north and the emerging Dacian state in the east thrust against the Celts, causing further reverberations which were to be quieted only when Caesar intervened to extend Roman domination over the whole of Gaul as far north as the Rhine. Under Augustus and Tiberius the rest of Celtic Europe was subjugated, and new campaigns across the Rhine aimed at annexing yet more barbarian territory in the belief that the empire was ever expanding.

For a while Britain remained free, but the Romans could not be stopped—Caesar had shown the way and Claudius followed. By A.D. 84 the armies had reached the north of Scotland, leaving only the Highlands, the Western Isles, and Ireland to continue their old way of life undisturbed. It was from here, after the Roman Empire had collapsed, that Celtic culture reemerged.

SOCIETY IN CRISIS

In the fifth century B.C., early Celtic aristocratic society burst apart, unleashing waves of population across Europe, which smashed against the monoliths of Mediterranean civilization. So great was the disruption that repercussions were still felt as late as the first century B.C., long after the full force had been spent. It was these minor convulsions that provided Caesar with his excuse for moving against the Gauls in 58 B.C.

Population expansion, overpopulation, and the excessive consumption of the aristocratic class were among the factors which brought Celtic society to the point of crisis (pp. 40–41). In the areas of the aristocratic heartland—in Germany and northern France—the effects can be seen in the disappearance of the wealthy chieftains' graves and the abandonment of their fortified

When the three envoys asked
by what sort of justice they demanded land,
under threat of violence,
from its rightful owners,
and what business Gauls had to be in Etruria,
they received the haughty reply
that all things belonged to the brave
who carried justice
on the point of their swords.
Passions were aroused and a fight began—
and then it was that the envoys
took their fatal step.

Livy

The aggression and conflict which pervaded the Hallstatt and La Tène period are brilliantly captured on this belt clasp of the Hallstatt period from Vace in Yugoslavia. Two mounted warriors, each supported by foot soldiers, confront each other. Their dress and weapons reflect their different ethnic origins.

courts; but the actual processes of the dispersal elude us. Livy, however, offers a plausible hypothesis in his story of Ambitgatus, king of the Bituriges who, finding it difficult to rule his rich and populous land, "decided to relieve his kingdom of the burdensome excess of population." To do this he sent his nephews Bellovesus and Segovesus, "both adventurous young men, out into the world to find such new homes as the gods by signs from heaven might point the way to; he was willing to give

them as many followers as they thought would ensure their ability to overcome any opposition they might encounter." Here then is a historian of the first century B.C. looking back on the distant past and interpreting it according to traditional beliefs. He goes on to tell us that the gods directed Segovesus to the uplands of southern Germany, while Bellovesus was sent to Italy. Bellovesus collected the surplus population (Livy's phrase) from a number of tribes and set out with his "vast host, some mounted, some on foot, and reached the territory of the Tricastini at the foot of the Alps." Eventually they found a way through the mountains and emerged in the valley of the River Po to found the city of Mediolanum (Milan). In this way began the Celtic colonization of what soon became Cisalpine Gaul.

Livy's account should not, of course, be accepted as accurate history. It was little more than a rationalization of dimly remembered folk tradition, but it provides some indication of the processes which led to the great migration. Livy believed that the movement began during the reign of the Elder Tarquin (traditionally 614–576 B.C.). Polybius, on the other hand, writing in the middle of the second century B.C., tells us that the Celts did not arrive in northern Italy until about 400 B.C. and came not from the west but from the Danube Basin via the eastern Alps. The conflict is more apparent than real, since both accounts are likely to reflect isolated historical events in what was, in all probability, a long and complex process.

An amusing, but not irrelevant, aside to the problem of the migration is provided by the Greek playwright Aristides of Miletus. Etruscans were often portrayed as figures of fun. Such a man was Aruns of Chiusi, whose wife had been seduced by another Etruscan. To take his revenge on society, Aruns filled wagons with wine, oil, and figs and set off for the Alpine passes to display the riches of the south to the Celts. Thus he enticed them to migrate into Italy, bringing destruction (and retribution) with them. This literary invention is an interesting reminder that, to the Celts of the transalpine regions, the south was the source of great luxury. The gods, says Livy, directed Bellovesus along "the much pleasanter road into Italy."

The classical writers give the impression that the Celtic migrations were sudden and very rapid, but in reality this was not so. The initial movements were probably slow and deliberate—a kind of bow wave in advance of a greater displacement. We have already seen that during the period of the aristocratic chiefdoms, there appears to have been a gradual movement north and west of the main centers of power and wealth. This could be seen as a preliminary manifestation of the much greater disruptions which were soon to follow.

The initial stages of expansion to the south can be recognized in the archaeological evidence recovered from the cemeteries clustering in the valleys along the southern flanks of the Alps, in particular in the region of the Lombard lakes. Here, in the warrior burials of Sesto Calende and the wagon burial of Ca' Morta, it is possible to recognize distinct cultural links with the Celtic world of the north, dating to as far back as the seventh century B.C. The Ca' Morta cemetery continued in use and in the late fifth century served as the resting place for warriors clad in La Tène equipment. It was during the fifth century that the dead buried in other cemeteries in the region of Bellinzona began to be provided with objects of early La Tène type and were also graced with Etruscan wine flagons of the kind exported from the Etruscan workshops to the Celtic world. Although alternative explanations are possible, we could reasonably conclude that the Alpine population had become increasingly Celticized during the fifth century, quite possibly as the result of the infiltration of people southward into the valleys along the trade routes between north and south. Because objects of La Tène A type have been found south of the Po in the region of Marzabotto, the Celts may have penetrated this area in the

fifth century, decades before the main Celtic movements southward gained momentum. The second line of Celtic advance indicated by Livy, eastward into the mountainous region between the upper Rhine and the Carpathian Basin, does not appear to have been opened up by earlier Celtic settlers. At present, the earliest archaeological evidence suggests that the Celtic (La Tène) settlement of northeastern Hungary did not begin until about 400 B.C., by which time the migrations were in full swing.

The fifth-century B.C. social crisis coincided with a phase of growing Etruscan influence north of the Alps. At Hirschlanden, near Tübingen, the grave mound of a warrior of the early fifth century was found, capped with a remarkable stone figure *(above)* —a full-scale representation of a warrior—carved in a style reminiscent of Etruscan work.

THE GREAT DISPERSAL

It is difficult to judge how many men were involved in the migrations and to assess the composition of the migrating forces. Did these armies consist only of warriors, or were whole families on the move? The classical sources give some indication, but they were prone to exaggerate and to oversimplify. That the numbers were large is, however, certain.

Livy's account of Bellovesus's force is particularly interesting: he actually enumerates the tribes from which the "surplus population" was enlisted—some seven in all. While we cannot accept the list as necessarily accurate, it clearly implies that the migratory movements were not confined to

ing the Illyrians (in modern Yugoslavia) and by the beginning of the third century were ravaging Macedonia and Thrace, penetrating deep into Greece in 279. Other groups crossed to Asia Minor where they caused widespread disruptions, until they were finally brought to heel by the kings of Pergamum in the early second century. Thus in southeastern Europe and Asia Minor the main period of Celtic aggression lasted just over two centuries after about 400 B.C. By about 180 their energies were spent, and they had either settled in peace with their neighbors or had been driven back into central Europe to Hungary and Czechoslovakia.

The dislocations caused by this onslaught must have been considerable. One effect was on the Celtic hordes themselves. It seems that in many instances, the fragmentation of the group ensued, and not infrequently we read of Celtic mercenaries in the service of foreign rulers. As early as 369, Celtic mercenaries were employed in Greece by Dionysius I in his battle against the Boetians. Later, in 277, the Hellenistic ruler Antigonus Gonatas used Celtic mercenaries against Pyrrhus, king of Epirus, but Pyrrhus too employed Celts—apparently he kept them under control by allowing them to plunder the graves of the Macedonian kings. Celtic mercenaries also played a significant part in the conflicts among the different rulers of Asia Minor, but, frequently got out of hand. We also hear of them in the service of the Ptolemies in Egypt in the third century, and as late as 187–186 Celtic mercenaries were involved in suppressing a revolt in upper Egypt. There can therefore be little doubt that a considerable part of the force that poured into the Balkans in the fourth century, and their successors, found gainful employment in the conflicts consequent upon the interminable power struggles of the Hellenistic rulers. What percentage of the original horde found its way back into Europe we will never know.

The migration of the Celts southward and eastward into Italy, Greece, Macedonia, and Asia Minor is tolerably well recorded in the works of the Greek and Roman historians. Such is the quality of record that the individual events can be considered in some detail (pp. 132–139). But if the Celts were known to have migrated in these directions, is it not possible that they also

The migration of the central European Celts, by the second century B.C., spanned Europe. South into Italy and east into Greece and Asia Minor, their progress is recorded in some detail by the classical authors. The

CALEDONES
PARISII
ICENI
REGNI
NERVII
VOLCAE TECTOSAGES
VENETI TREVERI
AULERCI VINDELICI
BITURIGES SEQUANI
ARVERNI BOII
BOII
SCORDISCI
CELTIBERI SENONES
390
DARDANI
277
TROCMI
TECTOSAGES
279
TOLISTOBOGII

movement northeastward into Transylvania and beyond is well attested by the discovery of cemeteries of the La Tène culture; but western movements into Spain and Britain are more problematical, since the evidence could be interpreted as little more than intensified trading contacts. However, one group appears to have crossed the North Sea and settled in Yorkshire.

a single tribe but were confederacies of splinter groups enlisted from a number of regions.

The main force of the migration burst upon the classical world about 400 B.C. By 390 the Celts were at the gates of Rome, and they remained in Italy, a constant irritation to the Roman government, until the early decades of the second century B.C. In southeastern Europe they were no less a menace. In the mid-fourth century they were fight-

expanded to the northeast and northwest? To answer this question, it is necessary for us to examine the archaeological evidence, for upon these matters the classical writers are silent.

The eastward migration of Celts from the area of southern Germany, and possibly Switzerland, is well attested in the spread of cemeteries containing early La Tène objects (principally La Tène B). One possible line of advance led eastward along the Danube into the northwestern part of what is now Hungary. Once through the constrictions imposed by the Alps and the Little Carpathians (in the area of Vienna and Bratislava), the migrants spread out into Transdanubia, where the number of their cemeteries suggests that settlement was dense.

This may well have been the route taken by the hordes who attacked the Balkans. At the same time there was a separate movement eastward into Transylvania (the heart of modern Romania), where once more Celtic cemeteries attest settlement. These groups would have come into contact with local inhabitants, culturally related to the Scythians, contributing to an ethnic mix-

ture from which the Dacian state emerged. In the west, much of France was already settled by communities that had adopted a La Tène style of culture. Even remote areas of western Brittany were producing pottery decorated with elaborate La Tène motifs. While there is no direct evidence of folk movement, minor shifts and readjustments must have taken place. One of the principal areas of innovation at this time was the Marne region, where a vigorous La Tène culture developed, sufficiently distinctive to be called the Marnian culture in archaeological terminology. From here it seems that direct contact was established with parts of the Low Countries, and it may well be that small bands of settlers spread northward. It is, however, difficult to distinguish on archaeological grounds between distribution patterns created by folk movement and those resulting from exchange systems. Much the same problem is posed by the evidence from Britain. It used to be thought that bands of Marnian invaders poured across the Channel to colonize the south and spread northward into Yorkshire. More recent work, however, has emphasized that, while it is true that the southeast of the country was in direct contact with the Continent, that contact is simply a continuation of a long-established relationship which had already existed for half a millennium. Commodities were traded back and forth, but there was no recognizable change in settlement pattern or in burial ritual which would signal a folk movement—with one exception: Yorkshire. Here, in the late fifth or early fourth century, a novel burial rite was introduced: bodies were inhumed, sometimes with their two-wheeled carts or chariots, in graves which were often set in rectangular enclosures delimited by ditches. This style of burial, hitherto completely alien in Britain, is well known among the early La Tène cultures of France and Germany. Perhaps then we are seeing, dimly reflected in the archaeological evidence from the Yorkshire Moors, the trace of one of the most far-flung of the Celtic migrations, equivalent in its daring to the movement of the Celts into Anatolia but unsung in contemporary literature.

The following account has come down to us of the Gallic migration. During the reign of Tarquinius Priscus in Rome, the Celts, one of the three Gallic peoples, were dominated by the Bituriges, and their king was consequently a member of that tribe. At the time we are concerned with the king was one Amitgatus, who by his personal qualities, aided by the good luck which blessed both himself and his subjects, had attained to very considerable power; indeed under his rule Gaul became so rich and populous that the effective control of such large numbers was a matter of serious difficulty.

Livy

The great strength of the migrating Celtic force lay in its infantry. Most men, even the poorest, could arm themselves with a sword and shield. This Celt-Iberian warrior on a first-century B.C. relief from Osuna, Spain, wears a helmet typical of the region and holds the usual oval Celtic shield.

PILLAGERS OF ROME

The opposing forces in northern Italy were well matched. Etruscan warriors, like the one depicted in the second-century B.C. bronze *(far right)*, were armed in much the same way as the Celts; but their small round shields, for fending off the blow rather than protecting the whole body, were better designed for more open fighting than the massed onslaught of Celtic type.

Right: Celts occasionally wore body armor, as the warrior shown here from Grézan, Gard, France, but this was unusual and was more likely learned from contacts with their Mediterranean opponents.

Terrified townships
rushed to arms
as the avengers
went roaring by;
men fled from the field
for their lives;
and from all the immense host,
covering miles of ground
with its straggling masses
of horse and foot,
the cry went up
"To Rome!"

Livy

Throughout the fifth century, Celts (or Gauls, as they are frequently called by the classical writers) began to settle in the Po valley. According to the classical writers, the first to come were the Insubres, who captured and destroyed the Etruscan city of Milan. The Cenomani settled around Brescia and Verona, the Lepontii around Lake Maggiore, and the Libici and Salluvii on the banks of the Ticina. A little later the Boii and Lingones crossed the Alps to take up their position south of the Po, while the Senones, coming still later, passed farther south into Umbria to settle on the Adriatic coast. By about 400 B.C. the land was densely settled and incapable of absorbing more. Polybius, writing a little later, describes the small scattered farmsteads and the neat fertile fields growing wheat, barley, millet, vines, and figs.

The next stage of the advance came soon after 400 B.C. when tribes from the Po valley, possibly under pressure from further immigrants, decided to move southward, through the Apennines, to explore and plunder Italy.

In about 391 B.C. (the traditions of Livy and Polybius give slightly differing dates)

CELTAE

Bergamum

Mediolanum Brixia Verona

Po

MARE
SARDOUM

Clusium Tevere
390

Veii
Roma Allia 387
386

MARE
TYRRHENUM

thirty thousand Celts, led by Brennus, marched on the Etruscan town of Clusium, which had recently established a treaty relationship with Rome. "The plight in Clusium was a most alarming one: Strange men in thousands were at the gates, men the like of whom the townsfolk had never seen, outlandish warriors armed with strange weapons who were rumored already to have scattered the Etruscan legions on both sides of the Po; it was a terrible situation" (Livy). Rome sent envoys to negotiate peace, but the demands of the Celts—land upon which to settle—were unacceptable, and battle ensued in which, contrary to international convention, the envoys took part, one of them actually killing a Celtic chieftain. This is the reason given by Livy for the Celts' turning on Rome, but it is unlikely that they really needed political provocation; visions of plunder would have been quite sufficient. In four days the Celtic hordes, composed of Senones and Lingones, covered the eighty miles to Rome. The mood of the city was captured by Livy in a speech which he puts into the mouth of the consul M. Popillius Laenas: "You are not facing a Latin or Sabine foe

who will become your ally when you have beaten him: we have drawn our swords against wild beasts whose blood we must shed or spill our own."

On the eighteenth of July at Allia on the left bank of the Tiber, the Roman army was routed, leaving the city entirely undefended. The Celts entered and in a frenzy of destruction reduced everything to a heap of smoldering ruins: only the Capitol held out, its defenders remaining under siege for seven months. Eventually, after plague had ravaged the Celtic armies, terms were agreed and the Celts moved off, their booty almost intact.

For more than fifty years following the destruction of Rome in 390 B.C. the Celtic armies in Italy remained a serious threat to Rome, and their presence encouraged the allied cities of central Italy to revolt. Many battles were recorded. One, of particular interest, took place at Anio in 367. Polybius describes how a Roman, T. Manlius, confronted a Celt in single combat in front of both armies and killed him, taking his neck torque. Such was the magnitude of his achievement that he assumed the name of Torquatus. The 350s saw an intensification of the conflict, but in 349 the Celts suffered a resounding defeat and a general stampede from the Romans began. Raids ceased altogether by about 335, and in 332–331 a treaty was concluded between Rome and the Senones.

The Celts were now in full retreat; in 295 they suffered a major defeat at Sentinum, and in 225 at the famous battle of Telamon, so vividly described by Polybius, a Celtic army was cut to pieces.

The Celts of the Po valley continued to be an irritation to Rome, particularly during the Second Punic War when Hannibal used them as somewhat uncontrolled allies. By taking the Punic side, the Celts had sealed their own fate. In 197 in the battle of Lake Como they were defeated and Latin settlement began. The Boii rebelled, but in a series of encounters culminating in the battle of Bologna in 191 their resistance was destroyed; massive spoils passed to Rome; vast territories were annexed; and the tribe, having suffered great losses, moved away to find a new home north of the Alps. The wheel had come full circle.

The actual area from which the initial movement into the Po valley came is uncertain, and thus the arrow in the Alpine area of the map is hypothetical. Livy mentions that it was the Bituriges who migrated first. Several hundred years later this tribe was living in central France, but at the time of the migrations it may well have occupied land north of the Alps. Expansion through the Apennines began about 400 B.C. after the Po valley had been extensively settled.

The assault on Rome (around 390 B.C.) caught the city totally unprepared. Although an earthwork defense protected the eastern approach, the Celts had no difficulty in sweeping through the city, destroying and looting as they went. The debris of this destruction has been found below the Forum and on the Palatine.

After the Celtic threat had abated, a massive new defensive system was built to protect the city. The so-called Servian Wall, constructed of large blocks of tufa, was ten kilometers long and served Rome well for centuries.

Overleaf (pp. 134–135):
The conflict between barbarian Celt, fighting naked, and the Etruscan warrior is vividly portrayed on a relief found at Bologna dating to the fifth to fourth century B.C.

133

VIOLATION OF DELPHI

The Celts who penetrated southeastern Europe came into conflict first with the world of Alexander the Great and, after Alexander's death in 334 B.C., with the rival faction of the Hellenistic dynasty who succeeded him. In the confusion of the period, Celtic mercenaries were sometimes used by the rival Hellenistic leaders, but more often the Celts moved around in raiding bands, several of which combined in 279 for the concerted attack through Greece to Delphi.

Above: Coins of the Macedonian kings. Head of Alexander, on coin minted in 297–281 B.C. by Lysimachus, to demonstrate his legitimacy; and (at right) coin of Antigonus Gonatas, 277–239 B.C. It was the death of Lysimachus in 281 that opened up new opportunities for the Celts in Macedonia. Antigonus Gonatas employed Celtic mercenaries in his army, but in 277 was defeated by Pyrrhus, king of Epirus.

While the Senones and their confederates were plundering their way through Italy, other Celtic tribes traditionally led by the Sigoves were moving through the foothills of the eastern Alps and raiding both Pannonia (Hungary) and Illyria (Yugoslavia). In all probability, the Danube formed the boundary of their easterly advance, for beyond lay the powerful tribes of Scythian extraction. Apart from the movement into Transylvania (pp. 130–131), these eastern territories were avoided, and the main thrust of the advance was concentrated on the Balkans.

Celts were active in Illyrian territory in the mid-fourth century. In 358 clashes with the Illyrians were recorded, and in 335 we hear that Alexander the Great had to undertake campaigns in Bulgaria as the result of unrest caused by the displacement of tribes resulting from the Celtic advance down the Adriatic coast. Indeed he actually received Celtic envoys at this time.

The advance continued. In 310 Celtic raids created panic among the Illyrian tribes, and a few years later, in 298, one group of Celts had reached Bulgaria while another had penetrated Thrace. Fighting in Bulgaria intensified during the 280s.

The culmination of this gradual buildup of forces came in 279 when a vast Celtic horde marched into Macedonia to plunder and to settle. The attractions of Greece were many, not least the vast treasures at the great sanctuaries, of which Delphi was the most famous. At Delphi resided the oracle of Apollo, who through the accuracy of her prophecy had gained worldwide recognition. The shrine was sacrosanct and thus was the appropriate place for the city-states of the Greek world to deposit their treasures for safekeeping. Rumors of untold wealth would soon have reached the invading armies, and it is hardly surprising therefore that Brennus advanced with his thirty thousand men towards the shrine.

The route southward led through the famous pass of Thermopylae, which they found to be strongly held by the Greeks. A direct frontal attack showed that the Celts were no match for the spears of the Greek hoplites. Faced with repulse, one group of Celts decided to move off and plunder the territory of the Aetolians; they sacked the town of Callium and butchered its inhabitants. Their action drew the Aetolian contingent away from Thermopylae. The Greeks were bent on revenge, and using the tactics of guerrilla warfare, cut the Celtic raiders to pieces—but their absence from the pass gave Brennus and his warriors the opportunity to outflank the remaining defenders using unguarded mountain passes.

Delphi was reached in midwinter; but though without substantial defenses, its position high on the side of Mount Parnassus gave it a degree of protection. The events of that fateful winter are not recorded in detail, and obscurities remain; but it would seem that the Celts achieved some measure of success. Strabo tells us that one of the participating tribes, the Tectosages, carried off a huge quantity of

Triumphant, Brennus ravages
the whole of Macedonia
without hindrance.
Then, as if the spoils of men
have no further attraction
for him, he turns his eyes
to the temples
of the immortal gods,
joking that they, who are rich,
must make presents to men.
So he marches on Delphi....
The Gauls, still
under the influence of
the previous night's
drunkenness, hurl themselves
into battle, without
considering the danger.
The Delphians fight back,
trusting more in the God
than their own forces....
His presence is soon apparent:
rocks, split from the mountain
by an earth tremor,
crush the Gallic army,
and scatter the strongest units,
which at the same time
break under the blows
of the defenders.
Finally, a storm breaks
and hail and cold put
an end to the wounded.

T. Pompeius

spoils to the region of Toulouse, where they eventually settled. But other parts of the Celtic force fared less well.

The story is told that the Greeks asked the oracle of Apollo for advice and received a reply couched in the usual enigmatic terms: that the god would send white maidens to the aid of the Greeks. The white maidens turned out to be a blizzard accompanied by a monstrous thunderstorm causing rockfalls. Under this cover, the Greeks attacked the Celtic camp, raining arrows down on the invaders. The Celts, thoroughly demoralized and in complete disarray, retreated, having first killed off their wounded. The Celtic temperament could not sustain reverses of this magnitude. During the long, hard retreat northward, constantly harried and attacked, the wounded

leader Brennus committed suicide. The remainder of the force continued their retreat to join the melee of dispossessed warriors in Macedonia.

Some groups moved back westward along the Danube, settling in the region of Beograd: they were known as the Scordisci. Others moved farther north to join the Celtic groups already settled in Transdanubia. But a number of tribes decided to move off eastward. The Tolistoagii and the Trocini, who had separated from Brennus in Macedonia, reached the Dardanelles in 278 and crossed with difficulty into Asia Minor. Another group, the Tectosages, who had been with Brennus, followed them. In Asia the Celts were to find a congenial land in which to pursue their warlike activities.

Delphi claimed to be the center of the world. By the seventh century B.C. it had risen from obscurity to a position of dominance, largely as the result of the fame of its oracle at the shrine of Apollo. Excavations, which began in 1892, showed the sanctuary itself to have been quite small, ca. 200 by 150 meters, but a city of some proportions spread out in front of it. Nearby was the sanctuary of Athena Pronaia within which is the circular shrine (or *tholos*), shown above. It was built about 400 B.C. Some of the earlier buildings had been destroyed by landslides in ca. 480 and 373, similar to the landslide which so demoralized the Celts in 279.

A CELTIC KINGDOM IN ASIA

The growth of the kingdom of Pergamum was spectacular. A place of obscurity in the fourth century, it rose to dominance under Philetaeros, who inherited a vast fortune follow-

ing the death of Lysimachus in 281 B.C. The dynasty he founded began with his nephew Eumenes I, the first of the Attalid kings. Eumenes's son Attalus I beat the Gauls in a great battle in 230. Eumenes II *(above right)* ruled from 197 to 159, during which time he enslaved forty thousand Celts (Galatians).

The Celtic force that crossed into Asia Minor—in all some twenty thousand men, women, and children—were immediately enlisted into the service of two local rulers, Nicomedes of Bythinia and Mithridates of Pontus, who controlled the northwestern part of Anatolia. Those Celts without weapons were armed by their employers to prepare them for their new role. Quite simply, their function was to raid and plunder the lands to the south ruled by the Seleucid king, Antiochus—a task, one would imagine, not uncongenial to the Celtic mentality. The raids were well-organized affairs: the Tolistoagii took the wealthy lands of Aeolis and Ionia; the Trocini were given the Dardanelles; while the Tectosages were allowed the interior. The Celtic onslaught was quite unprecendented and threw the cities of Aegean

Turkey into turmoil. Whereas in Greece the city-states had combined to repel the invader, here in Anatolia there was no cohesive resistance; each city fended for itself, suspicious of its neighbors. One by one they came under attack. Some paid protection money; others, like Miletus and Ephesus, fought. Priene would do neither, but one of its citizens, Sotas, organized a private army and managed to save many of the inhabitants from the countryside around. Only Pergamum managed successfully to drive off the attackers—a success which brought the city renown.

The raids persisted over several years, but in 275 Antiochus, his armies strengthened with elephants, took the field and resoundingly defeated them. The Celts now withdrew to northern Phrygia, where they were

settled in a land which became known as Galatia, their presence on the northern fringe of Seleucid territory serving as a buffer between the two power blocks.

For some years, they continued to extract money from the Seleucid monarchy in payment for leaving the cities of the south unmolested, but the comparative calm was short-lived, and raids became increasingly persistent. Eventually, in the 230s, the kingdom of Pergamum felt strong enough to resist. Payments were stopped, with the inevitable result that the Celts marched on the city. In the great battle which ensued, the armies of Pergamum, led by their king Attalus, scored a spectacular victory, after which the Celts retreated to Galatia and Attalus assumed the title King and Savior. The political situation in Asia Minor now became even more complicated. By brilliant political maneuvering, Pergamum managed to involve Rome on her side against the Seleucids, and in 189 at the battle of Magnesia the army of Antiochus was defeated: at the same time forty thousand Galatians (as the Celts were now called) who served with him were enslaved—an act which effectively marked the end of the Celtic raids. The historian Polybius put events into perspective: "All those who dwelt on this side of the Taurus did not rejoice so much at the defeat of Antiochus as at their release from the terror of the barbarians."

To celebrate their great victory, and to demonstrate their leadership of western Anatolia, the Pergamenes erected an altar to Zeus high on their hilltop capital. The outer wall of its podium was decorated with a magnificent relief portraying the battle between the gods and earth-borne giants, a composition of great brilliance and originality symbolizing the success of the Pergamum kings (the gods) against the barbarian Celts. At about the same time (during the reign of Eumenes II, 197–159) the balustrade of the nearby temple of Athene Nikephoros was decorated with a relief illustrating piles of captured Celtic armor, presumably of the type in use at the end of the third and beginning of the second centuries. All the familiar items are there: the carnyx, mail armor, shields, spears, swords, helmets, and a yoke, either from a chariot or a baggage cart. The temple frieze is the last monument to Celtic aggression in Asia.

Although much is known of the Asian Celts (the Galatians) in their relationship to their neighbors, our knowledge of their social and economic organization in their own territory remains vague. Their land, although comparatively infertile, provided them with a convenient and well-protected referred to as kings, were elected for the purpose of leading a raid. Annual meetings of a council composed of three hundred elders were held at a location, called Dry-nemetos—the *nemeton* element of the name suggesting that it was a sacred clearing in a wood. These isolated scraps of evidence,

The great altar of Zeus dominated the hilltop city of Pergamum. Constructed between 180 and 160 B.C., it was decorated with a series of energetic sculptures showing the conflict of the gods and the earth-

base from which to raid. It appears that the indigenous Phrygian peasants continued to till the land, presumably serving as the clients of their Celtic masters and thus giving them the freedom of mobility they required. Each of the three tribes was ruled by four tetrarchs; but war leaders, gleaned from the classical writers, give the impression that the Celtic way of life had changed little in the migration. Indeed the Galatians still maintained a distinct identity into the first century A.D., when St. Paul could address them as "O foolish Galatians." born titans, symbolizing the battles of the Pergamum kings against the Celts. Only the foundation of the altar now remains. All the sculptures and architectural fragments, removed by the German excavators in the nineteenth century, are now displayed in a full-size reconstruction in Berlin.

THE GERMANIC THREAT

The Gauls in the Po valley (the Cisalpine Gauls) were a constant menace to Rome, and during the Second Punic War gave some assist-

ance to Hannibal *(coin, above)* after he had crossed the Alps in 218 and had beaten the Roman army, led by Scipio *(top)* at the River Ticinus. The Romans were haunted by the memory of their vulnerability from the north, and when, at the end of the second century, the Cimbri and Teutones began to threaten the region, Marius *(bottom)* attacked them with his reorganized Roman army.

Where the boundary between the Celts and the Germans lay is a matter of dispute. Caesar believed it to be the River Rhine, but this may be little more than the military commander's desire to use the river (a convenient military boundary) as the symbolic dividing line between his potential Gallic allies to the south and the Germanic enemy to the north. Indeed he himself admitted that there were groups of Germans settled on the left bank and reports the belief that both the Belgae and Treveri were ultimately of German origin. In other words, the boundary line had been so blurred and obscured by folk movements in the past that it could not be precisely defined.

Caesar's account of the tribes living north of the Rhine was designed to highlight their differences from the Celts. The economy was more pastorally based, the people less civilized, and because they were untouched by the luxuries of the south, they tended to be far more warlike. Although allowance must be made for some exaggeration, these generalizations are borne out by writers who observed the situation from closer quarters in the first century A.D., when the Roman armies were more intimately involved in the German problem. In 113 B.C. a hitherto unknown tribe, called the Cimbri, suddenly burst into Noricum, in the eastern Alps, and there defeated the Roman consul who had moved into the area to defend the Celtic inhabitants. The event took the Romans completely by surprise—that a barbarian horde could appear so close to Italy, and savage a Roman force, was a cause for considerable concern.

The identity of the Cimbri raises interesting questions. Having first appeared in southeastern Europe about 120 B.C., they attempted to settle in the land of the Boii, but their advances were repelled and they had to turn west through the land of the Scordisci into the territory settled by the Taurisci and Norici. Posidonius, who made a special study of the problem, admitted that he did not known who they were, but Caesar proclaimed them to be Germans, and it is now generally accepted that the migration started in Jutland and gathered strength as it moved south. That the personal names of their leaders are all purely Celtic would suggest, however, that the Cimbri acquired a strong Celtic contingent during their movements.

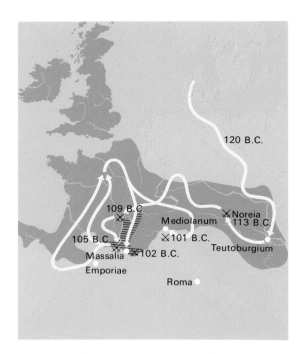

The origins of the Cimbri and Teutones is obscure. The homeland of the Cimbri may have been in Jutland, but as they moved south they gathered other groups to their cause. The Teutones, possibly a Celtic tribe, joined them at a later stage.

A few years later, in 109 B.C., they appeared in southern Gaul, their strength further augmented by another tribe, the Teutones. Although Caesar claimed that the Teutones were also of Germanic origin, their name contains the Celtic word meaning "the people" (the same as *túath* in Irish) and in all probability they were a northern Celtic tribe. Posidonius regarded them as a branch of the Helvetii who were of undisputed Celtic origin.

In southern Gaul the Cimbri and Teutones came into conflict with Rome, and after a number of undecisive battles they succeeded in annihilating a Roman army at Arausio, near Orange, in 105. Thereafter the two forces split up, the Cimbri moving south into Spain, while the Teutones caused havoc in northern Gaul. After a while the Cimbri returned, and the combined horde continued to ravage the Gaulish countryside. Finally they parted once more, the Teutones moving back to southern Gaul, where in 102 at Aquae Sextiae (Aix-en-Provence) they were met and destroyed by the Roman army of Marius. The Cimbri had meanwhile crossed the Alps into the Po valley but were intercepted by Marius, and at Vercellae (Vercelli) the barbarians were annihilated. It had been a frightening time for Rome, with the fearsome barbarian hordes on their very doorstep, and memories of the devastating Celtic invasion nearly three centuries earlier would have been very much in mind. Whatever the true ethnic origins of the invaders, to the Roman world they came from the north, from beyond the semi-civilized Celts with whom the Romans were becoming increasingly familiar. A few years later it was both convenient and politically expedient for Caesar to categorize them as Germans. The effects of the invasion on the Celts who were settled in Gaul were no less disruptive. The Helvetii, who at this time lived between the Rhine and the Danube, moved south into present-day Switzerland,

the tribes in Gaul only the Belgae of the north were strong enough to stand up to the invaders.

The overall situation in Gaul in the last decade of the second century B.C. was confused. The movement of the Cimbri and Teutones had caused widespread disruption among the Celtic tribes. Indeed it may have been at this time that groups of settlers crossed the Channel into southeastern Britain. But to present the situation as a German-inspired invasion (as the later Roman writers were inclined to do) is a gross oversimplification. Whatever the origins of the Cimbri, the majority of the tribes on the move were probably Celtic from the northern fringes of the Celtic world. Pressure from the north would make

Now the infantry of the Cimbri
began to move slowly forward
from behind their fortifications.
They marched in a square,
each side of which
was thirty furlongs in extent.
Their cavalry, 15,000 in number,
were a splendid sight
as they came riding out.
They wore helmets like the heads
and gaping jaws
of terrible wild beasts
and other strange creatures.

Plutarch, Life of Marius

The Germanic tribes shared many elements of culture and religion with the Celts. Their war god, Woden, was often depicted as a mounted warrior like his Celtic equivalent. *Left:* Germanic tombstone, eighth century A.D., representing Woden. It is quite possible that the *Germani* were originally a Celtic tribe living in the region beyond the Rhine. Indeed the author Dionysius of Halicarnassus, writing at the end of the first century B.C. but using older source material, says of Celtica that that part of it beyond the Rhine was called Germania. From Caesar's time onward, any tribe from across the Rhine was called German regardless of ethnic origins.

while the Tigurini, who were of Helvetian stock, joined the raiding hordes. Later another Celtic tribe, the Volcae Tectosages, joined the melee: it was they who, together with the Tigurini, in 107 B.C. near Bordeaux, defeated the Roman army led by Cassius Longinus and forced the humiliated troops to march under the yoke. Of all

the neighboring tribes of the south so vulnerable that a single, and possibly quite small-scale, event like the migration of a few Cimbri could cause sudden and widespread dislocations. It was a situation of instability that was to remain for more than six centuries.

THE RISE OF THE DACIANS

By the fifth century B.C., a people in Romania known as the Getae had developed an advanced and impressive civilization. Described by Herodotus as "the noblest as well as the most just of all the Thracian tribes," the Getae were also formidable as a fighting force. They opposed the advances of the Persian leader Darius and later were active against Alexander the Great as he marched northward to subdue an uprising among their southern neighbors, the Triballi. For decades they were a thorn in the flesh of the Macedonian rulers.

The Dacian state rose to power in the first century B.C. in central Romania—an area already crossed and fringed by migrating Celtic tribes. The white outline on the map shows Burebista's empire at its largest extent. The arrows indicate Celtic raids.

Below: Bronze boar, which once adorned a Celtic helmet from Bata, Hungary, first century B.C. or A.D.

The material culture of the Getic tribes was a complex amalgam—a long-established folk culture overlaid by Scythian and Greek influences—giving rise to a tradition of magnificent gold and silver work made to adorn the graves of the aristocrats. Indeed the characteristics of Getic society and art in the sixth to third centuries B.C. seem to have marked similarities to those of the Celts: the same love of display, the same powerful aristocracy, and the same warlike tendencies. This Geto-Dacian culture (as the Romanian archaeologists prefer to call it) formed the basis from which Dacian civilization was soon to emerge.

In the second century B.C. a shift of power can be detected. Until then, Geto-Dacian culture was centered upon the Dobruja and the plain of Wallacia, north of the lower Danube. In the early second century, however, Dacians are recorded within the arc of the Carpathians—the area now called Transylvania—and during the reign of King Rubobostes (before 168 B.C.) we learn of a further buildup of Dacian strength in this area. By the turn of the century, ascendancy had passed to Transylvania, and the Dacian state had begun to emerge.

Transylvania was a well-endowed region. It yielded a wide range of mineral deposits, including iron, copper, silver, and gold; the land was fertile, and it was well protected by the Carpathian range, defended moreover with strong Dacian fortifications. Their capital was centered in the Orăştie mountains, in the southeast of the region, within reach of the fertile valley of the Mureş.

In the eighties of the first century B.C., one of the Dacian tribes, led by Burebista, rose to a position of dominance and within twenty years or so had succeeded in establishing its preeminence over the rest of the Dacian communities of present-day Romania. Burebista, now extremely powerful (Strabo estimated that he had 200,000 troops at his command), began a policy of aggressive expansion. In 60 or 59 B.C. he marched westward against the Celts. First he overcame the Scordisci (in southern Hungary and northern Yugoslavia) and then turned northward through Hungary to attack the Boii and Taurisci. So successful were his campaigns that, according to Strabo, the devastation he wrought gave rise to the nickname "the Desert of the Boii" for the northern part of the Great Plain.

Burebista justified his attacks by claiming that he was simply winning back Dacian territory from the Celts. He was perhaps referring to the fact that the Celtic tribes in this area were relative newcomers, having arrived no more than three centuries before. The archaeological evidence shows that the sphere of Dacian influence now engulfed the region of the River Tisza (in the Great Hungarian Plain), spread across Slovakia, and extended west of the Danube, in the region of the Danube Bend (north of present-day Budapest). Even though Burebista died soon afterward and his kingdom began to fragment, the Celtic tribes had lost their driving energy and were unable to regain their former territories. In-

142

The Celtic tribes that occupied Transylvania were soon subsumed by emerging Dacian culture, but those that had settled along the lower Danube retained their own distinctive culture and issued coins of striking originality (below).

The capital of the Dacian state was the strongly fortified hilltop town of Sarmizegetusa, set at the end of a strongly protected valley in the Onesti mountains of Transylvania. The town was defended by a massive wall and was provided with a spacious religious precinct containing circular and rectangular temples (left). All were destroyed by the Roman armies led by Trajan early in the second century A.D.

stead they fell back westward. After having unsuccessfully besieged Noreia, the Boii joined forces with the Helvetii, who at this very moment had decided to move out of Switzerland to seek new lands in Gaul. In all there were 32,000 Boian refugees among the 368,000 migrants.

The Dacian advance was yet another example of the pressures which came to bear on the Celtic population. With the Atlantic in the west, the new vigorous Dacian state in the east, the Germanic buildup in the north, and the increasingly aggressive Roman presence in the south, it was only a matter of time before the Celts of the European mainland were squeezed out of existence.

A PYRRHIC VICTORY

On hearing of his arrival
the Helvetii sent an embassy,
composed of their
most illustrious citizens
and headed by Nammeius,
to say that they intended
to march through the Province
because there was no other
route open to them.
They promised to do no harm
and asked for his consent.
As Caesar remembered
that the consul Lucius Cassius
had been killed by the Helvetii,
and his army routed
and sent under the yoke,
he was not disposed
to grant their request.
If people so hostile to Rome
were permitted to go
through the Province,
he did not think they were
likely to refrain
from damage to persons
and property.

Caesar

The defeat of the Roman army of Cassius Longinus in 107 B.C. at the hands of the Volcae Tectosages was made more humiliating when the captured troops were forced to show their subservience by marching under the yoke. The event captured the imagination of nineteenth-century Swiss artist Charles Gleyre *(right)*.

The victory of the Volcae Tectosages over the Roman army in 107 B.C. is noteworthy in one important sense. It was the only significant battle fought against Romans on Gallic soil which was won by Celts. Although spectacular, the event was an isolated incident of no lasting significance. Roman authority was already well established in Provence, and within sixty years the whole of Gaul was to be in Roman hands.

The Roman foothold in Gaul was established between 125 and 121 B.C. It came about not as the result of outright aggression, but simply because the Celts had attacked the territory of Massilia, a Greek foundation which for centuries had been on friendly terms with Rome.

The political situation in barbarian Gaul in the middle of the second century was changing fast: a degree of unity was emerging under the leadership of the Arverni, a powerful tribe which occupied the Massif Central. Together with their allies, the Allobroges of the Rhone valley and the Saluvii who lay to the southeast, they constituted a political and military force of potential danger to the civilized Mediterranean coastal region. In 125 the Saluvii attacked the territory of Massilia. Rome responded immediately by sending an army, which the next year decisively defeated the Saluvii and destroyed their stronghold at Entremont.

The presence of Rome introduced a new factor into Celtic politics: allegiance with Rome could be used as a vital bargaining counter in the intertribal power struggle. The Aedui whose territory lay to the north of the Arverni (in the region of Autun) rapidly concluded a treaty with Rome and the next year asked for Rome's protection against the Arverni. Once more the Roman armies moved in. The Celts were soundly beaten, with casualties amounting to twenty thousand. The final confrontation came in 121, when a combined force of Allobroges and Arverni, led by the Arvernian king Bituitus, met the consular army, only to be virtually annihilated.

The result of these first entanglements in Gaul was that Rome had gained a new territory—an arc of land stretching from the Pyrenees to Geneva—while the Celts of transalpine Gaul had been given a foretaste of what was to come.

Rome's new transalpine province was rapidly absorbed into the classical world; a new colony was founded at Narbonne, roads were laid out, the Celtic aristocracy were encouraged to assume the Roman way of life, and administrative abuses, so typical of the period, became rife. The situation in the seventies of the first century B.C. is eloquently summed up by Cicero in a speech made on behalf of M. Fonteius, expropraetor of Gaul who was impeached for extortion:

All Gaul is filled with traders, is full of Roman citizens. No Gaul does any business without the aid of a Roman citizen; not a single sesterce in Gaul ever changes hands without being entered in the account books of Roman citizens.

THE TURNING POINT

The appearance of Julius Caesar in the political arena in the middle of the first century B.C. had a dramatic effect on the history of the Celts. His rivalry with Pompey made it

essential for him to gain substantial victories in the west to outshine Pompey's achievements in the east. Moreover, all the time he was actively campaigning against the enemies of Rome, he could legitimately maintain a large army at state expense. A brilliant soldier and charismatic leader, his troops idolized him. His grasp of geography and his speed of movement brought him success in Gaul. The coin above was minted in Rome in 44 B.C., the year of his assassination.

An overstatement, no doubt, but a reminder of the energetic commercial activity which followed in the wake of the Roman army.

Apart from the chaos caused by the invasions of the Cimbri and Teutones in the last decade of the second century, and the momentarily successful revolt of the Volcae Tectosages in the region of Toulouse, the new province enjoyed a degree of peace and prosperity. There had been some territorial expansion. The Volcae Tectosages made a further bid for freedom but were finally subdued by Sulla, and Toulouse was incorporated into the province. But elsewhere the original frontiers remained, protected by treaty relationships with the neighboring tribes.

Among the newly conquered tribes, a spate of revolts was only to be expected. In 90 and 83 the Salluvii were up in arms, while in 66 and again in 62–61 it was the turn of the Allobroges to rebel; but to no avail. Each uprising was ferociously quashed. By 60 B.C. the province was firmly under Roman control and already largely integrated with the Roman world. No further problems were expected from within, nor were there any.

It was at this moment that three things happened: the Helvetii and their allies decided to move into Gaul in search of new lands; Ariovistus, king of the Germanic Suevi, began to interfere in Gaulish intertribal rivalries; and Gaius Julius Caesar took up what was to be a ten-year command in Gaul. The coincidence of these three events in the year 59 B.C. was to have a shattering effect on the Celtic world. It was indeed a turning point.

The three events were interlinked. Ariovistus and his tribe were evidently under pressure from tribes living to the north and were intent upon gaining new lands for themselves to the south. An occasion presented itself when the Sequani invited them to intervene in a dispute they were having with their old rivals the Aedui. Ariovistus readily agreed on condition that the Sequani provide him and his followers with a large part of their territory in present-day Alsace. When the Germanic settlers arrived, the Sequani panicked and began to resist. It was at this point that the neighboring Aedui called upon their ally, Rome, for help.

"I myself," said Ariovistus,
"am the only man
of the whole Aeduan nation
who could not be prevailed
upon to swear this oath
or to give my children as hostages.
That was why
I fled from my country
and went to Rome
to claim assistance from the Senate—
because I alone
was not restrained either
by an oath
or by the surrender of hostages."

Caesar

Meanwhile the Helvetii, in western Switzerland, had decided that their constricted territory was too small for them. Moreover, they feared German pressures from across the Rhine, and they must have watched the fortunes of Ariovistus with alarm. The only solution was to move off to new lands in the west. Thus, after a year

Caesar in his official guise: marble statue from Rome. Conquests, particularly in Gaul, brought him political power in Rome. This is his only surviving full portrait from Roman times.

of preparation, they and their allies (including Boian refugees fleeing from Burebista), numbering 368,000 men, women, and children in all, set out with the intention of passing through Roman-held territory near Geneva, en route to the land of the Santones in western France, where they hoped to settle.

Although these two events seemed menacing, they were after all only part of a pattern of migration that had been practiced by the Celts for centuries. If events had been left to take their own course, it is unlikely that any repercussions would have been felt in the Roman world. Yet for Caesar, proconsul of Cisalpine and Transalpine Gaul, it was as if history were playing into his hands. He could present the facts as a German threat to Rome (reminding his audience of the Cimbri and Teutones), an appeal for help from an ally, and the potential invasion of a Roman province. Armed with the righteousness of self-justification, he could plunge into Gaul with every expectation of successful campaigns, culminating in the victorious war he so desperately needed both politically and financially. The stage was set for the last act in the tragedy of the European Celts.

The immediate causes of Caesar's intervention in Gaul were comparatively easily dealt with. At the beginning of the campaigning season in 58, he made for Geneva to prevent the Helvetii from crossing the Rhone. Quite undeterred, the migrating hordes moved off to the north to outflank Roman territory by marching around the Jura through the territory of the Sequani with whom they first negotiated permission. It was at this stage that the Aedui, Caesar's principal allies in free Gaul, complained of Helvetic raiding parties pillaging their lands. The Allobroges too were suffering from the invaders. Caesar now summoned all his available troops, some six legions, and after dogging the steps of the Helvetii for a while, moved in for the kill. The campaign was short and totally effective. In the aftermath the stragglers were rounded up; and the Helvetii, Tulingi, Latovici, and Rauraci, supplied with grain, were sent back home to reoccupy and rebuild their farms and villages on the charred remains of those they had burned some months before. Only the Boii were allowed to stay, being settled on the fringe of

147

The migration of the Helvetii and their associates—368,000 men, women, and children who set out across France to escape German neighbors—is the theme of this modern sketch.

After a year of preparation, they were ready to leave their homes in western Switzerland, their last act being the burning of their homes and villages —to remove any incentive to return. Detailed lists in Greek of all the emigrants capable of bearing arms, as well as the numbers of old men, women, and children, were prepared. This attempted migration set off the Gallic wars in 58 B.C.

Aeduian territory, possibly to serve as a buffer against aggressive neighbors. Of the 368,000 migrants who had set out, less than a third survived to return home.

Caesar had tasted power in Gaul. At this moment he could have withdrawn, but the opportunity was too good to miss.

It was now the turn of Ariovistus. "The man was an ill-tempered, headstrong savage," according to the Gauls, "and it was impossible to endure his tyranny any longer." After desultory negotiation, Caesar marched to Vesontio (Besançon), the largest town in the territory of the Sequani, and there prepared to do battle. It was already autumn and with the campaigning season nearly over, a rapid conclusion to the affair was necessary. Six days of uninterrupted marching led Caesar to within a few miles of the German forces. Further negotiations were undertaken, but to no avail: in the ensuing battle, Ariovistus was routed, and the remnants of his army fled back northward into Germany in disarray.

In a single summer Caesar had dealt decisively with the immediate cause for concern in Gaul. Leaving his army, under the command of Labienus, quartered in Sequanian territory, he returned to Italy. Caesar could not, even had he wished, have proceeded farther, but it was now even more essential for him to gain further victories, and in Gaul, with its incessant intertribal rivalries, he could easily find an excuse to intervene. His reason for mounting a second campaign in 57 was that the powerful Belgic tribes of the north were organizing armed resistance to Rome. This was a sufficient excuse to return to Besançon the next spring with reinforcements. The nature of the opposition was carefully explained to him by ambassadors from the Remi, one of the Belgic tribes which intended to stay on good terms with Rome. In all, about a quarter of a million troops were being mustered under the direction of the most powerful tribe, the Bellovaci. The Bellovaci were providing 100,000 troops; while the Suessiones offered 50,000 but, by virtue of their prestige, were allowed to nominate their king, Galba, as the commander-in-chief of the operation. Twelve other tribes agreed to send levies. It was a formidable opposition but no match for the incisive speed with which Caesar acted.

Knowing that he had the support of the

Aedui at his rear and the Remi in the heart of the dissident territory, Caesar advanced quickly towards the massed Belgic forces on the Aisne, somewhere in the region of Bervy-au-Bac. In a massive engagement, the Belgic army was scattered, and without pause Caesar thrust forward into the land of the Suessiones storming their *oppidum* of Noviodunum near Soissons. Next in his line of advance were the Bellovaci and Ambiani, but before he could attack the Bellovacian capital, the tribe sued for peace. Leadership of the Belgic resistance now rested with the Nervii, an austere tribe who occupied the land between the Sambre and the Scheldt: "They were a fierce warlike people who bitterly reproached the other Belgae for throwing away their inheritance of bravery by submitting to the Romans."

In one of the most hard-fought encounters of the war, enacted in the valley of the Sambre, Caesar met the combined force of Nervii, Atrebates, and Viromandui. It was a vicious, long drawn out, engagement, as the result of which "the tribe of the Nervii was almost annihilated and their name almost blotted out from the face of the earth." The pathetic remnants were allowed to retain their territory and *oppida*, protected from the depredations of their neighbors by Caesar's authority.

It remained, now, only to deal with the

Atuatuci, a remnant of the Cimbri and Teutones, who had settled in the middle Meuse region. They had retired to a strongly defended hillfort which Caesar proceeded to storm. Resistance was short-lived, and the army smashed down the gates, capturing the entire population. Caesar laconically sums up the encounter by saying that he "sold all the inhabitants of the place by auction in one lot. The purchasers reported that the number of persons included in the sale was 53,000."

While these events were being played out in the north, Publius Crassus, with a single legion, was sent to demand the formal submission of the tribes of Lower Normandy and Brittany: this was obtained without difficulty. It was now autumn, so, putting his legions into winter quarters among the newly conquered tribes, leaving one on the Loire to keep an eye on the Armorican tribes, he left for Italy. "All Gaul was at peace": his primary task had been accomplished.

During the winter of 57–56 a serious revolt broke out among the tribes of Armorica led by the Veneti who controlled the maritime trade in the region. Hearing of these events, Caesar sent word to Crassus that a fleet should be constructed on the Loire in readiness for the spring campaign. Meanwhile the Celts "fortified their strongholds, stocked them with corn from the fields, and assembled as many ships as possible." As these preparations proceeded, the tribes of Normandy joined the rebels. For Caesar the situation was dangerous, but once more the brilliance of his strategy and speed of his response saved the day. His main concern was to contain the revolt. Accordingly Labienus, with a force of cavalry, was sent among the Belgae, equipped for rapid movement should rebellion spark; Crassus moved to the land of the Aquitani on the Atlantic coast to prevent reinforcements coming through from the south, while Sabinus made a show of strength with three legions in Normandy and northern Brittany. Meanwhile the Loire fleet was nearing completion. The rebels, now isolated, were Ceasar's personal concern. The campaign began on land with Caesar taking a number of Celtic hillforts, but little progress could be made all the time that the rebels had command of the sea. Accordingly Caesar waited for his fleet to be completed and then in a decisive sea battle,

fought off Cape Quiberon, destroyed the Venetic navy. The victory ended the uprising, but to make an example of the rebels, all the senior Celts were executed and the rest of the population were sold as slaves. At the time of this confrontation, Sabinus was smashing the resistance of the tribes of Normandy. The year ended with the submission of the inhabitants of Aquitania and

In the famous opening passage to his *Gallic Wars*, Caesar tells us that Gaul was divided into three parts: the Belgae in the north, the Aquitani in the west, and the remainder "who call themselves Celts though we call them Gauls." Of these the fiercest were the Belgae who lived in constant warfare with their northern neighbors. On the map opposite the principal tribes and battle sites are shown.

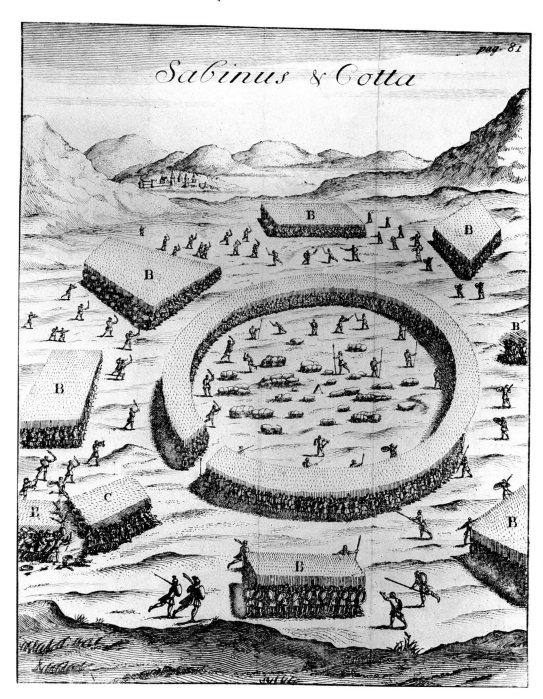

a late and indecisive campaign against the Morini and Menapii in Artois and Belgium. After burning farms and villages, Caesar withdrew his troops to their winter quarters in Normandy.

The battle scenes were much loved by book illustrators. Here is a romantic eighteenth-century interpretation of the defensive tactic employed by Cotta, one of Caesar's generals.

THE LAST HOPE

Two Gaulish resistance leaders stood up against Caesar in the latter stages of his war in Gaul. Ambiorix, chief of the Eburones (seen below through romantic nineteenth-century eyes, in a statue at Tongres), led the Belgic tribes in revolt in 54–53 B.C. but

failed and escaped into obscurity. In the next year Vercingetorix *(right)* staged a far more serious uprising in central Gaul but was forced to surrender and was eventually strangled in Rome at Caesar's triumph. The revolt led by Vercingetorix was the last chance for any united defense on the part of the fragmented, feuding Gauls.

The campaigns of 56 left Gaul firmly under Roman control. So sure was Caesar of his position that in 55 and 54 B.C. he pushed beyond Gaul to explore Britain and Germany. To the Roman audience in Italy these feats of military daring must have been almost unbelievable; in reality they were of little significance.

Gaul had still not been fully stabilized. Caesar returned from his second British expedition late in 54 B.C. to a situation of unrest in northern Gaul. The dissidents were headed by Ambiorix, king of the Eburones, who occupied land along the Meuse in the region of Namur. The spread of this revolt involved Caesar in protracted campaigns throughout Belgica from the land of the Senones and Carnutes, south of the Seine, to beyond the Rhine. Eventually, in the summer of 53 he set out through the Ardennes to attack Ambiorix. The king escaped into obscurity, but his land and people suffered the fury of the Romans. Every village and building was destroyed, animals were slaughtered, and crops consumed. Even if some tribesmen had escaped, "it seemed certain," wrote Caesar, "that they must die of starvation." The revolt had been long drawn out and viciously suppressed, but it was but a prelude for what was to follow.

The dissident Gauls desperately needed a war leader to match Caesar. In Vercingetorix they were to find one. Vercingetorix was the son of an Arvernian aristocrat named Celtillus, whose ambitions of kingship had led to his assassination. Vercingetorix was a headstrong young man whose outspoken anti-Roman feelings led to his expulsion from Gergovia. Undeterred, he gathered a band of followers and returned to the capital to oust the resistance and install himself as king. Caesar describes him thus: "A man of boundless energy, he terrorized waverers with the rigors of an iron discipline." Through sheer force of personality he had secured the allegiance of many tribes in the center and west of Gaul who had previously taken little part in resistance. For Caesar the situation was particularly dangerous: not only was he facing a far more widespread rebellion then ever before, but the rebels lay between him and his legions stationed in the still unstable north. At last, after six years of uncertainty, it looked as if the Gauls stood a chance of success.

151

THE FINAL DISASTER

The last rebellion began dramatically with the massacre of the Roman traders who had congregated in the town of Cenabum. Caesar was not to be deflected, and with his customary drive outflanked the rebels in order to join his legions in the north. Speed was now even more vital: one after another, native strongholds fell to his attack: Vellaunodunum of the Senones, Cenabum of the Carnutes, and Noviodunum of the Bituriges. Then, after a prolonged and bitter siege, Avaricum was taken. The Roman soldiers had no mercy: old men, women, and children were slaughtered, and of the forty thousand inhabitants only eight hundred escaped to join Vercingetorix who was camped nearby.

The first was unthinkable: accordingly, after a series of extraordinarily long marches, he joined Labienus, who had just succeeded in stamping out trouble among the Parisii on the Seine. His army reunited, he then prepared to meet Vercingetorix in open battle. Somewhere in the territory of the Sequani, a cavalry engagement took place at which the Gauls were routed. It was a staggering blow for Vercingetorix, for the Gauls regarded their cavalry with particular pride. Shaken, Vercingetorix

Right: A contemporary coin depicting a Celt, quite possibly Vercingetorix.

Below: Gallo-Roman statue from Vachères in Southern France showing a noble Gallic warrior.

The siege works of Alesia, shown in outline.

Outer siege works, 22 kilometers long.

Inner siege works, 14 kilometers long.

Fortifications of Vercingetorix.

Roman camps placed on high points to oppose Gaulish reinforcement forces from outside.

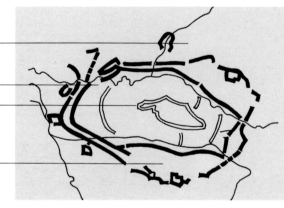

After a brief rest at Avaricum, enjoying the ample supplies found there, the Roman army moved off to capture the Arvernian town of Gergovia, situated on a steep hilltop difficult of access and guarded by Vercingetorix. In front of Gergovia, after a lengthy encounter, the Romans were forced to retreat, severely mauled. The extent of their defeat can be gauged from Caesar's reference to the loss of forty-six centurions —the backbone of the Roman army. The effect of the reverse was dramatic: At last, it seemed as though the Gauls had hope, and even the Aedui, long-standing allies of Rome, transferred their allegiance to Vercingetorix, seizing Caesar's principal supply base at Noviodunum.

For Caesar the situation was highly dangerous; he had two alternatives, either to retire to Provence or to strike at the enemy before they could build up reinforcements.

"I did not
undertake the war
for private ends,
but in the cause of
national liberty.
And since I must now
accept my fate,
I place myself
at your disposal.
Make amends to the Romans
by killing me
or surrender me alive
as you think best."

Caesar, quoting Vercingetorix

made for the defended hilltop of Alesia, where he set up camp to await Caesar's arrival. No doubt, in choosing Alesia he was mindful of his successes some weeks earlier when, from a similar position of strength at Gergovia, he had put Caesar to flight. He must have been well aware that the Gauls were no match for the Romans in the open field.

As soon as he arrived, Caesar decided to surround the hilltop with a complex of

siege works, realizing that direct attack was doomed to failure; and in spite of constant harassment by the Gallic cavalry, the first stage of the works were soon completed. A second series of defenses was then undertaken, facing outward to protect the besieging force from attack from the countryside around. This outer circuit, complete with forts and lookout posts, was 22.5 kilometers in length.

Vercingetorix was relying on the arrival of a relieving force which he had sent his messengers to summon. Eventually a vast army of Gauls approached, recruited from all parts of the country—some quarter of a million men in all. Three times they flung themselves at the Roman defenses, but on the last occasion, after a close-run encounter, they were soundly defeated. The

years of almost constant fighting, the Gauls were too exhausted to continue: their submission to the Roman will was now final.

The site of Alesia (Mont Auxois) is an extensive diamond-shaped plateau protected by river valleys on both sides. To the north and south rise steep hills, but to the west is open countryside where the Gallic reinforcements mustered.

Map opposite: Caesar's problem was twofold: He had to prevent the rebels from escaping and, at the same time, protect his rear from attack by the Celtic relief forces whom Vercingetorix had summoned. To do this he constructed two massive complexes of siege works (shown here in a reconstruction), an inner series facing Vercingetorix, and an outer line rising up onto the crests of the nearby hills where forts and watch towers were built.

Top and bottom: The siege works (shown in full-size reconstruction) were very complex. The main rampart, four meters high, was reinforced with an embattled breastwork. In front of it was a V-sectioned ditch. In front of this were trenches filled with sharpened saplings interleaved to form an entanglement, and farther out rows of circular pits were dug with sharpened stakes projecting upward from their bottoms. Finally the defenses were completed by a zone of iron spikes set in wooden blocks.

situation was lost: Vercingetorix surrendered, and his starving supporters filed out of their stronghold under Caesar's supervision.

The capitulation of Alesia was not quite the end. Caesar remained in Gaul throughout the winter and the next year (51) put down a revolt among the Bellovaci and besieged a group of dissidents in Uxellodunum. Their heroic stand was the final death agony of the free Celts. After eight

BRITANNIA

Caesar could not resist the opportunity of crossing to Britain—it was a place of mystery, a land of legendary mineral wealth, and a haven for dissidents. The purpose of his campaigns in 55 and 54 B.C. is unclear. Curiosity, combined with the quite unprecedented prestige which the expeditions brought him, would have been sufficient motive. The outcome was that the Romans had established, by treaties, a political toehold on the island.

For the next ninety years, the effects of Caesar's expedition continued to be felt. Traditional trading links between southern Britain and Armorica seem suddenly to have ceased, and instead the Trinovantes, who occupied part of southeastern Britain north of the Thames—the tribe with whom Caesar had concluded a treaty of friendship —began to grow rich by controlling what appears to have been a profitable trading

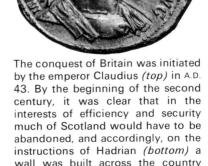

The conquest of Britain was initiated by the emperor Claudius *(top)* in A.D. 43. By the beginning of the second century, it was clear that in the interests of efficiency and security much of Scotland would have to be abandoned, and accordingly, on the instructions of Hadrian *(bottom)* a wall was built across the country to divide barbarian from Roman *(center)*.

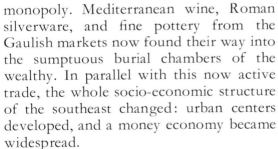

The initial stages of the conquest were soon over, and by A.D. 47 a frontier zone based on the Fosse Way had been established across Britain.

Between 47 and 51 the army extended its control over Cornwall and began to spread into Wales. In 51 the resistance leader Caratacus was captured in north Wales. Campaigning in Wales continued until A.D. 60, the year in which Boudicca rebelled.

From 71 to 74 large areas of the north of Britain were overcome and the hold on Wales tightened.

Agricola completed the conquest of north Wales in A.D. 78 and then turned his attention to Scotland, where his campaigns (A.D. 78–84) culminated in the battle of Mons Graupius.

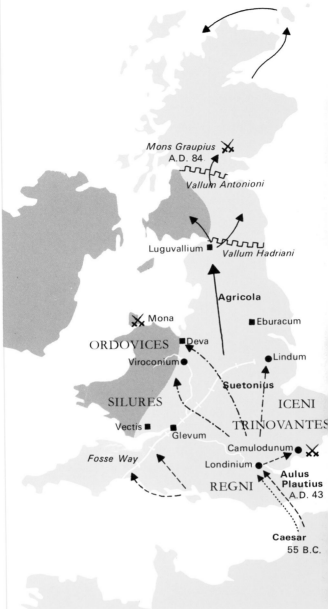

monopoly. Mediterranean wine, Roman silverware, and fine pottery from the Gaulish markets now found their way into the sumptuous burial chambers of the wealthy. In parallel with this now active trade, the whole socio-economic structure of the southeast changed: urban centers developed, and a money economy became widespread.

In A.D. 43 Rome looked once more to Britain as a place where its emperor, this time Claudius, could gain military prestige. Thus, under the command of Aulus Plautius, an invasion force once more set out for Kent intent to conquer. After the capitulation of the principal urban center at Camulodunum, the southeast was easily over-

run, only the Durotriges of Dorset putting up any concerted resistance. By the end of the first campaigning season, it was possible to begin work on the establishment of the frontier: a diagonal line marked by a road called the Fosse Way, which ran from Lincoln in the north to the vicinity of Exeter in the southwest. Behind that line the process of Romanization continued apace. The Fosse Way divided Britain into two very different halves: to the southeast was a settled semi-urbanized landscape dependent upon intensive grain production, while to the north and west social organization was more fragmented and the country mountainous, but there lay the mineral wealth.

Who the first inhabitants
of Britain were,
whether natives or
immigrants
is open to question:
one must remember
we are dealing
with barbarians.

Tacitus

Within a few years, the frontier was being so harassed by dissident tribesmen from the Welsh mountains, led by Caratacus, that further advance was essential. The Romans moved first into south Wales, then into the north, and finally, in A.D. 59, destroyed the druid center on Anglesey. It was at this moment that a highly dangerous rebellion broke out among the Iceni of Norfolk led by Queen Boudicca, and spread rapidly in the southeast, until even the Trinovantes took up arms against the Roman troops and administrators. The rebellion was contained, but it took ten years for the province to recover.

The early seventies saw a further advance in Wales, Yorkshire, and the north, culminating in a series of northern campaigns under the generalship of Agricola (A.D. 78–84). In the final great battle fought in the far north of Scotland, at Mons Graupius, in 84, the last Celtic army, still ferocious and unpredictable, still using chariots, was virtually annihilated. The conquest of the island was at an end—all but the Highland mountains and the Western Isles had been brought under Roman control. The only part of the Celtic world which had not experienced the force of Rome was Ireland. In 83 Agricola stood on the Scottish coast and looked across to Ireland thinking of conquest. This, however, was not to be.

During the Antonine period the northern frontier was calmed. To mark the satisfactory completion of the campaign a sesterce was issued A.D. 143–144 inscribed "Britannia."

THE ROMAN IMPRINT

Throughout the whole of Gaul
there were always
disputes and wars until
you passed under our control.
We ourselves,
despite many provocations
imposed upon you
by right of conquest
only such additional burdens
as were necessary
for preserving peace.
Stability between nations
cannot be maintained
without armies,
nor armies without pay,
nor pay without taxation.

Tacitus, Histories

Early in his governorship of Britain, Agricola devoted the winter, between campaigning seasons, to promoting schemes for the social betterment of the community. His object, so Tacitus tells us, was to accustom the natives to a life of peace and quiet by providing them with amenities such as elaborate public buildings. Gradually they came to appreciate the benefits of Roman life. They "spoke of such novelties as 'civilization,' when in fact they were only a feature of their enslavement." Tacitus could not resist the twist in the tail, but his statement of the process of Romanization, irrespective of region, cannot be bettered. Once the shock of the invasion was over, most tribes settled down to embrace the new way of life. For most of them it brought peace for the first time from the uncertainties and dangers of inter-tribal conflict.

The Roman administrators were careful to retain as much of the Celtic social and economic structures as possible. Tribal boundaries were formalized to become administrative boundaries, and many of the traditional *oppida* developed into thriving cities on the same spot or at a more convenient road nexus nearby. The old tribal aristocracy became the *equites* from among whom the town council, with its two chief magistrates *(duumvirs)*, were elected annually. Roman citizenship was readily bestowed on the worthy, and by the time of the emperor Claudius, Gauls were even admitted to the Roman Senate. The Roman desire to adapt native structures, rather than to replace, them is well demonstrated by the institution of the *Concilium Galliarum*. This was an annual gathering of representatives from all parts of Gaul held once a year at Lugudunum (Lyons). It was, in essence, a festival held in honor of the divine Augustus and was presided over by the high priest, or *sacerdos*, who was chosen from among the representatives. But it had other functions: provincial business could be discussed and representations made direct to the emperor. Although outwardly Roman in its appearance, the *concilium* was clearly little more than the old pre-Roman institution which used to meet annually at Chartres under the auspices of the archdruid. By focusing the religious fervor of the gathering on the person of the emperor, the Romans were able to harness Gallic energies to the good of the state.

Much the same procedure was attempted

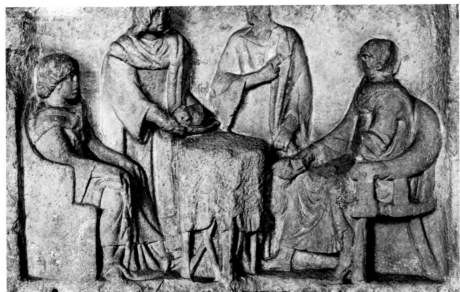

The adoption of the Roman way of life by the Gauls can most readily be appreciated by reference to the large collection of reliefs, which still survive, depicting everyday scenes.

Above left: An armorer at work, one of the many crafts depicted on Romano-Gaulish reliefs.
Above, center and right: On these two reliefs from Neumagen, near Trier, we can compare family life with that of a tavern. The domestic scene shows comfortable middle-class existence: the figure on the left sits in a basket-work chair, while the individual on the right occupies a well-carved wooden seat. Between them is what may be a folding table, on which fruit is being served. The postures, clothing, and furniture in this scene are purely Roman—a far cry from Strabo's description of the Celts sitting on dried grass at their feasts, only a few hundred years

Portraiture, whether of the gods or men, becomes far more naturalistic under Roman inspiration. Hermes *(far left)* is from Welschbilling near Trier; the young man is from Arles, southern France.

who seized the city. In the late third century it was still a flourishing concern, as is shown by the demands for its restoration after it had been destroyed in a siege in 272. Other famous schools grew up at Massilia, Toulouse, Lyons, Vienna, Reims, Bordeaux, Arles, and Trier. Of these, Massilia was perhaps the most famous, ranking with Athens, Rhodes, and Alexandria. It was renowned for its medical teaching, and it was here that Agricola, a native of Narbonnese Gaul was educated.

The quick-witted Celts were well known for their ability to learn, and it was for this reason that the Latin language spread so rapidly across Europe. Latin was a language that could be written; moreover, it was the language of education and of administration. Until the advent of Rome, Celtic writing was virtually unknown: If records had to be kept, then Greek was used; but after Caesar, Latin provided the means by which the ambitious young man could advance in the newly imposed social system.

Yet the Celtic language did not die out. It must have been widely spoken in rural areas, and indeed a few inscriptions in Celtic, but written in Latin or Greek letters,

at Camulodunum (Colchester), where a massive temple to the emperor Claudius was built; but the idea badly misfired. The native Britons resented the intrusion, and their resentment turned to outright aggression when the occasion for rebellion presented itself in A.D. 60.

Education, referred to by Tacitus above, was an important tool for Romanization. One of the earliest schools, for the sons of Gaulish aristocrats, was founded in Autun (the town which replaced the Aeduian capital of Bibracte). During a rebellion in A.D. 21 the scholars, all of wealthy parents, provided valuable hostages for the rebels

Everything else
is shared equally between us.
You often command
our legions in person,
and in person govern
these and other provinces.
There is no question
of segregation or exclusion.
Again, those emperors
who are well spoken
of benefit you
as much as they do us,
though you live far away,
whereas tyrants wreak
their will upon
such as are nearest to them.

Tacitus, *Histories*

earlier. The tavern scene is more rustic: the bearded figure wears a Celtic-style hooded cloak.

The imposition of Roman culture meant the adoption of a complicated way of life. Bartering and simple money exchanges gave place to involved transactions and record keeping. In this scene, *(above)* from Trier, the figure at far left holds open a wooden-based wax writing tablet, while the other two figures appear to be counting out money. A man at far right

enters bearing some merchandise (possibly grain) on his shoulder.

Above right: In another craft portrayal, a fuller is shown at work treading cloth in his vat. Other fabric is seen hanging up behind him, carved with realistic attention to the folds of the cloth.

are known. Some Celtic words were even taken into the Latin language—words for which no Roman equivalent existed, like *bracae* for trousers, and various specialist terms for types of wheeled vehicles. The Celtic *leuga* was still preferred to the Roman mile, and *vergebret* was sometimes used instead of *duumvir*. The survival of Celtic in the third century is shown by the emperor Severus's agreement that it could be used for wills. We must suppose, therefore, that most Roman Gauls, at least the educated ones, were bilingual, able to speak and write official Latin in their professional lives, but ready to relapse into patois whenever it was necessary.

The new regime provided ample scope for the native population to develop its various skills. The Celtic aristocracy became the urban rich. Strabo records that at Vienna, the new capital of the Allobroges, the chief men of the tribe soon moved into residence, no doubt administering their estates from the comfort of the city while serving the community in official positions. The more outstanding were able to play their part in world affairs. Domitius Afer, from Nimes, for example, became praetor in A.D. 25 and rose to the position of consul in 39; Valerius Asiaticus from Vienna was consul twice in the mid-first century.

For the lower classes there was of course the army. All provincials were eligible for service as auxiliary troops, and the Gallic cavalry was world famous. Having served his appointed term, a veteran would retire a Roman citizen, able to return with dignity to the land of his birth, if he wished to do so, to take up farming or become a trader. Manufacturing industries and trade developed rapidly, employing an increasingly large percentage of the population. Alongside a vast output of mass-produced goods, pottery, bricks, bronzework, and glass, the Celtic areas continued to produce their own specialities. Woolen goods were particularly popular in Rome; the hooded cloak from Britain, the *birrus britannicus*, was highly prized; so was the Gallic *sagum* of similar type. The poet Martial mentions that these Gallic garments were dyed in bright colors, a reminder of the Celtic love of display. Some cloth merchants, like the Secundinii from Trier, grew rich enough to build elaborate mausoleums for themselves.

Wherever one looks in those Roman provinces which were imposed on Celtic lands something of the Celtic spirit shines through, but nowhere is it better represented than in the religious art of the period. The gods were, after all, Celtic gods, and their shrines existed long before even Caesar was heard of. A sculptor who spent most of his life cutting ovolos and acanthus leaves on cornices, or churning out tombstones for the army, must have sighed with relief when he was asked to produce a triad of "mothers" or an Epona. The ambivalence attached to art, which persisted, in many areas, throughout the Roman period, has been demonstrated many times over by the pieces chosen to illustrate these pages. But nowhere is it better displayed than in the famous Gorgon's head relief from Bath (right). The Gorgon, so evidently a Celtic male with a mane of hair and drooping mustaches, stares out from the pediment of a purely classical temple, a dramatic reminder that one is here on the very fringe of the Roman empire, a few meters from the sacred spring over which the Celtic goddess Sulis presides. She may have been conflated with Roman Minerva, but her Celtic pedigree remains blazoned for all to see.

In spite of the Romanized life depicted on the reliefs shown on the previous pages, there were plenty of visual reminders of their Celtic heritage to be seen about the towns of Roman Gaul and Britain.

Below: On the arch of Narbonne, reliefs of Celtic armor—including helmets, shields, and a pig mounted on a standard—represent captured Celtic war gear, illustrating the troubled early history of the community.

Opposite: At Aquae Sulis (Bath), visitors and residents alike would have been reminded of Celtic antecedents of the shrine by the Gorgon's head which glowered down on them from the pediment of the temple—a fascinating conflation with a purely Celtic male face and the serpent-ridden hair of the classical gorgon.

Aerial view of the monastery of Skellig Michael, on an island off the Irish coast.

Opposite page: Moone Celtic cross, Kildare, Ireland.

THE ISLAND CELTS

Said Patrick to Kieran: "Precede me into Ireland…
and build thou a monastery;
there shall thine honor abide for ever
and thy resurrection be."

Seventeenth-century Irish poem

160

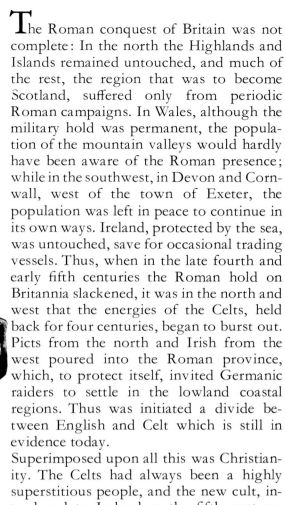

The long, dramatic saga of the Celts took a new turn soon after the fall of Rome and the disintegration of her Empire. Celtic invaders once more penetrated the heart of Europe, as if repeating history. But these were a new breed of warriors—soldiers of Christ, missionaries from Ireland who bore the Gospel and monasticism to the Continent, beginning in the sixth century A.D., to restore Christianity where Germanic marauders had wiped it out. Behind this wave of renewal there lay centuries of undisturbed Celtic survival in the western fringes of Romanized Europe. In Scotland, Wales, Cornwall, Brittany, and above all in Ireland, the Celts held on to their language and art, their spirit and their traditions. But remote as they were, they were not to remain untouched by Christianity. The Christianized Celts of the fringe lands created a remarkable culture, essentially Celtic in its expression and energy but motivated by the new religious force. Its influence went far and wide in medieval Europe, to spark the monastic movement and to inject Celtic myth—Camelot, the Grail, Tristan, and Parsifal—into the literature of many tongues.

The Roman conquest of Britain was not complete: In the north the Highlands and Islands remained untouched, and much of the rest, the region that was to become Scotland, suffered only from periodic Roman campaigns. In Wales, although the military hold was permanent, the population of the mountain valleys would hardly have been aware of the Roman presence; while in the southwest, in Devon and Cornwall, west of the town of Exeter, the population was left in peace to continue in its own ways. Ireland, protected by the sea, was untouched, save for occasional trading vessels. Thus, when in the late fourth and early fifth centuries the Roman hold on Britannia slackened, it was in the north and west that the energies of the Celts, held back for four centuries, began to burst out. Picts from the north and Irish from the west poured into the Roman province, which, to protect itself, invited Germanic raiders to settle in the lowland coastal regions. Thus was initiated a divide between English and Celt which is still in evidence today.

Superimposed upon all this was Christianity. The Celts had always been a highly superstitious people, and the new cult, introduced to Ireland in the fifth century, rapidly took root. Zealous enthusiasm fueled by their love of wandering ensured that missionaries spread into Wales, northern England, and Brittany, in the wake of settlers and thence, as the movement grew, to Gaul, Switzerland, and Italy. The Celtic Church—austere, highly individualistic, and organized like a Celtic tribe—came into inevitable conflict with the Roman Church, but by its sheer energy was able to maintain its distinctive character. Celtic love of oral learning and poetry, together with the Celtic feeling for design, found a willing patron in the monasteries. There these ancient skills flourished and were perfected. The verse composition, stone carving, fine metalwork, and manuscript illumination of the seventh, eighth, and ninth centuries were in the highest tradition of Celtic craftsmanship; while the "lives" of the saints provided a medium for storytelling, enlivened by miraculous events, in direct descent from the pagan sagas. In the Celtic Christian movement, then, the Celtic ethos was kept alive throughout the Dark Ages, to make its contribution to the culture of medieval Europe.

EVENTS ON EUROPE'S WESTERN FRINGE

From the middle of the third century A.D., the Roman frontier in Europe came under increasing pressure from the barbarian peoples of the north European plain. The buildup of population and the folk movements consequent upon it, with which Caesar dealt, were for a while counterbalanced by the energetic advances of the Roman Empire. But by the reign of Hadrian (A.D. 117–138) the Empire had reached its limits: frontiers were formalized and retrenchment set in. Freed from the necessity to respond to Roman aggression, the north European population could begin to organize aggressive campaigns of their own. For a while the Roman government

The legends surrounding St. Brendan became popular in the medieval period. They are a conflation of many stories, the oldest of which date back to the mid-sixth century. St. Brendan was a typical wandering monk seeking a life of austerity. He and his followers sailed across the western ocean in a curragh, visiting many islands, guided by a miraculous youth and nourished with supernatural fish and fruits. These fanciful stories were taken by some nineteenth- and twentieth-century romantics to mean that St. Brendan reached America.

Ireland had, in the third and second millennia, enjoyed a rich Neolithic and Bronze Age culture which left megalithic monuments, like this dolmen from Ballina, scattered across the countryside.

Right: Manuscript illustration of British coastal forts, erected by the Romans to withstand raids from Germanic pirates in the late third century A.D. These defenseworks remained in use into the fifth century. This title page from a Carolingian copy of the fifth-century *Notitia Dignitatum* shows the coastal forts under the command of the "Count of the Saxon Shore."

was able to maintain control, but gradually the barbarians gained the advantage. In the decade 250–260 a large tract of Roman territory north of the Rhine opposite Mainz was abandoned. Soon after, the province of Dacia was let slip.

The first major setback came in about 260 when, taking advantage of dissension in the Roman ranks, one of the Germanic tribes, the Alemanni, burst through the Rhine defenses and swept in a destructive wave through Gaul, reaching the Mediterranean. The incursion was quickly dealt with, but sixteen years later history was to repeat itself. This time the barbarian incursion was far more extensive. Franks crossed the lower Rhine and ravaged northern Gaul; the Alemanni swept triumphantly across the upper Rhine into Burgundy and central France; other tribes attacked Switzerland and Bavaria. The speed of the Roman response once more saved the situation, and the frontier defenses were patched up in readiness for the next onslaught.

Britain, though comparatively isolated, was not unaffected by these events. Franks and Saxons had taken to the sea and were raiding the coasts of the North Sea and the English Channel. To protect the island, coastal defenses on both sides of the Channel were put into good defensive order, and campaigns designed to rid the seas of pirates seem to have met with a degree of success.

An uneasy peace prevailed for some decades, but by the middle of the fourth century the Alemanni were again rampag-

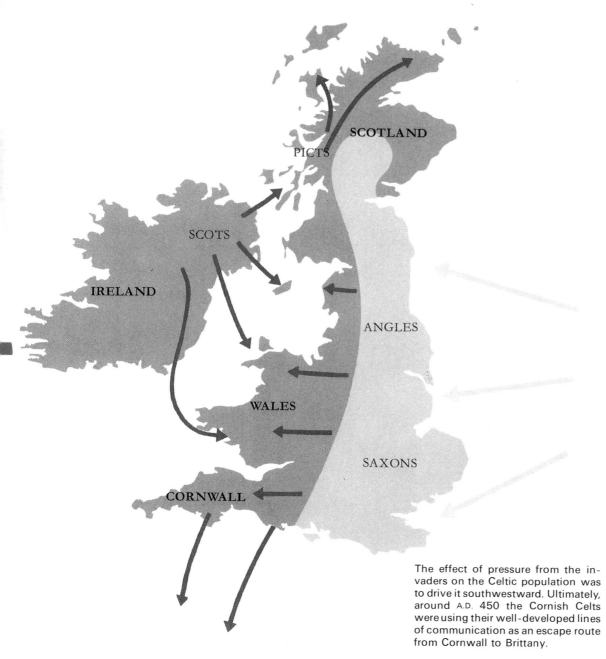

The enemies of Roman Britain came from all sides by land and by sea. The first great attack, called by classical writers the "barbarian conspiracy," took place in 367 and caused chaos south as far as the Thames. The period of folk movement during which Roman Britain was transformed to England was short: it began soon after 350 and was largely over by 450.

SCOTS

The Scotti was the name given to the peoples of northern Ireland, many of whom migrated to the western coasts of what became Scotland and also to north Wales. Other groups of Irish from the midland plain and the south settled in south Wales and in Cornwall.

PICTS

The Celtic and pre-Celtic peoples of Scotland became known to the Romans as Picti—"the painted ones." They were a constant menace to the northern frontiers in the fourth and early fifth centuries.

SAXONS, ANGLES, AND JUTES

The venerable Bede, in writing of the Germanic settlement of Britain, mentions these three tribes. It is not easy to distinguish them archaeologically. The situation in the migration period was more complex. In all probability settlers from the seaboard from Denmark to northern France all contributed to the Germanic settlement of Britain.

The effect of pressure from the invaders on the Celtic population was to drive it southwestward. Ultimately, around A.D. 450 the Cornish Celts were using their well-developed lines of communication as an escape route from Cornwall to Brittany.

Above: The Germanic raiders were warlike peoples not unlike the Celts of the pre-Roman period. This detail is taken from the helmet from Sutton Hoo (early seventh century A.D.).

Overleaf (pp. 164–165): The extreme western fringes of the Celtic world, the cliffs of Moher against which the Atlantic Ocean breaks.

ing through northeastern Gaul. Gradually the situation deteriorated as new peoples moved against the Empire: Visigoths, Ostrogoths, and Vandals. Unable to keep them out, successive emperors allowed groups across the frontier to serve as confederate troops—but the tide of invasion was impossible to stem. In December 406 vast numbers of Vandals, Alans, and Lugi crossed the frozen Rhine near Mainz and wandered through Gaul and Spain, while Burgundians moved into Alsace and Visigoths were allowed to settle in Narbonensis. In the first fifty years of the fifth century, Roman Gaul disintegrated.

Britain fared no better. A concerted attack of Saxons, Franks, Picts (from Scotland), and Attacotti (from the Western Isles)

poured into the province in 367 and caused chaos south to the Thames. Provincial government recovered, but it was seriously shaken. Then in the early fifth century Germanic invasion changed momentum. Previously there had been raids and some limited settlement in Britain under strict Roman supervision; now uncontrolled settlement began—Saxons, Franks, Jutes, and Angles pouring into the south and east of the country, totally obliterating Romano-British culture. Meanwhile the inhabitants of Ireland, unaffected by the Roman interlude and by the Germanic raiders, initiated folk movements of their own along the whole of the western seaboard of England and Wales, adding to the confusions of the age.

163

monthly supplies were not copiously contributed to them... and declared that, if larger munificence was not piled upon them they would break the treaty and lay waste the whole of the island." The threat soon became reality, the rebellious Saxons devastating cities and countryside alike "until [they] burned nearly the whole surface of the island and licked the western ocean with red and savage tongues." Some Britons retreated to the hills and forests of the west, others escaped overseas to Brittany; but eventually the rebellion was over, and the Saxons returned to their homes in eastern England.

Then followed a period of British resistance culminating in a decisive victory at Mount Badon in about A.D. 500, after which an uneasy peace was maintained between the two communities. But urban life was now a thing of the past: The cities "deserted and dismantled, they lie neglected because, although wars with foreigners have ceased, domestic wars continue" (Gildas). It sounds very much as though British society had reverted to the state of tribal warfare which existed when the Romans arrived five hundred years before.

In 549 a plague of considerable severity depopulated the land. Then began the inexorable western advance of the English settlers. After the battle of Dyrham fought in 577 just north of Bath, the English captured the old Roman cities of Bath, Cirencester, and Gloucester. Thus they arrived at the very boundaries of Wales and Dumnonia (Cornwall) which still retained their British-Celtic culture.

While Britain was experiencing the expansion of the English along its eastern coasts, the west coasts were being settled by the Irish. Irish raids were well underway by the end of the fourth century and continued well into the fifth. The Irish Sea had never been fully controlled by the Romans, and now with the decline of Roman power on land it became the link between Ireland and the adjacent coasts of Scotland, Wales, and Cornwall which received the immigrants.

The most intensive of the Irish settlements took place in southwestern Wales, in Pembrokeshire (the region recently renamed Dyfed after its ancient name). The settlers came from the dynasty of Leinster in sufficient numbers to set up a kingdom of their own and firmly to implant the Irish

For the British Isles the fifth century was a time of far-reaching and often violent change. The Roman province of Britannia remained under nominal Roman control until 410, in which year the emperor Honorius formally relinquished control of the province in a famous letter telling the inhabitants of the cities to look after their own defense. What then happened is obscure in detail, but with the complete breakdown of central authority and the collapse of the economic system, it seems that the country split into a number of self-contained kingdoms each with its own ruler or protector.

The principal threat in these early years came from the Picts, who occupied much of Scotland and who a few years before (in 367) had been involved in the devastating raid on the Roman province. As a protection against Pictish raids the Britons held a council at which the decision was taken to admit Saxons, presumably as settlers, who would be required to repel the attackers from the north. In making this decision the Britons were simply adopting a widely accepted policy which had been general practice throughout the Roman Empire for at least a century. Gildas, a western Briton writing soon after these events, explains what happened: "The barbarians, admitted into the island, succeeded in having provisions supplied them, as if they were soldiers and about to encounter... great hardships for their kind entertainers." After a while they complained that "their

Irish moved into Anglesey and northwest Wales.

A third force of Irish, emanating from Ulster, crossed into Scotland (incidentally giving the name to the country; for Scotti was the general name applied to the Irish immigrants). Their settlement extended along the west coast, to the north of the Antonine Wall (now Argyll), and was of sufficient intensity to create a strong and unified kingdom known as the Kingdom of Dálriata, which was to play a significant part in the subsequent history of the area. Finally there was the Irish settlement of Cornwall, a peninsula which retained its predominantly Celtic culture until the English penetration began in the ninth century. Judging by the memorial stones, carved with ogham inscriptions, found in the southwest, the Irish settlers came from southwest Wales during the fifth century: several of the Cornish inscriptions record the same names as those found on memorials in Dyfed.

The story of the fifth century in the British Isles is both complex and, in many areas, obscure, but the principal re-formations in society are tolerably clear. While the east was being absorbed by Germanic settlers from the Continent, largely (but not entirely) replacing the Romano-Celtic pop-

The various cultural influences which impinged on the British Isles are shown on these pages.

Far left: The Celtic cross from Carew, Wales (ninth century A.D.), is an example of the hybrid style brought about as the result of the Christianization of Celtic art.

Above: The inside of a broch in Glen Beg near Glenely, Scotland. Brochs were stone-built towers built in the first century B.C. to first century A.D. which continued to be occupied for several centuries. They represent the culmination of a traditional style of Celtic architecture extensively distributed in the far north of Britain.

language. Smaller bands moved west along the Bristol Channel, raiding the Romano-British countryside and causing widespread disruption. One band penetrated the mountainous center of Wales to set up a kingdom in Brecknock. The distribution of these early Irish settlers is shown by discoveries of their ogham inscriptions which cluster in Pembrokeshire and Carmarthenshire, where the densest settlement took place, but are scattered widely in the southwest. At about the same time another band of

ulation, the western peninsulas were being settled by peoples of pure Celtic descent from Ireland. Elsewhere, between these two opposed cultures, the descendants of the Romano-British population were maintaining a precarious hold; while in Scotland, north of the Antonine Wall, the Picts, substantially Celtic in origin and largely untouched by Rome, maintained and developed a distinctive culture of their own.

Above: The Welsh hillfort of Tre'r Ceiri within which the native population continued to live throughout the Roman period.

Above left: Invaders from abroad: Anglo-Saxon warriors seen in combat on the Franks casket (around A.D. 700).

Opposite page, top: Another hybrid, a repoussé bronze from the hillfort of South Cadbury dating to the end of the Iron Age or the beginning of the Roman period: a classicized version of a Celtic head.

BRITTANY

The Irish immigration from the west and the steady advance of the English settlement from the east caught the old Romano-Celtic population of western Britain in a kind of pincer movement. The result was inevitable: Large bodies of population moved south, across the Channel, to settle in the Armorican peninsula.

The principal causes of the migration is obscure. Gildas, however, implies that it was the revolt of the Saxon mercenaries, when, in describing the flight of the Britons, he describes how some refugees "with loud lamentations passed beyond the seas." He does not specifically mention Armorica, but movement in this direction seems a reasonable supposition. We should not, however, forget that Devon and Cornwall were also subject to immigration from Ireland in the fifth century, and there can be little reasonable doubt that the pressure on land caused by these incomings added to the flight of the Britons.

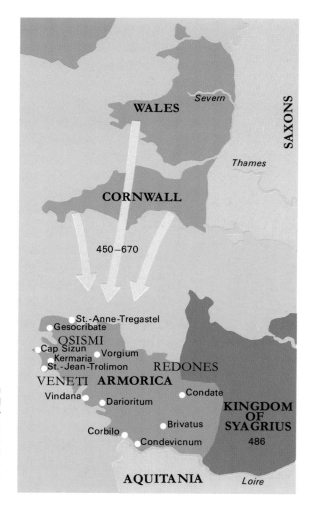

Traditional links between Armorica and western Britain can be traced back to the third millennium B.C. By the middle of the second millennium an extensive network of trade bound the two areas closely. It was during this period that the megalithic monuments in both countries developed a degree of similarity.

The migration southward appears to have been on a large scale. Substantial parts of Devon were stripped of their population, leaving the land open for the English settlers who moved in and imposed their own system of names on the empty countryside. The organization behind the exodus is indicated by the sixth-century writer Procopius of Caesarea, who describes how large numbers of Britons, ruled by their own kings, went annually to the land of the Franks where they were settled in thinly populated areas. It is very tempting to interpret this movement as the deliberate settlement of British mercenaries to serve the weakening Gallo-Roman state as confederates to drive off Saxon invaders. In other words, the initial British settlement of Armorica may well have been very

168

similar to the controlled settlement of Germanic peoples in the east of England to protect the land from the Picts.

Armorica at the time was in a state of almost constant rebellion against the central Roman authority. The first revolt took place in 409 when the local inhabitants, "encouraged by the example of the island Britons, had thrown off the Roman yoke" (Zosimus). A few decades later they were referred to as a "fickle and undisciplined people" prone to rebellion and in the throes of an active resistance movement. It was into this land, seething with discontent and lawlessness, threatened by the Saxons, and suffering from severe depopulation, that the British settlers moved in considerable numbers to create a new existence for themselves. The migration continued into the sixth century, by the end of which Armorica (or Gallia Ulterior as it is referred to in the *Gaulish Chronicle*) became Brittany. The Gallo-Roman language was replaced by a type of Celtic very similar to Cornish, and the peninsula was drawn back once more into the Celtic world to remain aloof from the rest of France for centuries to come. It was as if the clock had been put back five hundred years to the decades before Caesar:

The Veneti are the most powerful tribe on the Brittany coast. They have the largest fleet of ships, in which they traffic with Britain...and as the coast lies exposed to the violence of the open sea and has but few harbors, which the Veneti control, they compel nearly all who sail the waters to pay toll. Caesar, *Gallic Wars*

In Caesar's time the tribes of the two peninsulas were in active contact, and in both areas "cliff castles"—specialized defended enclosures on clifftop promontories—were being built as places of refuge.

Above: The Breton cliff castle at Cap Sizun.

169

ANCIENT IRELAND: THE BACKGROUND

While Britain was undergoing the traumas first of Roman invasion and later of the Germanic migrations, Ireland remained largely isolated, able to maintain its own Celtic tradition without hindrance. The great prose saga *Táin Bó Cualnge* (Cattle-Raid of Cooley) gives some indication of how the island was organized in the first centuries of the first millennium A.D. Ireland was at this stage divided into four parts—*Ulaid* (Ulster), *Connachta* (Connacht), *Laigin* (Leinster), and *Mumu* (Munster)—each of which was a large kingdom. Ulster was ruled by Couchobar macNessa from the court at Emain Macha; while Connacht, its great rival, was ruled by Queen Medb, whose rath was on the hill of Cruachain. At this stage the two southern kingdoms were of comparatively little significance.

Society was closely similar to that of the pre-Roman Celts of Europe—the same raiding, head-hunting, chariot warfare, the same exuberant boastfulness, and the same inability to work in larger groups for the common good.

In the period following that represented by the *Táin*, a new dynasty makes its appearance in Meath, in the Irish midlands, using as its royal center the much revered hill of

Niall—called Uí Néill—rapidly extended their power over most of the rest of northern Ireland, the most far-reaching change being their annexation and subsequent dismemberment of the ancient kingdom of Ulaid (Ulster) which stretched from Antrim to Donegal. This process took place in the middle of the fifth century. First the Airgialla of the central part of Ulster were subdued and the ancient site of Emain Macha was taken. Soon afterward, about 428, Donegal was taken, the newly won territories being divided by the two sons of Niall who ruled from Ailech. Niall's third

The sheela-na-gig represents the Irish goddess of Creation. The age of the megalithic tombs is well represented by great ritual monuments like New Grange *(above)*, third millennium B.C.); while the Iron Age, both pagan and Christian, has left innumerable defended enclosures. Of the royal sites, the hill of Tara *(above right)* is the most evocative.

Tara. Traditionally the founder of the dynasty was Niall Noígiallach (379–ca. 428) whose mother, "Cairenn, curly black-haired daughter of Sachell Balb of the Saxons," had probably been acquired in a raid on Roman Britain. The descendants of

son remained in the south to succeed his father at Tara. Thus the north of Ireland was divided into the kingdom of northern Uí Néill, with its center at Ailech, and that of the southern Uí Néill who were based on Tara. From 506 to 1036 the posi-

170

tion of head of the dynasty was shared alternately between these two centers.

While the conquest of Ulster was being undertaken in the north, there was continuous conflict in the south between the Uí Néill and the traditional rulers of Leinster who had occupied the midland plain before Niall's arrival. But by 513 local resistance had been overcome.

The southern half of Ireland was, at this time, more culturally advanced than the north, partly because contacts with Gaul, particularly with Aquitaine, had been maintained. The constant conflict between the Uí Néill of Tara and the people of Leinster greatly weakened the Leinster dynasty and enabled the Munster dynasty of Eóganacht (the descendants of Eógan) to emerge as leaders of the south, dominating the routes across Ireland from their royal capital established on the rock of Cashel in the plain of Tipperary. Although there were intermittent intertribal rivalries, the kingdom of Munster remained, by and large, peaceful, and it was here that the cultural life of Ireland flourished. The panegyric poetry of Munster was written down in the later sixth century, and by A.D. 600 vernacular writing had already begun. The density of ogham inscriptions in the area emphasize the development of its aristocratic culture. By the early Christian period, then, the old Ireland of the *Táin*, with its four kingdoms, had changed dramatically. Ireland was now divided into seven kingdoms: the recently established kingdom of the Uí Néill at Tara, together with Munster, Connacht, the remnants of Leinster, and the three separate kingdoms which emerged from the fragmentation of the old kingdom of Ulster. Each of these was composed of a number of tribes *(tuatha)*—about one hundred in all—whose chieftains owed allegiance to the regional king. Overall control of the south remained with the Eóganachta, while the north owed allegiance to the Uí Néill, who were accepted as the high kings of all Ireland throughout the rest of the first millennium.

Writing of the overlords in this way might give the impression of a sophisticated socio-political structure, yet the available evidence suggests that early Christian Ireland was still essentially a Celtic country organized in much the same way as the Celts of pre-Roman Europe.

⌐ Megalithic monuments

⋮ Celtic sanctuaries

◗ Hillforts

♜ Centers of royal power

⚲ Important monastic sites

The art of Ireland in the first millennium is a mixture of pagan Celtic themes and Christian symbolism.

Left: The enamel inlaid figure of a man from Email sits cross-legged in a position highly reminiscent of the gods on the Gundestrup caldron.

Opposite top: The brilliant sculpture of the tenth century is represented by the martyrdom of a Christian bishop—one of the narrative panels on the cross of Nuiredach, Monasterboice, County Louth.

171

Saint Patrick and the Irish Monks

The first firm date in Irish history is A.D. 431—the year in which, according to the *Chronicle* of Prosper of Aquitaine, Pope Celestine I sent Palladius to minister to "those of the Irish who believed in Christ." It was in the following year, so the *Annals of Ulster* record, that Patrick arrived in Ireland. Herein lies a problem: if the dates can be accepted, then the conversion of Ireland had begun some while before Patrick arrived. The matter is further confused by the *Annals'* treatment of Patrick's death, for which three dates are given: 457, 461, and 492. Such evidence leaves ample scope for interpretation and speculation. Some scholars believe there were two

A multitude of Irish artworks attest to the maintenance of the Christian traditions throughout the centuries in the Celtic fringe lands. The carved stone from Boa Island, County Fermanagh *(above)*, is believed to be a work of the seventh century A.D.

Patricks: the elder, known as Palladius, who died in 461; the younger, Patrick the Briton, would have arrived at about this time and died in 492. An alternative view is that Patrick the Briton preceded Palladius and died about 430. There are of course other possibilities, and the controversy is likely to continue, not least because, for some, it is a highly emotive issue.

That Patrick existed, and played a prominent part in spreading Christianity in Ireland, is not in dispute, but the fact that the early genealogies and lives of the saints imply that Christianity was already practiced among some of the communities of the south before the advent of Patrick, lends strong support to those who accept the activities of earlier missionaries.

Of Patrick's exploits we have two reliable sources—two letters written in Latin in the mid-fifth century, claiming to be by the saint himself. One of the letters, the *Confessio*, provides many details of his early life. He was, he claims, brought up in the

civilized countryside of Roman Britain but was captured by Irish raiders while still a boy and carried off to Ireland as a slave where he was forced to herd the flocks of his master. Six years later, guided by a voice from heaven, he made a two-hundred-mile trek to the coast, where he found a merchant ship bound for Gaul with a cargo of dogs (presumably hunting dogs). After a voyage of three days' duration, he landed in France, finding the country to be in a state of terror and desolation as the result of the barbarian raids. Eventually he returned to his family in Britain, but after a while he was again approached by heavenly messengers and heard the voice of the Irish crying out, "We beseech thee, holy youth, to come hither and walk among us." Realizing his duty, he became ordained and set off for Ireland, despite opposition from the Church authorities, to convert the heathen Irish.

The simple story is of outstanding interest. Patrick was probably born at the end of the fourth century when the fast collapsing Roman province of Britain was being wracked by Irish raids. He was presumably an educated Romano-British youth for whom the Church was the obvious vocation, and he would thus have carried to Ireland the traditions, learning, and prejudices of a provincial Roman. It is hardly surprising therefore that the Church which he founded in Ireland, no doubt modeled on the Church in Britain, was purely Roman in origin and episcopal in organization.

That many of the Irish kings accepted Christianity means that the new faith spread with little aggression or bloodshed. There were "countless numbers" of converts, and land was readily given by the local kings for the establishment of churches. These early complexes were simple circular enclosures, rather like the secular ring forts, containing a church or oratory, a priest's house, and a kitchen. They were governed by bishops and were called "cities"—a reminder that the Irish Church was modeled on the Roman, where episcopal seats were established in the *civitates*. But even at this early stage it is possible to recognize the beginnings of monasticism, which from the sixth century was to give the Celtic Church its special character.

The Lord will be with thee:
go thou
but straight before thee;
take to thee
first my little bell,
which until thou
reach the well
that we have mentioned
shall be speechless;
but when thou
attainest to it
the little bell will
with a clear melodious voice
speak out:
so shalt thou know the well,
and at the end
of nine years and a score
I will follow thee
to that place.

St. Patrick, Irish traditional

The stone carvings at center depict, respectively, a priest holding a crook and a bell that symbolizes the Gospel message (found on White Island, Lough Erne, Fermanagh), and St. Patrick in bishop's vestments, with a snake at his feet as in the legends (from a fifteenth-century grave slab).

THE NEW CULTURE

Patrick attempted the impossible: to implant upon a dispersed community with a simple, tribally organized economy a complex episcopal administration which had evolved in the thoroughly urbanized context of the Roman Empire. He was after all a provincial Roman, and to him the Roman system seemed appropriate. What is perhaps the most remarkable aspect of the mission is that it succeeded so dramatically.

Gradually throughout the fifth and early sixth centuries, the ecclesiastical organization established by Patrick became transformed to suit Irish society. The diocese, the administrative unit of the Church, disappeared and bishops lost their organizational duties. Instead, monasteries, following the teachings of their individual founders, became the dominant religious force. The Irish Church evolved in relative isolation, cut off from the great Christian centers of mainland Europe. The western sea routes, however, remained open, linking the countries surrounding the Irish Sea with the Mediterranean world. The wine trade continued to flourish, introducing into the western parts of the British Isles fine pottery and wine amphorae from North Africa. But alongside these luxuries came the knowledge of the monastic life which had developed so intensely in Egypt. All along the Atlantic seaboard monastic

life took root: in Spain, Aquitaine, western Britain, and Ireland. Irish monks also traveled to the west of Britain to study in the monasteries of Whithorn in Galloway and at St. David's in southwest Wales. There they learned the value of ascetism and returned to Ireland to build their cells in isolated locations in order to spend their lives in fasting and prayer. St. Enda, returning from Whithorn, moved far into the west to establish a cell on the bleak Aran Islands where he and his companions lived a life of hardship and simplicity—it was to mark the beginning of the wave of ascetism which swept Ireland and transformed the country's religious life. Irish monks congregated around the cells of the founders in large communities, and the idea of the monastic family was readily absorbed. The primatial see at Armagh became a mon-

174

astery at the end of the fifth century, while at Kildare a mixed community of monks and nuns was established by St. Brigid. At Clonard the church created by Patrick was transformed into a monastery by St. Finnian, who had been influenced by the monks of southern Wales. It soon became famous throughout Ireland.

It is easy to understand why the monastic system so rapidly replaced the episcopal system introduced by St. Patrick. Irish society was still organized in the Celtic manner, its basis being the tribe *(tuáth)* which was made up of a number of clans. The urban-derived episcopal system was both alien and inappropriate to Ireland; but the monastery was a concept which could readily be absorbed into the Celtic social organization. The monastery was, after all, a family governed by an abbot: it was little more than a religious version of the *tuáth* controlled by a chieftain. Thus the soil of Ireland, fertilized by St. Patrick's mission, provided a sympathetic environment for Mediterranean monasticism to take root. The ninth- or tenth-century *Catalogus Sanctorum*, looking back on the fifth and sixth centuries, divided the saints of Ireland into three "orders": the first was St. Patrick, the second were the saints who founded the great monasteries, the third "those who dwell in desert places and live on herbs, water, and alms and have nothing of their own." Although this threefold division should not be taken to imply a chronological evolution, the third order—the anchorites—do come comparatively late in the period. The life of the hermit, the ascetic who renounced everything, was a style of Christian behavior learned ultimately from Egypt via Spain and Gaul, but it became widespread in the Celtic west. To a Celt, membership of the family was an essential part of his well-being. It was logical, therefore, that in renouncing all

The tradition of erecting a simple engraved memorial stone over graves or a holy location was gradually transformed to give rise to the distinctive art of the High Cross. The inspiration for the style is quite clearly the work of the bronzesmith and the goldsmith whose intricate designs were copied in stone. Presumably these great crosses of the ninth and tenth centuries are copies of heavy wooden crosses whose arms were probably stabilized with cross braces at the angles—evolving into the highly distinctive form of the Irish High Cross.

One of the earliest groups, of which the Ahenny cross *(below, third from right)*, is a fine example, has a limited distribution in the south of Ireland. The bosses and interlace designs are a strong reminder of the metalwork tradition which they attempt to copy. This style dates to the eighth century.

A little later "Scripture Crosses" develop: the face of the cross was now divided into rectangular panels within each of which a different scene was depicted, some of which included nonreligious subjects. The tradition of the carved High Cross continues with some vigor into the twelfth century.

Crosses below, from left to right: Duvillaun, Kilnasaggart, Glendalough, Clonmacnoise, Clonmacnoise, Ahenny, Clonmacnoise, Monasterboice.

Early Christian architecture is widespread in Ireland. "St. Columba's House" (*right*), built of stone and mortar in 814 on the site of a wooden structure, is among the best preserved ruins of the St. Columba monastery at Kells.
The walls, more than a meter thick, surround a small cell-like room.

worldly possessions, he should also give up the luxury of community life. Thus many young men returning to Ireland from abroad shunned the comparative comfort of the well-established monasteries and made the ultimate sacrifice to be alone in the wilderness. Others made the same sacrifice—total divorce from family—by seeking solitude among strangers. Such men, in their quest of penance through exile, fueled the missionary movement which spread knowledge of the Celtic Church across the face of western Europe (pp. 186–189).

transcribed in Latin, they scribbled charming verses—influenced by Latin meter but redolent with a Celtic awareness of the natural world. That these great centers of learning could develop was in considerable part due to their Celtic heritage; for the tradition of druidic and bardic schools was strong in pagan Ireland, and the monasteries were their natural successors.

The early monasteries were modest structures, much like large homesteads, consisting of an enclosing wall and ditch within which were the principal buildings: the church or oratory, usually built of timber but sometimes of stone; the cells of the monks, which would often be simple circular structures of wattle and daub; the guest house; the refectory; and the school. Besides the buildings themselves, there might be various types of stone monuments. Memorial stones carved with ogham script were common, particularly in Munster, from the fourth to the seventh century. Simple roughly hewn slabs and pillars carved with the Christian symbol Chi-Rho and monograms in Greek and Latin also became popular to mark graves, and the grave slab of the founder frequently became the most revered spot in the monastic complex—the focus of the pilgrim's visit. These monuments were comparatively modest in execution: it was not until the eighth century that the elaborately carved high crosses began to be made to adorn the holy places. Together with fine metalwork and the magnificent manuscripts, they represent the artistic culmination of the Golden Age of early Christian Ireland.

My hand is weary with writing; my sharp great point is not thick; my slender-beaked pen juts forth a beetle-hued draught of bright blue ink.
A steady stream of wisdom springs from my well-colored neat fair hand;
on the page it pours its draught of ink of the green-skinned holly.
I send my little dripping pen unceasingly over an assemblage of books of great beauty, to enrich the possessions of men of art—whence my hand is weary with writing.

Irish traditional, eleventh century

Some monks spent much time in the scriptoria of the abbeys copying out the gospel books and transcribing other manuscripts thought useful. The twelfth-century miniature above shows the famous chronicler Bede at work.

Opposite: The circular tower developed late, partly as a response to Viking attack. Some towers were isolated, but sometimes they were attached to churches, as in this ninth-century example at Glendalough.

In spite of the harsh austerity practiced by the anchorites in the wilds, the monastic communities rapidly developed as centers of letters and learning. The culture practiced and taught was hybrid—a mixture of Roman superimposed on Celtic. The monks could write Latin, and many had a reasonable knowledge of classical authors. But in their art the Celtic freedom dominates, and in the marginal notes to the manuscripts which they so laboriously

In the *scriptoria* of the monasteries the skilled scribes spent their lives copying and illuminating manuscripts. The range of their work varied enormously—religious tracts, the lives of the saints, natural history, astronomy, and, of prime importance, the gospel books used at the altar, on which the greatest care and love were lavished. The monks transcribed in Latin and in Irish, sometimes to relieve the monotony, adding marginal notes of their own or composing lively poems in the vernacular. It is to the monastic scribes that we owe the survival of the ancient oral traditions of pagan Ireland. Painstakingly they transcribed the sagas to written form, censoring them of the worst excesses of heathenism. In collecting these old oral traditions, to which enormous prestige still attached,

GUARDIANS OF ANCIENT MYTHS AND LEGENDS

One of the most complete manuscripts of the famous pagan saga, the *Táin Bó Cualnge*, is contained in the Book of Leinster which was compiled in the twelfth century. The Leinster text is a corrected version of the story which was originally written down several centuries earlier. Several other, less complete, editions survive.

the monks preserved a record of pagan Celtic times quite unique in the ancient world.

Their attitude to this archaic record is amusingly summed up by the twelfth-century scribe who, having copied the whole of the *Táin Bó Cualnge*, could not resist adding a personal view: "But I, who have written this history, or rather fable, am doubtful about many things in this history or fable. For some of them are the figments of demons, some of them poetic imaginings, some true, some not, some for the delight of fools."

THE PILLOW TALK

Once when the royal bed was laid out for Ailill and Medb in Cruachan fort in Connacht, they had this talk on the pillows:

"It is true what they say, love," Ailill said, "it is well for the wife of a wealthy man."

"True enough," the woman said. "What put that in your mind?"

"It struck me," Ailill said, "how much better off you are today than the day I married you."

"I was well enough off without you," Medb said.

"Then your wealth was something I didn't know or hear much about," Ailill said. "Except for your woman's things, and the neighboring enemies making off with loot and plunder."

"Not at all," Medb said, "but with the high king of Ireland for my father—Eochaid Feidlech the steadfast, the son of Finn, the son of Finnoman, the son of Finnen, the son of Finngoll, the son of Roth, the son of Rigéon, the son of Blathacht, the son of Beothacht, the son of Enna Agnech, the son of Aengus Turbech. He had six daughters: Derbriu, Ethne, Ele, Clothru, Muguin, and myself Medb, the highest and haughtiest of them. I outdid them in grace and giving and battle and warlike combat. I had fifteen hundred soldiers in my royal pay, all exiles' sons, and the same number of freeborn native men, and for every paid soldier I had ten more men, and nine more, and eight, and seven, and six, and five, and four, and three, and two, and one. And that was only our ordinary household.

"My father gave me a whole province of Ireland, this province ruled from Cruachan, which is why I am called 'Medb of Cruachan.' And they came from Finn the king of Leinster, Rus Ruad's son to woo me, and from Coirpre Niafer the king of Temair, another of Rus Ruad's sons. They came from Conchobor, king of Ulster, son of Fachtna, and they came from Eochaid Bec, and I wouldn't go. For I asked a harder wedding gift than any woman ever asked before from a man in Ireland—the absence of meanness and jealousy and fear.

"If I married a mean man our union would be wrong, because I'm so full of grace and giving. It would be an insult if I were more generous than my husband, but not if the two of us were equal in this. If my husband was a timid man our union would be just as wrong because I thrive, myself, on all kinds of trouble. It is an insult for a wife to be more spirited than her husband, but not if the two are equally spirited.

The *Táin*

THE ROUND TABLE

The Arthurian legends, which relate back to events in the fifth century, were much loved in later times and were taken over by the more propaganda-conscious kings of England. There were many medieval accretions to the legend. The Round Table, for example, was added in the early Middle Ages, in the age of chivalry when the knights were considered equal. But the complex myth of the Holy Grail may have developed from an early story in which a magic caldron is mentioned—perhaps a distant reflection of the caldron associated with the pagan god Dagda.

Above: Twelfth-century miniature of the Last Supper: the round table here may have inspired the adoption of the Round Table in later Arthurian stories.

In the early twelfth century, Geoffrey of Monmouth, a minor ecclesiastic of Welsh descent, published his *History of the Kings of Britain*—a strange and fanciful compilation that begins with the settlement of the island by Brutus, great grandson of Aeneas, and ends with the Age of King Arthur. His source, he claims, was an ancient document in the British language given to him by one Walter, archdeacon of Oxford. Whether such a document existed we shall never know, but what is clear is that beneath the colorful fantasy and invention, of which Geoffrey's work is largely compiled, there are threads drawn from Welsh monastic writing and from Breton sources.

Geoffrey's book formed the foundation for the rich Arthurian tradition which grew by accretion throughout the Middle Ages, championed by the Plantagenet kings. It presented a highly respectable pedigree for the ruling house to adopt, and once Arthur could be freed from close association with the Welsh by dexterous manipulation— which involved some highly dubious medieval excavations at Glastonbury—then the British monarch could boast of origins quite as illustrious as those of his French rival. Politically acceptable and appealing to the romantic age of chivalry, Arthur was assured of a wide and highly uncritical audience: his exploits expanded with their constant retelling.

Yet behind all the nonsense lay some traditions which originated in the sixth century, when, evidently, the name of Arthur was revered throughout western Britain. Belief in him as a folk hero can be traced back to a compilation called the *History of the Britons*—a ragbag of folklore and other scraps gleaned from Welsh documents, put together in the ninth century by a Welsh cleric, Nennius. Arthur emerges simply as a war leader who spearheaded the British resistance against the Saxons in the years around 500, fighting a series of highly successful battles. The memory of these deeds lived long in the early Welsh literature. He is mentioned briefly in the long poem, *Gododdin*, composed about 600. Other early poems mention his followers, his horse, his kinsfolk, and his bards. In the famous Welsh legend the *Mabinogion*, Arthur occurs many times. Perhaps the most interesting story in this legend tells how a young man, Culhwch, in order to win Olwen as his bride has to perform a series of fantastic

tasks and enlists the aid of Arthur. The story provides the medium for the skills of the hero to be displayed, but it has all the verve and energy of the Irish sagas. The close relationship is further emphasized by the inclusion of famous figures from Irish mythology and by the strong similarities between the arrival of Culhwch at the court of Arthur and Lug's arrival at the court of Nuada in the Irish *Battle of Moytura*. This part of the *Mabinogion* is clearly in the same broad tradition as the early Irish sagas, reflecting the fabulous world of the pagan Celtic period seen through later eyes.

What emerges from the confusing detail of the Arthurian legends is that a folk hero or heroes, singly or collectively called Arthur, led a resistance movement against the Germanic settlers in western Britain in the late fifth and early sixth centuries. So great were his exploits, that the name of the hero was quickly absorbed into the traditions of Wales and merged with the older sagas and legends of the pagan Celtic period in stories

like that of Culhwch and Olwen. The name was also revered in later poetry. Thus when Geoffrey of Monmouth was searching for a basis for his mythical *History of the Kings of Britain*, there was ample material readily to hand. All he did was present Arthur in an updated guise which suited medieval susceptibilities. The Arthurian theme, then, bridges the gap between the Celtic saga tradition and medieval and modern romantic literature.

The developed myth—Round Table and Holy Grail—is shown in the fifteenth-century book illustration from *Les Chroniques de Hainaut (left)*. Many of the great literary works of the European Middle Ages are poetic elaborations of old Celtic legends. Marie de France and Chrétien de Troyes, writing in France in the twelfth century, acknowledged their debt to "Breton" or Celtic sources. Chrétien's *Parsifal*, in turn, with its retelling of the quest of the Grail, had a strong influence on medieval culture. The three miniature paintings here, from the fourteenth-century Manessa codex, are illustrations for works of three German poets.

Gottfried von Strassburg *(left)*, wrote the twelfth–thirteenth-century version of *Tristan and Isolde* that inspired Richard Wagner.
The minnesinger Wolfram von Eschenbach ca. 1170–1220, author of a Middle High German *Parsifal*, is shown in his armor.
Heinrich von Meissen, called Frauenlob, ca. 1250–1318 *(right)*, wrote courtly works in praise of women, partly inspired by old Celtic love poetry.

181

THE BARDS

The important role of the bard in early societies is very clearly shown in Ireland. Here the bardic tradition flourished, combining mythology, history, current events and poetry in a vast oral anthology. The poems,

often thousands of lines long, recited to music, were an important part of Celtic culture, and gave the bard the kind of semi-magical, semi-mythical status typified in Europe by the legend of Orpheus, shown here in a fifteenth century relief by Luca della Robbia.

In early Irish society there were two classes of men who were responsible for literary and musical composition: the bards, whose task it was to compose poems in praise of their masters, and the *filid*—a word which originally meant "seers"—who in addition to being poets were endowed with certain supernatural powers: they could, for example, hurt or even kill by satire. In the *Táin*, Medb sends "the druids and satirists and harsh bards" against Fer Diad to "make against him three satires to slay him and three lampoons, and that they might raise on his face three blisters, shame, blemish, and disgrace."

The *filid* and the bards were trained in specially organized schools. All teaching was oral and was accomplished by the simple procedure of the master intoning and the pupils repeating the matter in unison. Significantly the Old Irish verb "to teach" means "to sing over." Once quali-

fied, the *filí* would be free to travel, uttering panegyrics wherever he went, in expectation of reward. At the top of the poetic hierarchy was the *ollam*, who traveled and behaved in the manner befitting a minor king with a retinue of twenty-four men. No one could safely deny hospitality to such a man.

With the coming of Christianity, the magical attributes of the *filid* withered away, but the bardic tradition and the schools continued to flourish. The trade of the poet was still one of honor which required long years of apprenticeship to perfect. The principal difference was that, with Christianity, knowledge of Latin with its formal meter influenced the vernacular compositions, creating a new kind of syllabic lyric poetry.

The traditional schools of the bards and the *filid* were still active in the tenth century. Certain metrical tracts survive from this time prescribing the different meters to be practiced and the range of heroic literature which had to be studied in each year of the twelve-year apprenticeship. The length of the period of study is an interesting reminder of the twenty years which Caesar recorded to be the time needed to train a druid.

The twelfth century saw the beginnings of a renewed vigor in the bardic schools in Ireland, and it is in this period that much of the best Welsh poetry was written. The poetic renaissance may well be attributed to the patronage of the Welsh king Gruffudd ap Cynan, who, having spent his youth in Ireland, returned to his native Gwynedd, probably bringing Irish poets and musicians back with him. In both countries the twelfth century saw the beginnings of a stricter form of composition which was carefully preserved by families of hereditary bards, eventually giving rise to stereotyped and rather dull work bound by rigid conventions. The principal themes remained much the same as before: the patron was praised, the glory of his ancestors was paraded, and his personal generosity and bravery in battle were eulogized. Careful craftsmanship soon replaced freshness and originality, and the bardic tradition lapsed into mechanical dullness. Even so, bardic schools still flourished in Ireland as late as the seventeenth century.

SENILITY

Before I was bent-backed, I was eloquent of speech, my wonderful deeds were admired; the men of Argoed always supported me.

Before I was bent-backed, I was bold; I was welcomed in the drinking-hall of Powys, the paradise of Wales.

*Before I was bent-backed, I was handsome, my spear was in the van, it drew first blood—
I am crooked, I am sad, I am wretched.*

Wooden staff, it is Autumn, the bracken is red, the stubble is yellow; I have given up what I love.

Wooden staff, it is Winter, men are talkative over the drink; no one visits my bedside.

Wooden staff, it is Spring, the cuckoos are brown, there is light at the evening meal; no girl loves me.

Wooden staff, it is early Summer, the furrow is red, the young corn is curly; it grieves me to look at your crook.

Wooden staff, knotty stick, support the yearning old man, Llywarch, the perpetual babbler....

Boisterous is the wind, white is the hue of the edge of the wood; the stag is emboldened, the hill is bleak; feeble is the old man, slowly he moves.

This leaf, the wind drives it, alas for its fate! It is old—this year it was born.

*What I have loved from boyhood I now hate—
a girl, a stranger, and a gray horse; indeed I am not fit for them.*

The four things I have most hated ever have met together in one place; coughing and old age, sickness and sorrow.

I am old, I am lonely, I am shapeless and cold after my honored couch; I am wretched, I am bent in three.

I am bent in three and old, I am peevish and giddy, I am silly, I am cantankerous; those who loved me love me not.

Girls do not love me, no one visits me, I cannot move about; ah, Death, why does it not come for me!

Neither sleep nor joy come to me after the slaying of Llawr and Gwen; I an irritable carcass, I am old.

Welsh; attributed to "Llywarch Hen; ninth century

THE HARP OF CNOC Í CHOSGAIR

Harp of Cnoc Í Chosgair; you who bring sleep to eyes long sleepless; sweet, subtle, plangent, glad, cooling, grave.

Excellent instrument with the smooth gentle curve, trilling under red fingers, musician that has charmed us, red, lion-like, of full melody.

You who lure the bird from the flock, you who refresh the mind, brown spotted one of sweet words, ardent, wondrous, passionate.

You who heal every wounded warrior, joy and allurement to women, familiar guide over the dark-blue water, mystic sweet-sounding music.

You who silence every instrument of music, yourself a pleasing plaintive instrument, dweller among the Race of Conn, instrument yellow-brown and firm.

The one darling of sages, restless, smooth, of sweet tune, crimson star above the fairy hills, breast-jewel of High Kings.

Sweet tender flowers, brown harp of Diarmaid, shape not unloved by hosts, voice of the cuckoos in May!

I have not heard of music ever such as your frame makes since the time of the fairy people, fair brown many-colored bough, gentle, powerful, glorious.

Sound of the calm wave on the beach, pure shadowing tree of true music, carousals are drunk in your company, voice of the swan over shining streams.

Cry of the fairy women from the Fairy Hill of Ler, no melody can match you, every house is sweet-stringed through your guidance, you the pinnacle of harp-music ...

Irish, Gofraidh Fionn Ó Dálaigh, ca. 1385

WHERE ARE YOU GOING TO, MY PRETTY MAID?

*"Where were you going, fair maid," said he,
"with your pale face and your yellow hair?"
"Going to the well, sweet sir," she said,
"for strawberry leaves make maidens fair."*

*"Shall I go with you, fair maid," said he,
"with your pale face and your yellow hair?"
"Do if you wish, sweet sir," she said,
"for strawberry leaves make maidens fair."*

Cornish popular poem, seventeenth century

Overleaf (pp. 184–185): The Book of Kells is one of the great masterpieces of early Christian Ireland. It was probably written and illuminated in Iona early in the ninth century but carried from there, unfinished, to the new monastery of Kells, County Meath, where many of the monks fled from the Viking raiders. The book, comprising the four gospels, is elaborately ornamented. It is the culmination of Irish artistic development. Each gospel begins with a portrait page (St. John, on p. 185)—the frontal pose and wide-eyed face belying the ultimate Byzantine inspiration—but the Celtic spirit is everywhere to be seen in the intensely complex curvilinear style of the illumination.

The bards of the Irish royal houses composed countless songs which subsequently became part of the repertoire of the medieval troubadours (above). Celtic poetry dating back to the eighth century has survived by this means.

hgenerano

THE MISSIONARIES' FIRST STEP

The reconstruction shows a typical Irish monastery. Enclosed within a defensive wall or earthwork, it much resembled contemporary homesteads. The principal building was, naturally, the church or oratory; there could be more than one depending on the popularity of the establishment. Other buildings included the refectory and the guest house. The monks lived in individual cells of wickerwork or (in this case) corbeled stonework built around the perimeter wall. The round towers (of which

The desire for isolation through voluntary exile, which encouraged the Irish monks of the sixth century to seek solitude on remote islands or in the depths of the uninhabited countryside, led some men to cross the seas to Britain and mainland Europe, there to be alone among strangers. In this way the rigors of Celtic Christianity were introduced to a wider audience nearly a century after St. Patrick had first set foot in Ireland.

Among the first missionaries to leave Ireland was St. Columba, prince of the northern Uí Néill. In 563, with twelve companions, he set sail for Argyll, where one of the offshoots of his people, the Dálriata, had already settled, and there, on the remote offshore island of Iona, he founded a monastery. Iona was soon to become the ecclesiastical head of the Celtic Church in

political acts of this kind the prestige and patronage of the new establishment was firmly established.

Early in the seventh century Iona offered sanctuary to the exiled king Oswald of Northumbria, and when, in 634, he returned to his kingdom he invited the monks of Iona to settle among his people. Thus, the next year, Aidan, with twelve disciples, set out for Northumbria choosing as the site for their monastery the island of Lindisfarne, off the Northumberland coast in the North Sea. Lindisfarne and Iona were soon to become great cultural centers revered throughout the civilized world. Together they nurtured Celtic culture in the tranquillity and comparative safety of their island retreats.

Irish missionaries spread to all parts of Britain, some coming directly from Ireland,

about eighty survive in Ireland) were bell towers from which the monks were summoned to prayer, but they also served as secure places for monks and the monasteries' treasures in times of danger during the Viking raids. Towers were probably first built in the early tenth century.

Ireland, Scotland, and England. But it was more than that: it was a political center. At Iona he inaugurated Aidan king of the new territory of Dálriata, while at the same time establishing a peaceful relationship with the king of the northern Picts. Through

others from Iona. In the north they penetrated the Hebrides and sailed north to Orkney and Shetland reaching as far as Iceland. By the seventh century the Irish Celtic Church was known in all parts of the British Isles.

St. Brigid's monastery in Kildare was one of the most famous establishments in Ireland; founded in the late fifth century, it served both monks and nuns. It was a place of pilgrimage and grew rich. A seventh-century description of the church describes it as a many-windowed building, divided into three parts by screens which were ornamented by paintings and linen hangings, and with an ornate door. The fine tower *(left)* was added to the establishment in the tenth century.

The comparative comfort and opulence of St. Brigid's is in striking contrast to the monastery on barren, sea-battered Skellig Rock far out in

the Atlantic off the southwest coast of Ireland. The buildings—a group of beehive cells and two little oratories—are terraced into the side of the rock five hundred feet above the sea. There is a tiny cemetery with roughly inscribed grave slabs and protected garden plots where a few herbs and vegetables were persuaded to grow.

187

ST. COLUMBANUS

ST. FRIDOLIN

ST. CILIAN

ST. BONIFACE

Jesus be thanked,
to a foreign country
here have I come;
I will go on shore—
Lord Jesus, kind heart,
guide me to a good place
that I may worship
my dear Christ and Mary
the virgin flower.
I have come to land
and am weary with traveling.

THE RETURN TO THE CONTINENT

Mary, mother and maid,
if you have house
or mansion near here,
guide me to it,
for indeed I should greatly
wish to make me an oratory
beside Mary's house.

Cornish, fifteenth century

The Irish missionary settlement in Britain was only part of a much wider phenomenon. In the sixth century great numbers of missionaries crossed to Gaul, the Rhineland, Switzerland, and Italy. Some of them, like St. Gall, were hermits who sought nothing but the solitude of the Swiss mountains. Others were intent upon converting the heathen and setting up monasteries—men like St. Columbanus, who in 590 landed in Gaul and founded the famous abbey of Luxeuil. Men of such missionary zeal inevitably came into conflict with the secular authorities. St. Columbanus made a lifelong enemy of Queen Brunhilde of Burgundy, who eventually drove him from the country. However, he remained undaunted and continued his travels, arriving in northern Italy in 614 where he founded another abbey at Bobbio.

The energy and conviction of these men who were prepared to travel vast distances through dangerous and politically unstable territory is remarkable; but their faith was such that they were sustained and through their rigorous example encouraged others, heathen and Christian alike, to adopt their own demanding standards and regimes.

St. Columbanus Born in Leinster, he was a member of the religious community of St. Comgall of Bangor in County Down. About 590 he and twelve disciples set out for the Continent, traveled through western Gaul, and settled in Burgundy, where he founded abbeys at Luxeuil and Fontaine. He was forced to move on, through the court of Austria to Switzerland, and stayed for a while near Bregenz. Finally he traveled south through the Alps to Lombardy, where he founded a monastery at Bobbio.

St. Fridolin In his missionary wanderings in the sixth century, Fridolin founded a monastery and church on the island of Säckingen in the Rhine. He is still honored as the patron saint of Glarus, Switzerland.

St. Cilian The Irish bishop Cilian came to be called the apostle of Franconia for his work in that area of Germany. He died a martyr's death at Würzburg in the year 697.

St. Columba As a member of the royal house of the Uí Néill, Columba might have become king. Instead he chose the Church. He crossed to Argyll (western Scotland) where a branch of his people had recently settled, and there, on the island of Iona, founded a monastery which soon acquired great prestige. He served there as priest and abbot until his death in 597.

St. Cuthbert Born in about 634, Cuthbert spent his early life in England as a shepherd. In ca. 651 he entered the monastery at Melrose in Scotland, which followed the rule of St. Columba, and later moved to the Columban community at Lindisfarne, where he became abbot. From here he spent much of his time traveling about Northumberland spreading the gospel and converting the heathen.

St. Boniface Boniface was a West Saxon born ca. 675. He studied in monasteries at Exeter and Nursling, where he came under the influence of the teaching emanating from Canterbury. His first short missionary visit abroad was in Frisia (716–717). For twenty years he worked among the Germans and Franks.

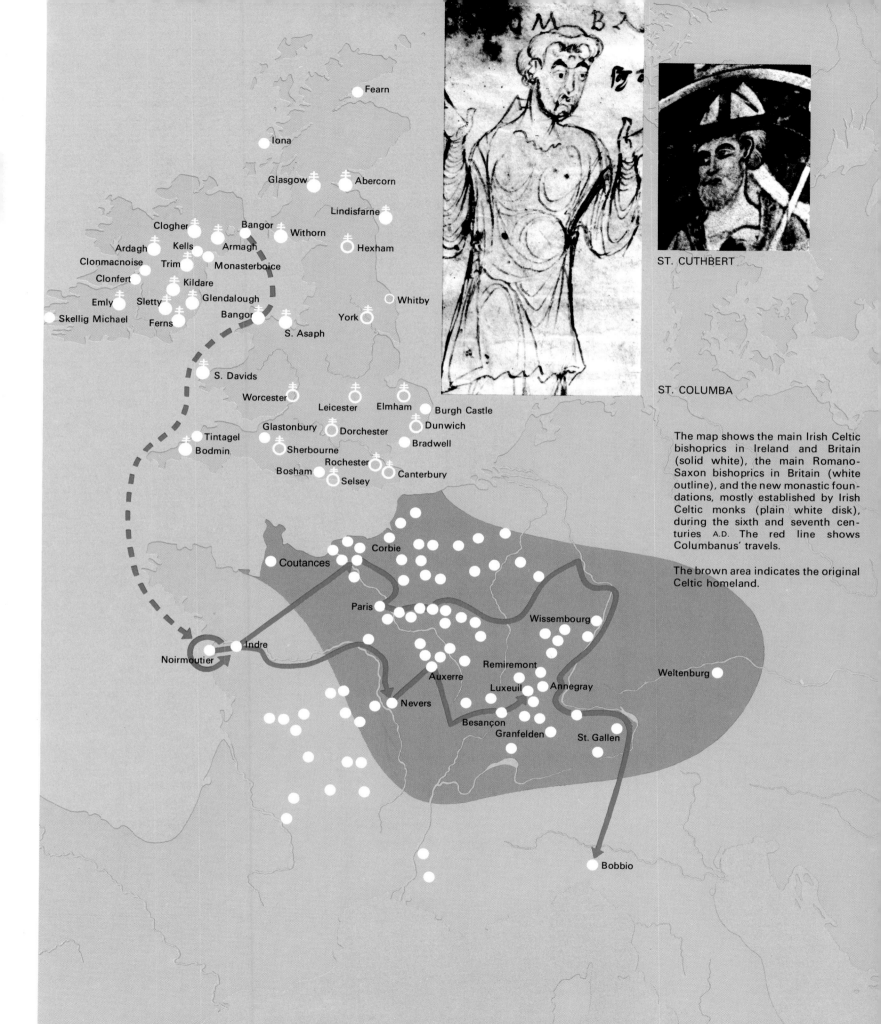

Fearn

Iona

Glasgow ⚕ Abercorn

Lindisfarne ⚕

Clogher ⚕ Bangor ⚕ Withorn
Ardagh ⚕ Kells Armagh ⚕ Hexham ⊕
Clonmacnoise ⚕ Trim Monasterboice
Clonfert
Kildare
Emly ⚕ Sletty Glendalough Whitby ⊕
Skellig Michael Ferns ⚕ Bangor ⚕ York ⊕
S. Asaph ⚕

S. Davids ⚕

Worcester ⚕ Elmham ⊕
Leicester ⊕ Burgh Castle
Glastonbury Dorchester ⊕ Dunwich
Tintagel Bradwell
Bodmin Sherbourne
Bosham Rochester ⊕ Canterbury ⊕
Selsey ⊕

ST. CUTHBERT

ST. COLUMBA

The map shows the main Irish Celtic bishoprics in Ireland and Britain (solid white), the main Romano-Saxon bishoprics in Britain (white outline), and the new monastic foundations, mostly established by Irish Celtic monks (plain white disk), during the sixth and seventh centuries A.D. The red line shows Columbanus' travels.

The brown area indicates the original Celtic homeland.

Corbie
Coutances

Paris
Wissembourg

Remiremont
Noirmoutier Indre Weltenburg
Auxerre
Luxeuil Annegray
Nevers Besançon
Granfelden St. Gallen

Bobbio

HEROES OF GOD

The Eastern Franks and the inhabitants of Thuringia were converted by the preaching of St. Cilian, who was subsequently martyred in Würzburg.

Below: Martyrdom of St. Cilian. ninth-century miniature, Landesbibliothek, Stuttgart.

Right: the twelfth-century miniature from Cîteau, France, recalls the felling of the Holy Oak of the Germans by St. Boniface, as a demonstration of the superior power of the Christian God.

In a Celtic society which so loved to hear stories of bravery and miraculous happenings, it was inevitable that the exploits of the early missionaries should come to be recorded for frequent retellings in the monasteries. Just as the daring of the chieftains had inspired the young men of the pagan Celtic world to deeds of valor, so the acts of the early saints edified their followers and reconfirmed them in their faith. Thus in the seventh century there came into existence a considerable body of literature describing the lives of the saints. It served many purposes: education and inspiration, certainly; but it was also an influential means of propaganda, particularly at a time when the Celtic Church was in conflict with the Church of Rome (pp. 192–193). Moreover, if a monastery wished to acquire popularity, it was essential for the exploits of its founding saint to be given wide publicity.

The early Lives derived ultimately from a literary form of which the Acts of the Apostles was the earliest example. Later the funeral oration formed the model. By the late fourth century the narrative style of presentation had evolved in Europe, and when in the seventh century Muirchu wrote the earliest surviving *Life of St. Patrick*, he noted in his introduction that he was composing in a new style which had been introduced into Ireland earlier that century. The classic Life is Adamnán's *Life of St. Columba*. It is divided into three parts: the saint's prophecies, his miracles, and his visions. Though composed about 685, it is already old-fashioned in its structure, the new narrative style of biography having by now gained widespread acceptance.

The Lives, then—mixtures of fable, fact, good sense, and wishful thinking—were avidly read for entertainment and inspiration. Today, while they provide only a skeletal history of the missionary movement, as a reflection of the aims and aspirations of the early Celtic Christian community they are of incomparable value.

ST. COLUMBA'S ISLAND HERMITAGE

Delightful I think it to be in the bosom of an isle, on the peak of a rock, that I might often see there the calm of the sea.

That I might see its heavy waves over the glittering ocean, as they chant a melody to their Father on their eternal course.

That I might see its smooth strand of clear headlands, no gloomy thing; that I might hear the voice of the wondrous birds, a joyful tune.

That I might hear the sound of the shallow waves against the rocks; that I might hear the cry by the graveyard, the noise of the sea.

That I might see its splendid flocks of birds over the fullwatered ocean; that I might see its mighty whales, greatest of wonders.

That I might see its ebb and its flood-tide in their flow; that this might be my name, a secret I tell, "He who turned his back on Ireland."

That contrition of heart should come upon me as I watch it; that I might bewail my many sins, difficult to declare.

That I might bless the Lord who has power over all, Heaven with its pure host of angels, earth, ebb, flood-tide.

That I might pore on one of my books, good for my soul; a while kneeling for beloved Heaven, a while at psalms.

A while gathering dulse from the rock, a while fishing, a while giving food to the poor, a while in my cell.

A while meditating upon the Kingdom of Heaven, holy is the redemption; a while at labor not too heavy; it would be delightful!

Irish; author unknown; twelfth century

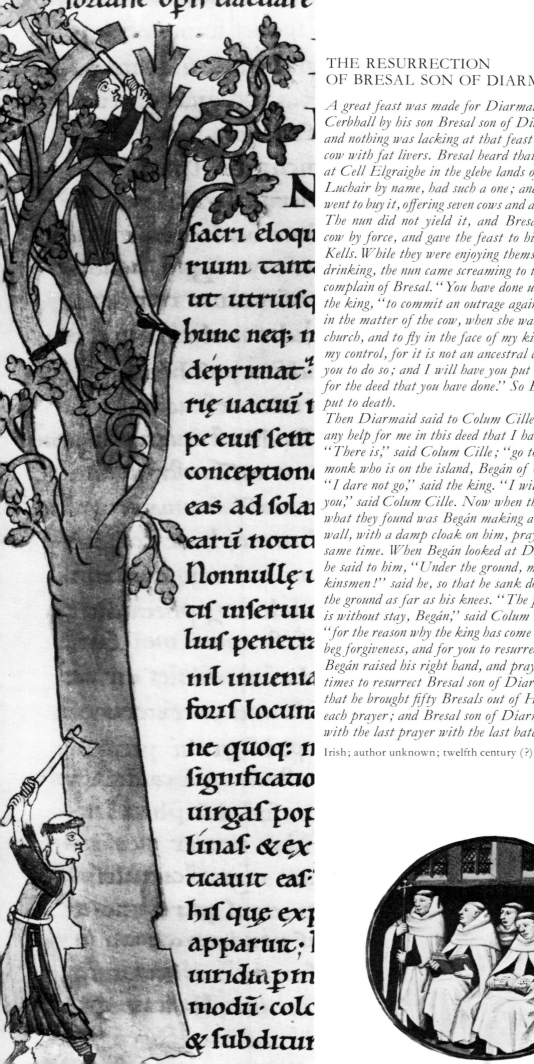

THE RESURRECTION OF BRESAL SON OF DIARMAID

A great feast was made for Diarmaid son of Cerbhall by his son Bresal son of Diarmaid; and nothing was lacking at that feast except a cow with fat livers. Bresal heard that a nun at Cell Elgraighe in the glebe lands of Kells, Luchair by name, had such a one; and Bresal went to buy it, offering seven cows and a bull for it. The nun did not yield it, and Bresal took the cow by force, and gave the feast to his father at Kells. While they were enjoying themselves drinking, the nun came screaming to the king to complain of Bresal. "You have done unjustly," said the king, "to commit an outrage against the nun in the matter of the cow, when she was in her church, and to fly in the face of my kingship and my control, for it is not an ancestral custom for you to do so; and I will have you put to death for the deed that you have done." So Bresal was put to death.

Then Diarmaid said to Colum Cille, "Is there any help for me in this deed that I have done?" "There is," said Colum Cille; "go to the old monk who is on the island, Begán of Ulster." "I dare not go," said the king. "I will go with you," said Colum Cille. Now when they arrived, what they found was Begán making a stone wall, with a damp cloak on him, praying at the same time. When Begán looked at Diarmaid, he said to him, "Under the ground, murderer of kinsmen!" said he, so that he sank down into the ground as far as his knees. "The protection is without stay, Begán," said Colum Cille, "for the reason why the king has come to you is to beg forgiveness, and for you to resurrect his son." Begán raised his right hand, and prayed three times to resurrect Bresal son of Diarmaid, so that he brought fifty Bresals out of Hell with each prayer; and Bresal son of Diarmaid came with the last prayer with the last batch of them.

Irish; author unknown; twelfth century (?)

I wish,
O son of the Living God,
ancient eternal King,
for a secret hut
in the wilderness
that it may be my dwelling.
A very blue shallow
well to be beside it,
a clear pool for washing away
sins through the grace
of the Holy Ghost.
A beautiful wood
close by around it
on every side, for the nurture
of many-voiced birds,
to shelter and hide it.

Irish, tenth century

The Celtic monastic tradition in Europe was eventually overshadowed by other styles of religious community which evolved in continental Europe—Benedictines, Cistercians, Carmelites, and Dominicans *illustrated in that order, left to right;* the roundels from the Book of Hours; the manuscript illumination is twelfth century.

The Benedictine order was instituted in Italy in the mid-sixth century following the rule of St. Benedict. It was introduced into the British Isles by St. Augustine. The Cistercians were a reformed order which took their name from the abbey of Cîteaux in Burgundy, founded 1098. The friars—Dominicans, Carmelites, and others—who became prominent in the medieval church believed that instead of isolating themselves in monasteries they should go out and preach to the world; their concept of religious life was therefore radically different from that of the earlier monks.

THE CHURCH IN CONFLICT

Behind the Easter controversy lay a split more fundamental than the simple calculation of a date. In the Celtic Church Easter was the time when man's quest for divine light came to the fore (symbolized by St. Christopher from Jerpoint Abbey, *top left*). In the Roman Church, however, it was firmly associated with the physical and metaphysical resurrection which was precisely dated to three days after the crucifixion (Resurrection by Verrocchio, *top right*). The Easter controversy was thus a battle of ideologies fought with symbols.

The individual
becomes a bearer of Christ,
that is, a bearer
of the spirit of the sun;
not a mere recipient
of the spirit, but one who
receives and radiates it,
as the full Moon reflects
the light of the sun.
Thus, the individual
becomes a bearer of Christ,
a Christoforus.

R. Steiner

The hermit cells on Skellig Michael *(above)* symbolize Celtic monasticism—small-scale, rigorous, and autonomous. Each monastery was self-contained and under the control of its own abbot. Although bishops existed in the Celtic Church, there was no episcopal administration. The Roman Church, on the other hand, reintroduced into Britain by St. Augustine at the end of the sixth century, was centrally organized and under the control of bishops who commanded substantial regional territories.

The settlement of the heathen Saxons in the east of Britain in the fifth century stifled the growth of Christianity, which had taken root during the Roman occupation. Only in the west of the island did it survive, where, as we have seen, having become firmly established in Ireland, the Celtic Church developed a distinctive character of its own. Meanwhile in the rest of Europe the Roman Church continued to flourish, largely out of touch with events in the west.

In 596 Pope Gregory decided to send a mission to the English. Augustine was chosen to head the group, and, after a show of reluctance, he landed in Kent in 597. There he was received by King Ethelbert (whose wife was a Christian) and was given permission to live and teach in Canterbury. Within a few months the king himself was converted. In 601 a second mission reached England with letters from the Pope confirming Augustine as archbishop, and within three years bishops were established in Rochester and in London following the conversion of the king of the East Saxons. Not long afterward, however, Augustine died, and the zeal of the early English Church began to lapse.

Elsewhere in England the Roman Church met with more success. Paulinus, based in York, established a strong presence in Yorkshire and Northumberland. Others followed, and within about forty years of Augustine's landing in Kent most of the English, with the exception of a few enclaves in the south, had been introduced to Roman Christianity.

The two powerful Christian churches, the Celtic and the Roman, met in Northumberland. The Roman mission had achieved success under the sponsorship of King Edwin, but on his death much was lost. The new king, Oswald, decided to invite the monks of the Celtic monastery of Iona (where he had taken temporary refuge) to restore Christianity to his kingdom. It was in this context that the community on Lindisfarne was established, whence the monks, borne on by missionary fervor, spread Celtic Christianity far beyond the borders of Northumbria. With the Roman Church of Paulinus firmly established in York, it was inevitable that the two churches, with their very different traditions, should sooner or later come into conflict.

The strength of the Celtic Church had been very much underestimated by Rome. In reply to one of the questions Augustine addressed to Pope Gregory concerning his relations with the Celtic Church, Gregory replied, "We commit them all to your charge, that the unlearned may be taught, the weak strengthened by persuasion, and the perverse corrected by authority." If these really were Gregory's words, then he showed an abysmal lack of understanding of the true situation. Augustine did meet twice with the Celtic bishops, but nothing

came of it. The long isolation of the Celtic Church had bred an independent spirit, and its teaching had diverged far from that of Rome. Yet neither Church could afford to ignore the other: Rome's power lay in its centralization, with the pope at its head, while the strength of the Celtic Church stemmed from its missionary zeal.

When eventually the conflict surfaced, it was presented around comparatively trivial points: the method of calculating the date of Easter, the procedure to be adopted in baptism, and the correct style of tonsure. In choosing these matters to try their strengths, it was almost as if the churches had decided to fall back on the ancient Celtic tradition of fielding heroes in single combat to avert an all-out fight which neither side wanted. The analogy is fanciful but not inappropriate.

The Easter conflict had complex origins. In order to determine the date of Easter it was necessary to relate certain calculations based on the lunar calendar with those based on the solar year, adopting different time cycles of 8, 11, 19, and 84 years. The scheme used by the Celtic Church involved the 84-year cycle which had been approved in the council of Arles held in 314. The Alexandrians, however, preferred the more accurate 19-year cycle. After some debate this was adopted by Pope Leo in the middle of the fifth century, and all the Roman churches followed suit. Thus the Celtic Church, in adhering to the old system, found itself out of step. The problem was discussed widely in the 630s, as the result of which the southern Irish Church decided to conform to Rome. The northern Irish Church and Iona and its dependencies remained aloof. The situation led to inconvenient anomalies: in Northumberland King Oswald, who followed the Celtic Church, found himself celebrating Easter, while his queen, who had been taught by Paulinus, was still observing Lent!

The dispute was finally referred to a synod held at Whitby in the autumn of 663. Although only the Easter question was debated, other differences cannot have been far from people's minds. The Roman case, eloquently put by bishop Wilfrid, won the day, but it was to take many generations before the two churches approached each other in anything like unity.

The acceptance by the Irish Church of the Roman method of calculating Easter marked the beginning of the dominance of the Roman Church

and the gradual loss of identity by the Celtic. Easter was calculated according to the Roman system (as in the Easter chart of the monk Byrthferth, A.D. 1011, shown here), and gradually the two churches came closer together.

The pope, Gregory I, the head of the Roman hierarchy, now became the symbolic head of the Celtic Church as well.

Left: The twelfth-century cross at Dysert O'Dea is a dramatic visual reminder of the influence of Rome on indigenous Irish culture. While the cross is in the Irish tradition, the symbolism of Christ dominant over his earthly vicar (the Pope) is Roman. In the late eleventh century a group of Irish monks went to the Continent to settle near Ratisbon. To begin with, they lived in their traditional cells, but after the death of their abbot they established a new foundation adopting the rule of St. Benedict—the first Irish Benedictine abbey on the Continent.

THE HEART
OF MEDIEVAL CULTURE

One of the companions of St. Columbanus was St. Gall. Both men left the monastery of St. Comgall of Bangor in County Down, Ireland, in about 590 to begin their wanderings in western Europe. Outspoken in their stand on the Easter controversy and rigorous in their demands for stricter discipline, they made enemies in the Burgundian court and were forced to move on to the neighborhood of Bregenz, Austria, where they parted. St. Columbanus passed through the Alps into Lombardy to found the monastery at Bobbio, while St. Gall, in 612, settled in Switzerland, where he was eventually buried.

Such was the fame of St. Gall that the monastery which was established at his tomb, in 720, soon developed into one of the greatest seats of learning in Europe, with a library of unsurpassed magnificence. St.

Key to the parts of the ninth-century plan for the abbey of St. Gall:

1. Hostels for servitors, sheep, pigs, goats, horses, cows.
2. Kitchen for guests and guest house.
3. Towers: St. Gabriel's and St. Michael's.
4. Western and eastern paradise (or atrium).
5. Kitchen.
6. Shops (of coopers, potters, grain, brewery, bakery, mill, press).
7. Refectory.
8. Cloister.
9. Cellar.
10. Infirmary and physician.
11. Novitiate.

The famous library at St. Gall contains a plan, drawn about 820, of an idealized Benedictine monastery *(right)*. The illustration on the left, a copper plate engraving, is an eighteenth-century view of the St. Gall monastery. The arrangement was dominated by the main church with its many altars and great western towers. To the south lay the cloister, with refectory and dormitory close by. Farther south were the domestic buildings and workshop, while the monastic farm lay to the west.

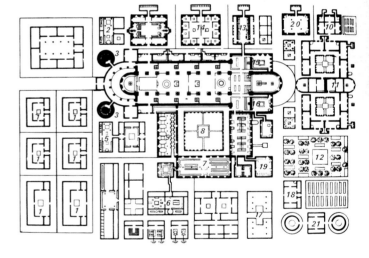

Gall, like Bobbio, lay close to the old road—the *via barbaresca* along which the Irish pilgrims passed en route to Rome. They were always eager to arrive at the monasteries along their way, to have access to the monastic libraries, while the monks, for their part, would have been glad to receive visitors to share their learning and hear news of the outside world. In this way, monasteries like St. Gall became the great cultural centers of Europe.

By the ninth century vast numbers of wandering Irish in organized bands were regularly crossing Europe—reflecting perhaps the innate love of migration which had so characterized their Celtic ancestors.

12. Cemetery.
13. Abbot's house.
14. School.
15. Scriptorium, Library.
16. Sacristy vestry.
17. Barn and threshing floor.
18. Gardener.
19. Baths.
20. Leeching.
21. Chickens, caretaker of fowl, geese, and latrina.

195

The world has laid low,
and the wind
blows away like ashes
Alexander, Caesar, and all who were
in their trust;

Irish fishermen set out for the
catch: a scene that has changed
little with the centuries.

Opposite page: The famous
Calvary from St. Thégonnec, Brittany.

THE CELTS TODAY

Grass-grown is Tara,
and see Troy now how it is—
And the English themselves,
perhaps they too
will pass!

Anonymous Irish poem, seventeenth-eighteenth century

They constitute a minority in the late twentieth-century Western world—a series of minorities scattered in diverse nations. From antiquity to the present, they have been tossed this way and that in the stormwinds of international politics. And "Celtic fringe"—the term used to describe them today—bespeaks fractionalism and political insufficiency.

Is there more to the Celtic revival than nostalgia, more to their identity than rhetoric and wishful thinking? The Celts of today can point as evidence to the languages they spoke: to Celtic, Irish, Welsh, and Breton, revived by poets and scholars and now spoken daily by many as living languages.

Another sign of Celtic life today, again in the cultural realm, is the survival of custom: dress, music, folklore, old Celtic place-names, and family traditions that derive from the old clans. But the Celts do not base their identity on language and folklore alone. The Celts today may be a fringe group in France and Britain, and a scattered minority in the vast United States—in Ireland they constitute a nation. Whatever the fate of the separatist movements in various nations today, the twentieth century has seen one example of a Celtic revival that is a political reality.

The desire of a people to recognize their oneness and to distinguish themselves by name and custom from other groups is a deep-seated human need. The Greeks might have called the barbarians *Keltoi*, but the Celts were concerned to recognize their membership in smaller groups—each of which had a distinctive name. It is most unlikely that the individual tribes believed themselves to be part of a larger ethnic entity. The growth and spread of the Roman Empire, the turmoil of migration which followed its collapse, and the emergence of modern Europe destroyed the old order, creating new nations and new loyalties. Nations tended to grow by agglomeration. Thus France absorbed Brittany in the sixteenth century, while Britain became, nominally, one nation as the result of Acts of Union from 1536 to 1801.

But these conflations, while in the spirit or postmedieval European development, were essentially political unions. The ethnic minorities of Ireland, Scotland, Wales, Brittany, the Isle of Man, and Cornwall still recognized their own uniqueness, and from the late eighteenth century they have sought, and sometimes fought, to preserve their individuality, first by saving their languages and customs from extinction and more recently by their increasingly loud calls for political independence. To what extent independence is economically practicable is highly debatable. A unified Ireland could, clearly, function efficiently if religious differences among its peoples could be overcome, but few would suggest that a free Cornwall could exist in isolation except as a tourist curiosity.

Devolution, self-determination, and local autonomy have become a significant political issue in the last decade. Sometimes it is confused by the excesses of revolutionary extremism; more often it is made to look irrelevant and ridiculous by the theatrical nostalgia encouraged by the tourist industry. But below these superficial excrescences there lies the simple human desire for identity—identity with a group of acceptable size distinguished by common culture, language, and history. It is in the Celtic fringes of Europe that these roots are most deeply embedded, unmoved by nearly two thousand years of political upheaval. Hardly surprising, therefore, that the call for devolution is a Celtic cry.

197

THE TRADITIONAL HOMELAND

In the Highlands and Islands of Scotland, Ireland, Wales, Cornwall, and Brittany, Celtic culture remains strong, despite centuries of attempted acculturation by the Vikings, the Normans, and more recently by the English and the French. Why these islands and peninsulas should retain so much of their indigenous culture is explained largely by their geography: they are remote, difficult of access, rugged, and comparatively easy to defend. Over much of the area the bedrock is old, extensively of igneous origin, and lacks the fertility of more easterly areas. Moreover, the comparatively high altitude of this fringe of Europe and its exposed position in relation to the Atlantic Ocean ensure an unusually

high rainfall. This in turn has affected soil and landscape.

Although there have been slight changes in climate over the last three thousand years, which have rendered some of the areas once farmed by man no longer desirable, and in the Highlands of Scotland the deliberate harassment of peasants has driven them from the land, the Celtic fringes were never densely populated nor were they highly productive of food. It was for this reason that the Romans cared little for them. Some roads were built and small provincial towns developed in the more accessible parts of those territories which were conquered; but so long as the scattered populations behaved and a constant supply of minerals was produced, the indigenous communities were left to themselves. The land was not productive enough to interest the speculators, who, in the more fertile areas, were developing large farming estates. Much the same was true for the post-Roman centuries, and it was not until union with England and France, in the last five hundred years, that real attempts to colonize the land from the east began.

Considerable areas of the "Celtic" lands are remote from centers of civilization. Large farming estates are still comparatively rare; more usually the land is farmed by family units living amidst their fields in the numerous farmsteads which pepper the landscape. The scene in parts of Wales or in Cornwall is strongly reminiscent of the pre-Roman Iron Age settlement pattern.

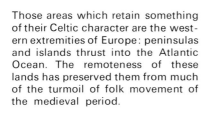

Those areas which retain something of their Celtic character are the western extremities of Europe: peninsulas and islands thrust into the Atlantic Ocean. The remoteness of these lands has preserved them from much of the turmoil of folk movement of the medieval period.

IRELAND

In 1801 Ireland was formally joined to the rest of the British Isles, but in 1921 after a serious uprising Southern Ireland (Eire) gained its independence. Northern Ireland still remains part of the United Kingdom. Population: N. Ireland, 1.54 million; Eire, 2.98 million. Gaelic is widely spoken, especially in the west.

SCOTLAND

Scotland was joined to England and Wales by the Act of Union, 1707. The Scottish National Party (SNP) is working towards the separation of Scotland from the rest of the British Isles but lacks majority support. Population: 5.18 million, of whom only 1.8 percent can speak Gaelic. (In 1971 there were 338 people who could speak only Gaelic.)

ISLE OF MAN

Though part of the British Isles, the Isle of Man is administered according to its own laws by the Court of Tynwald. The Island is not bound by British law unless it opts to be. Population: 0.05 million, of whom only 165 (in 1961) spoke Manx.

WALES

Wales was united with England in 1543 and has remained in the United Kingdom since then. The Welsh Nationalist Party (Plaid Cymru) seeks separation, but in 1979 the people voted overwhelmingly against devolution. Population: 2.64 million, of which 0.51 million can speak Welsh. In 1971 there were 32,725 people who were able to speak only Welsh.

CORNWALL

One of the counties of England largely untouched by the English emigrations of the period A.D. 400–1000. Some sporadic nationalist noises but no serious suggestion of separation. Population: 0.38 million. Cornish is a dead language, but there are signs of its academic revival.

BRITTANY

Brittany became part of France in 1532. Separatist movements, in particular the FLB (Front pour la Libération de la Bretagne), are working towards self-government though with little success. Population (Basse-Bretagne): 1.5 million, of which less than 50 percent can speak Breton.

The "Celtic lands" of western Europe have a tiny population (less than 14 percent of the population of France and Britain) and of this number probably less than half are indigenous. The Celtic languages are spoken by less than four million people.

HIGHLANDS

Edinburgh

SCOTLAND

NORTHERN IRELAND

Belfast

ISLE OF MAN

Galway

Dublin

EIRE

WALES

ENGLAND

Cardiff

London

CORNWALL

BRETAGNE

Rennes

FRANCE

WHO ARE THE CELTS OF TODAY?

The Celtic lands still show some continuity with long ago. The stone walls and houses of the bare, lonely Aran Islands (*right*) are centuries old; and the parceling up of the land, like the atmosphere of the place, appears to have changed very little since the early Middle Ages.

Traditional aspects of life in the Celtic fringes can still be found, but they are fast dying out except where nationalist movements or the tourist industry are working to maintain them. It is often difficult to distinguish between the genuine survival of traditions and their revival for emotional or political ends.

The traditional costumes of these Breton women are a survival. So too are the Breton bagpipes, but "traditional" music has become a political weapon.

The populations of the Celtic fringes are of course very mixed. Wales, Cornwall, and Brittany were subjected to a degree of Romanization. The Viking settlement in eastern Ireland introduced a new ethnic element, while in all regions an Anglo-Norman or Norman-French veneer can be traced. Yet in spite of this, indigenous Celtic traditions remain strong, and the great mass of the population is of Celtic origin.

The Celtic fringes can boast a strength of 13 to 14 million people—a not inconsiderable number when compared with 46 million for England and 50 million for the rest of France.

The individual characteristics of each Celtic region not only give it an identity but also serve as a reminder of the inheritance of the past. With the growth of nationalism in all areas, folk customs have been rescued from extinction and carefully nurtured to provide a new awareness of nationhood. In Wales, for example, interest in Welsh culture grew dramatically during the eighteenth century, frequently encouraged by the anglicized gentry. The Society of the Gwyneddigion, founded in 1771, was set up to foster an interest in Welsh literature and published much that was in danger of disappearing. Unfortunately, romantic fabrications were interspersed with genuine material. Much the same problem arose when the Eisteddfod (an annual gathering of bards) was revived in 1789. To give the proceedings a greater picturesqueness, a spurious neo-druidic charade was incorporated which still, sadly, is allowed to detract from the authenticity of the occa-

Economy is not easy to manipulate for nationalistic ends. Breton fishermen supply the markets today as they have always done.

sion. The contestants and audience are never allowed to forget their Celtic heritage; indeed, one of the subjects set in the Eisteddfod of 1858 was the capture of Rome by the Celtic chieftain Brennus.

In the Highlands and Islands of Scotland, echoes of the Celtic social structure can still be recognized, particularly in the clan system, which is avidly adhered to by a significant percentage of the community. The organization of the clan under a laird (chieftain) has much in common with the organization of the Celtic tribe, while the fierce loyalties and vicious blood feuds between clans, which so characterized the seventeenth and eighteenth centuries, are a direct reflection of the earlier Celtic way of life. So too are the Highland games—traditional gatherings of Highland peoples—which feature contests of strength such as throwing the hammer and tossing the caber, together with piping and dancing competitions. The need for a dispersed and tribally organized community to come together annually for competitive entertainments is very deep-rooted. On such occasions the gods would have been worshiped and political decisions taken. Now only the spectacle remains, for the amusement of tourists and nostalgic expatriates.

Each part of the Celtic fringe has its own very distinctive characteristics: the deep religious sensitivity of the Irish, the Welsh love of music and poetry, the austere aloofness of the Highlanders—characteristics which have become caricatures in the jokes of musical hall comedians but are not entirely mythical.

Irish villagers stand idly in typical pose, a sign of the times: many parts of Ireland today have a shortage of women.

Cattle rearing is still a vital part of the Irish economy. A form of wealth and status in the Celtic period, cattle now provide produce for export.

Contests of strength figure in the Highland games of Scotland. Much loved by tourists is tossing the caber.

201

Llanfairpwllgwyngyllgogerychwyrndrobwllllantysiliogogogoch

The Welsh are proud of what they claim to be the longest place name in the world, seen here in the railway station sign.

Above: The handwriting of a Gallo-Roman scratched on the base of a pottery vessel of the first century A.D.

Ogham was a type of script developed for ease of writing on stone or wood in the lands around the Irish Sea. It consisted simply of groups of lines inscribed on either side of the corner of a block, each group representing a letter. This example *(right)* comes from Balla-queeney in the Isle of Man.

The languages spoken by Celtic peoples today belong to two groups: Brythonic (or P-Celtic) and Goidelic (or Q-Celtic). Brythonic is called P-Celtic because *qu* appears as a *p* sound, whereas in Goidelic it remains *q*. The Goidelic dialects include Irish, Gaelic (spoken in the west coasts of Scotland), and Manx; while Welsh, Cornish, and Breton belong to the Brythonic branch. This distribution is the result of the migrations of the fifth and sixth centuries A.D. Before that the position was simpler: Brythonic was spoken in Britain and Goidelic in Ireland. The migration of the Irish westward introduced the Goidelic dialect into the western parts of Scotland, where it became known as Gaelic, and into the Isle of Man; while Brythonic remained in use in Wales and Cornwall and was carried to Brittany by the folk movements from Devon and Cornwall in the fifth and sixth centuries.

The Irish form of Celtic remained dominant in Ireland—in spite of the inroads of the Vikings, French, and English—until the sixteenth century, when English began to take over. But in Scotland the Celtic language had begun to be replaced by English somewhat earlier. In the Isle of Man, Manx was spoken extensively in the seventeenth century but has died out, apart from its use on ceremonial occasions. In Cornwall, too, Celtic expired in the eighteenth century, but in Brittany it has remained. Today about half of the population can speak Breton. Celtic can be heard widely throughout western Ireland though hardly at all in Ulster, while in Scotland only fifteen percent of the population are Gaelic speaking, but they are concentrated in the Hebrides.

In Wales, however, twenty-six percent of the population speak Welsh, and the Welsh Language Act of 1967, affirming the equal validity of Welsh and English, has ensured that in at least one area of the Celtic world the Celtic tongue will survive the inroads of alien languages.

AN NÁISIÚN

Airteagal 1

Deimhníonn náisiún na hÉireann leis seo a gceart do-shannta, do-chlaoite, ceannasach chun cibé cineál Rialtais is rogha leo féin do bhunú, chun a gcaidreamh le náisiúnaibh eile do chinneadh, agus chun a saol polaitíochta is geilleagair is saíochta do chur ar aghaidh do réir dhúchais is gnás a sinsear.

Airteagal 2

Is é oileán na hÉireann go hiomlán, maille lena oileáin agus a fharraigí teorann, na críocha náisiúnta.

Airteagal 3

Go dtí go ndéantar athchomhlánú ar na críochaibh náisiúnta, agus gan dochar do cheart na Párlaiminte is an Rialtais a bunaítear leis an mBunreacht so chun dlínse d'oibriú insna críochaibh náisiúnta uile, bainfidh na dlithe achtófar ag an bPárlaimint sin leis an límistéir céanna lenar bhain dlithe Shaorstát Éireann, agus beidh an éifeacht chéanna acu taobh amuigh den límistéir sin a bhí ag dlithibh Shaorstát Éireann.

THE NATION

Article 1

The Irish nation hereby affirms its inalienable, indefeasible, and sovereign right to choose its own form of Government, to determine its relations with other nations, and to develop its life, political, economic, and cultural, in accordance with its own genius and traditions.

Article 2

The national territory consists of the whole island of Ireland, its islands and the territorial seas.

Article 3

Pending the re-integration of the national territory, and without prejudice to the right of the Parliament and Government established by this Constitution to exercise jurisdiction over the whole of that territory, the laws enacted by that Parliament shall have the like area and extent of application as the laws of Saorstát Éireann and the like extra-territorial effect.

The writing of the Picts, living in Scotland, is uncommon. This inscription (left) appears on the base of the memorial stone from St. Vigeans, Angus, Scotland. The minuscule Pictish inscription contains the names Drosten Voret Forcus but cannot otherwise be read.

Text opposite: The first three articles of the Constitution of Ireland (Bunreacht na hEireann). The Constitution was enacted by the people on 1 July 1937 and came into operation at the end of that year.

Below: A page from a late thirteenth-century Welsh manuscript, the White Book of Rhyddech.

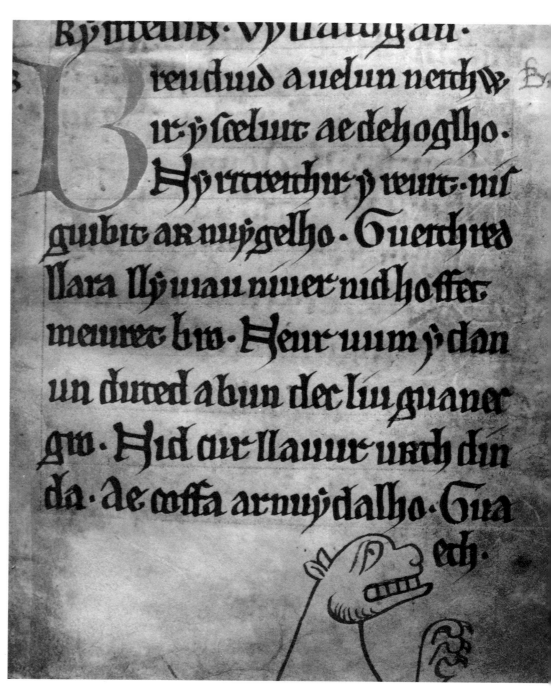

LITERATURE

The great literary traditions of Ireland and Wales could not have failed to make a profound impression on writers of the last three centuries. Patrick Kavanagh's poem (quoted far right) distills the essential truth: without a myth the poet is starved; his work becomes sterile. The Celtic west, with its enormously rich mythology, has sustained generations of exceptional writers, all of whom, knowingly or not, have derived strength from their native past.

In Scotland literary revival went hand in hand with fierce patriotism, but the leading men—Macpherson, Burns, Scott—remained dedicated Unionists. For them the noble Highlander, clinging desperately to the last remnants of his Celtic way of life, provided the literary stimulus. But swathed in nostalgia, the image was romantic rather than overtly political. Scotland had little ancient literature (in spite of Macpherson's dubious attempts to provide it with some), and this, combined with the rapid demise of Gaelic, goes some way towards explain-

Compared to the brilliant literary tradition of Ireland (and to a lesser extent Wales), Scotland and Brittany have contributed little to the modern literary scene. One reason may be that their mythologies had died before the age of enlightenment could give a new impetus to European culture. The thread with the past had been broken and could only be mourned.

In Ireland and in Wales the conscious nourishing of cultural traditions in the

The link between true Celtic literature and the literature of the more recent Celts is tenuous. In the conscious revival of the eighteenth century genuine Celtic literature was rescued from obscurity, but much that was spurious was mixed with it. James Macpherson's *Poems of Ossian* (1765), which he claimed were translations of the Gaelic poems of Ossian, a legendary warrior and bard, son of Finn, were substantially

JAMES MACPHERSON

F.R. CHATEAUBRIAND

LADY
AUGUSTA GREGORY

J.M. SYNGE

W.B. YEATS

composed by Macpherson himself. The spurious *Ossian* became famous internationally: it was well-known by Châteaubriand, republished by Goethe, and inspired the great Hungarian poet Sándor Petofi, who used the image of the Celt to symbolize freedom. Irish literature was more responsibly served (in the late nineteenth century) by Lady Gregory's fine translation *Cuchulain of Muirthemne*.

ing why the development of Scottish nationalism has not provided the stimulus for a reinvigorated literary tradition. Scotland has failed to produce modern writers of internationally recognized stature.

Much the same is true of Brittany. The savage repression of the Breton language by the French killed what little of the Celtic spirit may have survived the Middle Ages. Thus Chateaubriand was left to brood in melancholy on the past, inspired by Macpherson's "translations" of Celtic poetry and Rousseau's myth of the noble savage. He was alone, inspiring few, initiating no tradition.

seventeenth and eighteenth centuries ensured a continuity. The foundation of the Society of Gwyneddigion in 1771, dedicated to the study of Welsh literature, may have encouraged much revivalist nonsense, but it provided a real focus for the preservation of the Welsh language and the development of its literature.

If in Wales literary revival became enmeshed in a nostalgic antiquarianism, in Ireland it took a different course. From the time of Swift it was biting, political, and relevant, but it was not until the foundation of the Gaelic League in 1893—dedicated to keep the Irish language alive and to preserve Irish customs—that Irish literature came of age. In 1899 Lady Augusta Gregory, W. B. Yeats, and Edward Martyn founded the Irish Literary Theater and soon after, with Yeats and Synge, Lady Gregory set up the Abbey Theater in Dublin.

The atmosphere of innovation at the turn of the century encouraged many young writers, but it could not exert sufficient hold over James Joyce, for whom Paris, Trieste, and Zurich offered a more congenial home away from the claustrophobic censorship of the Irish Catholic Church. It is a sad comment on modern Ireland that until recently its most original writers have felt forced to flee to find freedom in which their creative abilities might develop.

Standing back from the great volume of literature produced by these writers, it is fair to ask what, if anything, the Celtic tradition has contributed to their work. There are three separate threads which we can distinguish: satire, saga, and language.

There could hardly be a more damning indictment of English attitudes to Ireland at the time and of the pseudoeconomic nonsense that was being put forward as policies. It was satire of a most powerful and dangerous kind, which would have done credit to a Celtic bard. The satirical tradition was to some extent continued by Shaw but his targets, the morals and manners of the London literary scene, were easy game.

The love of saga can most readily be seen in the works of Joyce and in particular in *Finnegans Wake*, published in 1939—an epic in all senses of the word. It is perhaps not too fanciful to see in its two principal characters—the Dublin publican, who is everyman, and his wife, the quintessential woman, or sometimes the River Liffey—something of the abstraction with which the Celt, listening to his sagas, would have been very much at home.

....I grew
Uncultivated and now the soil
turns sour,
Needs to be revived by a power
not my own.
Heroes enormous who
do astounding deeds—
Out of this world.

Patrich Kavanagh, "A Personal Problem"

G.B. SHAW

DOUGLAS HYDE

DYLAN THOMAS

JAMES JOYCE

SAMUEL BECKETT

Satire was perfected at an early date by Jonathan Swift—Anglican priest and essayist—whose vitriolic ink flowed against the bigotry of his times. To give one example, in a brilliantly cutting essay entitled "A Modest Proposal," he wrote,

I have been assured...that a healthy child well nursed is at a year old a most delicious nourishing and wholesome food whether steamed, roasted, baked, or boiled....I do therefore humbly offer it to public consideration that of the hundred and twenty thousand children already computed...[one] hundred thousand may at a year old be offered in sale to the persons of quality and fortune.

Finally, we can note language and the Celtic love of alliteration. Compare the sound of this eleventh-century Welsh verse,

Ar gad gad grendde, ar gryd
gryd graendde
Ac am Dâl Maelfre mil fanieri

with this description published in 1954:
It is spring, moonless night in the small town, starless and bible-black, the cobblestreets silent and the hunched courters-and-rabbits' wood limping invisible down to the sloe-black, slow, black, crowblack, fishing boat-bobbing sea.

The writer, Dylan Thomas, could not speak the Welsh language, but his spirit was Welsh.

St. Brendan's ancient voyage westward from Ireland, out into the Atlantic, was in many ways symbolic of what was to come. It achieved nothing, but then nothing was expected: the Atlantic coast was the limit of the real world.

The discovery of America at the end of the fifteenth century introduced a totally new dimension. For persons forced into a corner by political or religious persecution or by hunger, there was now another solution: to take ship for the new lands beyond the ocean. It was a way out which in the next four centuries was to be adopted by thousands of Celts in their last migration. Among the earliest causes of the Celtic exodus was religious persecution. The Civil War in Britain had brought the Puritans to power, but with the Restoration of the monarchy in 1660 their position became increasingly untenable, particularly in Wales where Presbyterians, who acted as a mediating influence in England, were few.

THE LAST MIGRATION

The setting of the sun in the west must have had the emotional appeal among primitive peoples that it still has today. The feeling that beyond the Atlantic Ocean there lay a miraculous land encouraged St. Brendan to make his voyage into the unknown. It also inspired hundreds of thousands of Celts to leave their homes to seek their fortunes in America.

In two years (1660–1661) ninety-three Puritan clergymen were ejected from their parishes. John Miles, for example, simply gathered his congregation around him and left for America to found a town of his own called Swanzey in Massachusetts. Other sects soon suffered from the displeasure of the crown. In 1677 it was the turn of the Quakers, who were imprisoned and even threatened with burning alive. So severe was the persecution that when William Penn acquired the grant of Pennsylvania from the King in 1681, the Welsh Quakers bought forty thousand acres of land from him and the next year set sail for their new land. In 1683 Arminian Baptists fled from Radnorshire to the outskirts of Philadelphia, and later, in 1701, Calvinistic Baptists joined them but soon moved to a new territory lower down the Delaware. The result of the exodus was twofold: at home the religious communities were so depleted of their active young men that they withered and died; while in Pennsylvania the Welsh community had grown to such proportions that in the early eighteenth century it was even commercially viable to publish books in the Welsh language.

Religious persecution of the late seventeenth century was replaced in the nineteenth century by agrarian poverty as the prime cause of migration. Nowhere is this better demonstrated than by Ireland in the 1840s and 1850s. In the forty years from the Act of Union in 1801 to the census of 1841, the population of Ireland had increased from five million to over eight million—an increase of exponential proportions. The holding capacity of the land could barely contain them, and as the population increased, so the lot of the agrarian poor became increasingly more wretched. Then in three successive years, 1845, 1846, and 1847, the potato crop, which had provided the staple diet of the Irish, failed. The result was misery and starvation, which could be alleviated only by mass migration. In the Great Famine alone, about a million people died, and an equivalent number migrated—most of them to America—cutting the population by twenty-five percent. While the British government can justly be accused of failing to take a sufficiently firm hold on the grossly inefficient Irish economy, no action could have prevented the famine and its consequences.

The Irish exodus to America was not confined to the famine years. Emigrants had left in the preceding decades and in the twenty years from 1841 to 1860 about 1.75 million people fled the country. The next forty years (1861–1900) saw the loss of about half a million a decade. Thereafter, until about 1940, the number gradually declined. In all, America received nearly 5 million Irish Celts in barely 120 years.

The situation in Scotland was somewhat different. Until about 1680 Scotland's prosperity had increased, but thereafter a decline set in, intensified by a series of poor harvests. Viewing the general economic situation, it seemed to many Scots that one way out of their troubles was to

emulate the English and, by founding colonies abroad, procure protected trading rights. Many Scotsmen had been included in English trading ventures earlier in the century; now it was Scotland's turn to look after her own interests. Thus, inspired by William Paterson, they decided to found a colony at Darien in middle America, close to the present day mouth of the Panama Canal. In the face of Spanish resistance and totally without the support of the English government, the venture was doomed to disaster. The difficulty of the excessively long sea journey and the fever-ridden landscape claimed several thousand

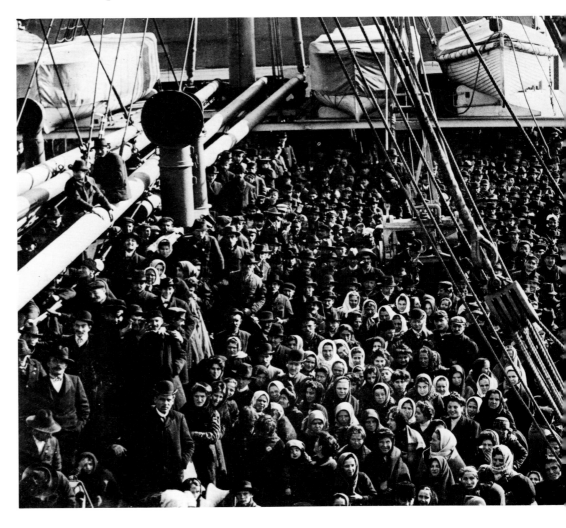

lives, and the venture collapsed in bankruptcy, leaving the country severely shaken and demoralized.

In 1707, within a few years of the end of the Darien fiasco, the Act of Union was passed binding Scotland with England and Wales. In the discontent which followed, culminating in the two great rebellions of 1715 and 1745, the Celtic social system of the Highlands came under increasing

The majority of the immigrants to America were from the lower levels of Old World society. They offered themselves as farm workers and laborers. Most of them were fleeing from religious persecution or from famine. Many came under some form of servitude, having sold themselves to ships' captains in exchange for the ocean passage. Migration was a hazardous business; in the eighteenth century, as many as one-third died at sea from the overcrowding and squalor of the ships. On arrival, the contracts which each of the "servants" had signed, binding himself to a period of four to seven years of work, were auctioned to the highest bidder. In the nineteenth century conditions for the migrants improved.

attack. The clan chieftains were stripped of their rights of "hereditary jurisdiction" and their followers disarmed, while the wearing of the kilt—the symbol of clanship—was forbidden. Even more insidious was the work of the Society for the Propagation of Christian Knowledge whose enthusiasm for setting up schools in the Highlands dealt a death blow to the Gaelic language. The dislocation caused by these sweeping social changes and the effects of the Highland clearances added to the grow-

The eviction of Irish peasants which gained momentum after the great famine of 1845–1847 contributed to the tide of emigrants fleeing Ireland. In 1878–1879 the Land League was founded by Michael Davitt to counter the extortions of the landlords. By mass meetings and social ostracism the League attempted to focus adverse publicity on landlords, agents, or those who rented land from which the previous tenant had been evicted. (The word "boycott" derives from one such agent, Captain Boycott, who became the focus of attention in 1880.) The Land League's success can in part be attributed to money sent home by Irish Americans.

Right: A family on the ferry to Ellis Island, the United States Bureau of Immigration's receiving station, about 1900. Migrating Celts, Welsh, Scots, and most of all Irish—arrived in rapidly growing numbers from the 1840's onwards.

ing number of Scots who saw salvation only in migration.

Farther north, in the Orkney Islands, remote from the political traumas which engulfed Scotland, emigration of a different kind was underway. In 1670 the Hudson Bay Company received its charter from Charles II giving it exclusive trading rights and administrative responsibilities for the vast area of Rupert's Land—the territory drained by the rivers flowing into Hudson Bay. The company's need for immigrant workers was met by the population of Orkney, since Stromness on Mainland (the largest of the Orkney Islands) was frequently the last port of call before the trading vessels faced the Atlantic. In 1702 Captain Grimmington was instructed to call at Orkney to enlist a dozen suitable men. Numbers were never great, and by 1800 there were only 416

Orkneymen serving in Canada, but that they constituted four-fifths of the company's employees gives some idea of the cultural impact. Thereafter about seventy men a year were enlisted to serve contracts of five or ten years. Although some returned home, many stayed, creating colonies in Manitoba, Saskatchewan, and Alberta. In these Canadian provinces familiar Orcadian place names—Scapa, Stromness, Kirkwall—can still be found. Although the company's ships ceased to call at the Islands in 1891 the century from 1850 to 1950 saw a constant migration westward to swell the already sizable Orcadian communities of Canada.

Many of the men who sailed from Stromness in the company's ships were craftsmen and specialists—bricklayers, boat builders, and sailors—the kind of men necessary for the well-being of the trading stations. Elsewhere in America in the industrial areas of the eastcoast a different kind of expertise was required which could not be supplied by the sailors of the Orkneys or the peasants of agrarian Ireland but which was fast developing in the coal fields of south Wales. The greatest advance was the development of a technique for using anthracite to smelt iron ore—a method pioneered by George Crane and David Thomas in the years following 1837. The new process at once attracted the attention of the American company that owned the great anthracite beds of Pennsylvania, and in 1839 Thomas

For many immigrants, the ocean passage to reach the New World was not the last journey. Although the Irish and other Celtic groups tended to settle in the cities of the eastern American seaboard, thousands of others pushed on westward across the continent in the now legendary wagon trains.

Migrants of Celtic origin made an impressive contribution to America's rise to industrial pre-eminence. The Scottish-born inventor Alexander Graham Bell made possible the transmission of verbal messages by electricity with his perfection of the tele-

A.G. BELL

S.M. JONES

A. CARNEGIE

H. LAUDER

J.M. CURLEY

J.F. KENNEDY

was persuaded to settle in Pennsylvania to develop the American anthracite iron industry. It was inevitable that large numbers of miners took the opportunity to escape from the south Welsh valleys to try their skills in the New World. In the later decades of the nineteenth century other skilled workers, including the tin platers from the Swansea area, followed.

Seen from an American point of view, the assimilation of huge numbers of immigrants posed serious problems. In 1840, 84,000 immigrants arrived, mostly from Ireland and Germany, but by 1854 the number had risen to 428,000. The problems of integration of so vast a number of aliens were enormous. Residents feared that they would be swamped, and since the majority of the immigrants were Catholic, anti-Catholicism began to take root. The influence of the Pope was seen as a threat to civil institutions and to republican government. But more pressing were the problems caused in the already overcrowded cities where employment was in short supply. Opposition soon became focused in a political association: the Know-Nothing, or Native America, movement. Few men of stature were attracted to such reactionary ideals—America was, after all, the place where the poor and oppressed of Europe could find freedom—and inevitably the movement failed, many of its supporters transferring to the Republican party.

By far the most numerous of the American Celtic minorities were the Irish. Loyalty borne of ethnic origins and a common religion, and intensified by the force of reaction against it, cemented the Irish-American population and created a powerful political lobby which no government could (or can) afford to overlook. When, in the 1880s, a British Home Secretary was heard to complain that the rebellious Irish were now out of reach of the British government, he was showing an awareness of

The period 1840–1925 saw the maximum influx of British and Irish to the United States. Less than half a million entered America in the period 1820–1840, but in the next twenty years the number had reached 2.4 million. The influx remained steady at about one million a decade until about 1900. The map shows the main centers of immigration from Scotland, Wales and Cornwall (regions shown in brown, cities as squares) and Ireland (regions outlined in white, cities shown as circles).

phone. Samuel Milton Jones devoted the fortune he made in the oil business to the reform of industrial practices. In the 1890s he introduced an eight-hour day and a minimum wage for his employees. Andrew Carnegie, of Scottish extraction, was the key figure in the American steel industry from 1873 to 1901. He used his great wealth to support many cultural and scientific institutions. Harry Lauder exemplifies the "Celtic" contribution to American show-business, and through it, to the entertainment business worldwide. J.M. Curley became a symbol of the emergence of the Irish from their

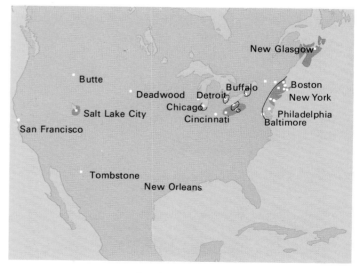

the new political reality. Forty years later Lloyd George could not fail to take note of the opinions of the New York Irish when formulating his policy on Ireland.

proletarian status to political eminence. The 35th President of the United States, John Fitzgerald Kennedy, himself of Irish descent, was also the first Roman Catholic to hold the office.

Celtic separatist movements are opposed to attempts on the part of central government to represent their specific interests. As a protest against such efforts, Breton separatists placed a bomb in the palace of Versailles on 26 June 1978, which exploded, causing considerable damage.

THE CRY FOR FREEDOM

In Northern Ireland thirty-three percent of the population is Catholic. As a minority they have suffered economically from the policies of the Protestant majority, which have, over the years, encouraged the Catholics to emigrate. The Civil Rights movement of the 1960s attempted to right the wrongs by securing civil rights for all. In August 1969 the Catholic quarter of Derry refused entry to the police; the sectarian fighting which ensued marked the beginning of a new era of violence.

Each of our Celtic countries has had a distinctive history which has fashioned its political climate and its aspirations, but all are now on the threshold of some degree of independence.

Brittany was first to be integrated with its larger neighbor, France, at the Treaty of Vannes in 1532; Wales followed soon after and became part of Britain as the result of a series of acts of parliament passed between 1536 and 1543. Scotland was added following the Act of Union in 1707, and on the first of January 1801 the United Kingdom of Great Britain and Ireland came into being.

In Ireland pro- and anti-British feeling polarized—Catholics demanded repeal of the Act and "Home Rule," while the Protestants favored "Unionism." By 1913 a Home Rule Bill looked likely to pass through the British parliament. The Protestant majority of Ulster reacted by setting up a paramilitary Ulster Volunteer Force to counteract the Citizen Army of the Catholics. Matters came to a head on Easter Sunday 1916 when the Irish Republican Brotherhood rose up to declare the Irish Republic, but the movement was smashed with ill-considered ferocity by the British troops. All fifteen leaders, having surrendered, were court martialed and executed.

The rising was a turning point: appalled by the severity of the British action, moderate opinion swung behind the Republicans, while Irish-American attitudes hardened against Britain.

In the General Election of December 1918 the reorganized Sinn Fein won 73 of the 105 Irish seats, but instead of sending its representatives to Westminster, it set up its own Republican party in Ireland—the Dail Eireann—whose first step was to ratify the Republic proclaimed in 1916. "The evacuation of our country by the English garrison" was its first objective, and for the next two and a half years it pursued this end by guerrilla warfare with the aid of its own Irish Republican Army (IRA). Repression and counter measures instituted by Britain brought widespread revolt. It was clear to most observers that the only solution was partition, since the Protestant north steadfastly refused to be separated from the rest of Britain. After protracted negotiation held in 1921, the Anglo-Irish Treaty was signed setting up an Irish Free State in the south. Many Irish could not tolerate the compromise: the IRA removed its support, and a period of civil war ensued which lasted until May 1923. It was a confused period in which the different factions maneuvered for power, but out of the massacres and reprisals a mature nation —Eire—emerged. There the situation was to remain until 1969—Eire, a free nation, overwhelmingly Catholic, committed to the unification of Ireland, and Ulster, predominantly Protestant, wishing to remain in the United Kingdom: the tensions and instability of the situation were all too evident.

Compared with Ireland, the rise of nationalism in Scotland and Wales has been a subdued and stately affair. The Welshness of Wales focused, in the eighteenth and nineteenth centuries, on the revival of Welsh culture from which emerged the National Library, the National Museum, and the University of Wales, together with emotional trappings such as the Eisteddfod, larded with its spurious druidic nostalgia. But in 1886 events began to take a political turn with the formation of the Young Wales movement (Cymru Fydd) dedicated to ensuring that the Liberal Party pay greater attention to Welsh affairs. However, lack of leadership and the absence of a well-defined political philosophy led to the rapid collapse of the party. It was not until 1925 that nationalism once again

Central to the problem of devolution, nationalism, and separatism is whether or not a region seeking to break away is economically viable. Ireland, with its rich farming system, has shown itself to be so, but other regions are less well endowed. The coal and steel industries of Wales are suffering decline, or at least a temporary setback, leading to pit closures and unemployment. In the north, however, the oil and gas deposits of the North Sea are bringing a new prosperity to Scotland, encouraging some to argue that Scotland would benefit from separation from the rest of Britain.

Left: The Welsh slag heap at Ffestiniog.

The Celtic regions underline their desire for independence by the use of their own flags and emblems. *Above:* The flag of Cornwall, the Irish Harp, and the Breton flag, carried by Bretons in a demonstration.

assumed a political image with the foundation of the Welsh Nationalist party (Plaid Cymru), whose avowed aim was to make Wales a self-governing domain within the Commonwealth. As agitation for Home Rule mounted, so the British government responded. A Ministry of Welsh Affairs had been created in 1951, and in 1964 a Secretary of State for Wales was appointed; thus by constitutional methods the Welsh nation was beginning to gain recognition. Meanwhile cultural nationalism gained strength particularly after the foundation of the Welsh Language Society in 1963, which aimed at giving the Welsh language equal status with English. The election of 1967, in which Plaid Cymru gained seats in Westminster for the first time, marked the beginning of a new era.

In Scotland the many small nationalist groups which had emerged out of nineteenth-century unrest came together in 1928 to create the National Party for Scotland, whose aim it was to press for Home Rule. Further amalgamation led to the formation of the Scottish National Party in 1934, but it was not until the 1960s that the party emerged from political obscurity:

But it would be
a great mistake to believe
that peace
can be achieved
simply by the
elimination of violence.
Those who hold that view
are condemned
to repeat the past.
The sort of trouble
we have seen in
Northern Ireland
has occurred there now
in almost every decade
for the past sixty years.
Can we not learn
from this?
The damage to
Northern Ireland
is great. It is not
measured simply in terms
of lives and suffering
though there
the tragedy has been
on an appalling scale.
It is not simply in the
damage to property
and the bitterness
which follows
from communal strife.
It is also in the entire
fabric of
Northern society.

John Lynch, TD,
Fianna Fail Annual Conference,
18 February 1978

In the last decade separatist movements have been more active in all
the Celtic countries. To the earlier
concern with cultural identity has
been added a move towards political
action, ranging from protest to terrorism.
In Northern Ireland, 1,889 people
have been killed (1,396 civilians, the
rest military or constabulary), while
Provisional IRA bombings in England have killed 61 civilians. Financial
support from American Irish is a
significant factor in maintaining the
state of aggression.
Opposite: The burial of an IRA
volunteer.

in 1962 it had less than 2,000 members;
in 1968 there were over 100,000.
Nationalism in Brittany is strongly linked
with the desire to preserve the language.
Hep Brezhoney, Breizh ebet—"Without Breton, no Brittany"—sums up the spirit precisely; but enforced *francisation* in the eighteenth and nineteenth centuries has so
permeated Brittany with French language
and culture that separation seems highly
unrealistic. The FLB *(Front pour la Libération de la Bretagne)* is, however, active
particularly in the university, while the
PDG *(Le Poing dans la Gueule)*, an extreme
group with close links with the IRA, takes
a more anarchistic line, demanding "a fight
to the death against the French state."
Neither is yet a significant political force.
The last decade has seen the intensification
of separatist ideals. In Northern Ireland the
Civil Rights movement of the 1960s, encouraged by the IRA and by left-wing
activists, has developed a revolutionary
fervor which has stimulated an equally violent opposition among the Protestant
majority. In August 1969 sectarian fighting
in the Bogside—the Catholic quarter of
Derry—led to the intervention of the
British government. Since then British
troops have been stationed in Northern
Ireland in an attempt to control sectarian
strife, but the battle between Protestant and
Catholic continues amid demands that the
British troops be withdrawn and Ireland be
united as a nation wholly separate from the
rest of Britain.
In Scotland calls for independence have
gained an impetus from the discovery of
North Sea oil. Believing themselves now to
be economically self-sufficient, some na-
tionalists have pushed for complete separation from England. However, since the
inhabitants of Orkney and Shetland, off
whose coasts most of the oil lies, wish to
remain part of Great Britain, the economic
viability of a Free Scotland is debatable.
The Welsh are under no delusions about
their economic dependence on a united
Britain. It is in this light that we must
interpret the results of the referenda held in
March 1979 offering a degree of political
autonomy to Wales and Scotland. The
Welsh overwhelmingly rejected the idea,
while only about one-third of the Scottish
voters were in favor. It remains to be seen
what the next steps towards the re-creation
of separate Celtic nations will be.

THE CELTS IN RETROSPECT

The Celts succeeded,
under the stimulus
which came to them
from Etruria and Macedon
and Marseilles,
in developing a style
of their own
which is
sufficiently distinctive
to enable our modern
Western archaeologists
to plot out the course
and extent of
these Celtic migrations
on the basis
of the remains
of the Celtic culture
which have come
to light.

Arnold J. Toynbee

The two things, according to Cato the Elder, which the Gauls valued, were glory and wit. The Celts shook the foundations of all the states of Antiquity, but they founded none of lasting importance. The superficial way in which they settled their newly-won territories, no less than their avoidance of water travel and mastery of the sea... demonstrates that this was not their historical destiny. They were bad citizens, but good mercenaries and excellent subjects; they submitted to the Romans with as little difficulty as they conquered in Asia Minor. The national history of the Gauls comes to an end with the death of Vercingetorix, just as that of the Galatians does with the death of Mithridates.

Theodor Mommsen

The Celtic culture as a whole, developing very early on, about 1000 B.C., and reaching its finest expression around 500 B.C., is a fundamental part of Europe's past. This is not to underrate the subsequent influence of the Latin and Germanic peoples on this part of Europe. But the Celtic foundation was already present.
Thus, European culture is inconceivable without the Celtic contribution. Even when the presence of the Celts in their original territory is no longer obvious, we must acknowledge the fact: they are at the root of the Western European peoples who have made history.

Hermann Noelle

The Celts have contributed something that we find nowhere else in the art of Antiquity: translation to, and development in, the third dimension of very largely non-representational decoration, based on a calculated play with curves. It is the finest achievement of their period of maturity. This relief art which, for want of a better name, we describe as plastic, displays the characteristics of molding as well as those of carving and chasing. It has, particularly in the Islands, a softness which suggests polishing; slopes which evoke sand dunes, with their shadows and their sinuous ridges; imperceptible changes of plane, which facilitate the creation and transformation of mass. This

intermediate zone between the linear and the dimensional, between "geometric" curves and the relief figure or motif, is the exclusive property of the Celts.

J. M. Duval

The most striking quality about the early medieval Celtic literatures, the more striking when one compares other contemporary literatures of Europe, is their power of vivid imagination and freshness of approach; as if every poet, gifted with a high degree of imaginative insight, rediscovered the world for himself. Where other medieval literatures are conventional and even hackneyed, early Celtic literature is capable of being highly original. This is not true of that genre which was most esteemed by the Celtic peoples themselves, the official "bardic" poetry, though even there the irrepressible vividness of Celtic thought breaks through. Fortunately other kinds of poetry were composed apart from the bardic, and it is there that the qualities referred to are mainly found.

K. H. Jackson

The ancient Celts bequeathed more than language, literature, and works of art to European civilization: They gave it the heritage of a sensitivity and an intellectual disposition which, down the centuries, remains the protagonist in a continuing dialogue with the various manifestations of the classical tradition. These two intellectual concepts only appear to oppose each other: two systems of thought and expression of differing nature, they are to some extent complementary. A study of the relationship between the Celtic art of the second Iron Age and contemporary Mediterranean art demonstrates this with particular clarity.
Not to recognize the validity of the specific characteristics of the historic Celts is to deny the existence of a deep-rooted dialectic system which has, with remarkable energy over the ages, given form to a European culture, which is an integral part of our inheritance.

M. Szabo

What remains from the military campaigns which periodically
shook ancient Europe, and which brought the Celts
to the conquest of part of Europe,
which, by the workings of their own particular destiny,
they had to relinquish under pressure
from the Romans and the Germanic tribes?
Only one of their states was to be reestablished:
namely Ireland.
All their other efforts to establish political entities
belong among the greatest failures
in the history of ancient Europe.
Their adventure,
made up of bloody defeat and glorious
but transitory revival,
and continuous wrangling dispute, reflects the nature of a people,
born rebels against any rigid order,
who could never manage to attain the concept of a state.
And yet the Celts played a great part in history.
Their opponents themselves were fully aware of their importance....

In the course of their turbulent history,
made up of short-lived successes and crushing reversals,
the Celts effectively worked like yeast on European culture,
despite the shortcomings
which prevented them establishing a state of their own.
The rich variety of their artistic achievement, highly developed
both in conception and execution—rational,
but also, as antithesis to the classical, irrational—is a substantial contribution
to the genesis of European art.
Of what survives of the Celts,
their sculptures and decorative art are still today
the most eloquent
and vivid evidence of the culture which united this restless people.

R. Lantier, *The Celts*, from vol. 3 of *Historia Mundi* (Berne, 1954)

So time in its passing
draws each thing forth, with benefit
to men, and Reason
bears each thing
into the realms of light.
For, seeing in their mind how
one thing illuminates
another, men reached the summit
of perfection in the arts.

Lucretius

QUOTATION SOURCES

Caesar, *De bello gallico* (quoted on pages 29, 126, 144, 146, 152, 168, 169). From Julius Caesar, *The Conquest of Gaul*, © 1951 by S.A. Handford. Quoted by permission of Penguin Books Ltd.
— *De bello gallico* (quoted on pages 48, 75, 108, 110). From B. Tierney, ''The Celtic Ethnography of Posidonius: Translation of the Texts by Athenaeus, Diodorus Siculus, Strabo, Caesar'', *Proceedings of the Royal Irish Academy* 60 (1960): 247 ff. Quoted by permission.
Diodorus Siculus, *Bibliotheca historica* (quoted on pages 5, 38, 50, 57, 82, 83, 96). From B. Tierney, ''The Celtic Ethnography of Posidonius'' (see above). Quoted by permission.
Livy, *Historae* (quoted on pages 83, 128, 131, 132). From Livy, *The Early History of Rome*, © 1960 by the Estate of Aubrey de Sélincourt. Quoted by permission of Penguin Books Ltd.
Strabo, *Geographica* (quoted on pages 28, 29, 56, 67, 94, 108). From B. Tierney, ''The Celtic Ethnography of Posidonius'' (see under Caesar, above).
Tacitus, *Historae* (quoted on pages 29, 155, 156, 157). From *The Histories*, © 1976 by Kenneth Wellesley. Quoted by permission of Penguin Books Ltd.
Táin Bó Cuailnge (quoted on pages 70, 77, 178). From *The Tain, Translated from the Irish Epic*, © 1969 by Thomas Kinsella. Reprinted by permission of the Dolmen Press and Oxford University Press.
Additional Celtic literature (quoted on pages 98, 183, 188, 190, 191, 196). From *A Celtic Miscellany: Translations from the Celtic Literatures*, © 1951, 1971 by Kenneth Hurlstone Jackson Reprinted by permission of Penguin Books Ltd.

BIBLIOGRAPHY

GENERAL

Allen, Derek. *An Introduction to Celtic Coins*. London, 1978.
Cunliffe, B. *Iron Age Communities in Britain*. 2d ed. London, 1978
Daicoviciu, C., and Condurachi, E. *Rumänien*. (*Archaeologia Mundi* series.) Geneva, 1972.
Dillon, Myles, and Chadwick, Nora K. *The Celtic Realms*. London, 1967.
Duval, Paul-Marie. *Les Celtes*. Paris, 1977.
— *Paris Antique des origines au 3e siècle*. Paris, 1961.
— and Kruta, V., eds. *Les mouvements celtiques du 5e au 1er siècle avant notre ère*. Paris, 1978.
Filip, Jan. *Celtic Civilization and Its Heritage*. 2d ed. Prague, 1977.
— ed. *The Celts in Central Europe*. Scékesfehérvar, Czechoslovakia, 1975.
— *Enzyklopädisches Handbuch zur Ur- und Frühgeschichte Europas*. 2 vols. Stuttgart, 1966, 1969.
Forrer, Robert. *Keltische Numismaten der Rhein- und Donaulande*. Strasbourg, 1908.
Hatt, Jean-Jacques. *Kelten und Gallo-Romanen*. (*Archaeologica Mundi* series.) Geneva, 1970.
Herm, Gerhard. *Die Kelten: Das Volk, das aus dem Dunkel kam*. Düsseldorf, 1975.
Hubert, Henri. *Les Celtes depuis l'époque de La Tène et la civilisation celtique*. Paris, 1974.
Kraft, Georg. *Beiträge zur Kenntnis der Urnenfelderkultur in Süddeutschland*. Bonn, 1927.
Kruta, Venceslas, and Lessing, Erich. *Les Celtes*. Paris, 1978.
Moreau, Jacques. *Die Welt der Kelten*. Paris, 1978.
Nash, D. *Settlement and Coinage in Central Gaul, ca. 200–50 B.C.* Oxford, 1978.
Pobe, Marcel, and Roubier, Jean. *Kelten – Römer*. Olten, Switzerland, 1974.
Powell, T.G.E. *The Celts*. London, 1958.
Raftery, Joseph, ed. *The Celts*. Cork, 1967.
Ross, Anne. *Everyday Life of the Pagan Celts*. London, 1970.
Szabo, M. *The Celtic Heritage in Hungary*. Budapest, 1971.
Todorović, J. *Kelti u Jugoistočno j Europi*. Belgrade, 1974.
— *Skordisci: Istorija i Kultura*. Belgrade, 1974.
Wyss, René. *Der Schatzfund von Erstfeld*. Zurich, 1975.

CELTIC SOCIETY

Cunliffe, B., and Rowley, T. *Lowland Iron Age Communities in Europe*. Oxford, 1978.
— *Oppida: The Beginnings of Urbanization in Barbarian Europe*. Oxford, 1976.
Duval, P.M., and Kruta, V. *L'Habitat et la nécropole à l'âge du fer en Europe occidentale et centrale*. Paris, 1975.
Hallstatt Archaeological Society. *Hallstatt: Kultur und Natur einer 4000jährigen Salzstätte*. 2 vols. Hallstatt, Austria, 1953–1954.
Jacobi, Gerhard. *Werkzeug und Gerät aus dem Oppidum von Manching*. Wiesbaden, Germany, 1974.
Jacobsthal, Paul. *Early Celtic Art*. 2 vols. Oxford, 1944.
Joffroy, René. *La tombe princière de Vix*. In *Monuments et Mémoires de la fondation Eugène Piot*, vol. 47. Paris, 1968.
Kimmig, Wolfgang. *Die Heuneburg an der oberen Donau*. Stuttgart, 1968.
Kraemer, Werner, and Schubert, Franz. *Die Ausgrabung in Manching, 1955–1961*. Wiesbaden, Germany, 1974.
Markale, Jean. *Les Celtes et la civilisation celtique*. Paris, 1970.
— *La Femme celte: Mythe et sociologie*. Paris, 1973.

Megaw, John V.S. *Art of the European Iron Age*. Bath, England, 1970.
Noelle, Hermann. *Die Kelten und ihre Stadt Manching*. Pfaffenhofen, Germany, 1974.
Normand, B. *L'âge du fer en Basse Alsace*. Strasbourg, 1973.
Norton-Taylor, Duncan. *The Celts*. Amsterdam, 1975.
Penninger, Ernst. *Der Dürnnberg bei Hallein*. 2 vols. Munich, 1972.
Piggott, Stuart. *Ancient Europe from the Beginnings of Agriculture to Classical Antiquity*. Edinburgh, 1965.
Spindler, Konrad. *Der Magdalenenberg bei Villingen*. Stuttgart, 1976.
Vasic, R. *The Chronology of the Early Iron Age in Serbia*. Oxford, 1977.
von Reden, Sibylle. *Die Megalith-Kulturen: Zeugnisse einer verschollenen Urkultur*. Cologne, 1978.
Wheeler, R.E.M., and Richardson, K.M. *Hill-forts of Northern France*. London, 1957.

RELIGION AND MYSTERY

de Vries, Jan. *Keltische Religion*. Stuttgart, 1961.
Duval, P.M. *Les Dieux de la Gaule*. Paris, 1976.
Le Roux-Guyonvarc'h, Francoise. *Keltische Religion*. In *Handbuch der Religionsgeschichte*, vol. 1. Göttingen, Germany, 1971.
MacCana, P. *Celtic Mythology*. London, 1970.
Ross, Anne. *Pagan Celtic Britain*. London, 1967.
Sharkey, John. *Celtic Mysteries: The Ancient Religion*. London, 1975.
Sjoestedt, Marie-Louise. *Dieux et héros des Celtes*. Paris, 1940.

THE GENIUS OF THE CELTS

Chadwick, Nora K. *The Druids*. Cardiff, 1966.
Duval, P.M., and Hawkes, C. *Celtic Art in Ancient Europe*. London, 1976.
Jacobsthal, J. *Early Celtic Art*. Oxford, 1944.
Piggott, Stuart. *The Druids*. London, 1968.
Szabo, Miklos, and Petres, E. *Eastern Celtic Art*. Szekesfehérvar, 1974.
Varagnac, André, and Fabre, Gabrielle. *L'art gaulois*. Paris, 1964.

THE DESTINY OF THE CELTS

Birley, Anthony: *Life in Roman Britain*. London, 1968.
de Beer, Gavin. *Hannibal: The Struggle for Power in the Mediterranean*. London, 1969.
Ebel, C. *Transalpine Gaul: The Emergence of a Roman Province*. Leiden, 1976.
Grant, Michael. *Julius Caesar*. London, 1969.
Le Gall, Joël. *Alésia, archéologie et histoire*. Paris, Fayard, 1963.
Schlette, F. *Kelten zwischen Alesia und Pergamon*. Leipzig, 1976.
Todorovic, J. *Skordisci*. Novi Sad and Belgrade, 1974.

THE ISLAND CELTS

Alcock, Leslie. *By South Cadbury, Is That Camelot...* London, 1972.
Bieler, Ludwig. *Irland. Wegbereiter des Mittelalters*. Olten, Switzerland, 1961.
Bowen, G.G. *The Settlements of the Celtic Saints in Wales*. Cardiff, 1954.
Chadwick, N. *Early Brittany*. Cardiff, 1969.
de Paor, M., and de Paor, L. *Early Christian Ireland*. London, 1960.

Dillon, Myles. *Early Irish Literature*. Chicago, 1948.
— *Early Irish Society*. Dublin, 1954.
— *Irish Sagas*. Cork, 1970.
Gsaenger, Hans. *Irland, Insel des Abels*. 2 vols. Freiburg Br., Germany, 1969–1970.
Hibert, Christopher. *The Search for King Arthur*. New York, 1977.
Jackson, K.J. *A Celtic Miscellany*. London, 1951.
— *The Oldest Irish Tradition: A Window on the Iron Age*. Cambridge, 1964.
Kinsella, T. *The Tain*. London, 1970.
Laing, L. *Late Celtic Britain and Ireland. ca. 400–1200 A.D.* London, 1975.
Markale, Jean. *L'épopée celtique en Bretagne*. Paris, 1975.
— *La tradition celtique en Bretagne armoricaine*. Paris, 1975.
O'Rahilly, T.F. *Early Irish History and Mythology*. Dublin, 1946.
Rhys, John. *Celtic Folklore, Welsh and Manx*. Vol. 1. Oxford, 1901.
Severin, Tim. *The Brendan Voyage*. London, 1978.
Thomas, Charles. *Britain and Ireland in Early Christian Times, A.D. 400–800*. New York, 1975.
Thurneysen, R. *Die irische Helden- und Königssage*. Halle, Germany, 1921.

THE CELTS TODAY

Greene, David. *The Irish Language*. Reprinted. Cork, 1977.
Howarth, Herbert. *The Irish Writers, 1880–1940*. New York, 1959.
Hyde, Douglas. *A Literary History of Ireland from Earliest Time to the Present Day*. London, 1899.
Jones, Maldwyn A. *Destination America*. New York, 1976.
MacLiammoir, Michael. *Ireland*. London, 1977.
Marzio, Peter C., ed. *A Nation of Nations: The People Who Came to America* (Smithsonian Institution). New York, 1976.
Merian (monthly publication). Issue on Ireland. Vol. 29, No. 5. Hamburg, 1976.
— Issue on Wales. Vol. 27, No. 6. Hamburg, 1974.
Rother, Frank, and Rother, A. *Die Bretagne: im Land der Dolmen, Menhire und Calvaires*. Cologne, 1978.
Smith, Edwin, and Cook, Olive. *Scotland*. London, 1967.
Uris, Leon, and Uris, Jill. *Ireland: A Terrible Beauty*. New York, 1976.

PICTURE CREDITS

Abbreviations

P: Photo
c.: Century
mill.: Millennium
Ms.: Manuscript
fol.: Folio
v.: Verso
r.: Recto

2 Helmeted goddess. Bronze. Kerguilly en Dinéault (Finistère, France). 1st c. A.D. Musée de Bretagne, Rennes.
4 Detail of bronze flask. Dürrnberg (Austria). Late 5th–early 4th c. B.C. Salzburger Museum Carolino-Augusteum, Salzburg.
6 Celtic warrior in battle. Bronze. Rome (Italy). Late 3rd c. B.C. Staatliche Museen, Berlin.
7 Celtic warrior. Relief. Detail of silver plated caldron. Gundestrup (Himmerland, Denmark). Mid–1st c. B.C.–3rd c. A.D. (date controversial). Nationalmuseet, Copenhagen.
9 Statuette of goddess. Clay. Cirna (Romania). ca. 1500 B.C. Muzeul de Istorie al R.S.R., Bucharest. P: Erich Lessing/Magnum.
10–11 Landscape. P: Hanspeter Renner.
12 Cattle. Detail of a seal stamp. Mesopotamia (Iraq). Late 5th mill. B.C. Musée du Louvre, Paris. P: Hirmer Fotoarchiv.
13 Dairy. Frieze. Tell al'Ubaid, Mesopotamia (Iraq). 4th mill. B.C. Museum of Baghdad. P: Georg Gerster.
14 *Top*: Stonehenge. Megalithic ceremonial ruin. Wiltshire (England). ca. 2500 B.C. P: Aerial Photography, University of Cambridge.
Middle left: Cremation urn from Singen (Germany). ca. 1200 B.C. Badisches Landesmuseum, Karlsruhe.
Middle right: Cremation urn from Ihringen (Baden-Württemberg, Germany). ca. 1200 B.C. Museum für Urgeschichte, Freiburg im Breisgau.
Bottom left: Bell-shaped beaker. Goodmanham (Humberside, England). ca. 2000 B.C. British Museum.
15 *Top right:* Belt boss. Bronze. Langstrup (Zealand, Denmark). 15th–14th c. B.C. Nationalmuseet, Copenhagen.
Middle right: Neolithic axe-blades. Auvernier (Switzerland). Schweizerisches Landesmuseum, Zurich.
16 *Left:* Horse rider on bronze axe. Hallstatt (Austria). 600 B.C. Prähistorische Abteilung, Naturhistorisches Museum, Vienna.
Center: Bronze pail. Hallstatt (Austria). 7th–6th c. B.C. British Museum.
Right: Bronze figure. Idrija (Yugoslavia). 8th–5th c. B.C. Prähistorische Abteilung, Naturhistorisches Museum, Vienna.
17 *Top:* Hallstatt site (Austria). Painting by Isidor Engl. Prähistorische Abteilung, Naturhistorisches Museum, Vienna.
Bottom, left to right:
Detail of bracelet. Gold. Reinheim (Germany). Late 5th–early 4th c. B.C. Landesmuseum für Vor- und Frühgeschichte, Saarbrücken. P: Staatliches Konservatoramt.
Iron spearhead. La Tène, Marin-Epagnier (Switzerland). ca. 250–120 B.C. Schweizerisches Landesmuseum, Zurich. P: From René Wyss, *Funde der jüngeren Eisenzeit, Aus dem Schweizerischen Landesmuseum*, Bern, 1957.
Detail from cart handle. Bronze and enamel. Thames, Brentford (England). Late 3rd c. B.C. Museum of London.
Brooch terminal in shape of human head. Bronze. Oberwittighausen (Baden-Württemberg, Germany). Late 5th–early 4th c. B.C. Badisches Landesmuseum, Karlsruhe.
20–21 Hill fort Old Oswestry (England). P: Aerial Photography, University of Cambridge.
22 Burial practices, Hallstatt cemetery (Austria). Painting by Isidor Engl. Prähistorische Abteilung, Naturhistorisches Museum, Vienna.
23 *Top, left to right:*
(All from Musée des Antiquités Nationales, St. Germain-en-Laye.)
Shell-shaped vessel. Terra-cotta. Thuisy (Marne, France).
Pottery vessel. Bergères-les-Vertuses (Marne, France).
Vessel with engraved ornaments. Prunay (Marne, France).
Vessel with painted decoration. Tourbe (Somme, France).
Right, top to bottom:
Ring from Edingen (Germany). Drawing by Franz Coray after G. Kraft.
Clasp and needle. From a grave near Egg (Switzerland). 1200–800 B.C. Schweizerisches Landesmuseum, Zurich.
Ring from Edingen (Germany). Drawing by Franz Coray after G. Kraft.
24 *Above:* Animal ornament. Detail of bronze situla. Este (Italy). 4th c. B.C. Museo Nazionale Atestino, Este.
25 *Top left:* Horse rider. Detail of Gundestrup caldron. See page 7.
Right, top to bottom:
Iron spearhead with short socket. La Tène, Marin-Epagnier (Switzerland). 250–120 B.C. Schweizerisches Landesmuseum, Zurich. P: From René Wyss, *Funde der jüngeren Eisenzeit, Aus dem Schweizerischen Landesmuseum*, Bern, 1957.
Iron spearhead with long socket. La Tène. See above.
Iron slashing sword. Grandson (Switzerland). 8th c. B.C. Schweizerisches Landesmuseum, Zurich.
Redrawing of military scenes on Hallstatt sword. (Damaged original in Naturhistorisches Museum, Vienna.) P: Römisch-Germanisches Zentralmuseum.
Iron spearhead with long blade. La Tène, Marin-Epagnier. 250–120 B.C. See above (iron spearhead).
Iron spearhead with narrow blade. La Tène, Marin-Epagnier. 250–120 B.C. See above (iron spearhead).
26 *Top left:* Gallic coin with lion. Silver. ca. 2nd c. B.C. Bibliothèque Nationale, Cabinet des Médailles, Paris.
Top right: Gallic coin of Redones tribe with rider. Gold. ca. 1st c. B.C. See above (*top left*).
Bottom left: Musician. Bronze statuette. Neuvy-en-Sullias (Loiret, France). 1st–3rd c. A.D. Musée Historique et Archéologique de l'Orléanais, Orléans. P: Jaques.
Bottom right: Druid. Bronze statuette. Neuvy-en-Sullias (Loiret, France). 1st–3rd c. A.D. See above (*bottom left*).
27 *Left:* Carved pillar. Sandstone. Pfalzfeld (Germany). 5th–4th c. B.C. Rheinisches Landesmuseum, Bonn. P: SCALA.
Top left: Roman coin with Gallic battle equipment. Denarius. ca. 48 B.C. British Museum, Department of Coins & Medals.
Top right: Gallic coin of Aulerci Cenomani with wreathed head. Gold. ca. 1st c. B.C. Bibliothèque Nationale, Cabinet des Médailles, Paris.
Bottom right: Dancing female figurine. Bronze. Neuvy-en-Sullias (Loiret, France). 1st c. A.D. Musée Historique et Archéologique de l'Orléanais, Orléans. P: Jaques.
28 *Top right:* Medieval scribe. Miniature. Bibliothèque Nationale, Paris, P: Giraudon.
Middle left: Virgil between two muses. Mosaic. Sousse (Tunesia). Museum Tunis. P: Giraudon.
Bottom center: Herodotus. Marble bust. Benha (Egypt). 2nd c. A.D. The Metropolitan Museum of Art, Gift of George F. Baker, 1891, New York.
29 *Top to bottom:*
Strabo. From Theret's *Les Vrais Portraits et Vies des Hommes Illustres*, 1584. P: Radio Times Hulton Picture Library.
Julius Caesar. Marble bust. Museo Nazionale, Naples. P: Alinari.
Pliny the Elder. Engraving. Bibliothèque Nationale, Paris. P: Lauros-Giraudon.
Posidonius. Bust. Museo Nazionale, Naples. P: Alinari.
30 *Top right:* Queen Medb (?). Detail of Gundestrup caldron. See page 7.
Middle: Colophon to Saint Matthew. Detail. The Durham Gospel Fragment I. Ms. A.II.10, fol. 3v. Durham Dean and Chapter Library. P: Courtesy of the Dean and Chapter of Durham Cathedral.
31 The Book of Durrow. Ms. fol. 3v. 7th c. A.D. Trinity College, Dublin. P: Courtesy of the Board of Trinity College, The Green Studio.
32 Rosmerta and Mercury. Gallo-Roman sculpture. Musée des Antiquités Nationales, St. Germain-en-Laye.
33 *Middle above:* Celtic coin with lancer. Silver. Hungary. ca. 1st c. B.C. National Museum, Budapest. P: Erich Lessing/Magnum.
Bottom: Ornate sword handle. Bronze. Châtillon-sur-Indre (Indre, France). 1st c. B.C. Musée Archéologique Thomas Dobrée, Nantes.
34 *Middle right:* Scythian horseman. Detail of collar. Gold. Kul Oba (Ukraine, Russia). 4th c. B.C. The Hermitage, Leningrad.
Bottom left: Bronze hydria. Grächwil (Switzerland). 6th c. B.C. Historisches Museum, Bern. P: Schweizerisches Landesmuseum.
35 *Middle above:* Burial chamber of *Hohmichele*, Heuneburg. Hundersingen (Baden-Württemberg, Germany). Reconstruction sketch. P: Courtesy Institut für Vor- und Frühgeschichte der Universität Tübingen.
Bottom, left to right:
– Dagger in sheath.
– Dagger. Iron and bronze.
– Sheath, back.
Magdalenenberg near Villingen (Baden-Württemberg, Germany). ca. 6th c. B.C. P: Institut für Ur- und Frühgeschichte der Universität Erlangen-Nürnberg.
36 *Top right:* Floor plan of tomb at Vix. Châtillon-sur-Seine (Côte-d'Or, France). From *Monuments et Mémoires* publié par l'Académie des Inscriptions et Belles-Lettres. Fondation Eugène Piot. Presses Universitaires de France, Paris, 1954. Tome 48ᵉ. Fascicule 1.
Middle left: Bronze krater of Vix (Côte-d'Or, France). Late 6th c. B.C. Musée Archéologique, Châtillon-sur-Seine. P: Lauros-Giraudon.
Middle right: Detail of Vix krater. See above.
37 *Middle above:* Heuneburg. Hundersingen (Baden-Württemberg, Germany). P: Institut für Vor- und Frühgeschichte der Universität Tübingen.
Below right: Reconstruction sketch of the Heuneburg. Franz Coray after W. Kimmig.
38 Wine transport. Relief from Cabrières-d'Aygues (Vaucluse, France). Musée Calvet, Avignon.
41 St. Gotthard pass (Switzerland). P: Erich Lessing/Magnum.
42 Celtic fireplace. La Tène period. Reconstruction. Open-air museum Asparn a.d. Zaya (Austria). P: Courtesy Niederösterreichisches Landesmuseum, Museum für Urgeschichte Asparn a.d. Zaya.
43 Celtic feast. Reconstruction drawing by Mark Adrian. From Arnold Jaggi, *Helvetier, Römer, Alamannen...*, Paul Haupt Verlag, Bern, 1962.
44 *Top:* Small silver disk. Villa Vecchia, Manerbio sul Mella (Italy). 3rd–2nd c. B.C. Museo Civico Romano, Brescia. P: Rapuzzi.
Middle left: Head of woman. Detail of a statue. 1st c. B.C. or A.D. Musée de Bourges. P: G. Franceschi-Zodiaque.
45 Head of young man. Bronze. Prilly (Switzerland). 1st c. A.D. Historisches Museum, Bern.
46 *Top left:* Small man's mask. Bronze. Welwyn (Hertfordshire, England). 1st c. B.C. British Museum.
Middle left: Bronze belt-hook. Hölzelsau (Kufstein, Austria). Early 4th c. B.C. Prähistorische Staatssammlung, Museum für Vor- und Frühgeschichte, Munich.
Bottom left: Textile fragment. *Hohmichele*, Heuneburg. Hundersingen (Baden-Württemberg, Germany). Early 6th c. B.C. Römisch-Germanisches Zentralmuseum, Mainz.
Right: Celtic clothing. Reconstruction sketch by Franz Coray.
47 *Top left:* Gold bracelet. Waldalgesheim (Rheinland-Pfalz, Germany). 4th c. B.C. Rheinisches Landesmuseum, Bonn.
Top right: Silver torque with iron core. Trichtingen (Germany). 2nd c. B.C. Württembergisches Landesmuseum, Stuttgart.
Middle, left to right:
Silver brooch. Schosshalde, Bern (Switzerland). 4th c. B.C. Historisches Museum, Bern.
Bronze brooch. Oberwittighausen (Baden-Württemberg, Germany). Late 5th–early 4th c. B.C. Badisches Landesmuseum, Karlsruhe.
Bronze brooch. Conflans (Aube, France). 3rd c. A.D. Musée des Beaux-Arts et d'Archéologie, Troyes. P: Jean Bienaimé.
Two gold bracelets. Erstfeld (Switzerland). 4th c. B.C. Schweizerisches Landesmuseum, Zurich.
Middle, below right: Short sword from Hallstatt (Austria). Drawing by Friedrich Simony. From *Die Altertümer vom Hallstätter Salzberg und dessen Umgebung* by Friedrich Simony. Aus der Kaiserlichen-Königlichen Hof- und Staatsdruckerei, Vienna, 1851.
Bottom, left to right:
Scottish cloth. P: Publisher's Archives.
Gaul. Limestone figure. Auxerre (Yonne, France). 2nd–3rd c. A.D. Musée Archéologique, Auxerre.
Helvetian. Tile antefix. Vindonissa (Switzerland). Late 1st c. A.D. Vindonissa-Museum, Brugg. P: C. Holliger.
Female head with torque. Tile antefix. Vindonissa (Switzerland). Late 1st c. A.D. Vindonissa-Museum, Brugg. P: C. Holliger.
48 *Top right:* Three mother-goddesses. Relief. Vertillum (Côte-d'Or, France). Musée Archéologique, Châtillon-sur-Seine. P: Jean Roubier.
Bottom left: Coin of the Andecavi. Gold stater. Bibliothèque Nationale, Cabinet des Médailles, Paris.
Bottom right: Mother-goddess. Detail. See *top right.*
49 Cloaked figures. Relief. Housesteads (Northumberland, England). 3rd c. A.D. P: Department of the Environment, Crown Copyright.
50 *White Horse.* Uffington (Berkshire, England). ca. 1st c. A.D. P: A. Howarth, Daily Telegraph Colour Library.
51 Gallo-roman sculpture from Portieux (Vosges, France). Mid–3rd c. A.D. Musée Départemental des Vosges, Epinal. P: J.-C. Voegtlé, © 1979 Copyright by SPADEM, Paris and Cosmopress, Geneva.
52 *Top left:* Epona. Relief. Limestone. Altbachtal (Rhineland, Germany). Early 3rd c. A.D. Rheinisches Landesmuseum, Trier.
Top right: Rider god. Relief. Whitecombe Farm (Dorset, England). P: National Monuments Record.
Middle left: Gallic horse trader. Relief from tombstone. Musée Archéologique, Dijon.
Bottom left: Foal. Bronze. Catalaunum, Châlons-sur-Marne (France). Musée Municipal, Châlons-sur-Marne. P: Jean Roubier.
Bottom right: Foal. Bronze. Aventicum (Switzerland). Kunsthistorisches Museum, Geneva. P: Jean Roubier.
53 *Coins, left to right and top to bottom:*
Coin of the Unelli. Gold. Cotentin (Normandie, France). Early 2nd c. A.D.
Coin of the Parisii. Gold. Early 1st c. A.D.
Coin of the Atrebates. Gold. 1st c. A.D.
Coin of the Jura area. Gold. 1st c. A.D.
These four from Bibliothèque Nationale, Cabinet des Médailles, Paris.
Coin from Transylvania (Romania). Silver. Mid–3rd c. B.C. British Museum.
Bottom: Cult wagon. Bronze. Mérida (Spain). 2nd–1st c. B.C. Musée des Antiquités Nationales, St. Germain-en-Laye.
54 *Above right:* Coin with chariot driver.

Silver. 1st c. B.C. British Museum.
Below left: Horse-drawn chariot. Clay. Pitigliano (Italy). 9th c. B.C. Römisch-Germanisches Zentralmuseum, Mainz.

55 *Top:* Coin with chariot driver. Silver. 1st c. B.C. British Museum.
Bottom left: Coin of the Turones. Gold. 150–121 B.C. Bibliothèque Nationale, Cabinet des Médailles, Paris.
Bottom right: Reconstruction of war chariot from Llyn Cerrig Bach (Anglesea, England). National Museum of Wales, Cardiff.

56 Celtic warriors with trumpets. Detail of Gundestrup caldron. See page 7.

57 *Left to right:*
Celt with shield. Limestone sculpture. Mondragon (Vaucluse, France). Musée Calvet, Avignon. P: G. Franceschi/Zodiaque.
Bronze shield with enamel or glass inlay. River Witham near Washingborough (Lincolnshire, England). 3rd–2nd c. B.C. British Museum.
Reconstruction of Gallic shield. Horath (Germany). Rheinisches Landesmuseum, Trier.
Bronze shield with glass inlay. River Thames at Battersea (Middlesex, England). 1st c. A.D. British Museum.

58 *Top, left to right:*
Sword from Hallstatt (Austria). Iron and bronze. 6th c. B.C. Prähistorische Abteilung, Naturhistorisches Museum, Vienna. P: Schweizerisches Landesmuseum.
Iron sword with bronze handle. Found near Mainz (Germany). Mittelrheinisches Landesmuseum, Mainz.
Dagger and sheath. Bronze. *Römerhügel,* Ludwigsburg (Germany). 7th–6th c. B.C. Württembergisches Landesmuseum, Stuttgart.
Bronze dagger sheath. Hallstatt (Austria). Drawing by Friedrich Simony. From *Die Altertümer vom Hallstätter Salzberg und dessen Umgebung* by Friedrich Simony. Aus der Kaiserlichen-Königlichen Hof- und Staatsdruckerei, Vienna, 1851.
La Tène sheath. Buthorpe (Yorkshire, England). 1st c. B.C. British Museum.
Iron spearhead with long socket. La Tène, Marin-Epagnier (Switzerland). ca. 250–120 B.C. Schweizerisches Landesmuseum, Zurich. From René Wyss, *Funde der jüngeren Eisenzeit, Aus dem Schweizerischen Landesmuseum,* Bern, 1957.
Lance head. Bronze. *Talhau,* Hundersingen (Baden-Württemberg, Germany). Württembergisches Landesmuseum, Stuttgart.
Two-edged dagger with bronze handle. Hallstatt (Austria). Drawing by Friedrich Simony. From *Die Altertümer vom Hallstätter Salzberg...* (see above).
Chisel. Hallstatt (Austria). Drawing by Friedrich Simony. From *Die Altertümer vom Hallstätter Salzberg...* (see above).
Iron sword. *Ferme Rouge,* La Quenique, Court-St-Etienne (Belgium). 5th c. B.C. Musée Royaux d'Art et d'Histoire, Brussels.
Middle left: Horseman. Detail of bronze cult chariot. Strettweg (Austria). 7th c. B.C. Landesmuseum Joanneum, Graz. P: Foto Fürböck.

59 *Top, left to right:*
Bronze helmet. Filottrano, near Ancona (Italy). 4th c. B.C. Museo Nazionale, Ancona. P: Soprintendenza Archeologica delle Marche.
Bronze and iron helmet. Amfreville (Eure, France). Later 4th c. B.C. Musée du Louvre, Paris. P: Giraudon.
Iron helmet. Giubiasco (Switzerland). 2nd c. B.C. Schweizerisches Landesmuseum, Zurich.
Cone-shaped helmet. Bronze. La Gorge-Meillet (France). ca. 450–300 B.C. Musée des Antiquités Nationales, St. Germaine-en-Laye. P: Lauros-Giraudon.
Iron helmet with bronze and coral decoration. Canosa di Puglia (Italy). Later 4th c. B.C. Staatliche Museen, Berlin. P: Bildarchiv Preussischer Kulturbesitz.
Iron helmet with bronze covering. Umbria (Italy). Late 4th c. B.C. Staatliche Museen, Berlin. P: Bildarchiv Preussischer Kulturbesitz.
Bottom: Iron helmet with bronze crest. Ciumeşti (Romania). 3rd c. B.C. Muzeul de Istorie al R.S.R., Bucharest.

60 *Top left:* Beehive-shaped stone dwelling. Pre-Celtic. Plateau des Claparèdes (Vaucluse, France). P: Jean Roubier.
Top right: Celtic house. La Tène-period, ca. 100 B.C. Reconstruction. Open-air museum, Museum für Urgeschichte, Asparn a.d. Zaya. P: Foto Nechuta, Courtesy Niederösterreichische Landesregierung.
Bottom left: Plan of farmstead. Little Woodbury (Wiltshire, England). Franz Coray after Bersu.

61 *Top:* Celtic house. Hallstatt-period. Reconstruction. Open-air museum, Museum für Urgeschichte, Asparn a.d. Zaya. P: Foto Nechuta, Courtesy Niederösterreichische Landesregierung.
Center: Fortification at Burgenrain (Switzerland). Reconstruction sketch. Franz Coray after A. Müller.
Bottom: Rampart of Wittnauer Horn (Switzerland). Sketch by Franz Coray.

62 Hill fort Maiden Castle (Dorset, England). P: Aerial Photography, University of Cambridge.

62–63 Fort of Dun Aengus, Aran Islands (Ireland). P: John Bulmer.

62 *Right:* Plan of gates. Danebury hillfort (Hampshire, England). Franz Coray after B. Cunliffe.

64 Part of Murus Gallicus. Reconstruction sketch Franz Coray after H. Noelle.

65 *Above:* Main entrance of oppidum at Manching (Germany). Reconstruction sketch after D.D.A. Simpson and Stuart Piggott.
Below: Aerial view of the oppidum at Manching (Germany). P: Archivbild Deutsches Archäologisches Institut.

66 God of hunt. Statue from La Celle-Mont-Saint-Jean (Sarthe, France). Musée des Antiquités Nationales, St. Germain-en-Laye.

67 View of La Tène, near Marin-Epagnier (Switzerland). P: Robert Tobler

68 Mother-goddesses. Gallo-Roman relief. Alésia (France). Musée Archéologique, Dijon. P: Pamir.

69 Stele with head of Janus. Limestone. Holzgerlingen (Baden-Württemberg, Germany). Württembergisches Landesmuseum, Stuttgart.

70 Three mother-goddesses. Engraved on stone. Burgundy (France). Musée des Antiquités Nationales, St. Germain-en-Laye.

71 Three-headed god. Terra-cotta. Detail of vase from Bavay (France). 2nd c. A.D. Bibliothèque Nationale, Paris.

72 *Left: Radiate* deity. Armagh (Northern Ireland). Ulster Museum, Belfast.
Right: Sheela-na-gig, Celtic fertility goddess. Relief. Detail on a corbel, Church of St. Mary and St. David, Kilpeck (Herefordshire, England). P: National Monuments Record.

73 *Left:* Antler-god. Detail of Gundestrup caldron. See page 7.
Right: Dis Pater. Bronze. Prémeaux (Côte-d'Or, France). Musée des Beaux-Arts, Beaune.

74 *Top right:* Rider god. Bronze. Willingham Fen (England). 2nd c. A.D. Cambridge Museum of Archaeology and Ethnology, Cambridge.
Bottom left: Taranis with Jupiter attributes. Bronze. Gallo-Roman statuette. Le Châtelet (Haute-Marne, France). Musée des Antiquités Nationales, St. Germain-en-Laye.

75 *Left:* Dis Pater. Bronze. Gallo-Roman statuette. Visp (Switzerland). Musée d'Art et d'Histoire, Geneva.
Right: Esus. Limestone relief. Trier (Germany). 1st c. A.D. Rheinisches Landesmuseum, Trier.

76 *Top:* Epona. Gallo-Roman statuette. Alesia (France). Musée Alesia, Alise-Sainte-Reine. P: Jean Roubier.
Bottom left: Boar-god from Euffigneix (Haute-Marne, France). Limestone. Gallo-Roman period. Musée des Antiquités Nationales, St. Germain-en-Laye. P: Jean Roubier.
Bottom right: Mother-goddess with fruits and foliage. Relief. Caerwent, Monmouth (Wales, England). ca. 1st–2nd c. A.D. National Museum of Wales, Cardiff.

77 *Top:* Esus cutting the willow tree. Relief. Paris (France). 1st c. A.D. Musée de Cluny, Paris. P: Jean Roubier.
Bottom, left to right:
Cross-legged sitting god. Bronze and enamel. Bouray-sur-Juine (Essone, France). Late 1st c. B.C.–early 1st c. A.D. Musée des Antiquités Nationales, St. Germain-en-Laye.
Hunting god. Touget (Gers, France). 1st–2nd c. A.D. Musée des Antiquités Nationales, St. Germain-en-Laye.
Horned, armed god from Burgh-by-Sands (Cumberland, England). Relief. P: Robert Hogg.
Goddess of serpents. Relief from a Roman altar, Church of all Saints. Ilkley (Yorkshire, England). P: National Monuments Record.
God with torque. Limestone. Rodez (Aveyron, France). Musée Fenailles, Rodez. P: G. Franceschi/Zodiaque.

78–79 Detail of cult wagon. Bronze. Strettweg (Austria). 7th c. B.C. Landesmuseum Joanneum, Graz. P: Erich Lessing/Magnum.

80 *Top:* Bear-goddess Artio. Bronze. Muri (Switzerland). 2nd–3rd c. A.D. Historische Museum, Bern.
Middle, left to right:
Bull. Bronze. Lillebonne (France). Gallo-Roman period. Musée Départemental, Rouen.
Horse. Bronze. Freisen (Saarland, Germany). 4th c. B.C. Rheinisches Landesmuseum, Trier.
Dog. Bronze. Moudon (Switzerland). Historisches Museum, Bern.

81 *Top right:* Bird-god Abraxas. Relief. Nyon (Switzerland). Gallo-Roman period. Historisches Museum, Bern.
Bottom: Boar. Bronze. Neuvy-en-Sullias (Loiret, France). 1st c. A.D. Musée Historique et Archéologique de l'Orléanais, Orléans. P: Jaques.

82 Three details of the pillar porch of the temple at Roquepertuse (Bouches-du-Rhône, France). 1st c. B.C. Musée Borély, Marseille.
Left: P: Belzeaux-Rapho.
Center and right: P: Lauros-Giraudon.

83 Pillar with schematized masks from the temple at Entremont (Bouches-du-Rhône, France). 2nd c. B.C. Dépôt des fouilles, Entremont. P: Centre Camille Jullian, Université de Provence.

84 *Top:* Cave entrance of *Dame Jouanne.* Larchant (Seine-et-Marne, France). From Marie E.P. König, *Am Anfang der Kultur,* Gebrüder Mann Verlag, Berlin, 1973.
Middle: Doorway. Church Dysert O'Dea (Ireland). P: Arnold Hintze.

85 Portal of cloister church. Clonfert (Ireland). P: Arnold Hintze.

86 *Top right:* Group of four heads. Limestone. Entremont (Bouches-du-Rhône, France). 3rd–2nd c. B.C. Musée Granet, Aix-en-Provence.
Middle, left to right:
Female head. Detail of caldron. Bronze. Kraghede (Denmark). ca. 1st c. B.C. Nationalmuseet, Copenhagen.
Male head. Bronze mount for wooden flagon. Dürrnberg (Austria). ca. 400 B.C. Keltenmuseum, Hallein.
Male deity. Detail from Pfalzfeld pillar. See page 27.
Bottom left: Coin of the Parisii. Gold. Early 1st c. B.C. Bibliothèque Nationale, Cabinet des Médailles, Paris.
Bottom right: Fragmentary stone head. Sandstone. Heidelberg (Baden-Wurttemberg, Germany). Late 5th–early 4th c. B.C. Badisches Landesmuseum, Karlsruhe.

87 *Top right:* Bronze disc. Ireland? 1st–2nd c. A.D. British Museum.
Middle left: Limestone double-head. Roquepertuse (Bouches-du-Rhône, France). 3rd c. A.D. Musée Borély, Marseille.
Middle right: Three-headed god. Reims (France). Gallo-Roman period. P: Schweizerisches Landesmuseum.
Bottom, left to right:
Virile mask. Bronze. Montsérié (Hautes-Pyrénées, France). 3rd–2nd c. B.C. Musée Massey, Tarbes. P: YAN.
Ragstone head. Mšecké Zehrovice, near Prague (Czechoslovakia). ca. 150 B.C. National Museum, Prague. P: SCALA.
Female head. Detail of a statue. 1st c. B.C. or A.D. Musée de Bourges. P: G. Franceschi/Zodiaque.
Head of a divinity. Detail of Gundestrup caldron. See page 7.

88–89 Source of the river Seine. Saint-Germain, Source de la Seine (Côte-d'Or, France). P: Erich Lessing/Magnum.

89 *Top right:* Water-goddess Coventina with two waternymphs. Relief. Museum of Antiquities, Newcastle-upon-Tyne.

90 *Top right:* Water-goddess Coventina. Relief. Detail of a stele. Carrawburgh (Northumberland, England). ca. 2nd–3rd c. A.D. Museum of Antiquities, Newcastle-upon-Tyne.

90 *Middle left:* Blind girl. Votive offering. Gallo-Roman stone sculpture. Shrine of the Source of the Seine (Côte-d'Or, France). Musée Archéologique, Dijon.
Middle right: Wooden leg. Votive offering. Shrine of the source of the Seine. See above. ca. 1st c. A.D.

91 *Left to right:*
(Unless indicated otherwise, all are from:
Shrine of the source of the Seine [Côte-d'Or, France]. Musée Archéologique, Dijon.)
Votive relief of kilted deity. Wilsford (Lincolnshire, England). P: Society of Antiquaries of London.
Wooden ex voto from Montbouy (Loiret, France). ca. 1st c. A.D. Musée Historique et Archéologique de l'Orléanais, Orléans. P: Jaques.
Limestone pilgrim figure. Ex voto. ca. 1st c. A.D.
Figure of a man. Wooden ex voto. ca. 1st c. A.D.
Bronze votive of Minerva. Ehl, near Strasbourg (France). 2nd c. A.D. Musée Archéologique, Strasbourg.
Female statue. Wooden ex voto. 1st c. A.D.
Pilgrim figure holding an offering. Ex voto. ca. 1st c A.D.

92 *Left:* Bronze terrier from Coventina's Well. Carrawburgh (Northumberland, England). Museum of Antiquities, Newcastle-upon-Tyne.
Right: Shaft at Holzhausen (Germany). From *Kölner Römer Illustrierte* No. 2, 1975, published by Historische Museen der Stadt Koln.

93 *Top, left to right:*
Sketches of Celtic shafts by Franz Coray after K. Schwartz.
– Shaft from the Vendée (France).
– Other shaft from the Vendée.
– Northern shaft at Holzhausen (Germany).
– Southwestern shaft at Holzhausen.
– Northwestern shaft at Holzhausen.
Bottom center: Face pot from Coventina's Well. Carrawburgh (Northumberland, England). Museum of Antiquities, Newcastle-upon-Tyne.

94 *Top:* Roman Celtic temple. Reconstruction sketch by Franz Coray after Wheeler.
Center: Cromlech of Castlerigg, Keswick (Cumberland, England). P: Edwin Smith.
Bottom: Diagram of Iron Age temple. Heathrow (Middlesex, England). Franz Coray after B. Cunliffe.

95 *Top:* 4th c. Romano-Celtic temple. Lydney Park (Gloucestershire, England). Reconstruction sketch by Franz Coray after Wheeler.
Bottom: Celtic forest place of worship. Reconstruction sketch by Franz Coray.

96 Wheel. Reconstruction of a La Tène original. Schweizerisches Landesmuseum, Zurich.

97 *Top:* Open bronze plaque of horse harness. London (England). 1st c. A.D. British Museum. P: Erich Lessing/Magnum.
Center: Reverse side of mirror. Desborough (Northamptonshire, England). 1st c. A.D. British Museum. Drawing by Franz Coray.
Bottom: Ornamental piece of a horse harness. Enameled. British Museum. P: Erich Lessing/Magnum.

98 Cock shaped brooch. Bronze and coral. Reinheim (Germany). Late 5th–early 4th c. B.C. Landesmuseum für Vor- und Frühgeschichte, Saarbrücken. P: Römisch-Germanisches Zentralmuseum.

99 Reverse side of decorated mirror. Bronze. Old Warden (Bedfordshire, England). Early 1st c. A.D. Bedford Museum, Bedford.

100 *Left:* Back view of dancing female figurine. See page 27.
Right: Front view of dancing female figurine. See page 27.

101 *Top right:* Figurine of a juggler. Bronze. Neuvy-en-Sullias (Loiret, France). 1st c. A.D. Musée Historique et Archéologique de l'Orléanais, Orléans. P: Jaques.
Bottom, left to right:
(All from Neuvy-en-Sullias, Loiret, France. Musée Historique et Archéologique de l'Orléanais, Orléans. P: Jaques.)
Back view of dancing female figurine. Bronze. 1st c. A.D.
Front view of dancing female figurine. See above.
Figurine of dancing man. Bronze. 1st c. A.D.
Figurine of a musician. Bronze. 1st c. A.D.

102 Bronze leaf. La Tène, Marin-Epagnier (Switzerland). 3rd–2nd c. B.C. Musée Cantonal d'Archéologie, Neuchâtel.

103 Detail of a bronze hammered shield with red inlaid glass-panes. Thames, near Battersea (Middlesex, England). Early 1st c. A.D. British Museum.

104 *Top left:* Cup with gold openwork. Schwarzenbach (Rheinland-Pfalz, Germany). Late 5th–early 4th c. B.C. Antikenmuseum, Staatliche Museen, Berlin. P: Isolde Luckert, Bildarchiv Preussischer Kulturbesitz.
Top right: Upper part of bronze flagon. Basse-Yutz (Moselle, France). Early 4th c. B.C. British Museum.
Center: Electrum torc. Snettisham (Norfolk, England). Mid–1st c. B.C. British Museum.
Bottom: Gold band., Fragment. Eigenbilzen (Limbourg, Belgium). Late 5th–early 4th c. B.C. Musée Royaux d'Art et d'Histoire, Brussels.

105 Head of cross-legged sitting god. See page 77.

107 Tarasque. Limestone statue of human heads. Noves (Bouches-du-Rhône, France). 2nd c. B.C. Musée Calvet, Avignon.

109 Great God. Detail of Gundestrup caldron. See page 7.

110–111 Bronze calendar. Coligny (Ain, France). Late 1st c. B.C. Musée de la Civilisation Gallo-Romaine, Lyon.

112 Smith-god Vulcan. Romano-British relief. P: Brian Brake.

113 Two men holding a spoked wheel. Detail of iron and bronze sword scabbard. Hallstatt (Austria). ca. 400 B.C. Prähistorische Abteilung, Naturhistorisches Museum, Vienna.

114 Swordsmith's trademark. Detail of bronze La Tène sword blade. Port (Switzerland). Schweizerisches Landes-

museum, Zurich.

115 *Left:* Salt mining. Reconstruction sketch by Mark Adrian.

Right: Copper mining by fire-setting at Mühlbach-Bischofhofen (Austria). Diagram by Franz Coray after J.G.D. Clark.

116 Wheelwright at work. 17th–c. engraving by J.F. Bénard. P: Publisher's Archives.

117 *Top right:* Cast bronze wheels from ritual wagon from Trebnitz (Germany). Lithography by M.A. Meyn. From *Zeitschrift für Ethnologie*, vol. V, Verlag von Wiegandt, Hempel & Parey, Berlin 1873.

Far left: Genius with wheel, altar and cornucopia. Relief. Carlisle (England). P: Robert Hogg.

Center: Reconstruction of cult-chariot. Dejbjerg (Denmark). Nationalmuseet, Copenhagen.

Bottom right: Barrels. Detail of wine transport relief. See page 38.

118 *Top left:* Funerary cart from Ohnenheim (Alsace, France). Reconstruction sketch.

Below: Bronze hub from cart of Vix (Burgundy, France). ca. 500 B.C. Both from *Monuments et Mémoires*, Fondation Eugène Piot, Tome 48e. Presses Universitaires de France, Paris 1954.

119 Cult chariot. Bronze. Glasinac (Bosnia, Yugoslavia). Hallstatt period, ca. 700–500 B.C. Prähistorische Abteilung, Naturhistorisches Museum, Vienna.

120 *Far left:* Plowing scene after the rock engraving of Bedolina, Val Camonica (Italy). Drawing by R. Lunz.

120–121 Plowstone of late La Tène period. Sketches by Franz Coray after G. Jacobi.

Left to right:

– from Dornburg (Germany)
– from Unterach am Attersee (Austria)
– from Dünsberg (Germany)
– from Unterach am Attersee (Austria)
– from Idrija (Yugoslavia)
– from Mukachëvo (Russia)

121 *Top left:* Scottish crotter using foot plow. P: C. Curwen.

Middle right: Modern plow. P: Gebrüder Ott AG Maschinenfabrik.

122 *Top right:* Plaque in shape of a horse's head. Bronze. Stanwick (Yorkshire, England). 1st c. A.D. British Museum.

Middle row, left to right:

Linchpin from a chariot. Enameled iron and bronze. King's Langley (Hertfordshire, England). Early 1st c. A.D. British Museum.

Detail from a bridle. Bronze. Attymon (Galway, Ireland). National Museum of Ireland, Dublin.

Chariot mount. Bronze. Waldalgesheim (Rheinland-Pfalz, Germany). Late 4th c. B.C. Rheinisches Landesmuseum, Bonn.

Phalera. Bronze on iron. Horovicky (Bohemia, Czechoslovakia). Late 5th–early 4th c. B.C. Nàrodní Muzeum v Praze, Prague.

Detail from a bronze shield. Thames, Wandsworth (England). 3rd–2nd c. B.C. British Museum. P: Erich Lessing/Magnum.

Bottom right: Harness of Hallstatt period. Reconstruction drawing by Franz Coray after D.D.A. Simpson and Stuart Piggott.

123 *Far left:* Silver phalera. Villa Vecchia, Manerbio sul Mella (Italy). 3rd–2nd c. B.C. Museo Civico Romano, Brescia. P: Rapuzzi.

Top right: Reconstructed harness after fragments from La Tène, Marin-Epagnier (Switzerland). Reconstruction by Prof. Dr. E. Vogt. Schweizerisches Landesmuseum, Zurich.

Middle right: Detail of harness mount. Enameled bronze. Santon (Norfolk, England). 1st c. A.D. Cambridge Museum of Archaeology and Ethnology, Cambridge.

Bottom right: Detail of harness plaque. Bronze and enamel. Polden Hill (Somersetshire, England). 1st c. A.D. British Museum.

124 *Top:* Tools from La Tène period. Reconstructions. Museum für Urgeschichte, Asparn a.d. Zaya. P: Erich Lessing/Magnum.

124–125 *Bottom row, left to right:*

(Unless indicated otherwise, all are from Schweizerisches Landesmuseum, Zurich.)

Tweezers. La Tène, Marin-Epagnier (Switzerland). Musée Cantonal d'Archéologie, Neuchâtel.

Shears. La Tène, Marin-Epagnier. Musée Cantonal d'Archéologie, Neuchâtel.

Fishing trident. La Tène, Marin-Epagnier.

Two knives. La Tène, Marin-Epagnier.

Two edge-tools. La Tène, Marin-Epagnier.

File. La Tène, Marin-Epagnier.

Awl for leather manufacturing. La Tène, Marin-Epagnier.

Needle for leather manufacturing. La Tène, Marin-Epagnier.

Cutter for leather manufacturing. La Tène, Marin-Epagnier.

Pick. La Tène, Marin-Epagnier. Musée Cantonal d'Archéologie, Neuchâtel.

Saw. La Tène, Marin-Epagnier.

Edge-tool. La Tène, Marin-Epagnier.

Pointed hook. Port, near Bern.

Pruning-knife. La Tène, Marin-Epagnier.

Pruning-knife. Port, near Bern.

Sickle. Port, near Bern.

Two mattocks. Giubiasco (Switzerland).

125 *Top:* Representations of women, incised on pottery from Sopron (Hungary). 6th c. B.C. Drawing by Franz Coray after a copy in the Museum für Urgeschichte, Asparn a.d. Zaya.

Above center: Snaffle bit. La Tène, Marin-Epagnier (Switzerland). Musée Cantonal d'Archéologie, Neuchâtel.

Above right: Modern snaffle bit. P: Ursula Perret.

126 Rider and two men fighting. Clasp from St. Margarethen (Austria). Hallstatt period. Prähistorische Abteilung, Naturhistorisches Museum, Vienna.

127 *Above:* Head of a Gaul. Denarius. Rome, ca. 48 B.C. Collection ESR, Zurich. P: Leonard von Matt.

Bottom: Praetorian guard. Detail of a relief. Early 2nd c. A.D. Musée du Louvre, Paris. P: Réunion des Musées Nationaux.

128 Horsemen fighting. Belt clasp from Vace (Yugoslavia). Hallstatt period. Prähistorische Abteilung, Naturhistorisches Museum, Vienna.

129 *Top right:* Warrior. Stone stele from Hirschlanden (Germany). Early 5th c. B.C. Wurttembergisches Landesmuseum, Stuttgart.

Below right: Grave mound at Hirschlanden (Germany). P: Landesdenkmalamt Baden-Württemberg.

131 Celt-Iberian warrior. Relief from Osuna (Spain). 1st c. B.C. Museo de Arqueología Nacional, Madrid.

132 *Left:* Warrior. Limestone bust. Grézan (Gard, France). Musée Archéologique, Nîmes.

Right: Etruscan warrior. Bronze. Cagli (Italy). 2nd c. B.C. Museo Nazionale di Villa Giulia, Rome. P: Leonard von Matt.

133 Servian Wall. Rome, section near the Central Station. 6th c. B.C., rebuilt 4th c. B.C. P: Fototeca Unione.

134–135 Etruscan and Celtic warrior fighting. Limestone relief. Detail of tombstone from Bologna (Italy). 5th–4th c. B.C. Museum Bologna. P: Leonard von Matt.

136 *Left:* Head of Alexander. Tetradrachma from Pergamum (Asia Minor). ca. 297–281 B.C. British Museum.

Center: Macedonian shield with head of Pan. Coin of Antigonos Gonatas. Tetradrachma. 277–239. B.C. British Museum.

137 Tholos of the Athena temple. Delphi (Greece). ca. 370–360 B.C. P: Erich Lessing/Magnum.

138 Coin of Eumenes II. of Pergamum. Tetradrachma. 197–159 B.C. British Museum.

139 Fight of the giants. Detail of the great altar of Zeus from Pergamum (Asia Minor). 180–160 B.C. Staatliche Museen, Berlin. P: Bildarchiv Preussischer Kulturbesitz.

140 *Top to bottom:*

Scipio Aemilianus. Bronze bust. Musée du Louvre, Paris. P: Giraudon.

Hannibal. Silver coin from Carthage (Tunisia). 220 B.C. British Museum.

Gaius Marius. Bust. Museo Pio Clementino, Vatican. P: Alinari.

141 Woden. Relief. Detail of tombstone from Hornhausen (Germany). 7th–8th c. A.D. Landesmuseum für Vorgeschichte, Halle. P: Bildarchiv Foto Marburg.

142 Bronze boar. Bata (Hungary). 1st c. B.C. or A.D. Magyar Nemezeti Muzeum, Budapest. P: Erich Lessing/Magnum.

143 *Left:* Lesser sanctuaries inside the fortress at Sarmizegetusa (Romania). P: Roger Wilson.

Right, top to bottom:

Celtic silver coin. Tetradrachma from Dacia (Romania).

Celtic copy of a silver tetradrachma of Philippe II. of Macedonia. Lower Danube.

Celtic billon coin. Tetradrachma from Dacia (Romania). All three from Scnweizerisches Landesmuseum, Zurich.

144–145 Defeat of Roman army. Painting by Charles Gleyre. 19th c. Musée des Beaux-Arts, Lausanne. P: André Held.

146 Julius Caesar. Denarius from Rome (Italy). 44 B.C. Collection ESR, Zurich. P: Leonard von Matt.

147 Julius Casear. Marble statue. Palazzo Senatorio, Rome. P: Leonard von Matt.

148 Migration of the Helvetii. Drawing by Mark Adrian. From Arnold Jaggi, *Helvetier, Römer, Alamannen...*, Verlag Paul Haupt, Bern, 1962.

149 Defensive tactic by Cotta. Engraving from an 18th–c. edition of Caesar's *Commentaries*. P: Radio Times Hulton Picture Library.

150 Statue of Ambiorix. Tongres (Belgium). P: Studio Christiaens.

150–151 Vercingetorix. Coin of the Arverni. Gold stater. Bibiliothèque Nationale, Cabinet des Médailles, Paris.

152 *Far left:* Gallic warrior. Limestone statue. Vachères (Basses-Alpes, France). Late 1st c. B.C. Musée Calvet, Avignon. P: Roger-Viollet.

Center: Outline of siege works of Alesia (France). From Barry Cunliffe, *Rome and Her Empire*, McGraw-Hill Book Co., 1978.

Above right: Coin. See page 127.

153 *Top:* Roman fortification of Caesar's siege at Alesia. Full-scale reconstruction located at the Beaune *Archéodrome* on the Paris-Lyon expressway, France. P: Philippe Katz, Musée Archéologique de Dijon.

Center: Aerial view of Alesia (France). P: Photothèque française.

Bottom: See above (*top*).

154 *Top to bottom:*

Claudius I. Roman emperor. Aureus. Rome (Italy). A.D. 41–42. Collection ESR, Zurich. P: Leonard von Matt.

Hadrian's Wall. England. P: Brian Brake.

Hadrian. Roman emperor. Sesterce. Rome (Italy). A.D. 119–138. Collection ESR, Zurich. P: Leondard von Matt.

155 *Top left:* Defeated Britons. Stone relief on distanceslab from Bridgeness on the Antonine Wall (Scotland). Mid–2nd c. A.D. P: National Museum of Antiquities of Scotland.

Bottom right: Britannia. Sesterce. Rome (Italy) ca. A.D. 143–144. British Museum.

156 *Left to right:*

Armorer. Tombstone relief. Original in Musée de Sens, molding in Musée des Antiquités Nationales, St. Germain-en-Laye. P: G. Franceschi, exclusive Editions Arthaud, Paris.

Domestic scene. Tombstone relief. Neumagen (Rheinland-Pfalz, Germany). 2nd–3rd c. A.D. Rheinisches Landesmuseum; Trier.

Tavern scene. Tombstone relief. See above.

157 *Top left:* Hermes. Welschbillig (Rheinland-Pfalz, Germany). Late 4th c. A.D. Rheinisches Landesmuseum, Trier.

Top right: Boy. Marble bust. Musée Lapidaire, Arles. P: Jean Roubier.

Bottom left: Tribute payment. Relief. Neumagen (Rheinland-Pfalz, Germany). 2nd–3rd c. A.D. Rheinisches Landesmuseum, Trier.

Bottom right: Fuller at work. Tombstone relief. Original in Musée de Sens, molding in Musée des Antiquités Nationales, St. Germain-en-Laye. P: G. Franceschi, exclusive Editions Arthaud, Paris.

158 Celtic armor. Limestone relief on arch of Narbonne (Aude, France). Musée Régional de l'Histoire de l'Homme, Narbonne.

159 Head of Gorgon. From the pediment of the Sulis Minerva temple. Bath (Somerset, England). Roman Baths Museum, Bath.

160 Monastery of Skellig Michael (Kerry, Ireland). P: Ludwig Wüchner.

161 High-cross of Moone (Kildare, Ireland). 8th–9th c. P: P. Belzeaux/Zodiaque.

162 *Top right:* St. Brendan. Detail from 16th–c. engraving. P: Mansell Collection.

Bottom left: Dolmen from Ballina (Mayo, Ireland). P: Wolfgang Fritz.

Bottom right: Saxon shore-forts. From *Notitia Dignitatum*, 1436, after a Carolingian copy of a 5th–c. original. Ms. Canon Misc. 378, fol. 153v. Bodleian Library, Oxford.

163 God with horned headdress. Detail of helmet from Sutton Hoo (England). Early 7th c. British Museum.

164–165 Cliffs of Moher (Clare, Ireland). P: Wolfgang Fritz.

166 *Top:* Bronze face plaque. Cadbury Castle (England). P: Courtesy of Prof. Leslie Alcock.

Bottom left: High-cross near Carew (Wales, England). 9th c. P: Werner Neumeister.

167 *Top right:* Inside of a broch. Glen Beg (Wicklow, Ireland). P: Werner Neumeister.

Bottom left: Anglo-Saxon warriors in combat. From a whalebone casket. ca. A.D. 700. British Museum.

Bottom right: Diagram of hillfort of Tre'r Ceiri (Wales, England). Franz Coray after R.C.A.M.

168–169 Breton cliff castle. Cap Sizun, Finistère (France). P: Erich Lessing/Magnum.

170 *Top right:* Martyrdom of Christian bishop. Relief panel from Muiredach cross. Monasterboice (Louth, Ireland). Early 10th c. P: Wolfgang Fritz.

Above left: Sheela-na-gig. Relief from Errigal (Keeroge, Ireland). Ulster Museum, Belfast.

Bottom left: Spiral design on stone grave covering. New Grange (Meath, Ireland). 3rd mill. B.C. P: Edwin Smith.

Bottom right: Hill of Tara, near Dublin (Meath, Ireland). P: Aerial Photography, University of Cambridge.

171 Enameled bucket handle in shape of squatting figure. Oseberg (Norway). University Museum of National Antiquities, Oslo.

172 *Left:* Carved stone from Boa Island, Lough Erne (Fermanagh, Ireland). ca. 7th c. A.D. P: Edwin Smith.

Right: Priest holding crock and bell. Stone carving. White Island, Lough Erne (Fermanagh, Ireland). 9th c. P: Impartial Reporter.

173 St. Patrick. Grave slab carving. 15th c. Louth (Ireland). P: National Museum of Ireland, Dublin.

174 *Top right:* Monastery of Skellig Michael (Kerry, Ireland). P: Picture Archives of the Archaeological Department of University College Dublin, photo F. Henry.

Bottom left to right:

Warrior. Relief from pillar of Carndonagh (Donegal, Ireland). P: National Monuments, Commissioners for Public Works in Ireland.

Stele of Duvillaun (Mayo, Ireland). P: Picture Archives of the Archaeological Department of University College Dublin, photo F. Henry.

Stele of Kilnasaggart (Armagh, Ireland). P: Edwin Smith.

Stele of Glendalough (Wicklow, Ireland). P: Wolfgang Fritz.

Cross of Clonmacnoise (Offaly, Ireland). P: P. Belzeaux/Zodiaque.

175 *Left to right:*

High-cross of the Scriptures. Clonmacnoise (Offaly, Ireland). 10th c. P: Werner Neumeister.

Cross of Ahenny (Tipperary, Ireland). 8th c. P: P. Belzeaux/Zodiaque.

Flan's Cross. Clonmacnoise (Offaly, Ireland). 9th c. P: Werner Neumeister.

High-cross of Muiredach. Monasterboice (Louth, Ireland). Early 10th c. P: Werner Neumeister.

176 *Top right:* St. Columba's House. Kells (Meath, Ireland). Early 9th c. P: Werner Neumeister.

Left: Beda Venerabilis. From a 12th–c. edition of Beda's *Vita Sancti Cuthberti*. Ms. Add. 39943 fol. 2r. British Library, London.

177 St. Kevin's Kitchen. Glendalough (Wicklow, Ireland). 9th c. P: Wolfgang Fritz.

179 The Book of Leinster. 12th–c. Ms. Trinity College, Dublin.

180 *Left:* Last Supper of Jesus and his disciples. Miniature from a 12th–c. Syriac codex. Ms. Add. 7169 fol. 2r. British Library, London.

Right: Vision of the Holy Grail appearing at Arthur's court. French Ms. 112 fol. 5. 1470. Bibliothèque Nationale, Paris. P: Courtesy of Robert Harding Assoc.

181 *Left to right:*

Illuminations from the Manessa Codex. 14th c. Ms. 848. Universitätsbibliothek, Heidelberg.

– Gottfried von Strassburg. Fol. 364r.
– Minnesinger Wolfram von Eschenbach. Fol. 149b.
– Meister Heinrich Frauenlob. Fol. 399r.

182 Orpheus playing the lute. Marble relief by Luca della Robbia. 1437–1439. Museo dell'Opera del Duomo, Florence. P: SCALA.

183 Medieval troubadours. Drawing by Franz Coray.

184 The Incarnation Initial. The Book of Kells. Fol. 34. Early 9th c. Trinity College, Dublin.. P: Courtesy of the Board of Trinity College, The Green Studio.

185 Portrait of St. John. The Book of Kells. Fol. 291v. See page 184.

186 Typical Irish monastery. Reconstruction sketch by Franz Coray after B. O'Hattrian.

187 *Left:* Tower in the cemetary of St. Brigid's Cathedral. Kildare (Ireland). 10th c. P: Edwin Smith.

Right: Skellig Rock in the Atlantic Ocean (Kerry, Ireland). P. Ludwig Wüchner.

188 *Left to right:*

St. Columban. Engraving. P: Publisher's Archives.

St. Fridolin. Detail on Glarus national banner (Switzerland). 15th c. Freulerpalast, Näfels. P: Foto Schönwetter.

St. Cilian. See page 190.

St. Boniface. From *Liber pontificarum* of Bishop Gundekar. 1071–1072. Gundekarianum, Eichstätt. P: Bildarchiv Foto Marburg.

189 *Left:* St. Columba. Pen-and-ink drawing. From Adamnans' Ms. *Vita Sancti Columbae*. 9th c. Ms. 555 fol. 166. Stiftsbibliothek, St. Gallen.

Right: St. Cuthberg shown as a bishop. Detail of a 12th–c. fresco in the Cathedral of Durham (England).

P: Courtesy of the Dean and Chapter of the Cathedral of Durham.

190 *Left:* St. Cilian. Miniature of the Codex bil. fol. 56. Landesbibliothek, Stuttgart. P: Bildarchiv Foto Marburg.
Right: Benedictine friars. Marginal roundel from the *Book of Hours.* French, ca. 1470. Ms. lat. 1176 fol. 132r. Bibliothèque Nationale, Paris.

191 *Left to right:*
Felling of the Holy Oak. Initial from *Moralia in Job* by Gregory the Great. French, ca. 1111. Ms. 173 fol. 41r. Bibliothèque de Dijon. P: Minirel Création.
Carmelite friars. Roundel from the *Book of Hours.* See page 190.
Franciscan friars. Roundel from the *Book of Hours.* See page 190.

192 *Top left:* St. Christopher. Relief from Jerpoint Abbey (Kilkenny, Ireland). 15th c. P: Arnold Hintze.
Top right: The Resurrection. Terra-cotta by Andrea del Verrocchio. 1465–1475. Museo Nazionale, Florence. P: Alinari-Brogi.
Middle left: Hermit cells on Skellig Michael (Kerry, Ireland). P: Franco Cianetti.

193 *Left:* High-cross of Dysert O'Dea (Clare, Ireland). 12th c. P: Franco Cianetti.
Right, above: Easter chart. From Byrhtferth's *Compendium of Science.* 1011. Bodleian Library, Oxford.
Right, below: Pope Gregory I. Fresco in the Monastery of Sacro Speco, Subiaco (Italy). Early 13th c. P: Leonard von Matt.

194–195 Copper engraving of the Abbey of St. Gall (Switzerland). From *Idea Sacra Congregationis Helveto Benedictinae anno jubilei saecularis...,* 1702. Stiftsarchiv St. Gallen.

195 Simplified plan of the Abbey of St. Gall (Switzerland). Stiftsarchiv St. Gallen.

196 Irish fishermen. P: Anita Volland-Niesz.

197 Calvary from St. Thégonnec (Brittany, France). P: Josef Jeiter.

198–199 Landscape. From *Ireland, A Terrible Beauty,* by Jill and Leon Uris. P: Jill Uris.

200 *Bottom, left to right:*
Breton women. P: Elliott Erwitt/ Magnum.
Breton bagpipers. P: Léo Pélissier.
Breton fishermen. P: Leni Iselin.

200–201 *Top:* Aran Islands (Ireland). P: Anita Volland-Niesz.

201 *Bottom, left to right:*
Irish villagers. P: Anita Volland-Niesz.
Cattle-market at Cahir (Tipperary, Ireland). P: Theo Frey.
Tossing the caber. Scottish Highland game. P: Publisher's Archives.

202 *Top right:* Longest place name. Wales (England). P: Werner Neumeister.
Middle left: Handwriting on a Gallo-Roman pottery vessel. La Granfesenque (France). 1st c. A.D. Musée de Rodez.
Bottom right: Ogham inscribed stone. Ballaqueeney, Isle of Man (Ireland). The Manx Museum and National Trust, Douglas.

203 *Top:* Stone from St. Vigeans, Angus (Scotland, England). P: Scottish Development Department.
Bottom: Page from the White Book of Rhyddech. ca. 1275–1300. National Library of Wales, Cardiff. P: Werner Neumeister.

204 *Top right:* Cattle-raid of Cooley. Illustration by John P. Campbell from a modern English translation of the

Táin bó Cuailnge. From Bernhard Fehr, *Die englische Literatur des 19. und 20. Jahrhunderts,* Berlin, 1923.
Middle, left to right:
James Macpherson (1736–1796). After a picture by Sir Joshua Reynolds. From Fehr, *Die englische Literatur...,* (see above).
René de Chateaubriand (1768–1848). Lithography by Achille Devéria. P: Roger-Viollet.
Lady Augusta Gregory (1852–1932). From Fehr, *Die englische Literatur....,* (see above).
John Millington Synge (1871–1909). After a drawing by Robert Gregory. From Fehr, *Die englische Literatur...,* (see above).
William Butler Yeats (1865–1939). 1932 photograph by Pirie MacDonald. P: The New York Historical Society.

205 *Left to right:*
George Bernard Shaw (1856–1950). P: Camera Press.
Douglas Hyde (1860–1949). P: Radio Times Hulton Picture Library.
Dylan Thomas (1914-1953). P: Camera Press.
James Joyce (1882–1941). 1928 photograph by Berenice Abbott. P: Collection, The Museum of Modern Art, New York. Stephen R. Currier Memorial Fund.
Samuel Beckett (born 1906). P: Camera Press.

206 Sunset at Land's End (Cornwall, England). P: Fritz Prenzel.

207 Crowded deck of the immigrant liner *Patricia* arriving in New York harbor, 1906. P: Edwin Levick, Courtesy of Library of Congress.

208 *Middle left:* Eviction of Irish peasants, 1848. Engraving. P: Mary Evans Picture Library.
Bottom right: Woman with child on the ferry to Ellis Island (USA), ca. 1900. P: Lewis Hine, Courtesy of International Museum of Photography, George Eastman House.

209 *Top:* Migrant wagon train P: Courtesy of the Smithsonian Institution.
Below, left to right:
Alexander Graham Bell (1847–1922). P: Radio Times Hulton Picture Library.
Samuel Milton Jones (1846–1904). P: City of Toledo Public Information Department.
Andrew Carnegie (1835–1919). P: Brown Brothers.
Harry Lauder (1870–1950). P: Courtesy of Library of Congress.
James Michael Curley (1874–1958). P: Courtesy of Library of Congress.
John F. Kennedy (1917–1963). P: Votava.

210 *Top:* Castle of Versaille (France). Engraving. P: Réunion des Musées Nationaux.
Bottom left: Catholic quarter of Derry (Ireland). From *Ireland, A Terrible Beauty,* by Jill and Leon Uris. P: Jill Uris.

211 *Left:* Slag heap at Ffestiniog (Wales, England). P: Werner Neumeister.
Right, top to bottom:
Cornish flag. P: Publisher's Archives.
Irish Harp. Artwork Franz Coray.
Breton demonstration in Rennes (France). P: Agence de Press SYGMA.

212–213 Burial of an IRA volunteer. From *Ireland, A Terrible Beauty,* by Jill and Leon Uris. P: Jill Uris.

215 High-cross of the Scriptures. Clonmacnoise (Offaly, Ireland). 10th c. P: Werner Neumeister.

216–217 Dolmen at Pentre Ifan, near Nevern, Pembroke (Wales, England). P: Werner Neumeister.

INDEX

223

PREFERENTIAL TRADE AGREEMENT POLICIES FOR DEVELOPMENT

PREFERENTIAL
TRADE AGREEMENT
POLICIES FOR
DEVELOPMENT
A HANDBOOK

Jean-Pierre Chauffour and Jean-Christophe Maur, Editors

THE WORLD BANK
Washington, D.C.

ISBN: 978-0-8213-8643-9
eISBN: 978-0-8213-8644-6
DOI: 10.1596/978-0-8213-8643-9

Library of Congress Cataloging-in-Publication Data.

Preferential trade agreement policies for development : a handbook / Jean-Pierre Chauffour, Jean-Christophe Maur, editors.
    p. cm.
    Includes bibliographical references and index.
    ISBN 978-0-8213-8643-9 — ISBN 978-0-8213-8644-6 (electronic)
    1. Developing countries—Commercial policy. 2. Developing countries—Foreign economic relations. 3. Tariff preferences—Developing countries. 4. Free trade—Developing countries. 5. Economic development—Developing countries. I. Chauffour, Jean-Pierre. II. Maur, Jean-Christophe. III. World Bank.
    HF1413.P69 2011
    382'.9091724—dc22

2011014920

Cover illustration: Barrie Maguire, NewsArt.com
Cover design: Drew Fasick

CONTENTS

Boxes

Figures

Tables

FOREWORD

Regional integration is increasingly recognized as a key avenue for promoting economic growth and reducing poverty. Preferential trade agreements (PTAs) have become a central instrument of regional integration in all parts of the world. Beyond market access and the progressive elimination of barriers at the border, PTAs are increasingly being used to address a host of behind-the-border issues, also known as "deep integration" issues, in order to promote cooperation in the areas of investment, trade facilitation, competition policy, and government procurement, as well as wider social issues related to the regulation of the environment and the protection of labor and human rights.

While the multilateral route to trade integration remains the first-best option, the stalling of the Doha Round of negotiations has led to a temporary impasse. Countries—developed and developing alike—have turned to the regional or bilateral route. With close to 300 PTAs notified to the World Trade Organization, regionalism has become a reality on the ground. Many countries are members of multiple PTAs, and the pace of negotiations on new agreements is accelerating. While it has been known for a long time that the traditional preferential market access elements of PTAs are likely to be suboptimal from a welfare perspective, as compared to multilateral or even unilateral liberalization, and that third parties often suffer from these arrangements, policy makers around the world expect these costs to be dwarfed by the deep integration benefits of modern PTAs.

The purpose of this handbook on preferential trade agreement policies for development is to explore the various ways in which policy makers and trade negotiators in the developing world can limit the costs and maximize the benefits of their regional integration efforts. Today's modern PTAs are shaping a broad and comprehensive reform agenda that developing countries can adopt and implement with full ownership and mutual accountability. Preferential market access is no longer the predominant motive. Increasingly important is the use of PTAs to promote competitiveness, upgrade production standards, liberalize services, modernize regulatory regimes, promote labor mobility, protect intellectual property, improve governance, and foster transparency and the rule of law; and, in time, to help build common regional values and norms for a more peaceful and prosperous world.

Open regionalism as a complement to a freer and more transparent, rules-based multilateral trading system has been promoted by the World Bank for many years. Regional integration continues to play a positive transformational role in Europe, North America, East Asia, and Latin America, and the same forces are poised to deepen integration in the Middle East and North Africa, South Asia, and Sub-Saharan Africa. In the course of wide-ranging consultations on the World Bank's upcoming international trade strategy, regional integration and cross-border trade cooperation emerged as one of the four main themes.

I hope that this handbook—the collective effort of some of the world's most renowned trade economists—enhances the understanding of various institutional arrangements and their possible development implications, thereby helping realize the promise of open regionalism and trade for poverty reduction.

Mahmoud Mohieldin
Managing Director
World Bank Group

ACKNOWLEDGMENTS

This handbook is the product of a rich and fruitful collaboration among an outstanding set of distinguished individuals—economists, lawyers, and professional practitioners from around the world on the challenges and opportunities of preferential trade agreements (PTAs) for developing countries. This collaboration was made possible by the support of the Multi-Donor Trust Fund for Trade and Development (MDTF-TD) financed by contributions from the governments of Finland, Norway, Sweden and the United Kingdom.

The editors would like to extend their special thanks to the 26 authors who contributed to this volume for the quality of their research, their professional insights, and their patience in dealing with our multiple requests from the initial conceptual stages, first drafts, lectures, and final assembly of the material. Without their unique knowledge and expertise, the preparation of this handbook would simply not have been possible.

This book is the result of the close cooperation of two World Bank vice-presidencies: Otaviano Canuto, vice-president of the Poverty Reduction and Economic Management (PREM) Network, and Sanjay Pradhan, vice-president of the World Bank Institute (WBI). Strong support from the Development Economics and Africa vice-presidencies must also be acknowledged, in particular through substantive contributions to chapters of this book and insightful comments.

The World Bank project on preferential trade agreements was originally the brain child of Uri Dadush, director of the World Bank International Trade Department, who in the *Global Economic Prospects 2005: Trade, Regionalism, and Development* (Washington, DC: World Bank, 2005) rightfully identified regionalism as an increasingly complex yet potentially productive avenue for promoting trade, economic integration, and development. When Bernard Hoekman took over the direction of the department, he not only provided the overall intellectual guidance for this project but also magnified its reach and helped us assemble the best possible crew of advisers and reviewers. Among them, we are particularly grateful to Richard Baldwin, Clem Boonekamp, Olivier Cattaneo, Jaime de Melo, Antoni Estevadeordal, Carsten Fink, Caroline Freund, Daria Goldstein, Mona Haddad, Gary Hufbauer, Nuno Limão, Patrick Low, Richard Newfarmer, Marcelo Olarreaga, and Sherry Stephenson for their overall guidance and support in various phases of this project.

This endeavor was complemented by a World Bank Institute initiative, under the lead of Roumeen Islam, manager of the Poverty Reduction team, to bring focus and an entirely new program of activities on regional integration. This initiative turned out to be instrumental in the conception of this handbook.

Notwithstanding fierce competing work priorities, Mona Haddad, sector manager (PREM), and Raj Nallari, manager (WBI), provided constant support without which the realization of this large project would not have been feasible.

The editors would also like to acknowledge the contributions of many reviewers of individual chapters: Susan Aaronson, Rolf Adlung, Julia Almeida Salles, Bruce Blonigen, Olivier Cadot, Steve Charnovitz, Meredith Crowley, Jaime de Melo, Daria Goldstein, Lee-Ann Jackson, Steven Jaffee, Michael Jensen, Muthukumara Mani, Toni Matsudaira, Gerard McLinden, Roberta Piermartini, Daniel Sokol, and Jon Strand. Other colleagues at the World Bank have volunteered to share their knowledge and enthusiasm and provided invaluable advice and recommendations throughout the process, including Jean-François Arvis, Aaditya Mattoo, Maurice Schiff, Ravindra Yatawara, and Gianni Zanini.

A special appreciation goes naturally to our experienced team of peer reviewers, who shared their international expertise and helped improve both the scope and focus of the entire manuscript: Ndiame Diop, Antoni Estevadeordal, and Richard Newfarmer.

A book cannot exist without an effective production team. This book benefited from the impeccable professionalism of the World Bank's Office of the Publisher. Stephen McGroarty and Mark Ingebretsen managed the publication process in the smoothest possible way. Nancy Levine did an outstanding job at copyediting the entire volume. She deserves most of the credit for ensuring the readability of the technical parts of the book, and for making it, if not a page turner, an accessible tool for experts. We would also like to thank the dedicated and professional support provided by the administrative team in the International Trade Department and WBI, including Cynthia Abidin-Saurman, Anita Chen, Nene Mane, Rebecca Martin, Anita Nyajur, Vasumathi Rollakanty, and Amelia Yuson. Special thanks also to Charumathi Rama Rao, who provided support on the financial management aspects of the project, and to Stacey Chow, who effectively coordinates the International Trade Department's publication program.

The editors would also like to thank the participants in the conference on the European and Asian approaches to Deep Integration co-hosted by the Centre for the Analysis of Regional Integration at Sussex (CARIS) at Sussex University on September 14–15, 2009; in particular, Michael Gasiorek, Peter Holmes, Jim Rollo, Zhen Khun Wang, and Alan Winters for useful and constructive feedback on early drafts of the chapters.

Our thanks also go to the participants to the 2009–10 WBI courses on PTA and Development in Washington, DC, Dakar, and Arusha, and particularly to those who have contributed to their success: Raymond Boumbouya, Caiphas Chekwoti, Göte Hansson, Peter Kiuluku, Tharcisse Ntilivamunda, and Ina Hoxha Zaloshnja. A particular thought goes to the late Dipo Busari and his family. We owe a lot to the excellence of instructors and speakers who contributed to the courses: Richard Baldwin, Paul Brenton, Nora Dihel, Kimberley Elliott, Simon Evenett, Carsten Fink, Caroline Freund, Larry Hinkle, Bernard Hoekman, Peter Holmes, Gary Hufbauer, Oliver Jammes, Tim Josling, Charles Kunaka, Thea Lee, Javier Lopez, Aadittya Mattoo, Bonard Mawpe, Mary Mbithi, Abdoulaye Ndiaye, Ibrahima Bouna Niang, Tom Prusa, Andrew Roberts, Sebastian Sáez, Pierre Sauvé, Ben Shepherd, Yolanda Strachan, David Tarr, and Gianni Zanini.

These thanks should not associate in any way our collaborators and partners in the production of this book to any remaining errors and shortcomings, which remain solely those of the editors.

ABOUT THE EDITORS AND CONTRIBUTORS

The Editors

Jean-Pierre Chauffour is lead economist in the World Bank's International Trade Department, Poverty Reduction and Economic Management (PREM) network, where he works on regionalism, competitiveness, and trade policy issues. Prior to joining the Bank in 2007, he spent 15 years at the International Monetary Fund (IMF) where he held various positions, including mission chief in the African Department and representative to the World Trade Organization (WTO) and United Nations (UN) in Geneva. Mr. Chauffour has extensive economic policy experience and has worked in many areas of the developing world, most extensively in Africa, the Middle East, and Eastern Europe. He holds master's degrees in economics and in money, banking, and finance from the Panthéon-Sorbonne University in Paris, France. He is the author of *The Power of Freedom: Uniting Human Rights and Development* (Washington, DC: Cato Institute, 2009).

Jean-Christophe Maur is senior economist in the growth and competitiveness practice of the World Bank Institute and a fellow with the Group d'Economie Mondiale at the Institut d'Etudes Politiques de Paris. His current areas of work cover regional integration issues, services liberalization, and contributing to the World Bank's Development Debates platform. Mr. Maur joined the World Bank in 2008 from the U.K. Department of International Development, where he participated in U.K. trade negotiations in trade facilitation and goods market access. He was also tasked to manage the multilateral trade assistance cooperation with the World Bank and contributed to create the multi-donor trust fund for trade and development. His research interests cover regional trade integration and public goods, trade facilitation, standards, and intellectual property rights. He holds a doctorate in economics from Institut d'Etudes Politiques de Paris, and is a graduate of the ESSEC Business School. He was also a visiting fellow at Harvard University.

The Contributors

Susan Ariel Aaronson, associate research professor of international affairs, George Washington University, Washington, DC, and research fellow, World Trade Institute, Bern.

Rohini Acharya, chief of regional trade agreements section, World Trade Organization, Geneva.

Soamiely Andriamananjara, senior economist, Growth and Competitiveness Practice, World Bank Institute, Washington, DC.

Richard Baldwin, professor of international economics, Graduate Institute of International and Development Studies, Geneva.

Paul Brenton, lead economist (Trade and Regional Integration), Poverty Reduction and Economic Management, Africa Region, World Bank, London.

Jo-Ann Crawford, counselor, World Trade Organization, Geneva.

Kamala Dawar, Graduate Institute of International and Development Studies, Geneva.

Kimberly Ann Elliott, senior fellow, Center for Global Development, Washington, DC.

Simon Evenett, professor of international trade and economic development, University of St. Gallen, Switzerland.

Carsten Fink, chief economist, World Intellectual Property Organization, Geneva.

Caroline Freund, chief economist, Middle East and North Africa Region, World Bank, Washington, DC.

Bernard Hoekman, sector director, International Trade Department, World Bank, Washington, DC.

Peter Holmes, Jean Monnet Reader in the Economics of European Integration, University of Sussex, Brighton, U.K.

Gary Hufbauer, Reginald Jones Senior Fellow, Peterson Institute for International Economics, Washington, DC.

Tim Josling, professor emeritus, Food Research Institute, Stanford University, Stanford, California.

Maryla Maliszewska, economist, Development Prospects Group, World Bank, Washington, DC.

Aaditya Mattoo, research manager, Trade and International Integration, World Bank, Washington, DC.

Sébastien Miroudot, trade policy analyst, Organisation for Economic Co-operation and Development (OECD), Paris.

Amelia Porges, principal, Law Offices of Amelia Porges PLLC, Arlington, Virginia.

Thomas Prusa, professor of economics, Rutgers University, Brunswick, New Jersey.

Anuradha R.V., partner, Clarus Law Associates, New Delhi.

Christelle Renard, RTA database administrator, World Trade Organization, Geneva.

Pierre Sauvé, deputy managing director and director of studies, World Trade Institute, University of Bern.

Ben Shepherd, principal, Developing Trade Consultants Ltd., New York City.

Sherry Stephenson, head, institutional relations, Organization of American States, Washington, DC.

Andrew Stoler, executive director, Institute for International Trade, University of Adelaide, Australia.

ABBREVIATIONS

AB	Appellate Body (WTO)
ACP	African, Caribbean, and Pacific (States)
ACWL	Advisory Centre on WTO Law
ADR	alternative dispute resolution
AFAS	ASEAN Framework Agreement on Services
AFTA	ASEAN Free Trade Area
AGOA	African Growth and Opportunity Act (U.S.)
ANZCERTA	Australia–New Zealand Closer Economic Relations Trade Agreement
ANZGPA	Australia and New Zealand Government Procurement Agreement
APEC	Asia-Pacific Economic Cooperation
APTA	Asia-Pacific Trade Agreement
ASEAN	Association of Southeast Asian Nations
ATIGA	ASEAN Trade in Goods Agreement
ATJ	Andean Tribunal of Justice
AUSFTA	Australia–U.S. Free Trade Agreement
BIT	bilateral investment treaty
BLA	bilateral labor agreement
BTA	bilateral trade agreement
CACJ	Central American Court of Justice
CACM	Central American Common Market
CAFTA	Central America Free Trade Agreement
CAFTA–DR	Dominican Republic–CAFTA
CAN	Comunidad Andina (Andean Community)
CAP	Common Agricultural Policy (EU)
CARICOM	Caribbean Community
CARIFORUM	Caribbean Forum of African, Caribbean, and Pacific (ACP) States
CEC	Council for Economic Cooperation (NAFTA); Commission of the European Communities
CEFTA	Central European Free Trade Agreement
CEMAC	Economic and Monetary Community of Central Africa (Communauté Économique et Monétaire de l'Afrique Centrale)
CEPA	Closer Economic Partnership Agreement (China)
CEPAL/ECLAC	Comisión Económica para América Latina/Economic Commission for Latin America and the Caribbean
CEPT	common effective preference tariff
CET	common external tariff
CIF	cost, insurance, and freight
CIS	Commonwealth of Independent States
COMESA	Common Market for Eastern and Southern Africa
CTC	change of tariff classification

CUSFTA	Canada–U.S. Free Trade Agreement
CVD	countervailing duties
DDA	Doha Development Agenda
DSB	Dispute Settlement Body (WTO)
DSM	Dispute Settlement Mechanism (WTO)
DSU	Dispute Settlement Understanding (WTO)
DTT	double-taxation treaty
EAC	East African Community; environmental affairs council
EBA	Everything But Arms (EU)
ECJ	European Court of Justice
ECLAC/CEPAL	Economic Commission for Latin America and the Caribbean/ Comisión Económica para América Latina
ECO	Economic Cooperation Organization
ECOWAS	Economic Community of West African States
EDI	electronic data interchange
EEA	European Economic Area
EEC	European Economic Community (for historical references)
EFTA	European Free Trade Association
EGS	environmental goods and services
EIA	economic integration agreement; environmental impact assessment
ENP	European Neighborhood Policy
EPA	economic partnership agreement
ESM	emergency safeguard mechanism
EU	European Union
FAO	Food and Agriculture Organization (of the United Nations)
FDI	foreign direct investment
FOB	free on board
FTA	free trade agreement; free trade area
FTAA	Free Trade Area of the Americas
FTC	Free Trade Commission (NAFTA)
GAFTA	Greater Arab Free Trade Agreement
GATS	General Agreement on Trade in Services
GATT	General Agreement on Tariffs and Trade
GCC	Gulf Cooperation Council
GDP	gross domestic product
GI	geographical indication
GNP	gross national product
GPA	Government Procurement Agreement (WTO)
GSP	generalized system of preferences
HS	Harmonized System
ICCPR	International Covenant on Civil and Political Rights
ICESCR	International Covenant on Economic, Social and Cultural Rights
ICN	International Competition Network
ICSID	International Centre for the Settlement of Investment Disputes
ICT	information and communication technology
ICTSD	International Center for Trade and Sustainable Development
IMF	International Monetary Fund
IPR	intellectual property right
ISO	International Organization for Standardization
IT	information technology
ITO	International Trade Organization

LAIA/ALADI	Latin American Integration Association/Asociación Latinoamericana de Integración
Mercosur	Southern Cone Common Market (Mercado Común del Sur)
MFA	Multifibre Arrangement
MFN	most favored nation
MLAT	mutual legal assistance treaty
MNC	multinational corporation
MNE	multinational enterprise
MRA	mutual recognition agreement
MTN	multilateral trade negotiation
NAAEC	North American Agreement on Environmental Cooperation (side agreement to NAFTA)
NAALC	North American Agreement on Labor Cooperation (side agreement to NAFTA)
NACEC	North American Commission for Environmental Cooperation
NAFTA	North American Free Trade Agreement
NGO	nongovernmental organization
NTM	nontariff measure
OAS	Organization of American States
OCT	Overseas Countries and Territories
OECD	Organisation for Economic Co-operation and Development
OSBP	one-stop border post
PAFTA	Pan-Arab Free Trade Area
PICTA	Pacific Island Countries Trade Agreement
PRTR	pollutant release and transfer registry
PTA	preferential trade agreement
REIO (clause)	regional economic integration organization
ROO	rule of origin
RoW	Rest of the World
RTA	regional trade agreement; reciprocal preferential agreement
SAARC	South Asian Association for Regional Cooperation
SACU	Southern African Customs Union
SAD	single administrative document
SADC	Southern African Development Community
SAFTA	South Asian Free Trade Area; Singapore–Australia Free Trade Agreement
SAR	special administrative region
SIA	sustainability impact assessment
SME	small and medium-size enterprise
SPARTECA	South Pacific Regional Trade and Economic Co-operation Agreement
SPS	sanitary and phytosanitary
TBT	technical barriers to trade
TDCA	Trade, Development, and Cooperation Agreement (EU–South Africa)
TEC	Treaty establishing the European Community
TFAP	trade facilitation action plan
TIFA	trade and investment framework agreement
TPA	Trade Promotion Act of 2002 (U.S.)
TPR	Tribunal Permanente de Revisión (Mercosur)
TPRM	Trade Policy Review Mechanism (WTO)
TPSEP	Trans-Pacific Strategic Economic Partnership
TRIMS	Trade-Related Investment Measures
TRIPS	Trade-Related Aspects of Intellectual Property Rights
TRQ	tariff-rate quota
TWP	temporary worker program
UDHR	Universal Declaration of Human Rights

UNCITRAL	United Nations Commission on International Trade Law
UNCTAD	United Nations Conference on Trade and Development
USITC	U.S. International Trade Commission
USTR	United States Trade Representative
VER	voluntary export restraint
WAEMU/UEMOA	West African Economic and Monetary Union/Union Économique et Monétaire Ouest-Africaine
WCO	World Customs Organization
WIPO	World Intellectual Property Organization
WTO	World Trade Organization

OVERVIEW

Jean-Pierre Chauffour and Jean-Christophe Maur

Preferential trade agreements (PTAs) have become a cornerstone of the international trade system. The surge in their number and scope is fast reshaping the architecture of the world trading system and the trading environment of developing countries. The integration of these diverse agreements into a multilateral framework that facilitates the expansion of trade is likely to be one of the main challenges facing the world trading system in the coming years.

Hundreds of preferential agreements—free trade agreements and customs unions that involve reciprocal tariff reductions—are currently in force, including close to 300 that had been notified to the World Trade Organization (WTO) as of end-2010. Such a proliferation of regional and bilateral PTAs, together with the sluggishness of Doha Round negotiations toward a new multilateral trade agreement, pose serious challenges to the promotion of a more open, transparent, rules-based multilateral trading system. Although PTAs may promote development, they necessarily discriminate against nonmembers and can therefore lead to trade diversion in a way that hurts both member countries and excluded countries. At the same time, PTAs create larger and more competitive markets and benefit producers and consumers through economies of scale and lower prices, among other effects. Beyond market access motives, PTAs are increasingly used as engines of change in many developing countries, to promote, implement, and lock in reforms in a wide range of policy areas such as investment regimes, competition rules, and government procurement.

In many developing countries, regional integration has become a key means of promoting economic growth and fighting poverty. In fact, no low-income country has managed to grow and sustainably reduce poverty without global or regional trade integration. In the short term, regional trade contributes to growth by expanding markets for goods and services. In the medium to long term, regional integration contributes to growth through improvements in productivity brought about by the transfer of improved technology, learning by doing, and increased competition. Bilateral or regional integration can be an important engine of trade competitiveness, both for small, very poor, landlocked countries and for less regionally integrated or diversified middle-income countries.

At the same time, the multitude of PTAs is becoming cumbersome to manage for many developing countries. As agreements proliferate, countries become members of several different agreements. The average African country, for instance, belongs to four different agreements, and the average Latin America country belongs to seven. This creates what has been referred to as a "spaghetti bowl" of overlapping arrangements, often with different tariff schedules, different exclusions of particular sectors or products, different periods of implementation, different rules of origin, different customs procedures, and so on. The proliferation of bilateral and regional PTAs may undermine progress toward a more open, transparent, and rules-based multilateral trading system.

This Handbook offers an introduction to the complex world of modern PTAs. It follows in the steps of earlier, seminal World Bank publications on the economics and practice of PTAs, notably *New Dimensions in Regional Integration* (De Melo and Panagariya 1996), *Trade Blocs* (World Bank 2000), and *Regional Integration and Development* (Schiff and Winters 2003). Supplementing these earlier publications, this volume aims at taking its audience beyond the traditional market access paradigm to consider more broadly and systematically the numerous regulatory policy dimensions that are contained in modern PTAs. In particular, it offers a framework for understanding a number of behind-the-border policies typically covered in PTAs, including labor mobility, investment, trade facilitation, competition, and government procurement, as well as other societal and more normative policies related to intellectual property, environment, labor rights, and human

1

rights. These latter are increasingly among the policies driven by powerful trading blocs as they strive to influence developing countries and the evolution of the global trading system.

The Handbook is also inspired by the numerous requests received by the World Bank from developing countries or groups of developing countries worldwide for advice on PTAs, including those currently being negotiated, as an aid in understanding the obligations and the possible economic and development implications of various provisions. In light of these requests, and in view of the growing but fragmented knowledge on PTAs, the Handbook seeks to provide a first point of entry into the issues, to inform the policy debate in this area, and to help trade policy makers, researchers, and practitioners, among others, better understand and navigate the world of PTAs. In particular, the book has been written with a view to informing policy makers and trade negotiators in developing countries about the economic and development implications of different approaches to the most important sectoral provisions in PTAs. The ultimate objective of the Handbook is to help developing countries use PTAs proactively, as instruments to bolster their trade competitiveness and leverage the global economy to promote growth and poverty reduction.

The content of the Handbook is largely nontechnical and has been written to be accessible for a large audience of policy makers, general academics, and other stakeholders who are not necessarily economists or legal specialists. It is designed to be used for both graduate and undergraduate teaching in economics, international relations, political science, and law, but it may also be of special interest to informed readers who may not have detailed knowledge of all aspects of PTAs. One of its key objectives is to offer an entry point to specialized areas covered in PTAs. For this reason, each chapter can be read independently, as a guide to the most salient issues arising in PTAs today. Given the rapidly evolving nature of many issues discussed in the Handbook, the volume is to be regarded as a window into the issues covered by PTAs, not as a definitive appraisal.

Although the global evolution of preferentialism betrays the influence of particular countries and integration initiatives, the Handbook purposely chooses not to discuss as stand-alone issues important bilateral or plurilateral initiatives led by large economies such as the European Union (EU) and the United States. Rather, it refers throughout to specific relevant examples. The focus is chiefly to promote understanding, from an analytical perspective, of the links between sectoral issues in deep integration and preferential liberalization and the implica-

tions of these links for development, rather than to assess the individual merits of given PTA initiatives.

The remainder of this overview offers a brief survey of the contents of the Handbook to help readers navigate among the topics and to put the various parts in perspective.

A Road Map of the Handbook

This volume consists of 22 mostly original and unpublished chapters written by renowned international trade academics and experts. They originate from the course on preferential trade agreements designed by the World Bank Institute and from the regional integration work of the World Bank's International Trade Department.

Chapter 1 highlights the main theme and raison d'être of the Handbook: that modern PTAs are essentially preoccupied by a wide range of behind-the-border and deep integration issues that represent considerable opportunities and challenges for low-income countries, beyond the benefits of market access. Chapter 2 maps the landscape of regionalism, chapter 3 presents the economic theory of PTAs, and chapter 4 describes the characteristics of potentially development-friendly PTAs. Chapter 5 examines the specificities of customs unions, one of the most advanced forms of PTA. Chapter 6 discusses the tension between regionalism and multilateralism. Next, chapters 7 through 17 survey current practice in the main policy areas typically covered in PTAs: agriculture policy, rules of origin, product standards, technical barriers, trade remedies, services, labor mobility, and deep integration areas related to investment, trade facilitation, competition policy, and government procurement. Chapters 18 through 21 review a number of more normative issues that are increasingly incorporated into PTAs—intellectual property, environment, labor rights, and human rights. Chapter 22 closes the volume with a discussion of the cross-cutting issue of dispute settlement in PTAs.

From a methodological standpoint, each policy area has been researched with a set of generic questions in mind. How do provisions in a given policy area compare across selected relevant PTAs and (when applicable) with WTO rules? What are the legal and economic implications of different formulations? Are there particular economic development benefits or costs associated with different approaches? To what extent are third parties being discriminated against, and are PTA provisions conducive to open regionalism? How binding are the provisions in the short term and the longer term? What dispute settlement mechanisms would be used in case of disagreements, and how? Are there particular approaches (e.g., hard law versus soft law) that can be advocated or that should be avoided? What are the implications of the provisions for building up institutions and for technical assistance needs? To what extent do the provisions help deliver regional public goods or tackle market failures that are regional in nature?

Beyond Market Access

Beyond market access, PTAs have become potential instruments of choice for many developing countries for promoting wide-ranging reforms and promoting ownership, mutual accountability, and results. In chapter 1, Jean-Pierre Chauffour and Jean-Christophe Maur discuss why, for many low-income countries, PTAs are increasingly the core of a credible development strategy for accelerating economic growth and reducing poverty. Choosing meaningful issues, with the right partner, with adequate technical assistance, and employing a cooperative approach, may bring about substantial progress toward liberalization and can serve as a positive signal or trigger for more challenging areas. To be sure, the maintenance of high border barriers toward third parties entails discrimination and costs, and traditional PTAs clearly represent an inferior solution compared with multilateral liberalization. But market access is no longer the only or even the main item on the agenda of negotiators, especially those of developing countries, since deep integration really involves the contemplation of a domestic reform strategy. In this respect, prioritization of core objectives should be a central consideration of negotiators.

From a theoretical standpoint, the economic paradigm of traditional or shallow PTAs does not necessarily apply to deep and comprehensive PTAs. Concepts such as mercantilist reciprocal liberalization, trade creation and diversion, or a textual approach toward the design of PTAs may still underpin the reasoning of many policy makers, but they are often not valid, or only partially explanatory, for deep integration liberalization. Discrimination is still an issue in deep PTAs, but it may not be the pervasive problem it is in goods-only PTAs, especially if the principle of open access to any regulatory treatment is respected.

More worrying than discrimination, perhaps, in view of the desirable objective of multilateral liberalization, is the inherent complexity created by overlapping and conflicting regulatory regimes in the myriad of PTAs. This concern is already clearly identified, and the call for multilateralizing regionalism already voiced, in the WTO. Complexity requires that some core principles should be followed. The key to making PTAs complementary to a nondiscriminatory multilateral system and supportive of development is to strive for open regionalism in the shape of agreements

characterized by low external barriers to trade, liberalized services markets, nonrestrictive rules of origins for services as well as for goods, a focus on reducing transaction costs at borders, and transparency and the availability of due process.

Another answer to complexity, and one not sufficiently considered, according to the authors, by developing countries, is selectivity. Liberalization is a complex matter, not only from a capacity standpoint, but also politically. Overloading the negotiating agenda (which will later become the implementing agenda) creates a distraction from what may be achievable and where gains may be the most important. Agreements bloated by too many issues may lose significance and fail to achieve much.

Finally, the dynamics of North-South, South-South, and North-North PTAs differ considerably. Asymmetric agreements make cooperation less easy and may provide less scope for transnational public goods and mutual recognition but may open greater prospects for lock-in and for access to imported regulatory regimes, when needed. Market access considerations will dominate for the small partner, whereas the larger partner will seek, beyond that, to diffuse its regulatory norms, including values norms, and to trigger competitive liberalization effects in partner countries.

Landscape

Today's multilateral trading system is characterized by a criss-crossing web of ever more complex PTAs. In chapter 2, Rohini Acharya, Jo-Ann Crawford, Maryla Maliszewska, and Christelle Renard survey the landscape of PTAs and note that recent developments and trends can be summed up in a number of stylized facts:

- PTAs have become ubiquitous, and participation in PTAs is becoming more diverse, spreading to most geographic regions, especially East Asia and the Pacific. North-South preferential partnerships are on the rise, as a number of developing countries elect to forgo unilateral programs such as the generalized system of preferences (GSP) in favor of reciprocal agreements. Cross-regional agreements are also expanding, in an attempt to keep on a level playing field with other countries that are also gaining preferences.
- There is some consolidation of PTA networks as bilateral relationships are replaced by plurilateral PTAs among the same partners. This is the case, for instance, in Latin America. Agreements between regional blocs—for example, between the European Free Trade Association (EFTA) and the Southern African Customs Union (SACU)—are

also on the increase. In Asia, countries long resistant to preferential trade liberalization are catching up, with the emergence of plurilateral PTAs that coexist alongside bilateral PTAs involving the same sets of partners.

- The structural configuration of PTAs is changing, with bilateral PTAs becoming increasingly the norm. Such PTAs can be concluded more rapidly, and they confirm a shift away from using PTAs as a means of forging traditional regional partnerships among geographically proximate countries and toward using them to negotiate strategic, bilateral market access, often among countries in different regions. Indeed, cross-regional PTAs account for two-thirds of those currently under negotiation.
- The regulatory scope of PTAs is rapidly becoming broader and deeper. On issues that fall under the current mandate of the WTO, some countries have elected to take on bilateral commitments that exceed those they have accepted at the multilateral level—that are "WTO+." In addition, some countries are undertaking "WTO-extra" commitments in PTAs on issues that lie outside the current WTO mandate.
- For a number of plurilateral PTAs, intra-PTA imports as a share of total imports have increased, and both intra-PTA exports and total exports have grown. PTA partners in selected plurilateral PTAs seem to trade more internally than would be expected in the absence of a PTA, and the impact on extra-PTA exports and imports is largely positive.

Economics

The theoretical effect of PTAs depends on the efficiency with which economic resources are allocated within and among countries as a result of partial trade liberalization, as opposed to full and multilateral liberalization. Chapter 3, by Richard Baldwin, provides a comprehensive review of the theoretical economic foundation of PTAs. PTAs generate a number of static effects that lead to a one-time reallocation of resources. The first effect is that exporters from a country that is enjoying lower (preferential) tariffs will benefit from the improved market access. A second, opposite, effect is that countries left outside the preferential trade area will lose out as their trade with PTA members is displaced by trade between members. A third, and largely uncertain, static effect is that PTAs may divert trade and enable producers from within the PTA to displace other, more efficient producers that had been able to serve the market when all faced the same tariff regime. Diversion concerns can be addressed through lump-sum transfers

within the PTA to ensure welfare gains for all. The potential negative effect of PTAs on third countries could be addressed by lowering PTA external tariffs to leave the third countries' trade levels unchanged. Even though this is rarely how PTAs operate in practice, they are, in theory, not necessarily bad for world welfare, from a static perspective.

There is more to the economics of PTAs than the mere mechanistic static effects. PTAs can generate complex dynamic gains that operate by changing the rate at which new factors of production, mainly capital, are accumulated. Signers of regional trade deals have long emphasized the importance of the dynamic, or growth, effect of PTAs, which may sensibly alter the economic benefits of preferential liberalization. One of the mainstay justifications for PTAs is the belief that uniting small economies will make regional firms more efficient and more competitive by allowing them access to a bigger market. Indeed, in the presence of imperfect competition and economies of scale, the size of the market matters. Preferential liberalization and defragmentation of national markets lead immediately to more competition because more firms are present in the market. This, in turn, results in industrial restructuring and upgrading because firms need to grow to cover their costs in the more competitive environment, and the least efficient firms exit the market. In the end, the region is left with a more efficient industrial structure, with fewer, bigger, more efficient firms competing more effectively with each other.

A further dynamic effect from preferential liberalization may stem from the location decisions of firms in the PTA—a source of potential distributional impact within the preference zone. Firms may benefit from the existence of positive externalities (or agglomeration forces) associated with being located close to where markets and other producers are. However, there are also negative externalities (or dispersion forces) linked with geographic concentration, such as higher cost for land or labor. The balance of agglomeration and dispersion forces is altered with preferential liberalization, but in a complex way. In theory, lowering trade costs reduces dispersion forces but also diminishes agglomeration forces. The alteration of the balance has implications that are potentially important—but are indeterminate in theory and case-specific—for the location decisions of firms. Members of a PTA are thus likely to benefit unequally from these complex dynamic gains.

North-South PTAs

Issues related to the distributional effects of PTAs among their members are of particular concern in the context of agreements between developed and developing countries. In chapter 4, Bernard Hoekman discusses the key development policy challenges associated with North-South PTAs and offers a number of rules of thumb and approaches for making these PTAs development friendly. North-South PTAs should strive to remove barriers to trade in the developed country for the products that the developing country produces; to lower trade barriers in the developing country partner or partners that raise the prices of goods and services consumed by firms and households; to promote more general liberalization based on the most favored nation (MFN) principle, as this best serves global development prospects; to support the adoption of complementary measures and actions that allow the potential benefits of trade opportunities to be realized; and to create mechanisms through which the private sector can be regularly informed of progress with implementation of the PTA and can provide feedback to authorities.

Achieving these objectives requires that changes be made in the way North-South PTAs are usually designed. If the goal is development, a first overarching objective should be far-reaching liberalization. This can be achieved through a redesign of the approach to PTAs: high-income countries should liberalize in all sectors (not just "substantially all"), on a preferential basis, with liberal and simple rules of origin. Developing-country signatories should reduce their tariffs and apply negotiated trade policy commitments on an MFN (nondiscriminatory) basis.

A second necessary change is to build in significant policy flexibility, as well as stronger accountability mechanisms. The goal should be to use PTAs as a tool for helping developing-country governments pursue priority national regulatory policy objectives, rather than have these objectives dictated by the trade partners. Economic cooperation based on institutions that help identify good practices would be a desirable and risk-free way forward. An important corollary is that governments should be held accountable for performance and outcomes. This requires mechanisms that generate the necessary information—an area in which the private sector has an important role to play.

A third plank of a development-focused approach is expanded development assistance. Such aid should not be limited to the issues that are covered by an agreement, and it should be aimed at improving trade-related regulation and its implementation, as well, including services inputs, both public (government services such as customs and trade facilitation) and private (transport, distribution, finance, etc.). The extension of the PTA agenda to regulatory issues can be beneficial to developing countries, especially if accompanied by financial transfers and technical assistance

that help implement PTA disciplines and enhance their credibility. But deep and comprehensive PTAs between developed and developing countries also bring new risks. The proposed norms will not necessarily benefit the developing countries if the provisions limit policy freedom in inappropriate ways or lead to the allocation of resources to activities that yield few immediate benefits or are complex and costly to implement.

Customs Unions

A customs union (CU) is a trade agreement whereby countries preferentially grant tariff-free market access to imports from each other and agree to apply a common external tariff (CET) to imports from the rest of the world. It is one of the most advanced forms of PTA and generally requires considerable coordination among members. In chapter 5, Soamiely Andriamananjara observes that CUs have recently become less popular than simple free trade agreements (FTAs). This trend reflects the nature of the current wave of regionalism, which is characterized by smaller cross-regional deals, flexibility, selectivity, and, most important, speed. Recent FTAs tend to be more pragmatic than their precursors and to focus more on strategic commercial market access and less on geographic considerations or political ambitions. By contrast, CUs are usually set up by a relatively large number of geographically contiguous countries and involve a certain loss of policy-making autonomy.

When a country joins a CU, it agrees to relinquish some of its national sovereignty over the formulation and implementation of trade policy. The implication is that a CU member considers the loss of some autonomy to be more than offset by the economic benefits of securing access to a larger and more harmonized regional market and of enhancing the depth and effectiveness of the ongoing regional integration process. Some regional groupings consider the establishment of a CU a prerequisite or a necessary step toward the future establishment of some deeper form of economic integration, such as a common market. Other groups regard a CU as a useful way of pooling countries' market power, coordinating their trade policies, and combining their negotiating powers to deal advantageously with the rest of the world.

The establishment of a CU involves reaching consensus on three other important issues not relevant to PTAs. First, members need to agree on a CET. The economic impact of the CU will be closely related to the degree of discrimination it entails, which depends on the selected tariff level. A higher CET entails more trade diversion and greater net welfare loss (although different economic agents will be affected differently). Whether CUs lead to higher external tariffs remains an open question. A number of arguments seem to suggest that CUs engender more protectionist pressures than PTAs, but this is an empirical question to which the existing literature has not been able to provide an unequivocal answer.

Second, members need to decide where and how to collect CET duties: at the initial port of entry into the CU, or at the final import destination. Collecting import duties at the first port of entry could facilitate freer movement of goods within the CU and minimize intra-CU border controls, but it requires the appropriate institutional capacity to administer the revenues and, most important, a high level of trust among members. Most existing CUs allocate revenues according to the final destination principle, which requires sophisticated administrative measures for identifying the end destination of each shipment entering the union.

Third, members have to decide which mechanism to use for managing CET revenues. In some cases, the CU allocates (a fraction of) these revenues to a joint fund to finance regional development initiatives. Pooling customs revenues presupposes a high level of coordinating capacity and a certain degree of trust among members and is more likely to be sustainable when tariff revenues do not constitute an important part of government revenue for individual members. In other cases, customs revenues are treated as the property of individual members and are allocated either according to the final destination or in line with an agreed sharing formula.

The collection and allocation of customs revenues in a CU setting is clearly an area in which harmonization of border management (e.g., customs procedures), cooperation, and modernization, along with capacity building, could be critical.

PTAs and Multilateral Liberalization

In chapter 6, Richard Baldwin and Caroline Freund discuss the relative merits of preferential liberalization and the circumstances under which PTAs are more likely to serve as building blocks for greater multilateral trade liberalization than to pose stumbling blocks. On the positive side, PTAs have offered a popular way for countries to liberalize their trade policies and gain market access. Countries are often unwilling to liberalize on their own because they count on tariffs to raise tax revenues and, at times, protect domestic sectors. Reciprocal liberalization in the context of PTAs makes liberalization easier because the increased market access may counter the political-economy forces opposing liberalization. PTAs do, however, generate trade diversion and trade preference rents and these distortions alter the

trading partners' incentives for further liberalization. A key question about the proliferation of PTAs, beyond their direct welfare impact for the countries signing them, therefore relates to their systemic effects on the world trading system. Are PTAs—leaving aside the objective of mutually beneficial multilateral reduction of trade barriers—a force for good or for bad? This question raises the more general question of the interaction between PTAs and the multilateral trade system. Do PTAs influence multilateral liberalization, or is it the other way round? Or do they influence each other?

A traditional view among economists is that PTAs form a stumbling block in the path to freer multilateral trade. First, market access preferences granted in PTAs create incentives to resist multilateral liberalization, which would erode these preferences by reducing external MFN tariffs. Second, market access preferences are used as bargaining chips by preference-granting nations against nontrade concessions. Third, countries tend to choose to pursue liberalization with trade partners in areas that are less likely to affect politically sensitive sectors, while still offering liberalization gains. Moving toward further liberalization may mean undertaking much more politically difficult liberalization that will affect the sensitive sectors.

At the other end of the spectrum of economic analysis are theories supporting the idea that PTAs could be building blocks for overall freer trade. Liberalization would beget liberalization in reciprocal negotiations, generating a virtuous circle, as exporters are transformed from bystanders in the tariff debate to antiprotectionists motivated by the prospect of market access. The initial reciprocal tariff cuts in PTAs may start a liberalization juggernaut rolling.

So far, there is little systematic empirical evidence that regionalism is overwhelmingly bad for the multilateral trade system, as some had feared. Analyses tend to show complementarity between PTA and multilateral tariff liberalization. Most empirical studies find trade creation effects in PTAs, with trade diversion as the exception. According to the natural trading partner hypothesis, countries tend to engage in PTAs with only those partners that can offer positive welfare gains. Among the selection criteria for such natural partners are geography and lower trade costs, large economic size, and economic complementarities (e.g., factor endowments and difference in economics size). The complementarity effect is stronger in sectors in which trade bloc partners are more important suppliers, which is precisely where trade discrimination would be more disrupting.

There is, however, also evidence of PTAs' acting as stumbling blocks. The United States and the European Union liberalized less during the Uruguay Round of multilateral trade negotiations in sectors in which preferences were granted.

Agriculture

Turning to the key chapters of PTAs, a first consideration is often to decide whether to include agriculture as part of the negotiations and PTA commitments. In chapter 7, Tim Josling discusses the challenges and opportunities associated with the incorporation of agriculture into PTAs. The challenges have to do with the additional competition faced by domestic agriculture from regional partners that may be lower-cost producers or that, in the case of bilateral agreements with developed countries, may have significantly better marketing and trade infrastructure. The policy dilemma is whether to subject domestic agriculture to further competition in the hope that the farm sector will respond by undertaking structural and technological change and becoming competitive regionally and, eventually, globally. Given adequate safeguards—in particular, to avoid import surges—the better strategy would be to attempt to develop a competitive agricultural sector, but the political economy does not always allow it.

As with other PTA chapters, the opportunities from incorporating agriculture in PTAs go far beyond the gains from trade creation. They include collective action on research, market development, and health and safety regulations, as well as cooperation on trade policy and on approaches to development agencies and donors. Where these arrangements have worked well, regional markets have been established, health and safety regulations have been harmonized or made more compatible, and trade has developed through investment, as firms have realized the potential of closer market integration. By contrast, when PTAs opt to exclude some or all agricultural sectors from the pressures and opportunities that come with freer regional trade, agricultural markets often remain confined within national borders or focused on traditional trade exchanges with overseas partners.

Overall, the dearth of empirical studies on economic integration in agricultural markets makes for a lack of clear guidance for policy makers. To help close that gap, the chapter provides a brief review of experience with agricultural provisions in selected PTAs. The issues common to all PTAs, as they contemplate the agricultural component of the agreement, include the way in which tariffs are cut, the use of tariff-rate quotas to open up markets on a progressive basis, the employment of safeguards to help domestic sectors cope with import surges, the treatment of subsidies (both domestic and on exports), and the provision of public goods. In the case of regional PTAs, the treatment of these issues will determine the extent to which the expansion of intrabloc markets can lead to scale economies and the rationalization of production and investment. In the case of bilateral PTAs among countries that are not in the same region, there is less potential for economies of scale and productivity gains, but PTAs could still offer a way to secure market access for agricultural exports and to benefit from (at least temporary) advantages over excluded competitors.

Rules of Origin

At the heart of the preferential regime of PTAs are the rules of origin (ROOs) that determine the eligibility of products to receive preferential access. In chapter 8, Paul Brenton reviews the rationale and practice of rules of origin in PTAs. The justification for preferential rules of origin is to prevent trade deflection or simple transshipment, whereby products from nonparticipating countries are redirected through a free-trade partner to avoid the payment of customs duties. These rules, however, can be manipulated to achieve other objectives, such as protecting domestic producers of intermediate goods. Restrictive rules of order that go beyond what is necessary to prevent trade deflection could raise the economic costs of supplying the markets of preferential partners and the administrative costs of proving conformity with the rules. These costs will constrain market access relative to what is promised on paper in the trade agreement. The rules of origin are therefore a key element determining the magnitude and distribution of the economic benefits that accrue from PTAs.

There is no simple and standard set of rules of order that can be identified as performing the task of preventing trade deflection. Three main criteria are used to establish whether a product imported from a partner that contains inputs from other countries has undergone sufficient processing or a substantial transformation: (a) a change of tariff classification; (b) a minimum amount of domestic value added; or (c) use of a specific manufacturing process. No one method is dominant; each has its advantages and disadvantages, and different rules of origin can lead to different determinations of origin. Other features of the rules of origin that can influence whether origin is conferred on a product include cumulation, which allows producers to import materials from a specific country or regional group of countries without undermining the origin of the product; tolerance, or de minimis, rules, which allow a certain percentage of nonoriginating materials to be used without affecting the origin of the final product; and the absorption principle, which provides that parts or materials that have acquired originating status by satisfying the relevant rules of origin for the particular product can be treated as being of domestic origin in any further processing and transformation.

Restrictive rules of origin constrain international specialization and discriminate against small, low-income countries where the possibilities for local sourcing are limited. Simple, consistent, and predictable rules of origin are more likely to foster the growth of trade and development. Rules of origin that vary across products and agreements add considerably to the complexity and costs of participating in and administering trade agreements. The burden of such costs is particularly heavy for small and medium-size firms and for firms in low-income countries. Complex systems of rules of origin add to the burdens of customs services and may compromise progress on trade facilitation. Specification of generally applicable rules of origin, with a limited number of clearly defined and justified exceptions, is appropriate if the objective is to stimulate integration and to minimize the burdens on firms and customs services in complying with and administering the rules. Producers should be given flexibility to meet origin rules by, for example, specifying in the rules that the products may satisfy either a change of tariff requirement or a value added criterion.

Preferences granted by member countries of the Organisation for Economic Co-operation and Development (OECD) would be more effective in stimulating exports from developing countries if they were governed by less-restrictive rules of origin; ideally, specific rules of origin should be designed, and producers in developing countries should be able to gain preferential access to all developed-country markets if their product satisfies a single origin test. Restrictive rules of origin should not be used as tools for achieving economic development objectives—they are likely to be counterproductive. The potential benefits of trade agreements among developing countries can be substantially undermined if those agreements contain restrictive rules of origin.

Trade Remedies

The diversity of PTA types, ranging from goods-only agreements to customs unions, means that the political and economic demands for trade remedy provisions vary greatly across PTAs. In chapter 9, Thomas Prusa shows that the proliferation and diversity of PTAs have produced a complicated pattern in the use and inclusion of trade remedy provisions across PTAs that defies simple characterization. Whereas some PTAs contain long discussions of trade remedy rules, others do not even mention trade remedies.

Furthermore, provisions differ significantly for the same country across different PTAs, and countries do not commonly incorporate the same trade remedy provisions in all their PTAs. In some cases, trade remedy provisions in PTAs make protection easier, but in most cases, the additional rules in PTAs tend to make protection harder to impose. Any country considering entering into a PTA should therefore consider carefully what provisions potential partners have included in prior agreements.

Another finding of the chapter is that PTAs are less likely to alter existing countervailing duty provisions than they are either antidumping or global safeguard rules. This is partly because few PTAs have created common policies on subsidies and state aid. Without such rules, and given the global nature of subsidy distortions, there appears to be little motivation for PTAs to limit the application of countervailing duties against members. PTA provisions regarding antidumping, countervailing duties, and global safeguards generally make protection more difficult to impose than do the existing WTO rules; that is, these provisions are WTO+. They work against protection through a combination of additional specific rules that relax the threshold and duration of application of measures and through the creation of institutions that help to defuse disputes. By contrast, PTA provisions on bilateral safeguard actions (e.g., transition safeguards and special industry safeguards) offer new avenues for PTA members to restrict intra-PTA trade.

Overall, the evidence shows that PTAs reduce the incidence of intra-PTA antidumping and safeguard disputes. At the same time, there appears to be an increase in actions against non-PTA members. So, although the liberalization effects of PTA tend to be reinforced by global safeguard and antidumping rules in PTAs, the trade diversion effects can also potentially be reinforced. In addition to the discrimination introduced by preferential tariffs, PTAs can lead to increased discrimination against nonmembers through more frequent trade remedy actions against them. Overall, the chapter calls for vigilance about the impact of trade remedy provisions in PTAs. The sheer number of PTAs with trade remedy rules is heightening the prominence of the issue.

Standards

Provisions relating to the management of standards for protection of human, animal, or plant life or health are now a common feature of most PTAs. In chapter 10, Jean-Christophe Maur and Ben Shepherd discuss the unique role that PTAs can play in reducing standards barriers to trade through the recognition of equivalence of rules and procedures. They observe that standards provisions in PTAs are likely to have welfare-enhancing effects on participating members. Although standards are classified as one of many nontariff barriers—the relative importance of which is growing with the decline in tariff duties—an important economic distinction is that standards serve a different policy objective than simple discrimination against foreign goods. Standards represent a quasi-regulatory means of pursuing important public policy objectives such as environmental protection, consumer safety, food quality, and compatibility between different types of apparatus. The policy objective should therefore not be to eliminate standards but to make them more efficient and cost effective.

Harmonization to international standards is an effective way of reducing the duplication of costs of complying with different sets of standards. Standards harmonization may also facilitate market access and enable countries with no or inefficient standard policies to put better practices in place. But it does mean compromising governments' ability to set national standards that may better fit the needs of local industries and consumers.

There are, broadly, two models for dealing with standards measures in PTAs. Where the European Union is involved, the agreement often expects the EU partner country to harmonize its national standards and conformity assessment procedures with those of the EU. PTAs in the Asia-Pacific region and those in which the United States is a partner typically address problems resulting from different national standards and conformity procedures through a preference for international standards or the use of mutual recognition mechanisms. Both approaches can be successful in reducing the negative impact of different standards and conformity assessment procedures, but there is a risk that they can introduce into global markets de facto discrimination, particularly against developing countries, because achieving conformity in technical standards requires capacity and resources.

Standards indeed have the potential to discriminate against nonmember countries when mutual recognition agreements are not open to third countries or when harmonization is not carried out on the basis of internationally agreed standards. As in the case of contingent protection measures and restrictive rules of origin, standards may end up raising external barriers against countries outside the PTA, thus eroding some of the benefits of multilateral liberalization. Good practices regarding standards in PTAs usually promote institutional arrangements to supervise the effective implementation of standards provisions. Important objectives of such arrangements are, most frequently, transparency, the diffusion of expertise,

and consultations on legal and administrative matters through regular dialogue.

Standards, in Practice

Andrew Stoler, in chapter 11, discusses specific best-practice provisions in PTAs concerning the treatment of technical barriers to trade (TBTs) and sanitary and phytosanitary (SPS) measures. He recommends that the parties to a PTA aim at using international standards whenever possible because doing so guarantees a high level of protection in the integrated market and makes it easier for third parties to trade into that market. If the parties to the PTA decide to pursue harmonization of their standards and conformity assessment procedures, they should accept that it might be necessary to limit harmonization to essential health and safety standards and to rely on mutual recognition and equivalence techniques for other areas. Where one partner is less developed than the other, the PTA will have to include technical assistance and capacity-building measures to assist the institutions and exporters of the developing-country partner in adjusting to harmonization.

If technical regulations and conformity assessment procedures cannot be harmonized, it is important for the purposes of the PTA that the parties work to eliminate requirements for duplicate or multiple measures or tests for the same product. This is particularly important for small and medium-size enterprises that cannot afford the high cost of meeting differing regulations and testing regimes. Mutual recognition agreements (MRAs) are important tools in this respect.

Transparency is important for business and consumers in this area of international trade. PTA partners should consider incorporating WTO+ notification obligations and a commitment not to implement any technical regulation or SPS measure until it has been published and comments by the PTA partner have been taken into account.

It is recommended that the PTA be drafted as a "living agreement" with a commitment to a work plan or prioritization of problem resolution through harmonization, mutual recognition, equivalence measures, and other policy tools that enable elimination or mitigation of trade-related problems over time. PTA provisions on TBTs and SPS measures should be legally binding, through a judicious combination of "soft" and "hard" law. The provisions should provide a pathway that permits integration to evolve and deepen over time by allowing the gradual resolution of TBT and SPS issues in the bilateral relationship. Such a pathway should be considered an integral part of any PTA that aims to deal effectively with standards, certification, and conformity assessment problems. Eventual recourse to the PTA dispute settlement provisions should be an option, along with recourse to the WTO Dispute Settlement Understanding (DSU).

Finally, PTA parties should agree to an overall commitment always to apply technical regulations and conformity assessment procedures on a national treatment basis and to allow third parties whose technical regulations and conformity assessment procedures can be demonstrated as being equivalent to the level agreed to by the PTA partners to benefit from the arrangements between the partners. A commitment to open regionalism would help ensure that the PTAs support the multilateral system.

Services

In recent years, increasing numbers of PTAs have sought to include provisions on liberalizing cross-border trade in services, investments in goods- and services-producing activities, and the temporary movement of business people. In chapter 12, Aaditya Mattoo and Pierre Sauvé show that liberalization of trade in preferential services differs fundamentally from liberalization of trade in goods in that the effect of many restrictive measures in services trade (given their regulatory nature) is to increase the costs of operation faced by foreign providers without necessarily generating equivalent domestic rents. There is therefore little or no cost to granting preferential access for services trade because there is little or no revenue to lose. In such circumstances, preferential liberalization will necessarily be welfare enhancing, but countries outside the preferential arrangement may lose.

PTAs covering services tend to follow two broad approaches with respect to liberalization of services trade and investment. Some PTAs tend to replicate the use, found in the General Agreement on Trade in Services (GATS), of a positive-list or hybrid approach to market opening whereby agreements list sectors, subsectos, and modes of supply in which governments are willing to make binding liberalization commitments; others pursue a negative-list approach, in which exceptions to liberalization are listed. More than half of all the PTAs concluded to date that feature services provisions use a negative-list approach. Such agreements are more prevalent in the Western Hemisphere, reflecting the influence of the North American Free Trade Agreement (NAFTA), and in agreements conducted along North-South lines (with the exception of the EU and EFTA agreements). Although both approaches can in theory generate broadly equivalent outcomes with respect to liberalization, as a practical matter, a negative-list approach can be more effective in locking in the regulatory status quo. In addition, the process of "getting there" tends to differ; a number of good governance–enhancing features are associated with negative

listing, most notably in the area of transparency. Studies devoted to the practice of preferential market opening suggest that North-South PTAs based on a negative-list approach tend to achieve the deepest, WTO+ liberalization.

The chapter also shows that gains from PTAs are likely to be significant in services areas where there is scope for reaping large economies of scale. In principle, these gains can also be realized through MFN liberalization, but in practice the full integration of markets may require a deeper convergence of regulatory regimes. Regulatory cooperation may be more desirable, and probably more feasible, within a subset of countries than if pursued on a global scale. Regional or international harmonization or standardization can be an important and cost-effective way of improving national standards. Yet the best partners for regulatory cooperation are likely to be those with the soundest regulatory frameworks, and they may not always be found within regional compacts.

There are gains from regulatory cooperation, but also costs. The former will dominate where national regulation can be improved and where regulatory convergence or harmonization can be carried out, taking into account local circumstances. The costs are likely to be smallest when foreign regulatory preferences are similar and regulatory institutions are broadly compatible.

Unless there are liberal rules of origin for investment that confer the full benefits of an integration scheme on third-country investors, the establishment of preferences may result in entry by inferior suppliers. Because the most efficient suppliers may also generate the greatest positive externalities, the downside risks of preferential liberalization may be greater, especially in crucial infrastructural services. This is particularly the case in services sectors with high location-specific sunk costs that need to be close to consumers. Preferential liberalization may then exert more durable effects on the nature of competition than in the case of trade in goods. For instance, concluding an agreement that allows second-best providers to obtain a first-mover advantage may imply that a country could be stuck with such providers, even if it subsequently liberalizes on an MFN basis.

Finally, PTAs have generally made little progress in tackling the interface between domestic regulation and trade in services (e.g., subsidies). Despite the greater initial similarities in approaches to regulation and greater cross-border contact between regulators that geographic proximity can afford, progress in the area of domestic regulation has been slow and generally disappointing, even at the PTA level.

Labor Mobility

The temporary movement of natural persons is a key mode of service delivery across borders. In chapter 13, Sherry

Stephenson and Gary Hufbauer show that, notwithstanding the strong sensitivity that surrounds the movement of people and the confusion about the fine line between temporary movement of workers and permanent migration, PTAs are increasingly being used as vehicles for dealing with labor mobility issues. Several PTAs between developed and developing countries have included new categories of labor, such as technicians, nurses, and health care workers, in their trade agreements or have offered an expanded number of categories for service suppliers, combined with expanded quotas. Other PTAs have eliminated the quotas altogether for certain categories of services suppliers (usually, professionals). To date, nearly all PTAs that cover services focus either exclusively or primarily on professional services suppliers.

Members of South-South regional integration groupings of geographically contiguous countries in Africa, Asia, and Latin America and the Caribbean often contemplate completely liberalized labor markets as part of their agreements. Progress is slowly being made toward the implementation of these commitments for all categories of workers, both for temporary movement and for permanent settlement. The chapter confirms the intuition that the countries that have gone furthest in opening their markets to temporary labor movement under PTAs are the ones that are experiencing a relative shortage of labor supply at home (e.g., Canada, Japan, and New Zealand). Conversely, the countries that have been most reluctant to open their market to temporary labor movement under PTAs are those that are experiencing a strong wave of migration pressure—notably, from Mexico, in the case of the United States, and from new EU members in Eastern Europe, for the EU.

Looking forward, the chapter observes that developed countries should proactively search for labor market niches in which additional temporary workers can become valued members of the workforce and the community. In that respect, there has been some progress within a new generation of bilateral labor agreements (BLAs) and temporary worker programs (TWPs). In the case of workers with lower skill levels, the best vehicle for promoting greater labor mobility may not be a formal PTA but, rather, the more flexible instrument of a TWP that specifies the length of stay for a certain number of workers in a specific economic activity. TWPs have the advantage that both governments are better able to enforce the clauses, and they can be more easily adapted to the cycle of economic fluctuations. Canvassing the extent of TWPs in the world economy today is challenging, as no one organization is responsible for maintaining an inventory of these agreements, but their numbers appear to be increasing.

Investment

As trade and investment become more and more intertwined in the context of international supply chains and firms' strategies of vertical specialization, countries are increasingly incorporating investment provisions into PTAs instead of negotiating bilateral investment treaties (BITs). In chapter 14, Sébastien Miroudot presents the salient features of investment provisions in PTAs. By combining trade liberalization provisions with investment liberalization and protection, PTAs emphasize the complementary relationship between trade and foreign direct investment (FDI). In contrast to BITs, investment provisions in PTAs ensure that disciplines are not limited to investment in the postestablishment phase but also deal with the preestablishment stage (i.e., market access, national treatment, and most favored treatment), thus providing economic incentives for investors, in the form of market access, in addition to the legal incentives (the protection of investment, once established). Given liberal rules of origin, investment provisions in PTAs do not seem to introduce severe distortions among investors; and developing countries have usually been able to maintain some of the restrictions needed for legitimate policy considerations.

Investment disciplines hold an important place in PTAs that they have not found in the multilateral negotiations. This is one of the four "Singapore issues" that were supposed to become the new additions to the WTO in the Doha negotiations. (The other three—trade facilitation, government procurement, and competition policy—are discussed in the following chapters). There are two main models of investment provisions in PTAs, one inspired by NAFTA, which places investment in goods and services industries in the same chapter, and one that follows the GATS model for part of the provisions on investment in services. Despite important differences, these two types of agreement offer the same degree of protection for investment and are equally liberalizing of investment, even if, empirically, NAFTA-inspired agreements are more ambitious in their scope and sectoral coverage. For developing countries, North-South PTAs with substantive investment provisions are found to positively affect FDI flows. They can also offer an opportunity to address concerns about dispute settlement for countries that are not ready to face commercial arbitration.

Trade Facilitation

Trade facilitation is a relatively recent domain of international trade cooperation, and countries are still very much in the process of learning how to design the best approach.

In chapter 15, Jean-Christophe Maur notes that the current approaches to trade facilitation in PTAs are mainly extensions of customs cooperation provisions, with some variations depending on the signatory countries. Trade facilitation provisions are also closely related to the proposals in the Doha Round of trade negotiations concerning trade facilitation involving developed countries. Good practice in this area seems to be to strive for living agreements, whereby institutional arrangements are set up for promoting exchange and joint initiatives with a view to possibly amending agreements through new provisions on trade facilitation. In addition, PTA signatories should extend their trade facilitation commitments beyond the sole remit of customs administration to include other border agencies (largely ignored in existing agreements) and services and standards, which are often treated separately. Indeed, recent PTAs that incorporate more advanced trade facilitation provisions demonstrate the increased interest in using PTAs to reduce transaction costs.

The trade facilitation agenda in PTAs remains largely driven by the most developed partners, which tend to set the agenda and to propose terms of agreement (e.g., ambitious reforms such as risk management) that may not necessarily reflect the needs and capacity of their less-developed partners. Reflecting this relative lack of consideration, there are few examples of special and differential treatment by trading partners, or of clear commitments on provision of technical assistance.

More generally, PTAs seem to fail to capitalize on opportunities to provide value added: that is, domains of potential regional cooperation are not always given priority. For instance, PTAs could have a much more active role in implementation through mutual recognition and assistance, the eventual sharing of resources, and joint efforts to improve the trade supply chain. Trade facilitation provisions that focus on reform on the ground, implementation, and monitoring of measurable objectives, as in Asia-Pacific Economic Cooperation (APEC), seem to deliver more effective and successful reforms. Such agreements tend to be pragmatic, flexible, and country specific and are generally well suited to the type of reforms required in the context of regional trade facilitation.

Competition Policy

The lack of a multilateral competition framework has coincided with a surge in PTAs that contain competition provisions intended to address market failures that national competition laws cannot remedy. In chapter 16, Kamala Dawar and Peter Holmes discuss how well-designed regional competition arrangements can help developing

countries deal with competition problems, including those emanating from international trade, such as import distribution monopolies and cartels, overseas export cartels, and the abuses of dominant firms from abroad. They observe that international trade presents complex competition policy issues because an abuse of market power can occur unevenly across several markets and jurisdictions, with consequences for the jurisdictional limits of a national authority.

Effectively enforced regional competition provisions may serve to lock in reforms that are politically difficult to sustain because of the influence of strong domestic lobbying groups that do not immediately benefit from competition law. PTAs can also pioneer or test-run provisions and so facilitate their negotiation at a multilateral level at a later date. Finally, regional competition regimes offer a demonstration effect of the positive gains to be had from effective national cooperation to underpin and improve the market liberalization process.

In the case of North-South PTAs, greater development benefits can be reaped if the more developed party offers appropriate technical assistance and capacity building. For developing countries with little experience in implementing competition rules, the PTA provisions should initially be limited to the exchange of information, technical assistance, and capacity-building support, as it may be more beneficial at first to focus on establishing a culture that values competition at the national or subregional level. Subsequent negotiations could expand the agreement. The use of soft law could be beneficial if governments are uncertain of the underlying technical issues and the consequences of the provisions. Other nonjudicial mechanisms, such as voluntary peer review and consultations, may also be appropriate.

The economic and human resources necessary to implement even a minimal regional decentralized competition regime arrangement are significant for both developed and developing countries. Nevertheless, the emerging evidence shows that the economic and welfare costs associated with cross-border anticompetitive practices are higher. Short-term political costs should be weighed against the understanding that the long-term and sustainable benefits of a strongly enforced regional competition regime will almost always outweigh its costs.

Decentralized agreements that only require the existence of a local competition law and authority to apply the law, such as NAFTA, are not as economically demanding as a regime that establishes a fully centralized law with a supporting regional authority, such as the EU or the Common Market for Eastern and Southern Africa (COMESA). Competition provisions in customs union agreements are, in general, more specific and demand higher commitments. The economic burdens of implementation can be offset if the parties are able to exchange information effectively and avoid duplications and conflicting decisions. For instance, the competition regime in the Caribbean Community (CARICOM) points to potential economies of scale from regional cooperation; the provisions allow for resource pooling among neighboring countries when national capacity is not adequate to implement and enforce the regional framework.

Government Procurement

In the same vein, according to Kamala Dawar and Simon Evenett, in chapter 17, government procurement provisions may have received greater attention in PTAs because of the prospects they offer for reforming national procurement systems, The authors note that all the PTAs that include government procurement provisions promote a liberal agenda, acknowledging the benefits of transparent nondiscriminatory and competitive procurement markets. Agreements differ in the scope and strength of their commitment to progressive liberalization of procurement markets, but the provisions typically cover a dozen aspects of procurement policies, including nondiscrimination principles, procedural rules, dispute settlement mechanisms, commitments to cooperation and further negotiations, state entities and sectors covered, and special exceptions know as offsets.

For many countries, government procurement outlays are a sensitive matter, making for reluctance to take on strong and legally binding international obligations. The desire for value for money from public purchasing has often been tempered by other objectives, such as support for specific domestic industries and interests. Accordingly, in many PTAs, particular attention has been paid to eliminating the more transparent forms of discrimination, such as price preferences. This may have had the unintended consequence of driving discrimination into nontransparent forms such as contract thresholds, limitation on number of bidders, exclusion of sensitive sectors, and the like. Yet the rules governing procurement provisions in PTAs appear less discriminatory than the provisions governing market access. One reason is that government is only one among numerous national buyers, which limits the impact on market outcome of its decisions to award specific preferences. Another focus of attention in PTAs has been improvement of the transparency of those public institutions in signatory countries that are responsible for state purchasing.

Transparency provisions in PTAs tend to generate benefits for nonmembers of the PTA, as well as members.

A government that has improved its national procurement procedures in compliance with PTA provisions may not find it worthwhile to maintain separate procurement processes for bidders from PTA signatories and nonsignatories. Government procurement provisions therefore offer the prospect of being implemented across-the-board and more formally, on an MFN basis. Third-party MFN rules are an important way of furthering nondiscriminatory liberalization over time and of diffusing good practices.

Although improvements to procurement regimes required by PTAs, such as increased transparency, may be costly, the expense could be mitigated through technical assistance and capacity-building programs negotiated as part of the PTA. Flexibilities are available to negotiators, including exclusion of certain entities from the agreement, the threshold set in order for procurement to be covered by the agreement, the exclusion of sectors such as defense and financial services, and the use of offsets or set-asides to accommodate domestic policies such as the promotion of indigenous communities or small businesses.

Intellectual Property

As Carsten Fink shows in chapter 18, rules for the protection of intellectual property rights (IPRs) have become a common, albeit controversial, feature of PTAs, especially those involving developed partners. Over the past decade or so, the United States has negotiated numerous PTAs that contain ambitious IPR chapters. These chapters introduce standards of protection for all types of IPRs that exceed those of the WTO Agreement on Trade-Related Aspects of Intellectual Property Rights (TRIPS)—that is, they are TRIPS+. The most prominent, and sometimes most controversial, standards include patent term extension, patenting of life forms, patent-registration linkage for pharmaceutical products, exclusive rights to test data, prolonged copyright protection, rules on technological protection measures and the liability of Internet service providers, and more stringent requirements for the enforcement of IPRs. These rules seek to deepen and update preexisting multilateral IPR rules, as embedded in the TRIPS Agreement. In May 2007 the United States adopted a new trade framework, the Bipartisan Agreement, to roll back some of the TRIPS+ provisions as they relate to pharmaceutical products. Although the Bipartisan Agreement covers only three PTAs, it marks an important shift in U.S. trade policy toward greater sensitivity with respect to the implications of global IPR rules for public health concerns.

Until recently, the agreements concluded by the EU were less far-reaching than those of the United States. In the past, the main TRIPS+ element of the EU's PTAs took the form of separate agreements on wines and spirits that included lists of geographic names to which signatories had to apply rigorous geographical indication protection. In 2006 the EU embarked on a new set of negotiations, and it is demanding the inclusion of more comprehensive IPR chapters in these new agreements. The EU's economic partnership agreement (EPA) with the Caribbean Forum of African, Caribbean, and Pacific (ACP) States (CARIFORUM), gives a sense of the new EU approach, including as it does TRIPS+ provisions not only on geographical indications but also in other areas, notably IPR enforcement. Future EU agreements with more developed trading partners may well be more ambitious than the agreement with CARIFORUM.

TRIPS+ standards of protection are found in several PTAs that do not involve the United States or the EU. Notably, several trade agreements negotiated by EFTA provide for patent term extension and exclusivity of pharmaceutical test data. Although agreements among developing countries usually do not go beyond TRIPS, several of the PTAs signed by Chile and Mexico include lists of geographical indications that benefit from protection in the signatory countries.

The adoption of TRIPS+ standards is often an important element in the overall package of quid pro quos necessary to conclude a preferential trade deal, reflecting the importance of IPRs as a market access concern for developed countries. Yet the logic of negotiating new IPR standards differs from the traditional logic that economists have applied to the reciprocal dismantling of tariff barriers, in several ways:

- Optimizing the degree of IPR protection entails striking a proper balance between the interests of IPR owners and the public at large. There is no guarantee that ever-higher standards of IPR protection will necessarily improve economic welfare.
- Because of the MFN obligation under TRIPS, PTA parties usually cannot implement TRIPS+ standards in a preferential way, which affects the bargaining incentives of countries that are engaged in multiple PTA negotiations.
- IPRs have been included in the definition of investment in many PTA investment chapters and in BITs. Such a broad definition of investment raises the possibility that private rights holders may directly challenge government measures affecting IPRs under the terms of an investment accord. Although there has been no investment

dispute in this area so far, the rapid spread of PTAs and BITs may well lead to the initiation of arbitration claims in the future.

Environment

Practically all countries recognize the critical importance of environment, but many do not believe that dealing with environment issues under trade agreements is necessarily the best approach. In chapter 19, Anuradha R. V. does not seek to build a rationale for the trade-environment linkage or to discuss whether environmental issues should be addressed in trade agreements or in stand-alone environmental agreements. Instead, she focuses on the main contours of the trade and environment debate at the multilateral level and on how environmental provisions are increasingly being incorporated into PTAs, especially by major developed economies.

The United States, the EU, Canada, and New Zealand are the principal proponents of environmental provisions in PTAs. On the basis of a review of existing agreements, it would appear that the key issues in the negotiation of environmental provisions in a PTA include an understanding of (a) the nature of legal obligations emerging from provisions relating to the environment under a PTA; (b) the potential economic costs of specific environmental requirements; (c) areas where technical assistance and capacity building would be necessary to ensure compliance with environmental obligations; (d) the nature and extent of the financial assistance required; and (e) the nature of dispute settlement and enforcement mechanisms.

Even before negotiations, pre-PTA impact assessments could provide important benchmarks for assessing the scope of the trade-environment linkage. For instance, the EU's use of sustainable impact assessments (SIAs) to appraise the environmental implications of the PTA for both parties offers a basis for addressing the linkages between environmental provisions and sustainable development in the trading partners. Technical and financial assistance and capacity-building support by the party that has more experience with such assessments should be a necessary aspect of the PTA process.

Labor Rights

Provisions on labor rights in PTAs are becoming increasingly common, particularly in PTAs between large, powerful, developed countries and smaller, poorer developing countries. In chapter 20, Kimberly Ann Elliott observes that demands to include labor rights in PTAs began with the United States and have since been taken up, albeit in somewhat different forms, by Canada, Chile, and, more recently, the EU. The definition of labor standards in PTA negotiations usually refers to the International Labour Organization (ILO) Declaration on Fundamental Principles and Rights at Work. That document lists four core labor standards as deserving of universal application: freedom of association, and "effective recognition" of the right to collective bargaining; abolition of forced labor; effective abolition of child labor; and elimination of discrimination in employment. Notwithstanding this common definition, the negotiating stances of the main demandeurs differ widely, especially on questions of implementation and enforcement. Overall, it is difficult to assess the implications of these agreements for developing countries because sustained attention to implementation is rare. PTA negotiations with the United States have led to changes in existing labor laws in several cases in which those laws were deemed inadequate, but monitoring and enforcement after agreements are signed are sporadic, at best.

Four key findings emerge from the review of labor provisions in PTAs: (a) enforceable provisions for labor standards are a condition for negotiating a PTA with the United States and are likely to remain so; (b) labor provisions in PTAs not involving the United States or Canada are unusual and are almost always hortatory, rather than legally binding or enforceable; (c) the EU appears to be joining the trend, if the model used in its EPA with CARIFORUM is replicated in other similar agreements, but the language on labor, although nominally binding, includes no sanctions for noncompliance; and (d) even in U.S. PTAs—which have the strongest language, on paper—enforcement is rare, sanctions have never been applied, and financial, technical, and capacity-building assistance to improve implementation of labor standards is uncommon.

Human Rights

The growing number and scope of PTAs containing human rights provisions reflects a new reality: policy makers perceive that economic integration will not be successful without a stronger focus on improving governance among trade partners. In chapter 21, Susan Ariel Aaronson notes that the United States, Canada, the EU, and the members of EFTA are the main demandeurs of human rights language in PTAs. The EU and EFTA focus on human rights under the Universal Declaration on Human Rights (UDHR), but they rely on aspirational language and on dialogue. Canada and the United States focus on specific human rights, embed these provisions in the body of the trade agreement, and often make them binding. These approaches have become more similar over time, but they remain distinct.

Although growing numbers of countries include or accept human rights provisions, the trend has limits. Many policy makers in middle-income countries and in the developing world are reluctant to use trade policies to change the behavior of other countries. As countries grow richer and more influential, however, these policy makers may become more willing to accept or to demand human rights provisions. Nevertheless, some industrial countries, such as Australia, that themselves have strong human rights records have refused to include human rights requirements in trade agreements. Other nations, such as China, have accepted such provisions.

The human rights embedded in these PTAs exhibit a great variety; they include civil and political rights to privacy, political participation, due process, and access to information, but also economic, social, and cultural rights, rights of indigenous peoples, and access to affordable medicines. Although countries with interests in promoting human rights may prod their trade partners to change their laws or devote greater resources to human rights, little is known about the actual effect of provisions in PTAs on human rights conditions. These provisions, especially the more positive economic, social, and cultural rights, are probably expensive for developing countries to implement—just like IPRs. Developing countries must devote scarce resources to human rights, perhaps before they have the national income or will to do so. If human rights provisions are carefully designed, they can focus on improving governance (the supply side), as well as on empowering people to demand their rights.

If these rights provisions are to be workable and lasting, policy makers will need to understand their effects on trade and governance. Policy makers, scholars, and activists should use human rights impact assessments, as well as widely accepted datasets, to gain greater understanding of how to make the match between trade and human rights effective and enduring.

Dispute Settlement

In theory, the parties to a PTA are the masters of their own treaty and could design an original dispute settlement mechanism from the ground up, or have no dispute settlement mechanism at all. In chapter 22, Amelia Porges observes that, in practice, almost all PTAs employ one of three general types of dispute settlement mechanism: diplomatic settlement, use of standing tribunals, or a WTO-type system in which ad hoc panels determine whether disputed measures are in conformity with the PTA's obligations.

Dispute settlement is useful in several ways. A PTA must provide an orderly way for its members to settle disputes and move on, or the disputes will poison bilateral relations, reduce the benefits from the PTA, and perhaps even lead to the demise of the agreement. Dispute settlement is also essential to ensure that the promises set forth in a PTA are kept. By participating in a PTA with strong dispute settlement provisions, a government signals its level of commitment to private and public interests at home and abroad. Even if no disputes are anticipated, enforcement provisions in a PTA reinforce the governments' precommitments, make their promises more credible, and signal that the PTA is a sound platform for investment that will create jobs and economic growth. Solid dispute settlement is even more important in North-South (or South-South) PTAs with asymmetrical power relations. Recently concluded PTAs in Latin America, Europe, and Asia demonstrate to a striking extent that as PTA obligations deepen, become more complex, and provide more value, PTA partners seek more certainty than purely diplomatic dispute settlement can provide.

The WTO-type ad hoc panel model is an often-used option, but some PTAs employ a standing tribunal instead. A tribunal may involve more fixed investment in infrastructure than ad hoc panels, but its permanence may make it available to take on more functions for the integration process. Thinking ahead toward coexistence and even multilateralization of PTA networks, however, it may be easier to mesh ad hoc panel systems than court-based systems.

In doing so, one should be aware that even an ad hoc system involves many procedural choices:

- Should the PTA limit panels to determining whether a PTA government has violated PTA law? Some PTAs follow the General Agreement on Tariffs and Trade (GATT) by making provision for disputes about government measures that do not violate the rules but still frustrate reasonably expected PTA benefits.
- Should the PTA provide that all of its obligations are subject to dispute settlement? Some do, whereas others exclude particular areas (for instance, soft law or competition law).
- How should the PTA deal with overlap between PTA obligations and those of the WTO or other PTAs? In practice, most give the complaining party the right to ask for consultations in either or both forums, but they prohibit a second panel process after a panel has been requested in one forum.

The parties to a PTA will also need to consider how they want dispute settlement to operate. Institutions are a threshold question: if negotiators want greater consistency and predictability in panel decisions, the support of a secretariat

will be helpful, but it will require an up-front investment. The details of panel procedures can be left to be agreed later, although negotiators can set key parameters in advance. Various approaches exist for dividing the expenses of disputes, handling translation and documentation issues, and regulating presentation of evidence and arguments.

PTAs with dispute settlement experience have sought (like the WTO negotiators) some way to ensure sound and consistent panel decisions: almost all ad hoc panel systems allow the parties to comment on panel reports in draft form, and two PTAs have committed to appellate mechanisms. Then there is the question of participation in the process. Who are the decision makers? Every PTA has a process for selecting members of panels or standing tribunals and ensuring their impartiality. Who (other than the governments) may provide input into this process? Every government that engages in dispute settlement relies on its private sector to identify problems, to provide relevant factual information, and to identify commercial priorities. Will the PTA permit panels to consider input from civil society in general? Must submissions and hearings be open to the public?

Finally, it is important to have some mechanism for determining whether government measures breach PTA obligations—but formal dispute settlement is not always the quickest way to resolve a measure that is causing a commercial problem. The committees and other institutions created by a PTA provide a practical setting for addressing and resolving such issues. Some PTAs go further and build in a role for mediation, conciliation, or other rule-agnostic practical settlement methods. The benefits of such mediation are sure to exceed its costs.

The final, and unavoidable, problem is compliance. Unless a PTA's dispute settlement instruments can (like the European Court of Justice) impose fines on members for noncompliance, PTAs' leverage to obtain compliance consists of authorizing withdrawal of PTA benefits or exercising moral suasion. To the extent that a PTA's preference margin is low relative to MFN benefits in the WTO, a PTA member may have much more leverage litigating in the WTO, if it can. Indeed, the record of experience with PTA disputes shows that except in the Southern Cone Common Market (Mercosur), where MFN tariffs are high, many PTA parties have chosen to turn to the WTO.

References

De Melo, Jaime, and Arvind Panagariya, eds. 1996. *New Dimensions in Regional Integration.* Cambridge, U.K.: Cambridge University Press.
Schiff, Maurice, and L. Alan Winters. 2003. *Regional Integration and Development.* Washington, DC: World Bank.
World Bank. 2000. *Trade Blocs.* Washington, DC: World Bank.

BEYOND MARKET ACCESS

Jean-Pierre Chauffour and Jean-Christophe Maur

Economists have repeatedly warned against them, nongovernmental organizations (NGOs) have fought them, and some governments have signed them begrudgingly (at least in appearance). Yet in the past 20 years, preferential trade agreements (PTAs) have multiplied unremittingly. What is even more striking is that their scope has broadened at the same time as their numbers have grown. Deep integration provisions in PTAs have become ubiquitous.

This first chapter looks at the background of the drive toward deep integration PTAs and at how they differ, in content and implications, from traditional market access agreements. It then discusses the theoretical and practical motivations behind today's deep PTAs. Finally, it highlights key areas for policy makers to consider as they contemplate their future PTA strategies.

A Preference for Deep Integration

Gaining market access or preserving a level playing field has remained an important motivation for entering into PTAs. But with the liberalization of trade around the world and the related diminishing size of preferential rents, the growing success of PTAs cannot be explained by traditional market access motives alone (even factoring for the possible substitution of tariffs for less transparent forms of protection). Countries are also interested in a host of other objectives—importing higher policy standards, strengthening regional policy coordination, locking in domestic reforms, and even addressing foreign policy issues (see Schiff and Winters 2004; Hoekman, ch. 4 in this volume).

All this translates into a beyond-market-access vision for PTAs that includes a broad set of rules and disciplines governing areas such as investment regimes, technical and sanitary standards, trade facilitation, competition policy, government procurement, intellectual property, environment protection, migration, labor rights, human rights, and other "behind the border" issues.

This vision is expressed in two ways in recent PTAs. The first is the pursuit of what can be termed a "WTO+" agenda, focusing on disciplines already espoused by the World Trade Organization (WTO) but often expanding their depth and breadth and seeking enforceability. The second is through rules and disciplines that are not covered by the WTO, or are covered very imperfectly (WTO extra). In practice, PTAs often pursue both objectives, to varying degrees. North American PTAs, for instance, focus more on WTO+ disciplines, while adding a few WTO extras to the mix. By contrast, European PTAs include numerous WTO-extra aspects. Horn, Mavroidis, and Sapir (2010) identify no fewer than 38 areas in U.S. and European Union (EU) PTAs that aim to go beyond WTO disciplines.

The proliferation and deepening of PTAs may offer developing countries vast opportunities to modernize and upgrade their rules and disciplines with a view to greater economic efficiency. At the same time, these trends pose a serious challenge for policy makers, especially in low-income countries, because of the added burden of covering an increasingly large and complex set of issues with limited administrative resources for negotiation and implementation, and frequently with no preexisting experience.[1]

Indeed, PTAs are increasingly addressing policy areas that are entirely new to developing countries. These broader agreements may deeply affect countries' development processes. To take an often-cited example, it is possible that the inclusion in PTAs of the most advanced forms of intellectual property rights (IPR) protection may require an alternative economic development model whereby knowledge and know-how are no longer acquired through imitation and reverse engineering (as happened with the generic pharmaceutical industries in middle-income countries), but through a less optimal, more demanding, and yet-unproved process of accumulation of capital and knowledge.

The deep integration commitments in new PTAs, with their concomitant challenges, stand in sharp contrast to older trade agreements, which chiefly had to do with dismantling barriers to trade and making trade policy simpler to administer. Although multilateral trade agreements under the WTO have pursued a similar path toward greater complexity—for instance, with the 1994 agreement on Trade-Related Aspects of Intellectual Property Rights (TRIPS) agreement—nowhere is the policy ambition as sweeping as in PTAs, under which regulatory disciplines are spreading to nontrade areas.

Before looking at the issues in detail, it is useful to try to capture the essence of the difference in the nature of the liberalization challenge posed by the new disciplines in PTAs. The trade literature usually characterizes this process in terms of positive versus negative integration and of behind-the-border versus at-the-border integration.

Positive versus Negative Integration

The first Nobel laureate in economics, Jan Tinbergen, articulated the notions of positive and negative integration in characterizing the process of international economic integration (Tinbergen 1954). Negative integration refers to the removal of trade barriers and the principle of nondiscrimination. This is the traditional remit of trade negotiations.[2] Tinbergen defines positive integration as

> [the] creation of new institutions and their instruments or the modification of existing instruments. . . . More generally, positive integration should consist of the creation of all institutions required by the welfare optimum which have to be handled in a centralized way. (Tinbergen 1954, 79)

Analysts have often retained the first part of the definition—that integration is not just about removal of barriers to trade flows but about "rule making" to facilitate these flows. Interestingly, though, Tinbergen offers in the second part of the definition a vision that suggests that the creation of intergovernmental public goods could also be welfare enhancing. This is an important aspect, to which we will return.

Various interpretations of the Tinbergen characterization have survived in the literature (e.g., Pelkmans 1984; Hoekman and Kostecki 2009; Ortino 2004, 18–34; Torrent 2007). We take from Tinbergen's definition the basic intuition that positive integration calls for public intervention to tackle market failures that would otherwise prevent economically optimal levels of integration.

Positive and negative integration have substantively different implications for the process of integration. Negative integration would mainly seek the prohibition of a narrow set of policies, as well as joint surveillance and, eventually,

mechanisms for redress, whereas positive integration requires taking active steps toward integration by defining common policies and setting up the legal and administrative framework to implement them. The difference is, however, not as clear-cut as it appears at first (see, e.g., Ortino 2004; Torrent 2007). In both cases, a certain degree of legal alignment is required, as is the establishment of minimal common institutions. For instance, agreeing on new rules that limit the way governments can intervene in markets could be seen as an instance of either positive or negative integration.[3]

Nevertheless the distinction remains useful for thinking broadly about important characteristics of deep integration, because new dimensions of PTAs clearly imply greater retooling of legal frameworks at the domestic level. Positive integration can be conducted in various ways, depending on how it is legally instrumentalized. Torrent (2007) notes, for instance, the substantive differences between U.S. and EU agreements regarding procurement provisions. The U.S. approach is more normative in that it inserts the rules in the agreement, whereas the EU adopts a more progressive approach by defining the rules through specialized organizations such as expert committees. Relative to negative integration, positive integration entails substantial differences in the drafting of language in agreements (the instruments of implementation being more complex) and therefore in negotiations and, probably, in the predictability of implementation. For instance, when tackling trade facilitation issues, it is not sufficient to agree on items that should be prohibited (e.g., the use of consular fees) or on simple positive obligations such as transparency; countries must also agree on standards for procedures, such as use of risk management screening at borders, and must monitor agency conduct. These obligations are not easily incorporated into normative commitments in trade agreements—Messerlin and Zarrouk (2000), for example, take the view that they should not be. Beyond adopting new policies designed to open markets, positive integration also seeks coordination of policies with trading partners, which may imply some form of institutional arrangements.

Behind-the-Border versus At-the-Border Policies

Another important dimension is characterized in the literature as behind-the-border versus at-the-border measures. National treatment and uniformization of obligations indeed differ in substance from most favored nation (MFN) obligations in that they require countries to change policies that affect internal transactions that are not necessarily related to trade.

The question of the impact of domestic regulations on trade is not new and is well recognized in the WTO. Domestic policies have the potential to be designed so as to discriminate against foreign producers. Article III of the General Agreement on Tariffs and Trade (GATT) accordingly requires that internal regulations comply with the national treatment principle, which states that other nationals should be treated the same as one's own. Beyond addressing discrimination per se through the national treatment principle, there is also a desire on the part of policy makers to reduce the costs of having to comply with multiple and heterogeneous requirements. As the world economy becomes more integrated and supply chains incorporate sourcing from many countries, the calls for some uniformization are growing. This is an area in which PTAs play an increasing role.

Behind-the-border policies directly affect domestic transactions and thus have obvious direct welfare implications that differ from the indirect effect through prices and volumes of trade goods. Their effect also implies a different political-economy equilibrium. Moreover, as we will see later, the notion of behind-the-border measures could be expanded to measures that are included in trade agreements not because of their direct or indirect effects on trade, but merely because trade agreements provide a convenient vehicle for international negotiation or enforcement.

In sum, deep integration measures may impinge on domestic policies that are not necessarily directly trade related. They require more advanced reform of the legal environment and, generally, a more complex set of instruments for implementation. They also may involve active supranational coordination. It is not hard to imagine how demanding and complex liberalization of these measures might be.

Motivations for Deep Integration

The reality of the new PTA landscape raises questions about the motives for entering into regional agreements. Why would policy makers around the world invest time, political capital, and resources in negotiating trade arrangements that discriminate among trading partners and offer uncertain welfare benefits, when a multilateral approach of nondiscriminatory market access provides a superior solution? The answer can only be that policy makers are looking for benefits that extend beyond market access for goods and services.

Krugman (1993) assumed that one reason for the success of PTAs was the convenience of dealing with the variety, complexity, and opacity of modern trade barriers in a bilateral or regional setting rather than at the multilateral GATT or WTO level. Implied by his analysis was a sense that the removal of traditional trade barriers was not necessarily solving the issue of market access. Schiff and Winters (2004) subsequently reviewed alternative rationales for PTAs. These rationales, either nonstandard or not well represented by traditional theoretical models, include domestic policy anchoring, importation of good regulatory practices, supranational coordination to achieve regional policy goals, export of regulatory standards by hegemons, and foreign policy considerations. These economic, societal, and political-economy motives for concluding a PTA are discussed in detail next.

Economic Motives

Market access mercantilism is the traditional force behind the push for trade liberalization. Led by the false logic that import barriers should be lowered only if reciprocal access for exports is granted, countries mutually agree to liberalize their markets, and in most cases, the result is welfare-enhancing liberalization. In a globalized world, countries seek to gain competitive advantage over their neighbors by negotiating special (preferential) market access with key destination markets.

Several facts challenge this traditional explanation. Preferences, to start with, may not be as important as in the past. Tariffs have been falling worldwide (figure 1.1), and in a very general sense, even the most protected markets now tend to exhibit tariff levels that are moderate compared with those of 15 years ago. There are obviously many exceptions at the product level. Developed economies and middle-income countries exhibit, on average, lower levels of protection than low-income countries.

Moreover, as PTAs grow in number, so does the number of recipients of preferences, leading to the erosion of the preference margins held over competitors. Carrère, de Melo, and Tumurchudur (2010) construct an adjusted market access measure of what countries receiving EU preferences actually enjoy when the preferences given to other partners are taken into account. When this measure is compared with the unadjusted measure of preference over the MFN tariff, it turns out that real market access is often much lower—for example, less than half for Cambodia, a recipient of the EU's Everything But Arms (EBA) preferences. In some instances, as in the case of a generalized system of preferences (GSP) recipient, such as Indonesia, there is no effective market access preference at all. As noted by Levy (2009), the reciprocal incentive apparently fails to explain the rationale behind asymmetric North-South types of agreement. Many developing countries

Figure 1.1. Most Favored Nation (MFN) Tariff Rates, Weighted Mean, All Products

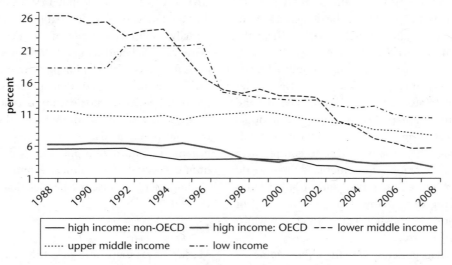

Source: World Bank, World Development Indicators database, http://data.worldbank.org/data-catalog/world-development-indicators.
Note: OECD = Organisation for Economic Co-operation and Development.

already benefit from very good market access in their northern partner countries.

To sum up: there is a tendency toward diminishing MFN tariffs; preference margins are actually smaller than they appear; and some developing countries already enjoy virtually tariff-free access to major markets under the GSP, EBA, and other preferential regimes. Under those circumstances, can market access incentives alone explain reciprocal liberalization in the PTA context?

Market access may persist as a motive in North-North and South-South agreements. In the global South, in particular, tariffs remain fairly substantial. Other incentives may also be in play. Countries at the periphery of a network of agreements (for instance, the partners of the EU and the United States) may suffer because industries shift toward the hub of the network and away from peripheral countries (the spokes) and because of erosion of the outlying countries' preferential access, since location in the hub provides preferential access to many more markets. This reality is what has led countries such as Chile, Mexico, and Singapore to pursue "spoke-spoke" strategies by mirroring their large trading partners' PTA policies and pursuing agreements with the same partners, even though their trade with such distant partners might be small. The strategy of the European Free Trade Association (EFTA) in parallel to the EU, and the accession of new countries to the EU, might be seen as being driven by a similar motive (see Baldwin 1994). Bhagwati (2008) also argues that even modest margins of preference have a sizable impact in a globalized world in which overall transaction costs are

decreasing and sources of comparative advantage can be found in small cost differences ("thin" margins of comparative advantage). Even preferences that are small on paper may become attractive for prospective partners.

Market access conditions are not determined only by tariffs. First, customs procedures and other domestic policies, such as standards, may affect foreign exporters' costs of access to the market. As noted by Bagwell and Staiger (2001), when governments choose these policies unilaterally, there is a possibility that market access might be set at a lower and less optimal level than under reciprocal liberalization negotiations.

Second, the market access question is not limited to goods. Foreign investment is another way of gaining access to foreign markets, and the inclusion in agreements of disciplines relating to investment can be an additional motive for reciprocal liberalization commitments.[4] Many PTAs now include investment disciplines that go beyond those of the WTO. WTO rules are limited to the supply of services following an investment (commercial presence), as specified in the General Agreement on Trade in Services (GATS), and to the trade-related investment measures (i.e., the Trade Related Investment Measures [TRIMS] agreement). Moreover, GATS relies on an "enterprise-based" definition of investment, whereas bilateral rules generally refer to a broader "asset-based" definition that covers portfolio investment and different forms of tangible and intangible property (Miroudot, ch. 14 in this volume).

Third, because traditional PTA analysis focuses on trade in goods, trade in services is often omitted from the discussion. Yet the services sector represents the largest, and a growing, share of gross domestic product (GDP) in many developed and developing countries; many services (e.g., electricity, telecommunications, transport, and professional services) are key inputs into the production of goods and other services; and the information technology (IT) revolution has increased the tradability of services. In these circumstances, services liberalization may offer considerable gains, both from increased trade flows and from reduced input costs for firms.[5] For some country groupings, such as South-South agreements, preferential integration in goods may bring little benefit; small countries with similar production structures and with small and inefficient manufacturing sectors might not have much to gain from engaging in goods-only PTAs. A promising next step might be to explore other integration dimensions in which complementaries might be beneficial, such as services (Mattoo and Sauvé, ch. 12 in this volume), investment (Miroudot, ch. 14 in this volume), and labor mobility (Stephenson and Hufbauer, ch. 13 in this volume). Hoekman and Sekkat (2010) examine this option in the case of the Pan-Arab Free Trade Area (PAFTA).

Yet the reality is that even if some limited sectoral advances (on movement of professionals, for instance) have been recorded in recent agreements, PTAs have made only modest inroads where access to services markets is concerned. Regulatory policies tend to pursue noneconomic objectives along with economic concerns (such as lowering the costs of barriers and compliance), and this, Hoekman, Mattoo, and Sapir (2007) remark, makes for a particularly complex political-economy calculus. As with tariffs, the transaction costs imposed by deep integration policies will lead incumbent services industries sheltered by regulatory protection to resist liberalization.

The bias against liberalization can be reinforced in the case of services by reluctance on the part of consumers and government. Consumers may fear that regulatory liberalization will affect their well-being—for instance, through slacker standards and lower quality of products and services.[6] Government and regulatory agencies may also view liberalization reluctantly, for several reasons: (a) regulation may be a source of indirect taxation, in that governments benefit from rents generated by regulatory protection (as is common in the area of standards); (b) governments may fear that their latitude to pursue regulatory objectives will be curtailed because cross-border supply could undermine local suppliers while being subject to different (lower) regulatory requirements; and (c) governments also pursue redistribution objectives by, for instance, imposing requirements for universal provision (e.g., in water supply, telecommunications, and postal services) and for

pricing below cost for the poorest customers in such services sectors as water, electricity, finance, and transport. Hoekman, Mattoo, and Sapir (2007) observe that not only do political-economy calculations become more complex in this environment, but also the usual reciprocity mechanism of trade liberalization may not work any more because of the difficulty of clearly separating measures that promote market access from measures that pursue legitimate regulatory objectives.

Aside from market access considerations, PTAs have a role to play in transnational regulation. This involvement reflects the standard economic-efficiency motive for regulation—addressing market failures. Three often-cited market failures are in the areas of monopoly power, externalities and the provision of public goods, and information asymmetries.

1. *Monopoly power and supranational competition.* Economies of scale and, more generally, market failures give rise to the possibility of monopoly power and abusive conduct by private firms. Trade liberalization may go some way toward creating competition by making markets contestable, but this will not always be sufficient. Domestic enforcement of competition rules is linked to market access. If, in a national jurisdiction, competition is weak because of lack of enforcement, market concentration and collusion in the domestic market may deter entry by foreign suppliers. In such instances, competition policy should complement trade liberalization to secure the gains from the opening of markets.

The threats of market power and abusive conduct may not justify the inclusion of competition rules and discipline in a PTA on economic grounds alone. After all, countries can individually opt to implement competition policies unilaterally. But such policies may not be effective in dealing with the risk of cross-border externalities and the abusive behavior of exporters abroad. Competition rules may be particularly relevant in PTAs where the risk of abuse of market power or collusive practice involves more than one national jurisdiction and where international legislation and cooperation could effectively curb anticompetitive behavior. For instance, a firm may use its market power in one market to extract monopoly rents in another; a dominant position may span several countries (as with Microsoft), potentially leading to anticompetitive market conduct; or firms may have agreed in one jurisdiction to collude in another, making it necessary for authorities to cooperate in order to collect evidence.

Because such competition issues are related to trade and investment, there are complementarities in dealing with them in the same forum as trade arrangements. PTAs offer a scope for creating disciplines that the WTO does not.

Arguably, the degree of cooperation in international competition arrangements will depend on the size of individual economies, the level of trade, and the enforcement capacity of the actors.

2. *Externalities and provision of public goods.* An externality (or transaction spillover) is a cost or benefit, not transmitted through prices, which is incurred by a party that did not participate in the action causing the cost or benefit. As the examples of climate change and the depletion of fish stocks show, externalities are not necessarily confined within the borders of a given country. In some cases, externalities may be best tackled by a small group of countries; for instance, river management and some transport issues should involve neighboring countries. Externalities are closely related to the need to provide public goods—that is, goods that are nonrivalrous and nonexcludable.[7] In the presence of externalities, markets may not spontaneously provide goods, such as clean air, that are socially desirable.

Addressing regional externalities should logically be a priority of regional PTAs, given the need for some form of supranational coordination to help internalize the externalities or share them fairly. Coordination can take several forms:

- *Alignment (for instance, through mutual recognition agreements) or harmonization of policies.* These measures eliminate segmentation of markets and duplication of the costs generated by barriers at the border.
- *Alignment and harmonization of policies to avoid leakage.* Leakage is a concern when, for instance, one jurisdiction in the PTA has lower regulatory standards that might undermine the regulatory efforts of its trading partners. An example is a country's deficient control of animal epizooties or pests that spill over to neighbors. (Animal border crossings cannot be totally controlled.)
- *Alignment and harmonization of policies to create networks and to facilitate information exchange.* This method essentially refers to the adoption of common standards and regulatory language in order to facilitate flows within the region (for instance, ensuring interoperability of national networks at a regional level). Such alignment is of particular relevance for services sectors such as finance and insurance, IT, professional services, transport, and electricity.
- *Pooling of efforts to create infrastructure or pooling financial and human resources to provide a regional public good.* For example, combined financing might be needed for a large infrastructure serving a region, such as a hydroelectric dam, or for a large port.

- *Joint decision making to ensure that national policies are coordinated at the regional level (e.g., management of food stocks).*
- *Transfer of resources to solve externality problems when contributions by individual member states are required.* A common instance is when institutions are weak and capacity building is needed to bring a partner country to a higher standard for the regional common good (e.g., customs enforcement).

Regional externalities should arguably be dealt with in those jurisdictions in which they occur, and they therefore require transnational mechanisms of cooperation. It is not entirely clear whether regional externalities (positive or negative) should necessarily be addressed in the specific context of a PTA (Schiff and Winters 2002). There is always the possibility (as for all commitments agreed in PTAs) of addressing these issues through dedicated agreements and transnational institutions such as bilateral customs or water management agreements. Historically, many such problems have been addressed in this way.

3. *Information asymmetries.* Sometimes goods characteristics may not be discernible to buyers before consumption. Credence goods do not—for example, chemicals may be harmful to health, unbeknownst to the people exposed to them; thus regulation is needed to inform consumers before purchase. Information asymmetries may affect producers themselves in situations where consumers' characteristics are hidden (e.g., in the insurance market). In most instances, the market itself deals with these information asymmetries through information dissemination and brand signaling. When, however, the asymmetries are not addressed, the market outcome is suboptimal. The problem of information is particularly acute for services because of their intangibility, which makes it harder for the buyer to learn about quality prior to consumption (Hoekman, Mattoo, and Sapir 2007). Regulation may then be called for—perhaps through licensing or the imposition of compulsory standards. International cooperation may help reduce the overall complexity of the regulatory framework for international traders by aligning and harmonizing regulations. Failure to tackle issues of this kind in a coordinated fashion may generate negative externalities.

In the specific PTA context, the challenge will be to assess whether information asymmetry problems are best tackled at the bilateral or regional level, rather than in other international forums. In most instances, this will be a question of judging the trade-offs between the transaction costs of cooperating with a limited number of countries, as against the international community, and between the benefits of coordination at the PTA versus the global level. There is a clear risk, for example, that regional standards in PTAs may exclude third, nonadhering, countries. Nevertheless, it may be much easier to agree on a common approach with a small number of countries and with countries with similar preferences. Finally, in some cases (e.g., regional epizooties), a neighboring-country approach will be appropriate.

Societal Motives

Beyond the economic motives, a PTA can be driven by societal motives or, as Bhagwati (2008) calls them, value-related demands. Each society has moral and social norms and preferences that may be undermined by market forces left to operate on their own. For instance, trade in dangerous weapons or in morally or religiously reprehensible material may need to be restricted. What is considered dangerous or morally reprehensible will vary significantly according to country and culture.

Social norms and values may be undermined by trade liberalization; after all, it is easier to control borders than to control a whole territory, and foreign producers may not hold themselves to a particular country's standards. This issue has long been recognized in multilateral trade agreements, leading to the inclusion of safeguard provisions and general exceptions (on moral grounds, for instance). Safeguard mechanisms and the language of general exceptions may, however, prove insufficient, and countries may want to negotiate sector-specific conditions in PTAs, such as reservations concerning universal provision of services.

Conversely, trade agreements may help further societal objectives. Development policy concerns, for example, are increasingly present in agreements such as the EU-sponsored economic partnership agreements (EPAs). Northern partners also push for provisions related to good governance, democracy, labor rights, and human rights (Elliott, ch. 20 in this volume; Aaronson, ch. 21 in this volume).

What is the specific value added of PTAs in helping to achieve these objectives? One motivation might be that threats to societal preferences are localized in a limited number of partners, and thus it makes sense to deal with those countries directly. Some PTAs, for example, have been specifically linked to measures for fighting narcotics production and trafficking; an example is the Central America Free Trade Agreement and the U.S. stipulations concerning narcotics in that PTA (Hornbeck 2003).

PTAs might be seen as a locus of positive spillovers between trade and societal policy issues. For instance, provisions on governance (e.g., open and transparent procedures) in international flows arising from the trade agreement would spill over into other domestic areas.[8] Clearly, in the case of trade and development, there are complementarities between openness and poverty-alleviating growth, and PTAs help target specific countries. In other instances, and more prosaically, there might merely be a quid pro quo between market access in the North and concessions on other fronts in the South.

Another motivation relates to the search for the best available forum for promoting the international sharing of societal norms, focusing on issues that are not already present in other agreements such as the WTO (for instance, labor rights or environment protection) or pushing for higher standards than currently exist in the international community. (See also "Institutions for reform," below.) This is a clear objective of the new U.S. trade policy of pursuing PTAs that was initiated under the George W. Bush administration. In a 2001 speech, Robert Zoellick, then U.S. trade representative, noted that "we need to align the global trading system with our values. . . . We can encourage respect for core labor standards, environmental protection, and good health . . . And we must always seek to strengthen freedom, democracy and the rule of law" (quoted in Evenett and Meier 2008). Related to this objective is the desire to use every trade forum to reaffirm these choices, with a view toward mutual complementarity and reinforcement between the different instruments.

Political-Economy Motives

Beyond the need for coordinating policy making with trading partners, PTAs also serve as forums for policy objectives that are strictly related neither to exchanges nor to the preferential nature of PTAs. PTAs can be seen as efficient forums for achieving broader geopolitical, institutional, and policy-anchoring objectives.

Geopolitical objectives. Geostrategic considerations have historically commanded the formation of PTAs. There are numerous examples of trade agreements that have been used to promote peace. Chief among them is the EU, which was born from the desire to prevent war from happening again in Europe. Winston Churchill called in 1946 for a "United States of Europe," but it was with economic integration and the 1951 European Coal and Steel Community that European integration began (Winters 1997; Baldwin 2008).[9] Other examples of agreements used for stability purposes, as noted by Bergsten (1996) include the Southern Cone Common Market (Mercosur, Mercado Común del Sur) and Asia-Pacific Economic Cooperation (APEC). More recently, the push by the United States to conclude PTAs has had foreign policy motives (Bhagwati 2008; Evenett and Meier 2008), as has Europe's neighborhood policy (European Commission 2007).[10]

Thus, PTAs can contribute to delivering peace and stability as a regional public good (Schiff and Winters 2004; World Bank 2005, box 2.6). Two mechanisms may come into play. First, trade exchanges increase economic interdependence and, thus, act as a disincentive for conflict. They may also help increase familiarity and trust and defuse trade-related disputes.[11] Second, and more specific to PTAs, institutions themselves serve as a conduit for diplomacy, allowing for frequent and repeated interaction among officials and for better exchange of information (Haftel 2007). Deep PTAs seem more attractive in this respect because they have more sophisticated institutions.

Empirically, Mansfield and Pevehouse (2000) have found that membership in a PTA significantly decreases the likelihood of armed conflict. More recently, Lee and Pyun (2009) provide statistically significant evidence that PTA institutions decrease the probability of conflict between members, whereas WTO membership seems only marginally significant. Martin, Mayer, and Thoenig (2010) test the interaction between conflict and PTAs over the period 1950–2000 and find that the hypothesis of geopolitical motivations behind the agreements is supported by evidence. Yet for PTAs to help ease the probability of conflict, there must be sufficiently large trade gains between the partners. Economics and political motives thus complement each other.

Institutions for reform. By offering a different set of institutions and related services from those of other forms of international agreements, PTAs provide an infrastructure for institutional dialogue and cooperation. As noted by the World Bank (2005), many issues covered by PTAs, such as the externality problems described earlier, could well be handled without a trade agreement. If PTAs are used, this must be because they are perceived as offering a good framework for achieving progress.

PTAs are relatively flexible instruments insofar as they allow for various levels of legal commitment and offer nearly infinite ways of creating policy space. For example, the options with dispute settlement are numerous: there may be no mechanism at all, or one or several dispute settlement mechanisms (Porges, ch. 22 in this volume). Each PTA can come with its own ad hoc instruments, which may be sector specific or may refer to external mechanisms such as international arbitration or WTO dispute settlement. Various ways of reaching settlement before recourse to formal dispute settlement are available, such as good offices, third-party mediation, and conciliation. Indirect evidence of legal flexibility is also provided by Horn, Mavroidis, and

Sapir (2009), who show that binding and nonbinding provisions coexist in agreements on nearly all the issues covered. Such flexibility, it should be noted, might appear as a virtue to policy makers but may not necessarily contribute to factual reform.

In contrast to multilateral forums, PTAs often feature innovative institutions. One innovation is the involvement of the private sector, from participation in stakeholder forums to the possibility of lodging complaints in, for example, the European Court of Justice, the General Secretariat of the Andean Community, or under the investment provisions of the North American Free Trade Agreement (NAFTA). Some PTAs offer more substantial transfers of sovereignty. Governments can also opt to devolve some of their authority to institutions created by PTAs, such as regional competition authorities, as described by Dawar and Holmes (ch. 16 in this volume).

The transaction costs of agreement are lower in PTAs with a small number of participating countries. In addition, small PTAs do not lend themselves to free riding, which is a practice that poses a key obstacle to successful global liberalization (Krugman 1993). Lower transaction costs allow for more binding constraints on each partner (noncooperation is more difficult) and for legal flexibility. Since the number required to reach consensus is lower, the agreement could be amended and revisited more often than is the case with multilateral agreements. A smaller number of participant countries enables more frequent and probably less formal interactions, which can contribute to problem solving and deeper relations. That seems an important feature for the regulatory aspects, which require agreement on complex issues (such as mutual recognition arrangements) and the setting up of expert bodies. This is the road followed by the EU under the Florence Forum.[12]

Resource transfers are more likely to occur in the framework of PTAs than in other international agreement settings. Many PTAs—North-South ones, in particular—do incorporate such transfers. Agreements signed by the EU are the most striking examples; other cases include U.S. free trade agreements (FTAs) with Latin American partners and South-South agreements such as the Common Market for Eastern and Southern Africa (COMESA). Resource transfers matter, in particular, for deep and asymmetric PTAs. Arguably, deep integration places heavier demands on capacity. Less developed trade partners may have difficulties in, for example, meeting the regulatory standards of their partners and thus obtaining effective market access. They may lack capacity to compensate for some of the adjustment costs of reform; to contribute effectively to the production of regional public goods; and, even more broadly, to help achieve geopolitical and societal objectives (development, conflict prevention, and so on).

Policy anchoring. A traditional political-economy explanation for a country's entering into binding international trade commitments is the pursuit of a domestic reform agenda and the use of external commitments to lock in progress and prevent future reversals. The opportunity to lock in is also a motive for including behind-the-border aspects in agreements. PTAs may be perceived as more effective lock-in mechanisms than other international agreements, and they may complement other external instruments in the process of reinforcing and consolidating domestic reforms.

By extending their reach to regulatory issues, PTAs offer a way of improving policy credibility (Hoekman, ch. 4 in this volume). What are the differences, then, between the sort of anchor offered by PTAs and that provided by the WTO? Aside from the obvious point that PTAs may offer commitments in WTO+ and WTO-extra areas, they may have specific advantages. The possibility of picking a partner may help reinforce credibility, as the partner of choice may be perceived as a strong proponent of reform. The EU, the United States, and other developed countries do, in fact, promote various agendas through their respective PTAs. Picking a partner or a group of partners may also signal a preference for a certain regulatory approach. In addition, lock-in through PTAs can be complemented by transfers of finance and knowledge.

An argument put forward by Schiff and Winters (1998) is that PTAs may actually be well suited for locking in policies because of the credibility of enforcement in these agreements. Incentives to enforce commitments are greater in a PTA because there is less possibility of free riding and fewer of the coordination problems that may arise in multilateral forums. In addition, there is more scope for retaliation because concessions in a PTA may go beyond just tariffs. Schiff and Winters note, however, that the disciplining effect is limited to the partner countries in the PTA, not third-country members. (They cite the peso crisis of 1994–95, when Mexico raised its tariffs on 500 items for non-NAFTA suppliers.) These dynamics are echoed by the conclusion reached by Prusa (ch. 9 in this volume), that PTAs tend to discipline the use of contingent protection measures among partners while, at the same time, the use of protection against third countries seems to be increasing.

There are several recent examples of countries that have used PTAs to pursue an ambitious domestic agenda; Schott (2003) cites Mexico and Chile. Similarly, the accession of Eastern European countries to the EU was strongly motivated by the desire to break irrevocably with socialism and consolidate market economy reforms. More recently, Costa Rica and Peru used their FTA negotiations with the United States to push domestic reforms. Levy (2009) does not find much in the way of market access motives for Peru, except a desire for greater certainty about future access (trading temporary preferences for more permanent ones), but the agreement did help the country cement its economic policy reforms. Some of these reforms, notably in the areas of services and investment, were part of the FTA implementation program, but the agreement also helped lock in prior policy reforms, such as tariff reductions. Another motivation for signing the FTA with the United States, Levy notes, may have been the hope that it would generate broader positive spillover effects on Peru's governance and the rule of law. By imposing good disciplines to protect foreign investors and market access, the FTA would signal a commitment to a better legal environment, in general.

In sum, there are strong rationales for policy makers to embark on deep and comprehensive PTAs, but the relative merits of regional integration are also issue specific and country specific. The choice of whether to include regulatory aspects in PTAs is essentially dictated by a dual concern: securing market access and addressing market failures, whether national (through the lock-in effect of policy reform and policy upgrading) or regional. Market failures will be of different natures and will involve different sets of countries, depending on the sector and the issue at hand—hence the need, as with any regulation, for a case-by-case approach. Other noneconomic considerations, such as fostering societal choices, may apply to some issues of a regulatory nature. Finally, specific institutional characteristics and advantages may motivate the choice of PTAs as adequate forums for reform.

Specificities of Deep Integration

The increased scope and depth of PTAs create opportunities but also pose extra challenges to policy makers as they negotiate and implement the complex market-access and regulatory web of these agreements. Policy makers may have to reevaluate their approach when negotiating and implementing deep integration PTAs. In particular, to what extent are the multiple goals of PTAs consistent and congruent? Do the new disciplines incorporated in PTAs create a different category of obligations? Does the deepening and popularity of PTAs create new challenges for the multilateral trading system? In this section, we suggest four major areas of emphasis for policy makers, especially in developing countries, as they refine their regional trade strategies: reexamining the question of discrimination and preferential access, adopting a holistic approach, building in flexibility, and focusing on implementation.

Preferences

Are the traditional concerns of discriminatory liberalization valid for the new areas of deep commitments in PTAs? Do deep integration measures generate trade diversion? Can they harm the liberalizing country? Do they act as stumbling blocks to further liberalization? These issues—in particular, those related to the impact of deep integration on multilateral architecture—have generated considerable interest as of late (OECD 2003; Baldwin, Evenett, and Low 2009; Estevadeordal, Suominen, and Teh 2009), thanks to mounting evidence provided by new PTAs. The new regulatory commitments found in today's PTAs are discussed here in light of the three classical economic concepts for analyzing market access discrimination in PTAs: trade diversion, third-party effects, and systemic effects.

Trade diversion. Discrimination in deep integration agreements can secure the benefits of market access without generating the potential cost of trade diversion. In this sense, regulatory discrimination does not raise the same concerns as tariff discrimination would. The certitude that better market access will be beneficial and that no diversion costs will occur leads to an important consideration for policy makers: all things being equal, PTA partners will unambiguously gain in preferential deep integration efforts. This may explain why deep integration issues are winning popularity in PTAs. (See Baldwin, ch. 3, and Baldwin and Freund, ch. 6, in this volume.)

Protection afforded by lack of regulatory openness is not necessarily protectionist in intent. Regulatory requirements often impose a transaction cost on the exporter without generating rents for the home country.[13] A case in point is superfluous or antiquated border controls, which create additional costs without any corresponding benefits.[14]

In such instances, liberalization of services, harmonization of standards, trade facilitation, investment liberalization, and openness of government procurement can generate benefits even if carried out preferentially. It is, however, important to stress that this positive effect only occurs if there is no sizeable rent transfer from domestic to foreign producers.[15] In trade in services, for instance, the impact of preferential liberalization will be determined by the nature of the regulatory barriers present. If lack of competition is an issue, regulatory liberalization may well replace a domestic monopolist practice with a foreign one (Mattoo and Sauvé, ch. 12 in this volume). Similarly, where access to services markets is subject to some form of licensing, rents may arise, and with them, the cost of trade diversion. In the case of government procurement, there is an additional aspect at work: restrictive and discriminatory

government procurement rules do not affect the market as a whole, and therefore, exclude suppliers only from serving the public share of the domestic demand (Dawar and Evenett, ch. 17 in this volume). Depending on the size of public markets, this may not be enough to exclude foreign suppliers from the market altogether.

Impact on third parties. The standard effect of discrimination will still be harmful for third parties (the excluded countries). This is, for instance, the case when countries adopt European standards instead of international ones (Maur and Shepherd, ch. 10 in this volume; Stoler, ch. 11 in this volume). It is important to ask, however, whether preferential measures are always discriminatory.

An important characteristic of regulatory measures is that de jure preferential treatment might be difficult to apply, making de facto MFN liberalization a preferable option. That is, devising a new regulatory regime applicable to each PTA may be impracticable, or the concept of rules of origin that applies to product characteristics simply cannot be as easily applied to regulations or intangible transactions.[16] For instance, provisions on protection of intellectual property rights apply equally to all origins, including domestic ones. Carving out specific regimes for some countries (as in the case of the WTO Article 6 exception for least-developed countries) requires complex legal and practical arrangements. Similarly, for customs procedures, although trade rules may differ depending on the origin of the product, it makes sense to maintain, as much as possible, similar procedures regardless of the origin of the good because most objectives of border controls apply to all imports. Those examples show that the concern about negative impact on excluded parties can largely disappear in the case of deep commitment provisions and that preferential liberalization could generate positive externalities for third countries.[17]

This is, however, not a universal rule. A characteristic of deep integration liberalization is that there are instances in which discrimination is inevitable and even necessary. The main illustration of this conclusion is provided by mutual recognition agreements (MRAs). MRAs can be negotiated in any regulatory area and are basically a way of lowering barriers to entry into the domestic market for foreign producers without outright harmonization of rules, thus preserving regulatory diversity and allowing countries to maintain national objectives and preferences. Under this principle, parties agree, in essence, to maintain their own regulatory procedures provided that they meet minimum common objectives. Recognition can be agreed both for regulatory standards and for their testing and can be applied in several areas: services (e.g., professional standards and transport), trade facilitation (e.g., declarations made with foreign customs), and technical trade barriers and phytosanitary measures. Another instance in which discrimination is needed relates to customs controls. Modern and efficient, risk-based border management calls for the selective control of imports, focusing on categories that present the highest risk of noncompliance. Risk criteria discriminate, for instance, by product category, country of origin, and identity of shipper, allowing simplified controls for authorized economic operators and express shippers.

Finally, the fact that liberalization in preferential settings could de facto lead to MFN liberalization has profound implications for overall liberalization negotiating strategy. Concessions given to one partner cannot be offered again to another when they are nondiscriminatory and are implicitly offered to the rest of the world. One implication might be that such liberalization is more difficult to achieve because it is more likely to be resisted by domestic firms that would lose not only to the preferential partners, as would be usually the case in a trade-diverting PTA, but also to the world as a whole (Krishna 1998). The reciprocity rationale for signing North-South agreements would also be undermined because offsetting market access preferences for goods (the objective of the South) against deep regulatory commitments (the objective of the North) seems to make little sense for developing countries. Preferences are bound to be eroded over time, but regulatory commitments are both permanent and MFN. Alternatively, as argued by Limão (2007), this asymmetry could provide an incentive for PTAs to maintain high barriers against third countries (through high preferences), in order to provide greater incentives for cooperation in nontrade areas and postpone to a distant future the threat of preference erosion.

Another related consideration is that parties that want to export a certain regulatory model—one more advantageous to their own firms—could gain from being the first to negotiate with a given country. This may be one aspect of the competitive liberalization framework described by Bergsten (1996).

Systemic effects: Deep integration as a building block. Are deep commitments in PTAs building blocks or stumbling blocks with respect to multilateral liberalization? This is a legitimate question, given that the slew of new commitments in PTAs makes these agreements much more invasive and, by adding new dimensions, may create even more hurdles for the welfare-superior objective of multilateral liberalization. Even when the more traditional aspect of tariff preferential liberalization is considered, the answer to this question is not entirely clear, with some analysts arguing that PTAs fundamentally undermine the multilateral system (Bhagwati's "termites") and others seeing in PTAs a

component of an overall dynamic of liberalization (Baldwin and Freund, ch. 6 in this volume).

In the context of deep integration, similar concerns prevail. How do complex and largely ad hoc PTAs touching on services and behind-the-border measures interplay with the multilateral order? Part of the answer was provided in the previous section, where the point was made that liberalization is often MFN in nature, thereby removing concerns about stumbling-block effects in these instances. There is also more to this story, as discussed by Baldwin, Evenett, and Low (2009) and in OECD (2003). Several mechanisms that support further liberalization are actually found in PTA provisions:

- PTAs may enforce or encourage adherence to international standards in, for example, sanitary and phytosanitary measures and technical barriers to trade (Lesser 2007). Numerous PTAs also refer directly to WTO rules.
- Third-party, nonparty MFN clauses are often found in services provisions (Fink and Molinuevo 2007) and in government procurement (Baldwin, Evenett, and Low 2009). According to third-party MFN rules, future and more advantageous commitments with other partners should be granted to PTA partners as well, thus triggering automatic liberalization. A benefit of such rules is that small countries avail themselves of the bargaining power of more powerful countries with common trade partners and so gain increased market access (Baldwin, Evenett, and Low 2009).
- When regimes operate under liberal rules of origin (ROOs) or liberal "denial of benefits" provisions, the provisions are applied not only to preferential trade in goods but also in any instance requiring the establishment of the origin of the partner subject to preferential rules. There are various instances in PTAs; they include access by third parties to MRAs, ROOs that apply to foreign firms that establish local presence in the partner country (Mattoo and Sauvé, ch. 12 in this volume),[18] and government procurement (Dawar and Evenett, ch. 17 in this volume). ROOs applying to regulations often happen to be liberal either because they otherwise become complex to administer or because, as we saw earlier, it does not make sense to operate parallel regulatory systems instead of an MFN system.
- The diffusion of identical and liberalizing rules in PTAs has been particularly noted in "contiguous" PTAs having one partner in common. This occurrence can be seen in investment provisions in agreements in North and South America, in procurement provisions, and in contingent protection (Baldwin, Evenett, and Low 2009). There could, however, be a downside, as large

trading powers export their own—and not necessarily compatible—vision of a liberalization agenda. Prusa (ch. 9 in this volume) describes a phenomenon of rules diffusion in which the EU and the United States act as spokes in their respective networks. More broadly, template approaches to liberalization are often used in PTAs. Rules relating to investment, services liberalization, or standards tend to replicate one of two or three existing models.

In sum, discrimination in the implementation of deep commitments in PTAs should not be underestimated, but there are ways of dealing with it. It should not be underestimated because deep integration creates stealthier and more complex ways to discriminate. Trade partners can push for specific regime designs with the aim of carving out more favorable market access conditions. One example is the insistence by the United States on including customs rules in its FTAs that allow for preferential treatment for express carriers—an industry in which the United States is well represented. However, the parallel with the tariff analysis of preferential liberalization does not necessarily hold because there is less risk of trade diversion, and the welfare implications of preferential liberalization are then necessarily positive. In such cases, PTAs would contribute to overall welfare gain. Moreover the rather complex nature of regulation tends to work to the advantage of MFN liberalization because managing multiple regulatory regimes to create specific preferences is often too complicated.

Policy Complementarities: Taking a Holistic Approach

The expansion of PTAs into new disciplines implies that policy makers are confronted with multiple policy choices with different objectives and complex interactions. In essence, new PTAs capture a broader paradigm than traditional ones. Evans et al. (2006) characterize one aspect of this expanded paradigm by pointing out that, unlike traditional trade liberalization that focuses chiefly on goods trade, deep integration aims at broad factor mobility, including liberalization of investment (capital movement), trade in services, and migration and labor standards. Perhaps nowhere are all the liberalization dimensions explored as deeply and comprehensively as in PTAs. The complementarities created might explain the attraction of PTAs (Mattoo and Sauvé, ch. 12 in this volume). A good example is the trade facilitation agenda, which embraces such goals as the streamlining of numerous border measures (all of which have specific regulatory objectives in sectors such as health, immigration, and security controls); the inclusion of services sectors that facilitate trade (transport, logistics, insurance, and so on);

rules concerning movement of persons; and standards policies.

The other aspect of the broader agenda is, of course, the regulatory one and the inclusion of domestic and other policies that have the objective not of protection but of remedying some sort of market failure. Such policies are included in PTAs at least in part because trade liberalization interacts with their objectives in ways that may often seem to make these objectives more difficult to achieve. Trade policies can no longer be designed on the assumption of their separability from other policies.[19]

Deep integration is as much about trade as it is about other dimensions of economic management and public policy. Starting with liberalization of services, all deep integration policies meet specific objectives, and the liberalization question cannot be divorced from the consideration of these goals. Policy makers should carefully think about why and how trade agreements should serve these objectives in the specific context of PTAs. Table 1.1 offers a snapshot of the variety of such objectives.

In *Termites in the Trading System* (2008), Bhagwati pointedly mocks the ever-expanding notion of trade-related policies: "If I sneeze and use imported cough syrup, that immediately affects imports; if I use domestic cough syrup, that potentially reduces exports of the syrup I have used up." It is true that by pushing the logic ad absurdum, every issue becomes trade related and has a trade effect. Although this does not mean that the impact of non-trade-related policies on trade (and vice versa) should be ignored, it is important to be clear about the primary objectives of policies and how to achieve them. The question for regulatory issues, which are, in essence, behind the border and not unique or specific to traded goods, is of three orders:

1. What are the issues of true international dimension that can *only* be addressed through international agreements?
2. How should behind-the-border rules in PTAs be designed to minimize trade-distorting effects?
3. How should policy makers prepare themselves to negotiate or resist such rules?

The first two questions roughly ask, what is the actual link with trade issues? On the first question, as was seen earlier, market failures and externalities of a supranational nature can be addressed using PTAs; for instance, international transit is a trade facilitation concern that clearly has a regional dimension. Arguably, these issues can also be addressed in separate, dedicated agreements such as bilateral cooperation treaties for competition law or stand-alone transit agreements (see Maur 2008; Dawar and

Table 1.1. Types and Scope of Regulatory Objectives in Selected Areas Covered by Trade Liberalization Agreements

Area	Regulatory objectives
Services	Universal provision (access, prices)
	Standards (professional, safety, interconnection of networks)
	Prudential regulations (banking)
	Cultural exceptions (media)
Standards for goods	Human, plant, and animal health
	Safety
	Network economies
Intellectual property rights (IPRs)	Innovation and creativity
Trade facilitation	Fiscal revenue
	Border security
	Prohibitions
	Immigration control
	Enforcement of domestic laws with respect to foreign goods
	Transit
Government procurement	Preference for national goods
	Protection of sensitive sectors (defense)
Consumer law	Consumer information and protection
Labor and human rights	Minimum standards
Environment	Public goods
	Minimum standards
Movement of persons	Immigration management

Source: Authors' compilation.

Holmes, ch. 16 in this volume). International trade may be an important source of market failure—for instance, with respect to environmental protection (Anuradha, ch. 19 in this volume).[20] Because of the binding nature of international agreements and the international trade dimension of externalities and market failures, there is a space for regulatory frameworks in the context of PTAs. Issues that were previously dealt with under dedicated bilateral instruments, such as bilateral investment treaties, customs cooperation agreements, and cooperation on competition policy, are now increasingly incorporated into PTAs. Although the jury is still out as to the most effective instrument for implementation, PTAs may be superior because of the possibility of issue links and institutional-savings costs, given that one body serves several purposes (Devlin and Estevadeordal 2006).

On the second question, that of reducing distortionary effects, the approach should be to minimize the conflicts between regulatory and trade liberalization objectives. For instance, harmonization to a low standards level would maximize trade liberalization objectives but clearly would not meet regulatory objectives. (Low standards may not meet a country's preferred level of enforcement.) An obvious approach is to ensure that the clarity of regulatory objectives is such that protectionist intents cannot hide themselves behind the disguise of rules. Hidden protectionism operates by raising the costs of (foreign) rivals, by imposing discriminatory rules at home (e.g., by designing

standards in such a way as to exclude foreign products), or by raising standards abroad (e.g., by exporting new regulatory requirements that increase the cost of production abroad and shift comparative advantage patterns).

On the third question, that of negotiating or resisting such rules, a first step is to clarify the policy-making process involved in making future commitments—to begin with, by involving the key ministries and administrations that oversee the nontrade objectives and by ensuring mutual understanding and coherence of objectives. Historically, PTA negotiations have typically been led by finance, foreign affairs, or trade ministries. These ministries would seldom coordinate with other ministries or specialized bodies of government, and sometimes their understanding of the issues at stake is limited. Another step is to minimize the costs of meeting the regulatory objectives, with reasonable statistical confidence. This step is often not done; instead, solutions that meet the objective of regulation irrespective of the costs caused by trade distortions are chosen. The notion of risk is often not embedded in the regulatory design because agencies have no direct interest in considering the costs borne by other parts of the economy in meeting their objectives and naturally opt for regulatory solutions that minimize risk rather than costs. An example is border controls, where 100 percent checking of consignments is not rare, to the exclusion of economically efficient methods of targeting only risky shipments. The marginal costs of meeting regulatory objectives (in particular, the costs for trade) should be balanced against the marginal expected benefits. (Maur and Shepherd, ch. 10 in this volume, discuss this issue in the context of standards.)

An important aspect that may justify resisting the incorporation of regulatory objectives into PTAs is the importance of national endowments and preferences, which will differ among countries. Bhagwati (2008) suggests that the rationales for different labor standards apply to countries that are at different stages of development and have different economic contexts. Although harmonization eliminates the costs associated with duplication and complexity, it can undermine national objectives by departing too much from these aims, and in the case of upward harmonization to stricter regulatory levels, it can raise the costs faced by some countries—often, the poorest ones. The exportation of (higher) regulatory standards and practices has been flagged in the recent literature as integral to the strategy of the two biggest proponents of PTAs, the United States and the EU (Maur 2005; Bhagwati 2008; Horn, Mavroidis, and Sapir 2009). A closer examination of PTA disciplines suggests that template approaches to PTA liberalization are indeed promoted by both hubs. This is worth highlighting because the EU and U.S. approaches generally differ quite substantially. In this volume, the influence of the EU and U.S. hubs is noted, for instance, for contingent protection rules (Prusa, ch. 9), the use of mutual recognition versus equivalence for standards (Maur and Shepherd, ch. 10; Stoler, ch. 11), differing areas of focus regarding IPR protection (Fink, ch. 18), and the diffusion of procurement and investment rules (Miroudot, ch. 14; Dawar and Evenett, ch. 17). PTAs—and bilateral agreements in general—offer a means of dealing with heterogeneity of preferences through the principle of equivalence, which often takes the form of mutual recognition, as was discussed earlier.

Flexibility and Customized Problem Solving

The flexibility offered by PTAs in terms of tailoring the level of ambition of given disciplines to particular trading partners is one finding from the early work on the new wave of PTAs (Heydon 2003). Although special and differential treatment and policy space are important features of modern trade negotiations involving developing countries, here we take the logic farther, arguing that it is not only the nature of partner countries and their capacity that dictate the need for such flexibility but also the regulatory issues themselves.

Many of the new policies captured in the latest generation of PTAs do not lend themselves to reduction to standalone legal language in a trade agreement. Rather, deep integration requires flexibility and customization in the way provisions are drafted:

- Provisions in the agreement compose only one of the building blocks of broader cooperation, which may include institutional arrangements, whether hard (e.g., a common institution) or soft (e.g., expert consultations), as well as technical assistance and capacity building.
- Gradual implementation is advisable, as reform may not be carried out overnight and will present unique challenges in a given country context.
- Flexibility is necessary for joint projects such as harmonization work and creation of common regional tools.
- Areas of cooperation will need to be reexamined as regulatory needs change over time.
- Deep integration areas will have to be revisited as understanding of how best to address regulatory dimensions evolves.
- Implementation of policy has to be monitored.
- Recourse to venues other than dispute settlement is needed.

Reliance on a rigid interpretation of an international agreement and on enforcement through dispute settlement is insufficient for the deep integration dimensions of liberalization (Hoekman, ch. 4 in this volume). Deep integration requires a combination of hard and soft law and enhanced capacity. The reasons for this are (a) practicalities, (b) uncertainty, and (c) political economy.

The first problem is practical and procedural: the appropriate implementation of behind-the-border policies requires a set of actions, ranging from enactment of legal provisions to establishment of adequate structures, including appropriate governance and rules, material and personnel for operationalizing the policies, and reporting mechanisms. All this is highly complex and is difficult to specify in full in an international agreement, and it might as well be left to domestic authorities to work out.

The second problem arises from the fact that there is uncertainty about the most appropriate design for regulatory policies and their implementation, since these aspects probably depends on country circumstances. A good example is the variety of competition provision rules and setups in PTAs (Dawar and Holmes, ch. 16 in this volume). Configurations of common competition regimes and provisions are greatly influenced by national regimes and by partners' size and level of development. Another source of uncertainty is time, because technological changes, for instance, may fundamentally affect the nature of the goods and services exchanged and the way markets, market operators, and government bodies conduct their work (in, for example, telecommunication services, standards policies, and border controls).

Finally, the political economy of PTAs that rely on soft-law mechanisms might be more supportive of actual liberalization than is the case with a top-down approach in which rules are rigidly imposed by a powerful trade partner. Ownership can be enhanced through cooperation and stakeholder involvement, which would be part of a process of identifying appropriate regulatory solutions for liberalization (Hoekman, ch. 4 in this volume). This is related to respect for country preferences while reducing differences with a view toward mutual recognition of regulations.

Thus, flexibility seems to be an important dimension to be considered in deep integration. This recognition gives rise to a recommendation for "living agreements" that incorporate a work program and for associated institutions that establish a pathway allowing deeper integration over time and the resolution of standards issues. Hoekman (ch. 4 in this volume) similarly argues in favor of a constructive rather than adversarial process in North-South PTAs. A problem with purely adversarial procedures is that they tend to leave unaddressed public good issues, whereas supranational institutions have an incentive to pursue such matters. PTAs then become instruments of cooperation, in addition to integration, and can provide a problem-solving forum for countries that are undertaking reform and upgrading their regulatory capacities.

Another aspect of the flexible approach toward deep integration is the implication for approaches to dispute settlement. On the one hand, negotiating and implementing deep integration dimensions is costly, creating a motive for ensuring a return on this investment by the establishment of strong dispute settlement mechanisms (Porges, ch. 22 in this volume). This may explain the observed trend toward more legalistic forms of dispute resolution, replacing the more diplomatic approaches of older agreements. In this regard, WTO-like ad hoc panels (which, among other things, permit recourse to the expertise of specialists) are often preferred. On the other hand, dispute settlement is only one of the several mechanisms in PTAs contributing to enforcement. Panel-type disputes only occur in exceptional cases, and smaller disagreements are resolved through other channels established in the PTAs. The latter approach is what can be described as soft law. In this respect, common institutions play an important role, allowing technical and ad hoc approaches to solving what are often complex issues and facilitating the involvement of third parties, such as the private sector.

As has already been indicated, the extent to which a PTA is symmetrical or not—that is, the degree to which the partners are equal or similar in level of development or economic size—has implications for the choice of degree of flexibility and informality. In this sense, a flexible approach can be seen as a building block for more formal arrangements down the line. Porges (ch. 22 in this volume) notes that dispute settlement tends to become more legalistic when the relationship is symmetric, whereas when it is asymmetric, political and diplomatic approaches are preferred. Although the softer structure may be seen as a way of affording flexibility to smaller partners and as reflecting the unequal balance of power, it leaves the solving of disputes to less transparent conduits in which power may be more easily wielded.

Implementation

The inadequacy of a solely legalistic approach to commitments implies that negotiations will not settle every issue and that, in addition to the ex ante work of negotiators, an important ex post agenda awaits countries signing PTAs. It can be argued that the implementation agenda is *on paper* more important in the case of PTAs than in the WTO. There are essentially two reasons for this. The first is that PTAs commit parties to effective liberalization, whereas the WTO often merely commits parties to bind only maximum levels of protection and provides numerous exemptions and exceptions for developing countries.[21] The second reason is that deep PTAs cover newer and more ambitious ground than does the WTO.

In some areas, the track record of PTAs in implementation has been relatively poor. Reviews of services (Mattoo and Sauvé, ch. 12 in this volume), and of competition provisions (Dawar and Holmes, ch. 16 in this volume) suggest unimpressive results, while in areas that have seen more pressure toward implementation, such as IPRs, the evidence shows much more substantial changes (Biadgleng and Maur forthcoming). The different treatment for IPRs is the direct result of the greater prominence of implementation and enforcement in recent PTAs involving the United States and Europe.

Dealing with deep integration issues requires preparedness that goes well beyond the negotiation stage, and most likely it entails the dedication of some permanent resources to managing the agreement. The resource and policy implications of deep integration agreements are likely to be, in part, unforeseen, as Hoekman (ch. 4 in this volume) suggests, and the problems may be compounded by countries' lack of preparedness. Examples of possible unintended consequences of commitments include incompatibilities between PTA commitments and the existing (domestic and international) legal environment;[22] political-economy constraints, where commitments are not accepted by domestic constituencies, including legislators who may have to vote on new laws; limitations on regulatory freedom; inefficiency in implementing the new regulatory environment; and economic implications that are less beneficial than initially thought.

Beyond the principle of liberalization agreed in the PTA, a work program of implementation must be devised in order to make liberalization a reality. The implementation of the provisions of an agreement may require different levels of intervention. First, institutional changes may be necessary because the implementation of new areas of policy may call for the establishment of new regulatory agencies or the reorganization of existing institutions. Second, new laws for regulatory reform will be required to reflect PTA commitments. The need for such legislation will vary, depending on the legal standing of international commitments in domestic law: some commitments require translation into domestic law, while others have direct effect, and some law systems rely more on a case law approach. The third dimension of implementation consists of the administrative, procedural, and operational changes required to comply with the new regulatory framework. This can include the management of the agreement itself, including transparency and monitoring requirements. Finally, enforcement of the newly adopted regulations needs to be considered; the requisite staff and resources will have to be allocated. Attention should be given to the quality of enforcement and to measures for assessing the effectiveness of the application of the laws (Biadgleng and Maur forthcoming).

The text of the PTA is only one initial element of the process of integration. Implementation issues must also be carefully examined to determine whether liberalization is effective. Monitoring and accountability matter. This is a more complex process than verifying that trade barriers are effectively dismantled, and the necessary information is often not readily available. In general, implementation in PTAs is not a very transparent process, and sustained attention to implementation is rare. This is an additional reason for the constructive cooperative approach recommended by Hoekman (ch. 4 in this volume), given the complementarity between information generation and exchange and the process for discovery of the best trade-facilitating regulatory solution.

In spite of some evidence that monitoring is taking place, information about implementation remains scarce, and most of the analysis of PTAs rests on the evidence provided by the agreements themselves and on some measures of outcomes such as trade flows.[23] Although such analysis provides useful insights, the policy recommendations that can be drawn from it are limited. Little is known about which liberalization strategies work best as agents of change

and which of the hard-law–soft-law approaches, or combinations thereof, contribute most to liberalization. The inference from the above discussion is that although many examples and many distinctive approaches to integration now exist, there is still relatively little basis for recommendations on how to appropriately implement deep integration provisions in PTAs, beyond a core set of principles.

For developing countries, one attraction of PTAs with more developed partners, at least in theory, is the prospect of access to capacity building and transfer of resources. Yet whether and how development assistance contributes to implementation is generally difficult to assess, and is even more so in the context of PTAs, given the naturally non-transparent nature of institutions.

An important issue that appears prominently in the discussion on competition policy, government procurement, and standards is to what extent the process of implementation should be run from the center. For instance, competition regimes in PTA contexts range from regional institutions to national institutions that cooperate on international issues. Several considerations affect whether the implementation process will be left to national government or devolved to a transnational body (Dawar and Evenett, ch. 17 in this volume).

The first, obvious point is that a prerequisite for common institutions or rules is the willingness of trade partners to abandon some of their sovereignty. When this does not happen (often, in the context of North-South agreements), only "lighter" options remain, and only core principles guaranteeing good policy and governance can be agreed. This is the solution chosen for procurement provisions. A related concern is the choice between maintaining national preferences and adopting international standards. In this area, the answer to the question of harmonization versus recognition depends on whether the benefits of harmonization outweigh the costs of loss of preferences. National ability to issue regulations is also a parameter to be taken into account. In particular, one motivation for preserving diversity in regulation and implementation is to derive the benefits from competition between different regulatory solutions and procedures. Messerlin and Zarrouk (2000) advocate less centralization in the context of conformity assessment in order to promote competition between different conformity bodies and their services (e.g., testing, surveillance, inspection, certification, etc.).

A second point is the degree of coordination that is required by the integration policy. For some transnational public goods, common institutions and a top-down approach may be preferable in order to solve the coordination problems that lead to inadequate supply of the goods.

Beyond public goods per se, common institutions appear particularly necessary when frequent interactions, decision making, adjudication, and exchange of information are needed, as in customs unions. (See Andriamananjara, ch. 5 in this volume.) A related dimension is the desire to achieve certain scale or efficiency effects. Competition policy illustrates the possibility of opting for a common, centralized competition regime—as in the cases of the EU, the Caribbean Community (CARICOM), COMESA, and the Andean Pact—when parties to a PTA do not differ much in their preferences regarding the type of competition enforcement.

For developing countries in particular, a top-down approach may prove attractive. A first incentive might be to improve governance. By decentralizing decision making within a PTA, member countries may be better able to shield policies from the risk of reversal and guarantee their independence. This strategy may be helpful, for example, for competition policy, where it might be difficult in some countries to escape the influence of particularly large firms and to discipline them. More generally, as discussed earlier, countries with weak judicial systems might find it advantageous to rely on supranational judicial institutions as a way of anchoring or locking in policies. Poor administrative resources at the country level could also motivate the pooling of resources among a group of countries—something small island countries have done.

Finally, a third consideration is efficiency motives, which may lead some countries to seek to replace their existing regulations with superior systems "imported" from partner countries and, through the institutional mechanisms of the PTA, to obtain access to the superior expertise and systems of the partner country.

Conclusions

Modern PTAs are evolving rapidly. They are increasingly deep, and they affect all countries and regions of the world, including the most remote quarters. As academics and policy makers try to deal with this new generation of PTAs, four tentative conclusions can be suggested regarding this changing landscape.

1. *Deep integration introduces a change of paradigm.* To be sure, PTAs still have to do with preferences, discrimination, and exclusion. They may lead to suboptimal outcomes and could complicate and even undermine progress toward a more open, rules-based, and nondiscriminatory multilateral trading system. More worrying than discrimination, perhaps, is the additional inherent complexity that is created by the overlapping and conflicting regulatory regimes promoted by myriads of PTAs. This concern has

already been clearly articulated, and a call for multilateralizing regionalism has been voiced in the WTO (Baldwin and Low 2009). The concern that PTAs "compete" with multilateral negotiations for the attention of negotiators and represent an untidy way of proceeding to liberalization remains legitimate.

Yet, an important emerging lesson is that the economic paradigm of shallow PTAs does not necessarily apply to deep and comprehensive PTAs. "Old" concepts such as mercantilist reciprocal liberalization, trade creation and diversion, or a textual approach to negotiating PTAs may still underpin the reasoning of many policy makers but are often archaic or incomplete for deep integration liberalization. Failure to understand the new paradigm of preferential integration may, in turn, explain why most PTAs either have not fully exploited the liberalization opportunities of behind-the-border measures or have not prioritized the opportunities closest to the parties' interests—although it might be naïve to attribute lack of progress solely to a lack of understanding.

2. *Deep integration PTAs are potentially powerful tools for pushing wide-ranging government-owned reforms.* Beyond market access, deep integration PTAs create opportunities to complement trade liberalization with other behind-the-border reforms. In addition, they offer unique instruments for promoting bilateral or plurilateral cooperation and resource transfers, transparency mechanisms, mutual equivalence, informal mechanisms for dispute resolution, in-depth and expert dialogue, and deeper liberalization among the willing parties. These are not approaches that can be easily, if at all, replicated in the large and formal setting of multilateral institutions.

Yet PTAs are worthwhile only if governments are themselves committed to reform and liberalization. PTAs offer a variety of mechanisms by which the process of reform will become more effectively and irremediably set in motion, but a prerequisite is that meaningful commitments be agreed to in the first place. Deep integration PTAs should therefore strive to provide open access to regulatory rules and disciplines in order to ensure equality of treatment of all members and nonmembers and so minimize the occurrence of "regulatory preferences." This means—beyond national treatment—liberal rules of origin, transparency, and the availability of due process. Good regulatory practice should lead de jure preferential liberalization to become, in effect, MFN liberalization. The question of discrimination in deep PTAs is likely to remain convoluted. Discriminatory regulations could take many forms, whether codified in rules or not. De facto preferences can arise from rules that look nonpreferential on paper, or from preferential enforcement. Furthermore, discrimination may, paradoxically, be the only form of acceptable liberalization, as parties mutually agree to accept each other's rules.

3. *Deep integration should be pursued strategically and selectively.* Another answer to complexity that is, in our view, not sufficiently considered by developing countries, is selectivity. (This is also suggested by Hoekman and Sekkat 2010.) Liberalization is a complex matter, not only from a capacity standpoint but also from a political one. The political economy of deep integration involves many (often opposing) interests and a large set of potential stakeholders. Overloading the negotiating agenda (which will later become the implementing agenda) diverts the focus from what may be achievable and from the areas where gains may be the most important. Agreements bloated by too many issues may lose significance and fail to achieve much.

Picking meaningful issues with the right partner, along with having adequate technical assistance and a cooperative approach, may bring about substantial progress on liberalization and serve as a positive signal or trigger for more challenging areas. Market access should not be the only item on the agenda of negotiators, especially those of developing countries, since deep integration really entails thinking about a domestic reform strategy. Prioritization of core objectives and sequencing should be central concerns of negotiators. Sound regulatory practice should underpin liberalization to minimize the prevalence of regulatory preferences and ensure the overall consistency of liberalization and regulatory objectives.

4. *There is no one-size-fits-all model of deep integration.* As policy makers more and more integrate these new dimensions, we can expect that they will use PTAs more intensively to further liberalization objectives—it may be hoped, in a way complementary to multilateral efforts. Liberalization in any sector is not a simple matter. It escapes easy characterization, as well as one-size-fits-all types of answers. This complexity means that there are few universal rules to follow; rather, carefully designed and specific solutions are needed. Deep integration is essentially a sui generis process, as is illustrated by Winters (2010) in the case of the EU. Yet complexity means that some core principles should be followed in order to promote, to the extent possible, market-based solutions.

The dynamics of North-South, South-South, and North-North PTAs differ considerably. Asymmetric agreements make cooperation less easy and may provide less scope for transnational public goods and mutual recognition but offer more prospects for lock-in and greater access to imported regulatory regimes, when needed. Market access considerations will be paramount for the small partner, whereas the larger partner will seek, beyond market access, to diffuse its regulatory norms, including values

norms, and to trigger competitive liberalization effects in partner countries. A related logic can be observed in the EU, which, as Maur (2005) notes, is attempting to leverage its PTAs to shape South-South agreements in its recent wave of agreements with the Mediterranean countries, the Balkans, and the African, Caribbean, and Pacific (ACP) countries.

Notes

The authors thank Jaime de Melo, Ndiame Diop, Bernard Hoekman, and Richard Newfarmer for helpful comments and suggestions.

1. In a WTO working paper, Fiorentino, Verdeja, and Toqueboeuf (2006) note that country negotiating resources are being shifted away from multilateral negotiations toward negotiations on PTAs.

2. The General Agreement on Tariffs and Trade (GATT) architecture was historically built, essentially, around the notion of negative integration and the prohibition of the most detrimental policies through elimination of border trade barriers and the espousal of nondiscrimination principles (Hoekman and Kostecki 2009). Recently, however, new forms of economic integration have been included in the multilateral trade framework, starting with the Kennedy Round and the General Agreement on Trade in Services (GATS) in 1979 and continuing with the WTO (and the incorporation of TRIPS, in particular). The WTO incorporates much more significant elements of positive integration than previously. PTAs follow the same trend and go even further in many instances.

3. Torrent (2007) provides the following example: "The European Community directives on the liberalization of movements of capital seem to be a clear example of 'negative' integration, but they were enacted according to what, in Tinbergen's terms, would be a clear example of 'positive integration' (and they would be defended in this way by many in the European Commission). In political terms, NAFTA's [North American Free Trade Agreement's] Chapter XI on investments would be looked at by many around the world as a typical example of 'negative integration' that sharply reduces the capacity of Governments to intervene in the economy. It is also an example of 'positive integration' that creates common rules that go beyond the liberalization of access (for example on protection of investments)."

4. According to Ethier (1998) and, subsequently, Levy (2009), attracting foreign direct investment (FDI) is one of the main incentives for entering into PTAs.

5. Technology allows services to be traded under several modal forms; for instance, medical diagnostics can now be provided at a distance, thanks to electronic imagery.

6. Note that well-being can be understood in broad terms as including not only economic welfare but also value-related preferences.

7. In economics, nonrivalry means that consumption of the good by one individual does not reduce the availability of the good for consumption by others. Nonexcludability means that no one can be effectively excluded from using the good.

8. According to Levy (2009), several mechanisms could be in play: (a) once a bureaucracy commits to good governance in a trade agreement, it may make little sense to maintain a different attitude for the domestic market; (b) good governance with respect to international flows could serve as a signal, spurring reform on the domestic front; and (c) if the rule of law is not followed within the country, there might be costly and adverse reputational spillovers that could affect the decisions of foreign investors and traders.

9. The decision to focus on coal and steel came about not only because of the economic importance of the two sectors but also because these materials were considered the main inputs for making weapons. "The pooling of coal and steel production should immediately provide for the setting up of common foundations for economic development as a first step in the federation of Europe, and will change the destinies of those regions which have long been devoted to the manufacture of

munitions of war, of which they have been the most constant victims" (Robert Schuman, Declaration of 9 May 1950).

10. "The EU can make an important contribution by working around the conflict issues, promoting similar reforms on both sides of the boundary lines, to foster convergence between political, economic and legal systems, enabling greater social inclusion and contributing to confidence building" (European Commission 2007).

11. World Bank (2005), however, notes that some wars began partly as trade disputes; examples are the U.S. Civil War (1861–65) and the Soccer War of 1969 between El Salvador and Honduras.

12. The Electricity Regulatory Forum, or Florence Forum, was set up to discuss the creation of a true internal electricity market in the EU. Since 1998, the forum has met once or twice a year, formerly in Florence and now in Rome. Further information on the Florence Forum is available on the Web page of the European Commission's Directorate General for Energy; see http://ec.europa.eu/energy/gas_electricity/forum_electricity_florence_en.htm. A similar body, the Madrid Forum, has been established for natural gas markets.

13. Thus, regulation does not necessarily generate positive terms-of-trade effects for the home country (e.g., customs duties revenues, in the case of tariff protection).

14. In most cases, the situation is not that clear-cut. Regulatory burdens often create additional jobs for administrations and provide opportunities for graft.

15. In normal circumstances, there should be no prior rent capture by domestic interests, since the objective of regulatory controls is not to raise revenue or afford protection.

16. The distinction is often blurred, and when identification methods are imperfect, origin is often used as a very imperfect proxy for other characteristics (as is country of citizenship for migrants).

17. This claim was tested empirically by Czubala, Shepherd, and Wilson (2009) in the context of adoption of international standards.

18. Baldwin, Evenett, and Low (2009) cite the example of ROOs in East Asian PTAs as particularly liberal, since they only require incorporation under the laws of the trade partner and do not impose any other nationality requirements on the entity, regarding, for example, the nationality of the people controlling the firm.

19. Although separability never really existed in practice, the traditional approach was to consider trade policy in relative isolation from other policies, including other economic policies.

20. Environmental externalities could also stem from purely domestic economic activities.

21. In terms of liberalization, PTAs will at least lock in the status quo if disciplines in an area are included. This is furthered by the use of negative-list approaches, as in some services provisions. Thus, the value of commitments in PTAs is higher than in the WTO. In this sense PTAs are more rigid. This may be a reason developed countries have intensively used PTAs with smaller developing countries as a way to lock in liberalization in a way that was not necessarily happening in the WTO. But with stricter commitments looming, resistance to liberalization may also be stronger.

22. Biadgleng and Maur (2010) cite the example of commitments made by the Arab Republic of Egypt with the EU to ratify, in contradiction to its own law, the Convention for the Protection of New Varieties of Plants established by the International Union for the Protection of New Varieties of Plants (UPoV).

23. Examples of different approaches to monitoring implementation are seen in the United States, which "certifies" implementation of FTAs before congressional approval; the EU, which reports regularly in the case of accession and in more ad hoc fashion with other partners on implementation; APEC implementation action plans; and South-South agreements such as COMESA, for which the secretariat monitors country progress.

References

Bagwell, Kyle, and Robert Staiger. 2001. "The WTO as a Mechanism for Securing Market Access Property Rights: Implications for Global Labor and Environmental Issues." *Journal of Economic Perspectives* 15 (3): 69–88.

Baldwin, Richard E. 1994. "Towards an Integrated Europe." Centre for Economic Policy Research, London. http://heiwww.unige.ch/~baldwin/.

———. 2008. "Sequencing and Depth of Regional Economic Integration: Lessons for the Americas from Europe." *World Economy* 31 (1): 5–30.

Baldwin Richard, Simon Evenett, and Patrick Low. 2009. "Beyond Tariffs: Multilateralizing Non-Tariff RTA Commitments." In *Multilateralizing Regionalism: Challenges for the Global Trading System*, ed. Richard Baldwin and Patrick Low, ch. 3. Cambridge, U.K.: Cambridge University Press.

Baldwin, Richard, and Patrick Low. 2009. *Multilateralizing Regionalism: Challenges for the Global Trading System*. Cambridge, U.K.: Cambridge University Press.

Bergsten, Fred. 1996. "Globalizing Free Trade." *Foreign Affairs* 75 (3): 105–20.

Bhagwati, Jagdish. 2008. *Termites in the Trading System: How Preferential Agreements Undermine Free Trade*. Oxford, U.K.: Oxford University Press.

Biadgleng, Ermias Tekeste, and Jean-Christophe Maur. Forthcoming. "The Influence of Preferential Trade Agreements on Implementation of Intellectual Property Rights in Developing countries: A First Look." Issue Paper (forthcoming), ICTSD Programme on Innovation, Technology, and Intellectual Property, International Centre for Trade and Sustainable Development, Geneva, Switzerland.

Carrère, Céline, Jaime de Melo, and Bormolaa Tumurchudur. 2010. "Disentangling Market Access Effects of Preferential Trading Arrangements with an Application for ASEAN Members under an ASEAN-EU FTA." *World Economy* 33 (1): 42–59.

Czubala, Witold, Ben Shepherd, and John S. Wilson. 2009. "Help or Hindrance? The Impact of Harmonized Standards on African Exports." *Journal of African Economies* 18 (5): 711–44.

Devlin, Robert, and Antoni Estevadeordal. 2006. "Trade and Cooperation: A Regional Public Goods Approach." In *Multilateral and Regional Frameworks for Globalization: WTO and Free Trade Agreements*, ed. Wonhyuk Lim and Ramon Torrent. Seoul: Korea Development Institute.

Estevadeordal, Antoni, Kati Suominen, and Robert Teh. 2009. *Regional Rules in the Global Trading System*. Cambridge, U.K.: Cambridge University Press.

Ethier, Wilfred J. 1998. "The New Regionalism." *Economic Journal* 108 (449): 1149–61.

European Commission. 2007. *A Strong Neighbourhood Policy*. Communication COM(2007)774 final. Brussels: European Commission.

Evans, David, Peter Holmes, Leonardo Iacovone, and Sherman Robinson. 2006. "Deep Integration and New Regionalism." In *Assessing Regional Trade Agreements with Developing Countries: Shallow and Deep Integration, Trade, Productivity, and Economic Performance*, ch. 2. Report for DFID Project Number 04 5881, University of Sussex, U.K.

Evenett, Simon, and Michael Meier. 2008. "An Interim Assessment of the US Trade Policy of 'Competitive Liberalization.'" *World Economy* 31 (1): 31–66.

Fink, Carsten, and Martin Molinuevo. 2007. "East Asian Free Trade Agreements in Services: Roaring Tigers or Timid Pandas?" World Bank, Washington, D.C.

Fiorentino, Roberto V., Luis Verdeja, and Christelle Toqueboeuf. 2006. "The Changing Landscape of Regional Trade Agreements: 2006 Update." WTO Discussion Paper 12, World Trade Organization, Geneva.

Haftel, Yoram Z. 2007. "Designing for Peace: Regional Integration Arrangements, Institutional Variation, and Militarized Interstate Disputes." *International Organization* 61 (1): 217–37.

Harrison, Glenn W., Thomas Rutherford, and David Tarr. 2002. "Trade Policy Options for Chile: The Importance of Market Access." *World Bank Economic Review* 16 (1): 49–79.

Heydon, Ken. 2003. "Key Findings. Regionalism: A Complement, Not a Substitute." In *Regionalism and the Multilateral Trading System*. Paris: OECD Publishing.

Hoekman, Bernard, Aaditya Mattoo, and André Sapir. 2007. "The Political Economy of Services Trade Liberalization: A Case for International Regulatory Cooperation?" CEPR Discussion Paper 6457, Centre for Economic and Policy Research, London.

Hoekman, Bernard, and Michel Kostecki. 2009. *The Political Economy of the World Trading System,* 3rd ed. Oxford, U.K.: Oxford University Press.

Hoekman, Bernard, and Khalid Sekkat. 2010. "Arab Economic Integration: The Missing Links." CEPR Discussion Paper 7807, Centre for Economic and Policy Research, London.

Horn, Henrik, Petros C. Mavroidis, and André Sapir. 2010. "Beyond the WTO? An Anatomy of EU and US Preferential Trade Agreements." *The World Economy* 33(11), 1565–88.

Hornbeck, J. F. 2003. *The U.S.–Central America Free Trade Agreement (CAFTA): Challenges for Sub-Regional Integration.* Report for the U.S. Congress, RL31870. Washington, DC: Government Printing Office.

Krishna, Pravin. 1998. "Regionalism and Multilateralism: A Political Economy Approach." *Quarterly Journal of Economics* 113 (1): 227–50.

Krugman, Paul. 1993. "Regionalism versus Multilateralism: Analytic Notes." In *New Dimensions in Regional Integration*, ed. Jaime de Melo and Arvind Panagariya. Cambridge, U.K.: Cambridge University Press.

Lee, Jong-Wha, and Ju Hyun Pyun. 2009. "Does Trade Integration Contribute to Peace?" Asian Development Bank Working Paper on Regional Integration 24, Asian Development Bank, Manila.

Lesser, Caroline. 2007. "Do Bilateral and Regional Approaches for Reducing Technical Barriers to Trade Converge towards the Multilateral Trading System?" OECD Trade Policy Working Paper 58, Organisation for Economic Co-operation and Development, Paris.

Levy, Philip I. 2009. "The United States–Peru Free Trade Agreement: What Did You Expect?" American Enterprise Institute Working Paper Series on Development Policy 1, American Enterprise Institute, Washington, DC.

Limão, Nuno. 2007. "Are Preferential Trade Agreements with Non-trade Objectives a Stumbling Block for Multilateral Liberalization?" *Review of Economic Studies* 74 (3): 821–55.

Mansfield, Edward D., and Jon C. Pevehouse. 2000. "Trade Blocs, Trade Flows, and International Conflict." *International Organization* 54 (4): 775–808.

Martin, Philippe, Thierry Mayer, and Mathias Thoenig. 2010. "The Geography of Conflicts and Free Trade Agreements." CEPR Discussion Paper 7740, Centre for Economic and Policy Research, London.

Maur, Jean-Christophe. 2005. "Exporting Europe's Trade Policy." *World Economy* 28 (11): 1565–90.

———. 2008. "Regionalism and Trade Facilitation: A Primer." *Journal of World Trade* 42 (6): 979–1012.

Messerlin, Patrick, and Jamel Zarrouk. 2000. "Trade Facilitation: Technical Regulations and Customs Procedures." *World Economy* 23 (4): 577–93.

OECD (Organisation for Economic Co-operation and Development). 2003. *Regionalism and the Multilateral Trading System.* Paris: OECD Publishing.

Ortino, Federico. 2004. *Basic Legal Instruments for the Liberalisation of Trade: A Comparative Analysis of EC and WTO Law.* Oxford, U.K.: Hart.

Pelkmans, Jacques. 1984. *Market Integration in the European Community.* Studies in Industrial Organization, vol. 5. The Hague: Martinus Nijhoff.

Schiff, Maurice, and L. Alan Winters. 1998. "Regional Integration as Diplomacy." *World Bank Economic Review* 12: 271–95.

———. 2002. "Regional Cooperation, and the Role of International Organizations and Regional Integration." Policy Research Working Paper 2872, World Bank, Washington. DC.

———. 2004. *Regional Integration and Development.* Oxford, U.K.: Oxford University Press.

Schott, Jeffrey J. 2003. "Assessing US FTA Policy." In *Free Trade Agreements: US Strategies and Priorities*, ed. Jeffrey Schott, ch. 13. Washington, DC: Institute for International Economics.

Tinbergen, Jan. 1954. *International Economic Integration.* Amsterdam: Elsevier.

Torrent, Ramon. 2007. "The Legal Toolbox for Regional Integration: A Legal Analysis from an Interdisciplinary Perspective." Prepared for the Euro-Latin Study Network on Integration and Trade (ELSNIT) Conference, Barcelona, October 26–27.

Winters, L. Alan. 1997. "What Can European Experience Teach Developing Countries About Integration?" *World Economy* 20 (7): 889–911.

———. 2010. "Europe Is Sui Generis—But It Provides Lessons for Developing Countries." Prepared for the Annual Conference of the Global Development Network, Prague, January 16–18.

World Bank. 2005. *Global Economic Prospects: Trade, Regionalism, and Development.* Washington, DC: World Bank.

2

LANDSCAPE

Rohini Acharya, Jo-Ann Crawford, Maryla Maliszewska,
and Christelle Renard

Preferential trade agreements (PTAs) are an enduring feature of the contemporary multilateral trading system. Sixty years after the founding of the General Agreement on Tariffs and Trade (GATT), the global trading landscape has changed beyond recognition. Membership in the World Trade Organization (WTO) continues to grow steadily, but meanwhile, participation in PTAs is expanding at an unprecedented rate. Slow progress in the Doha Round trade negotiations has no doubt contributed to this growth trend. As of February 2010, 266 PTAs were in force, and this figure did not include a significant number of agreements (mostly among developing countries) that had not yet been notified to the WTO, or the many PTAs still in the pipeline. As a consequence, a growing proportion of world trade is, or has the potential to be, conducted under preferential terms rather than under the nondiscriminatory regime of the WTO. In addition, trade conducted under preferential rules is increasingly subject to a plethora of crisscrossing regulatory regimes that modify and complicate the WTO's multilateral regulatory regime.

All but one of the WTO's 153 members is a party to at least one PTA (Mongolia is the exception), and most countries are parties to several. Today's PTAs are characterized by diverse geographic and physical configurations and differing regulatory content. Although PTAs offer the potential for increased trade and investment among their members through enhanced market access, they do so at the cost of introducing multiple layers of complexity into the global trading landscape, rendering trade relations less transparent and more unpredictable.

The aims of this chapter are (a) to provide a snapshot (as of February 2010) of recent developments and trends with respect to the number and scope of PTAs, (b) to analyze the types of PTA initiatives that are currently under negotiation in each geographic region, and (c) to assess the possible impact of a selection of plurilateral PTAs on trade

developments. Unless otherwise stated, the data presented take account of all bilateral, regional, and plurilateral trade agreements of a preferential reciprocal nature that have been notified to the GATT/WTO (see box 2.1 for definitions). The focus is on free trade agreements (FTAs), customs unions (CUs), partial-scope agreements in the area of trade in goods, and economic integration agreements (EIAs) in the area of trade in services.[1]

Trends among PTAs

Recent developments and trends are shaping a PTA landscape that presents a number of significant features.

The first is *ubiquity.* PTA participation is becoming more diverse, spreading to most geographic regions, but especially to East Asia and the Pacific. North-South preferential partnerships are on the rise, with a number of developing countries electing to forgo unilateral programs—such as the generalized system of preferences (GSP) or trading arrangements previously conducted under a WTO waiver—in favor of reciprocal agreements. These developments are testing the negotiating capacity of developing countries, particularly where they have to deal with issues for which no multilateral rules currently exist or where the negotiating framework differs from that of the WTO. Such is the case, for instance, in PTAs covering trade in services.

The second is *consolidation.* Bilateral relationships are being replaced by plurilateral PTAs among the same partners, and agreements between regional blocs are on the increase. In Asia, countries long resistant to preferential trade liberalization are catching up, and plurilateral PTAs coexist alongside bilateral PTAs among the same sets of partners. Notwithstanding some consolidation, the growing number of overlapping plurilateral PTAs—particularly in Africa and Central Asia but also, increasingly, in the Americas and Asia—points to a further fragmentation of

Box 2.1. Typology of Preferential Trade Agreements

Care should be taken when categorizing preferential trade agreements (PTAs), given the differences in terminology used by institutions and researchers. In this study, we use the generic term PTA to refer to all reciprocal preferential agreements. The World Trade Organization (WTO), however, uses the term regional trade agreements (RTA) for all reciprocal preferential agreements and reserves PTA for nonreciprocal preferential agreements such as the generalized system of preferences (GSP) and the African Growth and Opportunity Act (AGOA). The terminology employed in this chapter is explained below.

Free trade agreement (FTA). An agreement between two or more parties in which tariffs and other trade barriers are eliminated on most or all trade. Each party maintains its own tariff structure relative to third parties. Examples are the North American Free Trade Agreement (NAFTA) and the Japan–Singapore New-Age Economic Partnership Agreement.

Customs union (CU). An agreement between two or more parties in which tariffs and other trade barriers are eliminated on most or all trade. In addition, the parties adopt a common commercial policy toward third parties that includes the establishment of a common external tariff. Thus, products entering the customs union from third parties face the same tariff regardless of the country of entry. Examples are the Southern Cone Common Market (Mercosur, Mercado Común del Sur) and the agreement between the European Union (EU) and Turkey.

Partial-scope agreement. An agreement between two or more parties that offer each other concessions on a selected number of products or sectors. Examples are the Asia-Pacific Trade Agreement (APTA) and the agreement between the Lao People's Democratic Republic and Thailand.

Economic integration agreement (EIA). An agreement covering trade in services through which two or more parties offer preferential market access to each other. Examples are the U.S.–Peru and Thailand–Australia PTAs. Typically, services provisions are contained in a single PTA that also covers goods. An EIA may be negotiated some time after the agreement covering goods; for example, the Caribbean Community (CARICOM) and the European Free Trade Association (EFTA) have negotiated separate services protocols.

Preferential trade agreement (PTA). The generic term used in this study to denote all forms of reciprocal preferential trade agreements, including bilateral and plurilateral agreements.

The figure shows the breakdown of PTAs covering trade in goods notified to the WTO and in force as of February 2010. FTAs are by far the most common type, accounting for 83 percent of all PTAs. Customs unions, a deeper form of integration, require significant policy coordination between their parties. They are more time consuming to negotiate, are less common, and make up only 10 percent of all PTAs. Partial-scope agreements account for the remaining 7 percent.

Types of PTAs Notified to the WTO

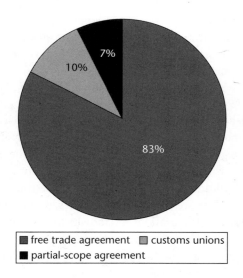

Legend: free trade agreement   customs unions   partial-scope agreement

Source: WTO Secretariat.

trading relations and to complications for traders, exporters, and customs authorities alike.

The third is the changing *structural configuration* of PTAs. Bilateral PTAs are increasingly becoming the norm. Such PTAs are concluded more quickly than those involving multiple partners. More significantly, they are indicative of

a shift away from viewing the agreements as a means of forging traditional regional partnerships among several geographically proximate countries and toward employing them, instead, as instruments for negotiating strategic, bilateral market access, often among countries in different regions. Indeed, cross-regional PTAs account for two-thirds of those currently under negotiation. Bilateral partnerships have the potential to generate further fragmentation of global trading rules because each PTA maintains its own distinct regulatory framework. Initiatives to alleviate fragmentation by harmonizing preferential rules of origin are little in evidence outside the pan-European system of cumulation of origin.

The fourth is the broadening and deepening of the *regulatory scope* of PTAs. Increasingly, PTAs include a services component, in addition to the traditional exchange of preferences on goods. On issues that fall under the current mandate of the WTO, some countries have elected to undertake bilateral commitments going beyond those they have accepted at the multilateral level (WTO+ provisions) and some are undertaking commitments on issues that lie outside the current WTO mandate (WTO-extra provisions).

The fifth is the *impact* of PTAs. As discussed later in this chapter, trade flow data indicate that for a number of plurilateral PTAs, intra-PTA imports have increased as a share of total imports, and growth in intra-PTA exports is associated with growth in total exports. PTA partners in selected plurilateral PTAs trade more internally than would be expected in the absence of a PTA, and the impact on extra-PTA exports and imports is largely positive.

The PTA Kaleidoscope

This section expands and updates an earlier study conducted by the WTO in 2008 (Fiorentino, Crawford, and Toqueboeuf 2009). As in that study, we map PTA proliferation and examine the trends and characteristics of PTAs with respect to their type, physical composition, scope, and geographic spread. The focus is on PTAs notified to the WTO and in force, and on those currently being negotiated.

Quantifying and Qualifying the Proliferation of PTAs

PTAs continue to be a prominent feature of most countries' commercial policy, and we expect the current sharp upward trend in the number of new PTAs to continue for the foreseeable future. Although the multilateral tariff reductions that would accompany successful completion of the Doha Round of trade negotiations may dull countries' appetite for the negotiation of further PTAs in the medium term, we think it is likely that the number of PTAs will continue to increase in the short term as those PTAs already signed or under negotiation enter into force and those further down the pipeline, in the proposal or study phase, come on line. Also, to the extent that PTAs are

a manifestation of motivations that may not be addressed in multilateral global economic integration efforts (for example, geopolitical concerns, the diffusion of social preferences, and the establishment of regional public goods), the successful conclusion of the Doha Round trade negotiations—despite the inherent preference erosion that will result—may not be sufficient to diminish the appeal of these agreements. Figures 2.1–2.4 trace the chronological development of PTAs within the WTO framework.

Figure 2.1 shows the number of PTA notifications received by the GATT/WTO each year between 1948 and February 2010. In the five-year period 2000–04, 15 PTAs were notified annually, on average. In 2005–07, notifications declined from the 2004 level, to an average of 24 per year. In 2009, 37 notifications were received, 20 covering trade in goods, and 17 covering trade in services. This was the highest number of notifications received in a single year.

The growth in PTA notifications should be interpreted with caution because it reflects accession commitments made by WTO members.[2] Following its accession to the WTO in 2008, Ukraine notified 10 PTAs, some of which had been in force for 10 years or more. Given that many of the countries in the WTO accession process (for example, the Russian Federation and the other successor states to the Soviet Union) are active PTA players, future accessions to the WTO will lead to periodic spurts in PTA notifications. In addition, recent efforts by the WTO membership to encourage notification of PTAs already in force but not yet notified appears to be producing results, because several PTAs that had been in force for some time were notified in the course of 2009.[3]

Figure 2.2 shows the total number of PTAs notified to the GATT/WTO according to the year in which they entered into force or became inactive.[4] As of February 2010, 457 PTAs had been notified, of which 266 (including accessions to existing agreements) are currently in force; of these, 191 are in the area of goods and 75 in services. The two significant dips in the cumulative active number of PTAs shown in the figure are a result of the consolidations of PTA networks in the European region following the enlargements of the European Union in 2004 and 2007 and among Balkan countries in the enlarged Central European Free Trade Agreement (CEFTA). These periodic consolidations, while reducing the total number of active PTAs, are not indicative of a decrease in the amount of trade that is subject to preferences; preferential trade continues to be conducted among the countries concerned, but under a different relationship or configuration. A similar process of consolidation is expected to take place in Central America, where bilateral agreements being concluded between

Figure 2.1. Total PTA Notifications Received by the World Trade Organization, by Year, 1949–2009

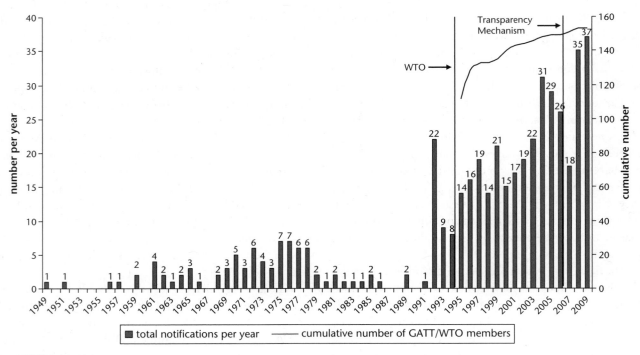

Source: WTO Secretarlat.
Note: GATT, General Agreement on Tariffs and Trade; PTA, preferential trade agreement; WTO, World Trade Organization.

Figure 2.2. All PTAs Notified to the GATT/WTO, by Year of Entry into Force, 1949–2009

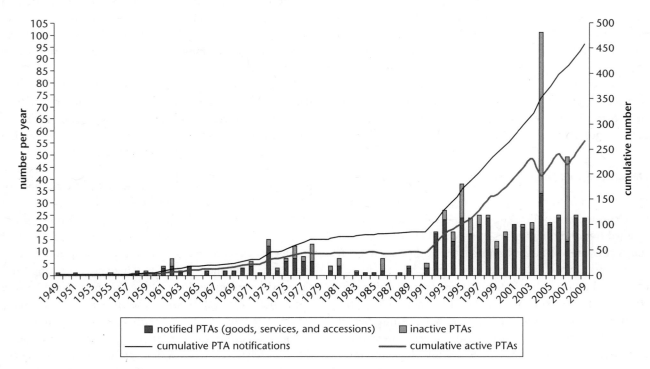

Source: WTO Secretariat.
Note: GATT, General Agreement on Tariffs and Trade; PTA, preferential trade agreement; WTO, World Trade Organization.

Figure 2.3. PTAs Notified to the GATT/WTO and in Force, by Year of Entry into Force, 1959–2009

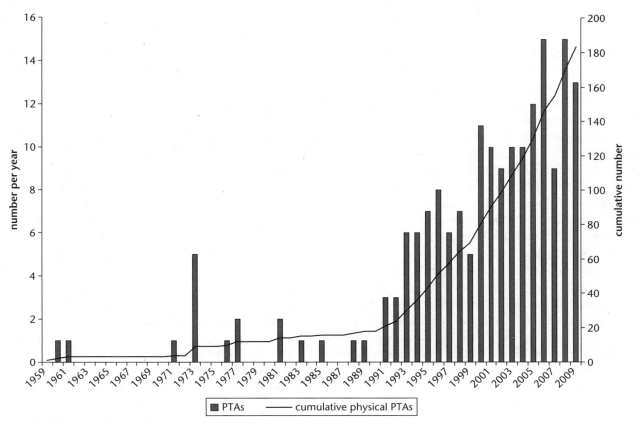

Source: WTO Secretariat.
Note: GATT, General Agreement on Tariffs and Trade; PTA, preferential trade agreement; WTO, World Trade Organization.

Figure 2.4. PTAs Notified to the GATT (Pre-1995) and the WTO (Post-1995), by Legal Provision

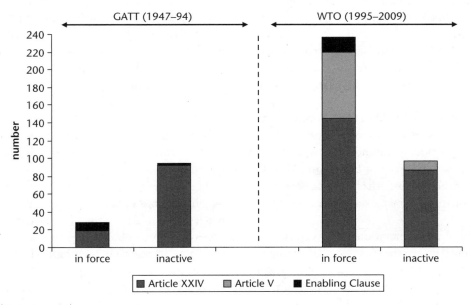

Source: WTO Secretariat.
Note: GATT, General Agreement on Tariffs and Trade; PTA, preferential trade agreement; WTO, World Trade Organization.

Chile, Panama, and individual Central American Common Market (CACM) countries will be replaced by a series of PTAs that link all CACM members with a respective Latin American partner.

Asia, by contrast, exhibits a layering effect whereby countries are members of both plurilateral and bilateral PTAs. For example, a preexisting PTA between New Zealand and Singapore coexists alongside the plurilateral PTA linking the same parties, the Trans-Pacific Strategic Economic Partnership (SEP). Similarly, the PTA between the Association of Southeast Asian Nations (ASEAN) and Japan coexists with bilateral PTAs between Japan and individual ASEAN members such as Indonesia, Malaysia, the Philippines, Singapore, Thailand, and Vietnam. This adds to the complexity of trading relations because agreements may contain different schedules for tariff elimination, rules of origin, and regulatory provisions.

The upward trend in the number of PTAs is evident in figure 2.2. Not only is the number of PTAs increasing, but the number of countries involved continues to diversify. During the 1990s, much of the proliferation of PTAs took place in Europe and Central Asia as the countries of those regions forged new trading relationships following the breakup of the Soviet Union. Since 2000, PTA participation has become more diverse, spreading to all geographic regions, particularly East Asia and the Pacific. PTA activity is increasingly concentrated in developing countries.

Figure 2.3 distinguishes between the number of physical PTAs and the number of PTA notifications.[5] The number of services PTAs has been increasing, particularly since 2000. For instance, of the 14 distinct PTAs that were notified and entered into force in 2009, 11 had a services component, and almost three-quarters of all PTAs in force and notified to the WTO contain provisions on trade in services. Also of note is the fact that developing countries are increasingly negotiating PTAs that include both goods and services components.

A total of 183 physical PTAs have been notified to the WTO (as of February 2010) and are currently in force. This figure does not include the hundred or so PTAs that are currently in force but have not been notified to the WTO. Such PTAs are almost exclusively among developing countries, and most are bilateral agreements involving two parties.

Figure 2.4 looks at the proliferation of PTAs chronologically, differentiating between the PTAs notified during the GATT years and those notified since the establishment of the WTO, according to the relevant legal provision.[6] Of the 123 PTAs notified during the GATT years, only a quarter remain in force. In many cases, older PTAs have been superseded by newer ones between the same signatories or have been consolidated into larger geographic groupings. Of those that remain in force, a third were notified under the GATT Enabling Clause, which allows preferential treatment among developing countries. Of the PTAs covering trade in goods notified to the WTO, 90 percent were notified under GATT Article XXIV, which permits PTAs as an exception to most favored nation (MFN) rules.

Of the 334 PTAs notified to the WTO, 70 percent remain in force. As we shall see, much of the recent growth of PTAs is accounted for by agreements among developing countries, many of which have notified the goods provisions of their PTAs under GATT Article XXIV, rather than exercising their option to notify them under the Enabling Clause.

Continuing Evolution of the Composition of PTAs

The past 15 years or so have witnessed changes in the dynamics of trading relationships between developed and developing countries.[7] Figure 2.5 shows how participation in PTAs has evolved over time.

Among PTAs concluded since the establishment of the WTO, the number with exclusively developing-country members rose initially and has since remained fairly steady; those exclusively among developed countries fell during the first five years of the WTO and have risen slightly since; and those between developed and developing countries show the most marked increase. In part, this mirrors the growing membership of developing countries in the WTO and the fact that developing countries outnumber developed countries in our classification by a ratio of about 2:1. However, it also reflects the fact that preferential trade relations between developed and developing countries are increasingly becoming reciprocal, in part because of the need to fulfill WTO legal obligations. In addition, a growing number of developing countries are choosing to forge reciprocal trading relationships with developed countries rather than rely on nonreciprocal preferential trading relationships such as GSP programs.

Figure 2.6 analyzes the hundred or so PTAs under negotiation and signed (but not yet in force), based on the parties' level of development.[8] The data shown in the figure confirm our observation that North-South PTAs are becoming increasingly prevalent. They constitute 69 percent of the PTAs under negotiation, whereas those exclusively between developing countries account for 22 percent and those exclusively between developed countries account for 9 percent.

Figure 2.5. Evolution of Notified PTAs in Force, by Type of Partner, 1958–2009

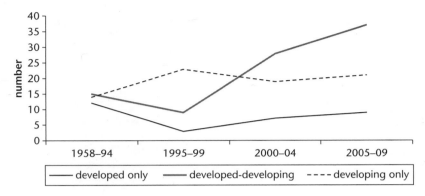

Source: WTO Secretariat.
Note: PTA, preferential trade agreement.

Figure 2.6. Number of PTAs under Negotiation and Signed, by Type of Partner, as of February 2010

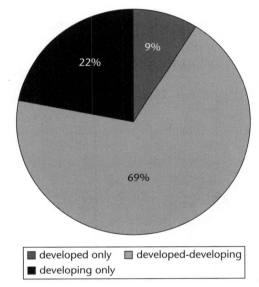

Source: WTO Secretariat.
Note: PTA, preferential trade agreement.

Structural Configuration of PTAs

As can be seen in figure 2.7, which differentiates between bilateral and plurilateral PTAs notified and still in force, plurilateral PTAs accounted for two-thirds of all PTAs notified during the GATT years.[9] Since the establishment of the WTO, bilateral PTAs have increasingly become the norm, making up more than 80 percent of all PTAs notified during this period and roughly 90 percent of those currently under negotiation. This confirms the observation by Fiorentino, Crawford, and Toqueboeuf (2009) that PTAs are less used as instruments for promoting intraregional

integration in the traditional sense—as with EFTA, ASEAN, and the Southern African Customs Union (SACU), which by definition are plurilateral partnerships—and more as tools for negotiating strategic, bilateral, and more flexible market access.

A related development is the emergence of PTAs in which all the parties are themselves members of PTAs. The first PTA of this kind notified to the WTO was that between EFTA and SACU, linking the four EFTA countries with the five-member SACU customs union. More PTAs of this type are currently under negotiation—for example, those between the European Union (EU) and the Southern Cone Common Market (Mercosur, Mercado Común del Sur) and between the Gulf Cooperation Council (GCC) and Mercosur.

Geographic Configuration of PTAs

Countries seeking preferential partners have tended recently to look beyond their regional neighbors and farther afield.[10] As figure 2.8 shows, as of February 2010, cross-regional PTAs accounted for 28 percent of PTAs notified to the GATT and for 34 percent of those notified to the WTO. The tendency toward the negotiation of PTAs across regional boundaries is more pronounced for PTAs currently being negotiated; cross-regional PTAs account for two-thirds of the total in this group.

Figure 2.9 presents the geographic regions represented in PTAs that have been established over the past 10 years. Countries in Europe and Central Asia, particularly members of EFTA and of the Commonwealth of Independent States (CIS), were active PTA players during the period. Also notable is the growing PTA participation of countries in East Asia and the Pacific; no new PTAs came into force in this region in 2000, but a yearly average of more than

Figure 2.7. Bilateral versus Plurilateral PTAs Notified to the GATT/WTO

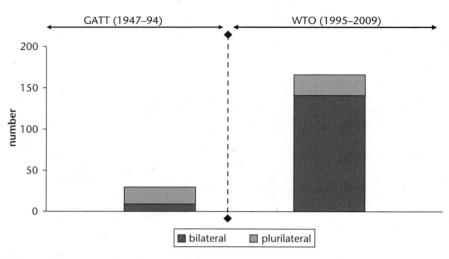

Source: WTO Secretariat.
Note: GATT, General Agreement on Tariffs and Trade; PTA, preferential trade agreement; WTO, World Trade Organization.

Figure 2.8. Cross-Regional and Intraregional PTAs Notified to the GATT/WTO

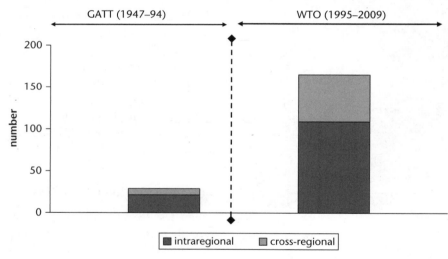

Source: WTO Secretariat.
Note: GATT, General Agreement on Tariffs and Trade; PTA, preferential trade agreement; WTO, World Trade Organization.

five new PTAs did so in the period 2005–09. In 2009, most PTA activity was conducted by countries in the Americas and the Caribbean, led by Canada, Chile, Peru, and the United States. By contrast, South Asia and Sub-Saharan Africa, home of some of the world's poorest countries, witnessed much less PTA activity during this time, indicating that they may risk becoming further marginalized in their pursuit of PTA partners.

Figure 2.10 shows PTAs under negotiation and signed but not yet in force, by geographic region. Cross-regional

PTAs consisting of parties in two or more geographic regions account for the largest share, 67 percent of the total. Intraregional PTAs under negotiation among countries in the Americas and the Caribbean make up the second largest group, followed closely by the East Asia and the Pacific region.

Another view of PTAs in force and under negotiation for a number of selected countries is shown in figure 2.11. The EU continues to be the dominant PTA player, with 29 PTAs in force and another 14 under negotiation. Chile, EFTA,

Figure 2.9. PTAs, by Region and by Year of Entry into Force, 2000–09

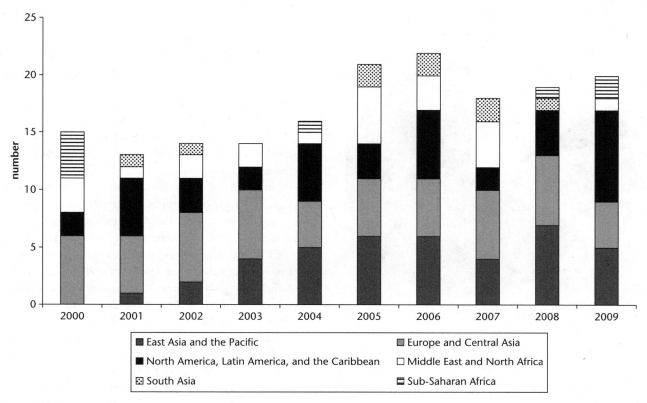

Source: WTO Secretariat.
Note: PTA, preferential trade agreement. An effort was made to classify each PTA according to the regions of its individual parties and to avoid the use of the cross-regional category. A degree of double-counting therefore arises because, for example, an intraregional PTA is counted once, whereas a PTA involving two or more regions is counted once for each region.

Singapore, and Turkey constitute the second most active group. Also of interest are Australia, Canada, the GCC, and the Republic of Korea, which have only a handful of PTAs in force but are actively negotiating a number of others.

Deepening Scope of PTAs

PTAs are increasingly covering more than trade in goods and services; they extend to rules and disciplines on various regulatory border and behind-the-border policies.[11] For the purposes of this chapter, we define such agreements as deep PTAs. These might contain

- Provisions that come under the current mandate of the WTO but only reaffirm the existing multilateral commitments
- Provisions within the current mandate of the WTO but in which the parties to a deep PTA undertake commitments beyond those accepted at the multilateral level (WTO+)

- Qualitatively different and new provisions lying outside the current WTO mandate (WTO extra).

PTA commitments that are also covered at the multilateral level include provisions concerning sanitary and phytosanitary (SPS) measures, technical barriers to trade (TBT), antidumping, state aid, and obligations already covered by the General Agreement on Trade in Services (GATS), Trade-Related Aspects of Intellectual Property Rights (TRIPS), and Trade-Related Investment Measures (TRIMS) arrangements. WTO-extra obligations deal with environmental provisions, labor laws, and movement of capital and also with competition policy, intellectual property rights (IPRs) not referenced in the TRIPS agreement, and so forth.

As figure 2.12 shows, the number of PTAs that include deep provisions has been steadily increasing since the early 2000s.[12] The most prevalent of these provisions usually concern customs cooperation, IPRs, competition policy, TBT and SPS measures, government procurement, and investment. Assessing such evolution is far from an exact

Figure 2.10. PTAs in Force and under Negotiation, by Region

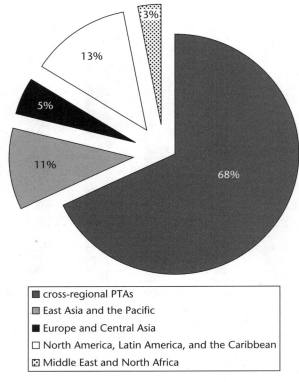

- ■ cross-regional PTAs
- ▨ East Asia and the Pacific
- ■ Europe and Central Asia
- □ North America, Latin America, and the Caribbean
- ▨ Middle East and North Africa

Source: WTO Secretariat.
Note: PTA, preferential trade agreement.

science. The WTO regional trade agreement (RTA) database currently includes only the commitments undertaken in PTAs notified to the WTO following the introduction of the Transparency Mechanism in 2006 and, to a lesser extent, agreements notified before December 2006. (The Transparency Mechanism calls for early announcement of negotiations to set up an RTA and early notification of the RTA's creation.) As a result, the database currently covers about 45 percent of the PTAs notified to the WTO. Figure 2.12 attempts to supplement the WTO information with other sources to provide a more accurate picture of the basic trends in the inclusion of additional commitments in PTAs. Although the cumulative rise in agreements that include such commitments is partly the outcome of the sample composition, the sheer volume of agreements containing such provisions (compared with the total number of PTAs) in recent years indicates the level of interest in deeper integration in the context of preferential trading.

Although it is difficult to be precise about the share of agreements containing provisions that go beyond existing commitments at the multilateral level, research on recent bilateral PTAs signed by the United States and the EU shows that there is an increasing tendency for their agreements to exceed existing WTO commitments. The United States and the EU are the main players on the international trade scene, and the bilateral agreements signed by them often constitute a benchmark for other PTAs. It has been

Figure 2.11. PTAs in Force and under Negotiation by Selected Countries and Groupings, as of February 2010

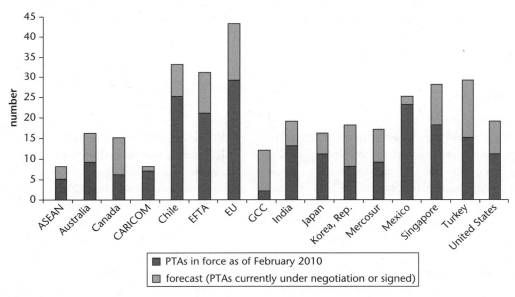

- ■ PTAs in force as of February 2010
- ▨ forecast (PTAs currently under negotiation or signed)

Source: WTO Secretariat.
Note: ASEAN, Association of Southeast Asian Nations; CARICOM, Caribbean Community; EFTA, European Free Trade Association; EU, European Union; GCC, Gulf Cooperation Council; Mercosur, Southern Cone Common Market (Mercado Común del Sur); PTA, preferential trade agreement.

Figure 2.12. Issues Covered in Regional Trade Agreements, 1989–2009

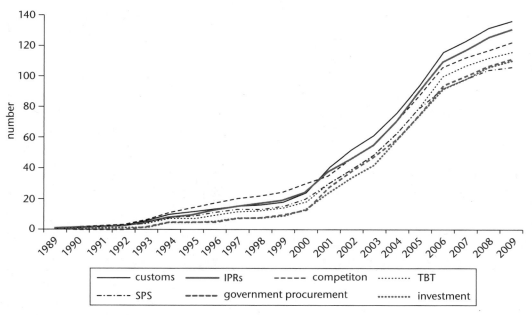

Source: WTO RTA database; World Bank Global Preferential Trade Agreements database; *Global Economic Prospects* (World Bank 2005); and additional observations based on Horn, Mavroidis, and Sapir 2010.
Note: IPRs, intellectual property rights; SPS, sanitary and phytosanitary; TBT, technical barriers to trade.

estimated that these two parties account for about 80 percent of the rules that regulate the functioning of world markets (Sapir 2007).

Horn, Mavroidis, and Sapir (2010) review provisions in 28 EU and U.S. PTAs with developed and developing countries. Table 2.1, which is based in part on their findings, indicates a high degree of coverage of WTO+ areas in both EU and U.S. agreements. Provisions on customs cooperation, TBT, and public procurement are included in most EU and U.S. agreements. By contrast, provisions on trade in services are included in all but one of the U.S. agreements but in only four of the EU agreements. Similarly, most U.S. agreements include obligations on TRIPS and on regulation of export taxes, whereas no EU agreements include such provisions.

It often proves in EU agreements that either the language regarding WTO+ obligations is not sufficiently precise to be legally enforceable, or no dispute settlement mechanism is available for enforcing the commitment. Areas that are often unenforceable because of imprecise language include public procurement, TBT and SPS provisions, and environmental laws; in U.S. agreements, SPS and competition provisions tend to have this shortcoming. Overall, however, the U.S. agreements contain substantially fewer areas with legally unenforceable language.

The depth of the commitments with respect to nontariff measures (NTMs) is increasingly substantial and in most

agreements goes beyond multilateral commitments. For example, in the case of customs administration, the EU favors the establishment of a framework for negotiation that aims at simplifying customs procedures and reducing deadweight costs. The United States also seeks to establish a framework for cooperation in customs administration, typically requesting that the other party increase transparency and publish all customs-related laws and regulations.

Enforceable provisions concerning SPS and TBT measures appear in fewer than half of the EU agreements under review. Typically, on top of reinforcing the commitments of the WTO TBT and SPS agreements, the EU establishes a forum designed to promote unilateral or mutual recognition of standards and conformity assessment. These commitments are deeper than in the case of U.S. PTAs, which usually reconfirm the parties' WTO obligations.

In the area of services, the obligations can be quite substantial. In at least one case (the U.S. PTA with Chile), the United States has adopted regulatory provisions that do not exist in the GATS. One such provision requires the parties to communicate their services-related laws at the draft stage, before they are actually enacted. Although the other party's comments are not binding, an active integration process is thus established.

The EU and U.S. PTAs contain a number of WTO-extra measures. In the area of competition, the EU generally includes legally enforceable provisions in its PTAs, whereas

Table 2.1. Deep Commitments in Selected EU and U.S. PTAs, by Type of Provision

Parties to PTA	Customs cooperation	SPS	TBT	Public procurement	Competition	IPRs	Investment	Services	Labor market regulations	Environmental laws
EEA	Yes	Yes	Yes	Yes	Yes	Yes	Yes	Yes	Yes	Yes
EU–Albania	Yes	No	Yes	Yes	Yes	Yes	Yes	No	No	Yes
EU–CARIFORUM	Yes	Yes	Yes	Yes	Yes	Yes	Yes	Yes	No	Yes
EU–Chile	Yes	Yes	Yes	Yes	Yes	Yes	Yes	No	No	Yes
EU–Croatia	Yes	Yes	Yes	Yes	Yes	Yes	Yes	No	No	Yes
EU–Egypt, Arab Rep.	Yes	No	Yes	Yes	Yes	Yes	Yes	No	No	Yes
EU–Israel	Yes	Yes	Yes	Yes	Yes	Yes	No	No	No	Yes
EU–Jordan	Yes	Yes	Yes	No	Yes	Yes	Yes	No	No	Yes
EU–Macedonia, FYR	Yes	Yes	Yes	Yes	Yes	Yes	Yes	No	No	Yes
EU–Mexico	Yes	Yes	Yes	Yes	Yes	Yes	Yes	Yes	No	Yes
EU–Morocco	Yes	No	Yes	Yes	Yes	Yes	Yes	No	No	Yes
EU–South Africa	Yes	No	Yes	Yes	Yes	Yes	Yes	No	No	Yes
EU–Tunisia	Yes	No	Yes	Yes	Yes	Yes	Yes	No	No	Yes
EU–Turkey	Yes	No	Yes	Yes	Yes	Yes	No	No	No	No
Total provisions	14	8	14	13	14	14	12	4	2	13
Legally enforceable provisions	13	3	5	7	13	11	8	4	2	2
NAFTA	Yes	Yes	Yes	Yes	Yes	Yes	Yes	Yes	Yes	Yes
United States–Australia	Yes	Yes	Yes	Yes	Yes	Yes	Yes	Yes	Yes	Yes
United States–Bahrain	Yes	Yes	Yes	Yes	No	Yes	No	Yes	Yes	Yes
United States–CAFTA-DR	Yes	Yes	Yes	Yes	No	Yes	Yes	Yes	Yes	Yes
United States–Chile	Yes	Yes	Yes	Yes	Yes	Yes	Yes	Yes	Yes	Yes
United States–Colombia	Yes	Yes	Yes	Yes	Yes	Yes	Yes	Yes	Yes	Yes
United States–Israel	No	Yes	No	Yes	No	No	No	No	No	No
United States–Jordan	Yes	No	No	Yes	No	Yes	No	Yes	Yes	Yes
United States–Korea, Rep.	Yes	Yes	Yes	Yes	Yes	Yes	Yes	Yes	Yes	Yes
United States–Morocco	Yes	Yes	Yes	Yes	No	Yes	Yes	Yes	Yes	Yes
United States–Oman	Yes	Yes	Yes	Yes	No	Yes	Yes	Yes	Yes	Yes
United States–Panama	Yes	Yes	Yes	Yes	No	Yes	Yes	Yes	Yes	Yes
United States–Peru	Yes	Yes	Yes	Yes	Yes	Yes	Yes	Yes	Yes	Yes
United States–Singapore	Yes	No	Yes	Yes	Yes	Yes	Yes	Yes	Yes	Yes
Total provisions	13	12	11	13	7	13	11	13	13	13
Legally enforceable provisions	13	2	11	13	0	13	11	13	13	13

Source: World Bank 2005; Horn, Mavroidis, and Sapir 2010; WTO RTA database; Tuck Trade Agreements Database, Center for International Business, Dartmouth College (http://www.dartmouth.edu/~tradedb/trade_database.html).

Note: The inclusion of deeper provisions in PTAs is shown whether or not the commitments go beyond existing commitments under the relevant WTO agreements. In addition, such provisions may or may not be legally enforceable. CARIFORUM, Caribbean Forum of African, Caribbean, and Pacific (ACP) States; EEA, European Economic Area; CAFTA-DR, Central America Free Trade Agreement–Dominican Republic; IPR, intellectual property rights; NAFTA, North American Free Trade Agreement; SPS, sanitary and phytosanitary; TBT, technical barriers to trade.

only about half of the U.S. PTAs considered by the Horn, Mavroidis, and Sapir (2010) study contain such provisions, and none is legally enforceable. Most EU PTAs prohibit agreements between enterprises that have the object or effect of prevention, restriction, or prohibition of competition, and most bar, as well, the abuse of a dominant position by one or more enterprises in activities affecting trade between parties. The agreements also stipulate that the competition authorities of the PTA parties cooperate to ensure that such prohibitions are enforced. Many EU PTAs also prohibit public aid that distorts or might distort competition by favoring certain enterprises or the production of certain goods. Legal enforceability varies among EU PTAs. For example, obligations of this kind in EU PTAs with Latin American countries are less far reaching than those signed with other countries. The EU–Mexico PTA does not refer to prohibitions, as do other agreements, but simply mandates that the parties agree on the appropriate measures for preventing distortions or restrictions of competition that could significantly affect trade between the EU and Mexico.

In the case of investment, most EU and U.S. PTAs contain legally enforceable obligations, but of quite different kinds. Typically, the EU agreement refers only to cooperation to promote investment between parties through the establishment of mechanisms to provide information on investment rules, development of a bilateral legal framework to promote

and protect investment, technical assistance, and so on.[13] The U.S. agreements, by contrast, generally include legally enforceable rules whereby parties agree to extend MFN and national treatment to each other and provide mechanisms for compensation in case of expropriation, as well as detailed rules for arbitration in case of conflict.

As for IPRs, all of the EU and U.S. PTAs listed in table 2.1 contain legally binding clauses that oblige the parties to become signatories to various intellectual property agreements not covered by the TRIPS agreement. The obligations under the U.S. agreements tend to be more comprehensive and to cover more aspects of intellectual property rights than do EU agreements.

Global Landscape of PTAs: State of Play and Future Regional Developments

Figures 2.13 and 2.14 show the participation of individual countries in PTAs covering trade in goods and services that had been notified and were in force as of February 2010. As regards trade in goods, the EU is engaged in the highest number of PTAs, followed by the United States, Chile, Mexico, and the EFTA states, which are members of 10 to 19 PTAs. Canada, Australia and most countries in Asia participate in five to nine PTAs, whereas most African countries and some Latin American countries are involved in one to four. The map does not show the hundred or so

Figure 2.13. Participation in Notified PTAs as of February 2010 (Goods)

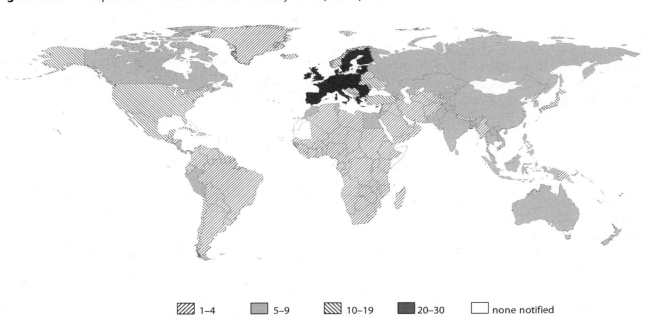

1–4   5–9   10–19   20–30   none notified

Source: WTO Secretariat.
Note: PTA, preferential trade agreement.

Figure 2.14. Participation in Notified EIAs as of February 2010 (Services)

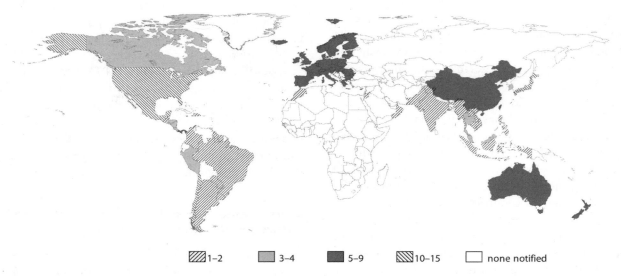

1–2   3–4   5–9   10–15   none notified

Source: WTO Secretariat.
Note: EIA, economic integration agreement.

PTAs, mostly involving developing countries, that are in force but have not been notified to the WTO.

The situation with regard to trade in services is somewhat different. Most countries in Africa and the Middle East have not yet notified PTAs involving trade in services. Interestingly, Chile, Mexico, Singapore, and the United States are engaged in more PTAs involving services than are the EU and the EFTA states.

This section examines the PTAs in force and under negotiation in each of five geographic regions. Figures 2.15–2.18 show the networks of plurilateral groupings in Europe and Central Asia; the Americas and the Caribbean; South Asia, East Asia, and the Pacific; the Middle East and North Africa; and Sub-Saharan Africa. What is immediately clear from these diagrams is the degree of overlapping plurilateral PTAs, particularly in Central Asia and Africa, but also increasingly in the Americas and Asia. For ease of reference, bilateral relationships are not shown but are discussed in the text. Even when only plurilateral relationships are shown, the complexity of trade relations faced by a number of countries is clearly evident. This complexity manifests itself in the resources necessary to administer and implement the PTA; the burden placed on customs officials charged with applying differing tariff schedules depending on the good and its origin; and the dilemma facing exporters who supply their goods in different markets and are confronted with different regulatory regimes such as rules of origin and product standards, according to the destination of the good.

Europe and Central Asia

On the European continent, the largest network of PTAs revolves around the European Union. The EU itself, by virtue of successive enlargements (most recently, from 25 to 27 in 2007), has been part of a changing network of PTAs in the region.[14] In addition to its own enlargements, its longest-standing relations in the region are with the EFTA states (Iceland, Liechtenstein, Norway, and Switzerland), beginning with PTAs in goods in the early 1970s and in services in 1994, and with Turkey, with which it has had a customs union since January 1996. The EFTA states and Turkey, by virtue of their association with the EU, have continued to expand their own PTA networks both within and outside the region.

Since enlarging to 27 member states, the EU has continued to expand its relationship with southeastern Europe and with countries in the Mediterranean Basin. In southeastern Europe, the EU has PTAs in force with Albania, Bosnia and Herzegovina, Croatia, the former Yugoslav Republic of Macedonia, and Montenegro. All these, together with Serbia, the United Nations Interim Administration Mission in Kosovo (UNMIK), and Moldova, are also members of the Central European Free Trade Agreement (CEFTA), which entered into force on May 1, 2007. With the inauguration of that agreement, a number of bilateral agreements between CEFTA's members were terminated.[15] The EU launched negotiations with Ukraine in February 2008.

Figure 2.15. Network of Plurilateral Groupings in Europe and Central Asia

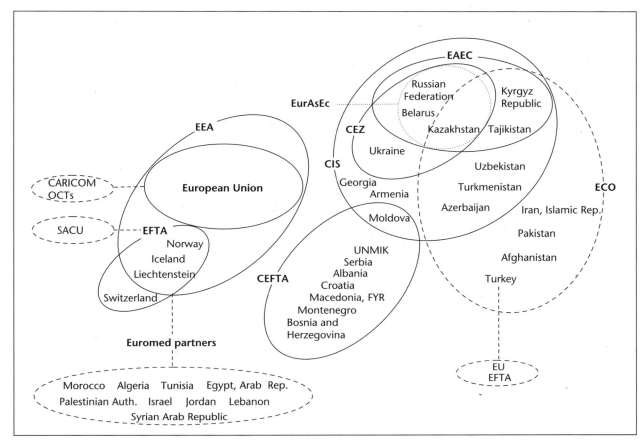

Source: WTO Secretariat.
Note: CARICOM, Caribbean Community; CEFTA, Central European Free Trade Agreement; CEZ, Common Economic Zone; CIS, Commonwealth of Independent States; EAEC, Eurasian Economic Community; ECO, Economic Cooperation Organization; EEA, European Economic Area; EFTA, European Free Trade Association; EU, European Union; OCTs, Overseas Countries and Territories; SACU, Southern African Customs Union; UNMIK, United Nations Interim Administration Mission in Kosovo.

Progress is being made toward the formation of a European Union–Mediterranean PTA, which was expected to be completed by 2010 but is not yet complete with respect to geographic coverage or scope. The EU has signed Euromed association agreements with all its Mediterranean partners. The most recent, with the Syrian Arab Republic, was expected to be completed in 2010 but is not yet in force.[16] Efforts are also under way to deepen agreements with the Arab Republic of Egypt, Israel, Lebanon, the Palestinian Authority, and Syria, through the addition of services chapters, and to enhance agricultural liberalization commitments in a number of the agreements. The EFTA states and Turkey, through their agreements with the EU, are following suit. EFTA has thus far notified agreements (in goods) to the WTO with all the Mediterranean partners except Algeria and Syria. Turkey has notified agreements in goods with Egypt, Israel, Morocco, the Palestinian

Authority, Syria, and Tunisia, and it is currently negotiating agreements with Algeria, Jordan, and Lebanon. Once the PTA is completed, it will permit diagonal cumulation of origin across all the parties (the EU, EFTA, Turkey, and the Mediterranean partners) and the Faroe Islands.

Farther afield, the EU has increased its interest in PTAs in recent years. In the Americas, negotiations on an agreement with Canada, to include goods and services, were launched in May 2009, and negotiations have been ongoing with Central American countries. In early March 2010, the EU announced that it had concluded a PTA covering goods and services with Colombia and Peru. Negotiations with Mercosur, stalled since 2004, have recently restarted and may be concluded in 2010. Negotiations with Ecuador were suspended in July 2009.

In Asia, the EU's PTA with Korea was initialed in October 2009. Negotiations with ASEAN, which began in

Figure 2.16. Network of Plurilateral Groupings in the Americas and the Caribbean

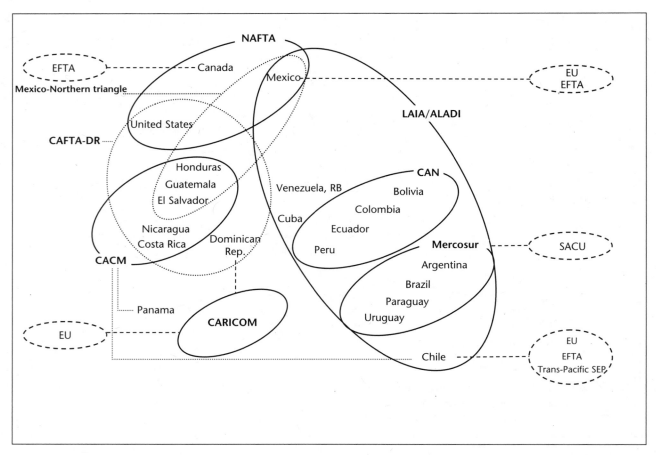

Source: WTO Secretariat.
Note: CACM, Central American Common Market; CAFTA-DR, Dominican Republic–Central America Free Trade Agreement; CAN, Andean Community; CARICOM, Caribbean Community; EFTA, European Free Trade Association; EU, European Union; LAIA/ALADI, Latin American Integration Association/ (Asociación Latinoamericana de Integración); Mercosur, Southern Cone Common Market (Mercado Común del Sur); NAFTA, North American Free Trade Agreement; SACU, Southern African Customs Union; Trans-Pacific SEP, Trans-Pacific Strategic Economic Partnership.

July 2007, are currently on hold while the EU pursues bilateral negotiations with each of the ASEAN member states, beginning with Singapore and Vietnam. Negotiations with India were launched in June 2007 and are currently in progress.

Following the expiration of the WTO waiver for the 2000 Cotonou trade preferences for the African, Caribbean, and Pacific (ACP) states, the EU has pursued negotiations for economic partnership agreements (EPAs) with these countries. On December 20, 2007, the EU adopted a market access regulation to grant duty-free and quota-free access to ACP countries that had concluded negotiations on agreements establishing or leading to the establishment of EPAs as of January 1, 2008, for all products except rice and sugar; the latter two products are expected to become duty-free in 2010 and 2015, respectively. Countries that have neither initialed an agreement nor have access to the EU's Everything

But Arms (EBA) scheme would be able to export to the EU under the GSP. The EU is conducting EPA negotiations with seven groups of countries: the Economic Community of West African States (ECOWAS), plus Mauritania; the Economic and Monetary Community of Central Africa (CEMAC, Communauté Économique et Monétaire de l'Afrique Centrale), plus São Tomé and Principe and the Democratic Republic of Congo; Eastern and Southern Africa (ESA); the East African Community (EAC); the Southern African Development Community (SADC); CARIFORUM (CARICOM and the Dominican Republic); and 14 Pacific countries. Agreements between the EU and the CARIFORUM states, Cameroon, and Côte d'Ivoire are already in force. Only the agreement between the EU and the CARIFORUM states includes services.

The EFTA states have also been very active in PTA negotiations in recent years, having notified 14 agreements in

Figure 2.17. Network of Plurilateral Groupings in South Asia, East Asia, and the Pacific

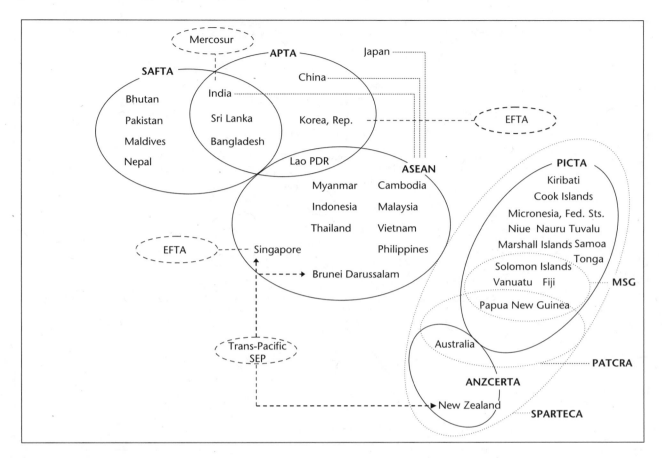

Source: WTO Secretariat.
Note: ANZCERTA, Australia–New Zealand Closer Economic Relations Trade Agreement; EFTA, European Free Trade Association; APTA, Asia-Pacific Trade Agreement; ASEAN, Association of Southeast Asian Nations; Mercosur, Southern Cone Common Market (Mercado Común del Sur); MSG, Melanesian Spearhead Group: PATCRA, Papua New Guinea–Australia Trade and Commercial Relations Agreement; PICTA, Pacific Island Countries Trade Agreement; SAFTA, South Asian Free Trade Arrangement; SPARTECA, South Pacific Regional Trade and Economic Cooperation Agreement; Trans-Pacific SEP, Trans-Pacific Strategic Economic Partnership.

goods and 5 in goods and services to the WTO. In addition, EFTA has signed agreements with Albania, Colombia, and Serbia. It is involved in negotiations with Algeria; Hong Kong SAR, China; India; Peru; Thailand; and Ukraine and is considering launching negotiations with Indonesia, Malaysia, Russia, and Vietnam. An interesting development was the decision by Switzerland to break ranks and separately negotiate PTAs with Japan and China; the former entered into force on September 1, 2009, and the latter is currently being negotiated. The other EFTA members have also launched separate negotiations with China.

In Central Asia, trade relations are still very much defined by historical linkages between the successor states to the former Soviet Union and with the bordering countries. The PTA set up by the CIS was negotiated in an attempt to maintain these links, but it has not been very successful, in that it has not been implemented by all the parties. Preferential trade liberalization in the region has therefore developed through a complex network of overlapping bilateral PTAs and plurilateral initiatives between the states of the region. For instance, Ukraine has notified PTAs with Armenia, Azerbaijan, Belarus, Georgia, Kazakhstan, the Kyrgyz Republic, FYR Macedonia, Moldova, Russia, Tajikistan, Turkmenistan, and Uzbekistan.[17]

In addition to the CIS PTA, other plurilateral agreements between the same parties include the Common Economic Zone (CEZ) between Belarus, Kazakhstan, Russia, and Ukraine and the Eurasian Economic Community (EAEC), made up of three CEZ parties (Belarus, Kazakhstan, and Russia), plus the Kyrgyz Republic and Tajikistan. In addition, Belarus, Kazakhstan, and Russia have formed the EurAsEc Customs Union, which entered into

Figure 2.18. Network of Plurilateral Groupings in Africa and the Middle East

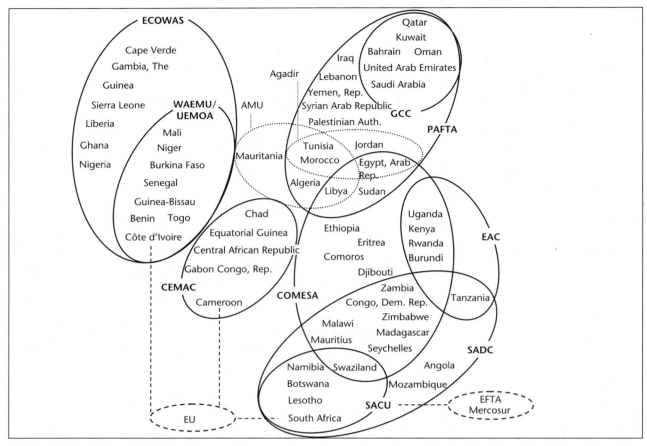

Source: WTO Secretariat.
Note: AMU, Arab Maghreb Union; CEMAC, Economic and Monetary Community of Central Africa (Communauté Économique et Monétaire de l'Afrique Centrale); COMESA, Common Market for Eastern and Southern Africa; EAC, East African Community; ECOWAS, Economic Community of West African States; EFTA, European Free Trade Association; EU, European Union; GCC, Gulf Cooperation Council; Mercosur, Southern Cone Common Market; PAFTA, Pan-Arab Free Trade Area; SACU, Southern African Customs Union; SADC, Southern African Development Community; WAEMU/UEMOA, West African Economic and Monetary Union/Union Économique et Monétaire Ouest-Africaine.

force in January 2010 and will be implemented over a five-year transition period. There is also an overlap between the EAEC, the CEZ, and the CIS, as some parties to these agreements are also members of the Economic Cooperation Organization (ECO), which consists of Afghanistan, Azerbaijan, the Islamic Republic of Iran, Kazakhstan, the Kyrgyz Republic, Pakistan, Tajikistan, Turkmenistan, Turkey, and Uzbekistan.

The Americas and the Caribbean

The Americas and the Caribbean continue to be actively involved in PTAs. In addition to NAFTA, the United States has agreements with numerous countries, including Chile and the Central America Free Trade Agreement plus the Dominican Republic (CAFTA-DR) in its own hemisphere;

Bahrain, Israel, Jordan, Morocco, and Oman in the Middle East and North Africa (MENA) region; and Australia and Singapore in the East Asia and the Pacific region. Agreements with Colombia, Korea, Panama, and SACU have been signed but have not yet entered into force pending congressional approval. Negotiations appear to be in progress with Malaysia, Thailand, and the United Arab Emirates, and an enlargement of the Trans-Pacific Strategic Economic Partnership (SEP) between Brunei Darussalam, Chile, New Zealand, and Singapore to include the United States has been proposed.

Canada has been less involved for a number of years but has recently stepped up its participation in PTAs. Agreements with EFTA and with Peru have been notified and entered into force in 2009. Agreements with Colombia and Jordan have been signed but have yet to enter into force, and negotiations with Panama were concluded in August 2009. Canada is also currently involved in negotiations with CARICOM, the Dominican Republic, four Central America countries, Singapore, Korea, and the EU, while PTAs have been proposed with India, Mercosur, Morocco, and Ukraine.

Mexico continues to expand its already substantial network of PTAs.[18] In addition to countries within the hemisphere, it has PTAs with EFTA, the EU, Israel, and Japan. Further expansion of its PTA network is planned, with negotiations in progress with Korea and Singapore. The Central and South American regions maintain complex intraregional and extraregional relations. Within the region, there are four customs unions at various stages of completion: CACM in Central America, CARICOM in the Caribbean, and the Andean Community (CAN) and Mercosur in South America. In addition, a large number of bilateral agreements, representing varying degrees of integration, have been negotiated within the Latin American Integration Framework (LAIA; in Spanish, ALADI, Asociación Latinoamericana de Integración). CACM members have also concluded PTAs with other countries in the region. Chile has bilateral protocols in force with all the members of the CACM except Guatemala and Nicaragua, where negotiations are still going on. Panama's individual bilateral protocols with CACM members are in force, and the country also has agreements in force with Chile, Colombia, the Dominican Republic, Mexico, Singapore, and Taiwan, China.[19] Agreements with Canada and the United States have been signed but have yet to enter into force, and Panama is considering negotiations with Mercosur. In the Caribbean, CARICOM, in addition to its PTAs with Colombia, Costa Rica, Cuba, the Dominican Republic, and the República Bolivariana de Venezuela, is negotiating with Canada and is considering an agreement with Mercosur. CARICOM members together with the Dominican Republic are parties to the EU–CARIFORUM EPA, which became effective at the end of November 2008.

In South America, two of the main regional blocs, Mercosur and the Andean Community, are pursuing a PTA. Individual Andean Community members are also negotiating PTAs, both within and outside the region. As of 2009, Peru had PTAs in force with Canada, Singapore, and the United States, and its agreement with China entered into force on March 1, 2010. It also has agreements under the LAIA/ALADI framework with Chile, Cuba, Mercosur, and Mexico and is currently negotiating with EFTA, Japan, Korea, and Thailand. Colombia, in addition to having agreements in force with CARICOM, Chile, Costa Rica, El Salvador, Guatemala, and Panama, has signed agreements with Canada, EFTA, and the United States and is currently

negotiating with Korea. Both Colombia and Peru have recently completed PTA negotiations with the EU.[20] Ecuador currently has agreements in force with Chile, Cuba, and Mercosur within the LAIA/ALADI framework.

Mercosur has signed several framework agreements aimed at establishing of PTAs but has only one partial-scope agreement in force, that with India, in addition to agreements under the LAIA/ALADI framework.[21] The group is currently negotiating agreements with Canada, the EU, and Turkey.

Chile has for several years been among the most active participants in PTA negotiations, and its agreements span all the continents. It has agreements in force with Australia, Canada, China, Colombia, Costa Rica, El Salvador, EFTA, the EU, Honduras, Japan, Korea, Mexico, Panama, Trans-Pacific SEP members (Brunei Darussalam, New Zealand, and Singapore), and the United States. It also has a partial-scope agreement in force with India and several agreements under the LAIA/ALADI framework.[22] In addition to these, it has signed an agreement with Guatemala in the context of its agreement with Central American countries and has extended the agreement with China to include services. Negotiations are ongoing with Malaysia, Nicaragua (under the Central American agreement), Thailand, Turkey, and Vietnam.

South Asia, East Asia, and the Pacific

After several years of resistance to signing PTAs, the Asia and the Pacific region has been playing catch-up and has become one of the most active regions in PTA negotiations, both among countries in the region and with extraregional partners. East Asia has been particularly active, with Japan and China taking the lead. Japan alone has 11 agreements in force, 8 of which have taken effect since 2007. Most of these agreements are with ASEAN and its members (Brunei Darussalam, Indonesia, Malaysia, the Philippines, Singapore, Thailand, and Vietnam), but agreements are also in force with Chile, Mexico, and Switzerland. An agreement with Peru entered into force on March 1, 2010, and Japan is negotiating with Australia, the GCC, India, and Korea. China currently has nine agreements in force: with ASEAN; with the Asia-Pacific Trade Agreement (APTA), which includes Bangladesh, India, Korea, the Lao People's Democratic Republic, and Sri Lanka; and with Chile; Hong Kong SAR, China; Macao, China; New Zealand; Pakistan; Peru; and Singapore. Negotiations with Australia, Costa Rica, the GCC, Iceland, Norway, and Switzerland are in progress. Korea, in addition to being a party to APTA, has agreements with ASEAN, Chile, EFTA, and Singapore, has signed agreements with the United States and the EU, and has launched PTA negotiations with a number of parties, including Australia, Canada, Colombia, the GCC, India, Japan, Mexico, New Zealand, and Peru. Taiwan, China, is expanding its network of PTAs, having notified agreements with Nicaragua and Panama to the WTO in 2009; agreements are in force with Guatemala and with Honduras–El Salvador. An agreement with the Dominican Republic is currently being negotiated, and discussions on a PTA with China began recently.

In Southeast Asia, the major trading bloc, ASEAN, is working toward the creation of an East Asian Economic Community by 2015. When fully implemented, this scheme is expected to form a single market in goods, services, and investment. ASEAN members are also negotiating PTAs with other parties, both as individual members and as a group. ASEAN itself has agreements in force with China, India, Japan, and Korea and with Australia and New Zealand. It is currently negotiating with the EU. Individually, Singapore has led the way, with 11 PTAs in force (with Australia, China, EFTA, Japan, Jordan, Korea, India, New Zealand, Panama, the Trans-Pacific SEP, and the United States), and it is negotiating another 7 (with Canada, Costa Rica, the EU, the GCC, Mexico, Pakistan, and Ukraine). Other active ASEAN members are Thailand, which has four agreements in force and five under negotiation, and Malaysia, with two in force and another six under negotiation.[23]

PTAs in South Asia have largely been confined to agreements among neighboring countries, although this is changing rapidly. India and Pakistan have both expanded their negotiations to countries outside the immediate region. In addition to agreements within the region, such as the South Asian Free Trade Area (SAPTA, which includes Bangladesh, Bhutan, Maldives, Nepal, Pakistan, and Sri Lanka) and PTAs with Afghanistan, Bhutan, Nepal, Pakistan, and Sri Lanka, India has PTAs with APTA, Singapore, and, more recently, ASEAN. It also has partial-scope agreements with Chile and Mercosur and is currently in negotiations with EFTA, the EU, the GCC, Japan, Korea, Mauritius, Thailand, and the Bay of Bengal Initiative for Multi-Sectoral and Economic Cooperation (BIMSTEC). Pakistan, in addition to being a party to SAPTA, the Protocol relating to Trade Negotiations among Developing Countries (PTN), and ECO, has notified agreements with China, Malaysia, and Sri Lanka to the WTO; PTAs with Mauritius and the Islamic Republic of Iran are also in force. Pakistan is negotiating agreements with the GCC and Singapore and is in negotiations to expand the ECO.

In the Pacific region, Australia and New Zealand, in addition to their long-standing Closer Economic Relations Agreement (ANZCERTA), in effect since 1983, have developed a significant list of preferential partners. Australia currently has PTAs with Chile, Singapore, Thailand, and the United States; a trilateral agreement with ASEAN and New Zealand has recently entered into force. Negotiations are being held with China, the GCC, Japan, Korea, and Malaysia, and entry into the Trans-Pacific SEP is being discussed. New Zealand's PTAs are with Australia, China, Singapore, and Thailand, and it is a party to the Trans-Pacific SEP. It has signed an agreement with Malaysia and has concluded agreements with the GCC countries and with Hong Kong SAR, China. Negotiations are ongoing with India and Korea. Australia and New Zealand are renegotiating their nonreciprocal agreement, the South Pacific Regional Trade and Economic Cooperation Agreement (SPARTECA), with the Pacific Island countries, with the aim of replacing it with a reciprocal PTA (PACER Plus). In the meantime, the Pacific Island Countries Trade Agreement (PICTA), which was notified to the WTO in August 2008, is being implemented by most of the parties. The PICTA countries are negotiating an EPA with the EU, but to date, only Fiji and Papua New Guinea have initialed interim EPAs.

The Middle East and North Africa

In the Middle East and North Africa, the key plurilateral agreements are the Agadir Agreement between Egypt, Jordan, Morocco, and Tunisia, in force since 2007; the Gulf Cooperation Council customs union, in force since 2003; and the Pan-Arab Free Trade Agreement (PAFTA), which has been in force since January 1, 1998, and includes members of the GCC and the Agadir Agreement, as well as other countries in the region. The Arab Maghreb Union (AMU) includes Agadir parties Tunisia and Morocco, as well as Algeria, Libya, and Mauritania. In addition, a crisscrossing network of bilateral agreements exists. For instance, Jordan has agreements with Bahrain, Egypt, Israel, Morocco, the Palestinian Authority, Sudan, Syria, Tunisia, and the United Arab Emirates and is negotiating with the GCC. Tunisia has agreements with Egypt, Iraq, Jordan, Libya, and Morocco. Egypt has agreements with Iraq, Jordan, Lebanon, Libya, Morocco, the Palestinian Authority, Syria, and Tunisia and has proposed negotiations with India.

Links with countries outside the region are also expanding. Several countries are part of the Euromed process of agreements with the EFTA and EU. The United States has agreements with Bahrain, Israel, Jordan, Morocco, and Oman, and is currently negotiating with the United Arab Emirates. The GCC as a group is also negotiating with a large number of partners across the world; an agreement with Lebanon is in force, and agreements have been signed with EFTA, Singapore, and Syria. The GCC's extensive negotiating agenda includes Australia, China, the EU, India, the Islamic Republic of Iran, Japan, Jordan, Korea, Mercosur, New Zealand, Pakistan, and Turkey.

Sub-Saharan Africa

Regional integration in Sub-Saharan Africa has, for the most part, taken the form of PTAs among geographically contiguous countries. SACU, the world's oldest customs union, is engaged in negotiating PTAs and recently notified an agreement with EFTA. Other efforts at creating intraregional and extraregional partnerships have fallen short of their ambitious statements of intent. In several cases, membership of regional groupings is defined by political alliances rather than market access goals, resulting in overlapping memberships that create difficulties in implementation.[24] Negotiations for an economic partnership agreement with the EU, although intended to strengthen regional integration, have created further confusion in eastern and southern Africa because memberships of the EPA groups and the regional agreements are different.[25] With regard to the current state of play of the EPA negotiations, in June 2009, an interim EPA was signed between the EU and Botswana, Lesotho, and Swaziland (part of the SADC EPA); Mozambique joined soon afterward. An interim EPA was initialed (but not yet signed) between the EU and the Seychelles, Zambia, and Zimbabwe in November 2007 and with the Comoros, Madagascar, and Mauritius in December 2007 for the Eastern and Southern Africa (ESA) EPA. An interim agreement was initialed between the EU and Uganda in November 2007 for the East African Community (EAC) EPA.

In West Africa, the main regional groups are the West African Economic and Monetary Union (WAEMU; in French, Union Économique et Monétaire Ouest-Africaine, UEMOA), ECOWAS, and CEMAC, all three of which are customs unions in force or in the making. The eight WAEMU members are all members of ECOWAS. The EU is negotiating EPAs with ECOWAS and CEMAC. With regard to the ECOWAS EPA, only Côte d'Ivoire and Ghana have initialed the interim agreement, in December 2007; the EU and Côte d'Ivoire notified the interim EPA in goods to the WTO in December 2008. In the case of the CEMAC EPA, the EU notified the WTO of the provisional application of the interim agreement in goods with Cameroon in October 2009.

Impact of PTAs on Trade

This next-to-last section examines the extent to which PTAs have contributed to the expansion of trade among PTA members and with the rest of the world. Several factors can contribute to the success or the failure of a PTA in stimulating trade flows. Coverage and the degree of liberalization are of crucial importance; clearly, agreements that cover substantially all trade, including agricultural products and services, and those that incorporate significant tariff and quota reductions are more likely to lead to higher trade flows among their members. If the barriers to trade with the rest of the world are kept low, as well, the risk of trade diversion is minimized, and trade with third parties is likely to be created as a result of the PTA.

The proliferation of PTAs that leads to overlapping agreements with varying rules of origin and diverse tariff schedules may complicate integration into global value chains and prove detrimental to trade. Hence, a successful PTA is likely to be associated with nonrestrictive rules of origin. In addition, trade facilitation measures, because of their effect on the costs of trade, are important to a successful PTA. Finally, the comprehensiveness of the PTA is of importance. The inclusion of behind-the-border regulatory measures that foster increased cross-border competition, including competition in services, and that establish rules governing investment and IPRs suitable to the partners' level of development contributes to the success of the PTA. Finally, even the best-designed agreements, if not implemented in full, will not bear the expected fruits. Often, the most effective PTAs have been those designed to complement a general program of economic reform.

This section surveys trade flows for a selection of major plurilateral PTAs; both intra-PTA and extra-PTA trade flows are included. Trade between members of the selected PTAs is equivalent to roughly 40 percent of world trade. A gravity model is developed to quantify the importance of these PTAs in stimulating trade among their members and with third countries.

Trade Developments for Selected Plurilateral PTAs

The most intuitive indication of the success of a PTA is the increase in trade among PTA partners as a share of total trade.[26] Even when the share of regional trade does not increase, it is possible that the volume of intra-PTA trade will rise if liberalization with respect to third partners leads to expansion of total trade.

As figure 2.19 shows, for most of the PTAs under consideration, intra-PTA imports as a share of total imports increased following the introduction of the PTA. (Extra-PTA trade and possible trade diversion are discussed below.) The most pronounced increases in the shares of intra-PTA imports were observed in the EU, ASEAN, the Andean Community (CAN), SAFTA, and, initially,

Figure 2.19. Evolution of the Share of Intra-PTA Imports in Total Imports, 1970–2008

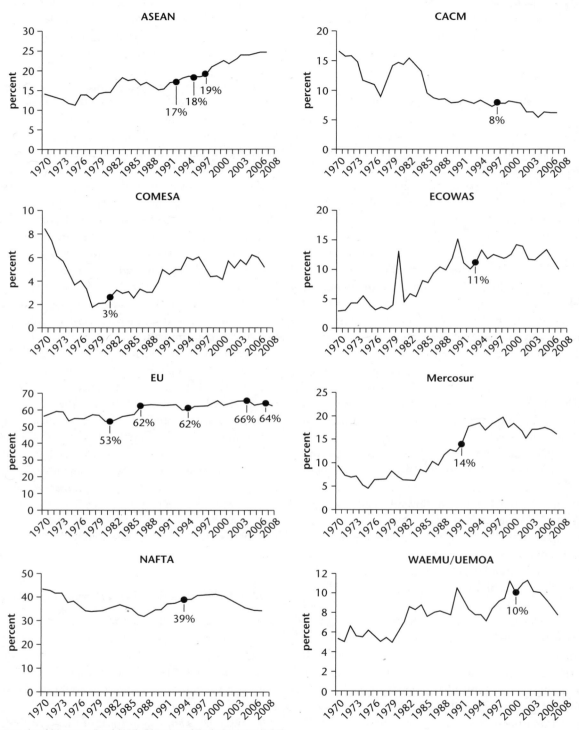

Source: International Monetary Fund (IMF), Direction of Trade Statistics (DOT).
Note: ASEAN, Association of Southeast Asian Nations; CACM, Central American Common Market; COMESA, Common Market for Eastern and Southern Africa; ECOWAS, Economic Community of West African States; EU, European Union; Mercosur, Southern Cone Common Market (Mercado Común del Sur); NAFTA, North American Free Trade Agreement; WAEMU/UEMOA, West African Economic and Monetary Union/Union Économique et Monétaire Ouest-Africaine. The dot on the plot line in each panel indicates the date of entry into force of the agreement (or enlargements, in the case of the EU).

NAFTA. The share of intra-NAFTA trade began to fall in the early 2000s, largely because increased imports from China replaced Mexican exports on the U.S. market (Batista 2008) and also crowded out domestic production in Mexico. The average share of intra-ASEAN imports in total imports increased from 17 percent in the 1980s to 25 percent in the 2000s; for intra-CAN trade during that period, the average share increased from 5 to 14 percent. The intra-Mercosur share increased substantially, from 9 percent in the 1980s to slightly more than 20 percent in the late 1990s. The rise, however, preceded the creation of the PTA by several years, and so it is uncertain to what extent Mercosur was responsible for increasing trade flows among its members. In many cases, increases in regional trade have been associated with unilateral or multilateral liberalization, as well, and with growing economic relationships with PTA partners.

For several PTAs, the share of intra-PTA imports in total imports has been falling or stagnant. These include EFTA, where the share of intra-PTA imports decreased from 22 percent in the 1980s to 17 percent in the early 2000s, and the CACM, with a drop from 12 to 7 percent over the same period. Several other PTAs, such as ANZCERTA, CEMAC, the GCC, the Papua New Guinea–Australia Trade and Commercial Relations Agreement (PATCRA), and SADC, experienced an increase in intra-PTA trade flows in the 1990s, followed by a decline in the early 2000s. The decrease in intra-PTA trade may be less worrying if the value of total trade is increasing. Figure 2.20 indicates that the share of intraregional trade (imports and exports) in gross domestic product (GDP) has indeed been growing in most of the sampled PTAs since the early 1970s. EFTA was the only PTA in which, on average, the share of intraregional trade in GDP was higher in the 1980s than in the early 2000s.

Moreover, for all the PTAs under review, the growth in intra-PTA exports has been associated with growth in total exports (table 2.2). The coefficient of correlation is positive for most PTAs and is quite high for several of them, such as ASEAN, EFTA, the EU, the GCC, and NAFTA. In the case of some African PTAs (Common Market for Eastern and Southern Africa [COMESA], ECOWAS, and WAEMU), the correlation is either negative or low, indicating that these may not have been successful in stimulating extra-PTA exports. These statistics, however, are mainly useful for understanding some basic associations; they do not permit inferences about the direction of causality between growth of intra-PTA trade and exports in general, or the importance of PTAs themselves in stimulating exports. We will return to the importance of intra-PTA trade below, using econometric analysis to establish the relationship between PTA membership and trade flows.

Next, we consider external protection as one of the likely factors determining whether the presence of PTAs might be an obstacle to growth of trade with external partners. Low external tariffs reduce the potential for trade diversion, ensure access to competitively priced inputs, and increase competition in the domestic market. The external protection of all PTAs under consideration has been falling over the past decade (see figure 2.21).[27] Several PTAs (EFTA, the EU, the GCC, and NAFTA) have an average MFN tariff of about 5 percent or lower. Most PTAs impose MFN tariffs that are, on average, less than 10 percent; these include ASEAN, CACM, CAN, CEFTA, Mercosur, SACU, and SADC. Preferential agreements with third parties and multilateral liberalization have also led to growth in the proportion of imports entering PTA markets tariff-free (see figure 2.22). The share in total imports of imports subject to zero MFN rates (calculated as an average for all members) has increased since 1995 for all PTAs except ECOWAS and WAEMU. On average, more than half of all imports enter the markets of developed countries at zero MFN tariffs. Several developing-country PTAs (ASEAN, CACM, EAC, SACU, and SADC) also have relatively open trade regimes.

In Latin America and Africa, only a low share of imports enters existing PTAs free of duty (figure 2.22). PTAs for which this is true, including CAN, CEMAC, the GCC, and WAEMU, are likely to perform worse with respect to creation of trade with nonmembers than PTAs that are more open. This result is consistent with the findings of *Global Economic Prospects 2005* (World Bank 2005), in which, on the basis of the gravity model, the authors concluded that several PTAs (CEMAC, CIS, COMESA, EAC, ECOWAS, SADC, and WAEMU) registered lower-than-expected overall exports.

Question of Intra- and Extra-PTA Trade Creation

A simple gravity model of trade could help insulate the effect of PTAs from all the other factors in play in explaining trade developments. Bilateral trade between any two countries depends on their market sizes measured by GDP (the equivalent of mass) and the distance between them. Because of their empirical robustness, gravity models have been extensively used to explain bilateral trade between countries and to estimate the impact of PTAs. Although early applications of gravity models have been criticized for their lack of theoretical foundations, later studies have shown that with special assumptions, a simpler version of the gravity model can be derived from the factor proportions model (Deardorff 1995), from increasing returns to scale and product differentiation

Figure 2.20. Evolution of the Share of Intraregional Trade in Gross Domestic Product, 1970–2008

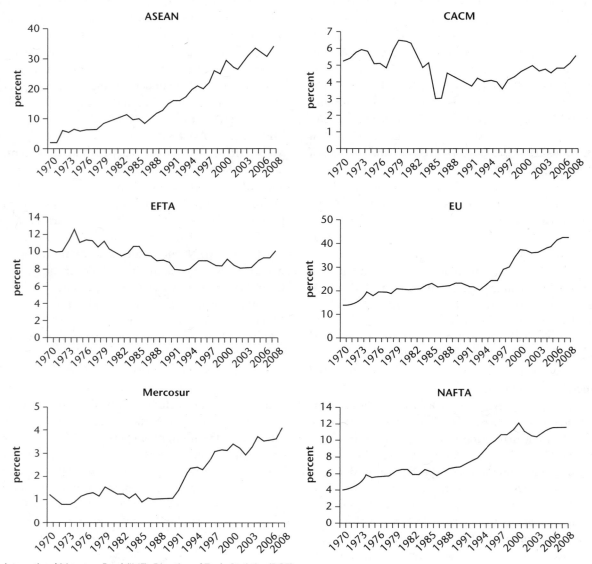

Source: International Monetary Fund (IMF), Direction of Trade Statistics (DOT).
Note: ASEAN, Association of Southeast Asian Nations; CACM, Central American Common Market; EFTA, European Free Trade Association; EU, European Union; Mercosur, Southern Cone Common Market (Mercado Común del Sur); NAFTA, North American Free Trade Agreement.

models, or from a combination of both (Shelburne 2000; Evenett and Keller 2002).

Typically, a gravity model equation explains the trade between two partners by using several factors: their income levels; a vector of explanatory variables that depend on the specific country pair but are constant over time (distance among trading partners, dummies for a common land border, a common language, a common colonizer, a current colonial relationship, a past colonial relationship, and an index of religious similarity); a set of time- and country-pair-varying explanatory variables (membership in the same PTA, membership in the same currency union); and

exporter and importer time dummies. In a refinement of the model, Baldwin and Taglioni (2006) suggest that biases from unobserved pairwise characteristics could be significant and proposed the inclusion of pair dummies to reduce the omitted-variables bias. Following this approach, the estimated gravity equation includes country-pair dummies and a time dummy instead of exporter and importer time dummies. It is worth noting that the inclusion of these dummies precludes the use of country-pair-specific variables such as distance between countries, contingency, common language, and colonial relationships.[28] The estimated coefficients of PTA dummies are presented in table 2.3.

Table 2.2. Correlation between Intra-PTA and Total Export Growth Rates, 1970–2008

PTA	Correlation coefficient
ANZCERTA	0.76
ASEAN	0.88
CACM	0.30
CAN	0.63
CARICOM	0.30
CEFTA	0.31
CEMAC	0.12
CIS	0.51
COMESA	−0.05
EAC	0.33
ECOWAS	0.03
EFTA	0.96
EU	0.98
Euromed	0.89
GCC	0.91
Mercosur	0.55
NAFTA	0.86
PATCRA	0.48
SADC	0.33
SAFTA	0.33
WAEMU/UEMOA	−0.08

Source: International Monetary Fund (IMF), Direction of Trade Statistics (DOT); authors' calculations.
Note: ANZCERTA, Australia–New Zealand Closer Economic Relations Trade Agreement; ASEAN, Association of Southeast Asian Nations; CACM, Central American Common Market; CAN, Andean Community; CARICOM, Caribbean Community; CEFTA, Central European Free Trade Agreement; CEMAC, Economic and Monetary Community of Central Africa (Communauté Économique et Monétaire de l'Afrique Centrale); CIS, Commonwealth of Independent States; COMESA, Common Market for Eastern and Southern Africa; EAC, East African Community; ECOWAS, Economic Community of West African States; EFTA, European Free Trade Association; EU, European Union; Euromed, European Union–Mediterranean Free Trade Area; GCC, Gulf Cooperation Council; Mercosur, Southern Cone Common Market (Mercado Común del Sur); NAFTA, North American Free Trade Agreement; PATCRA, Papua New Guinea–Australia Trade and Commercial Relations Agreement; SADC, Southern African Development Community; SAFTA, South Asian Preferential (Free) Trade Arrangement; WAEMU/UEMOA, West African Economic and Monetary Union/Union Économique et Monétaire Ouest-Africaine.

Table 2.3. Estimation Results of the Gravity Model of the Average Trade between Two Partners, Selected PTAs

	Intra-PTA trade	Extra-PTA exports	Extra-PTA imports
AFTA	1.556***	0.860***	0.745***
ANZCERTA	0.162	−0.0832**	−0.0191
CACM	−0.324	0.120***	0.314***
CAN	0.588***	0.120***	0.0254
CARICOM	−0.381***	−0.439***	−0.395***
CEFTA	0.0212	−0.110***	−0.0304*
CEMAC	0.364	0.164***	0.295***
CIS	−0.701***	0.208***	0.152***
COMESA	−0.155***	−0.318***	−0.269***
EAC	1.221***	0.0545**	0.137***
ECOWAS	0.514***	0.0484**	0.171***
EFTA	0.503***	0.149***	0.0768***
EU	0.472***	0.108***	0.00367
Euromed	0.124***	0.346***	0.217***
GCC	0.374***	0.413***	0.303***
Mercosur	0.689***	0.741***	0.645***
NAFTA	0.878***	0.192***	0.175***
PATCRA	0.339	0.158***	0.182***
SADC	0.842***	−0.134***	−0.0332
SAFTA	0.466***	0.506***	0.542***
WAEMU/UEMOA	0.465***	0.123***	0.00836

Source: Authors' calculations.
Note: AFTA, ASEAN Free Trade Area; ANZCERTA, Australia–New Zealand Closer Economic Relations Trade Agreement; ASEAN, Association of Southeast Asian Nations; CACM, Central American Common Market; CAN, Andean Community; CARICOM, Caribbean Community; CEFTA, Central European Free Trade Agreement; CEMAC, Economic and Monetary Community of Central Africa (Communauté Économique et Monétaire de l'Afrique Centrale); CIS, Commonwealth of Independent States; COMESA, Common Market for Eastern and Southern Africa; EAC, East African Community; ECOWAS, Economic Community of West African States; EFTA, European Free Trade Association; EU, European Union; Euromed, European Union–Mediterranean Free Trade Area; GCC, Gulf Cooperation Council; Mercosur, Southern Cone Common Market (Mercado Común del Sur); NAFTA, North American Free Trade Agreement; PATCRA, Papua New Guinea–Australia Trade and Commercial Relations Agreement; SADC, Southern African Development Community; SAFTA, South Asian Preferential (Free) Trade Arrangement; WAEMU/UEMOA, West African Economic and Monetary Union/Union Économique et Monétaire Ouest-Africaine.
* $p < 10\%$ ** $p < 5\%$ *** $p < 1\%$.

Overall, we find that the impact on intra-PTA trade of the PTAs covered in this study is positive. Almost all the PTA members seem to trade more with each other than would otherwise be expected from a typical trading relationship between countries with similar incomes and other characteristics. Our statistical analysis indicates that AFTA, CAN, EAC, ECOWAS, EFTA, EU, GCC, Mercosur, NAFTA, SADC, SAFTA, and WAEMU trade more internally than would be expected in the absence of a PTA.[29] The countries that belong to those PTAs seem to have adopted policies more conducive to bilateral trade expansion, but we cannot

infer whether it was the PTA alone that led to those policies. Again, AFTA seems to be the most successful, with the highest impact on bilateral trade (see figure 2.23). By contrast, CARICOM, CIS, and COMESA members seem to be trading with each other less than a normal trading relationship would predict. In the case of COMESA, the negative impact is rather small. Intra-COMESA trade is estimated to have been 14 percent smaller than expected under "normal" trading conditions.[30] The strong negative impact on CIS bilateral trade can be understood in the light of the dismantling of the Soviet Union and increasing openness to the rest

Figure 2.21. Most Favored Nation Applied Tariffs, Trade-Weighted Average of All PTA Members Selected Periods

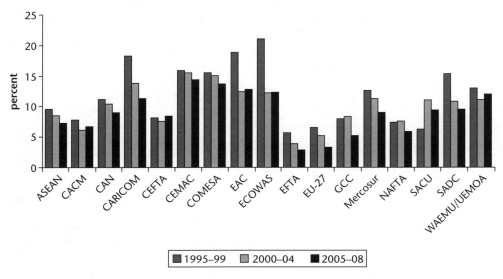

Source: World Bank, World Trade Indicators database.
Note: ASEAN, Association of Southeast Asian Nations; CACM, Central American Common Market; CAN, Andean Community; CARICOM, Caribbean Community; CEFTA, Central European Free Trade Agreement; CEMAC, Economic and Monetary Community of Central Africa (Communauté Économique et Monétaire de l'Afrique Centrale); COMESA, Common Market for Eastern and Southern Africa; EAC, East African Community; ECOWAS, Economic Community of West African States; EFTA, European Free Trade Association; EU-27, European Union after 2007 (27 members); GCC, Gulf Cooperation Council; Mercosur, Southern Cone Common Market (Mercado Común del Sur); NAFTA, North American Free Trade Agreement; SACU, Southern African Customs Union; SADC, Southern African Development Community; WAEMU/UEMOA, West African Economic and Monetary Union/Union Économique et Monétaire Ouest-Africaine.

Figure 2.22. Proportion of Tariff-Free Imports as a Share of Total Imports, All Goods, Selected PTAs and Periods

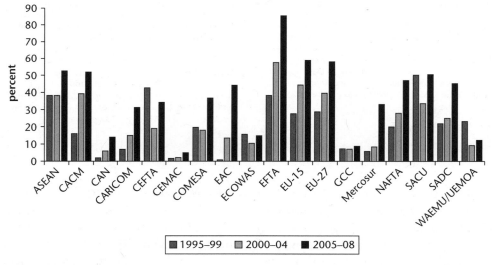

Source: World Bank, World Trade Indicators database.
Note: ASEAN, Association of Southeast Asian Nations; CACM, Central American Common Market; CAN, Andean Community; CARICOM, Caribbean Community; CEFTA, Central European Free Trade Agreement; CEMAC, Economic and Monetary Community of Central Africa (Communauté Économique et Monétaire de l'Afrique Centrale); COMESA, Common Market for Eastern and Southern Africa; EAC, East African Community; ECOWAS, Economic Community of West African States; EFTA, European Free Trade Association; EU-15, European Union before the 2004 enlargement (15 members); EU-27, European Union after 2007 (27 members); GCC, Gulf Cooperation Council; Mercosur, Southern Cone Common Market (Mercado Común del Sur); NAFTA, North American Free Trade Agreement; SACU, Southern African Customs Union; SADC, Southern African Development Community; WAEMU/UEMOA, West African Economic and Monetary Union/Union Économique et Monétaire Ouest-Africaine. Tariffs include ad valorem rates and ad valorem equivalents of specific tariffs.

Figure 2.23. Percentage Changes in Trade from Entry into Force of a Preferential Trade Agreement to 2008, Based on Gravity Model Estimates

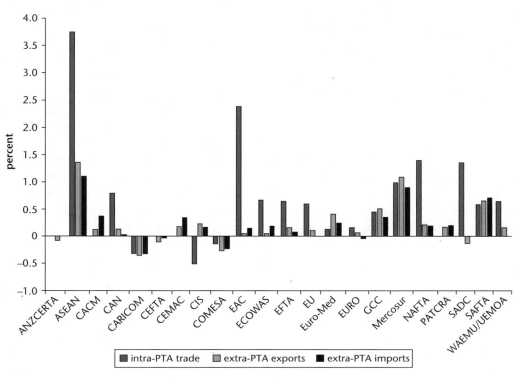

Source: Authors' calculations.
Note: ANZCERTA, Australia–New Zealand Closer Economic Relations Trade Agreement; ASEAN, Association of Southeast Asian Nations; CACM, Central American Common Market; CAN, Andean Community; CARICOM, Caribbean Community; CEFTA, Central European Free Trade Agreement; CEMAC, Economic and Monetary Community of Central Africa; CIS, Commonwealth of Independent States; COMESA, Common Market for Eastern and Southern Africa (Communauté Économique et Monétaire de l'Afrique Centrale); EAC, East African Community; ECOWAS, Economic Community of West African States; EFTA, European Free Trade Association; EU, European Union; Euromed, European Union–Mediterranean Free Trade Area; GCC, Gulf Cooperation Council; Mercosur, Southern Cone Common Market (Mercado Común del Sur); NAFTA, North American Free Trade Agreement; PATCRA, Papua New Guinea–Australia Trade and Commercial Relations Agreement; SADC, Southern African Development Community; SAFTA, South Asian Preferential (Free) Trade Arrangement; WAEMU/UEMOA, West African Economic and Monetary Union/Union Économique et Monétaire Ouest-Africaine. The bars show the magnitude of the impact of the respective PTAs on intra-PTA trade, calculated on the basis of statistically significant dummy variables from table 2.3.

of the world. Figure 2.23 translates the estimates presented in table 2.3 into the percentage impact on trade following the introduction of the PTA, up to 2008. For example, it is estimated that trade between AFTA members from its founding to 2008 was three times higher than would have been predicted by a typical trading relationship between countries with similar income and other characteristics.

We also analyze the impact of the introduction of PTAs on extra-PTA exports and imports and find that most of the PTAs considered here have been trade creating. The agreements whose members trade more with the rest of the world than would have been expected from a normal trading relationship include AFTA, Mercosur, and SAFTA. Members of CARICOM, CEFTA, COMESA, and SADC, however, are trading less with the rest of the world than our gravity model would have predicted in the absence of PTAs, indicating some degree of

trade diversion.[31] These results are broadly consistent with the findings of the previous sections and Baldwin and Freund, ch. 6 in this volume indicating that PTAs with higher external barriers are likely to be associated with trade diversion.

Conclusions

Today's multilateral trading system is characterized by a multiplicity of overlapping and intersection preferential trade agreements. The number of PTAs has grown markedly since 2000. PTAs offer members a means of securing enhanced market access and attracting investment, but at the cost of rendering the trading landscape less transparent and more unpredictable. Each PTA tends to create its own web of regulatory rules that coexist alongside multilateral rules.

The PTA landscape shows a number of distinctive features:

- *Ubiquity.* PTAs have spread to most geographic regions, especially East Asia and the Pacific, and North-South preferential partnerships are often chosen over unilateral programs, such as the GSP.
- *Consolidation.* In some cases, bilateral relationships are being replaced by plurilateral PTAs among the same partners.
- *Nature.* Bilateral PTAs are increasingly the norm. This movement corroborates the observation of a shift away from the use of PTAs to forge traditional regional partnerships among geographically proximate countries and toward their employment as instruments for negotiating strategic, bilateral market access, often among countries in different regions. This development risks generating further fragmentation of global trading rules, because each PTA maintains its own distinct regulatory framework.

- *Scope.* The regulatory scope of PTAs is broadening and deepening. Increasingly, PTAs include a services component, as well as commitments that exceed those they have accepted at the multilateral level or that lie outside the current WTO mandate.
- *Impact.* Analysis indicates that for a number of plurilateral PTAs, PTA partners trade more internally than would be expected in the absence of a PTA and the impact on extra-PTA trade is largely positive. Similar calculations to determine the effects of bilateral PTAs would be useful. In addition, the effects of PTAs on stimulating trade in services and investment is an area worthy of future study.

Annex

Annex Table 2A.1. Membership of Selected Plurilateral Preferential Trade Agreements

Abbreviation	Name of PTA	Members
AFTA	ASEAN Free Trade Area	Brunei Darussalam, Cambodia, Indonesia, Lao People's Democratic Republic, Malaysia, Myanmar, Philippines, Singapore, Thailand, Vietnam
ANZCERTA	Australia–New Zealand Closer Economic Relations Trade Agreement	Australia, New Zealand
APTA	Asia-Pacific Trade Agreement (Bangkok Agreement)	Bangladesh, China, India, Republic of Korea, Lao PDR, Sri Lanka
ASEAN	Association of Southeast Asian Nations	Brunei Darussalam, Cambodia, Indonesia, Lao PDR, Malaysia, Myanmar, Philippines, Singapore, Thailand, Vietnam
CACM	Central American Common Market	Costa Rica, El Salvador, Guatemala, Honduras, Nicaragua
CAFTA-DR	Central America–Dominican Republic–United States	Costa Rica, Dominican Republic, El Salvador, Guatemala, Honduras, Nicaragua, United States
CAN	Andean Community	Bolivia, Colombia, Ecuador, Peru
CARICOM	Caribbean Community	Antigua and Barbuda, The Bahamas, Barbados, Belize, Dominica, Grenada, Guyana, Haiti, Jamaica, Montserrat, St. Kitts and Nevis, St. Lucia, St. Vincent and the Grenadines, Suriname, Trinidad and Tobago
CEFTA	Central European Free Trade Agreement	Albania, Bosnia and Herzegovina, Croatia, former Yugoslav Republic of Macedonia, Moldova, Montenegro, Serbia, United Nations Interim Administration Mission in Kosovo (UNMIK)
CEMAC	Economic and Monetary Community of Central Africa/Communauté Économique et Monétaire de l'Afrique Centrale	Cameroon, Central African Republic, Chad, Republic of Congo, Equatorial Guinea, Gabon
CEZ	Common Economic Zone	Belarus, Kazakhstan, Russian Federation, Ukraine
CIS	Commonwealth of Independent States	Armenia, Azerbaijan, Belarus, Kazakhstan, Kyrgyz Republic, Moldova, Russia, Tajikistan, Turkmenistan, Ukraine, Uzbekistan
COMESA	Common Market for Eastern and Southern Africa	Burundi, the Comoros, Democratic Republic of Congo, Djibouti, Arab Republic of Egypt, Eritrea, Ethiopia, Kenya, Libya, Madagascar, Malawi, Mauritius, Rwanda, the Seychelles, Sudan, Swaziland, Uganda, Zambia, Zimbabwe
EAC	East African Community	Burundi, Kenya, Rwanda, Tanzania, Uganda

(continued next page)

Annex Table 2A.1. *(continued)*

Abbreviation	Name of PTA	Members
EAEC	Eurasian Economic Community	Belarus, Kazakhstan, Kyrgyz Republic, Russia, Tajikistan
ECO	Economic Cooperation Organization	Afghanistan, Azerbaijan, Islamic Republic of Iran, Kazakhstan, Kyrgyz Republic, Pakistan, Tajikistan, Turkey, Turkmenistan, Uzbekistan
ECOWAS	Economic Community of West African States	Benin, Burkina Faso, Cape Verde, Côte d'Ivoire, The Gambia, Ghana, Guinea, Guinea-Bissau, Liberia, Mali, Niger, Nigeria, Senegal, Sierra Leone, Togo
EEA	European Economic Area	European Union, Iceland, Liechtenstein, Norway
EFTA	European Free Trade Association	Iceland, Liechtenstein, Norway, Switzerland
EU	European Union	Austria, Belgium, Bulgaria, Cyprus, Czech Republic, Denmark, Estonia, Finland, France, Germany, Greece, Hungary, Ireland, Italy, Latvia, Lithuania, Luxembourg, Malta, Netherlands, Poland, Portugal, Romania, Slovak Republic, Slovenia, Spain, Sweden, United Kingdom
GCC	Gulf Cooperation Council	Bahrain, Kuwait, Oman, Qatar, Saudi Arabia, United Arab Emirates
LAIA/ALADI	Latin American Integration Association/ Asociación Latinoamericana de Integración	Argentina, Bolivia, Brazil, Chile, Colombia, Cuba, Ecuador, Mexico, Paraguay, Peru, Uruguay, República Bolivariana de Venezuela
Mercosur	Southern Cone Common Market/ Mercado Común del Sur	Argentina, Brazil, Paraguay, Uruguay
MSG	Melanesian Spearhead Group	Fiji, Papua New Guinea, Solomon Islands, Vanuatu
NAFTA	North American Free Trade Agreement	Canada, Mexico, United States
OCT	Overseas Countries and Territories	Anguilla, Aruba, British Antarctic Territory, British Indian Ocean Territory, British Virgin Islands, Cayman Islands, Falkland Islands, French Polynesia, French Southern and Antarctic Territories, Greenland, Mayotte, Montserrat, Netherlands Antilles, New Caledonia, Pitcairn, Saint Helena, Saint Pierre and Miquelon, South Georgian and South Sandwich Islands, Turks and Caicos Islands, Wallis and Futuna Islands
PAFTA	Pan-Arab Free Trade Area	Algeria, Bahrain, Egypt, Iraq, Jordan, Kuwait, Lebanon, Libya, Morocco, Oman, Palestinian Authority, Qatar, Saudi Arabia, Sudan, Syrian Arab Republic, Tunisia, United Arab Emirates, Republic of Yemen
PATCRA	Papua New Guinea–Australia Trade and Commercial Relations Agreement	Australia, Papua New Guinea
PICTA	Pacific Island Countries Trade Agreement	Cook Islands, Fiji, Kiribati, Federated States of Micronesia, Nauru, Niue, Papua New Guinea, Samoa, Solomon Islands, Tonga, Tuvalu, Vanuatu
PTN	Protocol relating to Trade Negotiations among Developing Countries	Bangladesh, Brazil, Chile, Egypt, Israel, Republic of Korea, Mexico, Pakistan, Paraguay, Peru, Philippines, Romania, Tunisia, Turkey, Uruguay, former Yugoslavia
SACU	Southern African Customs Union	Botswana, Lesotho, Namibia, South Africa, Swaziland
SADC	Southern African Development Community	Angola, Botswana, Democratic Republic of Congo, Lesotho, Madagascar, Malawi, Mauritius, Mozambique, Namibia, Seychelles, South Africa, Swaziland, Tanzania, Zambia, Zimbabwe
SAPTA/SAFTA	South Asian Preferential (Free) Trade Arrangement	Bangladesh, Bhutan, India, Maldives, Nepal, Pakistan, Sri Lanka
SPARTECA	South Pacific Regional Trade and Economic Cooperation Agreement	Australia, Cook Islands, Fiji, Kiribati, Marshall Islands, Federated States of Micronesia, Nauru, New Zealand, Niue, Papua New Guinea, Samoa, Solomon Islands, Tonga, Tuvalu, Vanuatu
Trans-Pacific SEP	Trans-Pacific Strategic Economic Partnership	Brunei Darussalam, Chile, New Zealand, Singapore
WAEMU/ UEMOA	West African Economic and Monetary Union/Union Économique et Monétaire Ouest-Africaine	Benin, Burkina Faso, Côte d'Ivoire, Guinea-Bissau, Mali, Niger, Senegal, Togo

Source: Authors' compilation.

Notes

1. The information used in this study is based on several sources: notifications to the WTO; documentation submitted to the WTO's Committee on Regional Trade Agreements (CRTA) or the Committee on Trade and Development (CTD); WTO accession documents; trade policy reviews; and other public sources. The information may not be exhaustive because, whereas it is possible to account accurately for all notified PTAs, information on nonnotified PTAs, agreements under negotiation, and agreements in the proposal stage is often scarce or inconclusive.

2. There is, of course, no obligation for nonmembers of the WTO to notify their PTAs, but PTAs that involve both members and nonmembers

of the WTO should be notified by the respective WTO member or members.

3. According to the WTO's Transparency Mechanism for Regional Trade Agreements (WTO document WT/L/671), notification is to take place as early as possible, no later than directly following the parties' ratification or application, and before the application of preferential treatment between the parties.

4. There is sometimes a significant time lag between the entry into force of a PTA and its notification. For instance, of the 37 PTA notifications received in 2009, 12 relate to PTAs that entered into force before 2009. Delays in notification may be caused by lengthy ratification procedures, countries' lack of knowledge of notification obligations, indecision about which legal provision (for example, Article XXIV or the Enabling Clause) to invoke (in the case of PTAs covering trade in goods), or recent accession to the WTO, creating notification obligations.

5. WTO statistics are based on notification requirements that do not reflect the physical numbers of PTAs and so tend to overstate the total number of PTAs. Notifications to the WTO include those made under GATT Article XXIV, General Agreement on Trade in Services Article V, and the Enabling Clause, as well as accessions to existing PTAs. The notification requirements contained in WTO provisions require that PTAs covering trade in goods and services be notified separately. For a complete list of PTAs notified to the GATT/WTO and in force, see the WTO's Regional Trade Agreements Database (http://rtais.wto.org/). The total number of notified PTAs in force minus economic integration agreements in services and accessions to existing PTAs yields the number of physical agreements.

6. Before the establishment of the WTO in 1995 and the negotiation of the General Agreement on Trade in Services (GATS), there was no obligation to notify PTAs with services provisions.

7. The World Bank's classification of developed countries includes all countries defined as high income, whether members of the Organisation for Economic Co-operation and Development (OECD) or non-OECD. This differs from the WTO classification, in which developing-country status is based on WTO members' self-selection.

8. Information on PTAs under negotiation and signed is based on available figures and is accurate to the best of our knowledge. Information on some geographic regions, such as Central Asia and the Middle East, is difficult to obtain and, thus, can only be considered a best estimate.

9. Bilateral PTAs may include more than two countries when one of the parties is itself a PTA. For example, for our purposes, EFTA-Chile is considered a bilateral PTA, although it involves the four countries of EFTA plus Chile. A plurilateral PTA refers to one in which the number of constituent parties exceeds two countries, such as Mercosur, CARICOM, and the SADC.

10. The World Bank regions used in this study are as follows: East Asia and Pacific; Europe and Central Asia; North America, Latin America, and the Caribbean; Middle East and North Africa; South Asia; and Sub-Saharan Africa. The regional classification of countries differs somewhat from that used in the WTO framework.

11. This section relies heavily on Horn, Mavroidis, and Sapir (2010).

12. Figure 2.12 shows the inclusion of such provisions in RTAs whether or not the commitments go beyond existing commitments under the relevant WTO agreements. In addition, such provisions may or may not be legally enforceable.

13. Until the conclusion of the Lisbon agreement, EU law did not cover investment provisions with third countries. Instead, this was a bilateral issue like double-taxation agreements.

14. The enlargement led to the termination of a number of bilateral agreements between the EU-25 (referring to the EU before the latest enlargement) and the new member states, and between the two new member states (Bulgaria and Romania) and third parties. The termination of these agreements was notified to the WTO (WT/REG/GEN/N/4).

15. The termination of these agreements was notified to the WTO (WT/REG/GEN/N/5).

16. The Mediterranean parties are Algeria, the Arab Republic of Egypt, Israel, Jordan, Lebanon, Morocco, the Palestinian Authority, the Syrian Arab Republic, and Tunisia. The agreement with Syria was adopted by the EU Council on October 27, 2009; signature of the agreement awaits further notice from Syria (European Commission, *Overview of PTA and other Trade Negotiations*, February 5, 2010).

17. Ukraine is also negotiating PTAs with EFTA, the EU, and Singapore, and an agreement with Canada has been proposed.

18. In addition to its plurilateral agreements such as NAFTA, LAIA/ALADI, the Protocol relating to Trade Negotiations among Developing Countries, the Global System of Trade Preferences among Developing Countries (GSTP), and the Mexico-Northern Triangle agreement (with El Salvador, Guatemala, and Honduras), Mexico has eight PTAs and another eight agreements under the LAIA/ALADI framework.

19. Panama's agreements with Guatemala and Nicaragua are in force but have not yet been notified to the WTO.

20. Colombia also has agreements with Cuba, Mercosur, and Mexico under the LAIA/ALADI framework.

21. The agreements are with the Andean Community, Bolivia, Chile, Colombia, Cuba, Ecuador, Mexico, Peru, and República Bolivariana de Venezuela.

22. The agreements are with Bolivia, Cuba, Ecuador, Mercosur, Peru, and the República Bolivariana de Venezuela,

23. Thailand has agreements in force with Australia, Japan, the Lao PDR, and New Zealand. Negotiations are ongoing concerning the Bangladesh, India, Myanmar, Sri Lanka, and Thailand Economic Cooperation (BIMSTEC) and with Chile, EFTA, India, and the United States. Malaysia has agreements in force with Japan and Pakistan and is currently negotiating with Australia, Chile, EFTA, India, New Zealand, and the United States.

24. Nowhere is overlapping membership more problematic than in simultaneous membership of multiple customs unions. For instance, Tanzania is a member of the East African Community (a customs union) and of SADC, a group that plans to become a customs union. Similarly, several countries are members of the SADC and of the Common Market for Eastern and Southern Africa (COMESA), both of which plan to become customs unions.

25. For example, Tanzania is negotiating under the EU-SADC EPA, although it is a member of the EAC, and a number of SADC and COMESA members are negotiating together under the EU-ESA EPA. (The Comoros, Djibouti, Eritrea, Ethiopia, and Sudan are COMESA members; Madagascar, Mauritius, the Seychelles, Zambia, and Zimbabwe are members of the SADC.)

26. This simple measure ignores the issue of preference utilization; that is, in some instances intra-PTA trade might not be conducted on a preferential basis. Furthermore, the growth of intra-PTA imports might, in some cases, be associated with trade diversion.

27. The reduction of external protection could be associated with the creation of this particular PTA or with other bilateral or plurilateral liberalization.

28. The sample covers all 179 countries available in the International Monetary Fund Direction of Trade statistics over the period 1970–2008. GDP data originate from the IMF's *World Economic Outlook* database. Dummies are included for the membership of the following PTAs: ASEAN, CACM, CAN, CARICOM, CEFTA, CEZ, CIS, COMESA, EAC, ECOWAS, EFTA, EU, GCC, Mercosur, NAFTA, PATCRA, SADC, SAFTA, and WAEMU/UEMOA.

29. These results are consistent with the gravity estimates of the impact of PTAs on intraregional trade found in *Global Economic Prospects 2005* (World Bank 2005). Although the World Bank analysis covers an earlier time period (1960–2000) and the gravity model specification is different, the relative values of the coefficients on intra-PTA trade are similar to our findings.

30. The impact on trade is equal to $e^{-0.155}-1 = -14$ percent.

31. The result for CEFTA is not easy to interpret because membership of the bloc has changed dramatically with EU enlargements.

References

Baldwin, Richard, and Daria Taglioni. 2006. "Gravity for Dummies and Dummies for Gravity Equations." NBER Working Paper 12516, National Bureau of Economic Research, Cambridge, MA.

Batista, Jorge Chami. 2008. "Competing for the US Import Market: NAFTA and Non-NAFTA Countries." In *Economic Integration in the Americas,* ed. Joseph A. McKinney and H. Stephen Gardner. London: Routledge.

Deardorff, A. V. 1995. "Determinants of Bilateral Trade: Does Gravity Work in a Neoclassical World?" NBER Working Paper 5377, National Bureau of Economic Research, Cambridge, MA.

Evenett, S. J., and W. Keller. 2002. "On Theories Explaining the Success of the Gravity Equation." *Journal of Political Economy* 110: 281–316.

Fiorentino, Roberto V., Jo-Ann Crawford, and Christelle Toqueboeuf. 2009. "The Landscape of Regional Trade Agreements and WTO Surveillance." In *Multilateralizing Regionalism: Challenges for the Global Trading System*, ed. Richard Baldwin and Patrick Low. Cambridge, U.K.: Cambridge University Press.

Horn, Henrik, Petros C. Mavroidis, and André Sapir. 2010. *Beyond the WTO? An Anatomy of EU and US Preferential Trade Agreements. The World Economy* 33(11), 1565–88.

Sapir, André. 2007. "Europe and the Global Economy." In *Fragmented Power: Europe and the Global Economy*, ed. André Sapir. Brussels: Bruegel. http://www.bruegel.org/publications/show/publication/fragmented-power-europe-and-the-global-econom.html.

Shelburne, R. C. 2000. *Intra-Industry Trade, the Gravity Model and Similarity in Endowments and Country Size.* Papers and Proceedings of the International Trade and Finance Association, San Diego State University, San Diego, CA.

World Bank. 2005. *Global Economic Prospects 2005: Trade, Regionalism, and Development.* Washington, DC: World Bank.

3

ECONOMICS

Richard Baldwin

Preferential trade agreements (PTAs) have been important features of the world trade system since the inception in 1947 of the General Agreement on Tariffs and Trade (GATT), which was succeeded in 1995 by the World Trade Organization (WTO). For the first 50 years of the GATT/WTO, PTAs dealt mainly, and often exclusively, with preferential tariff reduction. It is therefore natural that most economic analyses of PTAs focused on preferential tariffs. This view, however, has come to be outdated, as discussed by Chauffour and Maur, ch.1 in this volume.

The GATT/WTO's success in cutting developed countries' most favored nation (MFN) tariffs, coupled with rapid unilateral MFN tariff reductions by developing countries (Baldwin 2010b), means that today's margins of tariff preferences are relatively small. Carpenter and Lendle (2010), for instance, show that whereas almost half of world trade is between countries that share a PTA, only 16 percent is eligible for preferences, and most of these preferences are small; only 2 percent of world trade outside the EU has margins over 10 percent. The reason is that much of world trade is now granted MFN duty-free status, so that preference margins are zero by definition. Moreover, the preference margins that do exist are typically small. Less than 2 percent of world imports, excluding intra-EU trade, is eligible for preference margins that exceed 10 percent (Carpenter and Lendle 2010). As a result, analysis based on the traditional, preference-centric perspective is no longer sufficient. Nevertheless, the traditional view remains the core of received wisdom on PTAs, and so the bulk of this chapter deals with the economics of tariff preferences.

Specifically, this chapter examines the economics and political economy of preferential trade liberalization, starting with the elemental effects of preferential tariff cutting: the gain to partners receiving the preference (Smith's certitude); the loss to third countries that must compete with the preference-receiver (Haberler's spillover); and the ambiguous welfare impact on the nation granting the preferences (Viner's ambiguity). Issues related to scale economies and procompetitive effects are then explored. Finally, the discussion turns to the additional benefits that PTAs may offer in terms of learning effects, increased foreign investment, the provision of regional public goods such as transport networks, and other positive externalities. The annexes to the chapter contain technical explanations for interested readers.

Basic Economic Effects of Regionalism

The terminology behind the basic economics of discriminatory liberalization is marked by a conceptual tangle of conflicting, overlapping, and competing terminologies. To set the stage for discussion and analysis, we cover the three elemental effects at work. All have been known at least since 1950. To avoid creating yet another set of terms, we label them according to their intellectual fathers.

Smith's Certitude, Haberler's Spillover, and Viner's Ambiguity

Early contributions to the theory of preferential trade include Adam Smith, Robert Torrens, and Frank Taussig (see Pomfret 1997 for discussion and references). One of the most robust findings in the field is what might be called "Smith's certitude":

> When a nation "exempt[s] the good of one country from duties to which it subjects those of all others . . . the merchants and manufacturers of the country whose commerce is so favored must necessarily derive great advantage." (Pomfret 1997, quoting Smith 1776)

Much later, Gottfried Haberler (1936, 384) asserted that all members of a preferential trade agreement must gain, while third nations must lose. We now know that the first part of the assertion is wrong, but what might be called "Haberler's spillover"—the part about third nations losing—turns out to be almost as robust as Smith's certitude. Haberler's spillover and Smith's certitude are the linchpins of the political economy of preferential tariff cutting.

The only basic element added in the postwar period came with Jacob Viner's famous 1950 book, *The Customs Union Issue.* His key finding was that preferential tariff liberalization has ambiguous welfare effects on the preference-granting nation ("Viner's ambiguity"). Viner's ambiguity is quite general, yet one is hard pressed to see this from the analysis in his book. A preferential tariff is nothing more than a special case of nonuniform commodity taxation, but Viner did not have the benefit of modern economic tools for tax analysis. Rather, he relied on the enduring but imprecise concepts of "trade diversion" and "trade creation." These terms are misleading because they suggest that trade volumes are the key, even though Viner's words clearly indicate that cost changes are what matter. Moreover, they fail to cover all the effects generated by discriminatory tariff liberalization, even in a simple Walrasian setting. Given these shortcomings, and the decades-long debate on "what Viner really meant" (a debate in which Viner himself participated, without notable effect), it is curious that the terms have enjoyed such enduring success.[1]

The generality of Viner's ambiguity is glaringly obvious to readers schooled in the theory of the second-best (preferential liberalization induces new distortions while removing others), but Viner's book was a landmark. The theory of the second-best was unknown in 1950, and many of Viner's contemporaries—Haberler, for example—were muddled about the essential differences between general and preferential liberalization.

A fourth elemental effect in the regionalism literature concerns the interaction between preferential and multilateral tariff cutting. It is not really a basic economic effect but, rather, a specific combination of effects brought to prominence by the fact that the most important regional liberalizations over the past 60 years have been accompanied by multilateral liberalization. When thinking about this teaming of multilateral and regionalism liberalization, the guiding light is the Kemp-Wan logic, which is discussed next.

James Meade (1955) introduced analysis that led to one of the few general statements that can be made about PTAs—the Kemp-Wan theorem. Kemp and Wan (1976) demonstrated that PTAs could be designed to be Pareto improving for every member of the PTA and for the world at large. The logic is elegant. Assume that two nations sign a PTA and alter their external tariffs to freeze their external trade flows. The external trade flows can then be treated as part of the bloc's endowment. Removal of all intra-PTA barriers thus shifts the two-nation bloc from a second-best situation to a first-best situation (i.e., laissez-faire in goods

and factors, given tastes, technology, and endowments). The action of the free market, according to the first welfare theorem of Walrasian economics, guarantees an increase in economic efficiency, and lump-sum transfers within the PTA ensure welfare gains for all. Third nations are not affected because their trade vectors do not change. Dixit and Norman (1980) generalize the analysis, showing that the Kemp-Wan improvement can be obtained without lump-sum transfers; intra-PTA commodity taxes and subsidies are sufficient.

Of course, real-world PTAs do not adjust external tariffs in a Kemp-Wan manner, nor do they have access to large lump-sum transfers. Nevertheless, the theorem is important from a policy perspective; it proves that PTAs are not necessarily bad for world welfare. Moreover, it helps us think about why the combination of multilateral and preferential tariff cutting, which has been in operation since the 1950s, has had a relatively benign to date.

Illustration of Basic Economic Effects

Smith's certitude, Haberler's spillover, and Viner's ambiguity capture most of the basic economics of PTAs and, together with the Kemp-Wan logic, most of the political-economy reasoning in the "big-think" regionalism literature.[2] It is possible to deal with these mathematically. However, to demonstrate the basic interactions among the elemental effects and to facilitate the subsequent exposition of the logic of the big-think regionalism literature, a graphical analysis may be useful.

The simplest framework that meets the requirements is a Walrasian three-nation model (Home, Partner, and Rest of the World [RoW]) with three goods, numbered 1, 2, and 3. Each nation exports two goods and imports the other good (figure 3.1). Since each nation has two sources of

Figure 3.1. Trade Pattern for a Simple Preferential Trade Association

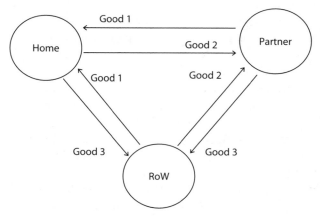

Source: Author's elaboration.

imports, tariff discrimination can be a real issue in all markets. To rule out Meade's secondary effects, tastes are assumed to be identical across nations and additively separable in all goods.[3] For simplicity's sake, the three nations are symmetric in size and with respect to the most favored nation (MFN) tariff they initially impose.[4]

The two trading equilibriums (regionalism versus multilateral free trade) in a typical market (Good 1) can be worked out with the help of the PTA diagram shown in figure 3.2. The analyses for imports of Good 2 (into Partner) and Good 3 (into RoW) are isomorphic because of the strong symmetry.

The diagram shows the export supply curves (marked XS, with the appropriate superscript to indicate the origin nation) for Home's two potential suppliers. The horizontal sum of the XS curves is shown as MS_{FT}, along with Home's import demand curve, MD. Under global free trade, the domestic and border price is P^{FT}, as shown in all nations for all goods. Assuming that all nations impose a specific tariff T on an MFN basis, the internal price in Home is driven up to P, while the border price is driven down to $P - T$ for both suppliers. Home imports drop, with the reduction divided equally between the two suppliers.

From MFN tariffs to preferential trade agreements. If a PTA is formed between Home and Partner, the total import supply curve becomes the kinked MS_{PTA} curve.[5] The resulting internal price falls to P', but there are now two border prices. The border price facing Partner-based exporters rises from $P - T$ to P', while the border price facing RoW firms falls from $P - T$ to $P' - T$. Partner exports expand, and RoW exports contract. Identical things happen in the market for Good 2, but here Home is the exporter and Partner is the importer. Nothing happens in the market for Good 3, where RoW is the importer: RoW maintains its MFN tariff, and the strong separability assumptions rule out Meade's secondary and tertiary effects.

We see Smith's certitude and Haberler's spillover immediately in figure 3.2. Smith's certitude shows up as Partner gains $a + b$ from the higher border price and the expansion of exports. Since the FTA is reciprocal and nations are symmetric, Home gains the same in Good 2. Haberler's spillover shows up in the fact that RoW loses area e because of the drop in the border price it faces (from $P - T$ to $P' - T$) and the reduction of its exports to Home and Partner.

The preference rent. A critical observation, as far as big-think regionalism is concerned, touches on a decomposition of Smith's certitude—that is, how PTA-based exporters gain from two distinct features of their improved market access. First, the removal of the intra-PTA tariff boosts their market access directly. Second, PTA-based exporters benefit from the reduction in RoW exports induced by the tariff discrimination. The second part of the gain—area a in figure 3.2—could be called the preference rent because if the tariff cutting were multilateral instead of preferential, PTA partners would gain only b, not $a + b$. This preference rent a is vulnerable to so-called preference erosion and thus plays a leading role in countries' resistance to moving from preferential tariff liberalization to multilateral liberalization.

On the import side (figure 3.3), Home gains a trade-volume effect, equal to area A, from expanding its imports; that is, from replacing high-cost domestic production with lower-cost imports. Home also gains from a border-price

Figure 3.2. Trading Equilibriums in a Preferential Trade Association

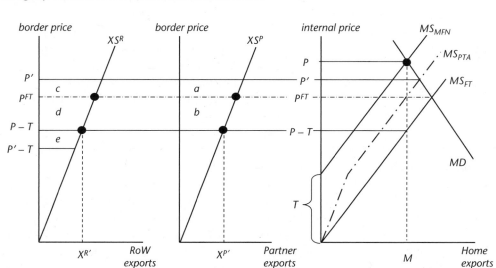

Source: Author's modification of figure in Baldwin and Wyplosz 2009, ch. 5.

Figure 3.3. Ambiguous Net Welfare Effects

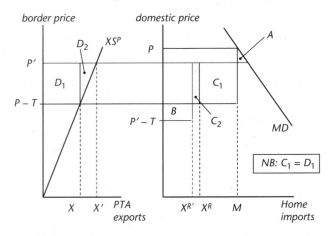

Source: Author's elaboration.

effect—the terms-of-trade improvement against RoW (area *B*)—while losing from the terms-of-trade loss against Partner (area $C_1 + C_2$). Home's terms-of-trade gain on the export side partly offsets the terms-of-trade loss on the import side ($D_1 = C_1$), so Home's net welfare change is $A + B + D_2 - C_2$.[6] As drawn, it looks as though Home and Partner gain, but whether they in fact do depends on elasticities and the initial MFN tariff. In general, Viner's ambiguity holds in this framework. As can be demonstrated mathematically, the PTA reduces welfare when the MFN tariff is sufficiently high (Baldwin and Venables 1995).

The net welfare impact on RoW is unambiguously negative (Haberler's spillover). RoW experiences no change on the import side but twice loses area *e* (shown in the leftmost panel in figure 3.2)—once on its exports of Good 1 to Home, and once on its exports of Good 2 to Partner. The Haberler spillover is an externality as far as the global trade system is concerned, and, as such, it plays a central role in the big-think regionalism literature.

A Note on Nontariff Barriers

The traditional view of regionalism focuses almost exclusively on preferential tariffs, but many PTAs also include liberalization of nontariff barriers. Here, we turn to the basic economics of technical barriers to trade (TBT) liberalization, or, more generally, frictional barrier liberalization. "Frictional," in this sense, means that the barriers impose a wedge between domestic and border prices, but the wedge is "burnt up" rather than collected as a rent by the government (as with a tariff) or by a quota holder (as with a quota).

Standards and regulations can influence economic activity and the structure of industry in ways too numerous to count. The World Bank, for instance, has conducted a large multiyear project studying the impact of standards on trade.[7] To focus on essentials, however, we abstract from many details and model TBTs as frictional barriers; that is, barriers that raise the marginal cost of selling a good internationally.[8] The effect of such frictional barriers is similar to that of a tariff except that no tariff revenue or other form of rent is generated. The gap between the prices of the good inside the importing nation and inside the exporting nation is burnt up by costly activities that are required to satisfy the TBT.

To keep things simple, consider again a three-nation world with TBT liberalization between two countries, Home and Partner; the third nation (RoW) remains outside the arrangement. We start by assuming that all three nations impose TBTs that have a specific-tariff equivalent of *T*. The policy change to be studied is a lowering of *T* to zero on all trade between Home and Partner, with no change in the barriers on trade between RoW and Home or between Partner and RoW.

The price and quantity effects of the preferential liberalization are very similar to those discussed above in the case of tariff liberalization; the only change concerns the border price. With frictional barriers, the domestic price is the border price for the importing nation, so the liberalization lowers Home's border price. At the same time, the exporter that benefits from the liberalization receives a higher price for its exports, and so the exporter's border price rises. The point is made concretely in figure 3.4.

Starting from the situation in which the TBT is applied to both Partner and RoW imports (i.e., when the equilibrium price is *P'*), the preferential liberalization shifts Home's import supply curve (*MS*) to MS_{PTA}, from MS_{MFN}. The internal Home price falls to *P"*, and this also becomes the price in Partner. The price that RoW exporters receive (net of the cost of the TBT) falls to $P" - T$. Partner exports expand and those of RoW contract, but the former contract less than the latter expand, so overall, Home's imports rise. The welfare implications are shown in figure 3.5.

As with preferential tariff cutting, the liberalization creates a positive trade volume effect for Home equal to area *A*. Since, however, the price that Home actually pays for its imports from Partner and RoW is Home's internal price (rather than the external price, as in the case of tariff protection), the liberalization leads to an unambiguous terms-of-trade gain. Home gets its imports—both from RoW and from Partner—for less, that is, for *P"* instead of *P'*. This gain corresponds to area *F* in figure 3.5. Thus, although the

Figure 3.4. Effects of Preferential Frictional Barrier Liberalization on Prices and Imports

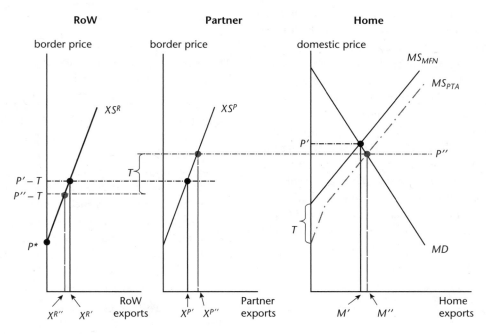

Source: Author's elaboration.

Figure 3.5. Welfare Effects of Preferential TBT Liberalization: Viner's Ambiguity Vanishes

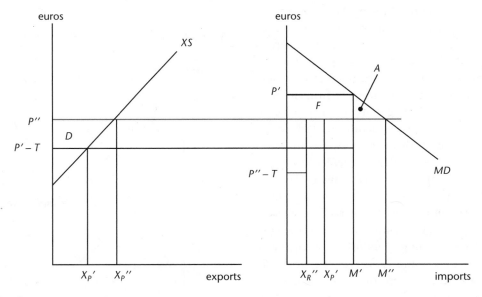

Source: Author's elaboration.
Note: TBT, technical barriers to trade.

discriminatory application of the TBT leads to supply switching from RoW to Partner, this "trade diversion" has no welfare consequences for Home.

As usual, Partner unambiguously gains from the preferences because it enjoys a positive trade volume effect (its exports expand) and a positive terms-of-trade effect.

Thus, in the market under study, the PTA partners unambiguously gain. Notice that Viner's ambiguity has disappeared. RoW unambiguously loses, for the usual reasons; that is, the heightened competition in Home's market induces RoW firms to sell less and to charge a lower net price.

Dynamic Gains of Regionalism

One of the principal justifications for PTAs, especially those involving developing countries, is the belief that uniting small economies will make regional firms more efficient and more competitive by allowing them access to a bigger market. The boost in efficiency would allow the firms to lower prices, raise quality, and increase their competitiveness, both internally and externally.

Plainly, this logic cannot work in the supply-and-demand-diagram world considered in the preceding section, since that worldview assumes that a firm's efficiency has nothing to do with market size. This section offers a window into the dynamic gains of regional integration and explains the logic of how regional integration could lead to a situation of fewer, larger firms operating on a more efficient scale and facing more effective competition.

Liberalization, Defragmentation, and Industrial Restructuring

National markets are separated by a very long list of barriers. These include tariffs and quotas, but also multiple technical, physical, and fiscal impediments that make it easier for companies to sell in their local market than in other markets. The typical outcome of these explicit and hidden barriers is that national firms can often be successful in their home markets while being marginal players abroad. This state of affairs, known as market fragmentation, reduces competition, which, in turn, raises prices and keeps too many firms in business. Keeping firms in business is not, of course, a bad thing in itself. The problem is that it results in an industrial structure marked by too many inefficient small firms that can get away with charging high prices to cover the cost of their inefficiency.

Tearing down regional barriers defragments the markets and generates extra competition. This procompetitive effect puts pressure on profits, and the market's response is "merger mania": the least efficient firms are squeezed out by the competition, prompting an industrial restructuring whereby weaker firms enter into mergers or are bought up. Schematically, the successive steps can be summarized as liberalization → defragmentation → procompetitive effect → industrial restructuring. The result is fewer, bigger, more efficient firms that face more effective competition from each other. All this means improved material well-being for all, as prices fall and output rises. In some industries, restructuring may be accompanied by a sizable reallocation of employment: firms cut back on redundant workers and close inefficient plants and offices (a painful process for workers who have to change jobs). In other industries,

however, liberalization can unleash a virtuous circle of more competition, lower prices, increased sales, and higher employment.

The Break-Even–Competition Curve Diagram in a Closed Economy

To study the logic of the effect of integration on scale and competition, we need a simple yet flexible framework that allows for imperfect competition. The break-even (*BE*)–competition curve (*COMP*) diagram employed here assumes a knowledge of simple imperfect-competition models. (Annex B provides an introduction for readers who are not familiar with such models.)

To study the effects of integration on firm size and efficiency, number of firms, prices, output, and the like, it is useful to consider a set of diagrams in which all these things are determined. To keep things simple, we begin with the case of a closed economy.

The key relationship is shown in figure 3.6, where the number of firms and the profit-maximizing price-cost margin are determined. As usual, the equilibrium will be the intersection of two curves, the *BE* curve and the *COMP* curve. To explain the economics of the diagram, we start with the *COMP* curve.

Figure 3.6. Competition (*COMP*) and Break-Even (*BE*) Curves

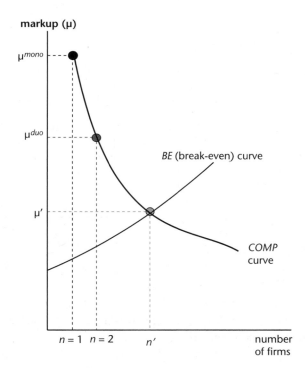

Source: Author's elaboration.
Note: The superscript *mono* refers to monopoly; *duo,* to duopoly.

The competition (COMP) curve. It is easy to understand that imperfectly competitive firms charge a price that exceeds their marginal cost; they do so in order to maximize profit. But how wide is the gap between price and marginal cost, and how does it vary with the number of competitors? These questions are answered by the *COMP* curve.

If there is only one firm, the price-cost gap—the markup of price over marginal cost—will equal the markup that a monopolist would charge. If more firms are competing in the market, competition will force each firm to charge a lower markup. This "competition-side" relationship between the markup and the number of firms is shown in figure 3.6 as the *COMP* curve. It is downward sloping because competition drives the markup down as the number of competitors rises, as explained above. We denote the markup by the Greek letter μ, ("mu," an abbreviation for markup). The size of the markup is an indicator of how competitive the market is.

The break-even (BE) curve. The markup and the number of firms are related in another way, summarized by the *BE* curve.

When a sector exhibits increasing returns to scale, there is only room for a certain number of firms in a market of a given size. Intuitively, more firms will be able to survive if the price is far above marginal cost, that is, if the markup is high. The curve that captures this relationship is called the zero-profit curve, or the break-even (*BE*) curve (figure 3.6). It has a positive slope because more firms can break even when the markup is high. That is, taking the markup as given, the *BE* curve shows the number of firms that can earn enough to cover their fixed cost—say, the cost of setting up a factory.

Equilibrium prices, output, and firm size. It is important to note that firms are not always on the *BE* curve, since they can earn above-normal or below-normal profits for a while. In the long run, however, firms can enter or exit the market, and so the number of firms rises or falls until the typical firm earns just enough to cover its fixed cost. By contrast, firms are always on the *COMP* curve, since firms can change prices quickly in response to any change in the number of firms.

With this in mind, we are ready to work out the equilibrium markup, number of firms, price, and firm size in a closed economy, using figure 3.7. The right-hand panel combines the *BE* curve with the *COMP* curve. The intersection of the two defines the equilibrium markup and the long-run number of firms. More specifically, the *COMP* curve tells us that firms would charge a markup of μ' when there are n' firms in the market, and the *BE* curve tells us that n' firms could break even when the markup is μ'. The equilibrium price is, by the definition of the markup, just the equilibrium markup plus the marginal cost, *MC*. Using the *MC* curve from the left-hand panel, we see that the equilibrium price is p' (μ' plus *MC*). The middle panel shows the demand curve, and this allows us to see that the total level of consumption implied by the equilibrium price is C'.

Figure 3.7. Prices, Output, and Equilibrium Firm Size in a Closed Economy

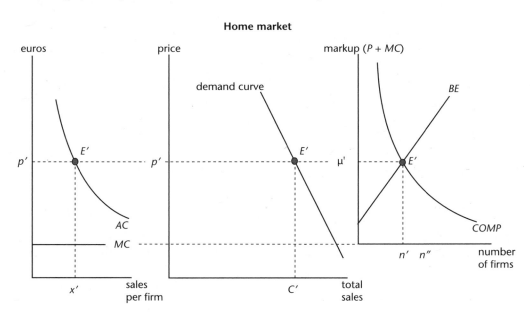

Source: Author's elaboration.

The left-hand panel helps us find the equilibrium firm size, that is, sales per firm, which we denote x. This panel shows the average and marginal cost curves of a typical firm. A typical firm's total profit is zero when price equals average cost. (When price equals average cost, total revenue equals total cost.) Since we know that total profits are zero at the equilibrium and that the price is p', the equilibrium firm size must be is x', which is where the firm's size implies an average cost equal to p'.

In summary, this three-panel figure lets us determine the equilibrium number of firms, markup, price, total consumption, and firm size, all in one diagram. With this in hand, we are now ready to study how regional integration—or indeed, any source of increase in market size—could lead to industrial restructuring.

The Impact of Regional Liberalization

Regional integration removes trade barriers gradually, but the basic economic effects can be better illustrated by considering a much more drastic liberalization—taking a completely closed economy and making it a completely open economy. To keep things simple, we suppose that there are only two nations, Home and Partner, and that they are identical. Since they are identical, we could trace the effects by looking at either market, but for convenience, we focus on Home's market.

The immediate impact of the no-trade-to-free-trade liberalization is to provide each firm with a second market of the same size and to double the number of competitors in each market. How does this change the outcome?

The competition aspect of the liberalization can be simply traced. The increased number of competitors in each market makes competition tougher. In reaction, the typical firm will lower its markup in each market to point A in figure 3.8.

The doubling of the market size facing each firm also has an important effect. The liberalization adds a new market for each firm, so it makes sense that more firms will be able to survive. To see how many more firms can survive, we work out the impact of the liberalization on the BE curve and find that the curve is shifted to the right, specifically, to BE^{FT}, as shown in the rightmost panel of figure 3.8. The shift means that at any given markup, more firms can break even. This is true because, as market size increases, sales per firm increase, providing a higher operating profit per firm at any given level of markup.

The size of the rightward shift is determined without difficulty. If there were no change in the markup, a doubling of the number of firms could break even, since each firm would be selling the same number of units. In other

words, the new BE curve must pass through point 1 in the figure. At that point, the markup is μ', the number of firms is $2n'$, and logic tells us that this combination of μ and n would result in all firms breaking even. Point 1, however, is merely an intellectual landmark used to determine how far out the BE curve shifts. It is not where the economy would be right after liberalization, since the markup would immediately be pushed down to μ^A.

Because the increase in competition would immediately push down the markup to μ^A, the two newly integrated markets will initially be at a point below the BE curve. We know that all firms will be losing money at point A because the actual markup (μ^A) is less than what would be needed to have all $2n'$ firms break even. This loss of profit is not a problem in the short run because firms only need to break even in the long run. Indeed, the profit losses are what would trigger the process of industrial restructuring that eventually reduces the number of firms.

The corresponding effect on prices is shown in the middle diagram, as the move from E' to A and then to E''. Before we explain this, observe that the middle panel shows the demand curve for Home only, so the no-trade-to-free-trade liberalization does not shift the demand curve. The Foreign market has an identical demand, but since exactly the same thing goes on in Foreign, we omit the Foreign demand curve to reduce the diagram's complexity.

As mentioned above, the initial impact of the extra competition ($2n'$ firms, rather than n', selling to the Home market) pushes the equilibrium markup down to μ^A, so the price falls to p^A. Thus, during the industrial restructuring phase, the price would rise to p'' (from p^A), but this rise does not take the price all the way back to its preliberalization level of p'.

The impact of this combination of extra competition and industrial restructuring on a typical firm is shown in the left-hand panel. As prices fall, firms that remain in the market increase their efficiency—that is, lower their average cost—by spreading their fixed cost over a larger number of sales. Indeed, since price equaled average cost before the liberalization and equals average cost in the long run after liberalization, we know that the price drop is exactly equal to the efficiency gain. In the left-hand panel, this is shown as a move from E' to E''. Increasing returns to scale are at the root of this efficiency gain. As the equilibrium scale of a typical firm rises from x' to x'', average costs fall.

To summarize, the no-trade-to-free-trade liberalization results in fewer, larger firms. The resulting scale economies lower average cost and thus make these firms more efficient. The extra competition ensures that these savings are passed on to consumers, so prices are lower.

Figure 3.8. Prices, Output, and Equilibrium Firm Size with Integration

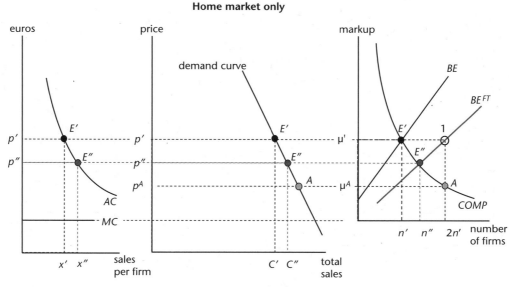

Source: Author's elaboration.

It is useful to think of the integration as taking place in two steps, as follows.

1. *Short term: Defragmentation and the procompetitive effect (from E′ to A).* We start with the short-term impact, that is to say, the impact before the number of firms can adjust. Before the liberalization, each market was extremely fragmented in the sense that firms in each country had a local market share of $1/n'$ and a zero share in the other market. After the liberalization, the market share of each firm is the same in each market, that is, $1/2n'$. This elimination of market fragmentation has a procompetitive effect, which is defined as a decrease in the price-cost markup, shown in the right-hand panel of figure 3.8 as a move from E′ to A. The short-term impact on prices and sales can be seen in the middle panel as a drop from p' to p^A.

2. *Long term: Industrial restructuring and scale effects (A to E″).* Point A is not a long-term equilibrium because the operating profit earned by a typical firm is insufficient to cover the fixed cost. We see this by noting that point A is below the *BE* curve, telling us that the markup is too low to allow $2n'$ firms to break even. To restore a normal level of profitability, the overall number of firms has to fall from $2n'$ to n''. In some cases, this process occurs via mergers and buyouts; in others, the number of firms is reduced by bankruptcies. As this industrial consolidation occurs, the economy moves from point A to point

E″. During this process, firms enlarge their market shares, the markup rises somewhat, and profitability is restored.

The welfare effects of this liberalization are straightforward. The four-sided area C marked out by p', p'', E′, and E″ in the middle panel of figure 3.9 corresponds to the gain in the Home consumer surplus. As usual, this gain can be broken down into the gain to consumers of paying a lower price for the units they bought prior to the liberalization and the gains from buying more (C″ versus C′). Exactly the same gain occurs in the Foreign market (not shown in the figure).

As it turns out, the four-sided region labeled C in figure 3.9 is Home's long-term welfare gain because there is no offsetting loss to producers and there was no tariff revenue to begin with. Firms made zero profits before liberalization, and they earn zero profits after liberalization. Note, however, that this long-term calculation ignores the medium-term adjustment costs.

The discussion above has shown that integration initially leads to big price reductions and large profit losses. These profit losses are eliminated as the number of firms falls and as profits are restored to normal levels. During this industrial restructuring process, prices rise slightly. This sequence of steps, sometimes called industrial consolidation or an industry shakeout, is relevant to some industries. In other industries, firms anticipate the increased competition

Figure 3.9. Welfare Effects of Complete Liberalization

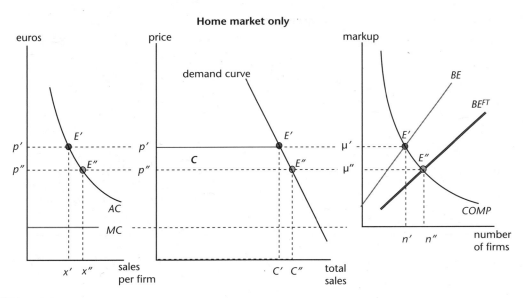

Source: Author's elaboration.

and undertake mergers and acquisitions quickly enough to avoid big losses. In figure 3.8, this would look like a move from E' directly to E''.

Agglomeration and the New Economic Geography

Industrialization and deindustrialization are core concerns of developing-country policy makers around the world. Or, to put it differently, policy makers care about the location of industry. Although a whole host of policies affects a nation's industrialization, trade policy has proved to be a critical element in industrialization in almost all countries. This section considers an analytical framework that permits us to think logically about several of the key forces affecting industrialization and how they interact with trade barriers. The framework is often called the new economic geography, following the terminology of 2008 Nobel laureate Paul Krugman.

The basic focus of the new economic geography is on whether firms would enter or exit a particular market. The key determinant, in this simplified view of the world, is the firms' profitability. If setting up a new firm in a particular country would be profitable, then the firm is created. If production in a particular country becomes unprofitable, the firm ceases production. The entry or exit decision rests on the balancing of two sets of forces: agglomeration forces and dispersion forces. Agglomeration forces promote the spatial concentration of economic

activity, whereas dispersion forces discourage such concentration. The spatial distribution of economic activity at any moment in time depends on the balance of the proconcentration (agglomeration) forces and the anticoncentration (dispersion) forces.

The main question in this section is, how does trade integration affect the equilibrium location of industry? To set the stage for the equilibrium analysis, we first consider dispersion and agglomeration forces in isolation. For better understanding of how trade arrangements affect profitability, and thus industrialization, it is convenient to employ a simple analytical framework, one constructed by Puga and Venables (1998). It focuses on four forces: two dispersion forces (factor-market competition and local-market competition), and two agglomeration forces (input-cost linkages and demand linkages).

Dispersion and Agglomeration Forces

Dispersion forces favor the geographic spreading out of economic activity. Land prices are the classic example. The price of land, and therefore the price of housing, office space, and so on, is usually higher in built-up areas such as central London than in rural areas such as northern Wales. If everything else were equal, firms and workers would prefer to locate in less built-up areas. (Of course, we know that other things are not equal.) The forces that make built-up areas more attractive are called agglomeration forces; we set them aside for the moment to concentrate on dispersion forces. Dispersion forces counteract agglomeration forces by increasing the attractiveness of less developed regions. In addition to land prices, there are several other forms of congestion-based dispersion forces, including wages, which tend to be higher in built-up areas.

In this section, we focus on only two dispersion forces. *Factor-market competition* captures the way that industrialization tends to push up wages. (That is, the competition is for labor and operates between industry and other sectors within a single country.) *Local-market competition* reflects the fact that the presence of many industrial firms in a particular country tends to increase the degree of competition for customers in the local market. An important point is that local-market competition depends on trade barriers. If a country's markets are perfectly open to international competition, the competition for local customers is a global competition. At the other extreme, if the country is completely closed off, local competition depends solely on the number of local firms. As trade barriers fall, the nature of competition shifts gradually from fully local to fully global.

Always assuming that other things are equal, factor-market competition means that countries with little industry tend to have low wages and are thus more attractive to industry. Local-market competition means that countries with little industry are markets in which the extent of competition is rather low, and they too are attractive to industry. Both types of competition are dispersion forces that tend to make firms want to avoid spatial concentration.

Agglomeration forces exist when the spatial concentration of economic activity creates forces that encourage further spatial concentration. This definition is more circular than the straight-line chain of causes and effects usually presented in economics, but its circularity is the heart of the subject.

There are many agglomeration forces, but some of them operate only on a very local scale. These explain, for instance, why banks tend to group together in one part of a city such as Paris or London and theatres cluster in another part of the city. The study of agglomeration at this level—it is called urban economics—is fascinating, but it is not the level of agglomeration that interests us. Trade arrangements affect agglomeration at the level of countries, and at that national level, city-level agglomeration forces are unimportant. The third and fourth forces we consider in this section are agglomeration forces that tend to encourage the clustering of industry in a single country.

Input-cost linkages capture the fact that a well-developed local network of suppliers can boost a country's attractiveness as a site for industrial production. This idea turns on the real-world fact that manufacturing firms require many intermediate inputs—parts and components. When these parts and components are produced locally, they tend to be cheaper and can be supplied in a timelier manner. Demand linkages reflect the attractiveness of a country that has easy access to customers, whether local or in a trading partner.

Demand-linked circular causality rests on market-size issues—hence its name. Firms want to locate where they have good access to a large market such as Japan or the United States. If a firm locates in the big market, it incurs shipping costs to sell to other markets, but its costs of selling to big-market customers are low. (It is cheaper to sell to nearby customers.) Since there are more customers in the big market, firms can reduce their shipping by moving there. This is where the circular causality of demand linkages starts. Other things being equal, firms want to be in the big market.

The causality becomes circular because the movement of firms from the small market to the big market makes the big market bigger and the small market smaller. The reason is that firms buy inputs from other firms. Thus, firms moving to the big market create more demand in the big market and less in the small one. We call this an agglomeration force, since spatial concentration of economic activity creates forces that encourage further spatial concentration.

The basic idea is illustrated in figure 3.10. It is useful to separate two things that are closely related: market size (big market as a share of total market, or the spatial distribution of demand), and firm location (share of firms in the big market, or the spatial distribution of firms).

Starting from the left-hand arrow, we see that market size affects the location of firms. The logic rests on firms' desire to minimize shipping costs. The right-hand arrow shows that the location of firms affects relative market size. The logic is simply that firms tend to buy inputs locally.

Figure 3.10. Demand-Linked Circular Causality

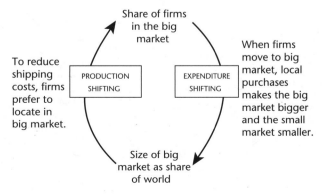

Source: Author's elaboration.

If no dispersion forces were in operation, this circular causality would continue until the small market was entirely empty of industrial firms.

This brings us to the second major type of agglomeration force. *Input-cost-linked circular causality* works in a fashion that is similar to demand-linked circular causality, but it involves production costs rather than market size.

In the modern economy, firms buy plenty of things from other firms. These range from raw materials and machinery to specialized services such as marketing, accounting, and information technology (IT) services. Since it is cheaper to find and buy such inputs from firms that are nearby, the presence of many firms in a location tends to reduce the cost of doing business in that location. Thinking this through, we can see that a similar circular causality will encourage agglomeration (see figure 3.11).

The figure separates two things that are closely related but are worth keeping distinct: firm location (share of firms in the big market, or the spatial distribution of firms), and the cost advantage of producing in the big market (cost of producing in the big market, or the spatial distribution of production costs).

Starting from the left-hand arrow, we note that if many firms are already in the big market, then doing business in the big market will, all else being equal, be cheaper than doing business in the small market. This production-cost differential influences the location of firms. The right-hand arrow shows how the relocation of firms tends to improve the business climate in the big market and worsen it in the small market, at least in terms of the range of available inputs. Again, if there were no dispersion forces, this circular causality would empty out the small market entirely. In other words, cost-linked circular causality describes the way in which firms are attracted by the

presence of many suppliers in the big market and how the movement of firms to the big market widens the range of supplies and thus makes the big market even more attractive from a cost-of-production point of view. This sort of logic is sometimes called "cluster economics."

Locational Effects of Liberalization

Trade integration affects the balance of agglomeration and dispersion forces in complex ways. Such complexity is important for understanding the real world, since trade liberalization has produced very different results in different developing countries. The best way to understand this complex logic is to follow the principle of progressive complexity. We start with a set of simplifying assumptions that allow us to focus on the critical logical relationships. Once we have understood this logic in a setting reduced to essentials, we add back complicating factors.

A simple diagram such as figure 3.12 helps with the study of the balance of the agglomeration and dispersion forces. In the figure, the strength of agglomeration and dispersion forces is plotted on the vertical axis, and the horizontal axis shows the share of all firms that are located in the big region—here, in the North.

- The agglomeration force line rises because of circular causality—that is, agglomeration forces become stronger as industry agglomerates.
- The dispersion force line rises because the benefit of staying in the small region increases as more firms move to the northern market. For example, as more industry moves to the North, the wage gap widens, and so does the difference in local competition.

The locational equilibrium in the left-hand panel is shown by point *E;* this is where the share of firms in the North rises to the point at which incentives to agglomerate are just balanced by incentives to disperse. It is instructive to consider why other points are not the equilibrium. For example, consider the point at which half the firms are in the North. For this equal distribution of firms, the strength of the agglomeration force is shown by point *a*, and the strength of the dispersion force is shown by point *b*. Because *a* is greater than *b*, we know that the agglomeration force—the force that tends to make firms want to move to the North—is stronger than the dispersion force, which tends to make firms want to move to the South. As a consequence, the situation in which only half the firms are in the North cannot be the equilibrium; with agglomeration forces stronger than the dispersion forces, some firms will move from South to North. As firms move northward,

Figure 3.11. Input-Cost-Linked Circular Causality

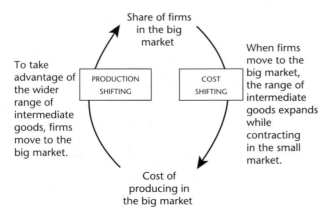

Source: Author's elaboration.

Figure 3.12. Locational Equilibrium Diagram

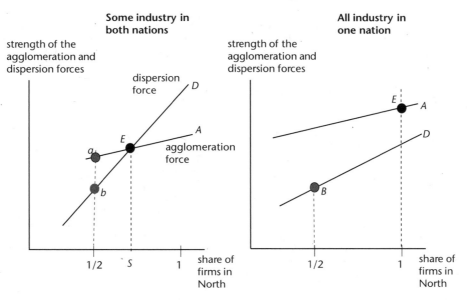

Source: Author's elaboration.

the gap between the agglomeration force and the dispersion force narrows. The location equilibrium is where the two forces just offset each other, that is, point E.

The example in the left-hand panel shows an equilibrium with some industry in both nations. The right-hand panel shows the situation in which agglomeration forces are so strong that all industry ends up in the North (full agglomeration). This is not a bad approximation of the situation that confronts many developing countries today (that is, they have essentially no competitive industry) and that faced almost all developing countries before the emergence of the newly industrializing countries in the 1980s.

Finally we come to the main subject of this section: how does tighter economic integration affect the location of industry across countries? Here, we view trade integration as simply reducing trade barriers such as tariffs and other restrictions. How do we show the trade-cost reduction in the locational equilibrium diagram?

As the discussion above suggests, lower trade costs between the two nations in our simple framework will weaken both the agglomeration forces and the dispersion forces. After all, at the extreme of costless trade, there is no advantage to being in any particular market, with the sole exception of that conferred by the factor-market competition dispersion force. The other three forces rely on differences that are created by costly trade. Factor-market competition, however, has nothing to do with trade costs; all that matters is how much industry is in each nation. The conclusion, then, is that if the world went to

costless trade, industry would spread out much more than is the case today.

This global statement—that lower trade costs foster the industrialization of poor countries—must be tempered, since partial removal of trade costs (e.g., the lowering of tariffs without removing natural trade barriers) can shift the locational equilibrium in either direction or may have no effect at all. What matters is whether the agglomeration forces fall sufficiently relative to the dispersion forces.

The basic idea is shown in figure 3.13. A trade liberalization will shift the agglomeration forces line down. If the liberalization has a big impact on the agglomeration forces, the line could shift to A_2; if the effect is more modest, the shift could be only to A_1. The liberalization also erodes the dispersion forces, and this is shown as the shift to D_1. (We could also consider large and small effects on the D curve, but that would clutter the diagram without adding insight.)

The key is that, in the case of A_1 and D_1, the liberalization has had no effect on industry location; industry is all in the North, before and after. In the A_2 and D_1 case, however, the liberalization has sparked some industrialization in the South; as the new equilibrium, E', implies a share of industry in the North (S') that is less than one.

Trade Arrangements

We now employ the tools presented above to organize our thinking about how preferential trade arrangements could affect the location of industrial production. Here we follow

Figure 3.13. Locational Equilibrium Diagram with Trade Liberalization

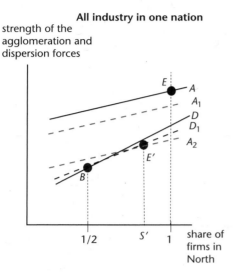

All industry in one nation

Source: Author's elaboration.

Figure 3.14. Trade Arrangements and Industrialization

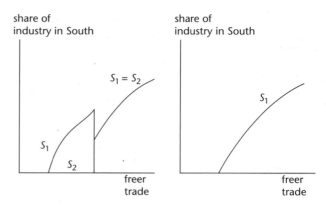

Source: Puga and Venables 1998.
Note: The notation $S_1 = S_2$ denotes that the two lines are identical and that both countries have an equal share of world industry.

the thinking of Puga and Venables (1998) who assume four nations: two northern nations with free trade in manufactured goods between them, and two southern nations whose exports face equal tariffs in all markets. In this model, initially, all industry is in the two northern nations. (Four nations are required if the intrinsic economic mass of the integrating area is to equal the intrinsic mass of the third nations when all nations are symmetric.)

The Puga and Venables framework is too complex to solve with paper and pencil, and so the effects are simulated with the use of a computer. The outcome is plotted in a diagram (figure 3.14) in which the share of world industry is on the vertical axis and the level of tariffs is on the horizontal axis. Because the focus is on the industry in the South, the paths of the industry share of the two southern nations are plotted as S_1 and S_2.

Global Multilateral Tariff Liberalization

To set the stage, consider the impact of a global reduction of tariffs (remember that North-North tariffs are already zero before starting). As global tariffs fall, the tendency for industry to disperse rises. At some point, it becomes profitable for some firms to relocate to the South. The local-market competition dispersion force is weakened, the factor-market dispersion force is unaffected, and both agglomeration forces are weakened as the advantages of being near customers (demand linkages) weaken and the advantages of being near suppliers (cost linkages) also weaken. At some point, the attractiveness of the South's

lower wages outweighs the demand and cost advantages in the North, and some firms move south.

Importantly, cluster economics continues to operate in the South, so industry initially only starts operating in one of the southern countries. In this exercise, the two southern countries are identical, so the choice of which starts first is entirely a matter of chance; to be concrete, this nation is labeled southern nation 1, and its industry share is marked S_1. The reason for this lumpy industrialization is that the first firms to set up create cost and demand linkages to other firms in the same country. They also raise wages, but the linkage effects are stronger, so what we see is a second industrial agglomeration forming in just one of the developing countries. This implication of cluster economics is both quite in line with real-world experience and somewhat unexpected for economists familiar with more neoclassical, marginalist reasoning, where things tend to change smoothly.

Notice that when the industrialization process spreads, the emergence of the second southern industry is initially harmful to the first because of the extra competition. (Think of the effect of the emergence of China on the exports of the Philippines and Thailand.) This is another implication of cluster economics that is not at first obvious.

Unilateral Liberalization

Next, consider unilateral liberalization in this simple Puga-Venables setup. We examine three types: only one southern nation liberalizes; both southern nations liberalize; and both northern nations liberalize.

Liberalization in a single southern economy. Here, only southern nation 1 engages in unilateral import tariff liberalization, with all other barriers held constant. The solid line marked S_1 in the right-hand panel of figure 3.14 shows the outcome, with the unilateral opening leading to industrialization. This is not always what happens, but it is certainly one possibility, and the one that actually occurs under the specific Puga-Venables setup.

The point is that although extra import competition from the North has a negative effect on industrial location in the South (the product-market local competition effect), the cheaper supply of imported intermediate goods becomes the dominant force at some point, and industry becomes established in southern nation 1. This result is not general; for example, if southern nation 1 were very small and faced high export barriers, unilateral liberalization would not induce industrialization. But where this is not the case, the combination of low wages and low-cost intermediates (resulting from import liberalization) eventually leads to industrialization, as is shown in the right-hand panel.

Unilateral liberalization by northern economies: The generalized system of preferences (GSP). Next, consider the case in which the North makes a gesture to the South by unilaterally removing tariffs on imports from the South. The outcome will be similar to that shown in the right-hand panel. The northern tariff cutting improves the prospects of locating industry in the South because it erodes the demand-linked causality that favors the North to begin with. However, since the South is not lowering its tariffs and much industry will remain in the North, the input-cost linkage continues to strongly favor a northern location. Moreover, as mentioned above, if the southern market is small enough, or the input-cost linkages are strong enough (or both), the North's unilateral tariff cutting may have no effect on industrialization. In terms of figure 3.13, we could have a situation like A_1 and D_1 where, despite the shift in attractiveness toward the small region, the balance of forces still favors full agglomeration in the North. Given how little most GSP programs have done to promote southern industry, this is not a case worth keeping in mind.

Liberalization by both southern economies. We now look at MFN liberalization by southern economies in tandem. All southern import tariffs are reduced in the same way, so only northern tariffs against southern exports remain. Initially, the outcome is like that of unilateral liberalization by a single southern nation. The lower southern tariffs heighten the anti-industrialization product-market competition from the North, but it encourages southern production by lowering the cost of inputs. If the southern markets are not too small and the importance of inputs is

sufficiently high, industrialization will start in one southern nation. As before, the logic of cluster economics tells us that the process begins in only one southern nation but then shifts to the other.

Preferential Liberalization

If the two southern nations sign a PTA and lower tariffs between themselves, something like multilateral liberalization occurs. As long as the two markets are not too small, the liberalization will cause industry to become established in the South, but the mechanism is completely different: the driving force here is the effective market enlargement caused by reducing intra-South barriers. This is, of course, the classic argument made in the 1960s and 1970s for South-South PTAs.

As in the multilateral case, the spread of industry to developing countries is uneven, initially taking place in one country and only spreading to the second when trade barriers are lower. Indeed, this sort of uneven development did occur in some early South-South PTAs. For example, in the East African Community, industry started to grow in Kenya at the expense of Uganda and Tanzania. The key difference is that the countries do not benefit from better access to northern markets or to North-produced intermediate inputs.

The impact of a North-South PTA is particularly interesting. Here, the southern nation obtains better access to the big northern market and benefits from lower-cost inputs, but in each case only with respect to the partner. The liberalizing southern economy suffers from more competition from northern firms, but because its wages are lower, the balance of better reciprocal market access is in favor of the South. This spread of industry is associated with a large decline in the North's share of industry. The loser is the other southern economy, which does not attract any industry and now has to contend with industrial clusters in both North and South. It is not difficult to see how a single North-South PTA such as the U.S.–Mexico agreement proposed in 1991 or the one between Japan and Malaysia could trigger a spate of requests from other southern nations.

Liberalization of Parts and Components But not Final Goods

A very common liberalization strategy among developing countries is to reduce tariffs unilaterally on inputs but not, or to a lesser degree, on final goods. This evokes the old measures of the effective rate of protection, whereby the actual protection provided by a nominal tariff of, say,

10 percent on automobiles can be vastly larger than 10 percent if the tariff on imported intermediates is zero. A numerical example will illustrate. Suppose a country can buy autos at US$10,000 and adds a 10 percent tariff, so that the auto sells for US$11,000 on the internal market. Furthermore, suppose the country charges no tariff on the parts needed to assemble an auto and can buy these parts for US$8,000. This implies that the cost of assembly, when it is done most efficiently, is worth US$2,000. But now we see that assembly of autos inside the country will be profitable as long as it costs less than US$3,000. Thus, in some sense, the effective rate of protection on the assembly activity is 50 percent, not 10 percent as the tariff on autos suggests. This is an old story, and countries around the world still keep up the fiction of having an automobile industry by maintaining a high tariff on autos and a low tariff on completely knocked down (CKD) autos—basically, kits that are opened and assembled like IKEA furniture.

Recently, however, the situation has become far more subtle. Many developing countries, especially in East Asia, are industrializing on the basis of parts and components manufacturing rather than final goods manufacturing. In essence, they industrialize by becoming part of the global supply chain. (Actually few of these supply chains are global; apart from some electronics, they are regional, in order to reduce transport cost and delays.)

For a wide range of countries, the import and export of parts and components are much more important than the export of final goods (Fukunari and Ando 2005). For the Philippines, for instance, 60 percent of the country's machinery exports consists of parts, as does 45 percent of its imports in this category. Plainly, the Philippines' industry is in the business of importing parts, adding some value, and then exporting the parts.

In terms of the Puga-Venables analysis, this uneven liberalization of parts and final goods fosters southern industry in that it reduces the cost of inputs without increasing the competition from northern industry in the final good. Of course, this might not work if the southern nation is too small.

The members of the Association of Southeast Asian Nations (ASEAN) are working on a slight variant of this uneven liberalization strategy. They are lowering regionally the within-ASEAN tariffs—the common effective preference tariffs (CEPTs)—on final goods, as well as on parts and components, but preferences only emerge on final goods as they are lowering their MFN applied tariffs on parts and components in line with their preferential cuts. This has made sales of ASEAN-assembled autos very attractive within the ASEAN group.

The point can be seen in table 3.1. Apart from Malaysia and Thailand, which have tried to build up more complete auto industries, the main ASEAN countries have lowered their MFN tariffs on engines to zero. More important, all of them also have lowered their preferential tariffs on engines to zero. Tariffs on autos are still very high (30 to 80 percent) on an MFN basis but are much lower (5 percent) on a preferential basis. Although these tariff cuts are impelled by the logic of supply-chain manufacturing in East Asia (much of this driven by Japanese firms), the cuts have also fostered such trade. From the perspective of the Puga-Venables analysis, this combination of regional preferences is a way of favoring agglomeration of parts and final goods industry at the regional level.

Regional Interindustry Trade

International trade occurs when a product is made in one country and purchased in another. In traditional trade theory, a country's production is thought of as stemming from its advantages, or, to be more precise, comparative advantages. Countries with abundant farmland would produce more cereal than they could consume and would thus be exporters of cereals, and the same logic would apply to the export patterns of countries that are especially well endowed with unskilled labor, high technology, or oilfields.

Table 3.1. ASEAN Tariffs on Engines and Automobiles, Most Favored Nation (MFN) Tariffs and Common Effective Preference Tariffs (CEPTs), 2008
(*percent*)

Item	Malaysia		Indonesia		Philippines		Thailand	
	MFN	CEPT	MFN	CEPT	MFN	CEPT	MFN	CEPT
Small-auto engines	25	0	0	0	0	0	10	0
Medium-size-auto engines	30	0	0	0	0	0	10	0
Automobiles	30	5	55	5	30	5	80	5

Source: ASEAN Secretariat Web site, http://www.aseansec.org/12025.htm.
Note: ASEAN, Association of Southeast Asian Nations. Small-auto and medium-size-auto engines correspond to ASEAN tariff lines 8407.31.00.00 and 8407.32.00.10. Automobiles correspond to 8703.21.29.10.

Much of the world's trade, however, involves two-way trade in similar goods—usually, manufactured goods—and often between countries that have similar comparative advantages. To account for this, Paul Krugman and a number of other theorists in the late 1970s and early 1980s developed the so-called new trade theory. This took a quite different view of the determinants of a country's exports.

The point of departure is firm-level scale economies that explain why the production of each good is spatially concentrated, not just in one country, but even in one factory. If the production of most goods is spatially concentrated but the customers for that good are spread across many countries, goods are made in one country but are bought in another, generating international trade. Moreover, scale economies tell us that no country can efficiently produce all goods, so each country specializes in a subset of the world's goods. Trade in similar products arises very naturally between similar countries. France and Germany, for example, both produce autos, and they both consume them. Since the production of each model of auto is spatially concentrated but the customers are spatially dispersed, the result is two-way trade in autos between countries that have quite similar comparative advantages.

Until recently, the focus of this intraindustry trade was between developed countries, to a large extent because they were the only ones that had significant and competitive manufacturing sectors. Since the mid-1980s, however, the so-called second unbundling phase of globalization has meant a rapid rise of industry in developing countries. A great deal of this new industry does not involve full production of goods; rather, it focuses on parts and components for export. The general trend is discussed in Brulhart (2009).

A good way to introduce the topic of this trade in parts and components is to tell the tale of how it started in East Asia. The phenomenal growth of Japanese incomes and wages in the 1980s and 1990s eroded the country's comparative advantage in manufacturing. Japanese businesses reacted by seeking lower-cost manufacturing sites for labor-intensive stages of production. The obvious solution was to offshore these stages to nearby East Asian economies.

This tendency started the development of what is called "Factory Asia." Instead of Japanese goods being made in Japan and sold in the United States or Europe, a new pattern of "triangle trade" emerged. Firms that were headquartered in Japan would produce certain high-technology parts in Japan, ship them to factories in ASEAN nations for labor-intensive stages of production (including assembly), and then ship the final products to Western markets or back to Japan. This division of East Asia into headquarters economies and factory economies

was strengthened as the latter—Hong Kong SAR, China; the Republic of Korea; Singapore; and Taiwan, China,—experienced their own "hollowing out" and followed the lead of Japanese manufacturing companies by offshoring the most labor-intensive production stages to East Asian countries that had a comparative advantage in such tasks (that is, countries whose low wages more than compensated for their low labor productivity).

Information technology advances and the falling costs of transportation, especially air freight, facilitated and accelerated the development of Factory Asia by making complex production structures easier and cheaper to manage, while at the same time making them more flexible and more reliable. China's opening up was another huge spur, bringing as it did something like a half-billion low-wage, low-productivity workers to the gates of Factory Asia. This accelerated the erosion of the headquarter nations' comparative advantage in labor-intensive production processes while simultaneously increasing the attractiveness of the offshoring solution.

Figure 3.15 shows the number of plants from Japanese electrical machinery and automobile industries that set up in the listed East Asian economies. (Plainly, the number of plants is only a rough indicator of the actual degree of offshoring.) The offshoring process started gradually but picked up speed in the late 1980s. Between 1975 and 1990, the total number rose three and a half times, with almost half of this increase coming between 1985 and 1990. The figure also shows that China was not a major player in the competition for plant locations before 1990. The plants

Figure 3.15. Location of Japanese Auto and Electrical Machinery Plants in East Asia, 1975–2004

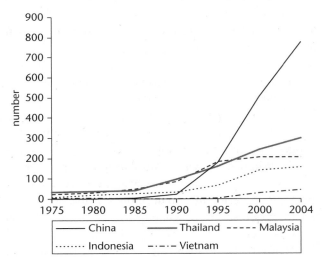

Source: Baldwin 2008.

Table 3.2. Intraindustry Trade as a Share of Internal and External Trade of PTAs
(percent)

	Internal	External
EU-15	46.6	24.8
CEMAC	1.2	0.1
WAEMU	0.9	0.4
EAC	0.3	0.4
SACU	0.3	9.0

Source: Brulhart 2009.
Note: CEMAC, Economic and Monetary Community of Central Africa (Communauté Économique et Monétaire de l'Afrique Centrale); EAC, East African Community; EU-15, European Union before the 2004 enlargement (15 members); SACU, Southern African Customs Union; WAEMU, West African Economic and Monetary Union.

generated new intraindustry trade, almost all of it in machinery and much of it in parts and components.

Intraindustry trade, however, is not universally important in PTAs. The two strongest contrasts are the EU and the African PTAs. As table 3.2 shows, the degree of two-way trade in similar products inside the EU is very high, almost 50 percent, but the share is much lower for the EU's external trade. Much of this intraindustry trade involves parts and components, and such trade tends to be regionalized in order to reduce the costs and difficulties of managing complex manufacturing processes at great distances. Among the African PTAs, two show higher intraindustry trade measures within the regional arrangement, and two exhibit the opposite. In all cases, the figures are quite low, reflecting the marginal role of manufacturing in these countries' exports.

Conclusions

For most of the history of the GATT/WTO, regionalism was all about tariff preferences. The literature has therefore focused primarily on the economics of preferential tariff liberalization. The first key concern—the issue facing nations in the early postwar period in Europe and Latin America—was whether an individual nation would gain from joining a PTA. The answer is unclear. Discriminatory liberalization is a synonym for preferential liberalization; this is both "liberalization"— which removes some price wedges and thus tends to improve economic efficiency— and "discrimination," which introduces new price wedges and thus tends to harm efficiency and welfare. From the 1990s on, concern shifted to the more systemic question of whether regionalism was good or bad for the multilateral trading system but the focus on tariffs remained.

More recently, fundamental changes in international commerce have led to a dramatic reduction in tariff preferences, but no reduction in worries that PTAs are

undermining the WTO. The new perspective, the so-called twenty-first-century regionalism, is really about defining the new international disciplines necessary to underpin twenty-first century international commerce—that is, international production networks and the flows of people, things, and information that they generate (Baldwin 2010a). Here, twenty-first century regionalism is defined as consisting of three parts: (a) the system of deep North-South agreements signed by the United States, the EU, and Japan; (b) the system of bilateral investment treaties and other facilitating agreements such as double-taxation treaties; and (c) the massive unilateral policy reform undertaken by emerging nations (of which unilateral tariff cutting is the most easily measured part).

This chapter has focused on the economics of the traditional view of PTAs: that they are mostly about preferential tariffs. As tariffs are just a form of tax, all of the traditional-view economics can be thought of as applied tax economics. A great part of the deeper disciplines involved in twenty-first-century regionalism, however, turns on regulation economics, and the regionalism literature has not focused much on this type of economics when it comes to PTAs. There is still much to be done.

Annex A. Policy Pitfalls of Classic but Incomplete Diagrammatic Analyses

Until the 1990s, the main points in the economic literature were presented using diagrammatic analysis. Two diagrams were particularly pivotal. The fact that they ignored some of the three elemental effects discussed in this chapter (Smith's certitude, Haberler's spillover, and Viner's ambiguity) distorted the direction of the literature and, with it, academic trade economists' perceptions of PTAs. Since these older, incomplete diagrams occasionally enter today's regionalism debate, it is worth presenting them briefly and highlighting their shortcomings. The first is the Johnson diagram that is still used in most undergraduate textbooks; the second is the Shibata "small PTA" diagram.

The Johnson (1960) Diagram and the Johnson-Cooper-Massell Proposition

Although economists have been well aware of the three effects since Meade (1955), this analysis was not integrated into mainstream trade theory, in part because it was marginal, whereas trade economists were interested in studying the discrete liberalization implied by PTAs. Viner (1950) provided no diagrams. Accordingly, customs union theory, as it was known at the time, was a distinctly wordy subject until Johnson (1960b) introduced his famous diagram that illustrated Viner's ambiguity in a manner that was immediately transparent to all economists (figure 3A.1). For policy analysis, Johnson's diagram is fatally flawed as it assumes that FTAs and the like only have welfare effects on the import side—export effects are assumed away.

In the diagram, Home imports can come from partner country A or B. Home's demand is an infinitely small share of world demand, so it faces perfectly elastic export supply curves from both sources (labeled XS_A and XS_B). We start with Home's imposing an MFN specific tariff of T, so that all imports come from the low-cost supplier, country A. The domestic price is $P^A + T$, and the border price is P^A.

Home can form a customs union with country A or B, so we consider both. The customs union with B would remove the tariff only on imports from B (the high-cost supplier), leading to supply switching. Home switches from importing everything from A to importing everything from B. Home's domestic price falls from $P^A + T$ to P^B. Assuming a utilitarian metric, the net welfare effects are $(B + D)$ minus E, which may be negative or positive depending on elasticities and the height of the initial tariff; this is Viner's ambiguity.[9]

The customs union with country B was termed "purely trade diverting," yet if the initial tariff was high and the $P^B - P^A$ border-price gap was small, it can be welfare improving for Home. This result—a welfare-improving but purely trade-diverting customs union—seemed to contradict Viner's reasoning, and it produced the first of what was to be a long series of ivory-tower debates over terminology; this one pitted Meade (1955) against Johnson (1960b) and Corden (1965).

If Home chooses to form a customs union with A, the ambiguity disappears. Such a customs union is unambiguously welfare improving, since its positive effects are identical to MFN free trade. (Both before and after, all imports would come from A.) Home's domestic price falls from $P^A + T$ to P^A, and the net welfare gain is $B + G + D + H$, in the right-hand panel.[10]

Readers will immediately note that Smith's certitude and Haberler's spillover are missing. Third nations are entirely unaffected by the trade policy of an infinitely small nation such as Home. In Johnson's diagram, the partner nations care no more about Home's trade policy than a perfectly competitive firm does about gaining or losing one atomistic buyer. This omission was an attractive feature when the pivotal question was whether a single nation would gain from joining a customs union, but it renders the diagram useless for consideration of systemic issues. The diagram *assumes* that Home's decision to form a PTA has no systemic effects at all. Also missing from the diagram is an analysis of the preferential access that Home's exports win in its partner's market.

For two decades, the Johnson diagram dominated economic analyses of PTAs to such an extent that Smith's certitude and Haberler's spillover came to be largely forgotten by academic trade economists. This went so far that many mainstream trade theorists came to view PTAs as economically irrational—a view encapsulated in the Johnson-Cooper-Massell proposition stating that a small nation should always prefer unilateral MFN liberalization to any PTA (Cooper and Massell 1965). The point is easily illustrated in figure 3A.1: cutting T to zero on imports from A and B will always yield net welfare gains that are at least as high as those from any customs union.

From the modern perspective, Johnson's analysis seems impossibly simplistic, and the disconnect between academic and real-world thinking is truly astounding. For instance, when the United Kingdom submitted its first

Figure 3A.1. Johnson's Diagram, Small Home and Partner Countries

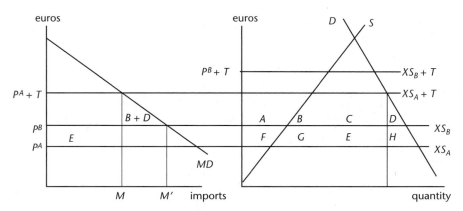

Source: For right-hand panel, Johnson (1960b); for left-hand panel, author's elaboration.
Note: The right-hand panel is the standard open-economy supply-and-demand diagram in price-quantity space for an infinitely small nation (Home). The left-hand panel transcribes the analysis into a more compact diagram in price-import space.

application for EU membership in 1961, better market access for U.K. exporters was the key concern, but academic economists were working with the Johnson diagram that assumed this away. Moreover, the main preferential trade agreement in existence at the time, the European Economic Community (EEC), accounted for a substantial fraction of world imports, and the key nations—France, Germany, and the United Kingdom—were far from atomistic. As Pomfret (1997) points out, a number of frameworks were developed at the time that would have allowed the necessary extension, including Johnson (1957, 1958), Humphrey and Ferguson (1960), and Blackhurst (1972), but the Johnson diagram's hold on the literature was so firm that the early efforts were obliged to stick with his small-country fiction.[11]

The "Small PTA" Diagram

An important analytical extension of the Johnson diagram came with the "small PTA" analysis (Shibata 1967). It allowed for Smith's certitude, although it still assumed away Haberler's spillover. The diagram continues to be used even today (e.g., Grossman and Helpman 1995), so it is worth presenting briefly.

The small PTA diagram shows somewhat different assumptions concerning the pattern of comparative advantage and the size of the two partners. The various combinations of assumptions yield a range of results that have been covered by three decades of literature. (See Panagariya 1999 for a comprehensive survey of literature using the small PTA diagram in recent decades.) Here we study a fairly standard case and illustrate the diagram's properties by demonstrating two classic results in the regionalism literature (figure 3A.2).

The diagram presumes that the two PTA partners, Home and Partner, import the same good from the RoW. Home and Partner are "small" with respect to RoW and so face a perfectly elastic RoW export supply curve, XS_{RoW}. This sets the initial border price to P_R in both nations. Home has a higher MFN tariff than Partner to start with (T_H, as opposed to T_P), so the pre-PTA price is higher in Home.

When Home and Partner form their PTA, Partner-based firms initially see a higher price in Home and so begin exporting to Home. In equilibrium, all post-PTA Home imports, M'_H, are supplied by Partner firms. Partner's internal price remains at $P_R + T_P$, so its consumption and production are unchanged, which means that the new exports to Home are replaced, one for one, by new Partner imports from RoW. In the case illustrated in figure 3A.2, Partner is large enough relative to Home to ensure that Home's entire demand can be satisfied by Partner's producers at $P_R + T_P$. In terms of welfare, the PTA results in a positive trade volume effect for Home but a negative border price effect. (Home pays $P_R + T_P$ for its imports instead of P_R.) Partner expands its imports across the tariff wedge, and this results in a positive trade volume effect equal to T_R times the expanded imports (M'_H).

Although it seems an odd objective from today's perspective, where rules of origin (ROOs) are a major barrier to trade, Shibata's goal was to illustrate the irrelevance of rules of origin. His point was that ROOs only prevent blatant trade deflection. Because goods from Partner and RoW are fungible, the equilibrium is the same with and without rules of origin, as long as Partner's supply is sufficient. If Partner's supply were not large enough to supply all of Home's imports at $P_R + T_P$, the PTA with ROOs would have somewhat higher prices than one without.

Figure 3A.2. The Small PTA Diagram: A Simple Case

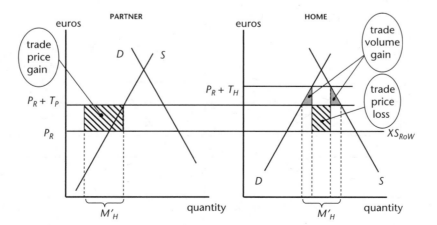

Source: Author's modification of a diagram in Pomfret (1997).

The use of this exercise in the big-think regionalism literature comes in the form of "imported liberalization/protection" (Grossman and Helpman 1995).

Another application that found popularity in the academic literature but seems odd today is the proposition that PTAs will always break down. Using a diagram similar to figure 3A.2, Vousden (1990, 234) argues that Home would be tempted to lower its MFN tariff to just under that of Partner in order to recapture the tariff revenue and that Partner would have an incentive to reply. The resulting race-to-the-bottom tariff cutting was viewed as making PTAs "unsustainable." Vousden (1990) did not attract much attention until Richardson (1995) extended and popularized his proposition. These two results (irrelevance of rules of origin and unsustainability of PTAs) are classic examples of how academic thinking on regionalism often followed literature-driven paths that had little relevance to real-world policy concerns.

Annex B. A Brief Review of Imperfect Competition Models

We start with the simplest problem: the decision faced by a firm that has a monopoly. The monopoly case is easy because it avoids strategic interactions. When a firm is the only seller of a product, it can choose how much to sell and what price to charge without considering the reaction of other suppliers. The only restraint a monopolist faces is the demand curve. A downward-sloping demand curve is a constraint because it forces the monopolist to confront a trade-off between price and sales; higher prices mean lower sales. When considering the impact of regional integration on imperfectly competitive firms, we need to determine how various policy changes will alter prices and sales. The first step in this direction is to see what determines a monopolist's price and sales in a closed economy. The natural question then is, what is the profit-maximizing level of sales for the monopolist?

An excellent way to proceed is to make a guess at the optimal level—say, Q' in the left-hand panel of figure 3B.1. Almost surely, this initial guess will be wrong, but what we want to know is whether it is too low or too high. To this end, we calculate the profit earned when Q' units are sold at the highest obtainable price, P'. The answer is $A + B$, since the total value of sales is price times quantity (area $A + B + C$) minus cost (area C).

Would profits rise or fall if the firm sold an extra unit? Of course, to sell the extra unit, the firm will have to let its price fall a bit, say, to P''. The change in profit equals the change in revenue minus the change in cost. Consider first the change in revenue. This has two parts. Selling the extra

unit brings in extra revenue (represented by areas $D + E$), but it also depresses the price received for all units sold initially, lowering revenue by an amount equal to area A. The net change in revenue, termed "marginal revenue," is given by areas $D + E$ minus area A. The change in cost, termed "marginal cost," is area E. Plainly, profit only increases if the extra revenue $D - A$ exceeds the extra cost E. As it is drawn, $D - A + E$ appears to be negative, so marginal revenue is less than marginal cost at $Q' + 1$. This means that raising output from Q' would lower profits, and so the initial guess of Q' turned out to be too high.

To find the profit-maximizing level using this trial-and-error method, we would consider a lower guess—say, Q' minus four units—and repeat the procedure applied above. At the profit-maximizing level, marginal revenue just equals marginal cost. This level must be optimal, since any increase or decrease in sales will lower profit. Increasing sales beyond this point will increase cost more than revenue, while decreasing sales would lower revenue more than cost. Both would reduce profit.

The right-hand panel of figure 3B.1 presents an easier way of finding the point at which marginal revenue equals marginal cost. The diagram includes a new curve, the marginal revenue curve, which shows how marginal revenue declines as the level of sales rises. (It declines because area A from the left-hand panel becomes very small for low levels of sales.) At the sales level marked Q^*, marginal revenue just equals marginal cost. The firm charges the most it can, P^*, at this level of sales. These are the profit-maximizing levels of sales and price.

Several aspects of imperfect competition come through even in the monopoly case. First, in setting up the problem, we had to make assumptions about the firm's beliefs concerning the behavior of other economic agents. In this case, the monopolist is assumed to believe that consumers are price takers and that the trade-off between prices and sales depends only on the demand curve rather than, for example, on the reaction of firms in other markets. Second, the critical difference between perfect and imperfect competition comes out clearly. As part of the definition, perfectly competitive firms are assumed to take the price of their output as given. (A classic example is a wheat farmer who cannot set his own price but just sells at the current market price.) This means that such firms are assumed to be ignorant of the fact that selling more will depress the market price. In terms of the diagram, perfectly competitive firms ignore area A, so they maximize profits by selling an amount at which price equals marginal cost. Of course, any increase in sales would have some negative impact on price, so it is best to think of perfect competition as a simplifying assumption that is close to true when all firms have

Figure 3B.1. Monopoly Profit Maximization

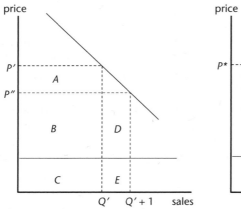
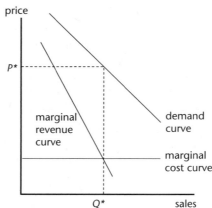

Source: Author's elaboration.

market shares which are close to zero. By stepping away from this simplification, imperfect competition allows firms to explicitly consider the price-depressing effect— area *A*—when deciding how much to sell.

The monopoly case is instructive but not very realistic; most firms face some competition. Taking account of this reality, however, brings us up against the strategic considerations discussed above. The convention we adopt to sort out this interaction is the so-called Cournot-Nash equilibrium that won John Nash a Nobel prize. That is, we assume that each firm acts as though the other firms' outputs were fixed. The equilibrium we are interested in is that in which each firm's expectations of the other firms' outputs turn out to be correct; that is, no one is fooled. This no-one-fooled notion proves to be somewhat difficult to comprehend in the abstract, but, as we shall see below, it is easy in specific applications.

Residual Demand Curve Shortcut

Since firms take as given the sales of other firms, the only constraint facing a typical firm is the demand curve shifted to the left by the amount of sales of all other firms. In other words, each firm believes it is a monopolist on the shifted demand curve. (We called the shifted demand curve the residual demand curve.) This realization is handy because it means that we can directly apply the solution technique from the monopolist's problem; the only change is that we calculate the marginal revenue curve on the basis of the residual demand curve instead of the demand curve.

This trick is shown in figure 3B.2 for a competition between two firms producing the same good—a situation

that economists call duopoly. For simplicity, we assume that the firms have the same marginal cost curves. Taking firm 2's sales as given at Q_2, firm 1 has a monopoly on the residual demand curve labeled RD_1. Firm 1's optimal output in this case is x_1', since at point A_1 the residual marginal revenue curve, RMR_1, crosses the marginal cost curve, MC. The right-hand panel shows the same sort of analysis for firm 2. Taking firm 1's output as fixed at Q_1, firm 2's optimal output is x_2'.

Note that the situation in the figure is not an equilibrium. To highlight the importance of the difference between expected and actual outcomes, the diagram shows the solutions of the two firms when expectations about the other firm's output do not match the reality. The consistent-expectations outcome (the Nash equilibrium) is shown in the next figure, but we first consider why figure 3B.2 is not an equilibrium.

As drawn, this is not a Cournot-Nash equilibrium because the firms' actual output levels do not match expectations: firm 1 produces x_1', which is greater than what firm 2 expected (that is, Q_1), and similarly, firm 2 produces x_2', which is greater than what firm 1 expected (Q_2). We can also see the problem by observing that the implied prices are not equal. If these quantities were actually produced by the firms, then firms would not be able to charge the prices they expected to charge. In other words, this is not an equilibrium because the outcome is not consistent with expectations.

Finding the Expectations-Consistent Equilibrium

The easiest way to find the expectation-consistent set of outputs is to exploit the assumed symmetry of firms. In

Figure 3B.2. Duopolist as Monopolist on Residual Demand: Example of a Nonequilibrium

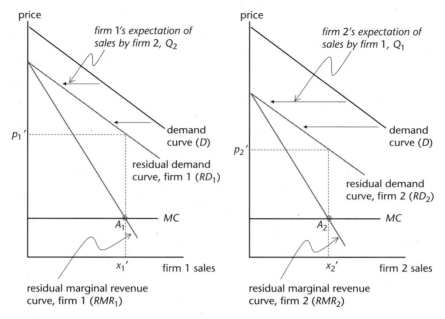

Source: Author's elaboration.

Figure 3B.3. Duopoly and Oligopoly: Expectation-Consistent Outputs

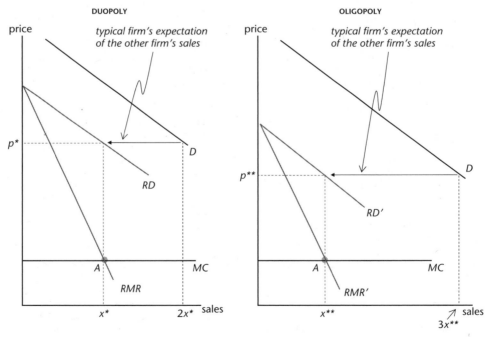

Source: Author's elaboration.

the symmetric equilibrium, each firm will sell the same amount. With this fact in mind, a bit of thought reveals that the residual demand curve facing each firm must be half of the overall demand curve. This situation is shown in the left-hand panel of figure 3B.3 for a duopoly. Some facts

to note are that (a) the optimal output for a typical firm is x^*, given by the intersection of RMR and MC; (b) total sales to the market are $2x^*$, and at this level of sales the overall market price (given by the demand curve D) is consistent with the price each firm expects to receive, given the residual demand curve, *RD;* and (c) the outputs of the identical firms are equal in equilibrium.

Although allowing for two firms is more realistic than allowing for only one firm, studying the impact of integration on mergers and acquisitions requires us to allow for an arbitrary number of firms. In economists' jargon, such a situation is called an oligopoly. As it turns out, this situation is straightforward in dealing with the case in which firms are symmetric. As more firms compete in the market (consider three instead of two), the residual demand curve facing each shifts inward, so that the residual marginal revenue curve also shifts inward. The implications of this shift for prices are clear. The new $RMR = MC$ point occurs at a lower level of per-firm output, implying a lower price. In equilibrium (i.e., where outcomes match expectations), each of the three firms produces an identical amount and charges an identical price. What happens is that as the number of firms continues to rise, each increase in the number of competitors shifts the *RD* facing each firm. This will inevitably lead to lower prices and lower output per firm.

Of course, this analysis simply formalizes what most readers would expect. If one adds more competitors to a market, prices will fall, along with the market share of each firm. As is so often the case, the brilliant concepts are simple.

Notes

1. The basic problem was that the profession found the simple trade creation–trade diversion paradigm to be effective in communicating the crucial welfare-ambiguity result, but the words did not fully capture all the basic economic effects. Arvind Panagariya suggests that the terms persist because they are "highly effective tools of focusing policy makers' attention on the ambiguous welfare effects of [regional trade associations]" (Panagariya 1999).

2. Of course, when considering the full economic impact, one must consider scale economies, procompetitive effects, variety effects, location effects, and growth effects (Baldwin and Venables 1995). Most of these, however, are not critical in the "big-think" regionalism literature.

3. Readers may mentally insert a fourth untaxed good that enters the utility function linearly, to formally eliminate Meade's tertiary effects.

4. The PTA diagram can be thought of as a modification of the Blackhurst (1972) diagram.

5. Given the symmetry, an FTA is automatically a customs union.

6. Area C_2 might be called the "trade diversion" effect, and $D_2 + A$ might be call the "trade creation" effect, but, as usual, the trade creation–trade diversion dichotomy is incomplete. Here, it omits the third-nation terms-of-trade gain, *B*.

7. For the results, see World Bank, Trade, http://www.worldbank.org/trade/standards.

8. In certain industries, the impact of TBTs is radically more complex. In industries with network externalities, such as mobile telephones, standards can be manipulated to throw up barriers against nonlocal firms. In industries with patent races (e.g., pharmaceuticals) a regulation that merely delays the introduction of foreign goods can radically alter the market outcome in favor of home firms. In industries with learning curves, product standards that apply to only a fraction of the market—government or military purchases, for example—can have large effects on

the market equilibrium. Modeling TBTs in such "sexy" industries will certainly be the subject of much future work, but in this chapter we focus on mundane industries in which TBTs act by raising the costs of foreign firms more than the costs of local firms.

9. The left-hand panel of figure 3A.1 translates the effects into Meade's two-part framework: $B + D$ is the trade volume effect (related to the change in the volume of imports), and E is the trade price effect (related to the change in the border price).

10. This contrast is the source of the rule of thumb that a PTA with your main trading partners is more likely to be welfare improving, since you are giving preferences to the partners that have demonstrated themselves to be the low-cost suppliers by winning the largest market share in an even competition with other suppliers.

11. The early 1980s saw a number of widely read studies that sought to reverse the Johnson-Cooper-Massell (JCM) proposition while retaining the small-country framework. These efforts (e.g., Wonnacott and Wonnacott 1981; Berglas 1983) strike the modern reader as awkward because of the small-nation assumption and the intricate diagrammatic analysis.

Bibliography

Balassa, Bela. 1967. "Trade Creation and Trade Diversion in the European Common Market." *Economic Journal* 77: 1–21.

Baldwin, Richard. 1989. "The Growth Effects of 1992." *Economic Policy* 9: 247–82.

———. 2008. "Managing the Noodle Bowl: The Fragility of East Asian Regionalism." *Singapore Economic Review* 53 (3): 449–78.

———. 2010a. "21st Century Regionalism: Filling the Gap between 21st Century Trade and 20th Century Trade Governance." http://eiitf.iift.ac.in/Richard%20Baldwin%20-%2021st%20Century%20Regionalism.pdf.

———. 2010b. "Unilateral Tariff Liberalisation." NBER Working Paper 16600, National Bureau of Economic Research, Cambridge, MA.

Baldwin, Richard, Simon Evenett, and Patrick Low. 2009. "Beyond Tariffs: Multilateralizing Non-Tariff RTA Commitments." In *Multilateralizing Regionalism: Challenges for the Global Trading System*, ed. Richard Baldwin and Patrick Low. Geneva: World Trade Organization. http://us-cdn.creamermedia.co.za/assets/articles/attachments/19838_multila_region_e.pdf.

Baldwin, Richard, and Anthony Venables. 1995. "Regional Economic Integration." In *Handbook of International Economics*, vol. 3, ed. Gene Grossman and Kenneth Rogoff, 1597–1644. Amsterdam: North Holland.

Baldwin, Richard, and Charles Wyplosz. 2009. *The Economics of European Integration.* 3rd ed. New York: McGraw-Hill.

Berglas, Eitan. 1983. "The Case for Unilateral Tariff Reductions: Foreign Tariffs Rediscovered." *American Economic Review* 73 (5): 1141–42.

Bhagwati, Jagdish. 1971. *The World Trading System at Risk.* Princeton, N.J.: Princeton University Press.

Blackhurst, Richard. 1972. "General versus Preferential Tariff Reduction for LDC Exports: An Analysis of the Welfare Effects." *Southern Economic Journal* 38: 350–62.

Brulhart, Marius. 2009. "An Account of Global Intra-Industry Trade, 1962–2006." *World Economy* 32 (3): 401–59.

Carpenter, Theresa, and Andrea Lendle. 2010. "How Preferential Is World Trade?" CTEI Working Paper.

Cooper, C. A., and B. F. Massell. 1965. "A New Look at Customs Union Theory." *Economic Journal* 75: 742–47.

Corden, W. Max. 1965. "Recent Developments in the Theory of International Trade." Special Papers in International Economics 7, International Finance Section, Princeton University, Princeton, N.J.

Dixit, Avinash, and Victor Norman. 1980. *Theory of International Trade.* Cambridge, U.K.: Cambridge University Press.

Fukunari, Kimura, and Mitsuyo Ando. 2005. "Two-Dimensional Fragmentation in East Asia: Conceptual Framework and Empirics." *International Review of Economics and Finance* 14 (3): 317–48.

Grossman, Gene M., and Elhanan Helpman. 1995. "The Politics of Free-Trade Agreements." *American Economic Review* 85: 667–90.

Haberler, Gottfried. 1936. *The Theory of International Trade with Its Applications to Commercial Policy.* New York: Macmillan.

Humphrey, D. C., and C. E. Ferguson. 1960. "The Domestic and World Benefits of a Customs Union." *Economia Internazionale* 13: 197–213.

Johnson, Harry G. 1953. "Optimum Tariffs and Retaliation." *Review of Economic Studies* 21 (2): 142–53.

———. 1957. "Discriminatory Tariff Reduction: A Marshallian Analysis." *Indian Journal of Economics* 5: 39–47.

———. 1958. "Marshallian Analysis of Discriminatory Tariff Reduction: An Extension." *Indian Journal of Economics* 6: 177–82.

———. 1960a. "The Cost of Protection and the Scientific Tariff." *Journal of Political Economy* 68: 327–45.

———. 1960b. "The Economic Theory of Customs Unions." *Pakistan Economic Review* 10: 14–30.

———. 1965. "An Economic Theory of Protectionism, Tariff Bargaining and the Formation of Customs Unions." *Journal of Political Economy* 73: 256–83.

Kemp, Murray C., and Henry Y. Wan, Jr. 1976. "An Elementary Proposition Concerning the Formation of Customs Unions." *Journal of International Economics* 6 (1): 95–97.

Meade, James E. 1955. *The Theory of Customs Unions.* Amsterdam. North-Holland.

Panagariya, Arvind. 1996. "APEC and the United States." CIES Discussion Paper 96/08, Center for International Economic Studies (CIES), University of Adelaide, Adelaide, Australia.

———. 1999. "Preferential Trade Liberalization: The Traditional Theory and New Developments." *Journal of Economic Literature* 39 (2): 287–331.

Panagariya, Arvind, and Ronald Findlay. 1994. "A Political-Economy Analysis of Free Trade Areas and Customs Unions." Policy Research Working Paper 1261, World Bank, Washington, DC.

Pomfret, Richard. 1997. *The Economics of Regional Trading Arrangements.* Oxford, U.K.: Oxford University Press.

Puga, Diego, and Anthony Venables. 1998. "Trading Arrangements and Industrial Development." *World Bank Economic Review* 12 (2, May): 221–49.

Richardson, Martin. 1995. "Tariff Revenue Competition in a Free Trade Area." *European Economic Review* 39: 1429–37.

Shibata, Hirofumi. 1967. "The Theory of Economic Unions: A Comparative Analysis of Customs Unions, Free Trade Areas and Tax Unions." In *Fiscal Harmonization in Common Markets,* ed. Call S. Shoup, vol.1, 145–264. New York: Columbia University Press.

Smith, Adam. 1776. *The Wealth of Nations.* Repr., Chicago, IL: University of Chicago Press, 1977.

Taussig, Frank. 1892. "Reciprocity." *Quarterly Journal of Economics* 7: 26–39.

Torrens, Robert. 1844. *The Budget: On Commercial and Colonial Policy.* London: Smith, Elder.

Viner, Jacob. 1950. *The Customs Union Issue.* New York: Carnegie Endowment for International Peace.

Vousden, Neil. 1990. *The Economics of Trade Protection.* Cambridge, U.K.: Cambridge University Press.

Wonnacott, Paul, and Ronald J. Wonnacott. 1981. "Is Unilateral Tariff Reduction Preferable to a Customs Union? The Curious Case of the Missing Foreign Tariffs." *American Economic Review* 71: 704–14.

4

NORTH-SOUTH PREFERENTIAL TRADE AGREEMENTS

Bernard Hoekman

This chapter argues that if preferential trade agreements (PTAs) are to be development-friendly, they must focus on complementing liberalization in trade goods with behind-the-border regulatory reforms that are supported through development assistance instruments and that engage the private sector. Such an extension of the PTA agenda to regulatory issues can be beneficial to developing countries. Yet deep and comprehensive PTAs between developed and developing countries bring new risks. The proposed norms may limit policy freedom in inappropriate ways or may result in the allocation of resources to areas that offer few immediate benefits or that are complex and costly to implement. A redesign of the approach to PTAs—to liberalize and expand market access, to build in policy flexibility and accountability, and to broaden technical assistance—is needed.

A basic premise is that a shift in objective from market access or market integration to development means that the modus operandi of negotiating and implementing trade agreements will have to change. One reason is that many of the poorest countries may not benefit much from a traditional trade agreement; they already have good access to major markets through nonreciprocal preference schemes, and they confront potential welfare losses if they pursue preferential liberalization in favor of PTA partners only. Another reason is that the priority needs in many poor developing countries are not related to trade policy but revolve around bolstering trade capacity, improving the investment climate, and maintaining a competitive real exchange rate. PTAs can help address some of these priorities, but only if they are appropriately designed and effectively implemented.

The next section provides a brief context for the trade-related reform agenda that confronts developing countries. Some rationales for and challenges facing North-South PTAs are then discussed from a development perspective, and the evolving status quo is described. Suggestions for further steps are presented, proceeding from the assumption that the focus of North-South trade agreements is to promote development. Given that preferential market access liberalization is a second-best exercise from a global welfare perspective, proposals are developed to encourage the pursuit of nondiscriminatory liberalization and a much more targeted focus on the key constraints that prevent developing countries from benefiting more from trade opportunities. Current approaches toward PTAs with developing countries that are being pursued by the European Union (EU) are assessed in light of these proposals. The intention is not to be comprehensive or to single out the EU; a similar analysis could be applied to recent U.S. PTAs. It is, however, true that the EU has been at the forefront in seeking to use PTAs as instruments for promoting development. Finally, the conclusions from the discussion are summarized.

Stylized Facts and Key Policy Challenges

Until the global economic crisis struck in 2008, the world had witnessed a rapid expansion in developing-country trade. The share of the developing economies in world trade increased from 20 percent in 2000 to 30 percent in 2008 (World Bank 2010b), and all regions experienced greater integration with the rest of the world. There are, however, important differences among developing countries with respect to both the growth in trade and its pattern and structure. The poorest countries generally did less well than middle-income economies in the 1990s, partly because of the dependence of their foreign exchange earnings on agricultural commodities. This helps explain why Sub-Saharan Africa's share of nonoil world trade remains far below the level that prevailed in the 1970s, despite relatively good growth and trade performance during most of the first decade of the twenty-first century.

Research suggests that a lack of diversification is associated with lower growth and greater output volatility. Africa is the least diversified region in the world today. Agricultural trade remains highly important for Sub-Saharan African countries, accounting for 25 percent or more of total exports. One consequence is that countries are subject to greater commodity price (terms-of-trade) volatility than are more diversified economies, and the effect of this volatility is more persistent (World Bank 2010a). Imbs and Wacziarg (2003) note that countries at early stages of development experience a positive relationship between export (output) diversification and growth, suggesting that from a development perspective, the policy focus should be on support for greater diversification (Newfarmer, Shaw, and Walkenhorst 2009; Haddad, Lim, and Saborowski 2010).

Existing programs that center on promoting trade of developing countries—especially nonreciprocal preferential access to Organisation for Economic Co-operation and Development (OECD) markets—have not been very effective.[1] Major reasons for this inefficiency include supply-side weaknesses, civil conflicts, macroeconomic policies that resulted in overvalued currencies, governance problems, corruption, and institutional weaknesses that inhibit local entrepreneurs from taking advantage of market opportunities. The question, then, is to identify what PTAs could do to help achieve progress on such issues.

Reform Priorities

Because average tariff barriers in developing countries remain higher than in industrial ones, much of the potential welfare gain from trade reforms will arise from their own liberalization. The reasons for imposing trade barriers vary; they include infant-industry protection (import-substitution industrialization), balance of payments considerations (concerns that liberalization will increase imports more than exports), and fiscal revenue objectives. (Tariffs are easy to collect and can be a significant source of government income.) All these reasons are second-best in most circumstances, in that a lower-cost domestic policy instrument can, in principle, be identified to satisfy the

objective at lower social cost, or complementary policies can be identified to address the by-product costs of openness.

The persistence of trade policies can be explained by political-economy reasons. Even though the aggregate income and wealth of a nation may be expected to grow when trade distortions are reduced, not everyone will gain. Owners of previously protected inefficient firms will lose, as may their workers, especially if there are doubts regarding the creation of new employment opportunities. Social insurance and adjustment assistance mechanisms may not exist or may be weak. These realities underline the importance of complementary reforms to increase the likelihood of realizing the benefits from trade reforms.

The list of beneficial concomitant reforms can be long and rather formidable. This, however, does not necessarily imply that there are difficult trade-offs to be made; most of the policies are essentially additive to trade liberalization in the sense that they do not give rise to trade-offs (Winters 2004).[2] Social costs may be lower if adjustment can be spread over a period of time, as long there is confidence that reform will actually occur. Without credible commitment to a clearly defined and commonly known final goal, investments and adjustments may look undesirable, and efforts may be diverted to lobbying. Trade agreements can play an important role in this connection by laying out a timetable for gradual liberalization that is credible because it is enforceable by trading partners.

Failure to maintain a realistic real exchange rate has been one of the main causes of unsuccessful trade liberalizations in developing countries (World Bank 2001). Another cause is failure to address the fiscal consequences of tariff revenue losses. These losses are far from inevitable, especially if nontariff barriers are converted into tariffs, exemptions are reduced, and tariff collections are improved. But they can pose a problem for poorer countries in which trade taxes account for large proportions of total revenue. Developing alternative sources of revenue may take time. Experience suggests, however, that moving toward a more uniform tariff structure and a concomitant elimination of exemptions may increase revenue collection, providing the space to develop alternative tax bases before undertaking more far-reaching liberalization.

A major area in which administrative constraints bind is institutional reforms. Given the importance of building up the legitimacy and ownership of these reforms among the population, not only significant "technical" setup time but also a good deal of "political" time is required. Getting institutions right the first time is very difficult, if not impossible, and continuing monitoring and adjustment are needed. There are often advantages to proceeding on a broad front in order to maintain some semblance of fairness, and extensive institutional reforms are likely to require time and considerable administrative skill to carry out. These observations apply, in particular, to regulatory policies and the agencies responsible for implementing them, because regulation can give rise to significant operating costs and entry barriers for firms in a given market once tariffs have been lowered. Tariff reforms can be executed at the stroke of a pen; regulatory reforms are much more complex.

Designing Successful Reforms

Governments have to build up support for their policies. Powerful interests will need to be assuaged—unless reforms are implemented in the context of major economic crises. Compensating these interests through the careful design of complementary policies is not just a matter of sordid logrolling.[3] Although any single efficiency-enhancing reform will hurt someone, if enough of them are packaged together, negative effects will be netted out, and many more people and interests will gain, on balance. This is one of the main reasons for proceeding on a broad front. It is of great importance to ensure that potential beneficiaries from trade-related reforms have the capacity to actually exploit new trade opportunities. This requires attention to the business environment and transaction costs, measures to enhance the productivity of firms and farms, improvement of connectivity to markets, steps to ensure access to finance, and the like. Specific areas for attention may include the following:

- *Infrastructure support.* Farmers need to be able to reach major market centers at reasonable cost, firms need access to a reliable and efficient power supply, and so on. In poor countries, transport (logistics) and transaction costs are often a multiple of any tariffs exporters confront. This is one explanation for the more limited participation of poor countries in the process of international specialization that was noted previously.
- *Credit markets.* Access to finance is a critical input, both for new start-ups and for the expansion of existing plants. For example, achieving minimum consignment size might entail hiring draft power or seasonal labor, but this is not possible without credit. Credit constraints are a major reason for limited adjustment to trade reforms.
- *Labor markets and mobility.* The primary vehicle for spreading widely the benefits of increased labor demand is labor mobility. If labor markets are segmented or distorted, benefits will be reduced.
- *Establishment of new businesses.* Cumbersome regulations for establishing new firms, constraints on access inputs (such as utilities), and restrictions on physical expansion or labor recruitment and separation can curtail the willingness of entrepreneurs to start or expand operations.

All these themes are highlighted in the research that focuses on the magnitude and determinants of adjustment costs and the factors that affect the size and distribution of the gains from trade reforms (Porto and Hoekman 2010). Thus, the benefits of trade liberalization depend, in part, on support from other policies and institutions. Openness can help induce improvements in these dimensions by making them more "visible" and by creating incentives to fix the problems, but additional investments and reforms will be required to address many of the constraints. For landlocked countries and poor, remote economies, reducing trade costs is often of critical importance. As discussed below, development assistance and mechanisms for monitoring impacts can help ensure that reforms are effective and can anchor expectations (i.e., increase credibility). Trade agreements can provide focal points, but only if they address national priorities—and are seen to do so—and are implemented.

Trade Liberalization Strategies: What Role Is for Preferential Agreements?

For governments that have decided to pursue opening of the economy, a practical question is how to do so. Starting in the 1960s, a number of economies were highly successful in increasing incomes and reducing poverty. Notable examples include Chile; Hong Kong SAR, China; the Republic of Korea; Singapore; and Taiwan, China. More recently, China, Malaysia, Mauritius, and Turkey, among others, have joined the list. All of them dramatically increased their ratio of trade to gross domestic product (GDP), but they pursued considerably different models of trade policy reform and economic integration. The success stories may be grouped into four broad categories:

- *Economywide trade liberalization.* Some economies have pursued very liberal, most favored nation (MFN) trade regimes, avoiding nontariff barriers and adopting either free trade (as did Singapore and Hong Kong SAR, China) or low, nonnegotiable, uniform tariffs (e.g., Chile and Estonia, before the latter's accession to the EU). Since the creation of the World Trade Organization (WTO) in

1995, a number of countries have pursued MFN liberalization in the context of accession to that body, using the WTO to anchor and precommit to reform; this was the case for China and Vietnam.

- *Protection with offsetting policies for exporters.* Other economies reduced the incentives created by protection to produce for the domestic market, employing elaborate systems that offset the bias against exports, including complex duty-drawback systems. Japan (in the early stages); Korea; and Taiwan, China, are examples.
- *Protection with export-processing zones.* Along with protection, exporters located in specific zones are offered tariff-free access to intermediate inputs, with better infrastructure and fewer regulatory requirements. The limited geographic scope of the zones makes them easier to manage, for countries with weak governance, than the "Asian" economywide model. Few countries have succeeded in stimulating exports substantially through this model. An exception is Mauritius, where the zones generated about two-thirds of gross exports and employed one-sixth of the workforce. Zones have also played a significant role in China.
- *PTAs.* An increasing number of countries are joining PTAs to provide a focal point or blueprint for reforms, a mechanism for increasing market size and enhancing the contestability of markets, and a means of overcoming political-economy resistance to reforms. Examples are accession to the EU by many Central and Eastern European countries, Turkey's entrance into a customs union with the EU, and Mexico's membership in the North American Free Trade Association (NAFTA). In all these instances, PTA membership complemented WTO accession or membership.

The first three approaches are unilateral. Trade liberalization by other countries is clearly desirable, however; trade negotiations are the time-honored mechanism for seeking such liberalization. In South-South agreements, the focus is increasingly on expanding the size of the market by not only abolishing trade barriers but also easing internal constraints on intraregional trade and investment through improvement of infrastructure trade facilitation and transit and corridor management. Given the large asymmetries in economic power (as indicated by market size), the challenge for small and poor countries in North-South agreements is to ensure that any negotiated outcome is in their interest. Such countries have very little scope to use their trade policies as an instrument for inducing other countries to open up their markets. There are two implications. First, unilateral reforms cost developing countries little in mercantilist terms—large (potential) PTA partner

countries simply will not be that interested because the developing countries' markets are too small. Second, and a related factor in PTA negotiations, quid pro quo "payments" are likely to be requested in nontrade areas such as regulatory regimes, investment policy, and so on (Schiff and Winters 2003; Limão 2007). That raises the issue of whether, in the negotiating process, governments lose access to potentially useful instruments for promoting development. (See, for example, Fink, ch. 18 in this volume.)

The Primacy of National Circumstances and Priorities

A challenge for developing-country governments is not only to generate better access to partner markets but also to use the PTA as a vehicle for promoting competition, reducing policy uncertainty, and improving the investment climate and business environment. Ensuring that deep integration will benefit developing-country PTA members requires that the specifics of regulation and cooperation reflect national circumstances. Regulatory standards and institutions need to be tailored to national circumstances to be effective and attain the desired objective. An increasing body of evidence has shown that a "one-size-fits-all" approach—including international best-practice norms—may not be appropriate. For example, Barth, Caprio, and Levine (2006), in a comprehensive cross-country assessment of the impact of the Basel Committee's standards for bank regulation, find no evidence that any single set of best practices will necessarily promote well-functioning banks. They argue that a high degree of country specificity may be needed, rather than mere adoption of international norms "off the shelf."

What may be most appropriate from an economic welfare (development) perspective is to create a framework for assisting governments in identifying good policies, rather than a system that is premised on negotiated harmonization or convergence. Instead of being (too) prescriptive ex ante, there is a case for maintaining flexibility conditional on ex post monitoring of outcomes. An important corollary of such an approach must be "restraint" on the part of large industrial partner countries in PTAs and accountability for performance and outcomes. Creating a focal point for constructive, as opposed to adversarial, interactions between governments on the competitive, market-segmenting effects of regulation—or lack of regulation—and on the costs and benefits of specific reforms could do much to mobilize the needed support by constituencies in developing-country PTA members. This is especially so if the high costs of adjustment and of subsequent compliance by developing-country members are recognized through increased technical assistance and investment to upgrade facilities (Hoekman and Winters 2009).

The Continuing Evolution of PTAs

The growth of PTAs has been significant. Recent PTAs tend to be more open than earlier vintages, many of which were designed to implement import-substitution strategies at the regional level. They also increasingly involve North-South cooperation and extend to behind-the-border regulatory policies relating to investment, labor, environment, and competition. Examples involving the United States include bilateral agreements with Australia, Chile, Central America, Jordan, and Morocco. Investment and competition policies are being discussed as part of the economic partnership agreement negotiations between the EU and the African, Caribbean, and Pacific (ACP) countries and are on the agenda of the EU's association agreements with non-ACP countries.[4]

Often, the implementation of such policies may entail pecuniary spillovers to other countries, providing a rationale for cooperation on, for example, tax or other incentive programs to attract foreign direct investment. In many cases, however, the purported rationale is that the disciplines themselves will promote development. From a development perspective, the extension of PTAs to regulatory issues can be beneficial if it improves policy credibility, thereby reducing risk premiums and helping attract investment. There is a prima facie case that regional cooperation on regulatory issues may be advantageous. Partners, to begin with, may be rather similar and may have common legal or administrative systems. North-South PTAs also tend to be associated with transfers of finance and knowledge (technical assistance), potentially helping reduce implementation and adjustment costs. In addition, high-income partners may provide offers of assistance in the form of implicit "insurance," as in the case of U.S. financial intervention to assist Mexico during the "tequila crisis."

In part, the expansion of the negotiating agenda is driven by a need to mobilize additional political support for abolishing the remaining trade-distorting policies in areas such as agriculture. The Uruguay Round was premised on such a grand bargain, with developing countries accepting new disciplines in a variety of areas, including intellectual property rights (IPRs) and services, in return for the elimination of the Multifibre Arrangement, the outlawing of voluntary export restraints, and inclusion of agriculture in the WTO.[5] A similar dynamic is driving PTAs today. The regulatory standards that are written into trade agreements generally start from the status quo prevailing in OECD countries, so that the lion's share of associated implementation costs—but presumably also of the benefits—lies with developing-country signatories. From a development perspective, the acid test is whether the proposed or negotiated rules in regulatory areas will improve the business environment and address supply-side priorities. Proponents of deep integration in North-South agreements argue that binding disciplines in areas such as competition and investment policy are critical for integrating markets. This point is discussed further below.

All this information may help explain why recent PTAs involving countries that object to the inclusion of issues such as investment and competition in the WTO—not to speak of more controversial subjects such as labor and environmental standards—may include disciplines in these areas at the regional level. Presumably the net balance is positive, in part, because the smaller number of negotiating parties makes it easier to exclude issues that are sensitive and to identify quid pro quo deals. But deeper integration may not be beneficial to all signatories. From a development perspective, the issue is not whether there are net benefits but how to maximize the potential payoffs. There may be cause for concern, in particular, about PTAs that offer partial access to large markets for goods in exchange for acceptance of regulatory norms that may do little, if anything, to increase the flow of investment to developing-country partners. The use, however, of PTAs as a framework to reduce the frictional costs of trade by harmonizing regulations and standards, increasing the credibility of reform initiatives, or acting as vehicles for governments to test the waters of freer trade may be very beneficial, even if they are difficult and complex to realize.

Summing up, there is a clear trend for PTAs to go beyond trade in manufactures. Recent U.S. PTAs include agriculture, and movement on this front is discernable in the EU; the Euro-Mediterranean negotiations include a proposal to pursue reciprocal liberalization of trade in agricultural products. Services, investment, and regulatory regimes are areas where, it can be argued, there is much to be gained by developing countries from policy reforms and liberalization. There are potential concerns about these areas insofar as developing countries perceive proposed or actual disciplines not to be in their interests but still necessary if these countries are to (continue to) gain preferential access to northern markets. Clearly, much depends on the coverage of the agreements and, in particular, on whether the regulatory disciplines for behind-the-border policies are appropriate in the sense that the benefits outweigh the costs of implementation. Much also depends on the extent to which merchandise trade is liberalized, through, for example, access to agricultural markets and removal of the threat of contingent protection, and whether services liberalization is covered, through all modes of supply, including mode 4 (temporary movement of service providers).

The tariff equivalents of the trade-restricting effects of domestic policies are a large multiple of the prevailing border tariffs today. Further services liberalization would have much greater positive effects on national welfare than would the removal of trade barriers—see, for example, Konan and Maskus (2006) on Tunisia, and Jensen, Rutherford, and Tarr (2007) on the Russian Federation. The "standard" increase in welfare from goods liberalization is 1 percent, but introduction of greater competition on services markets raises the gains to the 5–10 percent range or more. These large effects of services liberalization—for which there is increasing econometric evidence (Francois and Hoekman 2009)—reflect both the importance of services in the economy and the extent to which many sectors continue to be protected. There are, indeed, potentially large gains from reducing the prevalence and costs of differences in regulation, as well as the incidence of policies that simply prevent access to specific markets. A key question, however, is whether progress on liberalization can be, and is being, facilitated through PTAs, specifically.

A recent assessment by Roy, Marchetti, and Lim (2006) concludes that many of the trade agreements reported to the WTO since 2000 show a sectoral coverage that greatly exceeds the commitments the countries involved made in the General Agreement on Trade in Services (GATS). In areas where there are no WTO disciplines (e.g., on safeguards, subsidies, and procurement), there tend not to be PTA rules either. The same is true for domestic regulation; only one PTA (the Trans-Pacific Economic Partnership Agreement, between Brunei Darussalam, Chile, New Zealand, and Singapore) has established an across-the-board necessity test—that is, an assessment of whether the trade-restricting effects of a policy are necessary to achieve the underlying regulatory objective (Fink and Molinuevo 2007).

Harnessing Regional Integration for Development

It can be argued that, to be most beneficial to developing-country signatories, PTAs should

- Remove foreign barriers to trade in products in which developing countries have a comparative advantage.
- Lower domestic barriers that raise the prices of goods and services that firms and households consume.
- Promote more general MFN-based liberalization, which best serves global development prospects.
- Support the adoption of complementary measures, reforms, and investments that allow the potential benefits of trade opportunities to be realized.

The first two objectives are the bread and butter of PTAs. Their realization is constrained by political-economy forces. Small, poor countries have little to offer, in mercantilist terms, to induce large countries to remove policies that harm them. Such market access, however, is important for mobilizing political support for domestic reforms in the developing-country partner. A problem is that nonreciprocal preference programs may imply that exporters already have free access to the high-income market or markets. The third objective, MFN-based liberalization, does not, of course, drive PTAs, which revolve around *discriminatory* access.[6]

Realization of the fourth objective, adoption of complementary measures, is the key challenge, if North-South PTAs are to be most relevant from a development perspective. It may be impeded by the fact that the rules embedded (or proposed) in North-South PTAs tend to reflect the status quo in the high-income countries. From a development perspective, the extension of PTAs to regulatory issues can be beneficial if it improves policy quality or credibility, thereby reducing risk premiums and helping to attract investment. Regional cooperation may be more effective in this regard than multilateral cooperation because the partners may be more similar; for example, they may have common legal or administrative systems. As discussed below, North-South PTAs also tend to be associated with more extensive transfers of finance and knowledge (technical assistance), potentially helping to reduce implementation and adjustment costs. Proponents of deep integration in North-South agreements often argue that binding commitments in areas such as competition law and regulation are critical for integrating markets and that it is easier to envisage enforcement among the small number of partner countries. Although this can certainly be the case, the specific disciplines that are embedded in a PTA may not be a priority for development, implying that even if financial and technical assistance is made available, it could constitute diversion because the resources would have had a higher return elsewhere.

None of the four objectives is straightforward to achieve, explaining why many PTAs have partial coverage in market access terms and include rules that may not be first-best for developing-country members. If PTAs are to do more to satisfy the four criteria suggested, the modus operandi of designing and implementing them should give more weight to development considerations (economic efficiency and equity). Concretely, four changes could make North-South PTAs more development-friendly:

- Unconditional acceptance by all parties to a PTA of MFN liberalization of trade in goods *and* services by developing-country signatories, and preferential removal of *all* barriers by OECD partner countries—bound, in both cases, by an enforceable treaty instrument

- Construction of mechanisms to pursue priority national regulatory policy objectives in developing-country partners, as opposed to harmonization with the standards of OECD countries, while maintaining the role of PTAs as a commitment device
- Strengthened, grant-based financing mechanisms (aid for trade) to improve trade supply capacity and increase the benefits of trade reforms for poor households, using a local analysis of needs, with allocations determined by the country's overall development strategy
- Active engagement by and with the private sector in the surveillance and enforcement of the implementation of the various dimensions of the PTA, including the provision of financial and technical assistance.

Adjusting the Rules to Promote Market Access

PTAs are a steadily increasing source of discrimination in trade today. Lowering the external levels of PTA protection to reduce the extent of discrimination against nonmembers—which will often be developing countries—would promote the global public good. A solution offered by "realists" has been to point to MFN liberalization through WTO negotiating rounds, according to the fact that efforts to regulate PTAs through the WTO rule-making and enforcement process have been totally ineffective (Mavroidis 2005). In principle, however, if development were to be taken more seriously as a goal, changing the WTO rules on regionalism could help make the PTA process more development-friendly. Concretely, high-income countries would be required to liberalize in all sectors (not just "substantially all") on a preferential basis, with liberal and simple rules of origin.[7] Conversely, developing-country signatories would reduce their tariffs and apply negotiated trade policy commitments on an MFN basis. This MFN liberalization would not imply a requirement to move to zero tariffs across the board; instead, the goal would be a significant reduction in applied MFN tariffs by developing-country partners, bound by the WTO. This method would prevent trade diversion; reduce the administrative burden on customs authorities (as there would be no need to enforce rules of origin on imports); help ensure that the PTA benefits all trading partners, not just members; and allow governments more time to put in place alternative sources of fiscal revenue.

Large northern partners will not offer complete duty-free and quota-free access to large developing countries without a quid pro quo. In principle, such a quid pro quo

should be MFN reform as well—there is no reason to differentiate between developing countries. In effect, the MFN proposal implies emulation of the type of asymmetric liberalization that has been the norm in the General Agreement on Tariffs and Trade (GATT) and WTO, with the difference being that in the North-South PTA context, the northern countries "go all the way"—commit to free trade. Insofar as the North is not willing to do this for large developing countries, the WTO can and should be used as an instrument for reciprocal liberalization; the fact that the full preference rule might prevent PTAs from forming is, of course, not a problem from a global welfare perspective.

The "full Monty" rule for the North is consistent with the thrust of current WTO rules for regional agreements, except that it would go beyond the "substantially all trade" requirement to cover *all* trade. Although a formal rule change to this effect would be desirable, as noted by many—see, for example, Mavroidis (2005)—GATT Article XXIV (allowing an exception to the MFN rule to permit PTAs) and the Committee on Regional Trade Agreements are basically defunct. Absent effective enforcement of the rules, seeking to change them is a largely irrelevant exercise. Thus, in practice, full liberalization is an action that needs to be taken *unilaterally* by northern countries. There is no need to change Article XXIV to permit the implementation of this aspect of the proposal; what is needed is a meaningful commitment to take development seriously.[8] That cannot be said for the suggestion that developing country partners commit to MFN liberalization. Both Article XXIV and the Enabling Clause—which allows developing countries to liberalize less, especially where South-South agreements are concerned—would be implicated by an MFN rule. In terms of Article XXIV requirements, it may be easier to pursue a waiver for specific PTAs, as MFN-based reform implies that all WTO members stand to gain from the PTA. This solution leaves the inconsistency with the Enabling Clause to be resolved. Arguably, the economics here are clear: pursuing a MFN strategy has much less potential for welfare loss and can enhance benefits.[9]

The argument in favor of a MFN approach by developing-country PTA members extends to services. Although actual *additional* liberalization in the services area has not been great—with the exception of the EU, most PTAs have not gone much beyond the GATS—services and investment policies are very much on the PTA agenda. Multilateral liberalization opens the market to the largest number of competitors and gives consumers maximum choice. It also leads to a less complex policy regime than a preferential arrangement, implying lower administrative costs for the government and lower transaction costs for the private sector.

If the market access rule proposals outlined for PTAs are formalized in the WTO, then the next question is what to do about existing PTAs. In practice, the revealed preference of members of these PTAs is clear: full liberalization is often not the objective, and MFN is certainly not the goal. Seeking to change this status quo is unlikely to be fruitful. Existing PTAs will therefore need to be grandfathered, in the unlikely event that it proves possible to change the WTO rules. That said, there is no reason existing agreements could not be reopened by a developing-country government, assuming that development is indeed a major objective of the northern partner.

Policy Flexibility and Better Economic Governance

We next turn to the second element of a strategy for increasing the development-friendliness of North-South PTAs. The market access dimension of PTAs arguably should involve hard law—binding and enforceable commitments. As mentioned previously, a major element of the status quo is an increasing focus on harmonization and hard law for behind-the-border policies concerning services, investment, and regulation. This may well be beneficial to signatories, but much depends on country circumstances. What are the preconditions for such commitments to be beneficial? Have they been satisfied? Do the commitments remove access to policy instruments that are desirable or are the only ones a government can feasibly employ to address a market failure? Given that there is likely to be uncertainty with respect to these issues—and, often, differences in views between governments—an approach that allows for greater policy flexibility could do much to enhance the perceived benefits of engaging in PTA-based commitments.

A precondition for ownership of international agreements is that governments and stakeholders perceive the rules as benefiting the economy overall. A more economically based mode of cooperation—as opposed to a focus on harmonization-cum-approximation of laws—could help enhance such ownership. From an economic development perspective, a mechanism for identifying good practices makes sense, as these will often differ across countries. The focus would be on the provision of information and learning through regular interactions of relevant policy makers and constituents (stakeholders), peer review, and multilateral monitoring of the impacts of policies and their effectiveness in attaining stated objectives (see Chayes and Chayes 1995; Abbott and Snidal 2000; Helleiner 2000; Sabel and Reddy 2007). Rather than seek to impose existing

norms in OECD countries as examples of best practice, cooperation would be geared toward assisting countries in attaining their objectives efficiently. The specific content of regulation should reflect national (or local) circumstances. Thus, what may be most appropriate from an economic welfare (development) perspective is to create a framework for helping governments identify good policies, not a system that aims at harmonization.

An important corollary of such an approach must be accountability for performance and outcomes, generating information (based on analysis) on whether the policies employed are effective, what their costs and benefits are, and so on. The fact that trade agreements are binding contracts—that commitments are enforceable—gives them their value: traders have greater certainty regarding policy, and governments know what they are "buying" when they make commitments. Any approach toward recognizing differential capacities and identifying regulatory options and priorities should minimize uncertainty for traders and investors. Binding, enforceable disciplines on the use of trade policy are likely to be beneficial for development. The case for trade policies designed to deal with specific government and market failures that may prevent a supply response to reforms from emerging is very weak (Pack and Saggi 2006). It may not be obvious, however, what types of domestic policies might be most appropriate and effective, which suggests that experimentation and learning should be encouraged (see, for example, Rodríguez-Clare 2004; Rodrik 2004).

The prevalence of complicated trade policies in many countries is often driven by industrial policy objectives, which have a long history. They span not only trade protection but also subsidies and direct government involvement in industry. Although opinions differ, the weight of the evidence suggests that such policies are generally very costly, often prolong the adjustment period, and distort competition. That said, subsidies can facilitate learning, technology acquisition, and dynamic comparative advantage in situations where returns to such activities cannot be appropriated by private agents. Many commentators have argued that policy interventions, including implicit or explicit subsidies, lay behind the economic "miracles" in East Asia and were a major factor in the economic development of European states, the United States, and Japan in the 19th and 20th centuries. Their case is that import protection and carefully targeted subsidies allowed governments to stimulate key sectors that became efficient in their own right and provided positive spillovers for the economy as a whole.

In considering this infant-industry argument for government support, it is important to differentiate between sector-specific subsidies and policies aimed at facilitating learning and the development of private enterprise. The case for general policy support for certain types of activity, including innovation, education, transport infrastructure, and similar public goods, is uncontroversial. The same is true for policies aimed at promoting socially beneficial activities. Markets can and do fail. There may be good rationales for governments to provide incentives for firms and agents to undertake activities that would otherwise be undersupplied (Rodrik 2004). Specific interventions, however, will often get it wrong, in part as a result of rent seeking and in part because of general equilibrium effects (a subsidy for one activity implies a tax on all others).[10] Monitoring and analysis of impacts and of the performance of supported sectors and activities are therefore important, as is the establishment of credible exit mechanisms; governments need to be able to withdraw support for experiments that fail. Trade agreements offer a potential vehicle for supporting such mechanisms.

PTAs can help by creating institutional mechanisms that can assist in identifying policies that would be effective and efficient in attaining specific goals set by governments and by increasing the transparency of policies and their outcomes through joint monitoring and analysis. A first step is to identify the relevant policies via the equivalent of what is done at the WTO through the Trade Policy Review Mechanism and then to carry out an economic assessment of the rationale for and effectiveness of the relevant policies. An example of an institution that does the latter is the Productivity Commission in Australia. Assessment of whether instruments are achieving development objectives and whether less trade-distorting ones can be identified requires judgments regarding appropriate sequencing and the need for complementary reforms and investment. These judgments must be made by the government concerned but would benefit from inputs from other PTA members.[11]

Even if one is not convinced by the upside of pursuing greater flexibility on regulatory disciplines in PTAs, the downside risk is arguably limited. At worst, the cost is that PTA members conclude after a number of years that the approach is not beneficial. Such an attitude may, however, be too complacent. A case can certainly be made that if the raison d'être of a trade agreement is the negotiation of binding commitments, policy dialogue discussions may do more harm than good by increasing uncertainty; duplicating the efforts of the World Bank, the International Monetary Fund, and others; and incurring transaction costs. An alternative is to leave economic policy dialogue to international development and financial institutions. There is much to be said for this counterargument, but it ignores

the reality that PTAs are extending deeper behind the border. Moreover, with the exception of the WTO, trade policy is not a consistent focus of the activities of international organizations. A major advantage of a PTA is that the focus is on trade and trade-related policies. Creation of a focal point for a constructive, as opposed to adversarial, interaction between governments could do much to heighten the domestic profile of the trade agenda for developing-country PTA signatories. It would also increase information on the effects of existing policy instruments—a necessary condition for adopting better policies—and ensure that trade-related policy actions and investments are taken into consideration when decision makers allocate resources to public expenditures.

All these measures can be characterized as an effort to improve economic governance in partner countries and, in the process, enhance the ownership of PTAs. Clearly, the effectiveness of the implementation of the interactive mechanisms will be critical for their credibility. In the end, when governments (the partners jointly) deem that a binding commitment in an area makes sense, entering into such a commitment will increase the probability of enforcement. Insofar as cooperation in specific areas continues to be of the soft-law variety, legal enforcement mechanisms are not available. Here, accountability can only come from transparency, engagement, and publicly disseminated analysis of actions and impacts. Oversight by parliaments and analytical assessments by institutions in the North—the U.S. Congressional Budget Office and General Accountability Office; similar national institutions in the EU such as the French research institutions Centre d'Etudes Prospectives et d'Informations Internationales and the Centraal Plan Bureau in the Netherlands; and Australia's Productivity Commission—could help inform development assistance programs. But strengthening the capacity to undertake such analysis in developing-country partners is crucial.

Might such monitoring and interaction be better delegated to the WTO? Although non-PTA members may have little immediate interest in the policies pursued by a specific developing-country PTA member, the substantive coverage of PTAs will generally overlap to a great extent with the issues that are addressed by WTO agreements or that may be taken up in the future. There is much to be said for considering an expansion of the WTO Trade Policy Review Mechanism to enable it to undertake much more in-depth analyses of the impacts of policies pursued by PTA members and by customs unions (Hoekman 2005). An additional reason for establishing such a mechanism at the WTO is that the consultations and impact assessments associated with any policy flexibility mechanism will entail resource costs. These may be significant for poor countries with a scarcity of skilled personnel. If the required work is undertaken multilaterally, much of it could be carried out in the context of mechanisms such as the Enhanced Integrated Framework for Trade-Related Technical Assistance, reducing the costs. (See Prowse [2006] for a discussion.)

More regular interaction on trade policies would provide a framework for helping governments assess whether instruments are achieving stated objectives. The publication and dissemination in the countries concerned of the results and findings of reports and discussions would also increase the public profile of trade-related policies. More regular cooperative interaction by regulators and trade officials concerning trade policies and constraints on market integration could also improve communications between the development and trade communities, as the analysis and discussions might assist in identifying where development assistance has the greatest potential to help countries benefit more from trade agreements and cooperation.

Aid for Trade: Capacity Building for Competitiveness

The third plank of a development-focused approach is expanded development assistance to help address supply capacity constraints in poor countries—the types of measures briefly discussed in the section on trade liberalization strategies. This effort requires identifying and prioritizing needs and providing funds to address them. Especially in small, low-income countries that already have relatively free access to major markets, using aid to address constraints that reduce their competitiveness can have high payoffs and, indeed, may be the primary source of benefits. A major lesson of experience with projects and programs in the trade area (and in most others) is that country ownership and leadership at the highest levels are critical factors in ensuring concrete and sustained follow-up in removing constraints to trade expansion. The flexibility mechanism proposed above could help mobilize this follow-up by identifying where specific investments are likely to be needed, but it will need to be complemented by a comprehensive diagnostic analysis of factors that constrain supply responses and reduce competitiveness. Such diagnostics should feed into the process through which countries determine public investment allocations and policy reform priorities. In many low-income countries, this process increasingly centers on poverty reduction strategy papers, which form the basis for the provision of donor assistance at the country level. As discussed at greater

length by Prowse (2002 and 2006), trade-related funding should be allocated within the context of an overall country development program and an agreed macroeconomic policy framework. As a development tool, stand-alone specific funds and associated mechanisms are less likely to be effective than integration of the prioritization and resource allocation process into national poverty reduction and development strategies.

Trade policy often will not be the most important policy area from a growth perspective—and it should be borne in mind that many low-income countries have taken actions to move away from nontariff barriers and to reduce dispersion in tariffs. A fortiori, trade policies and institutions that are covered by PTAs may not be among the areas within the trade area where actions and investment are most needed. As stressed previously, the primary determinants of success in harnessing trade openness to deliver growth are concomitant policies and institutions in the developing countries themselves. Supply capacity is a necessary condition for exploiting market access opportunities, which will be determined by the prevailing investment climate and the trade and business environment. Much of the associated policy agenda extends beyond trade policies and cannot be addressed through trade agreements that are narrowly conceived. Measures to facilitate trade—to get goods and services in and out of the country for less cost—are likely to be particularly important in many of the poorest countries. Given that many of these countries are landlocked, cooperation with neighbors to reduce the costs of transit and transport and of access to ports may well generate a particularly high payoff. In general, measures aimed at improving the investment climate are likely to dominate trade policy, as are macroeconomic policies designed to ensure a realistic exchange rate and actions guaranteeing that markets exist and function.

The implication is that financial and technical resources made available by high-income countries to developing-country PTA partners should be allocated on the basis of national priorities and not tied to the narrow ambit of whatever is embodied in the PTA. As argued in the next section, a corollary of this is that it would be desirable to integrate PTA-based resources into the emerging multilateral mechanisms in order to assist poor countries in bolstering their trade capacity.

Private Sector Engagement in Implementation and Enforcement

To be credible and meaningful, PTA commitments must be enforceable. Signing a PTA is one thing, but implementing it and enforcing its provisions is quite another. Much of the literature on PTAs tends to focus on the texts and the coverage of disciplines; little attention is given to monitoring and assessing implementation. The same is true of enforcement, about which not much is known even in the best-documented PTAs. These are areas in which the private sector can play a major role. Mechanisms to encourage greater participation by firms, nongovernmental organizations (NGOs), and consumer groups need to be designed and incorporated into PTAs.

What matters to firms and consumer groups is whether market segmentation is being reduced. They have an interest in knowing about the removal of tariff and nontariff barriers and in having real-time information on what is happening at border crossings and how regulatory requirements are being enforced. Regular engagement between government and these groups—informed by an annual process through which information on the implementation of the PTA is generated (e.g., through a survey of exporters and importers)—would provide a valuable feedback loop and help increase ownership of the PTA.

Binding commitments (on market access, for example) need to be enforced. Dispute settlement provisions vary widely across PTAs but tend to be weak in many cases. This weakness reduces the relevance of the PTA for firms. The U.S., NAFTA-type PTAs are by far the most extensive in their dispute settlement provisions—not surprisingly, in the sectors where there are strong lobbies in the United States. These are, first and foremost, IPRs and investment protection and also areas such as product standards and conformity assessment. The latter is actually rather asymmetric. In the Central American Free Trade Agreement, signatories are subject to disciplines to enhance the likelihood that U.S. certification of goods will be accepted as equivalent, but there is no similar language on U.S. acceptance of the partners' certification. The seriousness of U.S. implementation is reflected not only with respect to formal, binding dispute settlement but also in terms of calling for, and setting up, bodies to monitor implementation. For example, the Web site of the Office of the U.S. Trade Representative contains documents on compliance by partners, and U.S. PTAs call for and have established performance benchmarks and contact points through which interested parties (citizens) can report perceived instances of noncompliance.[12]

Compared with the active caseload of the WTO, which has adjudicated more than 400 cases since 1995, for most North-South PTAs, there is very little evidence of enforcement action, even for U.S.-type PTAs (aside from NAFTA). Countries that are PTA members and could use

the dispute resolution mechanisms of the PTA often choose to resort to the WTO instead. The U.S.–Mexico Telmex dispute is an example. Piérola and Horlick (2007) provide other instances in which countries went to the WTO because PTA rules were ambiguous or nonexistent; they conclude that case law under NAFTA and similar agreements has entailed "little or no jurisprudential development" (Piérola and Horlick 2007, 891). Bown and Hoekman (2005 and 2008) discuss at greater length how PTAs can be complemented by mechanisms through which firms can more easily (i.e., at lower cost) obtain information on potential violations of agreements and on the way institutions might be designed so that the behavior of government agencies can be contested directly by the private sector.

The Proposed Approach and the Evolving Status Quo

The need for policy flexibility and aid for trade will vary by country: priorities differ, capacity differs, and the politics (what is feasible and to what extent there is a need to use trade agreements to pursue or lock in reforms) differs. Thus, differentiation in the agreements is called for. In practice, it is already applied in the PTA context. The front-runner is arguably the EU; the European Commission has stressed that development is an explicit objective underpinning its pursuit of PTAs with developing countries. The economic partnership agreements (EPAs) have attracted by far the most attention, but to date most EPAs have not addressed behind-the-border policies. (An exception is the agreement with the Caribbean countries, which has yet to be implemented.) More informative are the approaches the EU is pursuing with neighboring countries that are not accession candidates and with which it already has reciprocal free trade agreements. Cooperation with a number of these countries is now under the umbrella of the 2004 European Neighborhood Policy (ENP). The ENP has a threefold goal: (a) to support the national development strategy of a partner country; (b) to integrate partners into some EU economic and social structures (a stake in the Internal Market); and (c) to implement existing and future PTAs and association agreements. Technical and financial assistance (development cooperation) will focus on the areas that are identified as priorities under country-specific ENP action plans (CEC 2004).

A premise underlying the ENP is to pursue differentiated convergence with EU norms—competition policy, regulatory action for services liberalization, and so on. The

ENP's explicit recognition of differences in capacity and priorities in the context of bilateral economic cooperation with its neighbors, and of the need to complement binding treaties (PTAs) with soft law–type cooperation and technical and financial assistance, implies that the policy has parallels with the proposals set forth in "Harnessing Regional Integration for Development," an earlier section. Partner countries have to determine whether they want to pursue integration and, if so, in what areas and how. This presupposes an understanding of the benefits and costs of alternative instruments of cooperation, in particular, hard law (expansion of the coverage of binding treaties) versus soft law (economic cooperation).

As table 4.1 illustrates, this is a nontrivial challenge. The table maps two objectives—market integration and economic development—against EU instruments. It assumes that the EU cares about both the core objective of economic integration and economic development, whereas the partner country cares exclusively about national development. Thus, for the partner country, integration is an instrument, whereas for the EU it is a goal in itself, as well as an instrument. As can be seen from the first row, all the various EU instruments have the potential to contribute to achieving the goal of integration, although, in practice, much will also depend on the national policies that are pursued by partner countries (e.g., implementation). It is not obvious, however, that the instruments the EU has available will necessarily help achieve development objectives. With the exception of market access, whether this happens will depend very much on what a specific measure will do in or for the country concerned—the extent to which it addresses priority needs. The same point applies more generally to the question of whether actions to pursue integration will promote development.

There is tension between national development and integration, in that the latter constitutes a unique focal point which is defined by existing EU members, even if it is one that is constantly evolving. The former has no such focal point; both the goal and the metric used to assess progress will be idiosyncratic. Whether an instrument promotes development (growth, employment creation, and so on) will depend on what is done. Major questions, then, are whether deeper integration would help growth and, more important in the short run, in what areas integration will generate the highest payoffs. Table 4.1 simply indicates whether the expected sign is positive in terms of realizing the objective. From a practical policy-making perspective, it is also necessary to know the rank ordering of policy instruments, in which areas the goal should be to make binding commitments, and in which areas the focus should be on cooperation and aid.

Hard law—binding treaty instruments—involves the extension of association agreements to include services, agriculture, and possibly parts of the EU law (*acquis*). It is straightforward to conceptualize hard law with respect to simple market access—for example, reciprocal agreements to provide better access for agricultural and services flows, including the right of establishment (investment). There is, however, likely to be limited scope for reciprocity when it comes to the acquis, which is essentially nonnegotiable. Here, the issue is what will be asked of partner countries and the extent to which assistance is offered to achieve the required minimum standards. In practice, whether an à la carte approach is possible may depend importantly on the extent to which use is, or can be, made of the recognition principle, given that regulatory convergence (harmonization) may not be beneficial from a national development perspective. It also may or may not be necessary for effective access to the EU markets concerned (agriculture and services) or for the abolition of the threat of antidumping and safeguard actions.

Indeed, integration (defined by the acquis) may be second-order in terms of payoffs if the associated market access benefits are much smaller than gains from purely domestic reform. Take the example of services. The case for action to lower costs and improve quality is well known. There are also incentives for domestic agents to support services reform, especially in sectors (finance, transport,

Table 4.1. European Union (EU) Instruments and EU and National Objectives

Objective	EU instruments						National policies
	Treaties		Soft law		Aid		
	Border barriers	Internal market (acquis)	Economic cooperation	Participation in common programs	Grants	Loans	
Integration (EU)	X	X	X	X	X	X	X
Development (EU and partners)	X	?	?	?	?	?	X

Source: Author's elaboration.
Note: X = effective instrument; ? = sign of impact uncertain.

health, education, and so on) that are inputs into production and consumption and that, thus, affect large segments of the population. Although, in principle, the pursuit of market-opening reforms through trade agreements can be motivated on standard political-economy grounds, if there is not enough of a domestic constituency to support autonomous reform, it may be difficult to put this in practice. Thus, there may not be sufficient (or any) export interests, or alternatively, they may be concentrated in sensitive sectors—mode 4, for example—where the scope for the EU to make concessions is restricted, given the limited mercantilist value of access to the partner markets. This implies that it will be important to mobilize EU groups, such as NGOs, which attach value to the attainment of development objectives. There are also potential downsides insofar as partner countries are already pursuing unilateral services reforms, driven by a desire to improve international competitiveness. Putting the bilateral or regional opening of services on the negotiating table may slow desirable reforms if governments perceive more open markets as a bargaining chip.

Analysis aimed at prioritizing policy measures and related actions is therefore critical. Benefiting from North-South PTAs requires a coherent national development strategy in which trade-related and integration-related measures are part of a country's overall agenda. Hard law, soft law (economic cooperation), and financial and technical assistance options all need to be clearly mapped to the pursuit of national priorities. Hard law can be useful and beneficial for overcoming political-economy resistance to reform, reducing uncertainty, and locking in market access. But integration for its own sake, or the adoption of the EU model, is not necessarily going to be beneficial, and even if it is, it may not be a priority at a given point in time. Mechanisms to generate information and analysis of the impacts of different options, ex ante and ex post, are therefore of great importance. The lack of such mechanisms is perhaps the weakest element of the evolving status quo.

Conclusions

A precondition for benefiting from trade agreements is a clear understanding of the objectives to be achieved—in particular, the type of trade policy that the government wants to pursue. Trade agreements can play a useful role in the design and implementation of trade reforms, acting as a mechanism for locking in reforms, a focal point for future reforms, and a device to help overcome resistance by vested interests.

The PTAs that the EU and the United States are increasingly negotiating with developing countries can do much

good if they are designed in a way that puts development first. Taking development seriously has a number of implications, including identification of the most appropriate form of a PTA and its membership. The need to avoid trade diversion costs and attenuate tariff revenue losses is well known, as is the policy recommendation of complementing reciprocal liberalization with reductions in external (MFN) barriers to trade. The challenge is to move in this direction, which requires a willingness by the major traders to support MFN liberalization by developing-country counterparts as an appropriate quid pro quo for preferential access to their markets. Formally, this process will require a renegotiation of GATT Article XXIV (and of GATS Article V, which allows for agreements to liberalize trade in services) or a waiver. Although past experience does not furnish cause for great optimism that this is feasible, the effort would provide a signal that development concerns are being taken seriously. Given, however, that the WTO disciplines in this area are effectively redundant, in practice this may not be a serious possibility. Insofar as developing country partners do undertake MFN reforms, it may be easier to seek a waiver.

Market access commitments should be binding to ensure that they are credible. The acid test for whether regulatory disciplines in trade agreements should be binding is whether benefits outweigh costs. Often, there will be uncertainty as to whether this is the case. Mechanisms to exchange information on the effects of policies and the development of rules of thumb for behind-the-border, trade-related policies could be very beneficial for developing countries. That suggests that greater reliance on a soft-law approach that establishes broad guidelines and relies on transparency and accountability through regular (multilateral) monitoring of performance may be more effective in promoting development than harmonization, not least because it will enhance the eventual ownership of any specific norms that are adopted. Although detailed international harmonization through trade agreements may not be appropriate in many instances, one cannot generalize here except to note that careful, country-specific analysis and assessments are called for. International disciplines embedded in PTAs, starting with monitoring, analysis of impacts of policies, and information exchange, can help ensure transparency and promote increased accountability of governments.

The policy agenda confronting developing countries at the regional (PTA) level is similar to that at the multilateral level. A major difference is that in the case of North-South PTAs, more significant development assistance commitments are associated with the implementation of agreements. Trade-related assistance should focus on national, country-specific priorities; after all, there is only one national trade agenda. Technical and financial assistance should be managed accordingly.

In the past five years, much progress has been made by the international community toward improving aid effectiveness and prioritization of aid across sectors and uses. This also spans the trade area, the Enhanced Integrated Framework being a prominent example. Trade will be one priority among many and should, therefore, be considered in the context of the overall national development strategy. Ensuring that trade-related assistance provided in the context of PTAs conforms to this principle would further improve the potential development impact of PTAs, as it implies that national priorities come before PTA-defined requirements.

Indeed, much of what has been suggested in this chapter should be pursued multilaterally. There is only one domestic trade agenda in developing counties, one set of regulatory reform priorities, and one first-best trade policy. The rules of thumb proposed for PTAs are generalizable. In all the areas proposed, the WTO could play a supporting role—by requiring a shift from discriminatory to MFN reforms in a PTA context, by enhancing information on and analysis of the impacts of PTAs and national trade-related policies, and by encouraging donors to channel through multilateral aid mechanisms the resources that are mobilized to support PTA implementation.

Notes

This chapter draws on joint work with Alan Winters and is a substantially revised version of a paper presented at the International Trade Roundtable "The WTO at 10 Years: The Regional Challenge to Multilateralism," Brussels, June 27–28, 2005. Parts of that paper were subsequently published as Hoekman (2006) and Hoekman (2007).

1. There is extensive literature on the effect of preferences. See Hoekman and Özden (2007) for a survey and summary of both the old and more recent literature.

2. Of course, this is not always true. For example, a trade-off between trade liberalization and other objectives can arise in the short run if too large a shock would lead to the complete collapse of a market. Local labor markets may seize up in the face of large-scale redundancies because workers cease to leave their jobs speculatively for fear of not finding others. This is essentially a matter of timing—of staggering the trade liberalization (as is very common in practice) and ensuring that it is not accompanied by a negative macro shock.

3. In many countries, import-competing firms were compensated for trade reform by depreciation and other reforms that reduced their input costs—for example, measures to improve the efficiency of service providers.

4. Bilateral investment treaties (BITs) have been the primary vehicle for international cooperation in this area. BITs are, in part, designed to spur investment flows by providing recourse to international dispute resolution in the event of conflict with governments. Although some PTAs explicitly do not include investment policy disciplines because of preexisting BITs—an example is the 2000 Canada–Costa Rica PTA (Gestrin 2002)—most recent U.S. PTAs have more ample rights and coverage and generally subsume prior BITs.

5. The relevant agreements on IPRs and services are the Trade-Related Aspects of Intellectual Property Rights (TRIPS) agreement and the General Agreement on Trade in Services (GATS).

6. Recent empirical analysis, however, has begun to reveal evidence that PTAs generate incentives to pursue MFN liberalization once preferential market access reforms have been implemented. See Bohara, Gawande, and Sanguietti (2004) as well as Estevadeordal, Freund, and Ornelas (2008). The driver for such complementary MFN liberalization may be a desire to reduce the trade diversion costs of the PTA.

7. Although preferential liberalization by OECD members of PTAs is, of course, undesirable from a global welfare perspective, the solution is continued multilateral negotiations to remove trade-distorting policies on an MFN basis.

8. This commitment should not be difficult, insofar as partners are small, poor countries. Both the United States and the EU already give many of these countries duty-free access to markets.

9. If a North-South PTA has a South-South PTA as its partner (as opposed to only one developing country), then arguably the latter PTA also should completely liberalize trade to ensure that an integrated market is indeed being created. Rather than continuing to use trade policies (including nontariff barriers) to shelter local firms from competition, other policies should be used to address coordination problems, underprovision of public goods, and other market failures and to achieve equity objectives. Import-substitution policies that rely on trade protection have proved to be largely ineffective and costly.

10. In a comprehensive retrospective on the East Asian development experience, Noland and Pack (2003) argue that sector-specific policies did not result in high rates of total factor productivity growth for manufacturing. In the case of Korea and Taiwan, China, productivity growth was not much higher than in OECD economies. The authors argue that the primary reason these countries developed rapidly has more to do with economywide policies in areas such as education and infrastructure than with industrial targeting, not least because the government did not prove very effective in identifying winners.

11. International financial institutions could be brought into this process, in an advisory capacity. Their involvement would be desirable for at least two reasons. First, they have the mandate, experience, local presence, and capacity to provide policy advice. Second, these organizations generally take the lead in the development and financing of projects and programs in developing countries.

12. A noteworthy feature of recent U.S. PTAs is that dispute settlement makes provision for compensatory payments in lieu of implementation (or retaliation). In the U.S.-Chile agreement, in the case of nonimplementation of a panel finding, the losing party may offer to pay 50 percent of the damage caused. It appears that this penalty is open-ended, as the text speaks of annual payments. This PTA also provides for monetary fines of up to US$15 million per year in case of violations of labor or environmental provisions. Proceeds go into a fund earmarked for labor initiatives or green initiatives.

References

Abbott, Kenneth, and Duncan Snidal. 2000. "Hard and Soft Law in International Governance." *International Organization* 53 (3): 421–56.

Barth, James R., Gerard Caprio, Jr., and Ross Levine. 2006. *Rethinking Bank Regulation: Till Angels Govern.* Cambridge, U.K., and New York: Cambridge University Press.

Bohara, Alok, Kishore Gawande, and Pablo Sanguietti. 2004. "Trade Diversion and Declining Tariffs: Evidence from Mercosur." *Journal of International Economics* 64: 65–88.

Bown, Chad P., and Bernard Hoekman. 2005. "WTO Dispute Settlement and the Missing Developing Country Cases: Engaging the Private Sector." *Journal of International Economic Law* 8 (4): 861–90.

———. 2008. "Developing Countries and Enforcement of Trade Agreements: Why Dispute Settlement Is Not Enough." *Journal of World Trade* 42 (1): 177–203.

CEC (Commission of the European Communities). 2004. "European Neighbourhood Policy: Strategy Paper." COM(2004) 373 final, CEC, Brussels. http://ec.europa.eu/world/enp/pdf/strategy/strategy_paper_en.pdf.

Chayes, Abram, and Antonia Handler Chayes. 1995. *The New Sovereignty: Compliance with International Regulatory Agreements.* Cambridge, MA: Harvard University Press.

Estevadeordal, Antoni, Caroline Freund, and Emmanuel Ornelas. 2008. "Does Regionalism Affect Trade Liberalization Towards Non-Members?" *Quarterly Journal of Economics* 123 (4): 1531–75.

Fink, Carsten, and Martín Molinuevo. 2007. "East Asian Free Trade Agreements in Services: Roaring Tigers or Timid Pandas?" World Bank, Washington, DC. http://siteresources.worldbank.org/INTEAPSUMEASPR/Resources/2576847-1163691185244/East_Asian_FTAs_in_Services.pdf.

Francois, Joseph, and Bernard Hoekman. 2009. "Services Trade and Policy," CEPR Discussion Paper 7616, Centre for Economic Policy Research, London.

Gestrin, Michael. 2002. "The Relationship between Regional Trade Agreements and the Multilateral Trading System: Investment." TD/TC/WP(2002)18/FINAL, Organisation for Economic Co-operation and Development, Paris.

Haddad, Mona, Jamus Jerome Lim, and Christian Saborowski. 2010. "Trade Openness Reduces Growth Volatility When Countries Are Well Diversified." Policy Research Working Paper 5222, World Bank, Washington, DC. http://econ.worldbank.org/external/default/main?pagePK=64165259&theSitePK=469382&piPK=64165421&menuPK=64166093&entityID=000158349_20100226112948.

Helleiner, Gerald Karl. 2000. "Markets, Politics, and Globalization: Can the Global Economy be Civilized?" 10th Raúl Prebisch Lecture, United Nations Conference on Trade and Development, Geneva, December 11. http://www.unctad.org/en/docs/prebisch10th.en.pdf.

Hoekman, Bernard. 2005. "Operationalizing the Concept of Policy Space in the WTO: Beyond Special and Differential Treatment." *Journal of International Economic Law* 8 (2): 405–24.

———. 2006. "Trade Liberalization, Trade Agreements and Economic Development." In *The WTO Trade Remedy System: East Asian Perspectives,* ed. Mitsuo Matsushita, Dukgeun Ahn, and Tain-Jy Chen. London: Cameron May.

———. 2007. "Regionalism and Development: The European Neighborhood Policy and Integration à la Carte." *Journal of International Trade and Diplomacy* 1 (1): 1–55.

Hoekman, Bernard, and Çaglar Özden, eds. 2007. *Trade Preferences and Differential Treatment of Developing Countries.* Cheltenham, U.K.: Edward Elgar.

Hoekman, Bernard and L. Alan Winters. 2009. "Multilateralizing Preferential Trade Agreements: A Developing Country Perspective." In *Multilateralizing Regionalism: Challenges for the Global Trading System,* ed., Richard Baldwin and Patrick Low. Cambridge, U.K.: Cambridge University Press.

Imbs, Jean, and Romain Wacziarg. 2003. "Stages of Diversification." *American Economic Review* 93: 63–86.

Jensen, Jesper, Thomas Rutherford, and David Tarr. 2007. "The Impact of Liberalizing Barriers to Foreign Direct Investment in Services: The Case of Russian Accession to the WTO." *Review of Development Economics* 11 (3): 482–506.

Konan, Denise, and Keith Maskus. 2006. "Quantifying the Impact of Services Liberalization in a Developing Country." *Journal of Development Economics* 81 (1, October): 142–62.

Limão, Nuno. 2007. "Are Preferential Trade Agreements with Non-Trade Objectives a Stumbling Block for Multilateral Liberalization?" *Review of Economic Studies* 74 (3): 821–55.

Mavroidis, Petros. 2005. "Testing the Compliance of PTAs with the Multilateral Rules." Presented at the International Trade Roundtable 2005, "The WTO at 10 Years: The Regional Challenge to Multilateralism," Brussels, June 27–28.

Newfarmer, Richard, William Shaw, and Peter Walkenhorst, eds. 2009. *Breaking into New Markets: Emerging Lessons for Export Diversification.* Washington, DC: World Bank.

Noland, Marcus, and Howard Pack. 2003. *Industrial Policy in an Era of Globalization: Lessons from Asia.* Washington, DC: Institute of International Economics.

Pack, Howard and Kamal Saggi, 2006. "Is There a Case for Industrial Policy? A Critical Survey." *World Bank Research Observer* 21 (2): 267–97.

Piérola, Fernando, and Gary Horlick. 2007. "WTO Dispute Settlement and Dispute Settlement in the 'North-South' Agreements of the Americas: Considerations for Choice of Forum." *Journal of World Trade* 41 (5): 885–908.

Porto, Guido, and Bernard Hoekman, eds. 2010. *Trade Adjustment Costs in Developing Countries: Impacts, Determinants and Policy Responses.* Washington, D.C.: World Bank and Centre for Economic Policy Research (CEPR).

Prowse, Susan. 2002. "The Role of International and National Agencies in Trade–Related Capacity Building." *World Economy* 25 (9, September): 1235–61.

———. 2006 "Aid for Trade: Increasing Support for Trade Adjustment and Integration—A Proposal." In *Economic Development and Multilateral Trade Cooperation,* ed. Simon Evenett and Bernard Hoekman. Washington, D.C.: World Bank; Houndmills, Basingstoke, Hampshire, U.K: Palgrave Macmillan.

Rodríguez-Clare, Andres. 2004. "Clusters and Comparative Advantage: Implications for Industrial Policy." Inter-American Development Bank, Washington, DC.

Rodrik, Dani, 2004. "Industrial Policy for the Twenty-First Century." CEPR Discussion Paper 4767, Centre for Economic Policy Research, London.

Roy, Martin, Juan Marchetti, and Hoe Lim. 2006. "Services Liberalisation in the New Generation of Preferential Trade Agreements: How Much Further Than the GATS?" WTO Staff Working Paper ERSD-2006-07, World Trade Organization, Geneva.

Sabel, Charles F., and Sanjay G. Reddy. 2007. "Learning to Learn: Undoing the Gordian Knot of Development Today." *Challenge* 50 (5, Sept.–Oct.): 73–92.

Schiff, Maurice, and L. Alan Winters. 2003. *Regionalism and Development.* Oxford, U.K.: Oxford University Press.

Winters, L. Alan. 2004. "Trade Liberalization and Economic Performance: An Overview," *Economic Journal* 114 (February), F4–F21.

World Bank. 2001. *Global Economic Prospects and the Developing Countries 2002: Making Trade Work for the World's Poor.* Washington, DC: World Bank.

———. 2010a. *Global Monitoring Report 2010: The MDGs after the Crisis.* Washington, DC: World Bank.

———. 2010b. *World Trade Indicators 2009/2010: Trade under Crisis.* Washington, DC: World Bank.

5

CUSTOMS UNIONS

Soamiely Andriamananjara

A customs union (CU) is a form of trade agreement under which certain countries preferentially grant tariff-free market access to each other's imports and agree to apply a common set of external tariffs to imports from the rest of the world. That is, they enter into a free trade agreement (FTA) and apply a common external tariff (CET) schedule to imports from nonmembers.[1] A CU can be thought of as a deeper form of integration than an FTA, generally requiring more coordination and a greater loss of autonomy.

The aims of this chapter are to provide, from an economics perspective, an overview of the key features of CUs and to examine some design issues that may be of interest to policy makers and (nonspecialist) analysts. The discussions are meant to be relatively conceptual and nontechnical, but real-world illustrations are provided when available.

To begin with, the main economic costs and benefits of opting for a CU, relative to those for an FTA, are discussed, and selected issues regarding the design and determinants of a common external tariff are examined. Although a number of arguments seem to suggest that CUs may be subject to more protectionist pressures than FTAs, the existing literature does not provide an unequivocal answer. There then follows a conceptual discussion of the implications of the various administrative options related to the collection and sharing of customs duties; this, it is shown, is not only a technical issue, but also (and perhaps more important) a question of trust among member countries. The chapter concludes with an overview of a number of systemic aspects of CUs. Readers interested in the more operational and detailed aspects of CUs are referred to the excellent surveys in Development Network Africa (2007) and Keick and Maur (2011).

A Special Case of PTA

CUs have been around for a long time and were once more prevalent than FTAs. Early efforts toward economic integration were generally driven by the desire to establish a political union, and the members were willing to relinquish some political autonomy.[2] Early examples include the Zollverein, formed in 1834 by several German principalities, which turned out to be a step toward political unification, and the 1847 customs union between Moldavia and Walachia, a precursor to the creation of Romania.

More recently, CUs appear to have become less popular, at least with respect to the number of arrangements. As is thoroughly documented by Acharya et al. (ch. 2 in this volume), almost 85 percent of the regional integration arrangements notified to the World Trade Organization (WTO) through 2009 consisted of FTAs. This trend reflects the nature of the current wave of regionalism, which has been broadly characterized by smaller cross-regional deals, flexibility, selectivity, and, most important, speed.[3] Recent FTAs are inclined to be pragmatic and to focus more on strategic commercial market access and less on geographic considerations or political ambitions.[4] They generally involve a small number of partners (frequently, just two), which are often geographically distant from each other. They tend to achieve significant preferential and reciprocal trade liberalization within a short time while simultaneously preserving a member's sovereignty over its trade policy vis-à-vis the rest of the world, including its option of joining other preferential trade agreements (PTAs).

By contrast, CUs usually involve a relatively large number of geographically contiguous countries (see table 5.1 for a selected listing). They generally take longer to negotiate

Table 5.1. Selected Customs Unions, in Force and Planned

Agreement	Date
	In force
Southern African Customs Union (SACU)	1910
Switzerland–Liechtenstein	1924
European Union (EU)	January 1, 1958
Central American Common Market (CACM)	October 12, 1961
Caribbean Community (CARICOM)	August 1, 1973
Andean Community (CAN)	May 25, 1988
EU–Andorra	July 1, 1991
Southern Cone Common Market (Mercosur, Mercado Común del Sur)	November 29, 1991
Israel–Palestinian Authority	1994
EU–Turkey	January 1, 1996
Eurasian Economic Community (EAEC)	October 8, 1997
Economic and Monetary Community of Central Africa (CEMAC, Communauté Économique et Monétaire de l'Afrique Centrale)	June 24, 1999
West African Economic and Monetary Union/Union Économique et Monétaire Ouest-Africaine (WAEMU/UEMOA)	January 1, 2000
East African Community (EAC)	July 7, 2000
EU–San Marino	April 1, 2002
Gulf Cooperation Council (GCC)	January 1, 2003
Customs Union of Belarus, Kazakhstan, and Russia	July 1, 2010
	Planned
Arab Customs Union (ACU)	2010
Southern African Development Community (SADC)	2010
Economic Community of Central African States (ECCAS)	2011
Economic Community of West African States (ECOWAS)	2015
African Economic Community (AEC)	2019
Arab Common Market (ACM)	2020
Australia–New Zealand Closer Economic Relations Trade Agreement (ANZCERTA)	2020

Source: Author's compilation.

and implement than do PTAs, and they entail a certain loss of policy-making autonomy. By 2009, they accounted for less than 10 percent of the regional integration arrangements notified to the WTO. CUs are less numerous than PTAs, but they generally have much larger memberships. They also tend to cover much larger geographic areas. The four main CUs in Latin America—the Central American Common Market (CACM), the Andean Community (CAN), the Caribbean Community (CARICOM), and the Southern Cone Common Market (Mercosur, Mercado Común del Sur)—include almost all the region's economies. The existing and planned CUs in Sub-Saharan Africa—the Economic and Monetary Community of Central Africa (Communauté Économique et Monétaire de l'Afrique Centrale), the East African Community (EAC), the Southern African Customs Union (SACU), the West African Economic and Monetary Union (WAEMU), the Economic Community of West African States (ECOWAS), the Common Market for Eastern and Southern Africa (COMESA), the Southern African Development Community (SADC), and the Economic Community

of Central African States (ECCAS)—take in virtually every country in the region. Many countries in the Middle East and North Africa regions are members of the Gulf Cooperation Council (GCC), the Arab Customs Union (ACU), or both.

Although a CU is no longer the most popular option, it remains a central component of regional integration strategy in many developing regions. For many developing countries, the design and implementation of a CET, along with the elimination of intraregional trade barriers, continue to be key drivers of trade policy reform and to occupy an important place in policy debates. Given that customs duties constitute a significant source of government revenues in most of those countries, choosing the appropriate mechanism for collecting and allocating customs revenues is an important challenge for officials.

Economic Implications of Customs Unions

Chauffour and Maur (ch. 1 in this volume) discuss in detail the economic, societal, and political-economy motives for signing preferential trade agreements. A central issue is whether to opt for an FTA or a CU. By definition, both are preferential in nature and discriminate against third-party (nonmember) suppliers. The primary effect of a customs union, as with an FTA, is the expansion of trade flows among member countries, often at the expense of trade with nonmembers. This expansion, a consequence of the removal of the intraunion tariff barriers, can be decomposed into *trade creation* (more efficient suppliers in CU partners replace domestic suppliers of a given good) and *trade diversion* (more efficient third-party suppliers are displaced by less efficient suppliers located in partner countries, as a result of the discriminatory liberalization).[5] As is well established in the literature, when trade diversion dominates trade creation, CUs and FTAs tend to be welfare reducing (Viner 1950).[6] The likelihood of significant trade diversion is closely related to the degree of discrimination associated with the agreement (see Baldwin, ch. 3 in this volume).

Reasons for Choosing a Customs Union

There are many possible rationales for choosing a CU over an FTA, including political and economic ones. Some regional groupings consider the establishment of a CU a prerequisite for the future establishment of a political union, or at least some deeper form of economic integration, such as a common market.[7] The African Economic Community provides an illustration. The Abuja Treaty of 1991 envisaged gradual implementation in the following stages: (a) creation of regional blocs, by 1999; (b) strengthening of intrabloc integration and interbloc harmonization, by 2007; (c) establishment of an FTA and then a CU in each regional bloc, by 2017; (d) establishment of a continentwide customs union, by 2019; (e) realization of a continentwide African Common Market (ACM), by 2023; and (f) creation of a continentwide economic and monetary union (and thus also a currency union) and a parliament, by 2028.

Some groups, such as CARICOM, consider a CU to be a useful way of pooling market power, coordinating trade policies, and combining efforts to negotiate with the rest of the world. The more intense degrees of coordination and interaction associated with a CU can foster trust and familiarity among the parties and may even decrease the risk of conflicts, as has been the case with the European Union (EU). The fact that the external tariff is agreed with other parties through a legal agreement may help reform-minded governments lock in their trade policies and can shelter them from domestic lobbies.

On a lower level, a customs union can simply be a practical device for avoiding trade deflection while facilitating more fluid trade flows among member states. In the simplest form of an FTA, member countries grant free trade to each other but effectively maintain sovereignty over the conduct of trade policy vis-à-vis the rest of the world. Thus, the tariffs charged to nonmember suppliers will vary across members. This could lead to opportunities for trade deflection—a situation in which goods from outside the FTA are shipped to a low-tariff country and then transshipped tariff-free to the high-tariff country. Such roundabout shipping patterns, which have the sole purpose of exploiting the existing tariff differential, are inherently inefficient and can create friction among members.[8]

One way to avoid such wasteful trade deflection is for the members of the FTA to adopt a rules-of-origin system. Rules of origin can take various forms, but generally they require that goods (or value added) qualifying for tariff-free trade be produced within the FTA and that imports from outside the FTA pay the tariff of the final destination country, even if they pass through another member country (see Brenton, ch. 8 in this volume). In practice, rules of origin are particularly complex, and their implementation costs can be high.[9] They necessitate significant internal border controls to ensure compliance and to collect the relevant customs duties.

Another way to prevent trade deflection is to establish a customs union, which would require all members to apply the same external tariff to imports coming from outside the union. Because of the common external tariff (i.e., the absence of tariff differentials across members), the potential for trade deflection and the need for intraunion border inspections are, theoretically, minimized. In a fully implemented customs union, it is no longer necessary to maintain internal border controls for customs duty purposes or to design and implement the cumbersome and costly rules of origin that are necessary in a free trade area in which members have different external tariff structures.[10] The simplification offered by a CU can greatly facilitate cross-border trade, which is especially relevant because existing CUs generally involve geographically contiguous countries, reflecting the traditional objective of regional integration.[11] In this regard, a CU can approximate a larger single market (as compared with a number of separate markets in an FTA), which can generate greater economies of scale, as well as procompetitive pressures. These, in turn, can greatly benefit consumers and can translate into lower business costs and enhanced competitiveness for member countries.

Economic Implications of the Common External Tariff

As was mentioned earlier, the key difference between a CU and an FTA is the need to adjust the tariff structure applied to third-party suppliers, at least for some members. Countries that join an FTA are not required to change the tariffs they apply to imports from the rest of the world.[12] What will differentiate the effects of a CU from those of an FTA will be the extent to which the external tariff is increased or decreased by a given member with respect to a given good. The net economic effect of a CU crucially depends on how the adjustment of the external tariff affects the degree of discrimination vis-à-vis nonmember countries.

In order to isolate the impact of a CU, it is useful to start with a case in which an FTA is already in place (i.e., trade is already liberalized among the partners) and member countries are considering establishing a customs union by harmonizing their external tariff duties.[13] For ease of presentation, the following discussion assumes that two countries, A and B, are members of an FTA and have decided to form a customs union. Without loss of generality, it will be further assumed that, for a particular good, A has a low tariff and B has a high one. Two possible cases are relevant and are examined here.

One possibility is that the agreed common external tariff (CET) leads to a higher tariff rate for a given CU member (say, country A). The bloc's degree of discrimination is thus enhanced, and the negative impact of trade diversion caused by the FTA is exacerbated. This usually happens when a less advanced member has to implement a CET aimed at protecting the industries of a more developed member.[14] In this case, consumers in country A will lose because they have to pay higher prices for imports from the rest of the world or switch to less efficient suppliers from country B. Despite the higher external tariff, the government in country A could collect less tariff revenues if the higher degree of discrimination leads to a greater propensity for switching the sourcing of imports to duty-free, country B suppliers. Producers of the good in A face less competition from the rest of the world but more competition from B. In fact, the adoption of a high tariff by A effectively extends the protection received by country B producers to country A's markets. These producers may be the only ones to gain from the CU in this scenario. In some cases, and in a more dynamic setting, the expansion of the protected market may lead to some tariff-jumping types of investment in the customs union, motivated by the prospect of taking advantage of the larger, more protected market.

Joining a CU may offer a second possibility to consolidate the existing tariff schedule and adopt a more liberal trade regime. If the establishment of the CU yields a CET that is lower than the pre-CU tariff (say, in country B), the potential for trade diversion is reduced, or even reversed, because there is less potential for switching suppliers. The

discriminatory aspect of the FTA is, in a sense, diluted in this case. Starting from an FTA situation, a decrease in B's external tariff would have two effects, both working in the same direction. First, the liberalization will directly increase B's imports from the rest of the world (trade creation). Second, since it effectively dilutes the existing preference margin, it will reduce the attractiveness of sourcing from country A relative to sourcing from the rest of the world (less trade diversion). By reversing the trade diversion caused by the FTA (i.e., by inducing consumers to switch from less efficient suppliers in A to more efficient ones in the rest of the world), country B's tariff reduction will benefit its consumers. It could also help increase government revenues. as dutiable imports from the rest of the world expand (albeit at lower tariffs) and as country B shifts to dutiable imports and away from duty-free imports from A. Domestic producers will face more competition from nonmembers, but this will be offset by consumer gains resulting from lower prices and, potentially, by higher tariff revenues. Although adopting a lower CET may not lead to tariff-jumping investment, the higher returns associated with the more liberal economic environment could attract efficiency-seeking investments. Krueger (1995) has argued that if the CET level is chosen as the union's average tariff for a given commodity, an FTA will not lead to more net trade creation than a CU. Furthermore, as long as the CET is set below the tariff level of the high-cost country, an FTA will not be more welfare enhancing than a CU.

In the actual implementation of a CET, an individual CU member will generally have to increase its external tariffs on certain products while decreasing them on others. The overall impact will depend on the balance. Kemp and Wan (1976) demonstrate the existence of conditions that suffice to ensure that a CU is welfare enhancing. In particular, they show that if the CET is chosen so that trade with the rest of the world is kept unchanged, then following the establishment of a CU, welfare could potentially increase for all parties, including nonmembers, contingent on compensatory transfers. This increase occurs because any additional trade between CU members would be welfare-enhancing trade creation. Although this is an important result, it is a "possibility" and does not guarantee that the existing political-economy equilibrium will be a welfare-enhancing one.[15]

Factors Driving the Design and Level of the Common External Tariff

A well-designed and generally accepted CET is crucial for the sustainability of a customs union.[16] National tariffs must be harmonized at some agreed level, taking into account not only the often-conflicting positions of each member but also the various special interests within each member. Setting the level of the CET in a consensual manner could be a complex undertaking, entailing long and involved negotiations between member country governments, which are themselves subject to lobbying by different interest groups. For instance, it took the EU 11 years (1957 to 1968) to complete its CET, and Mercosur members took four years just to agree on their nonagricultural CET.

In many developing-country customs unions, the difficulties of agreeing on a common external tariff and on the distribution of revenues have proved to be so great that the resulting tariff schedules tend to include numerous country or sector-specific exceptions and sensitive lists. Although the CARICOM CET is largely in place, it allows broad scope for tariff reductions and suspensions, as well as for national derogations. The CET in Mercosur does not cover all sectors, and it includes special regimes for the automotive and sugar sectors.[17] In some CUs, temporary national exemptions are allowed—for example, EAC members Kenya and Tanzania were allowed to unilaterally reduce tariffs on selected grain imports. Derogations and safeguards are widely used in most CUs. Not only can these exceptions reduce the transparency and effectiveness of the CU, but they also can complicate trade negotiations and increase transaction costs. Furthermore, they reintroduce the potential for trade deflection—the very phenomenon that the CU is designed to prevent.

Like most other forms of regional integration agreements, a CU is inherently preferential and is, thus, discriminatory against third parties. As argued in the previous section, the economic impact of a CU will be closely related to the degree of discrimination, which depends on the CET level that is selected. The higher the CET, the more trade diversionary will the union be. An important question is thus whether a CU provides incentives for selecting higher or lower external tariffs than those in, say, an FTA.[18] The existing theoretical and empirical literature does not provide an unequivocal answer to this question. The result seems to depend on the way preferences (or objective functions) are aggregated across members and within each member.

A number of analysts have demonstrated that an FTA may create downward pressure on external tariffs. (See, for example, Richardson 1993; Bagwell and Staiger 1999; Freund 2000.) For instance, Baldwin and Freund (ch. 6 in this volume) argue that preferential trade liberalization in an FTA tends to make tariffs against nonmembers' third-nation tariffs more distortionary and that it creates an incentive for FTA members to reoptimize their most

favored nation (MFN) tariffs by making them more uniform and lower. (This is referred to as the "uniform tax rate principle.") In a related fashion, if trade diversion becomes apparent (i.e., if a country sees itself importing a good from a partner country at a higher cost than the cost of similar goods from nonmembers), an FTA member has the flexibility to cut tariffs on these third-party imports.[19] Similarly, the potential for trade deflection may lead high-tariff countries to cut tariffs to just below the level of their partners' rates to prevent imports from going through low-tariff countries that would otherwise capture the tariff revenue. In addition, lowering import tariffs on inputs used in producing exports to other FTA members can render exporters more competitive.[20] Do these arguments apply to CUs?

An often-stated objective of most customs unions among developing countries is to promote a harmonized reduction in internal and external trade barriers in order to better integrate the region into the multilateral trading system. There are, however, arguments that seem to suggest that CUs create pressures for more protectionism. Like other integration initiatives, CUs permit member countries to combine their market size and thereby increase their market power. Since trade policy is set jointly, this measure could strengthen their incentive to adopt high CETs in order to improve their terms of trade.[21] That is, they can reduce global demand for an imported product, and thereby decrease the import price, by charging higher tariffs. The larger the size of the union, the stronger this proprotectionist effect will be.

Furthermore, if CU members negotiate effectively as a bloc, they can pool their negotiating power and enhance it against the rest of the world, thus affecting the outcome of negotiations. Given the mercantilist nature of trade negotiations, increased negotiating power is likely to lead to a more protectionist outcome (in exchange for better market access). It could also be argued that nonmembers will act in a more conciliatory way when negotiating with a (single, large) customs union than with separate FTA members, and the result will be smaller requests for concessions.

The internal process of decision making within the CU could also place upward pressure on tariffs. The joint, consensual determination of the external tariffs may provide incentives to agree on higher CETs, since these imply higher preference margins and benefit partners' firms. (Protection is afforded to all producers in all CU member countries.) CU members will internalize this fact and will choose a higher external tariff (Freund and Ornelas 2010). Accordingly, one can think of a situation in which each CU member feels strongly about protecting a particular sector but would like lower tariffs on the other sectors. As

Winters (1996) argues, this may create a prisoner's-dilemma outcome under which the CET would provide high protection in all sectors, even though each country would be better off with low protection in all sectors.[22]

The establishment of a CU also changes the power of lobbies, but it is not clear whether the result will be stronger or weaker demand for protection. It is possible that lobbying pressure within a CU may be diluted, compared with national lobbying for protection within an FTA. As Winters (1996) suggests, it is more costly to lobby for a tariff increase in a CU than in an individual FTA member country because there may be more opposition to overcome or more representatives to influence. Moreover, the returns to lobbying activities are less under a CU, given that an extra 1 percent tariff protection becomes available to all members. Panagariya and Findlay (1996) provide a formal treatment of the argument that a customs union is a more effective instrument for diluting the power of interest groups than is an FTA. The high cost and low returns of lobbying under a CU could lead to a free-rider problem in lobbying, and all lobbying could end up taking place in one country. The author finds that such a process would yield a lower (common) external tariff under a CU than under an FTA. The larger the size of the customs union, the lower the resulting (lobbied) level of common external tariff would be.

The argument could, of course, cut in the other direction. In some sectors, lobbyists in different member countries may be able to overcome the free-rider problem, pool their resources, and cooperate. This is likely to happen in sectors in which they produce relatively similar goods (say, in agriculture) and where there is little intra-bloc trade flow. In this case, the national lobbies would be able to organize themselves into a regional lobby, and the resulting common external tariff would be higher in a CU relative to what would prevail in the individual markets under an FTA.

The degree of "permanence" of the policy outcomes will also affect the incentives for, and the amount of, lobbying. An FTA does not require member countries to immediately adjust their external tariffs, and it preserves discretion for a country to adjust its trade policy in the future. By contrast, a CU requires both tariff adjustments and a relatively longer-term commitment to the trade policy jointly agreed on by the CU members—the CET. It is therefore likely that lobbying for protection would be stronger during the negotiation and establishment of a CU than in the case of an FTA. Also, the difficulties in renegotiating or readjusting the CET could lead to the emergence of less transparent nontariff barriers that would be implemented at the national (instead of the regional) level.

Overall, whether opting for a CU leads to higher external tariffs remains an open question. A number of arguments seem to suggest that CUs may provide more protectionist pressures than FTAs. This, however, remains an empirical question to which the existing literature has not been able to provide an unequivocal answer.

Allocation and Collection of CET Revenue

For most CUs among developing economies, the potential for losses of tariff revenues constitutes an important negotiation issue. These losses may result from the liberalization of intraunion tariffs, from the adoption of the common tariff schedule, or from changes in trade patterns. Given the significance of tariff revenue for most developing countries, at least two issues need to be addressed when establishing a customs union: (a) Who has a claim on the collected customs duties? (b) Where and how should those duties be collected?

Ownership of the Collected Duties

The use or allocation of the collected duties is an important consideration. Should the customs revenues collected be treated as community property, or as income accruing to each member state? Generally, it is necessary to establish a regional, supranational institution or a secretariat to ensure smooth operations of the union. Although such an institution could be funded through direct contributions from members—for example, WAEMU provides for an additional tax of 1 percent on imports— treating customs revenues as the collective property of the union may be a more useful financing mechanism. In some cases, such as the EU, the union may decide to allocate (a fraction of) these revenues to a joint fund to finance regional development initiatives or to provide support to poorer CU members.[23] Of course, pooling customs revenues necessitates a high level of coordinating capacity and a certain degree of trust among members. This arrangement seems more likely to be sustainable when tariff revenues do not constitute an important part of government revenue for individual members—as is the case in the EU, but usually not for developing economies.

In other cases, CUs treat customs revenues as the property of individual members. Collected duties are allocated either according to the final destination or in line with an agreed sharing formula. Such a formula could provide for a simple reallocation based on negotiated and fixed shares, or it could involve a more complex range of economic and demographic variables. SACU, for instance, has a fairly complicated revenue-sharing system in which the share accruing to each member is calculated from three basic components: a customs pool, an excise pool, and a development component. The customs pool is allocated according to each country's share of total intra-SACU trade, including reexports. The excise component is allocated on the basis of gross domestic product (GDP). The development component (fixed at 15 percent of the total excise pool) is distributed to all SACU members according to each country's per capita GDP; that is, countries with lower per capita income will receive more (WTO 2003).

Most existing customs unions allocate revenues according to the final-destination principle. This method, although apparently simple in theory, requires a mechanism for identifying the final destination of each shipment entering the union; the destination country would then claim the appropriate duty amount. One way to handle this procedure is to keep the imported shipment in bonded facilities until it reaches the country of ultimate consumption. This may work for whole shipments of final goods that are entirely consumed in the destination country, but it may not be the appropriate mechanism for an imported shipment that undergoes transformation in an intermediate country before reaching its final destination. Indeed, incentives could emerge for some members to collect revenues on imports that are then wholly transshipped or minimally "transformed" or "repackaged" before being exported duty-free elsewhere in the CU. In such cases, burdensome internal border controls, guarantee mechanisms, or even some rules of origin are needed within the CU to determine what fraction of the collected duties should go to which member. This could be an important issue for small landlocked economies that rely on their larger coastal neighbors for transit and that could lose revenues as a result of leakages or fraud. When trade flows are sufficiently symmetrical, a member's losses could be offset by the gains it realizes when goods imported into its territory (for which it collects the tariff) are consumed in a neighbor's.[24]

Collection of Duties

At what point should customs duties be collected—at the initial port of entry into the CU or at the final import destination? Collecting import duties at the first port of entry into the CU (say, in the coastal member with the more developed port and transit facilities) could be one way of ensuring freer movement of goods within the CU and minimizing intra-CU border controls.[25] Indeed, if all trade taxes were collected at the point of first entry and administered or distributed centrally, member countries

would not need to monitor the passage across their borders of goods originating outside the CU for duty collection purposes.[26] This method would greatly enhance efficiency by reducing transaction costs at internal border posts, but it requires the existence of the appropriate institutional capacity to administer the revenues and, most important, a high level of trust among members. Both of these measures tend to be harder to achieve as the number and diversity of member states increase. The mechanism is more likely to be sustainable if customs duties are deemed to be community property of the CU and are used for collectively determined community purposes, or if members can devise a mechanism for identifying imports according to their final destinations.[27] A potential issue is the possibility of some diversion in revenue collections (and even economic activity) away from landlocked and less developed countries and toward the more developed trading hubs in the region.

Alternatively, customs duties could be collected at the final destination or the final consumption point.[28] Although conceptually straightforward, this type of agreement can be complex to implement and can be very costly. In fact, to be workable, it requires that significant border controls remain or that goods be shipped in some sort of transit and bonding facility all the way to the final destination, where duties would be collected.[29] Not only would the logistical costs of running such facilities be substantial, but they would also tend to diminish some of the expected gains from establishing a CU. For instance, they could discourage the establishment of regional value chains or processing chains (using imported inputs) or the generation of retail and wholesale services in intermediate locations between the initial port of entry and the final destination.

It is clear from the foregoing discussion that the collection and allocation of customs revenue in a customs union setting are not only technical issues, but also (perhaps more important) a question of trust. Good technical coordination and enforcement generally promote trust among CU members. Conversely, lack of trust would require more stringent and cumbersome controls on intrabloc transit and stricter application of the agreed disposition of revenue. This is clearly an area in which harmonization of border management (customs procedures), cooperation, modernization, and capacity building could be very useful (see Keick and Maur 2011; Dawar and Holmes, ch. 16 in this volume).

Conclusions

The conceptual discussions in this chapter demonstrate that CUs generally require a much greater degree of policy coordination among members than do FTAs. This is because they require member countries to agree to a common external tariff and to set up institutional mechanisms to collect and distribute the tariff revenue. When a country joins a customs union, it agrees to relinquish some of its national sovereignty with respect to the formulation and implementation of trade policy. The fact that a country is willing to surrender such autonomy over trade policy suggests that it considers this loss to be more than offset by the economic benefits of securing access to a larger and more harmonized regional market and of enhancing the depth and effectiveness of the ongoing regional integration. The loss of autonomy may also be acceptable to members because in most cases, CUs are driven by objectives that go beyond trade, such as economic and monetary unions or even political integration, and that require supranational institutions.

Ceding the control of some aspects of national trade policy may yield economic benefits, to the extent that it shelters the trade policy–making process from the influence of special interests, at least at the national level. Committing to a regionally agreed trade policy regime can serve as an effective lock-in mechanism for trade reform efforts and can send a strong signal to investors regarding the predictability of the policy environment.[30] In some cases, it may be more practical for a country to delegate the conduct of trade policy to another (larger) CU member or to a supranational agency. In others, a larger member country can impose its own trade policy or tariff structure on that of the union. In this case, there may be grounds for establishing a regional mechanism, such as a development fund, to compensate other member countries for adopting a tariff structure that is not inherently in their own economic interests.

It should be noted that the loss of autonomy implied by a CU also covers certain aspects of national trade policies, going beyond external tariffs. For instance, whereas FTA members retain full flexibility with regard to future PTA partners, CU members may be limited in their individual choices for future partners Indeed, membership in a CU, at least in principle, prevents an individual member from acting individually, since any agreement with a third party or any change to the CET needs to be decided by the CU as a whole. It can be argued that CUs could help prevent the emergence of a hub-and-spokes trading pattern (see the discussion in Baldwin and Freund, ch. 6 in this volume).

In a world of criss-crossing and overlapping trade agreements, the issue of the loss of autonomy can severely constrain members of CUs in using trade agreements as an effective commercial instrument—at least in theory. In the current wave of regionalism, in which flexibility and speed are valued, membership in a CU, if played by the rules, could constitute a straitjacket for some countries.

In reality, of course, there are numerous cases in which a CU member alone negotiates an FTA with a third party. Examples of such a situation include the FTAs between the EU and South Africa (a member of SACU) and between the United States and Bahrain (a member of the GCC). Similarly, Bolivia, Colombia, Ecuador, Peru, and the República Bolivariana de Venezuela form the Andean Pact (a CU), while Colombia and the República Bolivariana de Venezuela have joined with Mexico to make up the Group of Three, an FTA. In some instances, one CU may overlap another. For example, Lesotho, Namibia, and Swaziland belong to COMESA while also belonging to SACU, and Tanzania is a member of both the SADC and the EAC. Multiple and overlapping memberships in regional trade agreements can create difficulties because different groups can have conflicting operational or liberalization modalities, and so member countries will have to make different, incompatible commitments. This not only could render CUs less effective but could also confuse traders (and even customs officers) as to which commitments or tariff schedules apply to a particular shipment. Unnecessary transaction costs will be created because traders are obliged to find their way around a number of trade regimes with different tariff schedules, different rules of origin, and different procedures.

Notes

The author thanks Jean-Christophe Maur and anonymous reviewers for their helpful comments and suggestions.

1. GATT Article XXIV:8(a) defines a customs union as a single customs territory substituting for two or more customs territories and having two characteristics: (a) duties are eliminated on substantially all trade between the constituent territories, and (b) substantially the same duties are applied by each member to trade with nonmembers.

2. Historically, the early academic literature on regional integration tended to focus on customs unions; classic works are Viner's *The Customs Union Issue* (1950) and Meade's *The Theory of Customs Unions* (1955).

3. Fiorentino, Verdeja, and Toqueboeuf (2007) suggest that CUs are "out of tune with today's trading climate."

4. In some cases, PTAs are driven by narrow foreign policy or diplomatic considerations.

5. In practice, tariff liberalization could be accompanied or complemented by a rationalization of border management policies. See Keick and Maur (2010) for a thorough survey of the border management issues facing CUs.

6. Interestingly, although the seminal work by Viner (1950) focused on CUs, the analysis studied the removal of the intrabloc tariff while assuming that other policies (e.g., external tariffs) remained constant. Thus, it was more a study of FTAs than of CUs.

7. In the traditional literature on regionalism, the degrees of economic integration correspond to different stages: preferential trading area, free trade area, customs union, single market, economic and monetary union, and complete economic integration. These stages were generally thought to be a progression, with political union as the ultimate

objective. Nowadays, this progression seems a bit outdated, as many existing FTAs have no ambition to move to the next stage.

8. This situation effectively reduces the tariff of every FTA member to that of the lowest (plus the transport cost involved in roundabout importing).

9. Given that rules of origin have to take into account tariffs on imported intermediate goods used in the products manufactured within the FTA, as well as the extent of value addition, they tend to be complex to administer. Rules of origins also raise other issues; they can, for instance, create incentives for regional buyers to purchase high-cost inputs from partner countries, thus exacerbating trade diversion, and they can be captured by interests that favor protection in the form of stringent requirements. Robson (1998) argues that even with rules of origin, the problem of trade deflection is not entirely solved, as the low-tariff partner may meet its own requirements for a product from the rest of the world and can then export a corresponding amount of its own production to its partners.

10. The implementation of a customs union does not necessarily mean the abolition of border posts. These facilities serve many other (trade-related or nontrade-related) purposes, including collecting other taxes, controlling the movement of persons, and enforcing compliance with domestic standards and health and safety requirements.

11. The contiguous pattern of CU formation contrasts with the proliferation of cross-regional PTAs that characterizes the current wave of regionalism.

12. Although PTA members are not required to change their external tariffs, there may be strong political-economy pressures or incentives for adjusting them after the removal of intrabloc tariffs. See Winters (1996) and Freund and Ornelas (2010) for useful reviews of the literature on this topic.

13. This method is of course a simplification. In many CUs, many transitional tariffs and not-so-transitional nontariff barriers on intrabloc trade remain. Even the EU only removed the last physical, technical, and tax-related obstacles to intraunion trade in 1993, 36 years after the community was founded. The free trade area component of the East African Community (EAC) completely abolished tariffs on trade between Tanzania and Uganda and on exports from these two countries to Kenya. Many goods exported from Kenya to Tanzania or Uganda, however, continue to be subject to tariffs (Development Network Africa 2007). In Mercosur, there is not yet free internal trade in sugar, and most favored nation tariffs are applied with a 20 percent preference for intrazone trade.

14. In Mercosur, for instance, the smaller economies (Paraguay and Uruguay) preferred a CET structure with low tariffs, whereas Argentina and Brazil successfully pressed for higher rates.

15. As Hoekman argues in chapter 4 of this volume, real-world PTAs do not select their CETs in a Kemp-Wan manner, nor do they have access to large compensatory or lump-sum transfers.

16. A poorly designed CET can create divisive tensions among CU members. Adams (1993) provides an interesting example of how external tariffs triggered conflicts between the North and the South in the antebellum United States.

17. Mercosur allows members to temporarily deviate from CET rates under specific conditions and with some limitations. Following the peso crisis, Argentina raised tariffs to 35 percent on numerous consumer goods and cut the tariff on capital goods to zero.

18. Note that CETs are, in principle, subject to multilateral rules. GATT Article XXIV:5(a) stipulates that the duties (in this case, the CET) and other trade regulations imposed on trade of nonmembers shall not, on the whole, be higher or more restrictive than the general incidence of duties and other trade regulations applicable in the participants prior to the formation of the CU. Under the usual interpretation, this implies that the common tariff of a CU should not be higher than the preunion average.

19. Bohara, Gawande, and Sanguinetti (2004) provide some empirical evidence for this argument in the context of Argentina's external tariffs under Mercosur.

20. Winters (1996) suggests that Canada's decision to reduce 1,500 tariffs on inputs shortly after the initiation of the North American Free Trade Agreement was driven by this consideration.

21. This possibility is demonstrated, for instance, by Kennan and Riezman (1990) and by Krugman (1990).

22. This situation is illustrated by the disproportionate influence of EU members on policy in sectors in which they claim "vital interests." Other members strategically and willingly accommodate, in anticipation that the favor will be returned when their own "vital interests" come up.

23. It should be noted that in the case of the EU, tariff revenues constitute a small portion of government revenue, which is why EU members are more willing to forgo them and cede them to the commission.

24. On a related note, Dawar and Holmes (ch. 16 in this volume) argue that CUs provide incentives for stronger regional cooperation in the area of trade facilitation. Indeed, there is a need for harmonization of the quality of border enforcement across CU members to ensure that the weaknesses of one member do not undermine the tax collections of other members (since imports may be diverted to the border where enforcement is weakest).

25. In SACU, for instance, most customs duties are collected by South Africa, the dominant economy and trading hub of the bloc.

26. In this context, it should be noted, again, that in addition to import duties, other taxes may be collected by customs at the border and that the establishment of a CU does not mean abolition of all border controls. Keick and Maur (2010) discuss the issues related to border management in the context of CUs.

27. Of course, no existing customs union allocates tariff revenues according to where imports first enter the union. The EU allows member states to keep 10 percent of the tariffs they collect.

28. Conceptually, setting up a CU among countries that have already established an FTA among themselves does not necessarily require any changes in the procedure for collecting customs duties. In most cases, duties are collected on a destination basis before and after the establishment of a customs union.

29. Some customs unions allow for members to establish customs facilities in the territories of other member states in order to collect the customs that are due to them at the first point of entry. In practice, duties paid on imports from the rest of the world could still be collected by the country of final destination.

30. This argument is generally true for international trade agreements, whether bilateral, regional, or global. The need for agreeing on the CET makes it stronger in the case of customs unions.

References

Adams, Charles. 1993. *For Good and Evil: The Impact of Taxes on the Course of Civilization.* Lanham, MD: Madison Books.

Bagwell, Kyle, and Robert Staiger. 1999. "Regionalism and Multilateral Tariff Cooperation." In *International Trade Policy and the Pacific Rim*, ed. John Piggott and Alan Woodland. London: Macmillan.

Bohara, Alok K., Kishore Gawande, and Pablo Sanguinetti. 2004. "Trade Diversion and Declining Tariffs: Evidence from Mercosur." *Journal of International Economics* 64 (1, October): 65–88.

Development Network Africa. 2007. "Evaluation of an Appropriate Model for a SADC Customs Union." Report commissioned by the SADC Secretariat, Southern African Development Community, Gaborone.

Fiorentino, Robert, Luis Verdeja, and Christelle Toqueboeuf. 2007. "The Changing Landscape of Regional Trade Agreements: 2006 Update." WTO Discussion Paper 12, World Trade Organization, Geneva.

Freund, Caroline. 2000. "Different Paths to Free Trade: The Gains from Regionalism." *Quarterly Journal of Economics* 115 (4): 1317–41.

Freund, Caroline, and Emanuel Ornelas. 2010. "Regional Trade Agreements." Policy Research Working Paper 5314, World Bank, Washington,

DC. http://www-wds.worldbank.org/external/default/WDSContent Server/IW3P/IB/2010/05/19/000158349_20100519101328/Rendered/PDF/WPS5314.pdf.

Keick, Erich, and Jean-Christophe Maur. 2010. "Regional Integration and Customs Unions." World Bank, Washington, DC.

Kemp, Murray C., and Henry Y. Wan, Jr. 1976. "An Elementary Proposition Concerning the Formation of Customs Unions." *Journal of International Economics* 6 (1, February): 95–98.

Kennan, John, and Raymond Riezman. 1990. "Optimal Tariff Equilibria with Customs Unions." *Canadian Journal of Economics* 23: 70–83.

Krueger, Anne O. 1995. "Free Trade Agreements versus Customs Unions." NBER Working Paper 5084, National Bureau of Economic Research, Cambridge, MA.

Krugman, Paul. 1990. "Is Bilateralism Bad?" In *International Trade and Policy*, ed. Elhanan Helpman and Assaf Razin. Cambridge, MA: MIT Press.

Meade, James. 1955. *The Theory of Customs Unions*. Amsterdam: North-Holland.

Panagariya, Arvind, and Ronald Findlay. 1996. "A Political Economy Analysis of Free Trade Areas and Customs Unions." In *The Political Economy of Trade Reform: Essays in Honor of Jagdish Bhagwati*, ed. Robert C. Feenstra, Gene M. Grossman, and Douglas A. Irwin. Cambridge, MA: MIT Press.

Richardson, Martin. 1993. "Endogenous Protection and Trade Diversion." *Journal of International Economics* 34 (3–4, May): 309–24.

Robson, Peter. 1998. *The Economics of International Integration*. 4th ed. London: Routledge.

Viner, Jacob. 1950. *The Customs Union Issue*. New York: Carnegie Endowment for International Peace.

Winters, L. Alan. 1996. "Regionalism versus Multilateralism." Policy Research Working Paper 1687, World Bank, Washington, DC. http://www-wds.worldbank.org/external/default/WDSContentServer/IW3P/IB/1996/11/01/000009265_3970311114958/Rendered/PDF/multi0page.pdf.

WTO (World Trade Organization). 2003. "Trade Policy Review: Southern African Customs Union." Press release, April 25. WTO, Geneva. http://www.wto.org/english/tratop_e/tpr_e/tp213_e.htm.

6

PREFERENTIAL TRADE AGREEMENTS AND MULTILATERAL LIBERALIZATION

Richard Baldwin and Caroline Freund

With the Doha Round of trade negotiations ailing, the future of multilateral liberalization in the near term looks bleak. By contrast, preferential trade agreements (PTAs) continue to multiply (see Acharya et al., ch. 2 in this volume), making regionalism the most active mode of trade liberalization. The regionalization of trade is of serious concern to many international economists who view multilateralism as far superior to regionalism for improving welfare. At issue is the preferential nature of regional agreements, which could divert trade and reduce the potential for future multilateral liberalization.

The multilateralists argue that, although regionalism may increase trade, its effects on welfare and on the world trade system are likely to be harmful. There are two main concerns.[1] The first is trade diversion: preferential trade agreements, by diverting trade away from the most efficient global producers in favor of regional partners, may prove welfare reducing. The second concern, which is of greater importance, is that regionalism may hinder multilateralism, leading to a bad equilibrium in which several regional trade blocs maintain high external trade barriers. Regionalism can also undermine multilateralism simply by diverting limited government resources from multilateral negotiations.

These two concerns are related: in a highly regionalized world, there is likely to be significant trade diversion and hence lower welfare. Still, this feature of the bad equilibrium makes it less likely in practice. It is precisely because the trade diversion is costly to bloc members that there is an incentive to reduce external tariffs. As tariffs fall, trade diversion disappears, and regionalism becomes a force for general liberalization. Thus, despite the potential for a grim

outcome from high-tariff regional blocs and for large amounts of trade diversion, the theoretical literature shows that incentives to reduce external trade barriers so as to limit costly diversion are likely to be present.[2] The nascent empirical literature is tackling the question of how trade liberalization has been affected by the formation of PTAs. Although the verdict is not yet in, the evidence indicates that regionalism is broadly liberalizing.

This chapter summarizes the available theoretical and empirical evidence on the relationship between regionalism and multilateralism, with the aim of discerning whether the spread of regionalism is likely to be a threat to, or an opportunity for, broader trade liberalization. The next section identifies the distortions that generate a need for regional and multilateral trade agreements. There follows an overview of the available theoretical work on whether regionalism constitutes a stumbling block or a building block on the path to trade liberalization. The effect of regionalism on world welfare is then examined, the empirical literature is surveyed, and conclusions are drawn.

Reciprocal Trade Agreements

If there is one thing economists agree on, it is that free trade is best. Why, then, do we need trade agreements to lower tariffs? In fact, although global free trade may be good for world welfare, countries nevertheless have reasons to maintain tariffs. There ensues a prisoner's dilemma: each country may be unilaterally better off with a tariff, but jointly they are worse off. Cooperation through a trade agreement is necessary to liberalize trade.

Countries have tariffs for three main reasons. First, terms-of-trade considerations may induce a country to use tariffs to drive down the price of its imports relative to the price of its exports, thus raising welfare for the nation as a whole. For example, suppose a large country exports wine and imports cheese. By placing a tariff on imported cheese, the country increases domestic demand for wine relative to cheese, and if the country is large enough, this practice raises the world price of wine relative to cheese. If both the importing and the exporting country impose tariffs, however, the relative world prices of wine and cheese remain roughly unchanged, leaving consumers in both countries worse off because domestic prices are distorted. Consumers in both countries are consuming more of the domestic good than is ideal (given world prices), terms-of-trade gains do not materialize, and world welfare is reduced.

Second, there may be political constraints. Tariffs can be used as an internal redistribution tool by governments—typically to shift income to some favored industry, region, or group of voters or political contributors. For example, many economies tend to protect steel because production is commonly concentrated regionally and the workers and firm owners tend to be politically organized. This combination of political organization and geographic concentration often means that the sector's concerns may receive much greater weight in political decisions than would be suggested by its share of employment or output. Similarly, certain industries may receive special treatment if the owners of capital are connected to the government. Protection reduces consumer welfare, since consumers are forced to pay more than the world price, but governments cannot credibly commit to withholding protection of the special sectors.[3] In addition, protection may be in place because of historical reasons and can be politically difficult to remove because industry has adapted to it.

Third, countries, especially developing countries, may rely on tariffs for a share of the tax revenue they need to fund general government expenditures. Border transactions are an easy way to collect revenue when income tax systems are weak. This motive tends to be more important in developing countries, where other forms of revenue collection are difficult.

Reciprocal liberalization helps neutralize the first two forces described above: terms-of-trade motivations are neutralized, and joint welfare is higher because, with lower tariffs, consumption patterns are less distorted. Reciprocity in tariff cutting makes it easier to form a proliberalization coalition because the political strength of the domestic losses from tariff cutting can be balanced against the political strength of the exporters that gain from foreigners'

reciprocal tariff cutting. Moreover, once the agreement is in place, the reciprocity can help lock in the reform—can tie the government's hands, so to speak—in a way that helps governments resist special-interest pressures for protection. Even if domestic consumers do not object to new protection, the export interests of the foreign trade partner will.

The third reason for tariffs, revenue generation, is slightly different, as the government faces a loss of income with no offsetting added source of revenues if tariffs are reduced. Trade agreements with the World Trade Organization (WTO), or bilateral agreements with industrial countries, therefore often include provisions to help countries adjust to revenue loss.

Both the WTO and PTAs allow countries to cooperate and commit to reducing trade barriers, but there is an important distinction between the two types of agreements. In particular, PTAs go against the principle of nondiscrimination that is at the heart of the multilateral system. The first article of the General Agreement on Tariffs and Trade (GATT) concerns nondiscrimination, or most favored nation (MFN) treatment. MFN means that every time a country lowers a tariff, it has to offer the same treatment to all its trading partners. The purpose of this clause is to prevent trade diversion and the cumbersome tariff structure that would likely prevail in the absence of MFN.

By offering preferences to specific countries, PTAs definitively violate MFN treatment. Yet they are allowed, in part, because the MFN clause creates a free-rider problem. MFN means that countries in the WTO must offer the same tariff to all members. But if only a subset of members agrees on significant tariff reduction, other members can "free ride"—they get expanded market access without new commitments. If all members participated equally in MFN tariff reduction, PTAs might not be needed. PTAs enable countries that want to pursue deeper trade liberalization to evade the free-rider problem. Snape (1993) discusses the history of GATT Article XXIV, which allows for an exception to nondiscrimination, and argues that this article is vital for maintaining the multilateral club because some members might opt out if it were not included. (In particular, the United Kingdom, which was the largest importer at the time, insisted on keeping its Commonwealth preferences.) Summers (1991) asserts that all types of liberalization, whether unilateral, bilateral, or multilateral, are very likely to be good and that regionalism gives governments a way to maintain progress on liberalization.

This section has shown that reciprocal liberalization is usually necessary for removal of barriers to international trade. Although multilateral liberalization is preferable, regional liberalization is ubiquitous and cannot be ignored. The key question is whether this advancement of regionalism is broadly beneficial or detrimental to global trade and welfare (see box 6.1). In the next section, we discuss the recent rise of regional liberalization and how, in theory, it may affect the multilateral trade system.[4]

Stumbling Blocks and Building Blocks

From 1960 to the late 1980s, regionalism was a simple matter. It was represented by the European Economic Community (EEC), which encompassed a third of world trade in a highly effective customs union, and by a slew of PTAs among developing nations that covered a trivial fraction of world trade and in any case never operated effectively. The systemic implications of regionalism were simply not an issue.

Regionalism became complicated in the late 1980s when Canada and Mexico changed their minds about regionalism (Krugman 1991b, 7).[5] The United States had long been interested in regional preferential trade, but Canada and Mexico had resisted, fearing domination by their giant neighbor. In 1985, Canada proposed a free trade agreement (FTA) with the United States that entered into force in 1989. In 1990, Mexico, too, proposed an FTA with the United States. This initiative evolved into the North American Free Trade Agreement (NAFTA) at the insistence of Canada, which wished to safeguard its Auto Pact arrangement with the United States for tariff-free trade in automobiles and parts. The U.S.–Mexico initiative triggered a wave of Latin American requests for bilateral trade agreements with the United States and gave greater urgency to arrangements among Latin American

countries, most notably members of the Southern Cone Common Market (Mercosur, Mercado Común del Sur).[6]

The rise of North American regionalism coincided with two other major developments in the world trade system. First, GATT negotiations lurched from crisis to crisis in the late 1980s and then seemed to die with the acrimonious collapse of the Uruguay Round's "final" summit in December 1990. Second, European regionalism was reignited by the Single European Act and the collapse of the Soviet Union.

Many respected thinkers looked at this temporal correlation and saw causality. They feared that the spread of regionalism might kill the world trade system. These fears are easy to understand. Two-thirds of world imports went to North America and Europe; 40 percent of this total was intrabloc trade that was soon to be covered by discriminatory liberalization schemes. Still more worrisome, North American and European countries were the stalwarts of the GATT system. If regionalism weakened their support of multilateralism, the GATT was indeed in deep trouble. Spreading regionalism had become much more than a small-think "should I join?" question.

These fears promoted regionalism to a prominence on the world's policy agenda that it had not enjoyed since the 1950s. The shift naturally attracted paradigm-setting efforts by the profession's leading international economists.

Krugman (1991b) is clearest in rejecting the relevance of the 1950s small-think approach, which focused on static welfare issues and delineating the outlines of a new line of inquiry—what we call big-think regionalism:

> In a fundamental sense, the issue of the desirability of free trade areas is a question of political economy rather than of economics proper. While one could argue against the formation of free trade areas purely on the grounds that they might produce trade diversion . . . the real objection is a political judgment: fear that regional deals will undermine the delicate balance of interests that supports the GATT. (Krugman 1991b, 14–15)

Krugman's framing of what he identified as the key issue—the impact of regionalism on support for the GATT system—did not catch on, however.[7]

The focus of this part of the discussion is on what we consider to be the central theoretical question: does regionalism help or hinder multilateralism? Ultimately, this question is also empirical, but given the relative paucity of experience with the regionalism-multilateralism interface (only one multilateral trade negotiation has been completed since 1991), convincing empirics is at an early stage, with some tantalizing results just beginning to emerge (see "Welfare Consequences of PTAs," later in this

---

Box 6.1. Is Bilateralism Bad?

Paul Krugman, in a series of papers published in 1991, reframed the 1950s national welfare question as a global-level question. Krugman (1991a) introduced a new approach by asking whether the spread of regionalism raises or lowers world welfare. This discussion spawned a decade-long literature and continues to influence research even today. The "is bilateralism bad?" literature—also known as multilateralism versus regionalism literature—looks distinctly odd from today's perspective in that it tries to use simple theory to answer what is intrinsically a complicated empirical question. At the time, however, it was the best that economists could do; they had limited access to the necessary data and lacked the panel econometric techniques to exploit them. Moreover, spreading regionalism was at the time more of a threat than a reality, so there was little experience to support empirical tests. Baldwin (2009) offers a full discussion of the issue.

chapter). Moreover, given the complexity of the interlinkages, a clear theoretical understanding is a necessary condition for well-structured empirical work.

Are Regionalism and Multilateralism Friends or Foes?

Bhagwati, in *The World Trading System at Risk* (1991), does not focus on regionalism. In the first part of the book, "The GATT Architecture under Threat," he lists regionalism as one of four main threats. Nevertheless, his writing has helped establish big-think regionalism as the new paradigm. In the first paragraph of his chapter on regionalism, he writes, "These regional alignments have led to fears of fragmentation of the world economy into trading blocs in antithesis to GATT-wide multilateral free trade. Does such regionalism truly constitute a threat to multilateralism?" (Bhagwati 1991, 58). Although he does not set out an analytical framework for answering the question, his writing influenced the intellectual paradigm for more than a decade.

Theory requires explicit questions. Asking whether regionalism and multilateralism are friends or foes is not sufficient. Pure logic identifies three mutually compatible ways that regionalism and multilateralism could interact:

- Regionalism could affect multilateralism.
- Multilateralism could affect regionalism.
- Both multilateralism and regionalism could be driven by third factors.

The literature has looked at all three ways of framing the issue, but the first has dominated since Krugman (1991b, 1996) presented a simple analytical framework for posing the question. His explicit question was, How does an exogenous variation in regionalism (specifically, the formation of a new PTA) affect nations' incentives to cut tariffs multilaterally? Although most of the literature has followed Krugman's lead in asking how exogenous variations in regionalism affect multilateralism, authors have also discussed the specific effect of PTAs on multilateral trade negotiations (MTNs); the deeper forces driving PTAs and MTNs (Summers' notion that all the "isms" are good); and the effect of multilateralism on regionalism. These are discussed below.

Three Kinds of Stumbling Block Logic

In its cleanest form, the stumbling block logic asserts that if the stumbling block PTAs were forbidden, global free trade would be achieved, but that since they are permitted, global free trade becomes impossible. Weaker forms of this thesis

are put forward in the help-or-hinder literature (for example, PTAs may slow the achievement of global free trade), but the desire for clarity has led the profession to focus on the strong form.

In our opinion, only three forms of stumbling block logic are currently relevant to real-world policy analysis: the preference-erosion (exploitation), goodies-bag, and cherry-picking variants. (Many more will undoubtedly be illuminated in coming years.) For simplicity's sake, these possibilities are demonstrated under the naïve but transparent assumption that national governments choose tariffs to maximize national welfare.

Preference erosion, or exploitation. Starting from a world in which all nations have MFN tariffs, the question is whether some group of nations can raise its collective welfare above the free trade level by forming a trade bloc and thus exploiting other nations. If the answer is "yes," that bloc is a stumbling block on the road to multilateral free trade because the members would veto global free trade as undermining their exploitation of third nations.

In trade models, the answer is almost always "yes," but the answer may depend on the level of MFN tariffs when the bloc is formed.[8] Given Smith's certitude (briefly, that all parties to a preferential trade arrangement benefit) and Haberler's spillover (postulating that third nations must lose from such an arrangement), some combination of nations is bound to be better able to exploit third nations by acting as a bloc. This is almost trivially true if the bloc can violate its WTO tariff bindings by raising external tariffs. After all, the bloc as a whole has more buying power than its constituents do individually, so it can better exploit foreigners. Less obvious, but equally true, is that stumbling blocks can be found even when external tariffs are maintained (as has been the case for all the major postwar PTAs).

Consider the simple model presented in chapter 3 of this volume, with three symmetrical countries (Home, Partner, and Rest of the World, or RoW) and three goods. Home imports Good 1 and exports Good 2 to Partner; Partner imports Good 2 and exports Good 1 to Home; and Rest of the World exports Goods 1 and 2 to Home and Partner, respectively, and imports Good 3 from both (see figure 3.1, in ch. 3). The first welfare theorem tells us that global free trade is efficiency enhancing (a move to the first best), and symmetry ensures that each nation receives an equal slice of the gains.

This conclusion, however, can be reversed when we start from the situation in which Home and Partner have formed a PTA by eliminating tariffs among them. Taking the PTA as the base case, a move to global free trade eliminates the preference margin ($P' - P^{FT}$) that Home exporters

Figure 6.1. Net Welfare Effects, Preferential Trade Agreement to Global Free Trade

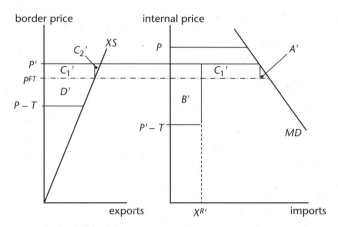

Source: Author's elaboration.

Figure 6.2. Relationship between MFN Tariffs and Home Welfare

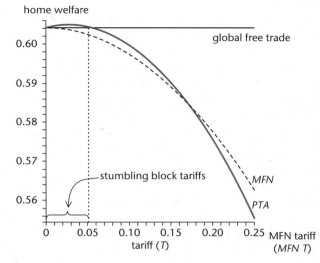

Source: Author's elaboration.
Note: Home welfare is plotted against the most favored nation (MFN) tariff for three trade regimes: *MFN* (all nations impose the same MFN tariff T on all goods); *PTA* (Home and Partner form a preferential trade agreement, PTA); and global free trade, which is the MFN regime with $T = 0$. The parameters chosen are $a = 1$, $b = 1/2$; the qualitative results are unaltered for other choices of parameters. Note that $T = 1/4$ is the prohibitive tariff with $a = 1$, $b = 1/2$. In ad valorem terms, the Viner crossing occurs at a tariff of about 27 percent of the free trade price, and the ad valorem tariff threshold for a stumbling block occurs at about 9 percent; the prohibitive tariff is about 42 percent for these parameter values.

enjoyed in Partner, thereby leading to a terms-of-trade loss of area $C_1{}'$ and a trade-volume loss of $C_2{}'$ (figure 6.1, left-hand panel).

On the import side, because of lower internal prices, from P' to P^{FT}, global free trade would win Home an additional trade volume gain of area A', a terms-of-trade improvement with respect to Partner exporters of area $C_1{}'$, and a terms-of-trade loss on imports from RoW, shown as area B' (right-hand panel). Global free trade would also improve Home exporters' market access to RoW, and this would boost Home welfare by area D'. Overall, the net welfare change of moving from the PTA to global free trade is $-C_2{}' - B' + D' + A'$; the sign of this is ambiguous.

It is straightforward to show that, in a simple model with linear demand, a low MFN tariff and a PTA with zero internal tariffs generate gains for the trade partners that exceed those from free trade. (This is shown in figure 3.2, in ch. 3; see Baldwin 2009, box 4, for further details of the model.) Figure 6.2 presents the Home welfare levels for different values of the MFN tariff.

For initial MFN tariff levels that are sufficiently low, we see that Home's welfare is higher with the PTA than it is with global free trade, even though Home would have agreed to global free trade starting from the initial situation without the PTA. (The line marked *MFN* is completely below the line marked "global free trade," but the *PTA* line is above the global free trade line for sufficiently low tariffs.)

Intuitively, the PTA allows Home to exploit RoW both on the import side (by pushing down the price it pays RoW exporters of Good 1) and on the export side (by raising the price in Partner at the expense of RoW exporters of Good 2). The move to global free trade undoes these two

forms of exploitation, but in exchange, it provides better access to the RoW market and more liberalization in Home's import market.

When the initial tariff T is low, the market access and home liberalization gains are modest, and so the net effect is negative. In other words, the basic logic of the stumbling block result turns on the way that a PTA allows the PTA partners to exploit excluded nations.

The model presented here is very special, but the heart and soul of the stumbling block effect—the exploitation of excluded nations—is a general result, and one that is surely an important consideration in the real world.

The opposition of small developing nations—especially those that benefit from European Union (EU) unilateral preferences—to agricultural liberalization in the WTO Doha negotiations is a classic example of the preference-erosion stumbling block. Had the EU not unilaterally granted preferences to these nations, they would probably have been pushing for opening of the EU market in sugar and other goods.

Goodies bag. The goodies-bag version follows closely the fundamental economic logic of the preference-erosion stumbling block.[9] Briefly, the rents corresponding to

Smith's certitude can be thought of as a set of "goodies" that can be used by one or both PTA parties to buy noneconomic benefits from its partners. Because the size of noneconomic benefits that can be "purchased" is linked to the richness of the goodies bag—that is, the margin of preferences—PTA members have an extra incentive to maintain high margins of preference by avoiding multilateral liberalization. The goodies-bag logic, however, extends to a far greater range of issues than the tariffs that are the focus of the preference-erosion stumbling block. In the case of a PTA between very large and very small nations—a case that is extremely common in the new century (e.g., the United States and Costa Rica; Japan and Singapore)—the large country's interest in the PTA can hardly be thought to be preferential market access.

The EU, for example, grants extensive preferences to its members' former colonies by using the justification of international solidarity. In other words, the economic gains to the EU's partners count as a plus inside the EU because they advance one of the EU's noneconomic objectives—fostering development. Similarly, but more explicitly, the United States justifies many of its PTAs with small, poor nations on the basis of noneconomic objectives, typically, antidrug or antiterrorism policies.

The earlier discussion illustrated how the desire to safeguard rents created by a PTA could make a nation reject global free trade when it would have embraced MFN free trade without the PTA. The goodies-bag stumbling block logic amplifies this mechanism by making both nations interested in each other's export rents—the area corresponding to C_1' in figure 6.1, with the link operating through the pursuit of noneconomic (in the narrow sense) objectives.

Cherry picking. An entirely distinct mechanism is at work in the cherry-picking stumbling block.[10] Assume that the trading environment is marked by both intraindustry trade in differentiated products and interindustry trade. In this world, trade liberalization will produce gains from trade because of the variety effect in the differentiated product sectors (as in Helpman-Krugman models) and because of comparative advantage effects. The comparative advantage gains, however, come bundled with politically difficult effects on domestic factor prices, which will be lower (e.g., lower wages).[11] Now suppose that two large nations have similar factor endowments. If they form a trade bloc, they will win a large share of the variety gains that would come with global free trade, and because of their similarity, they will experience little pain from lower factor prices.

Taking the trade bloc as the base case, the bloc members may find a move to global free trade unattractive. It would entail a good deal of pain in terms of factor prices

and only a modest amount of additional variety or comparative advantage gains. Depending on parameters, especially the political power of the sufferers, the gains may not be sufficient to make global free trade attractive to the bloc members.

Building Block Logic

Whereas many trade policy scholars, including Krugman (1991b) and Bhagwati (1991), worried that regionalism was a stumbling block to global free trade, others, such as Summers (1991) and Bergsten (1991), viewed regionalism as a largely benign or even constructive force in the world trade system.

Here, we consider the economic logic of the assertion that PTAs can foster multilateral liberalization. There are four main arguments in the literature. We begin with the one that permeates the rationales used by countries that simultaneously pursue regional and multilateral liberalization: the notion that preferential liberalization creates a political-economy momentum that makes multilateral liberalization easier (and vice versa).

Juggernaut. According to the juggernaut building block logic, liberalization begets liberalization. The logic comes in two parts that are most easily explained in the context of multilateral liberalization. When the GATT began in 1947, import duties were high worldwide, since they had been set without international coordination during the tariff wars named for the U.S. Smoot-Hawley Act. The tariffs balanced the supply of and demand for protection in the "political market" of each nation separately. The main *demandeurs* of import protection were import-competing firms and the workers they employed. Government was the supplier of protection, but concern for the country's general economic well-being meant that the government would set the protection level below what was lobbied for by special interests (the supply of protection being not perfectly elastic).

Starting from this situation of uncoordinated tariff setting, announcement of an MTN based on the principle of reciprocity alters the array of political forces inside each participating nation. The central point is reciprocity, which converts each nation's exporters from bystanders in the tariff debate to antiprotectionists. For exporters, lobbying against domestic tariffs becomes a means of lowering foreign tariffs. Because the MTN rearranges the political-economy forces inside each nation, all governments find it politically optimal to choose tariff levels that are lower than the unilaterally optimal tariffs.[12] This is the first part of the juggernaut theory.[13] The logic is not new.

Informed observers have long known that the GATT's reciprocal MTNs mostly had to do with helping nations internalize a political-economy externality inside their own polities, making it easier for national politicians to put together a national coalition in support of freer trade. Writers such as Robert Baldwin (1970, 1985) and Destler (1986) are explicit on this point, but historical accounts of the Cobden-Chevalier Treaties show that the use of external trade deals to realign domestic political forces was very much in the minds of nineteenth-century thinkers (Irwin 1996, 96). Even Krugman writes that "the process of multilateral negotiation . . . sets each country's exporting interests as a counterweight to import-competing interests; as trade negotiators bargain for access to each others' markets, they move toward free trade despite their disregard for the gains from trade as economists understand them" (Krugman 1991b, 17).

The second part of the juggernaut logic concerns the effects of the tariff cuts on openness. The cuts make all nations more open: export sectors expand with the foreign tariff cuts, and import-competing sectors contract with domestic tariff cuts. Assuming that political influence is linked to industry size, this economic relandscaping strengthens proliberalization forces and weakens antiliberalization forces in all nations—although, of course, such industrial restructuring takes years. In other words, the initial reciprocal tariff cuts start a liberalization juggernaut rolling. Because of the economic relandscaping that occurs during the phase-in of the initial tariff cuts, all governments find that their politically optimal tariff in the next MTN is below the levels that they found politically optimal during the previous MTN. These fresh tariff cuts continue the relandscaping, and the juggernaut continues to roll forward. Once the liberalization juggernaut starts rolling, it crushes all tariffs in its path.[14]

To the extent that regionalism can start the juggernaut rolling, PTAs can serve as building blocks.[15] The precise mechanism is a simple extension of the juggernaut logic. PTAs reconfigure members' economies, making export sectors larger and import-competing sectors smaller. Thus, the PTA can alter the member governments' stance toward MFNs, making it politically optimal to cut MFN tariffs to levels that would not have been politically optimal without the PTA. Of course, if a PTA results in higher external tariffs (as in the case of the EU's agriculture tariffs), then it can start the juggernaut rolling backward.

The basic idea is presented in figure 6.3. The two curves, *FE* (free entry) and *GFOC* (government first-order condition), show how the size of the import-competing sector depends on the tariff (free entry) and how that tariff depends on the size of the import-competing sector (n, for

Figure 6.3. Juggernaut Logic

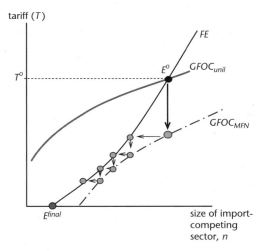

Source: Author's elaboration of figure 4 from Baldwin 2006.
Note: FE, free entry; *GFOC,* government first-order condition; *MFN,* most favored nation.

number of firms), via politics. The politically optimal tariff choice, which takes as given the size of the import-competing sector, is plotted as $GFOC_{unil}$, the solution to the government's first-order condition without MTN. The politically optimal tariff rises with n because the larger the import-competing sector, the higher the political benefit from a marginal increase in the tariff. The free entry curve, *FE,* relates the equilibrium number of firms to the tariff. As the tariff rises, more firms find it optimal to enter the market. These two relationships assume that the government and firms are shortsighted and that the government chooses T, taking n as given, while firms choose n, taking T as given. Note that the figure only captures the size of anti-trade forces; the size of the pro-trade export sector is suppressed to avoid the need for a three-dimensional diagram.

To see the two steps of the juggernaut effect, note that announcement of the MTN shifts the *GFOC* curve to $GFOC_{MTN}$. This curve is lower because the government finds it politically optimal to set a lower tariff for any given level of n when domestic protection is linked to foreign protection via reciprocity. As drawn, the new long-run equilibrium E^{final} entails free trade, but since entry and exit occur slowly, the tariff and the state of the import-competing industry do not jump to E^{final}. The figure illustrates one possible adjustment path. Each MTN results in an instantaneous drop in the tariff, but slow entry and exit mean sluggish movement of the state variable, as indicated by the horizontal arrows.

The juggernaut effect acts as a building block if the PTA reduces the importance of import-competing industry in governments' objective functions. In many models, a PTA between Home and Partner does reduce the size of the

Home import-competing sector, and then PTAs would be building blocks on the road to global free trade.

The *FE* curve in figure 6.3 was drawn for symmetric MFN tariffs. When the PTA is signed, the *FE* curve rotates inward, as shown in figure 6.4, because the additional competition from Partner producers lowers the Home price facing import-competing firms, and some of them exit. Consequently, the *GFOC* under reciprocal trade will yield a lower MFN tariff after a PTA (point E^2) than before (point E^1). Of course, if the PTA somehow increases protection of the Home import-competing sector, the effect is reversed, and the PTA acts as a stumbling block.[16]

Frankel and Wei momentum. Frankel and Wei (1998) illustrate another juggernaut-like mechanism. In their model, imperfect information makes workers uncertain as to whether they will win or lose from global free trade. Since a PTA is an intermediate form of liberalization, the authors show that a PTA could be politically feasible even when global free trade would not be. After the PTA is signed, the nation's true comparative advantage is revealed, and workers now know whether they will win or lose from free trade. If the parameters are chosen carefully, the certainty resolution may mean that global free trade is politically feasible only after the PTA. Thus, the PTA is a building block, and since it operates by altering the political-economy landscape, it can be thought of as a momentum-generating mechanism.

The juggernaut logic exploits the fact that nations do have preferences about trade arrangements, in the way that individual consumers have preferences about consumption

Figure 6.4. Juggernaut Building Block Logic

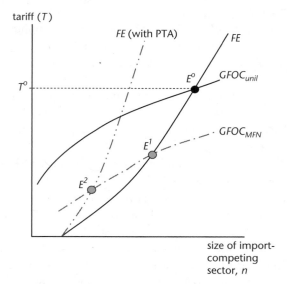

Source: Author's elaboration of figure 4 from Baldwin 2006.
Note: FE, free entry; GFOC, government first-order condition; PTA, preferential trade agreement.

bundles. The nature of the proposed trade deal can affect a nation's ranking of choices (unilateral versus reciprocal, for example). These rankings, unlike the rankings of a standard consumer, are path dependent because historical liberalization can affect the current political strength of various pro-trade and anti-trade special interest groups. A number of building block arguments assume, however, that nations, like consumers, have exogenous preferences about outcomes. We next consider the easiest of these arguments, which assumes a representative consumer and a government that acts to maximize the individual's well-being.

Kemp-Wan theorem. The assertion that trade blocs may be building blocks in a static world is as easy and as general as the assertion that they may be stumbling blocks. Starting from a world in which all nations have MFN tariffs, the question is: can some group of nations always raise its collective welfare by forming a trade bloc? If the answer is "yes," then a piecemeal enlargement of the bloc will raise bloc members' well-being monotonically. Bloc members attain the highest welfare when all nations are part of the bloc. In this world, the formation of a single bloc should trigger a domino effect that leads to worldwide free trade.

As seen in chapter 3, the Kemp-Wan theorem tells us that the answer to the above question is always "yes" when nations have access to international lump-sum transfers (Kemp-Wan 1976) or to a complete set of commodity taxes and subsidies (Dixit-Norman 1980). Kemp and Wan (1976), in probably the first formal contribution to the building block–stumbling block discussion, make exactly this point. (See Aghion, Antràs, and Helpman 2007 for an elaboration of the Kemp-Wan argument that uses modern cooperative game theory concepts.)[17]

Although the Kemp-Wan building block logic is flawless, it falls down in the face of the real-world problem that nations do not have access to massive lump-sum transfers. Indeed, the assumption that such international transfers are a realistic possibility basically assumes away most of the core difficulties facing the international trade system (and international relations more broadly). Without international transfers, the logic of preference-erosion stumbling blocks and cherry-picking stumbling blocks suggests that in many blocs, some members would eventually veto some enlargements.

Veto avoidance. The preference-erosion stumbling block logic discussed above rests on the fact that bloc members can veto the move to global free trade. The veto-avoidance building block logic points out that, although bloc members can veto multilateral trade liberalization, they cannot veto further PTAs that may eventually eliminate all tariffs globally. The explosion in the number of PTAs among small nations witnessed in the new century may very well be attributable to a combination of the juggernaut effect and veto-avoidance logic.[18]

We start by considering the development of an extremely common form of regionalism, hub-and-spoke PTAs. Here, one partner (e.g., the United States, the EU, or India) has a network of radial bilateral PTAs with some of its trading partners, but these trading partners do not have PTAs with each other. Simplicity dictates our continued use of the symmetric framework shown in figure 3.2 in chapter 3, so we arbitrarily bestow hub status on Home.

Roughly speaking, Home found the bilateral PTA with Partner attractive because the improved market access for Home exporters in Partner's market more than outweighed the potential welfare losses from trade diversion in Home's import market. This suggests that Home might also find a second bilateral PTA with RoW to be welfare enhancing.[19]

As it turns out, in the PTA diagram framework, Home always gains from signing a second PTA with RoW. Intuitively, the point is that Home gains the same preferential market access as it did from the first PTA, and it undoes the potentially harmful trade diversion by fully liberalizing its import market. To see this in more detail, we reinterpret figure 6.1. On the export side, Home's second PTA wins its preferential access to RoW's market without giving up its preferences in Partner; this has a net welfare value of areas $D' + C_1' + C_2'$ in the left-hand panel.[20] On the import side, the second PTA brings the price in Home's market for Good 1 to the global free trade level, P_{FT}. The welfare impact of this is the positive trade volume effect area A' plus the conflicting terms-of-trade effects, areas $-B'$ and $+C_1'$. (See Baldwin 2009, box 5, for a mathematical proof.)

Would RoW accept Home's offer of a second PTA? As it turns out, RoW gains from such a PTA as long as T is not too high (see Baldwin 2009 for details). That is, the hub-and-spoke situation is better for RoW than the initially disadvantaged position, when it was excluded from the Home-Partner PTA. On the export side, a PTA with Home would improve RoW's market access a great deal (its export price would rise from the depressed level of $P'-T$ to the free trade price, P_{FT}). The liberalization on the import side would have the usual positive trade volume effect and conflicting terms-of-trade effects, identical to those experienced by Home in its first PTA.

Plainly, Partner will be harmed by the formation of the hub-and-spoke system around Home; its preferences in Home are eroded, and it receives nothing in compensation. Partner would thus like to veto Home's second PTA, but except in extraordinary circumstances, third nations cannot veto PTAs. The main exception is customs unions, but functioning customs unions are quite rare in the modern world. Customs unions require supranational decision-making capacity to keep all external tariffs in line in the face of changes in antidumping duties; special unilateral preferences to third nations, such as the generalized system of preferences; and tariff changes in multilateral trade talks. The groups of nations that manage such coordination are of just two types: the EU, and nations involved in superhegemon relations (e.g., France and Monaco; Switzerland and Liechtenstein; and the South African Customs Union). Given that the real world is covered with hub-and-spoke trade arrangements, we assume henceforth that Partner has no veto over Home's PTA policy, and the hub-and-spoke system is indeed set up.

The story, however, is not finished. As it turns out, the two spokes may find a spoke-spoke PTA to be advantageous, and this would achieve global duty-free trade. (Trade, however, would not necessarily be free because of the exclusion of various sensitive sectors, rules of origin, and cumulation.)

The hub-and-spoke PTA puts Home in an enviable position, giving it the benefits of free trade for its imports and preferential market access for all of its exporters. In this sense, hub-and-spoke bilateralism might be thought of as another example of the preference-erosion stumbling block logic: Home would veto WTO talks aimed at achieving global free trade. This simple world, however, can attain global duty-free trade without multilateral talks—a PTA between Partner and RoW would do the job. So, would Partner and RoW be interested in a PTA?

Taking hub-and-spoke bilateralism as the point of departure, the spokes (in this case, Partner and RoW) clearly have a very different view of global free trade than does the hub. A move to global free trade would do nothing to erode Partner's preferences in Home, since those were already eroded by Home's second PTA. For Partner, the shift to the global free trade regime would involve a standard exchange of market access with RoW; Partner would see its export price to RoW rise from $P'-T$ to P_{FT} for Good 3, and RoW would see a symmetric border price rise for its exports of Good 2 to Partner (see figure 3.2) The attendant liberalization of the two nations' import markets would have the usual conflicting trade volume and terms-of-trade effects, but overall, the two nations could find the exchange to be welfare enhancing. In fact, Partner and RoW would always prefer global free trade to the hub-and-spoke situation.

This is certainly not to be taken as a general result. It does, however, illustrate how regionalism could be a building block in a world in which overall free trade would be in the interest of all nations, but achievement of the goal is blocked by nations that fear erosion of their preferences.

Related Logics: Induced Liberalization and Protection

Before ending this review of the helps-or-hinders literature, it should be useful to cover two economic mechanisms that link PTAs and MFN tariffs without formally making the connection with multilateral trade talks. Both consider the impact of PTAs on a nation's MFN stance in the absence of a new MTN. The first mechanism links PTAs to unilateral MFN liberalization; the second looks at how a PTA can lower or raise a nation's effective MFN tariff rate.

Unilateral liberalization. The building block logics examined earlier directly address the issue of whether PTAs help or hinder the attainment of global free trade. Here, we look at a related but logically distinct question: what is the impact of a PTA on the tariffs a nation would find unilaterally optimal to impose on third nations? Intuitively, the question is whether preferential tariffs are complements to or substitutes for MFN tariffs.[21] The easiest way to organize the various mechanisms is to start from the Meade (1955) formula for the welfare impact of any trade policy change in a Walrasian economy:

Net home welfare effect $= (\boldsymbol{p} - \boldsymbol{p}^{\star})d\boldsymbol{M} - (\boldsymbol{M})d\boldsymbol{p}^{\star}$ (6.1)

where $\boldsymbol{p}$ and $\boldsymbol{p}^{\star}$ are the vectors of internal and border prices (and $\boldsymbol{p} - \boldsymbol{p}^{\star} = T$, the tariff), $\boldsymbol{M}$ is the vector of bilateral imports (exports are negative imports), and $d\boldsymbol{M}$ and $d\boldsymbol{p}^{\star}$ are the vectors of changes in bilateral trade volumes and border prices, respectively.

A nation choosing its bilateral tariffs optimally would view this formula as a first-order condition and set it to zero to find its optimal tariff. The optimal bilateral tariffs are:

$$T_{od} = M_{od}\left(\frac{dp^{\star}}{dM}\right)_{od}$$ (6.2)

where o indicates the origin nation and d the destination nation (the nation choosing the tariffs). In general, anything can happen to T_{od} when the nation signs a free trade agreement, because, according to the Slutsky equation, the direct and cross-good income and substitution effects of the PTA-induced price changes could raise or lower the right-hand side of the equation (6.2). Real income is expanded because the price of the preferential good fell, raising demand and hence the optimal external tariff. However, there is also substitution toward the low-cost preferential good, reducing demand for other foreign goods and pushing the optimal external tariff down. Attempts to resolve the inherent ambiguity have led to the emphasis on several economic mechanisms in the literature.

Preferential and MFN tariffs as complements. If the PTA-induced price changes have little impact on the equilibrium slopes of the third-nation import supply curves, T_{od} is likely to fall because PTAs typically reduce PTA members' trade with third nations (Harberler's spillover); that is, M_{od} is likely to fall. For example, in the simple PTA diagram model presented in figure 3.2 in ch. 3, the import supply curves are linear, and so $dp^{\star}/dM$ does not change with preferential liberalization. However, Haberler's spillover effect lowers third-nation trade (M_{od}), and so Home's optimal tariff on RoW exports falls.

Another mechanism that yields complementarity turns on the general principle that taxes become more distortionary when the variance of rates across products increases. This is termed the uniform tax rate principle, and it is a feature of many economic models, especially when administrative and enforcement considerations are taken into account. It explains why most nations impose fairly even indirect tax rates across products. Since the PTA automatically makes the import tax structure more uneven, there is some presumption that the PTA makes the third-nation tariffs more distortionary. In models where this is true, nations are likely to lower third-nation tariffs when they reoptimize their trade tax structures. That is, PTAs encourage nations to reduce applied MFN tariffs.

Preferential and MFN tariffs as substitutes. The most obvious mechanism that suggests the substitutes result (i.e., nations find it optimal to raise third-nation tariffs after having signed a PTA) concerns the market power of the new bloc. If the PTA allows PTA members to better coordinate their third-country tariffs, the members are likely to raise external tariffs because they will have more purchasing power than before. This effect is only likely to be relevant in customs unions, where countries set tariffs jointly. Even so, two fairly unrealistic assumptions are required: that the governments share sufficiently similar objective functions, and that their external tariffs are not subject to WTO bindings (or that they are willing to violate their WTO commitments). Since most of the effective PTAs are among developed countries whose tariffs are almost universally bound at near-zero levels (apart from a few low-volume items) and since such countries rarely violate their WTO bindings, this mechanism is probably of little real-world relevance except for a few commodities (agriculture before the Uruguay Round) and a few low-trade-volume PTAs among developing countries.

Imported MFN liberalization and protection. A closely related line of reasoning considers the automatic impact of PTAs on the external protection of PTA members, when members impose different tariffs on third countries. Under some circumstances, the PTA effectively lowers the higher MFN tariff (imported MFN liberalization); in other circumstances, the PTA effectively raises the lower MFN tariff (imported MFN protection).[22]

A good example of imported MFN liberalization can be found in North-South PTAs. The concept can be explained intuitively with reference to Mexico's experience. In 1994, Mexico, along with Canada and the United States, formed NAFTA, which phased in tariff cuts over 10 to 15 years. Mexican MFN tariffs were (and still are) much higher than U.S. and Canadian MFN tariffs, but as NAFTA brought Mexican prices down to the U.S. internal level, domestic prices in Mexico came to resemble those that Mexico would have observed if it had lowered its MFN tariffs to U.S. levels. To put it differently, the high Mexican MFN tariffs became irrelevant because the same goods could be purchased from the United States duty-free, and the U.S. internal price was linked to the world price via its low MFN tariff (leaving aside the small sectors still protected by high U.S. MFN tariffs, such as clothing, textiles, and footwear). In this sense, Mexico ended up "importing" the low U.S. MFN tariffs.[23]

The argument can be illustrated more precisely by using figure 6.5, which shows import demand by the United States (left-hand panel), Mexico (middle panel), and the world market for the good under consideration (right-hand panel). The U.S. total supply curve is shown in Mexico's panel, for reasons that will become clear. The United States initially imposes a zero tariff on imports from the rest of the world, whereas Mexico imposes a tariff of T_{MX} on imports from both the United States and the rest of the world. When Mexico eliminates duties on U.S. imports, U.S.-made goods can enter Mexico duty-free. Since the Mexican internal price is initially above the U.S. internal price, U.S. firms sell to the Mexican market and, in doing so, drive down Mexico's internal price to the U.S. internal price—which, of course, is just the world price. U.S. production entirely displaces Mexican imports from the rest of the world, and the Mexican MFN tariff becomes irrelevant.

The feasibility of this outcome is established by noting that the U.S. supply at P^o is more than sufficient to cover the entire Mexican import demand (point 2 is to the right of point 1). Note that there is a secondary effect on world prices as the United States expands its imports. The new price is at the intersection of the dotted MD curve and the XS_{RoW} curve. For simplicity's sake, this second-order impact is not shown in the two leftmost panels.

If one combines this imported MFN liberalization with the juggernaut logic, the PTA can eliminate all the firms in Mexico that would otherwise have opposed MFN liberalization. That is, Mexican industry has no interest in lobbying for the maintenance of high Mexican MFN tariffs, which provide no protection to Mexican industry. In the case at hand, the Mexican government signed a vast array of PTAs to exchange its now politically useless MFN tariffs against preferential access for its exporters.

Since developed countries (the North) tend to have much lower MFN tariffs on most manufactured goods than developing countries (the South), the mechanism suggests that an important implication of North-South PTAs for the world trading system is their potential to lower the southern country's resistance to further liberalization. Given that most of the South does not participate in MTN tariff-cutting exercises on the basis of reciprocity, the North-South PTAs are one of the few ways of triggering juggernaut effects in developing countries.

Rules of origin and imported MFN protection. The opposite result, in which a PTA imports MFN protection to a country with low MFN tariffs, can occur when highly restrictive rules of origin are imposed. The argument can be illustrated with reference to NAFTA. Since the first U.S. foray into regionalism, the 1965 U.S.–Canada Auto Pact, U.S. and Canadian rules of origin on autos have been

Figure 6.5. Imported MFN Liberalization

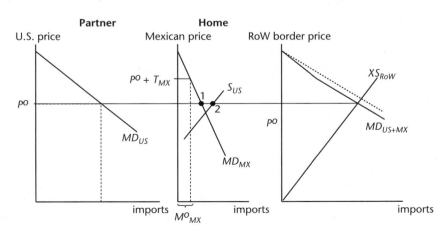

Source: Authors' elaboration.

highly restrictive. One of Canada's motives in pushing for the trilateralization of the U.S.–Mexico free trade agreement was to extend its restrictive rules of origin to Mexico and thereby avoid the undermining of the Auto Pact. The rules of origin forced Mexican-based car producers to import parts and components from the United States or Canada instead of from third countries. As before, NAFTA equalized U.S. and Mexican internal prices, but this meant that the Mexican prices were linked to the world prices via the higher MFN tariffs in Mexico's partners. In this way, "imported MFN protection" occurred. NAFTA, with its rules of origin, had effects that mimicked a rise in the Mexican MFN tariffs to U.S. and Canadian levels.

Although the distortionary impact of rules of origin is limited by the level of the MFN tariff, the all-or-nothing feature of rules of origin for final goods can lead to large effective rates of protection. For example, if a US$20,000 NAFTA-origin automobile pays zero tariff and the same non-NAFTA auto would pay 5 percent, a rule of origin stipulating that a particular component must be made within NAFTA could make it economical to pay up to US$1,000 more for the local versus the imported component. Although the distortion in the final good market is limited to 5 percent, the distortion in the component market can be much larger. (This distortion represents the traditional logic of effective rate of protection.)

Bargaining-Model Stumbling Block–Building Block Logic

The stumbling block–building block mechanisms discussed earlier resonate strongly with real-world considerations because they take advantage of the simple institutional features of real-world tariff cutting in PTAs and MTNs. This, however, is not how big-think regionalism started reasoning about the issue (Krugman 1991b, 1996).[24]

When Krugman wondered how regionalism would affect the GATT, the tool he grabbed for was simple bargaining-game theory, with two countries that are considering setting tariffs cooperatively (under GATT), or noncooperatively (Nash tariffs). As figure 6.6 shows, both countries prefer the cooperative outcome. Krugman observes, "Trade bargaining . . . is characterised by a Prisoners' Dilemma. This Dilemma arises in part from the terms of trade effect of conventional optimal tariff analysis, but also (and presumably in practice mostly) from the effect of each country's tariff on the other country's producer interests" (Krugman 1996, 72). He goes on to invoke all the usual theorems of repeated games to think about the building block–stumbling block issue and concludes, "Trade liberalisation must be supported by the belief of countries that if they cheat they will lose from the subsequent collapse

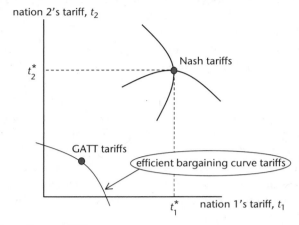

Figure 6.6. An Economic Theory of the GATT

Source: Krugman 1991a.

of the cooperative outcome" (Krugman 1996, 72).[25] The crux of his analysis is to examine the impact that an exogenously formed PTA has on the costs and benefits of cheating.

Much of Krugman's reasoning is informal, so it is worth spelling it out explicitly. The whole analysis turns on three equilibrium welfare levels:

- W^{GATT} is the level of a nation's welfare with global cooperation (GATT tariffs)
- W^{Nash} is national welfare under noncooperative tariffs
- W^{cheat} reflects the nation's welfare when its government "cheats"—that is, chooses a tariff to maximize its own welfare when the foreign government embraces its GATT tariffs.

There are two logical steps in the approach. The first step consists of the obvious point that, from a global perspective, tariffs are worse than a zero-sum game. Therefore, some form of cooperation could be Pareto improving, yet nations have an incentive to cheat. Formally, this is a prisoners' dilemma, and it arises when $W^{cheat} > W^{GATT} > W^{Nash}$. The second step involves a dynamic game that models the circumstances under which cooperation is sustained. As Krugman notes, cooperation is self-enforcing when the gains from cheating are more than offset by the losses from the (infinite) punishment. Taking δ as the discount factor, the present value of cooperating forever is $W^{GATT}/(1 - \delta)$. If cooperation is to be sustained, its value must exceed the one-period gain from cheating, W^{cheat}, plus the present value of the infinite sequence of the Nash outcomes that are felt in the next period, after the foreigners realize that cheating has occurred, $\delta W^{Nash}/(1 - \delta)$.

Clearing the $(1 - \delta)$ terms, the condition for self-sustaining global free trade is:

$$W^{GATT} > (1 - \delta)W^{cheat} + \delta W^{Nash}$$

In words, each nation compares the value of welfare under cooperation with a weighted average of the cheating outcome and the Nash outcome.

The contribution of this approach comes in considering how a PTA changes the three levels, W^{cheat}, W^{GATT}, and W^{Nash}. Krugman (1996) asks whether the formation of a trade bloc among nations makes them more or less able or willing to cooperate. His answer is that it can cut either way.

Krugman's core insight—one that has been followed up in a dozen subsequent articles—is that PTAs typically act to reduce their members' trade with the rest of the world and so reduce both the cost and the benefit of cheating. Since these work in opposite directions, some bargain-approach papers find that PTAs are building blocks (i.e., they make cooperation more likely), whereas others find they are stumbling blocks.

This approach works well for explaining strategic interactions among private agents, but it may be less useful for explaining trade negotiations among large countries. In particular, it requires two assumptions: that the cheating period is long enough to make it tempting, and that punishment can be usefully modeled as consisting only of tariff changes. Since tariff changes are immediately observable, the first assumption is problematic unless partner countries are very slow to respond, which may well reflect policy in small developing countries. Punishment is likely to include more than just tariffs; it may affect external development aid, treatment of expatriates, migration, military aid, political support in the international arena, participation in the North Atlantic Treaty Organization, and other concerns. With a shorter period of deviation and more tools of punishment available, as is the case for large developed countries, it is therefore likely that all welfare-improving agreements are enforceable. Thus, the effect of PTAs on the cost and benefit of deviating from cooperation is unlikely to have a first-order impact on multilateral cooperation when the major countries are involved. This type of model may help explain why some agreements among developing countries are never implemented and why some do not survive when external conditions change.

Other Links from PTAs to MTNs

A number of points made in the literature do not fit neatly into the stumbling block–building block framework as we have delineated it. One line of reasoning views a nation's MFN tariffs, or its stance favoring or against multilateral cooperation, as depending on the strength of various domestic special interest groups. The question here, in the big-think framework, is whether a PTA weakens or strengthens pro-trade and anti-trade interest groups. At one end, Winters (1993) argues that regionalism (e.g., in the EU, on agriculture) strengthened the hand of protectionists, since it worsened Olsen's asymmetry (which holds that winners from protection are few in number and are easy to organize, whereas losers are dispersed, numerous, and difficult to organize politically). Winters terms this the "restaurant bill" problem. Just as diners at a table where the bill will be split equally tend to order too much, the EU tended to grant too much protection to farmers. At the other end, Richardson (1994) and Panagariya and Findlay (1994) argue that a PTA tends to dilute the influence of special interest groups via various mechanisms.

Another important line of thinking asserts that the formation of PTAs creates forces that induce nations to begin or complete multilateral trade talks. For example, Lawrence (1991), WTO (1995), and Sapir (1996) all argue that the threat of regionalism was a critical element in inducing GATT members to initiate the Uruguay Round and to accept the final Uruguay Round agreement. Bergsten (1996) dubs this effect "competitive liberalization" and asserts that regionalism fosters multilateralism, and vice versa. Formalizing regional agreements as a force for competitive liberalization, Saggi and Yildiz (2008) study the role of PTAs in multilateral liberalization in the presence of a nondiscrimination constraint, such as the MFN rule in the WTO. They show that if PTAs are not permitted, a country with special interests aligned against free trade may oppose a multilateral free trade agreement because it can ride for free on the liberalization efforts of others. Nondiscrimination means that when any small group of countries liberalizes, all WTO members benefit from lower tariffs on their exports. The threat of PTAs can reverse that situation by offering the liberalizing countries a way to stop the outsider from free riding. In this model, competition to the multilateral system in the form of PTAs can make multilateral free trade feasible when it would not be feasible in the absence of that competition.

A somewhat related idea, which has not been formalized, is that PTAs are a testing ground for the GATT/WTO (Bergsten 1996; Lawrence 1996). The prime example here is the EU, which dealt with deeper-than-tariff-cutting liberalization for decades before the issues arrived on the GATT agenda in the Tokyo and Uruguay Rounds. (See Ludema 1996 for a partial formalization of this idea.)

Another line of thinking suggests that PTAs can provide commitments that boost the credibility of a country's policy reforms (Fernandez and Portes 1998). This was explicitly mentioned by Mexico in its request to the United States for an FTA and has been highlighted as an important reason that Eastern European countries have been keen to join the EU.

Finally, studying how regionalism affects multilateralism is not the only way to look at the relationship between the two. A few authors have examined it from the other direction: how multilateralism affects regionalism. Both Ethier (1998) and Freund (2000a) view regional initiatives as a consequence of the success of multilateralism. Ethier asserts that it is a benign consequence, since PTAs intensify world investment and create incentives for economic reforms in less developed countries. Freund studies the incentives for and the sustainability of preferential liberalization when multilateral tariffs are lower and finds that deeper multilateralism provides greater incentives to form PTAs. The intuition draws from the complementarity effect between internal and external tariffs. When external tariffs are low, the loss from trade diversion is small, but the gains to producers from preferential access and to consumers from lower prices remain. This reasoning could help explain, at least in part, the large increase in PTAs since the conclusion of the Uruguay Round and the formation of the WTO in 1995.

Regionalism Versus Multilateralism: Empirical Evidence

The empirical literature on regionalism as a building block or stumbling block with respect to free trade is small, compared with the theoretical literature, but interesting results are beginning to emerge. To date, there is no evidence that regionalism has been a major stumbling block to free trade and some evidence that it has promoted broad liberalization. On the question of whether regional agreements alter countries' willingness to move to free trade, there is only anecdotal evidence. PTA members have continued to participate in the WTO, with little evidence of a distinct change in priorities. Finally, on the welfare impact of regionalism, evidence of trade creation exceeds evidence of diversion.

History points to complementarity between PTAs and external liberalization. Irwin (1996) shows that bilateral agreements during the nineteenth century induced broader liberalization. The Anglo-French treaty of 1860 led to a host of bilateral agreements that were ultimately linked by the inclusion of an unconditional MFN clause. Precisely because trade diversion associated with high tariffs was costly, the French negotiated numerous such MFN-style agreements.

Using data on trade and trade policy in 50 countries between 1965 and 1995, Foroutan (1998) provides a general account of how countries forming regional trade blocs have adjusted their external tariffs. She finds that both integrating and nonintegrating countries have reduced their trade barriers, suggesting that regionalism is benign. However, Foroutan does not control for other factors that may have induced countries to behave as they did, making it impossible to disentangle the effects of trade agreements from those of other global, regional, or sectoral trends.

Baldwin and Seghezza (2010) study the relationship between preferential and MFN tariffs in 23 developed and developing countries and find a positive relationship, suggestive of the tariff complementarity discussed earlier. Because their dataset is a cross-section (for 2005), the authors note that they cannot assess whether their result arises from a causal relationship or is just a consequence of, say, fixed effects that affect both preferential and multilateral tariff levels. Still, their findings indicate that regionalism has not led to significantly higher external tariffs.

Using a detailed cross-industry dataset on Argentina for 1992, 1993, and 1996, Bohara, Gawande, and Sanguinetti (2004) examine the influence of imports from Mercosur's partner Brazil on Argentina's external tariffs. They find that increased preferential imports vis-à-vis the value added of the domestic industry led to lower external tariffs in Argentina, especially in industries that experienced trade diversion. This, again, is consistent with the complementarity of tariffs. Trade diversion is costly, and to minimize it, tariffs were lowered in precisely those industries with the most diversion. One issue is that the study concentrates on the effects of increases in preferential imports and does not address the direct effect of preferential tariffs.

Estevadeordal, Freund, and Ornelas (2008) offer the first attempt to evaluate empirically the effect of preferential tariffs on external trade liberalization in a large group of developing countries. They examine changes in preferential tariffs and MFN tariffs in 10 Latin American countries and 100 industries over 12 years. When countries form a PTA, they lower the tariffs they apply to each other, but the duties on imports from outside countries can increase, decrease, or remain unchanged. The authors look at how countries in Latin America, where regionalist forces have been particularly strong since the early 1990s, altered their trade policies vis-à-vis bloc outsiders after forming PTAs and, specifically, whether sectors with relatively large preferences have been liberalized or protected to the same extent as other sectors. If countries raise their external tariffs (or reduce them by less) as a result of regional liberalization, such preferential arrangements should indeed raise concerns about the recent trend. If, instead, preferences lead to relatively lower external tariffs, regional agreements should be accorded a more benign reputation than they currently have.

The results imply that regionalism is a building block for free trade. There is no clear evidence that trade preferences lead to higher tariffs or smaller tariff cuts, and there is strong evidence that preferences induce a more rapid decline in external tariffs in free trade areas. For example, if a country that follows a strict policy of nondiscrimination offers free access to another country in a sector in which it applies a 15 percent multilateral tariff, the country would tend to subsequently reduce that external tariff by more than 3 percentage points. As in the study by Bohara and colleagues, Estevadeordal, Freund, and Ornelas (2008) find that the complementarity effect is stronger in sectors where trade bloc partners are more important suppliers, which is precisely where trade discrimination would be more disruptive. Using a similar methodology for the Association of Southeast Asian Nations, Calvo-Pardo, Freund, and Ornelas (2009) also find evidence that regionalism is associated with unilateral tariff reduction.

Recent studies by Limão (2006) and Karacaovali and Limão (2008) address a related question: whether preferential liberalization by the United States and the EU hindered multilateral trade liberalization at the Uruguay Round. In the context of the theoretical literature described earlier, they examine the goodies-bag stumbling block and, specifically, whether commitments to liberalize were significantly different in goods that offered preferences and in goods that did not. These papers, however, do not take into account the size of the preferences or the importance of trade in the products that received preferential treatment. Both papers find that liberalization was relatively smaller in products where preferences were used. They argue that, intuitively, because the United States and the EU offer preferences on a unilateral basis to extract concessions from recipients in nontrade areas, they tend to resist liberalization to prevent erosion of preferences.

The evidence in Limão (2006) is widely misrepresented as showing that the United States raised tariffs in the Uruguay Round for items on which it granted PTA preferences. Of course, this cannot be correct, since MTN market access talks only involve tariff bindings, and the United States did not violate any of its bindings in the Uruguay Round. Indeed, the data show U.S. tariffs decreasing for all but 12 of the thousands of tariff lines, defined at the Harmonized System–8 product level in the WTO's database. Formally, Limão estimates an econometric model of U.S. tariff cuts during the Uruguay Round. His famous stumbling block finding is that the United States cut tariffs by less than his econometric model predicted they should have on items for which the United States had granted PTA preferences before the Uruguay Round. In short, he shows that the U.S. preferences acted as a "slowing block," not as a stumbling block.

The findings of Foroutan (1998), Bohara, Gawande, and Sanguinetti (2004), Estevadeordal, Freund, and Ornelas (2008), and Calvo-Pardo, Freund, and Ornelas (2009)—all of which imply that regionalism is a building block for external liberalization in developing countries—contrast sharply with those of Limão (2006) and of Karacaovali and Limão (2008), who find that the United States and the EU liberalized less during the Uruguay Round in sectors in which preferences were granted. One reason for differing results is that that the countries analyzed are very different. Since the multilateral system has not enforced much tariff reduction on developing countries, tariffs are relatively high among that group, creating a large potential for trade diversion. Lower external tariffs moderate that loss. The results of the first group of researchers named above suggest that this force is important in explaining changes in MFN tariffs of developing countries involved in free trade areas. In contrast, Limão's work focuses on industrial countries. Tariffs were already quite low in the United States and the EU at the onset of the Uruguay Round, thus reducing the importance of this channel. In addition, the theoretical underpinnings of Limão's analysis, which is used to justify the importance of preferences in North-South agreements, rely on the formation of PTAs for noneconomic reasons; preferential treatment is extended in return for noneconomic benefits, such as cooperation on migration, drug trafficking, or a global political agenda. This is not the case in South-South PTAs, where the goal is to exchange access to markets and improve regional economic cooperation.

Welfare Consequences of PTAs

A large portion of the empirical literature on trade diversion versus trade creation has attempted to provide answers to the question of whether bilateralism is bad (see box 6.1, above). If regionalism is moving world trade away from natural trade patterns, thus reducing world welfare, more diversion will be observed; if regionalism is pushing trade in the right direction, we should observe little diversion. The analyses also offer an indirect check on the effect of regional agreements on trade liberalization. If regional members tend to raise barriers to nonmembers, there should be strong evidence of trade diversion—increased trade with members at the expense of nonmembers. By contrast, if regional members tend to lower barriers to nonmembers in concert with PTAs, diversion should be limited.

Unfortunately, estimating trade diversion is no easy task. It requires knowledge of the counterfactual: what would have happened to trade if there were no trade agreement? Since this is unknown, assumptions must be made.

Most studies use a gravity equation (which predicts bilateral trade on the basis of income and other characteristics) and focus on variables that capture the extent to which PTA partners trade more or less than would otherwise be expected.[26] The key trade creation variable is a dummy that is equal to 1 if both countries are members of a common PTA; the key trade diversion variable is a dummy that is 1 if one country belongs to a PTA and the other does not. (See Frankel, Stein, and Wei 1995; Carrère 2006; Lee and Shin 2006.) A positive coefficient on the former offers evidence of trade creation; a negative coefficient on the latter offers evidence of diversion. Overall, the message from such studies is that trade creation predominates. In fact, a concern is that the estimates of the creation effect may be implausibly large, as well as too dependent on the sample of countries and variables included (Haveman and Hummels 1998).

Magee (2008) expands on the traditional approach with insights from the literature on the proper estimation of gravity models. He uses panel data for 133 countries between 1980 and 1998 and includes country-pair fixed effects, exporter-year fixed effects, and importer-year fixed effects to capture the counterfactual more accurately than standard gravity specifications would. The dyad effects pick up what is natural about the trade partners, and the exporter-year and importer-year effects pick up country-specific dynamics. Magee finds that the average impact of agreements on trade flows is small, only 3 percent. Moreover, on average, trade creation dominates trade diversion by about one order of magnitude.

Another strand of the literature uses more disaggregated data to examine specific agreements. Clausing (2001) develops an analysis at the product level of the 1988 Canada–U.S. Free Trade Agreement (CUSFTA). Using variations in liberalization across industries to identify trade creation and diversion, she finds that in most sectors trade creation tends to be the rule and trade diversion the exception. Taking a similar approach, Trefler (2004) finds both trade creation and trade diversion in CUSFTA but calculates positive welfare effects for the average Canadian. Romalis (2007) finds that the expansion of CUSFTA to Mexico, through NAFTA, has been trade diverting. Romalis's exercise is similar to Clausing's and Trefler's, but he uses changes in EU trade over the period to capture what would have happened in the absence of the agreement. Although this might create a better counterfactual if the NAFTA countries were very similar to the EU, it could lead to overestimates of trade diversion in NAFTA if the EU's trade with its own new and existing trade agreement partners were to expand more rapidly. Even so, Romalis's results suggest that the welfare costs of the agreement are tiny.

A different perspective is taken by Chang and Winters (2002), who study the effects of Mercosur—a trading bloc formed by Argentina, Brazil, Paraguay, and Uruguay in 1991—on export prices to Brazil. They find that Argentina's export prices increased, whereas the export prices of countries outside Mercosur fell. These price effects indicate that Mercosur has hurt outsiders while helping Brazil, a Mercosur partner.[27]

As Krugman (1991b) shows, whether an agreement is welfare improving also depends on trade costs. To determine whether nature plays a role in PTA formation, Frankel, Stein, and Wei (1995) examine whether regional trade is greater than could be explained by natural determinants—proximity, size, per capita gross national product, common border, common language, and so on. They find in favor of the formation of "natural" trade blocs.

Krishna (2003) tackles the natural trade bloc question by using detailed U.S. trade data to estimate the welfare effects from 24 hypothetical bilateral trade agreements in a general equilibrium framework and then correlating the estimated welfare changes with geographic variables and trade volumes. Neither geography nor trade volume is found to be significantly correlated with welfare gains, indicating that they are not good indicators of the gains from trade, as the natural trade bloc approach would suggest. Still, Krishna finds that 80 percent of the potential agreements he examines are welfare improving. Given the predominance of trade creation, it is not clear that a correlation between distance or trade volume and welfare is necessary to indicate that blocs are formed naturally. To determine which agreements are most natural, the costs of forming an agreement should also be included, and such costs are plausibly lower with a neighbor or with a large trade partner, as the relationship between the two countries is likely to be well developed.

Baier and Bergstrand (2004) develop a general equilibrium model to determine which country pairs would gain the most from forming PTAs. They then examine whether these dyads were actually linked by a PTA in a sample of 53 countries in 1996. They find that the likelihood of a PTA is larger the closer the two countries are to each other, the more remote they are from RoW, the larger their gross domestic products (GDPs), the smaller the difference between their GDPs, the larger their relative factor endowment difference, and the wider the (absolute) difference between their and RoW's capital-labor ratios. These variables predict the formation of 85 percent of the bilateral PTAs in their sample. Their results thus offer support for the natural trade bloc view.[28] In subsequent work, Baier and Bergstrand (2007) use the same approach to estimate the impact of PTAs on trade flows. Their key finding is that, once one takes into account the endogeneity of the agreements, the positive impact of PTAs on bilateral trade becomes more robust and much larger—in fact, five times larger—than in estimates that take agreements as exogenous. Thus, countries seem to form PTAs when there is much to be gained from liberalizing bilateral trade.

Proving that agreements are natural or unnatural is daunting, as it requires an assessment of many potential agreements and their welfare consequences—and calculating trade diversion and creation in even one agreement is already difficult. Nevertheless, there is solid empirical support for the more general premise of the natural trade bloc view: that trade blocs are formed by countries that have much to gain from freer trade.

The theoretical literature on static effects of trade agreements highlights the potential costs of preferential liberalization and the possibility that trade-diverting agreements may be more viable politically. The empirical literature is not entirely conclusive, but it does suggest that trade diversion is not a major concern, although in some agreements and sectors it may matter. Trade diversion may be less relevant than was initially thought because countries form trade agreements with "natural trading partners," where trade creation is the norm, or because governments may respond to trade diversion by reducing external tariffs.

Overall, the empirical literature shows that countries in regional agreements tend to liberalize trade broadly. There is evidence that regional agreement members tend to reduce external tariffs, and that this is especially true of members of free trade agreements (as opposed to customs unions). In addition, trade diversion tends to be small or nonexistent, which is consistent with endogenous tariff changes that reduce costly diversion. There is, however, some evidence that regional agreements may limit trade liberalization in the multilateral setting.

Conclusions and Rules for PTAs

In this chapter, we have examined the effect of regionalism on the multilateral trade system. The theoretical literature underscores the diverse mechanisms by which regionalism can be helpful or harmful to that system. So far, there is little evidence that regionalism is overwhelmingly bad for the multilateral trade system, as some had feared, and there is some evidence that regionalism is associated with general liberalization.

To ensure that regionalism is a positive force in the future, four ideal guidelines can be kept in mind:

1. Bind tariff rates at applied rates, leaving no room for tariff increases following a trade agreement. This measure

prevents countries from backtracking on previous liberalization. Although this would be difficult to accomplish, it is a worthwhile goal. Tariffs in most developing countries are set well below their bindings (by 20 to 30 percentage points!), making the term "binding" meaningless. A move toward more restrictive bindings would make regionalism less dangerous and would give member countries a lever against a potential increase in the political forces favoring protection.

2. Agree to lower multilateral tariffs partway, through the use of preferential tariffs. Even though empirical work has shown that regionalism tends to be a force for general liberalization, irrespective of restrictions, a commitment in this direction would ensure that regionalism serves as a building block for free trade.

3. Redefine North-South agreements to incorporate preferences from the North in response to MFN liberalization on the part of the South. In the developing countries, where tariffs are generally higher, this would prevent sizable diversion. In addition, it would be far easier to implement than a range of tariffs across various agreements.

4. Keep regional agreements open, extending eligibility to all countries willing to follow the rules.[29] This helps ward against a global outcome dominated by a handful of protective trade blocs.

Trade negotiators should have these guidelines in mind, but the WTO should also do its part to ensure a positive spread of regionalism. This can be accomplished by monitoring regional agreements among members, publishing reports on regional agreements that call attention to bad behavior, and securing the authority to impose more restrictions on regional agreements.

Given the concerns about regionalism, it is important to highlight where the long-run potential benefits can be found. The best way to ensure that regionalism is welfare improving is for countries to pursue serious deep integration agreements. Real resource gains are obtainable if countries integrate labor markets, combine regulatory institutions, harmonize standards, and cooperate extensively on trade facilitation. Removal of behind-the-border barriers will enhance trade and welfare without the traditional costs of PTAs in tariff revenue and trade diversion. The benefits of deep integration include real resource gains that will accrue to nonmembers as well as members. The focus should be on the quality, not the number, of agreements. There is a danger, however, that the present wave of PTAs is being generated by minor agreements that will not produce significant benefits, especially given their cost to the world trading system. How to achieve deeper integration in services, agriculture, transport, and other sectors will be the focus of most of the remaining chapters of this volume.

Notes

The authors are grateful for comments from Jean-Pierre Chauffour, Jaime de Melo, and Jean-Christophe Maur.

1. Bhagwati (1993, 2008) and Panagariya and Bhagwati (1999) provide in-depth discussions of these concerns.

2. Grossman and Helpman (1995), Levy (1997), and Krishna (1998) show that regionalism can lead to a reduction in support for multilateral liberalization. However, Bagwell and Staiger (1999), Freund (2000b), and Ornelas (2005b) find that the formation of a PTA can cause its members to lower tariffs. Panagariya (2000) offers an excellent survey of the literature.

3. A tariff can theoretically be used optimally to protect an infant industry until it is strong enough to compete. It is difficult, however, to identify the infants that have potential to grow, and it is often difficult to drop protection after it has served its purpose. Moreover, it is typically politically connected sectors, rather than growing sectors, that obtain protection.

4. The next two sections draw heavily on Baldwin (2009).

5. Bhagwati (1991, 71) ascribes the shift to the United States' conversion to regionalism, but this contradicts the judgments of trade policy scholars who were engaged in the details of policy at the time (Wonnacott 1987, 17; Schott 1988, 29; Whalley 1996; Hufbauer, Schott, and Clark 1994, 100). It also contradicts the facts. Bearing witness to the long-standing U.S. interest in regionalism is a string of deals that were struck, or almost struck, in 1854, 1874, and 1911. In March 1948 the United States and Canada concluded a secret draft protocol eliminating most tariffs and quotas bilaterally, but this was ultimately rejected by the Canadians. In 1958, U.S. government procurement was preferentially liberalized in Canada's favor, and in 1965, the U.S.–Canada Auto Pact came into force. The 1974 Trade Act authorized the U.S. president to negotiate an FTA with Canada, and the 1979 Trade Agreements Act required the president to study an FTA in North America.

6. See Baldwin (1993, 1997) and Serra et al. (1997) for an account of this domino effect.

7. Krugman argued that the multilateral process had run aground with the December 1990 failure of the Uruguay Round and was unlikely to get afloat any time soon because the system was plagued by profound problems. "While some kind of face-saving document will probably be produced, in reality the [Uruguay Round] has clearly failed either to significantly liberalize trade or to generate goodwill that would help sustain further rounds of negotiation" (Krugman 1991b, 5). Regionalism, however, was not one of those fundamental problems. "But while the move to free trade areas has surely done the multilateral process some harm, it is almost surely more a symptom than a cause of the decline of the GATT.... The problems of the GATT are so deep-seated that it is unlikely that a world without regional free trade agreements would do much better" (Krugman 1991b, 20). He closed his essay with a prediction that history falsified and with a faute de mieux view of regionalism:

> The world may well be breaking up into three trading blocs; trade within those blocs will be quite free, while trade between the blocs will at best be no freer than it is now and may well be considerably less free. This is not what we might have hoped for. But the situation would not be better, and could easily have been worse, had the great free trade agreements of recent years never happened. (Krugman 1991b, 20–21)

8. The logic of the preference-erosion or exploitation stumbling block was demonstrated in a Walrasian setting by Riezman (1985) and Kennan and Riezman (1990) and in a Brander-Krugman setting by Krishna (1998) and Freund (2000a). See also Goto and Hamada (1995),

Nordström (1995), and Bond and Syropoulos (1996a, sec. 3) for examples of preference-erosion stumbling blocks.

9. The theoretical notion was formalized by Limão (2007).

10. Levy (1997) illustrates a cherry-picking stumbling block in a highly stylized setup, but his main result is surely more general than his model.

11. This is called the Stolper-Samuelson effect in the economic literature.

12. More formally, without MTNs, governments maximize a politically weighted objective function that includes matters affected by the nation's own tariffs: profits of import-competing sectors, consumer surplus, and tariff revenue. During the negotiations, a nation's tariff affects all those things, but foreign tariff levels are linked to domestic tariffs via reciprocity, and the objective function now includes the effect of foreign tariffs on exporter's profits. Since this new impact is negative (higher domestic tariffs reduce exporter's profits via reciprocity), announcement of the MTN leads the government to find it politically optimal to choose a tariff that is lower than the politically optimal tariff before the MTN.

13. The word "juggernaut," defined as "any massive inexorable force that advances crushing whatever is in the path," stems from a British mispronunciation of the name of the Hindu deity of the Puri shrine, Jagannath. A festival held in Puri involves the "chariot of Jagannath," an enormous and unwieldy construction that requires thousands of people to get it rolling. Once started, however, it rolls over anything in its path.

14. The juggernaut logic is from Baldwin (1994, ch. 2.5); it is elaborated in Baldwin and Robert-Nicoud (2005) and Baldwin (2006) and formalized in part by Freund (2000b). The first part of the juggernaut mechanism—realignment of domestic special interests through reciprocity—has long been recognized in histories of trade liberalization—for example, by Bergsten (1996) and Destler (2005), under the name "bicycle theory and export politics." The point was also made by many others, including Robert Baldwin (1985). The basic idea dates much further back, as Irwin (1996) points out. More recently, the first half of the juggernaut logic has been studied formally by Grossman and Helpman (2001) and by Bagwell and Staiger (2002). Juggernaut-like mechanisms were discussed independently by Hufbauer, Schott, and Clark (1994, 164) and by Richardson (1993). Bergsten (1998) mentions an alternative source of political-economy momentum ("modest liberalization begets broader liberalization by demonstrating its payoff and familiarizing domestic politics with the issue"). Staiger (1995) uses a repeated game setting, with workers moving slowly out of the import-competing sector to generate gradualism, but MTNs and GATT reciprocity play no role. Milner (1997) and Oye (1992), working independently in the international political-economy context, discuss mechanisms by which PTAs can create a proliberalization political-economy momentum. More recently, Hathaway (1998) presents a similar logic in her positive-feedback model.

15. But multilateral tariff cutting may also lower tariffs to a level at which PTAs become feasible, when previously they were not; this may have been the case with the Canada–U.S. FTA.

16. Agriculture in Europe is a good example. Formation of the customs union realigned special interests in the European Economic Community (EEC) in a way that fostered higher agricultural tariffs. EEC tariffs on agricultural goods were not bound until the 1990s, and so the community was free to raise its agricultural tariffs without appealing to the Article 24 exception. Since EEC tariffs were bound for manufacturing goods, EEC members needed the Article 24 exception to establish the common external tariff (CET), and this led them to respect the article's requirement that the CET not be higher, on average. Roughly speaking, France lowered its tariffs; Germany raised its tariffs; and Belgium, Luxembourg, and the Netherlands did little, as their tariffs were initially between the French and German levels. In this way, the formation of the EEC customs union probably reduced the overall size of the EEC import-competing sector in manufacturing but raised it in agriculture.

17. The key concepts are "coalition externalities" (Haberler's spillover) and "grand-coalition superadditivity" (global free trade is first-best). The authors assume that one nation is the undisputed agenda setter and that

unlimited international transfers (transferable utility, in game theory parlance) are possible.

18. See Lloyd (2002) for a clear development of the veto-avoidance logic. This line of thinking is one strand in the widely discussed competitive liberalization logic advanced by Bergsten (1996).

19. This is especially true given all the separability that rules Meade's secondary and tertiary effects (see Meade 1955).

20. Given the separability of the markets, the second FTA with RoW would yield a price for Good 3 equal to P'.

21. Contributions to the literature that have looked at the complementarity versus substitutes effects include Riezman (1985), Kennan and Riezman (1990), Krugman (1991a, 1991b, 1996), Richardson (1993), Bond and Syropoulos (1996a), Freund (2000a), and Ornelas (2005b, 2007).

22. Shibata (1967), Vousden (1990), Krueger (1993), Richardson (1993, 1994, 1995), and Grossman and Helpman (1995) are all important contributors to or users of this line of analysis.

23. Extension of this analysis led to the proposition of the unsustainablity of FTAs. Vousden (1990, 234) argues that Home would be tempted to lower its MFN tariff to just under that of Partner in order to recapture the tariff revenue and that Partner would have an incentive to reply, with the resulting race-to-the-bottom tariff making FTAs "unsustainable." Richardson (1995) extended and popularized this result. The main results in Shibata (1967), Vousden (1990), and Richardson (1995)—the irrelevance of rules of origin and the unsustainability of FTAs—are of little relevance to real-world policy concerns. (Rules of origin are at the heart of many current policy debates, and FTAs, not customs unions, are by far the most prevalent form of PTA.)

24. This approach came to be known as the terms-of-trade approach after Kyle Bagwell, Robert Staiger, and their students formally modeled the issues, starting with Bagwell and Staiger (1993). For examples of this sort of application to regionalism questions, see Bond and Syropoulos (1996b); Bond, Syropoulos, and Winters (1996); Campa and Sorenson (1996); Yi (1996); Bagwell and Staiger (1999); Conconi (2000); Conconi and Perroni (2000); Freund (2000b); and Ornelas (2005a, 2007).

25. This is not a new point. It is very clear in the discussion of Johnson (1953) but probably dates much further back. Indeed, the notion that a quid pro quo would be mutually advantageous was probably well understood by trade diplomats as far back as Roman times.

26. An alternative is to use computable general equilibrium models to identify counterfactuals, but the results are highly dependent on the parameters assumed. See, for example, Brown, Deardorff, and Stern (1992).

27. Schiff and Chang (2003) find that the threat of duty-free exports from Argentina to Brazil, measured by Argentina's exports of the same good to another country, also lowers prices of exports by nonmembers of Mercosur to Brazil.

28. Egger and Larch (2008) confirm those findings in a larger sample, finding also that preexisting nearby PTAs increase the probability that a country pair will form a PTA.

29. Baldwin (2006) argues that the WTO can be involved, as was done in the Information Technology (IT) Agreement, which bound IT tariffs at zero for all countries willing to join. This is a way of "multilateralizing regionalism."

References

Aghion, Philippe, Pol Antràs, and Elhanan Helpman. 2007. "Negotiating Free Trade." *Journal of International Economics* 73, no.1 (September): 1–30.

Bagwell, Kyle, and Robert W. Staiger. 1993. "Multilateral Tariff Cooperation during the Formation of Regional Free Trade Areas." NBER Working Paper 4364, National Bureau of Economic Research, Cambridge, MA. http://www.nber.org/papers/w4364.

———. 1999. "Regionalism and Multilateral Tariff Cooperation." In *International Trade Policy and the Pacific Rim,* ed. John Piggott and Alan Woodland. London: Macmillan.

———. 2002. *The Economics of the World Trading System.* Cambridge, MA: MIT Press.

Baier, Scott L., and Jeffrey H. Bergstrand. 2004. "Economic Determinants of Free Trade Agreements." *Journal of International Economics* 64, no.1 (October): 29–63.

———. 2007. "Do Free Trade Agreements Actually Increase Members' International Trade?" *Journal of International Economics* 71, no.1 (March): 72–95.

Baldwin, Richard. 1993. "A Domino Theory of Regionalism." NBER Working Paper 4465, National Bureau of Economic Research, Cambridge, MA. http://www.nber.org/papers/w4465.

———. 1994. *Towards an Integrated Europe.* London: Centre for Economic Policy Research.

———. 1997. "The Causes of Regionalism." *World Economy* 20 (7): 865–88.

———. 2006. "Multilateralising Regionalism: Spaghetti Bowls as Building Blocs on the Path to Global Free Trade." *World Economy* 29 (11): 1451–1518.

———. 2009. "Big-Think Regionalism: A Critical Survey." In *Regional Rules in the Global Trading System,* ed. Antoni Estevadeordal, Kati Suominen, and Robert Teh. Cambridge, U.K.: Cambridge University Press.

Baldwin, Richard, and Frédéric Robert-Nicoud. 2005. "Juggernaut Model—The Lego Version." Graduate Institute of International Studies, Geneva.

Baldwin, Richard, and Elena Seghezza. 2010. "Are Trade Blocs Building or Stumbling Blocks?" *Journal of Economic Integration* 25, no.2 (June): 276–97.

Baldwin, Robert E. 1970. *Non-Tariff Distortions of International Trade.* Washington, DC: Brookings Institution.

———. 1985. *The Political Economy of U.S. Import Policy.* Cambridge, MA: MIT Press.

Bergsten, C. Fred. 1991. "Commentary: The Move toward Free Trade Zones." *Economic Review, Federal Reserve Bank of Kansas City,* 76 (November–December): 27–35.

———. 1996. "Globalizing Free Trade: The Ascent of Regionalism." *Foreign Affairs* 75, no.3 (May–June): 105–20.

———. 1998. "Fifty Years of the GATT/WTO: Lessons from the Past for Strategies for the Future." Working Paper 98-3, Peterson Institute for International Economics, Washington, DC. http://www.iie.com/publications/wp/wp.cfm?ResearchID=144.

Bhagwati, Jagdish N. 1991. *The World Trading System at Risk.* Princeton, NJ: Princeton University Press.

———. 1993. "Regionalism and Multilateralism: An Overview." In *New Dimensions in Regional Integration,* ed. Jaime de Melo and Arvind Panagariya. Oxford, U.K.: Oxford University Press.

———. 2008. *Termites in the Trading System.* Oxford, U.K.: Oxford University Press.

Bohara, Alok K., Kishore Gawande, and Pablo Sanguinetti. 2004. "Trade Diversion and Declining Tariffs: Evidence from Mercosur." *Journal of International Economics* 64 (1): 65–88.

Bond, Eric, and Constantinos Syropoulos. 1996a. "The Size of Trading Blocs: Market Power and World Welfare Effects." *Journal of International Economics* 40 (3–4): 412–37.

———. 1996b. "Trading Blocs and the Sustainability of Interregional Cooperation." *The New Transatlantic Economy,* eds. Matthew Canzoneri, Wilfred Ethier, and Vittorio Grillli. Cambridge, U.K.: Cambridge University Press.

Bond, Eric W., Constantinos Syropoulos, and L. Alan Winters. 1996. "Deepening of Regional Integration and External Trade Relations." CEPR Discussion Paper 1317, Centre for Economic Policy Research, London.

Brown, Drusilla K., Alan V. Deardorff, and Robert M. Stern. 1992. "North American Integration." *Economic Journal* 102, no.415 (November): 1507–18.

Calvo-Pardo, Hector, Caroline Freund, and Emanuel Ornelas. 2009. "The ASEAN Free Trade Agreement: Impact on Trade Flows and External

Trade Barriers." Policy Research Working Paper 4960, World Bank, Washington, DC. http://www-wds.worldbank.org/servlet/WDSContentServer/WDSP/IB/2009/06/10/000158349_20090610085729/Rendered/PDF/WPS4960.pdf. Forthcoming in *Quantifying the Costs and Benefits of Regional Economic Integration in Asia*, ed. Robert Barro and Jong-Wha Lee. Manila: Asian Development Bank.

Campa, José Manuel, and Timothy L. Sorenson. 1996. "Are Trade Blocs Conducive to Free Trade?" *Scandinavian Journal of Economics* 98 (2): 263–73.

Carrère, Cèline. 2006. "Revisiting the Effects of Regional Trade Agreements on Trade Flows with Proper Specification of the Gravity Model." *European Economic Review* 50: 223–47.

Chang, Won, and L. Alan Winters. 2002. "How Regional Blocs Affect Excluded Countries: The Price Effects of Mercosur." *American Economic Review* 92 (4): 889–904.

Clausing, Kimberly A. 2001. "Trade Creation and Trade Diversion in the Canada–United States Free Trade Agreement." *Canadian Journal of Economics* 34: 677–96.

Conconi, Paola. 2000. "Trade Bloc Formation under Imperfect Competition." The Warwick Economics Research Paper Series (TWERPS) 571, Department of Economics, University of Warwick, Coventry, U.K.

Conconi, Paoli, and Carlo Perroni. 2000. "Issue Linkage and Issue Tie-In in International Negotiations." The Warwick Economics Research Paper Series (TWERPS) 558, Department of Economics, University of Warwick, Coventry, U.K.

Destler, I. M. 1986. *American Trade Politics*. Washington, DC: Peterson Institute for International Economics.

———. 2005. *American Trade Politics*. 4th ed. Washington, DC: Peterson Institute for International Economics.

Dixit, Avinash, and Victor Norman. 1980. *Theory of International Trade*. Cambridge, U.K.: Cambridge University Press.

Egger, Peter, and Mario Larch. 2008. "Interdependent Preferential Trade Agreement Memberships: An Empirical Analysis." *Journal of International Economics* 76 (2): 384–99.

Estevadeordal, Antoni, Caroline Freund, and Emanuel Ornelas. 2008. "Does Regionalism Affect Trade Liberalization toward Nonmembers?" *Quarterly Journal of Economics* 123, no.4 (November): 1531–75.

Ethier, Wilfred J. 1998. "Regionalism in a Multilateral World." *Journal of Political Economy* 109 (6): 1214–45.

Fernandez, Raquel, and Jonathan Portes. 1998. "Returns to Regionalism: An Analysis of Nontraditional Gains from Regional Trade Agreements." *World Bank Economic Review* 12, no.2 (May): 197–220.

Foroutan, Faezeh. 1998. "Does Membership in a Regional Preferential Trade Arrangement Make a Country More or Less Protectionist?" *World Economy* 21: 305–35.

Frankel, Jeffrry A., and Shang-Jin Wei. 1998. "Regionalization of World Trade and Currencies: Economics and Politics." In *The Regionalization of the World Economy*, ed. J. A. Frankel, ch. 7. Chicago, IL: Chicago University Press.

Frankel, Jeffrey A., Ernesto Stein, and Shang-Jin Wei. 1995. "Trading Blocs and the Americas: The Natural, the Unnatural, and the Super-Natural." *Journal of Development Economics* 47: 61–95.

Freund, Caroline. 2000a. "Different Paths to Free Trade: The Gains from Regionalism." *Quarterly Journal of Economics* 115 (4): 1317–41.

———. 2000b. "Multilateralism and the Endogenous Formation of Preferential Trade Agreements." *Journal of International Economics* 52: 359–76.

Goto, Junichi, and Koichi Hamada. 1995. "EU, NAFTA, and Asian Responses: A Perspective from the Calculus of Participation." NBER Working Paper 5325, National Bureau of Economic Research, Cambridge, MA.

Grossman, Gene, and Elhanan Helpman. 1995. "The Politics of Free Trade Agreements." *American Economic Review* 85: 667–90.

———. 2001. *Special Interest Politics*. Cambridge, MA: MIT Press.

Hathaway, Oona. 1998. "Positive Feedback: The Impact of Trade Liberalization on Industry Demands for Protection." *International Organization* 52, no.3 (Summer): 575–612.

Haveman, Jon D., and David L. Hummels. 1998. "What Can We Learn from Bilateral Trade? Gravity and Beyond." Krannert School of Management—Center for International Business Education and Research (CIBER), Purdue University, West Lafayette, IN.

Hufbauer, Gary C., Jeffrey Schott, and Diana Clark. 1994. *Western Hemisphere Economic Integration*. Washington, D C: Institute for International Economics.

Irwin, Douglas. 1996. "Multilateral and Bilateral Trade Policies in the World Trading System: An Historical Perspective." In *New Dimensions in Regional Integration*, ed. Jaime de Melo and Arvind Panagariya. Cambridge, U.K.: Cambridge University Press.

Johnson, H. 1953. "Optimum Tariffs and Retaliation." *Review of Economic Studies* 21 (2): 142–53.

Karacaovali, Baybars, and Nuno Limão. 2008. "The Clash of Liberalizations: Preferential vs. Multilateral Trade Liberalization in the European Union." *Journal of International Economics* 74: 299–327.

Kemp, Murray C., and Henry Y. Wan, Jr. 1976. "An Elementary Proposition Concerning the Formation of Customs Unions." *Journal of International Economics* 6 (1): 95–97.

Kennan, John, and Raymond Riezman. 1990. "Optimal Tariff Equilibria with Customs Unions." *Canadian Journal of Economics* 23 (1): 70–83.

Krishna, Pravin. 1998. "Regionalism and Multilateralism: A Political Economy Approach." *Quarterly Journal of Economics* 113, no.1 (February): 227–50.

———. 2003. "Are Regional Trading Partners 'Natural'?" *Journal of Political Economy* 111 (1): 202–26.

Krueger, Anne O. 1993. "Free Trade Agreements Versus Customs Unions." *Journal of Development Economics* 54: 169–87.

Krugman, Paul. 1991a. "Is Bilateralism Bad?" In *International Trade and Trade Policy*, ed. Elhanan Helpman and Assaf Razin. Cambridge, MA: MIT Press.

———. 1991b. "The Move toward Free Trade Zones." *Economic Review, Federal Reserve Bank of Kansas City,* 76, no.6 (November–December): 5–25.

———. 1996. "Regionalism versus Multilateralism: Analytic Notes." In *New Dimensions in Regional Integration,* ed. Jaime de Melo and Arvind Panagariya. Cambridge, U.K.: Cambridge University Press.

Lawrence, Robert Z. 1991. "Emerging Regional Arrangements: Building Blocs or Stumbling Blocks?" In *Finance and the International Economy 5: The AMEX Bank Review Prize Essays,* ed. Richard O'Brien, 23–35. New York: Oxford University Press.

———. 1996. *Regionalism, Multilateralism, and Deeper Integration.* Washington, DC: Brookings Institution Press.

Leamer, Edward E. 1990. "The Structure and Effect of Tariff and Non-Tariff Barriers in 1983." In *The Political Economy of International Trade: Essays in Honor of Robert E. Baldwin,* ed. Ronald W. Jones and Anne O. Krueger. Cambridge, MA: Blackwell.

Lee, Jong-Wha, and Kwanho Shin. 2006. "Does Regionalism Lead to More Global Trade Integration in East Asia?" *North American Journal of Economics and Finance* 17: 283–301.

Levy, Philip I. 1997. "A Political-Economic Analysis of Free-Trade Agreements." *American Economic Review* 87 (4): 506–19.

Limão, Nuno. 2006. "Preferential Trade Agreements as Stumbling Blocks for Multilateral Trade Liberalization: Evidence for the United States." *American Economic Review* 96 (3): 896–914.

———. 2007. "Are Preferential Trade Agreements with Non-trade Objectives a Stumbling Block for Multilateral Liberalization?" *Review of Economic Studies* 74 (3): 821–55.

Lloyd, Peter John. 2002. "New Bilateralism in the Asia–Pacific." *World Economy* 25 (9): 1279–96.

Ludema, Rodney D. 1996. "Increasing Returns, Multinationals and Geography of Preferential Trade Agreements." *Journal of International Economics* 56 (2): 329–58.

Magee, Christopher S. P. 2008. "New Measures of Trade Creation and Trade Diversion." *Journal of International Economics* 75 (2): 340–62.

Meade, James E. 1955. *The Theory of Customs Unions*. Amsterdam. North-Holland.

Milner, Helen V. 1997. *Interests, Institutions and Information: Domestic Politics and International Relations.* Princeton, NJ: Princeton University Press.

Nordström, Håkan. 1995. "Customs Unions, Regional Trading Blocs and Welfare." In *Expanding Membership of the European Union,* ed. Richard E. Baldwin, Pertti Haaparanta, and Jaakko Kiander, 54–78. Cambridge, U.K.: Cambridge University Press.

Ornelas, Emanuel. 2005a. "Trade Creating Free Trade Areas and the Undermining of Multilateralism." *European Economic Review* 49: 1717–35.

———. 2005b. "Rent Destruction and the Political Viability of Free Trade Agreements." *Quarterly Journal of Economics* 120: 1475–1506.

———. 2007. "Exchanging Market Access at the Outsiders' Expense: The Case of Customs Unions." *Canadian Journal of Economics* 40 (1): 207–24.

Oye, Kenneth A. 1992. *Economic Discrimination and Political Exchange: World Political Economy in the 1930s and 1980s.* Princeton, NJ: Princeton University Press.

Panagariya, Arvind. 2000. "Preferential Trade Liberalization: The Traditional Theory and New Developments." *Journal of Economic Literature* 38: 287–331.

Panagariya, Arvind, and Jagdish Bhagwati. 1999, "Preferential Trading Areas and Multilateralism: Strangers, Friends or Foes?" In *Regionalism in Trade Policy: Essays on Preferential Trading,* ed. Arvind Panagariya, 47–111. Singapore: World Scientific Publishing.

Panagariya, Arvind, and Ronald Findlay. 1994. "A Political Economy Analysis of Free Trade Areas and Customs Unions." Policy Research Working Paper 1261, World Bank, Washington, DC.

Richardson, Martin. 1993. "Endogenous Protection and Trade Diversion." *Journal of International Economics* 34 (3–4): 309–24.

———. 1994. "Why a Free Trade Area? The Tariff also Rises." *Economics and Politics* 6 (1): 79–96.

———. 1995. "Tariff Revenue Competition in a Free Trade Area." *European Economic Review* 39: 1429–37.

Riezman, Raymond. 1985. "Customs Unions and the Core." *Journal of International Economics* 19 (3–4): 355–65.

Romalis, John. 2007. "NAFTA's and CUSFTA's Impact on International Trade." *Review of Economics and Statistics* 89 (3): 416–35.

Saggi, Kamal, and Halis Murat Yildiz. 2008. "Bilateral Trade Agreements and the Feasibility of Multilateral Free Trade." MPRA Paper 17561, Munich Personal RePEc Archive, Munich, Germany. http://mpra.ub.uni-muenchen.de/17561/.

Sapir, André. 1996. "Discussion" of ch. 7, L. Alan Winters, "The European Community: A Case of Successful Integration?" In *New Dimensions in Regional Integration,* ed. Jaime de Melo and Arvind Panagariya, Cambridge, U.K.: Cambridge University Press.

Schiff, Maurice, and Won Chang. 2003. "Market Presence, Contestability, and the Terms-of-Trade Effects of Regional Integration," *Journal of International Economics* 60, no.1 (May): 161–75.

Schott, Jeffrey. 1988. "The Free Trade Agreement: A US Assessment." In *The Canada–United States Free Trade Agreement: The Global Impact,* ed. Jeffrey J. Schott and Murray G. Smith. Washington, DC: Institute for International Economics.

Serra, Jaime, et al. 1997. *Reflections on Regionalism: Report of the Study Group on International Trade.* New York: Carnegie Endowment for International Peace.

Shibata, Hirofumi. 1967. "The Theory of Economic Unions: A Comparative Analysis of Customs Unions, Free Trade Areas and Tax Unions." In *Fiscal Harmonisation in Common Markets,* ed. Call S. Shoup, vol. 1, 145–264. New York: Columbia University Press.

Sinclair, P., and D. Vines 1995. "Bigger Trade Blocs Need Not Entail More Protection." University of Birmingham, U.K.

Snape, Richard. 1993. "History and Economics of GATT's Article XXIV." In *Regional Integration and the Global Trading System,* ed. Kym Anderson and Richard Blackhurst, 273–91. New York: Harvester Wheatsheaf.

Staiger, Robert W. 1995 "A Theory of Gradual Trade Liberalization" In *New Directions in Trade Theory,* ed. Alan V. Deardorff, James A. Levinsohn, and Robert M. Stern. Ann Arbor, MI: University of Michigan Press.

Summers, Lawrence. 1991. "Regionalism and the World Trading System." *Economic Review, Federal Reserve Bank of Kansas City,* 76, no.6 (November–December): 295–302.

Trefler, Daniel. 2004. "The Long and Short of the Canada–U.S. Free Trade Agreement." *American Economic Review* 94 (4): 870–95.

Vousden, Neil. 1990. *The Economics of Trade Protection.* Cambridge, U.K.: Cambridge University Press.

Whalley, John. 1996. "Regional Trade Arrangements in North America: CUSTA and NAFTA." In *New Dimensions in Regional Integration,* ed. Jaime de Melo and Arvind Panagariya, 352–81. Cambridge, U.K.: Cambridge University Press.

Winters, L. Alan. 1993. "The European Community: A Case of Successful Integration?" CEPR Discussion Paper 755, Centre for Economic Policy Research, London.

Wonnacott, Paul. 1987. "U.S. and Canadian Auto Policies in a Changing World Environment." Canadian-American Committee, C. D. Howe Institute and National Planning Association, Toronto, Canada.

WTO (World Trade Organization). 1995. *Regionalism and the World Trading System.* Geneva: WTO.

Yi, Sang-Seung. 1996. "Endogenous Formation of Customs Unions under Imperfect Competition: Open Regionalism Is Good." *Journal of International Economics* 41 (1–2): 151–77.

7

AGRICULTURE

Tim Josling

The links between regional integration and agricultural trade strategy are of increasing interest to developing countries as they confront the challenge of opening up their economies to competition while mitigating the associated adjustment costs. Countries around the world have stepped up their efforts to establish regional preferential trade agreements (PTAs) and to coordinate trade relations with other regions. Agricultural trade is a core component of many of these trade initiatives, and a large part of the gains from regional integration depends on the inclusion of agricultural and food products in PTAs. Agricultural trade policy and regional integration agreements can together serve as instruments for accelerating growth and contributing to poverty alleviation.

Although the motivation for PTAs is often political, these agreements have significant implications for agriculture and other sectors of the economy. Many North-South agreements were concluded after a country gained independence in order to maintain trading links developed in the colonial era—typically, for trade in raw materials and agricultural products. Other PTAs were instituted as part of the development of alliances and to bolster regimes that were under threat. Agricultural products often provided trade opportunities that reinforced such alliances. PTAs have long been used by developed countries to pursue overseas developmental objectives through the provision of preferential market access, often for primary products. Such access, however, has frequently been constrained when sensitive domestic agricultural products were involved.

More recent thinking has cast doubt on the longer-term benefits of PTAs on the grounds that they tend to lock exporting countries into a particular pattern of exports, often of unprocessed raw materials and farm products, while competitors develop other markets and diversify their range of export products. A further problem, from the viewpoint of developing countries, has been that the terms of the PTAs are largely at the discretion of the preference-granting country, with little guarantee that the agreements will not be changed if they lose domestic political backing. This asymmetry also implies that the granting country can continue to extract political benefits from the preference-receiving partner, including support for economic and political positions.

The role of PTAs in agricultural development varies greatly, from strategic and deliberate to largely passive and reactive. Countries can choose to plan their agricultural strategies on a regional basis to take advantage of scale economies and to overcome some of the constraints facing small national markets. Often, however, agriculture is brought into regional agreements through extraneous circumstances rather than careful planning; agriculture becomes one element in a broader set of complex trade-offs. PTAs often have an underlying rationale of contributing to increased regional cohesion and political integration, and the treatment of the agriculture sector becomes of interest, beyond strictly commercial considerations. Food security and the coordination of food policies and marketing infrastructure may be important reasons for the inclusion of a strong agricultural component in regional policies. Thus, the key issues in addressing agricultural trade in PTAs are whether regional integration promotes or hinders the development of a sustainable, competitive agriculture sector and whether agricultural trade considerations contribute to or detract from the benefits of regional integration.

This chapter attempts to put into perspective what we know and do not know about the economic impact of PTAs on agricultural development. The next section surveys the arguments for and against preferential trade integration as a development strategy for agriculture. These arguments relate, in general, to the effects of opening up trade among selected trade partners, as opposed to relying on either unilateral or multilateral actions. The rationales also cite possible economies in the joint production of public goods that benefit agriculture, ranging from research and extension to food security reserves. The second section then reviews what is known empirically about the impact of PTAs on agricultural trade. The third discusses some ways in which PTAs have dealt in practice with a set of problems that are commonly encountered when agriculture is included in PTA provisions. Both regional and bilateral PTAs are considered, as the agricultural problems differ somewhat in the two types of agreements.

Economics of Agricultural Trade in PTAs

In most respects, the economics of agricultural trade in PTAs is no different from the economics of nonagricultural trade. As with trade in nonfarm goods, agricultural trade in PTAs benefits from static gains related to expanded market access and from more dynamic gains related to the spread of ideas, innovations, and know-how (see Baldwin, ch. 3 in this volume).

Two important initial questions frame any agricultural trade strategy in PTAs: (a) how high are domestic (tariff and nontariff) barriers relative to those of regional partners and other countries, and (b) how efficient are the export sectors within the region? If the region includes suppliers of agricultural products whose costs are lower than those of more distant exporters, then the regional strategy carries benefits similar to the unilateral or multilateral lowering of tariff barriers. Regional supplies can be integrated into a country's food policy, and ensuring access to those supplies will be an element in food security policy. The higher the existing tariffs (and other trade barriers) that restrict regional trade in these products, the greater will be the benefits of preferential liberalization to consumers. But this also implies greater disruption to domestic producers, who presumably have not had to face regional competition. When there are other products that could gain from the export opportunities that would open up with regional trade, a beneficial transfer of resources from the import-competing to the exporting agriculture sector may be possible. But if the agriculture sector in the regional partner is not efficient, the reduction in trade barriers may merely substitute a high-cost partner product for a more efficient third-country supply. Under these conditions, the advantages are likely to be small and the costs high.

These considerations need to be seen in a dynamic context. Inefficient agricultural suppliers could become low cost if their inefficiencies had been the consequence of limited markets and diseconomies of scale. The extent to which regional integration can provide the scale needed for such cost reductions depends on specific circumstances, but, in principle, the achievement of economies of scale can be a positive argument for regional integration. If the partner with the inefficient agriculture sector can make use of scale economies to become efficient, costs will decrease. But to treat PTAs as a nursery for potentially competitive sectors is controversial at best: the infant may become dependent on the protected market within the PTA and may not have an incentive to become competitive outside the area. Moreover, import-competing sectors will tend to shrink with regional integration and may lose some benefits of scale. Thus, the larger question is whether there is a possibility of a broad restructuring of the agriculture sectors of each of the PTA partners so that economies of scale can be exploited and resources redeployed to take advantage of regional (as opposed to national) cost advantages.

Fluctuations in output often mark agricultural markets, and trade is a vital means for offsetting the impact on available consumer supplies. The easier trade is, the less is the cost of market disruption to consumers. Greater regional food security is thus another plausible argument for integration of the regional partners' food supply network. All parties to a PTA that includes an open internal agricultural market will enjoy the advantages of more secure access to regional supplies. Even where weather and other related determinants of yield variations are regionally correlated, there can still be benefits from pooling risks. Storage facilities can be collectively operated, and regionally coherent transportation systems can improve distribution. There may, however, be a political cost because of loss of the ability to control domestic markets.

Agricultural trade in PTAs can benefit from some of the considerations of spatial or economic geography that apply to trade in goods. Some of these have to do with the provision of public goods, where the good concerned is valued (and underprovided) across local jurisdictions. More generally, both public and private sector actions can be expanded to a regional scale with advantage. Greater coordination of export strategies, more reliable supply chains for buyers, shared control over the quality and safety of exports, a better bargaining position with importers in other countries, and the possibilities for branding and labeling of regional products are all likely to result in expansion of export markets.

Preferential Agricultural Trade and Multilateral Commitments

As noted by Baldwin and Freund (ch. 6 in this volume), a key tension between bilateral or regional trade rules and multilateral trade rules arises from the latter's requirement that PTAs eliminate tariffs and other trade measures on "substantially all trade" and that the level of preference be 100 percent. (The multilateral rules in question are those of the General Agreement on Tariffs and Trade, or GATT, as now embodied in the World Trade Organization, or WTO.)[1] Although there has as yet been no agreement on the interpretation of "substantially all trade," agriculture is the sector most often excluded or treated differently; manufactures are far more likely to benefit from tariff reductions in PTAs than are agricultural goods (Fiorentino 2005). The prospect that competing exporters will challenge the exceptional treatment of agriculture in PTAs is remote, however, because these competitors tend to benefit from it. Exporters within the PTA have implicitly agreed to the exclusion and would be reluctant to challenge a partner with respect to mutually agreed decisions.

The requirement for movement toward full internal free trade (100 percent preference) has also been problematic. In some PTAs, partners gain an advantage from preferential tariffs but still face nonzero rates. Despite the inconsistency with GATT Article XXIV, several of these preferential tariff schemes have been permitted. As noted, there would be little outside interest in challenging such schemes, given that the lack of 100 percent preference works to the advantage of the excluded supplier.[2] The WTO requirement that the free trade area encompass "substantially all trade" (which, for most developing countries, includes agriculture) imposes costs on PTAs that include high-cost agriculture sectors. It may be therefore better in economic terms for such PTAs to exclude highly protected sectors, including agriculture.

The complementarity of preferential tariff reduction with multilateral trade developments can be part of a positive strategy for agriculture: the multilateral system could work to lower most favored nation (MFN) tariffs and reduce trade-distorting subsidies, making it easier and less costly to negotiate PTAs. The coordination of multilateral strategy among the regional partners also offers other possibilities for regional negotiating strategies and negotiating groups and opens an opportunity to develop strategies that combine regional and multilateral integration.[3]

There are indications that PTAs may be more successful than multilateral agreements in opening markets for agricultural goods. It often seems easier to fine-tune market access within discriminatory agreements, through selective inclusions. The European Union (EU) provides limited access for sensitive agricultural products to the many countries that have signed such agreements, including the Mediterranean countries; the African, Caribbean, and Pacific (ACP) countries; South Africa; and Mexico.[4] Within the North American Free Trade Agreement (NAFTA), the United States is moving toward a free internal agricultural market with Mexico and Canada, with few exceptions. More recently, the United States has negotiated agreements with Chile, Central America, the Dominican Republic, and Australia, giving those countries preferred, although not free, access to U.S. markets. Less sensitive food products are also included in the generalized system of preferences (GSP) schemes. Substantial amounts of agricultural trade thus do face barriers less restrictive than MFN tariffs. Presumably, much of this trade is diverted from lower-cost suppliers.

Yet, the short-term market access gains from a PTA have to be weighed against the possible adverse effects on the multilateral trading system. Many of the problems that make the incorporation of agriculture in a PTA regime difficult also prevail in a multilateral context. A prominent issue in this regard is the extent to which disciplines on domestic farm subsidies can be included in PTAs. It is often assumed that the conduct of domestic policy is outside the realm of PTAs, but this is not always the case. The movement toward "decoupled" policies, encouraged by the WTO Agreement on Agriculture, has the advantage of making it easier to have free trade in a commodity and still maintain domestic support policies (box 7.1). Nevertheless, the existence of an active domestic support policy, involving subsidies and market management, complicates the negotiation of free trade in those products. If agricultural trade can be omitted from PTA provisions, the question of domestic support does not arise. Conversely, if agriculture cannot be excluded without violating WTO provisions, the potentially problematic issue of domestic support policies cannot be avoided.

The treatment of export subsidies in PTAs is similarly problematic. Various trade agreements include provisions that countries may not employ export subsidies in mutual trade. Although this stipulation sounds logical, it is not easy in practice to ban subsidies paid on internal trade without creating an incentive to import from outside and a disincentive to export within the PTA. In effect, export subsidies also have to be controlled at the WTO level.

The current Doha Round of WTO negotiations would, if successfully completed, make a significant difference to the ease with which agricultural trade could be opened up within PTAs. Under the provisions of the 2008 draft modalities, tariff levels for developed countries would decline by more than 50 percent for agricultural products, and tariff-rate quotas (TRQs) for sensitive commodities would be expanded. This would reduce both the degree of preference for partner suppliers (and hence the risk of trade diversion) and the adjustment for import-competing sectors. Under an agreed schedule of WTO tariff reductions,

---

Box 7.1. The WTO Agreement on Agriculture

The Agreement on Agriculture entered into force with the establishment of the WTO on January 1, 1995. The preamble to the document cites the agreed long-term objective of the Uruguay Round reform program: to establish a fair, market-oriented agricultural trading system. The program includes specific commitments to reduce support and protection in the areas of domestic and export subsidies and of market access and through the establishment of strengthened and more operationally effective GATT rules and disciplines. The Agreement on Agriculture also takes into account nontrade concerns, such as food security and the need to protect the environment, and it provides for special and differential treatment for developing countries, including an improvement in the opportunities and terms of access for agricultural products of particular export interest to these members.

In principle, all WTO agreements and understandings on trade in goods apply to agriculture. These include GATT (incorporated into the WTO agreements as GATT 1994) and WTO agreements on such matters as customs valuation, import-licensing procedures, preshipment inspection, emergency safeguard measures, subsidies, and technical barriers to trade. Where there is any conflict between these agreements and the Agreement on Agriculture, the provisions of the latter prevail. The WTO General Agreement on Trade in Services and the Trade-Related Aspects of Intellectual Property Rights Agreement are also applicable to agriculture.

Source: WTO Agreements series: Agriculture.

---

the marginal impact of quicker reductions for regional or bilateral partners may be more tolerable. In addition, export subsidies would finally be eliminated—a step that has proved difficult to accomplish within PTAs. But the main contribution that the WTO negotiations on agriculture can make to the process of regional and bilateral trade liberalization may be to push countries to abandon price supports in domestic markets and embrace direct payments for public goods or for income relief. Such policies will be more compatible with PTAs, as well as beneficial for the multilateral trading system.

Because of the slow pace of the Doha Round negotiations on agriculture, regional negotiations may have to bear the brunt of attempts to further liberalize agricultural trade and to open access to new markets for agricultural exports. Thus, in agriculture there is a strong degree of complementarity in trade negotiations. Plurilateral agreements can erode market access barriers, but they can also foster less advantageous trade flows by discrimination among suppliers. Multilateral talks can reduce the scope for such trade diversion. The multilateral process can handle subsidy reduction, which, in turn, makes it easier for countries to agree to opening up regional or bilateral trade. This complementarity, however, depends on progress at the multilateral level. Currently, that is the stumbling block.

Economic Integration as an Agricultural Strategy

Is regionalism a better approach to agricultural trade policy than reliance on improved market access through the multilateral system? PTAs may be better than tariff reductions through the WTO at improving market access for the preferred partner with less threat to domestic agriculture sectors. Regional and bilateral PTAs, however, cannot deal effectively with agricultural export subsidies and domestic farm support, and so it is likely that the WTO will continue to be needed as a complement (Josling 2009). Meanwhile, regionalism poses problems for the multilateral system. PTAs may pick the easiest agriculture sectors to liberalize, leaving the most difficult products to the WTO. PTAs can also lead to investment in the "wrong" countries, just to get access to their agricultural markets. Moreover, too many simultaneous negotiations can overstretch resources. Some PTAs can be "strategic": an example is the efforts of the Southern Cone Common Market (Mercosur, or Mercado Común del Sur) to get the rest of South America into its camp before dealing with the United States and NAFTA. Some PTAs can be competitive, as when the EU and the United States compete for the Mercosur market. Such activities are likely to distract from the WTO, or they might distort the multilateral nature of the Doha Round.

These issues have been discussed in the literature of trade strategy. Analyses by Zissimos and Vines (2000) and by Andriamananjara (2002) suggest that joining a PTA can be the best "safe-haven" strategy when other countries are also doing so. But this does not imply that the end result is one large free trade area, given that PTA membership confers a terms-of-trade gain on members at the expense of nonmembers. Some members, at least, will be better off by limiting PTA membership than by allowing expansion to cover the world as a whole. The effect is similar to that suggested by the domino theory of the dynamics of regional trade blocs (see Baldwin, ch. 3 in this volume). As PTAs expand, the attraction of being within the bloc (or the cost of being outside) increases, but the marginal gain to existing members of adding one more (small) market to the bloc, and the extra administrative and political cost of a large membership, will act as a brake. The implication is that each such agreement will tend to find its equilibrium size, where the costs and benefits of enlargement are in balance.[5]

So, is the pursuit of PTAs a short-term or a long-term strategy in agricultural liberalization? Pursuing bilateral North-South PTA arrangements at the regional level may lead to short-term benefits of access to agricultural markets for participating developing countries. But developing countries should be aware that preferential access is likely to be eroded as more countries sign such deals, reducing the value of preferences (García-Alvarez-Coque 2002). For PTAs to be beneficial in the longer term, governments and stakeholders should implement a set of reforms to help sustain the growth of domestic agriculture and reduce the poverty of the agricultural population.

As noted, this type of discriminatory trade agreement has both positive and negative aspects. On the positive side is the ease of reaching an agreement among a small group of adjacent countries. Often, the countries involved will share historical and social perspectives on trade and agriculture. But this ease of reaching agreement comes at a cost. PTAs tend to "cherry-pick" the easiest trade areas in which to conclude a deal, leaving the more difficult ones to the WTO. The ease of reaching an agreement may reflect the willingness of the parties to avoid hard decisions by excluding sensitive sectors such as agriculture from the deal.

Those PTAs that have been most effective in opening up agricultural markets have tended to include as members major agricultural exporters that see the advantages of expanding markets. Countries that are mainly importers of farm products are less likely to agree to open up markets, and hence the benefits to the sector may be small.

In PTAs among members in different regions, the temptation to exclude sensitive sectors of agriculture is even greater, as there is less probability that the deal will include provisions of benefit to agricultural export interests. Given that bilateral PTAs often involve countries that are not geographically close, there is often an opportunity to negotiate with a country with a complementary agricultural pattern to take advantage of trade opportunities. In practice, this often works in reverse, as countries cherry-pick partners so as to avoid conflicts over agriculture. The existence of political tensions in trade agreements usually indicates potential economic benefits that could be realized from changes in trade patterns.

The positive and negative aspects of PTAs are compounded by the apparent advantage that nonreciprocal preferences give to the recipient country relative to others. But overall, the limiting factors mentioned earlier, together with the restrictive rules of origin for many processed products, have severely limited the role of trade preferences in encouraging agricultural diversification in developing countries.

Tariffs introduce a wedge between the world price of a product and the price on the domestic market. Trade preferences allow products from the beneficiary country to enter the partner country with lower import duties than are applied to other countries' products under the partner country's MFN tariffs and hence capture some of the wedge. They give suppliers in beneficiary developing countries access to part or all of the price premium that normally accrues to the importing country government as tariff revenue. The acquisition of these rents raises returns in the developing country and, depending on the nature of competition in domestic product and factor markets, stimulates expansion of the activity concerned, with implications for wages and employment.

Developing countries, especially the least developed countries, face much higher trade-related costs than other countries in getting their products into international markets. Some of these costs may reflect institutional problems within the countries themselves, such as inefficient practices and corruption, and they require a domestic policy response. But some reflect weak transportation infrastructure and firms' lack of access to standard trade-facilitating measures such as insurance and trade finance.

Empirical Evidence on Agricultural Trade and PTAs

What might a theoretical approach to the issue of agricultural trade and regional agreements suggest? Would one expect the proliferation of PTAs to have brought about trade expansion in agricultural products? In his analysis of the economic impact of regional integration on agricultural trade, Goto (1997) concludes that the higher the level of preintegration protection, and the lower the degree of product differentiation, the greater the impact of regional integration. He hypothesizes that "regionalism has more [of an impact] on agricultural trade than on manufacturing [trade], because the initial level of protection is higher and the degree of product differentiation is lower for agricultural products." On the basis of this theoretical conclusion, PTAs could be expected to have a significant role in agricultural liberalization, and this hypothesis will be explored in the brief review of the empirical literature that follows.

The literature on agricultural trade issues in PTAs is thin and scattered, and there is very little by way of detailed and comparative analyses of the arrangements made for agriculture in regional PTAs. Bilateral PTAs are somewhat better documented, as they tend to be focused on a more limited number of products, and the trade flows and conditions of market access are watched closely by the domestic sectors concerned. Unilateral preferences are again the subject of study, in part because of their dependence on periodic renewal and in part because of their direct impact on competing suppliers. An example of a case for which there is adequate information and several empirical analyses is the EU's regime for bananas, where the WTO case has brought much transparency to the way in which the ACP countries sell their bananas to Europe and to the marketing choices of the excluded suppliers. Sugar sales to the United States and the EU under PTAs have also been closely analyzed, and adequate data exist for calculating the effects of such trade arrangements.

Absent such comprehensive and detailed studies dealing with the amount and type of agricultural products traded within PTAs, the assessment of the costs and benefits of agricultural trade in PTAs has tended to rely on more conceptual studies. These studies can be grouped by their focus on one of three questions:

- Has regional trade increased faster than trade with third countries?
- Does the existence of PTAs explain trade flows among the partners in such agreements?
- What are the gains and losses from participation in regional or bilateral PTAs?

The first group of studies essentially consists of explorations of the extent to which world trade is becoming more or less regionalized. It is difficult to derive direct implications from the outcome of such studies because regional trade could well increase rapidly even in the absence of regional agreements. The nature of agricultural and food trade itself is changing over time, and the goods and services that are traded across continents may vary with the regional composition of trade. But it is still useful to have these studies as a way of putting the regionalization of agricultural trade policy in context.

The second group of studies generally involves ex post explanations of trade flows. The most commonly used technique is a gravity model. By inserting dummy variables for the existence of PTAs in regression equations, this method aims to determine the significance of such trade policies in the explanation of trade flows. Agricultural trade flows can be isolated in these studies, and the importance of the trade policy for agriculture can be determined. One application has been to look at the implications of

health and safety regulations for regional trade. These models do not evaluate the trade policies themselves and cannot indicate whether a particular trade strategy is desirable.

The third group of studies consists of ex ante evaluations of prospective agreements. These studies often use computable general equilibrium (CGE) models to calculate trade flows and the welfare implications of policies. Most of the few studies that focus on agriculture take a similar approach, analyzing the significance of trade agreements for agricultural trade.

Each of the three sets of studies has strengths and weaknesses. The study findings are reviewed below, and issues of relevance to the specific question of the empirical evaluation of trade preferences are then addressed.

Regional Trade Flows

The steady growth in world trade in relation to world output is seen as an indicator of the success of the multilateral trade rules put in place by the GATT and reinforced by the WTO. The assumption has been that the elimination of trade barriers and the extension of trade rules have stimulated trade flows. But has trade tended to be concentrated among regions? The literature (e.g., Lloyd 1992; Anderson and Blackhurst 1993) tentatively concludes that the trading system has not developed into a series of intensively trading blocs, with decreased interbloc trade.[6] Trade among blocs remained resilient, despite the burst of "regionalism" in trade policy that characterized the decade from 1985 to 1995. Nevertheless, evidence of increased intrabloc trade has been a widespread, if not a dominant, feature of the trading system.

Several studies find that intraregional trade in agricultural and food products grew during the 1980s and 1990s (Vollrath 1998; dell'Aquila and Kuiper 2003). With regard to the effects of particular trade blocs, Diao, Roe, and Somwaru (2001) find that, on average, agricultural trade under NAFTA, the EU (then consisting of 15 countries), Mercosur, and Asia-Pacific Economic Cooperation grew more rapidly than did total world agricultural trade.[7] In particular, growth in intraregional agricultural trade exceeded the growth in extraregional agricultural trade for these PTAs.

Trade Flows and Preferences

A PTA increases trade among members through preferential treatment. The question is whether that growth comes at the expense of the rest of the world. Despite a number of theoretical and empirical contributions in recent years, the effects of PTAs on trade in agrifood products have not been evident from the literature because most of the studies have dealt with merchandise trade. To what extent agrifood trade among PTA partners has increased and how much of the increase could be attributed to trade diversion remained for some time an open empirical question.

Recently, researchers have tried to answer this question but have come to mixed conclusions. Jayasinghe and Sarker (2008) analyzed NAFTA's trade creation and trade diversion effects on trade in six selected agrifood products from 1985 to 2000. The results show that the share of intraregional trade within NAFTA is growing and that NAFTA has displaced trade with the rest of the world. Countries participating in NAFTA have moved toward a diminished degree of relative openness in their agrifood trade with the rest of the world. Grant and Hertel (2005), however, find, with only a few commodity exceptions, that PTAs have increased trade with nonmembers even as members have increased trade among themselves. As these examples show, the impact of PTAs on agriculture varies among regions and among agricultural products.

Evaluating Trade Preferences

A major problem with the standard databases on tariff levels is that they rarely incorporate preferential tariffs. Given the amount of world trade that enters countries under preferential (or zero) tariffs, the picture of market access presented in these databases is misleading. This omission is gradually being rectified; one notable advance has been the development by the French research organization Centre d'Études Prospectives et d'Informations Internationales of a database that includes full information on the preferential tariffs accorded developing countries. Analysis of the extent to which PTAs promote the development of agriculture by opening up markets remains difficult but is now subject to empirical exploration.

Trade preferences, both reciprocal and nonreciprocal, can provide the premium over the normal rate of return that is required to encourage investment in developing economies. The increase in agricultural trade attributable to preferences leads to more output and, if there are scale economies, to lower costs, stimulating further trade. Thus, the search for preferential access to foreign markets is naturally a component of national trade policy. The degree of preference, however, can be fleeting if others are also negotiating market access. The benefits may be those of the first mover and can be eroded steadily over time.

The granting of trade preferences is also a policy decision subject to evaluation. The key question is whether the partner receiving the preference is able or likely to be able to meet import requirements at a reasonable cost. Lowering tariffs against third countries, even if done unilaterally, is a strategy that would minimize the cost of giving preference to high-cost imports. Making exceptions for tariff-free access for high-cost partner supplies would seem less desirable. Too stringent rules of origin will also add to the possibility of trade diversion because they will discourage processing of third-country raw materials in the partner country.

The main drawback to relying on preferences for export products for agricultural development is the effect on the pattern of domestic agricultural production. A few export commodities will benefit from preferences, but this will set the economic context for other products that have to compete for land and labor. In addition, the guarantee of access under unilateral preference schemes may be a Faustian bargain, as the supplying economy becomes more dependent over time on the continuation of the preference margin. Preferences can create a degree of dependence that constrains flexibility and diversification and results in high-cost production of preferred products (Topp 2001). Moreover, other countries will have an interest in reducing those preference margins over time. The most highly protected products have the highest potential margins of preference, but these are also the products that are likely to lose the most protection through WTO negotiations.

Many preferences are, in any case, quantity constrained. When preferences are granted on products for which domestic prices in industrial countries are much higher than world prices, such as sugar in the EU and the United States, quantities are limited, to avoid undermining the distortionary policies that generate the large divergence between domestic and world prices. In these instances, preferential access can lead to substantial gains for preferred suppliers but little hope of market expansion and high probability that the gains will be eroded.

In addition, some of the preference rents may not be available for development. How much of the available rent is actually obtained by suppliers in developing countries depends on the nature of competition in the industry and the regulations governing the granting of preferential access, among other factors. If there is little effective competition among buyers, exporters may be unable to capture much of the price premium. Olarreaga and Özden (2005) find that only a third of the available rents for African exports of clothing to the United States under the African Growth and Opportunity Act actually accrue to exporters. Furthermore, satisfying the rules governing preferences raises costs and reduces the extent to which the preferences increase actual returns. The costs of satisfying the rules of origin in preference schemes have been cited as a major reason for low use of preferential access in some cases (UNCTAD 2001; Brenton and Ikezuki 2005; and Brenton, ch.8 in this volume).

Tariff preferences can lead to other adverse effects that need to be taken into account. Negotiations in the Doha Round have shown that existing preferences can lead to support for highly protectionist policies in industrial countries and can weaken proposals that would substantially reduce such levels of protection. This not only causes a rift among developing-country negotiating positions but also perpetuates policies that depress world markets and reinforce dependence on preferences for export revenue.

Differences and inconsistencies between preference schemes can prevent developing-country suppliers from evolving global market strategies. Furthermore, the preference schemes may not be directly consistent with poverty reduction objectives: beneficiaries of trade preferences are not always the poorest constituents in developing countries. Although rents do accrue to the developing country, they will tend to benefit the owners of the most intensively used and the most limiting factors.

Relatively few studies have directly measured the value of preferences. The value depends on the difference in returns in different markets. The rents accrue to the holder of the preference, but those rents are usually subject to the trade policy of the preference-giving country. A recent example of this view of preferences is given in Paggi, Yamazaki, and Josling (2005): the value of improved access to Central American markets by U.S. exporters as a result of the Central America Free Trade Agreement (CAFTA) and its extension to the Dominican Republic (CAFTA–DR) depends on who else has such preferences in those markets and how long any advantage over other competitors will last. The United States competes with the Mercosur countries and with the EU in Central American agricultural markets, and evaluation of the value of CAFTA for U.S. exporters is as much a function of the state of trade relations among these other countries as of the details of CAFTA as such.[8]

One problem with calculating the value of regional and bilateral preferences in agriculture is that the models traditionally used do not adapt well to such questions. The study of trade flows and the impact of regionalism may not capture the strategic and dynamic aspects of PTAs. A country contemplating joining a PTA does not need to know whether that PTA has been trade creating or trade diverting; the issue is whether acceding to the agreement creates beneficial trade flows, either from better market access or from reliable low-cost imports. In the case of a customs union, the height of the common tariff holds the key—for some countries, accession will lead toward liberalization, whereas for others, it will be a move toward greater protection (see Andriamananjara, ch.5 in this volume).

Gravity models and other models that seek to "explain" trade flows are of limited use in evaluating the value of preferences. Ex post analysis of why trade has taken place does not answer the fundamental question of whether differentiating one's own tariff schedule in exchange for similar differentiation by others is beneficial. If the gravity model identifies "natural" trade partners, then the question is, why is that natural trade, based on proximity and income, not taking place already? The answer could be that the trade policy of the partner country precludes such trade, but many other explanations could intrude. And the "best" trade partners may well be on other continents. So, gravity models are an interesting way of looking at trade patterns, but a shaky guide to policy action.

CGE models also have drawbacks for the evaluation of preferences, although they do address the key issue of the economic benefits and costs. The difficulties stem from whether the situation to be analyzed can be specified in enough detail. The trade policy question may require knowledge of particular market conditions, such as quality and production cost. The device of assuming that each country produces a somewhat different version of traded products masks the question of whether and how such differentiation can be created and exploited. An exporter will ask, "What are the regional markets that can open up for my product, and how can I adjust to meet the market requirements?" The CGE model will reply that the relevant substitution elasticity is already in the model and is not a part of the policy space.

Therein lies the dilemma facing analysts in this area. Every PTA is different in its coverage and treatment of products. Moreover, members' motivations and interests can differ widely, making the overall analysis of the agreement of limited use to individual countries. And within each country, the calculation of costs and benefits will be specific to conditions in particular sectors. In brief, the task of analyzing any particular decision for a country on the basis of the benefits to be gained from a trade agreement is heavily data intensive, context specific, and time related. It is not surprising that the models do not produce satisfying answers to such questions.

Does this mean that the study of PTAs and their variations is pointless? Clearly, one needs to continue to evaluate the overall impact of a fragmentation of the rule system in world trade and the ways in which regional and multilateral trade can coexist and become more complementary. But in addition to that work, there is considerable scope for focusing on the practical issues of decision making in the area of trade policy. Such work would help countries—in particular, those with limited internal analytical capacity— face the challenges of the day.

The Practice of Agricultural Trade in PTAs

Regional PTAs have the capacity to develop strong regional agricultural systems, but the path may be politically difficult. Bilateral PTAs are free of the problem of regional competition, but they often have issues with the liberalization of trade in particular products, where there may be links between the two economies concerned. Regional PTAs are considered first because most of the difficult questions surrounding the incorporation of agriculture arise in these cases. The EU, the European Free Trade Association (EFTA), NAFTA, and Mercosur provide rich examples of the ways in which the issues have been tackled. The recent growth of bilateral PTAs across regions offers many other cases of the treatment of agriculture. In particular, the bilateral PTAs negotiated with the EU and with the United States represent (different) standards for the way in which developing countries can seek to gain secure market access in major developed-country markets. These bilateral agreements tend to be "lighter" in the area of agricultural policy, avoiding the problems that accompany the development of regional agricultural and food markets (Josling 2009).

Agricultural Provisions in Regional PTAs

The inclusion of agricultural trade in a regional PTA is a challenge for negotiators. Relatively high levels of protection in agricultural markets, combined with a heightened sensitivity to issues bearing on the maintenance of a domestic production base for staple foods, make for tensions. Countries in the same region are likely to have similar production patterns. Where there has been a history of agricultural trade among the countries, the tensions may be a minor political problem, but in many cases, trade with neighbors in a regional group may raise major concerns.

Some PTAs have chosen to omit agriculture from their provisions. EFTA was created in 1960 by seven countries that had opted out of the European Economic Community (EEC, the precursor of the EU). Several members (Austria, Finland, Sweden, and Switzerland) had high-cost farming sectors because of climate or topography and did not wish to compete directly with the United Kingdom or Denmark. EFTA accordingly chose to exclude agriculture (and fisheries) from the free trade provisions. Each country was able to maintain its own agricultural policy through tariff provisions and domestic support.[9]

The decision to leave agriculture and fisheries out of the EFTA agreement led to the exclusion of the sector from the terms of the European Economic Area (EEA), the set of bilateral PTAs that the EU negotiated with EFTA members as a way of keeping them close to the EU in terms of economic regulation and price levels. The EEA allowed for free trade in manufactured goods and cooperation in regulatory issues. In effect, it extended the previous bilateral PTAs to several aspects of trade that had been incorporated into the 1992 Single Market of the EU. Although some quotas on agricultural goods were expanded, there was no progress toward incorporation of the rural sector into economic integration, as would be stimulated by enlargement. Later, EFTA countries found themselves unable to include agriculture in bilateral agreements that they negotiated with countries such as Canada and had to settle again for small bilateral trade deals.

At the other extreme, the countries that formed the EEC (later, the European Union) made a conscious decision to include all trade, including agriculture, in their trade liberalization. As integration progressed, more internal agricultural trade took place, some of it displacing lower-cost imports. In addition, the agricultural market became more integrated as firms were able to locate in other member states, and a European food industry began to emerge. The development of a Common Agricultural Policy (CAP), with common financing and uniform support mechanisms, advanced further in the EU than in other PTAs. More recently, harmonized regulations on food safety and quality controls have reinforced the development of a regional industry.

The polar cases of EFTA and the EU bracket the degree of incorporation of agriculture in PTAs. Almost all other PTAs have included agricultural trade in the liberalization process, to varying degrees. The agricultural content of the PTAs can be explored by identifying some issues that arise in most cases. These categories are not confined to agricultural trade, but they do form a set of negotiating issues that frame the agricultural agenda. They include the schedule for cutting tariffs and the use of TRQs as a way of increasing access; safeguards against import surges; subsidies to domestic firms and to firms dependent on exports; the provision of public goods, both environmental and related to food security; and market structures and institutions.

Tariff cutting. Elimination of tariffs among partners is the defining feature of a PTA, and the inclusion of agricultural tariff lines in the reduction schedules is a key decision. For some products, the tariff cuts are made at the time the PTA enters into force; for others, a schedule of reductions is agreed on. Agricultural tariff cuts, at least for sensitive products, are usually introduced over time. The timetable for liberalization in NAFTA provides an example.

NAFTA set in process the removal of all trade barriers to goods moving between countries in North America. The detailed market access provisions were embedded in three bilateral agreements (the one between the United States and Canada essentially continued a previous bilateral agreement). For the U.S.–Mexico bilateral agreement, the time period for most sectors to achieve market integration was 10 years, but markets for some sensitive agricultural products (beans and corn for Mexico, and tomatoes and citrus products for the United States) were given 15 years to adjust. The adjustment period has ended, and the U.S.–Mexico agricultural market is now effectively open.[10]

Another success in removing tariff barriers on trade in farm products has been in the Australia–New Zealand regional market.[11] The Australia–New Zealand Closer Economic Relations Trade Agreement (ANZCERTA) takes the two countries further toward effective market integration than does NAFTA in North America, although by no means as far as the EU. Both countries are major agricultural exporters. The product mix of exports is somewhat similar, reducing the scope for trans-Tasman trade, but there are natural trade flows based on climatic differences, such as sales of Australian wheat to New Zealand and exports of New Zealand dairy goods to Australia. These flows were hampered by tight restrictions on trade within domestic marketing legislation. It took bold political decisions, coupled with a significant reduction in the power of the marketing agencies, to allow trade in agricultural products to flow freely.

In most respects, tariff cutting in agricultural markets has been successful in Latin American PTAs. Among Mercosur countries, agricultural trade is nominally free; indeed, agricultural products are widely traded among the member states, notably from Argentina to the others. Mercosur has relatively few provisions that apply specifically to agriculture. There are two likely reasons for this relatively liberal treatment of the sector. First, Mercosur includes major exporters of temperate agricultural products, each of which would like to strengthen its agriculture industry and promote regional exports. Second, as a result of sweeping structural reforms, the countries concerned have eliminated many of the state marketing monopolies that previously controlled trade.[12] This, together with the reduction of subsidies and support prices, has allowed a fuller incorporation of agriculture within Mercosur than in many other PTAs.

Safeguards. As a complement to tariff cutting, PTAs frequently include safeguards that allow temporary increases in tariffs should imports surge (see Prusa, ch.9 in this volume). Agricultural products in PTAs are often subject to specific safeguard provisions to help guard against sudden shifts in trade patterns. The nature of the safeguards for agriculture is usually in the form of a "snapback" to a previous tariff, no higher than the MFN tariff rate, for a limited period of time. Similar provisions in NAFTA were used on several occasions during the transition period to react to trade surges. Countries generally reserve the right to take action under WTO safeguard provisions, although not in addition to regional safeguards. The EU is again an exception; its regulations prohibit safeguard action against trade from another member state.

Domestic and export subsidies. The thorny issue of domestic subsidies in PTAs has been dealt with in two different ways. Generally, the decision is made in negotiations not to attempt any constraints on subsidies. Indeed, it is usually assumed that PTAs could not regulate domestic subsidies because to do so on inter-PTA trade but not on extra-PTA sales would be impractical at best and self-defeating at worst. The emphasis in several PTAs is, accordingly, on acknowledging the multilateral process as the location of decisions on subsidy reduction. Hence, NAFTA contains the injunction to "endeavor to work towards domestic support measures" that have minimal trade-distorting effects or that would be exempt under a future GATT agreement (the so-called "green box" policy instruments). It recognizes, however, the right of parties to change domestic support measures subject to GATT obligations. This light treatment of a contentious area enabled negotiators to say that they were not altering domestic policy.

The EU took a different tack. All subsidies by member states are constrained by the competition regulations of the EU, and farm subsidies are not excluded from this provision. The CAP became (in principle) the only vehicle for granting agricultural subsidies, although some exceptions have survived the attempts by the European Commission to enforce this regulation. One result of the common nature of the CAP has been that the EU can negotiate reductions in domestic support as a single WTO member, which individual members of other PTAs are not in a position to do.

Export subsidies for agricultural products pose similar issues. Several PTAs have contemplated banning export subsidies on intrabloc trade, but this is easier said than done. The NAFTA provisions again give a good example of the dilemma facing PTA negotiators. The text states that parties "share the objective of the multilateral elimination of export subsidies for agricultural goods" and promises cooperation in the GATT to this end. The zeal for multilateral elimination of such policies does not, however, extend to their internal use. Article 705.2 of NAFTA merely holds it "inappropriate" for a party to grant export subsidies on sales to another party unless the importing country is benefiting from export subsidies paid by other countries.[13] In other words, matching of EU export subsidies in Mexico is allowable by the United States and Canada until such practices are stopped multilaterally. Indeed, if the exporting and importing parties agree to an export subsidy on intra-NAFTA trade, that subsidy is allowed. This provision, no doubt, was included to take account of the considerable importance to the United States of retaining the means to stay competitive with EU export subsidies in the Mexican market.

PTA discussions about the impact of different marketing structures and institutions raise some interesting issues. This is particularly true for state marketing institutions in agricultural products, where historical differences in policies can lead to problems for integration. An early example was the difficulty posed for the EU at the time of U.K. accession (1973) by the existence in England and Wales of the Milk Marketing Board (MMB), which held a monopoly on milk sales and on imports of milk products. This situation was clearly inconsistent with the competition regulations of the EU, and so the MMB had to change its policies and give up its control over the milk market. A more recent example appears in the 1986 U.S.–Canada free trade agreement. Canada was able to exclude from the free trade provisions the products of its supply-managed sectors, primarily dairy and poultry, which were managed largely by provincial marketing boards. Neither the United States nor Canada wished to face the task of harmonizing marketing systems for these products, and it was felt that the operation of the boards required control of all imports, including those from the United States. As a result, the integration of these sectors was delayed indefinitely.

Public goods. It is widely recognized that agriculture provides certain public goods (as well as negative externalities in the way of water and soil pollution). In rich countries, these public goods are often identified as the stewardship of the landscape and the provision of locally grown healthy foods; in less affluent societies, the benefits are food security, rural development, and poverty alleviation. Whether society is adequately compensating the farm sector for the provision of these public goods is a subject of debate in many countries. The collective provision of a public good within a PTA can sometimes be advantageous, in particular where agricultural and environmental conditions are defined more by geography and climate than by political boundaries. Similarly, coordination of rural infrastructure within a regional PTA could

form the basis for improvement of the economic capacity of an agricultural area.

One particular public good associated with agriculture deserves separate mention. Food security refers to the ability of a country to provide the conditions under which food is available to (and relatively affordable by) the population. Economic, social, and political imperatives converge here. The contribution of PTAs to the attainment of this objective is generally positive, as discussed earlier, but the issue does pose some challenges for negotiators. A balance has to be struck between the benefits of open trade for the regionwide sharing of risk and the ultimate national responsibility for ensuring food supplies. The issue that may cause regional friction is whether a partner in a PTA may restrict supplies to another partner when its own supplies are scarce. The stronger PTAs, with regional food markets and coordinated policy reactions, will tend to restrain the ability of one country to impose an export ban on a partner, whereas the weaker agreements tend to leave this possibility open.

Many PTAs include provisions that relate to the health and safety aspects of agricultural and food trade, such as the harmonization (or the mutual recognition of) health and safety regulations. (See, in this volume, Maur and Shepherd, ch. 10, and Stoler, ch. 11, on standards in PTAs.) Most such provisions are based on the WTO Sanitary and Phytosanitary Agreement and do not require members to go far beyond those standards. In some cases, however, such as ANZCERTA, the establishment of joint agencies to oversee such regulations acts as a guard against trade frictions (Almeida, Gutierrez, and Shearer 2009).

Institutions. Institutional innovations are also common, although some of the bodies set up seem to have little role in policy decisions. The NAFTA trilateral agricultural agreement, for instance, set up a Committee on Agricultural Trade to administer the arrangements and an Advisory Committee on Private Commercial Disputes regarding Agricultural Goods to deal with private disputes. But there is little evidence that these bodies have had any significant impact on agricultural trade policy over the 15 years of their existence.

Agricultural Provisions in Bilateral PTAs

The treatment of agriculture in bilateral PTAs is often markedly different from that in regional agreements.[14] The motivation for such PTAs ranges from strategic to practical, but most often it is the exchange of preferential access for goods and services, with little regard for the longer-run economic relationship. No regional integration of the agriculture sectors is envisaged, and many of the tensions around farm policies that occur in regional pacts are absent. The main characteristics of bilateral PTAs are usually determined by the dominant partner, often a developed country, and the discussion of these PTAs is therefore conveniently organized according to the dominant partner—in these examples, the EU and the United States.

EU agreements. In the network of agreements involving the EU and nonmembers, agriculture is still treated as being largely outside the realm of unrestricted free trade. The Euro-Mediterranean free trade agreements (Euromed FTAs) now being finalized between the EU and the countries of North Africa and the Middle East have so far avoided including unrestricted access for sensitive agricultural products, and the same is true for the customs union that was negotiated with Turkey. The negotiation of a free trade agreement between the EU and South Africa was held up by the reluctance of the EU to grant improved access to goods that would have directly competed with those covered by the CAP. The agreement between the EU and Mexico was also difficult to negotiate until Mexico abandoned its attempt to win easy access to the EU market for a full range of agricultural products.

Similarly, Mercosur and the EU are finding it difficult to overcome the problems that improved access to the EU market would seem to pose for European agriculture. The Cotonou Agreement between the EU and ACP countries, which mandated the negotiation of a transformation of the existing nonreciprocal agreements into full free trade areas after eight years, attempted to address agricultural trade issues, but these negotiations were hampered by inconsistency with the CAP. The unilateral PTA between the EU and the least developed countries (the Everything But Arms agreement) broke significant new ground in this respect by providing duty-free and quota-free access for agricultural goods, with only temporary derogations for the most sensitive commodities—rice, sugar, and bananas.

Traditionally, the EU has used the policy of trade preferences as a strategy of cooperation for development and has unilaterally granted trade concessions to other countries. Now, Euromed agreements are taking further steps toward trade liberalization on a bilateral and reciprocal basis. Since the first Euro-Mediterranean Conference in November 1995, the EU and 12 Mediterranean countries have been engaged in negotiating association agreements (the Barcelona process). The overall objective is to form, eventually, a single Euro-Mediterranean free trade area from the separate agreements in place. Yet, trade in agriculture is subjected to weak liberalization within the present framework of the association agreements. No explicit liberalization road map has been defined for the agriculture sector as a whole; only for certain products have specific concessions for liberalization been determined. A concern for the non-EU Mediterranean countries is that, with the conclusion of PTAs between the EU and other countries in Asia and Latin America, the competitive advantage that they themselves used to enjoy in EU markets may be eroded, and they may become marginalized.

The deferral of substantive negotiations on liberalization of trade in agricultural products has been a constant feature of the Euro-Mediterranean partnership (Asbil 2005). The principal reason has been the reluctance on the part of European farmers to compete with Mediterranean countries that are not EU members. The southern enlargement of the EU in the 1980s redefined its relation with the Mediterranean partners. Greece, Portugal, and Spain compete directly in agricultural products with the countries of North Africa, and these members' political influence largely explains the limits on trade concessions through tariff quotas and reference quantities (García-Alvarez-Coque 2002). Agriculture has become a key sector in the debate between the EU and its Mediterranean trade partners because it is seen as a necessary element in the establishment of a balance of commercial opportunities through increases in both industrial and agricultural exports from the region.

The other problem that Mediterranean countries need to consider is the shortcomings in the diversification and competitiveness of their production structures. Several Mediterranean countries have very similar product compositions of exports. Algeria, Cyprus, Israel, Morocco, and Spain all have agriculture sectors oriented toward specialty products—mainly, fresh fruit and nuts, olive oil, and wine. The similarity of agricultural products means that, especially since the enlargement of the EU to include Cyprus, Greece, Malta, Portugal, and Spain, EU members find it easy to replace supplies from nonmember Mediterranean countries with supplies from EU members.

The current negotiations between the EU and the ACP countries (the signatories to the Lomé and Cotonou Agreements) have advanced through six regional talks. The EU has succeeded in agreeing on a comprehensive economic partnership agreement (EPA) with Caribbean ACP countries through CARIFORUM and the Caribbean Community (CARICOM) Regional Negotiating Mechanism.[15] In the case of the African countries, negotiations are being channeled through four of the main regional agreements. The Economic Community of West African States (ECOWAS), in collaboration with the West African Economic and Monetary Union (WAEMU), is the negotiating partner for 16 West African states. Eight Central African states have been negotiating through the Economic and Monetary Community of Central Africa (CEMAC, Communauté Économique et Monétaire de l'Afrique Centrale) in conjunction with the Economic Community of Central African States (ECCAS), which CEMAC has plans to merge with. Seven Southern African states are negotiating through the Southern African Development Community (SADC), although some of those states are not SADC members. Another 15 are represented by the Common Market for Eastern and Southern Africa (COMESA), even though some of them do not participate in other COMESA activities. With the exception of the agreement with the Caribbean, the EPAs are still not fully in operation. Some countries have signed partial ("goods only") agreements, but more than half of the ACP countries failed to reach an agreement before the January 1, 2008, deadline, when the WTO waiver that allowed the EU to negotiate these agreements expired. Renewal of the waiver would encounter some opposition. Countries that have shown opposition to the EPAs include South Africa, which already has a free trade agreement with the EU, and Nigeria, with its oil-based economy. A bold move by China to develop trade and investment links with African countries appears to be causing a rethinking of the desirability of continuing close ties with the EU if those ties come with political constraints.

U.S. agreements. U.S. policy toward regional and bilateral PTAs changed dramatically in the mid-1980s. Long a champion of the multilateral system and of nondiscrimination, the United States has now become an active supporter of bilateral PTAs as a complement to its commitment to the WTO and its membership in NAFTA. The United States has completed, or is currently in the midst of, trade negotiations with 27 countries aimed at creating about 20 separate PTAs.[16] The United States has economic and geopolitical reasons for expanding its commercial ties; the attraction for other countries is to secure preferred access to the large U.S. market.[17]

The first of these recent PTAs was signed with Israel in 1985 as an expression of political and economic support for that country. The free trade agreement with Canada followed in 1986, largely at Canada's request. It was designed to consolidate existing sector agreements, encourage U.S. investment north of the border, and give Canadian firms some protection from aggressive use of trade remedy provisions (i.e., antidumping and countervailing duty measures). In 1990, Mexico requested similar conditions, to ensure overseas investors' access to the large U.S. market. Canada opted to join the United States and Mexico in NAFTA, which incorporated the earlier bilateral agreement with Canada. A free trade agreement with Jordan

was concluded in 2001, again as a show of political support and economic assistance.

The United States began to negotiate additional bilateral PTAs in 2002 as an expression of a policy of "competitive liberalization" articulated by the U.S. trade representative. This policy consisted of offering swift negotiations to any country that was willing to conform to terms consistent with the mandate of the U.S. administration, as specified in the Trade Promotion Authority Act. The list of willing trade partners with which PTAs were concluded includes Bahrain, Morocco, Oman, Peru, and Singapore. Among other completed bilateral PTAs with a more significant agricultural component were those with Chile and Australia. Talks with Bolivia, Ecuador, Peru, the Southern African Customs Union, and the United Arab Emirates (UAE) are currently suspended.[18] Agreements with Colombia, the Republic of Korea, and Panama await ratification. A new front has been opened up in the Asia-Pacific region as the United States has begun to explore the possibility of a Trans-Pacific Partnership (TPP) agreement to include Australia, Brunei Darussalam, Chile, New Zealand, Singapore, and possibly Malaysia and Thailand. Recent agreements have often been designed as "templates" for future PTAs within a region. Thus, the PTAs with Bahrain, Oman, and the UAE are seen as building blocks toward a Middle East free trade area, and the negotiations with Malaysia and Thailand (along with the one already in place with Singapore) were originally supposed to pave the way for other bilateral PTAs with countries in the Association of Southeast Asian Nations—although this prospect has been overtaken by the TPP. The PTAs themselves usually follow from trade and investment framework agreements (TIFAs) and bilateral investment treaties (BITs). The United States has a considerable number of TIFAs and BITS in place that would form the basis for bilateral PTAs.

Although all the PTAs have provisions for tariff reductions that affect many food and agricultural goods, the agreements, with few exceptions, control trade in a range of products considered politically sensitive in one or both partners. For the United States, these sensitivities include sugar, citrus fruits, peanuts, and dairy products; for the partners, the list includes corn, beans, and rice.

Three current agreements have the greatest actual or potential impact on U.S. agricultural markets and hence on the environment in which policy is formed: the recent PTAs with Chile and Australia, and the CAFTA–DR agreement. Table 7.1 summarizes the main characteristics of each agreement.

The United States and five Central American countries— Costa Rica, El Salvador, Guatemala, Honduras, and Nicaragua—began negotiations on CAFTA in 2003, and the agreement took effect in 2006. Negotiations with the

Table 7.1. Summary of Provisions Affecting Agriculture in NAFTA, U.S.–Chile, U.S.–Australia, and CAFTA Agreements

Provision	NAFTA	Chile FTA	Australia FTA	CAFTA
Tariff cuts	Some tariffs eliminated; others staged over 5, 10, and 15 years	Some tariffs eliminated; others staged over 4, 8, 10, and 12 years; some cuts delayed for 2 and 4 years	Most tariffs eliminated; others staged over 4, 10, and 18 years	Some tariffs eliminated; others staged over 5, 10, and 15 years; other cuts delayed for 6 or 10 years; duty-free status after 15 or 20 years
TRQs	TRQs introduced during transition period for sensitive products	No use of TRQs introduced	TRQs for imports of avocados, cotton, peanuts, tobacco, beef, and dairy products into the United States expanded; above-quota duties for beef phased out over 18-year period; current sugar TRQs not increased: no cuts in above-quota tariff	TRQs for sensitive products in Annex 3.3 imposed; rules on administration of TRQs (in addition to GATT Article XIII) put in place
Agricultural safeguards	TRQs allowed as special safeguard for horticultural crops (Annex 703.3)	Additional duties linked to price trigger (Article 3.18) for goods listed in Annex 3.18; total duties not to exceed MFN rate; safeguard not operative after 12 years, or when zero-duty stage reached	Additional customs duties linked to price trigger for horticultural products (Annex 3-A, section A) and to quantity triggers for beef (Annex 3-A, section B); price triggers used for beef in 19th year of agreement (Annex 3-A, section C); safeguard not operative when zero-duty stage reached	Additional duties linked to trigger quantities (Article 3.14) for products listed in Annex 3.14; total duties not to exceed MFN rate; safeguard not operative when zero-duty stage reached
Other safeguards	Safeguards (Chapter 8A) stipulated: snapback to previous year's tariff on bilateral trade or MFN tariff	Trade remedies (Chapter 8) stipulated; GATT 1994 Article XIX safeguards adhered to	Safeguards (Chapter 9) stipulated; GATT 1994 Article XIX safeguards adhered to	Trade remedies (Chapter 8) stipulated; GATT 1994 Article XIX safeguards adhered to
Export subsidies	Agreement reached to avoid use of export subsidies on bilateral trade unless third countries subsidized exports to NAFTA markets; agreement reached to work together for elimination in the GATT	Agreement reached to avoid use of export subsidies on bilateral trade unless third countries subsidized exports to Chile or the United States; agreement reached to work together for elimination in the WTO	Agreement reached to avoid use of export subsidies on bilateral trade unless third countries subsidized exports to Australia; agreement reached to work together for elimination in the WTO	Agreement reached to avoid use of export subsidies on bilateral trade unless third countries subsidized exports to CAFTA markets; agreement reached to work together for elimination in the WTO
Domestic support	Agreement reached to work together in GATT for reduction of domestic support levels and to shift to less-trade-distorting instruments	Agreement reached to work together in WTO for reduction of domestic support levels and to shift to less-trade-distorting instruments	Agreement reached to work together in WTO for reduction of domestic support levels and to shift to less-trade-distorting instruments	Agreement reached to work together in WTO for reduction of domestic support levels and to shift to less-trade-distorting instruments
SPS measures	Precursor of WTO SPS agreement (Chapter 7B)	Affirm commitment to SPS agreement	Work to resolve trade conflicts over SPS barriers	Affirm commitment to SPS agreement
Dispute settlement	Dispute settlement mechanism for matters arising from agreement (Chapter 20) put in place; separate procedures for review of antidumping and countervailing actions (Chapter 19) put in place	Dispute settlement mechanism for matters arising from agreement (Chapter 22) put in place	Dispute settlement mechanism for matters arising from agreement (Chapter 21) put in place; provision for monetary penalties put in place	Dispute settlement mechanism for matters arising from agreement put in place
Institutions	Committee on Agricultural Trade; Working Group on Agricultural Subsidies; Advisory Committee on Private Commerce Disputes Regarding Agricultural Goods	Working Group on Agricultural Trade; Committee on Sanitary and Phytosanitary Matters	Committee on Agriculture; Standing Technical Working Group on Animal and Plant Health Measures	Committee on Agricultural Trade; Agricultural Review Commission; Committee on Sanitary and Phytosanitary Matters

Source: Author's compilation from texts of agreements.

Notes: CAFTA = Central America Free Trade Agreement; FTA = free trade agreement; GATT = General Agreement on Tariffs and Trade; MFN = most favored nation; NAFTA = North American Free Trade Agreement; SPS = sanitary and phytosanitary; TRQ = tariff-rate quota; WTO = World Trade Organization. Citations of specific provisions refer to the respective agreement.

Dominican Republic that would fully integrate that country into CAFTA were concluded in 2004. In addition, ratification of the pending agreement with Panama, if successful, would round off the establishment of free trade agreements between the United States and almost all of the countries of Central America (see Paggi, Yamazaki, and Josling 2005).

CAFTA is intended to help foster economic growth and improve living standards in the Central American region by reducing and eliminating barriers to trade and investment. It essentially converts the nonreciprocal and discretionary benefits that these countries derive from the Caribbean Basin Initiative (CBI) into permanent and reciprocal access to the U.S. market. CAFTA covers all trade, but the agricultural component is one of its most important aspects (see table 7.1). The key to the agricultural agreement is market access; the arrangement contains relatively few provisions in the areas of export subsidies and sanitary and phytosanitary regulations, and it does not cover domestic subsidies.

Agricultural trade barriers in the Central American countries are higher than those for manufactured goods, and CAFTA will create improved market opportunities for U.S. agricultural products and for related goods and services. CAFTA locks in the applied duty rates for many products and ensures that permanent U.S. access to the market is preserved. Its short-term impact on U.S. exports may, however, be modest because the terms of the agreement delay the full benefits of increased access to the countries of the region for U.S. agricultural products of interest. The lengthy phase-in period for increased market access and the back-loading of commitment levels suggest that the benefits of the agreement may only be realized many years in the future.

Increased access to the U.S. market for Central American goods will also be a consequence of CAFTA. Here, however, the effect is likely to be even more limited because most CAFTA countries have had permanent duty-free access to the U.S. market since the late 1960s under the GSP and since 1990 under the provisions of the Caribbean Basin Initiative (CBI) and the Caribbean Basin Economic Recovery Act (CBERA), which implements the CBI. The CBI was enhanced in 2000 under the terms of the Caribbean Basin Trade Partnership Act (CBTPA) to grant access more equivalent to that enjoyed by Mexico under NAFTA. In fact, approximately 99 percent of CAFTA exports already enter the U.S. market duty-free. Duties are paid only on over-quota imports, as part of the U.S. tariff-rate quota regimes for sugar, dairy products, cotton, meats, and peanuts.[19]

The bilateral PTA with Chile was easier to negotiate than either NAFTA or CAFTA. Chile is an important exporter of agricultural products, particularly fruits, vegetables, and wine, but the different seasonality makes the produce complementary to rather than competitive with U.S. production. The beneficiaries were supermarkets, which gained the assurance of year-round supplies. Chile is one of the more liberal Latin American countries, even on agricultural products, so that opening up to U.S. exporters was not such a big move for its farmers. Aside from some controversy over wine labels, the talks went smoothly. It may have helped that Chile is not a significant sugar exporter.

The U.S. agreement with Australia also involved a Southern Hemisphere country and thus offered some advantages of complementary production. Australia, however, is a major exporter of meats, dairy products, cereals, and sugar, and so tight rules had to be built in to the agreement to protect U.S. farmers from competition from imports. Reluctantly, Australia accepted long transition periods for dairy products and beef, and an exclusion altogether of any relaxation of protection for the U.S. sugar sector. This decision may have an effect on the politics of future bilateral PTAs.

The most ambitious bilateral agreement to have been negotiated since NAFTA is still awaiting approval by Congress at present. The Korea–U.S. Free Trade Agreement (KORUS) would establish a free trade area between the United States and a major economy in East Asia. There was no doubt from the beginning of the talks that agriculture would be a stumbling block, with the Korean government, in particular, not wishing to open up its highly protected rice market to U.S. exports. The U.S. position had been to include rice, even if access for U.S. rice were to be introduced slowly over a transition period. In the end, the rice sector was essentially excluded from the agreement. This establishes a precedent in case KORUS were to act as a template for an agreement with Japan.

Conclusions

Agricultural trade is becoming increasingly governed by conditions negotiated in preferential trade agreements (PTAs), whether regional or bilateral. Regional integration of agricultural markets through open trade can have a positive effect on the development of a competitive and sustainable agriculture sector, although complementary policies at the multilateral level are needed to prevent trade diversion. PTAs can yield benefits in the area of food security and the provision of public goods, but the empirical analyses required to quantify these benefits are scarce, in part because of the very diverse treatment of agriculture in PTAs. If concluded with the right partner countries, PTAs can avoid the disadvantages of trade diversion. If the terms of the agreements are appropriate, such PTAs can further full integration into the global economy and stimulate needed investment and the transfer of technology.

Notes

1. A full account of the interpretation of GATT Article XXIV is provided in Hudec and Southwick (1999). Srinivasan (1998) presents a critique of the systemic issues posed by PTAs. A type of agreement not considered in this chapter is the partial-scope agreement, which covers only a subset of goods. These agreements are not generally notified under Article XXIV.

2. It is perhaps ironic that the insistence on both the inclusion of substantially all trade and 100 percent preference increases the likelihood of trade diversion. Exclusion of those sectors where protection is high, and the partial liberalization of internal trade in those high-cost sectors that are covered, would reduce trade diversion, although it would also limit trade creation. The strict rules were presumably inserted to discourage trade agreements that merely "picked low-hanging fruit" by confining themselves to nonsensitive sectors or small reductions in tariffs.

3. For a discussion of the benefits of coordinating trade strategies for small countries, see Schiff (1997, 2002); Andriamananjara and Schiff (1998).

4. Adjustment of market access provisions is made easier by the negotiation in the Uruguay Round of tariff-rate quotas (TRQs) that ensure continued access for those countries with negotiated quotas. Allocation to preferred partners of TRQs allowed in WTO schedules is a principal link between the multilateral and preferential trade regimes. These allocations appear contrary to the spirit of Article XIII of the GATT, which provides that the distribution of quotas should be nondiscriminatory and should reflect market conditions.

5. Analytical devices such as that applied here are sometimes difficult to reconcile with a world of actual countries and diverse trade strategies. In fact, some new members may be willing to pay the price for entry, and some old members may have strong reasons for excluding newcomers.

6. The "completion" of the European Community's (EC's) internal market reform, which was incorporated in the 1992 program, was the product of an attempt to remove remaining barriers between EC members in goods, services, labor markets, and capital markets. The success of the European Commission in pushing through this program caused a stir of interest in other regions.

7. The inclusion of APEC in this list is of interest, as no preferential tariff reductions were specified in that agreement. APEC's modus operandi was and is a loosely coordinated process of unilateral liberalization among its members, with no discrimination against outsiders.

8. This analysis also points up the importance of timing in trade agreements. The advantage of being first to reach a deal may be considerable. And the negotiation of long transition periods may be of little value in easing adjustments if other countries can enter into agreements with a shorter time horizon.

9. A side agreement guaranteed access for Denmark to the British market for pigmeat products and for limited quantities of dairy goods.

10. Canada declined to join the open market between Mexico and the United States because that would have required liberalization of the supply-managed sectors (dairy products and poultry), as well as sharply increased prices for sugar in Canada.

11. The original ANZCERTA suffered from a lack of ambition and political support (Lloyd 1991). A 1988 review of its operations led to an acceleration of the process of liberalization, with July 1990 set as the date for the removal of remaining tariff and nontariff barriers. In addition, export subsidies on intrabloc trade were to be removed.

12. In 1991, Argentina eliminated export taxes on agricultural goods, which had long been a source of government revenue. A small tax on oilseed exports remained, together with a fee to pay for research. Argentina has essentially liberalized imports of agricultural goods, although some export taxes have reappeared in recent years.

13. The language about and treatment of export subsidies is much softer in NAFTA than in the U.S.–Canada Free Trade Agreement, which banned the use of export subsidies between the two countries.

14. Bilateral PTAs involving Singapore do not face the same political problems in including agriculture and food products as do most other agreements. Singapore has no significant agricultural production and no import barriers. Other countries, however, may be concerned about the possibility of trade deflection through Singapore. Japan, for instance, has not agreed to open its agricultural market to imports from Singapore in their bilateral free trade agreement.

15. CARIFORUM includes the Dominican Republic, as well as the CARICOM countries.

16. It is worth recalling that in the late 1930s, U.S. trade policy took a similar direction. The Reciprocal Trade Agreements Act of 1934 was an open-ended mandate to negotiate bilateral trade agreements with other countries, and about 30 such agreements were signed.

17. In many cases, access is already covered by existing agreements, but the negotiation of a formal PTA reduces uncertainty as to whether these preferences will continue.

18. SACU is made up of Botswana, Lesotho, Namibia, South Africa, and Swaziland.

19. For more details on CAFTA and its potential impact on U.S. agriculture, see Paggi, Yamazaki, and Josling (2005).

References

Almeida, Juliana Salles, Carlos M. Gutierrez, Jr., and Matthew Shearer. 2009. "The Treatment of Agriculture in Regional Trade Agreements in the Americas." Integration and Trade Sector, Inter-American Development Bank, Washington, DC.

Anderson, Kym, and Richard Blackhurst, eds. 1993. *Regional Integration and the Global Trading System.* New York: St. Martin's Press.

Andriamananjara, Soamiely. 2002. "On the Size and Number of Preferential Trading Arrangements." *Journal of International Trade and Economic Development* 11 (3): 279–95.

Andriamananjara, Soamiely, and Maurice Schiff. 1998, "Regional Groupings among Microstates." Policy Research Working Paper 1922, World Bank, Washington, DC. http://econ.worldbank.org/external/default/main?pagePK=64165259&theSitePK=469372&piPK=64165421&menuPK=64166093&entityID=000009265_3980625102911.

Asbil, Alexandre. 2005. "The Barcelona Process and Trade Liberalisation in Agriculture." Presentation to conference of the Food and Agriculture Organization of the United Nations (FAO), Rome, October 10–14.

Brenton, Paul, and Takako Ikezuki. 2005. "The Impact of Agricultural Trade Preferences, with Particular Attention to the LDCs." In *Global Agricultural Trade and Developing Countries*, ed. M. Ataman Askoy and John C. Beghin. Washington, DC: World Bank.

dell'Aquila, Crescenzo, and Marijke Kuiper. 2003. "Which Road to Liberalisation? A First Assessment of the EuroMed Association Agreements." Working Paper 2, European Network of Agricultural and Rural Policy Research Institutes (ENARPRI), Centre for European Policy Studies, Brussels.

Diao, Xinshen, Terry Roe, and A. Somwaru. 2001. "What Is the Cause of Growth in Regional Trade? Trade Liberalization or RTAs? The Case of Agriculture." *The World Economy* 24(1): 51–79.

Fiorentino, Roberto. 2005. "Regional Trade Agreements and the WTO: Theory and Practice of WTO Provisions on RTAs." Presentation to conference of the Food and Agriculture Organization of the United Nations (FAO), Rome, October 10–14.

García-Alvarez-Coque, José María. 2002. "Agricultural Trade and the Barcelona Process: Is Full Liberalization Possible?" *European Review of Agricultural Economics* 29 (3): 399–422.

Goto, Junichi. 1997. "Regional Economic Integration and Agricultural Trade." Policy Research Working Paper 1805, World Bank, Washington, DC. http://www-wds.worldbank.org/servlet/WDSContentServer/WDSP/IB/2000/02/24/000009265_3971110141344/Rendered/PDF/multi_page.pdf.

Grant, J., and Tom Hertel. 2005. "Regionalism in World Agricultural Trade: Lessons from Gravity Model Estimation." Global Economic Analysis conference, Lübeck, Germany, June.

Hudec, Robert, and James D. Southwick. 1999. "Regionalism and the WTO Rules: Problems in the Fine Art of Discriminating Fairly." In *Trade Rules in the Making: Challenges in Regional and Multilateral Negotiations,* ed. Miguel Rodríguez Mendoza, Patrick Low, and Barbara Kotschwar. Washington, DC: Brookings Institution Press.

Jayasinghe, Sampath, and Rakhal Sarker. 2008. "Effects of Regional Trade Agreements on Trade in Agrifood Products: Evidence from Gravity Modeling Using Disaggregated Data." *Review of Agricultural Economics* 30 (1): 61–81.

Josling, Tim. 2009. "Agriculture." In *Commentary and Analysis*. Book 1 of *Bilateral and Regional Trade Agreements: Commentary, Analysis and Case Studies,* ed. Simon Lester and Bryan Mercurio. Cambridge, U.K.: Cambridge University Press.

Lloyd, Peter. J. 1991. "The Future of CER: A Single Market for Australia and New Zealand." Committee for Economic Development of Australia (CEDA) and Institute for Policy Studies, Wellington.

———. 1992. "Regionalisation and World Trade." *OECD Economic Studies* 18 (Spring). Organisation for Economic Co-operation and Development (OECD), Paris.

Olarreaga, Marcelo, and Çaglar Özden. 2005. "AGOA and Apparel: Who Captures the Tariff Rent in the Presence of Preferential Market Access?" *World Economy* 28, no.1 (January): 63–77.

Paggi, Mechel S., Fumiko Yamazaki, and Tim Josling. 2005. "The Central American Free Trade Agreement: What's at Stake for California Agriculture?" Center for Agricultural Business, California State University, Fresno, CA.

Schiff, Maurice. 1997. "Small Is Beautiful: Preferential Trade Agreements and the Impact of Country Size, Market Share, Trade Policy, and Smuggling." *Journal of Economic Integration* 12, no.3 (September): 359–87.

———. 2002. "Regional Integration and Development in Small States." Development Research Group, Trade, World Bank, Washington, DC.

Srinivasan, T. N. 1998. "Regionalism and the WTO: Is Nondiscrimination Passé?" In *The WTO as an International Organization,* ed. Anne O. Krueger, 329–49. Chicago, Il: University of Chicago Press.

Topp, Vernon. 2001. "Trade Preferences: Are They Helpful in Advancing Economic Development in Poor Countries?" Australian Bureau of Agriculture and Resource Economics (ABARE), Canberra.

UNCTAD (United Nations Conference on Trade and Development). 2001. "Trade Negotiation Issues in the Cotonou Agreement: Agriculture and Economic Partnership Agreements." UNCTAD, Geneva.

Vollrath, Thomas L. 1998. "RTAs and Agricultural Trade: A Retrospective Assessment." In *Regional Trade Agreements and U.S. Agriculture,* ed. Mary Burfisher and Elizabeth Jones. Agricultural Economic Report 771. Economic Research Service, U.S. Department of Agriculture, Washington, DC.

Zissimos, Ben, and David Vines. 2000. "Is the WTO's Article XXIV a Free Trade Barrier?" CSGR Working Paper 49/00, Centre for the Study of Globalisation and Regionalisation, University of Warwick, U.K.

8

PREFERENTIAL RULES
OF ORIGIN

Paul Brenton

Preferential rules of origin are applied by countries that offer certain trade partners zero-duty or reduced-duty access for their imports as a means of determining the eligibility of products to receive such preferential access.[1] These rules of origin are required to prevent trade deflection or simple transshipment, whereby products from nonpreferred countries are redirected through a free trade partner to avoid the payment of customs duties. They are meant to ensure that only goods originating in participating countries enjoy duty preferences. Rules of origin are thus integral to preferential trade agreements such as bilateral and regional free trade agreements and to the nonreciprocal preferences that industrial countries offer to developing countries.

The nature of rules of origin and their application can have profound implications for trade flows and for the work of customs authorities. Rules of origin can be designed in such a way as to restrict trade and therefore can be used, and are being used, as instruments of trade policy. The proliferation of free trade agreements throughout the world, with the accompanying preferential rules of origin, is increasing the burden on customs services in many countries, with implications for the ease of trade. Perhaps surprisingly, given their potential to influence trade flows, preferential rules of origin are one area of trade policy that has been subject to very little discipline during the almost 50 years of the multilateral rules-based system now governed by the World Trade Organization (WTO).

Determining the country of origin of products has become more difficult over the past four decades as technological change, declining transport costs, and the process of globalization have led to the splitting up of production chains and the distribution to different locations of the various elements in the production of a good. The issue becomes which of these stages of production defines the country of origin of the good. This chapter argues that complex rules of origin, which differ across countries and agreements, can be a significant constraint on trade, a substantial burden on customs, and a hindrance to trade facilitation. The nature of the rules of origin can undermine the stated intentions of preferential trade agreements.

The next section discusses what is meant by "origin" and examines methods for determining where a substantial transformation of a product takes place. The second section elaborates on the definition of preferential rules of origin and looks at the rules of origin in existing preferential trade agreements. The third reviews the economic implications of rules of origin, examines the links between rules of origin and the use of trade preferences, estimates the costs of complying with rules of origin, and analyses the use of rules of origin as a tool for economic development. The final section provides some conclusions.

Defining Origin

When a product is produced in a single stage or is wholly obtained in one country, such that there are no imported components, the country origin of the product is relatively easy to establish. This applies mainly to "natural products" and to goods made entirely from them. Proof that the product was produced or obtained in the preferential trade partner is normally sufficient. For all other cases in which two or more countries have taken part in the production of the good, the rules of origin define the methods for ascertaining in which country the particular product has undergone sufficient working or processing or has been subjected to a substantial transformation. (In general, these terms can be used interchangeably.) A substantial transformation is one that conveys to the product its essential character. Unfortunately, there is no simple and standard rule of origin for identifying the "nationality" of a product.

Although rules relating to products that are wholly obtained are usually relatively straightforward, this is not always the case. A good example of how rules for products that appear to be in their natural state, and are therefore apparently wholly obtained, can become complex and restrictive is the case of fish—typically, a sensitive sector in many countries. There is no apparent import content of fish caught in the sea or ocean, yet the European Union (EU) rules for fish caught outside a country's territorial waters but within the exclusive economic zone of a country can be very complex and difficult to satisfy and to prove compliance with. To receive preferential access to the EU under the generalized system of preferences (GSP), all of the following conditions relating to the vessel that catches the fish and the crew that sails on it must be satisfied:

- The vessel must be registered in the beneficiary country or in the EU.
- The vessel must sail under the flag of the beneficiary or of a member state of the EU.
- The vessel must be at least 60 percent owned by nationals of the beneficiary country or the EU or by companies with a head office in either the beneficiary country or in an EU state, and the chairman and a majority of the board members must be nationals of the beneficiary country or the EU.
- The master and the officers must be nationals of the beneficiary country or of an EU member, and at least 75 percent of the crew must be nationals of the beneficiary country or of an EU country.

Under the EU's Cotonou Agreement, which gives preferential access to the EU market to African, Caribbean, and Pacific (ACP) countries, the rules of origin for fish are slightly different and a little more liberal than those for GSP countries:

- The vessel must be registered in the EU or in any ACP state.
- The vessel must sail under the flag of any ACP or EU country.
- The vessel must be at least 50 percent owned by nationals of any ACP or EU state, and the chairman and the majority of the board members must be nationals of any of those countries.

- Under certain conditions, the EU will accept vessels chartered or leased by the ACP state under the Cotonou Agreement.
- Under Cotonou, the master, the officers, and 50 percent of the crew must be nationals of any ACP state or the EU.

So, identifying the nationality of fish can be a demanding task! More important, these rules have important economic implications for countries that wish to attract foreign direct investment (FDI) into their fisheries sectors and for small island economies that may have great difficulty in meeting the crew and officer requirements.

Methods for Determining Substantial Transformation

The three main criteria for determining origin are change of tariff classification, value added, and specific manufacturing process. We discuss each in turn.

Change of tariff classification. Origin is granted if the exported product falls into a different part of the tariff classification from any imported inputs that are used in its production. Application of this "tariff-shift" method has been facilitated by the widespread adoption of the Harmonized System (HS), under which most of the world's more than 190 countries are now classifying goods according to the same harmonized categories. The level of classification of the HS at which change is required remains an issue, however. Typically, it is specified that the change should take place at the heading level (that is, at the four-digit level of the HS).[2] Examples of simple HS headings are "beer made from malt" (HS 2203) and "umbrellas and sun umbrellas" (HS 6601). But headings can be more sophisticated:

> Machinery, plant or laboratory equipment, whether or not electrically heated (excluding furnaces, ovens and other equipment of heading 8514), for the treatment of materials by a process involving a change of temperature such as heating, cooking, roasting, distilling, rectifying, sterilizing, pasteurising, steaming, drying, evaporating, vaporizing, condensing or cooling, other than machinery or plant of a kind used for domestic purposes; instantaneous or storage water heaters, non-electric. (HS 8419)

The HS, however, was not designed specifically as a vehicle for determining country of origin; its purpose is to provide a unified commodity classification for definition of tariff schedules and for statistical purposes. Thus, in particular cases it can be argued that a change of tariff heading will not identify substantial transformation, whereas in other cases, substantial transformation may occur without change of tariff heading. As a result, schemes utilizing the criterion of change of tariff heading usually provide for a wide range of exceptions that need to satisfy other criteria for determining country of origin.

The change of tariff classification may be used to define both a positive test of origin, by stating the tariff classification of imported inputs that can be used in the production of the exported good (for example, those under a different heading), and a negative test, by stating cases in which change of tariff classification will not confer origin. For example, the North American Free Trade Agreement (NAFTA) rule of origin for tomato ketchup states that a change to ketchup (HS 210320) from imported inputs of any chapter except subheading 200290 (tomato paste) will confer origin. In other words, any ketchup made from imported fresh tomatoes will confer origin, but ketchup made from tomato paste imported from outside the area will not qualify for preferential treatment, even though the basic change of tariff classification requirement has been satisfied.[3] In the EU's preferential rules of origin, bread, biscuits, and pastry products (HS 1905) can be made from any imported products except those in chapter 11, which include flour—the basic input to these products.

The WTO Agreement on Rules of Origin stipulates that preferential and nonpreferential rules of origin should be based on a positive standard, but it allows the use of negative standards (a definition of what does not confer origin) if they "clarify a positive standard." The latter condition is so vague as to have had very little effect, and EU and NAFTA rules of origin, for example, are rife with negative standards.

Thus, although in principle the change of tariff classification can provide a simple, uniform method of determining origin, in practice, instead of a general rule, there are often many individual rules. Nevertheless, the rule on change of tariff classification, once defined, is clear, unambiguous, and easy for traders to learn, and it is relatively straightforward to implement. In terms of documentation, it requires that traders keep records showing the tariff classification of the final product and of all the imported inputs. This may not be a demanding requirement if the exporter directly imports the inputs, but it may be more difficult if inputs are purchased from intermediaries in the domestic market.

Value added. When the value added to a product in a particular country exceeds a specified percentage, the goods are defined as originating in that country. This criterion can be defined in two ways: as the minimum percentage of the value of the product that must be added in the country of origin, or as the maximum percentage of imported inputs in total inputs or in the value of the product.

As in the case of change of tariff classification, the value added rule has the advantage of being clear, simple, and unambiguous as stated. In application, however, it can become complex and uncertain. First, there is the issue of the valuation of materials, which may be based on several prices: ex works (from factory); free on board (FOB); cost, insurance, and freight (CIF); or into factory. Each method yields a different (in this instance, ascending) value of nonoriginating materials. Second, the application of this method can be costly for firms that will require sophisticated accounting systems and the ability to resolve often-complex accounting questions. Finally, under the value added method, origin is sensitive to changes in the factors that determine production cost differentials across countries, such as exchange rates, wages, and commodity prices. For example, operations that confer origin in one location may not do so in another because of differences in wage costs, and an operation that confers origin today may not do so tomorrow if exchange rates change.

Specific manufacturing process. This criterion delineates for each product or product group certain manufacturing or processing operations that define origin (positive test) and manufacturing or processing procedures that do not confer origin (negative test). The rules may require the use of certain originating inputs or prohibit the use of certain nonoriginating inputs. For example, EU rules of origin for clothing products stipulate manufacture from yarn, while the rule for sodium perborate requires manufacture from disodium tetraborate pentahydrate.[4]

The main advantage of specific manufacturing process rules is that, once defined, they are clear and unambiguous so that, from the outset, producers are able to clearly ascertain whether their product is originating or not. There are, however, a number of drawbacks to this system, including obsolescence (as a consequence of changes in technology) and documentary requirements, such as an up-to-date inventory of production processes, which may be burdensome and difficult to comply with.

Table 8.1 summarizes the main advantages and disadvantages of these various methods of determining sufficient processing or substantial transformation. No one rule dominates others as a mechanism for formally identifying the nationality of all products, and each has its advantages and disadvantages. It is clear, however, that different rules of origin can lead to different determinations of origin.

Producers who are eligible for preferential access to different markets under different schemes with different rules of origin may find that their product qualifies under some schemes but not others. For example, a company in a developing country may find that the product it produces qualifies for preferential access to the EU market under the EU's GSP scheme but that the same product does not satisfy the rules of origin of the U.S. GSP scheme.

Table 8.1. Summary of Methods for Determining Origin

Rule	Advantages	Disadvantages	Key issues
Change of tariff classification in the Harmonized System	Consistency with nonpreferential rules of origin. Once defined, rule is clear, unambiguous, and easy to learn. Relatively straightforward to implement.	Harmonized System not designed for conferring origin; as a result, there are often many individual product-specific rules, which can be influenced by domestic industries. Documentary requirements may be difficult to comply with. Conflicts over the classification of goods can introduce uncertainty about market access.	Level of classification at which change required; the higher the level, the more restrictive. Test may be positive (e.g., which imported inputs may be used) or negative (e.g., definition of cases where change of classification will not confer origin); negative test more restrictive.[a]
Value added	Clear, simple to specify, and unambiguous. Allows for general rather than product-specific rules.	Complex to apply; requires firms to have sophisticated accounting systems. Uncertainty resulting from sensitivity to changes in exchange rates, wages, commodity prices, and so on.	Level of value added required to confer origin. Valuation method for imported materials: methods that assign a higher value (e.g., CIF) will be more restrictive with respect to use of imported inputs.
Specific manufacturing process	Once defined, clear and unambiguous. Provides for certainty if rules can be complied with.	Documentary requirements can be burdensome and difficult to comply with. Leads to product-specific rules. Domestic industries can influence the specification of the rules. Can quickly become obsolete due to technological progress and therefore require frequent modification.	Formulation of the specific processes required; the more procedures required, the more restrictive. Use of negative test (processes or inputs which cannot be used) or positive test (what can be used); negative test more restrictive.

Source: Author's compilation.
Note: CIF, cost, insurance, and freight.
a. A positive determination of origin typically takes the form of "change from any other heading," as opposed to a negative determination of origin, such as "change from any other heading except for the headings of chapter XX." It is worth noting that change of tariff classification, particularly with a negative determination of origin, can be specified to have an effect identical to that of a specific manufacturing process.

Best-Practice Suggestions for the Design of Rules of Origin

Although it is difficult to derive specific recommendations with regard to the best-practice approach to the design of rules of origin, certain general propositions can be advanced that apply to both preferential and nonpreferential rules:

- The rules of origin should be simple, precise, easy to understand, transparent, predictable, and stable. They should avoid or minimize scope for interpretation and administrative discretion.
- The rules should be designed to have the least trade-distorting impact and should not become disguised nontariff barriers to trade. Protectionist lobbying should not compromise the specification of the rules of origin.
- As much as possible, the rules should be consistent across products and across agreements. The greater are the inconsistencies, the greater will be the complexity of the system of rules of origin, both for companies and for officials administering the various trade schemes.

Rules of Origin and Trade Preferences

Preferential rules of origin define the conditions that a product must satisfy to be deemed as originating in a country that is eligible for preferential access to a partner's market—not simply transshipped from a nonqualifying country or subject to only minimal processing. In practice, the greater the level of work that is required by the rules of origin, the more difficult it is to satisfy those rules, and the more restrictive the rules are in constraining market access relative to what is required simply to prevent trade deflection. This is particularly true for small, less diversified developing economies. The higher the amount of domestic value added that is required by a value added rule, the more difficult compliance will be, since there will be less scope for the use of imported parts and materials. A rule of origin that prevents the use of imported flour in the production of pastry products such as biscuits, for example, will be very restrictive for countries that do not have a competitive milling industry.

With regard to requirements relating to sufficient processing, change of tariff classification is the most frequently used criterion in current preferential trade agreements, and it features in both EU agreements and NAFTA. WTO research (WTO 2002) shows that of 87 free trade agreements (FTAs) and other preferential trade agreements investigated, 83 used change of tariff classification in the determination of origin. Most agreements specify that the change should take place at the heading level (that is, at the four-digit level), but in many agreements, especially those involving the EU and NAFTA, the tariff-shift requirement varies by product. For example, Estevadeordal and Suominen (2003) show that, although in NAFTA about 40 percent of tariff lines requires change of tariff heading, most tariff lines (54 percent) are subject to the more restrictive requirement of change of chapter (two-digit level). For a small number of products, only a change of subheading (six-digit level) is required.

Although change of tariff heading is used in most preferential trading agreements, it is seldom the only method applied. It is also important to note that in some agreements, such as those involving the EU, change of tariff classification is applied to some products, but the value added and specific manufacturing process methods are used for others. In NAFTA, rules of origin tend to require at least change of tariff classification, but the level at which change is required varies across products. This typically leads to considerable complication for customs officials in determining origin in preferential agreements. By contrast, many agreements between developing countries tend to specify general rules of origin and eschew the detailed product-by-product approach adopted by the EU and NAFTA.

Furthermore, in EU agreements and in NAFTA for certain products, rules are stipulated that require satisfaction of more than one method to confer origin. This is clearly more restrictive than a requirement to satisfy a single method. For example, in NAFTA's rules of origin, the requirement for passenger motor vehicles (HS 870321) reads, "A change to subheading 8703.21 from any other heading provided there is a regional value content of not less than 50 percent under the net cost method."

In some agreements for certain products, two or more methods will be stipulated, and satisfaction of *any one* of the methods will be sufficient to confer origin. For example, in the EU rules of origin, the requirements for wooden office furniture (HS 940330) are "manufacture in which all the material used is classified within a heading other than that of the product" or "manufacture in which the value of all the materials used does not exceed 40 percent of the ex-works price of the product." The provision of alternative means of satisfying origin requirements gives exporters, especially small firms, greater flexibility and will facilitate trade under preferential trade agreements.

With respect to value added requirements, the WTO views a threshold for domestic content of between 40 and 60 percent as the norm, with a typical average import requirement of between 60 and 40 percent. The EU agreements identify various thresholds on import content, ranging from 30 to 50 percent. NAFTA has a domestic content requirement of either 50 or 60 percent, according to the method used to value the product. A value added requirement of 50 percent can be very demanding in the globalized world of today, in which production has become split among (perhaps many) countries.

A further feature of globalization is that, for such products as clothing, computers, and telecommunication equipment, much of the value added lies in the intermediate products. High value added requirements therefore become particularly difficult for developing countries to satisfy, since it is the final, labor-intensive stage that they host. In this way, restrictive rules of origin act to constrain specialization at the country level. The available evidence suggests that for many products, value added in low-income countries is substantially less than 30 percent. When the final stage of production involves labor-intensive activities applied to relatively high-value imported inputs, it is more difficult for low-wage countries to satisfy a particular value added requirement than it is for higher-wage countries.

In general, these percentage value rules are rarely applied as the sole test of origin and are typically employed with the change of tariff classification. Exceptions among agreements are the Australia–New Zealand Closer Economic Relations Trade Agreement (ANZCERTA), the South Pacific Trade and Economic Co-operation Agreement (SPARTECA), and the Association of Southeast Asian Nations (ASEAN) Free Trade Agreement (AFTA), which have percentage requirements without any additional need for change of tariff heading. All three agreements do require that the last process of manufacture be undertaken in the exporting country.

As noted earlier, under the value added method, origin is sensitive to changes in factors such as exchange rates, wages, and commodity prices. The value added method thus tends to penalize low-labor-cost locations, which will find it more difficult than higher-cost locations to add the necessary value. It is likely to cause particular problems of compliance for companies in developing countries that lack the sophisticated accounting systems necessary under this method.

Rules based on specific manufacturing processes are widely used (in 74 of the 83 preferential trade agreements analyzed by the WTO), often in conjunction with the change of tariff classification criterion, the value added criterion, or both. They are a particular feature in the textiles and clothing sectors. Some examples of the application of the rules follow:

- A producer imports cotton fabric (HS5208), which is then dyed, cut, and made up into cotton shirts (HS6105). The value of the imported materials amounts to 65 percent of the value of the shirts. In this case, origin would come under a change of tariff heading rule, but not under a value added rule, which requires an import content of not more than 60 percent or a domestic content of more than 40 percent. A specific manufacturing process requirement that the products have been manufactured from yarn (the production stage before fabric) would mean that the product would not be originating.[5]
- A doll (HS9502) is made from imported plastics and imported ready-made garments and footwear. The value of the imported materials amounts to 50 percent of the value of the doll. In this case, the doll would be originating under a value added rule requiring an import content of no more than 60 percent; it would not be originating under the change of tariff heading because garments and accessories for dolls are classified under the same tariff heading as dolls.

Most preferential trade agreements also specify types of operations that are deemed to be insufficient in working or processing to confer origin. Typically, they include (a) simple packaging operations, such as bottling, placing in boxes, bags, and cases, and simple attachment on cards and boards; (b) simple mixing of products and simple assembly of parts; and (c) operations to ensure the preservation of products during transport and storage. The requirements act to ensure that these basic operations do not confer origin even if the basic rule of origin, such as change of tariff heading, has been satisfied.

Several other typical features of the rules of origin of preferential trade schemes can influence whether origin is conferred on a product and can hence determine the effect of the scheme on trade flows. These are cumulation, tolerance rules, and absorption. The treatment of duty drawback and of outward processing outside the free trade partners or preferential trade partners can also be important.

Cumulation

The basic rules of origin define the processing that has to be done in the individual beneficiary or partner to confer origin. Cumulation allows producers to import materials from a specific country or regional group of countries without undermining the origin of the final product. In effect, the imported materials from the identified countries are treated as being of domestic origin in the country requesting preferential access. There are three types of cumulation: bilateral, diagonal (or partial), and full.

The most basic form, *bilateral cumulation,* applies to materials provided by either of two partners of a preferential trade agreement. In this case, originating inputs (i.e., materials) that have been produced in accordance with the relevant rules of origin and imported from the partner, qualify as originating materials when used in a country's exports to that partner. For example, under the EU's GSP scheme, the rule of origin for cotton shirts states that origin is conferred to a beneficiary country if the shirt is manufactured from yarn. Nonoriginating yarn may be imported, but the weaving into fabric, the cutting, and the making up into a shirt must take place in the beneficiary. The EU's GSP scheme allows for bilateral cumulation so that fabric that originates in the EU (that is, fabric produced in accordance with the rule of origin for fabric—in this case, produced from the stage of fibers) can be treated as originating in the beneficiary country. Thus, originating fabrics can be imported from the EU and used in the production of shirts for export that will qualify for preferential access to the EU. The EU, however, is often not the least-cost supplier of inputs, and so the benefits of this type of cumulation can be limited. If the extra cost of using EU-sourced inputs rather than the lowest-cost inputs from elsewhere exceeds the available benefit from preferential access, cumulation will have no effect, and there will be no improvement in market access.

Diagonal cumulation takes place on a regional basis. Qualifying materials from anywhere in the specified region can be used without undermining preferential access. In other words, parts and materials from anywhere in the region that qualify as originating can be used in the manufacture of a final product, which can then be exported with preferences to the partner country's market. Diagonal cumulation is widely used in EU agreements but is not applied by NAFTA. In Europe, a pan-European system of rules of origin with diagonal cumulation has been developed to govern EU free trade agreements with countries of the European Free Trade Association (EFTA) and with countries in Central and Eastern Europe. Diagonal cumulation is allowed under the EU's GSP scheme, but within a limited set of regional groups that have pursued their own regional trade agreements. For example, diagonal cumulation can take place within four regional groupings: ASEAN, the Central American Common Market (CACM), the Andean Community, and the South Asian Association for Regional Cooperation (SAARC).

Diagonal cumulation allows originating materials from regional partners to be further processed in another country in the group and treated as though the materials originated in the country where the processing is undertaken.[6] This flexibility in sourcing is, however, constrained by the further requirement that the value added in the final stage of production exceed the highest customs value of any of the inputs used from countries in the regional grouping. Thus, for example, with diagonal cumulation, shirt producers in Cambodia can use fabrics from Indonesia (provided that they are originating—that is, produced from the fiber stage) and still receive duty-free access to the EU, but the value added in Cambodia must exceed the value of the imported fabric from Indonesia. Similarly, producers in Nepal can import originating fabric from India and still qualify for preferential access to the EU if the value added in Nepal is sufficient.

As demonstrated in a report by the United Nations Conference on Trade and Development (UNCTAD) and the Commonwealth Secretariat (2001), the value added requirement can render regional cumulation of little value. For example, value added in the making up of clothing in Bangladesh ranges from between 25 and 35 percent of the value of the product, so the import content of the fabrics that come from India is around 65 to 75 percent. In this case, the value added requirement placed on regional cumulation is not met, and origin of the made-up clothing is conferred not on Bangladesh, but on India. Regional cumulation still allows clothing that is produced in Bangladesh from Indian fabrics preferential access to the EU, but not at the zero rate for which Bangladesh is eligible. Rather, the rate for which India is eligible—a 20 percent reduction from the most favored nation (MFN) rate—is applied. Thus, instead of the zero duty, which is in principle available to Bangladesh under the Everything But Arms regulation, a tariff of more than 9 percent would be levied on these exports from Bangladesh to the EU.

In *full cumulation,* any processing activities carried out in any participating country in a regional group can be counted as qualifying content, regardless of whether the processing is sufficient to confer originating status on the materials themselves. Full cumulation allows for greater fragmentation of production processes among the members of the regional group and so stimulates increased economic linkages and trade within the region.

Under full cumulation, all the processing carried out in participating countries is assessed in deciding whether there has been substantial transformation. Full cumulation therefore encourages deeper integration among participating countries. Full cumulation is rare. It is currently applied in the EU agreements with the EFTA countries;

with Algeria, Morocco, and Tunisia; and, under the Cotonou Agreement, with the ACP countries. It is also available in the GSP schemes of Japan and the United States; among countries within specified groupings; and, on a global basis, among all developing-country beneficiaries in the schemes of Australia, Canada, and New Zealand, as well as the ANZCERTA and SPARTECA regional agreements.

Under full cumulation, it may be easier for more developed, higher-labor-cost countries to outsource labor-intensive, low-technology production stages to less developed, lower-wage partners while maintaining the preferential status of the good produced in low-cost locations. Diagonal cumulation, by requiring that more stages of production or higher value added be undertaken in the lower-cost country, may make it more difficult for the products produced by outsourcing to qualify for preferential access. The documentary requirements of full cumulation may be more onerous than those required under diagonal cumulation. Detailed information from suppliers of inputs may be required under full cumulation, whereas the certificates of origin that accompany imported materials may suffice to show conformity under diagonal cumulation. For this reason, it is desirable that traders be offered a choice between diagonal or full cumulation.

To illustrate the alternatives, a clothing product made in one country from fabric produced in a regional partner and made from nonoriginating yarn would be eligible for duty-free access to the EU under full cumulation but not under diagonal cumulation, since the fabric would not be deemed to be originating. (The rule of origin for the fabric requires manufacture from fibers.) Or, country A provides parts (say, chassis for bicycles) to country B, where they are processed (painted and prepared) and sent to country C for final assembly, using locally produced parts (tires and seat), before being exported to country D. Countries B, C, and D participate in the same FTA; country A is not a member. The value of the final product (the bicycle) exported from country C to country D consists of 25 percent parts from country A, 25 percent value added in country B, and 50 percent parts from and value added in country C. The value of parts from country A makes up 50 percent of the value of the intermediate product exported from country B to country C. If there were a 40 percent maximum import content for all products, the bicycle exported from country C to country D would qualify for preferential access under full cumulation. (Only the 25 percent of parts from country A is nonoriginating.) It would not, however, qualify under diagonal cumulation because the value of nonoriginating materials in the product exported by country B exceeds 40 percent. This intermediate product would not be treated as originating, and the total of nonoriginating materials in the final product would now be calculated as 50 percent of the final price of the bicycle (the value from both country A and country B).

Tolerance Rules

Tolerance, or de minimis, rules allow a certain percentage of nonoriginating materials to be used without affecting the origin of the final product. The tolerance rule can make it easier for products with nonoriginating inputs to qualify for preferences under the change of tariff heading rule and the specific manufacturing process rule. This provision does not affect the value added rules. The tolerance rule does not act to lower the limitation on the value of imported materials; the nonoriginating materials will always be counted in calculating import value content.

In NAFTA, nonoriginating materials can be used even if the rule on sufficient processing is not fulfilled, provided that the value of these materials does not exceed 7 percent of the value of the final product. Under the EU's GSP scheme, the threshold is 10 percent, but under the Cotonou Agreement between the EU and the ACP countries, the tolerance rule allows 15 percent of nonoriginating materials that would otherwise not be accepted. For example, in the case of the doll described earlier, in which the use of dolls' clothing accessories denied origin to the final product under the change of heading rule (since the accessories are classified under the same heading), origin would be conferred under the EU GSP if the value of the dolls' clothing and accessories is less than 10 percent of the value of the doll.

The tolerance rules applied to the textiles and clothing sector are often different and are generally less favorable than the general rules on tolerance. In many cases, the rule is applied in terms of the maximum weight rather than the value of the nonoriginating materials that are tolerated, and in cases in which the value threshold is maintained, it is set at a lower level than in the general rule.

Absorption (Roll-Up) Principle

According to the absorption principle, parts or materials that have acquired originating status by satisfying the relevant rules of origin can be treated as being of domestic origin in any further processing and transformation. This is of particular relevance to the value added test. For example, in the production of a particular part, origin is conferred because imported materials constitute 20 percent of the final price of the part and are less than the maximum, say, 30 percent required by an import content rule of origin. This part will then be treated as 100 percent originating when incorporated into a final product. The 20 percent

import content of the part is not taken into account when assessing the import content of the final product. The converse of this is that if the part does not satisfy the relevant rule of origin, it is deemed to be 100 percent nonoriginating ("roll-down"). Ideally, if the part or the materials fail to satisfy the relevant rule of origin, the portion of value added domestically should still be counted in the determination of the origin of the final product.

Duty Drawback and Outward Processing

Provisions relating to duty drawback can lead to the repayment of duties on nonoriginating inputs used in the production of a final product that is exported to a free trade or preferential trade partner. Some agreements contain explicit no-drawback rules that will affect decisions relating to the sourcing of inputs by firms exporting within the trade area, reducing the incentives for the use of imported inputs from nonparticipating countries and encouraging the use of originating inputs from participating ones. Increasingly important are rules concerning territoriality and the treatment of outward processing by companies based within the free trade area that is undertaken in countries that are not members of the agreement. These rules determine whether processing outside the area undermines the originating status of the final product exported from one partner to another.

Rules of Origin in Existing Preferential Trade Agreements

Preferential rules in EU and U.S. agreements. All three methods of determining origin are employed in agreements involving the EU and NAFTA. A key feature of the EU and NAFTA models of rules of origin is that these rules are specified at a very detailed level on a product-by-product basis and can be very complex—they often run to well over 200 pages! The rules for clothing products under NAFTA provide an example of very complex and restrictive rules of origin. The following summarizes the rules for men's or boys' overcoats made of wool (HS620111), which are typical of the nature of the rules for a wide range of clothing products:

> A change to subheading 620111 from any other chapter, except from heading 5106 through 5113, 5204 through 5212, 5307 through 5308 or 5310 through 5311, Chapter 54 or heading 5508 through 5516, 5801 through 5802 or 6001 through 6006, provided that the good is both cut and sewn or otherwise assembled in the territory of one or more of the Parties.

The basic rule of origin stipulates change of chapter but then provides a list of headings and chapters from which imported inputs cannot be used. In effect, the overcoat must be manufactured from the stage of wool fibers forward, since neither imported woolen yarn (HS5106–5110) nor imported woolen fabric (HS5111–5113) can be used. However, the rule also states that neither imported cotton thread (HS5204) nor imported thread of man-made fibers (HS54) can be used to sew the coat together. This rule in itself is very restrictive, and the rule for this product is further complicated by requirements relating to the visible lining:

> Except for fabrics classified in 54082210, 54082311, 54082321, and 54082410, the fabrics identified in the following sub-headings and headings, when used as visible lining material in certain men's and women's suits, suit-type jackets, skirts, overcoats, car coats, anoraks, windbreakers, and similar articles, must be formed from yarn and finished in the territory of a party: 5111 through 5112, 520831 through 520859, 520931 through 520959, 521031 through 521059, 521131 through 521159, 521213 through 521215, 521223 through 521225, 540742 through 540744, 540752 through 540754, 540761, 540772 through 540774, 540782 through 540784, 540792 through 540794, 540822 through 540824 (excluding tariff item 540822aa, 540823aa or 540824aa), 540832 through 540834, 551219, 551229, 551299, 551321 through 551349, 551421 through 551599, 551612 through 551614, 551622 through 551624, 551632 through 551634, 551642 through 551644, 551692 through 551694, 600110, 600192, 600531 through 600544 or 600610 through 600644.

This stipulates that the visible lining used must be produced from yarn and finished in either party. The rule may well have been introduced to constrain the effect of the tolerance rule, which would normally allow 7 percent of the weight of the article to be of nonoriginating materials. In overcoats and suits, the lining is probably less than 7 percent of the total weight. Finally, it is interesting to note that the rules of origin also provide very specific exemptions to the rules of origin for materials that are in short supply or are not produced in the United States—reflecting firm-specific lobbying to mitigate the restrictiveness of the original NAFTA rules of origin. The most specific example is where apparel is deemed to be originating if assembled from imported inputs of "fabrics of subheading 511111 or 511119, if hand-woven, with a loom width of less than 76 cm, woven in the United Kingdom in accordance with the rules and regulations of the Harris Tweed Association, Ltd., and so certified by the Association." The task facing importers, and the relevant customs officials, in checking consistency with such rules is clearly not a simple one!

Preferential rules in other agreements. This detailed, product-specific approach to rules of origin of the EU and NAFTA can be contrasted with most of the agreements involving developing countries, such as AFTA, the Common Market for Eastern and Southern Africa (COMESA), and the Southern Cone Common Market (Mercosur, Mercado Común del Sur), where rules are typically general and there are no, or very few, product-specific rules of origin. This suggests that domestic industry did not play a significant role in the specification of these rules. Some agreements, such as AFTA, rely solely on the value added method. The COMESA rules of origin require satisfaction of a value criterion (either the CIF value of imports must not exceed 60 percent of the value of all materials used, or domestic value added should be at least 35 percent of the ex-factory cost of the goods) or a change of tariff heading.[7]

What are the merits of these different approaches to the specification of preferential rules of origin? Detailed product-by-product rules can leave very little scope for interpretation. Indeed some argue that a product-by-product approach based on input from domestic producers is the best way of dealing with the specification of rules of origin. But, as the examples of fish and clothing show, product-specific rules can become very complex and restrictive. The more complex and the more technical the rules become, the greater is the scope for the participation of domestic industries in setting restrictive rules of origin (see Hoekman 1993). Indeed, "the formulation of product specific rules of origin is, by its nature, very much out of the practical control of generalists, which is to say government officials at the policy level, and very much in the practical control of specialists, which is to say the representatives of concerned industries" (Palmeter 2003, 159). Other interests, such as consumers of the relevant product, are effectively excluded from discussion concerning the rules of origin.

Those who lobby hardest for trade policy interventions are not altruistic, and their objectives with regard to rules of origin are likely to be to restrict competition from imports and to expand their own exports within a free trade area at the expense of third-country suppliers. Such objectives can be more effectively pursued when policy is determined in an environment that lacks transparency and openness, as can easily occur when rules of origin are determined product by product.

From a trade policy perspective, the restrictiveness of a value added rule, in terms of its impact on trade, is clearer and more apparent than is the case for the change of tariff classification and specific manufacturing process rules. It is relatively straightforward to compare alternative proposals concerning a value added rule. The extent of protection engendered by complex and technical rules of origin that differ across products is much more difficult to detect. This asymmetry of information is one reason why those groups seeking protection will push for complex rules of origin and why the change of tariff classification and specific manufacturing process rules may be more susceptible to capture by protectionist domestic interest groups (see Hirsch 2002). Adopting a product-by-product approach to rules of origin will tend to lead to rules that are more restrictive than is necessary to prevent trade deflection—to protectionist rules of origin—and that can lead to an overly complex system that is difficult for traders to implement and that adds considerably to the burden on customs services.

More general rules of origin can allow greater scope for interpretation, as noted by Izam (2003). In Asia, there are some suggestions of underutilization of AFTA preferences, reflecting uncertainties concerning the rules of origin. It appears that differing interpretations of the rules in ASEAN countries lead to inconsistent application of the rules within the region. This suggests the need for more effective coordination between customs and other relevant authorities in partner countries, with the aim of clarifying existing rules and regulations rather than applying more restrictive rules of origin. It is also important that alternative rules be considered so that producers are allowed some flexibility in proving origin. Giving producers the option of satisfying either a value added rule or a change of tariff classification rule is likely to be trade facilitating.

There is substantial variation in the permitted amount of nonoriginating import content under value added requirements in different agreements. In the Canada–Chile agreement, for example, products are typically subject to a change of tariff classification (where the level of change required varies by product) and a domestic value added requirement that varies between 25 and 60 percent, according to the product and the method of valuation used. In the U.S.–Chile agreement, where the rules are similar to those of NAFTA but not identical for all products, the required domestic content is between 35 and 55 percent. Under the Canada–Chile agreement, plastic products (HS39), for example, must satisfy the requirements of change of tariff heading and between 50 and 60 percent of domestic value added, depending on the method of valuation. Under the U.S.–Chile agreement, most plastic products need only satisfy the requirement of change of subheading to be originating. To be originating under the U.S.–Chile agreement, nonelectrical engineering products (HS84) must satisfy a change of subheading and a domestic value content of between 35 and 45 percent, whereas under the Canada–Chile agreement, such products need to satisfy change of subheading but only a 25 to 35 percent content requirement (always depending on the valuation method). Thus, certain products produced in Chile that are granted duty-free access to Canada may not receive such treatment

in the United States because of the more liberal rules of origin applied in the Canada–Chile agreement for those products, whereas other products may satisfy U.S. but not Canadian rules of origin requirements.

Most free trade and nonreciprocal trade preference schemes contain provisions for cumulation, but there is considerable variation in its nature. For example, the EU allows for diagonal cumulation in the Pan-European Area of Cumulation, encompassing the EFTA, Central and Eastern European, and Balkan countries, whereas under the Cotonou Agreement, there is full cumulation among African and Caribbean countries. Similarly, for tolerance rules, which are widely applied in agreements that are not based on the sole use of the value added method, there are considerable differences across agreements, even those involving the same country. Under the EU–Mexico Free Trade Agreement, nonoriginating materials can constitute up to 10 percent of the value of the final product, while under the agreement between the EU and South Africa, the level of tolerance is set at 15 percent. Different rules of tolerance are often established for certain sectors, especially textiles and clothing.

Measures of the restrictiveness of different origin regimes. Estevadeordal (2000) introduced an ordinal index (the R-index) to capture the overall restrictiveness of a set of rules of origin. The index is derived from data at the tariff-line level and is based on an observation rule, with the following two assumptions:

- For a change of tariff classification (CTC), change at the chapter level is more difficult to satisfy than a change at the heading level; a change at the heading level is stricter than at the subheading level; and a change at the subheading level is more stringent than at the tariff-line or item level.

- Additional criteria usually imply a more restrictive rule. When a CTC is accompanied by a value added requirement, a specific technical process, or both, the rule is more difficult to meet. Allowances (tolerance) and cumulation, by contrast, will tend to diminish the restrictiveness of a given rule.

Higher values are assigned more demanding rules, with a maximum value of 7. Figure 8.1 provides a simple summary of the outcome of applying this index to a number of free trade agreements by using information presented in Estevadeordal and Suominen (2006). The index shows that agreements involving the United States and the EU tend to have more restrictive rules of origin than do agreements among developing countries, such as COMESA and the Economic Community of West African States (ECOWAS). Agreements involving the EU and the United States tend to

Figure 8.1. Restrictiveness (R-Index) of Rules of Origin in Free Trade Agreements

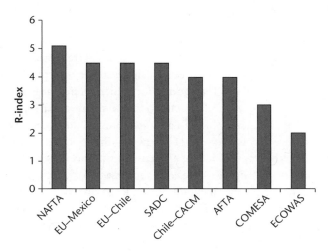

Source: Derived from Estevadeordal and Suominen 2006.
Note: AFTA, ASEAN Free Trade Agreement; ASEAN, Association of Southeast Asian Nations; CACM, Central American Common Market; COMESA, Common Market for Eastern and Southern Africa; ECOWAS, Economic Community of West African States; EU, European Union; NAFTA, North American Free Trade Agreement; SADC, Southern African Development Community. For derivation of the R-index, see the discussion in the text.

have complex product-specific rules of origin, whereas the COMESA and ECOWAS agreements have simpler rules that are common across products.

Although agreements between developing countries often have less restrictive rules of origin on paper, in practice their implementation can be highly restrictive. For example, to be able to use the ECOWAS trade liberalization scheme, companies must obtain, for each and every product that they wish to export, approval from their national ministry and then from ECOWAS. This is in addition to the requirement of a certificate of origin for each shipment. The whole process apparently takes between four to six months. Indeed, exporters registering for the first time are advised to state the names of future products to be exported under the scheme. If not, they will have to apply again for each new product they wish to export!

Economic Implications of Rules of Origin

The specification and implementation of rules of origin can be a major determinant of the impact of free trade and preferential trade agreements. In practice, rules of origin are controversial because the available evidence suggests that the utilization of preferences tends to be less than full. That is, substantial proportions of actual exports that are eligible for preferences do not enter the partner's market with zero or reduced duties but actually pay the MFN tariff.[8] Sapir (1998) shows that 79 percent of EU dutiable

imports from GSP beneficiaries in 1994 qualified for preferential access to the EU market, yet only 38 percent actually entered the EU market with a duty less than the MFN rate. The reasons for this difference are the effects of rules of origin and tariff quotas for particular products, which set limits on the amount of imports that can receive beneficial access to the EU market. The gap also reflects the treatment of textiles and clothing products, which accounted for more than 70 percent of EU imports from countries covered by the GSP but for which the utilization rate (the ratio of imports receiving preferences to eligible imports) was only 31 percent.

Rules of Origin and the Utilization of Trade Preferences

Under the EU's Everything But Arms Agreement for the least developed countries, which offers duty-free access for all products, almost all of Cambodia's exports to the EU are eligible for zero duty preferences, yet in 2001, only 36 percent of those exports obtained duty-free access. Brenton (2003) shows that this failure to utilize preferences meant that, on average, Cambodia's exports to the EU paid a tariff equivalent to 7.7 percent of the value of total exports. Again, the main suspect for this underutilization of trade preferences is the rules of origin, particularly since Cambodia specializes in the production of clothing products, for which EU rules of origin are very restrictive, requiring production from yarn.

Brenton and Manchin (2003) show that large amounts of EU imports from Eastern European countries of clothing products made from EU-produced fabrics still enter the EU market under an alternative customs regime—outward processing—even though there is no fiscal incentive to do so, since EU tariffs have been removed under free trade agreements. This probably reflects the costs and uncertainties in proving origin that would be necessary under the normal preferential customs procedures. Estevadeordal and Miller (2002) demonstrate that, in the transition from the U.S.–Canada free trade agreement to NAFTA, rules of origin for certain sectors, such as textiles, became more restrictive and that, as a result, the utilization of the available preferences declined.

Compliance with rules of origin entails costs that can affect the sourcing and investment decisions of companies.[9] If the optimal input mix for a firm involves the use of imported inputs that are proscribed by the rules of origin of a free trade agreement in which the country participates, then the rules of origin will reduce the value of the available preferences. The firm will have to shift from the lowest-cost source of inputs to a higher-cost source in the domestic economy, reducing the benefits of exporting under a lower tariff. In the extreme, if the cost difference exceeds the size of the tariff preference, the firm will prefer to source internationally and pay the MFN tariff. The ability to cumulate inputs from a partner under bilateral, diagonal, or full cumulation will tend, in increasing order, to open the possibilities for identifying low-cost sources of inputs that do not compromise the qualifying nature of the final product. Nevertheless, if the lowest-cost supplier is not a member of the area of cumulation, the benefits of the preferential scheme will always be less than indicated by the size of the preferential tariff.

Rules of origin can also distort the relative prospects of similar firms within a country. For example, a clothing producer in Moldova may have established an efficient manufacturing process on the basis of importing fabrics from Turkey. A less efficient producer that uses imported EU fabrics may be able to expand production on the basis of preferential access to the EU market under the GSP (with bilateral cumulation). The more efficient firm may not be able to expand, since its product does not qualify for preferences because of the use of nonqualifying fabrics and there may be substantial costs in changing suppliers of fabrics.

These problems will be exacerbated in sectors in which economies of scale are important. Producers that supply both preferential and nonpreferential trade partners, or that face different rules of origin in different preferential partners, will have to produce with a different input mix for different markets if they are to receive preferential access. This may undermine the benefits from lower average costs that would arise if total production were to be based on a single set of material inputs and a single production process.

Rules of origin may be an important factor in determining the investment decisions of multinational firms. Such firms often rely on imported inputs from broad international networks that are vital for supporting firm-specific advantages such as a technological edge in the production of certain inputs. More generally, if the nature and application of a given set of rules of origin increase the uncertainty concerning the extent to which preferential access will actually be provided, the level of investment will be less than if such uncertainty were reduced.

For companies, there is not only the issue of complying with the rules on sufficient processing but also the cost of obtaining the certificate of origin, including any delays that arise in obtaining it. The costs of proving origin include satisfying a number of administrative procedures, so as to be able to provide the required documentation, and maintaining systems that accurately account for imported inputs from different sources, in order to prove consistency with the rules. The ability to prove origin may well require

the use of what are, for small companies in developing and transition economies, sophisticated and expensive accounting procedures. Without such procedures, it is difficult for companies to show precisely the geographic breakdown of the inputs they have used.

An important feature of most preferential trade schemes is the requirement of direct consignment or direct transport. It stipulates that goods for which preferences are requested are shipped directly to the destination market. If they are in transit through another country, documentary evidence may be requested to show that the goods remained under the supervision of the customs authorities of the country of transit, that they did not enter the domestic market there, and that they did not undergo operations other than unloading and reloading. In practice, it may be very difficult to obtain the necessary documentation from foreign customs offices.

Finally, it is important to note that customs authorities are typically responsible for implementing the system of rules of origin. Customs usually has the responsibility for checking the certificate of origin and may also be involved in issuing origin certificates for local exporters. Rules of origin, although an essential element of preferential trade agreements, add considerable complexity to the trading system for traders, customs officials, and trade policy officials.

Implementation of preferential trade agreements increases the burden on customs. Limited resources and weak administrative capacity in many developing countries mean that these trade agreements have inevitable repercussions for trade facilitation. At the very least, when designing trade agreements, issues of administrative capacity in customs need to be taken into account. Complicated systems of rules of origin increase the complexity of customs procedures and the burden on origin-certifying institutions.

In general, rules of origin that are clear, straightforward, transparent, and predictable and that require little or no administrative discretion will place less of a burden on customs than will complex rules. The use of general rather than product-specific rules appears to be most appropriate for preferential rules of origin applied by and to developing countries. Less complicated rules of origin stimulate trade between regional partners by reducing the transaction costs of undertaking such trade, in comparison with more complex and restrictive rules of origin.

WTO members have recognized that rules of origin are an important factor affecting the ability of exporters to exploit market access opportunities. At the sixth WTO ministerial meeting, held in Hong Kong SAR, China, in December 2005, ministers declared that "developed-country Members, and developing-country Members declaring themselves in a position to do so, agree to implement duty-free and quota-free market access for products originating from [least-developed countries (LDCs)]" and that "members shall take additional measures to provide effective market access, both at the border and otherwise, including simplified and transparent rules of origin so as to facilitate exports from LDCs."

Quantifying the Costs Associated with Rules of Origin

The costs of complying with rules of origin can be decomposed into distortionary costs (caused by changes in the production structure to enable compliance) and administrative costs (to prove origin). Information on these costs is limited. Early studies suggested that the costs of providing the appropriate documentation to prove origin could be about 3 percent or more of the value of the export shipment for companies in developed countries (Herin 1986).[10]

Recently, efforts have been made to derive cost estimates for various product-specific rules of origin by linking the index of the restrictiveness of rules of origin developed by Estevadeordal (2000) to rates of utilization of preferences, after controlling for the size of the preferential margin. Cadot et al. (2006) find utilization rates of preferences to be positively related to preferential margins and negatively related to the restrictiveness of the rules of origin, as proxied by the R-index. They then proceed to use the R-index and the information on utilization of preferences to carry out nonparametric estimation of the upper and lower bounds of the costs of complying with the rules of origin. By revealed preference, when utilization rates are 100 percent, the preference margin provides an upper bound for compliance costs. When utilization rates are zero, the preference margin provides a lower bound of the costs of complying with the rules of origin. For intermediate rates of utilization, the average rate of preference is taken to capture the costs of compliance. The trade-weighted average of compliance costs is found to be 6.8 percent for NAFTA and 8 percent for EU rules of origin.

Cadot et al. (2006) also use the information on utilization rates to break down the estimate of compliance costs into the costs attributable to the costs of administration and those attributable to the distortionary element. They assume that low values of the R-index will tend to be associated with low administrative costs. (For example, the requirement to satisfy only change of tariff heading will require little paperwork.) Hence, preference margins for high utilization rates and a low value of the R-index will set an upper bound on the distortionary element of the compliance costs. The authors conclude that administrative

costs for NAFTA are around 2 percent and those for EU rules, about 6.8 percent, which reflects the more demanding certification procedures of EU schemes.

Finally, Estevadeordal and Suominen (2006) include the R-index in a standard gravity model of bilateral trade flows. Their econometric analysis leads them to conclude that restrictive, product-specific rules of origin undermine overall trade between the partners in a free trade agreement and that provisions such as cumulation and tolerance rules, which increase the flexibility of application of a given set of processing requirements, act to boost intraregional trade. By applying this approach at the sectoral level, they find support for the hypothesis that the restrictiveness of rules of origin for final goods stimulates trade in intermediate products between preferential partners.

It is useful to complement these econometric studies with case studies, and there is one product-specific case that clearly highlights how restrictive rules of origin can constrain the ability of beneficiaries to exploit trade preferences (Brenton 2006). Both the EU and the United States have schemes that offer duty-free access to low-income countries in Africa. A key sector is clothing. Most of today's developed countries and newly industrialized countries have used the clothing sector as a gateway to industrial development. The sector has very low entry barriers: it is labor intensive, the technology is relatively simple, start-up costs are comparatively low, and scale economies are negligible. The industry generates employment for large magnitudes of unskilled labor. Finally, the clothing sector is still subject to high tariffs in rich countries, so that there are large margins of preference for low-income countries in Africa.

Exports of apparel from African least-developed countries to the EU and to the United States were almost equal in 2000, but, by 2005, the value of exports to the United States was more than three times greater than the value of exports to the EU. The key factor explaining this increase is the rules of origin. EU rules stipulate production from yarn. This means that a double-transformation process must take place in the beneficiary; the yarn is woven into fabric, and then the fabric is cut and made up into apparel. The rules prohibit the use of imported fabric, although cumulation provisions allow for the use of inputs produced in other ACP countries. To obtain preferences, apparel producers must use local, EU, or ACP fabrics; they may not use fabrics from the main fabric-producing countries in Asia and still qualify for EU preferences. This is a binding restriction, since few countries in Africa have competitive fabric industries. The rules of origin under the U.S. African Growth and Opportunity Act (AGOA) allow African clothing exporters to use fabrics from any country (the so-called third-country fabric rule). The EU rules do not allow producers in African least-developed countries the flexibility they currently have under the U.S. scheme to source fabrics globally.

De Melo and Portugal-Pérez (2008), controlling for other relevant factors, find that, although Sub-Saharan African countries were offered similar preferential margins of around 10 percent in both EU and U.S. markets under Everything But Arms (EBA) and AGOA, the U.S. third-country fabric rule was associated with an increase in apparel exports from the seven main African exporters of about 300 percent. The removal of tariffs on imports of apparel from Sub-Saharan African countries was estimated to have led to a 96 percent increase in exports.

It is worth remembering that the EU has granted preferences to African countries for apparel, subject to these strict rules of origin, for more than 20 years under the Lomé and Cotonou Agreements and now EBA. These strict rules, however, have done little to encourage the development of an efficient fabric industry in Africa and are likely to have severely constrained the impact of preferences in stimulating the apparel industry. (See Brenton and Özden 2009 for a more detailed analysis of the impact of the EBA and AGOA on apparel exports from African least-developed countries and the role of the rules of origin.)

The specific justification for constraining access to third-country fabrics through the use of restrictive rules of origin is to encourage the expansion of fabric production in Africa, consistent with the view that vertical integration in Africa is crucial to survival in a world in which competitors in Asia are no longer constrained by quotas. However, the basis for this view is not well founded (see Stevens and Kennan 2004), since restrictive rules of origin will not lead to the emergence of competitive textile producers in Africa and will actually undermine the prospects of the sector. Textile capacity will only emerge if production of apparel continues. Lack of access to competitively produced fabrics undermines the viability of the apparel sector, so that there will be no demand for locally produced yarns and fabrics. Substantial improvements in infrastructure, especially in power and transport, together with a better climate for investment, are essential requirements for significant investments in textile production.

The European Commission now appears to have accepted the need for less restrictive rules of origin for clothing in its negotiations on economic partnership agreements (EPAs) with countries in Africa, the Caribbean, and the Pacific. For the interim EPAs that have been signed with African countries, the rules of origin for clothing have been relaxed to allow African exporters to use imported fabrics from any country and to qualify for preferential access to the EU market.

Rules of Origin and Economic Development

Can and should rules of origin be used as tools for stimulating economic development within a regional grouping? The draft ministerial text for the Cancún meeting of WTO members as part of the Doha Development Round of trade negotiations proposes, under provisions for special and differential treatment, that "developing and least-developed country Members shall have the right to adopt preferential rules of origin designed to achieve trade policy objectives relating to their rapid economic development, particularly through generating regional trade." Strict rules of origin are viewed by some as a mechanism for encouraging the development of integrated production structures within developing countries to maximize the impact on employment and to ensure that it is not just low value added activities that are undertaken.

There are problems with this view. First, such rules discriminate against small countries where the possibilities for local sourcing are limited or nonexistent. Since most developing countries are small, they are particularly disadvantaged by restrictive rules of origin relative to larger countries. Second, there is no evidence that the application of strict rules of origin over the past 30 years has done anything to stimulate the development of integrated production structures in developing countries. In fact, such arguments have become redundant in the light of technological changes and global trade liberalizations that have led to the fragmentation of production processes and the development of global networks of sourcing. Globalization and the splitting up of the production chain do not allow the luxury of establishing integrated production structures within countries. Strict rules of origin act to constrain the ability of firms to integrate into global and regional production networks and, in effect, act to dampen the location of any value added activities. In the modern world economy, flexibility in the sourcing of inputs is a key element in international competitiveness. Thus, it is most likely that restrictive rules of origin, rather than stimulating economic development, will raise costs of production by constraining access to cheap inputs and will undermine the ability of local firms to compete in overseas markets.

Flatters (2002) and Flatters and Kirk (2003), documenting the evolution of the rules of origin in the South African Development Community (SADC), show that the adoption of restrictive rules of origin is more likely to constrain than to stimulate regional economic development. This example provides a salutary lesson on how sectoral interests and misperceptions of the role and impact of rules of origin can undermine regional trade agreements.

SADC initially agreed to simple, general, and consistent rules of origin similar to those of the neighboring and overlapping COMESA. The initial rules required a change of tariff heading, a minimum of 35 percent of value added within the region, or a maximum import content of 60 percent of the value of total inputs. Simple packaging and the like were defined to be insufficient to confer origin. Subsequently, however, these rules were revised, and there are now more restrictive sector- and product-specific rules, with the change of tariff heading requirement being supplanted by detailed technical process requirements and rules with much higher domestic value added and lower permitted import content. The rules became much more similar to those of the EU and of NAFTA, reflecting, in part, the influence of the recently negotiated EU–South Africa agreement and the rules of origin governing EU preferences for ACP countries:

> The EU–South Africa rules were often invoked by special interests in South Africa as models for SADC. Such claims were too often accepted at face value and not recognized as self-interested pleading for protection by already heavily protected domestic producers. There were few questions about the appropriateness of the underlying economic model (whatever it might be) for SADC. (Flatters and Kirk 2003, 7)

Flatters (2002) points out that, in the SADC case, it has been argued that the weakness of customs administrations in the region makes it likely that low-cost products from Asia could enter through porous borders and then claim tariff preferences when exported to another member state. It is then suggested that restrictive rules of origin are required to prevent this from happening. There is no reason, however, to expect that weak customs administrations would be better able to enforce strict rules of origin than less restrictive rules. In fact, in many cases, the rules of origin are so strict that no producers in the region can satisfy them and therefore no discretion on the part of customs is required; preferences are not granted, and the preferential trade agreement has no impact. A better approach is to adopt economically sensible rules of origin and a program for improving administrative capacities in customs. Clearly designed safeguard measures can also be adopted to deal with surges of imports entering via partner countries.

To conclude, rules of origin are an inefficient tool for achieving development objectives; better policies are available. Rules of origin should be used as a mechanism for preventing trade deflection. Restrictive rules of origin that

go beyond this function and seek to force use of local content are likely to prove counterproductive, since they undermine the competitiveness of downstream industries (see Flatters 2001). If the objective is to stimulate regional trade, it is best achieved by adopting simple, clear, consistent, and predictable rules of origin that avoid administrative discretion and onerous burdens on customs and that minimize the costs of compliance for businesses.

Conclusions

The nature of rules of origin typically reflects the purpose that is set for them, the transparency of the process by which they are determined, and the composition of the group involved in that process. Within preferential trade areas, complex and restrictive rules of origin act to dampen competition for final producers within a country from suppliers in partner countries and to stimulate intra-area exports of intermediate products by diverting demand away from third-country suppliers. Such rules typically emerge when the process by which they are determined lacks transparency and openness and is dominated by input from domestic industry. If the purpose of preferential rules of origin is simply to prevent trade deflection, then a simple and less restrictive set of rules of origin implemented through general rather than product-specific rules is appropriate. In the current globalized world market, less restrictive rules are more likely to stimulate trade and investment in the partner region by giving producers as much flexibility as possible in sourcing their inputs without compromising the ability to prevent transshipment of goods from third countries that are not members of the agreement. If the objective of the trade agreement is to foster trade and development, it is best achieved through simple and liberal rules of origin, rather than by using rules of origin as opaque measures of trade protection. The analysis in this chapter leads to the following broad conclusions:

1. Rules of origin that vary across products and agreements add considerably to the complexity and costs of participating in and administering trade agreements. The incidence of such costs falls particularly heavily on small and medium-size firms and on firms in low-income countries. Complex systems of rules of origin add to the burdens on customs and may compromise progress on trade facilitation.
2. Restrictive rules of origin constrain international specialization and discriminate against small, low-income countries, where the possibilities for local sourcing are limited.

3. Simple, consistent, and predictable rules of origin are more likely to foster the growth of trade and development. Specifying generally applicable rules of origin, with a limited number of clearly defined and justified exceptions, is appropriate if the objective is to stimulate integration and minimize the burdens on firms and customs in complying with and administering the rules.

4. Producers should be accorded flexibility in meeting origin rules, for example, by specifying that *either* a change of tariff requirement *or* a value added rule can be satisfied.

5. Preferences granted by developed countries would be more effective in stimulating exports from developing countries if they were governed by less restrictive rules of origin. Ideally, these schemes should have common rules of origin. Producers in developing countries should be able to gain preferential access to all developed-country markets if their product satisfies a single origin test.

6. Restrictive rules of origin should not be used as tools for achieving economic development objectives; they are likely to be counterproductive. The potential benefits of trade agreements among developing countries can be substantially undermined if those agreements contain restrictive rules of origin.

Notes

This chapter is based on Brenton and Imagawa (2005).

1. Countries also apply another set of often different nonpreferential rules of origin in applying basic trade policy measures such as tariffs, quantitative restrictions, antidumping measures and countervailing duties, and safeguard measures, as well as to fulfill requirements relating to country-of-origin marking and public procurement and for statistical purposes.

2. The Harmonized System comprises 96 chapters (two-digit level), 1,241 headings (four-digit level), and about 5,000 subheadings (six-digit level).

3. The apparent reason for this rule in NAFTA is to protect producers of tomato paste in Mexico from competition from producers in Chile; see Palmeter (2003).

4. The EU rule of origin for sodium perborate also allows satisfaction of a maximum import content rule of 40 percent.

5. This yarn-forward rule is common in EU agreements for all clothing products. The United States typically applies an even stricter process rule requiring that the clothing be made from fibers, which means that the processes of spinning fiber into yarn and weaving yarn into fabric, as well as making up fabric into clothing, have to be undertaken in the exporting country to confer origin on the product.

6. For both bilateral and regional cumulation, there can be an additional requirement that the processing carried out be more than "insufficient working or processing." This addition, which is typical in EU agreements but not in those of other countries, requires that more than packing, mixing, cleaning and preserving, and simple assembly of parts take place.

7. The COMESA agreement also specifies that a range of goods deemed to be of particular importance to economic development need only satisfy a 25 percent domestic value added criterion.

8. For many years, UNCTAD has been highlighting the relatively low levels of utilization of preferences granted by developed countries to developing countries. For a recent discussion of utilization rates of GSP schemes and rules of origin, see Inama (2002).

9. Economists have generally given little attention to rules of origin within the voluminous literature on free trade areas. The key initial contributions on rules of origin are Krueger (1997) and Krishna and Krueger (1995); these authors demonstrate how rules of origin can act as "hidden protectionism" and can induce a switch in demand in free trade partners from low-cost external inputs to higher-cost partner inputs to ensure that final products actually receive duty-free access. Falvey and Reed (1998) show how rules of origin can be used to protect a domestic industry from unwanted competition from a partner, even in conditions where trade deflection is unlikely.

10. Herin (1986) also found that as a result of the costs to EFTA producers of proving origin, one-quarter of EFTA exports to the EU paid the applied MFN duties.

References

Brenton, Paul. 2003. "Integrating the Least Developed Countries into the World Trading System: The Current Impact of EU Preferences under Everything But Arms." *Journal of World Trade* 37: 623–46.

———. 2006. "Enhancing Trade Preferences for LDCs: Reducing the Restrictiveness of Rules of Origin." In *Trade, Doha and Development*, ed. Richard Newfarmer. Washington, DC: World Bank.

Brenton, Paul, and Hiroshi Imagawa. 2005. "Rules of Origin, Trade and Customs." In *The Customs Modernization Handbook*, ed. Luc De Wulf and José B. Sokol. Washington, DC: World Bank. http://siteresources.worldbank.org/INTEXPCOMNET/Resources/Customs_Modernization_Handbook.pdf.

Brenton, Paul, and Miriam Manchin. 2003. "Making EU Trade Agreements Work: The Role of Rules of Origin." *World Economy* 26 (5): 755–69.

Brenton, Paul, and Çağlar Özden. 2009. "Trade Preferences for Apparel and the Role of Rules of Origin: The Case of Africa." In *Trade Preference Erosion: Measurement and Policy Response,* ed. Bernard Hoekman, Will Martin, and Carlos A. Primo Braga, 401–24. Washington, DC: Palgrave Macmillan and World Bank.

Cadot, Olivier, Celine Carrère, Jaime de Melo, and Bolormaa Tumurchudur. 2006. "Product-Specific Rules of Origin in EU and US Preferential Trading Arrangements: An Assessment." *World Trade Review* 5 (2): 199–224.

De Melo, Jaime, and Alberto Portugal-Pérez. 2008. "Rules of Origin, Preferences and Diversification in Apparel: African Exports to the US and to the EU." CEPR Discussion Paper 7072, Centre for Economic Policy Research, London. http://www.cepr.org/pubs/new-dps/dplist.asp?dpno=7072.

Estevadeordal, Antoni, 2000. "Negotiating Preferential Market Access: The Case of NAFTA." *Journal of World Trade* 34 (1): 141–66.

Estevadeordal, Antoni, and Eric Miller. 2002. "Rules of Origin and the Pattern of Trade between US and Canada." Inter-American Development Bank (IADB), Washington, DC.

Estevadeordal, Antoni, and Kati Suominen. 2003. "Rules of Origin in FTAs in Europe and the Americas: Issues and Implications for the EU–MERCOSUR Inter-Regional Association Agreement." In *Market Access for Goods and Services in the EU–Mercosur Negotiations*, ed. Alfredo G. A. Valladão and Roberto Bouzas. Paris: Chaire Mercosur de Sciences Po.

———. 2006. "Rules of Origin: A World Map and Trade Effects." In *The Origin of Goods: Rules of Origin in Preferential Trade Agreements*, ed. Olivier Cadot, Antoni Estevadeordal, Akiko Suwa-Eisenmann, and Thierry Verdier. Oxford, U.K.: Oxford University Press.

Falvey, Rod, and Geoff Reed. 1998. "Economic Effects of Rules of Origin." *Weltwirtschaftliches Archiv* 134: 209–29. http://www.springerlink.com/content/g638k36612659n59/.

Flatters, Frank. 2001. "The SADC Trade Protocol: Which Way Ahead?" *Southern African Update* 10: 1–4.

———. 2002. "SADC Rules of Origin: Undermining Regional Free Trade." Presented at the Trade and Industrial Strategies (TIPS) Forum,

Johannesburg, September. http://qed.econ.queensu.ca/faculty/flatters/writings/ff_sadc_roo_tips_forum.pdf.

Flatters, Frank, and Robert Kirk. 2003. "Rules of Origin as Tools of Development? Some Lessons from SADC." Presented at Institut National de la Recherche Agronomique (INRA) Conference on Rules of Origin, Paris, May.

Herin, Jan. 1986. "Rules of Origin and Differences between Tariff Levels in EFTA and in the EC." European Free Trade Association (EFTA) Secretariat, Geneva.

Hirsch, Moshe. 2002. "International Trade Law, Political Economy and Rules of Origin: A Plea for a Reform of the WTO Regime on Rules of Origin." *Journal of World Trade* 36 (2): 171–88.

Hoekman, Bernard. 1993. "Rules of Origin for Goods and Services: Conceptual and Economic Considerations." *Journal of World Trade* 27: 81–99.

Inama, Stefano. 2002. "Market Access for LDCs: Issues to be Addressed." *Journal of World Trade* 36 (1): 85–116.

Izam, Miguel. 2003. "Rules of Origin and Trade Facilitation in Preferential Trade Agreements in Latin America." Presented at the International Forum on Trade Facilitation, Geneva, May.

Krishna, Kala, and Anne Krueger. 1995. "Implementing Free Trade Areas: Rules of Origin and Hidden Protection." NBER Working Paper 4983, National Bureau of Economic Research, Cambridge, MA. http://www.nber.org/papers/w4983.

Krueger, Anne. 1997. "Free Trade Agreements versus Customs Unions." *Journal of Development Economics* 54: 169–87.

Palmeter, David. 2003. *The WTO as a Legal System: Essays on International Trade Law and Policy.* London: Cameron May.

Sapir, André. 1998. "The Political Economy of EC Regionalism." *European Economic Review* 42: 717–32.

Stevens, Christopher, and Jane Kennan. 2004. "Comparative Study of G8 Preferential Access Schemes for Africa: Report on a DFID-Commissioned Study." Institute of Development Studies, Brighton, U.K.

UNCTAD (United Nations Conference on Trade and Development) and Commonwealth Secretariat. 2001. "Duty and Quota Free Market Access for LDCs: An Analysis of Quad Initiatives." UNCTAD, Geneva; Commonwealth Secretariat, London. http://r0.unctad.org/ditc/tab/publications/duty_quota_free.pdf.

WTO (World Trade Organization). 2002. "Rules of Origin Regimes in Regional Trade Agreements." WT/REG/W/45, WTO, Geneva.

9

TRADE REMEDY
PROVISIONS

Thomas J. Prusa

The question of whether preferential trade agreements (PTAs) are good or bad for the global trade system has always been contentious. As experience has accumulated, our understanding of the consequences of PTAs has evolved. The traditional worries about welfare impacts associated with trade creation and diversion have been augmented by a multitude of new and unanticipated concerns.[1]

Most countries have been reducing tariffs across the board for all partners on a nondiscriminatory basis, and the value of PTA preferences has, as a consequence, steadily fallen. How much trade creation or diversion can be expected when preferential rates are essentially the same as most favored nation (MFN) rates?[2] For many PTAs, therefore, the main welfare consequences are likely to stem from nontariff provisions. Indeed, as emphasized in this handbook, PTAs have increasingly come to address many issues beyond tariffs—government procurement, labor standards, environmental protection, and so on.

This chapter examines the potential effects of one such beyond-tariffs area, trade remedy provisions. The focus is on the most frequently used of these provisions: antidumping measures, countervailing duties (CVDs), and safeguard measures. Antidumping measures and countervailing duties are designed to sanction exporters who engage in "unfair" trading practices that cause material injury to domestic producers. These unfair practices can take the form of selling products below their "normal" price (dumping) or of benefiting from government-provided subsidies (the situation that CVDs are meant to address). By contrast, safeguard actions are designed to deal with unexpected circumstances arising in the course of "fair" trade. They can be imposed even if there has been no unfair trade practice, as long as imports have increased to such an extent that domestic producers have suffered serious

injury. Because this material injury standard is considered weaker, and because antidumping measures and CVD protection are country specific, sanctions against unfair trade practices are generally easier to apply. World Trade Organization (WTO) rules require that, for all of the trade remedies discussed here, there be a link between change in trade volume and the imposition of trade protection; the existence of a causal link is generally determined by an administrative body in the importing country.

An important precursor to the analysis reported here was the development of a database of PTA provisions. As of early 2009, the database contained detailed information on trade remedy provisions in 74 PTAs. The longer-run goal is to survey all PTAs reported to the WTO.

Some PTAs include no language concerning specific trade remedies; others prohibit trade remedies against members. Often, PTAs allow trade remedies but add extra rules. The database permits us to dig deeper and look at which rules were actually included in the agreements. We are then able to determine whether certain rules are more common than others and whether countries that are involved in many PTAs are consistent in the provisions they enact in different agreements.

The next section surveys some of the political and economic justifications for including trade remedy provisions in PTAs. The subsequent sections take advantage of the database to survey the provisions contained in the PTAs included. As a first step, the PTAs are divided into three groups: those with trade remedy rules, those that prohibit the use of trade remedies, and those without any trade remedy rules. Specific provisions are then scrutinized in greater detail. Next, the hub-and-spoke pattern of PTAs is discussed, along with the hubs' use of trade remedy provisions. Despite considerable variation in rules within hubs, there is evidence of different North American and

European philosophies regarding trade remedies. The set of PTAs that have managed to prohibit one or more trade remedies is then examined. Finally, the chapter concludes with an analysis of the important issue of protection diversion.

Before moving to the main discussion, a comment on terminology is useful: the terms "trade remedies," "contingent protection," and "administered protection" are employed interchangeably in this chapter.

The Political Economy of the Need for Trade Remedies in PTAs

The rationale for the inclusion of preferential tariff schedules and definitions of rules of origin in PTAs seems clear. It is less obvious why most PTAs devote significant language to amending and qualifying the use of trade remedies.

One explanation for the widespread presence of trade remedies in PTAs is the political economy of protectionism (Tharakan 1995). The long-term process of tariff liberalization in the post–World War II era has reduced tariff rates to very low levels worldwide. Import-competing sectors, however, still have an incentive to secure protection through whatever means they can find. With the most direct route (tariffs) eliminated, these interests turn to the next best alternative, contingent protection (trade remedies).

A second, related argument is that contingent protection acts as a pressure-release valve that enables continued liberalization (Jackson 1997). Trade liberalization often imposes costs of adjustment on uncompetitive industries, and the incorporation of trade remedy measures in PTAs may be thought of as a way of managing the political consequences of these costs through a temporary reversal of liberalization.

Empirically, it turns out that the trade remedy rules in PTAs often make granting protection more difficult. A third rationale explains why this might be so. The inclusion of PTA provisions that restrict the use of trade remedies is consistent with the view that contingent protection is necessary because countries are insufficiently open to trade. For example, Mastel (1998) argues that dumping is driven by closed home markets. The elimination of barriers to intra-PTA trade reduces the ability of firms to dump, as they no longer have a protected home market where they can earn supernormal profits.[3] This third explanation is also consistent with the lack of rules on countervailing duties in PTAs. Specifically, given that most PTAs have failed to strengthen antisubsidy rules, the notion that there

will be fewer subsidies and thus less need for countervailing duties is not supported.

Each of the three explanations suggests that PTAs may alter the demand for trade remedy protection. On the one hand, import-competing sectors need to be assured that they can protect themselves from the unanticipated consequences of the regional liberalization program. Retaining trade remedies in the PTA helps maintain political support for the agreement. On the other hand, regional liberalization might eliminate unfair trade.

To the extent that PTA trade remedy provisions offer new forms of protection or make existing forms of protection easier to obtain, they are similar to provisions in PTAs for long transition periods, complicated rules of origin, and carve-outs for sensitive sectors—all of which result in slower liberalization for import-competing sectors. Instead of directly cushioning the effects of the PTA by drawing out the process of tariff elimination, trade remedies achieve a different cushioning effect by specifying a set of conditions—injury to the domestic industry—under which regional liberalization may be temporarily suspended or partially reversed. Bilateral safeguard rules are an example of rules that temporarily reverse preferential concessions. Such rules may hurt PTA partners and moderate beneficial trade creation, but they may be beneficial from a global perspective if they serve to lessen trade diversion.

PTA provisions that make contingent protection more difficult to grant have more subtle effects. Abolishing or restricting the use of trade remedies with respect to PTA partners' trade will most likely increase intrabloc trade. The welfare effects, however, are uncertain. The ambiguity stems from the well-known insight that preferential trade arrangements have both trade creation and trade diversion effects (Viner 1950). Rules on contingent protection can clearly both create and divert trade (Bown and Crowley 2007).

The danger is that, as intraregional trade expands because of preferential tariffs, contingent protection will be increasingly directed at the imports of nonmembers. Bhagwati (1996) and Bhagwati and Panagariya (1996) foresaw this danger, arguing that the elastic and selective nature of contingent protection increases the risk that PTAs will lead to trade diversion.[4] As specific provisions are discussed in what follows, it is important to consider the conflicting motivations countries may have when negotiating agreements. If trade remedies serve primarily as pressure-release valves, PTAs should include provisions that make it easier for domestic industries to raise barriers, but if PTAs open up closed home markets, then, arguably, some trade provisions are not needed.

Incidence of Trade Remedy Actions

Before discussing the role of trade remedies in PTAs, it is useful to review the incidence of trade remedy actions over the past decade. Table 9.1 presents data from notifications made by members to the WTO over the 1995–2007 period. Whereas the other WTO exceptions—infant industries, balance of payments, national security, and so on—are rarely invoked, the provisions studied in this paper have been used literally hundreds (or, in the case of antidumping measures, thousands!) of times.[5]

Countries' clear preference for using antidumping rather than countervailing duty measures or safeguards is striking. As shown, there were nearly nine times more initiations of antidumping measures (3,220) than of countervailing duty (201) and safeguard (163) actions combined.[6] A similar discrepancy is seen in the number of measures applied.

There has been a significant change in the use of these remedies. The four major users—Australia, Canada, the European Union (EU), and the United States—accounted for more than 90 percent of the contingent trade initiations during the 1980s and were the targets in more than 75 percent of the investigations (Prusa 2001).[7] By contrast, countries from all parts of the world are now active users and targets of contingent protection (Prusa 2005). Since 1995, 43 countries have initiated antidumping cases, 18 have initiated countervailing duty cases, and 30 have initiated global safeguard cases. Nearly 100 countries have been the subject of antidumping investigations, and 40 have been targeted in countervailing duty investigations.[8] The broadened set of uses and targets of trade remedies reflects increased globalization.

Trade remedies can reinforce the trade diversion effects of a PTA: on average, the imposition of antidumping and countervailing duty measures reduces subject imports from the targeted country by about half (Prusa 2001). When faced with contingent protection measures, non-PTA members will be at an even greater disadvantage than under preferential tariffs. The potential for such discrimination is clear for country-specific measures such as antidumping

and countervailing duty measures, but it is also a major concern for global safeguards because provisions in PTAs often allow PTA members to be excluded from these safeguards (Bown 2004).

Trade Remedy Provisions in PTAs

PTAs vary in size, degree of integration, geographic scope, and members' level of economic development, and the political and economic demands for trade remedy provisions across PTAs also necessarily vary. The proliferation and diversity of PTAs has produced a complicated pattern in the use and inclusion of trade remedy provisions across PTAs that defies simple characterization.

Some PTAs contain long discussions of trade remedy rules; others do not even mention trade remedies. For some PTAs, the trade remedy provisions make protection easier, but in most cases they make it more difficult to impose.

A simple characterization is impossible, not only because trade remedy provisions vary from one PTA to the next but also because provisions differ for the same country across different PTAs. For example, PTAs entered into by the United States have no specific antidumping provisions except for the North American Free Trade Agreement (NAFTA), which contains a number of these provisions—notably, the creation of binational panels that review antidumping determinations made by national authorities. Similarly, the EU has entered into PTAs that have no antidumping rules, others that contain many antidumping rules, and even some that prohibit the use of antidumping.

Diversity among PTAs

Tables 9.2 and 9.3 present a summary of the 74 PTAs surveyed and their characteristics. With only four exceptions, the PTAs mapped were notified to the WTO. The database includes PTAs with members in Europe, North America, the Caribbean, Latin America, Asia and the Pacific, Africa, and the Middle East. The sample reflects the economic diversity of PTAs, covering as it does North-North, South-South, and North-South agreements. Most (46) of the sampled PTAs have a mix of developed and developing countries in their membership; 22 have only developing countries as members, and 6 have developed members only.[9] The sample is dominated by free trade agreements: 80 percent of the PTAs in the sample are free trade areas, 10 percent are customs unions, and 10 percent are preferential trade areas.[10]

Table 9.1. Trade-Contingent Initiations and Measures in PTAs, 1995–2007

Trade-contingent instrument	Initiations	Measures
Antidumping measures	3,220	2,052
Countervailing duties	201	119
Safeguards	163	83

Source: WTO Secretariat.

Table 9.2. Contingent Protection Rules in Selected PTAs

PTA	Entry into force	Relevant GATT provision	Type[a]	Development status of members	Antidumping	Countervailing duty	Global safeguards	Bilateral safeguards
						Trade remedy		
AFTA	1992	Enabling Clause	FTA	Developing	No rules	No rules	No rules	Rules
Andean Community	1993		CU	Developing	Rules	Rules	No rules	Rules
ANZCERTA	1990	Article XXIV	FTA	Developed	Disallowed	Rules	No rules	Rules
Australia–Singapore	2003	Article XXIV	FTA	Mixed	Rules	Rules	No rules	Disallowed
Australia–Thailand	2005	Article XXIV	FTA	Mixed	Rules	Rules	Rules	Rules
Australia–United States	2005	Article XXIV	FTA	Developed	No rules	No rules	Rules	Rules
CACM	1961	Article XXIV	CU	Developing	Rules	Rules	No rules	No rules
Canada–Chile	1997	Article XXIV	FTA	Mixed	Disallowed	No rules	Rules	Rules
Canada–Costa Rica	2002	Article XXIV	FTA	Mixed	Rules	No rules	Rules	Rules
Canada–Israel	1997	Article XXIV	FTA	Mixed	No rules	Rules	Rules	Disallowed
CARICOM	1973	Article XXIV	CU	Developing	Rules	Rules	No rules	Rules
CEMAC	1999	Enabling Clause	PTA	Developing	No rules	No rules	No rules	No rules
China–Hong Kong SAR, China	2004	Article XXIV	FTA	Developing	Disallowed	Disallowed	No rules	Rules
China–Macao SAR, China	2004	Article XXIV	FTA	Developing	Disallowed	Disallowed	No rules	Rules
COMESA	1994	Enabling Clause	PTA	Developing	Rules	Rules	No rules	Rules
EEA	1994	Article XXIV	FTA	Developed	Disallowed	Disallowed	No rules	Rules
EFTA	2001	Article XXIV	FTA	Developed	Disallowed	Disallowed	No rules	Rules
EFTA–Chile	2004	Article XXIV	FTA	Mixed	Disallowed	Rules	Rules	Rules
EFTA–Croatia	2002	Article XXIV	FTA	Mixed	Rules	Rules	No rules	Rules
EFTA–Israel	1993	Article XXIV	FTA	Mixed	Rules	Rules	No rules	Rules
EFTA–Jordan	2002	Article XXIV	FTA	Mixed	Rules	Rules	No rules	Rules
EFTA–Macedonia, FYR	2001	Article XXIV	FTA	Mixed	Rules	Rules	No rules	Rules
EFTA–Morocco	1999	Article XXIV	FTA	Mixed	Rules	Rules	No rules	Rules
EFTA–Palestinian Authority	1999	Article XXIV	FTA	Mixed	Rules	Rules	No rules	Rules
EFTA–Singapore	2003	Article XXIV	FTA	Mixed	Disallowed	Rules	No rules	Rules
EFTA–Tunisia	2005	Article XXIV	FTA	Mixed	Rules	Rules	Rules	Rules
EFTA–Turkey	1992	Article XXIV	FTA	Mixed	Rules	Rules	No rules	Rules
EU	1958	Article XXIV	CU	Developed	Disallowed	Disallowed	No rules	Disallowed
EU–Algeria	1976	Article XXIV	FTA	Mixed	Rules	Rules	Rules	Rules
EU–Andorra	1991	Article XXIV	CU	Mixed	No rules	No rules	No rules	No rules
EU–Chile	2003	Article XXIV	FTA	Mixed	Rules	Rules	Rules	Rules
EU–Croatia	2002	Article XXIV	FTA	Mixed	Rules	Rules	No rules	Rules
EU–Egypt, Arab Rep.	2004	Article XXIV	FTA	Mixed	Rules	Rules	Rules	Rules
EU–Faeroe Islands	1997	Article XXIV	FTA	Mixed	Rules	No rules	No rules	Rules
EU–Macedonia, FYR	2001	Article XXIV	FTA	Mixed	Rules	No rules	No rules	Rules
EU–Israel	2000	Article XXIV	FTA	Mixed	Rules	No rules	No rules	Rules
EU–Jordan	2002	Article XXIV	FTA	Mixed	Rules	No rules	No rules	Rules
EU–Lebanon	2003	Article XXIV	FTA	Mixed	Rules	Rules	Rules	Rules
EU–Mexico	2000	Article XXIV	FTA	Mixed	Rules	Rules	No rules	Rules
EU–Morocco	2000	Article XXIV	FTA	Mixed	Rules	No rules	No rules	Rules
EU–OCT	1971	Article XXIV	FTA	Mixed	No rules	No rules	No rules	Rules
EU–Palestinian Authority	1997	Article XXIV	FTA	Mixed	Rules	No rules	No rules	Rules
EU–South Africa	2000	Article XXIV	FTA	Mixed	Rules	Rules	Rules	Rules
EU–Switzerland–Liechtenstein	1973	Article XXIV	FTA	Developed	Rules	No rules	No rules	Rules

(continued next page)

Table 9.2. *(continued)*

PTA	Entry into force	Relevant GATT provision	Type[a]	Development status of members	Antidumping	Countervailing duty	Global safeguards	Bilateral safeguards
							Trade remedy	
EU–Syrian Arab Republic	1977	Article XXIV	FTA	Mixed	Rules	Rules	No rules	Rules
EU–Tunisia	1998	Article XXIV	FTA	Mixed	Rules	No rules	No rules	Rules
EU–Turkey	1996	Article XXIV	CU	Mixed	Rules	No rules	No rules	Rules
GCC	1981	Enabling Clause	PTA	Developing	No rules	No rules	No rules	No rules
Group of Three (Colombia, Mexico, and Venezuela, RB)	1995		FTA	Developing	Rules	Rules	Rules	Rules
Japan–Singapore	2002	Article XXIV	FTA	Mixed	No rules	No rules	Rules	Rules
Korea, Rep.–Chile	2004	Article XXIV	FTA	Developing	Rules	Rules	Rules	Rules
LAIA/ALADI	1981	Enabling Clause	PTA	Developing	No rules	No rules	No rules	Rules
Mercosur	1991	Enabling Clause	CU	Developing	Rules	Rules	No rules	Disallowed
Mexico–Chile	1999	Article XXIV	FTA	Developing	No rules	No rules	Rules	Rules
Mexico–EFTA	2001	Article XXIV	FTA	Mixed	Rules	Rules	No rules	Rules
Mexico–Israel	2000	Article XXIV	FTA	Developing	Rules	Rules	Rules	Rules
Mexico–Japan	2005	Article XXIV	FTA	Mixed	No rules	No rules	Rules	Rules
Mexico–Nicaragua	1998	Article XXIV	FTA	Developing	Rules	Rules	Rules	Rules
Mexico–Northern Triangle	2001		FTA	Developing	Rules	Rules	Rules	Rules
Mexico–Uruguay	2004		FTA	Developing	Rules	Rules	Rules	Rules
NAFTA	1994	Article XXIV	FTA	Mixed	Rules	Rules	Rules	Rules
New Zealand–Singapore	2001	Article XXIV	FTA	Mixed	Rules	No rules	No rules	Disallowed
SADC	2000	Article XXIV	FTA	Developing	Rules	Rules	No rules	Rules
SAFTA	1995	Enabling Clause	PTA	Developing	Rules	Rules	No rules	Rules
SPARTECA	1981	Enabling Clause	PTA	Mixed	Rules	No rules	No rules	Rules
Turkey–Israel	1997	Article XXIV	FTA	Developing	Rules	No rules	No rules	Rules
United States–Bahrain	2006	Article XXIV	FTA	Mixed	No rules	No rules	Rules	Rules
United States–CAFTA-DR	2006	Article XXIV	FTA	Mixed	No rules	Rules	Rules	Rules
United States–Chile	2004	Article XXIV	FTA	Mixed	No rules	Rules	Rules	Rules
United States–Israel	1985	Article XXIV	FTA	Mixed	No rules	No rules	No rules	Rules
United States–Jordan	2001	Article XXIV	FTA	Mixed	No rules	No rules	Rules	Rules
United States–Morocco	2006	Article XXIV	FTA	Mixed	No rules	No rules	Rules	Rules
United States–Singapore	2004	Article XXIV	FTA	Mixed	No rules	No rules	Rules	Rules
WAEMU/UEMOA	2000	Enabling Clause	PTA	Developing	Rules	No rules	Rules	Rules

Source: Author's compilation.

Note: Blank cells under "Relevant GATT provision" indicate PTAs not notified to the WTO. AFTA, ASEAN Free Trade Area; ANZCERTA, Australia–New Zealand Closer Economic Relations Trade Agreement; ASEAN, Association of Southeast Asian Nations; CACM, Central American Common Market; CAFTA-DR, Dominican Republic–Central America Free Trade Agreement; CARICOM, Caribbean Community; CEMAC, Economic and Monetary Community of Central Africa (Communauté Économique et Monétaire de l'Afrique Centrale); COMESA, Common Market for Eastern and Southern Africa; EEA, European Economic Area; EFTA, European Free Trade Association; EU, European Union; GCC, Gulf Cooperation Council; LAIA/ALADI, Latin American Integration Association/Asociación Latinoamericana de Integración; Mercosur, Southern Cone Common Market (Mercado Común del Sur); NAFTA, North American Free Trade Agreement; OCT, Overseas Countries and Territories; SADC, Southern African Development Community; SAFTA, South Asian Free Trade Area; SAR, special administrative region; SPARTECA, South Pacific Regional Trade and Economic Cooperation Agreement; WAEMU/UEMOA, West African Economic and Monetary Union/Union Économique et Monétaire Ouest-Africaine.

a. CU, customs union; FTA, free trade area; PTA, preferential trade agreement.

Table 9.3. Characteristics of PTAs

Characteristic	Number	Percentage of total	Intra-PTA imports, 2005 (billions of U.S. dollars)
Relevant GATT provision			
Article XXIV	61	82.4	
Enabling Clause	9	12.2	
Unknown	4	5.4	
Type of agreement			
Customs union	7	9.5	
Free trade agreement	60	81.1	
Preferential trade agreement	7	9.5	
Development status of members			
Developed	6	8.1	2,932.4
Developing	22	29.7	501.0
Mixed	46	62.2	1,307.7

Source: Author's compilation.
Note: GATT, General Agreement on Tariffs and Trade. Numbers may not sum to totals because of rounding.

The substantial variation in trade remedy provisions across PTAs likely reflects the diversity among PTAs.

Size. Many PTAs involve fairly small amounts of intraregional trade; these include the Economic and Monetary Community of Central Africa (CEMAC, Communauté Économique et Monétaire de l'Afrique Centrale); the agreements between the European Free Trade Association (EFTA) and Tunisia, Mexico, and Uruguay and between the United States and Bahrain; and the West African Economic and Monetary Union/Union Économique et Monétaire Ouest-Africaine (WAEMU/UEMOA). Others, including the EU, the European Economic Area (EEA), and NAFTA, involve substantial amounts of trade. PTAs with a great deal of trade may well have greater political demands for trade remedies than those with less trade. It is clear, however, that although size may matter, it is not the only determinant of trade remedy rules: the two largest PTAs, the EU and NAFTA, have very different philosophies about trade remedy rules, as do two of the smallest PTAs, CEMAC and EFTA–Tunisia.

Integration. There is no clear definition of integration with respect to PTAs, and PTAs differ greatly as to their degree of integration. Clearly, however, the extent to which PTAs go beyond simple tariff reductions influences the type of trade remedy provisions and the approach toward them. PTAs with deeper integration have adopted harmonized or common behind-the-border measures, they have allowed for free or freer movement of capital and labor, and some have even adopted a single currency. PTAs that aim at deeper integration are more likely to do away with trade remedy measures.

Development status. Many PTAs have a mixed membership of developed and developing countries; others have only developing or developed countries as members. Developed countries such as Canada, the United States, and EU members have a long history with trade remedies that might change their political willingness to restrict or prohibit the use of these instruments.

Legal basis. The PTAs in our survey represent about half of the total number of PTAs notified to the WTO under the General Agreement on Tariffs and Trade (GATT) Article XXIV and the Enabling Clause of 1979.[11] As shown in table 9.3, about 82 percent of the PTAs in our sample were notified under Article XXIV of GATT and about 12 percent under the Enabling Clause.[12] Given its roots, PTAs notified under the Enabling Clause may have fewer rules.

A First Look at the Provisions

For this analysis, three key trade remedy provisions were mapped: antidumping measures, countervailing duties, and global safeguards. In addition, information was gathered on the provisions regarding bilateral safeguards. These are found in most PTAs and are meant to apply only to the trade of other PTA members. They provide a temporary escape hatch from PTA commitments. Generally, bilateral safeguards require evidence of increased imports from regional partners and of serious injury to the domestic industry. In this sense, they are similar to the other forms of contingent protection.

A two-level template was adopted to facilitate the analysis and comparison of PTAs. First, for each provision, PTAs were mapped into three distinct groups:

- Those that disallow the remedy among the members
- Those with no language regarding the remedy
- Those with specific rules regarding the remedy.

A quick glance at table 9.2 shows that there is considerable variation, both among PTAs and within provisions. Some PTAs prohibit the use of antidumping and countervailing duty remedies against members; in this group are the agreements between China and Hong Kong SAR, China, and between China and Macao SAR, China; the EEA; EFTA; and the EU. Others have no language for any of the main trade remedy laws, and some have no language for antidumping and countervailing duty measures but contain special provisions for global safeguards. Finally, many PTAs have extra rules for all the provisions studied.

Some key differences among PTAs and trade remedy provisions emerge from the analysis:

- Antidumping is by far the most likely provision to be prohibited (see table 9.4).[13]

Table 9.4. Summary of Contingent Protection Rules in PTAs

Provision	Antidumping	Countervailing duty	Global safeguards	Bilateral safeguards
Disallowed				
Number	9	5	0	5
Percent	12.2	6.8	0.0	6.8
No rules				
Number	18	30	45	4
Percent	24.3	40.5	60.8	5.4
Rules				
Number	47	39	29	65
Percent	63.5	52.7	39.2	87.8

Source: Author's compilation.

- PTAs are most likely to have no special rules concerning global safeguards.
- PTAs often have additional rules for antidumping and bilateral safeguards.
- Most PTAs either have no specific countervailing duty provisions or have very weak CVD rules. A reason may be that the economic impact of subsidies is rarely confined to intra-PTA trade; subsidies affect global trade. Accordingly, there may be little economic justification for their inclusion in a PTA.

What Provisions Are Included?

As seen in table 9.4, PTAs often include rules for trade remedies. Details about the key rules contained in the PTAs are presented next, following which I discuss how often specific rules are included in the agreements.

Antidumping. Box 9.1, point C, outlines specific categories of rules related to antidumping that may be included in PTAs. PTAs have modified four key requirements in antidumping investigations: de minimis dumping margins, de minimis dumping volumes, the lesser-duty rule, and the duration of final antidumping duties.

Under WTO rules, an antidumping investigation is to be terminated immediately if the dumping margin is found to be less than 2 percent of the export price or if the volume of dumped imports from a particular country is less than 3 percent of imports. PTA provisions that specify higher de minimis dumping margins or higher de minimis volumes than the WTO benchmarks will treat PTA partners more favorably. This is because even though exports from PTA and non-PTA sources may be found to have the same dumping margin, the investigation against the PTA member will terminate, while the investigation against non-PTA sources will continue

if the margin turns out to be higher than the WTO benchmark but less than or equal to that prescribed in the PTA.

Multilateral rules encourage but do not mandate the application of an antidumping duty that is less than the dumping margin if a lesser duty would be adequate to remove the injury to the domestic industry. A lesser-duty rule or mandate in a PTA can provide a significant advantage to members. In the event that an antidumping action is taken by a country against a group of suppliers, some of which happen to be PTA members and others not, PTA partners will face a lower antidumping duty, even though the antidumping investigation might have found the same dumping margin against all suppliers.

Under multilateral rules, definitive antidumping duties are to be terminated within five years from their imposition. Thus, PTAs that impose a shorter termination period on regional partners will give an advantage to exporters from those countries. Antidumping duties against exports from PTA partners will already have been phased out, while exports from non-PTA partners can continue to be restrained by the duties.

These four provisions (C.2–C.5 in box 9.1) modify existing WTO antidumping provisions. By contrast, the establishment of a regional body that has the power to conduct investigations, or the authority to review or remand final determinations of national authorities, is a unique innovation in PTAs. The PTA literature suggests that a regional institution can have a significant effect on the frequency of antidumping initiations and measures against PTA partners. The best-known example of such a regional institution occurs in Chapter 19 of NAFTA, which allows a binational panel to review the final antidumping or countervailing duty determination made by the authority of another NAFTA partner.

Box 9.1. Antidumping Template

A. Antidumping actions disallowed
B. Antidumping actions allowed, but with no specific provisions
C. Antidumping actions allowed, with specific provisions
  1. Mutually acceptable solution
  2. Different de minimis dumping margin
  3. Different de minimis dumping volume
  4. Lesser-duty rule
  5. Different duration of antidumping duty
  6. Regional body or committee
    a. Conducts investigations and decides on antidumping duties
    b. Reviews or remands final determinations
    c. Other

Box 9.2. Countervailing Duties Template

A. Subsidies: Export subsidies on agriculture prohibited
B. State aid: Incompatible if it distorts competition
C. Countervailing duties
  1. Disallowed
  2. Allowed, but with no specific provisions
  3. Allowed, with specific provisions
    a. Mutually acceptable solution
    b. Regional body or committee
    • Conducts investigations and decides on countervailing duties
    • Reviews or remands final determinations
    • Other

Box 9.3. Global Safeguards Template

A. Rights and obligations under GATT Article XIX/Safeguards Agreement retained
B. PTA members excluded from global actions under defined conditions
  1. Grounds for exclusion
    a. Imports from the other party do not account for a substantial share of total imports
    b. Imports from the other party do not contribute to serious injury or threat thereof
  2. Definitions
    a. Substantial share
    • Imports are among the top five suppliers during the most recent three-year period
    • Exports jointly account for 80 percent of the total imports of the importing country
    b. Contribute importantly to serious injury
    • Growth rate of imports from a party is lower than the growth rate of imports from all sources

There are differing views on the impact of this specific provision. Using a time dummy to control for the pre-PTA versus post-PTA effect, Jones (2000) finds a statistically significant reduction in both U.S. antidumping filings against Canada and Canadian antidumping filings against the United States after NAFTA took effect. Blonigen (2005), however, incorporates information on actual panel activity and finds no evidence that binational reviews under Chapter 19 of NAFTA affected the frequency of U.S. filings or affirmative determinations against Canada and Mexico. The fact that the United States has refused to include a similar provision in any subsequent PTAs suggests that U.S. policy makers believe that the binational panels have altered the pattern of protection.

Countervailing duties. In contrast with the provisions on antidumping, which address key statutory criteria, the provisions concerning countervailing duties include very few substantive rules (see box 9.2). As previously discussed, this absence is probably related to the lack of limits on state aid and subsidies in PTAs.

Two provisions regarding countervailing duties appear noteworthy. First, some PTAs specify a series of steps that members are first required to take to try to reach a mutually satisfactory outcome before the countervailing duty investigation begins. Such provisions might lead to fewer disputes, although to date there is no empirical evidence regarding their impact.

Second, provisions giving regional bodies the ability to conduct countervailing duty investigations or to review and remand final determinations have received significant attention, and there is some empirical support for the hypothesis that they do reduce the number of disputes.

Global safeguards. Provisions that allow PTAs to exclude members from global safeguard actions have received considerable attention. Imports from PTA members may be excluded from a global safeguard action if those imports do not account for a substantial share of total imports and if they do not contribute to serious injury or the threat thereof (box 9.3). Most PTAs describe very precisely what is meant by "substantial share" of total imports and "contribute importantly to serious injury." For example, a number of PTAs state that imports from a PTA partner do not constitute a substantial share of total imports if that partner is not among the top five suppliers during the most recent three-year period. Similarly, imports from a PTA partner do not contribute importantly to serious injury or threat thereof if the growth rate of those imports during the period of serious injury is appreciably lower than the growth rate of total imports from all sources.

The WTO Appellate Body has repeatedly rejected safeguard actions from which PTA partners are excluded. As noted earlier, these exclusions are highly contentious and have prompted non-PTA members to file multiple WTO dispute cases. In each case, the Appellate Body had ruled against the WTO member's exclusion of PTA partners.

Bilateral safeguards. There are two types of bilateral safeguards: transition safeguards and special safeguards. Transition safeguards are designed to mitigate the costs incurred as industries adjust to the preferential tariffs and often can only be imposed during the transition period. Special safeguards are provisions for products or sectors that are politically sensitive.

PTAs often include extensive language defining when and for how long bilateral safeguards can be imposed (see box 9.4). Part of the reason for this detail might be the absence of analogous WTO provisions specifying the default behavior—unlike the case with the other trade remedies.

The role of regional bodies in bilateral safeguard actions is noteworthy. Regional institutions might have a coordinating function, serving for example, as clearinghouses for information on emergency action. Alternatively, regional authorities could conduct safeguard investigations or review safeguard measures taken by national authorities.

Box 9.4. Bilateral Safeguards Template

A. Safeguard measures disallowed
B. Safeguard measures allowed, but with no specific provisions
C. Safeguard measures allowed, with specific provisions
  1. Conditions for application of safeguard
    a. Increasing imports cause serious injury to domestic industry
    b. During transition period, reductions in tariffs lead to increased imports and to serious injury
    c. Other
  2. Mutually acceptable solution
  3. Investigation
  4. Application of safeguard measures
    a. Only to the extent necessary to remedy serious injury and facilitate adjustment
    b. Suspension of concessions, tariff reduction, or reversion to most favored nation rates
    c. Other
  5. Provisional measures
  6. Duration and review of safeguard measures
    a. Less than four years' duration
    b. Not allowed beyond transition period
  7. Maintenance of equivalent level of concessions (compensation)
  8. Suspension of equivalent concessions (retaliation)
  9. Regional body or committee
    a. Conducts investigations and decides on safeguard duties
    b. Reviews or remands final determinations
    c. Other
  10. Notification and consultation
  11. Special safeguards

The special safeguard provisions in the PTAs are usually applied to agricultural products and textiles and clothing, which in many countries are the most difficult sectors to liberalize. Products or sectors that are hard to liberalize at the multilateral level are also hard to liberalize in PTAs and require special safeguard treatment.

Hub-and-Spoke Pattern

A review of the list of PTAs in table 9.2 shows that the proliferation of PTAs has not happened by chance; rather, a small set of countries recurs as members of most PTAs. Put differently, there is a pronounced hub-and-spoke and cross-regional pattern in the PTAs in the sample. The largest constellations are grouped around the EU, EFTA, and the United States (figure 9.1), but there are other active PTA players, including Mexico, with 9 PTAs, Singapore (6), Australia (5), Chile (5), and Canada (4).

The prominent hub-and-spoke and cross-regional pattern of the PTAs in the sample raises the question of whether there are identifiable features in the trade remedy provisions negotiated by the hubs. The hypothesis is that each major hub negotiates according to certain key principles. The rules and philosophy may vary across hubs, but we expect consistency within a hub.

Table 9.5 presents a summary of the provisions in each PTA. Looking first at the antidumping provisions, we see that EFTA and the EU have a different philosophy than the other major hubs, notably the United States. Among the EU's PTAs, 90 percent either prohibit antidumping measures or limit their use. All of EFTA's agreements either prohibit or limit the use of antidumping. By contrast, almost 90 percent of U.S. PTAs contain no language on antidumping, and, indeed, it is clear that the United States is the least open of all hubs to the inclusion of antidumping provisions in PTAs.

This does not imply that any of the hubs consistently incorporates the same rules in each (or even most) agreements. Table 9.6 shows whether a rule is included in the majority of each hub's agreements. When the hubs are inspected more closely, there is little evidence that any of them negotiate the same rules in all their PTAs. For instance, for only five hubs—the EC, EFTA, Mexico, Australia, and Canada—are there antidumping rules in most of the agreements, and only in the EC and EFTA do most agreements contain the same substantive provision. Moreover, this provision (regarding a mutually acceptable solution) involves rather weak language. The other three hubs often have antidumping rules, but for no hub is a particular rule included in most of the agreements. Thus, while it is fair to say that the Europeans are more

Figure 9.1. Hub-and-Spoke and Cross-Regional Arrangement of PTAs

EU	EFTA	Mexico	United States	Singapore	Chile	Australia	Canada
EU	EFTA–Turkey	NAFTA	U.S.–Singapore	U.S.–Singapore	U.S.–Chile	SPARTECA	NAFTA
EEA	EFTA–Tunisia	Mexico–Uruguay	U.S.–Morocco	New Zealand–Singapore	Mexico–Chile	ANZCERTA	Canada–Israel
EU–Turkey	EFTA–Singapore	Mexico–Northern Triangle	U.S.–Jordan	Japan–Singapore	Korea, Rep.–Chile	Australia–U.S.	Canada–Costa Rica
EU–Tunisia	EFTA–Palestinian Authority	Mexico–Nicaragua	U.S.–Israel	EFTA–Singapore	EU–Chile	Australia–Thailand	Canada–Chile
EU–Syrian Arab Republic	EFTA–Morocco	Mexico–Japan	U.S.–Chile	Australia–Singapore	Canada–Chile	Australia–Singapore	
EU–Switzerland–Liechtenstein	EFTA–Jordan	Mexico–Israel	Australia–U.S.	AFTA			
EU–South Africa	EFTA–Israel	Mexico–EFTA	U.S.–CAFTA-DR				
EU–Palestinian Authority	EFTA–Macedonia, FYR	Mexico–Chile	U.S.–Bahrain				
EU–OCT	EFTA–Croatia	Group of Three	NAFTA				
EU–Morocco	EFTA–Chile						
EU–Mexico	EFTA						
EU–Lebanon	EEA						
EU–Jordan							
EU–Israel							
EU–Faeroe Islands							
EU–Macedonia, FYR							
EU–Egypt, Arab Rep.							
EU–Croatia							
EU–Chile							
EU–Andorra							
EU–Algeria							

Source: Author's compilation.
Note: AFTA, ASEAN Free Trade Area; ANZCERTA, Australia–New Zealand Closer Economic Relations Trade Agreement; ASEAN, Association of Southeast Asian Nations; CAFTA-DR, Dominican Republic–Central America Free Trade Agreement; EEA, European Economic Area; EFTA, European Free Trade Association; EU, European Union; Mercosur, Southern Cone Common Market (Mercado Común del Sur); NAFTA, North American Free Trade Agreement; OCT, Overseas Countries and Territories; SPARTECA, South Pacific Regional Trade and Economic Cooperation Agreement.

open than the United States to incorporating antidumping provisions in PTAs, there is not compelling evidence that the European PTAs are consistent in the precise rules they negotiate.

Ironically, PTAs appear to have a more unified approach toward countervailing duties. The commonality seems to be that extra provisions are not included in regional agreements. With the exception of EFTA and, to a lesser extent,

Table 9.5. Cross-Tabulation of Contingent Protection Rules, by Hub
(percent)

Provision	Full sample (74 PTAs)	EU (21 PTAs)	EFTA (12 PTAs)	Mexico (9 PTAs)	United States (9 PTAs)	Singapore (6 PTAs)	Chile (5 PTAs)	Australia (5 PTAs)	Canada (4 PTAs)
Antidumping									
Disallowed	12.2	9.5	33.3	0.0	0.0	16.7	20.0	20.0	25.0
No rules	24.3	9.5	0.0	22.2	88.9	50.0	40.0	20.0	25.0
Rules	63.5	81.0	66.7	77.8	11.1	33.3	40.0	60.0	50.0
Countervailing duties									
Disallowed	6.8	9.5	16.7	0.0	0.0	0.0	0.0	0.0	0.0
No rules	40.5	52.4	0.0	22.2	66.7	66.7	40.0	40.0	50.0
Rules	52.7	38.1	83.3	77.8	33.3	33.3	60.0	60.0	50.0
Global safeguards									
Disallowed	0.0	0.0	0.0	0.0	0.0	0.0	0.0	0.0	0.0
No rules	60.8	76.2	83.3	11.1	11.1	66.7	0.0	60.0	0.0
Rules	39.2	23.8	16.7	88.9	88.9	33.3	100.0	40.0	100.0
Bilateral safeguards									
Disallowed	6.8	4.8	0.0	0.0	0.0	33.3	0.0	20.0	25.0
No rules	5.4	4.8	0.0	0.0	0.0	0.0	0.0	0.0	0.0
Rules	87.8	90.5	100.0	100.0	100.0	66.7	100.0	80.0	75.0

Source: Author's compilation.
Notes: EFTA, European Free Trade Association; EU, European Union; PTA, preferential trade agreement.

Table 9.6. Antidumping Template for Selected PTA Hubs

Provision	EU	EFTA	Mexico	United States	Singapore	Chile	Australia	Canada
A. Antidumping actions disallowed								
B. Antidumping actions allowed, but with no specific provisions				X	X			
C. Antidumping actions allowed, with specific provisions	X	X	X				X	X
1. Mutually acceptable solution	X	X						
2. Different de minimis dumping margin								
3. Different de minimis dumping volume								
4. Lesser-duty rule								
5. Different duration of antidumping duty								
6. Regional body or committee								
a. Conducts investigations and decides on antidumping duties								
b. Reviews or remands final determinations								
c. Other	X	X						

Source: Author's elaboration.
Note: EFTA, European Free Trade Association; EU, European Union; PTA, preferential trade agreement. Regional hubs are checked if at least 50 percent of their PTAs include the specific provision.

Mexico, there is little support for prohibiting countervailing duties or even including CVD provisions in regional agreements.

Of the five hubs that tend to have countervailing duty rules—EFTA, Mexico, Chile, Australia, and Canada—four have also negotiated restrictions on agricultural subsidies (table 9.7). As discussed earlier, developments on countervailing duties may depend on progress on subsidization, and it is likely that substantial progress on subsidization will only come via a multilateral format.

Interestingly, only two hubs (EFTA and Mexico) include the same provision in most of their agreements. By chance, the one provision again involves rather weak language about a "mutually acceptable solution." This

Table 9.7. Countervailing Duties Template for Selected PTA Hubs

Provision	EU	EFTA	Mexico	United States	Singapore	Chile	Australia	Canada
A. Subsidies: Export subsidies on agriculture prohibited			X	X		X	X	X
B. State aid: Incompatible if it distorts competition	X	X						
C. Countervailing duties								
1. Disallowed								
2. Allowed, but with no specific provisions	X			X	X			X
3. Allowed, with specific provisions		X	X			X	X	X
a. Mutually acceptable solution		X	X					
b. Regional body or committee								
• Conducts investigations and decides on antidumping duties								
• Reviews or remands final determinations								
• Other		X						

Source: Author's elaboration.
Note: EFTA, European Free Trade Association; EU, European Union; PTA, preferential trade agreement. Regional hubs are checked if at least 50 percent of their PTAs include the specific provision.

provision does not impinge on any decision criteria once a case is initiated.

A survey of global safeguards supports the view that the hubs strive for a consistent approach across PTAs. Only four hubs (Mexico, the United States, Chile, and Canada) include additional rules in most of their agreements, but they tend to include similar provisions across PTAs.

All four of these hubs allow PTA members to be excluded from global actions (table 9.8). We also see some consistency in how the exclusions are incorporated: three of the four exclude on the basis of market share and three of the four, on the basis of lack of impact.

As has been mentioned, the exclusion provisions have been the subject of repeated WTO disputes (Argentina–Footwear; United States–Wheat Gluten; United States–Line Pipe; and United States–Steel). In each case, the investigating authority included imports from all sources in making the determination that imports were entering in such increased quantities as to cause serious injury to the domestic industry, but, instead of applying safeguard measures to all imports irrespective of their source, the country invoking the safeguard action excluded its PTA partners. In all four cases, the Appellate Body ruled against the WTO member that included its PTA partners in the safeguard investigation but excluded them in the application of the safeguard measure.[14]

The provisions excluding PTA partners from global safeguard actions once again raise concerns about increased discrimination against nonmembers and the welfare impacts of trade diversion. Although WTO dispute settlement panels have consistently ruled against excluding PTA partners from safeguard measures, they have done so on quite narrow grounds. Conceivably, under a different set of circumstances, exclusion of PTA partners from safeguard measures could pass muster.

Bilateral safeguards display more consistency across hubs than do the other three statutes. All eight major hubs have bilateral safeguard rules (table 9.9). Indeed, there appears to be more commonality across the precise rules than for the other three trade remedy statutes combined.

Nevertheless, there again appears to be some evidence of distinct European and North American approaches toward bilateral safeguard rules. Although there is considerable consistency across EC and EFTA PTAs, the precise rules differ from those in the other hubs.

PTAs That Prohibit Trade Remedies

Thirteen of the surveyed PTAs have abolished the application to intraregional trade of one or more trade remedies. What distinguishes these PTAs? Why have they been able to abolish trade remedy measures against members' trade?

The depth of market integration incorporated in the PTA is the leading candidate for explaining the abolition of trade remedy measures, particularly antidumping. A common subsidy policy is one example of a policy reflecting deeper integration, and, as was previously discussed, there is some evidence that a common subsidy policy influences countervailing duty provisions. De Araujo, Macario, and Steinfatt (2001) have argued that the implementation of

Table 9.8. Global Safeguards Template for Selected PTA Hubs

Provision	EU	EFTA	Mexico	United States	Singapore	Chile	Australia	Canada
A. Rights and obligations under GATT Article XIX/Safeguards Agreement retained			X	X		X		X
B. PTA members excluded from global actions under defined conditions			X	X		X		X
1. Grounds for exclusion								
a. Imports from the other party do not account for a substantial share of total imports			X			X		X
b. Imports from the other party do not contribute to serious injury or threat thereof			X	X				X
2. Definitions								
a. Substantial share								
• Among the top five suppliers during the most recent three-year period			X			X		X
• Exports jointly account for 80 percent of the total imports of the importing country								
b. Contribute importantly to serious injury								
• Growth rate of imports from a party is lower than the growth rate of imports from all sources			X					X

Source: Author's elaboration.

Note: EFTA, European Free Trade Association; EU, European Union; PTA, preferential trade agreement. Regional hubs are checked if at least 50 percent of their PTAs include the specific provision.

common macroeconomic and microeconomic policies in the EU reduced the social and political cost related to the removal of antidumping provisions. Wooton and Zanardi (2002) link the phasing out of antidumping measures with the creation of a single market. Taken together, these support the view that PTAs which go beyond the elimination of border measures or adopt common internal regulations are more likely to do away with trade remedy measures.

The adoption of a common competition policy might also permit the elimination of certain trade remedies. It might, for example, make antidumping redundant. Of course, the two explanations are not mutually exclusive, since a common competition policy may not make sense until a sufficiently high level of integration is achieved. Hoekman (1998), however, dismisses the notion of a link between the adoption of a common competition policy and the abolition of antidumping in a PTA by arguing that the adoption of a common competition policy in a PTA is often motivated by the need to manage the consequences of deeper integration.[15]

A third factor might be the development status of the members of the PTA. Development status could proxy for a wide set of political-economy factors that might affect the ability to prohibit trade remedies. Over the past two decades, developing countries have become more frequent users of antidumping and safeguard actions, and their embrace of antidumping might make it difficult for them to give up such remedies. Indeed, we find that only two developing-economy PTAs, those between China and Hong Kong SAR, China, and between China and Macao SAR, China, have prohibited antidumping measures.

Table 9.10 brings together background data on those PTAs that have abolished trade remedies. On average, such PTAs enjoy greater intra-PTA trade (both in value and share) and are more likely to have a competition policy provision in the PTA and to have achieved deeper integration. There does not seem to be any difference with respect to the adoption of a common external tariff. PTAs that have disallowed trade remedies and PTAs that retain the instruments appear equally likely to have a common external tariff.

Trade and Protection Diversion

A concern about PTAs that prohibit trade remedies or add additional rules regarding them is that having such provisions does not guarantee that disputes will not occur. The rules may mean that fewer cases will be filed against PTA members, but that tells us little about what may happen to

Table 9.9. Bilateral Safeguards Template for Selected PTA Hubs

Provision	EU	EFTA	Mexico	United States	Singapore	Chile	Australia	Canada
A. Safeguard measures disallowed								
B. Safeguard measures allowed, but with no specific provisions								
C. Safeguard measures allowed, with specific provisions	X	X	X	X	X	X	X	X
1. Conditions for application of safeguard								
a. Increasing imports cause serious injury to domestic industry		X			X		X	X
b. During transition period, reductions in tariffs lead to increased imports and to serious injury			X	X		X	X	X
c. Other	X	X						
2. Mutually acceptable solution			X	X	X	X	X	X
3. Investigation	X	X						
4. Application of safeguard measures								
a. Only to the extent necessary to remedy serious injury and facilitate adjustment	X	X						
b. Suspension of concessions, tariff reduction, or reversion to most favored nation rates			X	X	X	X	X	X
c. Other								
5. Provisional measures	X	X					X	
6. Duration and review of safeguard measures								
a. Less than four years' duration			X	X	X	X	X	X
b. Not allowed beyond transition period				X		X		X
7. Maintenance of equivalent level of concessions (compensation)			X	X	X	X		X
8. Suspension of equivalent concessions (retaliation)			X	X	X	X		X
9. Regional body or committee								
a. Conducts investigations and decides on safeguard duties								
b. Reviews or remands final determinations								
c. Other	X	X			X			
10. Notification and consultation	X	X	X	X	X	X	X	X
11. Special safeguards				X		X		X

Source: Author's elaboration.

Note: EFTA, European Free Trade Association; EU, European Union; PTA, preferential trade agreement. Regional hubs are checked if at least 50 percent of their PTAs include the specific provision.

other countries. The PTA provisions might simply lead to fewer intra-PTA disputes but to just as many (or even more) cases against non-PTA members.

Bhagwati (1996) and Bhagwati and Panagariya (1996) argue that the elastic and selective nature of administered protection makes "protection diversion" a particularly pernicious and unforeseen consequence of PTAs. Administered protection is elastic because it is arbitrary and the targets can be easily manipulated. So, apart from the discrimination introduced by preferential tariffs, PTAs can lead to more discrimination against nonmembers of the PTA through more frequent trade remedy actions against them: trade diversion begets protection diversion, which begets more trade diversion.

The issue is clearest regarding global safeguards. Fifteen PTAs allow members to be excluded from safeguard protection.[16] Once safeguard protection is enacted, another form of PTA-induced discrimination is introduced. Even if the PTA discriminatory tariff preferences are modest, global safeguard duties often exceed 10 percent. Thus, the secondary trade diversion stemming from safeguards may surpass the primary trade diversion resulting from tariff preferences.[17]

Protection diversion is also relevant for antidumping provisions. Unfair trade is poorly measured according to WTO rules; often, all exporters to a market might be found guilty of dumping. Over the past decade, it has become increasingly rare for authorities to fail to determine that

Table 9.10. Characteristics of PTAs That Have Disallowed Trade Remedies

PTA	Development level	Disallowed			Intra-PTA imports		Common external tariff (percent)	Competition chapter	Integration
		Antidumping	CVD	Bilateral safeguards	Value (billions of U.S. dollars)	Share of trade (percent)			
ANZCERTA	Developed	X			10.1	6.9		X	X
Australia–Singapore	Mixed			X	9.9			X	
Canada–Chile	Mixed	X			4.7	1.4		X	
Canada–Israel	Mixed			X	3.9	1.1		X	
China–Hong Kong SAR, China	Developing	X	X		202.4	21.1			X
China–Macao SAR, China	Developing	X	X		55.4	8.4			X
EEA	Developed	X	X		301.4	7.3		X	X
EFTA	Developed	X	X		1.4	0.8		X	X
EFTA–Chile	Mixed	X	X		0.3	0.2		X	
EFTA–Singapore	Mixed	X			3.1	0.8		X	
EU	Developed	X	X	X	2,419.0	61.1	X	X	X
Mercosur	Developing			X	22.1	20.1	X	X	
New Zealand–Singapore	Mixed			X	1.3	0.6		X	
Group average					233.5	10.2	15.40	11 (of 13)	6 (of 13)
Group average, excluding EU					51.3	6.0			
Average of other PTAs					28.9	3.1	13.10	43 (of 61)	4 (of 61)

Source: Author's compilation.
Note: ANZCERTA, Australia–New Zealand Closer Economic Relations Trade Agreement; CVD, countervailing duty; EEA, European Economic Area; EFTA, European Free Trade Association; EU, European Union; Mercosur, Southern Cone Common Market (Mercado Común del Sur); PTA, preferential trade agreement; SAR, special administrative region.

unfair pricing exists.[18] Unfair trade may be practiced by suppliers within as well as outside the trade bloc. But, given that PTA rules on antidumping measures make it impossible (if the measures are abolished by the PTA) or more difficult (if the PTA rules tighten discipline on their use) to apply that remedy to intrabloc members, antidumping duties might be applied only to countries outside the bloc. Antidumping duties are rarely less than 10 percent, so, as with global safeguards, it is quite possible that the secondary trade diversion may surpass the primary trade diversion. Moreover, as Bhagwati (1996) has argued, the source of injury might be truly rooted in the PTA preferences, but the PTA rules may result in the antidumping duties being imposed on non-PTA sources.

To get a sense of the extent of the diversion, I augmented the PTA database with information on worldwide antidumping activity since 1980. The earlier years of data were gathered to allow a better comparison of pre-PTA and post-PTA filing patterns. Altogether, I have information on 4,805 antidumping cases initiated by WTO countries that belong to at least one PTA.

The annual number of antidumping disputes initiated by PTA members against PTA members (intra-PTA filings) is calculated for each importing country. Because PTAs are enacted over a variety of years, I abstract from calendar time and instead consider time as measured relative to the year the PTA was enacted. For each PTA, year zero is the year the PTA was enacted, year $t-1$ is the year before establishment, year $t-2$ is two years before, year $t+1$ is the year after establishment, and so on. This view of time allows us to conveniently aggregate across PTAs.

In figure 9.2, the aggregate number of antidumping disputes is plotted in relation to each PTA's inception. The chart is compelling. During the years prior to the creation of the PTA, intra-PTA antidumping activity increases. In the year the PTA is enacted (time = 0), the number of antidumping disputes drops sharply, and it remains much lower than the pre-PTA level. On average, during the 10 years prior to the PTA, there were 29.5 antidumping cases per year; by contrast, during the 10 years following the PTA, there were just 23.6 cases per year.

Figure 9.2. Intra-PTA Antidumping Filings, Sample of 74 PTAs

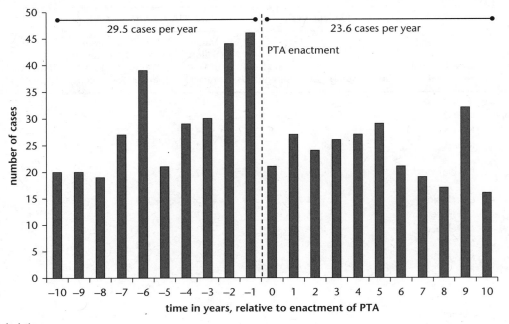

Source: Author's calculations.
Note: PTA, preferential trade agreement.

Although the results are persuasive, the analysis does not control for the possibility that antidumping activity in general—against both members and nonmembers of the PTA—may have fallen coincidentally with the enactment of the PTA. That is, the analysis is not able to distinguish the PTA effect from some other trend. For instance, given that the Uruguay Round was concluded in 1994 and that many PTAs were enacted in the mid-1990s, it is possible that the observed decline in antidumping activity might be a result of antidumping provisions in the Uruguay Round rather than of the PTA provisions.

To control for this possibility, a difference-in-difference analysis is needed. The general idea is to identify the effect of a specific treatment by comparing the treatment group, after treatment, with the same group before treatment and with some other control group. In this case, the "treatment" group is composed of countries that join a PTA, and the "control" group is made up of countries not in a PTA. The comparison will therefore involve antidumping filings against PTA members and nonmembers both before and after each PTA is enacted.

In table 9.11, the protection diversion effect is clearly seen. Of the cases filed during the pre-PTA period, 58 percent were against non-PTA countries and 42 percent were against PTA members. By contrast, during the post-PTA period, 90 percent of the cases were against non-PTA coun-

Table 9.11. Antidumping Activity, by PTA Status

	Target		
Time	Non-PTA member	PTA member	Total
Pre-PTA			
Number of cases	506	370	876
Percent	58	42	
Post-PTA			
Number of cases	3,554	375	3,929
Percent	90	10	
Total			
Number of cases	4,060	745	4,805
Percent	84	16	

Source: Author's calculations.
Note: PTA, preferential trade agreement.

tries, and only 10 percent were against PTA members. So, during the "before" period, the difference between PTA members and nonmembers is 16 percentage points, but in the "after" period, the difference is 80 percentage points, yielding a difference-in-difference result of 64 percentage points. The implied change in filing patterns is quite large: the results suggest that almost 1,300 antidumping cases, or about one-third of the 3,929 cases filed during the post-PTA period, were diverted away from PTA members.

The results clearly raise the specter of protection diversion and more subtle forms of trade diversion. It is true that tariff preferences are small and might result in only modest amounts of trade diversion. This does not imply, however, that trade diversion is not a concern; rather, it appears that other provisions of the PTA might be a greater source of discrimination.

Conclusions

Overall, the findings highlight the need to be vigilant about the impact of trade remedy provisions in PTAs. These provisions vary greatly across PTAs and increase the overall complexity of the world trade environment. Pricing behavior that is perfectly fine when the product is exported to one country may be sanctioned when the product is exported to another country.

Trade remedy provisions in PTAs have a mixed welfare impact. This ambiguous finding partly reflects the existence of trade creation and trade diversion within the PTA. In some cases, PTA rules appear mostly to promote trade creation; at other times, the rules seem simply to constitute trade diversion.

Some PTA rules make it easier to restrain intra-PTA imports. Such provisions may benefit global welfare by mitigating trade diversion stemming from preferential tariffs. More often, PTA rules either prohibit contingent protection against PTA members or make contingent protection harder to apply against members. This raises the very real possibility that PTAs induce protection diversion, which, in turn, produces more trade diversion.

There are other possible consequences of including trade remedy provisions in PTAs. For instance, PTAs might serve as small-scale experiments that allow countries to better understand the practical effect of certain provisions. If parties find certain new rules attractive, those rules might be incorporated in future WTO negotiations. In this sense, PTAs might act as "beta" testing for the larger-scope WTO rounds. By giving members experience with new provisions, PTA rules could streamline future WTO negotiations.

Conversely, the trade remedy provisions in PTAs may erode the market access that nonmembers thought they had secured in prior WTO rounds. The erosion is not limited to trade diversion stemming from preferential tariffs but also comes about because of selective use of contingent protection rules. As a result, PTAs may make it more difficult for non-PTA members to agree to future WTO liberalization out of concern that the requisite quid pro quo by PTA members may not be realized. The complicated pattern of inclusion of these provisions threatens the delicate give-and-take balancing of incentives that is at the crux of the GATT or WTO agreements.

Notes

The author thanks Robert Teh and the staff of the WTO Secretariat for their assistance in developing the trade remedy database.

1. World Bank (2005) contains an excellent discussion of the myriad of effects associated with the proliferation of PTAs.

2. There is growing evidence that a high percentage of PTA tariff preferences are never utilized. Brenton and Ikezuki (2005), Amiti and Romalis (2007), and Dean and Wainio (2009) discuss utilization for different countries, products, and time periods. Francois, Hoekman, and Manchin (2005) find a threshold preference margin of 4 percent below which preference margins are irrelevant, probably because of high compliance costs such as the cost of paperwork and red tape.

3. This third rationale does not explain why PTAs simply do not prohibit the use of trade remedies against PTA members. After all, from Mastel's (1988) perspective, the elimination of intraregional tariffs and other border barriers also means that the raison-d'être for trade remedies is eliminated.

4. Bhagwati writes, "My belief that [free trade agreements] will lead to considerable trade diversion because of modern methods of protection, which are inherently selective and can be captured readily by protectionist purposes, is one that may have been borne out in the [European Economic Community, EEC]. It is well known that the European Community has used antidumping actions and [voluntary export restraints] profusely to erect Fortress Europe against the Far East. Cannot much of this be a trade-diverting policy in response to the intensification of internal competition among member states of the European Community?" (Bhagwati 1996, 37).

5. Official statistics on other border measures are not widely published. From my review of WTO and U.S. reports, I doubt that there have been more than a few hundred disputes involving all other trade remedies *combined*.

6. The context should be taken into account in looking at the small number of safeguard initiations and actions, compared with the other trade remedy measures, since a safeguard action may involve multiple import sources.

7. In this paper, European Union is regularly used when discussing the pre-1993 European Community. The European Community enacted many PTAs before 1993.

8. The four traditional users now account for only about one-third of antidumping initiations and less than one-tenth of safeguard initiations. Traditional users still account for about three-fourths of all countervailing duty initiations.

9. The category "developed countries" refers to Australia, Canada, the EU, EFTA members, Japan, New Zealand, and the United States. All other countries are classified as "developing."

10. Free trade areas account for a comparably large share of all notified PTAs.

11. As of July 18, 2007, 157 PTAs in force had been notified to the WTO under either GATT Article XXIV or the Enabling Clause.

12. These percentages are very comparable to those for all notified PTAs. Of the 157 PTAs notified to the WTO under either Article XXIV or the Enabling Clause, 82 percent were notified under Article XXIV.

13. In the case of the EEA, the prohibition on antidumping applies only to intraregional trade in goods that fall under chapters 25 to 97 of the WTO's Harmonized Tariff System. In other words, antidumping measures can still be taken against agricultural and fishery goods.

14. The key concept that underlines all these cases has been called "parallelism." In brief, parallelism prohibits any asymmetry in the application of safeguard measures. The Appellate Body's decisions have been carefully worded; the panel has avoided ruling on whether GATT Article XXIV permits the exemption from a safeguard measure of imports originating in a member of a free trade area. The decisions have all been

crafted so as to address only the specific facts and circumstances of the case at hand.

15. Hoekman (1998) defines deep integration as consisting of explicit actions by governments to reduce the market-segmenting effect of differences in national regulatory policies that pertain to products, production processes, producers, and natural persons. In practice, this will require decisions (a) to regard a partner's policies as equivalent (mutual recognition) or (b) to adopt a common regulatory stance in specific areas (harmonization).

16. The PTAs are United States–Singapore; United States–Jordan; United States–CAFTA-DR (Central America Free Trade Agreement plus Dominican Republic); NAFTA; Mexico–Uruguay; Mexico–Northern Triangle; Mexico–Nicaragua; Mexico–Israel; Mexico–Chile; Group of Three; EU–Chile; Canada–Israel; Canada–Chile; Australia–United States; and Australia–Thailand.

17. Bown (2004) shows that the exclusions incorporated into the U.S. steel safeguard created significant discrimination and that developed and developing countries differed in their ability to adjust to the tariffs.

18. For the United States, the U.S. Department of Commerce finds unfair pricing in more than 95 percent of all firms investigated; Blonigen (2003) finds that the average U.S. dumping margin exceeds 60 percent.

References

Amiti, Mary, and John Romalis. 2007. "Will the Doha Round Lead to Preference Erosion?" *IMF Staff Papers* 54 (2): 338–84.

Bhagwati, Jagdish. 1996. "Regionalism and Multilateralism: An Overview." *New Dimensions in Regional Integration*, ed. Jaime de Melo and Arvind Panagariya. Cambridge, U.K.: Cambridge University Press.

Bhagwati, Jagdish, and Arvind Panagariya, eds. 1996. *The Economics of Preferential Trade Agreements*. Washington, DC: AEI Press.

Blonigen, Bruce A. 2003. "Evolving Discretionary Practices of US Antidumping Activity." NBER Working Paper 9625, National Bureau of Economic Research, Cambridge, MA.

———. 2005. "The Effects of NAFTA on Antidumping and Countervailing Duty Activity." *World Bank Economic Review* 19 (December): 407–24.

Bown, Chad P. 2004. "How Different Are Safeguards from Antidumping? Evidence from U.S. Trade Policies toward Steel." Working Paper, Brandeis University, Waltham, MA.

Bown, Chad P., and Meredith A. Crowley. 2007. "Trade Deflection and Trade Depression." *Journal of International Economics* 72 (1): 176–201.

Brenton, Paul, and Takako Ikezuki. 2005. "The Value of Trade Preferences for Africa." Trade Note 21, World Bank, Washington, DC.

Dean, Judith M., and John Wainio. 2009. "Quantifying the Value of US Tariff Preferences for Developing Countries." In *Quantifying the Value of Preferences and Potential Erosion Losses,* ed. Bernard M. Hoekman, Will Martin, and Carlos Alberto Primo Braga. Washington, DC: World Bank.

De Araujo, José Tavares, Jr., Carla Macario, and Karsten Steinfatt. 2001. "Antidumping in the Americas." *Journal of World Trade* 35: 555–74.

Fiorentino, Roberto V., Luis Verdeja, and Christelle Toqueboeuf. 2007. "The Changing Landscape of RTAs: 2006 Update." WTO Discussion Paper 12, World Trade Organization (WTO), Geneva.

Francois, Joseph, Bernard Hoekman, and Miriam Manchin. 2005. "Preference Erosion and Multilateral Trade Liberalization." *World Bank Economic Review* 20 (2): 197–216.

Hoekman, Bernard. 1998. "Free Trade and Deep Integration: Antidumping and Antitrust in RTAs." World Bank Policy Research Working Paper 1950, World Bank, Washington, DC.

Jackson, John H. 1997. *The World Trading System: Law and Policy of International Economic Relations.* Cambridge, MA: MIT Press.

Jones, Kent. 2000. "Does NAFTA Chapter 19 Make a Difference? Dispute Settlement and the Incentive Structure of US/Canada Unfair Trade Petitions." *Contemporary Economic Policy* 18: 145–58.

Mastel, Greg. 1998. *Antidumping Laws and the U.S. Economy.* Armonk, NY: M. E. Sharpe.

Prusa, Thomas J. 2001. "On the Spread and Impact of Antidumping." *Canadian Journal of Economics* 34 (3): 591–611.

———. 2005. "Antidumping: A Growing Problem in International Trade." *World Economy* 28: 683–700.

Tharakan, P. K. M. 1995. "Political Economy and Contingent Protection." *Economic Journal* 105: 1550–64.

Viner, Jacob. 1950. *The Customs Union Issue.* New York: Carnegie Endowment for International Peace.

Wooton, Ian, and Maurizio Zanardi. 2002. "Trade and Competition Policy: Antidumping versus Anti-Trust." Discussion Paper in Economics 02-06, University of Glasgow, Glasgow, Scotland.

World Bank. 2005. *Global Economic Prospects 2005: Trade, Regionalism, and Development.* Washington, DC: World Bank.

10

PRODUCT STANDARDS

Jean-Christophe Maur and Ben Shepherd

With the decline of many tariffs in recent decades as a result of successive waves of unilateral, regional, and multilateral liberalization, nontariff measures have become important barriers to trade. The multilateral trading system, and an increasing number of preferential trade agreements (PTAs), has been paying greater attention to product standards as an important type of potential non-tariff barrier.

The World Trade Organization (WTO) agreements set out general rules for the design and implementation of product standards, but it has been in regional contexts that the main instruments of liberalization in this area—harmonization and mutual recognition—have been deployed. These instruments, however, are not free of risk regarding their compatibility with the broader aim of multilateral liberalization. Preferential agreements involving both developed and developing countries (North-South PTAs) can lead to specifications that are overly complex or burdensome from the point of view of many developing countries. Indeed, they could be perceived as locking these countries out of vital international markets (Baldwin 2000). It is therefore important for policy makers and trade policy practitioners to understand the issues that product standards raise in a regional integration context and, in particular, the challenges developing countries can face in dealing with foreign standards as they become increasingly integrated into the world economy.

Although product standards are widely recognized as having potential effects on regional and international trade flows, their motivation and impact are fundamentally distinct from those of traditional trade barriers such as tariffs. Whereas tariffs are mainly protectionist in intent and effect, product standards are not always protectionist from either point of view. Indeed, even when standards have protectionist effects, they are rarely motivated solely by protectionist considerations. Product standards often represent a quasi-regulatory means of promoting an important public policy objective, such as environmental protection, consumer safety, food quality, or compatibility between different technical norms and standards.

This chapter addresses issues arising from the treatment of product standards in PTAs. A unique feature of preferential liberalization is that it offers an alternative means, complementary to multilateral efforts, of diminishing through bilateral mutual recognition efforts the costs associated with compliance with standards. This prospect, and the presumption that standards are not necessarily established for protectionist purposes, suggest that preferential liberalization can be a force for good. The effect on third countries and the lack of international coordination may, however, carry significant costs.

The next section provides a brief overview of the relationship between product standards and trade.[1] Following that, we consider in greater detail the policy measures available for dealing with standards in PTAs, in particular, mutual recognition and harmonization, and look at broader issues of institutional coordination and regional cooperation. Finally, we address the interface between regional and multilateral approaches to standards.

Product Standards and Trade: An Overview

It is common to distinguish three broad groups of standards, based on the types of activities to which they apply, as defined by the International Organization for Standardization (ISO): product standards, process standards, and management systems (see ISO 2006, 2008). *Product standards* have to do with the characteristics of goods or services, in particular with respect to aspects such as quality, safety, and fitness for purpose. A simple example of a product standard is the limit, set by the U.S. Food and Drug Administration (FDA), of one part per million of methyl mercury (a potential toxin) in fish marketed for human consumption. *Process standards* apply to the conditions under which goods or services are produced, packaged, or refined. An example is the production of dairy products without hormones: milk from hormone-free cows is indistinguishable from milk from cows treated with hormones, but only farms that meet a particular set of production conditions can describe their milk as "hormone free." *Management systems* assist organizations in running their operations and create a framework within which the requirements of product and process standards can be consistently met. Management systems are often referred to as meta-standards; an example is the ISO 9000 series of quality standards (see box 10.1).

A well-functioning standards system will usually incorporate elements of all three groups of standards. This chapter focuses mainly on the first group—the product standards that apply to everything from primary produce and agricultural products to sophisticated manufactured goods such as electrical equipment (box 10.2). The remainder of this section briefly discusses the rationale for product standards before moving to a more detailed discussion of how they are designed and implemented.

Economic Rationale for Product Standards

Why are product standards necessary at all? Broadly speaking, standards can be seen as a way of bringing the outcomes of a decentralized market economy more closely into line with social objectives that may not otherwise be achieved (see, for example, Maskus, Otsuki, and Wilson 2000; Ganslandt and Markusen 2001). Two of the most common reasons why standards might be necessary relate to spillover effects (externalities) from certain activities and to information asymmetries between buyers and sellers. These effects are clearly relevant for standardization at the national level, but they also set the scene for regional and global coordination on standards.

Externalities. Packaging is an example of an externality. In the absence of any rules or standards, producers and consumers do not directly pay the cost of disposing of packaging materials after the product has been bought and unpacked. These materials must be taken away to a landfill, where they will break down over time, perhaps releasing pollutants into the environment. A standard setting out biodegradability requirements for packaging materials can help reduce this problem and limit the negative environmental spillovers from useful economic transactions. Social objectives such as environmental protection and public health are common externality-based rationales for the development of product standards.

Another example of externalities relates to network effects and interoperability (see, for example, David and Greenstein 1990; Gandal and Shy 2000; Barrett and Yang 2001).

Box 10.1. What Are Meta-Standards?

Closely associated with standards are the quality assurance processes that users employ to effect and manage compliance. Indeed, a "new" category of standards has evolved that defines and describes such meta-systems. Meta-standards do not concern a specific product or production process but, rather, set overall principles and rules to be followed in broad areas of activity. Examples include the ISO 9000 series of standards for quality management systems and the ISO 14000 series for environmental management systems. In certain industries, compliance with these standards is itself becoming a commercial necessity, alongside more traditional product and process standards. For instance, in the area of food safety, meta-standards include hazard analysis and critical control point (HACCP) standards, good manufacturing practices (GMP), good agricultural practices (GAP), and ISO 22000 on food safety management systems.

Source: Henson and Jaffee 2007.

Box 10.2. Proliferation and Growing Importance of Product Standards

Product standards represent an important and constantly growing set of regulatory measures that have potential effects on trade. The available evidence suggests that these standards cover all sectors, from simple agricultural products (Disdier, Fontagné, and Mimouni 2008) to the most complex electronic goods (Moenius 2007). Many countries produce their own standards but are also increasingly involved in efforts aimed at regional or international standardization. Before looking in more detail at the regional dimension of standards and their trade effects, it is useful to get an idea of the phenomenon's extent and development over recent years through a few stylized facts:

- The International Organization for Standardization comprises 3,000 working groups and committees.
- The ISO has issued about 15,000 international standards (WTO 2005).
- A survey of national product standards in a selection of member countries of the Organisation for Economic Co-operation and Development (OECD) identified a total of nearly 300,000 documents (Moenius 2005). The Perinorm database on which Moenius drew contains about 650,000 standards from 21 countries (WTO 2005).
- In 1975 there were only 20 Europe-wide standards, but by 1999 the number had grown to 5,500 (Moenius 2005).
- The number of Europe-wide standards in the agricultural and textiles and clothing sectors grew at a rate of nearly 20 percent per year over the period 1995–2003 (Shepherd 2006).

The high-definition DVD (HDDVD) market has recently seen the emergence of Blu-ray as the de facto dominant standard over the alternative HDDVD system. DVD players can usually display only one of these two formats, and the more consumers buy a particular type of player, the greater is the incentive for firms to release a wider range of movies in the corresponding format. Each consumer's purchase therefore has an externality—a spillover effect—in the sense that it increases the value for every other customer of having a player of the same format. At the same time, consumers may be reluctant to purchase a player of either format while there is uncertainty as to which will become dominant in the future. Standardization makes it possible to overcome this reluctance and develop the spillovers more completely than would be possible if each equipment manufacturer adopted its own technology standard.

Information asymmetries. Information asymmetries refer to the availability of product-related information to buyers and to sellers. For example, a consumer wants to buy a car that is safe and has a certain level of fuel efficiency, but until she actually acquires it and starts using it, it is very difficult to tell to what extent it meets those requirements. The carmaker is in a much better position to know the car's true characteristics. An unscrupulous manufacturer might advertise a car as being safe and fuel efficient when in fact it is not.[2] How can the consumer go about finding the desired type of car when she knows that advertisements may not always be truthful? Standards can offer a way out of this set of difficulties: if the consumer sees that an independent testing authority has certified that a car meets a particular safety standard, then she can be confident about its characteristics. Objectives such as quality and fitness for purpose are commonly pursued through these kinds of standards. Alternatively, standards can be seen as a way of reducing the costs a consumer must bear in searching for the product that best matches her preferences (see, e.g., Jones and Hudson 1996).

Producers also need information on consumer tastes to manufacture profitable products. Gathering such information can be costly, especially for overseas firms that may be unfamiliar with local preferences and practices. Standards can help make this process simpler and less costly, to the extent that they summarize a set of characteristics considered to be valuable in the local market. (See Swann, Temple, and Shurmer 1996 and Moenius 2005 for a discussion of this mechanism.)

Designing and Implementing Product Standards

Given the role that standards play in the economy, they should be set up to promote the desired social objectives while minimizing costs to the extent possible. Standards may be mandatory or voluntary. Mandatory standards (also referred to as technical regulations) must be met by firms as a matter of law, and penalties are set for nonconforming products. Compliance with voluntary standards remains a matter of commercial choice for individual firms. In practice, both types of standards exist side by side, although the bulk of standards-related activity in most countries now consists of voluntary standards. Mandatory standards tend to be mostly confined to core public health and consumer safety areas, such as requirements governing food and medicines. This coexistence is also apparent at the regional level—for example, in the European Union's (EU) "New Approach" to harmonization. (See European Commission 2000 and WTO 2005 for a discussion.)

Given the coexistence of mandatory and voluntary standards, the responsibility for meeting those standards is increasingly shared between the public and private sectors. In most cases, standards are set up in a complex environment characterized by interplay between private and public interests and agents (Casella 2001). In the United States, for instance, the FDA is a public body (part of the executive branch), and its standards are mandatory and enforceable through the executive branch and the courts. At the same time, the American National Standards Institute (ANSI), a nonprofit organization, develops and promulgates voluntary standards in a wide range of areas. Sometimes the boundaries between public and private organizations can become blurred. ANSI, for example, is a private law body, but its members include government agencies, as well as private sector organizations.

In this public-private partnership, the state often finds itself at an informational disadvantage with respect to the private sector when it comes to designing and implementing particular standards. It is therefore important for policy makers to find the right balance between public and private initiatives and to ensure that they work together. For instance, in the European Union's New Approach to harmonization, the public sector takes the lead in enacting mandatory core standards in certain sectors, but private standards organizations such as the European Committee for Standardization (CEN) remain responsible for developing detailed voluntary standards setting out particular ways in which products can be designed and built to meet the mandatory standards (European Commission 2000).

Of course, drafting the documents containing product standards is only part of the process. National standards systems require supporting infrastructure to ensure the effective implementation of standards. Figure 10.1 presents the infrastructure components of a "farm-to-fork" national quality system. All standards systems need a solid basis in

Figure 10.1. Elements of a Standards Infrastructure

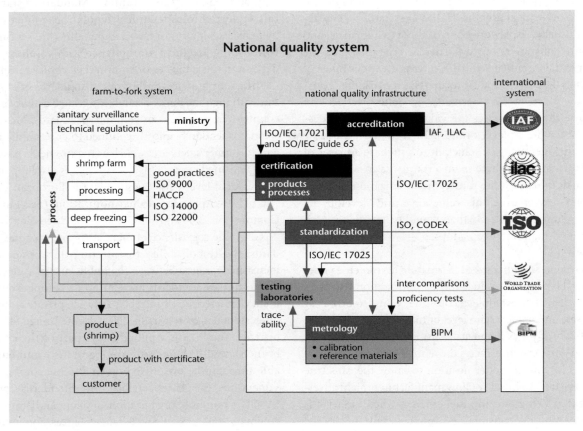

Source: Sanetra and Marbán 2007.
Note: The figure represents the infrastructure in developed countries. Accordingly, the term "national" infrastructure is used, but in practice, although all the elements of the standards infrastructure are necessary, functions can sometimes be distributed among countries

metrology—the establishment of accurate, reliable, and traceable measurements. Without reliable means of measurement, product standards become meaningless, since there is no way of assessing a product's performance in relation to the set of benchmarks set out in a standard.

A sound basis in metrology makes it possible to demonstrate whether specified requirements relating to a product have in fact been met. This process, known as conformity assessment, can be completed either through a supplier's declaration of conformity, in which the seller states that the product meets certain requirements, or through a third-party conformity assessment. In the latter case, an independent laboratory tests whether the product meets certain requirements, and if it does, the laboratory certifies conformity.[3] In some cases, conforming products may receive the right to display a particular logo or label, such as "CE" for certain European standards, or they may be included in an official register of conforming goods. For third-party conformity assessment to be reliable, testing laboratories must themselves be subject to independent

assessment of their equipment and processes. Accreditation of testing laboratories serves this purpose.

Standardization involves a complex and technically sophisticated set of organizations and processes. Depending on their level of development, countries, especially developing countries, may need to be selective when they adopt standards infrastructure. Regional cooperation offers a way for countries to share the burden and spread the costs of setting up standards infrastructure. The creation of regional agencies for metrology, testing and conformity assessment, accreditation, and standardization is an example of a concrete approach to cooperation. Use of foreign conformity assessment mechanisms is another possibility, where domestic capacity is weak.

Regional and International Dimensions of Standardization

The rationales for standards discussed above also apply in a cross-border setting. Asymmetries of information between consumers and producers are even more serious in a traded-goods context because of the ineffectiveness on the international plane of signaling mechanisms that work domestically, such as firm reputations built up over a long period. In addition, a number of important public policy goals—concerning environmental protection, for example—are now recognized as having regional and even global dimensions. In these and other areas, countries are increasingly keen to cooperate on standards, at least to some extent, at the transnational level, through PTAs or the WTO.

The ISO is just one among many transnational entities that issue standards. It is a network of national standards institutes, and, in keeping with the private-law character of many of these institutes, it is a nongovernmental organization. Its standards are, accordingly, private and voluntary.

Another example of international standardization is the Codex Alimentarius Commission, a public organization created as a joint venture between the World Health Organization (WHO) and the Food and Agriculture Organization of the United Nations (FAO). Unlike the ISO, the commission deals with only one area of standardization, food safety.[4] Although its standards do not have direct legal force, they serve as the basis for legally binding rules in many countries (see box 10.3, below).

In addition to international structures such as the ISO and the Codex Alimentarius Commission, some regional bodies deal with standardization. Among them is CEN, which has a regionwide standardization function in the EU. Its members are the national standards bodies of 30 European countries; CEN itself is a private nonprofit organization. Although the standards CEN issues are voluntary, member organizations are required to issue its standards as national standards and to withdraw any inconsistent national standards. CEN's standards are therefore often referred to as being "European standards" or "harmonized European standards" because they are expected to apply with equal force in all member countries.

Cost Effects of Standards

Policy makers need to be aware of the costs entailed by standards and of their potential to distort regional and global trade relations. The implementation of standards policies might lead to discrimination between national and foreign suppliers or between different categories of foreign suppliers. From the point of view of foreign exporters, product standards in an importing country can sometimes represent an additional source of costs (Maskus, Otsuki, and Wilson 2005). Moreover, even though national standards may be legitimate, their multiplicity and diversity can mean duplication of market access costs that may be inefficient from a global perspective. These effects can put foreign competitors at a disadvantage and generate—intentionally or not—a form of protection for domestic industries.[5] Coordination among countries in implementing their standards policies may yield harmonized policies, reducing the cost of market access while preserving regulatory objectives. A potential difficulty with this kind of coordination—discussed in more detail below—is its assumption that it is optimal for the same standard to apply across a wide range of countries. In fact, however, different economic and social conditions may call for different standards.

What kinds of costs can compliance with product standards impose on manufacturers? It might, for example, be necessary to redesign a product, in whole or in part. New machinery may have to be purchased, or a new production process may have to be set up. All these adaptations are associated with increased fixed costs of production (including sunk ones), in the sense that they largely involve a one-off payment rather than a recurring expense.

In some cases, adaptations to deal with product standards can affect the level of variable production costs, as well. If the new production process uses more expensive inputs, or if the new machinery is more costly to run, the unit cost of production will increase. It might

Box 10.3. Do Voluntary Standards Have Cost Effects, Too?

At first glance, it might seem that only mandatory standards would have measurable cost impacts. After all, manufacturers are, in principle, free not to comply with voluntary standards if they so choose. Legally speaking, they are not required to pay additional costs to access a particular market. In practice, the situation is not that straightforward. If compliance with voluntary standards is a commercial imperative, even if not a legal one, we might still expect to see some evidence of cost effects. Is this, in fact, the case?

As it turns out, there is substantial evidence that voluntary standards do indeed affect trade flows, which is consistent with their having a significant impact on cost. Two studies that look into voluntary standards find significant impacts of standards on trade—negative in the work of Czubala, Shepherd, and Wilson (2009), and a mix of sector-specific negative and positive results in the case of Moenius (2005). In addition, Shepherd (2007) finds evidence that voluntary standards affect export diversification in partner countries, which may be indicative of an effect on fixed, not just variable, costs of production. These findings, taken together, suggest that although compliance with voluntary standards may not be necessary as a matter of law, it is still of sufficient commercial importance to produce important links with production costs and trade flows.

also be necessary to formally demonstrate compliance with a particular standard, in which case additional testing and certification procedures might be needed. These procedures also increase variable production costs.

Maskus, Otsuki, and Wilson (2005) collected data from nearly 700 firms in 17 developing countries, as part of an effort to better understand the cost effects of foreign standards. The authors' findings are in line with the types of effects discussed above. In their sample, the fixed costs of compliance with foreign standards are, on average, nearly 5 percent of firm value added. Moreover, increased compliance investment is associated with a small but significant effect on variable production costs.

In assessing the supply-side effects of standards, the distinction between fixed and variable costs is important. Recent advances in the theory of international trade (Chaney 2008) suggest that higher variable costs primarily affect trade by reducing exports per firm among the small subset of firms that already exports to foreign markets. Higher fixed costs, by contrast, tend to force some firms out of export markets entirely, thus altering the range of products exported, or the set of foreign markets served, or both.

The costs and benefits of standards will also depend on their dynamic effects in the long run. For instance, Jaffee (2003) shows how the horticultural industry in Kenya has used changing European regulations as a stimulus to innovation, competitive repositioning, and industrial upgrading. Diaz Rios and Jaffee (2008) find that developing-country firms responded differently to stricter aflatoxin regulations in the EU. The new rules only exacerbated the commercial difficulties of some exporters, but they offered an opportunity for others to upgrade their production techniques and gain additional market share. The reallocation of resources over time from small and relatively inefficient firms to larger, more efficient ones is associated with gains in sectoral productivity—a kind of technological upgrading that holds significant development promise.

Consolidation: Trade Effects of Product Standards

This brief discussion shows that the overall economic impacts of product standards are difficult to assess. From the producer's point of view, there are two opposite forces at play in the short term: possible cost increases stemming from the need to adapt production processes and demonstrate conformity, and possible cost savings through the transmission of market-specific information that would otherwise be costly to obtain. Over the longer term, there is also potential for technological progress induced by standards. At the industry level, standards may lead to a reorganization of firms and of the sector around more efficient production methods. (See, for instance, Maertens and Swinnen [2009] on how the Senegalese vegetable export chain reacted to the tightening of European standards.) The overall impact on producers is therefore ambiguous and depends on the relative strength of these two effects in particular cases.

Because of this theoretical ambiguity, empirical work to assess the trade impacts of standards is difficult to interpret, since there is no simple way of distinguishing results that are consistent with theory from those that are not. Although empirical work emphasizes the relative size and significance of these different effects, it remains difficult to identify them separately in a satisfactory manner. Even apart from this issue, empirical work is hampered by the need to rely on very rough proxies to measure the costs associated with standards: only in rare cases is a direct measure of restrictiveness possible (see box 10.4).

A comprehensive economic assessment of product standards couched in terms of a measure of aggregate welfare could not, of course, be limited to the supply side. It would need to take into account the extent to which a particular standard reduces social costs (e.g., less dangerous products) or creates social benefits (e.g., compatible systems) and thus brings the economy closer to its welfare optimum. Such a comprehensive analysis is at the core of the concept of a regulatory impact assessment (see, e.g., Hahn and Litan 2005) and could easily be extended to the regional context by explicitly considering costs and benefits with cross-border dimensions. However, to take up the issue of internalization and aggregate welfare would be to go beyond the scope of this chapter. Hence, the next sections will deal exclusively with observable trade effects, and largely with the supply-side effects discussed above.

A final observation, however, points toward what are likely to be efficiency costs. The implementation of national standards policies is, by and large, rarely coordinated with trading partners, and it would be surprising if this shortcoming did not lead to more complex and costly standards systems than are strictly necessary. In particular, developing countries may not have available to them the best standards technology, and they may consequently implement inefficient policies—policies that are too costly or do not achieve their objectives. Furthermore, because national policies, even if they incorporate some form of regulatory impact assessment, are decided without consideration of cross-border effects and externalities, it is likely that duplication and incompatibility of standards and practices will create systemic costs.

Disdier, Fontagné, and Mimouni (2008) employ the so-
called inventory method of measuring standardization,
using data from the Trade Analysis and Information System
(TRAINS) database to tally the number of standards that
potentially affect trade in agricultural products. (The
TRAINS database is maintained by the United Nations
Conference on Trade and Development [UNCTAD].) From
these tallies, they construct coverage ratios—the percentage
of products (tariff lines) in the sample that is subject to
product standards. In the aggregate, they find that higher
coverage ratios—that is, a larger inventory of standards—
tend to be associated with reduced exports from developing
countries to member countries of the Organisation for
Economic Co-operation and Development. Trade between
OECD countries appears to be relatively unaffected. This
result would be consistent with a situation in which
adjustment costs are higher or more difficult to cover in the
developing world than in rich countries. In line with the
results of Moenius (2005), Disdier, Fontagné, and Mimouni
(2008) report that this aggregate impact tends to mask
considerable cross-sectoral heterogeneity: in some cases,
standards have a negative impact, consistent with the
dominance of cost increases, whereas in others, they have a
positive impact, consistent with the dominance of cost-
reducing information effects.

There are very few examples of applied work in which it
has proved possible to compare directly the substantive
content of standards, rather than just their numbers. Otsuki,
Wilson, and Sewadeh (2001) do this for the standards
governing acceptable levels of aflatoxin in African groundnut
exports to the EU. They assess restrictiveness directly in terms
of the maximum permissible aflatoxin content of groundnuts,
measured in parts per billion. Their gravity model results
suggest that tighter aflatoxin regulations are associated with
fewer groundnut exports from African countries to the EU,
which is consistent with increased compliance costs. As a
rough order of magnitude, they find that a proposed new EU
aflatoxin regulation would result in trade flows 63 percent
lower than those that would be observed under a less
restrictive Codex Alimentarius standard. This very strong
result needs to be nuanced, however, in light of the
conflicting case study evidence presented by Diaz Rios and
Jaffee (2008).

Dealing with Standards in PTAs

Having set out the general context, we now turn to look
more closely at the particular issues raised by product standards in PTAs.

First, it should be clear from the discussion above that
regional standards can produce economic effects similar to
those associated with national standards. The essential
dynamic is one of insiders and outsiders: members of a
PTA may benefit from a liberalization of product standards
that, at the same time, creates costs for countries outside
the agreement.

Second, agreed disciplines on standards in PTAs should
be viewed in the context of the overall bargain leading to
the agreement, including the mercantilist objectives that
may motivate the negotiations. It is not a given that provisions on standards in a PTA necessarily improve on existing national policies; countries may negotiate preferential
market access in exchange for nonoptimal standards policies set by their trading partners. (See Fink, ch. 18 in this
volume, for a discussion in the context of intellectual property rights.)

Third, PTAs offer a specific mode of trade liberalization
when it comes to standards: the recognition (often mutual)
of standards and procedures. This approach to liberalization is specific in the sense that it is difficult to achieve it
multilaterally. The mutual recognition of standards and
procedures requires a case-by-case approach that only
seems practical in PTAs consisting of a select number of
trading partners with reasonably similar economic and
social characteristics. A case-by-case approach is also often
required in light of the political sensitivities generated by
changes in product standards in areas such as environmental protection and public health.

The importance of these effects is demonstrated by the
prominence product standards have been receiving in
PTAs: Budetta and Piermartini (2009) find that 58 of the
70 PTAs in their sample contain provisions on product
standards. In this section, we briefly examine the economics of preferential standards liberalization and then discuss
two of the main approaches that have been adopted within
regional forums and that have also influenced developments at the multilateral level: harmonization and mutual
recognition (Nicolaïdis 2001).

The Economics of Preferential Standard Liberalization

Liberalization of standards in PTAs is not necessarily de
jure discriminatory, and when it is, it is not necessarily de
facto discriminatory. This point is clearly made, for
instance, by Baldwin, Evenett, and Low (2009) for several
deep integration dimensions. Thus, a PTA on standards
does not translate automatically into a preferential liberalization of standards; in some instances preferential liberalization is equivalent to multilateral liberalization. We
return to this issue in the last section of this chapter.

As we shall see below, there are different routes to liberalization of standards in PTAs. Some of these—mutual recognition agreements and harmonization with standards of the
preferential trading partner that differ from international
standards—are distinctly preferential. A parallel can be
drawn with preferential liberalization of tariffs: standards,

like tariffs, create compliance costs for business that liberalization can reduce. A key difference is that standards do not raise revenue (see "A note on nontariff barriers" in Baldwin, ch. 3 in this volume). Or, rather, standards are not supposed to bring in revenue, but there are instances in which fees must be paid—for example, for the certification process or for laboratory examination costs.[6] These processes of certification and accreditation may create rents that are captured by public or private domestic interests. In this case, the analysis of preferential liberalization is similar to that of the tariff case, with the exception that the tariff revenue is replaced by the rent capture. In strict welfare terms, if domestic interests are benefiting from this implicit tax on importers, it is possible that preferential liberalization may generate the negative effects due to trade diversion.

Even when undertaken on a discriminatory basis, preferential liberalization may nevertheless contribute to kick-starting a process of reform of national standards policies. By introducing more rigorous processes in standards infrastructure operations, PTAs can make it more difficult to use standards for purposes other than consumer protection, even when the standards are not internationally harmonized.[7]

It is also the case that the gap between the prices of the good inside the importing nation and the exporting nation is dissipated by costly activities that are required to satisfy the standards. As shown in more detail in chapter 3, there is no possible negative impact on the importer. Preferential liberalization is unambiguously beneficial in this respect because it generates an economy for both exporter and importer of not having to pay the costs of meeting the standards—even though trade diversion may still occur, since a preference is created. Thus, there is a favorable presumption toward discriminatory liberalization of standards in the absence of rent capture.

Harmonization of Standards

As noted above, the need for producers to comply with multiple, different standards to access different markets could act as a barrier to trade. One response to this problem is to seek to remove the differences between national standards through a process of harmonization. In this context, harmonization means the convergence of national standards toward a common set of requirements (box 10.5). The question of whether it is optimal for a particular set of countries to adopt the same standard depends on the balance between two effects: the potential for increased trade thanks to reduced cost multiplicity, and the likelihood that different national preferences and resource endowments will

---

Box 10.5. Facilitating Market Access: Harmonization, Equivalence, and Mutual Recognition

Part of the international effort around standards and technical regulations aims at reducing the overall burden on traders. Coordinating policies to make them more "alike," or more "compatible," is one way of reducing the costs of compliance. There are three ways of achieving this: harmonization, equivalence, and mutual recognition.

Harmonization is straightforward; it simply means replacing two or more rules or procedures with a single one. Nevertheless, the term can be somewhat misleading because there are degrees of harmonization, involving rules alone, procedures alone, both rules and procedures, or even higher-level objectives only (essential requirements), as in the EU's New Approach.

The aim of the other processes, equivalence and mutual recognition, is to preserve diversity of rules and procedures, provided that "equivalent" or "like" objectives are met. Nicolaïdis and Egan (2001, 456) offer the following definition:

> Recognition refers to the acceptance of equivalence of selected foreign standards or regulations. Mutual recognition establishes the general principle that if a product or a service can be sold lawfully in one jurisdiction, it can be sold freely in any other participating jurisdiction, without having to comply with the regulations of these other jurisdictions. This involves a transfer of regulatory authority from the host jurisdiction to the home jurisdiction from which a product, a person, a service or a firm originates. The "recognition" involved here is of the "equivalence," or at least "compatibility" of the counterpart's regulatory system; the "mutual" part indicates that the reallocation of authority is reciprocal and simultaneous.

Thus, one difference is that mutual recognition can be broken down into two components: the "recognition" of the equivalence of a partner's regulatory system, and the "mutual" aspect, which indicates that both parties simultaneously recognize the other (Nicolaïdis and Shaffer, 2005). Equivalence can thus in principle be asymmetric and unilateral as in U.S. PTAs, where the approach is that parties can decide to accept the other party's regulations as equivalent.

Equivalence can be achieved if the outcome of two standards is identical, even though the means of reaching it differ. Veggeland and Elvestad (2004) quote the example of hard cheese, the manufacturing of which in Australia requires the heating of milk, whereas Switzerland achieves the same levels of pathogen destruction through other production methods, using raw, unpasteurized milk. Equivalence is thus the acceptance that a third party's standards or procedures, in effect, fulfill national requirements.

Mutual recognition normally refers to the acceptance of certification of a partner country. It can also be used to refer to agreements on specific sectors or on specific instances of application, or to agreements between specific partners of the "principle of mutual recognition" (Nicolaïdis and Egan 2001).

interact to produce different optimal regulations in each closed economy. For example, Norway and Zambia might be able to realize some trade gains by adopting the same standards for environmentally friendly packaging materials, but their technological and enforcement capacities differ greatly, and it could be very difficult to ensure that the standard is in fact implemented. Moreover, the differences in income levels and relative land abundance might suggest that Norwegians and Zambians could legitimately have different preferences in relation to the trade-off between the cost and the environmental properties of packaging materials. These issues are extremely complex to resolve but need to be kept in mind when examining harmonization efforts. (See Bhagwati 1996 for a review.)

Harmonization of standards can take place in two ways. Unilateral harmonization occurs when one country or group of countries simply adopts a standard prevailing in another country. More common is concerted harmonization, whereby countries work together to identify a set of requirements that is acceptable to all parties. Concerted harmonization can be a lengthy and uncertain process, requiring extensive negotiations among the parties concerning every standard in each jurisdiction. The more divergent the parties' interests and approaches to standardization, the more difficult it is likely to be to negotiate a set of harmonized standards. Successful harmonization therefore tends to involve countries at reasonably close levels of development, and with some broad similarities in their preferences and their general approaches toward regulation.

Trade effects of harmonization: Insiders versus outsiders. With respect to trade effects, the distinction between countries inside the harmonizing region and those outside is crucial. Ordinarily, the cost-reducing effects of harmonization accrue primarily to firms within the region where standards are harmonized. Foreign exporters still must satisfy the importing region's standards, in addition to whatever requirements may prevail in their home country. They therefore face some level of cost multiplicity (albeit lower than the levels that pertained prior to harmonization). In the case of "harmonizing-up" by the preferential area— that is, the adoption of a stricter standard than prevailed prior to harmonization— it may even be more difficult to access some markets (box 10.6).

At the same time, however, harmonization allows foreign exporters to realize economies of scale by granting them access to a larger market. Exporters have to meet only one type of standard for the whole region, and this reduces the fixed costs of compliance. The balance between cost and scale effects is an empirical issue that must be resolved case by case. The currently available evidence suggests that the cost effect sometimes dominates in the case of regional

---

Box 10.6. Trade Effects of Harmonization: Empirical Evidence

There is substantial empirical evidence to the effect that harmonized standards are often associated with increased trade among harmonizing countries. For instance, Henry de Frahan and Vancauteren (2006) find that harmonization of standards across Europe tends to boost trade among European Union (EU) members: bilateral exports in sectors with harmonized food regulations are, on average, 253 percent higher than in nonharmonized sectors. The tariff equivalent of nonharmonization ranges from 73 to 97 percent, depending on the sector. These findings are consistent with the cost-based analysis presented above: a single, harmonized standard avoids the cost multiplicity that arises from multiple standards, making it easier for producers to access an expanded market within the harmonization zone. Of course, this dynamic must be nuanced in certain cases because of the possibility that information effects will work in the opposite direction: Moenius (2005) shows that the effect of harmonization on trade is not always positive, even for the harmonizers, and suggests that the reason could be the dominance of information effects in some sectors.

For countries outside the harmonization zone, the picture is not generally so rosy. Empirical work suggests that there is considerable scope for a kind of trade diversion effect: the cost reductions implicit in harmonization can lead to a switch in demand to a relatively high-cost supplier within the harmonization zone, to the detriment of lower-cost suppliers elsewhere. In the case of the EU, Baller (2007) and Chen and Mattoo (2008) show that harmonization under the EU's New Approach directives can sometimes have a negative impact on trade with third countries. It is plausible that the EU's harmonization program involves a significant degree of harmonizing-up to a higher standard, which would also tend to have negative trade consequences for excluded countries. Developing countries are more likely to be affected than developed ones, presumably because adaptation costs are higher in a technology-scarce environment.

---

harmonization but that harmonization with international standards generally leads to dominance of the scale effect. In other words, the net effect of harmonization on the exports of excluded countries tends to be negative for regional harmonization but positive for international harmonization.

One way of dealing with the difficulties created by this insider-outsider dynamic is the hybrid approach adopted by the members of the Asia-Pacific Economic Cooperation (APEC). APEC is a particularly heterogeneous regional grouping that includes developed countries such as Australia, Japan, and the United States; developing countries at various income levels (e.g., China, Peru, and Thailand); and transition countries (the Russian Federation and Vietnam). Such a diverse membership would seem to suggest that concerted harmonization could be a particularly long and uncertain process. Similarly, the presence of a number of large countries makes it unlikely that unilateral harmonization by all members except one would be a possibility.

Consistent with its commitment to "concerted unilateralism" and "open regionalism," APEC has therefore adopted an intermediate approach. APEC member economies commit to increasing harmonization of their own national standards with international standards, such as those issued by the ISO; they identify priority sectors in which harmonization should be pursued first; and they undertake to participate actively in the work of international standards bodies. As with other APEC commitments, member economies must make public progress reports (individual action plans) each year. Helble, Shepherd, and Wilson (2007) show that substantial progress appears to have been made on these points.

Trade effects of international harmonization. The empirical literature discussed above examined the impact of regional harmonization on outside countries. In addition, there is now a growing body of empirical evidence suggesting that harmonization with international standards can mitigate the costs that foreign exporters might otherwise face.[8] Czubala, Shepherd, and Wilson (2009) find that EU standards that are not harmonized with international (ISO) norms have a negative and significant impact on exports of African clothing to the EU; internationally harmonized EU standards have no statistically significant impact.

These results are confirmed by Shepherd (2007), who focuses on the fixed-cost effects of standards. A 10 percent increase in the total number of EU standards leads to a 6 percent reduction in the variety of products exported by non-EU partner countries. This finding is consistent with the idea that standards tend to generate fixed costs that exporters must pay to access foreign markets. By contrast, a 10.0 percentage point increase in the proportion of those standards that are harmonized with ISO standards is associated with a small (0.2 percent) but significant increase in partner-country export variety. These results suggest that convergence of regional standards to international norms can be an effective way of limiting the potential for negative trade effects in excluded countries, in particular, developing countries.

Mutual Recognition of Standards or Conformity Assessments

Another way of dealing with the cost issues raised by divergent national standards is mutual recognition of standards.[9] Whereas harmonization eliminates the costs associated with different standards by reducing multiplicity, mutual recognition allows each country to maintain potentially different standards but requires each country to accord equal treatment to goods produced in partner countries, even though standards might be different. If South Africa and Nigeria decide to harmonize standards, they adopt a single set of requirements that applies equally in both countries. If they agree to mutual recognition of standards, South African products that conform to local standards can be put on the Nigerian market, even if they do not comply with Nigerian standards (and vice versa). Of course, it is possible for recognition to be unilateral (equivalence) rather than mutual; for example, Nigeria may decide to treat products conforming to South African standards as equivalent to those conforming to its own standards.

An advantage of mutual recognition of standards over harmonization is that once the principle has been agreed on, it is not necessary to engage in long and complex negotiations over each individual standard; the rule simply applies across the board. National standards agencies continue to go about their work as usual, the only difference being that nonconforming products from foreign markets might now appear on the domestic market.

In fact, however, mutual recognition can be extremely difficult to implement among countries with markedly different social preferences or with fundamentally different approaches toward regulation. Although the rule is relatively easy to apply in practice, it is usually difficult for countries to reach agreement as to whether it should be applied at all. Mutual recognition can be seen as creating a risk that one country's standards might be undermined by another country's different—perceived as lower—standards. In an environment of mobile capital, the fear is that a sharp difference in standards might create an incentive for production to relocate from high-standard to low-standard countries. This would, in turn, provide a motive for authorities in the high-standard country to lower standards in a "race to the bottom."

Although there is considerable debate as to the empirical relevance of this dynamic, there is no doubt as to its political relevance. (See Drezner 2006 for a review.) As a result, mutual recognition is generally only seen among relatively similar countries. European countries, for instance, adopted a form of mutual recognition rule as set out in the *Cassis de Dijon* decision: products that comply with mandatory regulations in one European country cannot usually be prevented from accessing markets in other European countries. But even within a relatively homogeneous grouping such as the EU, the idea of adopting a type of mutual recognition rule for services trade—the "country of origin" principle—proved so controversial that it had to be largely shelved (box 10.7).

Another form of mutual recognition applies to conformity assessments. Under such a regime, countries agree to recognize the results of testing and certification procedures conducted in other countries, even though there is no harmonization or mutual recognition of the underlying standards themselves. For example, if the EU and Australia agree to mutual recognition in the area of conformity assessments, European exporters can have local laboratories certify their compliance with Australian standards. Since the question of recognition is limited to the performance of scientific tests and the certification of results, this procedure should be considerably easier for countries to negotiate than full-scale mutual recognition of standards. Fundamentally, all that is required is that the recognizing countries have a certain level of trust concerning the quality of testing and certification authorities overseas.

A Review of Standards in PTAs

How commonly is each of the above approaches actually applied in practice? Recent work by Budetta and Piermartini (2009) provides some useful first results (see table 10.1). The authors analyze the texts of 70 regional and bilateral PTAs, of which 58 contain some kind of provision related to product standards. Interestingly, harmonization appears to be much more common than mutual recognition of standards: 29 agreements provide for harmonization of mandatory standards, and 25 provide for harmonization of voluntary standards. By contrast, only 5 agreements include mutual recognition of voluntary standards, and 15 provide for mutual recognition of mandatory standards.

Mutual recognition is the most frequent approach for conformity assessment, perhaps because it is easier to achieve mutual recognition of conformity than of standards. Instead of implying equivalence of regulatory objectives, which is a sensitive issue in many cases, recognition of conformity assessment only looks at whether the ways in which tests are performed and certification is granted are equivalent in the countries concerned.

Legally, there is an important difference between the structural patterns of the two types of obligation. Agreements to pursue harmonization can sometimes impose a relatively small number of up-front obligations, and it is common for the parties to commit to ongoing negotiations with a view to harmonization. The devil is thus in the details, since the extent of harmonization that in fact takes place depends on the outcome of a long and complex process. Moreover, Budetta and Piermartini (2009) point out that the majority of agreements with harmonization obligations include the EU as a party, and most of them require harmonization with EU standards. This dynamic reflects both a long-term dynamic within the EU and the fact that most of these agreements involve much smaller and less developed economies. Thus, the figures cited above also reflect the influence of different "models" of treatment of standards and technical regulations in preferential agreements.

Box 10.7. Trade Effects of Mutual Recognition: Empirical Evidence

The available empirical evidence on the effects of mutual recognition is much more limited than in the case of harmonization. Chen and Mattoo (2008) look at the effects of European mutual recognition agreements (MRAs) with other (non-EU) countries that cover conformity assessments. They find that conformity assessment MRAs uniformly promote trade between the parties. Baller (2007) confirms that result for a wider range of countries. An and Maskus (2009) find similar evidence, using firm-level survey data, and suggest that their results would be consistent with a stronger beneficial effect on developing-country exporters from MRAs than from international harmonization of standards.

Chen and Mattoo (2008), however, demonstrate that the impact of conformity assessment MRAs on third countries depends crucially on the nature of the rules of origin that accompany them. Rules of origin set out the conditions under which a product is treated as originating in a particular country, for the purposes of applying the specific regime under an agreement; in this case, a rule of origin would preclude third countries from accessing the mutual recognition regime. For instance, whereas a product in country A, a member of the agreement, could have local conformity assessment accepted as valid in other countries participating in the agreement, the product from a third country would have to be certified following the practices of the country where the product is being sold.

MRAs with relatively open rules of origin tend to be trade promoting for all countries, but the presence of restrictive rules of origin can reverse that effect. In addition, Amurgo-Pacheco (2006) finds evidence that conformity assessment MRAs can have negative trade impacts on excluded developing countries.

Table 10.1. Prevalence of Harmonization and Mutual Recognition in Preferential Trade Agreements
(number, out of sample of 58 PTAs)

	Voluntary standards	Mandatory standards	Conformity assessment
Harmonization	25	29	25
Mutual recognition	5	15	39

Source: Adapted from Budetta and Piermartini 2009, table 2.

Mutual recognition, by contrast, tends to impose stronger obligations up front: countries sometimes immediately commit to give full force to each other's standards, although this may in some cases be limited to particular sectors. The extent to which individual agreements result in the removal of multiple standards-related barriers is therefore an empirical question that needs to be examined in detail in each case.

Many regional and bilateral PTAs contain additional provisions related to the design and management of regional standards systems (see table 10.2). Usually, a cluster of obligations concerning the transparency of standards and their administration forms a key component. For instance, Budetta and Piermartini (2009) find that 21 of the 58 PTAs dealing with product standards impose a requirement of prior notification on the parties. This means that new standards, or modifications of existing ones, must be notified prior to their entry into force; in many cases, there is also an obligation to allow time for comments. Another common example of a transparency obligation is the creation of a national contact point or the establishment of a consultation system. Twenty of the agreements surveyed by Budetta and Piermartini (2009) contain such obligations.

Table 10.2. Content of Preferential Trade Agreements Relating to Provisions on Standards *(percent)*

Provision	Lesser, based on 24 case studies	Budetta and Piermartini, based on 58 PTAs
Reference to WTO TBT Agreement	86	52
Harmonization of standards, technical regulations, and conformity assessment	47	46
Harmonization to regional technical regulations and standards	34	45
Equivalence of technical regulation and standards	33	26
Recognition of conformity assessment	77	67
Transparency	80	52
Joint committee or regional body	80	62
Dispute settlement	80	50
Technical assistance	47	38
Metrology	14	29

Source: Lesser 2007; Budetta and Piermartini 2009.
Note: TBT, technical barriers to trade; WTO, World Trade Organization.

Some PTAs go even further in their treatment of product standards and incorporate institutions designed to make the process of standard setting and administration work more smoothly between trading partners. Of the agreements reviewed by Budetta and Piermartini (2009), 34 provide for some kind of regional administrative body to deal with the administration of standards systems, and 24 include a dispute settlement mechanism. Interestingly, 22 agreements have provisions relating to technical assistance. This last point is consistent with the increasing trend toward North-South integration agreements and suggests that the parties are aware of the asymmetric challenges that can arise when trading partners at different levels of development pursue integration bilaterally. It is impossible, however, to draw any general conclusion as to the effectiveness of these provisions because the way they are implemented is so important. Legal provisions of agreements tell us about the intentions of their drafters but not about the actual implementation.

Still, there is evidence in Europe, in the Southern Cone Common Market (Mercosur, Mercado Común del Sur), and in the Andean countries that PTAs generate actual changes in standards policies. Aldaz-Carroll (2006) reports that by 2004, Mercosur had developed about 370 regional voluntary standards and 407 regional technical regulations and sanitary and phytosanitary (SPS) measures. The Andean Community has harmonized technical regulations for 31 agricultural products representing about 60 percent of intraregional trade. An additional piece of indirect evidence of the attention paid to implementation issues is provided by Budetta and Piermartini (2009), who examine WTO disputes concerning technical regulations and find that a number of them involve PTA partners, suggesting that such disputes are linked to the agreements they have signed.

What do existing regional experiences tell us about the ingredients of a successful approach to standards? Aldaz-Carroll (2006) reviews the evidence from Asia and Latin America, and concludes that the following aspects are crucial:

- Building trust among parties to the PTA
- Building regulatory capacity among parties
- Focusing on simplification, transparency, and dynamism in the standards-upgrading process
- Allowing for gradual reform where appropriate
- Promoting mutual recognition of conformity assessments as a first step
- Identifying priority sectors for harmonization.

Lessons from the Standards Provisions in PTAs

The examination of specific provisions in agreements confirms that countries seek to use PTAs to help with market access and implementation of compliance with foreign standards. Chapter 11, which takes up the practice of product standards in PTAs, provides additional empirical information. The establishment of institutions to help with implementation is widespread and is often coupled with transparency requirements (box 10.8). These features suggest that regional institutions can contribute to making standards less burdensome to trade. Access to information, trust, and capacity building all matter. The need to coordinate national, regional, and multilateral efforts on standards might, however, place a significant strain on resources and capacity in some poorer countries.

The treatment of standards in PTAs is highly dependent on the type of agreement. First, agreements involving the EU and the United States each propose different models, and it is still unclear which advantages each partnership may or may not yield. Take, for instance, the question of

recognition. Some U.S. agreements use the concept of equivalence, which can be pursued unilaterally by each partner without reciprocity. The EU on the other hand, focuses on mutual recognition or harmonization. It is also unclear which model is superior. Where the advantage lies is most likely to vary depending on the partner country (and the similarity of regulatory preferences). Second, agreements between partners at similar development levels (North-North or South-South) are more likely to lead to deep integration measures such as mutual recognition; Lesser (2007) cites the example of the Trans-Pacific Strategic Economic Partnership Agreement between Brunei Darussalam, Chile, New Zealand, and Singapore. Third, technical assistance dimensions are more prevalent in North-South agreements, where upgrading of capacity may be needed before regulatory reform takes place.

Finally, the agreements contain examples of good practice. Among them are, obviously, support for the multilateral WTO framework and, to the extent that it is consistent with the adoption of optimal standards, international harmonization efforts. Advance notification to trading partners is another. The approach favored by the United States

---

Box 10.8. How Small ASEAN Countries Manage to Access Certification and Accreditation Services

The absence of internationally recognized public laboratories need not act as a binding constraint on the implementation of mutual recognition agreements, provided that the private firm can either use a private company or obtain access to the testing infrastructure of neighboring countries. Permitting the efficient operation of private testing service providers (local and foreign) can enable export-ready firms to access testing services at low cost. In the presence of internationally recognized third-party certifiers, the absence of a national accreditation agency or office need not be a serious constraint. The major export markets will accept certification from these third-party certifiers.

Although the small size of the market in the Lao People's Democratic Republic and in Cambodia might discourage foreign testing companies from establishing local branches and offering services across a wide range of sectors, at least one foreign third-party certification company has begun operating in Cambodia. Intertek, an internationally recognized testing company, has opened an office in Phnom Penh and is offering testing and certification services to exporting companies. The service conducts tests for companies that export garments to the U.S. and EU markets. Since the advent of Intertek, inspection costs have declined. Intertek has no contact with the government of Cambodia, but it works closely with foreign buyers. This example illustrates the importance of private sector third-party certifiers in enabling exporters to obtain the necessary documentation to prove they meet international standards.

East Asia is developing a network of calibration laboratories with traceability to physical measurement standards at the national level or to the internationally recognized national physical standards of another country. Most members of the Association of Southeast Asian Nations (ASEAN) have both privately and publicly owned laboratories that are accredited by a government accreditation service. The original six ASEAN members (Brunei Darussalam, Indonesia, Malaysia, the Philippines, Singapore, and Thailand) have entered into MRAs on laboratory accreditation with other ASEAN members. In the newer members of ASEAN, the CLMV countries (Cambodia, Lao PDR, Myanmar, and Vietnam), individual laboratories engage in MRAs with foreign counterparts; this is the case for Intertek in Cambodia.

In countries without a national accreditation agency, the government may contract a foreign accreditation body to carry out national accreditation activities on its behalf. Within ASEAN, the Brunei Ministry of Development has an agreement with the Singapore Accreditation Council (SAC) that includes the use of SAC accreditation of laboratories and of certification and inspection bodies and that, in addition, provides for training to build up capacity in Brunei Darussalam. A government can also allow foreign accreditation bodies to provide services directly to laboratories in a foreign country without any formal arrangement with the government. Although this would work for many markets, it would not assist with improved market access to the EU under any of the EU's MRAs because, under those agreements, the exporting country is required to endorse the accreditation service.

Source: World Bank 2008.

to request justification for decisions to refuse equivalence also stems from the right kind of principles, as does the promotion of suppliers' declarations of conformity. Finally, the establishment, in the context of agreements, of institutions such as specialized committees that meet regularly seems to offer a good venue for dialogue and exchange of information, enabling learning by doing, monitoring of implementation, and defusing of possible disputes.

Regional Standards in a Multilateral World

Standards in the WTO are disciplined by the Agreement on the Application of Sanitary and Phytosanitary Measures (SPS Agreement) and the Agreement on Technical Barriers to Trade (TBT Agreement). The WTO agreements do not force countries to adopt standards, but they do provide disciplines to be adopted when applying standards. For example, the SPS Agreement states a specific preference for the Codex Alimentarius. One very specific dimension of the two agreements is, therefore, to aim for a balance (some will see it as a tension) between countries' autonomy to pursue domestic regulatory objectives and the objective of nondiscrimination.

WTO Disciplines on Regional Standards

Unlike other trade policies in which regional and bilateral PTAs may be seen as an exception to multilateralism, the SPS and TBT Agreements incorporate the regional dimension into their provisions:

- Articles 4.1, 9.2, and 9.3 of the TBT Agreement address PTA issues.
- Article 2.4 of the TBT Agreement recognizes that in some instances, international standards may not be appropriate means of fulfilling certain objectives because of "fundamental climatic, geographical, or fundamental technological problems."
- Article 2.7 of that agreement seeks to promote recognition of other members' equivalence of technical regulations.
- The TBT Agreement suggests that members seek mutual recognition agreements on conformity (Article 6.3).[10]
- The TBT Agreement refers to international and regional standards-setting bodies (Article 4.1), as well as regional certification bodies (Articles 9.2 and 9.3), although not to regional standards.
- Article 13 of the SPS Agreement refers to the applicability of the agreement to regional bodies.
- The SPS Agreement recognizes that national boundaries are not necessarily relevant for the application of SPS measures and refers to regional conditions (Article 6).

- Article 4 of the SPS Agreement suggests that members seek mutual recognition agreements on SPS measures.[11]

The fact that regional aspects are so explicitly mentioned in the TBT and SPS Agreements reflects the nature of standards, which must meet regulatory objectives such as protecting the environment. Meeting these regulatory objectives, by definition, creates barriers to trade. The role of the WTO is to help minimize any excessive burden on trade created by such regulations and to ensure that no discrimination arises from them. This requires that the need for regulation, as well as the principle of nondiscrimination, be taken into account (Trachtman 2003).[12]

In some instances, necessity may be compatible with regional interventions. At the same time, it has to be acknowledged that there is an immediate tension between the risk of discrimination created by any agreement between a select few and the pursuit of legitimate objectives of protection through regional standards interventions.

There is a certain lack of clarity as to how WTO disciplines apply to regional TBT and SPS measures because of the need to interpret the relation between the provisions of the General Agreement on Tariffs and Trade (GATT)—in particular, Article XXIV, on preferential trade agreements, and Article I, on the most favored nation (MFN) obligation—and the provisions of the SPS and TBT Agreements themselves. Trachtman (2003) is of the opinion that the WTO language does not require harmonization or mutual recognition within PTAs. He notes that a specific area of uncertainty relates to mutual recognition agreements, in particular, the potential that they create for discrimination toward nonparticipating trading partners; unlike the General Agreement on Trade in Services (GATS), the TBT and SPS Agreements do not suggest that recognition be offered on an open basis (i.e., that third-party countries be allowed to obtain recognition). A too strict application of the MFN principle, however, could prevent legitimate liberalization of trade in PTA through harmonization and recognition.

Regional Standards Systems and Multilateralism

As we saw earlier, regional standards and bodies are an important layer of the international trade system and are recognized as such in the WTO texts. In what way can regional initiatives be compatible with multilateral, nondiscriminatory, and open-trade objectives?

The first contribution of PTAs might be their role in enforcing multilateral disciplines, providing, in a way, some redundancy in enforcement. Multilateral and preferential agreements have different enforcement mechanisms that may strengthen each other. Concessions in PTAs may also be perceived as more valuable to trading partners than multilateral concessions, and infringement of commitments as thus more costly. PTAs offer more possibilities for "soft" dispute resolution through dialogue and information sharing at an expert level that can help defuse many disputes. In some cases, too, PTAs offer more stringent arbitration rules than the WTO, foreshadowing, for instance, the repeal of offending standards. In some agreements, such as the North American Free Trade Agreement (NAFTA), the possibility of resorting to both the WTO and PTA dispute settlement mechanisms is explicitly mentioned (Budetta and Piermartini 2009).

Second, PTAs can offer scope for further autonomous liberalization in the area of standards by promoting harmonization in areas not explicitly covered by the WTO, contributing to the elimination of national standards, or promoting provisions that are stricter than WTO language. In the first instance, given that standards are generally designed to be MFN—that is, the standards specification is the same for products from all origins—regional standards design or discipline can complement multilateral disciplines (Lesser 2007; see also the further discussion below).[13] Mercosur provides an example of harmonization of regional standards. In addition, as Trachtman (2003) notes, agreements among countries with more homogeneous regulatory preferences may render the reduction of standards barriers easier. In this second instance, principles similar to those professed by the WTO are adopted, but in a more binding way.

In some instances, national systems may not be adapted to guarantee the correct application of a given standard. The economic reason for such a situation is the existence of cross-border externalities or cross-border economies of scale. In such circumstances, transnational cooperation may be called for. The SPS Agreement mentions regional conditions with respect to diseases and pests that may require cross-country coordination to ensure control or eradication. (This is an example of an externality.) Small countries may also lack the resources to develop adequate institutions to manage standards. In particular, accreditation and metrology bodies may not be available in some countries, or it might not make economic sense to have such services in small markets, and access to regional facilities in a partner country is therefore needed (an example of economies of scale). Thus, international cooperation might help implement a "division of labor" among countries according to their specific comparative capacities in certification (Aldaz-Carroll 2006).

A related point is the capacity of PTAs or regional institutions to help with the implementation of standards and, more generally, with the sharing of experience. This may go beyond deeper harmonization, to the definition of common procedures (e.g., risk management, testing protocols). Mutual recognition, or, in WTO language, equivalence of measures, in standards or in the testing and certification of trade partners, is a facilitating practice that is implemented through specific ad hoc agreements (e.g., the EU–U.S. agreement on mutual recognition of conformity assessment) or as part of PTAs.[14] This process is essentially bilateral or, in some rarer cases (the EU, Mercosur) regional, since relatively intensive cooperation among the parties is required if it is to be acknowledged that foreign standards or testing systems are equivalent to national ones and go toward meeting the same regulatory objectives.

Finally, regional cooperation can also involve the provision of technical assistance and transfer of knowledge (see box 10.8, above). Such a level of cooperation can be easier to attain and can be more flexible than in international agreements.

Regional Standards: Stumbling Blocks, or Building Blocks?

Like two sides of the same coin, the characteristics of preferential cooperation that could favor multilateral liberalization are often the same that could hinder it. At the heart of this paradox is the fact that cooperation creates a "special relationship" to which other trading partners lack access. Two cases can arise. The first is that this preferential relationship is used to raise the standards applied to the rest of the world (without a justifiable change in the regulatory objectives). This can occur when a regional standard that is used as the basis of harmonization is protectionist in intent. An example of a protectionist regional standard is Mercosur's prohibition of imports in wine in barrels (Nofal 2004).

The second, more common, occurrence is when the preferential relationship, while leaving standards outside the PTA unchanged or improved and trade within the parties to the agreement liberalized, provides preferential access to products from within the PTA but not to third parties, leading to trade diversion. This is what happens with "nonopen" MRAs that are confined to members of the agreement only and cannot be extended to third countries. The economic incentives so created are the same as for other forms of preferential access; they generate market access rents that may act in the future as stumbling blocks to further liberalization.

There is also the related question of whether regional standards systems produced by preferential agreements may, as they grow in size, create disincentives for progress toward greater international harmonization, as the cost of changing standards rises in relation to the marginal benefit of increased market access.

The cost of switching to more open international standards and certification can be increased in two ways. First, problems of compatibility and complexity can arise when a country belongs to many standards systems. Second, regional systems may alter incentives for further liberalization. Once a country joins a regional standards system, changing to an international system may not be attractive enough because the costs would be too high and the marginal benefit of extra market access too small. There is also the possibility that a regional standards group may become large enough to exert market power and affect the terms of trade, thus providing incentives to exclude nonmembers. Finally and perhaps closer to reality, large economic areas that are producing standards have an incentive to export their own policy models. The EU and the United States, for example, are known to be pushing to spread their trade policy norms (Maur 2005; Horn, Mavroidis, and Sapir 2010), as is discussed next.

What the Texts of Agreements Tell Us

Lesser (2007) and Budetta and Piermartini (2009) examine the legal provisions relating to TBTs in PTAs notified to the WTO with a view to assessing, in particular, whether these provisions promote convergence toward the multilateral system. Some dimensions reviewed by the two studies convey a positive picture, in that PTAs do not overtly conflict with the WTO disciplines:

- Of 70 surveyed PTAs, 58 have TBT provisions, and 30 (51 percent) make explicit reference to the WTO TBT Agreement (Budetta and Piermartini 2009).
- Lesser (2007) finds that 86 percent of the PTAs in a sample of 24 refer to the WTO TBT Agreement.

A mere reference to the WTO TBT Agreement would not be sufficient to justify a conclusion that PTAs constitute a building block for a liberal multilateral system. The researchers therefore look at several other dimensions of PTAs that may contribute to greater or less convergence. On the whole, a picture of agreements that, by and large, act as potential complements to international initiatives emerges. For instance, when PTAs seek harmonization of standards, technical regulations, and certification procedures among partners (about half of PTAs reviewed do so), in about 60 to 70 percent of these cases, the use of international standards is encouraged (Lesser 2007).

Similarly, transparency measures often echo those contained in the WTO, such as advance notification of new regulations.

Although PTAs seem to promote aspects of multilateral standards disciplines, these same agreements are pushed by large economies with relatively idiosyncratic and distinct approaches. Budetta and Piermartini (2009) conclude their investigation on a note of caution, observing that harmonization seems generally favored over mutual recognition, especially for standards setting. (Mutual recognition of certification is more widespread.) This opens the possibility of the strong party's imposing its vision of standards policy—formally, as part of the agreement, or perhaps more subtly, through technical assistance, for example. Harmonization to EU or international standards is, for instance, a distinct feature of EU agreements. Moreover, the fact that regional standards are promoted alongside or instead of international ones (again, the EU has promoted the use of its standards in several agreements) adds to the risk that different hubs will pull partner countries in separate directions incompatible with a multilateral vision.[15]

Beyond the WTO Provisions

PTAs also predictably focus on areas in which multilateral initiatives cannot or do not yet offer disciplines. Two main models of recognition prevail. One, promoted in some U.S. PTAs, is the recognition of conformity assessment conducted in the territories of partner countries as equivalent to one's own. As noted by Lesser (2007), the U.S. agreements often go beyond WTO rules by stating that any refusal to authorize certification performed in the partner country has to be justified on request. This contrasts with the softer language in the WTO TBT agreement, which merely encourages equivalence. Another feature of the U.S. agreements is their promotion of private sector self-certification through supplier declarations of conformity assessment. The second model is that of the European Union, which insists more on MRAs on conformity. Generally, this translates into separate bilateral MRAs. To date, these agreements involve partners at similar development levels; apparently PTAs between developed and developing partners, even when calling for such MRAs, have not led to any being signed yet.

A desire to go beyond the WTO agreements is one motivation of PTA provisions on TBTs. Transparency provisions in PTAs are in some instances more onerous than those required by the WTO, with longer notification times (90 days). In the case of harmonization to regional standards and certification, the rationale is often to fill gaps where international standards do not exist or are inappropriate; this is the case with the Common Market for Eastern and Southern Africa (COMESA), APEC, and the Andean Community (Lesser 2007).

The second motivation in PTAs is to promote implementation and enforcement. Such agreements often create enforcement and implementation institutions for standards. Most PTAs call for the establishment of a committee, body, or network in charge of TBTs (Lesser 2007). The functions of such bodies can be varied: exchange of information, monitoring of implementation, consultation, and in the more advanced cases, harmonization and legal enforcement. Examples of regional organizations for standards include the Caribbean Regional Organization for Standards and Quality (CROSQ, established by the Caribbean Community, CARICOM); the African Regional Organization for Standardization (ARSO, set up by COMESA); and the Mercosur Standardization Association (AMN). An initiative worth noting is the Standardisation, Quality Assurance and Metrology (SQAM) initiative by the Southern African Development Community (SADC); the initiative encompasses cooperation on standards management, accreditation, and metrology.[16]

Dispute settlement is another dimension in which some PTAs create mechanisms supplementing or going beyond what is foreseen in the WTO. Numerous PTAs contain some form of dispute resolution arrangement (as does over half the sample reviewed by Lesser 2007). The Andean agreement is an example of one in which the revocation of infringing TBT measures can be ordered and in which dispute settlement measures provide for alternative mechanisms of redress to those offered by the WTO.

We cannot really draw conclusions here as to whether these added disciplines have a measurable positive impact on developing countries' ability to meet standards and their standard systems. More detailed sector-level studies would be required to determine whether these disciplines promote more effective and less costly use of standards.

We have so far presented evidence about TBTs only. We can presume that similar regional provisions relating to SPS standards and measures are strongly linked to international harmonization efforts. Casual evidence is provided by references in PTAs to the Codex Alimentarius (see box 10.9), which is mentioned in 20 agreements in the World Trade Law database.

Conclusions

Product standards are an important fact of commercial life and in many instances are justified—at least in part—by

---

Box 10.9. The Codex Alimentarius and Preferential Trade Agreements

The North American Free Trade Agreement (NAFTA) between Canada, Mexico, and the United States; the Treaty of Asunción, which established the Southern Cone Common Market (Mercosur, Mercado Común del Sur) between Argentina, Brazil, Paraguay, and Uruguay; and the Asia-Pacific Economic Cooperation (APEC), with 21 members, have all adopted measures consistent with principles embraced by the Uruguay Round agreements and related to Codex Alimentarius standards.

NAFTA includes two ancillary agreements dealing with sanitary and phytosanitary (SPS) measures and technical barriers to trade (TBT). In connection with SPS measures, Codex standards are cited as basic requirements to be met by the three member countries with respect to the health and safety aspects of food products. Mercosur's Food Commission has recommended a range of Codex standards for adoption by member countries and is using other Codex standards as points of reference in continuing deliberations. APEC has drafted a mutual recognition arrangement on conformity assessment of foods and food products. It calls for consistency with SPS and TBT requirements and with Codex standards, including the recommendations of the Codex Committee on Food Import and Export Certification Systems. EU directives also frequently refer to the Codex Alimentarius as the basis for their requirements.

Source: Web site of the Food and Agriculture Organization of the United Nations (FAO).

---

economic analysis because of spillover effects or information asymmetries. Since these effects are not limited by national borders, they can serve as a basis for regional and global cooperation on product standards. Policy makers, however, need to be aware that product standards also impose costs and that multiple or conflicting standards can create an overly burdensome cost environment for business and international trade. Like any regulatory instruments, standards are open to capture by vested interests and may in some cases act as a form of protectionist measure.

There is a clear tension between, on the one hand, the legitimate protection of important social goals, and the promotion of economic efficiency in some areas, and, on the other, the costs that standards can entail both inside and outside national borders. These costs can be particularly severe for firms in countries that are excluded from common approaches to standards, as well as in developing countries where technical and financial constraints can make it difficult to comply with burdensome standards abroad. The economic costs and benefits of product standards need to be carefully assessed in each case, paying particular attention to the possibility of cross-border impacts and to whether individual countries are in a position to build a satisfactory national standards infrastructure or whether cross-border cooperation is needed.

PTAs can provide an answer to regional cooperation problems. Moreover, they are at the heart of liberalization efforts regarding standards and technical regulations. This is partly because core measures such as harmonization and mutual recognition of standards or of conformity assessment are much easier to negotiate and implement among groups of countries with relatively similar development levels and institutional settings. As with other types of preferential liberalization, however, it is important for policy makers to ensure that such efforts work in tandem with and do not undermine the broader multilateral agenda expressed in the WTO SPS and TBT Agreements.

Indeed, most PTAs do not seem to be designed with the objective of taking a different path from the one agreed in the WTO. WTO disciplines, however, remain relatively general, so PTAs should ensure that they adopt disciplines that reduce the risks of exclusion of third-country traders. This chapter has reviewed a number of possible approaches, such as a focus on international harmonization and inclusion of open rules of origin regarding certification. Both instruments can be seen as ways of multilateralizing PTAs. Of course, it is also important for PTA groupings to retain sufficient flexibility to allow standards to evolve in line with international developments and not to lock participants into a particular set of norms that is difficult to modify.

For parties to a PTA, harmonization and mutual recognition seem to have positive effects on the volume of trade. Choosing between harmonization and mutual recognition is, however, important because the countries' level of development and their regulatory objectives will influence which approach is better suited to their particular circumstances. In general, harmonization seems suitable for a minority of cases. Whether to pursue commonality in standards definition or simply in conformity assessment is another consideration. Cooperation on conformity assessment is arguably a more accessible first step for many countries.

Product standards raise a number of important issues in the context of North-South PTAs, which are becoming steadily more common. Adoption of identical standards by countries at very different development levels raises serious questions as to whether either country, and in particular the less developed partner, will achieve a socially optimal level of regulation. In addition, developing countries can face particularly severe technical and financial obstacles when it comes to undertaking the investments necessary to bring about compliance with some developed-country standards. This analysis suggests that technical assistance, capacity building, and aid for trade might have important

roles to play in supporting the development of standards infrastructure within PTAs.

The next chapter reviews in greater depth actual practice with respect to product standards in a selected number of representative PTAs.

Notes

The authors are grateful to Juliana Salles Almeida, Silja Baller, Michael Friis Jensen, and Roberta Piermartini for suggestions and sharing of results.

1. For an overview of policy issues in this area and a review of empirical work, see WTO (2005).

2. This is a variant of the "lemons" problem discussed by Akerlof (1970).

3. In some cases the declaration of conformity can be made by the purchaser, as well. A supplier's declaration regime can potentially lead to significant cost savings for business and government. Fleiss, Gonzales, and Schonfeld (2008) find some empirical evidence in Europe to support the view that a shift from third-party certification to a supplier-declaration system can be trade promoting.

4. The WTO agreements maintain a distinction between standards broadly related to food safety and those related to more general issues in the area of manufactured goods. The former are largely dealt with under the Agreement on the Application of Sanitary and Phytosanitary Measures (the SPS Agreement); the latter come under the Agreement on Technical Barriers to Trade (the TBT Agreement).

5. The empirical literature offers little evidence that protectionism may be a motivation behind some standards (see Kono 2006). The financial crisis and measures taken by some countries to protect domestic industries have, however, raised again the specter that standards may be used as protectionist devices. An example is India's recent decision to ban Chinese toys on safety grounds ("Downturn Heightens China-India Tension on Trade." *Wall Street Journal*, March 20, 2009, http://online.wsj.com/article/SB123749113639187441.html).

6. WTO Article VIII states, "All fees and charges of whatever character (other than import and export duties and other than taxes within the purview of Article III) imposed by contracting parties on or in connection with importation or exportation shall be limited in amount to the approximate cost of services rendered and shall not represent an indirect protection to domestic products or a taxation of imports or exports for fiscal purposes."

7. This happens when agreements are signed with the EU, which requires strict standards. Countries have to meet the safety expectations set by EU legislation if they want to be able to export foods to the EU. In some African, Caribbean, and Pacific (ACP) countries, this requirement has been met with resistance by policy makers, who see a traditional sphere of influence being undermined by the new regime (Doherty 2008).

8. As noted above, harmonization is not always optimal in a welfare sense because countries (and regions) can differ in their preferences and resource endowments. Thus, while adoption of internationally harmonized standards can often be beneficial from a trade point of view, policy makers need to ensure that the overall welfare effect is positive. This question is particularly important for developing countries and regions, given the technical and financial burdens that international standards can impose.

9. Harmonization and mutual recognition should generally be viewed as complements, not substitutes. In the EU's New Approach, for instance, both instruments work together.

10. TBT Article 6.3 states, "Members are encouraged, at the request of other Members, to be willing to enter into negotiations for the conclusion of agreements for the mutual recognition of results of each other's conformity assessment procedures. Members may require that such agreements fulfill the criteria of paragraph 1 and give mutual satisfaction

regarding their potential for facilitating trade in the products concerned."

11. SPS Article 4 states, "Members shall, upon request, enter into consultations with the aim of achieving bilateral and multilateral agreements on recognition of the equivalence of specified sanitary or phytosanitary measures."

12. It is worthwhile at this stage to mention another area in which the question of (regional) standards applies: that of services. Authorization, certification, licensing of services suppliers, and recognition of qualifications are areas in which the question of standards arises and regional integration prospects may have a role to play. The WTO General Agreement on Trade in Services resembles the TBT and SPS Agreements in recognizing this, although in a quite different way. Trachtman (2003) notes that GATS Article VII provides specifically for the autonomous or mutual recognition of standards of other trade partners. It thus clearly views mutual recognition as an acceptable exception to MFN treatment.

13. Note, however, that the existence of a uniform standard does not guarantee nondiscrimination: the standard may be so designed as to target a particular source of imports (by including a characteristic specific to that source only) or may be implemented in a discriminatory fashion through testing and certification procedures.

14. The EU–U.S. agreement covers telecommunication equipment, electromagnetic compatibility (EMC), electrical safety, recreational craft, manufacturing practices for pharmaceutical goods, and medical devices. MRAs have also been concluded with Australia, Canada, Japan, New Zealand, and Switzerland; see http://ec.europa.eu/enterprise/international/index_en.htm.

15. See table 10.2, above. The diffusion of EU standards is actually clearly advocated in the European Commission (2001), which states as an aim, "to promote where possible, the adoption of overseas standards, and regulatory approaches based on, or compatible with, international and European practices, in order to improve the market access and competitiveness of European products."

16. A recent review of standard provisions in African PTAs can be found in Meyer et al. (2010).

References

Akerlof, George A. 1970. "The Market for Lemons: Quality Uncertainty and the Market Mechanism." *Quarterly Journal of Economics* 84 (3): 488–500.

Aldaz-Carroll, Enrique. 2006. "Regional Approaches to Better Standards Systems." Policy Research Working Paper 3948, World Bank, Washington, DC.

Amurgo-Pacheco, Alberto. 2006. "Mutual Recognition Agreements and Trade Diversion: Consequences for Developing Nations." Working Paper 20/2006, Graduate Institute of International and Development Studies, Geneva.

An, Galina, and Keith E. Maskus. 2009. "The Impacts of Alignment with Global Product Standards on Exports of Firms in Developing Countries." *World Economy* 32 (4): 552–74.

Baldwin, Richard E. 2000. "Regulatory Protectionism, Developing Nations, and a Two-Tier World Trading System." In *Brookings Trade Forum, 2000,* ed. Susan Collins and Dani Rodrik. Washington, DC: Brookings Institution.

Baldwin, Richard E., Simon Evenett, and Patrick Low. 2009. "Beyond Tariffs: Multilateralizing Non-Tariff RTA Commitments." In *Multilateralizing Regionalism: Challenges for the Global Trading System,* ed. Richard E. Baldwin and Patrick Low. Cambridge, U.K.: Cambridge University Press.

Baller, Silja. 2007. "Trade Effects of Regional Standards Liberalization: A Heterogeneous Firms Approach." Policy Research Working Paper 4124, World Bank, Washington, DC.

Barrett, Christopher B., and Yi-Nung Yang. 2001. "Rational Incompatibility with International Product Standards." *Journal of International Economics* 54 (1): 171–91.

Bhagwati, Jagdish. 1996. "The Demands to Reduce Domestic Diversity among Trading Nations." In *Fair Trade and Harmonization: Prerequisites for Free Trade?,* ed. Jagdish Bhagwati and Robert E. Hudec. Cambridge, MA: MIT Press.

Budetta, Michele, and Roberta Piermartini. 2009. "A Mapping of Regional Rules on Technical Barriers to Trade." In *Regional Rules in the Global Trading System,* ed. Antoni Estevadeordal, Kati Suominen, and Robert Teh. Cambridge, U.K.: Cambridge University Press.

Casella, Álessandra. 2001. "Product Standards and International Trade: Harmonization through Private Coalitions?" *Kyklos* 54 (2/3): 243–64.

Chaney, Thomas. 2008. "Distorted Gravity: The Intensive and Extensive Margins of International Trade." *American Economic Review* 98 (4): 1707–21.

Chen, Maggie X., and Aaditya Mattoo. 2008. "Regionalism in Standards: Good or Bad for Trade?" *Canadian Journal of Economics* 41 (3): 838–63.

Czubala, Witold, Ben Shepherd, and John S. Wilson. 2009. "Help or Hindrance? The Impact of Harmonised Standards on African Exports." *Journal of African Economies* 18 (5): 711–44.

David, Paul A., and Shane Greenstein. 1990. "The Economics of Compatibility Standards: An Introduction to Recent Research." *Economics of Innovations and New Technologies* 1: 3–41.

Diaz Rios, Luz B., and Steven Jaffee. 2008. "Barrier, Catalyst, or Distraction? Standards, Competitiveness, and Africa's Groundnut Exports to Europe." Agriculture and Rural Development Discussion Paper 39, World Bank, Washington, DC.

Disdier, Anne-Célia, Lionel Fontagné, and Mondher Mimouni. 2008. "The Impact of Regulations on Agricultural Trade: Evidence from the SPS and TBT Agreements." *American Journal of Agricultural Economics* 90 (2): 336–50.

Doherty, Martin. 2008. "The Importance of Sanitary and Phytosanitary Measures to Fisheries Negotiations in Economic Partnership Agreements." ICTSD Issues Paper 7, International Centre for Trade and Sustainable Development, Geneva.

Drezner, Daniel W. 2006. "The Race to the Bottom Hypothesis: An Empirical and Theoretical Review." Fletcher School, Tufts University, Medford, MA. http://www.danieldrezner.com/policy/RTBreview.doc.

European Commission. 2000. *Guide to the Implementation of Directives Based on the New Approach and the Global Approach.* Luxembourg: Office for Official Publications of the European Communities. http://ec.europa.eu/enterprise/newapproach/legislation/guide/index.htm.

———. 2001. "Implementing Policy for External Trade in the Fields of Standards and Conformity Assessment: A Tool Box of Instruments." Commission Staff Working Paper SEC(2001)1570, European Commission, Brussels.

Fleiss, Barbara, Frederic Gonzales, and Raymond Schonfeld. 2008. "Technical Barriers to Trade: Evaluating the Effects of Supplier's Declaration of Conformity." Trade Policy Working Paper 78, Organisation for Economic Co-operation and Development, Paris.

Gandal, Neil, and Oz Shy. 2000. "Standardization Policy and International Trade." *Journal of International Economics* 53 (2): 363–83.

Ganslandt, Mattias, and James R. Markusen. 2001. "Standards and Related Regulations in International Trade: A Modeling Approach." NBER Working Paper 8346, National Bureau of Economic Research, Cambridge, MA.

Hahn, Robert W., and Robert E. Litan. 2005. "Counting Regulatory Benefits and Costs: Lessons for the US and Europe." *Journal of International Economic Law* 8 (2): 473–508.

Helble, Matthias, Ben Shepherd, and John S. Wilson. 2007. *Transparency and Trade Facilitation in the Asia-Pacific: Estimating the Gains from Reform.* Canberra: Department of Foreign Affairs and Trade.

Henry de Frahan, Bruno, and Mark Vancauteren. 2006. "Harmonization of Food Regulations and Trade in the Single Market: Evidence from Disaggregated Data." *European Review of Agricultural Economics* 33 (3): 337–60.

Henson, Spencer, and Steve Jaffee. 2007. "Public and Private Food Safety Standards: Compliance Costs and Strategic Opportunities." World Bank Institute, Washington, DC.

Horn, Henrik, Petros C. Mavroidis, and André Sapir. 2010. "Beyond the WTO? An Anatomy of EU and US Preferential Trade Agreements." *World Economy* 33 (11): 1565–88.

ISO (International Organization for Standardization). 2006. *Metrology, Standardization, and Conformity Assessment: Building an Infrastructure for Sustainable Development.* Geneva: ISO.

———. 2008. *Fast Forward: National Standards Bodies in Developing Countries.* Geneva: ISO.

Jaffee, Steven. 2003. "From Challenge to Opportunity: Transforming Kenya's Fresh Vegetable Trade in the Context of Emerging Food Safety and Other Standards in Europe." Agriculture and Rural Development Discussion Paper 1, World Bank, Washington, DC.

Jones, Philip, and John Hudson. 1996. "Standardization and the Costs of Assessing Quality." *European Journal of Political Economy* 12 (2): 355–61.

Kono, Daniel. 2006. "Optimal Obfuscation: Democracy and Trade Policy Transparency." *American Political Science Review* 100 (3): 369–84.

Lesser, Caroline. 2007. "Do Bilateral and Regional Approaches for Reducing Technical Barriers to Trade Converge towards the Multilateral Trade System?" OECD Trade Working Paper 58, TAD/TC/WP(2007)12/FINAL, Organisation for Economic Co-operation and Development, Paris.

Maertens, Miet, and Johan F. Swinnen. 2009. "Trade Standards and Poverty: Evidence from Senegal." *World Development* 37 (1): 161–78.

Maskus, Keith, Tsunehiro Otsuki, and John S. Wilson. 2000. "Quantifying the Impact of Technical Barriers to Trade: A Framework for Analysis." Policy Research Working Paper 2512, World Bank, Washington, DC. http://go.worldbank.org/FS4JCCSV10.

———. 2005. "The Cost of Compliance with Product Standards for Firms in Developing Countries: An Econometric Study." Policy Research Working Paper 3590, World Bank, Washington, DC. http://www-wds.worldbank.org/servlet/WDSContentServer/WDSP/IB/2005/05/15/000090341_20050515133900/Rendered/PDF/wps3590.pdf.

Maur, Jean-Christophe. 2005. "Exporting Europe's Trade Policy." *World Economy* 28 (11): 1565–90.

Meyer, Nico, Tamas Fenyes, Martin Breitenbach, and Ernst Idsardi. 2010. "Bilateral and Regional Trade Agreements and Technical Barriers to Trade: An African Perspective." OECD Trade Policy Working Papers 96, Organisation for International Co-operation and Development, Paris.

Moenius, Johannes. 2005. "Information versus Product Adaptation: The Role of Standards in Trade." University of Redlands, Redlands, CA. http://ssrn.com/abstract=608022.

———. 2007. "Do National Standards Hinder or Promote Trade in Electrical Products?" University of Redlands, Redlands, CA. http://www.iecchallenge.org/papers/pdf_iecchallenge/moenius.pdf.

Nicolaïdis, Kalypso. 2001. "Harmonisation and Recognition: What Have We Learned?" In *Trade and Regulatory Reform: Insights from Country Experience.* Paris: Organisation for Economic Co-operation and Development.

Nicolaïdis, Kalypso, and Michelle Egan. 2001. "Transnational Market Governance and Regional Policy Externality: Why Recognize Foreign Standards?" *Journal of European Public Policy* 8 (3): 454–73.

Nicolaïdis, Kalypso, and Gregory Shaffer. 2005. "Managed Mutual Recognition Regimes: Governance without Global Government." *Law and Contemporary Problems* 68: 263–318.

Nofal, Beatriz. 2004. "Constructing a Deeper Integration in MERCOSUR." Background paper for *Global Economic Prospects 2005*, World Bank, Washington, DC.

Otsuki, Tsunehiro, John S. Wilson, and Mirvat Sewadeh. 2001. "What Price Precaution? European Harmonization of Aflatoxin Regulations and African Food Exports." *European Review of Agricultural Economics* 28 (3): 263–84.

Sanetra, Clemens, and Rocío M. Marbán. 2007. "The Answer to the Global Quality Challenge: A National Quality Infrastructure." Organization of American States, Washington, DC; International Trade Centre, Geneva; Physikalisch-Technische Bundesanstalt, Braunschweig. http://www.ptb.de/en/org/q/q5/docs/OAS_EN07.pdf.

Shepherd, Ben. 2006. "The EU Standards Database: Overview and User Guide." World Bank, Washington, DC. http://siteresources.worldbank.org/INTRES/Resources/469232-1107449512766/EUSDB_Overview_UserGuide_021306.pdf.

———. 2007. "Product Standards, Harmonization, and Trade: Evidence from the Extensive Margin." Policy Research Working Paper 4390, World Bank, Washington, DC.

Swann, Peter, Paul Temple, and Mark Shurmer. 1996. "Standards and Trade Performance: The UK Experience." *Economic Journal* 106 (438): 1297–1313.

Trachtman, Joel P. 2003. "Towards Open Recognition? Standardization and Regional Integration under Article XXIV of GATT." *Journal of International Economic Law* 6 (2): 459–92. http://jiel.oxfordjournals.org/cgi/reprint/6/2/459.

Veggeland, Frode, and Christel Elvestad. 2004. "Equivalence and Mutual Recognition in Trade Arrangements: Relevance for the WTO and the Codex Alimentarius Commission." NILF-Report 2004-9, Norwegian Agricultural Economics Research Institute, Oslo.

World Bank. 2008. *Overcoming Trade Barriers from Standards and Technical Regulations.* Policy Research Report, East Asia and Pacific Region Poverty and Economic Management. Washington, DC: World Bank.

WTO (World Trade Organization). 2005. *World Trade Report 2005: Trade, Standards and the WTO.* Pt. 2. Geneva: WTO. http://www.wto.org/english/res_e/publications_e/wtr05_e.htm.

11

TBT AND SPS MEASURES, IN PRACTICE

Andrew L. Stoler

In recent years, the number of technical regulations and standards adopted by countries has grown significantly. More stringent regulatory policy can be seen as impelled by higher standards of living worldwide, which have boosted consumers' demand for safe, high-quality goods, and by growing problems of water, air, and soil pollution that have encouraged modern societies to explore environmentally friendly products.

Measures related to technical barriers to trade (TBTs) and to sanitary and phytosanitary (SPS) standards and regulation have become important dimensions of preferential trade agreements (PTAs) (see Maur and Shepherd, ch. 10 in this volume). Governments seek to act through their PTAs, as well as through the World Trade Organization (WTO), to protect human, animal, or plant life or health. Such efforts are within WTO guidelines, provided that they are not discriminatory and that regulations and standards are not used as disguised protectionism. In a number of instances, PTA members seek to go beyond the broad rules-based approach followed in the WTO and to reduce differences in national standards and certification processes that impede trade.

There are, broadly, two models for dealing with standards measures in PTAs. Where the European Union (EU) is a party to a PTA, the agreement often calls for the partner country to harmonize its national standards and conformity assessment procedures with those of the EU. PTAs in the Asia-Pacific region and those in which the United States is a partner typically seek to address problems resulting from different national standards and conformity procedures through a preference for international standards or through the use of mutual recognition mechanisms.

Both approaches can be successful in reducing the negative impact of a multiplicity of standards and conformity assessment procedures. There is, however, a risk that they can introduce de facto discrimination in global markets, particularly against developing countries, because achieving conformity in technical standards requires capacity and resources.

This chapter looks at the experience of representative PTAs with TBT and SPS provisions, with a view to identifying common characteristics of, and differences between, their basic approaches to standards.

Standards and International Trade

The aims of SPS regulations and standards are to protect human beings or animals from risks arising from additives, contaminants, toxins, and disease-causing organisms in their food; to protect human life from plant- or animal-carried diseases; to protect animal or plant life from pests, diseases, or disease-causing organisms; and to prevent or limit other damage to a country from the entry, establishment, or spread of pests.[1]

TBT technical regulations and standards set out specific characteristics of a product, such as its size, shape, design, functions, and performance, or the way it is labeled or packaged before it is put on sale. In certain cases, how a product is made can affect these characteristics, and it may then prove more appropriate to draft technical regulations and standards on the basis of process and production methods rather than of the product's characteristics per se.

In all the PTAs reviewed in this chapter, members use the PTA to go beyond what is achievable through the multilateral instruments of the WTO (box 11.1). They appear to recognize that only by avoiding a situation in

---

Box 11.1. WTO Standards and Guidelines on TBT and SPS Measures

Article XX of the General Agreement on Tariffs and Trade (GATT) allows governments to enact trade measures to protect human, animal, or plant life or health, provided that the provisions do not discriminate and are not used as disguised protectionism. In addition, two specific World Trade Organization agreements deal with food safety, animal and plant health and safety, and product standards in general. Both seek to identify how to meet the need for standards and at the same time avoid protectionism in disguise. These issues are becoming more important as tariff barriers fall.

The WTO Agreement on the Application of Sanitary and Phytosanitary Measures (the SPS Agreement) lays out the basic rules on food safety and on animal and plant health standards. It allows countries to set their own standards, but it stipulates that regulations must be based on science and should be applied only to the extent necessary to protect human, animal, or plant life or health. Furthermore, such regulations should not arbitrarily or unjustifiably discriminate between countries where identical or similar conditions prevail. Member countries are encouraged to use international standards, guidelines, and recommendations where these exist. When this practice is followed, the measures are unlikely to be challenged legally in a WTO dispute. Members, however, may impose measures that result in higher standards if there is scientific justification; they may set higher standards on the basis of appropriate assessment of risks, so long as the approach is consistent and not arbitrary; and they can, to some extent, apply the "precautionary principle"—a kind of safety-first approach—to deal with scientific uncertainty.

The agreement allows countries to use different standards and different methods of inspecting products. If an exporting country can demonstrate that the measures it applies to its exports achieve the same level of health protection as in the importing country, the importing country is expected to accept the exporting country's standards and methods. The SPS Agreement includes provisions on control, inspection, and approval procedures. Governments must provide advance notice of new or changed sanitary and phytosanitary regulations and establish a national enquiry point to provide information. The agreement complements the WTO Agreement on Technical Barriers to Trade (the TBT Agreement).

The TBT Agreement seeks to ensure that technical regulations, standards, and testing and certification procedures do not create unnecessary obstacles. The agreement does recognize countries' rights to adopt the standards they consider appropriate—for example, to protect human, animal, or plant life or health; to safeguard the environment; or to meet other consumer interests. Furthermore, members are not prevented from taking measures necessary to ensure that their standards are met. But the agreement also lays down disciplines. A myriad of regulations can be a nightmare for manufacturers and exporters. Life can be simpler if governments apply international standards, and the agreement encourages them to do so. In any case, whatever regulations countries use should not discriminate. The agreement also sets out a code of good practice for both governments and nongovernmental or industry bodies in preparing, adopting, and applying voluntary standards, and more than 200 standards-setting bodies use this code. Under the agreement, the procedures used to decide whether a product conforms with relevant standards have to be fair and equitable, and any methods that would give domestically produced goods an unfair advantage are discouraged.

The agreement also encourages countries to recognize each other's procedures for assessing whether a product conforms. Without recognition, products might have to be tested twice, first by the exporting country and then by the importing country. Manufacturers and exporters need to know what the latest standards are in their prospective markets, and, to ensure that this information is made available conveniently, all WTO member governments are required to establish national enquiry points and to keep each other informed through the WTO. About 900 new or changed regulations are notified each year. The Technical Barriers to Trade Committee is the main clearinghouse for sharing information among members and the primary forum for discussing concerns about the regulations and their implementation.

Source: World Trade Organization documents, http://www.wto.org.

---

which producers have to manufacture to different standards in different national markets, or have to test the same product repeatedly, will the parties be able to foster more deep-seated economic integration.

PTAs that include TBT and SPS provisions normally incorporate an active work program of cooperation on standards, certification, and conformity assessment issues. This produces a stronger economic development focus, in contrast to the way these issues are treated in WTO agreements. The latter are designed to set standards and guidelines, whereas the PTAs examined here go beyond that objective to contribute to economic integration through the phased elimination of standards-related barriers. Some of the most ambitious PTAs in this regard are South-South

agreements among developing countries; these include the Association of Southeast Asian Nations (ASEAN) and the Southern Cone Common Market (Mercosur, or Mercado Común del Sur).

There are different models for dealing with the elimination of the employment of TBT and SPS measures as trade barriers in PTAs. In PTAs involving the EU, there is a strong preference for harmonization of standards and for conformity assessment procedures. As a trade-off, the EU typically supports, both technically and financially, significant technical assistance programs to assist developing-country partners with the harmonization effort. When the EU concludes an agreement with more distant countries, such as Chile, there is not normally an obligation to harmonize completely with EU standards and procedures; instead, the agreement calls for the promotion and use of both EU and international standards.

Agreements concluded among Asian countries and those involving the participation of the United States take a different approach from that of the EU. Rather than require harmonization, these PTAs typically seek to facilitate mutual recognition agreements and approaches based on equivalence of different approaches in different countries. The U.S. PTAs normally include the establishment of a committee charged with addressing TBT measures or SPS rules that are seen to be creating trade problems.

In chapter 10 in this volume, Maur and Shepherd observe that it is unclear which advantages each model may or may not yield and that any judgment as to which model is superior may well depend on the particular partner country and the similarity of regulatory preferences. In the sections that follow, the main features of TBT and SPS provisions in 11 representative PTAs are reviewed, taking first North-North PTAs and then North-South and South-South agreements. Experience with the cost of implementing TBT and SPS measures and the role of technical assistance are then discussed. Table 11.1 provides a summary of the main features of the 11 agreements with respect to TBT and SPS measures.

North-North PTAs: The Example of AUSFTA

As a benchmark for a discussion of North-South and South-South PTAs in the area of TBT and SPS measures,

this section briefly reviews the Australia–United States Free Trade Agreement (AUSFTA) as illustrative of North-North PTAs.

After relatively brief negotiations, the AUSFTA entered into force in 2005. The agreement was not the outcome of an attempt to solve any significant trade issues between the two countries; rather, it was seen by both Canberra and Washington as a demonstration of how two like-minded developed countries could move ahead with significant trade liberalization in a period when multilateral progress in the Doha Round was stalled. That said, both U.S. and Australian exporters did face some difficulties with SPS measures in their bilateral export markets, and it was natural to build into the agreement provisions addressed to both SPS and TBTs.

Both Australia and the United States accepted as the basis for their obligations the provisions of the WTO SPS and TBT Agreements. The chapters of the agreement build on these basic obligations by establishing bilateral institutions and procedures designed to further facilitate trade between the parties.

Chapter 7 of the AUSFTA establishes a bilateral committee with a mandate of facilitating bilateral information exchange and bilateral consultations on SPS measures that could affect bilateral trade; on technical cooperation activities and issues; and on positions and agendas in multilateral SPS forums, including the WTO's SPS Committee. The committee is supplemented by a Standing Technical Working Group on Animal and Plant Health Measures. The mandate of the working group includes resolving specific

Table 11.1. Comparison of Main Features Relating to TBT and SPS Measures, 11 PTAs

PTA	Use of international standards	"Living agreement" institutions	Provisions on TBT issues	Provisions on SPS issues	WTO+ transparency	Technical assistance provisions	Binding with dispute settlement
ASEAN Trade in Goods Agreement (ATIGA)	Yes	Yes	Yes	Yes	Yes	Unclear	Yes
Australia–United States FTA (AUSFTA)	Yes	Yes	Yes	Yes	Yes	No	Not for SPS
Chile–China	Unclear	Yes	Yes	Yes	Unclear	No	Yes
Chile–United States	Yes	Yes	Yes	Yes	Yes	No	Not for SPS
China–New Zealand	Yes	Yes	Yes	Yes	Yes	Yes	Yes
EU–Chile	Yes	Yes	Yes	Yes	No	Yes	No
EU–Morocco	Yes	Yes	Yes	Yes	No	Yes	No
EU–South Africa TDCA	Yes	Yes	Yes	Yes	No	Yes	No
Mercosur	Unclear	Yes	Yes	Yes	Unclear	No	Yes
Singapore–Australia FTA (SAFTA)	Yes	Yes	Yes	Yes	Yes	No	Yes
Thailand–Australia FTA (TAFTA)	Yes	Yes	Yes	Yes	No	Yes	Not for SPS

Source: Author's compilation.
Note: ASEAN, Association of Southeast Asian Nations; FTA, free trade agreement; PTA, preferential trade agreement; SPS, sanitary and phytosanitary; TBT, technical barriers to trade; TDCA, Trade and Development Cooperation Agreement.

SPS issues, engaging in bilateral scientific and technical exchange on risk assessment and regulatory processes, and considering measures relating to SPS that affect or are likely to affect bilateral trade. The working group is also to establish specific work plans to address any SPS issues in the bilateral relationship.

The TBT chapter of the PTA differs from the SPS chapter in that it creates TBT chapter coordinators that are responsible for coordinating TBT matters with the other party and for consulting with the other side should a TBT issue arise in the bilateral relationship. Where an issue cannot be resolved through the efforts of the coordinators, the PTA provides for the establishment of ad hoc technical working groups charged with identifying workable and practical solutions that would facilitate trade.

The parties to the agreement obligate themselves to use relevant international standards to the extent provided in the WTO Agreement and to give positive consideration to accepting as equivalent the technical regulations and conformity assessment procedures of the other party. The transparency provisions of the WTO Agreement are backed up by bilateral TBT notification obligations.

According to Article 7.2.2 of the agreement, the entire SPS chapter is off-limits with respect to dispute settlement action. Thus, although the SPS provisions impose a kind of "best-efforts" obligation on the parties, they are not binding over the longer term. A different approach is taken in the TBT chapter; only one article addressed to technical regulations (Article 8.5) is exempt from recourse to dispute settlement. This implies that the remainder of the chapter—in particular, its obligations regarding conformity assessment and transparency—are legally binding on the parties and that this binding nature applies in both the short and long terms.

The provisions of the AUSFTA have been fully implemented with respect to TBT and SPS measures. Implementation, however, has not been problem free. U.S. exporters now enjoy relatively uninhibited (in terms of quarantine restrictions) access to the Australian market for stone fruit, table grapes, and citrus fruit, but this access has not put an end to U.S. complaints about the overly restrictive nature of Australian quarantine measures at the WTO SPS Committee.[2] For its part, Australia still complains about the effect of certain American SPS measures on its exports.

North-South PTAs

The impact on international trade of the need to comply with different foreign technical regulations and standards may be more significant in the case of "asymmetrical" North-South agreements where one party is economically dominant. Meeting TBT and SPS regulations and standards in those circumstances could involve significant costs for producers and exporters located in the less developed country. These costs typically arise from the translation of foreign regulations, the hiring of technical experts to explain foreign regulations, and the adjustment of production facilities to comply with the requirements. In addition, there is the need to prove that the exported product meets the foreign regulations. The high costs involved may discourage manufacturers from trying to sell abroad. In the absence of international disciplines, a risk exists that technical regulations and standards could be adopted and applied solely to protect domestic industries.

The remainder of this section reviews the treatment of TBT and SPS provisions in seven PTAs representative of the variety of North-South agreements: EU–Morocco, EU–Chile, EU–South Africa, Singapore–Australia, Thailand–Australia, Chile–United States, and China–New Zealand.

EU–Morocco: A Euro-Mediterranean Agreement

The EU–Morocco PTA is representative of the approach to TBT and SPS provisions in the Euro-Mediterranean agreements. The agreement action program is aimed at eliminating trade barriers associated with standards and conformity assessment. It obliges the parties to the PTA to take appropriate steps to promote the use by Morocco of EU technical rules and EU standards for industrial and agricultural products and certification procedures. A system of accreditation of conformity assessment procedures based on international and EU standards is also foreseen for Moroccan adoption. A separate mutual recognition agreement (MRA), the Agreement on Conformity Assessment and Acceptance of Industrial Products, is intended to implement this aspect of the PTA (Lesser 2007).

In 2003, at the Palermo Euro-Med ministerial meeting, Euro-Med participants agreed to address the approximation of legislation in the field of standards, technical regulations, and conformity assessment procedures, through a six-point program.[3] That program calls for

- Identifying priority sectors
- Building acquaintance with applicable EU legislation and conducting a gap analysis
- Transposing necessary framework legislation and sectoral legislation
- Creating or reforming institutions
- Setting up necessary certification and conformity assessment bodies
- Identifying technical assistance needs.

Perhaps because of the gap between the two countries' relative levels of economic development, it has been difficult for Morocco to harmonize its standards with those of the EU or even to develop acceptable approaches to the development of mutual recognition agreements. A 2007 document of the Moroccan government comprehensively lays out the steps that Morocco needs to take to realize the objectives of the 2005 EU–Morocco Plan of Action, which covers a period of three to five years.[4] Among the actions deemed necessary in the short term are the reinforcement of local institutions charged with standardization, conformity assessment, metrology, and market surveillance. The document notes that it will be particularly important for Morocco to reinforce its conformity assessment structures and guarantee their competence in areas covered by regulation. Although it is clear from both the 2007 government paper and the action plan that harmonizing national standards with EU and international standards remains an important medium-term goal, there is little evidence that Morocco has as yet been successful in these efforts.

Working with representatives of Moroccan industry and the Commerce and Industry Ministry, the Moroccan Office of Standardisation and Quality Promotion has identified a number of priority sectors for the conclusion of conformity assessment recognition agreements with the EU. The choice of priority sectors (electrical appliances, construction machinery, and building products) stemmed partly from a desire to ensure that certain products were safe to use in the Moroccan market and partly from knowledge of where national testing capacity is already in place in the country.[5]

The EU has worked to support Morocco through technical assistance. A document of the Directorate General for Trade lists 53 instances of SPS-related technical assistance provided to Morocco during the period 2001–05.[6] But although this assistance has undoubtedly been helpful, Morocco faces other important problems in selling its products on the EU market.

A major problem relates to the increasing need for producers and exporters to meet private quality control standards in the EU, many of which differ greatly from one member state market to another. For instance, a 2005 World Bank case study notes that producers and exporters of citrus and tomatoes have to meet six different quality control standards: of these, two are recognized worldwide, three are European retailers' individual standards, and one relates to organic and biodynamic standards (Aloui and Kenny 2005). Just how much the machinery of the PTA can help Moroccan exporters in areas like this is unclear. Furthermore, compliance has proved not only technically difficult, but also costly (see "Implementation Costs and Technical Assistance Needs," below).

EU–Chile Free Trade Agreement

The EU–Chile Free Trade Agreement (FTA) is representative of a looser EU approach to TBT and SPS standards and regulations. Here, the focus is on the use of technical regulations and conformity assessment procedures based on international standards, unless those standards are judged to be ineffective or inappropriate for fulfilling legitimate objectives. The parties also agree to work toward compatibility or equivalence of their respective technical regulations, standards, and conformity assessment procedures, and the agreement establishes a special committee on these matters. The committee has identified the need for a technical assistance program and has launched such a program, funded by the EU.

The special committee is cochaired by Chile and the EU. Its work program aims at

- Monitoring and reviewing the implementation and administration of the TBT chapter of the agreement
- Providing a forum for discussing and exchanging information on any matter related to the TBT chapter, in particular as it relates to the parties' systems for technical regulations, standards, and conformity assessment procedures, as well as developments in related international organizations
- Providing a forum for consultation and prompt resolution of issues that act or can act as unnecessary barriers to trade
- Encouraging, promoting, and otherwise facilitating cooperation between the parties' organizations, whether public or private, for metrology, standardization, testing, certification, inspection, and accreditation
- Exploring any means for improving access to the parties' respective markets and enhancing the functioning of the TBT chapter.

The committee has met regularly. According to a joint communiqué issued following the seventh meeting, held in 2009, "the overall working of the committee was considered highly satisfactory by the parties."[7]

Information about the details of the agendas and the results of the meetings of the committee is not readily available. A specific working group on animal welfare was established in 2003 by the Joint Management Committee for SPS, with the aim of achieving the objectives of SPS provisions in the EU–Chile PTA. According to the information available, this working group has developed its activities on the basis of an annual action plan that has been agreed jointly. At the beginning, it was focused on practices relating to the stunning and slaughter of animals. In 2006 both parties decided to incorporate animal transport as a new issue to work on in the context of the agreement (Benavides and Jerez 2007). The European Commission approved a financial contribution to a maximum amount of 35,000 euros for the organization of an international seminar on animal welfare in the framework of the PTA. A series of seminars grew out of conclusions reached in the working group on how better to reach the objectives of the agreement through exchange of information on scientific expertise and the establishment of active contacts between scientists from both parties.[8]

An operational fund was established to facilitate the implementation of the EU–Chile Association Agreement. Five of 13 projects covered by these funds involved TBT and SPS issues. These were related to

- International traceability and comparability of chemical measurements and supervision of market risk for the main exported food products
- Creation of a Web site on Chilean and European technical regulation, including the EU's environmental and quality requirements
- Requirements of standards and conformity assessment in the EU market
- Harmonization of SPS regulations
- A project to establish mutual recognition of testing standards by Chile's farming and stockbreeding service (Servicio Agrícola y Ganadero) and by agricultural laboratories in the EU.

The benefits of these projects have been recognized by Chilean and EU authorities. For instance, Chile created a Web site, "Chile–UE: Requerimientos de Mercado, Más Información Mejores Negocios," that was expected to facilitate trade through improved transparency relating to technical and environmental regulations in both Chile and the EU and through the reduction of the costs of access to the information.[9]

Another good example of the progress achieved in the context of this operational fund is related to the international traceability and comparability of chemical measurements and supervision of market risk for the most important exported food products. Advances here have contributed to the international recognition of Chile's Center of Chemical Metrology and are expected to benefit Chilean export sectors.[10]

Finally, it is important to note an observation in Annex 2, on policy coherence analysis, of the EU–Chile country strategy paper for 2007–13:

> The EU/Chile Association Agreement represents the most ambitious FTA that the EU has signed with a third party up to now. A similar level of ambition should be pursued in harnessing the potential created by the Agreement for expanding EU interests into the surrounding countries. Full use should be made of the action agreed and cooperation tools envisaged, particularly in the following areas: ....[11]

It appears that Chile has, to some extent, been caught in a bind resulting from differing obligations in the PTAs it has concluded with the EU and the United States. The passage continues, concerning standards and technical regulations:

> The EU observed with concern a marked tendency for the Chilean standardisation process to incorporate solely a reference to the US standards, particularly when no agreed international standards exist. The immediate effect of such behaviour is to divert trade to imports of non-EU origin or to give rise to additional costs to adapt products made in the EU. The EU will focus on increased cooperation and pay political attention to the promotion of international standards, or in their absence, to double recognition of both US and EU norms. Such an approach should be followed, in particular, for new technologies where the EU local value added is still prominent.

On SPS, the annex adds:

> In the sanitary and phytosanitary area the objectives are to implement the EC/Chile SPS Agreement fully and effectively. The EU's potential to export food products and semi-processed agricultural products in order to complete the national product range on offer should be supported by smooth SPS administration.

EU–South Africa Trade and Development Cooperation Agreement

The 1999 EU–South Africa Trade and Development Cooperation Agreement (TDCA) is another illustration of the EU's approach to TBT and SPS standardization and conformity assessment, this time in a low-income country. Under the agreement, the parties pledge to cooperate on

- Measures, in accordance with the provisions of the WTO TBT Agreement, to promote greater use of international technical regulations, standards, and conformity assessment procedures, including sector-specific measures
- Development of agreements on mutual recognition of conformity assessment in sectors of mutual economic interest
- Cooperation in the area of quality management and assurance in selected sectors of importance to South Africa
- Facilitation of technical assistance for Southern African capacity-building initiatives in the fields of accreditation, metrology, and standardization

- Development of practical links between South African and European standardization, accreditation, and certification organizations.[12]

In comparison with other agreements signed by the EU—for instance, the EU–Chile Association Agreement—the TDCA is less ambitious in the TBT and SPS areas. In fact, there is just one provision on TBTs that appears in the section related to other trade-related matters, while SPS is referred to in the general provisions on agriculture (Article 61) within the section on economic cooperation.

There is no ready evidence on the extent to which implementation of TBT and SPS provisions has been achieved. According to an official communication from the European Commission, it became clear to the Commission that TBT and SPS provisions were not being implemented fully when it recognized that bilateral cooperation on some topics, including SPS, was mostly limited and ad hoc. In addition, the Commission pointed out,

> As regards the provisions that have not been implemented yet, there seems to be a strong interest in deepening cooperation in the following areas: trade and related-trade areas, intellectual property rights, customs, competition policy, regional policy, *sanitary and phytosanitary measures, technical barriers to trade, . . .* (italics added)[13]

This situation seems to explain the initial interest in including both TBT and SPS issues in the TDCA review.[14] According to another European Commission communication, the parties should consider a new orientation and possible revision of the TDCA.[15] The Commission identified some provisions in the PTA that might need to be amended. In effect, it suggested new commitments and enhanced cooperation in trade-related areas and mentioned, among other articles, Article 47, which is related to standardization and conformity assessment.

The communication suggested, concerning a revision of the economic cooperation text: "updated wording must be considered for cooperation in the fields of energy, transport, agriculture and *sanitary and phyto-sanitary matters*" (italics added). On SPS, said the communication, a more substantial change was recommended because SPS measures had become "an important impediment to trade and therefore required enhanced cooperation."

The negotiations on an agreement amending the TDCA, which started formally in 2007, did not in the end include negotiations on trade and trade-related matters. In a European Commission communication concerning a proposal for an EU–South African agreement amending the TDCA, it was acknowledged that

From the start of the negotiations it was clear that all trade and trade-related issues would be discussed in the context of the talks on the future Economic Partnership Agreement (EPA) with the countries of Southern Africa. The TDCA negotiations on trade and trade-related matters were therefore immediately suspended, pending the outcome of the EPA talks.[16]

Trade and trade-related issues seem to be handled more effectively under the EPA between the EU and the Southern African Development Community (SADC). According to a trade cooperation report, "the revision of the trade chapter of the TDCA continued to be dealt with within the framework of the negotiations for an EU–SADC [EPA]."[17]

The EU's interest seems to be to try to achieve meaningful coexistence between the TDCA and the EU–SADC EPA. That, however, may take longer than expected because the regional context in southern Africa is particularly complex. In general terms, it is known that the EPA's objectives are to develop a more predictable and rules-based regional market for goods and services with a view toward fostering regional integration; to harmonize trade rules within the region; and to create a simple trading framework between the countries of southern Africa and the EU.

In the relationship between the SADC, the Southern African Customs Union (SACU), and the TDCA, a number of issues appear to require urgent attention. At the Second South Africa–EU Summit, it was noted,

> The experience of the EU is witness to the benefit of strong regional integration. We recognise that the Regional Economic Communities (RECs) are key pillars for deeper integration in Africa and therefore support greater political cohesion and stronger economic integration in [SACU and the SADC].
>
> In this context, we engaged in a frank and open discussion on the EU–SADC Economic Partnership Agreement and on the implications that these negotiations, at all its stages, have on current processes of regional integration in Southern Africa. We agreed to urgently pursue the negotiation and resolution of all outstanding issues with a view to a prompt and mutually satisfactory conclusion that supports regional integration and development in Southern Africa.[18]

Cooperation on SPS measures is one of the areas explicitly identified as a priority for treatment in the joint action plan of the EU–South Africa Strategic Partnership, established May 14, 2007.[19] This inclusion is important because the joint action plan and the TDCA constitute the groundwork for enhanced and deepened political dialogue and cooperation.

The trade cooperation report mentioned above contains a section on SPS matters. Within it, both parties express their commitment to conduct "open and transparent collaboration and communication" and "to avoid or minimise trade obstacles in the future." This commitment followed an earlier South African ban on imports of EU meat. During early 2009, close contacts between both parties continued, with a view to ensuring SPS protection and doing so in "a way, which prevents any undue trade restrictions between the EU and SA." The report points out that

> the European Commission continued to extend SPS training opportunities to the competent South African authorities. For example, on 25–27 November 2008, a regional training workshop was held in Johannesburg on EU legislation for Bovine Spongiform Encephalopathy (BSE). The South African authorities were also invited to participate in a training course in Austria on 2–5 March 2009 for veterinarians at border inspection posts at airports. An invitation has also been extended to a forthcoming training programme for laboratory experts in the area of aflatoxins/ochratoxins. Another meeting on food analysis will take place in Munich on 3–14 August 2009.[20]

The EU also funded a South Africa Pesticide Initiative Program (SA PIP), which, although related to SPS matters, was developed in the context of the private sector development program. It was reported that the program has had good results:

> The South Africa Pesticide Initiative Program (SA PIP) has successfully hosted training workshops throughout the years, disseminating information to emerging farmers; grower associations and various stakeholders. . . . The Programme's two main focus areas are to assist exporting producers to comply with the EU's legal food safety requirements; and to support and develop emerging farmers through training and empowerment initiatives, and so to grow the South African export volume destined for Europe.[21]

Within the context of the TDCA framework, South Africa and the EU jointly developed a country strategy paper (CSP) and a European Commission multiannual indicative program (MIP) for the period 2007–13. At least 5 percent of this 980 million euro funding allocation will go toward supporting a TDCA facility program. A development cooperation report indicates that the EU will contribute 5 million euros to the project, to help with the implementation of the TDCA and the joint action plan.[22]

Singapore–Australia Free Trade Agreement

The Singapore–Australia Free Trade Agreement (SAFTA), signed in 2003, was Australia's first PTA since the conclusion of an agreement with neighboring New Zealand 20 years earlier. (Singapore, by contrast, was already one of

the most active negotiators of PTAs at the time.) The bilateral relationship underlying this PTA is significant both economically and politically, and each party had something to offer the other through additional liberalization. In particular, through a process of annual reviews, the agreement has helped considerably to facilitate trade between Australia and Singapore, including trade affected by TBT and SPS measures, as exemplified by the Sectoral Annex on Horticultural Goods (box 11.2).

The TBT and SPS chapter of SAFTA builds on an earlier bilateral mutual recognition agreement on conformity assessment. The chapter includes best-efforts obligations on harmonization of mandatory requirements, acceptance of the equivalence of each other's mandatory requirements, and cooperation on SPS questions that might arise in the bilateral relationship. The core purposive policy in this PTA is found in its provisions related to the negotiation of sectoral annexes, which are, in effect, the implementing arrangements for the chapter. For SAFTA, the sectoral annexes are intended to resolve specific issues in the bilateral relationship over time.

The conformity assessment procedure has had effects in other market sectors. This includes the restriction on imports of cars that are more than three years old, a way of ensuring that Singaporean road safety standards are met. It is further illustrated by the removal of technical barriers to Australian electrical exports to Singapore. In the past, such goods had to be inspected and approved by two separate Singaporean agencies before they could be approved for sale. Since the implementation of SAFTA, Singapore recognizes Australian conformity assessment procedures.[23]

Box 11.2. Success Story: Orchids to Australia

The Sectoral Annex on Horticultural Goods of the Singapore–Australia Free Trade Agreement establishes the concept of "accredited exporter," defined as "an exporter of the scheduled horticultural goods who has demonstrated to its regulatory authority that it possesses the necessary technical capabilities, management competence, facilities, equipment and production systems required to meet the mandatory requirements of the importing Party." In an early success story, Australia and Singapore agreed that Australia will minimize import control and inspection and approval procedures when orchids shipped by accredited Singaporean exporters are accompanied by the required certificates and reports. Other horticultural goods are similarly subject to reduced import control, and goods can be added to the coverage of the annex by mutual agreement of the SAFTA parties.

Sources: "Singapore-Australia Free Trade Agreement (SAFTA)—A Business Guide" (http://www.dfat.gov.au/trade/negotiations/safta/ch3_safta_guide.html), and SAFTA Annex 5-B, text (http://www.dfat.gov.au/ta/safta).

Although SAFTA's provisions are not very binding, as the obligations are nearly all of a best-efforts nature, the PTA has produced some worthwhile short-term results. In the longer term, the agreement is likely to progressively take on a more binding character, as sectoral annexes are negotiated and implemented to deal with specific issues and problems in bilateral trade. It is unlikely that the specific best-efforts obligations of SAFTA Chapter 05 could be the basis for a successful action under the PTA's own dispute settlement procedures. However, Article 10.1 of Chapter 05 makes it clear that implementing arrangements for the chapter are intended to be reflected in sectoral annexes with more operational legal content. Failure to abide by the terms of a negotiated sectoral annex would appear to give cause for invocation of the PTA's dispute settlement provisions. By their very nature, obligations under a sectoral annex could not be the cause for action under the WTO's Dispute Settlement Understanding (DSU) because they do not fit the definition of a "covered agreement."

Thailand–Australia Free Trade Agreement

The Thailand Australia Free Trade Agreement (TAFTA), which entered into force in 2005, resulted from a negotiation that was much more problematic than the Singapore–Australia negotiations. Given Thai resistance to hard-law obligations in many areas of the agreement, Australia was often willing to settle for looser language and weaker obligations. In a number of areas in which it proved too difficult to reach agreement, the two sides pledged to return to the negotiating table in 2008. Political issues have since interfered with that second stage of negotiations.

Against this background, it is not surprising that TAFTA incorporates a number of best-efforts obligations on the parties in respect of industrial standards, including obligations to endeavor to harmonize technical regulations and to give positive consideration to accepting as equivalent the technical regulations of the other party. For TBT matters, the parties agree to work together to resolve problems resulting from differing conformity assessment procedures and to share information through contact points established for the purpose. In the SPS area, obligations are more significant, and the parties have created a standing Expert Group on Sanitary and Phytosanitary Measures and Food Standards. This body is charged with consulting on requests for recognition of equivalence of SPS measures and promoting resolution of disputes that arise in connection with SPS measures. A unique and apparently valuable feature of the SPS chapter is its provision, in Article 607.4, for cooperation on a product trace-back system for notification of noncompliance of imported consignments for commodities subject to SPS measures.

In most important areas, TAFTA obligations do not take the form of binding hard law. Generally, the obligation is for best efforts. In addition, the fact that the SPS chapter is specifically excluded from recourse to the PTA's dispute settlement mechanism also loosens the binding nature of the PTA. Mandated, more binding, obligations exist in areas in which compliance are easiest, such as information sharing and cooperation on procedural questions.

By virtue of its Article 610:2, TAFTA's SPS provisions cannot give rise to invocation of the bilateral PTA's dispute settlement provisions. Part of the mandate of the SPS Expert Group, however, is "progressing resolution of disputes that arise in connection with the matters covered by this Chapter." The TBT chapter is silent on the question of dispute settlement, but its best-efforts obligations would be difficult to litigate successfully under most dispute resolution systems. In all likelihood, serious disputes between Australia and Thailand would need to be adjudicated under the WTO DSU.

Cooperation under the PTA has been unable to resolve Thailand's long-standing complaints about lack of access to the Australian poultry market. Australia cites concerns over infectious bursal disease virus (IBDV) as necessitating SPS measures that exclude the importation of fresh poultry. An Australian risk assessment procedure in 2006 has had the effect of making the Australian SPS measures more severe. Market access has improved with the implementation of TAFTA because of the utilization of TBT-related mechanisms designed to promote world best practices in transparency, quarantine, and industrial standards.[24]

Chile–United States Free Trade Agreement

Chile and the United States have long had one of the best economic and political bilateral relationships in the Western Hemisphere. Originally, the plan was for Chile to join the North American Free Trade Agreement (NAFTA), and there was strong support from both Mexico and Canada for this idea. Opposition from several quarters in the United States sidetracked that plan, and both Canada and Mexico negotiated separate bilateral PTAs with Chile before the United States and Chile sat down at the negotiating table. The PTA entered into force in 2004. Agricultural trade issues and quarantine questions are important to both parties in this agreement, and it is altogether natural that forums would be established through the PTA to address these issues.

The Chile–United States PTA relies on a living agreement approach to resolving SPS and TBT issues, in both cases establishing committees mandated to enhance mutual understanding, consult on matters related to the development and implementation of TBT and SPS matters, and coordinate technical cooperation programs. The SPS committee is also charged with reviewing progress on addressing SPS matters arising in the bilateral relationship. The TBT committee's responsibilities include consulting on matters that come up under the agreement, and where such consultations relate to a dispute between the parties, they constitute consultations for the purpose of the operation of the PTA dispute settlement chapter.

The PTA's TBT chapter also contains provisions designed to facilitate negotiations on recognition of conformity assessment procedures, and it enhances transparency over and above that provided through the multilateral TBT Agreement in the WTO.

The PTA affirms that the basic binding obligations of the parties are those of the WTO TBT and SPS Agreements. Instead of hard-core binding obligations, the PTA's provisions in these areas establish cooperative frameworks for discussion and resolution of problems that might arise in bilateral trade.

Recourse to the PTA dispute settlement provisions is not permitted for any matter that might arise under the SPS chapter, meaning that all serious SPS disputes would need to be dealt with only under the WTO DSU. Obligations under the TBT chapter could presumably be taken to the PTA-specific dispute settlement provisions, but hard obligations exist only with respect to transparency and national treatment in accreditation of conformity assessment bodies.

Discussions in the context of the PTA's SPS Committee reportedly led to the easing of Chilean SPS restrictions on citrus fruits, creating a new market opportunity for Sun Pacific Shippers Sales, a company that is now able to access the Chilean market in the off-season for citrus.[25] Similarly, the agreement allowed Chile to raise issues concerning plant registration in exportation, where a certification system has been established to address SPS matters.[26]

China–New Zealand Free Trade Agreement

In the Asia-Pacific region, China has been actively pursuing a program of negotiating PTAs with its main trading partners. Part of China's motivation for these agreements is to gain formal recognition from its partners of its market economy status, an acknowledgment that it sets as a precondition for the commencement of PTA negotiations. For China's partners, of course, the motivation is access to the huge Chinese market. In its negotiations with China, New Zealand was keenly aware that Australia was also negotiating a PTA with the Chinese. New Zealand won the race, and its PTA entered into force in 2008. SPS measures are a critically important trade concern in both China and New Zealand, so

it is not surprising that the chapters dealing with SPS and TBT matters in this PTA are more detailed than in some other agreements and that the PTA has an important proactive character.

The SPS chapter establishes a joint management committee charged with overseeing implementation of the chapter, with responsibilities that include drawing up for each party a priority order for consideration of market access requests by the other party, including the undertaking of risk analyses. Areas addressed in considerable detail include adaptation to regional conditions; the acceptance of the other party's measures as equivalent; verification, certification, and import check procedures; and a well-developed cooperation plan. Because the PTA entered into force relatively recently, China and New Zealand are still negotiating certain aspects of the implementing arrangements, but concrete results have already been achieved (box 11.3).

The PTA created a joint TBT committee to oversee implementation, identify priority sectors for enhanced cooperation, monitor the progress of work programs, and facilitate technical consultations. Other provisions in the TBT chapter favor the use of international standards, where possible, and the acceptance of each others' technical regulations and conformity assessment procedures. Provision is also made for regulatory cooperation in a number

Box 11.3. Impact of SPS Measures in the China–New Zealand PTA

In the Joint Report prepared by China and New Zealand on the occasion of the Two Year Review of the Free Trade Agreement, the Parties note that the following are among the arrangements concluded on new or improved market access:

- Arrangement on New Zealand Product Process Hygiene Requirements for Processing Edible Tripe Products for Export from New Zealand to the People's Republic of China;
- Cooperation Arrangement on Management of Sanitary Measures Regulating the Import of Dairy Products from New Zealand;
- Official Assurance Programme (OAP) for the Export of Pears from China to New Zealand;
- Agreed electronic certificate for live seafood exports from New Zealand to China;
- Official Assurance Programme for the Export of Table Grapes (Vitis vinifera) from the People's Republic of China to New Zealand; and,
- Official Assurance Programme for the Export of Fresh Processed Onions (Allium cepa) from the People's Republic of China to New Zealand.

Source: "China–New Zealand Free Trade Agreement, Two-Year Review: Joint Report," p. 15, at http://www.chinafta.govt.nz/3-Progressing-the-FTA/3-Moving-forward/index.php.

of important areas, for enhanced transparency, and for technical assistance.

The PTA contains an agreement on mutual recognition of conformity assessment for electrical and electronic equipment (EEEMRA). Before the implementation of that agreement, Chinese exports to New Zealand had to be tested against New Zealand standards, and New Zealand exports to China had to be tested, inspected, and certified by Chinese conformity assessment bodies. The EEEMRA gives suppliers in both countries an alternative way of demonstrating compliance with electrical safety and electromagnetic compatibility regulatory requirements.[27]

The SPS and TBT provisions of this PTA are considered binding by the parties and are subject to dispute settlement. Implementation of plans and work programs still under discussion are likely to make the PTA provisions even more binding over time, as the parties progressively adopt measures to further facilitate trade between them.

Although the TBT and SPS chapters lack dispute settlement provisions, the obligations of those chapters appear to be fully subject to recourse under the dispute settlement provisions in Chapter 16 of the PTA. There appears to be a soft-law option for both SPS and TBT issues. One function of the Joint Management Committee for SPS is consultation with a view to resolving SPS issues arising in bilateral trade; a similar provision exists with respect to the Joint TBT Committee. For TBTs, there is also an option for specialized technical consultations, which are explicitly stated not to prejudice rights under Chapter 16. The dispute settlement language of the PTA indicates that the complaining party can choose to turn to either the PTA or the WTO forum for dispute resolution.

South-South PTAs

When TBT and SPS provisions are present in South-South PTAs, they tend to refer mainly to the WTO Agreements. This is shown here by the review of three representative South-South PTAs: Mercosur, ASEAN, and the Chile–China FTA.

Mercosur

Mercosur, which links Argentina, Brazil, Paraguay, and Uruguay, dates from the December 1991 Treaty of Asunción. The economic aspects of the arrangements in the group have evolved over time, and significant amendments were made to Mercosur's regional rules after the conclusion of the Uruguay Round of multilateral trade negotiations. Mercosur's basic approach to TBT and SPS matters has been to use the WTO Agreements in these areas as the basis

for Mercosur-specific work plans and decisions affecting intra-Mercosur trade.

Before the end of the Uruguay Round, for example, Mercosur's member countries adopted, through Mercosur Decision 6/93, their own agreement on SPS measures (Acuerdo Sanitario y Fitosanitario entre los Estados Partes del Mercosur, ACSAFIM). The agreement contained provisions on harmonization with international standards for SPS protection, a provision facilitating acceptance of other countries' measures as equivalent, rules on risk assessment and regionalization, and other provisions that later appeared in the WTO SPS Agreement. When the WTO SPS Agreement was adopted by Mercosur member countries, the Mercosur Council approved the WTO Agreement as the operative agreement in Mercosur and denounced ACSAFIM.

For SPS measures, Mercosur Resolution 60/99 sets out principles, directives, criteria, and parameters for SPS equivalence agreements among Mercosur member countries. The resolution starts with an indication that the basic principles to be applied in the Mercosur environment are those of the WTO and the WTO SPS Agreement. Key principles specifically referred to are the desirability of acceptance of others' measures as equivalent where the protection level is as high as that in the importing country; the need to facilitate reasonable access for inspectors from the importing country; nondiscrimination; and proportionality in measures, which should in all cases be science based. Referenced international norms for the purpose of equivalence agreements include those of the Codex Alimentarius, the World Organisation for Animal Health (OIE), and the Plant Health Committee of the Southern Cone (COSAVE, Comité de Sanidad Vegetal del Cono Sur).[28]

In the TBT area, the Mercosur countries decided to build on the basics of the WTO Agreement through an internal work program aimed at reducing intraregional barriers to trade by harmonizing technical regulations and setting up procedures to govern the recognition of different conformity assessment processes as equivalent (Decision 56/02). Key terms in this decision are taken directly from the WTO TBT Agreement. (A Mercosur technical regulation has the same meaning as a technical regulation as defined in Annex 1 of the TBT Agreement.) A basic principle of the Mercosur decision is that in the elaboration or revision of Mercosur technical regulations and conformity assessment procedures, the PTA partners must take as the basis of their work the general principles and rules of the TBT Agreement. The decision also obliges Mercosur countries to take international standards into account where applicable and to apply adopted technical regulations in the same way to commerce among Mercosur states and to imports from third countries (the national treatment principle).

The binding provisions in Mercosur appear to be more or less those of the WTO TBT and SPS Agreements. The decisions and resolutions specific to Mercosur are more process oriented and focus on practical steps, such as how to develop a Mercosur technical regulation.

Mercosur's basic approach to dispute settlement is governed by Decision 37/03, which sets out the rules and regulations of the Olivos protocol for the settlement of disputes. Interestingly, Article 1 of the annex to that decision indicates that Mercosur members have the option of choosing the forum for settlement of their disputes. Evidently, they have the option of pursuing dispute settlement under Mercosur rules or taking the matter up under the WTO DSU.

When a dispute is submitted to resolution under Mercosur rules, a number of options are open to the parties: direct negotiations between the disputing parties; the intervention of the Grupo Mercado Común (which is optional); a WTO-like ad hoc arbitration procedure; and, finally, a review procedure by the Tribunal Permanente de Revisión del Mercosur. If judgments under the arbitration procedure selected are not adhered to by the losing party, the Mercosur dispute settlement procedure provides for compensatory measures, which must be proportional to the harm suffered by the winning party.

Research undertaken in 2003–04 for Mercosur identified more than 110 TBT and SPS practices in the region that acted as barriers to trade (Zago de Azevedo 2004). To address these issues, the Mercosur countries embarked on a harmonization and mutual recognition project. Hundreds of Mercosur technical regulations exist today, and guidelines and guides have been developed for the mutual recognition of conformity assessment procedures. Considerable progress has been made in harmonizing SPS regulations in the region.

In the Mercosur Trade Commission, consultations have been initiated between and among members with a view to exchanging information in an effort to resolve standards disputes.[29] Two recent cases illustrate the process:

- Argentina initiated a complaint concerning unilateral modifications by Brazil and Uruguay to a Mercosur technical regulation dealing with toys.[30] In Argentina's view, the actions by its Mercosur partners negatively affected the harmonization process in Mercosur and prejudiced the interests of Argentine manufacturers.
- In another case, Paraguay requested consultations with Brazil regarding the negative impact on its exports of

plastic chairs of Brazil's adoption of legislation requiring mandatory quality certification.[31]

ASEAN Trade in Goods Agreement

The countries of the Association of Southeast Asian Nations (ASEAN) have not had generally applicable mutual obligations with respect to SPS and TBT matters, apart from the WTO Agreements. They have relied instead on the negotiation and implementation of sectoral MRAs. This changed with the implementation of the new ASEAN Trade in Goods Agreement (ATIGA), which contains new obligations in both the TBT and SPS areas.

In the TBT area, for example, ATIGA obligates ASEAN member governments to follow the TBT Agreement's Code of Good Practice, to use international standards where possible, and to ensure that technical regulations are not adopted in ways that frustrate trade within ASEAN. Technical regulations, where applicable, must be applied in ways that facilitate the implementation of any ASEAN sectoral MRAs, and conformity assessment procedures are expected to be consistent with international standards and practices. A unique feature of ATIGA is the establishment of a postmarket surveillance system that is supported by alert systems designed to ensure ongoing compliance on the part of producers.

In the SPS area, ATIGA obligates members of ASEAN to be guided by international norms and standards in their SPS-related activities and encourages member governments to develop equivalence agreements and explore additional opportunities for intra-ASEAN cooperation.

The new agreement is generally considered to be binding in nature. Its provisions make frequent use of the word "shall," which is interpreted within ASEAN as a mandatory obligation that must be complied with. Where it was felt that commitments could be less rigid, other expressions, such as "endeavor to," were used in place of "shall." Examples of such wording are, "Member States shall develop and implement a Marking Scheme, where appropriate, for products covered under the ASEAN Harmonised Regulatory Regimes or Directives," but "Member States are encouraged to actively participate in the development of international standards."

With the entry into force of ATIGA, its obligations are subject to potential dispute settlement action under the ASEAN Protocol on Enhanced Dispute Settlement Mechanism, signed in 2004. Although this is considered a hard-law agreement, backed by dispute settlement, it is also the case that ASEAN traditionally favors resolution of problems through consultation—an approach explicitly referred to in the description of the mandate of the

ASEAN Committee on SPS Measures established by Article 82 of ATIGA.

Chile–China FTA

Chile is among the most active countries in the world when it comes to pursuing PTAs. The Chileans saw a PTA with China as helping to lock in Chile's important position in China as a copper supplier and as an opportunity for China to use the PTA with Chile as a gateway for Chinese business in South America. The PTA between Chile and China, in operation since October 2006, is a modern agreement in which the SPS and TBT provisions are tied closely to those in the WTO Agreements. This extends to the adoption of WTO definitions, phrases, and principles. In both the SPS and TBT sections, the PTA addresses such issues as the recognition of equivalence in technical regulations and conformity assessment, as well as notification and transparency provisions.

The parties to the PTA consider that it is legally binding on both countries' central governments and regional authorities. Should a dispute arise under the agreement, the parties may have recourse to the PTA dispute settlement provisions, ensuring the legally binding nature of the TBT and SPS provisions.

As with China's PTA with New Zealand, the SPS and TBT obligations can give rise to a complaint under the PTA's dispute settlement chapter even if the SPS and TBT sections themselves make no provision for dispute resolution. The complaining party has the option of choosing whether to pursue a complaint under the WTO DSU or under the PTA dispute settlement provisions.

The implementation of the SPS chapter in the Chile–China FTA seems to have helped facilitate bilateral trade in certain products through expanded trade opportunities. Chile and China have successfully conducted their first bilateral meeting on the implementation of the SPS chapter. Three protocols on quarantine were signed during the official visit of the Chilean president to China in 2008; they deal with quarantine for exports of cherries and plums from Chile to China and for exports of citrus and shallots from China to Chile, and with inspection and quarantine for imports and exports of pork, milk, and dairy products between China and Chile.[32]

Chile considers the conclusion of these protocols very positive developments in the relationship, since they formally open the Chinese market to Chilean exports of cherries, plums, and milk and dairy products and define the sanitary requirements for pork exports.[33] For their part, the Chinese expect to see a growth in their exports to Chile of shallots and citrus.

Implementation Costs and Technical Assistance Needs

Implementing TBT and SPS provisions could be costly, especially for exporters. If a firm has to adjust its production facilities to comply with diverse technical requirements in individual markets, production costs per unit are likely to increase. This imposes handicaps, particularly on small and medium-size enterprises. Conformity assessments are also costly. Compliance with technical regulations generally needs to be confirmed, and this may be done through testing, certification, or inspection by laboratories or certification bodies, usually at the company's expense. Information needs impose other costs, including the costs of evaluating the technical impact of foreign regulations, translating and disseminating product information, training experts, and so on. Finally, exporters may be subject to surprise costs because they are usually at a disadvantage vis-à-vis domestic firms, in terms of adjustment costs, when confronted with new regulations.

The major costs to governments and exporters in the TBT and SPS areas do not arise out of the technical implementation of the WTO or PTA agreements themselves but from compliance with trading partners' SPS and TBT measures. Although data on the actual cost of compliance with PTA partner measures are not readily available, examples of the cost of compliance with specific TBT and SPS measures, and of the cost of technical assistance provided pursuant to specific PTAs, could be cited.

For instance, earlier in this chapter, mention was made of the need of Moroccan citrus and tomato exporters to meet various nongovernment standards in the EU market. One of these standards is the private standard GLOBAL-GAP, relating to good agricultural practices; its certificates are increasingly required by European retailers as a condition for accepting Moroccan products.[34] Aloui and Kenny (2005) estimated the cost to a 10-hectare tomato farm of meeting the standard at US$71,000, or 3 percent of the free on board (FOB) value of the farm's exports; of this amount, US$20,000 represents annually recurring costs.

The WTO Secretariat has attempted to measure more systematically the cost and need for technical assistance related to compliance with standards-related measures. The data collected show that these costs can be substantial but also that the costs to developing countries can be mitigated to a significant degree by technical and capacity-building assistance provided by developed countries (box 11.4).

Many of the PTAs reviewed in this chapter are living agreements in the sense that they create bilateral or regional institutions, such as the committees and working groups established in the U.S.–Australia FTA, the

Box 11.4. WTO Assessment of TBT
Implementation Costs

In 2002, the World Trade Organization (WTO) surveyed 45
developing countries' priorities for technical assistance and
capacity building in the area of technical barriers to trade
(TBTs). Although the survey was conducted with reference
to the implementation of the multilateral TBT Agreement,
in many cases the survey results would apply as well to the
implementation of TBT provisions in PTAs.

The responses enabled the WTO Secretariat to identify
seven main areas of needs and specific technical assistance
activities to help meet these needs. In the order of frequency
of response, the perceived needs are:

- Assistance in infrastructure and capacity building: 43 out
  of 45 responses (96 percent)
- Improved knowledge of the TBT Agreement, including
  Annex 3 (the Code of Good Practice for the Preparation,
  Adoption and Application of Standards), and dissemination
  and increased awareness of the agreement: 33 responses
  (73 percent)
- Exchange of experience among members, and bilateral
  contact and cooperation: 33 responses (73 percent)
- Assistance with the effective implementation of the TBT
  Agreement: 32 responses (71 percent)
- National and regional coordination and strategy:
  29 responses (64 percent)
- Assistance in participating in the work of the WTO
  TBT Committee and other organizations: 20 responses
  (44 percent)
- Help with market access questions arising out of TBT
  measures: 16 responses (36 percent).

Source: For the survey, G/TBT/W/178, July 18, 2002; for the results,
G/TBT/W/193, February 10, 2003.

Box 11.5. Using the PTA's Living Agreement
Institutions for Capacity Building: An Example

The United States has entered into a PTA with the Central
America Free Trade Agreement plus the Dominican Republic
(CAFTA-DR). Article 7.8 of this PTA establishes a Committee
on Technical Barriers to Trade. Among the explicitly stated
functions of the committee are "enhancing cooperation in
the development and improvement of standards, technical
regulations, and conformity assessment procedures and, as
appropriate, designing and proposing mechanisms for
technical assistance of the type described in Article 11 of the
TBT Agreement, in coordination with the Committee on
Trade Capacity Building, as appropriate."

The scope of assistance referred to in Article 11 of the
TBT Agreement is very broad and includes assistance with
the preparation of technical regulations, support for the
establishment of national standardizing bodies, and
assistance with conformity assessment procedures.

The committee's discussions and procedure are
supplemented by regularly updated national action plans
for trade capacity building prepared by the developing-
country parties to the PTA. As TBT and SPS issues or
implementation problems arise, they can be added to the
updated action plan.

Sources: Lesser 2007, 24–25; http://www.ustr.gov/trade-
agreements/free-trade-agreements/cafta-dr-dominican-republic-
central-america-fta/cafta-dr-tcb; http://www.ustr.gov/trade-
agreements/free-trade-agreements/cafta-dr-dominican-republic-
central-america-fta/final-text.

New Zealand–China FTA, and others. Another good example is described in box 11.5. Often, the PTA committees are
tasked with drawing up work plans or prioritizing issues
for resolution.

Effective participation in the bilateral process implies
the need for a certain amount of capacity building, at least
in those developing countries that have less experience
with TBT and SPS measures. For example, before ATIGA
entered into force on 17 May 2010, according to the
ASEAN Secretariat, a significant amount of technical assistance was already taking place within ASEAN to prepare
for the implementation phase.

Over time, as government officials gain greater experience with implementation of the TBT and SPS provisions
in PTAs, the incremental effect of participation in a new or
expanded PTA should decrease considerably. For example,
as Chinese officials become familiar with the operation of
the agreement with New Zealand and their responsibilities
under that PTA, they will be that much more prepared to
take on whatever provisions are eventually agreed in their
PTA negotiations with Australia.

In nearly all of the PTA provisions examined in this
chapter, frequent reference is made to the WTO SPS and
TBT Agreements and to the desirability of relying on
international standards and procedures. In a very real
sense, the many years of work and cooperation at the multilateral level in these areas have made it easier to manage
implementation of PTA-level provisions. Of course, fundamentally different climatic, geographic, or technological
factors in different countries will always limit the appropriateness of international standards and harmonization
to some degree, particularly when the PTA partners are
not neighbors.

In only about half of the PTAs surveyed for this chapter
did the parties make the agreements' TBT and SPS provisions legally binding and enforceable through dispute settlement, and in a number of cases, provisions relating to
SPS were specifically excluded from the possibility of dispute settlement. Where dispute settlement does apply to
TBT or SPS provisions, the parties to the agreement
usually have the choice of bringing a dispute before the
WTO DSU or the PTA-specific dispute settlement mechanism. Parties to the Andean Community, for instance,
have relied heavily on the Community settlement mechanism for their TBT and SPS disputes (box 11.6). Yet, in
general, PTAs favor dispute avoidance (i.e., working out

Box 11.6. Dispute Settlement of TBT and SPS Measures in the WTO and within the Andean Community

Over the period 1995–2004, just 12 cases involving TBT or SPS measures were brought under the WTO's Dispute Settlement Understanding. In a roughly comparable period (1997–2004), 24 cases out of a total of 104 legal cases brought to dispute settlement in the Andean Community involved TBT or SPS measures, with 88 percent of these disputes related to SPS matters. Commonly noted procedural issues at dispute included

- Delays of more than five months in granting SPS permissions, whereas the maximum time frame for granting permission is 10 days
- Validity limited to 60 days on SPS permissions, although the minimum validity period established by Andean Community regulations is 90 days
- Establishment of complementary requirements for granting SPS permission, beyond Andean Community legislation
- Grants of permissions for only a small portion of the products, with other products subject to indefinitely pending deliberation without any stated objections on SPS grounds.

In some instances, it was indicated that the complainant perceived the procedural problem in granting SPS approval as intentional or as a hidden restriction.

Source: Fliess and Lejarraga 2005, 246–47.

differences through consultation or within a technical group) over litigation, even if litigation is an option. In some cases, implementing committees are charged with pursuing resolution of disputes—implicitly, through cooperative consultation.

Conclusions

Research into the practice of addressing TBT and SPS measures in PTAs suggest that such agreements converge with, and support, the multilateral trading system. To ensure that this does happen, PTAs should include, where feasible, a number of important best-practice provisions.

1. The parties to the PTA should undertake to use international standards whenever possible, as doing so guarantees a high level of protection in the integrated market and makes it easier for third parties to trade in that market.
2. If the parties to the PTA decide on an approach of harmonizing their standards and conformity assessment procedures, they should accept that it might be necessary to limit harmonization to essential health and safety standards and rely on mutual recognition and equivalence techniques for other areas.

3. If one partner is less developed than the other, the PTA should incorporate technical assistance and capacity-building measures to assist the institutions and exporters of the developing-country partner. In negotiating a PTA, governments should recognize that deeper integration and the resolution of standards-related problems will take time and will require considerable bilateral work. A PTA that aims to be effective should incorporate bilateral institutions (committees and the like) that have a mandate to deal with standards-related questions over time through harmonization, equivalence, or mutual recognition techniques. Ideally, the institutions established in the PTA should also be capable of helping to resolve trade-related problems arising out of exporters' need to comply with private standards in an importing country's market.
4. If technical regulations and conformity assessment procedures cannot be harmonized, it is important for the purposes of the PTA that the parties work to eliminate duplicate or multiple measures or mandatory tests for the same product. This is particularly crucial for small and medium-size enterprises that cannot afford the high cost of meeting differing regulations and testing regimes. Mutual recognition agreements are important tools in this respect.
5. Transparency regarding SPS standards in international trade is very important for businesses and consumers. PTA partners should consider enacting WTO+ notification obligations and a commitment not to implement any technical regulation or SPS measure until it has been published and comments from the PTA partners have been taken into account.
6. The PTA should be a living agreement with a commitment to a work plan or to prioritization of problem resolution through harmonization, mutual recognition, equivalence measures, and other policy tools that enable elimination or mitigation of trade-related problems over time. Ideally, the work program should also be capable of addressing problems relating to compliance with private standards.
7. PTA provisions on TBT and SPS matters should be legally binding through a judicious combination of soft and hard law. The agreement should provide a pathway that permits an evolution and deepening of integration over time by allowing the gradual resolution of TBT and SPS issues in the bilateral relationship. Such a pathway should be considered an integral part of any PTA that aims to deal effectively with standards, certification, and conformity assessment problems. Eventual recourse to the PTA dispute settlement provisions should be an option, in addition to recourse to the WTO Dispute Settlement Understanding.

8. PTA parties should agree to an overall commitment whereby technical regulations and conformity assessment procedures are always applied on a national treatment basis. Third parties whose technical regulations and conformity assessment procedures can be demonstrated as being equivalent to the level agreed to by the PTA partners should be permitted to benefit from the arrangements between the partners. A commitment to open regionalism would help to ensure that PTAs support the multilateral system.

Notes

1. The terms "standard" and "technical regulation" are used throughout this chapter. The difference is that whereas conformity with standards is voluntary, technical regulations are by nature mandatory. The two types of provision have different implications for international trade. If an imported product does not fulfill the requirements of a technical regulation, it will not be allowed to be put on sale. In the case of standards, noncomplying imported products will be allowed on the market, but their market share may be affected if consumers' prefer products that meet local standards, such as quality or color standards for textiles and clothing. The WTO Web site pages offer a detailed presentation of technical barriers to trade (http://www.wto.org/english/tratop_e/tbt_e/tbt_info_e.htm) and of sanitary and phytosanitary measures (http://www.wto.org/english/tratop_e/sps_e/spsund_e.htm).

2. Office of the U.S. Trade Representative, "U.S.-Australia Free Trade Agreement, Report of the Agricultural Technical Advisory Committee in Fruits and Vegetables," http://ustraderep.gov/Trade_Agreements/Bilateral/Australia_FTA/Reports/Section_Index.html, accessed January 1, 2009.

3. *Euromed Report* 64, July 9, 2003, 3-4.

4. Morocco, "Fiche signalétique de projet de jumelage: appui a la direction de la normalisation et de la promotion de la qualite dans l'harmonisation et la mise en oeuvre de la legislation technique," final version, May 2, 2007, Rabat.

5. Ibid., 6.

6. European Commission, Directorate General for Trade, "Inventarisation of Technical Assistance Provided to Third Countries in the Area of SPS by the European Union and Its Member States," October 15, 2009, Brussels.

7. European Union, "Joint Communiqué, VII EU-Chile Association Committee, 2009," http://www.delchl.ec.europa.eu/en/whatsnew/NEWS_2009_15_10_association_comittee.htm.

8. EUR-Lex, Access to European Union Law, http://eur-lex.europa.eu/LexUriServ/LexUriServ.do?uri=CELEX:32004D0907:EN:NOT.

9. Chile, Dirección General de Relaciones Económicas Internacionales (DIRECON), "Relaciones Multilaterales: Noticias," http://www.direcon.cl/index.php?accion=prensaArticulo&id_prensa=153.

10. Fundación Chile, "Presidenta Bachelet Inauguró Moderno Centro de Medición de Residuos de Fundación Chile," http://www.fundacionchile.cl/portal/page?_pageid=113,232271&_dad=portal&_schema=PORTAL&p_item_id=5166352&p_area_id=206271.

11. European Commission, "Chile Country Strategy Paper 2007–2013," ec.europa.eu/external_relations/chile/csp/07_13_en.pdf.

12. *Official Journal of the European Communities,* L 311/18, December 12, 1999.

13. European Commission, "Toward an EU-South Africa Strategic Partnership," communication to the European Council and European Parliament, COM(2006) 347 final, Brussels, June 28, 2006, http://eur-lex.europa.eu.

14. Article 103 provided for a review of the TDCA within five years of the agreement's entering into force.

15. European Commission, communication to the European Council, COM(2006) 348 final, Brussels, June 28, 2006, http://eur-lex.europa.eu.

16. European Commission, "Proposal for a Council Decision on the Signing of an Agreement between the European Community and its Member States, of the one part, and the Republic of South Africa, of the other part, amending the Agreement on Trade, Cooperation and Development," COM(2008)50 final, Brussels, February 4, 2008, 2.

17. European Commission, "Cooperation between the European Union and South Africa," Brussels, July 23, 2009. UE-ZA 4903/09, http://register.consilium.europa.

18. Council of the European Union, "Second South Africa-European Union Summit," Kleinmond, South Africa, September 11, 2009, 13231/09 (Presse 266), http://register.consilium.europa.

19. Council of the European Union, "South Africa–European Union Strategic Partnership Joint Action Plan," Brussels, May 15, 2007, http://register.consilium.europa.

20. Ibid., 5.

21. "Europe and South Africa Development Partners, 2007/8," http://www.eusa.org.za/en/eu_and_country/EU20078.pdf.

22. Council of the European Union, "Cooperation between the European Union and South Africa," Brussels, November 24, 2008, UE-ZA 4904/09, http://register.consilium.europa.

23. Ibid.

24. Australia, Department of Foreign Affairs and Trade, "Thailand Country Brief," December 2008, Canberra, http://www.dfat.gov.au/geo/thailand_thailand_brief.html, accessed February 23, 2009.

25. Office of the U.S. Trade Representative, "The U.S.–Chile Free Trade Agreement: An Early Record of Success," http://www.ustr.gov/Document_Library/Fact_Sheets/2004/The_US-Chile_Free_Trade_Agreement_An_Early_Record_of_Success.html, accessed February 20, 2009.

26. Office of the U.S. Trade Representative, "The U.S.–Chile Free Trade Agreement: Excerpts from Trade Advisory Committee Reports," http://www.ustr.gov/assets/Trade_Agreements/Bilateral/Chile_FTA/Reports/asset_upload_files85_4956.pdf, accessed February 22, 2009.

27. Ministry of Foreign Affairs and Trade, "Guide to the New Zealand-China Free Trade Agreement," Wellington, 2008, 34.

28. The Codex Alimentarius, which comes under the auspices of the Food and Agriculture Organization of the United Nations (FAO) and the World Health Organization (WHO), is a collection of internationally recognized standards, codes of practice, guidelines, and other recommendations relating to foods, food production, and food safety. OIE is the intergovernmental organization responsible for improving animal health worldwide. COSAVE is a regional organization established by agreement between the governments of the Mercosur parties within the framework of the International Plant Protection Convention.

29. The Trade Commission assists the Mercosur executive body in applying the instruments of common trade policy agreed to by the member states for the operation of customs unification.

30. For Brazil, CCM XCVII, Acta No 06/08, Consultation No 08/07; for Uruguay, CCM XCVII, Acta No 08/07; http://www.mercosur.int/msweb/portal%20intermediario/es/index.htm.

31. CCM CV, Acta No 08/08, Consultation No 06/08, http://www.mercosur.int/msweb/portal%20intermediario/es/index.htm.

32. "Communiqué between the People's Republic of China and the Republic of Chile," http://hr.china-embassy.org/eng/zxxx/t427229.htm.

33. "Visita de Estado de S.E. la Presidenta de la República Michelle Bachelet a la República Popular China," http://www.echilecn.com/eg/html/31/2008-5/78.html.

34. The standard had been called EUREPGAP; the name was changed in 2007.

Bibliography

Aloui, Omar, and Lahcen Kenny. 2005. "The Cost of Compliance with SPS Standards for Moroccan Exports: A Case Study." Agriculture and Rural Development Discussion Paper, World Bank, Washington, DC.

APEC (Asia-Pacific Economic Cooperation) Secretariat. 2000. "Information Notes on Good Practice for Technical Regulation." APEC, Singapore.

Benavides, Daniela, and Sandra Jerez. 2007. "Bienestar animal (BA): responsabilidad ética, exigencia commercial y atributo de valor." *Boletin Veterinario Oficial* 8 (1 semestre). http://www2.sag.gob.cl/Pecuaria/bvo/BVO _8_I_semestre_2007/articulos/bienestar_animal .pdf.

Budetta, Michelle, and Roberta Piermartini. 2009. "A Mapping of Regional Rules on Technical Barriers to Trade." In *Regional Rules in the Global Trading System*, ed. Antoni Estevadeordal, Kati Suominen, and Robert Teh. Cambridge, U.K.: Cambridge University Press.

Fliess, Barbara, and I. Lejarraga. 2005. "Looking beyond Tariffs: Nontariff Barriers of Concern to Developing Countries," ch. 7. OECD Trade Policy Studies, Organisation for Economic Co-operation and Development, Paris.

Lesser, Caroline. 2007. "Do Bilateral and Regional Approaches for Reducing Technical Barriers to Trade Converge towards the Multilateral Trading System?" OECD Trade Committee Working Paper 58, TAD/TC/WP(2007)12/FINAL, Organisation for Economic Co-operation and Development, Paris.

Maskus, Keith, Tsunehiro Otsuki, and John S. Wilson. 2000. "Quantifying the Impact of Technical Barriers to Trade: A Framework for Analysis." Policy Research Working Paper 2512, World Bank, Washington, DC.

Nidhiprabha, Bhanupong. 2002. "SPS and Thailand's Exports of Processed Food." Revised version of a paper presented at the Project Launching Workshop, Royal Princess Hpoteh, Bangkok, October 1–3.

Turner, J., F. Maplesden, B.Walford; and S. Jacob. 2005. "Tariff and Nontariff Barriers to New Zealand's Exports of Wood-Based Products to China." *New Zealand Journal of Forestry* 50 (1).

WTO (World Trade Organization). 2005. *World Trade Report 2005: Trade, Standards and the WTO.* Pt. 2, Geneva: WTO.

Zago de Azevedo, André Filipe. 2004. "Mercosur: Ambitious Politics, Poor Practices." *Brazilian Journal of Political Economy* 24 (4, October–December): 584–601.

12

SERVICES

Aaditya Mattoo and Pierre Sauvé

An extensive literature exists on the costs and benefits of integration agreements concerning trade in goods, but hardly any analysis of the implications of such agreements on trade in services has been carried out. Such a gap is surprising, given the strong growth witnessed since the mid-1990s in the number of preferential trade agreements (PTAs) featuring detailed disciplines on trade and investment in services. The recent proliferation of PTAs covering services is evidence of heightened policy interest in the contribution of efficient services sectors to economic development and of a growing appreciation of the gains likely to flow from the progressive dismantling of impediments to trade and investment in services.

To date, 76 PTAs featuring provisions on trade and investment in services have been notified to the World Trade Organization (WTO), as shown in annex tables 12A.1 and 12A.2. This number represents 28 percent of all notified PTAs, a proportion slightly higher than the share of services in world trade (figure 12.1). As figure 12.2 illustrates, developed countries are party to just under two-thirds (62 percent) of all PTAs featuring services provisions, commensurate with their aggregate share in world services trade. North-South agreements, with both developed and developing countries as members, account for 49 percent of such PTAs, and North-North agreements among developed countries, for 13 percent. Services-related South-South PTAs have grown noticeably in number and today account for 38 percent of notified agreements. From a political-economy perspective, the predominance of services-related PTAs involving developed-country partners is consistent with the aggregate pattern of specialization and the direction of trade and investment in services trade today.

If all trade agreements can, in essence, be likened to "incomplete contracts," the incipient multilateral regime for services is arguably the most incomplete of all. That consideration greatly heightens the salience of studying the relationship between preferential and multilateral regimes for services trade. This chapter considers a number of questions—both theoretical and policy related—arising from the study of the PTA-WTO divide in services trade. Do the tools of economic analysis developed for studying the effects of preferences in goods trade yield meaningful insights in the services field? To what extent, and in what form, can developments in preferential agreements inform approaches to rule making and market opening under the General Agreement on Trade in Services (GATS)? Do the observed differences in negotiating architectures across services-related PTAs matter? What is the likelihood that such differences may inform the evolution of the WTO's architecture of services rules following the completion of the Doha Development Round of trade negotiations? Does the issue of preference erosion arise in services trade, and if so, what is its sectoral or modal incidence? Does the practice of liberalization of services markets suggest that PTAs can be likened to "optimal regulatory convergence areas"—groups of countries whose aggregate welfare is maximized by regulatory convergence?

Regional and bilateral attempts at developing trade rules for services continue to parallel efforts at framing similar disciplines in the WTO, under the aegis of GATS. For this reason, regional and multilateral efforts at services rule making are closely—indeed, increasingly—intertwined processes, with much iterative learning by doing, imitation, and reverse engineering. Experience gained in developing the services provisions of PTAs has expanded negotiating capacity in participating countries and has built up expertise that is available for deployment in a multilateral setting. GATS itself remains incomplete, with negotiations pending or stalled in such important areas as emergency safeguards, subsidies, government procurement, and domestic regulation, but regional and bilateral experimentation has generated useful policy lessons in comparative negotiating and rule-making dynamics. In

Figure 12.1. Services-Related PTAs as a Share of Total PTA Notifications to the WTO, 2010

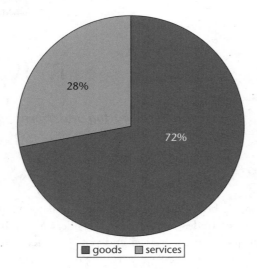

Source: World Trade Organization, Regional Trade Agreement (RTA) database, http://rtais.wto.org/UI/PublicMaintainRTAHome.aspx.

Figure 12.2. Services-Related PTAs Notified to the WTO, by Country Group

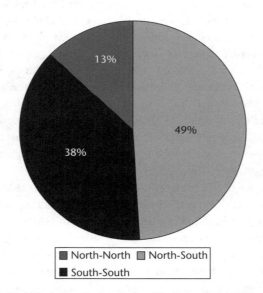

Source: World Trade Organization, Regional Trade Agreement (RTA) database, http://rtais.wto.org/UI/PublicMaintainRTAHome.aspx.

addition, developments in WTO jurisprudence in the services field have begun to be reflected in patterns of market-opening commitments found in PTAs—a trend that can be expected to deepen as judicial activism under GATS increases.[1]

The efforts that countries devote to developing rules governing the process of services trade liberalization at the regional level typically follow in the wake of the far-reaching changes in services and investment policy frameworks that have taken hold in many countries in the post–Uruguay Round period. PTA negotiations offer the opportunity to pursue, deepen, or lock in some (or many) of the policy reforms put in place domestically in recent years and to reap the benefits likely to flow from such policy consolidation—notably, in the form of improved investment climates.

This chapter takes stock of the more recent wave of PTAs with a view to informing some of the policy choices developing countries will typically confront in negotiating regional regimes for services trade and investment. Although a country's choice of integration strategy will in most instances be dictated by political considerations, there remains a need for a careful assessment of the economic benefits and costs of alternative approaches to services liberalization.

The chapter focuses on two core issues. The first is the economics of regional integration in services. Does services trade differ sufficiently from trade in goods as to require different policy instruments and approaches in the context of preferential liberalization? Do PTAs allow deeper forms of regulatory cooperation to occur, and in what way? The discussion highlights the importance for third countries of multilateral disciplines on PTAs and the criteria for preventing PTAs from being detrimental to nonmembers.

The second concern is the political economy of regionalism in services trade. Here, the discussion highlights lessons arising from the practice of preferential liberalization in services, drawing on a sample of 55 of the 76 services-related PTAs notified to date in the WTO. Within the sample, 3 PTAs are North-North agreements, 27 are classified as North-South, and 25 as South-South.

The Economics of Services Trade in PTAs

The economic effects of preferential tariff arrangements are generally well understood (see Baldwin, ch. 3 in this volume) and form the core of conventional trade theory. Such, however, is hardly the case with services. The analysis of preferential agreements in services trade requires an extension of conventional trade theory in two ways, both of which relate to core distinguishing features of services: first, the manner in which trade in services occurs and, second, the form that trade protection takes in the sector.

Since services trade often requires proximity between the supplier and the consumer, the analysis has to take account of preferences extended not just to cross-border trade but also to foreign direct investment (FDI) and to individual foreign services providers. Another point is that preferential treatment in services is granted not through tariffs but through discriminatory restrictions on the movement of labor and capital (e.g., on the quantity or share of foreign ownership) and through a variety of domestic regulations such as technical standards and licensing and qualification requirements.

Given such differences, can one say that trade in services differs enough from trade in goods as to modify the accepted conclusions regarding the economic effects of preferential liberalization? In particular, what would happen if a country liberalized services trade faster in a regional or bilateral context than at the multilateral level? To answer such questions, we next review the costs and benefits of trade preferences arising in services trade and examine the scope for regional or bilateral regulatory cooperation in this sector.

Costs and Benefits of Preferential Treatment in Services Trade

The manner in which privileged access is granted in services markets depends on the instruments of protection that are in use. By imposing quantitative restrictions on services output or on the number of service providers, a country can allocate a larger proportion of the quota to a preferred source. For example, countries often preferentially allocate freight and passenger quotas in air, land, and maritime transport, limit the airtime allocated to foreign broadcasts, and restrict the numbers of foreign telecommunications operators, banks, or professionals.

Another common means of restricting access to service markets that lends itself to preferential treatment is to place conditions on foreign ownership, the type of legal entity permitted, and branching rights. Most host-country governments accord national treatment to foreign investors after their establishment, but national treatment rarely applies before establishment. Host countries are therefore able to impose performance requirements on prospective foreign services providers with respect to such things as training, or employment in managerial-level positions. These requirements can easily be waived for members of a preferential arrangement.

Preferences can also be granted through taxes and subsidies. Foreign providers may be subject to different taxes from nationals and may be denied access to certain subsidy programs. These forms of discrimination, too, can be waived selectively, as is the case, for example, with coproduction agreements in audiovisual services.

Countries can and do impose on foreign providers qualification and licensing requirements that may be more burdensome than is necessary to satisfy otherwise legitimate public policy objectives. When these are waived selectively in favor of members of a PTA and denied to nonmembers that would otherwise qualify for the benefits, de facto preferences result. Regulatory preferences may arise in all sectors, but they are especially prevalent in professional and financial services, where domestic regulatory requirements and licensing regimes respond to information asymmetries.

Measures affecting variable costs. A common effect of many restrictive measures in services trade is to increase the variable costs of operation faced by foreign providers without necessarily generating equivalent rents. In such cases, the analysis of discriminatory regulation can proceed in a manner analogous to that for tariffs. When tariffs are the instruments of protection, the costs of trade diversion can be an important disincentive to concluding preferential liberalization agreements. Despite the increase in consumer surplus from any liberalization, there may still be an aversion to such agreements because the displacement of high-tariff imports from third countries by low- or zero-tariff imports from preferential sources implies lost revenue.

The situation may differ when the protectionist instrument is a regulatory barrier that imposes a cost on the exporter without necessarily yielding corresponding revenues for the government or any other domestic entity. Under such circumstances, which characterize much of services trade (given the regulatory nature of impediments), there may be little or no cost to granting preferential access because there is little or no revenue to lose. In such circumstances, preferential liberalization will necessarily be welfare enhancing.

Countries outside the preferential arrangement may, however, lose. Exemption from a needlessly burdensome regulation implies reduced costs for a class of suppliers and hence a decline in prices in the importing countries. This decline may hurt third-country suppliers, who may suffer reduced sales and a decreased producer surplus.

The analysis of discriminatory regulation is also relevant to quantitative restrictions on the sale of services. In the case of goods, the quota rents can be appropriated by domestic intermediaries such as the importer, rather than by the foreign exporter. For many services, intermediation is difficult because the service is not always storable and is directly supplied by producers to consumers. Rents are therefore usually appropriated by exporters rather than by domestic importers. As in the case of frictional measures that increase variable costs, there is typically no cost of trade diversion to the preference-granting country.

The main policy implication that emerges from the above discussion is that when a country maintains regulations that impose a cost on foreign providers without generating any benefit (such as improved quality) or revenue for the government or other domestic entities, welfare is necessarily enhanced by preferential liberalization. Nonpreferential liberalization, however, would yield an even greater increase in welfare, both nationally and globally, because the service would then be supplied by the most efficient providers.

Measures affecting fixed costs. Some regulatory measures can have the effect of increasing the fixed costs of entry or establishment in services markets. Examples include mandatory establishment of a local presence, license fees for entry into the market, and the need to requalify to provide professional services. As with measures affecting variable costs, a country is likely to benefit from eliminating, even on a preferential basis, excessive fixed costs of entry by removing unnecessary burdensome qualification, licensing, and local establishment requirements for professional and financial services.

Regardless of the chosen partners, the presumption that a country will benefit from such initiatives is greater if agreements are not exclusionary but are open to all parties able to satisfy the regulatory requirements maintained within the integrating area. The greatest benefits arise if agreements to recognize professional qualifications include all countries that have comparable regulations. The benefits in such instances stem both from increased competition and from greater diversity of services.

Measures restricting the number of service providers. The norm in many service industries is for the level of competition to be restricted by government regulation. There may be legitimate reasons to do so: significant economies of scale may be possible, and some industry segments, such as network-based energy, water distribution, and transport services, have natural monopoly features. In such circumstances, the manner in which entry is allowed—by mergers and acquisitions, or through greenfield (de novo) investments—can assume considerable significance.

Interestingly, allowing limited new entry by foreign firms, whether this is done preferentially or on a most favored nation (MFN) basis, may not be welfare enhancing. The main reason is that even though consumers may benefit from the increased competition, the gain may be offset by the transfer of rents from domestic to foreign oligopolists.

Restrictions on de novo entry are often imposed with a view to channeling new foreign capital into weak or undercapitalized domestic institutions (as is common in financial services, for example) and so assist with restructuring in the context of progressive liberalization. These considerations may affect the preferred mode of entry: acquisition implies less competition than greenfield entry, but it allows domestic firms to extract some rents through the disposal of their assets.

Liberalization tends to generate gains when all barriers to entry are removed. If only limited entry is allowed, then open, nondiscriminatory access—through, for example, the global auctioning of licenses—would have an edge over preferential access, which cannot guarantee that preferential (i.e., insider) investors will be the most efficient ones. Absent liberal rules of origin for investment, the establishment of preferences may indeed result in entry by inferior suppliers. Because the most efficient suppliers (in terms of costs, quality, or both) may generate the greatest positive externalities, including the dynamic learning properties associated with knowledge flows and the associated rise of total factor productivity, the downside risks of preferential liberalization are magnified (Mattoo and Fink 2002). The ability of nonpreferential liberalization to more readily secure access to the most efficient suppliers of services is a matter of some importance, given the crucial infrastructural role many services perform and the strong influence of their intermediate inputs on economywide performance.

Preferential liberalization of entry barriers may also lead to higher prices for consumers, lower takeover prices for domestic assets, or lower license fees for the government (because the pool of potential buyers is limited). These concerns are likely to be compounded in concentrated markets, which are common in many services industries in the developing world.

Sunk costs and the sequence of liberalization. Sunk costs are important in goods and services industries alike, but location-specific sunk costs—those incurred in supplying a particular market—are arguably higher in a number of services sectors, insofar as their provision requires proximity between suppliers and consumers. One consequence (which is closely related to the above discussion on barriers to new entrants) is that preferential liberalization may have more durable effects on the nature of competition than in the case of goods. For instance, under an agreement that allows inferior providers to establish, a country could be stuck with such providers even if it subsequently liberalizes on an MFN basis.

Sunk costs matter because they have commitment value and can be used strategically by first movers to deter new entrants (Tirole 1998). A firm that establishes a telecommunications or transport network signals that it will be around tomorrow, since it cannot easily dispose of its assets. The commitment value is stronger, the more slowly capital depreciates and the more firm specific it is.

Firms allowed early entry into such markets may accumulate a quantity of capital sufficient to limit the entry of new rivals. These incumbency effects may be stronger in services with network externalities, such as telecommunications, where new entrants must match the technical standards of the incumbent—standards that the latter may have played a large part in defining. The incumbent may also be able to assure itself of the services of the best franchisees by selecting them early on and imposing exclusivity arrangements on them. Each of these forms of capital accumulation enhances first-mover advantages and allows established firms to prevent, restrict, or retard competition.

Because of the importance of sunk costs in many services industries, sequential entry (which preferential liberalization with restrictive rules of origin may entail) can produce very different results from simultaneous entry. If entry is costly, an incumbent may be able to completely deter entry, leading to greater market concentration. Furthermore, the first-mover advantage may be conferred on an inferior supplier, which may naturally exploit such advantages to establish a position of market dominance, insulated from more efficient third-country competitors. How durable such a position may be in practice will depend on the importance of sunk costs relative to differences in price and quality.

There are two important qualifications to the above reasoning. First, subsequent entry by a more efficient firm can take place by acquisition, circumventing some of the problems linked to first-mover advantages. This has notably happened in a number of countries in the financial sector, especially where first movers may have overbid or sunk excessive costs into setting up their operations in the early stages of liberalization. Second, in certain services sectors, firms may learn by doing: the experience acquired by established operators may reduce their current costs, enhancing their profitability and discouraging others from entering. Caveats aside, a country needs to carefully evaluate not just the static costs of granting preferential access to a particular partner country but also how the eventual benefits from multilateral liberalization are likely to be affected.

Static and dynamic economies of scale. Combining services markets through a regional integration agreement can lead to gains arising from a combination of scale effects and changes in the intensity of competition. In a market of a given size, there is a trade-off between scale economies and competition: if firms are larger, there are fewer of them, and the market is less competitive. Enlarging the market shifts this trade-off, as it becomes possible to have both larger firms and more competition (World Bank 2000).

Regional liberalization can also act as an inducement to FDI. Apart from changing the organization of local industry, if PTAs create large markets and do not impose stringent ownership-related rules of origin, they may help attract foreign investment when economies of scale matter. For example, a foreign transport service provider might not find it worthwhile to establish in Latin America if each country market were segmented, but it might find a continentwide integrated market attractive.

One rationale for coverage of services in PTAs is a variant of dynamic economies of scale, or of the infant-industry argument. South-South PTAs, in particular, are seen as a means of gradual liberalization. Exposure to competition at first in the more sheltered confines of a regional market may help firms prepare for global competition. This approach improves on traditional protection of infant industries because the integration process promotes some degree of international competition. Furthermore, firms that have become more competitive at the regional level are less likely to resist broader liberalization. They may even champion subsequent MFN liberalization as they begin to reap the benefits of open markets and encounter the constraints of a regional market. In this sense, as noted by Baldwin and Freund (ch. 6 in this volume), PTAs can be seen as building blocks toward multilateral liberalization (Bhagwati 1990; Lawrence 1991). There is, however, a risk that regional liberalization might create a new constellation of vested interests that could resist further market opening, raising the concern that regionalism could prove a stumbling block to further multilateral liberalization. GATS offers a way out of this dilemma by allowing member countries to precommit to future multilateral liberalization, signaling a time frame over which regional preferences may be progressively eroded or eliminated.

Regionalism and Regulatory Cooperation

The gains from PTAs are likely to be significant in areas where there is scope for attaining economies of scale, as in certain international transport and financial services, and for promoting increased competition, as in business or professional services. In principle, these gains can also be realized through MFN liberalization, but in practice, the integration of markets often requires a convergence of regulatory regimes. Such convergence might well be more feasible in a bilateral or regional context—for instance, where proximity, whether geographic or in terms of income levels or legal traditions, implies closer institutional and regulatory ties. The regulatory intensity of services trade makes it necessary to consider whether and how

PTAs can be conduits for trade- and investment-facilitating convergence in domestic regulatory practices. Simply put, under what circumstances is a country more likely to benefit from cooperation in a plurilateral or regional forum than in a multilateral one?

Addressing the regulatory intensity of services trade. The economic case for regulation in services arises essentially from market failure attributable to three kinds of problems: (a) asymmetric information, especially in knowledge-intensive industries such as financial or professional services; (b) externalities, as in tourism, transport, and water supply; and (c) natural monopolies or oligopolies, especially in network-based services for which access to essential facilities is a critical ingredient.

In the first two cases, national remedies can themselves become impediments to trade if domestic regulatory requirements are needlessly burdensome or are framed so as to tilt competitive conditions in favor of domestic suppliers. The institution of some variant of a necessity test in services agreements (the purpose of which, as in goods trade, is to ensure a broad measure of proportionality between regulatory objectives and the means of pursuing them), together with strengthened disciplines on transparency, would enable exporters to challenge the appropriateness of regulatory regimes abroad. Doing so would help ensure that domestic regulations serve legitimate objectives, rather than mask protectionist interests, and would thus create benefits for domestic consumers and users of services.

In the third case, that of natural monopolies and oligopolies, it is the *absence* of regulation (typically, procompetitive regulation) that can lead to trade problems and directly inhibit or nullify negotiated market access. As negotiations on basic telecommunications services have shown, international rules on access to essential facilities, and on means of ensuring that dominant suppliers do not abuse their market advantages to deter entry and stifle competition, can provide significant benefits to consumers and users of telecommunications services.

To ensure that domestic regulations at home and abroad support trade, a country must decide on the appropriate level of coordination (multilateral, regional, or bilateral), the appropriate mechanism (such as international rules or standards), and the appropriate approach (mutual recognition or harmonization) to be pursued in individual services sectors. International rules can do little to address impediments to trade arising from fundamental differences among countries in regulatory standards. In such circumstances, two approaches can be envisaged: harmonization and mutual recognition. These approaches are often presented as alternatives, but in fact, the former tends to be either a precondition or a result of the latter. Where differences in mandatory quality standards matter, mutual recognition may be feasible only when there is a certain degree of prior harmonization of mutually acceptable minimum standards. A similar logic applies to compatibility standards—although there may be no alternative to full harmonization if differences matter, as in the cases of road-safety standards, railway gauges, and legal procedures.

Regulatory cooperation may be more desirable, and is likely to be more feasible, among a subset of countries than if pursued on a global scale. There is, however, little, if any, empirical guidance on the payoffs to regulatory cooperation—on the costs and benefits of mutual recognition agreements or the deeper harmonization of regulatory standards. The lack of empirical evidence complicates the task of deciding on the scope and depth, as well as the geographic reach and the optimal institutional forms, of regulatory cooperation.

If national standards are not optimal or are insufficiently developed, regional or international harmonization or standardization can be a way of improving such standards, as has happened in the financial services field with the Basel Accord on capital adequacy. In such situations, the best partners for regulatory cooperation are likely to be those with the soundest regulatory frameworks. Such partners may not always be found within regional compacts. Moreover, the standard-setting process can at times be captured by protectionist interests, in which case convergence around "best" regulatory practice can serve a useful liberalizing purpose.

Another consideration is that there are gains from regulatory cooperation, but also costs. The former will dominate where national regulation can be improved. The aggregate adjustment cost of regulatory convergence depends on the degree of differences between the policy-related standards of the countries involved in an integration area. The costs are likely to be smallest when foreign regulatory preferences are similar and regulatory institutions are broadly compatible. The benefits of eliminating policy differences through harmonization depend on the prospects of creating a truly integrated market, and that depends on the "natural distance" between countries and, ultimately, on factors such as levels of development, physical distance, legal systems, and language.

If national standards optimally serve national objectives, there is a trade-off between the gains from integrated markets and the costs of transition and of departing from optimal domestic standards. For instance, a poor country may prefer to maintain a low mandatory standard for certain services because that reflects the socially optimal trade-off between price, quality, and implementation capacities, whereas the socially optimal trade-off in a rich country may lead to a preference for and the adoption of a higher standard. Under such circumstances, harmonization of standards could create benefits in the shape of increased competition in integrated markets, but it would necessarily impose a social cost in at least one country. This matter may be nontrivial in the growing number of integration agreements concluded along North-South lines (see box 12.1).

PTAs as optimal regulatory areas for services. An optimal regulatory area can be thought of as defining the set of countries whose aggregate welfare would be maximized by regulatory convergence. Such an area would balance the benefits and costs of participation. The gains from eliminating policy differences through harmonization depend on the prospects for creating truly integrated markets, which are conditioned by natural ties between countries and on factors such as geographic and linguistic proximity. The costs depend on the ex ante similarity of regulatory preferences and the compatibility of regulatory institutions.

In the definition of an optimal regulatory area, it must be recognized that cooperation can be a vehicle for exchanging information on experience with regulatory reform and identifying good regulatory practices. This form of cooperation can be especially useful for regulating new services in sectors characterized by continuous technical change. Developing countries may have a particular interest in cooperating with advanced industrial countries that have the longest experience with regulatory reform and in which the newest technologies and their regulatory implications are often first introduced.

Whether or not an individual country benefits from regulatory convergence or harmonization, its willingness to participate in this effort may hinge on where the standard is set, the level at which it is set, and the regulatory environment to which the standard responds. The latter factors will in turn determine who will bear the costs of transition toward the adoption of the standard. The incentive to make regulations converge may depend on the relative size of markets, and small countries often have more to gain. This may explain why small countries acceding to the European Union (EU) accept that they will bear the full cost of transition.

It should be noted that the process of regulatory convergence can itself involve sunk costs of transition. The

---

Box 12.1. WTO+ and WTO-Extra Provisions in U.S. and EU PTAs

Horn, Mavroidis, and Sapir (2010) compare the substantive differences in the preferential trade agreements (PTAs) of the United States and the European Union (EU). Their work draws attention to the distinction between "WTO+" provisions, referring to PTA-induced outcomes that build on existing World Trade Organization (WTO) disciplines and commitments, and "WTO-extra" provisions, which involve disciplines or commitments that have yet not been agreed at the WTO level. The authors further highlight the issue of "legal inflation," distinguishing those provisions that are legally binding and enforceable from those that are merely hortatory.

Both EU and U.S. preferential trade agreements contain a significant number of WTO+ and WTO-extra obligations, but EU agreements go much further in their WTO-extra coverage. U.S. agreements, however, typically contain more legally binding provisions, both in WTO+ and WTO-extra areas, than do EU agreements. Horn, Mavroidis, and Sapir conclude that the two have chosen markedly different strategies for including provisions in their PTAs that go beyond the WTO agreements—in particular, where legal inflation, which is almost totally absent in U.S. agreements, is concerned.

The authors are not able to draw from their analysis precise conclusions about this asymmetry of behavior, but the fact that much of the legal inflation occurs in development-related provisions, which are unique to the EU agreements, suggests that the EU has a greater need than the United States to portray its PTAs as not driven solely by commercial interests. The authors speculate that this pattern may reflect a lack of consensus among EU member states about the ultimate purpose of these PTAs and that the wide variety of provisions of weak legal value may represent a compromise among various interests in the EU.

Although both EU and U.S. preferential trade agreements go significantly beyond the WTO agreements, these PTAs contain only small numbers of legally enforceable WTO-extra provisions. Very few provisions can be regarded as breaking new ground: mainly, these are environment and labor standards in U.S. agreements, and competition policy in EU agreements. All such provisions can be seen as dealing with regulatory matters. Other enforceable WTO-extra provisions found in both EU and U.S. PTAs concern domains that are closely related to existing WTO disciplines. Such disciplines are dealt with in the General Agreement on Trade in Services (GATS), for investment and capital movement matters, and in the agreements on Trade-Related Investment Measures (TRIMS) and on Trade-Related Aspects of Intellectual Property Rights (TRIPS).

The fact that the new, legally enforceable WTO-extra provisions all deal with regulatory issues suggests that EU and U.S. agreements can be regarded as vehicles of "regulatory projectionism," or means for the two trade powers to export their own regulatory approaches to their PTA partners. Developing countries' costs and benefits in assuming such regulatory obligations require closer analytical scrutiny.

Source: Horn, Mavroidis, and Sapir 2010.

sequence in which a country chooses to harmonize (or progressively align) its regulations with those its trading partners is thus a relevant consideration. One reason is that the sequence of harmonization may influence the bargaining power of different country groupings in the negotiation concerning the level at which the harmonized standard should be set. For example, the countries in Eastern Europe that acceded to the EU individually could arguably have had a greater say in the EU-wide standard in specific areas if they had been original members, had negotiated collectively, or both. Similarly, harmonization first conducted at the level of the Southern Cone Common Market (Mercosur, Mercado Común del Sur) and then at the level of the Free Trade Area of the Americas (FTAA) or the WTO, could imply different costs and produce a different outcome from direct harmonization at the higher level.

A final consideration concerning preferential regulatory convergence is the administrative burden that may be implied by the maintenance and administration of distinct regulatory requirements and procedures by members and nonmembers of a PTA. Such costs may be so acute for a number of developing countries as to tilt negotiating incentives in favor of multilateral undertakings. It may also encourage the multilateralization of norms first brokered at the regional level or incite countries to simply extend to all third countries treatment similar to that afforded to PTA members, bearing in mind the limits of MFN-based outcomes on regulatory issues.

Third-Country Effects

PTAs between countries that are WTO members or are accessing the WTO can be potentially harmful to nonmember countries because they imply preferential liberalization in favor of certain member states. Such discrimination violates one of the central obligations imposed by both the General Agreement on Tariffs and Trade (GATT) and GATS: the MFN treatment rule. GATS is similar to the GATT in permitting signatories to pursue preferential liberalization arrangements, subject to a number of conditions that are intended to minimize potential adverse effects on nonmembers and on the multilateral trading system as a whole.

In the context of agreements liberalizing trade in goods, a sufficient condition for preferential liberalization to be deemed multilaterally acceptable is that it not have detrimental impacts on third countries. That is, the volume of imports by member countries from the rest of the world should not decline on a product-by-product basis after the implementation of the agreement (Kemp and Wan 1976;

McMillan 1993). Although in principle this is a simple enough criterion, its implementation is not straightforward because the focus is on trade flows at the individual product level.

The liberalization of services trade implies not only that measures restricting the ability of foreign suppliers to engage in cross-border trade are reduced or eliminated but also that factor mobility, including, especially, the establishment of a commercial presence, is allowed. In determining the welfare implications for third parties of regional integration agreements covering services, account therefore needs to be taken of the impact on both trade and factor flows (capital and labor). Both flows are endogenous and interdependent, so that simple prescriptions or criteria along Kemp-Wan lines are no longer applicable (see Baldwin, ch. 3 in this volume).

If trade and factor flows are substitutes, a decline in trade in products need not necessarily be detrimental to an outside country because larger factor flows substitute for trade. This is the standard case in neoclassical trade theory, assuming constant-returns-to-scale technology. With increasing returns, the relationship between factor movements and product-trade flows may well be complementary; that is, an increase in one may be associated with an increase in the other. Although the presumption is that by liberalizing both product and factor markets, the aggregate benefits for participants will increase and that this in turn will be beneficial for the rest of the world (partly through induced growth and investment effects), straightforward criteria with which to evaluate such integration effects ex ante do not exist. These problems are compounded by the difficulty of establishing clear-cut criteria for product likeness in services, given the far greater degree of product differentiation and customer tailoring arising in services markets.

The Practice of Services Liberalization in PTAs

In theory, the inclusion of services trade in PTAs can help achieve greater transparency by means of rules that require mutual openness, heightened credibility of policy through legally binding commitments, and more efficient protection and regulation through rules favoring the choice of superior policy instruments. Relatively little, however, is known about the actual practice of services liberalization in PTAs. What can be learned from experience with PTAs governing services trade? Does the bilateral or regional route to services trade and investment liberalization actually offer significant prospects for speedier or deeper liberalization and more comprehensive rule making than does a multilateral framework?

This section examines the manner in and the degree to which PTAs covering services have achieved the theoretical objectives enumerated above. Substantive provisions and negotiated outcomes under GATS are compared with the progress made under a broad sample of PTAs featuring disciplines on trade in services.

Key Disciplines

Although PTAs covering services come in many different shapes and sizes, they tend to share with GATS a common set of key disciplines governing trade and investment in services, although the burdens of obligation differ (table 12.1). The areas of greatest rule-making convergence between the multilateral and PTA levels relate to scope of coverage. Most commonly found in both sets of agreements, and typically drafted in an identical manner, are disciplines on transparency, national treatment, MFN treatment, payments and transfers, and monopolies and exclusive services providers, as well as general exceptions. Considerable similarities also exist between the multilateral and PTA levels as regards the need for sectoral specificity (i.e., individual sectors or horizontal issues such as labor mobility that require special treatment in annexes). Less convergence (and more limited PTA progress) can be observed in areas of rule making that have posed recurring difficulties in the GATS setting. These include issues such as domestic regulation, emergency safeguards, and subsidy disciplines for services.

Most favored nation and national treatment. The principles of most favored nation and national treatment constitute two of the basic building blocks for any agreement on services, just as they do in the goods area. As with GATS, very few PTAs set out such principles in unqualified form, regardless of whether they are framed as general obligations (which is the case for MFN in virtually all agreements and for national treatment in agreements pursuing a negative-list approach to liberalization) or as obligations that apply solely in sectors where liberalization commitments are positively undertaken.[2]

One can easily understand that within agreements among more than two parties, MFN is required to ensure equality of preferential treatment among all signatories. But why should an MFN obligation be embedded in PTAs concluded among bilateral partners? Part of the reason lies in the principle, first addressed in NAFTA, that members of a given PTA automatically secure any PTA+ benefits that any one party to the original PTA may be willing to accord to a third party in a subsequent PTA. For example, any NAFTA+ commitment that Canada or Mexico might be willing to grant to the EU in the context

of a subsequent PTA would have to be granted to the United States.

The issue of MFN treatment in services sector PTAs has generated much policy controversy in the context of the economic partnership agreements (EPAs) that member states of the EU have entered into with members of the Caribbean Forum of African, Caribbean, and Pacific (ACP) States (CARIFORUM) and plan to conclude with other ACP country groupings. Fears are expressed that such a clause, which would apply only to agreements involving partners accounting for more than 1 percent of world trade, could reduce incentives for South-South PTAs in services if the benefits of such integration automatically flow (for free) to EU members. (For a fuller discussion, see Messerlin 2009.) Such a debate seems to ignore an important political-economy consideration: third-country MFN rights allow smaller countries to benefit from the negotiating clout of larger partners that sign agreements with common partners (see Baldwin, Evenett, and Low 2009).

A weaker variation of the above discussion can be found in the recently concluded free trade agreement (FTA) between India and the Republic of Korea, which stipulates that if any party subsequently enters into another agreement offering more favorable treatment to a nonparty, then that party is to give consideration to a request by the other party for the incorporation of such treatment into the PTA. Any such incorporation should maintain the balance of concessions in the overall agreement. Similarly, in the FTA between the Association of Southeast Asian Nations, Australia, and New Zealand (AANZ), if any more favorable treatment is granted in a future trade agreement by one party to a nonparty to the FTA, then the other parties may request consultations to discuss the possibility of extending no less favorable treatment. In addition, the requested party is to enter into consultations with the requesting party, bearing in mind the overall balance of benefits.[3] (On the related issue of MFN clauses in the context of investment provisions, see Miroudot, ch. 14 in this volume.)

Transparency. As may be expected, given the regulatory intensity of services trade, transparency disciplines are common to all PTAs covering services. These typically stipulate, as is the case under GATS, an obligation to publish relevant measures, to notify new (or changes to existing) measures affecting trade in services, and to establish national enquiry points to provide on request information on measures affecting services trade. One innovation beyond GATS is the provision in some PTAs that members afford the opportunity (to the extent possible, i.e., on a "best-endeavors" basis) for prior comment on proposed

Table 12.1. Key Disciplines in PTAs That Cover Services

Agreement	MFN treatment	National treatment	Market access (nondiscriminatory quantitative restrictions)	Domestic regulation	Emergency safeguards	Subsidy disciplines	Government procurement	Rule of origin (denial of benefits)
GATS (1994)	Yes	Yes	Yes	Yes	Future	Future negotiations	Future negotiations	Yes
Andean Community	Yes	Yes	Yes	Yes[a]	No	No	No	Yes
ASEAN Framework Agreement on Services (1995)	Yes	Yes	Yes	Not specified	Yes	No	No	Yes
ASEAN–Australia (2009)	Consideration on request	Yes	Yes	Yes	No	No	No	Yes
ANZCERTA (1988)	MFN for excluded sectors	Yes	Yes	Yes	No	Export subsidies prohibited; Other subsidies excluded	No	Yes
Bolivia–Mexico (1994)	Yes	Yes	Yes	Yes[a]	Future	No	Separate chapter	Yes
CAFTA–Chile (1999)	Yes	Yes	Yes	Yes[a]	No	No	Separate chapter	Yes
CAFTA–Dominican Republic (1998)	Yes	Yes	Yes	Yes[a]	Future	Future negotiations	Separate chapter	Yes
CAFTA–Dominican Republic–U.S. (2004)	Yes	Yes	Yes	Yes	No	No	Separate chapter	Yes
Canada–Chile (1996)	Yes	Yes	Yes	Yes[a]	No	No	No	Yes
Canada–Colombia (2008)	Yes	Yes	Yes	Yes	No	No	Separate chapter	Yes
Canada–Peru (2008)	Yes	Yes	Yes	Yes	No	No	Separate chapter	Yes
CARICOM (2001)	Not specified	Yes	Not specified	Yes[a]	Yes	No	No	Yes
CARICOM–Dominican Republic (1998)	Yes	Yes	Yes	Yes[a]	Future	No	Separate chapter	Yes
CARIFORUM–EU (2008)	Yes	Yes	Yes	Yes	No	No	Separate chapter	Yes
Central American Economic Integration	Not specified	No general article	No	No	No	No	No	Not specified
Chile–Colombia (2006)	Yes	Yes	Yes	Yes	No	No	Separate chapter	Yes
Chile–Mexico (1998)	Yes	Yes	Yes	Yes[a]	No	No	No	Yes
China–ASEAN (2007)	No	Yes	Yes	Yes	No	No	No	Yes
China–Singapore (2008)	No	Yes	Yes	Yes	No	No	No	Yes
Costa Rica–Mexico (1994)	Yes	Yes	Yes	Yes[a]	Future	No	Separate chapter	Yes
EEA	Yes	Yes	No	Yes	No	Yes (covered under competition disciplines)	No	Beneficiaries specified through definition of "undertakings"
EFTA–Colombia (2008)	Yes	Yes	Yes	Yes	No	No	Separate chapter	Yes

Agreement							
EFTA–GCC (2009)	Yes	Yes	Yes	No	No	Separate chapter	Yes
EFTA–Mexico (2000)	Yes	Yes	Yes	No	No	No	Not specified
EFTA–Singapore (2002)	Yes	Yes	Yes	No	Requests for consultations to be given sympathetic consideration	Separate chapter	Yes
El Salvador–Taiwan, China (2007)	Yes	Yes	Yes	No	No	No	Yes
EU (1957)	Yes	Yes	Yes	No	Yes (covered under competition disciplines)	Yes	Yes
EU–Mexico (1997)	Yes	Yes	No (provisions on regulatory carve-out and recognition)	No	No	Separate chapter	Yes
Group of Three (1994)[b]	Yes	Yes	Yes[a]	No	No	Separate chapter	Yes
Guatemala–Taiwan, China (2005)	Yes	Yes	Yes	No	No	No	Yes
India–Korea, Rep. (2009)	Consideration to be given to request for MFN treatment	Yes	Yes	No	No	No	Yes
India–Singapore (2005)	Consideration to be given to request for MFN treatment	Yes	Yes	No	No	No	Yes
Japan–Chile (2007)	Yes	No (only in relation to financial services)	Yes	No	No	Separate chapter	Yes
Japan–Indonesia (2007)	Yes	Yes	Yes	No	No	No	Yes
Japan–Malaysia (2005)	Yes	Yes	Yes	Future	No	No	Yes
Japan–Philippines (2006)	Yes	Yes	Yes	No	No	Future	Yes
Japan–Singapore (2002)	No	Yes	Yes	No	No	Separate chapter	Yes
Japan–Switzerland (2009)	Yes	Yes	Yes	Future	No	No	Yes
Japan–Thailand (2007)	Yes	Yes	Yes	Future	No	Separate chapter	Yes
Korea, Rep.–Singapore (2005)	Yes	Yes	Yes	No	No	Separate chapter	Yes
Malaysia–Pakistan 2007)	Yes	Yes	Yes	Future	No	No	Yes
Mercosur (1997)	Yes	Yes	Yes	No	Future negotiations	Future negotiations	Yes
Mexico–Nicaragua (1997)	Yes	Yes	Yes[a]	No	No	Future negotiations	Yes
Mexico–Northern Triangle (2000)[c]	Yes	Yes[a]	Yes[a]	Future	No	No	Yes

(continued next page)

Table 12.1. Key Disciplines in PTAs That Cover Services (*continued*)

Agreement	MFN treatment	National treatment	Market access (nondiscriminatory quantitative restrictions)	Domestic regulation	Emergency safeguards	Subsidy disciplines	Government procurement	Rule of origin (denial of benefits)
NAFTA (1992)	Yes	Yes	Yes	Yes[a]	No	No	Separate chapter	Yes
New Zealand–China (2008)	Yes	Yes	Yes	Yes	No	No	No	Yes
Singapore–Jordan (2005)	No	Yes	Yes	Yes	No	No	No	Yes
Singapore–Panama (2006)	Yes	Yes	Yes	Yes	No	No	Separate chapter	Yes
Taiwan, China–Nicaragua (2006)	Yes	Yes	Yes	Yes	No	No	No	Yes
U.S.–Chile (2003)	Yes	Yes	Yes	Yes[a]	No	No	Separate chapter	Yes
U.S.–Colombia (2006)	Yes	Yes	Yes	Yes	No	No	Separate chapter	Yes
U.S.–Jordan (2000)	Yes	Yes	Yes	Yes	No	Future negotiations	Yes	Yes
U.S.–Oman (2006)	Yes	Yes	Yes	Yes	No	No	Separate chapter	Yes
U.S.–Panama (2007)	Yes	Yes	Yes	Yes	No	No	Separate chapter	Yes
U.S.–Singapore (2003)	Yes	Yes	Yes	Yes[a]	No	No	Separate chapter	Yes

Source: Authors' compilation.

Note: ANZCERTA, Australia–New Zealand Closer Economic Relations Trade Agreement; ASEAN, Association of Southeast Asian Nations; CAFTA, Central America Free Trade Agreement; CARICOM, Caribbean Community; CARIFORUM, Caribbean Forum of African, Caribbean, and Pacific (ACP) States; EEA, European Economic Area; EFTA, European Free Trade Association; EU, European Union; GATS, General Agreement on Trade in Services; GCC, Gulf Cooperation Council; Mercosur, Southern Cone Common Market (Mercado Común del Sur); MFN, most favored nation; NAFTA, North American Free Trade Agreement; PTA, preferential trade agreement.

a. Rules on domestic regulation are set out more narrowly; in most cases they apply only to the licensing and certification of professional services suppliers.

b. Colombia, Mexico, and República Bolivariana de Venezuela.

c. The Northern Triangle countries are El Salvador, Guatemala, and Honduras.

changes to services regulations. Increasingly, such provisions are becoming legally binding. This is notably the case in North-South PTAs, following a trend initiated by the FTAs between the United States and Chile and between the United States and Singapore. The latter development offers an interesting example of what could be described as "tactical" or "demonstration-effect" regionalism, with advances at the PTA level creating precedents that their proponents hope will facilitate their subsequent replication at the multilateral level.[4]

Market access. PTAs covering services typically address nondiscriminatory quantitative restrictions that impede access to services markets (and which are partly dealt with under GATS Article XVI). A number of earlier PTAs, however, particularly those concluded in the Western Hemisphere and modeled on North American Free Trade Agreement (NAFTA), were actually weaker than GATS, committing parties solely to making such restrictions fully transparent in annexes listing nonconforming measures and to a best-endeavors approach to their progressive dismantling in the future. (In contrast, under GATS, WTO members undertake policy bindings in sectors, subsectors, and modes of supply against which market access commitments are scheduled.) The WTO-minus provisions of earlier agreements are no longer found in the newest-generation PTAs entered into by the United States, Canada, and other countries that had initially agreed to the lower standard of treatment. The newer language is similar to that found early on in Mercosur and in the various PTAs to which EU members are party; it prohibits the introduction of new nondiscriminatory quantitative restrictions on any scheduled commitments and sectors, mirroring the similar requirement in GATS Article XVI.

Domestic regulation. The assumption behind the argument, discussed above, that PTAs in the services field provide scope for creating optimal regulatory areas, is that the aggregate adjustment costs of regulatory convergence and policy harmonization are likely to be smaller when foreign regulatory preferences are similar and regulatory institutions are broadly compatible. Both sets of conditions are likelier, on balance, to obtain among countries that are "closer" geographically, linguistically, culturally, or historically (Mattoo and Fink 2002). In practice, the broad intersect between domestic regulation and services trade has tended to prove intractable (just as it has under GATS), even among the smaller subset of countries engaging in PTAs.

In many instances, PTAs address domestic regulation in a manner analogous to that found in GATS Article VI—that is, with a focus on procedural transparency and on ensuring that regulatory activity does not lead to unduly

burdensome restrictions on trade or investment in services, or to disguised ones. With the exception of the EU itself and of agreements reached between the EU and countries in Central and Eastern Europe before accession to the EU, no PTA to date has made tangible progress in delineating the elements of a necessity test aimed at ensuring broad proportionality between regulatory means and objectives, as contemplated under the GATS Article VI:4 mandate (see Delimatsis 2008). Neither NAFTA nor the many NAFTA-type agreements reached in the Western Hemisphere contain in their services chapters an article on domestic regulation per se. Instead, these agreements feature more narrowly drawn disciplines relating to the licensing and certification of professionals.[5]

On most matters relating to rules governing domestic regulation in services trade, progress has been greater at the multilateral than at the PTA level. Such progress has been evident in the Doha Round discussions on licensing and qualification requirements and procedures, technical standards, transparency, and special and differential treatment. The disciplines on licensing procedures found in a number of recent PTAs entered into by members of the Friends of Domestic Regulation (the main *demandeurs* for domestic regulation disciplines at the multilateral level) reflect the progress made in the Doha Round negotiations. For instance, Article 65:3(a) of the China–Singapore FTA makes specific provision allowing applicants to remedy deficiencies in their applications. In addition, in cases where an application was denied or terminated, the applicant is afforded the possibility of resubmitting a new application at its own discretion. Similar provisions are found in Article 10:5 of the AANZ FTA and Article 111:3 of the New Zealand–China FTA. Although the provisions on licensing procedures in these PTAs do not go as far as the draft Doha Round proposals, they do offer an interesting illustration of the iterative relationship between PTAs and the WTO and of the way in which PTAs can reverse-engineer developments originating at the multilateral level. The area of domestic regulation is one in which increasing numbers of PTAs embed existing GATS provisions and signal members' desire to incorporate by reference the ultimate outcome of the ongoing GATS Article VI:4 negotiating mandate. In so doing, PTAs cease to assume the role of rule-making laboratories. This trend is most common with regard to the "unfinished agenda" of GATS (apart from government procurement, where significant PTA-induced movement has occurred in the services area).

Harmonization, mutual recognition, and regulatory cooperation. With a few notable exceptions—notably, the EU and Australia–New Zealand Closer Economic Relations Trade Agreement (ANZCERTA), both of which involve a level of integration that extends to a common labor market—tangible progress on matters of regulatory harmonization or mutual recognition within PTAs has generally proved more arduous than might be expected in theory (see box 12.2).

Although a number of PTAs call on members to recognize—at times, on the basis of explicit timetables—foreign educational credentials and professional qualifications in selected professions, progress in concluding mutual recognition agreements has often proved slow, difficult, and partial. This is particularly noteworthy in agreements between countries with federal political regimes and systems

in which authority is delegated to licensing bodies at the subnational level.

Still, in comparison with the progress registered under GATS Article VII (recognition), reliance on the subsidiary approaches afforded by PTAs has led to some tangible progress. Such advances appear more pronounced within South-South PTAs such as Mercosur and the Association of Southeast Asian Nations (ASEAN) Framework Agreement on Services (AFAS), both of which have seen the conclusion of mutual recognition agreements in several regulated professions—for example, for nurses, engineers, accountants, architects, and lawyers.

Box 12.2. Harmonization and Mutual Recognition in Services: Promise and Pitfalls

The pessimism that often greets calls for regulatory harmonization is based on the absence of widely accepted international standards in services. Where such standards do exist, as in financial services and maritime transport, meeting them tends to be seen as a first step toward acceptability, rather than as a sufficient condition for market access. The General Agreement on Trade in Services (GATS), like the General Agreement on Tariffs and Trade (GATT), does not specifically require the use of international standards. It generally provides weaker incentives for the use of such standards than do the Sanitary and Phytosanitary (SPS) and Technical Barriers to Trade (TBT) Agreements, and it does not include a presumption of compliance; those agreements do.

It is unlikely that meaningful international standards for most services will be developed soon. Still, in those areas in which global standards do exist, the likelihood of disguised or needlessly restrictive impediments to trade and investment may be significantly lessened. The presumption must also be that the existence of such standards may significantly facilitate trade and investment by promoting cross-border trade and by helping to overcome the various information asymmetries that hold back such trade and its commensurate liberalization under GATS.

Accordingly, efforts should be directed toward ensuring that trade agreements create a stronger presumption in favor of genuinely international standards in services trade. As with recognition agreements, efforts to develop international standards for services trade will likely require greater doses of technical assistance and capacity building. This may be usefully done at the national and regional levels, particularly because proximity, whether geographic, historical, or cultural, may be expected to facilitate regulatory convergence.

Efforts to promote the adoption of international standards will invariably be carried out outside a trade policy framework. Contrary to much popular belief, trade agreements are not in the business of making regulatory standards. Rather, they specify how such standards are to be implemented, should they affect trade. The relevant institutions for promoting international standards for services are to be found in the various specialized regulatory institutions, such as the Bank for International Settlements for banking standards, the International Telecommunications Union for telecommunications, and the International Standardization Organization (ISO) for various categories of services, including the means of producing and supplying them.

A multilateral agreement such as GATS cannot mandate countries to conclude MRAs. As in the case of regional agreements, multilateral disciplines can be more or less permissive with regard to mutual recognition. The practice of MRAs suggests that their scope is often quite limited; they are invariably concluded between very similar countries. Even in a region with as strong an integrationist dynamic as Europe, and despite a significant level of prior or complementary (minimal) regulatory harmonization, the effect of MRAs has been limited by the unwillingness of many host-country regulators to cede full control. It should come as no surprise that MRAs have yet to exert significant effects on services trade.

Such an outcome in turn raises the question of the benefits and costs of MRAs. Here, the analogy with regional integration agreements is again useful, as MRAs can be likened to sector-specific preferential arrangements. Where regulatory barriers are prohibitively high—one can imagine autarky as the ultimate example—recognition can only be trade creating. If they are not, selective recognition can have discriminatory effects and can lead to trade diversion. The result may well be to create trade according to a pattern of mutual trust rather than on the basis of the forces of comparative advantage.

GATS Article VII (recognition) strikes a delicate balance by allowing such agreements, provided that third countries have the opportunity to accede or to demonstrate equivalence. Article VII thus has a desirable open-ended aspect that Article V (dealing with integration agreements) does not. This makes it particularly worrisome that many MRAs have been notified by WTO members under Article V rather than Article VII. In any case, the key concern for any multilateral agreement should be not how those who enjoy preferential access are treated, but how those who do not enjoy such access are treated. Ironically, the only line of defense of the rights of third countries could well come from a necessity test aimed at ensuring that such countries are not subjected to unnecessarily burdensome regulation even if they are not parties to an MRA.

Because of the potential of MRAs to create trade and investment distortions, bilateral or plurilateral recognition agreements should respect the nondiscrimination principle, as mandated by Article VII of GATS. Such agreements should not, as a rule, be notified under GATS Article V but should, rather, be open to all eligible participants under the terms of Article VII.

Source: Mattoo and Sauvé 2003.

Most PTAs feature provisions calling for greater institutional cooperation between the parties' domestic regulators in implementing agreements, typically setting up joint regulatory commissions and periodic meetings at the senior or ministerial level. Such cooperation, even though it proceeds from soft-law undertakings, can still yield important trade- and investment-facilitating benefits and can help build trust, enhance enforcement capacities, and identify postnegotiation implementation bottlenecks. All of these may be key ingredients—indeed, preconditions—for regulatory harmonization and effective mutual recognition initiatives.

Emergency safeguard mechanisms, subsidy disciplines, and government procurement. With few exceptions, PTAs have made little headway in tackling the key "unfinished" rule-making items on the GATS agenda. This is most notably the case for disciplines on an emergency safeguard mechanism (ESM) and subsidy disciplines for services trade, where governments confront the same conceptual challenges, data limitations, feasibility challenges, and political sensitivities at the regional level as they do on the multilateral front. For example, the countries of Southeast Asia, which until recently were among the most vocal proponents of an ESM in GATS, have yet to adopt such a provision within AFAS. To date, in the Western Hemisphere, only members of the Caribbean Community (CARICOM) have adopted (but have not yet used) such an instrument, and questions remain as to the necessity and the operational feasibility of an ESM in services trade, given the flexibilities embedded in the very conduct of market opening under most agreements.

NAFTA provides one example of sector-specific experimentation with safeguard-type measures. Under the terms of the agreement's chapter on financial services, Mexico was allowed to impose market-share caps if the specific foreign ownership thresholds agreed to (25 percent for banks and 30 percent for securities firms) were reached before 2004. Mexico could have recourse to such market-share limitations only once during the transition period and could only impose them for a three-year period. Under no circumstances could such measures be maintained beyond the end of the transition period foreseen for market opening under NAFTA (e.g., 2001). Mexico, in fact, never made use of such provisions even as the aggregate share of foreign participation in its financial system became significantly higher than the specified thresholds (Sauvé and Gonzalez-Hermosillo 1993; Sauvé 2002). It is interesting, if somewhat surprising, that no further attempt has been made, either in PTAs or at the WTO level, to consider the scope for, and the practical means of, replicating the Mexican financial

services example on a sectoral basis for areas in which market opening may be prone to unanticipated dislocations, with injurious consequences for smaller domestic firms—in distribution, for instance. The quest for a generic emergency safeguard measure applicable to all sectors and predicated on the GATT model has led to a negotiating stalemate at both the PTA and WTO levels. (For a fuller discussion, see Sauvé 2002; Marconini 2005; Pierola 2008.)

On the issue of disciplines for service-related subsidies, with the exceptions of the EU (including its preaccession agreements with countries in Central and Eastern Europe) and of ANZCERTA, the quest for rule-making advances has proved just as elusive at the PTA as at the WTO level. This is particularly so within countries with federal systems of governance.

Whereas a number of PTAs (e.g., Mercosur) replicate the exhortation in GATS to develop future disciplines on subsidies in services trade, most PTAs that cover services specifically exclude subsidy practices. Paralleling provisions found in GATS, the FTA between the European Free Trade Association (EFTA) and Singapore requires that sympathetic consideration be given to requests by a party for consultations in instances where subsidy practices affecting trade in services may be deemed to have injurious effects. The area of subsidy disciplines, like that of domestic regulation, is one in which many PTAs signal a desire to incorporate by reference the outcome of any agreed outcome from ongoing (but largely stagnant) discussions at the WTO level. (For a fuller discussion, see Sauvé 2002; Adlung 2007; Poretti 2008.)

More progress has been made at the PTA level in opening up government procurement markets in services. This has typically been achieved through negotiations in the area of government procurement per se—as with the WTO's Government Procurement Agreement (GPA)—rather than through services negotiations.[6]

The approach taken in PTAs is for the most part very similar to that adopted in the WTO; that is, nondiscrimination among members within the scope of scheduled commitments, and procedures to enhance transparency and due process. PTAs whose members are all parties to the GPA, such as EFTA and the Singapore–Japan FTA, specifically mention that the relevant GPA articles apply, and most agreements concluded in the Western Hemisphere basically replicate GPA disciplines at the regional level. In contrast to the GPA, which applies in principle to purchases by both central and subnational governments, most PTAs provide for binding government procurement disciplines at the national level only (OECD 2002c; see also Dawar and Evenett, ch. 17 in this volume).

Investment. A policy domain in which PTAs have achieved considerable progress, while forward movement has stalled in the WTO, is that of investment rule making. Most PTAs feature comprehensive disciplines on the protection and liberalization of cross-border investment activity. There is scope in this area for investor-state arbitration alongside WTO-like state-to-state dispute settlement, together with extensive liberalization commitments, most often brokered on a negative-list basis. Given the central role assumed by investment as the most important mode of service supply, such developments are of some significance for the operation of services markets and for the promotion of more contestable entry conditions in them. (For a fuller discussion of the evolution of international rules on investment, see Beviglia Zampetti and Sauvé 2007.) The extent to which PTAs featuring comprehensive investment norms might influence the WTO's evolving architecture of rules will very much depend on prospects for crafting a multilateral regime for investment. Any such agreement at the WTO level would likely raise a number of intractable questions regarding the scope of GATS—notably, its coverage of commercial presence as a mode of supplying services. Starting with NAFTA in 1994, a large and growing number of PTAs has shown how the treatment of investment in services need not be distinguished from that in other sectors subject to trade disciplines. The issue of preferential advances in investment rule making is taken up by Miroudot, ch. 14 in this volume.

Rules of origin and denial of benefits. A final area of rule making concerns rules of origin, which determine who ultimately qualifies for preferential treatment under PTAs. In services agreements, this matter is generally addressed under provisions dealing with denial of benefits (see Beviglia Zampetti and Sauvé 2007).

The literature on rules of origin has focused almost exclusively on merchandise trade flows and hence on policies for determining the origin or nationality of tangible *products*. Much less attention has been paid to the increasingly important issue of how to determine the origin of *producers*, which is the primary concern of the study of rules of origin in services trade and investment. The ability to contest services markets often requires the physical presence of suppliers in the territory of consumers, either in the form of individual services providers performing cross-border transactions on a temporary (contract) basis, or as entities servicing a foreign market on the basis of a commercial presence in that market. Governments that are signatories of trade and investment agreements may, accordingly, need to ascertain whether suppliers originate

in other countries, with a view to extending or denying the benefits foreseen under such agreements.

Experience shows that rules of origin for services and investment can play a significant role in determining the degree to which regional trading arrangements discriminate against nonmember countries, and hence the extent of potentially costly trade and investment diversion. When levels of protection differ among participating countries, the effective preference granted to a trading partner will depend on the restrictiveness of the applied rule of origin. In the extreme, if one participant has a fully liberalized market, the adoption of a liberal rule of origin by the other participants can be likened to MFN liberalization because services and services suppliers can enter or establish themselves in the liberal jurisdiction and from there move to, or service, the partner countries.

From an efficiency perspective, origin rules for services should allow for third-country services suppliers, particularly those operating through a commercial presence (via mode 3 entry) to take advantage of, and contribute to, the benefits of an integrating area. Under a liberal rule of origin for services and investment aimed at ensuring that established foreign operators are not mere shell companies but conduct substantial business operations in the host-country market, third-country investors and service providers can take full advantage of the expanded market opportunities afforded by the creation of a PTA by establishing a commercial presence within the integration area.[7] Not surprisingly, participants that seek to benefit from preferential access to a protected market and deny benefits to third-country competitors are likely to argue for the adoption of restrictive rules of origin. This may be the attitude, in particular, of regionally dominant but nonglobally competitive service providers toward third-country competition within a regionally integrating area.

The adoption of restrictive rules of origin is permissible under GATS Article V:3, which allows PTAs concluded between developing countries (South-South PTAs) to restrict the benefits of integration to service suppliers that are owned and controlled by citizens of the integrating area. It is not clear whether such flexibility serves the development interests of those that use the rules. Several South-South PTAs, notably ASEAN, Mercosur, the Andean Pact, and the FTAs between China and Hong Kong SAR, China, and between China and Macao SAR, China, have opted for a restrictive policy stance in this area.

The policy stance on rules of origin for services and investment in a PTA can play an important role in promoting or inhibiting access to the most efficient suppliers of services. In many services sectors, the most efficient (or most globally competitive) suppliers tend to be either developed-country firms or firms originating outside an integrating area. Accordingly, the adoption of rules of origin that restrict benefits to nationals of member states can have detrimental effects by potentially locking integrating partners into suboptimal patterns of production and consumption. This problem may be compounded, and may generate longer-term deadweight losses, because many services, particularly network-based services, involve significant location-specific sunk costs, such that first movers (even if relatively inefficient) can exert long-term dominance and extract monopolistic rents. Then, a country may be stuck with inferior suppliers for a long time even if it subsequently liberalizes on an MFN basis. Indeed, because of the importance of sunk costs in many services industries, sequential entry (which preferential liberalization with restrictive rules of origin can easily promote) can produce very different results from simultaneous entry. If entry is costly, an incumbent may indeed be able to deter entry, leading to greater market concentration and a reduction in consumer welfare. (For a fuller discussion, see Mattoo and Fink 2002.) Some measure of solace can be taken from the observation, confirmed in this chapter's sample of reviewed PTAs, that to date, most preferential agreements have adopted the most liberal rule of origin for mode 3 suppliers, whereby any juridical person incorporated in any party to an integration agreement and conducting substantial business operations there receives full treaty benefits.

Modalities of Liberalization: Negative-List versus Positive-List Approaches

Two major approaches toward the liberalization of trade and investment in services have been manifest in PTAs and in the WTO: (a) the positive-list, or "bottom-up," approach (typically, a hybrid approach featuring a voluntary, positive choice of sectors, subsectors, and modes of supply in which governments are willing to make binding commitments, together with a negative list of nonconforming measures to be retained in scheduled areas), and (b) the negative-list, or "top-down/list it or lose it," approach. Although both negotiating modalities can be made to produce broadly equivalent liberalization outcomes, the two approaches may generate qualitative differences that may be significant from both a domestic and an international governance point of view.[8] Even though the debate over these competing approaches appears settled at the level of GATS, it is useful to recall these differences because the issue is still very much alive in the PTA context, and WTO members

are contemplating the scope that may exist in the current negotiations for making possible improvements to the GATS architecture.

Under a GATS-like positive or hybrid approach to scheduling liberalization commitments, countries agree to undertake national treatment and market access commitments specifying (through reservations in scheduled areas) the nature of treatment or access offered to foreign services or foreign service suppliers.[9] Countries retain the full right to undertake no commitments. In such instances, they are under no legal obligation to supply information to their trading partners on the nature of discriminatory or access-impeding regulations maintained at the domestic level.

A related feature of GATS that tends to be replicated in PTAs that espouse a bottom-up or hybrid approach to liberalization is that countries have the possibility of making commitments that do not reflect (i.e., are made below) the regulatory status quo—a long-standing practice in tariff negotiations that was replicated in a GATS setting.

The alternative, top-down approach to liberalization of services trade and investment is based on the concept of negative listing, whereby all sectors and nonconforming measures are to be liberalized unless otherwise specified in a transparent manner in reservation lists appended to an agreement. Nonconforming measures contained in reservation lists are then usually liberalized through consultations or, as in GATS, periodic negotiations.

It is interesting to note that despite the strong opposition that such an approach generated when first mooted by a few GATT contracting parties during the Uruguay Round, the negative-list approach to services liberalization has recently been adopted by a majority of PTAs covering services that have been notified to the WTO. In the sample of 55 PTAs under review in this chapter, 33 (60 percent of the total) follow a negative-list approach.

First used (for trade in services only, in the absence of an investment chapter) by Australia and New Zealand in ANZCERTA, the approach was further developed by Canada, Mexico, and the United States in NAFTA in 1994. Mexico has played a pivotal role in extending this liberalization approach and similar types of services disciplines (i.e., right of nonestablishment) to other PTAs it has signed with countries in South and Central America.[10] The pattern has been replicated in PTAs signed between Central and South American countries, on the one hand, and Asian economies, on the other hand, particularly in PTAs involving the region's most advanced partners— among them, Australia, Japan, Korea, New Zealand, Singapore, and Taiwan, China.

A number of distinguishing features of negative listing can be identified. First, such an approach enshrines and affirms the up-front commitment of signatories to an overarching set of general obligations (subject to reservations). This is currently the case under GATS, primarily with respect to the agreement's provisions on MFN treatment (Article II, with scope for one-time exceptions) and transparency (Article III). Most other disciplines apply in an à la carte manner to sectors and modes of supply on the terms inscribed in members' schedules of commitments.[11]

A second, and perhaps more immediately operational, defining characteristic of negative listing lies in its ability to generate a standstill—that is, to establish a stronger floor of liberalization by locking in the statutory or regulatory status quo. Such an approach avoids the GATS pitfall of allowing a wedge to arise between applied and bound regulatory or statutory practices.[12] An important caveat concerns the propensity of negative-list agreements to allow parties to lodge reservations that preserve future regulatory freedom in a manner analogous to unbound or nonscheduled commitments under GATS. Here again, and unlike GATS, which yields no information on the nature of nonconforming measures retained in what are typically sensitive sectors, negative-list agreements oblige signatories to reveal the nature of existing nonconforming measures in such reserved sectors.

The main governance-enhancing feature arising from the adoption of a negative-list approach is thus the greater level of transparency it can generate if adhered to properly.[13] The information contained in reservation lists will be important to prospective traders and investors, who value the one-stop shopping attributes of a comprehensive inventory of potential restrictions in foreign markets. Such an inventory is also likely to benefit home-country negotiators, assisting them in establishing a hierarchy of impediments to tackle in future negotiations. This information can in turn lend itself more easily to formula-based liberalization—for instance, by encouraging members to agree to reduce or progressively phase out "revealed" nonconforming measures that may be similar across countries, such as quantitative limitations on foreign ownership in selected sectors (see Sauvé 1996).

The production of a negative list may also help generate a useful domestic policy dialogue between the trade-negotiating and regulatory communities, thereby encouraging countries to perform a comprehensive audit of existing trade- and investment-restrictive measures, benchmark domestic regulatory regimes against best international practices, and revisit the rationale for, and the most efficient means of, satisfying domestic policy objectives.[14]

A further liberalizing feature found in a number of PTAs using a negative-list approach to liberalization consists of a ratchet mechanism (table 12.2), whereby any autonomous liberalization measure undertaken by a PTA member between periodic negotiating rounds is automatically reflected in that member's schedule of commitments or lists of reservations. A provision of this kind typically aims at preventing countries from backsliding with respect to autonomously decreed policy changes. It may also provide negotiating credit for autonomous liberalization by developing country members, an issue currently under discussion in the GATS context.

Such ratchet provisions are found in many South-South PTAs covering services in the Western Hemisphere. For instance, Article 10 of the Andean Community's Decision 439, on services, applies to all new measures adopted by member countries that affect trade in services and does not allow for the establishment of new measures that would increase the degree of nonconformity or fail to comply with the commitments contained in Article 6 (market access) and Article 8 (national treatment) of the decision. Article 36 of the CARICOM Protocol, another status quo or standstill provision, prohibits members from introducing any new restrictions on the provision of services in the community by CARICOM nationals.

A provision of this type can exert positive effects on the investment climate of host countries by signaling to foreign suppliers the host countries' commitment not to reverse liberalization (see Hoekman and Sauvé 1994; Stephenson 2001c). Such credibility-enhancing provisions may be especially important for smaller countries that often find it difficult to attract larger doses of foreign direct investment.

A recent comprehensive review of East Asian PTA commitments in services suggests that some qualification is required to the common belief that negative listing inherently yields greater transparency (see Fink and Molinuevo 2007). Some agreements that use negative listing provide a clearer road map of existing regulatory impediments, but others fall short of the expected transparency because, as noted above, they use sweeping sectoral or mode-specific carve-outs or exclude entire categories of measures, such as subnational measures.[15]

Evidence on the impact of negative listing on induced levels of liberalization is also mixed. Some parties have concluded hybrid-list agreements that achieve greater liberalization than their negative-list agreements with other partners. For example, Singapore's positively listed commitments in its PTA with Japan provide significantly greater coverage than its negatively listed commitments in its PTA with Australia. There is little doubt, however, that when done properly, negative-list agreements may yield

Table 12.2. Negotiating Approaches in Services Trade

Main features	GATS-like (hybrid approach)	Negative-list approach
General description	Schedule of commitments positively lists sectors, subsectors, and modes of supply in which commitments on market access, national treatment, and any additional commitments are undertaken and negatively lists any nonconforming treatment or measures retained therein.	Free trade and investment in services are assumed unless specific existing measures are inscribed in reservation lists indicating the sector, subsector, industrial classification, nature of the treaty provision that is violated, description of the measure in question, and nature of the measure's nonconformity with regard to specific treaty provisions.
	A la carte liberalization: members retain the right to choose sectors, subsectors, and modes of supply in which they are prepared to undertake legally binding market access, national treatment, and any other additional commitments.	List or lose: all nonconforming measures not notified at the moment of a PTA's entry into force are automatically bound as "free" (signatories lose the right to invoke nonconforming measures that are not inscribed in their lists of reservations on an agreement's entry into force).
Locking in of regulatory status quo	Not guaranteed unless otherwise specified. Members are typically allowed to schedule commitments below the regulatory status quo, regardless of the level of market openness flowing from existing domestic regulatory measures.	Generally guaranteed.
Transparency	Generally more limited, as signatories retain the flexibility not to schedule commitments or to schedule commitments below the regulatory status quo.	Generally greater, given focus on reserving existing nonconforming measures, but some agreements allow signatories to lodge sweeping reservations (e.g., all nonconforming measures that exist at the subnational level).
Scope for introducing future nonconforming measures	Can be secured either by omitting a sector, subsector, or mode of supply from a member's schedule of commitments or by scheduling an unbound commitment. No information on the nature of nonconforming measures is generated in nonscheduled or unbound sectors, subsectors, or modes of supply.	Specific annexes allow signatories to a negative list PTA to retain future policy flexibility in sectors, subsectors, and modes of supply. These become the GATS equivalent of unbound measures. Parties are normally required to describe the current level of nonconformity prevailing in such reserved areas.
Ratchet mechanism	None.	Many negative-list PTAs feature a ratchet provision aimed at ensuring that any autonomous measure of a liberalizing nature enacted after a PTA's entry into force or, where envisaged, between periodic negotiating rounds, becomes the liberalizing party's commitment under the PTA, with market-opening benefits automatically extended to PTA partners on an MFN basis in the case of plurilateral PTAs.

Source: Authors' compilation.
Note: GATS, General Agreement on Trade in Services; MFN, most favored nation; PTA, preferential trade agreement.

important benefits in regulatory transparency and locking-in of the regulatory status quo.

Two potential pitfalls arising from the use of negative listing can be identified. First, such an approach may be administratively burdensome, particularly for developing countries. The burden may be mitigated by allowing for progressivity in the completion of members' negative lists of nonconforming measures.[16] The costs of compliance must also be weighed against some of the benefits in governance and best regulatory practices described above. A second concern is that the adoption of a negative list implies that governments ultimately forgo the right to introduce discriminatory or access-impairing measures in the future—even in sectors that do not yet exist or are not regulated at the time of an agreement's entry into force.

To assuage the latter concerns while promoting the transparency-enhancing properties associated with the use of negative listing, a suggestion has been made that countries be encouraged (possibly in the WTO context) to exchange comprehensive and nonbinding lists of nonconforming measures—something that has been done in the Andean Community and is being considered for Mercosur. (See Sauvé and Wilkie 2000 for a fuller description of such a proposal.)

In an important new development along the above lines, exemplified in the most recent Japanese PTAs, negotiators have sought to combine the best properties of negative and hybrid listing. Recent Japanese PTAs maintain a GATS-like hybrid approach to scheduling, preserving the right of countries to pick and choose those sectors, subsectors, and modes of supply in which they desire to make commitments. The country's PTAs balance this flexibility with the twin obligations of scheduling the regulatory status quo (to prevent members from offering less access than currently exists) and exchanging nonbinding lists of nonconforming measures, to promote greater regulatory transparency. The economic partnership agreement between the EU and CARIFORUM takes a similar approach by allowing parties to schedule status quo commitments on a GATS basis. (For a fuller discussion, see Sauvé 2009; Sauvé and Ward 2009b; Marconini and Sauvé 2010.)

PTAs have become more flexible, and important variations are being introduced, depending on the negotiating partners. For instance, Japan's PTAs with Indonesia, Malaysia, the Philippines, and Thailand have been conducted along positive-list lines, while those with Chile and Switzerland take a negative-list approach. PTAs increasingly mix positive- and negative-list approaches within the same agreement. Recourse to negative listing is particularly pronounced in the investment area. Some agreements use both approaches, depending on the sector or mode of supply (e.g., positive listing for cross-border trade and negative listing for commercial presence, or negative listing for banking services and positive listing for insurance services).

Assessing the Depth of Preferential Liberalization in Services Trade

The depth of services liberalization varies considerably across PTAs, with notable differences across sectors, modes of supply, and approaches to scheduling commitments (i.e., hybrid versus negative-list approaches), as well as across country groups (North-North, North-South, and South-South) and partner pairings. This chapter does not attempt a comprehensive assessment of the market-opening advances achieved in services-related PTAs across the sample of agreements under review, but it does draw on a number of important recent contributions to the literature to offer stylized facts about the WTO+ nature of PTAs in services trade.

Sequencing

Preferential market opening in services rarely, if ever, predates preferential talks in goods trade. Countries that engage in services-related PTAs either conduct such negotiations alongside merchandise trade negotiations in a manner analogous to the WTO's single undertaking approach or pursue services talks sequentially once a PTA in goods trade has been agreed.[17] The latter approach is more common among South-South PTAs, whereas agreements involving members of the Organisation for Economic Co-operation and Development (OECD) typically espouse the single undertaking route.

Countries preferring sequential liberalization may wish to test the waters in goods trade first, raising comfort levels with new trading partners. They may also wish to limit the scope for bargaining across several policy areas that takes place in WTO-type negotiations, although that choice may well constrain negotiations, given the narrowness of the resulting negotiating remit. Sequential liberalization may also allow partners to identify key services inputs and address potential services sector bottlenecks holding back trade in manufactured products or primary commodities. The greater degree of liberalization achieved to date under North-South PTAs, particularly those based on a negative-list approach, helps explain why PTAs predicated on a single undertaking approach have tended to attain greater levels of market opening.

The fact that PTAs have achieved significant progress in market-opening terms when compared with GATS should come as no surprise when one considers that the WTO commitments under GATS were brokered in the early 1990s—in the case of telecommunications and financial services, where the most progress was made, in 1997. By far the greatest number of services-related PTAs postdates the entry into force of GATS. Such agreements have taken advantage of the rising comfort levels afforded by the pedagogical journey undertaken during the Uruguay Round, the increased services-specific trade-related technical assistance dispensed at both the multilateral and PTA levels in the post–Uruguay Round period, and the far-reaching degree of unilateral liberalization in services markets that characterized the period and which the WTO-GATS has not yet been able to catch up with and consolidate. A more analytically meaningful comparison would thus be one

Table 12.3. Key Features of PTAs That Cover Services

Agreement	Scope or coverage[a]	Negotiating approach	Treatment of investment in services	Right of nonestablishment	Ratchet mechanism
GATS	Universal	Positive list	Covered as "commercial presence" (mode 3)	No	No
Andean Community	Universal	Negative list	Covered as "commercial presence"	No	No
ANZCERTA	Universal	Negative list	Covered as "commercial presence" but no common disciplines on investment	Yes	No
ASEAN–Australia–New Zealand	Universal	Positive list	Covered as "commercial presence" and under investment	No	No
ASEAN Framework Agreement on Services	Universal	Positive list	Covered as "commercial presence" and under a separate investment chapter	No	No
Bolivia–Mexico	Universal	Negative list	Separate chapter	Yes	Yes
CACM	Construction services	Positive list	Not specified	No	No
CAFTA–Chile	Universal	Negative list	Separate chapter	Yes	Yes
CAFTA–Dominican Republic	Universal	Negative list	Separate chapter	Yes	Yes
CAFTA–Dominican Republic–U.S.	Universal	Negative list	Separate chapter	Yes	Yes
Canada–Chile	Universal	Negative list	Separate chapter	Yes	Yes
Canada–Colombia	Universal	Negative list	Separate chapter	Yes	Yes
Canada–Peru	Universal	Negative list	Separate chapter	Yes	Yes
CARICOM	Universal	Negative list	Covered as "commercial presence" and in separate chapters (on right of establishment and movement of capital)	No	No
CARICOM–Dominican Republic	Universal	Negative list	Separate chapter	Yes	No
CARIFORUM–EU	Universal (audiovisual services explicitly excluded)[a]	Positive list	Covered as "commercial presence"	No	No
Chile–Colombia	Universal	Negative list	Separate chapter	Yes	Yes
Chile–Mexico	Universal	Negative list	Separate chapter	Yes	Yes
China–ASEAN	Universal	Positive list	Covered as "commercial presence"	No	No
China–Singapore	Universal	Positive list	Covered as "commercial presence"	No	No
Costa Rica–Mexico	Universal	Negative list	Separate chapter	Yes	Yes
EEA	Universal	Negative list	Separate chapter	Yes	No
EFTA–Colombia	Universal	Positive list	Covered as "commercial presence"	No	No
EFTA–GCC	Universal	Positive list	Covered as "commercial presence"	No	No
EFTA–Mexico	Universal	Positive list	Covered as "commercial presence" and under a separate investment chapter	No	No
EFTA–Singapore	Universal	Positive list	Covered as "commercial presence" and under a separate investment chapter	No	No
El Salvador–Taiwan, China	Universal	Negative list	Separate chapter	Yes	Yes
EU	Universal	Negative list	Treated as freedom to establish	Yes	No
EU–Mexico	Universal (audiovisual services explicitly excluded)	Standstill (+ future negotiation of commitments, as in GATS)	Covered as "commercial presence" and under a separate investment chapter	No	No

(continued next page)

Table 12.3. Key Features of PTAs That Cover Services (*continued*)

Agreement	Scope or coverage[a]	Negotiating approach	Treatment of investment in services	Right of nonestablishment	Ratchet mechanism
Group of Three[b]	Universal	Negative list	Separate chapter	Yes	Yes
Guatemala–Taiwan, China	Universal	Negative list	Separate chapter	Yes	Yes
India–Korea, Rep.	Universal	Positive list	Covered as "commercial presence" and under a separate investment chapter	No	No
India–Singapore	Universal	Positive list	Covered as "commercial presence"	No	No
Japan–Chile	Universal	Negative list	Separate chapter	Yes	Yes
Japan–Indonesia	Universal	Positive list	Covered as "commercial presence" and under a separate investment chapter	No	No
Japan–Malaysia	Universal	Positive list	Covered as "commercial presence" and under a separate investment chapter	No	No
Japan–Philippines	Universal	Positive list	Covered as "commercial presence" and under a separate investment chapter	No	Yes
Japan–Singapore	Universal	Positive list	Covered as "commercial presence" and under a separate investment chapter	No	No
Japan–Switzerland	Universal	Negative list	Covered as "commercial presence" and under a separate investment chapter	No	Yes
Japan–Thailand	Universal	Positive list	Covered as "commercial presence"	No	No
Korea, Rep.–Singapore	Universal	Negative list	Separate chapter	Yes	Yes
Malaysia–Pakistan	Universal	Positive list	Covered as "commercial presence" and under a separate investment chapter	No	No
Mercosur	Universal	Positive list	Separate protocols	No	No
Mexico–Nicaragua	Universal	Negative list	Separate chapter	Yes	Yes
Mexico–Northern Triangle[c]	Universal	Negative list	Separate chapter	Yes	Yes
NAFTA	Universal	Negative list	Separate chapter	Yes	Yes
New Zealand–China	Universal	Positive list	Covered as "commercial presence"	No	No
Singapore–Jordan	Universal	Positive list	Covered as "commercial presence"	No	No
Singapore–Panama	Universal	Negative list	Separate chapter	Yes	Yes
Taiwan, China–Nicaragua	Universal	Negative list	Separate chapter	Yes	Yes
U.S.–Chile	Universal	Negative list	Separate chapter	Yes	Yes
U.S.–Colombia	Universal	Negative list	Separate chapter	Yes	Yes
U.S.–Jordan	Universal	Positive list	Covered as "commercial presence"	No	No
U.S.–Oman	Universal	Negative list	Separate chapter	Yes	Yes
U.S.–Panama	Universal	Negative list	Separate chapter	Yes	Yes
U.S.–Singapore	Universal	Negative list	Separate chapter	Yes	Yes

Source: Authors' compilation.

Note: ANZCERTA, Australia–New Zealand Closer Economic Relations Trade Agreement; ASEAN, Association of Southeast Asian Nations; CACM, Central American Common Market; CAFTA, Central America Free Trade Agreement; CARICOM, Caribbean Community; CARIFORUM, Caribbean Forum of African, Caribbean, and Pacific (ACP) States; EFTA, European Free Trade Association; EU, European Union; GATS, General Agreement on Trade in Services; GCC, Gulf Cooperation Council; Mercosur, Southern Cone Common Market (Mercado Común del Sur); NAFTA, North American Free Trade Agreement.

a. Except for CACM (construction services), excludes air transport, and in certain cases, maritime cabotage (transport of goods or passengers between two points in the same country by a vessel registered in another country).

b. Colombia, Mexico, and República Bolivariana de Venezuela.

c. The Northern Triangle countries are El Salvador, Guatemala, and Honduras.

between the level and nature of PTA commitments and of negotiating offers made by WTO members in the ongoing Doha Development Agenda (DDA).

Comparison with the WTO

Today's PTAs may have taken services liberalization further than the situation prevailing at the end of the last round of multilateral negotiations, but there are marked differences in outcomes that bear noting, Using a sample of 28 PTAs concluded among 29 WTO members, Roy, Marchetti, and Lim (2008) identify differences in the level of commitments scheduled under GATS for modes 1 (cross-border supply) and 3 (commercial presence) and those flowing from GATS offers made, as of January 2008, under the Doha Development Agenda or included in PTAs. In computing sector coverage, the authors look at the best commitments undertaken by each country in any of its agreements. The results are summarized in figure 12.3.

Figure 12.3 shows that the average level of subsectors bound in the prevailing GATS schedules is rather low (31 percent for mode 1 and 44 percent for mode 3), reflecting the caution that characterized the first-ever multilateral negotiation in the services field. The figure further reveals that DDA offers have not modified this landscape in a dramatic fashion; mode 1 increases 7 percentage points, to 38 percent, and mode 3 gains 9 percentage points, to 53 percent. The value added of PTAs is significant. For mode 1, coverage is 73 percent, on average—almost double

that achieved by the latest DDA offers. For mode 3, it reaches 85 percent, almost double the average proportion of sectors covered by existing GATS commitments and significantly higher than what has been offered in the DDA to date.

The study by Roy, Marchetti, and Lim (2008) of the WTO+ nature of PTA commitments regarding mode 3 (commercial presence)—by far the most important means of accessing services markets—reveals significant variance across country groupings (table 12.4). Despite the considerable diversity in additional sectoral coverage for individual countries, PTAs are found to go beyond existing GATS commitments and DDA offers across all country groupings. The PTA-induced jump in sectoral coverage for developing countries is much larger than for developed countries, which had higher sectoral coverage levels to start with under their GATS schedules.

Table 12.4 further highlights sizable differences in mode 3 liberalization patterns between agreements pursuing hybrid and negative-list approaches to liberalization, with far greater commitments scheduled under the former. It also shows that PTAs conducted along North-South lines achieve deeper liberalization than those involving South-South partnerships. Such a result is broadly commensurate with the continued dominance of OECD countries in world services trade and investment, even as a growing number of developing countries are fast acquiring significant levels of comparative advantage across a wide range of sectors. The findings may also confirm the superior negotiating leverage that large countries have in preferential confines relative to what is possible at the WTO level.

Several PTAs, particularly (but not only) those negotiated along South-South lines, show a tendency to deepen liberalization commitments only marginally beyond the GATS. This raises serious questions about the agreements' very rationale, all the more so when signatories resort to the GATS framework for rule-making purposes without attempting to craft new or PTA-specific rules to govern services trade and investment among themselves.[18]

A factor that clearly influences the level of commitments undertaken in services-related PTAs is the economic importance of the trading partners involved. Marchetti and Roy (2008) and Roy, Marchetti, and Lim (2008) show how the United States invariably secures from its trading partners greater commitments than those the same countries are willing to undertake in PTAs with other trading partners, including OECD countries. Marchetti and Roy (2008) argue that such a finding can be traced to a mix of political influence and foreign policy factors and to the relative importance of the U.S. market for its trading partners' key goods exports, as in the cases of the Central

Figure 12.3. Sectoral Coverage of PTAs and of GATS Offers and Schedules, Selected Countries

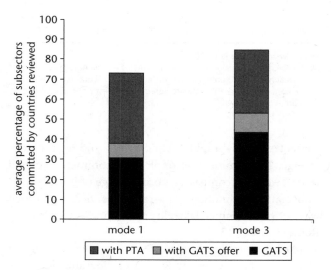

Source: Roy, Marchetti, and Lim 2008.
Note: GATS, General Agreement on Trade in Services; PTA, preferential trade agreement.

Table 12.4. Average Percentage of Subsectors Subject to Market Access Commitments on Mode 3, Selected Country Groupings *(percent)*

Item	GATS	With GATS DDA offer	With PTA	Difference from best WTO treatment
All	44	53	85	32
Developing countries	36	46	86	40
Developed countries	67	74	82	8
Hybrid listing	57	66	69	3
Negative listing	37	47	93	46
U.S. PTA partner	30	39	93	54
Non-U.S. PTA partner	56	66	76	10

Source: Adapted from Roy, Marchetti, and Lim 2008.
Note: DDA, Doha Development Agenda; GATS, General Agreement on Trade in Services; PTA, preferential trade agreement; WTO, World Trade Organization.

American countries, the Dominican Republic, and the Andean countries.

Sectoral and modal patterns. Turning to sectoral patterns of liberalization, the available empirical evidence attests to significant WTO+ advances across the full range of traded services. Using an index that ranks scheduled commitments on a scale from 1 to 100, Marchetti and Roy (2008) show how PTAs have registered far-reaching advances in comparison with GATS commitments and DDA offers across all sectors (see table 12.5). These include sectors that have attracted fewer commitments and DDA offers under GATS, such as audiovisual services, as well as those that have generally proved more attractive in a multilateral setting, including computer, tourism, and telecommunications services.

With the notable exception of land transport issues, where physical proximity stands out as a determinative trade-facilitating feature driving cross-border liberalization, PTAs continue to encounter resistance in opening up those services sectors that have proved difficult to address at the multilateral level. Thus, most PTAs tend to exclude from their coverage the bulk of air transport services (with the notable exception of the EU for intra-EU traffic), as well as a broad swath of public services.

Relatively limited progress—although still WTO+ in most areas—has similarly been achieved in PTAs in sectors in which particular policy sensitivities arise, such as maritime transport, audiovisual services, energy, and, to some extent (though more so for some countries than others), the movement of services suppliers. Other sectors that generally fit this overall pattern include postal and courier services (but not express delivery) and health and education services.

By contrast, PTAs have proved useful settings in which to advance liberalization prospects in market segments

Table 12.5. GATS Commitments, GATS DDA Offers, and "Best" PTA Commitments for All Members Reviewed, Selected Sectors *(scale: 1–100)*

Sector	GATS	GATS DDA offers	PTAs
Professional	30	39	67
Computer	55	74	93
Postal and courier	14	20	53
Telecommunications	51	58	80
Audiovisual	17	20	50
Construction	40	46	75
Distribution	32	41	76
Education	18	25	57
Environment	20	30	62
Financial	36	40	53
Health	8	11	34
Tourism	51	61	83
Maritime	12	23	57
Rail	14	20	52
Road	16	18	56
Auxiliary transport	21	24	58

Source: Marchetti and Roy 2008.
Note: DDA, Doha Development Agenda; GATS, General Agreement on Trade in Services; PTA, preferential trade agreement. Scores for modes 1 and 3 are combined. PTA data are based on the best (most liberalizing) PTA commitments.

characterized by rapid technological and commercial change. A prominent example is e-commerce (digital trade), which encompasses a broad range of business and information technology (IT)–related services and which was not yet a commercial reality at the time of the Uruguay Round (see box 12.3).

Market-opening advances are also notable in sectors in which new post–Uruguay Round proliberalization constituencies have emerged that seek to use trade agreements to secure expanded opportunities in world markets. This

---

Box 12.3. PTAs and Digital Trade

Increasingly, preferential trade agreements (PTAs) acknowledge the growing cross-border electronic delivery of services and digital products (e.g., software) by incorporating trade rules for e-commerce. A nonbinding e-commerce chapter in the U.S.–Jordan PTA of 2000 was followed by the first legally binding U.S. e-commerce chapter in bilateral trade agreements—in the 2003 free trade agreement (FTA) between the United States and Singapore—and by a further flurry of U.S.-led bilateral PTAs incorporating e-commerce chapters subject to dispute settlement provisions.

The trend has spread, and PTAs between Singapore and Australia, Thailand and Australia, India and Singapore, and other parties contain digital trade rules. Other PTAs—the Maghreb Arab Union and agreements between, among others, India and Thailand, Japan and Mexico, Japan and the Association of Southeast Asian Nations (ASEAN), India and ASEAN, and China and ASEAN—contain binding and nonbinding pledges related to information and communication technology (ICT) and e-commerce, as do trade-related statements by Asia-Pacific Economic Cooperation (APEC) and other cooperation agreements. PTAs thus function as a laboratory for digital trade rules, with a demonstration effect that is potentially useful for future multilateral or other preferential trade negotiations.

Digital products. E-commerce chapters of PTAs that follow the U.S. model formalize a definition of digital content products; confirm the applicability of World Trade Organization (WTO) rules to e-commerce and the applicability of provisions on cross-border trade in services to electronically supplied services; ensure a zero-duty rate on the content of digital trade; and provide for nondiscriminatory and most favored nation (MFN) treatment for digital products such as music, films, and software (see table 12.1). Interestingly, from the point of view of rules of origin, in this template digital products, to benefit from nondiscrimination or MFN, must not be fully created in and exported by a contracting party of the PTA.

Electronic trade in chapters on cross-border trade in services. The cross-border trade in services chapters of newly agreed U.S.-led PTAs also innovate to the benefit of the digital delivery of services. These PTAs use a negative-list approach to schedule services trade commitments. Assuming that no reservations are made, this top-down approach guarantees that narrow or outdated classification schemes and uncertainties relating to the mode of delivery do not limit the applicability of commitments to digitally delivered services. Importantly, the PTAs specify that "neither Party may require a service supplier of the other Party to establish or maintain a representative office or any form of enterprise, or to be resident, in its territory as a condition for the cross-border supply of a service." MFN exemptions are ruled out. Again the devil is in the details, in the form of specified nonconforming measures. (For example, in the case of U.S.-led PTAs, U.S. state-level regulations are sometimes listed as exceptions.) On the side of services rules, the PTAs introduce strengthened transparency requirements, sector-specific mutual recognition annexes (e.g., for professional services), and binding rules on domestic regulation useful for digital trade.

"Deep" digital trade rules. Two other developments in PTAs foster digital trade rules:

- *Nonbinding joint understandings* on e-commerce calling for liberal digital trade principles and rules that foster the diffusion of ICT and e-commerce. A number of PTAs spell out a cooperation agenda on various aspects of the information society—in particular, in areas such as telecommunications policy, ICT standards and conformity assessments, interconnection and interoperability issues, cybersecurity, electronic signatures, the balance between privacy protection and the free cross-border flow of information, intellectual property rights, and consumer confidence in e-commerce.
- *Incorporation of "deep integration" digital trade principles* as an integral component of bilateral trade agreements, with digital trade sometimes subject to dispute settlement provisions. Such deep digital trade provisions may relate to, for example, domestic regulation, transparency, consumer protection, data protection, authentication and digital signatures, and paperless trading.

Source: Wunsch-Vincent 2008.

---

is notably the case for express delivery services, which feature prominently in a number of recent PTAs. Similarly, many recent PTAs, including South-South agreements, are giving greater attention to new areas of financial services such as asset management and financial services delivered through electronic means; to trade in some segments of higher education and related services (e.g., vocational training and educational testing); and to the wellness industry situated at the interface of tourism and health services.

In some cases, market-opening advances rest on a complementary set of new disciplines. Such a trend is most visible in the field of investment, where PTAs have achieved significant forward movement over the WTO. It is also notable in the area of procurement liberalization. A further example of the close nexus between market

opening and novel (procompetitive) rule making can be found in the tourism sector, where the EPA between the EU and CARIFORUM recently blazed a new trail (see box 12.4). It is possible that many such advances could be replicated at the WTO level in the Doha Round or beyond, all the more so as most of them are being actively discussed in ongoing negotiations under the GATS and have been the object of collective requests advanced by various coalitions of like-minded WTO members.

The sectoral patterns of PTA-induced market opening in services trade described above appear to hold at the regional level. This is evidenced, for instance, in the work of Fink and Molinuevo (2007), which offers an aggregated measure of the GATS+ nature of market-opening commitments in a sample of service-related PTAs concluded among Asian countries (see figure 12.4). Such findings

Box 12.4. Tourism Liberalization in the EU–CARIFORUM EPA

The tourism sector stands out as one in which developing countries possess clear comparative advantages in services trade. Accordingly, several developing-country governments have for some time been clamoring for provisions in trade agreements dedicated to the sector and its specificities. Such calls led, in the course of the World Trade Organization (WTO) Doha Round of trade negotiations, to the formulation of a draft annex to the General Agreement on Trade in Services (GATS) covering tourism services and to a collective request sponsored by a majority of developing-country members of the WTO, several of them in the Caribbean region. The collective inability of WTO members to complete the Doha Round has so far stymied progress in this area. Not surprisingly, proponents of tourism trade liberalization have taken their case to subsidiary settings.

The precedent set in the EPA between the European Union (EU) and the Caribbean Forum of African, Caribbean, and Pacific (ACP) States (CARIFORUM) is likely to influence the treatment of tourism in other PTAs involving developing countries, as well as at the WTO level.

Initially, CARIFORUM members had proposed the inclusion of a distinct tourism annex in the EPA. The origin of this initiative seems to have been the WTO Doha Round proposal submitted in 2001 by several Latin American and Caribbean countries. That proposal was the inspiration for the draft text on tourism formulated by the Caribbean Hotel and Tourism Association and adopted by the Caribbean Regional Negotiation Machinery in the EPA context.

Mutual recognition. On the question of the negotiation of a mutual recognition agreement (MRA) for tourism service providers, the EPA states, in Article 114, that "the Parties shall co-operate towards the mutual recognition of requirements, qualifications, licenses or other regulations in accordance with Article 85 . . ." Article 85, which deals with mutual recognition in general, reaffirms the parties' right to require that natural persons possess the necessary qualifications or professional experience (or both) to supply covered services. It also commits the parties to encourage the relevant professional bodies in their respective territories to jointly develop and propose recommendations on mutual recognition to the CARIFORUM–EU Trade and Development Committee to determine the criteria to be applied by the parties for the authorization, licensing, operation, and certification of investors and services suppliers. Tourism is identified, in Article 85(3), as one of the priority sectors for the development of mutual recognition arrangements under the agreement. The EPA specifically mandates the EU and CARIFORUM to encourage the relevant professional bodies in their territories to start negotiations three years after the EPA's entry into force in order to jointly develop and propose recommendations on mutual recognition; this represents a hortatory, or "best-endeavors," commitment.

Competition policy disciplines. An important element of the Doha Development Agenda proposal which the Caribbean Hotel and Tourism Association retained in its EPA draft was the creation of a competitive safeguard for tourism. The inclusion of disciplines on anticompetitive practices was of key importance to CARIFORUM states because the global tourism industry is characterized by vertically integrated market structures and consolidated distribution channels controlled by a limited number of large international players, many of them based in the EU. Specifically, in accordance with the chapter dealing with competition policy, Article 111 of the EPA commits the parties to maintain or introduce measures designed to prevent suppliers from materially affecting "the terms of participation in the relevant market for tourism services by engaging in or continuing anti-competitive practices, including, *inter alia,* abuse of dominant position through imposition of unfair prices, exclusivity clauses, refusal to deal, tied sales, quantity restrictions or vertical integration." The EPA provision on the prevention of anticompetitive practices, unlike other provisions on the tourism sector, is legally binding.

Trade-related capacity building. The EPA's treatment of tourism services features distinct development cooperation provisions, in contrast to other sectors, where such issues are addressed generically. The EPA contains an explicit commitment by the EU to help advance the tourism sector in the CARIFORUM states, as well as a nonexhaustive list of specific areas in which the parties agree to cooperate. Among these areas are capacity building for environmental management and the development of Internet-based marketing strategies for small and medium-size tourism enterprises. Also included is the upgrading of national accounts systems with a view toward facilitating the introduction of tourism satellite accounts (statistical instruments for analyzing the economic importance of tourism) at the regional and local levels.

Source: Sauvé and Ward 2009b, 2009c; World Trade Organization, "Communication by Bolivia, Dominican Republic, Ecuador, El Salvador, Honduras, Nicaragua, Panama, Peru, and Venezuela: Draft Annex on Tourism," S/CSS/W/107, September 26, 2001.

reveal that although GATS+ advances are significant across all sectors, they are particularly noticeable in the areas of business services (reflecting the emergence of digital trade, e-commerce, and the outsourcing revolution in services); distribution; and education, health, and transport services—all areas that proved difficult in the WTO context during the Uruguay Round and in the more recent context of the Doha Development Agenda.

Less progress, relatively, has been seen in Southeast Asian PTAs in areas such as telecommunications and financial services. These are precisely the sectors in which GATS

negotiations have to date been most successful. Perhaps the GATS advances lessened the scope or the perceived need for significant new advances in PTAs.

Using the Fink-Molinuevo methodology and applying it to the four largest members of CARIFORUM in the context of the EPA with the EU, Sauvé and Ward (2009b) reveal a broad pattern of WTO+ or WTO-extra advances arising at the preferential level (see annex figures 12A.1–12A.4).

The East Asian PTA experience described in Fink and Molinuevo (2007) confirms the partial, incremental nature of market opening in services trade. This feature

Figure 12.4. GATS+ Advances in East Asian PTAs with Services Provisions, by Sector

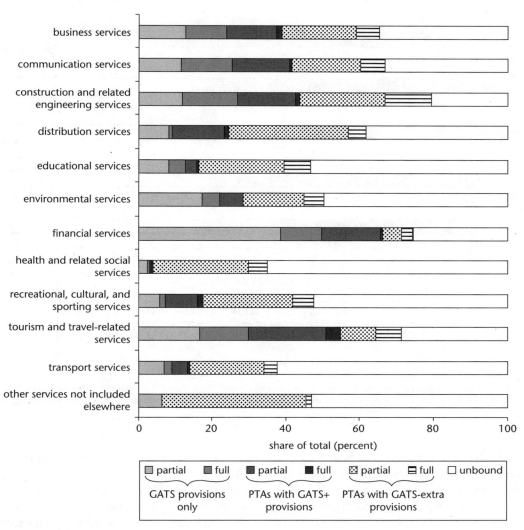

Source: Fink and Molinuevo 2007.
Note: GATS, General Agreement on Trade in Services; PTA, preferential trade agreement. "Partial" and "full" refer to the degree of market opening.

is particularly apparent when commitments are analyzed on a modal basis (see figure 12.5). On the positive side, the most significant GATS+ advances in East Asian PTAs relate to the two modes of supply likely to generate the strongest developmental returns. These are mode 4 (movement of natural persons), the least committed of all modes under GATS, and mode 3 (commercial presence), the most committed of the modes subject to GATS bindings, and the principal means through which services are traded internationally. This outcome is not entirely surprising, given the reluctance of countries to contemplate mode 4 liberalization on an MFN basis in the WTO.[19]

As in other preferential settings and at the WTO level, less progress has been made in East Asian PTAs on mode 1 (cross-border supply) than mode 3 (commercial presence). This difference reflects the generally greater caution shown toward transactions that many host countries feel they cannot regulate, or at least, not easily.

Evidence of iterative learning by doing. The relationship between PTAs and the WTO is not unidirectional in character but involves iterative, two-way interaction between the two layers of trade governance in ways that can inform subsequent patterns of rule making and market opening at both levels. Examples of such interaction are notably found in areas in which WTO jurisprudence has clarified

Figure 12.5. GATS+ Advances in East Asian PTAs with Services Provisions, by Mode

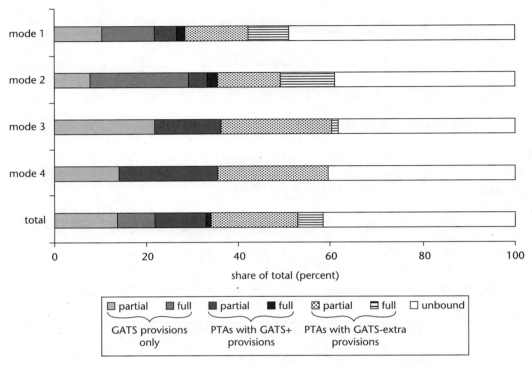

Source: Fink and Molinuevo 2007.
Note: GATS, General Agreement on Trade in Services; PTA, preferential trade agreement. "Partial" and "full" refer to the degree of market opening. Modes are defined as follows: mode 1, cross-border supply of services; mode 2, consumption abroad; mode 3, commercial presence; mode 4, movement of natural persons.

or interpreted the scope of key provisions governing services trade that are typically found both in the WTO-GATS and in the services and investment chapters of PTAs. Baptista Neto (2009), for instance, has found evidence of NAFTA-minus treatment of recreational services in U.S. reservation lists following the decision by the WTO's Dispute Settlement Body and Appellate Body (DSB and AB) concerning online gambling (United States–Gambling Services). Similarly, the most recent DSB and AB decisions in the China–Publications and Audiovisual Products dispute have prompted some observers to note the need for China to adjust its future PTA commitments with a view to ensuring the preservation of adequate policy space within which to pursue cultural policy objectives (Chen and Shi 2011).

Coexistence of hard- and soft-law provisions. A final, salient, trend that emerges from the most recent generation of PTAs and that has both rule-making and market-opening

dimensions is the increasing reliance, particularly in agreements brokered by the EU, on nonbinding provisions embedded in PTAs alongside treaty provisions that are legally binding and enforceable. Advances of this type reflect the ever-broadening remit of trade rule making and the commensurate desire of parties to assign to regulatory cooperation a number of trade- and investment-facilitating roles. For various reasons, such PTA advances may well be limited to preferential settings and may encounter difficulties in being agreed in the WTO. This may notably be the case when parties harbor concerns over MFN-induced free riding, when particular policy sensitivities arise at the WTO level that can be contained or addressed in a PTA setting, or when parties may simply not desire binding and enforceable obligations. Cultural cooperation appears to correspond to the former category of policy domains, while aid for trade and its design in the services field likely falls more within the latter category (see box 12.5).

Box 12.5. Cultural Cooperation and Aid for Trade in the EU–CARIFORUM EPA

Cultural cooperation

A novel feature of the economic partnership agreement (EPA) between the European Union (EU) and the Caribbean Forum of African, Caribbean, and Pacific (ACP) States (CARIFORUM) is its inclusion of a protocol on cultural cooperation between the parties. The protocol establishes a clear precedent for addressing matters relating to cultural industries within preferential trade agreements (PTAs), laying the basis for the incorporation of similar provisions in other EPAs. The inclusion of language on cultural cooperation matters marks a significant evolution in EU attitudes toward the subject in a trade policy context. Earlier, the EU had tried to preserve maximum policy autonomy toward cultural industries by eschewing any commitments in trade agreements and, in the case of the Doha Development Agenda (DDA), by refusing to direct negotiating requests to its trading partners or to entertain offers in response to requests by trading partners. The advances made in the protocol respond to CARIFORUM members' strong offensive interests in this area, notably the music industry.

The EPA protocol establishes a framework within which the parties can work together to facilitate exchanges of cultural activities, goods, and services, as well as the movement of artists and other cultural professionals, and to improve cinematographic cooperation. The protocol can be viewed as the first concrete response to Article 16, on preferential treatment, of the United Nations Educational, Scientific, and Cultural Organization (UNESCO) Convention on the Protection and Promotion of the Diversity of Cultural Expressions. According to CARIFORUM officials, the conclusion of the coproduction agreements called for under the protocol will enable Caribbean audiovisual producers to access new sources of funding for creative projects. Given the EU's long-standing sensitivities in the audiovisual sector, the protocol likely comes as close to opening new market access opportunities as the EU's EPA partners could have hoped, without actually resulting in new liberalization commitments on national treatment or market access.

Aid for trade

The cooperation elements of the EU–CARIFORUM EPA reflect the desire of EU members to infuse the agreement with a concrete development dimension. In so doing, the EPA charts useful new territory at a time when the multilateral community is struggling to give operational meaning to the concept of aid for trade.

The EPA text does not contain explicit language on the level of development financing to be made available overall, nor does it spell out the specific issues and sectors subject to coverage by the agreement. These omissions have sparked much criticism throughout the CARIFORUM region over the allegedly unbalanced nature of the agreement, in that its development provisions remain somewhat abstract and not legally enforceable, while its liberalization commitments are up front, legally binding, and enforceable. Responding to such critiques, the Caribbean Regional Negotiating Machinery (CRNM), which led the negotiations on the CARIFORUM side, cautioned that "any perceptions about the EPA's practical deficiencies with respect to the treatment of development and development cooperation and assistance should first be tempered by the recognition that as a trade agreement, the EPA should not be perceived to be the primary vehicle through which development may be achieved." Rather, it should be considered "one strategic instrument in a range of economic development strategies."

According to the Joint Declaration on Development Co-operation, which is annexed to the EPA and constitutes an integral part of it, a package of 165 million euros has been set aside for the six years following the agreement's entry into force to fund activities that are identified and rank-ordered in the Caribbean regional indicative plan. In addition to funding for that plan, each CARIFORUM state will receive funds for its national indicative plans (NIP); two priority projects must be identified for such additional funding. The Dominican Republic and Jamaica announced that they would be using some of the financing under their respective NIPs for purposes of EPA implementation.

The minimum cost of implementing the EPA's provisions on investment, trade in services, and e-commerce and of addressing capacity constraints at the national and regional levels has been estimated at 15.6 million euros. The constraints identified include insufficient numbers of specialists and experts; limited human resources within both public and private sectors; the absence of an organized services sector body through which stakeholders can be mobilized; general absence of infrastructure; and inadequacy of financial resources. Key tasks include building regulatory capacity, overcoming information asymmetries to assist CARIFORUM firms and entities in identifying business opportunities in the European market, and developing productive capacity in goods and cultural services.

Specific technical assistance efforts are to be directed at the following objectives: (a) improving the ability of CARIFORUM service suppliers to gather information on and to meet EU members' regulations and standards; (b) increasing the export capacity of local services suppliers; (c) facilitating interaction and dialogue between services suppliers in both parties; (d) addressing quality and standards in those areas in which the CARIFORUM states have undertaken commitments; (e) developing and implementing regulatory regimes for specific services at the CARIFORUM level and in the signatory CARIFORUM states; (f) establishing mechanisms for promoting investment and joint ventures between service suppliers of the parties; and (g) enhancing the capacities of investment promotion agencies in CARIFORUM states.

Source: Sauvé and Ward 2009b. The quotation from the CRNM is from RNM Update 0802, http://www.crnm.org/documents/updates_2008/rnmupdate0802.htm (accessed April 19, 2008). The information on costs is from CARICOM Secretariat 2008, 10, and the listing of objectives is from CARICOM Secretariat 2008, Article 121 (2).

Annex

Annex Table 12A.1. Preferential Trade Agreements (PTAs) That Include Provisions on Trade in Services

Agreement	Type[a]
ANZCERTA (S)	EIA
ASEAN–China (S)	EIA
CARICOM (S)	EIA
EFTA (S)	EIA
Mercosur (S)	EIA
Australia–Chile	FTA, EIA
Brunei Darussalam–Japan	FTA, EIA
CAFTA–DR	FTA, EIA
Canada–Chile	FTA, EIA
Canada–Peru	FTA, EIA
Chile–Colombia	FTA, EIA
Chile–Costa Rica (Chile–Central America)	FTA, EIA
Chile–El Salvador (Chile–Central America)	FTA, EIA
Chile–Japan	FTA, EIA
Chile–Mexico	FTA, EIA
China–Hong Kong SAR, China	FTA, EIA
China–Macao SAR, China	FTA, EIA
China–New Zealand	FTA, EIA
China–Singapore	FTA, EIA
Costa Rica–Mexico	FTA, EIA
EEA (S)	EIA
EFTA–Chile	FTA, EIA
EFTA–Korea, Rep.	FTA, EIA
EFTA–Mexico	FTA, EIA
EFTA–Singapore	FTA, EIA
EU–Albania	FTA, EIA
EU–CARIFORUM EPA	FTA, EIA
EU–Chile	FTA, EIA
EU–Croatia	FTA, EIA
EU–Macedonia, FYR	FTA, EIA
EU–Mexico	FTA, EIA
Iceland–Faroe Islands	FTA, EIA
India–Singapore	FTA, EIA
Japan–Indonesia	FTA, EIA
Japan–Malaysia	FTA, EIA
Japan–Mexico	FTA, EIA
Japan–Philippines	FTA, EIA
Japan–Singapore	FTA, EIA
Japan–Switzerland	FTA, EIA
Japan–Thailand	FTA, EIA
Japan–Vietnam	FTA, EIA
Jordan–Singapore	FTA, EIA
Korea, Rep.–Chile	FTA, EIA
Korea, Rep.–Singapore	FTA, EIA
Mexico–El Salvador (Mexico–Northern Triangle)	FTA, EIA
Mexico–Guatemala (Mexico–Northern Triangle)	FTA, EIA
Mexico–Honduras (Mexico–Northern Triangle)	FTA, EIA

(continued)

Annex Table 12A.1 *(continued)*

Agreement	Type[a]
Mexico–Nicaragua	FTA, EIA
NAFTA	FTA, EIA
New Zealand–Singapore	FTA, EIA
Nicaragua–Taiwan, China	FTA, EIA
Pakistan–Malaysia	FTA, EIA
Panama–Chile	FTA, EIA
Panama–Costa Rica (Panama–Central America)	FTA, EIA
Panama–El Salvador (Panama–Central America)	FTA, EIA
Panama–Honduras (Panama–Central America)	FTA, EIA
Panama–Singapore	FTA, EIA
Panama and Taiwan, China	FTA, EIA
Peru–China	FTA, EIA
Peru–Singapore	FTA, EIA
Singapore–Australia	FTA, EIA
Thailand–Australia	FTA, EIA
Thailand–New Zealand	FTA, EIA
Trans-Pacific Strategic Economic Partnership	FTA, EIA
U.S.–Australia	FTA, EIA
U.S.–Bahrain	FTA, EIA
U.S.–Chile	FTA, EIA
U.S.–Jordan	FTA, EIA
U.S.–Morocco	FTA, EIA
U.S.–Oman	FTA, EIA
U.S.–Peru	FTA, EIA
U.S.–Singapore	FTA, EIA
EU-15 enlargement	CU, EIA
EU-25 enlargement	CU, EIA
EU-27 enlargement	CU, EIA
EU Treaty	CU, EIA
Total number of services PTAs	76
Total number of services-only PTAs	6
Total number of goods PTAs	196
Total number of PTAs in force	272
Total number of services PTAs as a percentage of total PTAs in force	27.94

Source: World Trade Organization, Regional Trade Agreement (RTA) database, http://rtais.wto.org/UI/PublicMaintainRTAHome .aspx.
Note: The notation (S) after an agreement denotes services only. WTO statistics on PTAs are based on notification requirements rather than on physical numbers of PTAs. Thus, for a PTA that includes both goods and services, two notifications are counted (one for goods and the other services), even though there is actually only one PTA. ANZCERTA, Australia–New Zealand Closer Economic Relations Trade Agreement; ASEAN, Association of Southeast Asian Nations; CAFTA–DR, Dominican Republic–Central America Free Trade Agreement; CARICOM, Caribbean Community; CARIFORUM, Caribbean Forum of African, Caribbean, and Pacific (ACP) States; EEA, European Economic Area; EFTA, European Free Trade Association; EU, European Union; Mercosur, Southern Cone Common Market (Mercado Común del Sur); NAFTA, North American Free Trade Agreement. EU-15 refers to the EU after the 1995 enlargement; the members were Austria, Belgium, Denmark, Finland, France, Germany, Greece, Ireland, Italy, Luxembourg, Netherlands, Portugal, Spain, Sweden, and the United Kingdom. EU-25 and EU-27 refer to successive enlargements of the EU, in 2004 and 2007.
a. CU, customs union; FTA, free trade agreement; EIA, economic integration agreement.

Annex Table 12A.2. Classification of Preferential Trade Agreements (PTAs) Featuring Services Provisions by Country Group

North-North	North-South	South-South
ANZCERTA	Australia–Chile	ASEAN–China
EEA	Brunei Darussalam–Japan	CARICOM
EFTA	CAFTA–DR	Chile–Colombia
EU-15 enlargement	Canada–Chile	Chile–Costa Rica (Chile–Central America)
EU-25 enlargement	Canada–Peru	Chile–El Salvador (Chile–Central America)
EU-27 enlargement	Chile–Japan	Chile–Mexico
EU Treaty	China–New Zealand	China–Hong Kong SAR, China
Iceland–Faroe Islands	EFTA–Chile	China–Macao SAR, China
Japan–Switzerland	EFTA–Korea, Rep.	China–Singapore
U.S.–Australia	EFTA–Mexico	Costa Rica–Mexico
	EFTA–Singapore	India–Singapore
	EU–Albania	Jordan–Singapore
	EU–CARIFORUM EPA	Korea, Rep.–Chile
	EU–Chile	Korea, Rep.–Singapore
	EU–Croatia	Mercosur
	EU–Macedonia, FYR	Mexico–El Salvador (Mexico–Northern Triangle)
	EU–Mexico	Mexico–Guatemala (Mexico–Northern Triangle)
	Japan–Indonesia	Mexico–Honduras (Mexico–Northern Triangle)
	Japan–Malaysia	Mexico–Nicaragua
	Japan–Mexico	Nicaragua–Taiwan, China
	Japan–Philippines	Pakistan–Malaysia
	Japan–Singapore	Panama–Chile
	Japan–Thailand	Panama–Costa Rica (Panama–Central America)
	Japan–Vietnam	Panama–El Salvador (Panama–Central America)
	NAFTA	Panama–Honduras (Panama–Central America)
	New Zealand–Singapore	Panama–Singapore
	Singapore–Australia	Panama–Taiwan, China
	Thailand–Australia	Peru–China
	Thailand–New Zealand	Peru–Singapore
	Trans-Pacific Strategic Economic Partnership	
	U.S.–Bahrain	
	U.S.–Chile	
	U.S.–Jordan	
	U.S.–Morocco	
	U.S.–Oman	
	U.S.–Peru	
	U.S.–Singapore	

Source: World Trade Organization, regional trade agreement (RTA) database, http://rtais.wto.org/UI/PublicMaintainRTAHome.aspx.
Note: PTAs include all categories of preferential agreements. ANZCERTA, Australia–New Zealand Closer Economic Relations Trade Agreement; ASEAN, Association of Southeast Asian Nations; CAFTA–DR, Dominican Republic–Central America Free Trade Agreement; CARICOM, Caribbean Community; CARIFORUM, Caribbean Forum of African, Caribbean, and Pacific (ACP) States; EEA, European Economic Area; EFTA, European Free Trade Association; EU, European Union; Mercosur, Southern Cone Common Market (Mercado Común del Sur); NAFTA, North American Free Trade Agreement. EU-15 refers to the EU after the 1995 enlargement; the members were Austria, Belgium, Denmark, Finland, France, Germany, Greece, Ireland, Italy, Luxembourg, Netherlands, Portugal, Spain, Sweden, and the United Kingdom. EU-25 and EU-27 refer to successive enlargements of the EU, in 2004 and 2007.

Annex Figure 12A.1. GATS and EU–CARIFORUM Commitments Compared: Barbados

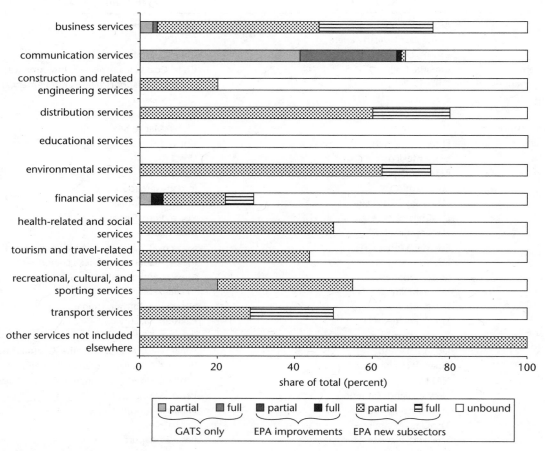

Source: Sauvé and Ward 2009b.

Annex Figure 12A.2. GATS and EU–CARIFORUM Commitments Compared: Dominican Republic

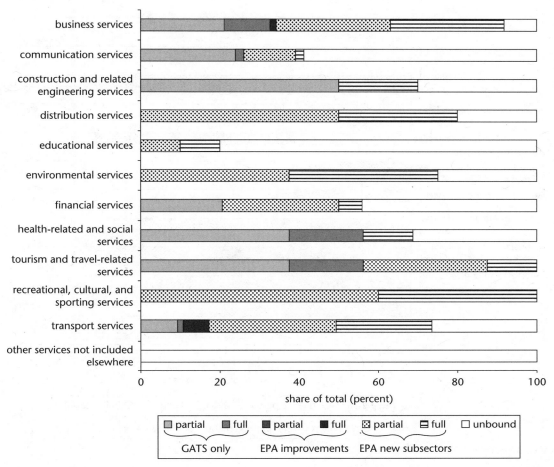

Source: Sauvé and Ward 2009b.

Annex Figure 12A.3. GATS and EU–CARIFORUM Commitments Compared: Jamaica

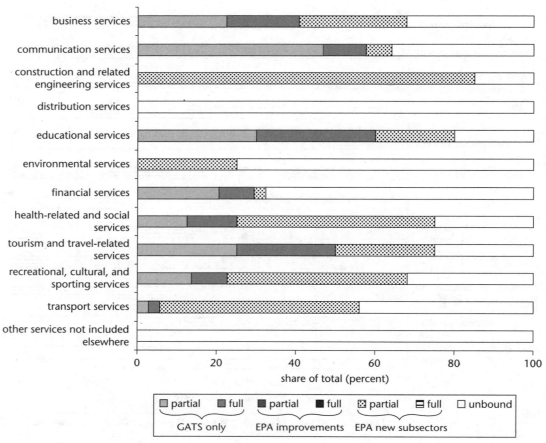

Source: Sauvé and Ward 2009b.

Annex Figure 12A.4. GATS and EU–CARIFORUM Commitments Compared: Trinidad and Tobago

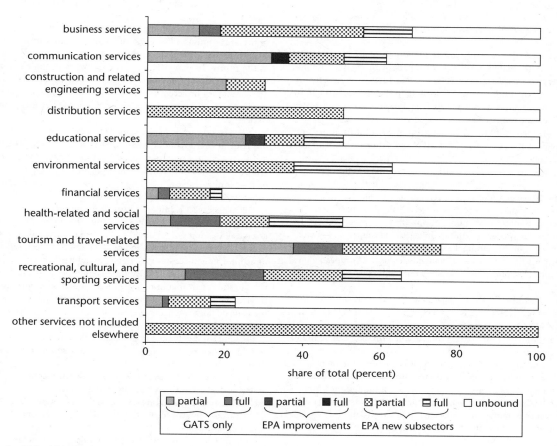

Source: Sauvé and Ward 2009b.

Notes

The authors are grateful to Natasha Ward and Sacha Wunsch-Vincent for their valuable comments on and written contributions to an earlier draft of this chapter.

1. Evidence of such causality can be found in recent PTAs involving the United States, notably in reservations made with regard to online gambling services (Baptista Neto 2009). It may further be expected in the aftermath of the most recent WTO ruling in the dispute brought by the United States against China in the area of publications and audiovisual products (Chen and Shi 2011).

2. Only the Mercosur Protocol and Decision 439 of the Andean Community provide that no deviation from MFN and national treatment is to be allowed among members.

3. There is a measure of asymmetry in this provision, as the obligation does not apply to bilateral or plurilateral agreements between an Association of Southeast Asian Nations (ASEAN) state or the ASEAN states, on the one hand, and a nonparty or Australia or New Zealand, on the other.

4. Other examples of demonstration-effect or precedent-setting regionalism are the provisions on the linkages between trade and labor standards inserted in the waning days of the Clinton administration into the U.S.–Jordan FTA and the recurring tendency of the European Commission to insert disciplines on trade and competition into the EU's PTAs with developing countries.

5. Whereas similar GATS language states that the measures in question should not restrict the supply of a service under any of the four GATS modes, the NAFTA-type agreements narrow this requirement to the cross-border supply of a service. No comparable provision can be found in these agreements' investment chapters.

6. Despite notable progress in PTAs, government procurement practices continue in most instances to be the province of discriminatory practices. In the case of NAFTA, for instance, even though the scope of covered purchases was quadrupled from that in the 1987 Canada–U.S. FTA, covered entities represented only a tenth of North America's civilian procurement market at the time of the agreement's entry into force. See Hart and Sauvé (1997).

7. More restrictive rules of origin conditioning the receipt of preferences may relate to factors such as local incorporation (if it denies benefits to branches of third-country invested entities), place of incorporation or location of headquarters or ownership, and control tests aimed at limiting PTA benefits to local juridical persons. Examples of the latter can be found under Mercosur and the Andean Pact.

8. The purpose of the discussion here is to note such differences without advocating any implicit hierarchy of policy desirability. Both approaches have strengths and weaknesses. The governance-enhancing aspects of negative listing have, however, been noted by several observers. See, in particular, Sauvé (1996); Snape and Bosworth (1996); WTO (2001); Stephenson (2002). For a fuller discussion of the good-governance-promoting aspects of PTAs, see Baldwin, Evenett, and Low (2009), as well as Chauffour and Maur, ch. 1 in this volume.

9. Members of Mercosur adopted a slightly different version of the positive-list approach, with a view toward liberalizing services trade within the region. According to Mercosur's Protocol of Montevideo on Trade in Services, annual rounds of negotiations based on the scheduling of increasing numbers of commitments in all sectors (with no exclusions) are to result in the elimination of all restrictions on services trade among members within 10 years of the entry into force of the protocol. The latter has yet to enter into force. See Peña (2000); Stephenson (2001b).

10. The Andean Community has adopted a somewhat different version of the negative-list approach. Decision 439, on trade in services, specifies that the process of liberalization is to begin when comprehensive (nonbinding) national inventories of measures affecting trade in services for all members of the Andean Community are finalized. Discriminatory restrictions listed in these inventories were to be lifted gradually through a series of negotiations, ultimately resulting in a common market free of barriers to services trade by a target date (set initially at 2005 but not yet achieved).

11. Most PTAs that employ a negative-list approach to liberalization feature unbound reservations listing sectors in which members wish to preserve the right to introduce new nonconforming measures in the future. In many PTAs, particularly those modeled on NAFTA, such reservations nonetheless oblige member countries to list existing discriminatory or access-impairing measures whose effects on foreign services or service suppliers might in the future become more burdensome.

12. The suggestion has been made that WTO members could address this issue in GATS without revisiting the agreement's negotiating modality by agreeing to a new framework provision designed to encourage governments to reflect the statutory or regulatory status quo in their scheduled commitments, while retaining the voluntary nature of such commitments. See Sauvé and Wilkie (2000).

13. This caveat is important because a number of PTAs, particularly those conducted along North-South lines, have seen powerful partners reserve all measures of a subnational nature through one sweeping reservation that yields no information on the nature and sectoral incidence of nonconforming measures maintained by subnational governments. Such reservations also greatly reduce the potential scope of the PTA in question, to the extent that in many federal countries, important pockets of services regulation apply at the subnational level. The insurance sector in the United States and many energy-related services in Canada are cases in point.

14. For a fuller discussion of the modalities and uses to which a trade-related regulatory audit may be put, see Marconini and Sauvé (2010); Sauvé (2010).

15. One troubling example is recent PTA practice by the United States, which increasingly uses sweeping negative-list reservations that exclude all measures affecting services at the subnational level. Recent U.S. PTAs are also notable for excluding mode 4 (movement of natural persons) commitments.

16. In NAFTA, for instance, subnational governments were initially given an extra two years to complete their lists of nonconforming measures pertaining to services and investment. The NAFTA parties subsequently decided not to complete the lists at the subnational level, opting instead for a standstill on existing nonconforming measures. Compliance with the production of negative lists has been similarly problematic elsewhere in the Western Hemisphere, as a number of agreements were concluded without such lists being finalized and without firm deadlines for doing so. The inability of users to access the information contained in the negative lists to such agreements deprives the latter of an important good-governance-promoting feature.

17. In trade negotiations, the term "single undertaking" means that participants accept or reject the outcome of multiple negotiations in a single package, rather than select among them.

18. Countries reluctant to go beyond GATS include, for instance, EFTA countries; India; the EU prior to the EPA with CARIFORUM and, to some extent, the FTA with Chile; and the ASEAN countries other than Singapore. In some particular cases, the reason for these more limited advances may be that PTA negotiations took place before the last DDA offer, and what was conceded in the PTA may later find its way into a revised GATS offer.

19. An example drawn from the Asian experience relates to the labor mobility provisions found in recent Japanese PTAs. These include novel features aimed at assisting partner countries with training in the home country prior to their admission as professionals in the Japanese labor market, with a view to meeting Japanese licensing requirements in nursing and other health-related occupations. Although the numerical quotas agreed by Japan in these areas remain low relative to the supply capacity (and negotiating interests) of sending countries, such provisions

nonetheless represent a step forward in the treatment of mode 4 issues in a context of population aging and labor market shortages in OECD countries.

Bibliography

Abugattas Majluf, Luis, and Sherry M. Stephenson. 2003. "Liberalization of Trade in Services: Options and Implications for Latin American and Caribbean Countries." In *Trade Negotiations in Latin America: Problems and Prospects*, ed. Diana Tussie. Houndsmills, Basingstoke, Hampshire, U.K.: Palgrave Macmillan.

Adlung, Rudolf. 2007. "Negotiations on Safeguards and Subsidies in Services: A Never-Ending Story?" *Journal of International Economic Law* 10 (2, June): 235–65.

Baier, Scott L., and Jeffrey H. Bergstrand. 2001. "International Trade in Services, Free Trade Agreements, and the WTO." In *Services in the International Economy*, ed. Robert M. Stern, ch. 7. Ann Arbor, MI: University of Michigan Press.

Baldwin, Richard E. 2000. "Regulatory Protectionism, Developing Nations and a Two-Tier World Trade System." CEPR Discussion Paper 2574, Centre for Economic Policy Research, London.

———. 2006. "Multilateralising Regionalism: Spaghetti Bowls as Building Blocs on the Path to Global Free Trade." 2006 World Economy Annual Lecture, Nottingham, England, June 22.

Baldwin, Richard, Simon Evenett, and Patrick Low. 2009. "Beyond Tariffs: Multilateralizing Non-Tariff RTA Commitments." In *Multilateralizing Regionalism: Challenges for the Global Trading System*, ed. Richard E. Baldwin and Patrick Low. Cambridge, U.K.: Cambridge University Press.

Baptista Neto, J. A. 2009. "United States Preferential Trade Agreements in Services: How Far Beyond the NAFTA?" Master in international law and economics thesis, World Trade Institute, University of Bern, Bern.

Beviglia Zampetti, Americo. 2000. "Market Access through Mutual Recognition: The Promise and Limits of GATS Article VII." In *GATS 2000: New Directions in Services Trade Liberalization*, ed. Pierre Sauvé and Robert M. Stern, 283–306. Washington, DC: Brookings Institution Press.

Beviglia Zampetti, Americo, and Pierre Sauvé. 2006. "Rules of Origin for Services: Economic and Legal Considerations." In *The Origin of Goods: Rules of Origin in Regional Trade Agreements*, ed. Olivier Cadot, Antoni Estevadeordal, Akiko Suwa Eisenmann, and Thierry Verdier, 114–45. Oxford, U.K.: Oxford University Press.

———. 2007. "International Investment." In *Research Handbook in International Economic Law*, ed. Alan O. Sykes and Andrew Guzman, 211–70. London: Edgar Elgar.

Bhagwati, Jagdish. 1990. "Multilateralism at Risk: The GATT Is Dead, Long Live the GATT." *World Economy*, 13 (2): 149–69.

CARICOM (Caribbean Community) Secretariat. 2008. "Implementation of the CARIFORUM-EC Economic Partnership Agreement." CARICOM Secretariat, Georgetown.

CEC (Commission of the European Communities). 2002. "The State of the Internal Market for Services: Report from the Commission to the Council and the European Parliament, Presented under the First Stage of the Internal Market Strategy for Services." COM(2002)41 Final, July 30, Commission of the European Communities, Brussels.

Chen, Weidong, and Jingxia Shi. 2011. "The 'Specificity' of Cultural Products versus the 'Generality' of Trade Obligations: Reflecting on 'China–Publications and Audiovisual Products.'" *Journal of World Trade* 45 (1): 159–86.

Coe, David T., Elkanah Helpman, and Alexander W. Hoffmaister. 1997. "North-South R&D Spillovers." *Economic Journal* 107 (440): 134–49.

Copeland, Brian R. 2001. "Benefits and Costs of Trade and Investment Liberalization in Services: Implications from Trade Theory." Paper prepared for the Department of Foreign Affairs and International Trade, Government of Canada, Ottawa.

Curzon, Gerard. 1965. *Multilateral Commercial Diplomacy: The General Agreement on Tariffs and Trade and Its Impact on National Commercial Policies and Techniques.* London: Michael Joseph.

Dam, Kenneth W. 1970. *The GATT: Law and International Economic Organization.* Chicago, IL: University of Chicago Press.

Delimatsis, Panagiotis. 2008. "Towards a Horizontal Necessity Test for Services: Completing the GATS Article VI:4 Mandate." In *GATS and the Regulation of International Trade in Services,* ed. Marion Panizzon, Nicole Pohl, and Pierre Sauvé, 370–96. Cambridge, U.K.: Cambridge University Press.

Doove, Samantha, Owen Gaabitas, Duc Nguyen-Hong, and Joe Owen. 2001. "Price Effects of Regulation: Telecommunication, Air Transport and Electricity Supply." Productivity Commission Working Paper 1682, AusInfo, Canberra.

Ethier, Wilfred J. 1982. "National and International Returns to Scale in the Modern Theory of International Trade." *American Economic Review* 72 (3, June): 389–405.

Evenett, Simon J. 2005. "'Competitive Liberalization': A Tournament Theory-Based Interpretation." University of St. Gallen, St. Gallen, Switzerland. http://www.alexandria.unisg.ch/publications/22172.

Evenett, Simon J., and Michael Meier. 2007. "An Interim Assessment of the U.S. Trade Policy of 'Competitive Liberalization.'" University of St. Gallen Discussion Paper 2007-18, St. Gallen, Switzerland. http://ssrn.com/abstract=985521.

Feketekuty, Geza. 1998. "Setting the Agenda for Services 2000: The Next Round of Negotiations on Trade in Services." Presented at conference on "The Future of Services Trade Liberalization: Services 2000," sponsored by the Coalitions of Service Industries, Ditchley Park, England, April.

———. 2000a. "Assessing Improving the Architecture of GATS." In *GATS 2000: New Directions in Services Trade Liberalization*, ed. Pierre Sauvé and Robert M. Stern, 85–111. Washington, DC: Brookings Institution Press.

———. 2000b. "Regulatory Reform and Trade Liberalization in Services." In *GATS 2000: New Directions in Services Trade Liberalization*, ed. Pierre Sauvé and Robert M. Stern, 225–40. Washington, DC: Brookings Institution Press

Findlay, Christopher, and Tony Warren. 2000. *Impediments to Trade in Services: Measurement and Policy Implications.* London and New York: Routledge.

Finger, J. Michael. 1992. "GATT's Influence on PTAs." Presented at a World Bank and Centre for Economic Policy Research (CEPR) conference on "New Dimensions in Regional Integration," Washington, DC, April 2–3.

Fink, Carsten. 2007. "Liberalizing Services Trade in the ASEAN Region." In *A Handbook of International Trade in Services*, ed. Aaditya Mattoo, Robert M. Stern, and Gianni Zanini. Oxford, U.K.: Oxford University Press.

———. 2008. "PTAs in Services: Friends or Foes of the Multilateral Trading System?" In *Opening Markets for Trade in Services: Countries and Sectors in Bilateral and WTO Negotiations*, ed. Juan A. Marchetti and Martin Roy, 113–47. Cambridge, U.K.: Cambridge University Press.

Fink, Carsten, and Marion Jansen. 2008. "Services Provisions in Regional Trade Agreements: Stumbling Blocks or Building Blocks for Multilateral Liberalization?" *Multilateralizing Regionalism: Challenges for the Global Trade System*, ed. Richard Baldwin and Patrick Low, 221–61. Cambridge U.K.: Cambridge University Press.

Fink, Carsten, and Martin Molinuevo. 2007. "East Asian FTAs in Services: Roaring Tigers or Timid Pandas?" East Asia and Pacific Region, Report 40175, World Bank, Washington, DC. http://siteresources.worldbank.org/INTEAPSUMEASPR/Resources/2576847-1163691185244/East_Asian_FTAs_in_Services.pdf.

Frankel, Jeffrey A., Ernesto Stein, and Shang-Jin Wei. 1995. "Trading Blocs and the Americas: The Natural, the Unnatural, and the Super-Natural." *Journal of Development Economics* 47: 61–95.

Glassman, Cynthia A. 2000. "Customer Benefits from Current Information Sharing by Financial Services Companies." Study for the Financial Services Roundtable, Washington, DC.

Greenaway, David. 1993. "Study on Regional Integration: Third Country Responses." Background paper for the OECD Trade Directorate project on "Regional Integration," Organisation for Economic Co-operation and Development, Paris.

Hamilton, Bob, and John Whalley. 1984. "Efficiency and Distributional Implications of Global Restrictions on Labour Mobility: Calculations and Policy Implications." *Journal of Development Economics* 14 (1): 61–75.

Hardin, Alexis, and Leanne Holmes. 1997. "Service Trade and Foreign Direct Investment." Industry Commission Staff Research Paper, Productivity Commission, Government Publishing Services, Canberra.

Hart, Michael, and Pierre Sauvé. 1997. "Does Size Matter? Canadian Perspectives on the Development of Government Procurement Disciplines in North America." In *Law and Policy in Public Purchasing: The WTO Agreement on Government Procurement*, ed. Bernard M. Hoekman and Petros C. Mavroidis, 203–21. Ann Arbor, MI: University of Michigan Press.

Hoekman, Bernard. 1996. "Assessing the General Agreement on Trade in Services." In *The Uruguay Round and the Developing Countries*, ed. Will Martin and L. Alan Winters. Cambridge, U.K.: Cambridge University Press.

Hoekman, Bernard, and Carlos A. Primo Braga. 1997. "Protection and Trade in Services: A Survey." *Open Economies Review* 8 (3, July): 285–308.

Hoekman, Bernard M., and Pierre Sauvé. 1994. *Liberalizing Trade in Services*. World Bank Discussion Paper 243. Washington, DC: World Bank.

Holmes, Leanne, and Alexis Hardin. 2000. "Assessing Barriers to Services Sector Investment." In *Impediments to Trade in Services: Measurement and Policy Implications,* ed. Christopher Findlay and Tony Warren. London and New York: Routledge.

Horn, Henrik, Petros C. Mavroidis, and André Sapir. 2010. "Beyond the WTO? An Anatomy of EU and US Preferential Trade Agreements." *World Economy* 33 (11): 1565–88.

IADB (Inter-American Development Bank). 2002. *Beyond Borders: The New Regionalism in Latin America.* Economic and Social Progress in Latin America, 2002 Report. Washington, DC: IADB.

Iida, Keyia, and Julia Nielson. 2003. "Strengthening Regulatory Transparency." In *Domestic Regulation and Service Trade Liberalization,* ed. Aaditya Mattoo and Pierre Sauvé, 7–26. Washington, DC: Oxford University Press for the World Bank.

IMF (International Monetary Fund). 2009. *Balance of Payments Manual.* 6th ed. Washington, DC: IMF. http://www.imf.org/external/pubs/ft/bop/2007/bopman6.htm.

Kalirajan, Kaliappa. 2000. "Restrictions on Trade and Distribution Services." Productivity Commission Staff Research Paper, AusInfo, Canberra.

Kemp, Murray C., and Henry Y. Wan, Jr. 1976. "An Elementary Proposition Concerning the Formation of Customs Unions." *Journal of International Economics* 6 (1): 95–97.

Kemp, Steven. 2000. "Trade in Education Services and the Impacts of Barriers on Trade." In *Impediments to Trade in Services: Measurement and Policy Implications,* ed. Christopher Findlay and Tony Warren. London and New York: Routledge.

Kessides, Ioannis N., Roger G. Noll, and Nancy C. Benjamin. 2009. "Regionalizing Telecommunications Reform in West Africa." Policy Research Working Paper 5126, World Bank, Washington, DC. http://go.worldbank.org/31T8TCK3G0.

Koncz, Jennifer, and Anne Flatness. 2008. "U.S. International Services: Cross Border Trade in 2007 and Services Supplied through Affiliates in 2006." In *Survey of Current Business* (October), U.S. Department of Commerce, Bureau of Economic Analysis, Washington, DC. http://www.bea.gov/scb/pdf/2008/10%20October/services_text.pdf.

Kowalczyk, Carsten. 1990. "Welfare and Customs Unions." NBER Working Paper 3476, National Bureau of Economic Research, Cambridge, MA.

Lawrence, Robert Z. 1991. "Emerging Regional Arrangement: Building Blocks or Stumbling Blocks?" In *Finance and the International Economy 5: The AMEX Bank Review Prize Essays,* ed. Richard O'Brien, 23–35. New York: Oxford University Press.

Leebron, David. 2003. "Regulatory Discrimination in Domestic United States Law: A Model for the GATS?" In *Domestic Regulation and Service Trade Liberalization,* ed. Aaditya Mattoo and Pierre Sauvé, 43–56. Washington, DC: World Bank and Oxford University Press.

Leroux, Eric. 1995. *Le libre-échange nord-américain et les services financiers.* Collection Minerve. Montréal: Editions Yvon Blais.

Low, Patrick, and Aaditya Mattoo. "Is There a Better Way? Alternative Approaches to Liberalization under GATS." In *GATS 2000: New Directions in Services Liberalization,* ed. Pierre Sauvé and Robert M. Stern. Washington, DC: Brookings Institution Press.

Lumengo-Neso, Olivier, Marcelo Olarreaga, and Maurice Schiff. 2001. "On 'Indirect' Trade-Related Research and Development Spillovers." Policy Research Working Paper 2580, World Bank, Washington, DC.

Marchetti, Juan A. 2004. "Developing Countries in the WTO Services Negotiations." ERSD Staff Working Paper ERSD-2004-06, Economic Research and Statistics Division, World Trade Organization, Geneva.

Marchetti, Juan A., and Martin Roy. 2008. "Services Liberalization in the WTO and in PTAs." *Opening Markets for Trade in Services: Countries and Sectors in Bilateral and WTO Negotiations,* ed. Juan A. Marchetti and Martin Roy, 61–112. Cambridge, U.K.: Cambridge University Press.

Marconini, Mario. 2005. "Emergency Safeguard Measures in the GATS: Beyond Feasible and Desirable." UNCTAD/DITC/TNCD/2005/4, United Nations Conference on Trade and Development (UNCTAD), Geneva.

Marconini, Mario, and Pierre Sauvé. 2010. "Negotiating Trade in Services: A Practical Guide for Developing Countries." In *Trade in Services Negotiations: A Guide for Developing Countries,* ed. Sebastián Sáez, 19–86. Washington, DC: World Bank.

Markusen, James. 1983. "Factor Movements and Commodity Trade as Complements." *Journal of International Economics* 14: 341–56.

Mattoo, Aaditya. 1998. "Financial Services and the WTO: Liberalization in the Developing and Transitional Economies." Presented at workshop on "Measuring Impediments to Trade in Services," Productivity Commission, Canberra, April 30–May 1.

Mattoo, Aaditya, and Carsten Fink. 2002. "Regional Agreements and Trade in Services: Policy Issues." Policy Research Working Paper 2852, World Bank, Washington, DC.

Mattoo, Aaditya, and Pierre Sauvé. 2002. "Regionalism and Trade in Services in the Western Hemisphere: A Policy Agenda." Prepared for forum on "FTAA and Beyond: Prospects for Integration in the Americas," organized by the Inter-American Development Bank and Harvard University, Punta del Este, December 15–16.

———. 2003. "Domestic Regulation and the GATS: Looking Ahead." In *Domestic Regulation and Service Trade Liberalization,* ed. Aaditya Mattoo and Pierre Sauvé. Washington, DC: Oxford University Press for the World Bank.

———. 2008. "Regionalism in Services Trade." In *A Handbook of International Trade in Services,* ed. Aaditya Mattoo, Robert M. Stern, and Gianni Zanini. Oxford, U.K.: Oxford University Press.

Mattoo, Aaditya, Randeep Rathindran, and Arvind Subramanian. 2001. "Measuring Services Trade Liberalization and its Impact on Economic Growth: An Illustration." World Bank Policy Research Working Paper 2380, World Bank, Washington, DC.

McGuire, Greg, and Michael Schuele. 2000. "Restrictiveness of International Trade in Banking Services." In *Impediments to Trade in Services: Measurement and Policy Implications,* ed. Christopher Findlay and Tony Warren. London and New York: Routledge.

McGuire, Greg, Michael Schuele, and Tina Smith. 2000. "Restrictiveness of International Trade in Maritime Services." In *Impediments to Trade in Services: Measurement and Policy Implications,* ed. Christopher Findlay and Tony Warren. London and New York: Routledge.

McLaren, John. 1997. "Size, Sunk Costs, and Judge Bowker's Objection to Free Trade." *American Economic Review* 87 (3, June): 400–20.

———. 1999. "A Theory of Insidious Regionalism." Department of Economics, Columbia University, New York.

McMillan, John. 1993. "Does Regional Integration Foster Open Trade? Economic Theory and GATT's Article XXIV." In *Regional Integration* and the Global Trading System, ed. Kym Anderson and Richard Blackhurst. London: Harvester Wheatsheaf.

Mengozzi, Paolo. 1993. "Trade in Services and Commercial Policy." In The European Community's Commercial Policy after 1992: The Legal Dimension, ed. Marc Maresceau. Dordrecht: Martinus Nijhoff.

Messerlin, Patrick. 2009. "Economic Partnership Agreements: How to Rebound?" In Updating Economic Partnership Agreements to Today's Global Challenges, ed. Emily Jones and Marti F. Darlan, 22–27. Economic Policy Paper Series 09. Washington, DC, and Brussels: German Marshall Fund of the United States. http://www.gmfus.org/publications/index.cfm.

Monge-Naranjo, Alexander. 2003. "Lessons from the NAFTA for Latin America and the Caribbean." World Bank, Washington, DC.

Nguyen-Hong, Duc. 2000. "Restrictions on Trade in Professional Services." Productivity Commission Staff Research Paper, AusInfo, Canberra.

Nicolaïdis, Kalypso, and Joel P. Trachtman. 2000. "From Policed National Treatment to Managed Recognition: Mapping the Boundary in GATS." In GATS 2000: New Directions in Services Trade Liberalization, ed. Pierre Sauvé and Robert M. Stern, 241–82. Washington, DC: Brookings Institution Press.

Nielson, Julia, and Daria Taglioni. 2004. "Services Trade Liberalisation: Identifying Opportunities and Gains." OECD Trade Policy Working Paper 1, Organisation for Economic Co-operation and Development, Paris. http://www.oecd.org/officialdocuments/displaydocumentpdf/?cote=td/tc/wp%282003%2923/final&doclanguage=en.

OAS (Organization of American States). 1998. Sectoral Agreements on Services in the Western Hemisphere. Washington, DC: OAS.

———. 1999. "Provisions on Trade in Services in the Trade and Integration Agreements of the Western Hemisphere." OAS, Washington, DC.

OECD (Organisation for Economic Co-operation and Development). 2002a. GATS: The Case for Open Services Markets. Paris: OECD.

———. 2002b. "Labor Mobility in PTAs." TD/TC/WP(2002)16, OECD, Paris.

———. 2002c. "The Relationship between the Multilateral Trade System and Regional Trade Agreements: Government Procurement." TD/TC/WP(2002)24, OECD, Paris.

———. 2002d. "The Relationship between Regional Trade Agreements and the Multilateral Trading System: Investment." TD/TC/WP(2002)18, OECD, Paris.

———. 2002e. "The Relationship between Regional Trade Agreements and the Multilateral Trading System: Services." TD/TC/WP(2002)21, OECD, Paris.

———. 2002f. "Service Providers on the Move: Taking a Closer Look at Labor Mobility and the GATS." OECD Trade Directorate, Paris.

———. 2003. "Quantifying the Benefits of Liberalising Trade in Services." OECD, Paris.

———. 2007. "The Services Trade Restrictiveness Index: Issues and Challenges in Its Design." Meeting of the Experts on the STRI, TAD/TC/SXM(2007)2, OECD, Paris.

———. 2009. "Assessing Barriers to Trade in Services in the MENA Region." OECD Trade Policy Working Paper 84, TAD/TC/WP(2008)25/FINAL, OECD, Paris.

Panagariya, Arvind. 2000. "Preferential Trade Liberalization: The Traditional Theory and New Developments." Journal of Economic Literature 38 (2): 287–331.

Patterson, Gardner. 1966. Discrimination in International Trade: The Policy Issues, 1945–1965. Princeton, NJ: Princeton University Press.

PECC (Pacific Economic Cooperation Council). 1995. "Survey of the Impediments to Trade and Investment in the APEC Region." PECC, Singapore.

Peña, María-Angélica. 2000. "Services in MERCOSUR: The Protocol of Montevideo." In Services Trade in the Western Hemisphere: Liberalisation, Integration, and Reform, ed. Sherry M. Stephenson, 154–68. Washington, DC: Brookings Institution Press.

Pierola, Fernando. 2008. "A Safeguards Regime for Services." In GATS and the Regulation of International Trade in Services, ed. Marion Panizzon, Nicole Pohl, and Pierre Sauvé, 434–65. Cambridge, U.K.: Cambridge University Press.

Poretti, Pietro. 2008. "Waiting for Godot? Subsidy Disciplines in Services Trade." In GATS and the Regulation of International Trade in Services, Regulation and Development, ed. Marion Panizzon, Nicole Pohl, and Pierre Sauvé, 466–88. Cambridge, U.K.: Cambridge University Press.

Prieto, Francisco Javier. 2000. "The GATS, Subregional Agreements, and the FTAA: How Much Is Left to be Done?" In Services Trade in the Western Hemisphere: Liberalization, Integration, and Reform, ed. Sherry M. Stephenson, 217–41. Washington, DC: Brookings Institution Press.

Primo-Braga, Carlos Alberto. 1992. "NAFTA and the Rest of the World." In North American Free Trade: Assessing the Impact, ed. Nora Lustig, Barry Bosworth, and Robert Z. Lawrence, 210–49. Washington, DC: Brookings Institution.

Qian, Ying. 2000. "Analysis of the Commitments under the GATS and the World Trade Organization." World Bank, Washington, DC.

Robert, Maryse, Pierre Sauvé, and Karsten Steinfatt. 2001. "Negotiating Investment Rules: Possible Scenarios for an EU-MERCOSUL Agreement." Institut d'Etudes Politiques, Paris.

Robinson, Sherman, Zhi Wang, and Will Martin. 1999. "Capturing the Implications of Services Trade Liberalization." Presented at the Second Annual Conference on Global Economic Analysis, Ebberup, Denmark, June 20–22.

Roy, Martin, Juan Marchetti, and Hor Lim. 2006. "Services Liberalization in the New Generation of Preferential Trade Agreements: How Much Further than the GATS?" WTO Staff Working Paper ERSD-2006-07, World Trade Organization, Geneva.

———. 2008. "The Race towards Preferential Trade Agreements in Services: How Much Further Than the GATS?" In GATS and the Regulation of International Trade in Services, ed. Marion Panizzon, Nicole Pohl, and Pierre Sauvé, 77–110. Cambridge, U.K.: Cambridge University Press.

Salazar-Xirinachs, José M., and Maryse Robert. 2001. Toward Free Trade in the Americas. Washington, DC: Brookings Institution Press.

Sapir, Andre. 1998. "GATS 1994–2000." Journal of World Trade 33: 51–66.

Sauvé, Pierre. 1996. "Services and the International Contestability of Markets." Transnational Corporations 5 (1, April): 37–56.

———.1997. Preparing for Services 2000. CSI Occasional Paper 4. Washington, DC: Coalition of Services Industries.

———. 2000. "Making Progress on Trade and Investment: Multilateral vs. Regional Perspectives." In Services Trade in the Western Hemisphere: Liberalization, Integration, and Reform, ed. Sherry M. Stephenson, 72–85. Washington, DC: Brookings Institution Press.

———. 2002. "Completing the GATS Framework: Safeguards, Subsidies and Government Procurement." In Development, Trade and the WTO: A Handbook, ed. Bernard Hoekman, Aaditya Mattoo, and Philip English, 326–35. Washington, DC: World Bank.

———. 2003. "Assessing the General Agreement on Trade in Services: Half-Full or Half-Empty?" In Trade Rules behind Borders: Essays on Services, Investment and the New Trade Agenda, ed. Pierre Sauvé. London: Cameron May.

———. 2009. "Trade and Investment in Services: An ADB-ITD Training Module for the Greater Mekong Sub-Region." Asian Development Bank, Manila, and International Institute for Trade and Development, Bangkok. http://www.adb.org/Documents/Guidelines/Trade-Investment-services/default.asp.

———. 2010. "Conducting a Trade-Related Regulatory Audit in Financial Services." In Financial Services and Preferential Trading Arrangements: Lessons from Latin America, ed. Mona Haddad and Constantinos Stephanou. Directions in Development series. Washington, DC: World Bank.

Sauvé, Pierre, and Denis Audet. 2009. "The Treatment of Trade in Services in Economic Partnership Agreements: Implications for Prospective EPA Partners." In Updating Economic Partnership Agreements to Today's Global Economic Challenges, ed. Emily Jones and Darlan

F. Marti, 85–91. Economic Policy Paper Series 09, German Marshall Fund of the United States, Washington, DC and Brussels. http://www.scribd.com/doc/38477671/Updating-Economic-Partnership-Agreements-to-Today-s-Global-Challenges-Essays-on-the-Future-of-Economic-Partnership-Agreements.

Sauvé, Pierre, and Brenda Gonzalez-Hermosillo. 1993. "Implications of the NAFTA for Canadian Financial Institutions." In *C. D. Howe Commentary* 44 (April). Toronto, Canada: C. D. Howe Institute.

Sauvé, Pierre, and Karsten Steinfatt. 2001. "Financial Services and the WTO: What Next?" In *Open Doors: Foreign Participation in Financial Systems in Developing Countries*, ed. Robert E. Litan, Paul Masson, and Michael Pomerleano, 351–86. Washington, DC: World Bank Group, International Monetary Fund, and Brookings Institution Press.

Sauvé, Pierre, and Natasha Ward. 2009a. "The EC–CARIFORUM Partnership Agreement: Assessing the Outcome on Services and Investment." ECIPE Discussion Paper. European Centre for International Political Economy, Brussels. http://www.ecipe.org/publications/ecipe-working-papers/the-ec-cariform-economic-partnership-agreement-assessing-the-outcome-on-services-and-investment.

———. 2009b. "Services and Investment in the EC–CARIFORUM Economic Partnership Agreement: Innovation in Rule-Design and Implications for Africa." In *Beyond Market Access for Economic Development: EU–Africa Relations in Transition*, ed. G. Faber and J. Orbie, 137–72. London: Routledge.

———. 2009c. "Tourism Services Liberalization: The Role of Business Advocacy in the Caribbean–European Union Economic Partnership Agreement." Business and Trade Policy Case Study, International Trade Centre, Geneva. http://www.intracen.org/btp/business_advocacy/publications/tourism_services_liberalization..pdf.

Sauvé, Pierre, and Christopher Wilkie. 2000. "Investment Liberalization in GATS." In *GATS 2000: New Directions in Services Trade Liberalization*, ed. Pierre Sauvé and Robert M. Stern, 331–63. Washington, DC: Centre for Business and Government, Harvard University, and Brookings Institution Press.

Schiff, Maurice, and W. Chang. 2003. "Market Presence, Contestability, and the Terms-of-Trade Effects of Regional Integration." *Journal of International Economics* 60 (1, May): 161–75.

Schott, Jeffrey, ed. 1989. *Free Trade Areas and U.S. Trade Policy*. Washington, DC: Institute for International Economics.

Silver, Sara. 2002. "US under Pressure over Mexican Trucking." *Financial Times* (November 4).

Snape, Richard. 1993. "History and Economics of GATT's Article XXIV." In *Regional Integration and the Global Trading System*, ed. Kym Anderson and Richard Blackhurst. London: Harvester Wheatsheaf.

Snape, Richard, Jan Adams, and David Morgan. 1993. *Regional Trading Arrangements: Implications and Options for Australia*. Canberra: Australian Government Publishing Service.

Snape, Richard, and Malcolm Bosworth. 1996. "Advancing Services Negotiations." In *The World Trading System: Challenges Ahead*, ed. Jeffrey Schott, 185–203. Washington, DC: Institute for International Economics.

Stephenson, Sherry M. 1999. "PTAs on Services within APEC and Disciplines of the Multilateral Trading System." Presented to the meeting of the Asia-Pacific Economic Cooperation (APEC) Group on Services, Wellington, February.

———. 2000. "PTAs on Services and Multilateral Disciplines: Interpreting and Applying GATS Article V." In *GATS 2000: New Directions in Services Trade Liberalization*, ed. Pierre Sauvé and Robert M. Stern. Washington, DC: Brookings Institution Press.

———. 2001a. "Deepening Disciplines for Trade in Services." *OAS Trade Unit Studies: Analyses on Trade and Integration in the Americas* (March). Washington, DC: Organization of American States.

———. 2001b. "Multilateral and Regional Services Liberalization by Latin America and the Caribbean." OAS Trade Unit Studies, OEA/Ser.D/XXII, SG/TU/TUS-9, Organization of American States, Washington, DC.

———. 2001c. "Services." In *Toward Free Trade in the Americas*, ed. José M. Salazar-Xirinachs and Maryse Robert, 163–85. Washington, DC: Brookings Institution Press.

———. 2002. "Regional versus Multilateral Liberalization of Services." *World Trade Review* 1 (2): 187–209.

Stephenson, Sherry M., and S. Yi. 2002. "Transparency in Regulation of Services." Presented to the meeting of the Asia-Pacific Economic Cooperation (APEC) Group on Services, Mexico City, February.

Thompson, Rachel. 2000. "Formula Approaches to Improving GATS Commitments." In *GATS 2000: New Directions in Services Trade Liberalization*, ed. Pierre Sauvé and Robert M. Stern, 473–86. Washington, DC: Brookings Institution Press.

Tirole, Jean. 1998. *The Theory of Industrial Organization*. Cambridge, MA: MIT Press.

Trachtman, Joel P. 2003. "Lessons for the GATS from Existing WTO Rules on Domestic Regulation." In *Domestic Regulation and Service Trade Liberalization*, ed. Aaditya Mattoo and Pierre Sauvé. Washington, DC: Oxford University Press for the World Bank.

United Nations. 2002. *Manual on Statistics of International Trade in Services*. Geneva: United Nations. http://unstats.un.org/unsd/tradeserv/TFSITS/manual.htm.

United Nations and World Bank. 1993. *Liberalizing International Transactions in Services: A Handbook*. Geneva: United Nations Conference on Trade and Development.

U.S. Coalition of Service Industries. 2003. "Reports of ISAC 13 on the US–Chile and US–Singapore Free Trade Agreements." http://www.uscsi.org.

Viner, Jacob. 1950. *The Customs Union Issue*. New York: Carnegie Endowment for International Peace.

Walmsely, T., and L. Alan Winters. 2002. "Relaxing the Restrictions on the Temporary Movement of Natural Persons: A Simulation Analysis." University of Sussex, Brighton, U.K.

Warren, Tony. 2000. "The Identification of Impediments to Trade and Investment in Telecommunications and Financial Services." *Impediments to Trade in Services: Measurement and Policy Implications*, ed. Christopher Findlay and Tony Warren. London and New York: Routledge.

Winters, L. Alan. 1996. "Regionalism versus Multilateralism." Policy Research Working Paper 1687, World Bank, Washington, DC.

———. 2001. "Harnessing Trade for Development." University of Sussex, Brighton, U.K.

Wonnacott, Paul, and Ronald J. Wonnacott. 1981. "Is Unilateral Tariff Reduction Preferable to a Customs Union? The Curious Case of the Missing Foreign Tariffs." *American Economic Review* 71 (4, September): 704–14.

World Bank. 2000. *Trade Blocs*. New York: Oxford University Press.

———. 2002. *Global Economic Prospects and the Developing Countries 2002: Making Trade Work for the Poor*. Washington, DC: World Bank.

———. 2003. *Global Economic Prospects and the Developing Countries 2003: Investing to Unlock Global Opportunities*. Washington, DC: World Bank.

———. 2004. *Global Economic Prospects and the Developing Countries 2004: Realizing the Promise of the Doha Round*. Washington, DC: World Bank.

WTO (World Trade Organization). 1995. *Regionalism and the World Trading System*. Geneva: WTO.

———. 1999. "The Fundamental WTO Principles of National Treatment, Most-Favored-Nation Treatment and Transparency." WT/GTCP/W/114, WTO, Geneva.

———. 2001. *Market Access: Unfinished Business—Post–Uruguay Round Issues*. Special Study 6. Geneva: WTO.

———. 2003. *Regional Trade Agreements*, Geneva: WTO.

Wunsch-Vincent, Sacha, 2003. "The Digital Trade Agenda of the U.S.: Parallel Tracks of Bilateral, Regional and Multilateral Liberalization." *Aussenwirtschaft* 58: 7–46.

———. 2006. *The WTO, the Internet and Digital Products: EC and US Perspectives*. Oxford, U.K.: Hart Publishing.

———. 2008. "Trade Rules for the Digital Age." In *GATS and the Regulation of International Trade in Services*, ed. Marion Panizzon, Nicole Pohl, and Pierre Sauvé, 497–529. Cambridge, U.K.: Cambridge University Press.

Zoellick, Robert B. 2001. "Free Trade and the Hemispheric Hope." Remarks to Council of the Americas, Washington, DC, May 7.

13

LABOR MOBILITY

Sherry Stephenson and Gary Hufbauer

Of all the liberalization dimensions of international trade, the opening of labor markets is probably the most sensitive. As a result, agreements to open (generally, only partially) labor markets are not as plentiful as other liberalization agreements, and they are typically more restrictive. They are also less well surveyed. This chapter presents an overview of provisions for opening labor markets that are found in preferential trade agreements (PTAs).

Movement of labor is one of the four fundamental economic freedoms, along with free movement of goods, services, and capital. Of the four, it has met with the least receptivity on the part of countries in the international economy, whether developed or developing. Even the most spirited free traders—Chile; Singapore; the United Kingdom; and Hong Kong SAR, China, for example—have been reticent about opening their borders more to admit labor from abroad. These economies and many others shy away from significant opening for natural persons from other countries, even in the face of labor shortages at home.

The contrast between the desire to promote capital mobility and investment flows and the reluctance to envisage corresponding labor mobility is stark. More than 2,800 bilateral investment treaties have been signed to date, but nothing equivalent exists in the area of labor (Vis-Dunbar and Nikiema 2009). The number of trade agreements covering services is growing rapidly, yet willingness to incorporate meaningful provisions on labor mobility into the services package is limited, and most agreements contain very modest market access opportunities for foreign workers. Several recent free trade agreements (FTAs) contain no provisions at all in this area. Leaving aside formal bilateral and regional trade agreements, it is extremely difficult to determine the number of bilateral agreements worldwide that incorporate arrangements for temporary worker programs. There appears, however, to be not more than a handful. Information is scarce, and no single

institution has been designated as a repository of agreements and promoter of labor mobility. And whereas most governments sponsor investment promotion agencies to encourage inward flows of capital and foreign direct investment, there is no similar institution for workers. In nearly all countries, the agency that deals with the influx of foreign labor is the immigration authority, whose concern is to regulate and restrict, not to promote. To complicate matters further, immigration authorities are primarily focused on setting rules for permanent rather than temporary migration. Temporary migration, however, is the object of international trade policy and is the focus of this discussion.

The problems with the present situation are twofold. The first has to do with its unbalanced nature. Developed economies have a comparative advantage in the export of capital and thus benefit tremendously from the openness of capital markets and the welcoming character of most investment regimes. That kind of receptiveness does not exist for labor movements. Developing countries have a comparative advantage in the export of their people, but they are constrained from realizing the gains from trade that they might otherwise enjoy.

The second problem is that the entire world suffers from a loss of potential income that could be realized through greater mobility. Depending on what assumptions are made by researchers, the potential gains could be quite substantial and could easily surpass the combined gains anticipated from freer trade in agriculture and manufactured goods—as currently proposed in the Doha Development Round sponsored by the World Trade Organization (WTO). Nevertheless, proposals for greater market access for foreign workers are limited, and this has been a central obstacle to progress in the services component of Doha Round negotiations.

It has been argued by many, including, prominently, Lant Pritchett and L. Alan Winters, that greater mobility of labor would be the first-best development promotion strategy (Pritchett 2006; Winters 2008). Pritchett writes that it is hard to imagine a policy more directly at odds with poverty reduction or pro-poor growth objectives than one limiting the demand for lower-skilled labor. This limitation can be viewed as the principal way that rich countries are currently inhibiting the development possibilities of poorer countries—much more than through restrictive agricultural policies or nontariff barriers.

In such a challenging and often hostile environment for labor mobility, what options might developing countries have for increasing the scope for the movement of their workers? Given the impasse in the Doha Round and the lack of any progress on services in multilateral negotiations for the past several years, preferential trade agreements might offer a more promising channel for greater labor mobility, even if among a limited number of partners. Other options that have been relatively unexplored to date may also be available, such as the promotion of circular migration through temporary worker agreements—time-bound instruments that allow greater flexibility for both labor-sending and labor-receiving countries.

In this chapter, we do not delve into the Doha quagmire but, rather, explore these other options. We first discuss the concept and magnitude of labor mobility and the potential benefits from greater liberalization. We then review the various ways in which members of PTAs have treated the issue of labor mobility to assess whether these preferential agreements have effectively promoted temporary entry. Only PTAs between developed and developing countries are examined.

The questions we attempt to answer are the following: Which developed countries are more amenable to greater openness for natural persons, and what are the possible reasons? Can recent PTAs be emulated? What have temporary worker programs in bilateral and plurilateral agreements with developing-country partners achieved, and could such agreements usefully supplement the PTA approach? After exploring these issues, we look at policy suggestions that might be implemented by the World Bank to promote labor mobility for its developing-country members.

We recognize that developed countries are currently experiencing very high levels of unemployment and that these conditions will probably continue through 2011 and possibly into 2012. Accordingly, political resistance to all forms of labor mobility is extremely high. This chapter, however, is written with a view to the longer term, when normal economic conditions will have been restored.

The Concept of Labor Mobility

In international services trade, labor mobility is conceptualized as the temporary movement of natural persons and is categorized as mode 4. Article I.2 (d) of the WTO General Agreement on Trade in Services (GATS) defines mode 4 as the supply of a service "by a service supplier of one Member, through presence of natural persons of a Member in the territory of any other Member." (See box 13.1 for estimates of the size of this mode.) A natural person of another member is defined as

a natural person who resides in the territory of that other Member or any other Member, and who under the law of that other Member:
(i) is a national of that other Member; or
(ii) has the right of permanent residence in that other Member . . ." (Article XVIII[k])

Temporary versus Permanent Workers

For services trade, and for our purposes here, labor mobility is understood as the movement of workers to carry out employment in another country for a time-limited period. Although the term "temporary" is not defined under GATS, the notion of moving in order to work for a limited period, as opposed to moving with the intention of emigrating permanently, is what distinguishes mode 4. This is affirmed in the GATS "Annex on Movement of Natural Persons Supplying Services under the Agreement," which specifies that GATS shall not apply "to measures affecting natural persons seeking access to the employment market of a Member, nor shall it apply to measures regarding citizenship, residence or employment on a permanent basis." All subsequent trade agreements, following the WTO approach, consider only the temporary movement of workers, but governments have been unwilling to define in precise terms what period of time is meant by "temporary." The official statistical definition of temporary migration is a stay of less than one year, but for trade policy purposes, a temporary stay can vary anywhere from a few weeks to a few years, depending on the commitments governments are prepared to undertake. This lack of precision has been both a strength and a weakness in defining mode 4 treatment within trade agreements.

The great political sensitivity surrounding international labor mobility is not helped by the very frequent confusion, in both statistical analysis and political debate, between temporary and permanent migration. Immigration authorities deal with both simultaneously, and at times the character of "temporary" labor movement is disregarded and all immigrants are treated as though

Box 13.1. Labor Mobility in Statistical Terms

Historically, one of the main ways that temporary labor migration has been captured in the data is through recorded "transfers and payments" in balance of payments statistics; this category is what we and others term "remittances." According to the International Monetary Fund (IMF) *Balance of Payments Manual,* "remittances" mainly comprise "compensation of employees" and "personal transfers" (IMF 2010). Transactions are recorded in the balance of payments when money is paid by residents to nonresidents, or vice versa. Determining the magnitude of mode 4 (temporary movement of services providers) by examining transactions is problematic, since remittances are made by both temporary and permanent migrants and by workers in the manufacturing and agricultural segments of the economy, as well as in services sectors. In addition, payments to undocumented foreign workers are not captured statistically when they are spent in the country in which the person works (see also Carzaniga 2008).

Looking at volume rather than value is hardly more satisfactory. The Organisation for Economic Co-operation and Development (OECD) collects information on the number of temporary foreign workers in surveys of firms, visas, border crossings, and so on. These data cover intracorporate transferees and other temporary workers. They are, however, far from a perfect match for mode 4. Furthermore, the scope may differ from one country to another, and in any event, figures are only available for a subgroup of OECD members.

Karsenty (2000) calculated services trade through mode 4 to be no more than 1 to 2 percent of total two-way trade in services. Applying this range to the most recent trade data available (2008) would put the value of services trade through mode 4 somewhere between US$70 billion and US$150 billion annually. Those figures may underestimate the actual value of this form of services trade, since remittances alone in 2007 amounted to more than US$200 billion. Remittances, however, likely overestimate mode 4 services trade.

Source: Karsenty 2000; OECD data.

they were seeking permanent status. Moreover, inside the host country, the line between permanently and temporarily resident migrants often becomes blurred.

Categories of Labor Included in Trade Agreements

Although the GATS text does not define specific categories of labor, WTO members have accepted four widely used categories for the purpose of inscribing commitments under mode 4. These categories are not comprehensive, as they cover only skilled professionals. In a few recent trade agreements, as we will see in the next section, countries have begun to move beyond this limited range of categories to broaden their consideration of labor categories for market access. The four traditional mode 4 categories are the following:

- *Business visitors and salespersons* (BVs). Foreign nationals who travel abroad to negotiate the sale of a service or to explore the possibility of making a foreign direct investment (of establishing a commercial presence, in GATS terminology) for their company in the destination country. Their main purpose is to facilitate future transactions rather than actually to carry out transactions.
- *Intracorporate transferees* (ICTs). Employees of a foreign services company that has set up a commercial presence abroad and that transfers these employees to its foreign location.
- *Independent professionals* (IPs). Self-employed persons who are supplying a service to a company or an individ-

ual in a host country. In most trade agreements, these have been limited to professional workers, but commitments can also be extended to lower-skilled categories of workers.

- *Contractual services suppliers* (CSSs). Employees of a foreign services company with no local presence or commercial presence in the host country who are engaged under contract to provide a service to a firm in the destination country.[1]

Developing countries' interest in promoting greater labor mobility most concerns the independent professional and contractual services supplier categories, rather than employees of multinational corporations (MNCs). This is because most developing countries, with notable exceptions such as Brazil, China, and India, have not yet become home bases for MNCs. Greater flexibility in the independent professional and contractual services supplier categories would allow most developing countries to send a larger number of professionals abroad for temporary employment. The business visitor and intracorporate transferee categories are of interest to successful emerging countries such as Brazil, China, and India.

Potential Economic Gains from Greater Labor Mobility

The fact that we cannot accurately know the real statistical importance of temporary workers in the world economy is secondary to the fact that impediments to labor mobility suppress trade to the disadvantage of everyone, but particularly developing countries. Goods move freely in response to price differentials, and capital flows effortlessly around the globe in response to profit and interest rate differentials, but workers are not allowed to move readily in response to wage differentials. Consequently, very large wage differentials exist in the world today, as shown in figure 13.1. The benefit to be derived from the exploitation of comparative advantage is directly proportional to the size of wage, price, or profit differences prior to trade or investment liberalization; thus, considerable gains could be realized if workers were permitted to exploit wage differentials among countries. (See box 13.2 for estimates of these gains.)

Theoretical Model of the Distributional Effects of Mode 4 Liberalization

Like trade in goods, labor mobility can create losers as well as winners. In the overall balance, gains usually exceed losses by a wide margin, but political sensitivities focus on those who lose. In simple theoretical terms, migration can be modeled as an increase of supply in the labor markets of developed countries and a decrease of supply in developing countries. Here, we use that framework to examine the effects of those supply changes on the incomes of capitalists and workers, in both the sending and the host countries, and on the incomes of the migrants themselves.

Effect in developed countries. Given the restrictions on labor mobility, the equilibrium in the labor market is at point *A* in figure 13.2. After liberalization, the equilibrium moves to point *B*, reflecting an increase in the number of hours worked and a decrease in the wage per hour. The loss

for native workers is shown by area *ACDE*. The gain for capitalists is shown by area *EABD*, with most of this gain coming from the loss for native workers. Since the gain for capitalists is larger than the loss for native workers, the liberalization of mode 4 leads to an overall gain, shown by area *ABC*.

Effect on developing countries. The effect of the liberalization of mode 4 on developing countries is the exact opposite to that for developed countries. With restrictions on mode 4, the equilibrium in the labor market is at point *B* in figure 13.3. After liberalization, the equilibrium point moves to point *A*, reflecting an increase in the wage per hour and a decrease in the number of hours worked.

As will be apparent later, the gains for migrants in developed countries are much larger than the loss that their departure inflicts on developing countries. Nonmigrant workers also experience gains, shown by area *ACDE* in figure 13.3, since the wage rate has increased in developing countries. But nonmigrant capitalists experience a very large loss, shown by area *ABDE* (most of the loss corresponds to the wage gain for nonmigrant workers). Because the loss for nonmigrant capitalists is larger than the gain for nonmigrant workers, the group of nonmigrants as a whole experiences an overall loss of income, shown by area *ABC*. In other words, the effect on total welfare of liberalizing mode 4 is negative for nonmigrants in developing countries. Income per capita, however, is likely (although not guaranteed) to rise as marginal productivity increases.

Overall outcome. Migrants lose their erstwhile wages in developing countries but enjoy larger wages in developed countries. They therefore experience a gain, measured by the wage difference between the destination and source countries.

Figure 13.1. Theoretical Gains from Liberalization of Mode 4

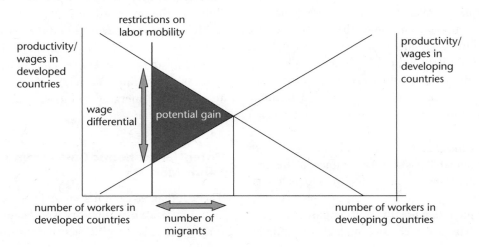

Box 13.2. Quantitative Estimates of Overall Gains from Greater Labor Mobility

Complete liberalization of mode 4 would result in very large gains.
Hamilton and Whalley (1984) use a partial equilibrium (PE) model and 1977 data to estimate the benefits from the complete elimination of all immigration restrictions, for skilled and unskilled labor alike. The potential gains are enormous, ranging from 60 to almost 205 percent of world gross domestic product (GDP). Millions of workers would move from low-productivity to high-productivity jobs in countries with high salaries, until wages in labor-sending and labor-receiving countries equalized. Iregui (1999) revisits the question using a computable general equilibrium (CGE) model and more precise measures of elasticities and population characteristics. Here again, the gains are large, ranging from 15 to 67 percent of world GDP. Moses and Letnes (2004), using more precise values for productivities, confirm large gains, ranging from 4.3 to about 112 percent of world GDP in 1977. According to these authors, the "most reasonable" gain would be 7.5 percent of world GDP.

The large differences between these estimates, both within and between studies, can be explained by the differences in modeling frameworks (partial versus general equilibrium) and assumed parameters. Some estimates assume that migrants can achieve the average productivity of workers in the destination country; others assume that additional education and training will be needed.

Gains from less than complete liberalization of mode 4 are still large.
Because full liberalization is politically unacceptable, some economists have estimated the potential outcome of more modest liberalization of mode 4. Moses and Letnes (2004) estimate the gains from eliminating 10 percent of the wage inequality between countries and find that potential gains would still be large, corresponding to around 2.2 percent of world GDP. Walmsley and Winters (2002) estimate the potential gain from a 3 percent increase in the workforce in developed countries, a movement of 14.2 million workers, and a 50 percent increase in the current number of immigrants in developed countries at US$156 billion in 2002, representing 0.6 percent of world GDP. World Bank (2006) reaches a very similar result.

Most of the gains come from the movement of unskilled labor.
According to Iregui (1999), the potential gains from the migration of skilled labor only are much smaller: 3 to 11 percent of world GDP, in comparison with 13 to 59 percent for all skills. Walmsley and Winters (2002) show that the potential gain from the movement of unskilled workers would account for US$110 billion, or 70 percent of the total. This reflects the fact that inequality in wages worldwide is larger for unskilled than for skilled workers.

Source: Annex table 13A.1.

Figure 13.2. Theoretical Effect on Developed Countries of Liberalization of Mode 4

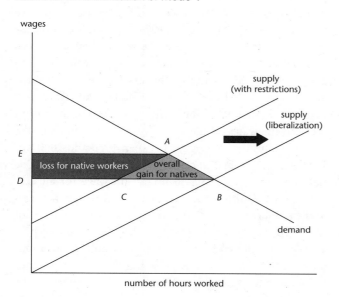

Figure 13.3. Theoretical Effect on Developing Countries of Liberalization of Mode 4

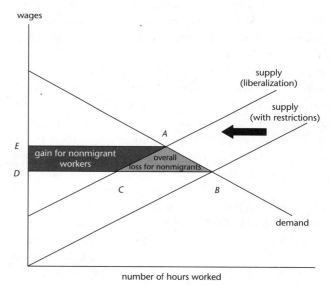

According to the theoretical model, the liberalization of mode 4 has the following distributional consequences:

• In developed countries, most of the gains for capitalists are balanced by losses to native workers.

• In developing countries, most of the losses to capitalists are mirrored by gains to nonmigrant workers.

• In developed countries, the gains for capitalists are larger than the losses for native workers. Therefore, total income in developed countries rises.

- In developing countries, the losses for capitalists are larger than the gains for nonmigrant workers. Therefore, total income in developing countries falls.

Distributional Effects of Mode 4 Liberalization

The theoretical and empirical prediction of large gains from full or partial liberalization of mode 4 outlined in box 13.2 do not hide the fact that labor mobility will have distributional consequences. Migrants are the main winners; the results for natives in both the sending and the host countries are mixed.

Gains for migrants. Walmsley and Winters (2002) calculate that benefits to migrants (US$171 billion) actually account for more than the total gain from increased labor mobility (US$156 billion). Total gains are smaller than the gains to migrants because of the losses to the sending countries, discussed below.

Losses for developing countries, before remittances. The departure of migrants reduces the number of workers in the sending countries, which increases hourly wages of nonmigrant workers but diminishes total output. Walmsley and Winters (2002) calculate that Brazil would see its welfare reduced by US$7 billion if the workforce going to developed countries increased by 3 percent, and China would experience a decline of US$2 billion, notwithstanding the compensation received from remittances. The authors' calculations suggest that unskilled workers in India would see a wage increase of 0.7 percent and that skilled workers in Mexico would enjoy an increase of 4.5 percent. Returns to capital would, however, decrease by, for example, 0.4 percent in Mexico. Exploring a more extreme scenario, Moses and Letnes (2004) arrive at similar results. In their calculations, a 10 percent elimination of wage inequality leads to an 11.4 percent increase in the wages of nonmigrant workers in the poorest countries in 1998, while the return to capital in those countries falls like a stone, by 21 percent.

The importance of remittances for developing countries. If the gains to migrants themselves are included in the overall balance sheet for developing countries, the picture changes completely. (Pritchett 2006 makes this point.) When the gains to migrants are combined with the national income losses to the sending countries, the developing countries experience a significant gain in plausible scenarios—the equivalent of 1.8 percent of their gross domestic product (GDP), according to the World Bank's *Global Economic Prospects 2006*, which explores the "3 percent scenario."

World Bank estimates of global remittances show that globally, compensation and remittances increased sixfold between 1990 and 2008, rising from US$69 billion to US$397 billion (adjusted for inflation). In 2007, migrant compensation and remittances accounted for around 0.7 percent of world GDP, but for developing countries, the relative importance of remittances in GDP in 2007 was much higher. Remittances were 2.1 percent of the GDP of developing countries as a whole, but 1.9 percent of the GDP of middle-income countries and 5.8 percent of the GDP of the least-developed countries (a UN category).

An increasing share of remittances goes to developing countries, which accounted for 46 percent of this flow in 1990 but for 76 percent by 2007. It is estimated that remittances touch 1 in 10 people worldwide. Dependence on remittances is especially high in certain countries. The main receiving countries in absolute terms are India (US$27 billion), China (US$26 billion), Mexico (US$25 billion), and the Philippines (US$17 billion). For many smaller countries, remittances represent a very large fraction of GDP, accounting for more than 36 percent of the GDPs of Moldova and Tajikistan and about 25 percent of the GDPs of Guyana, Honduras, and Lesotho.

Mixed picture in developed countries. Outcomes of migration for the developed countries are mixed, although slightly positive. Workers, especially unskilled ones, face increased competition from migrants and see their wages decline. For example, Hatton and Williamson (1998) estimate that in 1910, American wages would have been 11 to 14 percent higher in the absence of the immigration wave that set in after 1870. Borjas (1999) calculates that immigration to the United States between 1980 and 1998 resulted in a decrease in native wages amounting to 1.9 percent of GDP and that the losses were concentrated among low-skilled U.S. workers, whereas skilled workers actually benefited from immigration. Immigration reduced the wages of native high-school dropouts in the United States by 8.9 percent between 1980 and 2000 but increased the return to capital by 2 percent of GDP. The net gain from the 1980–98 migration wave for all U.S. natives is the difference between the decrease in wages and the increase in returns to capital, or 0.1 percent of U.S. GDP per year over the period. This net gain represents about US$10 billion a year, accounting for about 5 percent of U.S. economic growth over a 20-year period.

Moses and Letnes (2004) find the same pattern in the case of a 10 percent elimination of wage inequality. They calculate that liberalization of this magnitude would reduce wages in developed countries by 3.1 percent, while increasing the return to capital by 7.2 percent. Walmsley and Winters (2002) reach similar results in the case of a 3 percent increase in the workforce of developed countries: that scenario leads to a 0.8 percent decrease in U.S. and European wages and a 0.8 percent increase in return to capital in the United States. The World Bank's *Global Economic Prospects 2006* study shows that in the 3 percent scenario, the incomes of all natives combined in developed countries would rise by 0.4 percent (World Bank 2006).

Labor Mobility in Preferential Trade Agreements

A stalemate on services liberalization at the multilateral level has clouded the Doha Round for the past several years, with no moves to put new services offers on the table or to improve existing ones made since the end of 2005.[2] In contrast, an increasing amount of activity has taken place at the regional level, with the negotiation of numerous PTAs, a large number of which have incorporated mode 4 as part of the package.[3]

The members of some recent PTAs have accepted greater labor mobility at the regional level. Although progress is still relatively modest, interesting initiatives have been taken. Developing countries in the Americas and in Asia have entered into several free trade agreements that contain provisions to facilitate procedures for temporary labor movement and open up market access opportunities. Some agreements include guaranteed numerical quotas for certain categories of skilled labor. In this section, we compare approaches to labor mobility in PTAs. Only PTAs between developed and developing economies, and only those negotiated since the entry into force in January 1994 of the North American Free Trade Agreement (NAFTA), which signaled an era of deeper and more comprehensive preferential trade agreements, are considered.

Our discussion is divided along geographic lines, distinguishing between PTAs negotiated by the United States, Canada, the European Union (EU), Japan, and Australia and New Zealand. Annex tables 13A.2–13A.6 summarize the salient provisions of the PTAs that are examined.

Before delving into the details, a broad overview may be useful. NAFTA and other first-generation U.S. PTAs allowed limited mobility for professional workers, but second-generation U.S. PTAs are quite restrictive, as a result of congressional opposition. Canadian PTAs are much more liberal for skilled workers, as well as professionals, and contain some innovative provisions. Early EU agreements with developing countries did not have provisions allowing labor mobility because the subject was reserved to the competence of member states, but more recent EU agreements with Chile and the countries of the Caribbean Forum of African, Caribbean, and Pacific (ACP) States

(CARIFORUM) do permit limited access. Japanese PTAs allow the usual professional categories and contain innovative provisions for semiskilled workers. Australia and New Zealand have negotiated highly innovative agreements with China and Chile. By contrast, the Trans-Pacific Strategic Economic Partnership Agreement between Brunei Darussalam, Chile, New Zealand, and Singapore is quite restrictive. This feature may ease future accession by Australia, Japan, the United States, and Vietnam, but it does nothing for labor mobility among the Pacific members.

PTAs Negotiated by the United States and Canada

NAFTA was the pioneer agreement and template for many subsequent PTAs. It contains a chapter entitled "Temporary Movement of Business Persons," designed to facilitate temporary entry to member countries for business people involved in goods or services trade or in investment activities. The categories defined under NAFTA are traders and investors, business visitors, intracorporate transferees, and professionals. There is no limit on the number of visas for business visitors, and a work permit is not required. According to Martin and Lowell (2008), the novel migration component of NAFTA is the Trade NAFTA, or TN, visa (see Stephenson 2007 for a summary). This visa was uncapped in 1994 for Canadians and has been uncapped for Mexicans since 2004. When proof of a job offer is demonstrated, the TN visa permits employment for one year, with unlimited renewal.

In addition to the chapter on temporary entry, NAFTA, like subsequent agreements with a similar structure, contains an annex on professionals that is specifically targeted at professional services suppliers. These annexes are intended to promote the development of mutually acceptable standards and criteria for licensing and certification of professional services suppliers, on the basis of factors such as educational background, qualifying examinations, and experience. In addition, the NAFTA annex encourages members to submit recommendations for furthering the process of mutual recognition. A qualifying list of 62 professions is set out in an appendix to the agreement; applicants must fulfill the necessary qualification requirements. The United States originally placed a quota of 5,500 per year on the number of professionals who could be admitted from Mexico, but that quota has been eliminated.

Besides NAFTA, the United States has negotiated several other bilateral free trade agreements with developing countries. The agreements selected for examination are those with Chile, the five-country Dominican Republic–Central America Free Trade Agreement (CAFTA–DR), Morocco,

Peru, and Singapore (annex table 13A.2). Bilateral agreements with Colombia, the Republic of Korea, and Panama have been finalized but are awaiting ratification by the U.S. Congress.

Under the agreements with Chile and Singapore, both of which were concluded in 2002 and entered into force in 2004, labor mobility was expanded slightly for professional workers, and a path to a special visa for professionals (the H-1B1 visa) was created. The visa provided for an initial stay of 18 months, but with unlimited extensions. In addition, an annual quota of 1,400 visas for professionals from Chile was granted, as was an annual quota of 5,400 visas for professionals from Singapore, on top of the fixed total of H-1B visas from all countries. The new visa category created under these agreements is meant for temporary migrants, for stays of up to 18 months initially, but with the possibility of unlimited extensions.

In brief, the current provisions governing labor movement to the United States under NAFTA and the agreements with Chile and Singapore are as follows:

- NAFTA: TN visa; uncapped for both Canadians and Mexicans
- Chile FTA: H-1B1 visa; capped at 1,400 professionals
- Singapore FTA: H-1B1 visa; capped at 5,400 professionals.

As mentioned, these visa numbers are additional to whatever entries occur under other visa categories, most importantly, the H-1B visa for skilled workers and professionals.

Unfortunately, the opposition of the U.S. Congress to these arrangements, and in particular to the agreements with Chile and Singapore, was loud and clear. Key members of Congress objected that the trade agreements had encroached on the realm of immigration matters. As a consequence of this outcry, no free trade agreement negotiated by the United States since 2002 has contained a chapter to facilitate the temporary movement of skilled workers.[4] Thus, the FTAs with Morocco, with the CAFTA–DR members, and with Peru, like those negotiated with Colombia, Korea, and Panama, contain no chapter on temporary entry. Each does contain an annex on professionals, with objectives similar to those set out in NAFTA, but these annexes explicitly state that "no provision shall impose any obligation on a party regarding its immigration measures," and they contain no market access commitments. Thus, public and official attitudes in the United States with respect to labor mobility have regressed since 2002. Until political opinion changes, it will be close to impossible for developing countries to

negotiate greater labor mobility in trade agreements with the United States.

In Canada, the situation has evolved in the opposite direction (see annex table 13A.3). Interestingly, and perhaps because of pressures from the private sector and apparent labor shortages in the Canadian market prior to the current economic crisis, the government has negotiated recent FTAs that go quite far toward providing increased access not only for professionals but also for semiskilled foreign workers. Although the FTA that Canada negotiated with Chile in 1997 looks very much like NAFTA, with the only categories of workers covered being investors, traders, business visitors, intracorporate transferees, and professionals, it is notable in that no numerical limits were placed on 72 of these categories of professional labor.

Strikingly, the two very recent FTAs negotiated by Canada with Colombia (2008) and Peru (2009) go much farther. They cover all professional categories, with no numerical limits and no specified length of stay, meaning that visas could in theory be renewed indefinitely. For the first time, they also expand coverage of worker categories beyond highly trained professionals to include "technicians." In both the Colombia and Peru FTAs, Canada has listed 50 categories of technicians to be admitted into the Canadian market with no specified length of stay. These workers must have a high school degree, with two years of technical training. Technician categories include, among others, mechanics, construction inspectors, food and beverage supervisors, chefs, plumbers, and oil and gas well drillers. This recent development constitutes a major step forward for the expansion of temporary entry in trade agreements.

PTAs Negotiated by the European Union

In this section, we examine PTAs between the EU and third countries (see annex table 13A.4) Total labor mobility is guaranteed within the EU itself, although only after 10 years for some of the newest members.

The form of PTAs negotiated by the EU differs from that pioneered by the United States. Provisions for services and investment liberalization are set out in a title (or section) of the EU agreements entitled "Trade in Services and Establishment." The European Commission does not as yet have negotiating authority from the EU member states in all service areas.[5] The European Commission consequently always follows a positive-list approach in its trade agreements, with lists of commitments attached to the main text of the agreements. Thus, in terms of market access, mode 4 is brought within the scope of EU PTAs in a way similar to that followed under GATS. Categories of workers included in mode 4 commitments by the EU include the four that are traditional for PTAs: traders and investors, business visitors, intracorporate transferees, and independent professionals. The EU has negotiated relatively few PTAs with developing countries that cover services. Although it has numerous association agreements in place with neighboring Mediterranean countries (the Arab Republic of Egypt, Jordan, Morocco, the Syrian Arab Republic, Tunisia, Turkey, and others), these agreements focus on goods and have not yet incorporated services provisions.

The EU has negotiated association agreements with Mexico and Chile and has more recently finalized an economic partnership agreement (EPA) with CARIFORUM. There are no in-depth services provisions in the EU agreement with Mexico, which was concluded in March 2000 when the GATS negotiations were just beginning, but the PTA with Chile is substantial. In addition to the coverage of mode 4 in the text of the agreement, there is a specific article entitled "Movement of Natural Persons" in the EU–Chile association agreement, as well as an annex on professionals.[6] In the annex, the EU specifies 33 categories of professional services providers that it will accept from Chile without numerical limit, for a time period of three months, subject to the "necessary academic qualification and experience." Interestingly, Chile did not commit reciprocally to accepting any professionals from the EU.

The more recent EU–CARIFORUM economic partnership agreement follows a similar structure, but, in addition to the usual categories of workers defined under mode 4, the EU has expanded coverage of workers to three additional categories important for CARIFORUM members: contractual services suppliers, independent professionals, and graduate trainees. The following applies to these three categories:[7]

- *Contractual services suppliers.* This category applies to a specific list of activities and permits temporary entry for a cumulative period of six months. A contractual services supplier must fulfill certain requirements; the terms and conditions are set out in EU schedules for its member states.
- *Independent professionals.* The provisions for the CSS category also apply to independent professionals, again, subject to EU schedules.
- *Graduate trainees.* Graduate trainees, a new category, are workers from CARIFORUM states who have a university degree and are temporarily transferred to the parent company or to a commercial establishment for career development or to obtain training in business methods. They may enter for a period of up to one year.

In the annex on professionals attached to the CARIFORUM agreement, the European Union committed to accept 29 categories of professional services providers without numerical limit, provided that they have a university degree and three years' experience. The CARIFORUM members did not commit reciprocally to accept any EU professionals.

PTAs Negotiated by Japan

Japan has negotiated four PTAs that are of interest for the question of labor mobility. These are summarized in annex table 13A.5. The PTAs with Mexico and Chile are very similar in form and content to the NAFTA-type approach and agreements, with a negative list of nonconforming measures and with mode 4 treated in a chapter on temporary movement of business persons. That chapter defines movement for the same four categories usually seen in trade agreements: traders and investors, business visitors, intracorporate transferees, and independent professionals. Japan has set a time limit of three years for three of these categories (all except business visitors), which is a fairly generous interpretation of length of stay.

The two more recent PTAs negotiated by Japan with countries in Southeast Asia—those with Indonesia and the Philippines—are notable for their innovations in covering, for the first time, specific categories of nurses and health care workers. These PTAs have also expanded the categories of workers in the chapter on mode 4 to include "professionals with personal contracts" (essentially, the same as independent professionals). All these categories (except for business visitors) are allowed a stay of up to three years. Japan has also increased the number of professional categories covered in the annex on professionals in these two PTAs, to 14 in the case of Indonesia and 10 for the Philippines. No numerical limits are placed on these professional categories, except for nurses and health care workers, for whom an annual quota is in effect. For those professions, specific educational and training requirements are included in the agreements: a health degree plus two years of prior work experience and six months of language training in Japanese. The specification of particular categories of work with annual quotas and training requirements is an innovative approach that has not yet been seen in other PTAs.

PTAs Negotiated by Australia and New Zealand

Four PTAs negotiated by Australia and New Zealand are relevant for this study (annex table 13A.6). One PTA was negotiated jointly by the two countries with the 10-member

Association of Southeast Asian Nations (ASEAN). Three of the four are very recent, having been signed or having entered into force since the end of August 2008. The oldest of the four, and the one with the least ambitious provisions for labor mobility, is the Trans-Pacific Strategic Economic Partnership Agreement between Brunei Darussalam, Chile, New Zealand, and Singapore. This agreement, which entered into force in 2006, follows a NAFTA-type structure, but with lighter content. The only category of workers specified in the temporary entry (or labor mobility) chapter is that of professionals, and no length of stay is specified. The annex on professional services primarily sets out a best-endeavors clause for the development of "mutually acceptable standards and criteria for licensing and certification of professional service providers." No professional categories of services providers are listed, and so the annex has no market access component.

In the New Zealand–China PTA that entered into force in October 2008, the chapter on labor mobility specifies five categories of labor: business visitors, investors, intra-corporate transferees, contractual services supplies, and a new category of "installers." The CSS category includes artisans with Chinese cultural expertise such as theater artists, Mandarin language teachers, and Chinese medical specialists. China made no commitment with regard to professional service providers; New Zealand allows entry of designated professionals from China for up to three years. Intracorporate transferees from China are also permitted a three-year stay. The new category of installers is allowed a three-month stay.

The Australia–Chile PTA that entered into force in March 2009 follows a NAFTA-type structure, and the chapter on temporary entry specifies the four usual categories of labor. An annex on professional services does not include a market access component, and no numbers are attached to any category of worker. Australia allows intracorporate transferees a stay of up to four years and contractual services suppliers, a stay of one year, with the possibility of renewal. This recent PTA is quite original in its treatment of spouses and accompanying family members; they are granted the right to join the worker after he or she has been in Australia for more than one year. Dependents and spouses of corporate executives, intracorporate transferees, and contractual services suppliers from the other party to the agreement are allowed to enter and reside in Australia or Chile. Moreover, the spouse is given the right to enter, stay, and work, for a period of time equal to that of the national.

The ASEAN–Australia–New Zealand PTA, signed in August 2008, contains a chapter on temporary entry, which includes the four usual categories of labor plus the additional category of "installers" added by New Zealand. The length of stay offered by the partners to the PTA is variable, with Australia and New Zealand allowing the longest stay, of three or four years, respectively, for intracorporate transferees and one year for independent professionals and contractual services suppliers. It is notable that the ASEAN members committed to much less generous durations of stay for all labor categories than did their developed partners. In another innovative decision, Australia also included "spouses" in its categories of temporary labor permitted entry.

Comparison and Assessment of PTAs

An overall comparison of the PTAs negotiated with developing countries by the United States, Canada, the EU, Japan, and Australia and New Zealand is shown in the bar graphs set out in annex figures 13A.1–13A.6. The bars indicate the relative magnitude of the developed economies' commitments on labor mobility. The higher the bar for a particular agreement, the more access it provides for workers from its developing-country partner. The number of categories of workers encompassed within the chapter on temporary entry or movement of natural persons is indicated, as well as the number of professionals allowed, under specified quotas or without numerical limitation, through the annex on professionals.

In general, it can be said that trade agreements concluded by developed countries with developing countries focus almost exclusively on professional services providers. Many, however, go well beyond GATS in providing access for a greater number of categories of professional services, through expanded numbers of covered categories or through the provision of unlimited access. They also often offer the possibility of long-term visa renewals once professionals are settled in the country. Thus, distinct progress has been made with respect to professional services.

A few developed countries have been willing very recently to go beyond the expansion of access for professional services providers. These include, notably, Canada, in two recent FTAs negotiated with Colombia and Peru that extend access to the Canadian market to 50 categories of technicians. The innovative group also includes the EU's EPA with CARIFORUM, which extends market access to contractual services suppliers and independent professionals (for stays of six months) and to graduate trainees (for stays of one year). Japan has moved to liberalize access to its labor market for nurses and health care workers in its recent EPAs with Indonesia and the Philippines. Finally, both Australia and New Zealand have expanded the categories of labor in their PTAs to include contractual service suppliers and "installers" (for New Zealand) in their recent agreement with ASEAN members and in the New Zealand PTA with China. The latter also contains novel provisions for artisans who are proficient in Chinese cultural occupations, such as theater, language, and medicine. Australia's PTA with Chile covers the spouses and dependents of intracorporate transferees and contractual services suppliers residing in the country longer than one year. Thus trade agreements have moved over the past two years beyond the purely professional categories of labor to include within their scope contractual services suppliers, semiprofessionals and technicians, nurses and health care workers, and even spouses and dependents.

The trading partners that have been the most willing to open their markets wider for foreign workers from developing PTA partners have been countries that face considerable labor shortages. Canada has shown itself the most generous in this respect, with Japan being selective and sector-specific in responding to its labor market needs. Australia has been willing to consider family dependents as part of the labor categories defined under its most recent PTA. The United States and the EU have faced heavy inward migration flows, both documented and undocumented, from Latin America (in the U.S. case) and from North Africa and Eastern Europe (for the EU), and they are less willing to contractually bind greater market openness for foreign workers in their PTAs.[8] Nonetheless, the EU did expand its coverage of labor categories in the recent EPA with CARIFORUM members. In the United States, official and public attitudes have turned sour, and no agreements have been negotiated containing mode 4 coverage since 2002.

The story of labor mobility within trade agreements is still being written; the situation continues to evolve. Currently, several PTAs between developed and developing economies are under negotiation. The EU is negotiating with ASEAN, Colombia, Ecuador, India, Korea, Peru, five countries in Central America, and the four members of the Southern Cone Common Market (Mercosur, Mercado Común del Sur). Canada is negotiating with the Caribbean Community (CARICOM), four countries in Central America, the Dominican Republic, Jordan, Korea, Panama, and Singapore. Japan is negotiating with India and Peru, and Australia is negotiating with China, the Gulf Cooperation Council (GCC), Korea, and Malaysia. Only the United States is currently abstaining from further involvement in regional trade negotiations. Thus, the sample for evaluating the treatment of labor mobility in PTAs will continue to expand in the coming years. Developing countries that are able to proactively define and push their interests with

developed-country trading partners should find opportunities that did not exist in the past.[9]

PTAs Negotiated among Developing Countries

Labor mobility is not confined to PTAs involving developed countries; it is also an important feature of several South-South PTAs. This section presents a brief overview of labor mobility provisions in several agreements.

The Caribbean Community (CARICOM) has had one of the most successful experiences with liberalizing the movement of service providers at the regional level, dating from the signing in 1998 of Protocol II, on "Establishment, Services and Capital." The objective of the protocol is to bring the CARICOM Single Market Economy into effect. (For further discussion, see Stephenson 2007.) CARICOM provisions rest on two pillars: (a) facilitation of travel, common travel documents, and national treatment at the port of entry (Article 46 of the CARICOM Single Market Economy treaty) and, since 2005, a common passport; and (b) the free movement of skilled persons within the community (Articles 32, 34d, 35d, 36, 36a, and 37 of the treaty). Five categories of skilled workers were initially identified:

- Graduates of the Universities of the West Indies, Guyana, and Suriname
- Graduates of approved universities outside the region
- Media workers
- Musicians
- Artists
- Sports persons
- Workers in the tourism and entertainment industries
- Any other skilled person eligible under Articles 35d and 36a of Protocol II.

Effective January 1, 2010, domestic helpers were added to the list.[10] Since 2007, discussions have been under way on adding teachers and nurses.

A certificate of recognition must be obtained from the respective national labor ministries by those wishing to move abroad. A six-month temporary residency permit is issued while the certificate is reviewed by the receiving country, after which an indefinite work and residence permit is granted. CARICOM has recognized the importance of transferability of social security benefits, but progress on this matter has been slower than expected.

Achieving the free movement of workers is also stated as a goal of the East African Economic Community in its protocol on establishing a common market, expected to enter into force on July 1, 2010. Many hurdles remain, however, on the path to full free movement. Work permits are not harmonized across countries; they are relatively restrictive and remain difficult to obtain; they are subject to delays and administrative requirements; and rejections are numerous. Portability of social benefits is very limited. Progress has been made on harmonization of standards and mutual recognition for graduates, but much less so for technical and vocational training.

The treaty of the Economic Community of West African States (ECOWAS) requires the community to ensure the removal of obstacles to the free movement of persons, goods, services, and capital and to guarantee the right of residence and establishment. To date, ECOWAS has signed three supplementary protocols on this subject. The first provides for the free entry of community citizens for a period of 90 days without a visa, provided that they possess travel documents, and also grants them the rights of entry, residence, and establishment.[11] The second protocol allows community residents to reside, seek employment, and engage in income-earning employment in any member state.[12] The protocol specifically refers to migrant workers, defined as nationals of community member states who seek or propose to hold employment, are already holding employment, or have in the past held employment in a member country. Special provisions are made for four protocol categories: migrant workers, itinerant workers, seasonal workers, and border workers (Mattoo and Sauvé 2010).

Despite early provisions on the free movement of persons, implementation within ECOWAS has been slow—hampered, in particular, by the efforts of young member states to affirm their sovereignty. At times, slow progress in other areas of economic integration and adverse reactions to the influx of foreign labor in periods of recession have hindered implementation (OECD 2008). In recent years, several measures have been undertaken—in particular, since 2000, in the harmonization of passports, as well as joint border operations by customs and migration offices.[13]

An interesting development took place in January 2008 when ECOWAS adopted a common approach to migration, clearly influenced by the European model (OECD 2008). The approach consists of two parts, the first devoted to the legal framework and key principles, and the second to a regional migration and development action plan.

For countries that are also members of the West African Economic and Monetary Union/Union Économique et Monétaire Ouest-Africaine (WAEMU/UEMOA), the treaty confers the right of free movement of people, the right to provide services, the right of establishment of persons carrying out an independent or salaried activity, and the right of residence.[14] It further provides for nondiscrimination with respect to the right to seek and engage in employment. In 2005 the conference of WAEMU/UEMOA heads of state and government approved a progressive approach toward the implementation of freedom of movement for persons, the right of residence, the provision of services, and the right of establishment. This suggests the adoption of regional codes of freedoms and rights of movement, as well as harmonization measures. The codes concern four areas (OECD 2008):

- Right of establishment for the freedom to carry out self-employed professions
- Under equal conditions, access to higher-education establishments
- Establishment of a community visa for nationals of countries outside the WAEMU/UEMOA or ECOWAS zones
- Building of control posts juxtaposed on both sides of the border of member countries.

In 2006 regulations were adopted on free movement and right of establishment for workers in specific professions (for example, accountants and pharmacists). Today, the commission is working on a draft common policy in the areas of movement and stay by third-country nationals.

In Latin America, as in Southeast Asia, progress in liberalizing labor mobility has been slow within regional arrangements. Mercosur members have included freedom of movement among their integration goals. In theory, Mercosur nationals may currently move among member states, although the right to work is regulated by host governments. Progress in liberalizing labor mobility has been sluggish. A Mercosur social security agreement was signed in 1997, but many of the steps aimed at facilitating migration within the community are taking far longer to be implemented than planned. Much of the migration that occurs in the Mercosur region is outside formal channels. In December 2002, Mercosur leaders signed an Agreement on Residency for Mercosur Nationals aimed at giving migrants "equal civil, social, cultural, and economic rights and freedoms" with the citizens of the Mercosur country in which they are living, "particularly the right to work and to carry out any legal activity." The related Agreement on Regulating the Migration of Mercosur Citizens encouraged Mercosur governments to legalize unauthorized nationals of Mercosur members (World Bank 2010).

In October 2003, ASEAN members raised their ambitions from the formation of a free trade area to the creation of an ASEAN Economic Community (AEC), in the

Declaration of the ASEAN (Bali) Concord II, which was subsequently endorsed by summits of ASEAN leaders (Soesastro 2005). Nevertheless, the liberalization of labor movement still has a very long way to go before achievement of this objective. Currently, ASEAN members have made only very modest commitments on mode 4 in their respective schedules of services commitments, which have now undergone five rounds of negotiations under the ASEAN Framework Agreement on Services since that pact went into effect in January 1996. Many of the mode 4 commitments go no farther than what is set out in members' WTO schedules. ASEAN has, however, made more progress with the realization of mutual recognition agreements (MRAs) than any other regional grouping, having signed six MRAs to facilitate the movement of professional services suppliers through the recognition of their professional accreditations. These agreements cover engineering services, nursing services, architectural services, medical practitioners, dental practitioners, and accountancy services.

Bilateral Labor Agreements

Efforts to manage labor mobility among developing countries at the regional level have been consequential, although progress has not matched aspirations. The most notable efforts have taken place in agreements aiming for a common market; these generally go beyond simply managing labor mobility to encompass migration dimensions. The examples reviewed above all concern countries that are regional neighbors with a significant history of population migration. It is worth highlighting some interesting initiatives, which include coverage of recent graduates, common migration policies, and common passports to facilitate border crossings.

As was noted above, the treatment of labor mobility in formal PTAs has focused overwhelmingly on skilled labor categories, with only a few recent agreements moving to cover certain types of semiskilled workers. Against this background, can other vehicles be used to promote labor mobility? Bilateral labor agreements (BLAs) are alternatives to the more legalistic and rigid PTAs and can serve both to promote and to regulate the flow of unskilled or semiskilled workers.

Short History

Bilateral labor agreements have provided a means for employing seasonal and low-skilled foreign labor on a temporary basis. They allow industrial countries that need foreign labor to design labor exchange programs that steer inward flows to specific areas of labor demand. For destination countries, the primary aim is to address skill gaps in the local labor market, whether for seasonal workers (often in the agricultural sector) or low-skilled labor. Occasionally, BLAs also deal with higher-skilled workers in areas of labor shortages such as health or information technology.[15]

Bilateral labor agreements have had an interesting history. They were popular in the United States and Europe in the 1960s but fell into disfavor in the 1970s and 1980s, affected by the adverse combination of inflation and high unemployment that came to be known as "stagflation." For 22 years, beginning in 1942, the United States had a *bracero* program to admit temporary agricultural workers from Mexico. Admissions under this program peaked at more than 450,000 a year but began to shrink because of the enforcement of labor market regulations, combined with technological changes. Nonetheless, the program continued to admit more than 200,000 Mexican temporary workers a year until it ended in 1964. In Western Europe, temporary worker programs were peaking when they were ended unilaterally in 1973–74. European temporary worker programs differed from the Mexico–U.S. program in several important respects, including the locus of employment (nonfarm manufacturing, construction, and mining, rather than agriculture), as well as in their policies toward settlement. Unlike Mexicans who filled seasonal U.S. jobs and were expected to return to Mexico every year, migrants in Europe filled year-round jobs and earned rights to unify their families and settle with work and residence permits.[16]

Several developed countries have entered into second-generation bilateral labor agreements (as of the turn of the millennium), although many of these were in the form of memoranda of understanding, rather than more formal contractual arrangements. BLAs do not take any one set form; in fact, there is such a variety of agreements that international organizations have developed a "Compendium of Good Practice Policy Elements in Bilateral Temporary Labour Arrangements" as a follow-up activity to the first Global Forum on Migration and Development (GFMD), held in 2007.

BLAs have been increasing in number over recent years, but no single institution is responsible for collecting and maintaining information on them. Neither the ILO nor the IOM (International Organization for Migration) has information on BLAs at the country level.[17] It is therefore extremely challenging to collect these data, and what is presented in this section will certainly be incomplete. Although many countries have entered into bilateral labor agreements, others prefer to channel their temporary labor needs through their more formal immigration channels. In the United States, most temporary admission programs are open to citizens of all countries. The range of temporary visa programs includes both skilled professionals (e.g., H-1B visas) and other kinds of temporary labor (e.g., H-2A temporary agricultural workers).

In examining the panorama of bilateral labor agreements that we have been able to identify for this study and that are set out in table 13.1, it is interesting to note that such agreements have now been signed by countries in all regions of the world. In the Americas, Canada has been very active in developing bilateral temporary worker programs and has concluded agreements with Barbados, Colombia, Guatemala, Jamaica, Mexico, Trinidad and Tobago, and the countries of the Eastern Caribbean. In Europe, the governments of Germany, Italy, Spain, and the United Kingdom have actively negotiated bilateral labor agreements with developing countries around the world. In Africa, South Africa has pursued such arrangements, mainly with neighboring countries. In Asia, China has concluded BLAs with several developed- and developing-country partners.[18]

Terms of Coverage

The coverage of the bilateral labor agreements varies. Canada's agreements cover exclusively the agricultural sector. The Seasonal Agricultural Workers Program (SAWP) is based on bilateral memoranda of understanding and is managed by Human Resources and Skills Development Canada (HRSDC). Canadian employers submit requests, which have to be approved by the HRSDC, for foreign

agricultural workers. The approved requests are then communicated via Canadian network contacts in Mexico to private recruitment agencies in the participating Caribbean countries. Finding the workers to fill the required demand is then the responsibility of the countries of origin. In 2000 about 7,300 Mexicans were among the 16,900 foreign farmworkers admitted to Canada; the other workers were from Barbados, Colombia, Jamaica, Trinidad and Tobago, and six other Eastern Caribbean islands.[19] The BLA with Colombia is the result of demands by Canadian companies in Alberta and Manitoba for Colombian workers in the food-packing industry.

The BLAs concluded by Spain provide for a selection committee that is made up of representatives of the participating governments and is responsible for selecting the best-qualified workers for existing job offers and for conducting training courses that may be needed. In these agreements for regulating labor migration flows, the Spanish authorities, through Spanish embassies in origin countries, notify authorities in the origin country of the number and types of workers needed. There is no set quota. Origin countries in turn notify the Spanish authorities of the possibility of meeting this demand with their nationals willing to go to Spain.

Spain's bilateral agreement with Colombia covers agricultural workers who are selected to work temporarily in fruit harvesting in the Catalonia region. Within the framework of the temporary and circular labor migration mode that implements this agreement, the National Training Institute in Colombia designs training programs for the labor migrants so that, on their return to their communities of origin, they can transfer the skills and know-how

Table 13.1. Bilateral Labor Agreements with Developing-Country Partners: Government Programs for Temporary Workers

Region and country	Developing-country partners
Americas and the Caribbean	
Canada	Barbados, Colombia, Guatemala, Jamaica, Mexico, Organization of Eastern Caribbean States, Trinidad and Tobago
Europe	
France	Mauritius
Germany	Bulgaria, Croatia, Czech Republic, Poland, Romania, Slovak Republic, Slovenia, Ukraine
Greece	Albania, Bulgaria
Italy	Albania, Moldova, Sri Lanka, Tunisia
Spain	Bulgaria, Colombia, Dominican Republic, Ecuador, Mauritania, Morocco, Philippines, Romania, Senegal
United Kingdom	India, Philippines, Spain
Asia	
China	Australia; Japan; Jordan; Korea, Rep.; Mauritius; South Africa; Spain; United Arab Emirates
Africa	
South Africa	Botswana; Cuba; Iran, Islamic Rep.; Lesotho; Malawi; Mozambique; Swaziland; Tunisia

Source: ILO, IOM, and OSCE, "Compendium of Good Practice Policy Elements in Bilateral Temporary Labour Arrangements," revised version, December 2, 2008.
Note: ILO, International Labour Organization; IOM, International Organization for Migration; OSCE, Organization for Security and Co-operation in Europe.

acquired in Catalonia. Under this BLA, less than 10 percent of selected Colombian workers have failed to return home. In Ecuador a Migration and Control Unit was created in 2002 within the Ministry of Foreign Affairs to receive job vacancy notices from Spanish enterprises and match the job offers with the most appropriate candidates through a large database. Spain has similar BLA programs with Bulgaria, the Dominican Republic, Mauritania, Morocco, Romania, and Senegal. Under the Spain–Philippines BLA, nurses and other Filipino workers are allowed into Spain and are afforded the same protections as Spanish workers.

The bilateral labor agreements signed by the United Kingdom with India, the Philippines, and Spain enable the United Kingdom to recruit registered nurses and other health care professionals (physiotherapists, radiographers, occupational therapists, biomedical scientists, and other workers regulated by appropriate professional bodies in both countries) for work on a temporary basis. The U.K.–Spain agreement provides for recognition of Spanish nursing skills in the United Kingdom.

Greece has signed BLAs in the agriculture and fisheries sectors. Under the agreements with Albania and Bulgaria, Greek authorities assess the annual need for seasonal agricultural workers and grant residence and permits to workers from these countries according to demand from Greek employers. Under the BLA with Egypt, which covers the fisheries sector, temporary labor migrants are subject to specific regulations regarding the possibility of changing employers and the extension of their stay in the country, and they are eligible for the transfer of social security rights and pensions on a mutual basis.

South Africa has negotiated several bilateral agreements with neighboring countries in response to its growing labor crisis. The Joint Initiative for Priority Skills Acquisition (JIPSA) Act of 2004 acknowledged that particular sectors require skills from outside the country. South African mining companies fought hard to keep their right to hire foreign contract workers, and the 2002 Immigration Act was modified to accommodate this pressure. Bilateral agreements are focused on recruiting workers from Botswana, Lesotho, Malawi, Mozambique, and Swaziland to work in the mines and farms of South Africa. The share of foreigners in the mines' workforce rose from 47 percent in 1990 to 60 percent in 2000, but this share has declined recently in response to efforts to hire locally.

China has negotiated several BLAs with willing partners experiencing labor shortages, including Australia, Japan, Jordan, Korea, Mauritius, South Africa, Spain, and the United Arab Emirates. These agreements are very diverse, cover a wide range of topics on labor cooperation, and list specific numbers of recruited workers. The number of Chinese citizens working as temporary laborers abroad has increased substantially, from 63,200 in 1987 to more than half a million in 2004.[20]

The BLAs in which China is a partner cover diverse labor sectors. Chinese labor cooperation with the United Arab Emirates takes place in the areas of construction, factories, medical care centers, and maritime activities. With Australia, the BLA centers on nursing and a few other sectors, and an attempt is made to curb the excessive fees charged by the recruitment agencies by offering the alternative of government employment offices. Under the BLA with Mauritius, Chinese workers may be recruited only from companies that are on an established, government-approved list. The BLA with Jordan concerns the textile and construction sectors. An agreement with South Africa was concluded in 2002 and was extended in 2006 to focus on human resources development and job creation strategies, in addition to worker recruitment. A successful pattern for the bilateral labor agreement has been the agreement between China and Japan, under which more than 30,000 Chinese trainees are sent to Japan every year in temporary labor (trainee) cooperation programs.[21]

The advantages of BLAs or temporary worker programs, particularly for lower-skilled categories of workers, are numerous. First, and most important, is the flexibility they offer with respect to the management of the labor market by the countries involved. Such agreements can be negotiated in response to the economic cycles of the market.[22] As is seen in the examples cited, they can be targeted to specific sectors and can even be firm based, if necessary. Monitoring of such agreements can be carried out on both sides as a joint responsibility, rather than putting the burden entirely on the destination country to determine the legality of the worker. Guarantees can be designed and written into the agreements in the form of bonds or fines for noncompliance, to encourage respect for the provisions by private parties. Incentives can be built in on both sides of the agreement. Workers are more willing to respect the contract and return home if there are prospects of an opportunity (based on performance and need) to go back to the host country for future employment. Most participants in the BLAs that have functioned to date have found that the agreements have fulfilled the expectations of both sides.[23]

The disadvantage of bilateral labor agreements is that, unlike PTAs, they are single-issue instruments. This limitation means that developing-country partners do not have scope within a BLA to trade their "offensive" interests in labor mobility for the "offensive" interests of their developed-country trading partners.

Multilateral and MFN Considerations

It must be recognized that bilateral labor agreements represent an important derogation from the most favored nation (MFN) principle that is the core of the world trading system. The same is true of bilateral investment treaties (BITs) and double-taxation treaties (DTTs), of which there are many thousands in the world today. None of these pretend to treat all countries on equal terms; partners are favored over nonpartners. Of course PTAs also discriminate between partners and outsiders, and those inside the PTA receive more favorable treatment than those outside. From the perspective of true multilateralism ("no discrimination is the first-best policy"), these various forms of bilateral and regional agreements clearly occupy a second-best world. The tension that characterizes negotiations over trade liberalization, as well as over investment and labor mobility, is between a first-best multilateral approach, which may be stalled because of lack of agreement among countries worldwide, and a second-best regional or bilateral approach that achieves liberalization between the partners but creates discrimination against the rest of the world. A large and robust literature has developed around the debate as to which approach will engender the most liberalization and the greatest gains over the horizon of a decade or longer. We will not rehearse the arguments here, since they are familiar to most readers; we simply observe that the issue is certainly not settled. For the past decade, however, most governments have been "voting with their feet" by placing more emphasis on bilateral and regional agreements. This trend seems very likely to continue.

What about the consistency of BLAs with GATS? This question has not been litigated in the WTO and is not likely to be litigated any time soon, so a definitive answer cannot be given. Three considerations, however, would probably have weight in the WTO Appellate Body's reasoning, if a nonparty to a BLA did claim that its GATS rights to labor mobility (mode 4) were violated by the bilateral agreement.

First, GATS Article II(1) establishes the MFN principle for services, including mode 4. Under Article II(2), MFN can be waived for a BLA, as for any other GATT or GATS obligation, but this requires a favorable vote by three-fourths of WTO members. In any event, there are no extant waivers for BLAs or BITs.[24]

Second, under GATS Article V(1), two or more countries can enter into an economic integration agreement to liberalize trade in services and thereby avoid the MFN requirement. The agreement should have "substantial sectoral coverage" and should eliminate "substantially all discrimination" between the parties. These conditions are to be applied with "flexibility" when a developing country is a party to the economic integration agreement, under the provisions of Article V(2). In our judgment, the Appellate Body would give great weight to Article V(2) in evaluating a BLA. In fact, we think the "flexibility" provision would be decisive.

Third, there is the matter of negotiating history. As our discussion shows, BLAs, like BITs, have been around for a very long time, predating the original GATT (signed in 1947) by decades. A strong argument can be made that if the Uruguay Round negotiators had meant to impose an MFN requirement on these agreements, they would have said so in very explicit terms. After all, important economic arrangements would have been upset by an MFN requirement. Silence seems to indicate assent to the status quo ante.

One of the main reasons that countries enter into BLAs is that these agreements are flexible and short term and appear to escape the long-term contractual constraints of GATS. The large majority of bilateral labor agreements cover a different category of worker than do the formal services agreements (PTAs or GATS); they focus on unskilled (agricultural) or lower-skilled workers, whose movements governments have not been willing to liberalize in the context of either GATS or regional services agreements. We conclude, from this brief and sketchy review, that the Appellate Body would very likely respect the special status of BLAs if a claim were ever brought. As a practical matter, no WTO member has much interest in bringing a claim, and the possibility of litigation seems remote.

Conclusions

This chapter has examined how recent preferential trade agreements (those concluded since 1994 between developed and developing trading partners, as well as some South-South PTAs and labor agreements) have dealt with labor mobility. It has shown that some of the most recent PTAs have innovated in interesting ways to promote labor mobility, either by expanding the number of services suppliers accepted under particular categories (for example, without numerical quotas) or by creating new space for specifically defined categories of labor, such as technicians, nurses and health care workers, and sporting and cultural occupations. To date, however, all but a very few PTAs that cover services focus on professional services suppliers. A new generation of less formal temporary worker programs is paying more attention to the needs of lower-skilled and semiskilled temporary workers. Some of the regional integration groupings among developing countries in Africa, Asia, and Latin America and the Caribbean are making progress toward the opening of labor markets at the regional level to all categories of workers, both for temporary movement and for permanent settlement. Members of these groupings appear willing to go farther in their ultimate objectives than is the case under the North-South PTAs, where the norm is to cover prescribed and limited, although often expanded, categories of workers.

Thus, while the latest steps are positive and encouraging for developing countries, they leave much work for future negotiators. In our view, patience should be the watchword of negotiators based in developing countries. They should take heart and guidance from the long experience of developed and developing countries in crafting the liberalization of trade in textiles and clothing. This was a supersensitive industry as early as the late 1950s, when the Eisenhower administration in the United States negotiated the first restraint agreement with Japan, and it remained sensitive for the next 50 years. Eisenhower's accord with Japan was followed by the Short-Term Cotton Agreement and the Long-Term Cotton Agreement in the Kennedy and Johnson administrations, and then three generations of the Multifibre Arrangement (MFA) under GATT auspices.

The complexity of bilateral textiles and clothing quotas under these agreements was truly bewildering and, from an economist's viewpoint, highly distortive. But within this complex framework, over the span of five decades, trade in the sector was greatly liberalized and grew enormously. The secret, if there was a secret, was that negotiators of good will, representing both developed and developing countries, discovered niches of textiles and clothing trade where the political costs of further liberalization, combined with suitable safeguard mechanisms, were not insurmountable. At every stage of this long process, the economic gains from liberalization were enormous; the "magic," if there was any magic, was to focus attention on products and mechanisms that did not encounter overwhelming resistance in the developed countries. We think the same approach commends itself to labor mobility negotiations—a long, persistent, and patient search for niches in the labor markets of developed countries where greater entry of migrants is not only tolerated but welcomed.

On the basis of this overview, we offer four sets of recommendations.

1. *Concerning professional workers*
When developing countries are able to define their interests well and are willing and able to pursue bilateral trade agreements with the major developed trading partners reviewed in this study (other than the United States, at present), they should be able to obtain expanded market access. Labor markets worth exploring are opportunities for firms and individuals that offer unique cultural talents or specialized skills, as well as for some independent professionals, and geographic or occupational niches of the industrial developed economies that suffer from labor shortages. If developing countries wish to promote exports of services providers in the health services, this is certainly an area that offers a large potential for expansion. For this market, it might be advisable to develop local training programs for the specific skills required in the target market, in the way that the Philippines has done and Indonesia is currently doing.

2. *Concerning semiskilled and lower-skilled workers*
In the case of workers with lower skill levels and less formal educational training, the best vehicle for promoting greater labor mobility is not formal PTAs but the more flexible instrument of temporary worker programs (TWPs). These programs can be designed to promote circular migration in a way that benefits the labor-sending and labor-receiving countries, as well as the workers themselves. TWPs are extremely flexible in both design and execution and allow the parties involved to design the clauses covering length of stay, nature and place of employment, and appropriate guarantees. They also offer governments the possibility of adjusting in a responsive manner to the cycles of their domestic labor markets. Such agreements must elicit the positive involvement of parties on both sides, making this a framework with buy-in, where all parties to the agreement have an interest in seeing it succeed. Although these agreements have been successfully promoted so far by only a handful of countries, primarily China and the Philippines, there is tremendous scope for their further application in the world economy.

3. *For developing-country governments and negotiators*
Developing country governments and negotiators should bear six precepts in mind:

- Developing-country negotiators should approach the discussions of labor mobility with a positive attitude and should emphasize the gains to the destination country. The economic gains are invariably large, and the political costs are often exaggerated, so it is useful for negotiators from developing countries to research particular labor markets and lay the facts on the table.
- To better serve their negotiators, developing-country governments should conduct in-depth research on the labor markets of potential destination countries with the aim of discovering promising niches. This will require the services of specialized officers or contractors working in the destination countries.

- Developing-country specialists should work with educational and credentialing authorities in the developed countries to lay the groundwork for mutual recognition agreements for the benefit of their independent professionals and other highly skilled workers.
- When multinational corporations seek to expand their operations abroad, whether in a developed or a developing country, government negotiators should team up with the corporations to ensure agreement on the requisite number of visas for intracorporate transferees and contractual services suppliers to support the new operation. This needs to be done whether or not a PTA is in place.
- Developing-country negotiators should seek agreement on the status of mode 4 workers, meaning their rights as to visas, working conditions, social security contributions, unemployment compensation, and ability to remit funds. To some extent, these matters are covered in TWPs, but important elements are often not addressed.
- Above all, senior officials in the developing country must attend to the "image" of their migrants abroad—doing whatever is possible to ensure that their migrants convey an impression of hard-working, law-abiding,

respectful people. When adverse incidents happen, as they will, the government of the developing country should cooperate as appropriate, through revocation of visas and other measures.

4. *For developed-country governments and negotiators*
Like developing countries, developed countries should proactively search for labor market niches where additional temporary workers will become valued members of the workforce and the community. Developed-country officials must not surrender to arguments that the labor market is an undifferentiated mass, or succumb to the anti-immigrant voices of a vocal minority. They should hammer home the distinction between permanent immigration, which remains under sovereign control, and temporary workers who are subject to negotiated agreements. They should seek to build flexible responses not only into TWPs but also into the quota and time clauses of PTAs. Most important, they should put some effort into seeking out and conveying positive messages about the contributions and accomplishments of temporary workers.

Annex

Annex Table 13A.1. Quantitative Estimates of Gains from Increased Labor Mobility

Authors	Region covered	Assumption or situation	Gains	
Borjas (1999)	United States	U.S. 1980–2000 immigration wave, with immigrants representing roughly 10 percent of the U.S. workforce	*Large redistributive effect:* return to capital, +2 percent of GDP; labor wages, –1.9 percent of GDP[a]	*Small net gains for natives:* US$10 billion a year (0.1 percent of U.S. GDP), or roughly 5 percent of average economic growth over past 20 years
Hamilton and Whalley (1984)	World	Elimination of all restrictions on labor mobility (1977 data)	60.1–204.6 percent of 1977 world GDP in 1977[b]	
Iregui (1999)	World	Elimination of all restrictions on labor mobility (between 37 and 53 percent of the labor endowment of developing regions migrates)	*Nonsegmented labor market:* 15–67 percent of world GDP *Segmented labor market (skilled versus unskilled):* 13–59 percent of world GDP	*If only skilled labor migrates:* 3–11 percent of world GDP
Moses and Letnes (2004)	World	Elimination of all restrictions on labor mobility (1977 and 1998 data)	*For 1977, with 100 percent elimination of wage differential:* US$0.34 trillion–US 11.27 trillion (1977 dollars) (more probably, US$0.58 trillion); 4.3–111.6 percent of 1977 world GDP (more probably, 7.5 percent of 1977 world GDP) *For 1977, with 10 percent elimination of wage differential:* 22 percent of total potential gain; wages, +4.1 percent in poorest countries; +3.3 percent in middle-income countries; –2.5 percent in richest countries; return to capital, –8.3 percent in poorest countries; –6.9 percent in middle-income countries; +5.7 percent in richest countries	*For 1998, with 100 percent elimination of wage differential:* US$1.97 trillion–US$55.04 trillion (1998 dollars) (more probably, US$3.4 trillion); 5.6–155 percent of 1998 world GDP (more probably, 9.6 percent of 1998 world GDP) *For 1998, with 10 percent elimination of wage differential:* 23 percent of total potential gain; wages, +11.4 percent in poorest countries; +2.1 percent in middle-income countries; –3.1 percent in richest countries; return to capital, –21.0 percent in poorest countries; –4.4 percent in middle-income countries; +7.2 percent in richest countries

(continued next page)

Annex Table 13A.1. (*continued*)

Authors	Region covered	Assumption or situation	Gains	
Walmsley and Winters (2002)	World	Increase in migration from developing countries to high-income countries sufficient to increase labor force in the host countries by 3 percent in 2002	*Total:* +0.6 percent of world GDP (US$156 billion in 2002, or 1.5 times the expected gains from liberalization of all remaining goods) *Movement of unskilled workers (accounting for most of the gains):* +US$110 billion versus +US$46 billion for the movement of skilled workers *Migrants' welfare:* +US$171 billion (+US$73 billion in the United States, +US$25 billion in Japan, +US$68 billion in the EU) *Resident welfare:* net, –US$15 billion; developing countries, in some cases, gain if remittances are high (+US$16 billion in India), but most lose (–US$7 billion in Brazil); developed countries, small gains (+US$3.9 billion in EU)	*Change in real wages of unskilled workers:* increase in developing countries (+0.7 percent in India); decrease in developed countries (–0.6 percent in the United States) *Change in real wages of skilled workers:* dramatic increase in developing countries (+4.5 percent in Mexico); decrease in developed countries (–0.8 percent in the United States) *Change in rental price of capital:* decrease in developing countries (–0.4 percent in Mexico); increase in developed countries (+0.8 percent in the United States)
World Bank (2006), 31	World	Increase in migration from developing countries to high-income countries sufficient to increase the labor force in the host countries by 3 percent by 2025 (revision of Walmsley and Winters 2002)	+0.6 percent of world GDP, (US$356 billion in 2025); +0.4 percent of developed-country GDP; +1.8 percent of developing-country GDP (including migrants' income)	

Source: Studies listed under "Authors"; see the bibliography for details.
Note: EU, European Union; GDP, gross domestic product.
a. Hatton and Williamson (1998) find similar results on wages when studying the 1870–1910 migration wage in the United States; they estimate that U.S. wages in 1910 would have been 11 to 14 percent higher in the absence of immigration after 1870.
b. The large differences in estimates, both within and between studies, can be explained by differences in modeling frameworks (partial versus general equilibrium), production elasticities, productivity, cost of movement, or workforce size.

Annex Table 13A.2. Agreements between the United States and Developing Countries

Provision	U.S.–Singapore	U.S.–Chile	U.S.–Morocco	CAFTA–DR	U.S.–Peru
Entry into force	January 1, 2004	January 1, 2004	January 1, 2006	March 1, 2006	February 1, 2009
Chapter on trade in services	Ch. VIII	Ch. 11	Ch. 11	Ch. 11	Ch. 11
Treatment of foreign services					
National treatment	Yes (Art. 8.3)	Yes (Art. 11.2)	Yes (Art. 11.2)	Yes (Art. 11.2)	Yes (Art. 11.2)
Most favored nation	Yes (Art. 8.4)	Yes (Art. 11.3)	Yes (Art. 11.3)	Yes (Art. 11.3)	Yes (Art. 11.3)
Local presence required	No (Art. 8.6)	No (Art. 11.4)	No (Art. 11.5)	No (Art. 11.4)	No (Art. 11.4)
Provisions on mode 4					
Chapter	Ch. 11	Ch. 14	None	None	None
Committee	Yes (Art. 11.7)	Yes (Art. 14.5)	Joint committee to review the implementation of the annex on professionals	Commission to review the implementation of the annex on professionals	—
Dispute settlement	Yes (Art. 11.8)	Yes (Art. 14.6)	—	—	—
Transparency of regulation	Yes (Art. 11.5)	Yes (Art. 14.4)	—	—	—

(*continued next page*)

Annex Table 13A.2. *(continued)*

Provision	U.S.–Singapore	U.S.–Chile	U.S.–Morocco	CAFTA–DR	U.S.–Peru
Side letters	Yes (professionals must comply with certain labor and immigration laws and have an employer in the United States)	Yes (professionals will obtain visa through the U.S. H-1B program)	None	Yes ("No provision shall impose any obligation on a party regarding its immigration measures")	—
Worker categories covered	Investors, traders, intracorporate transferees, professionals	Investors, traders, intracorporate transferees, professionals	—	—	—
Specification of length of stay	None	None	—	—	—
Provisions on professionals					
Annex on professionals	App. 11.A.2	Annex 14.3.D	Annex 11.B	Annex 11.9	Annex 11.B
Number of professional categories covered	2 (disaster relief claims adjuster, management consultant)	4 (disaster relief claims adjuster, management consultant, agricultural manager, physical therapist)	0 (pledge to work on)	0 (pledge to work on)	0 (pledge to work on)
Specified quotas	*Singapore:* no numerical limit *United States:* 5,400	*Chile:* no numerical limit *United States:* 1,400	—	—	—
Postsecondary degree required	Yes: 4 years or more	Yes: 4 years or more	—	—	—
Specification of length of stay	None	None	—	—	—

Source: Authors' compilation.
Note: — = no provisions; CAFTA–DR, Dominican Republic–Central America Free Trade Agreement.

Annex Table 13A.3. Agreements between Canada and Developing Countries

Provision	NAFTA	Canada–Chile	Canada–Colombia	Canada–Peru
Entry into force	January 1, 1994	July 5, 1997	Signed November 21, 2008	January 1, 2009
Chapter on trade in services	Ch. 12	Ch. H	Ch. 9	Ch. 9
Treatment of foreign services				
National treatment	Yes (Art. 1202)	Yes (Art. H-02)	Yes (Art. 902)	Yes (Art. 903)
Most favored nation	Yes (Art. 1203)	Yes (Art. H-03)	Yes (Art. 903)	Yes (Art. 904)
Local presence required	No (Art. 1205)	No (Art. H-04)	No (Art. 905)	No (Art. 907)
Provisions on mode 4				
Chapter	Art. 16	Ch. K	Ch. 12	Ch. 12
Side letters	None	None	None	None
Committee	Yes (Art. 1605)	Yes (Annex K-05)		
Dispute settlement	Yes (Art. 1606)	Yes (Art. K-06)	Yes (Art. 1206)	Yes (Art. 1206)
Transparency of regulation	Yes (Art. 1604)	Yes (Art. K-04)	Yes (Art. 1204)	Yes (Art. 1204)
Worker categories covered	Investors, traders, intracorporate transferees, professionals	Investors, traders, intracorporate transferees, professionals	Investors, traders, intracorporate transferees, professionals, technicians, spouses	Investors, traders, intracorporate transferees, professionals, technicians

(continued next page)

Annex Table 13A.3. (*continued*)

Provision	NAFTA	Canada–Chile	Canada–Colombia	Canada–Peru
Specification of length of stay	None	None	None	*Peru:* investors, 1 year; traders, 90 days; intracorporate transferees, 1 year; professionals, 1 year; technicians, 1 year
				Canada: investors, 1 year; traders, 1 year; intracorporate transferees, 3 years; professionals, 1 year; technicians, 1 year
Provisions on professionals				
Annex on professionals	App. 1603.D.1	App. K-03.IV.1	App. 1203.D	App. 1203.D
Number of professional categories covered	63 (accountant, architect, medical professional, scientist, teacher, others)	72 (accountant, architect, medical professional, scientist, teacher, others)	All categories of professionals except health, sports, art, education, legal, and management services; 50 categories of technicians (mechanical and avionics technician, construction inspector, food and beverage supervisor, textiles specialist, electrician, plumber, oil and gas well driller, chef, others)	All categories except health, sports, art, education, legal, and management services; 50 technicians (mechanical and avionics technician, construction inspector, food and beverage supervisor, textiles processing, electrician, plumber, oil and gas well driller, chef, others)
Specified quotas	No numerical limit except for the United States: 5,500	No numerical limit	No numerical limit	No numerical limit
Postsecondary degree required	Yes: 4 years or more	Yes: 4 years or more	Yes: professionals, 4 years; technicians, 2 years	Yes: professionals, 4 years; technicians, 1 year
Specification of length of stay	None	None	None	1 year

Source: Authors' compilation.
Note: NAFTA, North American Free Trade Agreement.

Annex Table 13A.4. Agreements between the European Union and Developing Countries

Provision	EU–Chile	EU–CARIFORUM	EU–Turkey	EU–Morocco
Entry into force	February 1, 2003	December 29, 2008	December 31, 1995	March 18, 2000
Chapter on trade in services	Title III, Ch. I	Pt. II, Title II, Ch. 3	None	Title III (pledge to work on)
Treatment of foreign services				
National treatment	Yes (Art. 98)	Yes (Art. 77)	—	—
Most favored nation	No	Yes (Art. 79)	—	—
Local presence required	No (Art. 97)	—	—	—
Provisions on mode 4				
Chapter	Art. 101	Pt. II, Title II, Ch. 4	None	None
Side letters	None	None	—	—
Committee	Yes (Art. 100)	Yes (Art. 85)	—	—

(*continued next page*)

Annex Table 13A.4. (*continued*)

Provision	EU–Chile	EU–CARIFORUM	EU–Turkey	EU–Morocco
Dispute settlement	None	Pledge to create one (Art. 87)	—	—
Transparency of regulation	Yes (Art. 105)	Yes (Art. 86)	—	—
Worker categories covered	Investors, intracorporate transferees, business sellers, professionals	Investors, intracorporate transferees, business sellers, professionals, graduate trainees	—	—
Specification of length of stay	*EU:* professionals, 3 months	Investors, 90 days; intracorporate transferees, 3 years; business sellers, 90 days; independent professionals, contractual services suppliers, 6 months; graduate trainees, 1 year	—	—
Provisions on professionals				
Annex on professionals	Annex VII	Annex IV	None	None
Number of professional categories covered	*EU:* 33 (engineer, accounting, construction, mining, computer, legal services, others) *Chile:* 0	*EU:* 29 (architectural, legal, accounting, engineering, computer, management services) *CARIFORUM:* 0	—	—
Specified quotas	No numerical limit	No numerical limit	—	—
Postsecondary degree required	"Necessary academic qualification and experience"	University degree + 3 years experience	—	—
Specification of length of stay	*EU:* 3 months	*EU:* 6 months	—	—

Source: Authors' compilation.
Note: — = no provisions; CARIFORUM, Caribbean Forum of African, Caribbean, and Pacific (ACP) States; EU, European Union.

Annex Table 13A.5. Agreements between Japan and Developing Countries

Provision	Japan–Mexico	Japan–Chile	Japan–Indonesia	Japan–Philippines
Entry into force	April 1, 2005	Signed March 27, 2007	July 7, 2008	December 11, 2008
Chapter on trade in services	Ch. 8	Ch. 9	Ch. 6	Ch. 7
Treatment of foreign services				
National treatment	Yes (Art. 98)	Yes (Art. 107)	Yes (Art. 79)	Yes (Art. 73)
Most favored nation	Yes (Art. 99)	Yes (Art. 108)	Yes (Art. 82)	Yes (Art. 76)
Local presence required	No (Art. 100)	No (Art. 109)	No (Art. 78)	No (Art. 72)
Provisions on mode 4				
Chapter	Ch. 10	Ch. 11	Ch. 7	Ch. 9
Side letters	None	None	None	None
Committee	Yes (Art. 117)	None	Yes (Art. 96)	Yes (Art. 113)
Dispute settlement	Yes (Art. 118)	Yes (Art. 133)	Yes (Ch. 14)	Yes (Ch. 15)
Transparency of regulation 4	Yes (Art. 116)	Yes (Art. 132)	Yes (Art. 95)	Yes (Art. 111)
Worker categories covered	Investors, business visitors, intracorporate transferees, professionals	Investors, business visitors, intracorporate transferees, professionals	Investors, business visitors, Intracorporate transferees, professionals, professionals with "personal contracts," nurses and care workers	Investors, business visitors, intracorporate transferees, professionals, professionals with "personal contracts," nurses and care workers

(*continued next page*)

Annex Table 13A.5. (*continued*)

Provision	Japan–Mexico	Japan–Chile	Japan–Indonesia	Japan–Philippines
Specification of length of stay	*Japan:* business visitors, 90 days; other categories, 3 years *Mexico:* business visitors, 30 days; other categories, 1 year	*Japan:* business visitors, 90 days; other categories, 3 years *Chile:* business visitors, 30 days; other categories, 1 year	*Japan:* business visitors, 90 days; other categories, 3 years *Indonesia:* business visitors, 60 days; other categories, 1 year	*Japan:* business visitors, 90 days; other categories, 3 years *Philippines:* business visitors, 59 days; other categories, 1 year
Provisions on professionals				
Annex on professionals	Annex 10	Annex 13	Annex 10	Annex 8
Number of professional categories covered	*Japan:* 2 (engineer, specialist in humanities or international services) *Mexico:* 42 (accountant, engineer, lawyer, scientist, nurse, others)	*Japan:* 2 (engineer, specialist in humanities or international services) *Chile:* 41 (accountant, engineer, lawyer, scientist, nurse, others)	*Japan:* 14 (legal and accounting services, engineer, specialist in humanities or international services, nurse, health care worker) *Indonesia:* 4 (mechanical and electrical engineer, nurse, health care worker)	*Japan:* 10 (legal and accounting services, engineer, specialist in humanities or international services' Japanese university graduate nurse, health care worker) *Philippines:* 4 (mechanical and electrical engineer, nurse, health care worker)
Specified quotas	No numerical limit	No numerical limit	No numerical limit except for nurses and health care workers	—
Postsecondary degree required	4 years or more	4 years or more	Professionals, 4 years; nurses and health care workers, public health degree + 2 years work experience + 6 months language training	Professionals, 4 years; nurses and health care workers, national health degree + 3 years work experience + 6 months of training in the host country to pass the host-country certification exam
Specification of length of stay	*Japan:* 3 years *Mexico:* 1 year	*Japan:* 3 years *Chile:* 1 year	*Japan:* 3 years *Indonesia:* 1 year	*Japan:* 3 years *Philippines:* 1 year

Source: Authors' compilation.
Note: — = no provisions.

Annex Table 13A.6. Agreements between Australia and New Zealand and Developing Countries

Provision	Trans-Pacific SEP (Brunei Darussalam, Chile, New Zealand, Singapore)	ASEAN–Australia–New Zealand	New Zealand–China	Australia–Chile
Entry into force	May 28, 2006	Signed August 28, 2008	October 1, 2008	March 6, 2009
Chapter on trade in services	Ch. 12	Ch. 8	Ch. 9	Ch. 9
Treatment of workers				
National treatment	Yes (Art. 12-4)	Yes (Ch. 8, Art. 5)	Yes (Art. 106)	Yes (Art. 9-3)
Most favored nation	Yes (Art. 12-3)	Yes (Ch. 8, Art. 7)	Yes (Art. 107)	Yes (Art. 9-4)
Local presence required	No (Art. 12-7)	No (Ch. 8, Art. 4)	No (Art. 108)	No (Art. 9-5)
Provisions on mode 4				
Chapter	Art. 12-11	Ch. 9	Ch. 10	Ch. 13
Side letters	None	None	None	None
Committee	None	None	Yes (Art. 133)	Yes (Art. 13-6)
Dispute settlement	None	Yes (Ch. 9, Art. 9)	Yes (Art. 134)	Yes (Art. 13-7)
Transparency of regulation	None	Yes (Ch. 9, Art. 8)	Yes (Art. 131)	Yes (Art. 13-5)

(*continued next page*)

Annex Table 13A.6. (*continued*)

Provision	Trans-Pacific SEP (Brunei Darussalam, Chile, New Zealand, Singapore)	ASEAN–Australia– New Zealand	New Zealand–China	Australia–Chile
Worker categories covered	Professionals	Business visitors, investors, intracorporate transferees, contractual services suppliers, installers (to install purchased machinery—New Zealand only), spouses	Business visitors, investors, intracorporate transferees, contractual services suppliers, installers	Business visitors, investors, intracorporate transferees, contractual services suppliers, relatives
Specification of length of stay	No	*Indonesia:* business visitors, 60 days; investors, 60 days; others, 2 years *Australia:* intracorporate transferees, 4 years; investors, 2 years; business visitors, 6 months; professionals, 12 months *New Zealand:* business visitors, 3 months; investors, 3 months; intracorporate transferees, 3 years; installers, 3 months; professionals, 12 months *Philippines:* business visitors, 59 days; others, 1 year *Vietnam:* intracorporate transferees, 3 years; others, 90 days	*China:* business visitors, 6 months; investors, 6 months; intracorporate transferees, 3 years; professionals, —; installers, 3 months *New Zealand:* business visitors, 3 months; investors, 3 months; intracorporate transferees, 3 years; professionals, 3 years; installers, 3 months	*Australia:* business visitor, 1 year; investors, 90 days; intracorporate transferees, 4 years; professionals, 1 year *Chile:* —
Provisions on professionals				
Annex on professionals	Art. 12-11	Annex 4	Annexes 10 and 11	Annex 13-A
Number of professional categories covered	Pledge to "work on" 6 categories (engineer, architect, geologist, geophysicist, planner, accountant)	*Australia:* 0 *New Zealand:* 33 (engineering, legal, taxation, veterinary, computer, translation services) *Indonesia:* 13 (legal, tourism, restaurant, engineering, computer, R&D, maintenance services) *Philippines:* all persons "who occupy a technical, advisory, or supervisory position" *Vietnam:* 2 (computer and engineering services) *Singapore:* 0	*China:* 5 (education, medical, translation, hotel, computer) *New Zealand:* 6 (traditional Chinese medicine, Chinese chef, Mandarin teaching aide, martial arts coach, tour guide, skilled worker "in category identified as being in shortage")	"Subject to national criteria"
Specified quotas	—	Entry subject to national rules	*China:* no numerical limit *New Zealand:* traditional Chinese medicine, 200; Chinese chefs, 200; Mandarin teaching aides, 150; martial arts coaches, 150; tour guides, 100; skilled workers "in category in shortage," 1,000	—

(*continued next page*)

Annex Table 13A.6. (*continued*)

Provision	Trans-Pacific SEP (Brunei Darussalam, Chile, New Zealand, Singapore)	ASEAN–Australia– New Zealand	New Zealand–China	Australia–Chile
Postsecondary degree required		*New Zealand:* 3 years or more + 6 years experience *Indonesia:* "high qualification" *Philippines:* "knowledge at an advanced level" *Vietnam:* "university degree" + 5 years experience	*China:* "appropriate education level" + 2 years experience *New Zealand:* "appropriate education level" + experience	—
Specification of length of stay	—	*Vietnam:* 90 days *New Zealand:* 1 year *Philippines:* 1 year *Indonesia:* 2 years	*China:* — *New Zealand:* 3 years	*Chile:* — *Australia:* 1 year

Source: Authors' compilation.

Note: — = no provisions; ASEAN, Association of Southeast Asian Nations; R&D, research and development; SEP, Strategic Economic Partnership.

Annex Figure 13A.1. Provisions on Mode 4 in PTAs between the United States and Developing Countries

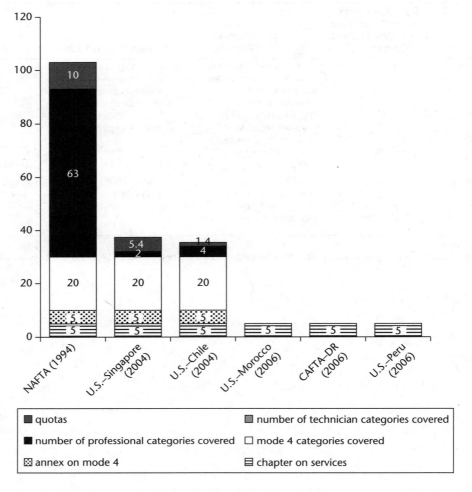

Source: Authors.
Note: CAFTA–DR, Dominican Republic–Central America Free Trade Agreement; NAFTA, North American Free Trade Agreement; PTA, preferential trade agreement. Mode 4 refers to the movement of natural persons to supply services. The height of the bars indicates the degree of access that PTA provides for workers from developing-country partners. Values are assigned to each component of access as follows (not all components may be applicable to a particular agreement):
Chapter on services in the PTA? If yes, 5 points.
Annex on mode 4 service supply? If yes, 5 points.
Mode 4 categories covered. Number of categories (shown on the bars) is multiplied by 5 to yield total points.
Number of professional categories covered. Shown on the bars.
Number of technician categories covered. Shown on the bars.
Quotas. If uncapped, 10 points. Otherwise, shown as the total number of workers allowed under the quota, in thousands.

Annex Figure 13A.2. Provisions on Mode 4 in PTAs between Canada and Developing Countries

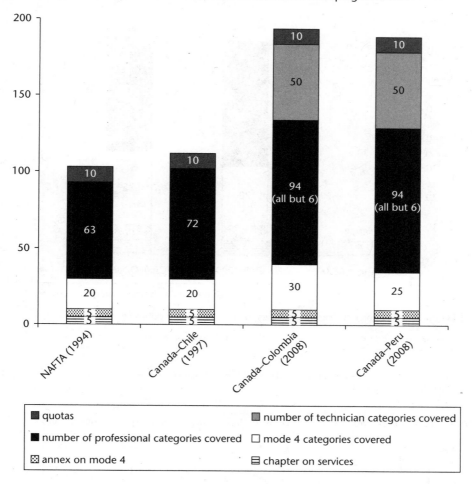

Source: Authors.
Note: NAFTA, North American Free Trade Agreement; PTA, preferential trade agreement. For the method of deriving the values for the bars, see the note to annex figure 13A.1.

Annex Figure 13A.3. Provisions on Mode 4 in PTAs between the European Union (EU) and Developing Countries

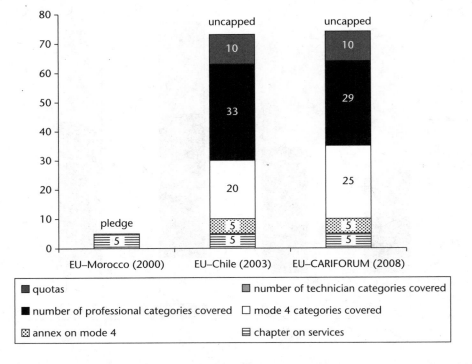

Source: Authors.
Note: CARIFORUM, Caribbean Forum of African, Caribbean, and Pacific (ACP) States; PTA, preferential trade agreement. For the method of deriving the values for the bars, see the note to annex figure 13A.1.

Annex Figure 13A.4. Provisions on Mode 4 in PTAs between Japan and Developing Countries

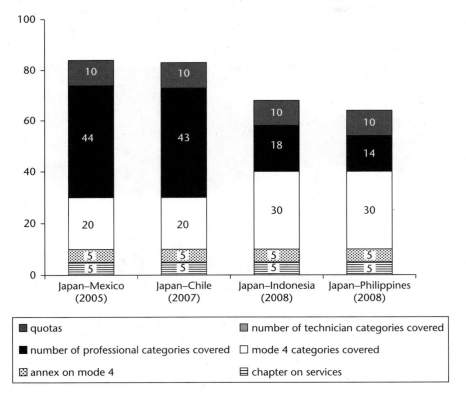

Source: Authors.
Note: PTA, preferential trade agreement. For the method of deriving the values for the bars, see the note to annex figure 13A.1.

Annex Figure 13A.5. Provisions on Mode 4 in PTAs between Australia and New Zealand and Developing Countries

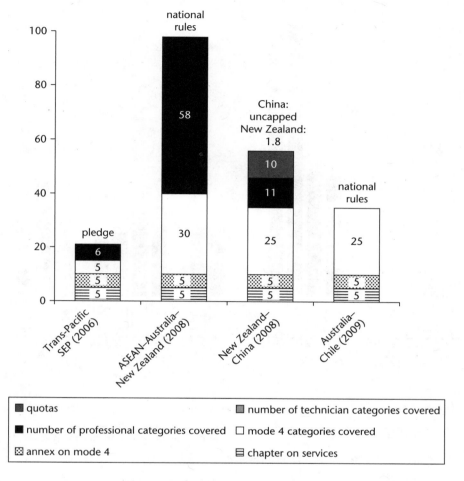

Source: Authors.
Note: ASEAN, Association of Southeast Asian Nations; PTA, preferential trade agreement; SEP, Strategic Economic Partnership. For the method of deriving the values for the bars, see the note to annex figure 13A.1.

Annex Figure 13A.6. Provisions on Mode 4 in PTAs between Developed and Developing Countries

Source: Authors.
Note: ASEAN, Association of Southeast Asian Nations; CAFTA–DR, –Dominican Republic–Central America Free Trade Agreement; CARIFORUM, Caribbean Forum of African, Caribbean, and Pacific (ACP) States; NAFTA, North American Free Trade Agreement; PTA, preferential trade agreement; TPSEP, Trans-Pacific Strategic Economic Partnership.

Notes

This chapter is a modified version of a chapter in Cattaneo et al. (2010). Thibaud Delourme, a student at the Maxwell School of Syracuse University, assisted with the research.

1. Carzaniga (2008, 478) points out that foreigners working for a host-country company on a contractual basis as independent services suppliers (ISS) are covered by GATS (and, in general, by trade agreements that include mode 4), whereas they would not be covered if they were employees of the company. What distinguishes their situation is the type of payment received: the foreign employee receives a domestic currency wage from the company in the host country, whereas the ISS is paid a fee and the contractual services supplier is paid foreign wages.

2. By December 2005, the total number of services offers had reached 69, involving 93 WTO members. Of the 69, 31 were revised offers. There has been very little change since; the number of initial offers has increased only to 71. Thus, one-third of WTO members have not put any initial offer for services forward since the beginning of the negotiations. The Doha Round was suspended in July 2006, without any revised offers having been submitted. Services negotiations were not actively taken up when

the round resumed in 2007. A "signaling conference" was held at the request of interested ministers in July 2008, but it did not elicit much enthusiasm.

3. For an earlier discussion examining treatment of mode 4 in PTAs, see Nielson (2003).

4. The only exception is the FTA with Australia. No market access provisions for labor mobility were included in the text itself, but a side letter was added after the conclusion of the negotiations that allowed an annual quota of 10,500 Australian professionals to enter the U.S. market. This was done in 2002, and it proved to be the final straw for members of the U.S. Congress.

5. Sáez (2009) explains that within the EU, issues concerning trade in services do not fall exclusively under the competence of the community because they go beyond Articles 113 and 238 of the treaty that accords supranational treaty-making powers to the community on behalf of all the member states. Thus, implementation of the services provisions and obligations of a trade agreement must be approved by each EU member state in accordance with domestic laws.

6. Article 101, on movement of natural persons, contains only a review requirement: "Two years after the entry into force of this

Agreement, the Parties shall review the rules and conditions applicable to movement of natural persons (mode 4) with a view to achieving further liberalisation."

7. It should be mentioned that several EU member states have attached economic needs tests (ENTs) to their commitments on mode 4 entry. Actual access provided, even under the expanded commitments, will depend on how these tests are interpreted and applied in practice. No definitions were supplied with the ENT entries, and some are applied quite restrictively.

8. Indeed, a very recent PTA between the members of the European Free Trade Association (EFTA)—Iceland, Liechtenstein, Norway, and Switzerland—and Colombia, signed on November 25, 2008, does not even include an annex on professional service suppliers, and the body of the agreement contains no mention of the movement of natural persons, other than their definition as mode 4. EFTA members are not facing labor shortages and, in the current hostile economic climate, did not feel any pressure to include liberalization of labor mobility in their agreement with Colombia. See http://www.sice.oas.org.

9. This approach is suggested by a paper by Henry Gao, "Report on China's Export Interests in Services in Australia," 2008, which was provided to the authors. The strategy calls for collecting information on the labor market and services export structure of the potential or current negotiating partner, carrying out surveys to identify those categories of labor with the greatest potential for expansion following the removal of trade-restrictive barriers, and building on achievements of previous PTAs in the area.

10. Two members, Antigua and Barbuda, and Belize, were allowed a five-year grace period to study the impact of free mobility for domestic helpers before adding them to their list.

11. Protocol A/P.1/5/79, relating to free movement of persons, residence, and establishment, in application of Article 27 of the treaty establishing ECOWAS. The successive texts complementing the free movement regime are Supplementary Protocol A/SP.1/7/85, on the code of conduct for the implementation of Protocol A/P.1/5/79; Supplementary Protocol A/SP.1/7/86, on the second phase (right of residence) of the aforementioned protocol; Supplementary Protocol A/SP.1/6/89, amending and complementing the provisions of Article 7 of the aforementioned protocol; and Supplementary Protocol A/SP.2/5/90, on the implementation of the third phase (right of establishment) of the aforementioned protocol.

12. Supplementary Protocol A/SP.1/7/86.

13. Eight countries use the regional passport: Burkina Faso, Côte d'Ivoire, The Gambia, Ghana, Guinea, Niger, Nigeria, and Sierra Leone.

14. Treaty Establishing the West African Economic and Monetary Union, 1996, Articles 4, 91–93.

15. Host countries typically act unilaterally in determining whether temporary workers may bring their families and settle. Most European countries allow temporary workers whose work permits have been renewed several times to obtain immigrant status after five years.

16. Between 1960 and 1973, the number of migrant workers in Western Europe jumped from 2 million to 7 million, and the total foreign population rose from 4 million to 12 million. Most of these workers came from geographically distant nations such as Turkey or Morocco, rather than neighboring countries. After the halt in temporary worker programs in the mid-1970s, the migrant workforce in Europe stabilized at around 5 million over the next decade. See Martin (2007); see also Council of Europe (1996).

17. The International Labour Organization (ILO) has developed a multilateral framework on labor migration that constitutes a comprehensive collection of principles, guidelines, and good practices on labor migration programs, including bilateral labor agreements; see ILO, http://www.ilo.org/public/english/protection/migrant/areas/multilateral .htm.

18. A few memoranda of understanding on migratory and labor cooperation have been signed recently by developing countries; they include those between Peru and Chile (2006), Peru and Ecuador (2006), and Peru and Mexico (2002). The aim of these memoranda is to provide for exchange of information and protection of the rights of migrant workers, in particular under the UN International Convention on the Protection of the Rights of Migrant Workers and Their Relatives. The memoranda do not include provisions for promoting labor mobility. The Philippines has signed bilateral memoranda with many destination countries to cover the flows, rights, and obligations of its temporary workers. A reciprocal temporary worker program agreed on by Argentina and Bolivia includes many of these protections.

19. As part of Canada's SAWP scheme with Caribbean countries and Mexico, the HRSDC cooperates closely with private agencies, including Foreign Agricultural Resource Management Services (FARMS) in Ontario and Nova Scotia and the Foundation of Enterprises for the Recruitment of Foreign Labor (FERME) in Quebec, New Brunswick, and Prince Edward Island. Guest workers in Canada are employed in four provinces: Ontario (two-thirds of the total), Quebec, Alberta, and Manitoba. Although the Mexican government tries to ensure that every worker returns to Mexico, independent researchers estimate that 15 percent of the Mexicans fail to return home every year. See http://migration.ucdavis .edu/RMN/more.

20. Gao, personal communication (see note 9). The data are from the *China Foreign Labor Cooperation Annual Report 2004*, issued by the China International Contractors Association, Beijing.

21. See http://www.jitco.or.jp for details on this program. Information on China's bilateral labor agreements was provided to the authors by Dr. Shu Bin, manager, Labor Department, China National Aero-Technology Import & Export Corporation, during a workshop held in Beijing under World Bank auspices, May 21–22, 2009.

22. A recent study by Persin (2008) compares the United Kingdom's responses concerning its labor market and immigration policies in the context of the eastern enlargement of the EU with its willingness to provide offers on mode 4 under the GATS. Persin finds that the government opted for managed migration through bilateral labor agreements and an employer-led system, rather than through more formal WTO commitments. The author concludes that the more flexible "bilateral or regional labor immigration schemes are preferred to a binding multilateral labor immigration scheme such as the GATS" because it is easier and less costly under the former to agree on rules and procedures, as well as to solve any problems jointly.

23. The Migration Policy Institute, based in Washington, DC, has done considerable work on the benefits and challenges of temporary worker programs and circular migration schemes. See Batalova (2006); Meyers (2006); Agunias (2007); Newland, Agunias, and Terrazas (2008).

24. Unlike BLAs and BITs, DTTs are specifically exempted from national treatment and MFN requirements by GATS Article XIV.

Bibliography

Agunias, Dovelyn Rannveig. 2007. "Managing Temporary Migration: Lessons from the Philippine Model." Insight. Migration Policy Institute, Washington, DC. http://www.migrationpolicy.org/pubs/Insight_POEA _Oct07.pdf.

Batalova, Jeanne. 2006. "The Growing Connection between Temporary and Permanent Immigration Systems." Task Force Insight 14. Migration Policy Institute, Washington, DC. http://www.migrationpolicy .org/ITFIAF/TFI_Batalova.pdf.

Borjas, George J. 1999. *Heaven's Door: Immigration Policy and the American Economy.* Princeton, NJ: Princeton University Press.

Carzaniga, Antonia. 2008. "A Warmer Welcome? Access for Natural Persons under PTAs." In *Opening Markets for Trade in Services*, ed. Juan A. Marchetti and Martin Roy, 475–502. London: Cambridge University Press.

Cattaneo, Olivier, Michael Engman, Sebastián Sáez, and Robert M. Stern. 2010. *International Trade in Services: New Trends and Opportunities for Developing Countries.* Washington, DC: World Bank.

Council of Europe. 1996. "Temporary Migration for Employment and Training Purposes." European Committee on Migration (CDMG),

Strasbourg. http://www.coe.int/t/dg3/migration/Documentation/Legal
_texts/CDMG_96_18e_Temporary_migration_employment_training
_purposes_en.pdf.

Hamilton, Bob, and John Whalley. 1984. "Efficiency and Distributional
Implications of Global Restrictions on Labor Mobility." *Journal of
Development Economics* 14: 61–75.

Hatton, Timothy, and Jeffrey G. Williamson. 1998. *The Age of Mass
Migration: Causes and Economic Impact.* New York and Oxford, U.K.:
Oxford University Press.

IMF (International Monetary Fund). 2010. *Balance of Payments Manual,
Sixth Edition.* Washington, DC: World Bank.

Iregui, Ana. 1999. "Efficiency Gains from the Elimination of Global
Restrictions on Labor Mobility: An Analysis Using a Multiregional
CGE Model." Estudios Economicos, Banco de la República, Bogota.

Karsenty, Guy. 2000. "Assessing Trade in Services by Mode of Supply." In
GATS 2000: New Directions in Services Trade Liberalization, ed. Pierre
Sauvé and Robert M. Stern. Washington, DC: Brookings Institution
Press.

Martin, Philip. 2007. *Towards Effective Temporary Worker Programs: Issues
and Challenges in Industrial Countries.* International Migration Papers
89. Geneva: International Labour Office. http://www.ilo.org/public/
english/protection/migrant/download/tempworkers_martin_en.pdf.

Martin, Susan, and B. Lindsay Lowell. 2008. "Examining Labor Mobility Provisions for the United States." Presented at the seminar on
"Demographic Change and International Labor Mobility in the
Asia Pacific Region: Implications for Business and Cooperation,"
organized by Korea National Committee for Pacific Economic Cooperation (KOPEC) and the Pacific Economic Cooperation Council
(PECC), Seoul, March 24–26. http://www.pecc.org/component/
eventlist/details/121-kopec-demographic-change-and-international-
labor-mobility-in-the-asia-pacific-region.

Mattoo, Aaditya, and Antonia Carzaniga, eds. 2003. *Moving People to
Deliver Services.* Washington, DC: World Bank.

Mattoo, Aaditya, and Pierre Sauvé. 2010. "Regionalism in Services Trade."
in *A Handbook of International Trade in Services,* ed. Aaditya Mattoo,
Robert M. Stern, and Gianni Zanini. 2nd ed. Oxford, U.K.: Oxford
University Press.

Meyers, Deborah W. 2006. "Temporary Worker Programs: A Patchwork
Policy Response." Task Force Insight 12, Migration Policy Institute,
Washington, DC. http://www.migrationpolicy.org/ITFIAF/TFI_12
_Meyers.pdf.

Moses, Jonathon, and Bjorn Letnes. 2004. "The Economic Cost to International Labor Restrictions: Revisiting the Empirical Discussion."
World Development 32 (10): 1609–26.

Newland, Kathleen, Dovelyn Rannveig Agunias, and Aaron Terrazas.
2008. "Learning by Doing: Experiences of Circular Migration." Insight,

Migration Policy Institute, Washington, DC. http://www.migrationpol-
icy.org/pubs/Insight-IGC-Sept08.pdf.

Nielson, Julia. 2003. "Labor Mobility in Preferential Trade Agreements." In
Moving People to Deliver Services, ed. Aaditya Mattoo and Antonia
Carzaniga, 93–113. Washington, DC: World Bank.

OECD (Organisation for Economic Co-operation and Development).
2007. *International Migration Outlook.* Paris: OECD.

———. 2008. *West African Mobility and OECD Migration Policies.*
Paris: OECD. http://www.oecd.org/document/29/0,3343,en_38233741
_38247095_41481445_1_1_1_1,00.html.

Persin, Daniela. 2008. "Free Movement of Labor: UK Responses to the
Eastern Enlargement and GATS Mode 4." *Journal of World Trade*
42 (5): 837–64.

Pritchett, Lant. 2006. *Let Their People Come: Breaking the Gridlock on Global
Labor Mobility.* Washington, DC: Center for Global Development.

Sáez, Sebastian. 2009. "The EU EPA Negotiations." Presented at a World
Bank training course on services, Washington, DC, March 21.

Soesastro, Hadi. 2005. "Accelerating ASEAN Integration: Moving Beyond
AFTA." CSIS Economics Working Paper Series 091, Centre for Strategic
and International Studies, Jakarta. http://www.csis.or.id/publications
_paper_view.asp?id=52&tab=1.

Stephenson, Sherry. 2007. "Mobility of Service Providers in the Caribbean
Region." Box 13.6 in L. Alan Winters, "The Temporary Movement of
Workers to Provide Services: GATS (Mode 4)." In *A Handbook of Inter-
national Trade in Services,* ed. Aaditya Mattoo, Robert M. Stern, and
Gianni Zanini, 535–37. Oxford, U.K.: Oxford University Press.

———. 2008. "Demographic Change and International Labor Mobility in
the Pacific Americas—Issues, Policies and Implications for Cooperation." In *Labor Mobility in the Asia-Pacific Region,* ed. Graeme Hugo and
Soogil Young, 171–201. Singapore: Institute of Southeast Asian Studies.

Vis-Dunbar, Damon, and Henrique Suzy Nikiema. 2009. "Do Bilateral
Investment Treaties Lead to More Foreign Investment?" *Investment
Treaty News,* April 30. International Institute for Sustainable Develop-
ment, Winnipeg, Manitoba, Canada.

Walmsley, Terri Louise, and L. Alan Winters. 2002. "Relaxing the Restric-
tions on the Temporary Movement of Natural Persons: A Simulation
Analysis." CEPR Discussion Paper Series 3719, Centre for Economic
Policy Research, London.

Winters, L. Alan. 2008. "The Temporary Movement of Workers to Provide
Services (GATS Mode 4)." In *A Handbook of International Trade in
Services,* ed. Aaditya Mattoo, Robert M. Stern, and Gianni Zanini,
480–96. Oxford, U.K.: Oxford University Press.

World Bank. 2006. *Global Economic Prospects 2006: Economic Implications
of Remittances and Migration.* Washington, DC: World Bank.

———. 2010. *Global Economic Prospects 2010: Crisis, Finance, and
Growth.* Washington, DC: World Bank.

14

INVESTMENT

Sébastien Miroudot

A distinguishing feature of the current wave of globalization is that trade and investment are more and more intertwined. Advances in technology and increased liberalization of trade in the second half of the twentieth century have reduced trade costs and allowed the "unbundling" of the production process (Baldwin 2006). Instead of producing in a single country, firms can offshore specific tasks and fragment production internationally, in vertically integrated chains (Jones and Kierzkowski 2001). A global production network enables firms to cut costs by taking advantage of differences in technology and factor prices across countries, leading to productivity gains that can translate into higher income for all the countries involved in the global supply chain. This fragmentation of production requires liberalization of both trade and investment.

As a consequence of these trends, countries are increasingly incorporating investment, traditionally dealt with in separate bilateral investment treaties (BITs), into their preferential trade agreements (PTAs). Not surprisingly, the number of new BITs concluded has been decreasing since 2001 (UNCTAD 2008), while the number of PTAs with investment provisions has been rising (figure 14.1).[1] Another reason for the slowdown in concluding new BITs is that more than 2,000 BITs are already in force, and most bilateral relationships are already covered.

The inclusion of investment provisions in PTAs has given birth to a new type of trade agreement that has no equivalent at the multilateral level. No multilateral agreement on investment exists, and rules on investment at the World Trade Organization (WTO) are limited to those in the General Agreement on Trade in Services (GATS), on the supply of services following an investment (commercial presence, mode 3), and in the Trade-Related Investment Measures (TRIMS) Agreement (box 14.1). GATS, moreover, relies on an enterprise-based definition of investment and thus applies only to business or professional establishments in which the investor has majority ownership or exercises

control (direct investment). Bilateral rules on investment, by contrast, generally rest on a broader, asset-based definition that extends to portfolio investment and various forms of tangible and intangible property (e.g., real estate).

Following the example of the North American Free Trade Agreement (NAFTA) in 1994, most PTAs combine provisions on the protection and promotion of investment, as traditionally found in BITs, with provisions on the liberalization of foreign investment and comprehensive trade in services disciplines. These agreements jointly liberalize trade and investment and are more advanced than multilateral rules. They take into account company strategies that combine foreign direct investment (FDI) and trade to create global supply chains that maximize productivity through the distribution of production among a number of countries.

From a political-economy perspective, there are several motivations for negotiating disciplines on trade and investment simultaneously. The first is that PTAs emphasize market access and investment liberalization more than they do investment protection and promotion. With the exception of agreements signed by the United States and, in some cases, by Canada and Japan, BITs do not include nondiscrimination provisions for the preestablishment stage. Moving from BITs to PTAs implies opening of markets and negotiations similar to those occurring in trade. Concessions on investment can be balanced by concessions on trade within the same agreement, and countries can deal in a more comprehensive way with market opening issues that today involve both trade and investment.

Another difference between BITs and PTAs is that PTAs cover an indefinite period, whereas BITs have a limited life span—10 years, for example. Unlimited commitments on trade and investment make PTAs more appealing for firms seeking opportunities in new markets. Policy makers may also be interested in a long-term commitment, especially where the ratification of trade and investment liberalization

Figure 14.1. Total Number of PTAs and Number with Investment Provisions, 1970–2009

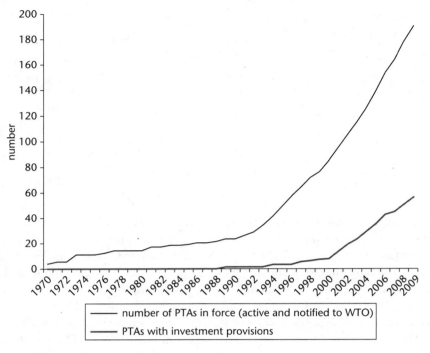

Source: World Trade Organization database and calculations by the author.
Note: PTA, preferential trade agreement; WTO, World Trade Organization.

Box 14.1. Rules on Investment at the WTO

World Trade Organization (WTO) rules on investment are found in the General Agreement on Trade in Services (GATS), which covers the supply of services following an investment (mode 3, commercial presence) and in the Trade-Related Investment Measures (TRIMS) Agreement.

GATS and mode 3
GATS includes schedules for specific commitments and lists of exemptions from most favored nation (MFN) treatment submitted by member governments. Only by reference to a country's schedule and (where relevant) its MFN exemption list is it possible to know to which services sectors, and under what conditions, the basic GATS principles of market access, national treatment, and MFN treatment apply within that country's jurisdiction. The schedules are complex documents in which the country identifies the services sectors to which it will apply the market access and national treatment obligations of the GATS, as well as any exceptions from those obligations it wishes to maintain. The commitments and limitations are in every case entered with respect to each of the four modes of supply that constitute the definition of trade in services in Article I of GATS: cross-border supply, consumption abroad, commercial presence, and presence of natural persons. Commercial presence (mode 3) describes the conditions under which foreign services suppliers may establish, operate, or expand a commercial presence, such as a branch, agency, or wholly owned subsidiary, in the member's territory.

TRIMS
The TRIMS Agreement provides that no contracting party shall apply any trade-related investment measure inconsistent with Articles III (national treatment) and XI (prohibition of quantitative restrictions) of the General Agreement on Tariffs and Trade (GATT). An illustrative list of measures agreed to be inconsistent with these articles is appended to the agreement. The list includes measures which require particular levels of local procurement by an enterprise (local content requirements) or which limit the volume or value of imports that such an enterprise can purchase or use to an amount related to the level of products it exports (trade-balancing requirements).

The TRIMS Agreement mandates notification of all nonconforming trade-related investment measures and requires their elimination within two years by developed countries, within five years by developing countries, and within seven years by least-developed countries. It establishes a committee that monitors the implementation of these commitments, among its other responsibilities. The agreement also provides for consideration, at a later date, of whether broader provisions on investment and competition policy should be added.

Source: World Trade Organization.

treaties is not politically easy. The initial political cost might be higher for the PTA, but the issue does not have to be reopened periodically, and once the agreement is concluded, investors benefit from long-term protection and a long-term guarantee of nondiscrimination. Given the stalemate of the Doha Development Agenda, with no multilateral agreement on investment and no progress on the liberalization of services trade, it is through PTAs that countries can expect to improve disciplines on investment.

Finally, because most of the remaining restrictions on investment are in the area of services, countries can find some advantage in dealing with bilateral investment liberalization in PTAs that grant preferential treatment under GATS Article V and for which no most favored nation (MFN) exemption is needed. Countries thus ensure that their bilateral obligations are not multilateralized and that consistency between investment rules and WTO obligations is guaranteed.[2]

The increase in the number of PTAs with investment provisions is thus driven by both economic and legal considerations. The remainder of this chapter examines PTAs and how their provisions have changed the landscape of investment rules. Because PTAs are being compared with multilateral rules in GATS and bilateral provisions in BITs, the full overview of disciplines that affect investment is presented. The focus is on services and GATS because more than 60 percent of current investment is in services and because GATS, although not explicitly an international investment agreement, has influenced the architecture and nature of bilateral investment measures found in PTAs.

The next section looks at the nature and scope of investment provisions in PTAs. Key issues related to the extent of investment liberalization are then discussed; they include the risk of an investment "spaghetti bowl," the scope for MFN guarantees in this accumulation of competing rules and commitments, and the degree of investment protection in PTAs. The final sections examine the economic impact of investment provisions in PTAs, from both a theoretical and an empirical perspective, and present conclusions.

Nature and Scope of Investment Provisions in PTAs

Investment provisions in PTAs are generally deep and comprehensive.[3] There are instances of agreements that cover investment marginally, in a few articles that contain no binding commitment but only refer in general terms to the promotion of investment between the parties. These agreements, however, are not representative of the recent trend toward PTAs that cover investment through a full package of disciplines and liberalization commitments. Annex table 14A.1 provides an overview of recent PTAs

containing substantive investment provisions. As discussed below (in "Three Types of PTA"), these PTAs fall into three categories: "NAFTA-inspired" agreements that tend to reproduce the architecture of NAFTA; "GATS-inspired" agreements in which investment provisions for services are in a separate chapter influenced by GATS; and "hybrids" that combine the other two approaches. The table also highlights the wide range of bilateral investment measures that are found in these PTAs.

Typology of Investment Measures

We first review the typology of investment provisions, examining, in turn, establishment, nondiscrimination, investment regulation and protection, dispute settlement, and investment promotion and cooperation.

Establishment. Establishment is the most critical component of market access for foreign investors. Concretely, establishment refers to either the creation of a new firm in the host country (greenfield investment) or the acquisition of an existing firm (through mergers and acquisitions). Provisions on establishment define the conditions under which foreign firms can invest, starting with the definitions of "investor" and "investment." The scope of the agreement depends on these definitions; all subsequent rules will apply only to investment covered in the PTA.

Generally, PTAs do not give investors a generic and unlimited right to set up a permanent presence in the host country. Only some agreements signed by the European Union (EU) mention a right of establishment. In GATS-inspired agreements, provisions on establishment are included under the market access principle. In NAFTA-inspired agreements, a reference to market access can also be found in some PTAs, but establishment is generally dealt with through nondiscrimination provisions relating to the preestablishment phase. Investors are granted national treatment and most favored nation treatment under the conditions for establishment, as discussed later in the chapter.

From the point of view of investors, there is no significant difference between these approaches. All agreements acknowledge the right of governments to regulate and to list reservations that allow countries to restrict establishment in specific sectors or under specific circumstances. In addition to general exceptions—including measures relating to the general public interest, such as national security and public health, order, and morals—agreements also include industry-specific limitations.

Nondiscrimination. Nondiscrimination provisions limit the discretion of the host country in distinguishing among categories of companies in applying regulatory and restrictive measures. National treatment means that domestic and foreign-owned companies must be treated the same; most favored nation treatment precludes discrimination among foreign companies. National treatment in the preestablishment phase can be particularly effective in liberalizing investment because it permits foreign investors to set up operations on an equal footing with domestic investors. Although MFN treatment is a core provision in any international investment agreement, not all PTAs grant it for investment. There are two types of MFN provisions in a preferential agreement. First, the provision can state that an investor from a party or its investment should be treated no less favorably than an investor from another party to the agreement. The provision ensures the same treatment for all parties within the agreement. This type of provision is of little relevance in the case of a bilateral agreement (and most PTAs with investment provisions are bilateral). The second type of MFN provision is called "nonparty" or "third-party" MFN treatment and grants to investors of other parties or to their investment a treatment no less favorable than the one granted to *any nonparty*. The aim is to guarantee that better treatment offered to a third party, through, for example, another PTA, is extended to the parties of the first agreement. This second type of MFN provision can be seen as an efficient liberalization mechanism that extends new commitments found in recent agreements to parties of former PTAs. Omission of an MFN treatment provision in a PTA is one way of preventing the multilateralization of investment obligations and can lead to investment diversion when some PTAs are more preferential than other investment agreements. (See the discussion of multilateralization, below.)

To the extent that domestically owned companies receive better treatment than foreign-owned ones, national treatment can be seen as the important discipline and MFN treatment can be regarded as superfluous. Some countries, however, provide investment incentives such as tax holidays or subsidies that target foreign investors specifically and are not offered to domestic companies. In that case, MFN treatment is better than national treatment for the investor. Accordingly, some agreements, such as NAFTA, in what is termed "standard of treatment" provisions, specify the "better of the treatment" required by national and MFN treatment.

There are qualifications to the application of national and MFN treatment. To begin with, national and MFN treatment are generally granted "in like circumstances." The foreign investor and the domestic investor (or another foreign investor, in the case of MFN treatment) have to be in comparable situations, and whether more favorable treatment has been accorded is analyzed case by case. Although some agreements (in particular, those signed by the United States) specifically mention "in like circum-

stances," this is also the interpretation of any MFN clause in international law: the more favorable treatment can only be granted to the "same subject matter," according to the *ejusdem generis* ("of the same kind") principle (see OECD 2005, ch. 4). The wording of national and MFN treatment clauses varies among agreements and can matter for their implementation. In addition, PTAs list limitations to national treatment, as well as exemptions from MFN treatment, at the industry level, and the detailed analysis of these reservations defines the extent of the preferential treatment granted in the agreement.

Investment regulation and protection. Bilateral investment treaties traditionally contain provisions that limit the ability of governments to restrict the activities of investors or to expropriate their investments. The most extensive package of such provisions can be found in the investment chapters of NAFTA and of subsequent NAFTA-inspired agreements.

A core provision is free transfer of funds, which allows for the unrestricted flow of investment-related transactions and capital movements. These transfers include all kinds of fees and returns to investment, such as profits, dividends, capital gains, royalty payments, management fees, technical assistance, payments related to the liquidation of the investment, payments made pursuant to a loan, and payments arising out of dispute settlement.

Fair and equitable treatment is another standard drawn from customary international law. In contrast to national treatment and most favored nation treatment, which are comparative standards based on the treatment afforded different groups of investors, fair and equitable treatment is an absolute standard.

A third set of rules pertains to expropriation. Because the threat of expropriation or nationalization can discourage investors, a core rule in investment agreements is that any expropriation should take place on a nondiscriminatory basis and with adequate compensation.

Two other types of provisions can have a positive impact on investors and help countries promote FDI. First, provisions prohibiting performance requirements prevent a country from imposing on investors measures that would, for example, force them to source locally. Such local content requirements can be highly trade restrictive, in addition to discouraging investment.[4] In the context of global production networks, these requirements are likely to leave a developing economy outside supply chains, as the objective of such networks is precisely to fragment the production process and to move inputs across countries. This is an area in which trade rules and investment rules overlap in the TRIMS Agreement and in its list of prohibited performance requirements.

Second, provisions on temporary entry and stay for key personnel facilitate investment, as there is hardly any FDI that does not imply movement of people, in addition to movement of capital. Because these provisions touch on sensitivities about migration laws, disciplines are very specific and are limited to investment-related temporary migration.

Dispute settlement. All PTAs include means for resolving disputes between states concerning the interpretation and implementation of the agreement. A smaller number of agreements introduces an investor-state dispute settlement mechanism that enables investors to make claims and defend their interests directly. Such a mechanism can provide an effective way of implementing investment provisions because it allows foreign investors to seek redress for damages resulting from host governments' breaches of their obligations. The investor-state dispute settlement mechanism relies either on ad hoc arbitration involving an independent arbitrator, generally under the rules of the United Nations Commission on International Trade Law (UNCITRAL), or on permanent arbitration, typically through the International Center for the Settlement of Investment Disputes (ICSID).

The investor-state dispute settlement provision comes from investment treaties and borrows its main elements from the system of commercial arbitration. In the universe of trade agreements, by contrast, the paradigm is state-state resolution of disputes, as exemplified by the WTO dispute settlement mechanism (Choi 2007). One of the first PTAs to include direct claims by investors was NAFTA. It is interesting that provisions which had been part of investment treaties for a long time became controversial in the context of the implementation of a trade agreement with investment provisions. Although many PTAs now contain an investor-state dispute settlement provision, some agreements modeled after NAFTA lack a mechanism of this kind; an example is the Australia–United States Free Trade Agreement (Dodge 2006). Even when the provision is present, negotiators have sometimes been reluctant to extend its coverage to new investment-related disciplines found in trade agreements. In particular, in agreements containing a separate chapter on services that covers market access and national treatment provisions for investment in services, investor-state dispute settlement does not apply.

So far, very few state-state disputes have been filed under PTAs; countries prefer to bring disputes to the WTO (Morgan 2008). By contrast, the number of investor-state disputes brought under international investment agreements has been rising, with a cumulative total of 255 known cases at the end of 2006 (UNCTAD 2006).

Investment promotion and cooperation. The last category of investment provisions focuses on the promotion of investment and the harmonization of certain rules. Rather than lay down binding commitments or disciplines protecting investors, these provisions tend to organize cooperation between countries through exchange of information or the creation of specific bodies or commissions. The agreement may mention a general objective of harmonization of investment rules and policies, but without specific provisions on how to achieve harmonization. Such provisions also include clauses foreseeing the future liberalization of investment.

Three Types of PTA

Although investment provisions in PTAs are diverse, two models can be identified, with very different approaches to the way investment commitments are scheduled and to the overall architecture of agreements. The first model is NAFTA, in which investment is dealt with in a single chapter that covers both investment in goods and investment in services and that includes broad provisions on the regulation and protection of investment, in addition to liberalization commitments. In the second model, investment provisions are split between two chapters: an investment chapter that sets out disciplines relevant for all investments (in goods and services industries) and a services chapter that contains liberalization commitments relevant for services, as well as other provisions on trade in services. This second model can be said to be GATS-inspired in that the provisions for services follow the approach of that WTO agreement. A third type of "hybrid" agreement combines the NAFTA and GATS approaches.

NAFTA-inspired agreements. The architecture of NAFTA is characterized by a clear separation between the investment chapter and the chapter on cross-border trade in services. Provisions relevant for investment in services and trade in services according to mode 3 (commercial presence) are part of the investment chapter; provisions regarding financial services are dealt with in a separate chapter. The definitions of investor and investment are far-reaching. Investment is not limited to FDI but also covers some types of portfolio investment, such as equity securities, as well as property, such as real estate.

NAFTA provides for national and MFN treatment in both the preestablishment and postestablishment phases. Nondiscrimination disciplines apply to "the establishment, acquisition, expansion, management, conduct, operation, and sale or other disposition of investments." In addition, the provision on standard of treatment grants the better of national or MFN treatment, and the clause on minimum standard of treatment provides for "fair and equitable treatment and full protection and security." The remainder of the investment chapter covers all relevant protection disciplines, such as free transfer of funds, provisions on expropriation and compensation, and investor-state dispute settlement.

The intention of the agreement to be far-reaching can also be seen in the way nondiscrimination commitments are treated. The approach is that of the negative list, whereby national treatment and MFN treatment are granted for all sectors, with two lists of reservations—one for existing measures that are not conforming at the date of the agreement, and another for future measures that gives the governments discretion to maintain or introduce restrictive measures after the agreement has entered into force. The negative-list approach is generally seen as the more favorable to liberalization in the sense that commitments are made for investments in all sectors, and only the exceptions listed at the time the agreement is signed can be maintained. There is, nonetheless, some discretion left for governments because of the practice of listing reservations for future measures. These reservations are thus not too different from unbound commitments under the GATS approach. In sectors in which reservations are made regarding future measures, there is a possibility of introducing new restrictive measures that are not listed in the agreement.

Empirically, negative-list PTAs are found to go further in their sectoral coverage (Fink and Molinuevo 2008). The proliberalization approach stems from another mechanism that complements the negative listing of restrictions. NAFTA-inspired agreements not only lock in the investment regime but also include as commitments under the PTA any new measure taken unilaterally by the parties that moves in the direction of liberalization. This creates a ratchet effect because investment restrictions, once removed, cannot be reintroduced.

Preferential trade agreements signed by Canada, Mexico, and the United States (the three parties to NAFTA) are, not surprisingly, NAFTA-inspired. The approach has also been exported to Asia, where a significant number of bilateral agreements follow the NAFTA model. Examples include the Chile–Republic of Korea, Korea–Singapore, and Singapore–Australia free trade agreements (FTAs).[5]

GATS-inspired agreements. GATS-inspired agreements contain an investment chapter that covers all investments and provides for the protection of investment through disciplines as far-reaching as those in NAFTA-inspired agreements. The difference is that the provisions of the investment chapter concerning market access, national treatment, and MFN treatment apply only to goods. The

analogous nondiscrimination principles for services are found in a separate chapter.

The treatment of investment is therefore influenced by services concepts that come from GATS. Whereas the investment chapter includes an asset-based definition of investment, on the basis of which investment protection measures apply, the trade in services chapter does not define investment but relies on the concept of commercial presence (mode 3 in GATS). Commercial presence is the supply of a service through a business or professional establishment in the territory of the country in which the service is supplied. In the case of services, market access, national treatment, and MFN treatment apply only to commercial presence.

As in GATS, the MFN principle is a general obligation and applies to all services sectors covered in the agreement. Exemptions can be enumerated in a negative list. For market access and national treatment, GATS-inspired agreements reproduce the format of GATS schedules of commitments. There is a positive list of sectors for which specific commitments are made, and limitations are listed for these commitments. Commitments and limitations are listed by mode of supply, according to GATS typology.

Some authors have pointed out that the GATS approach toward the scheduling of commitments lacks transparency (Hoekman 1996; Stephenson 2002; Mattoo 2005). For example, when sectors are unbound, there is no indication of the restrictive measures that apply. These sectors have to be identified by deduction, as only the ones with specific commitments are listed. The same criticism can apply to GATS-inspired PTAs. An advantage of these PTAs, however, is that they ensure the consistency of regional liberalization with multilateral disciplines. When PTAs explicitly refer to GATS articles to define the concepts that organize the liberalization of mode 3, it is easier to assess the preferential content of the PTA and to be sure that the provisions are not "GATS-minus" (less favorable than in GATS). The analysis is more complicated in the case of NAFTA-inspired agreements that are based on different concepts.

The straightforwardness and familiarity of the GATS approach may explain why it has been popular among PTA negotiators. They are on accustomed ground when working with GATS-like schedules of commitments, and they can more easily strike a deal on the basis of existing multilateral commitments augmented by preferential commitments.

Hybrid approaches. Most agreements can be clearly identified as GATS-inspired or NAFTA-inspired, but some depart from these two models. A very small number has adopted a scheduling approach that is modeled after neither. This is the case, in particular, for the agreements signed in the context of the European integration process, such as EU enlargement agreements that are notified to the WTO but are of a different nature from other PTAs. There are also PTAs without deep investment provisions in which investment promotion is mentioned only as a general objective, without any specific commitment.

Among PTAs with deep investment provisions, however, a significant number tends to combine the GATS and NAFTA approaches. These are designated as "hybrid" in annex table 14A.1. First, most of the agreements signed recently by Japan (with the exception of that with Chile) deal with both commercial presence and investment in services and include a GATS-like schedule of commitments, as well as a negative list of nonconforming measures. In coverage, they are comparable to NAFTA-inspired agreements in that they employ a broad, asset-based definition of investment that is extended to services with respect to national and MFN treatment (unlike GATS-inspired agreements) and include the mechanisms of the negative-list approach, such as the ratchet effect. At the same time, consistency with GATS commitments is improved. Restrictions on investment in services appear twice in these agreements: in the schedule of commitments for services under mode 3, and in the list of nonconforming measures in the investment chapter. The ratchet mechanism is transposed onto the GATS-inspired schedule of commitments through an additional column in which Japan commits to bind any new liberalization measure in specific subsectors.

Another hybrid approach can be found in the Australia–Chile FTA, which is mostly NAFTA inspired but in which a reservation on market access in the negative list reproduces the market access column usually found in GATS schedules. The architecture is quite convoluted: the agreement first grants market access for all investments but then adds a reservation for all services (negative listing) and an exception for a positive list of subsectors in a GATS format that includes reservations.

It is not certain that these agreements, with their complex structure, really afford the transparency that investors require. Their intent, however, is to combine the best of two worlds: the advantages of the negative list of NAFTA-inspired agreements, in which all restrictive investment measures are listed, and the consistency of GATS-inspired agreements with respect to multilateral commitments. In the future, such a combination could be useful in multilateralizing PTAs and harmonizing the treatment of investors and investment.

Key Issues

Some of the issues arising from the existence of two sets of disciplines were touched on above, but they need to be further elaborated. In particular, questions remain about the degree of liberalization achieved through the kind of disciplines found in PTAs. Moreover, the proliferation of international investment agreements and the coexistence of bilateral, plurilateral, and multilateral rules are key issues in the analysis of investment provisions in PTAs. How is bilateral investment liberalized in PTAs? Is there an investment "spaghetti bowl" comparable to the one for trade? What exactly is the role of MFN provisions in this accumulation of competing rules and commitments? As PTAs progressively replace BITs, will they offer the same degree of investment protection as do BITs?

Liberalization of Bilateral Investment in PTAs

It is common to refer to the liberalization of investment when discussing bilateral investment measures. As a general objective, most PTAs explicitly mention in their preambles the liberalization, expansion, and promotion of bilateral investment. Nevertheless, investment is liberalized in these agreements mainly through the nondiscrimination principles described above. Countries make commitments to grant the same treatment to foreign investors and domestic investors, or to different foreign investors, but they undertake no commitment to remove all existing barriers to investment. For example, countries can maintain an investment screening process through which they authorize or reject an investment, or they can impose specific conditions before approving the investment. To the extent that the same conditions apply to domestic and foreign firms, there is no discrimination, yet the investment regime can still be quite restrictive. In addition, countries generally maintain discriminatory measures through exemptions, reservations, and limitations with respect to national and MFN treatment. With the exception of provisions in a few agreements for phasing out commitments, these limitations are generally meant to stay, at least until further negotiations occur. PTAs generally have mechanisms for "encouraging" the progressive removal of remaining barriers but do not commit to their full elimination.

One important achievement in PTAs, in comparison with BITs, is that they include disciplines on market access.[6] In most BITs, national treatment and MFN treatment cover only the postestablishment phase, and there are no nondiscrimination obligations concerning the establishment of companies. Disciplines on market access are most important for the ability of foreign investors to enter the market and for the creation of a level playing field for domestic and foreign companies. In NAFTA-inspired agreements, these disciplines take the form of national and MFN treatment obligations toward the "establishment, acquisition, and expansion" of investments, whereas GATS-inspired agreements have a combination of market access and national treatment commitments for services. The difference is that market access in the sense of GATS Article XVI is defined by means of a list of six different types of prohibited quantitative restrictions (see Delimatsis and Molinuevo 2008). Some of these restrictions (e.g., foreign equity limits) are discriminatory and are also prohibited by the national treatment principle, but others, such as quotas that apply indifferently to domestic and foreign investors, are nondiscriminatory. The latter restrictions are not covered by national treatment obligations because they do not involve discrimination between domestic and foreign companies.[7]

In both types of agreement, countries can still maintain reservations or carve out specific sectors, but in sectors in which commitments are made, existing measures are locked in, creating a standstill. Countries cannot introduce new restrictive measures on investment in these sectors. This kind of guarantee is valuable for investors and generally has a positive impact on investment decisions, especially when the commitment is embedded in an international agreement.

In the case of NAFTA-inspired agreements, there is, in addition, the ratchet effect mentioned above. If a party decides to remove unilaterally some barriers to investment, the standstill of the agreement will apply to this new regime, and the country cannot revert to the restrictive measures—or, if it did, it would have to offer compensation and renegotiate with the other parties. This is clearly a pro-liberalization effect that is attached to NAFTA mechanisms rather than to the negative list. A similar ratchet effect can easily be incorporated into GATS-inspired agreements, as demonstrated in some of the PTAs signed by Japan.

An advantage specific to the negative listing is the automatic inclusion of new sectors under the disciplines of the agreement. As technological innovations take place, it is not unusual to see the emergence of new activities that do not fit into old classifications (such as new services provided online), and there may be legal uncertainty about the application of national treatment or MFN treatment to these innovations. In a negative-list agreement, these sectors are automatically covered, as the only reservations are those listed when the agreement was signed. This is not the case in GATS-inspired agreements, in which no specific commitment could have been made for these sectors, unless they clearly fit into an existing sector.

One should not overemphasize these differences between NAFTA-inspired and GATS-inspired agreements. In principle, the former should be more favorable to the liberalization of investment. In practice, the NAFTA-style agreements contain very broad reservations that often

return them to the status quo found in GATS-inspired agreements. For example, it is not uncommon to find a reservation for future measures saying that the country can adopt or maintain any measure related to new services. (Japan tends to introduce such measures in its PTAs.) Reservations for future measures give countries the opportunity to avoid the disciplines of the agreement in as many sectors as they wish.

This caution is certainly unavoidable if the agreements are to be signed and politically accepted. Legitimate concerns related to public interest or national security also lead to restrictions on foreign investment. It should be recognized, however, that agreements already include safeguards to deal with these concerns.

Restrictions on foreign investment are also generally found in services sectors that have traditionally been regulated and in which market imperfections can in some cases justify the existence of restrictions. In addition, there are many restrictions at the subfederal or subnational level that are not always clearly identified.[8]

An approach more favorable to the liberalization of investment would be to add, in addition to the standstill, the rollback principle So far, only the Organisation for Economic Co-operation and Development (OECD) Codes of Liberalisation of Capital Movements and Current Invisible Operations include such a principle. The codes provide for the periodic examination of remaining restrictive measures: countries have to justify the continuation of their measures, and other countries can try to persuade them to remove these barriers or suggest less restrictive ways to meet the objectives cited to justify the measures (OECD 2008). In the case of NAFTA, there is an element of rollback in the inclusion of phase-out commitments—a proviso whereby nonconforming measures are in force for a limited number of years and then disappear. Although NAFTA-inspired agreements include a ratchet mechanism, this mechanism is based on unilateral liberalization, with no obligation or commitment to achieve further progress. GATS-inspired agreements often include clauses on future liberalization, with a commitment to review the agreement (say, after three years), but in practice, there are few examples of agreements in which commitments have been updated.

From firms' point of view, what ultimately matters is the domestic investment regime. Countries can maintain very restrictive measures such as public monopolies, discriminatory licensing procedures, or foreign equity limits while still signing comprehensive PTAs. It is mainly through unilateral liberalization that firms can expect an improvement in market access for their investments. Sectors in which investment is regulated are generally reformed not when a PTA is signed but, rather, when there is a domestic consensus for reform. In that situation, all foreign countries are likely to benefit from new liberalization efforts, independent of PTAs.

It is important to understand that PTAs with respect to investment offer only preferential binding and not always preferential treatment. To begin with, the domestic investment regime can be more liberal than is suggested by the limitations listed in the PTA.[9] The limitations do not mean that the country actually has investment restrictions but only that it is allowed to maintain some restrictions within the legal framework of the agreement. The schedules of commitments provide an indication of the bound level of investment restrictiveness. Another reason that PTAs are sometimes not preferential in practice is that the investment regime is not discriminatory. For trade in goods, it is easy to discriminate between trade partners through the application of different tariffs (and the tariff already constitutes discrimination between domestic and foreign companies). In the case of investment, barriers are generally the same for all foreign countries; there are few exceptions to MFN treatment.[10] The barriers apply to foreign-owned companies established under domestic law—even though the rationale for discrimination is not very sound, as the companies generate jobs in the local economy.

For the reasons discussed above, the sectoral coverage of preferential investment provisions is generally quite extensive (Fink and Molinuevo 2008; Marchetti and Roy 2008; Miroudot 2009), although there are exceptions in key sectors. In "Economic Impact: Theory and Evidence," below, we will see that these provisions have been found to have a positive economic impact.

A "Spaghetti Bowl" of Investment Provisions?

According to the United Nations Conference on Trade and Development (UNCTAD 2009b), there were, at the end of 2008, a total of 2,676 BITs, 2,805 double-taxation treaties (DTTs), and 273 international agreements, other than BITs and DTTs, that contained investment provisions; this last category includes PTAs. International investment agreements are therefore proliferating even more than trade agreements, suggesting a giant "spaghetti bowl." One should, however, recall the exact meaning of this expression introduced by Bhagwati (see Bhagwati, Krishna, and Panagariya 1999). The "spaghetti bowl" is not the consequence of the sheer number of agreements in force but of differences in the depth and patterns of sectoral liberalization in PTAs, combined with diverse sets of rules of origin that create high trade costs for firms.

Rules of origin in PTAs define the national origin of products traded in order to determine whether the preferential treatment of the agreement applies to these products. In the case of investment, rules of origin apply to juridical persons (the companies) and define the conditions under which an investor from a third country can benefit from the investment provisions contained in the PTAs signed by the country where it has established. These rules are found either in the definition of the investor and the conditions of incorporation or in clauses on denial of benefits that specify who cannot benefit from the preferential treatment granted in the agreement.

Rules of origin for investment are generally quite liberal (Beviglia Zampetti and Sauvé 2006; Fink and Nikomborirak 2007). Most PTAs follow the GATS approach (which is also common in BITs), whereby the juridical person has to be incorporated under the law of the member party and engaged in "substantive business operations" in that party. This rule is part of the conditions set in GATS Article V for PTAs to be allowed as derogations to the MFN obligation of GATS. For this reason, there is little variation across PTAs on the rules of origin for juridical persons.

There are no criteria defining substantive business operations. According to Emch (2006), that requirement is aimed at ensuring that the link of the company to the territory of the party is "genuine." It is loose enough to not be interpreted by countries as giving them the opportunity to add strict criteria in order for business operations to be regarded as substantive.

The consequence of these liberal rules of origin is that the impact of divergent provisions across PTAs is reduced. If the investment regime is more liberal in one country because of a PTA, companies from third countries can invest in that market through any subsidiary established in a country belonging to the PTA. A concrete example is provided by Fink and Mattoo (2002), who describe how, following the adoption of NAFTA in 1994, several Spanish and Dutch banks established in Mexico through their U.S. subsidiaries. Financial liberalization had just started in Mexico, and U.S. (and Canadian) investors were the first to be able to invest in the Mexican banking industry. When the EU–Mexico agreement entered into force in 2000, offering provisions similar to those in NAFTA for financial services, some of these companies transferred the ownership of their Mexican subsidiaries back to the parent companies in Europe. This example illustrates how liberal rules of origin can compensate for the absence of MFN treatment. From the point of view of companies in third countries, however, this is only a second-best situation because of the cost associated with investment through a subsidiary.

Because of leaky rules of origin, the "spaghetti bowl" problem is not too severe in the case of investment (Baldwin, Evenett, and Low 2009).[11] There are, nonetheless, potential inconsistencies between the different types of international investment agreements when their provisions overlap. Inconsistency can also exist between provisions in PTAs and multilateral rules. In the case of investment, only services sectors have multilateral commitments in GATS. A certain number of PTAs are found to have GATS-minus commitments; they list nonconforming measures that have no equivalent in GATS. For example, in the economic partnership agreement between the EU and the Caribbean Forum of African, Caribbean, and Pacific (ACP) States (CARIFORUM) that entered into force in 2008, measures on subsidies are explicitly excluded from the scope of application of market access and national treatment provisions. There is no similar carve-out in the GATS schedule of the EU, where only subsidies on research and development are excluded from national treatment with respect to commercial presence.[12] PTAs do not prevent GATS commitments from applying, and so these GATS-minus provisions should have a limited impact, in practice. Nevertheless, such inconsistencies create legal uncertainty and send the wrong signals to investors.

Multilateralization of Investment Provisions through MFN Clauses

The most favored nation clause is a pillar of international trade law and has historically been a powerful tool for multilateralizing bilateral commitments. For investment in services, there is a general MFN obligation that applies to all sectors in GATS and covers, as a consequence, all disciplines related to mode 3 trade in services. The MFN principle is also found in bilateral investment treaties, but its scope is limited to postestablishment when these bilateral agreements contain no provision on the liberalization of investment in the preestablishment phase.

A PTA is an exception to the MFN principle because it grants preferential treatment to specific parties and breaks the equality in the treatment of economic partners that is precisely the objective of MFN clauses. The inclusion of MFN provisions within PTAs has two objectives. First, in the case of a regional or plurilateral agreement, it ensures that all parties to the PTA receive the same treatment. The relevance of MFN provisions is limited in the case of bilateral agreements, as there is only one partner, but MFN provisions are useful with respect to nonparties (also called third parties). If a new PTA is signed, the parties to the former agreement would like to benefit from any additional preferential treatment found in the new PTA.

Unfortunately, most PTAs tend to put limits on the benefits of the application of the MFN principle to parties when better treatment is offered to nonparties. First, some PTAs (such as the Korea–Singapore FTA) simply omit MFN treatment from their investment provisions. In other agreements, there is an MFN clause, *but other PTAs are excluded from the scope of the provision*. Parties can grant better treatment to third countries in another PTA without any obligation to extend this better treatment to the parties of the PTA that includes the MFN provision. This type of provision is referred to as a regional economic integration organization (REIO) exception clause. It can be limited to past agreements (as in the New Zealand–China FTA) or extended to future agreements—the case with the FTA between the European Free Trade Association (EFTA) and Korea. The latter situation differs from an agreement without an MFN clause in that the other party has an opportunity to negotiate the benefits granted in a new PTA signed with a third country. When there is an REIO exception, the agreement does not prevent the new preferential treatment granted to third parties from being extended to the parties of the current PTA, but the extension is not automatic. It can be done through a request, a review of commitments, renegotiation, or a party's unilateral decision, but the extension has to be agreed and made official in some kind of document complementing the original PTA.

In NAFTA and in NAFTA-inspired PTAs, there is generally an exception to MFN treatment regarding commitments made in PTAs signed earlier, but not for future agreements. Instead of an REIO exception clause, the exception is listed as a reservation in the annex on future measures or in a specific annex. Exceptions are also listed for future agreements. For example, in PTAs entered into by the United States, four sectors are excluded from the application of the MFN principle to future agreements: aviation; fisheries; maritime matters; and telecommunications and transport services, including transport networks.

The scope of application of MFN can also be limited. For example, PTAs often indicate that there is no requirement to extend dispute settlement procedures when these are more favorable in another PTA.

Most BITs also contain an MFN exemption for PTAs (Adlung and Molinuevo 2008). In this case, parties to a BIT cannot expect to benefit from the more favorable conditions granted by their partners in a PTA. There are, however, BITs in which such an MFN exemption is not found. The question remains open as to whether commitments made in the PTA should be extended to BIT parties: the more favorable treatment offered to third parties can only be granted "in like circumstances" to the parties covered by MFN treatment, and differences in the scope and objectives of the two types of investment agreement could lead to interpretations limiting the extension of the PTA disciplines to BIT parties. Another debate concerns GATS Article II and whether the MFN clause in GATS covers BITs. If it does, obligations incurred under any BIT might have to be extended to all WTO members. There is, however, no consensus about the interaction between BIT provisions and GATS, and there has been no dispute settlement or case that could throw light on these issues (see Adlung and Molinuevo 2008).

In conclusion, the role of the MFN clause in extending the benefit of PTAs to third countries seems limited. For some agreements, MFN mechanisms may apply, and new liberalization commitments can benefit nonparties, but this is not so in most cases. Moreover, studies show that countries tend to negotiate similar commitments across agreements (Fink and Molinuevo 2008; Marchetti and Roy 2008; Baldwin, Evenett, and Low 2009) or to introduce reforms unilaterally without discriminating between investment partners. Fink and Jansen (2008) note that unilateral commitments on services (including investment in services) are generally not discriminatory because countries seek to avoid the economic distortions associated with discrimination.

There are, however, sectors in which governments are found to discriminate; examples include air transport, which is generally excluded from GATS and from PTAs, and financial services, where the scope of nondiscriminatory disciplines in trade agreements is very limited. For these sectors, the liberal rules of origin mentioned above might be more efficient than MFN clauses for circumventing discriminatory policies.

Investment Protection in BITs and in PTAs

Provisions traditionally found in BITs now tend to be included in trade agreements, and so a legitimate question is whether PTAs provide the same degree of protection to foreign investors in terms of the extensiveness of the protection provisions described in "Investment regulation and protection," above. The answer depends primarily on the type of PTA and the existence or absence of a BIT between the PTA parties. Two cases can be identified:

1. No bilateral investment treaty exists between the signatories, and the PTA is their first investment agreement. The scope and depth of the rules introduced by the PTA depend on the outcome of the negotiation, but the PTA can potentially include any of the protections that would be found in a BIT. Examples include NAFTA and

the FTAs between the United States and Australia; Japan and Malaysia; and Korea and Singapore.

2. A BIT between the countries existed before the entry into force of the PTA. Some countries decide to maintain the existing BIT alongside the PTA, especially when the two sets of rules, in the PTA and in the BIT, tend to complement each other. The EFTA–Chile agreement and most of the agreements signed by the EU follow this approach. When the PTA is clearly superior to the existing BIT, with more comprehensive provisions, the latter can simply be replaced. Either the BIT is terminated (as with the Australia–Chile FTA), or the PTA can suspend part of the provisions of the BIT when it enters into force (e.g., the U.S.–Morocco FTA).

When PTAs include an investment chapter, the provisions on investment protection are generally equivalent to the content of similar BITs. The fact that some agreements are GATS inspired does not prevent investment in services from benefiting from the basic protections provided in the investment chapter. It should also be noted that, unlike the services chapter that refers to "commercial presence," the investment chapters of GATS-inspired PTAs use a broader, asset-based definition of investment, and the provisions on the protection of investment apply to this broad definition. "Commercial presence" is relevant in GATS-inspired PTAs only with respect to the level of liberalization in services, as defined in the services chapter and in the commitments annexed to the agreement. On the basis of an analysis of 20 PTAs, Houde, Kolse-Patil, and Miroudot (2007) show that there is no difference in the level of investment protection between GATS-inspired and NAFTA-inspired PTAs.

In conclusion, there is technically no impediment to the inclusion in PTAs of the provisions on investment protection usually found in BITs, and countries have generally adopted the same kind of provisions in both types of agreement. The remaining differences between BITs and PTAs result from the outcome of negotiations and the existence of a BIT already in force before the PTA was negotiated. Some countries have designed PTAs that can replace earlier BITs, while others maintain part of the guarantees offered to foreign investors in the BIT and have not duplicated the provisions in the PTA.

Economic Impact: Theory and Evidence

The two preceding sections examined the architecture of investment PTAs and the implications of their legal provisions. Little was said about the economic impact of bilateral investment measures. For a long time, this issue has been overlooked, in large part because of lack of data and of methods for precisely assessing the impact of PTAs on flows of trade and investment. Recent developments in economic theory, as well as new empirical tools, have to some extent enabled economic analysis to catch up. There is now empirical evidence on the positive impact of bilateral investment measures in PTAs. Studies have, however, shown that not all PTAs improve the investment climate and that other determinants of FDI are important as well and may condition the positive impact of PTA provisions.

Economic Benefits of PTAs with Investment Provisions: Theory

Trade and investment can be seen as two sides of market access. Firms have different means of serving foreign markets; in particular, they can choose between exporting (trade) and creating a subsidiary within the foreign economy for local production (international investment). The recent literature on firm heterogeneity and global sourcing (Antràs and Helpman 2004; Helpman 2006) focuses on the choice between exports and FDI. Not all firms follow the same path. Depending on their productivity, size, and structure of production, firms adopt different strategies that lead to different types of international activities such as offshoring, outsourcing, or vertical specialization. The least productive firms tend to stay in the domestic market, while more efficient companies can engage in international investment and become multinational enterprises (MNEs). There are also differences across sectors in the way firms organize their production, based on product characteristics and technologies.

The "proximity-concentration tradeoff" (Brainard 1997) describes a substitution effect between trade and investment. Market-seeking MNEs face trade costs when they export (all those costs related to sales overseas) but can save on production costs because of scale economies, as all the production is done in the home country. When they invest abroad and manufacture locally, MNEs no longer incur trade costs, but production costs can increase because production is now split between the home country and the host, diminishing scale economies. The outcome of this trade-off depends on the relative sizes of trade costs and investment costs. High border barriers such as tariffs may encourage the company to produce close to the consumers in the foreign economy—that is, to engage in tariff-jumping FDI.

In this theoretical framework, PTAs affect firms' strategies at several levels. First, the trade liberalization provisions in PTAs have an impact on trade costs. Reduced trade

costs can encourage trade rather than investment within the region where the PTA is signed. Conversely, to the extent that the PTA increases trade costs vis-à-vis third-party countries, it can promote tariff-jumping investment by these parties. An implication is that even an agreement with no investment provisions is likely to influence firms' decisions because of its impact on the trade-off between investment costs and trade costs. If, in addition, a PTA includes provisions that lower investment costs, it is likely to further encourage FDI over arm's length trade.

Because of the link between trade costs and investment decisions, the concepts of trade creation and trade diversion can be transposed into the realm of investment. A PTA that increases trade barriers relative to third countries can be investment creating, by encouraging FDI from these third countries. The same PTA can be investment diverting intraregionally because arm's length trade is less costly and firms liquidate former tariff-jumping FDI. Restrictive rules of origin for goods within the PTA can also lead to investment diversion, as manufacturers using third-country inputs concentrate their production in the country with the largest market and the lowest external tariffs (Estevadeordal and Suominen 2005).

The proximity-concentration trade-off is only one side of the complex relationship between trade and investment and is relevant only with respect to horizontal FDI. In the case of vertical FDI and vertical specialization leading to global value chains, trade and investment are complements rather than substitutes. Vertical FDI is associated with efficiency-seeking strategies whereby firms intend to benefit from locational advantages such as better or relatively cheaper factors of production or strategic resources. In this context, a PTA is likely to increase FDI through both its trade and its investment provisions. In particular, the reduction of barriers to imports of intermediate goods and services can encourage FDI (Ferrantino and Hall 2001).

The picture is further complicated by network effects and third-country effects that arise because firms choose their production location from among several countries that belong to different regional integration schemes. When economic integration is deepened in a group of countries, trade liberalization can have a redistributive effect on intraregional investment patterns; one country might attract more FDI and other countries, less.

In brief, whether a PTA eventually increases or reduces FDI flows is an empirical question. The answer depends on the relative strength of the decreases in trade costs and investment entry costs, as well as FDI motives (efficiency seeking or market seeking). Whether FDI is positive for the host country, and for developing countries specifically, is a broader question that is beyond the scope of this chapter. The answer is partly empirical, and an abundant literature has discussed the gains (or lack of gains) from FDI. Overall, however, FDI has consistently been found to be beneficial to developing countries, in particular because it transfers knowledge as well as capital, producing a long-term impact on economic growth.[13] FDI also leads to integration into world markets and is key to developing economies' participation in global value chains.

Empirical Studies

Although economic theories have recently shed light on firms' decisions to invest or to export, few empirical studies have investigated the role of PTAs in fostering trade and investment. A wider literature exists on the impact of BITs on FDI flows. Annex table 14A.2 summarizes the results of selected recent studies.

The earliest study to look at the impact of trade liberalization on investment is that by Jeon and Stone (2000). Focusing on the Asia-Pacific region, they find that the Association of Southeast Asian Nations (ASEAN) has increased intraregional trade but that its impact on intraregional investment is insignificant. This study uses a gravity model in which PTAs are included as dummy variables to identify differences between intraregional and extraregional bilateral investment flows. The dummy variable takes the value of 0 when there is no agreement and a value of 1 when countries have signed a PTA. Using a similar methodology, Hufbauer and Schott (2008) show that the most prominent PTAs, including NAFTA, the ASEAN Free Trade Area, the EU, and EFTA, have increased bilateral investment stocks between their members. One exception is the Canada–U.S. FTA, which preceded NAFTA and which seems to have led to decreased bilateral investment stocks. This could be interpreted as the unwinding of former tariff jumping between the United States and Canada once trade liberalization took place.

When using a dummy variable to account for the existence of the PTA, it is difficult to assess the exact role of investment provisions. The trade provisions, as we have seen, are likely to play an important role in FDI decisions, and the agreement itself, independent of its provisions, could increase bilateral investment—for example, by advertising to potential investors opportunities in the partner country. Furthermore, the dummy variables cannot distinguish between ambitious agreements with deep investment provisions and PTAs that only marginally address investment. Adams et al. (2003) were the first to control for this problem by introducing an index of liberalization that measures the breadth and depth of PTA provisions. The index is then used in a gravity model to assess the role of certain types of provisions that characterize new regionalism and, in particular, investment provisions. Lesher and Miroudot (2007) use a similar methodology to analyze the economic impact of North-South PTAs and find that the more extensive the provisions on investment are, the higher are trade flows and, to an even greater extent, investment flows.

More recent studies have tried to improve the theoretical framework by introducing a model that can better account for firms' decision to trade or to invest. Miroudot (2009) tests an index of investment provisions in FDI and trade equations derived from the knowledge capital model, which introduces horizontal and vertical MNEs, as well as consideration of the skill endowments of countries. The index of investment provisions is further refined by taking into account the sectoral coverage of investment provisions and the extent to which they go beyond GATS in the case of services, in order to measure the preferential content of the agreement. The impact of PTA investment provisions is lower than in previous studies but is still positive and economically significant. Dee (2006) proposes a model of "complex" FDI that also takes into account vertical and horizontal motivations for FDI and introduces third-country effects so that the bilateral investment relationship is influenced by the trade and investment regime in other countries, in particular, neighboring countries. In the case of Asia, Dee argues that patterns of investment are already explained by fundamentals and do not need the investment provisions of PTAs. When FDI and trade are not driven by size, income, and other market characteristics, the impact of PTA provisions is less obvious, but the author still finds positive effects for some economies.

The most recent studies thus introduce nuances in the role of investment PTAs. Some of these PTAs are signed by countries that are "naturally" inclined toward increased bilateral FDI flows, and the provisions of the PTA may play a minor role. For some other countries, the economic environment is not favorable to FDI, and the investment provisions of PTAs may not be enough to change this situation. Nonetheless, these provisions are solidly associated in empirical analysis with increased FDI flows; the studies include control variables such as gross domestic product (GDP) or GDP per capita that account for differences in growth and income.

The literature yields mixed results on the effect of BITs. Following Hallward-Driemeier (2003), several studies find weak evidence of a positive impact of BITs on investment. Gallagher and Birch (2006) point out that BITs signed by Latin American countries with the United States do not seem to attract U.S. investment, while the number of BITs signed by a country with other countries is positively correlated with the total amount of inward FDI. Aisbett (2007) identifies an endogeneity issue, in that BITs are first signed with countries with which there is already an important bilateral investment relationship. When the selection in BIT participation is controlled for, the correlation between BITs and investment flows is not robust.

Two studies provide evidence of a positive impact of BITs on FDI flows, in particular, to developing countries. Egger and Merlo (2007) propose a dynamic panel estimation and estimate that in the short run, BITs produce a 4.8 percent increase in FDI. The long-run impact is estimated at 8.9 percent. The authors stress that failure to account for the dynamic nature of FDI leads to biased results. Busse, Königer, and Nunnenkamp (2010) control for the endogeneity of BIT adoption and for unilateral investment liberalization and find a positive impact of BITs on FDI flows. Further investigation of the relationship shows that BITs can be a substitute for weak domestic institutions but not for unilateral capital account liberalization.

Recent studies on the impact of BITs on investment have gone further than PTA empirical studies by introducing a dynamic framework and by better taking into account the endogeneity issue. They have, however, not sufficiently distinguished the different types of BITs, in particular, those that include liberalization provisions in addition to protection disciplines—the case of some BITs signed by the United States, Canada, and Japan. An exception is a study by Berger et al. (2010), who look at the impact of specific types of provisions. Although, in the case of PTAs, the authors find that guarantees of market access and state-investor dispute settlement mechanisms have a positive impact on FDI flows, these provisions do not play a significant role in the case of BITs. Investors respond quite indiscriminately to BITs.

The fact that most BITs do not cover preestablishment could explain part of the mixed empirical results and the difference observed between BITs and PTAs. Moreover, about 2,500 BITs are in force, and the more common it is for two countries to share a BIT, the less one can expect the variable to explain differences in bilateral investment flows.

Conclusions

PTAs are more and more becoming "PTIAs"—preferential trade *and investment* agreements. Dealing with investment when opening markets becomes increasingly relevant in the context of the fragmentation of world production and global supply chains. Studies on globalization highlight the

regional dimension of international production networks (see, for example, Inomata et al. forthcoming). In Europe and North America, it is through comprehensive economic integration agreements such as NAFTA and the European Economic Agreement that global supply chains have emerged. In Asia, production networks preceded the introduction of PTAs, but countries are now engaged in multiple negotiations to ensure that policies can cope with the rapid growth of trade and investment. Some authors have pointed out that the distribution of intra-ASEAN investment flows has remained unchanged in the last decade, a situation perhaps related to the late adoption of the ASEAN Investment Agreement (AIA) and to its relatively loose disciplines (Jarvis et al. 2009).

Because of the importance of the relationship between trade and investment (whether as substitutes or complements), there is a rationale for introducing investment provisions in trade agreements, and it is not surprising to see more and more PTAs including deep investment commitments. PTAs generally do not improve on existing BITs with respect to protection of investment, but by adding the market access dimension and by regrouping trade and investment provisions under the same agreement signed for an indeterminate period, they offer a better package of disciplines for investors. BITs influence the policy determinants of FDI, but PTAs also improve the economic determinants and have been found to have a stronger impact on investment (UNCTAD 2009a).

Several lessons for developing countries emerge from the recent wave of trade and investment agreements. First, there are important economic gains in the negotiation of bilateral investment measures, and empirical studies show that these gains are higher for North-South PTAs. Developed countries already have among themselves instruments that grant national treatment and MFN treatment to investors and their investments (in particular, the OECD Codes of Liberalisation of Capital Movements and Current Invisible Operations, and the companion National Treatment Instrument). With no multilateral agreement on investment, and with GATS negotiations stalemated, PTAs are so far the only option for increasing market access for investors, for both inward and outward investment. Investment protection could be achieved for developing countries through BITs, but disciplines limited to postestablishment are not enough to realize the gains from the internationalization of production. Only BITs covering preestablishment and complemented by a PTA that liberalizes trade can offer the same attractiveness to foreign investors.

North-South PTAs with investment provisions are especially relevant when thinking about global value chains consisting of a parent company established in the North and subsidiaries created in the South to supply inputs or to perform final assembly of the product. In the context of vertical specialization, the prohibition of performance requirements, such as local content requirements, is particularly important because FDI is motivated by global production rather than being aimed at the local market. To the extent that the foreign affiliate does not compete with local companies, market access, not just nondiscrimination, is crucial in this context because the foreign investor will look for the lowest investment costs in all potential locations. As demand and global value chains shift to the South (Kaplinsky and Farooki 2010), the experience of successful North-South PTAs with investment provisions should now be reproduced in South-South PTAs. So far, there are fewer South-South PTAs with deep investment provisions, but their number has been increasing in Asia (Miroudot 2009).

The second lesson is that because of liberal rules of origin, not all developing countries have to sign a PTA with the main trading economies. Regional initiatives and the multilateralization of PTAs can guarantee that in the future all developing countries will become part of at least one regional agreement offering access to the main markets through the "spaghetti bowl" of investment PTAs. What is important is to promote multilateral-friendly provisions that can ensure the consistency of provisions across agreements. In particular, third-party MFN rules can help countries benefit from agreements signed by other countries and can be efficient in minimizing the costs associated with distortions in the preferential treatment granted. For developing countries that may lack the resources to negotiate multiple PTAs and may be afraid of bilateral negotiations with larger and more developed economies, these mechanisms should be emphasized and further strengthened.

The third lesson is that despite promotion of the liberalization of investment, these agreements have all preserved the right of countries to regulate. Countries can be reluctant to grant full national treatment and market access to foreign investors, but in practice, agreements allow for many exceptions and reservations that can lead to progressive liberalization, as well as the reservation of activities for public purposes. The economic gains measured in empirical studies are found in agreements that maintain nonconforming measures in key sectors and that have carved out certain sectors. For economic gains to be maximized, restrictive investment measures should be minimized, but this does not generally entail forgoing policies that may be desirable for development.

Finally, even if agreements with less ambitious provisions have been found to have a positive impact because of the signal they send investors, agreements with wide sectoral coverage and broad disciplines are associated with higher flows of FDI. The signaling effect is often related to a commitment to negotiate further, and the positive impact will be sustained if the countries effectively build on the initial agreement and expand the scope of investment commitments.

There is little evidence of asymmetric treatment in North-South PTAs: provisions tend to be the same for all parties. A difference can be seen in the sectoral coverage of agreements for investment in services. The developed economy generally has more subsectors with commitments, but fewer preferential commitments. The opposite holds for the developing economy: typically, fewer sectors are scheduled in the PTA than for the developed-country partner, but the commitments are more often preferential. This difference reflects the fact that GATS schedules of commitments for mode 3 are more extensive for developed countries. In terms of additional liberalization, the effort can be bigger for the developing country. This is in the country's self-interest, and an asymmetric treatment that would restrict the liberalization commitments of the developing country would limit its potential gains (Heydon and Woolcock 2009). Through symmetric provisions, investment PTAs can achieve a pro-development outcome.

For the least-developed economies, a concern that can be addressed through PTAs is the risk of facing costly compensation under commercial arbitration and having legitimate policy considerations overridden by direct claims of foreign investors. Although an investor-state dispute settlement mechanism is in the end desirable, in that it offers the highest guarantees to foreign investors, some authors have argued that such a mechanism could be premature for the least-developed economies.[14] Moreover, there is no multilateral institution for administering BITs and resolving disputes about the interpretation and application of investment treaties (Adlung 2009). By referring to WTO definitions and legal instruments (in particular, GATS), and by resorting to state-state dispute mechanisms in the tradition of trade agreements, PTAs can offer a better option for developing countries that are not ready for the commercial arbitration of BITs. In the future, however, the convergence of dispute mechanisms in international trade and economic law will be necessary (Choi 2007), and improvement of investor-state dispute settlement mechanisms could better serve the interests of developing economies, as well.

Table 14A.1. Overview of Recent PTAs Covering Investment

PTA	Year in force	Type	Establishment or market access	Nondiscrimination		Temporary entry for key personnel	Investment protection			Investor-state dispute settlement
				National treatment	MFN treatment		Fair and equitable treatment	Free transfer of funds	Expropriation and compensation	
Australia–Chile FTA	2009	Hybrid	Positive list	Negative list	Negative list	Yes	Yes	Yes	Yes	Yes
CAFTA–DR FTA	2006	NAFTA-inspired	Negative list	Negative list	Negative list	No	Yes	Yes	Yes	Yes
Canada–Peru FTA	2009	NAFTA-inspired	Negative list	Negative list	Negative list	Yes	Yes	Yes	Yes	Yes
Chile–Colombia FTA	2009	NAFTA-inspired	Negative list	Negative list	Negative list	Yes	Yes	Yes	Yes	Yes
China–Singapore FTA (services)	2009	GATS-inspired	Positive list	Positive list	No	Yes	Pending the conclusion of the ASEAN–China Investment Agreement			
EU–CARIFORUM EPA	2008	GATS-inspired	Positive list	Positive list	Negative list	Yes	No	No	No	No
EFTA–Korea, Rep. FTA	2006	GATS-inspired	Positive list (services), negative list (goods)	Positive list (services), negative list (goods)	Negative list	Yes	Yes	Yes	Yes	Yes
Japan–Brunei Darussalam EPA	2008	Hybrid	Positive list (commercial presence), negative list (investment)	Positive list (commercial presence), negative list (investment)	Negative list	No	Yes	Yes	Yes	Yes
Japan–Chile SEP	2007	NAFTA-inspired	Negative list (positive list for financial services)	Negative list (positive list for financial services)	Negative list	Yes	Yes	Yes	Yes	Yes
Japan–Indonesia EPA	2008	Hybrid	Positive list (commercial presence), negative list (investment)	Positive list (commercial presence), negative list (investment)	Negative list	Yes	Yes	Yes	Yes	Yes
Japan–Malaysia EPA	2006	Hybrid	Positive list (commercial presence), negative list (investment)	Positive list (commercial presence), negative list (investment)	Negative list	Yes	Yes	Yes	Yes	Yes
Japan–Philippines EPA	2008	Hybrid	Positive list (commercial presence), negative list (investment)	Positive list (commercial presence), negative list (investment)	Negative list	Yes	Yes	Yes	Yes	To be negotiated

Agreement	Year	Type	Positive list	Positive list	Through a request				
Japan–Thailand EPA	2007	GATS-inspired	Positive list	Positive list	Yes	Yes	Yes	Yes	Yes
Korea, Rep.–Singapore FTA	2006	NAFTA-inspired	Negative list (positive list for financial services)	Negative list (positive list for financial services)	No	Yes	Yes	Yes	Yes
New Zealand–China FTA	2008	GATS-inspired	Positive list (services), negative list (goods)	Positive list (services), negative list (goods)	Yes	Yes	Yes	Yes	Yes
Panama–Singapore FTA	2006	NAFTA-inspired	Negative list	Negative list	Yes	Yes	Yes	Yes	Yes
U.S.–Morocco FTA	2006	NAFTA-inspired	Negative list	Negative list	No	Yes	Yes	Yes	Yes
U.S.–Oman FTA	2009	NAFTA-inspired	Negative list	Negative list	No	Yes	Yes	Yes	Yes
U.S.–Peru PTA	2009	NAFTA-inspired	Negative list	Negative list	No	Yes	Yes	Yes	Yes

Source: Author's compilation.

Note: ASEAN, Association of Southeast Asian Nations; CAFTA–DR, Dominican Republic–Central America Free Trade Agreement; EFTA, European Free Trade Association; EPA, economic partnership agreement; EU, European Union; CARIFORUM, Caribbean Forum of African, Caribbean, and Pacific (ACP) States; FTA, free trade agreement; GATS, General Agreement on Trade in Services; MFN, most favored nation; NAFTA, North American Free Trade Agreement; PTA, preferential trade agreement; SEP, strategic economic partnership. The table includes only PTAs that entered into force between 2006 and 2009 and that contain substantive investment provisions covering both goods and services. In the case of the EFTA–Republic of Korea FTA, there is a separate agreement on investment in which Norway is not a party. In the China–Singapore FTA, provisions on investment are those of the ASEAN–China Investment Agreement when it enters into force. The term "positive list" means that the provision is included in the agreement for a positive list of sectors; "negative list" means that the provision applies to all sectors, except those specified in a list in which reservations are made by the parties.

Table 14A.2. Selected Empirical Studies on the Impact of Bilateral Investment Measures

Empirical study	Data coverage	Empirical model	Results
Investment provisions in preferential trade agreements			
Dee (2006)	Bilateral stocks of outward foreign direct investment (FDI) for up to 32 parent countries and 109 hosts (1988–97).	Model of "complex" FDI with third-country effects and an index of investment provisions for 38 preferential trade agreements (PTAs).	When FDI and trade are sufficiently driven by fundamentals (as in Asia), the resulting network patterns of investment do not need to be boosted by investment provisions of PTAs. When this is not the case, the investment provisions of PTAs signed with source countries have mixed effects. (A positive effect is found for PTAs signed by large economies.)
Lesher and Miroudot (2007)	Bilateral trade and investment flows of 51 reporter countries with 180 partner countries (1990–2004).	Gravity regressions for trade and FDI flows with an index for investment provisions in 24 North-South PTAs.	Investment provisions are positively associated with trade and, to an even greater extent, investment flows. Results are insignificant for bilateral investment treaties
Hufbauer and Schott (2008)	Bilateral FDI inward stocks for about 170 countries (1976–2005).	Gravity regressions with dummy variables for nine prominent PTAs.	Most PTAs have increased bilateral investment stocks between their members. The Canada–U.S. FTA has decreased bilateral FDI stocks (interpreted as the unwinding of former tariff-jumping FDI)
Miroudot (2009)	Bilateral trade and investment stocks of 18 Asian economies with 190 partner countries (1990–2006).	Gravity regressions derived from the knowledge-capital model for trade and FDI flows with an index for investment provisions in 22 Asian PTAs. (The index includes data on sectoral coverage.)	Preferential treatment for investment is associated with higher inward and outward investment stocks. The impact is lower than in previous studies but economically significant (about 14 percent more FDI for the most extensive investment provisions over the least extensive ones)
Investment provisions in bilateral investment treaties (BITs)			
Gallagher and Birch (2006)	Total FDI inflows and FDI from the United States in 24 Latin American countries (1980–2002).	Regression on total FDI inflows with a variable indicating the number of BITs with other countries and gravity regression for FDI inflows from the United States with a dummy variable for BITs.	BITs with the United States do not independently attract U.S. FDI, but a higher number of BITs with other countries is associated with more FDI inflows
Egger and Merlo (2007)	Bilateral stocks of outward FDI for 24 home and 28 host countries (1980–2001).	Dynamic panel estimation of an FDI equation derived from the knowledge-capital model; dummy variable for BIT ratification and signature.	The short-run impact of BITs on FDI is estimated at 4.8 percent and the long-run impact at 8.92 percent. Accounting for the dynamic nature of FDI leads to less biased results
Aisbett (2007)	Bilateral investment outflows of 24 OECD countries to 28 developing countries (1980–1999).	Model of host government's decisions whether to participate in a BIT and foreign investor's decision whether to invest in the host, controlling for endogeneity of BIT adoption.	The correlation between BITs and investment flows is not robust when selection into BIT participation is controlled for, and there is no evidence for the claim that BITs signal a safe investment climate
Busse, Königer, and Nunnenkamp (2010)	Three-year averages of bilateral FDI flows from 28 source countries into 83 developing host countries (1978–2004)	Gravity regressions on the share of bilateral FDI in total FDI outflows, with a dummy variable for BITs ratified and control variables for unilateral FDI liberalization; instrumentation of BIT and generalized method of moments (GMM) estimation to control for the endogeneity of BIT adoption.	BITs do promote FDI flows to developing countries and may even substitute for weak domestic institutions, although not for unilateral capital account liberalization
Investment provisions in BITs and PTAs			
Berger et al. (2010)	Three-year averages of FDI flows from 28 source countries into 83 developing host countries (1978–2004)	Gravity regressions on the share of bilateral FDI in total FDI outflows, with dummy variables for specific types of investment provisions; GMM estimation to control for the endogeneity of trade and investment treaties.	FDI reacts positively to PTAs only if they offer liberal admission rules. Dispute settlement mechanisms appear to play a minor role. The reactions to BITs are less discriminate, with foreign investors responding favorably to the mere existence of BITs

Source: Author's compilation.
Note: OECD, Organisation for Economic Co-operation and Development.

Notes

This chapter draws on Houde, Kolse-Patil, and Miroudot (2007); Lesher and Miroudot (2007); and Miroudot (2009). The author thanks Rudolf Adlung and Jean-Christophe Maur for their helpful comments and suggestions. The views expressed are those of the author and do not represent those of the Organisation for Economic Co-operation and Development (OECD) or its member countries.

1. In this chapter, we define PTAs with investment provisions as agreements that include provisions on the liberalization or protection of investment. In most PTAs, promotion of investment is among the objectives mentioned in the preamble or in a specific article on investment, but only agreements with substantive provisions for encouraging bilateral investment (through liberalization or protection) are taken into account.

2. Whether GATS MFN obligations apply to WTO members with no MFN exemption for their bilateral investment treaties under the GATS remains an open question. See Adlung and Molinuevo (2008) for a discussion.

3. For a recent stocktaking of investment provisions in PTAs, see Kotschwar (2009).

4. On the negative impact of local content requirements, see Moran, Graham, and Blomström (2005, ch. 11).

5. On the spread of specific NAFTA provisions to countries outside the Americas, see Baldwin, Evenett, and Low (2009).

6. As noted, BITs signed by the United States and some BITs signed by Canada and Japan cover the preestablishment phase and therefore deal with market access.

7. The possibility of de facto discrimination should be taken into account. The fact that the same measure applies de jure to both domestic and foreign investors does not mean that the impact of the measure is the same for the two. The treatment of the foreign company can still be regarded as "less favorable."

8. In NAFTA, for example, these restrictions are "grandfathered" but are not explicitly listed.

9. Studies suggest that this is often the case. See, for example, Barth et al. (2006), on the banking industry.

10. Some exemptions can, however, have an important impact on FDI in sectors such as financial services, audiovisual services, and professional services.

11. Fink and Jansen (2008) and Baldwin, Evenett, and Low (2009) study rules of origin for services providers, but their analysis regarding juridical persons is relevant for all investors. The rules of origins are the same for goods and services in the case of established companies.

12. This example and others can be found in Adlung and Morrison (2010).

13. On the determinants of FDI, see Blonigen (2005). On FDI spillovers and the benefits of FDI for development, see Moran, Graham, and Blomström (2005).

14. See UNCTAD (2008). The increased complexity of investment agreements and the larger number of arbitration cases necessitate capacity-building initiatives for developing economies.

References

Adams, Richard, Philippa Dee, Jyothi Gali, and Greg McGuire. 2003. "The Trade and Investment Effects of Preferential Trading Arrangements: Old and New Evidence." Australian Productivity Commission Staff Working Paper, Australian Productivity Commission, Canberra.

Adlung, Rudolf. 2009. "Trade in Healthcare and Health Insurance Services: The GATS as Supporting Actor?" WTO Staff Working Paper ERSD-2009-15, World Trade Organization, Geneva.

Adlung, Rudolf, and Martin Molinuevo. 2008. "Bilateralism in Services Trade: Is There Fire Behind the (BIT-) Smoke?" Journal of International Economic Law 11: 365–409.

Adlung, Rudolf, and Peter Morrison. 2010. "Less Than the GATS: 'Negative Preferences' in Regional Services Agreements." Journal of International Economic Law 13: 1103–43.

Aisbett, Emma Kate. 2007. "Bilateral Investment Treaties and Foreign Direct Investment: Correlation versus Causation." CUDARE Working Paper 1032, University of California Berkeley, Berkeley CA.

Antràs, Pol, and Elhanan Helpman. 2004. "Global Sourcing." Journal of Political Economy 112 (3): 552–80.

Baldwin, Richard. 2006. "Globalisation: The Great Unbundling(s)." Contribution to the project "Globalisation Challenges for Europe and Finland," Economic Council of Finland, Helsinki. http://www.vnk.fi/hankkeet/talousneuvosto/tyo-kokoukset/globalisaatioselvitys-9-2006/artikkelit/Baldwin_06-09-20.pdf.

Baldwin, Richard, Simon Evenett, and Patrick Low. 2009. "Beyond Tariffs: Multilateralizing Non-Tariff RTA Commitments." In Multilateralizing Regionalism: Challenges for the Global Trading System, ed. Richard Baldwin and Patrick Low, 79–145. Cambridge, U.K.: Cambridge University Press.

Barth, James R., Juan A. Marchetti, Daniel E. Nolle, and Wanvimol Sawangngoenyuang. 2006. "Foreign Banking: Do Countries' WTO Commitments Match Actual Practices?" WTO Staff Working Paper ERSD-2006-11, World Trade Organization, Geneva.

Berger, Axel, Matthias Busse, Peter Nunnenkamp, and Martin Roy. 2010. "Do Trade and Investment Agreements Lead to More FDI? Accounting for Key Provisions inside the Black Box." WTO Staff Working Paper ERSD-2010-13, World Trade Organization, Geneva.

Beviglia Zampetti, Americo, and Pierre Sauvé. 2006. "Rules of Origin for Services: Economic and Legal Considerations." In The Origin of Goods: Rules of Origin in Regional Trade Agreements, ed. Olivier Cadot, Antoni Estavadeoral, Akiko Suwa Eisenmann, and Thierry Verdier, 114–46. Oxford, U.K.: Oxford University Press.

Bhagwati, Jagdish, Pravin Krishna, and Arvind Panagariya, eds. 1999. Trading Blocs: Alternative Approaches to Analyzing Preferential Trade Agreements. Cambridge, MA: Massachusetts Institute of Technology.

Blonigen, Bruce A. 2005. "A Review of the Empirical Literature on FDI Determinants." NBER Working Paper 11299, National Bureau of Economic Research, Cambridge, MA.

Brainard, S. Lael. 1997. "An Empirical Assessment of the Proximity-Concentration Trade-off between Multinational Sales and Trade." American Economic Review 87: 520–44.

Busse, Matthias, Jens Königer, and Peter Nunnenkamp. 2010. "FDI Promotion through Bilateral Investment Treaties: More Than a Bit?" Review of World Economics 146 (1): 147–77.

Choi, Won-Mog. 2007. "The Present and Future of the Investor-State Dispute Settlement Paradigm." Journal of International Economic Law 10 (3): 725–47.

Dee, Philippa. 2006. "Multinational Corporations and Pacific Regionalism." Pacific Economic Papers 358, Australia–Japan Research Center, Australian National University, Canberra.

Delimatsis, Panagiotis, and Martin Molinuevo. 2008. "Article XVI: Market Access." Max Planck Commentaries on World Trade Law, WTO—Trade in Services 6: 367–426.

Dodge, William S. 2006. "Investor-State Dispute Settlement between Developed Countries: Reflections on the Australia–United States Free Trade Agreement." Vanderbilt Journal of International Law 39 (1): 1–38.

Egger, Peter, and Valeria Merlo. 2007. "The Impact of Bilateral Investment Treaties on FDI Dynamics." World Economy 30: 1536–49.

Egger, Peter, and Michael Pfaffermayr. 2004. "The Impact of Bilateral Investment Treaties on Foreign Direct Investment." Journal of Comparative Economics 32: 788–804.

Emch, Adrian. 2006. "Services Regionalism in the WTO: China's Trade Agreements with Hong Kong and Macao in the Light of Article V(6) GATS." Legal Issues of Economic Integration 33: 351–78.

Estevadeordal, Antoni, and Kati Suominen. 2005. "Rules of Origin in the World Trading System and Proposals for Multilateral Harmonization."

In *Quantitative Methods for Assessing the Effects of Non-Tariff Measures and Trade Facilitation,* ed. Philippa S. Dee and Michael J. Ferrantino, 337–410. Singapore: Asia-Pacific Economic Cooperation (APEC) Secretariat and World Scientific Publishing.

Ferrantino, Michael J., and H. Keith Hall. 2001. "The Direct Effects of Trade Liberalization of Foreign Direct Investment: A Partial Equilibrium Analysis." USITC Office of Economics Working Paper 2001-10-B, U.S. International Trade Commission, Washington, DC.

Fink, Carsten, and Marion Jansen. 2008. "Services Provisions in Regional Trade Agreements: Stumbling Blocks or Building Blocks for Multilateral Liberalization?" In *Multilateralizing Regionalism: Challenges for the Global Trading System,* ed. Richard Baldwin and Patrick Low, 221–61. Cambridge, U.K.: Cambridge University Press.

Fink, Carsten, and Aaditya Mattoo. 2002. "Regional Agreements and Trade in Services." Policy Research Working Paper 2852, World Bank, Washington, DC.

Fink, Carsten, and Martin Molinuevo. 2008. "East Asian Preferential Trade Agreements in Services: Liberalization Content and WTO Rules." *World Trade Review* 7: 641–73.

Fink, Carsten, and Deunden Nikomborirak. 2007. "Rules of Origin in Services: A Case Study of Five ASEAN Countries." Policy Research Working Paper 4130, World Bank, Washington, DC.

Gallagher, Kevin P., and Melissa B. L. Birch. 2006. "Do Investment Agreements Attract Investment? Evidence from Latin America." *Journal of World Investment and Trade* 7 (6): 961–74.

Hallward-Driemeier, Mary. 2003. "Do Bilateral Investment Treaties Attract FDI? Only a Bit . . . and They Could Bite." Policy Research Working Paper 3121, World Bank, Washington, DC.

Helpman, Elhanan. 2006. "Trade, FDI, and the Organization of Firms." *Journal of Economic Literature* 44: 589–630.

Heydon, Kenneth, and Stephen Woolcock. 2009. *The Rise of Bilateralism: Comparing American, European, and Asian Approaches to Preferential Trade Agreements.* Geneva and New York: United Nations University Press.

Hoekman, Bernard. 1996. "Assessing the General Agreement on Trade in Services." In *The Uruguay Round and Developing Countries,* ed. Will Martin and L. Alan Winters, 88–124. Cambridge, U.K.: Cambridge University Press.

Houde, Marie-France, Akshay Kolse-Patil, and Sébastien Miroudot. 2007. "The Interaction between Investment and Services Chapters in Selected Regional Trade Agreements." OECD Trade Policy Working Paper 55, Organisation for Economic Co-operation and Development, Paris.

Hufbauer, Gary, and Jeffrey Schott. 2008. "Fitting Asia-Pacific Agreements into the WTO System." In *Multilateralizing Regionalism: Challenges for the Global Trading System,* ed. Richard Baldwin and Patrick Low, 554–635. Cambridge, U.K.: Cambridge University Press.

Inomata, Satoshi, B. Meng, N. Yamano, and S. Zhu. Forthcoming. "Globalization and Regional Integration: A Study of International Production Networks." Institute of Development Economics, Japan External Trade Organization (IDE-JETRO), Chiba, Japan.

Jarvis, Darryl, Chen Shaofeng, Tan Teck Boon, and Lee Kuan Yew. 2009. "Investment Liberalization in the Association of Southeast Asian Nations: Progress, Regress or Stumbling Bloc?" In *Expansion of Trade and FDI in Asia: Strategic and Policy Challenges,* ed. Julien Chaisse and Philippe Gugler, 138–85. London: Routledge.

Jeon, Bang Nam, and Susan F. Stone. 2000. "Foreign Direct Investment and Trade in the Asian-Pacific Region: Complementarity, Distance and Regional Economic Integration." *Journal of Economic Integration* 15: 460–85.

Jones, Ronald W., and Henryk Kierzkowski. 2001. "A Framework for Fragmentation." In *Fragmentation: New Production Patterns in the World Economy,* ed. Sven W. Arndt and Henryk Kierzkowski, 17–34. Oxford, U.K.: Oxford University Press.

Kaplinsky, Raphael, and Masuma Farooki. 2010. "What Are the Implications for Global Value Chains When the Market Shifts from the North to the South?" Policy Research Working Paper 5205, World Bank, Washington, DC.

Kotschwar, Barbara. 2009. "Mapping Investment Provisions in Regional Trade Agreements: Towards an International Investment Regime?" In *Regional Rules in the Global Trading System,* ed. Antoni Estevadeordal, Kati Suominen, and Robert Teh, 365–417. Cambridge, U.K.: Cambridge University Press.

Lesher, Molly, and Sébastien Miroudot. 2007. "Analysis of the Economic Impact of Investment Provisions in Regional Trade Agreements." *Aussenwirtschaft* 62 (2): 193–232.

Marchetti, Juan A., and Martin Roy. 2008. "Services Liberalization in the WTO and in PTAs." In *Opening Markets for Trade in Services: Countries and Sectors in Bilateral and WTO Negotiations,* ed. Juan A. Marchetti and Martin Roy, 61–112. Cambridge, U.K.: Cambridge University Press.

Mattoo, Aaditya. 2005. "Services in a Development Round: Three Goals and Three Proposals." Policy Research Working Paper 3718, World Bank, Washington, DC.

Miroudot, Sébastien. 2009. "Impact of Investment Provisions in Asian RTAs." In *Expansion of Trade and FDI in Asia: Strategic and Policy Challenges,* ed. Julien Chaisse and Philippe Gugler, 186–211. London: Routledge.

Moran, Theodore H., Edward M. Graham, and Magnus Blomström, eds. 2005. *Does Foreign Direct Investment Promote Development?* Washington, DC: Peterson Institute for International Economics.

Morgan, David. 2008. "Dispute Settlement under PTAs: Political or Legal?" In *Challenges to Multilateral Trade: The Impact of Bilateral, Preferential and Regional Agreements,* ed. Ross P. Buckley, Vai Io Lo, and Laurence Boulle, 241–63. The Hague: Kluwer Law International.

OECD (Organisation for Economic Co-operation and Development). 2005. *International Investment Law: A Changing Landscape.* Paris: OECD.

———. 2008. *OECD Codes of Liberalisation: User's Guide 2008.* Paris: OECD.

Sauvant, Karl P., and Lisa Sachs. 2009. *The Effect of Treaties on Foreign Direct Investment: Bilateral Investment Treaties, Double Taxation Treaties, and Investment Flows.* Oxford, U.K.: Oxford University Press.

Sauvé, Pierre. 2007. "Investment Regulation through Trade Agreements: Lessons from Asia." In *Towards Coherent Policy Framework: Understanding Trade and Investment Linkages,* Economic and Social Commission for Asia and the Pacific (ESCAP), 27–64. Studies in Trade and Investment 62. Geneva and New York: United Nations.

Stephenson, Sherry M. 2002. "Regional versus Multilateral Liberalization of Services." *World Trade Review* 1: 187–209.

UNCTAD (United Nations Conference on Trade and Development). 2006. *Latest Developments in Investor-State Dispute Settlements.* IIA Monitor 4. New York and Geneva: United Nations.

———. 2008. *International Investment Rule-Making: Stocktaking, Challenges and the Way Forward.* UNCTAD Series on International Investment Policies for Development. New York and Geneva: United Nations.

———. 2009a. *The Role of International Investment Agreements in Attracting FDI to Developing Countries.* UNCTAD Series on International Investment Policies for Development. New York and Geneva: United Nations.

———. 2009b. *World Investment Report 2009: Transnational Corporations, Agricultural Production and Development.* New York and Geneva: United Nations.

15

TRADE FACILITATION

Jean-Christophe Maur

Regional cooperation on customs and the facilitation of trade goes hand in hand with preferential trade liberalization. Preferential regimes require specific customs arrangements and some degree of cooperation between partners' border agencies if trade creation between the partners to the agreement is to be achieved. Cooperation between neighboring countries to facilitate international trade goes back to antiquity. Regional trade facilitation efforts are thus not at all a new idea, but they have acquired in recent years a renewed dimension that invites further examination. Two concurrent dynamics are in play: the spread of preferential trade agreements (PTAs), and the rise of an international consensus on the need for modern border management tools.

Recently negotiated PTAs tend to incorporate, in addition to liberalization of trade in goods, numerous provisions on reciprocal regulatory reform and cooperation. Trade facilitation is one of these aspects, as shown in agreements on customs procedures, simplification, harmonization, and cooperation. This represents a significant change from earlier practice, when trade facilitation provisions were nearly absent from PTAs.

Since the late 1990s, new international efforts have been made to promote faster and easier movement of goods across borders, in order to reap the full benefits of the liberalization of policies affecting international trade. Notable in this respect are the initiatives undertaken in the World Trade Organization (WTO), starting in 1998 with a symposium on trade facilitation, and the work of the Asia-Pacific Economic Cooperation (APEC) in this area.[1]

The study of regional trade facilitation efforts is instructive and offers useful lessons from local successes regarding the approach to reform and the implementation of reforms. This chapter presents what we know about these issues. It asks the following questions: What are the factors behind the increase of facilitation provisions in regional PTAs? What are the specific advantages and drawbacks of each type of cooperation? What types of trade facilitation reform should be undertaken regionally?

Regional Trade Facilitation Initiatives: Background

Regional trade facilitation initiatives are numerous and varied. This variation is expressed in the scope of the agreements negotiated and in the institutions created to manage regional cooperation. Historically, cooperation on trade facilitation has taken place not so much in PTAs as through various kinds of bilateral cooperation arrangements, such as transit corridor agreements.

Scope

There is no common definition of trade facilitation in PTAs. An overview of selected agreements shows that trade facilitation is generally defined by the scope of the measures covered in the agreement rather than by a specific definition (box 15.1). This is not to say that there are no elements of commonality between the various definitions. The common elements have to do with procedures related to the importation and exportation of goods (e.g., customs, standards, and technical barriers to trade) and with their enforcement.

Trade facilitation provisions in PTAs vary mainly by the amount of detail and the scale of their aspirations. Certain agreements, such as APEC, are broad in scope and include, for instance, services trade. Detail and ambition seem also to have increased over time, as is shown by recent agreements signed by the United States and the European Union (EU).

As a first step toward understanding the scope of trade facilitation in trade agreements, we can examine the trade facilitation negotiations in the WTO Doha Round. The focus in the WTO is mainly on the revision of three articles of the

---

Box 15.1. Definition and Scope of Trade Facilitation in Selected PTAs

The excerpts that follow are from the texts of the respective preferential trade agreements (PTAs).

Asia-Pacific Economic Cooperation (APEC), 1999

Trade facilitation is defined as "the use of technologies and techniques which will help members to build up expertise, reduce costs and lead to better movement of goods and services."

APEC, 2002

"Trade facilitation generally refers to the simplification, harmonization, use of new technologies, and other measures to address procedural and administrative impediments to trade."

Common Market for Eastern and Southern Africa (COMESA), 1994; Southern African Development Community (SADC), 1996; East African Community (EAC), 2004

The three agreements use the same language: "'Trade facilitation' means the co-ordination and rationalisation of trade procedures and documents relating to the movement of goods from their place of origin to their destination"; "'trade procedures' means activities related to the collection, presentation, processing and dissemination of data and information concerning all activities constituting international trade."

European Union (EU)–Chile, 2003

No definition is given, but the objective of the agreement is "the facilitation of trade in goods through, inter alia, the agreed provisions regarding customs and related matters, standards, technical regulations and conformity assessment procedures, sanitary and phytosanitary measures and trade in wines and spirit drinks and aromatised drinks."

Caribbean Forum of African, Caribbean, and Pacific (ACP) States (CARIFORUM)–EU Economic Partnership Agreement (EPA), 2008

"Customs and trade facilitation" (not defined) covers customs legislation, procedures and administrative cooperation, including the establishment of a joint committee. Detailed provisions address, among other things, joint initiatives, additional facilitation measures for traders with high level of compliance; nondiscrimination and reasonableness principles; application of the EU's single administrative document; risk assessment and simplified measures; binding rulings; use of information technology; transparent and nondiscriminatory licensing of customs brokers; no mandatory use of preshipment inspection; facilitation of transit movement; reduction and simplification of documentation; rapid release of goods; right of appeal; standards of integrity; customs valuation; and relationships with business communities.

Dominican Republic–Central America Free Trade Agreement (CAFTA–DR), 2004

"Customs administration and trade facilitation" is not defined but covers the publication of customs laws, regulations, and general procedures; simplified procedures and rapid release of goods; automation; risk management; cooperation on exchange of information and advance information of regulation changes; express shipment; review and appeal procedures and customs penalties; advance ruling, and capacity building. Trade facilitation measures are only mentioned as they relate to future joint work in the field of standards, cooperation on regulatory issues such as convergence or equivalence of standards, international harmonization, and reliance on supplier's declaration of conformity.[a]

Canada–Costa Rica, 2002

"With the objectives of facilitating trade under this Agreement and cooperating in pursuing trade facilitation initiatives on a multilateral and hemispheric basis, Canada and Costa Rica agree to administer their import and export processes for goods traded under this Agreement on the basis that: (a) procedures be efficient to reduce costs for importers and exporters and simplified where appropriate to achieve such efficiencies; (b) procedures be based on any international trade instruments or standards to which the Parties have agreed; (c) entry procedures be transparent to ensure predictability for importers and exporters; (d) measures to facilitate trade also support mechanisms to protect persons through effective enforcement of and compliance with national requirements; (e) the personnel and procedures involved in those processes reflect high standards of integrity; (f) the development of significant modifications to procedures of a Party include, in advance of implementation, consultations with the representatives of the trading community of that Party; (g) procedures be based on risk assessment principles to focus compliance efforts on transactions that merit attention, thereby promoting effective use of resources and providing incentives for voluntary compliance with the obligations to importers and exporters; and (h) the Parties encourage cooperation, technical assistance and the exchange of information, including information on best practices, for the purpose of promoting the application of and compliance with the trade facilitation measures agreed upon under this Agreement."

Source: Author's compilation.
a. The scope of "customs administration" provisions in the U.S.–Chile (2004) and U.S.–Peru (2009) agreements is nearly identical (under the title of "customs administration") to that in the CAFTA–DR agreement, except that capacity building is not mentioned.

General Agreement on Tariffs and Trade (GATT)—dealing, briefly, with freedom of transit, fees and formalities, and procedures—and the emphasis is on rules and regulations, rather than on procedures (see box 15.2). Infrastructural aspects and services related to international trade are either excluded or are dealt with in different negotiations. A second approach is to refer to other international instruments, such as the Revised Kyoto Convention of the

Trade facilitation became a topic of discussion for the World Trade Organization (WTO) at the Singapore Ministerial Conference in December 1996, when members directed the Council for Trade in Goods "to undertake exploratory and analytical work . . . on the simplification of trade procedures in order to assess the scope for WTO rules in this area" (Singapore Ministerial Declaration, para. 21).

After several years of exploratory work, in July 2004 WTO members formally agreed to launch negotiations on trade facilitation on the basis of modalities contained in Annex D of the so-called "July package." Under this mandate, members are directed to clarify and improve General Agreement on Tariffs and Trade (GATT) Article V (freedom of transit), Article VIII (fees and formalities connected with importation and exportation), and Article X (publication and administration of trade regulations). The negotiations are also aimed at enhancing technical assistance and capacity building in this area and improving effective cooperation between customs and other appropriate authorities on trade facilitation and customs compliance issues.

To date, members have submitted a great number of proposals under the mandate, and these provide the basis for the ongoing negotiations. The negotiations are to be completed according to the overall Doha Development Agenda timeline.

Source: World Trade Organization.

World Customs Organization (WCO) and the standards of various specialized agencies and international organizations.[2] A third approach is to avoid all a priori definitions and to embrace whichever definition is provided in a given agreement.

In this chapter, trade facilitation encompasses all measures (often, but not always, enforced at the border) that can reduce the cost of policing international trade. Governments need to control international trade in various ways in order to manage externalities or meet core policy objectives such as consumer protection, national security, and revenue generation. The economic challenge is to ensure that such policies are enforced in the most efficient way. As discussed in the next section, this does not necessarily imply the removal of trade protection, but it does involve the minimization of costs that are directly related to the operations of international trade supply chains.

In the context of regional integration, deciding on trade facilitation reform policies involves the following two steps:

1. Identify the most cost-effective policies for regulating imports and exports and ways of implementing these policies. From an economic perspective, under what circumstances are regulations optimal, given market failures affecting the supply of trade facilitation services and regulations? Because markets are imperfect, governmental intervention is sometimes needed to deliver the optimal social outcome. When market failures cannot be remedied at the national level, addressing them becomes a transnational issue, and collective action is needed. Regional solutions should be sought when the failing markets correspond to a well-defined set of nations.

2. Determine which of these trade facilitation policies are best implemented at the regional level. When do regional approaches offer better and more cost-effective prospects than other means (regional, unilateral, or multilateral) for carrying out trade facilitation reform? A subsidiarity test needs to be applied: actions to achieve a given policy objective should be taken at the lowest level of government capable of effectively addressing the problem at hand (Sauvé and Zampetti 2000). Ideally, this level of action should correspond to the level affected by the need for the regional good—that is, the political jurisdiction should match the economic domain of benefits. Thus, the most appropriate participants will partake in the provision of regional trade facilitation, and transaction costs will be economized (Arce and Sandler 2002).

Cooperation for Regional Trade Facilitation

Trade facilitation reform is often a regional issue. By definition, the crossing of borders involves two trading partners, and the improvement of transport conditions often requires some form of regional infrastructure hub. Thus, a wide variety of regional cooperation efforts for trade facilitation exist, as described next.

Transit corridor management. Many regional organizations have been set up to guarantee the smooth and rapid flow of goods from gateway ports to the hinterland. Corridor management agreements typically deal with technical standards for vehicles, mutual recognition of drivers' licenses, and market access by transport services. The management structures require cooperation among private and public sector stakeholders operating in several countries and on issues that range from streamlining of regulatory requirements to improvement of infrastructure. An example of successful corridor management is the Trans-Kalahari corridor in southwestern Africa (box 15.3).

Sanitary and phytosanitary protection. Coordinated action by countries is required to prevent the spread of diseases borne by agents that easily cross borders. For example, Tanzania and its neighbors in the Southern African

---

Box 15.3. The Trans-Kalahari Corridor

The Trans-Kalahari Corridor (TKC) is a road route between South Africa's Gauteng province and Namibia's Walvis Bay, via Botswana. The corridor, which opened in 1998, replaced a longer route through western South Africa. In 1999, through the efforts of the Walvis Bay Corridor group—a public-private partnership that aims to make Namibia's Walvis Bay Port an international gateway to and from the South Africa Customs Union (SACU)—a rehabilitation project was carried out. The route already had fairly good connectivity and required a relatively small amount of capital investment. The main work program of the TKC Management Group—consisting of representatives from transport operators, infrastructure and transport authorities, port and customs authorities, freight forwarders, and other interested businesses—thus focused on facilitating agreements between the three member countries that would promote the simplification of border-crossing procedures. To this end, the TKC Management Group established partnerships with the customs agencies of Botswana, Namibia, and South Africa.

In August 2003 the group embarked on the pilot phase of a program to replace all existing transport documents with a single administrative document (SAD). In November 2003 the ministers of transport of Botswana, Namibia, and South Africa signed a broad memorandum of understanding that formally binds the signatories and the private sector to a program to deal with cross-border transport and trade issues such as border management, customs control, traffic regulation, and road transport policies.

Since these agreements were put in place, border processing times in the corridor have been cut from an average of 45 minutes to 10–20 minutes. Cost savings from the reduction in border delays are estimated at approximately US$2.6 million per year. Operators now move approximately 620,000 tons annually along the corridor, representing about 65 percent of expected capacity. By contrast, in 1999, before the improvements, only 15 percent of the route's capacity was utilized.

In February 2008 the Namibian roads authority announced that it would invest up to 310 million Namibian dollars in upgrading road infrastructure along the portion of the corridor that extends from Okahandja and Karibib. The work entails widening the road and was expected to take four years to complete. On February 8, 2008, the governments of Namibia and Botswana signed a memorandum of understanding concerning the creation of a new dry port facility at Walvis Bay that will be operated by Botswana. The acquisition of land in Namibia by Botswana under a 50-year lease is being carried out as part of the regional integration initiative of the Southern African Development Community (SADC). The initiative will increase use of the Trans-Kalahari Corridor, and it would probably not have been economically feasible before the regulatory overhaul of the corridor.

Source: Author's compilation from the following sources: M. Madakufamba, "Towards Seamless SADC Transport Corridors," *The Namibian*, March 3, 2008, http://www.namibian.com.na/index.php?id=28&tx_ttnews[tt_news]=48259&no_cache=1; A. Shilongo, "NAM, Bots Sign MoU," *New Era*, February 11, 2008; C. Tjatindi, "N$310-M Earmarked for Trans Kalahari Corridor Rehabilitation," *New Era*, February 7, 2008; U.S. Agency for International Development (USAID), "Trans-Kalahari Corridor Exemplifies Collaboration," USAID, Washington, DC., 2006; Arnold 2006; World Bank 2005; Adzibgey, Kunaka, and Mitiku 2007.

Development Community (SADC) have agreed on a five-year program of vaccination, surveillance, and control of animal movements across borders to combat highly contagious bovine diseases that persist in Tanzania (Tanzania 2005).

Regional standards and accreditation bodies. Accreditation bodies ensure that standards certification laboratories are able to assess conformance with standards. In many countries, the national standards infrastructure is not well developed, and the economy is too small to support such institutions. To overcome this problem, Brunei Darussalam (to give one illustration) has concluded an agreement with the Singapore Accreditation Council.

Guarantees. Regional guarantee and insurance mechanisms enable transporters to reduce costs by avoiding duplication and the need to make cash deposits. The Common Market for Eastern and Southern Africa (COMESA) has introduced a "yellow card," a third-party regional motor vehicle insurance scheme that allows traders to purchase insurance covering transport in the region (Arvis 2005). COMESA launched in 2010 a regional customs bond guarantee system that will be initially operational in Burundi, Kenya, Rwanda, and Uganda. Regional guarantees (to secure the payment of duty and taxes) can compensate

for the failure of national organizations to set up such systems, hampered as they are by the small scale of operations, underdeveloped national financial services, and the unwillingness of international insurers to face the political and commercial risks of developing markets. In Uganda the cost of customs bonds is estimated to amount to 4 percent of import and export costs. Uganda's Integrated Framework diagnostic study (Uganda 2006) recommends a regional approach toward reducing the incidence of these costs.

One-stop border posts (OSBP). Joint management of border posts on each side of the border can be the source of many benefits. In southern Africa, TradeMark Southern Africa is providing support for the establishment of several OSBPs along the North-South corridor, a major transit project.[3] Countries can align their procedures so as to ensure streamlined movement of goods across the border. Harmonization of some procedures, data exchange, unified documentation, and mutual recognition of findings allow the elimination of cost duplication. The sharing of facilities such as scanners and weighbridges is a potential additional source of cost saving. Finally, joint operations may enhance the overall efficiency of border agencies (information sharing, for example, improves intelligence) and may foster regulatory changes that will facilitate trade, such as allowing forms of extraterritoriality or the adoption of international norms.

Economic Dimensions of Trade Facilitation

The economic impact of facilitation of trade flows at the regional level is twofold. First, preferential trade facilitation measures have static efficiency effects because of better allocation of factors. Second, they have more systemic and dynamic effects that are associated with imperfect competition settings. Schiff and Winters (2002) note that "in the presence of economies of scale or inter-country externalities, market solutions are generally sub-optimal, and failing to cooperate can be very costly. However, regional cooperation is not the same as regional integration, and, indeed, there is generally rather little connection between them."[4]

Static Effects

Assuming for now that trade facilitation efforts are conducted on a preferential basis, what would be the trade and welfare effects of liberalization? The answer hinges on whether the implicit protection afforded to domestic industries by higher trade costs prior to liberalization generates domestic rents.

The first type of rent to be considered is tax revenue, and here different situations prevail according to the country. Sometimes border fees such as consular or transit fees are imposed with a revenue objective in mind—that is, fees are higher than what would be strictly necessary to cover the costs of services such as maintenance of transit corridors or the operational costs of border agencies. The Arab Republic of Egypt abolished its consular fees in the context of its regional agreements with the European Union (EU), COMESA, and the Greater Arab Free Trade Area (GAFTA). Although no cost estimates were made of the revenue that had been generated by these fees, Egypt acknowledged that the costs of services rendered had been only a fraction of the fee levied.[5]

The second type of rent is that captured by vested public and private interests. Lack of facilitation provides scope for such interests to levy surcharges on importers and exporters or to provide poor-quality services, resulting in delay, loss of goods, and corruption. In some instances, rents are directly created by the public sector: corrupt officials use the complexity and uncertainty of rules to extract "speed money" from traders. Exclusive licensing of some operations at the border, as illustrated by compulsory use of customs brokers, stifles competitive provision of services

and results in inefficiencies. In other cases, the complexity and lack of transparency of administrative processes indirectly favor the emergence of operators that can work the system and charge fees for facilitation services.

The existence of rents may create opposition to reform. For example, in a small project funded by the World Bank, an international mail service that offers highly simplified procedures for small exporters, Exporta Facil, was set up in Peru. The exporter using this service does not need to use a customs agent, logistics agent, or freight forwarder or to consolidate the merchandise, and even the packaging is provided for. The exporter only needs to go to a post office and complete the export declaration for the tax agency, using the Internet (Toledano and Ansón 2008). According to the project team, private customs agents put up some resistance to the initiative. A compromise was reached that set the maximum value of the packages to be exported at US$2,000, but with the proviso that the maximum value would be revised a year later. (The plan is to raise the maximum to US$10,000.)

The other effect of domestic rents is well known from the economic analysis of discriminatory trade liberalization: it can lead to trade diversion and to negative welfare effects if the loss of domestic rents to foreign exporters is not compensated by the benefits from lower prices resulting from the liberalization. In many situations, however, there are no such domestic rents, or they are small, and so the liberalization effects of trade facilitation, even on a preferential basis, will necessarily be welfare enhancing. This is an important difference from tariff liberalization, where the risks of trade diversion are much higher. Trade facilitation lowers trade costs and benefits the consumers of imported goods because larger and more affordable quantities of goods are available.

Under a preferential facilitation regime (e.g., a mutual recognition agreement on procedures, or a specific authorized traders' regime that gives some form of preferential treatment to exporters from the PTA partner country), the sources of supply may shift from the most efficient world supplier (if there were no discrimination) to the most favored one (the PTA partner). Trade facilitation, however, is often nondiscriminatory, eliminating the risk of trade diversion.

Even though the overall effects of trade facilitation are positive, the reforms can produce losers: the external trade partners that may be excluded from the preferential regime; the economic actors that had benefited from high trade costs; domestic producers that were protected from international competition; and private sector interests that were able to extract rents from the complexity of the trade environment.

Dynamic Effects

There are two main dimensions to the benefits of transnational cooperation, corresponding to the specific market or institutional failures faced by countries: (a) the realization of economies of scale through, for example, elimination of duplication and increased competition, and (b) the avoidance of negative externalities and the creation of positive externalities among neighbors.

Economies of Scale

Given the many interventions and parties in the international transport of goods, and perhaps the need to cross several borders, there is plenty of scope for trade operators to encounter cost duplication. Because an important portion of these costs is fixed, eliminating duplication will enable efficiency gains for firms and will allow smaller-scale operators to access export markets—an important consideration for developing countries.[6]

Duplication arises because similar requirements must be met repeatedly, but also because national rules differ, which increases search costs and associated uncertainties and creates further opportunities for rent seeking and corruption.[7] COMESA has reduced duplication through a regional license for carriers, obviating the need to pay for multiple licenses (Schiff and Winters 2003). Inspection of goods, if carried out in different places on each side of a border, also delays trade, and different national regulatory requirements force traders to meet two standards instead of one. To illustrate, in Tanzania, registration requirements for agrochemical pesticides are burdensome and subject to high fees, yet Tanzania's market for such pesticides is small, and meanwhile, equivalent and more efficient products have already been registered and tested in neighboring Kenya (Tanzania 2005).[8]

Methods of reducing duplication costs may involve:

- *Forming a common market within a customs union.* Intraunion borders are removed, and external borders are managed on behalf of the union.
- *Harmonization* through the use of identical templates and information fields for documentation. (Simplification of documentation, often pursued along with harmonization, is another measure for reducing duplication, although it is not intrinsically regional.)
- *Mutual assistance among authorities,* through meetings of experts, exchange of information and data, and assistance with extraterritorial investigations.[9]
- *Mutual recognition* of rulings (e.g., on customs control measures in transit operations) and of certification and testing.

- *Sharing of facilities* such as border posts and, possibly, gateway facilities such as airports and ports.

An important caveat is that some aspects of these cooperation mechanisms are not necessarily regional or bilateral and may be achieved multilaterally. For instance, harmonization is not necessarily optimal at the regional level; more broadly shared international standards may be more efficient. Still, a large part of these extra costs may be better addressed at the regional level, by a limited number of countries because of political-economy considerations and the complexity of arrangements such as mutual recognition.

Economies of scale can also be realized on administrative procedures and on the private services that deliver trade facilitation. Because the procedures and services that facilitate trade can involve large fixed, and possibly sunk, costs, full economies of scale in administrative procedures and services for international trade transactions may not be realized at the country level, especially in small and poor countries. It is unclear to what extent there is a scale barrier to efficient border administration that employs modern practices such as single windows and risk management. The extent to which economies of scale can be realized depends on the presence and size of fixed costs in the management of trade transactions. If these fixed costs are low, it is unlikely that regional economies of scale will be large enough to justify complex regional cooperation mechanisms. Customs reform projects have been shown to be sustainable at the country level (Moïsé 2005), but when fixed costs are important, it may be more cost-effective to share them regionally rather than incur them alone. It is then important to identify where the fixed costs lie.

For Finland, Norway, and Sweden, a motivation for entering into cross-border cooperation agreements (starting in 1960) was division of labor; that is, sharing of the cost of managing the 1,630-kilometer-long border between Norway and Sweden and the 739-kilometer-long border between Norway and Finland.[10] Another indication that small administrations may not be able to afford all the material and infrastructure necessary is seen in the current WTO negotiations; several members have called on "small, vulnerable economies" to undertake a regional approach toward implementing certain expected WTO commitments that will require capacity building and have made a specific submission regarding regional trade facilitation enquiry points.[11]

Standards and backbone services. Beyond customs operations, there are perhaps more acute problems in the implementation of standards. Many developing countries are too small to offer the full range of conformity assessment for standards, partly because of problems with access to accreditation. Small countries should thus benefit from regional integration (World Bank 2005).

Setting up regional certification and accreditation bodies, or opening regional markets for such bodies, could be a way to provide cheaper and better testing, building on scale economies and comparative advantage. Regional approaches can make sense for countries facing serious shortages in technical skills, which can be an issue for modern trade facilitation techniques.[12] For instance, Cambodia, the Lao People's Democratic Republic, and Vietnam are all deficient in standards infrastructure, and lack of certification and accreditation is a common problem (Haddad 2008).

Once again, solutions to national constraints are not necessarily regional; the opening of certification and accreditation markets to international companies may be enough to remedy the absence of national providers of such services. In some instances, however, market openness may not be enough, and access to regional providers (implying open access to testing and certification in neighboring countries and perhaps some form of formal arrangement) might be needed.

Another sector in which size can be an important constraint is the backbone services that are crucial to trade transactions: finance and insurance, transport and logistics, handling, measurement services, and communication services. The supply of these services for trade transactions can require a scale of production that extends beyond national borders.[13] Insurance and financial services (letters of credit, guarantees, insurance, and the like) constitute key inputs for the capacity to trade internationally. National operators in developing countries may not be able to provide these services, or only at noncompetitive prices.

According to the European Bank for Reconstruction and Development (EBRD 2003), national banking systems do not pool enough capital to underwrite trade transactions.[14] Small firms often lack access to the financial guarantees for payments that would allow them to export.[15]

Fixed costs and geographic factors confer natural monopoly characteristics on some modes of transport, particularly rail and maritime at the national level, that can be mitigated or even eliminated in a broader regional setting. For instance, regional transport hubs help realize economies of scale and create extra competition.[16] For freight transport, the emergence of multimodal hubs, generally located near important existing air, sea, or rail infrastructure, generates important economies of scale, through higher utilization of infrastructure, as well as efficiency gains (compared with point-to-point routes) through competition between modes of transport (Müller-Jentsch 2003). Transport hubs depend as much, and probably more, on the liberalization of regional transport services (through, e.g., relaxation of cabotage restrictions or expansion of air traffic rights) than on the availability of infrastructure. Indeed, transport hubs tend to be geographically mobile, suggesting the secondary importance of infrastructure as a determinant of their location.

Regional Cross-Border Externalities

Regional agreements can serve as a policy coordination mechanism to help prevent individual countries from adopting national strategies that fall short of optimal global outcomes. Lack of coordination is in some instances linked to externality problems—problems that affect the welfare of individual countries but cannot be handled by these countries alone. Although the distinction between positive and negative externalities is not really important from a strict analytical point of view, it may be useful from a policy viewpoint because each may raise different implementation challenges. Positive (or negative) externalities arise when actions by one or more countries create benefits (impose costs) that are not taken into account in the decision to perform that action. In other words, the private cost to the country that originates the action does not equal its social cost.

Negative externalities. Countries that carry on transit trade can be tempted to use trade-restricting policies such as setting revenue-maximizing fees for transit, imposing compulsory transit routes and checkpoints, limiting access to foreign transporters, or requiring securitized convoys. Fees and requirements may exceed the cost of the services provided (use of roads, provision of security, and so on) or go beyond the measures strictly necessary for secure transit.[17] In the worst cases, the motives behind these policies are protectionist; often, countries simply fail to consider the negative externalities imposed on neighbors.[18] The risk of negative spillovers is particularly important when alternative transit routes are few, as is frequently the case in Africa.[19] Domestic transport infrastructure constraints often have regional implications, justifying, from an economic perspective, regional ports or airport hubs. Landlocked countries depend on the quality of their neighbors' infrastructure.

To illustrate, Uganda's most important transport and trade facilitation issues are outside the country's direct control (Uganda 2006). Tanzania and Kenya, its coastal neighbors, offer poor trade facilitation—the Kenyan port of Mombasa, which handles 95 percent of Uganda's external trade traffic, is congested; transit bond regimes are financially burdensome; and rail transit does not offer a competitive alternative to poor road transport and expensive pipeline transport.[20] As Schiff and Winters (2002) note, this type of externality is often asymmetric: landlocked countries stand to gain a great deal from better transit, but the benefits for the coastal partner (i.e., improved access to the internal market) are much smaller. In practice, landlocked countries have not gained much from participation in regional trade agreements, probably because important trade obstacles have persisted (Yang and Gupta 2005).

Standards and phytosanitary (SPS) measures provide a further example of possible market failure. As was discussed earlier, weak or absent enforcement of SPS in one country can mean that negative consequences spill over to neighbors.

Positive externalities. Like the elimination of negative externalities, the creation of positive externalities such as network effects may justify regional intervention. Transport, electronic, and other information networks play an increasingly important role in trade facilitation reform. We distinguish here between two main forms of positive externalities: the establishment of shared facilities, and the creation of networks.

There are benefits for neighboring countries in joining existing networks rather than developing their own systems or multiplying bilateral channels of communication and information exchange. Southern African countries, for example, are planning to exchange electronic information on transit cargo on the basis of a system called Asycuda++. (Mozambique, however, has a proprietary system that is incompatible with its neighbors' software; see Mozambique 2004.) At the heart of network externalities lie the notions of adoption of common standards for operation and interoperability. By joining networks, countries may gain access to several markets while having to pay the cost of plugging into this network only once. This is a consideration in favor of adopting international standards, which will be accepted by all other countries belonging to the same network of standards.

The adoption of standards for border procedures may lead to regional practices that differ from internationally accepted norms. A good practice therefore is to base regional standards on international ones. Europe is pushing for the use of the single administrative document (SAD), but the SAD itself is based on an internationally accepted standard, the UN layout key. There is a solidly established culture of international customs and product standards that provides strong incentives for adopting these in regional trade agreements.

The European Union has developed several regional networks facilitating trade: the New Computerized Transit System (NCTS) for electronic transmissions, the Galileo satellite system for global navigation (GALILEO), and the Trans-European Networks on Transport. Similar aspirations are seen in trade action plans in developing countries, such as Uganda's recent Diagnostic Trade Integration Study (DTIS), which emphasizes the use of electronic data interchange (EDI) at the regional level; the development of a regional cargo-tracking system; and the interconnection of the East African Community's customs electronic systems (Uganda 2006). Transport hubs, mentioned above, also create positive externalities, such as access to multimodal transport platforms.

Positive externalities—beyond the realization of economies of scale—also arise from the provision of international finance and insurance. International provision of such services offers the possibility of mutualizing risks across a region and contributes to positive network effects, such as linking banks that do not usually do business with each other and diffusing skills through the network. The principle of mutualization is applicable to other trade-related financial instruments that are specifically relevant to trade facilitation and transit, such as guarantees for payment of taxes and insurance. COMESA, for example, plans to set up a regional transit bond scheme. Regional guarantees (to secure the payment of duty and taxes) can address the failure of national organizations to set up such systems. In Uganda, the cost of customs bonds is estimated to add up to 4 percent to import and export costs, and one recommendation of the Integrated Framework diagnostic study is to use a regional approach to reduce the incidence of these costs (Uganda 2006). Arvis (2005) argues that the lack of a regional customs guarantee explains why transit initiatives in developing countries to replicate the success of the TIR transit system have failed so far (see also Arvis 2010 for a detailed discussion of transit systems and the TIR).[21]

Systemic Effects of Regional Trade Facilitation

Trade facilitation is not an end in itself; rather, it is a means of fostering regional integration, and it can play a critical complementary role in regional integration strategies.

Trade facilitation as complementary to regional integration. PTAs create a potential loophole for tax evasion if producers and products outside the preferential agreement are able to take advantage of the exemption regime. It is therefore in the nature of PTAs to include provisions related to customs implementation and cooperation. First, regional PTAs require the establishment of a specific customs regime for the processing of goods benefiting from the preferential treatment. This requires, among other things, the provision of additional information and documentation by traders and additional verification work by customs. The most prominent implementation feature of regional trade agreements is seen in the criteria set out in rules of origin.[22] Second, enforcement of customs control at border is likely to become stricter as the trade tax base is reduced by the liberalization and because of the need to combat the incentives for tax evasion.

Paradoxically, PTAs may complicate rather than facilitate trade, in that they create additional administrative requirements for exporters who wish to benefit from the preferential regime. The costs of compliance are nontrivial and could amount to a significant share of trade. For instance, the compliance costs of rules of origin were estimated at around 2 percent of trade value for the North American Free Trade Agreement (NAFTA) and 6.8 percent for the EU (Cadot et al. 2006).

It could be argued that in the more complex environment of regional trade, PTAs create incentives for more efficient enforcement of customs procedures. To maximize market access, the authorities of the exporting country have an incentive to help the importing country manage its border controls efficiently. This can include mutual assistance in investigations and exchange of information.

The existence of complementarities between regional integration and trade facilitation is even more evident when a broader view of trade facilitation is taken. The narrow focus on border management enforcement was the main approach adopted in the older generation of PTAs (Moïsé 2005). Modern PTAs go beyond the promotion of intraregional trade; they are intended to further trade liberalization in general.

Interplay between regional and multilateral trade facilitation. Two concerns about PTAs are whether they are welfare enhancing and whether they represent a natural path toward broader liberalization. In both cases, the gold standard is multilateral liberalization. What is the role of regional trade facilitation provisions in the broader trade liberalization context? To what extent do regional trade facilitation provisions discriminate against third parties? Do they contribute to the "spaghetti bowl" problem?

As noted earlier, trade facilitation provisions in PTAs are likely to be nondiscriminatory, and any reform undertaken in the context of a specific agreement would be expected to benefit the rest of the world. The nondiscriminatory aspect of trade facilitation is apparent in the language of most agreements, which generally outline universal reforms. In any case, many dimensions of trade facilitation are, in the terminology of public goods, nonexcludable: for instance, once simplification or transparency is achieved, it does not make sense (and may not be feasible, in most cases) to exclude other countries from benefiting from it. Similarly, the improvement of border agencies' equipment through information technology yields benefits for all traders. In theory, it is always possible to manage access to such facilities, by, for example, charging different access fees, but in practice, this not done—it is probably pointless and may run afoul of WTO disciplines.

Some modern techniques of trade facilitation rely on special and differential treatment for specific categories of traders. This is particularly the case in the areas of risk management and authorized trader approaches to border management. Security is a growing concern in international trade, and PTAs may be used to set up specific regimes not accessible to all traders. Recent PTAs negotiated by the United States, for instance, contain obligations for more favorable treatment of express shipments, especially with respect to expedited clearance times. These measures bear a distinct risk of creating some form of discrimination that excludes countries or traders that do not have the capacity or possess the correct criteria to access these simplified regimes. In particular, it may be difficult for companies in developing countries to receive preferred trader status.

Although efforts to further simplify and speed border crossing should be encouraged, when special regimes are required, there is a need to be careful about the implications of creating incentives for rent seeking and for exclusion of certain operators. In the specific case of developing countries, firms may have more problems in complying with the requirements of authorized traders because their shipments are less regular or because they cannot put together the documentation necessary for accreditation. Similarly, risk management profiles may single out shipments from particular origins or in certain industries in a way that may be detrimental for countries exporting these goods. Parties to a PTA could also discriminate against third parties by granting preferential access to their most efficient screening facilities to PTA members. In fact, however, there is little evidence in existing PTAs of preferential treatment in trade facilitation.

On balance, it appears that trade facilitation provisions in PTAs are likely to impart additional momentum to reform and to benefit not only the PTA members but other traders, as well. In some dimensions of trade facilitation, nevertheless, discrimination remains a distinct possibility. For example, certain features of trade facilitation regimes could discriminate by type of operator or source of trade and thus undermine broader regional or multilateral liberalization. There seems, however, to be no evidence of this happening on a large scale now. Regional trade facilitation provisions therefore do not seem to pose a risk of undermining multilateral efforts, and PTAs could, indeed, complement the multilateral process.

Balancing the Benefits and the Costs of Implementation

The costs associated with trade facilitation reforms and projects are not confined to the costs of regional infrastructure (which are not intrinsically different from those in a nonregional setting) but also include the cost of regional coordination. The discussion focuses on the latter.

Regional coordination is not cost free. Anecdotal evidence suggests that the transaction costs of coordination rise sharply with the number of countries participating in a PTA. A review of transit corridors (Arnold 2006), for instance, finds that corridor management in large regional agreements has been difficult to achieve and has sometimes led to more cumbersome rules, compared with (probably more nimble) cooperation agreements and bilateral trade agreements. For trade facilitation, there may be many stakeholders involved, as well as numerous agencies on each side of the border that may need to be coordinated.

The heterogeneity of national interests is often an additional complicating factor. Border controls pursue multiple objectives—collecting revenues, guaranteeing the security of the home territory, protecting consumers, and, of course, facilitating trade. The nature of these objectives and the priority accorded them varies by country.

Some types of coordinated trade reform might make it more difficult to accommodate such particularities.[23] For instance, adoption of a strong harmonization rule in relation to customs information systems might bind all participating countries to use identical technology, leaving less space for adaptation to individual circumstances.

Finally, and linked to all these points, some forms of coordination can limit regulatory innovation at the country level. Given the changing business and economic context within which international trade transactions take place, it is by no means clear that what looks like an optimal regulation today will necessarily be seen as such in five years' time.[24] Governments can change national regulations relatively easily in the light of new circumstances, but the same is not true of regional or multilateral rules: consensus among all parties is usually required. International coordination of reforms can therefore run the risk of introducing too much rigidity and regulatory "stickiness." This would reduce the overall amount of regulatory experimentation and could retard the rate of learning and discovery. Flexible forms of regional cooperation may help lower the costs of future renegotiations and amendments.

Delivering Regional Public Goods

The existence of externalities points to the need to coordinate actions and ensure the delivery of public goods.

Regional cooperation yields mutual ("social") benefits that exceed the individual ("private") benefits that countries would derive by acting alone. Even in the rare cases in which a given country would not benefit or would lose from the cooperative action, it should be possible to compensate that country with part of the extra benefits generated by solving the externality problem. There are, however, situations in which this may not be possible—for example, where there are important transaction costs, as mentioned above, or where information is imperfect and countries may not fully realize the size of the gains from trade facilitation or may not be able to agree on the exact scope of reform to be carried out jointly.

Going some way toward solving the imperfect information problem are simple measures that may sow the seeds of future cooperation through generation and exchange of information. Such measures include raising awareness among groups of stakeholders to strengthen coalitions of reformers; creating formal or informal regional bodies (e.g., expert committees for government officials; regional trade associations) where stakeholders can meet and exchange ideas; and supporting research and analysis of issues to inform policy makers.

The nature of cooperation will be dictated by the type of regional trade facilitation policy needed. Depending on the type of policy, each participating country's level of contribution will differ. The first and most common way of producing a regional good is by the summation of countries' efforts: each country needs to contribute a similar amount to the joint effort. A regional agreement to harmonize border procedures and adopt common documentation is an example. The more countries that engage in harmonizing, the higher will be the benefits for the entire region because of the resulting access to a broader overall market. A variation of this situation is when countries' contribution levels are different. Facilities for which economies of scale are important, such as regional guarantees or testing laboratories, also need contributions from all countries in the region, but these may be uneven, related to the capacity of each country to contribute.

A second type of regional public good is produced by tackling the failures arising from the "weakest link." The inability of one country to adopt trade facilitation measures may have negative spillovers on neighbors, which then have an interest in assisting their weaker neighbor to upgrade its capacity. An example is the enforcement of rules of origin and other customs regulations in a regional PTA. Traders will rapidly "port-shop" to determine which customs authorities are the more lenient and whether this leniency justifies the added cost of rerouting goods through a specific border. Even relatively small differences in the level of implementation can create sizable losses for the region in the form of forgone tax revenue, lowered standards, and increased threats to health or security. Even worse, when border tax revenues are an important source of government revenue, there may be an incentive to practice beggar-my-neighbor tactics by attracting imports from partner countries in a PTA.

Finally, some public goods important for regional facilitation do not need to be supplied by each country; gateways such as ports, pipelines, and airport hubs can be used by all countries in the region but are not needed in each country. This does not have to be major infrastructure—specific equipment may also be shared among a group of countries. In such cases the challenge is for countries to agree not to duplicate efforts and instead to concentrate on a best-shot effort.

In summary, the promotion of regional trade facilitation requires a careful analysis of the types of regional efforts that are needed. The PTA provisions will need to reflect the various forms of cooperation that are required to supply the regional public goods. In some instances, coordination of policies will have to be the prime objective; in other circumstances, implementation will have to be carried out in only a subset of countries; and in still others, countries will have to make tangible contributions involving cross-border transfers of expertise, and funds will have to be designated. Finally, for some regional efforts, all of the above actions will be needed.

Institutional Arrangements for Facilitation of Regional Trade

The question of regional public goods raises implicitly the question of what institutional format would be best suited for delivering them. In fact, there is a varied array of regional institutional arrangements designed to tackle trade facilitation problems.

Bilateral cooperation agreements in the fields of customs, standards, and transit are common. These agreements aim primarily at improving specific areas of enforcement and generally have narrow objectives. Some recent agreements push new forms of cooperation. For instance, the United States and China have an agreement permitting U.S. officers stationed in China to perform inspections related to standards. This concept is similar to that of the container security initiative, under which U.S. customs officers are stationed in participating ports. In the case of the EU, customs cooperation agreements seem to be confined to those between large trading partners and developed or emerging partners, and their aim is essentially to develop advanced forms of cooperation.

Transit corridor agreements are ad hoc regional agreements that have the single objective of managing international trade corridors. They take very different forms, and, as shown in Arnold (2006), no single model prevails. The corridor arrangements are very much works in progress and have been influenced by the problems they were meant to address. In particular, the role of governments in corridor arrangements varies greatly, from that of sole parties to being only one actor. The active involvement of the private sector is an interesting feature of such arrangements.

A distinction can be made between shallow and deep PTAs. The former contain only very limited provisions related to customs enforcement of preferences, whereas the latter tend to increasingly include extensive trade facilitation provisions. The big differences between them and ad hoc cooperation agreements are that in deep PTAs other sectors are liberalized in parallel and the institutions behind the PTA tend to be more complex—providing, for example, for dispute settlement—and to be closer to political decision centers.

Customs unions enable a more advanced form of trade facilitation cooperation. The fundamental tenet of a customs union is the uniformity of the external tariff. This has implications for customs management: the quality of border enforcement has to be identical across the customs union to ensure that the weaknesses of one party do not undermine the tax collections of others (through the diversion of imports to the border where enforcement is the least stringent) or hinder the fulfillment of other border control objectives, since not all countries in the union may be concerned about the same issues.

Finally, there are single common markets, such as the EU. Although the experience of the EU is far removed from some of the preoccupations of developing countries, it shows that even in the context of a common market, where internal borders are dismantled, the management of external borders remains challenging, and the integration of border procedures is accompanied by significant reforms.

We next examine in more detail two forms of regional arrangements that are most relevant for regional trade facilitation reform: transit corridors and PTAs.

Transit Corridors

Access to global trade is an important development challenge, both for individual countries and for neighbors wishing to access their markets. This challenge is especially important for landlocked countries and land-based crossing of borders. Experience shows that trade facilitation projects and reforms are complex to design and carry out and that they are not always successful because they require the implementation of a wide range of consistent measures in several sectors and countries.

According to Arnold (2006), the source for much of the information in this section,

> So far, one of the most effective approaches is to focus on trade corridors. Indeed, one salient feature of overland trade, since the most ancient times, is its organization along linear corridors. The trade corridor is the natural entity to identify problems, bring together policy-makers and stakeholders, and implement concrete facilitation measures or investment. Corridors also bring together national reforms and regional policies. (Arnold 2006, vii)

Although transit corridors are generally relatively well defined geographically, there is no standard for their operations in practice or for institutional and regulatory arrangements. Different modes of transport may be involved, and the number of routes can vary. Institutional arrangements for corridors range from very informal arrangements, to official government management, to government bilateral agreements and sophisticated institutions and decision-making processes.

The scope of corridor management covers trade and transit agreements, infrastructure and facilities, transport and logistics services, standards, regulations and procedures, security, and overall performance of the corridor (table 15.1). Participants in transit corridors thus represent many different sectors, and the interface between the public and private sectors is particularly important.

The management of transit corridors is a relatively complex affair that requires three key ingredients: legal arrangements, the provision of physical infrastructure, and the operationalization of the transit itself. Legal arrangements

include the signing of international agreements and the establishment of the regulatory framework necessary for the provision of transport and logistics services across borders (see box 15.4). Provision of infrastructure concerns the physical facilities that make up the corridor—mainly, transport and border infrastructure. Operationalization includes the maintenance of the physical infrastructure, the monitoring of corridor operations, and stakeholder management.

These components can be delivered by various institutional structures, separately or together. In southern Africa, some corridor management structures are public-private partnerships and others are entirely government driven. Adzibgey, Kunaka, and Mitiku (2007) point out the variety of legal instruments employed in Africa: treaties (Northern Corridor), multilateral agreements (Central Corridor), memoranda of understanding (Trans-Kalahari), constitution (Dar es Salaam), and company registration (Maputo; Trans-Kalahari). The diversity of international corridor arrangements is interesting in that it seems to mirror the various degrees of formality in the levels of international cooperation. It would seem that a memorandum of understanding does not carry the same legal weight as a constitution. Formality can, however, come at a cost, as Adzibgey, Kunaka, and Mitiku (2007) note: the constitution of the Dar es Salaam corridor had not yet been signed by Zambia at the time of their writing. In some instances, there is no management structure at all.[25]

Recent studies of transit corridors have insisted on the central and important role of the private sector, whose dynamism has been seen as crucial for pushing important changes (Arnold 2006; Adzibgey, Kunaka, and Mitiku 2007; Arvis, Raballand, and Marteau 2010).

Table 15.1. Functions of Selected Corridors

Corridor	Functions
ASEAN	Trade and transit agreements; standards and procedures
Asian Highway	Trade and transit agreements; infrastructure and facilities; standards and procedures
Canada–Mexico (NAFTA)	Infrastructure and facilities
ECOWAS	Trade and transit agreements; standards and procedures
GMS Corridors	Trade and transit agreements; standards and procedures
Maputo	Infrastructure and facilities; transport and logistics services; overall performance
Mercosur	Trade and transit agreements; standards and procedures
Northern Corridor	Infrastructure and facilities; transport and logistics services; overall performance
Pan-American	Infrastructure and facilities
SAARC Corridors	Infrastructure and facilities
TEN	Trade and transit agreements; infrastructure and facilities; standards and procedures
TRACECA	Trade and transit agreements; infrastructure and facilities; standards and procedures
Trans-Kalahari	Standards and procedures; overall performance

Source: Arnold 2006.
Note: ASEAN, Association of Southeast Asian Nations; ECOWAS, Economic Community of West African States; GMS, Greater Mekong Subregions; Mercosur, Southern Cone Common Market (Mercado Común del Sur); NAFTA, North American Free Trade Agreement; SAARC, South Asian Association for Regional Cooperation; TEN, Trans-European Networks; TRACECA, Transport Corridor Europe-Caucasus-Asia.

Box 15.4. Mercosur's Transit and Cross-Border Transport Agreement

An agreement among the countries of the Southern Cone Common Market (Mercosur, Mercado Común del Sur) in Latin America has introduced a uniform legal regime for international transport by authorized transport companies. It provides for the development of an international transport document, sets up a customs regime modeled after Europe's TIR Convention (although it is not as complete because it lacks a guarantee mechanism), and binds the participants to implement an international third-party liability scheme. The agreement provides for standards regarding carrier responsibility for lost, damaged, and delayed goods. Among the general provisions is the opening of transport markets. According to the agreement,

> Each contracting Party undertakes to give, on the basis of reciprocity, national treatment to the transport companies authorized by other Parties to carry out international transport under the terms of the Agreement. Such transport companies from other countries can also be given exemption from domestic taxes duties and rates on a reciprocal basis.

The agreement contains provisions that apply to both bilateral and transit road transport and that provide for reciprocity in the allocation of passenger and goods traffic between the parties. It also distinguishes between goods carried on own account and those carried by third parties. Finally, it allows for temporary use of the vehicles of third countries by an authorized transport company.

Source: Arnold 2006.

A basic function of transit corridor management is to provide a large amount of coordination, and an essential dimension of that coordination is with neighboring countries. Another dimension is international advocacy, through regional groupings and associations of stakeholders. Finally, regional cooperation is required for joint efforts—the provision of common facilities, but also transfers of resources across countries to ensure better operation of transit.

In most corridors, the regional coordination function is likely to be essential for the delivery of legal, physical, and operational inputs into the management of the transit corridor. Where it matters most is in the legal and regulatory aspects, as the effectiveness of transit corridors depends on trade and transit agreements between the countries participating in the corridor. The scope of such agreements should be large. The list here is inspired by Arnold (2006):

Interconnection; removal of transit bottlenecks. Many actions, such as the elimination of unnecessary administrative requirements for transit, can be taken by governments alone, but in some instances, joint efforts may be required—for example, in establishing joint border posts or relocating border functions (when, for instance, customs officials are located in the ports of trading partners).

Simplification and harmonization of border and clearance procedures. Many actions can be carried out by governments unilaterally—including simplification of documentation requirements and adoption of modern border management techniques—but coordination of border operations can go a long way toward improving transit. Cooperative activities may include the adoption of common standards for documentation; transit agreements; cooperation agreements between border agencies on mutual assistance, exchange of data, and joint expert groups; and joint border posts and synchronization of border operations.

Interoperability through adoption of processes that enable transporters to operate across borders. The principles are similar to those of border cooperation. Governments must agree on common sets of standards for transport that avoid transshipment of cargo from one operator to another. In some instances, international and regional standards already exist. Certification that standards are being met is also necessary; here, the greatest challenges concern trucks and inland and coastal shipping, the standards for which are often determined by local bodies without any mutual recognition of neighboring countries' ability to certify such standards.

Promotion of market access, private sector participation, and competition. Transport services and ancillary services such as logistics, customs broking, freight forwarding, trade finance, and insurance are not always able to compete in foreign markets. Air and maritime transport are particularly subject to restrictions on the operations of foreign operators in domestic transport. Some countries mandate the use of national customs brokers and freight forwarders. The rationale is often the poor quality of documentation submission by traders, but the requirement ends up creating inefficiencies—and rents for local operators. Although in these situations, multilateral reform (services liberalization) or unilateral reform (elimination of monopolies and regulatory rents) would seem more appropriate, regional competition may be a step toward more cost-effective services if trade partners possess services industries that can provide effective competition. Allowing the private sector to operate transport infrastructure, or even some border management functions, may be a way of introducing modern, efficient management.

Extension of cost-effective and efficient guarantees against liabilities. Air and maritime transport tend to have access to regional or worldwide guarantees, but road transport often has to be insured by local suppliers in each country of transit. Regional insurance systems are one solution. Another type of liability is that arising from nonpayment of customs duties and taxes.

Improvement of corridor capacity. Gateways, roads, and border crossings require important infrastructure for transit. A hurdle to investment is that border crossings for transit may be located in remote regions that receive low priority in government funding, as is the case with the Pan-American Highway and border crossings to land-locked countries in Africa (Arnold 2006). In Asia, the Greater Sub-Mekong Region has been established partly to provide for joint regional infrastructure in transport and telecommunications (Brooks 2008).

Institutional Arrangements in PTAs

PTAs represent one of the fastest developing forms of regional cooperation and incorporate more and more provisions, in particular in regulatory areas (Horn, Mavroidis, and Sapir 2010). PTAs have so far not led to much trade facilitation reform (Moïsé 2005), but they are able to perform several functions that may be necessary for regional trade facilitation. We mentioned earlier the importance of coordination and transfer of resources—both functions that PTAs could assume. In addition, the newer PTAs offer prospects for reform beyond the WTO agenda, they incorporate possible institutional mechanisms for assisting with implementation, and they gather under one umbrella disciplines that can complement and reinforce each other.

Deep integration agreements offer the possibility of pursuing comprehensive trade facilitation, involving reforms in several sectors of the economy that can be incorporated into the new generations of PTAs. These agreements afford the opportunity to deal with sectors that are not well covered multilaterally, while providing efficient enforcement mechanisms. The wider remit of PTAs compared with multilateral approaches is reflected in the definitions reviewed in box 15.1, which are much broader for regional agreements than at the multilateral level. A good illustration is the adoption of flexible and harmonized policies on visas and the opening of services—dimensions that are usually out of reach of a multilateral agreement but that can be part of regional discussions. (The Economic Community of West African States [ECOWAS], for instance, has suppressed visas between member countries.) The political economy of PTAs makes dealing with migration issues easier because countries can exchange commitments on movements of natural persons—something not possible in the General Agreement on Trade in Services (GATS).[26]

By tackling many dimensions of trade facilitation, PTAs may be able to exploit natural complementarities between the different elements of trade facilitation reform.[27] A particular challenge for reform is to get all the agencies involved in border control to work toward a common objective of facilitating trade. Coverage in the same trade agreement of the policy areas implemented by these agencies (such as SPS measures and standards) could provide a useful venue for agreeing to common aims linking these policies, and the specific political-economy incentive behind each set of policies may be superseded by the overarching objective of the PTA itself.

Conceivably, all the facets of trade facilitation reform could be included in specifically designed cooperation agreements on, for instance, customs cooperation or transit. PTAs, however, generally offer scope for covering a wide spectrum of policies across which various concessions, including noneconomic ones, could be traded off (Devlin and Estevadeordal 2004). Although this broadening does increase the complexity of negotiations, PTAs can guarantee better commitments. In theory, any attempt to deny a trade facilitation concession by imposing other trade barriers (e.g., tariffs) should be more difficult because use of these measures is regulated by the agreement. By the same token, enforcement of trade facilitation measures will be guaranteed by the possibility that partners will withdraw other concessions.

PTAs are not infrequently complemented by resource sharing and redistribution mechanisms among partner countries, which may include financial and technical assistance. Trade facilitation reforms can be demanding, in both expertise and material. Regional efforts offer, in addition to other support, the possibility of benchmarking (as, for example, in the regional program for Trade and Transport Facilitation in Southeastern Europe; see De Wulf and Sokol 2005) and the sharing of good practice. The EU devotes considerable money and effort to assisting neighbor countries with which it has association agreements (OECD 2006). Similarly, APEC has developed a program of technical assistance under which members have drawn up both collective and individual country assistance plans, covering 16 subject areas.[28] Most of these plans are carried out individually by the countries. Participation is voluntary but is conducted in coordination with other APEC members, and closely related objectives are pursued in this way. Progress is monitored at the APEC level. Several funds financed by individual country members, such as Japan's Trade and Investment Liberalization Fund (TILF), provide limited support to members.

Regional capacity building also takes place in South-South agreements such as COMESA. The South African Revenue Service (SARS) provides direct technical assistance to regional trade partners. In particular, when the provision of better trade facilitation at the regional level is impaired by the some members' lack of capacity, with implications for the regional system, a regional group can assist the delivery of joint assistance by acting as a coordination mechanism and sharing the costs among members. Even in the absence of redistribution arrangements, PTAs potentially create beneficial access to external financial resources by increasing the credibility of the regional group in offering loan collateral and enhancing its ability to do so (Devlin and Estevadeordal 2004).

PTAs act as trust-building mechanisms, promoting interactions between officials and exchange of information (Schiff and Winters 1998). Trust is a vital aspect of trade facilitation cooperation, as it helps mitigate risk through increased confidence in shared information and systems. It thus contributes to reduction of physical constraints on the transport of goods in the form of, for example, inspections, or requirements to adhere to compulsory routes.

PTAs have a good track record in enabling trust building across partner countries' administrations, but attempts to involve businesses through such means as public-private partnerships have been much less successful. For instance, the European Union has had mixed success with its efforts to build ambitious public-private partnerships in the context of its European transport network policy.[29]

Customs cooperation committees are often established in PTAs to discuss enforcement issues and to help defuse disputes (World Bank 2005, 89). More informal expert groups have also been established in a regional integration context, such as the EU Florence process on infrastructure, which has been influential in promoting reform (Rufin 2004).

Regional trade integration implies the building of regional institutions that can promote certain policies on behalf of its members. PTAs offer a cost-saving institutional architecture (Devlin and Estevadeordal 2004; Sandler 2006) through which the demand for regional public goods can be more easily aggregated. Both the redistributive mechanisms discussed above and the cooperation mechanisms established through PTAs contribute to the delivery of public goods by limiting free riding and helping to improve capacity. It is also often thought that regional institutions are better placed to advance international harmonization agendas (World Bank 2005). Finally, the pooling of scarce resources can make regional institutions more efficient.

Trade Facilitation Provisions in PTAs

Trade facilitation provisions are relatively new elements in PTAs, but they are expanding rapidly. Several existing agreements involve major trading nations and contain sophisticated commitments.

How expansive trade facilitation measures in PTAs are is difficult to gauge, as it depends on the definition of what constitutes such measures. For instance, Bin (2008), looking at Southeast Asia and using a broad definition that includes standards and technical regulations, as well as customs cooperation (now a staple of most regional trade agreements), finds 34 agreements, out of a total of 134, that contain trade facilitation measures. Wille and Redden (2007) review some of the same agreements, employing a definition closer to what is being negotiated under the WTO, with more of a focus on customs operations.

Examples of agreements containing advanced provisions about border clearance and facilitation of trade are now relatively plentiful and can be found not only in PTAs in which the EU and the United States take part but also in agreements involving Japan and Southeast Asian countries and in several South-South agreements—the South Asian Free Trade Area (SAFTA), COMESA, and the Malaysia–Pakistan ECA.

EU Agreements

It is only recently that the EU has included more ambitious trade facilitation provisions in its agreements. Before that, trade facilitation–related measures were found only in the framework of customs cooperation (Fasan 2004), which really had to do with enforcing trade rules. Since the conclusion of the association agreements with Mediterranean countries, provisions on trade facilitation have been expanded, but only in the agreements with Chile (2002) and Mexico (2000) were comprehensive and more ambitious objectives set. After a short moratorium on the negotiation of preferential agreements, a new generation of agreements is under way that includes the economic partnership agreements with African, Caribbean, and Pacific (ACP) countries. The EPAs completed so far include large trade facilitation chapters.

The agreement with Chile is the first of its type to mention specifically modern and ambitious trade facilitation measures. Publication on the Internet, advance rulings, the single window, right of appeal, use of risk management techniques, simplification of formalities, including the use of the European single administrative document (SAD), automation, and mechanisms of cooperation are mentioned in the agreement.

The EPA agreements that have been signed also have a broad scope, although they contain variations that may have resulted from the negotiation process. Stevens et al. (2008) note that levels of ambition on some provisions vary somewhat across EPA agreements that have been negotiated or are under negotiation. For example, some EPAs, such as those with the Caribbean Forum of African, Caribbean, and Pacific (ACP) States (CARIFORUM) and

Pacific ACP countries, contain provisions for the use of the single administrative document; others do not. The latter include the agreements with the Economic and Monetary Community of Central Africa (CEMAC, Communauté Économique et Monétaire de l'Afrique Centrale), with SADC, and with Côte d'Ivoire and Ghana.[30] This difference occurs even though the backbone structure of the agreements remains the same. The reason remains unclear: does it reflect a unilateral evolution in the EU position, particular aspects that needed more emphasis because of specific characteristics of the partner country (including its level of development), or a truly negotiated outcome?

Several general remarks can be made about the EU agreements. First, the PTAs reflect the general ambitions of the EU in the WTO trade facilitation negotiations. The EU is among those WTO members that broadly support the current agenda of negotiations, with comparatively few narrow offensive interests. Its preferential trade facilitation agenda is therefore very similar to that prevailing at the multilateral level. The agreements also refer explicitly to international standards and organizations, suggesting that the EU is seeking complementarity between the different processes. Perhaps this complementarity could be enhanced by identifying exactly which areas need to be pursued jointly and as a matter of priority. (This is something that the committee established by the agreement might do.)

Second, agreements are used to help promote a European-sanctioned vision of trade facilitation. This is evident in the stated objective of developing common positions in international organizations, the diffusion of the SAD standard (which is based on an international standard), and strong institutional mechanisms.

Third, advanced agreements provide for the establishment of formal institutional mechanisms for cooperation, with special committees on customs and trade facilitation. Such committees have a broad remit: exchange of information, notification, monitoring, joint development of standards and policy positions, facilitation of the provision of technical assistance, and mutual assistance on enforcement. In addition, for rules of origin an agreement of this kind provides a consultative forum for dispute settlement and for amendment of the agreement's provisions.

In recent negotiations of EPA agreements, cooperation is becoming more coercive, with the possibility of retaliation in case of failure to comply with administrative cooperation. The importance of cooperation mechanisms may be linked to a fourth aspect of the agreements: in most cases, the language of provisions remains unspecific, giving the partner country the opportunity of choosing how to reform its procedures and, in most cases, of defining the objective of the reform.[31] The provisions thus correspond to the rather aspirational nature of the agreements rather than laying down binding disciplines. This is the result of the nature of trade facilitation measures, which tend to be context-specific and procedural rather than easily translatable into precise and uniform legal language. It may also reflect the newness of negotiations on trade facilitation among countries. Finally, one can question the relative absence of language relating to technical assistance, at least in the EPA agreements, given the need for technical, legal, and management upgrading to support trade facilitation reform.

U.S. Agreements

As with the EU agreements, recent agreements signed by the United States have greatly extended the trade facilitation provisions, in line with U.S. multilateral negotiating strategy.

The increased emphasis on customs procedures started with the PTA with Australia (2003). Since then, U.S. PTAs have followed a relatively uniform template, with both developing and developed countries. The customs administration chapter of early agreements (e.g., with Chile and Morocco) has been renamed "customs administration and trade facilitation" in recent agreements, but the content has remained substantively the same. This is indicative of an agenda that is driven largely by the United States and less by the trading partner. The most recent agreement, with Peru, displays very few variations from the agreement with CAFTA plus the Dominican Republic (CAFTA–DR).

Overall, the provisions of U.S. agreements seem slightly more binding than comparable provisions in European agreements. For instance, regarding the expedited release of goods, the agreements contain disciplines about release at point of arrival and separation of release and border clearance. The provisions are quite specific, indicating a desirable release time of no more than 48 hours, or 6 hours for express shipment. Similarly, dispositions on the use of electronic submission and computer-based systems are more prescriptive than the EU agreements, which suggest only cooperation.

The agreements also focus on a subset of disciplines that are of interest to the United States. Advance rulings and express shipment stand out. In both cases, the agreements provide for detailed rules that are not present in non-U.S. free trade agreements (FTAs). They also reflect current U.S. proposals in the WTO negotiations.[32]

Other Agreements

The trade facilitation agenda, unlike other subjects in PTAs such as intellectual property, is not entirely driven by the parallel efforts of the two hubs, Europe and the United States. There is a strong drive to promote trade facilitation in some countries in Asia and the Pacific. We review here some of what we believe are the most notable agreements, drawing largely on Wille and Redden (2007).

Asia-Pacific Economic Cooperation (APEC). In 2001 APEC adopted the Shanghai Accord, which stresses the importance of trade facilitation. The accord endorsed the APEC Principles on Trade Facilitation as part of a collective action plan and set a target of a 5 percent reduction in cross-border trade transaction costs by 2006.[33] A trade facilitation action plan (TFAP) followed in 2002. A second trade facilitation action plan (TFAP II) was agreed for the period 2007–10, with the target of a further 5 percent reduction in costs. The APEC Trade Facilitation Principles encompass a broad agenda: transparency; communication and consultation; simplification; practicability and efficiency; nondiscrimination; consistency and predictability; harmonization, standardization, and recognition; modernization and the use of new technology; due process; and cooperation.

Several characteristics of the APEC approach are worth highlighting. The first is that on the implementation side, actions are strictly voluntary, and therefore implementation has not been uniform. Wille and Redden (2007) report that 62 percent of the TFAP was completed in 2006. It is also unclear whether implementation was a direct consequence of APEC efforts, given the overlapping membership of various APEC members in other agreements, including NAFTA and ASEAN, as well as decisions to reform trade facilitation unilaterally.

The second point is that the menu of actions listed in the trade facilitation action plans is much more detailed and ambitious than in EU, U.S., or other binding agreements. One measure of the ambition of the action plan is the reference to agendas that go beyond customs to include, for instance, services, business mobility, and security, as under the 2002 Secure Trade in the APEC Region (STAR) initiative. Even within customs, the actions suggested are deep in nature, with detailed plans for paperless trading, single windows, and sophisticated risk management techniques, including advance lodging of information, scanning, and simplified clearance for authorized economic operators.

The TFAP II goes even further, exhibiting a third characteristic of APEC cooperation—the recent emphasis on multicountry reform initiatives known as collective actions/pathfinders. TFAP II lists the APEC single window as the joint effort for customs procedures under which a framework and lessons from country initiatives are to assist individual efforts to build single windows. Another joint effort concerns business mobility and the extension of the APEC business travel card scheme, which facilitates immigration procedures and eases entry for business travelers.

A fourth characteristic is the tendency to refer frequently to international and regional initiatives and standards, suggesting that the plans aim at promoting an open liberalization agenda.

ASEAN Free Trade Agreement (AFTA). Like APEC, AFTA is nonbinding.[34] As noted by Wille and Redden (2007), some elements of trade facilitation were present early on in the 1992 AFTA, although they were not explicitly identified as trade facilitation. Progress on these remained limited. The real focus on trade facilitation started in earnest with the ASEAN Vision 2020 plan, initiated in 1997. This was followed by a number of initiatives, the most recent of which is the Vientiane Action Programme of 2004. Among the actions that have been undertaken, the ASEAN single window, agreed in December 2005, is demonstrating some vision. Yet overall, ASEAN actions are fragmented, framed by a succession of initiatives and declarations and sometimes only aspirational. Individual countries have, however, made good progress on some fronts, such as reforming customs procedures in the spirit of the WCO revised Kyoto convention and standardizing information requirements (Wille and Redden 2007).

Australia–Singapore FTA. The FTA between Australia and Singapore was signed in November 2002 and came into force in July 2003. An interesting aspect of this agreement is that it involves two advanced nations. Trade facilitation measures are not grouped under a single heading and are not identified as such, but several provisions of the agreement nevertheless have trade facilitation as an aim. These include provisions on paperless trading, risk management, and publication of information. There are also interesting complementary provisions on business mobility and sharing of best practices.

Conclusions

There is a tendency toward greater sophistication in provisions concerning trade facilitation in regional trade agreements. The focus remains very much on customs procedures, even if the language used sometimes seems to relate to border agencies in general and in some rare instances is complemented by, for example, liberalization measures in services. Most often, provisions in PTAs remain relatively unspecific. In particular, clear and measurable objectives are largely absent. APEC is an exception in this respect.

The approach followed by agreements led by the United States and the EU are closely related to these actors' positions in the WTO negotiations. This is not necessarily a bad thing, as PTAs can be complementary to multilateral efforts (although they could also be used to circumvent these efforts). It is surprising that PTAs are not more diverse. As outlined earlier, there are specific areas where PTAs could serve to further trade facilitation reform, but it is not obvious that the agreements reviewed here are focusing on this potential.

There are two paths for reaching agreement on trade facilitation provisions in PTAs. The first is through the classic mercantilist approach to negotiations. It would seem that developing countries have much to gain from improved facilitation measures and may wish to negotiate these in exchange for concessions in other domains. This advice, however, should be qualified by the absolute need to ensure that any commitment on trade facilitation provisions is much more specific than is currently the case. The second path is through reciprocal benefits arising from cooperation. Here, the scope seems more promising for agreements among developing countries, and probably among geographically close trade partners. The broad precept behind such mutual cooperation is that it generates positive externalities. Of course, these two characterizations must not be taken wholesale; trade-offs can arise in South-South agreements (for instance, regarding transit between landlocked and coastal countries), and cooperation can take place in North-South agreements, on such matters as security issues and cooperation between customs authorities.

We found little evidence that existing trade facilitation provisions contradict nondiscrimination principles. On the contrary, PTAs often tend to reaffirm such principles and promote international standards. In some instances, however, PTAs are used to further specific preferred models in such areas as express shipment provisions (in U.S. agreements) and use of European standards.

Nonbinding agreements such as APEC have gone much further in promoting trade facilitation reform than have binding agreements. This is partly a reflection of the head start of APEC over many agreements in this area, but it may also highlight some limits in using binding language when conceiving international cooperation for trade facilitation. Soft law has an important role to play. Trade facilitation provisions that focus on reform on the ground, implementation, and monitoring of measurable objectives, as in APEC, seem to deliver more effective and successful reforms. Such agreements tend to be pragmatic, flexible, and country specific and are generally well suited to the type of reforms required in the context of trade facilitation.

Transit issues, a very important dimension for countries with limited or no geographic access to main trade routes, are rarely present in PTAs. The reason is that the PTAs with the most advanced trade facilitation provisions involve developed and developing countries that are distant from each others, whereas agreements among developing countries are not deep enough to cover such aspects satisfactorily. Furthermore, many transit dimensions have been managed outside trade agreements. Finally, cooperation on technical assistance, although present in some agreements, remains largely underdeveloped.

Notes

Comments from Toni Matsudaira are gratefully acknowledged.

1. For the symposium, see WTO Secretariat Background Note G/C/W/80 Rev.1 and Symposium Report G/C/W/115.

2. Among these bodies are the Confederation of British Industry (CBI); the International Civic Aviation Organization (ICAO); the International Maritime Organization (IMO); the International Road Transport Union (IRU); the United Nations Centre for Trade Facilitation and Electronic Business (UNCEFACT); and the United Nations Economic Commission for Europe (UNECE). Agreements may refer to some of these standards; for example, the Association of Southeast Asian Nations (ASEAN) Free Trade Area refers to the United Nations/Electronic Data Interchange For Administration, Commerce and Transport(UN/EDIFACT); CAFTA–DR cites the World Customs Organization (WCO) Customs Data Model; and the EC–CARIFORUM EPA refers to the Revised Kyoto Convention.

3. TradeMark Southern Africa website, http://www.trademarksa.org/.

4. On the substantive differences between regional trade and cooperation agreements, see Devlin and Estevadeordal (2004).

5. Communication from the Arab Republic of Egypt to the WTO Negotiating Group on Trade Facilitation, TN/TF/W/75, November 15, 2005, http://docsonline.wto.org/.

6. World Bank (2005, 85) notes, for instance, that the cost of certifying organic nut production in Moldova for export to Germany can come to US$18,000 per year, a not insignificant amount for firms in poor countries.

7. Arvis, Raballand, and Marteau (2010) examine the large impact associated with uncertainty along the supply chain because of nonharmonized regulations.

8. The Tanzanian certification and testing agency for pesticides "charges relatively high fees to register an agro-chemical and also requires three years of field testing. It does not recognize the testing done and registration of chemicals in neighboring countries, including Kenya. Hence, there are a broad range of newer, more effective and safer chemicals which do not get registered in Tanzania because of the high cost and which are prevented from being legally imported from Kenya or other neighboring countries. The chemical registration revenue imperative of the [testing agency] thus appears to take precedence over a feasible solution of mutual recognition of other (including more rigorous) testing and registration systems" (Tanzania 2005, 97).

9. This is an important facilitating practice for customs valuation. For a discussion, see De Wulf and Sokol (2005), ch. 8.

10. Communication by Norway to the WTO Trade Facilitation Negotiating Group on Border Agency Cooperation, TN/TF/W/48, June 9, 2005. In 1995 Norway calculated the savings associated with the two agreements: without them, 10 new customs offices would have had to be opened on the Norwegian side of the border, and 100 new customs officers would have been needed. The cost would have been about US$8 million in additional investment and US$8 million in recurring annual costs for new buildings, salaries, and so on. Businesses would have incurred an estimated US$39 million in additional annual costs because of longer waiting times and double stops at the border.

11. Communication from Barbados, Fiji, Papua New Guinea, and the Solomon Islands to the WTO Negotiating Group on Trade Facilitation, TN/TF/W/129, July 7, 2006.

12. An essential piece of the architecture for the enforcement of technical regulations and sanitary and phytosanitary (SPS) measures in international commercial exchanges is accreditation, which offers an internationally recognized guarantee that national processes of standards conformity assessment can be relied on. Holmes et al. (2006) offer a good overview of the issue. In Sub-Saharan Africa there was until recently only one accredited expert, located in South Africa, able to provide accreditation. Three additional experts, also in South Africa, have now been trained. This confirms the view that in many developing countries, markets for accreditation and certification bodies may be too small.

13. Arvis, Raballand, and Marteau (2010) show how advanced logistics services are inhibited by lack of trade facilitation: it is often impossible, note the authors, to maintain multicountry inventories or to avoid first clearance and then reexport to the gateway country.

14. Payment guarantee systems require less working capital than payment in advance (which is required when there is no guarantee), and thus they help smaller agents access international trade.

15. This shortcoming has prompted EBRD and the International Finance Corporation (IFC) to create international risk-sharing funds to provide small enterprises with access to trade finance. These funds help international banks (confirming banks) cover the political and commercial risk faced by local issuing banks when they guarantee international trade transactions.

16. As an instance of economies of scale, air transport hubs avoid the inefficiency of empty cargo capacity on incoming or outgoing freight, which is a problem for small, nondiversified economies.

17. McTiernan (2006) reports that Benin and Togo charge very high fees for transit, which gives an incentive for transport from Lagos to Accra to be carried out by ship instead of overland.

18. The failure stems not merely from oversight or neglect but also from lack of incentives for the country of transit to internalize the costs of more efficient transit.

19. A counterexample is Bolivia, which has several access roads to the sea (Schiff and Winters 2003).

20. Arvis, Raballand, and Marteau (2010) cite the poor performance and unpredictability of Tanzanian railways, which have an error margin of four to five days in predicting the arrival of a shipment, as a reason for the increase in road transit from Kenya to northern Tanzania. That traffic increased by 20 percent over five years. Similarly, 75 percent of Rwandan trade now transits through Kenya, whereas 50 percent went through Tanzania only three years prior to the authors' survey.

21. The TIR is an international transit regime adopted by 68 parties, primarily in Europe, the Middle East, North Africa, and Central Asia. It was initially known in French as Transport Internationaux Routiers but is now only referred to as TIR in legal texts.

22. Cooperation provisions on rules of origin have traditionally been included with the provisions on rules of origin; chapters on customs cooperation deal with other elements of cooperation.

23. Aldaz-Carroll (2006) provides an example of such difficulties for regional standards harmonization in sensitive sectors in Mercosur.

24. As noted by Arvis (2010), it may be desirable for the transit system to evolve according to the level of integration among countries. Transit can indeed work as a series of independent national systems, but there are significant gains from cooperation, such as harmonization and information sharing, which can be implemented gradually.

25. The Northern Corridor Transit Agreement (NCTA) was signed in 1985 by Burundi, Kenya, Rwanda, and Uganda to promote the use of the Northern Corridor as an effective route for the surface transport of goods between the partner states. The Democratic Republic of Congo joined the corridor group in 1987. Trade facilitation along the Central Corridor was until recently handled through bilateral agreements, mainly between Tanzania and the landlocked countries. In 2006 Burundi, the Democratic Republic of Congo, Rwanda, Tanzania, and Uganda signed a multilateral

agreement to form the Central Corridor Transit Transport Facilitation Agency (CCTTFA), which is modeled along the lines of the NCTA authority. The constitution establishing the Dar es Salaam Corridor Coordinating Committee involves stakeholders from Malawi, Tanzania, and Zambia. The Walvis Bay Corridor Group (WBCG), a nonprofit public-private partnership, was established in 2000 and incorporated in Namibia to coordinate and integrate public and private sector development efforts along the Walvis Bay Corridor (see box 15.3). Its initial business development efforts focused on the Trans-Kalahari Corridor, mainly to facilitate institutional cooperation between Botswana, Namibia, and South Africa through the Trans-Kalahari Corridor Management Committee (TKCMC). In 2003 the three governments signed a formal trilateral corridor agreement, and the TKCMC was established through a memorandum of understanding. The WBCG currently serves as the secretariat for the TKCMC. A similar body, the Walvis Bay-Ndola-Lubumbashi Corridor Committee, has been set up for the Trans-Caprivi Corridor, and an analogous approach is being taken toward the Trans-Cunene Corridor.

26. The exchange of commitments, however, is only likely when partner countries have similar levels of development and patterns of comparative advantage that make movements of natural persons relatively balanced. Bin (2008) finds that provisions on mobility of business persons are present in about one-third of PTAs containing trade facilitation provisions in Asia and the Pacific.

27. For instance, regional guarantee systems help establish global standards for documentary credit (EBRD 2003) and thus generate information that can be used for other purposes.

28. For the areas and state of progress, see APEC, Sub-Committee on Customs Procedures, "CAP Assessment/Evaluation Matrix, Summary by Economy, July 2009," 2009/SOM2/SCCp/016.

29. Another way to create ownership for businesses is to give them access to dispute settlement under the PTA, as NAFTA and CAFTA do for investment. Similar solutions could be envisaged in relation to trade facilitation, offering the possibility for the private sector to challenge governments that illegitimately restrict their business.

30. Similarly, provisions for common institutions are absent in the agreement with CEMAC but are quite developed in other agreements.

31. For example, according to Article 31 of the EU-CARIFORUM EPA, "[the parties] shall simplify requirements and formalities where possible, in respect to the rapid release of goods."

32. See the proposals to the WTO by Australia, Canada, Turkey, and the United States, TN/TF/W/153, and by the United States, TN/TF/W/144/Rev.2.

33. The parties are Australia; Brunei Darussalam; Canada; Chile; China; Hong Kong SAR, China; Indonesia; Japan; the Republic of Korea; Malaysia; Mexico; New Zealand; Papua New Guinea; Peru; the Philippines; the Russian Federation; Singapore; Taiwan, China; Thailand; the United States; and Vietnam.

34. The parties are Brunei Darussalam, Cambodia, Indonesia, Lao PDR, Malaysia, Myanmar, the Philippines, Singapore, Thailand, and Vietnam.

References

Adzibgey, Yao, Charles Kunaka, and Tesfamichael Nahusenay Mitiku. 2007. "Institutional Arrangements for Transport Corridor Management in Sub-Saharan Africa." SSATP Working Paper 86, Sub-Saharan Africa Transport Policy Program, World Bank, Washington, DC.

Aldaz-Carroll, Enrique. 2006. "Regional Approaches to Better Standards Systems." Policy Research Working Paper 3948, World Bank, Washington, DC.

Arce, Daniel G., and Todd Sandler. 2002. *Regional Public Goods: Typologies, Provision, Financing, and Development Assistance.* Stockholm: Almqvist and Wiksell International for Expert Group on Development Issues, Swedish Ministry of Foreign Affairs.

Arnold, John. 2006. "Best Practices in Management of International Trade Corridors." Transport Paper 13, World Bank, Washington, DC http://

siteresources.worldbank.org/INTTRANSPORT/Resources/336291-1227561426235/5611053-1229359963828/itc-1-11-07.pdf.

Arvis, Jean-François. 2005. "Transit and the Special Case of Landlocked Countries." In *Customs Modernization Handbook,* ed. Luc De Wulf and Jose B. Sokol, ch. 11. Washington, DC: World Bank.

———. 2010. "Transit Regimes." In *Border Management Modernization,* eds. Gerard McLinden, Enrique Fanta, David Widdowoson and Tom Doyle, ch. 7. Washington, DC: World Bank.

Arvis, Jean-Francois, Gael Raballand, and Jean-Francois Marteau. 2010. *The Cost of Being Landlocked: Logistics Costs and Supply Chain Reliability.* Directions in Development: Trade. Washington, DC: World Bank.

Bin, Peng. 2008. "Trade Facilitation Provisions in Regional Trade Agreements in Asia and the Pacific." Staff Working Paper 01/08, UNESCAP Trade and Investment Division, United Nations Economic and Social Commission for Asia and the Pacific, Bangkok.

Brooks, Douglas H. 2008. "Regional Cooperation, Infrastructure and Trade Costs in Asia." ADB Institute Working Paper 123. Asian Development Bank Institute, Tokyo.

Cadot, Olivier, Celine Carrère, Jaime de Melo, and Bolormaa Tumurchudur. 2006. "Product-Specific Rules of Origin in EU and US Preferential Trading Arrangements: An Assessment." *World Trade Review* 5 (2): 199–224.

Devlin, Robert, and Antoni Estevadeordal. 2004. "Trade and Cooperation: A Regional Public Goods Approach." In *Regional Public Goods,* ed. Antoni Estevadeordal, Brian Frantz, and Tam Robert Nguyen. Washington, DC: Inter American Development Bank and Asian Development Bank.

De Wulf, Luc, and Jose B. Sokol. 2005. *Customs Modernization Handbook.* Washington, DC: World Bank.

EBRD (European Bank for Reconstruction and Development). 2003. "Regional Trade Facilitation Programme: Fostering Transition through Documentary Credit." Evaluation Department, EBRD, London.

Fasan, Olu. 2004. "Comparing EU Free Trade Agreements: Trade Facilitation." ECDPM InBrief 6F, European Centre for Development Policy Management, Maastricht, Netherlands.

Haddad, Mona. 2008. "Trade Issues in East Asia: Overcoming Trade Barriers from Standards and Technical Regulations." Policy Research Report, East Asia and Pacific Region, World Bank, Washington, DC. http://www-wds.worldbank.org/external/default/WDSContentServer/WDSP/IB/2008/02/28/000333037_20080228050849/Rendered/PDF/427200WP0P10991port0ASEAN0Standards.pdf.

Holmes, Peter, Leonardo Iacovone, Rungroge Kamondetdacha, and Lara Newson. 2006. "Capacity Building to Meet International Standards as Public Goods." UNIDO Working Papers, United Nations Industrial Development Organization, Vienna.

Horn, Henrik, Petros C. Mavroidis, and André Sapir. 2010. "Beyond the WTO? An Anatomy of EU and US Preferential Trade Agreements." *World Economy* 33 (11): 1565–88.

McTiernan, Andrew. 2006. "Customs and Business in Africa: A Better Way Forward Together." Report prepared for Business Action for Improving Customs Administration in Africa (BAFICAA). http://webarchive.nationalarchives.gov.uk/20100918113753/http://www.sitpro.org.uk//policy/baficaa/baficaareport.pdf.

Moïsé, Evdokia. 2005. "Trade Facilitation Reforms in the Service of Development: Country Case Studies." OECD Trade Policy Working Paper 12, Organisation for Economic Co-operation and Development, Paris.

Mozambique. 2004. "Integrated Framework." Vol. 1 of "Mozambique: Diagnostic Trade Integration Study." World Trade Organization, Geneva.

Müller-Jentsch, Daniel. 2003. *Transport Policies for the Euro-Mediterranean Free-Trade Area: An Agenda for Multimodal Transport Reform in the Southern Mediterranean.* World Bank Technical Paper 527. Washington, DC: World Bank.

OECD (Organisation for Economic Co-operation and Development). 2006. "OECD/DAC Project on Trade Facilitation: Phase 1: A Review of Technical Assistance." *OECD Papers* 6 (2).

Rufin, Carlos. 2004. "Regional Public Goods and Infrastructure." In *Regional Public Goods: From Theory to Practice,* ed. Antoni Estevadeordal, Brian Frantz, and Tam Robert Nguyen. Washington, DC: Inter-American Development Bank.

Sandler, Todd. 2006. "Regional Public Goods and International Organizations." *Review of International Organizations* 1 (1, March): 5–25.

Sauvé, Pierre, and Americo B. Zampetti. 2000. "Subsidiarity Perspectives on the New Trade Agenda." *Journal of International Economic Law* 3 (1): 83–114.

Schiff, Maurice, and L. Alan Winters. 1998. "Regional Integration as Diplomacy." *World Bank Economic Review* 12: 271–95.

———. 2002. "Regional Cooperation and the Role of International Organizations in Regional Integration." Policy Research Working Paper 2872, World Bank, Washington, DC.

———. 2003. *Regional Integration and Development.* Washington, DC: World Bank.

Stevens, Christopher, Mareike Meyn, Jane Kennan, Sanoussi Bilal, Corinna Braun-Munzinger, Franziska Jerosch, Davina Makhan, and Francesco Rampa. 2008. "The New EPAs: Comparative Analysis of Their Content and the Challenges for 2008." Final Report, Overseas Development Institute and European Center for Development Policy Management, London.

Tanzania. 2005. "Integrated Framework." Vol. 1 of "Tanzania: Diagnostic Trade Integration Study." World Trade Organization, Geneva.

Toledano, Joëlle, and José Ansón. 2008. *Postal Economics in Developing Countries: Posts, Infrastructure of the XXIst Century?* Bern: Universal Postal Union.

Uganda. 2006. "Integrated Framework." Vol. 1 of "Uganda: Diagnostic Trade Integration Study." World Trade Organization, Geneva.

Wille, P., and J. Redden. 2007. "A Comparative Analysis of Trade Facilitation in Selected Regional and Bilateral Trade Agreements and Initiatives." In ESCAP, *Trade Facilitation beyond the Multilateral Trade Negotiations: Regional Practices, Customs Valuation and Other Emerging Issues—A Study by the Asia-Pacific Research and Training Network on Trade,* 27–76. New York: United Nations.

World Bank. 2005. "Beyond Trade Policy Barriers: Lowering Trade Costs Together." In *Global Economic Prospects 2005: Trade, Regionalism, and Development,* ch. 4. Washington, DC: World Bank.

Yang, Yongzheng, and Sanjeev Gupta. 2005. "Regional Trade Agreements in Africa: Past Performance and the Way Forward." IMF Working Paper WP/05/36, International Monetary Fund, Washington, DC.

16

COMPETITION POLICY

Kamala Dawar and Peter Holmes

There is general agreement that competition among firms enables consumers to enjoy freedom of choice, low prices, and good value for money, while at the same time promoting innovation and higher standards. On the national level, the need for regulation to prevent anticompetitive practices is, accordingly, widely accepted.

On the plane of international trade, the competition policy issues are more complex. Abuse of market power can span markets and national boundaries, and many countries lack a competition policy framework that would facilitate cooperation with other countries.

The inclusion of competition provisions in trade agreements is potentially beneficial—particularly for developing countries, which suffer disproportionately from cross-border anticompetitive practices. Competition law and policy inherently contribute to better balance between the rights of producers and protection for consumers and other members of society. A well-administered competition law will have positive spillover effects on the economy at large, not just the particular firms or groups that bring complaints.

The extent to which regional competition provisions in trade agreements can promote regional public goods and deal with market failures depends on the nature of the provisions and on their implementation and enforcement. A small group of countries has begun to develop cooperative practices and appears to be active in initiating such agreements. These are primarily developed countries with established national competition law, existing agencies, and a strong competition culture. In other regional competition regimes, such provisions are the beginnings of state-to-state practices that are likely to develop over time. The development and effective implementation of national law and policy regarding competition and consumer protection are essential complements to regional competition policy.

This chapter first discusses the economic case for including competition provisions in preferential trade agreements (PTAs) and the costs and benefits involved. It then surveys representative arrangements between countries in the global North and the global South and at differing stages of development. Finally, it analyzes the strengths and shortcomings of the several regional competition policy models and of specific agreements, explores questions of third-party discrimination and trade diversion, and looks at the practical implementation of the agreements.

The discussion leads to the conclusion that regional competition provisions can create an incentive for implementing national competition policy regimes, with a view toward locking in such policies, increasing foreign direct investment (FDI), and, in the case of North-South agreements, promoting technical assistance and learning by doing. All these interactions have the potential to generate beneficial regional public goods.

Competition Policy and Development: A Survey of the Literature

It is argued here that, in principle, PTAs can address market failures that national competition laws cannot and that they can offset, to some degree, the absence of an international regime. This conclusion is not self-evident. Even if it can be shown that optimal competition provisions in PTAs are beneficial, it does not follow that what has actually been negotiated is ideal. Nevertheless, the contention in this chapter is that existing competition provisions do have a potential for positive effects.

The desirability of competition is (mostly) taken for granted in advanced industrial economies. Some consensus exists that competition is good for economic development and that the natural selection process of the market cannot be entirely relied on to ensure that firms can enter and exit as freely as possible.

In developing countries, there are doubts about the ability of markets to function so as to deliver the gains from competition. There is suspicion of strong competition, on the grounds that it will merely ensure the "survival of the fattest" and lead to dominance by large firms. Some developing countries, in their early period of industrialization, tried to limit the severity of competition, especially from imports, to protect their own enterprises. Only the most dogmatic market fundamentalist could deny that there are models in which monopoly capitalism emerges and circumstances in which it might prove beneficial. Examples can always be selected in which intensified competition went wrong, and economists need to be modest in urging the gains for development to be had from strong competition.

In fact, however, recent research does support the thesis that competition is good for development, both stimulating new business and benefiting consumers. Dutz and Hayri (1999), after surveying the existing empirical evidence and conducting a major cross-country study, found a strong correlation between long-run growth and effective enforcement of antitrust and competition policy. A recent study by the United Nations Conference on Trade and Development (UNCTAD) reviewed the literature and commissioned case studies around the world. The results (Brusick et al. 2004) broadly support the view that competition is good for development, and the authors argue that competition policy is very much complementary to other instruments for encouraging enterprise development.

Skeptics argue that although competition is desirable, the difficulties, expense, and skilled-staff requirements involved in making competition policy work effectively render it unlikely that developing countries will see much benefit from it. At best, the effort will be an expensive waste; at worst, it will present a further opportunity for regulatory capture, as incumbents or other potential losers use competition policy to frustrate rather than foster competition. We cannot rule out this result a priori. There is, however, considerable evidence that if governments are willing to let their competition agencies act, these bodies can be effective. Extensive case studies that are reported in CUTS (2003) and Brusick et al. (2004) corroborate the findings of Dutz and Hayri's (1999) cross-sectional statistical analysis. The case studies suggest that competition policy can be made to work in developing countries to the benefit of both development and the consumer, at costs that, although not trivial, are modest in relation to the consumer savings from successful interventions. Dutz and Vagliasindi (2002) also find that effective enforcement of competition policy in transition economies is associated with more rapid entry of new firms. Competition policy offers more than just static gains from lower prices.

The international dimension of competition policy is clearly important to developing countries that are adversely affected by foreign firms' anticompetitive behavior. Evenett, Levenstein, and Suslow (2001) show that even in globalized markets, cartels do not necessarily collapse rapidly of their own accord. Many cartels are based in developed countries, where their activities are legal under the laws of the exporting countries, as long as the effects are confined to foreign markets.[1] Competition authorities in developed countries are largely forbidden to provide confidential information on cartel activity conducted abroad, without specific legal authority.[2] U.S. and European Union (EU) authorities have traditionally considered themselves capable of addressing foreign anticompetitive practices that affect their own interests, through appeal to the *effects doctrine*.[3] In practice, however, the difficulty and cost of obtaining evidence on the behavior of firms located in foreign jurisdictions can make it difficult to bring cases. As Phlips (1998) has argued, without clear evidence of motivation and collusion, the burden of proof in cases based on overseas evidence can be very hard to sustain. An example is the 1988 case in which the European Court of Justice rejected, on appeal, the European Commission's attempt to fine a cartel of foreign wood pulp producers for price-fixing (Vedder 1990). In the 1986 *Matsushita v. Zenith* case, the U.S. Supreme Court found cooperative conduct legal under antitrust law, although the actions did violate antidumping rules (Belderbos and Holmes 1995).

In fact, the absence of international rules on mandating cooperation on competition policy enforcement increases the temptation to resort to antidumping rules. An international agreement on competition policy would not mean, however, that antidumping rules would be superseded. These rules are designed to cover far more types of behavior than does competition policy (see Bourgeois and Messerlin 1999; Sykes 1999) and have overtly protectionist motives.

The case for some form of international cooperation on competition policy is very strong unless one is skeptical of antitrust policy as such.[4] The EU's experience with international restrictive business practices has contributed to the belief that reduction of trade barriers alone is inadequate. It became clear that oligopolistic firms were able to divide EU markets after border barriers were lifted and that anticompetitive price discrimination could occur. Given the propensity of member states to protect their own national champions, the EU's founders early on deemed a supranational competition policy necessary.

Anderson and Jenny (2005, 67) observe,

In the 1990s, extensive evidence surfaced that international cartels are alive and flourishing in the "globalising" economic environment. Investigations conducted by the US Department of Justice, the European Commission, the

Canadian Competition Bureau and authorities in other jurisdictions revealed the existence of major cartels in (to cite but a few of many examples) the following industries: graphite electrodes (an essential input to steel mini-mill production); bromine (a flame retardant and fumigant); citric acid (a major industrial food additive); lysine (an agricultural feed additive); seamless steel pipes (an input to oil production); and vitamins.

Levenstein and Suslow (2001) argue that reductions of 20–30 percent in the prices of developing-country imports of products known to be affected by cartels would yield benefits greater than those from a 50 percent cut in agricultural tariffs. Utton (2008) finds that a large share of the competition problems of most developing countries emanates from the international sector, from such sources as import distribution monopolies and cartels; the influence of dominant firms based in other countries, including neighbors; overseas export cartels; and regional market sharing. These market failures can be difficult to deal with unilaterally, depending on where the unlawful conduct takes place and where the evidence is located. If the conduct takes place abroad, prosecution becomes problematic. Export cartels are notoriously hard to chase because they deliberately collude outside the jurisdiction of the importing country, and the same goes for regional market sharing. Where, however, an abuse of dominant position extends beyond a national market, there is a clear administrative case for regional cooperation, as in the EU.

The anticompetitive practices of multinational corporations are disadvantageous to developing countries and have particularly detrimental consequences in a context of economic scarcity. Levenstein and Suslow (2001) examined 16 products that were cartelized during the 1990s and for which reasonably reliable trade data were available. They estimated that the total value of such "cartel-affected" goods imported to developing countries was US$81.1 billion, a sum equivalent to 6.7 percent of all imports to these countries and 1.2 percent of their combined gross domestic product (GDP).[5]

This evidence suggests that developing countries should actively work for international cooperation on competition policy. Interestingly, they did just that before the Uruguay Round of the General Agreement on Tariffs and Trade (GATT). Officials in India, to take one instance, have frequently expressed their support for UNCTAD's principles and rules for the control of restrictive business practices (UNCTAD 2000).[6] It is therefore surprising that so much controversy surrounds the link between trade policy and competition policy.

Many authors have, however, argued that free trade is itself the best competition policy and have, in particular,

opposed attempts to use trade agreements to press developing countries to adopt competition laws. Hoekman and Holmes (1999) contend that a major flaw in the EU proposals for a World Trade Organization (WTO) multilateral competition policy agreement was that the scheme would have imposed burdensome administrative requirements that were not worth the benefits, since the proposals on the table did not include any obligations by developed countries to provide assistance in cases against export cartels that affect developing countries. Nevertheless, Hoekman and Saggi (2004) argue that developing countries may be able to profit from bilateral deals in which they agree to the adoption of a competition regime in exchange for market access in the partner country. It should be evident that the most attractive deal is one in which a developed country agrees to make real cooperation available to a developing-country partner.

All in all, there is little doubt that global competition problems exist, and it is generally accepted that international cooperation is desirable. What is less clear is what shape such cooperation should take. What works and what does not is essentially an empirical matter. It is therefore necessary to identify and examine the form and history of competition provisions in PTAs.

Economics of Competition Provisions

Competition law and policy designed to regulate and curb anticompetitve practices are now common at the national level. Anticompetitive practices include abuse of market dominance, collusion between firms, mergers and acquisitions that secure a dominant market position, artificially restricted output that leads to artificially high prices, predatory pricing, and price fixing.

Competition policy issues are more complex under globalization because abuse of market power can occur unevenly across several markets and beyond the jurisdiction of a national authority. Restrictive business practices may be carried out by domestic producers on foreign markets, or by foreign producers on domestic markets. The effectiveness of the prohibition of these anticompetitive practices will depend on the engagement of the various competition agencies, on whether competition law embodies the extraterritoriality principle, and on the degree to which agencies cooperate in addressing behavior that only one jurisdiction may view as harmful.

The lack of a comprehensive and coherent approach toward cross-border competition issues has led to proposals for a binding multilateral competition regime. Such a framework is currently rejected within the WTO. Meanwhile, competition provisions are increasingly being included in regional trading agreements and bilateral competition arrangements, as a halfway house or stepping-stone toward agreement on the international level. This development has not been unanimously welcomed, partly because any form of regionalism creates trade diversion and preferentialism, and partly because of the costs of negotiating and implementing regional competition provisions, at a time when experience with the economic and welfare effects of such regimes is as yet inconclusive.

Some analysts favor the narrower but stronger option of negotiating a mutual legal assistance treaty (MLAT) that specifies how competition authorities may assist one another in securing and sharing evidence that is not readily obtainable. Under the MLAT between Canada and the United States, for example, Canada has requested that U.S. authorities obtain documentary evidence and testimony from U.S. corporate offices, using compulsory procedures. Canada has also assisted in the execution of search warrants at the premises of a firm in Canada that was allegedly party to felony violations of U.S. antitrust laws. The documentary and other evidence Canada provided to U.S. authorities contributed to the initiation of grand jury investigations in the United States.

Clearly, improvement of interagency relationships and cooperation mechanisms will facilitate coordination of competition investigations and prosecutions. But MLATs are not a complete solution; they cannot be applied in jurisdictions that lack competition agencies, and they are less effective where national agencies are unequal in expertise, resources, and enforcement mechanisms. More comprehensive regional competition regimes can potentially overcome some of these challenges and discrepancies, and to them we next turn.

Benefits of Various Types of Agreement

In principle, the economic rationale for including competition law and provisions in PTAs is to prevent liberalization from being undermined by anticompetitive business practices within the region, to the disadvantage of consumers and firms. Competition policy provisions in PTAs therefore have two aims: to ensure that the partner's enforcement (or nonenforcement) of competition policy does not undermine the market access preferences granted in the agreements, and to guarantee that cross-border competition policy issues are dealt with adequately through regulatory cooperation. Beyond this rule of thumb, there is little evidence to support definitive conclusions about the economic benefits of the different types of competition-related provisions found in PTAs. Although not enough is yet known about the relative merits of different measures

for promoting competition in regional trade agreements, some relevant issues can be raised.

Institutional and behavioral shortcomings—lack of the requisite competition culture or of the political will to promote domestic implementation—contribute to poor implementation of regional competition provisions. A well-designed regional competition agreement needs to take account of these local realities and to foster the national structural and behavioral environment necessary to draw benefits from the regional competition provisions.

In regional groupings where individual members are at very different stages of economic development, where some lack a competition law or functioning enforcement agency, and where approaches to sovereignty pooling differ, establishment of a strong regional enforcement mechanism can be beneficial. Examples of groups in this category are the Andean Pact, the Common Market for Eastern and Southern Africa (COMESA), and the Southern Cone Common Market (Mercosur, Mercado Común del Sur).

The case of Mercosur is instructive because its intergovernmental ministerial approach to regional competition law has not been implemented effectively. This kind of failure is usually attributed to the unwillingness of some members to enact national laws or to set up domestic regimes that can give effect to external regional obligations. De Araújo (2001) notes that the Mercosur competition policy agreement, the Fortaleza Protocol, requires member states to have a national competition law but creates no collective agency; Paraguay and Uruguay chose to ignore the protocol. The lack of effective regional competition remedies may have undermined some of the benefits expected from the free trade schedules for this common market. Some Mercosur members have developed competition law and policy, but unless all members of an agreement have an effective domestic law, there can be no legal basis for action by a member against practices organized in another member state.

North-North competition agreements are more conducive to cooperation and coordination of activities than other types of PTA and may generate more benefits, but there are gains to be had from North-South regional competition regimes, as well. Developing countries in these arrangements will tend to benefit from such competition provisions as cooperation in enforcement activities and technical assistance. The benefits have been notable in the case of the Brazil–U.S. competition cooperation agreement, which, among other things, provides for U.S. technical assistance that has helped improve Brazil's expertise in the field of competition law and policy. This has enabled Brazil to communicate and cooperate with the United States in confronting anticompetitive practices. In cases like this, consultations between the competition agencies provide an opportunity for one agency to offer its support, advice, and experience to its counterpart. Notification of enforcement actions enables authorities to compare information about particular cases, and the provisions for technical assistance can be very helpful in building up capacity and expertise in the field. A notable example was the extensive cooperation the South African competition authorities received from the EU regarding the international merger of SmithKline Beecham PLC and Glaxo Wellcome PLC. The South African Competition Tribunal explicitly noted that its decision against the merger proposal was largely based on the EU's stand, and both South Africa's Competition Commission and the EU found that the merger would significantly affect competition in similar markets. The merger was eventually approved subject to the merging parties' outlicensing some products in specific areas in order to reduce their post-merger market share (CUTS 2003).

North-South PTAs will yield greater development benefits and will have better implementation records when (a) the more developed party offers appropriate technical and capacity-building assistance to the less developed one, and (b) the less developed regional partner is able to benefit from the assistance. For those members with nascent or nonexistent competition regimes, technical assistance should aim to impart the required expertise and experience over the long term, so as to promote the generational behavioral changes necessary for a competition culture.

Constructing Effective Enforcement Mechanisms

PTAs that have a goal of deepening integration between the members through a customs union or common market may find it economically advantageous to design effective regional competition enforcement mechanisms. This will be in addition to efforts to promote competition on a national level in PTA members that are in the early stages of implementing competition. When, in highly centralized arrangements, a regional authority is established to assist implementation, it must be given (if it is not to be a paper tiger) strong investigative powers, adequate resources and expertise, and the ability to issue cease-and-desist orders and collect fines. Transition economies in deep integration PTAs facing a strong legacy of statist economies may find it economically useful to include, as well, effective regulations on state aid and antidumping policy. Even in those countries with experience of competition, implementation of regional competition law will be more successful if the provisions explicitly promote partners' existing domestic policy priorities, such as support for small businesses or disadvantaged communities.

Positive Spillovers

National competition law and policy constitute public goods. Notably, competition provisions respond to market failures such as cartel creation or abuse of dominant market position. The provisions are designed to ensure that the benefits of liberalization are not undermined by private restrictive business practices and to promote more efficient, fairer markets. This is in the interests of both businesses and consumers. Competition law and policy inherently help balance the rights of producers and the protection accorded to consumers and other members of society.

Strictly speaking, competition law is not a pure public good, in the sense that the use of competition agency resources to pursue a case brought by one set of interests occurs at the expense of those whose cases cannot be heard, and certain types of firm can be denied standing on the basis of nationality. There is no doubt, however, that a well-administered competition law will have positive spillover effects on the economy at large, and not just on those firms or groups whose cases are adjudicated.

At a regional level, competition provisions can produce regional public goods by regulating cross-border trade, as well as mergers and acquisitions. There is a growing need for regional cooperation to address cross-border anticompetitive practices. Unilateral competition measures undertaken by national governments will not yield the same magnitude of regional public goods. Cooperation and coordination will require an agreement between the parties and may lead to complementary regional institutional arrangements or mechanisms. The institutions that monitor and enforce regional competition rules and regimes will be shared among countries, as will the ensuing benefits. Countries, by working together, will induce beneficial cross-border spillover, through, for example, information provision or cooperation in enforcing competition law in the region. In addition, regional agencies are able to realize economies of scale: even if a competition agency with twice the economic or geographic reach as another costs more than the narrower one, the cost increase is less than proportionate.

PTA competition provisions, where they have been negotiated, generally insist on core principles that include nondiscrimination, due process, and transparency. Although these commitments are made regionally, there is a positive spillover, and their effect is multilateral (Kulaksizoglu 2004). For example, Turkey's competition policy was established as a result of a bilateral agreement with the EU, but a U.S. or Japanese firm operating in Turkey will benefit from it as much as will a Turkish or European firm.

The extent to which a regional competition regime can deal with market failures depends on the comprehensiveness of the provisions and the will to enforce them. Regional competition provisions that address cartels collectively will yield regional public goods. Those that do not explicitly prohibit such restrictive business practices will not produce any such benefits. Where the agreement deals with cartels, the publication and notification of cartel enforcement actions in one country will generally stimulate enforcement efforts in other countries—a form of competition advocacy. This effect is particularly germane where a formal framework exists that establishes a relationship between competition authorities. Cross-jurisdictional and multijurisdictional information exchange also promotes the investigation and successful prosecution of cross-border restrictive business arrangements such as international cartels.

Consumer Protection

Lack of adequate, comprehensive consumer protection is a detriment to the achievement of healthy, competitive markets, as well as of healthy consumers. If explicit consumer protection provisions are included in the regional competition regime, there is potential for realizing greater regional public goods. Such provisions can help preserve the dynamic potential of consumers, while ensuring that consumer protection measures do not become unnecessary barriers to trade and that they are consistent with international trade obligations. A regional arrangement to protect consumer welfare will prevent cross-border firms from locating in a jurisdiction with relatively lax consumer policy, which would make cross-border consumer complaints and redress difficult to enforce. A regional regime is also better able to cope with information asymmetries in such areas as registries of licensed businesses, e-commerce regulations, and so on.

Regional consumer policy can address the negative spillover effects of cross-border anticompetitive business practices and can also deliver economies of scale. In order to deal fully with regional market failures, however, complementary regional consumer policy that focuses directly on the cross-border demand side is needed. It must be geared toward collecting information and evidence about practices that may be particularly injurious to consumers, in a situation in which competitors can avoid harm because they are able to pass on the costs of restrictions to the ultimate consumers.

Domestic consumer agencies increasingly acknowledge their inability to identify legislative and enforcement gaps in cross-border consumer protection—particularly in e-commerce, but also with respect to other deceptive practices, scams, and spam. These domestic agencies have little or no basis for acting against domestic entities that are causing market injury to consumers outside the country (although domestic consumers may have effective recourse against the same practice). Similarly, the agencies may have no clear authority or capacity to take action against entities that are located, or conducting business from, outside the domestic territory and that are targeting or entering into transactions with domestic consumers. At the national level, the ability to enforce injunctions or cease-and-desist orders to protect consumers across national borders is very limited, leading to lack of consumer confidence in cross-border transactions.

Implementation Costs

The costs of implementing the competition provisions of PTAs will depend on their nature and objectives and on the existing domestic competition framework and level of competition culture. The challenge for negotiators and policy makers is to craft the competition provisions so that the accruing benefits are seen to exceed the implementation costs. Regional competition laws and provisions for cooperation between competition enforcement agencies can increase the success and efficiency of the parties' efforts to reduce the negative impact of restrictive business practices.

Those decentralized agreements which require the existence of local competition law and the authority to apply the law nationally, such as the North American Free Trade Agreement (NAFTA) and the U.S.–Chile agreement, will not be as economically demanding as a regime that establishes a fully centralized law with a supporting regional authority, as in the EU or COMESA. The provisions in customs union agreements are, in general, more specific and demand higher commitments from the parties because their goal is regional integration.

In North-South competition agreements in which cooperation is limited to the exchange of specified information and nonmandatory notification, the costs involved are those associated with human resources (technical assistance, capacity building, and so on), communication, and travel. These economic burdens will be offset if the parties are able to exchange information effectively (thus contributing, for example, to the successful conclusion of an investigation) and avoid duplication and conflicting decisions.

For developing countries, the preconditions for successfully implementing even the most minimal cooperation provisions come at a price. For example, a qualified staff supplied with adequate resources is needed; it has been estimated that if a country were to report every single investigation that might have an impact in a counterpart's jurisdiction, at least five staff members would be required (Rosenberg and de Araújo 2005). Even if developed countries entering into North-South agreements have well-established domestic competition frameworks, implementation of competition provisions still entails costs—both the costs related to human capacity and administration, and the political costs of alienating potential business support or releasing confidential or agency information.

The provisions of the Revised Treaty of Chaguaramas, which established the Caribbean Community (CARICOM), indicate the potential economies of scale offered by regional cooperation, by allowing for resource pooling among neighboring countries when national capacity is not adequate for implementing and enforcing the regional framework. These provisions have been imported into other arrangements negotiated by CARICOM, such as the competition chapter in the economic partnership agreement (EPA) between the EU and the Caribbean Forum of African, Caribbean, and Pacific States (CARIFORUM) (Dawar and Evenett 2008).

Many North-South regional competition regimes specify that the developed parties will provide technical assistance. The cooperation provisions tend to be used primarily as capacity-building tools, whereby the more mature agency helps develop the expertise of the newly established one, rather than as a way of effectively coordinating enforcement activities. Capacity-building activities involve monitoring, communication, travel, and staff costs, which are borne only by the northern parties to the agreements.

In North-North and South-South PTA competition chapters, the parties are generally at similar levels of institutional development. Such arrangements will not necessarily lead to the transfer of capacity-building activities, with their associated costs. If, however, a central authority is mandated, it may undertake internal capacity building. In 2005, the European Commission's Directorate General for Competition managed a program to train national judges in European Commission competition law. That initiative, which costs 800,000 euros annually, is perceived to be an important element in the promotion of a common competition culture in the EU.

Cost-Benefit Analyses

In agreements between parties at similar levels of institutional development, the costs of negotiating and implementing competition provisions will be seen as justified only if the agreement produces substantial and beneficial multijurisdictional cooperation between the parties. It has been reported, for example, that the notification procedure specified in the competition cooperation agreement between Argentina and Brazil is burdensome for both countries and that its application is not systematic (Botta 2009). In a context of scarce human and material resources, such a provision cannot be routinely carried out because its immediate costs exceed its perceived benefits.

In general, the costs should be proportionate to the benefits that can reasonably be expected. The provisions negotiated should be as simple as possible, focusing primarily on information exchange, technical assistance, and capacity building. Subsequently, the commitments can be expanded to include, for instance, provisions on mandatory notification and comity. Where developing countries with less well established domestic competition frameworks are parties to regional competition provisions, notification provisions should be mandatory only for the most important cases for both jurisdictions. More general commitments should be implemented only after the necessary expertise and cooperation mechanisms have been developed.

Many members of regional agreements are small economies with insufficient resources to fund national competition agencies. In some of the developing countries that have created a national competition law, the law is not always well understood or adequately enforced. Given the competing short-term pressures on scarce resources, national governments do not always look favorably on regional competition provisions that would yield benefits only in the longer term. It is for this reason that advocacy and promotion of a competition culture are so important in the early stages of implementation, when the economic costs are presumed to outweigh the gains.

Cost-benefit analyses are invaluable in persuading government officials of the long-term benefits to be had from competitive markets. Evidence is growing that the benefits of enforcing competition provisions against cartels go beyond increased economic efficiency and consumer welfare. In 2005 the EU adopted five decisions against cartels, and the fines imposed totaled 683 million euros. In 2006 the European Commission issued seven final decisions in which 41 undertakings were fined a total of 1.85 billion euros (European Commission 2007). This activity has resulted in substantial savings for EU consumers, since overcharges stemming from cartels are estimated to be typically about 20–30 percent of prices (Connor 2004). Heimler and Anderson (2007) note that the EU antitrust authorities' successes with anticartel enforcement suffice alone to justify the investment in the relevant institutions.

Evenett (2004) estimates the annual deterrent effect of anticartel laws in the EU prior to enlargement at 96 percent of enforcement outlays, in just one sector (see table 16.1). To date, very few cost-benefit analyses of the impact of competition law enforcement in cases other than anticartel enforcement (such as abuse of dominance) are available.

The economic and human resources necessary to implement even a minimal decentralized competition regime are significant for developed and developing countries alike. Nevertheless, the emerging evidence on the economic and welfare costs associated with cross-border anticompetitive practices shows that those costs are undoubtedly higher than the costs of competition enforcement. Short-term political costs should be weighed against the understanding that the long-term and sustainable benefits of a strongly enforced regional competition regime will almost always outweigh its costs.

Implications for Open Regionalism

There are reasons for believing that the inclusion of competition and consumer provisions in PTAs will benefit rather than hinder open regionalism—regional arrangements that do not discriminate against outside countries. This is particularly the case if the provisions are designed to harmonize national laws, rather than maintain separate and differentiated national laws. A properly written competition law is inherently neutral and nondiscriminatory, and so competition policy should always increase the free flow of trade and investment. If a regional member enhances its competition law as a result of a PTA provision, this change will have effects beyond the other regional members. Regional competition provisions monitor business behavior and evaluate the economic role of large foreign companies on a regional basis, without contradicting the principle of open regionalism.

A regional competition law may strengthen regional economic integration by prohibiting or controlling agreements restricting competition or by restraining abuse of dominant market positions across borders. Once internal tariff barriers are removed, firms should not be allowed to distort regional or member markets through cross-border anticompetitive practices. It is possible for competition laws to be operated in a distortionary way—for example, by ruling out perfectly normal vertical arrangements commonly employed by importers or by exempting certain practices used by local firms. Some critics of the trade and competition proposals at the WTO argue, however, that the converse can apply; competition provisions of PTAs may be specifically intended to enhance market access for foreign firms at the expense of local interests. Some competition officials, too, express concern that their offices may become antidumping agencies if they are given inappropriate rules on predatory pricing. These fears seem to be less problematic in practice than had been anticipated. India, for example, as far as we can tell, did not raise any formal objection to the inclusion of competition issues in the EU–India negotiations. Regional arrangements, anyway, are less subject to capture and distortion than purely national ones. Although one may have sympathy for the argument that competition rules in PTAs should not focus solely on market access, that focus is not unreasonable in a trade-related regime.

Again, although the empirical evidence is limited, we believe the inclusion of competition provisions at the regional level could offer an opportunity to promote open regionalism by addressing the negative impact of cross-border trade distortions. Effectively enforced regional competition provisions may be able to lock in reforms that are politically difficult to sustain because of strong domestic lobbying by interests that do not benefit immediately from competition law. Regional agreements can pioneer or test-run provisions and so facilitate their negotiation at a multilateral level at a later date. Finally, regional competition regimes can offer a demonstration effect of the positive gains to be had from effective

Table 16.1. Cartel Overcharges and Deterrent Effect, Vitamin Industry, 1990s

Country or group	Overcharges on vitamin imports, 1990–99 (millions of U.S. dollars)	Deterrent effect of anticartel laws (millions of U.S. dollars)	Annual average deterrent as a share of enforcement outlays (percent)
EC-10	660.19	1,220.78	96
Brazil	183.37	72.09	65
Mexico	151.98	44.59	46
Peru	18.91	6.98	7

Source: Evenett 2004.
Note: EC-10 refers to the 10 members of the European Community (now the EU) before the 1986 enlargement: Belgium, Denmark, France, Ireland, Italy, Germany, Greece, Luxembourg, the Netherlands, and the United Kingdom.

national cooperation to underpin and improve the market liberalization process.

Effects on Third Parties

As noted above, in practice, competition laws are unlikely to discriminate against third parties. Cooperation provisions and agreements could be viewed as excluding third parties, but in fact, they are unlikely to have any significant trade-diverting effects. Indeed, Brusick et al. (2004) have argued that a PTA which provides for members to adopt national competition laws and apply them in a nondiscriminatory manner vis-à-vis national, intra-PTA, and third-party firms will, other things being equal, have trade-creating effects.

In the case of regional competition provisions, the impact on third parties will depend to a large extent on the nature of the competition regime and is contingent on the character and existence of preexisting national competition laws and enforcement institutions. In many cases, as noted in the section on spillovers, regional competition laws can have a positive impact on third parties, as measures implemented to protect competition and consumers in one market will also benefit consumers elsewhere. Regional competition regimes increase the efficiency and quality of markets, while lowering prices for goods and services. Not only is the competition regime generally advantageous for markets and consumers; it can also provide information, demonstration effects, and cooperation to third-party agencies.

Nevertheless, a PTA designed to confront anticompetitive practices only insofar as they may affect trade between PTA members could in theory have a de jure discriminatory effect on non-PTA firms. At the national level, the remedies and institutional provisions included in the regional agreement will be made available only to member states, which may induce trade diversion against competitive third-party producers. Agreements that create common laws and policies with direct effect could theoretically treat third parties differently from those agreements which only commit members to ensure national treatment in competition rules. It is difficult to see, however, how discrimination could apply in practice in these agreements, since third-country firms that are established in one party are usually treated like any other firm in competition law, except sometimes with respect to mergers and takeovers.

Different approaches to the assessment of liability and, in particular, the imposition of different remedies can cause negative spillovers to third parties in the sense that measures adopted in one jurisdiction can affect commercial decisions and the welfare of consumers in another.

Heimler and Anderson (2007) note this potential in their discussion of the various jurisdictions that were involved in assessing the anticompetitive practices of the Microsoft Corporation. The breakup in one jurisdiction of a large international corporation as a result of a finding of abuse of dominant position might be seen as a negative development in another jurisdiction where behavioral remedies are viewed as adequate for handling cases of obstructive or distorting competition in a market. Yet, if a firm is broken up by the judgment of one jurisdiction, that could, in practice, lead to its dismantling elsewhere.

Another potentially negative effect on third parties is that if there is no law in the third-party jurisdiction prohibiting cartels, the third party may unknowingly serve as a safe haven for international cartels which collude to restrict the market in order to protect or increase their profit margins. Firms and consumers located in a jurisdiction with lax competition provisions will, nevertheless, benefit from the existence of a region with strong competition law enforcement that is able to successfully prosecute the cartel.

Some PTAs have addressed the discriminatory effects of regional competition regimes. The Canada–Costa Rica PTA provides that measures taken to proscribe anticompetitive activities are to be applied on a nondiscriminatory basis. The free trade agreement between Colombia, Mexico, and the República Bolivariana de Venezuela requires state-owned monopolies to act on the basis of commercial considerations in operations in their own territories and not to use their monopoly positions to engage in anticompetitive practices in a nonmonopolized market in such a way as to affect enterprises in other member states.

Another area with potential for trade distortions is the use of competition measures in place of antidumping measures in intraregional trade, in cases where the parties employ different criteria and conditions and where antidumping measures would still apply to third parties. In fact, however, PTAs rarely abolish antidumping provisions.

Regional Competition Policy in Practice

From a trade perspective, promoting competitive markets helps ensure access to those markets by foreign firms. The lack of a comprehensive multilateral competition agreement has drawn attention to regional provisions as a potential tool for controlling cross-border restrictive business practices. Because of the principles of nondiscrimination and national treatment, trade agreements can include competition objectives even without the negotiation of a competition chapter, but they will then not have a coherent, independent regime for directly tackling harmful, restrictive business practices (see box 16.1).

Box 16.1. Competition Policy and International Cooperation

The World Trade Organization (WTO) system contains binding rules that are designed to promote a competitive environment. General national treatment and most favored nation (MFN) obligations enjoin nondiscrimination in competition policy. The provisions for trade in goods in the General Agreement on Tariffs and Trade (GATT) address the activities of state enterprises and subsidies and prohibit state-initiated voluntary export restraints. The General Agreement on Trade in Services (GATS) competition rules go further toward regulating the operation of monopoly services providers, in that they incorporate provisions for resolving disputes where competition is restricted. The GATS Telecommunications Reference Paper contains competition provisions for the telecommunications market, committing the signatories to ensure that established suppliers with dominant market power do not prohibit potential competitors from entering the market. Finally, there are provisions for members to address anticompetitive licensing practices in the Trade-Related Aspects of Intellectual Property Rights (TRIPS) Agreement. These procompetition obligations do not, however, represent a comprehensive agreement by the parties to prevent cross-border restrictive business practices and to apply the same criteria across various sectors of the economy.

If governments are to tackle cross-border restrictions on competition effectively, they need to cooperate on law enforcement. Without policies to establish and develop cooperation and coordination among competition agencies, the challenges of addressing cross-border anticompetitive practices persist. Although bodies such as the Organisation for Economic Co-operation and Development (OECD) and the International Competition Network (ICN) are able to promote competition on a voluntary, intergovernmental level, their membership is largely made up of developed countries that are already engaged in these activities domestically, and they cannot offer any significant legislative push beyond this mandate. It can be argued that without effective competition laws to buttress markets, partial and discriminatory liberalization merely serves to protect emergent dominant firms or cartels in the region from external competition.

Regional Competition Models

A comparative survey of competition provisions at the regional level indicates great diversity. The overview in this section focuses on describing the legal obligations set out in the provisions of each agreement (see table 16.2); it does not attempt to assess the successfulness of implementation. Within each regime, associations are classified as North-North, South-South, and North-South.

Centralized regimes. The most comprehensive regional competition regime is the fully centralized system with supporting regional institutions. A supranational law addresses anticompetitive practices that affect trade between the members or that distort competition within the region and establishes a distinct regional jurisdiction. Regional and domestic laws may overlap, but only the regional laws can adequately address anticompetitive practices that affect trade between treaty members or anticompetitive practices that take place in the regional territory beyond the jurisdictional boundaries of any one member of the PTA. Without regional law, political entities may use the effects doctrine, as the EU and the United States have done, to respond to anticompetitive practices beyond their borders, but decisions against firms located elsewhere may be unenforceable.

Competition laws in the fully centralized model are directly applicable within the territory of a member and are superior to any national law or judgment that is inconsistent with the regional law. Regional competition laws may also have direct effect in members' jurisdictions, giving firms or citizens the right to invoke the regional law in the domestic courts of the member countries. Fully centralizing the regional competition law requires creation of a complementary regional institutional mechanism to conduct investigations, enforce actions, and assess and levy penalties. In addition, the uniformity of court rulings needs to be guaranteed, through a superior regional court, a process of binding preliminary opinions, or both.

The Treaty on the Functioning of the European Union (TFEU) is the leading example of a centralized regime among northern or developed-country partners. The competition provisions cover, among other things, agreements or concerted practices between enterprises (Article 101) and abuses of dominance by enterprises (Article 102). Article 107 prohibits state aid that distorts competition. Since 1989, the EU has had associated rules concerning concentrations that may affect trade between members. Parties do maintain separate and distinct national competition laws, as well as national competition authorities that may differ substantially from one another, but from the creation of the association, regional competition law has promoted a soft harmonization of member states' competition laws. The European Commission's Directorate General for Competition has primary competence for applying EU competition laws. The European Court of Justice has reaffirmed, through case law, the direct effect of European law and its superiority to national law.[7]

The Andean Pact; the West African Economic and Monetary Union (WAEMU; in French, UEMOA, Union Économique et Monétaire Ouest-Africaine); and COMESA are centralized South-South competition regimes. The Andean Pact system is based on supranational rules enforced by community bodies. Decision 608 empowers

Table 16.2. Models of Regional Competition Regimes

Model	North-North	South-South	North-South	Key characteristics
Centralized	EU	COMESA WAEMU/UEMOA Andean Pact		Regional authority Regional law Regional enforcement
Partially centralized	ANZCERTA	CARICOM		Regional authority Regional law Domestic enforcement
Partially decentralized		Mercosur	U.S.–Brazil EU–Jordan	No regional authority Regional law Domestic enforcement
Decentralized		SACU	NAFTA Canada–Chile Canada–Costa Rica	No regional authority No regional law Domestic law subject to harmonization criteria

Source: Authors' compilation.
Note: ANZCERTA, Australia–New Zealand Closer Economic Relations Trade Agreement; CARICOM, Caribbean Community; COMESA, Common Market for Eastern and Southern Africa; EU, European Union; Mercosur, Southern Cone Common Market (Mercado Común del Sur); NAFTA, North American Free Trade Agreement; SACU, Southern African Customs Union; WAEMU/UEMOA, West African Economic and Monetary Union/Union Économique et Monétaire Ouest-Africaine.

the General Secretariat to tackle cross-border anticompetitive practices more effectively by imposing sanctions. WAEMU competition law applies to practices that have an intraregional effect; countries that do not have national competition laws may apply regional competition law within their own boundaries.

COMESA's competition regulations and rules are derived from Article 55 of its association treaty. As in the EU, agreements or concerted practices between enterprises that restrict or are designed to restrict competition in the COMESA common market are generally prohibited.[8] Members may not grant, in the form of subsidies, state aid that restricts or threatens to distort competition between member states (Article 52). Article 49 mandates the elimination of quantitative and other restrictions between members. The regulation concerning abuse of dominant position requires the COMESA Competition Commission to assess vertical restraints on a rule-of-reason basis, and horizontal agreements are illegal. The regulations provide for a premerger notification system under which the commission scrutinizes larger mergers, above certain turnover thresholds. The cooperation provisions for the COMESA Commission and for member states specify the application and enforcement of the competition regulations and rules. Where there is concurrent jurisdiction of the commission and national courts, consistency in the application of competition law must be ensured. These regional regulations are directly, fully, and uniformly effective in all member states.

Partially centralized regimes. The second competition model establishes regional competition law but supports it with an only partially centralized agency. As with the fully centralized regime, the independent regional law has direct applicability and takes precedence over national laws and judgments that are inconsistent with it. Although the central agency has a mandate to receive complaints and initiate independent investigations, it must work with the member states' competition agencies and national courts to process case actions leading to enforcement and remedies.

In deep integration North-North arrangements such as the Australia–New Zealand Closer Economic Relations Trade Agreement (ANZCERTA), the main objective is to expand free trade by eliminating barriers to trade and promoting fair competition. In addition to coordinating bilateral trade in goods and services, ANZCERTA promotes integration in such areas as quarantine, customs, transport, standards, and business law. Antidumping measures have been removed, and the parties' competition authorities and courts have concurrent or overlapping jurisdiction. This enables either competition authority to control the misuse of market power in the trans-Tasman market without a need for independent supranational institutions. Complaints relating to the abuse of dominant market position can be filed and heard in either jurisdiction, and valid and enforceable subpoenas and remedial orders can be issued in the partner country. To underpin this arrangement, the parties have signed a separate bilateral enforcement agreement that provides for extensive investigatory assistance, the exchange of confidential information, and coordinated enforcement.

The rules governing competition policy within CARICOM, a South-South agreement, are contained in Chapter 8 of the Revised Treaty of Chaguaramas. That chapter establishes a Community Competition Commission (CCC) with jurisdiction over all cases of cross-border anticompetitive conduct. Article 30(b) obligates members to enact competition policy legislation and establish competition enforcement bodies. Chapter 8 requires members to cooperate in the determination of competition legislation; to take the necessary legislative measures to ensure consistency and compliance with the rules of competition; and to set penalties for anticompetitive business conduct. Provisions are made for cooperation between national authorities in member states and within the CCC so as to achieve compliance with the rules of competition. Under Article 173(e–h), it is the responsibility of the CCC to cooperate with national authorities, provide support, and facilitate exchange of information and expertise. The CCC is responsible for taking effective measures to ensure that nationals of other member states have access to competent enforcement authorities, including the courts, on an equitable, transparent, and nondiscriminatory basis.

Partially decentralized regimes. Further down the scale of centralization are regimes that have a regional law but no independent regional body with powers of investigation and enforcement. Thus, the application of the law is left entirely to the members. National competition authorities have the jurisdiction to bring cases, and they are also the recipients of complaints of any violation of the regional competition law.

An example is Mercosur, whose competition protocol provides for a regional competition framework without any central agency. This partly decentralized arrangement has had significant implications for the enforcement of the provisions. An intergovernmental committee assists cooperation and the allocation of investigations and cases among the members. To ensure some harmonization among the parties, Mercosur's competition provisions set out common principles to establish the minimum requirements for its members' domestic laws and procedures.

Decentralized regimes. In the least centralized regional competition regime, members do not create a regional law; instead, they agree to cooperation principles and criteria for national laws addressing anticompetitive practices that are detrimental to the functioning of the PTA.

NAFTA, a North-South arrangement that includes Canada, Mexico, and the United States, does not rely on any institutions for enforcement, nor are there detailed procedures for cooperation or for recourse to dispute settlement. NAFTA's Chapter 15, covering competition policy, monopolies, and state enterprises, requires members to adopt or maintain measures proscribing anticompetitive business conduct and to take appropriate action, but it does not set out any more specific competition rules. The provisions formalize existing consultations and cooperation between the parties on the effectiveness of their national competition laws, as well as cooperation on the enforcement of those laws via mutual legal assistance, notification, consultation, and exchange of information. The parties' rights to apply antidumping or countervailing measures are preserved (Article 1902).

Another North-South arrangement, the Canada–Costa Rica Free Trade Agreement, includes provisions that specify the substantive requirements of a satisfactory domestic law, along with matters of due process and transparency. Although a cooperation mechanism is not created, there is some potential for competition authorities to cooperate informally. Timelines are set for the establishment of national laws to address certain anticompetitive practices.

The treaty of the Southern African Customs Union (SACU), a South-South agreement, commits members to establish competition policies and to cooperate in the enforcement of competition laws and regulations (Article 40). Remedies relating to unfair trading practices are also provided for. Article 41 states that the SACU council shall develop, within the context of the larger customs union, policies and instruments to address unfair trade practices between member states, on the advice of the regional commission.

Scope

In addition to representing differing degrees of centralization, PTA competition provisions have substantive and procedural requirements that vary depending on how comprehensive the competition regime is. A full taxonomy of provisions, as outlined by Solano and Sennekamp (2006), could consist of measures and provisions on the following issues:

1. Adoption, maintenance, and application of competition law
2. Establishment of bodies for cooperation and coordination and for enforcing competition law
3. Anticompetitive acts, and measures to be taken against them
4. Nondiscrimination, due process, and transparency in the application of competition law

5. Prohibition of the use of antidumping measures against signatories' commerce

6. Permitted forms of recourse to trade remedies (e.g., antidumping measures, countervailing duties, and safeguards)

7. Application of dispute settlement procedures in competition matters

8. Flexibility and progressivity, or "special and differential" treatment.

For the purposes of this section, it is useful to identify two sets of competition provisions in PTAs: those that envisage harmonization of the competition rules of the contracting parties, and those that provide for cooperation on competition-related issues (Holmes et al. 2005). The main families of provisions can be divided according to representative parties—the EU, the United States, and Canada.

The EU has tended to negotiate PTAs that employ language similar to Articles 101, 102, and 106 of the TFEU, which implicitly promotes harmonization of dynamics even where no approximation is mandated (as in the EU–Jordan PTA). The PTA provisions generally prohibit anticompetitive agreements and abuse of dominant position that affect trade, but they do not provide commensurately robust provisions to ensure coordination and cooperation among the parties. The Euro-Mediterranean agreements are of this type, except for the one with Algeria, which has stronger provisions. Other, more elaborate EU agreements, such as that with Chile, include provisions that allow trade measures such as safeguards but prohibit the use of anticompetitive state assistance, require nondiscrimination on the part of state monopolies, and mandate notification of state aid.

The U.S. and Canadian PTAs with competition provisions prohibit anticompetitive behavior. The agreements can be divided into PTAs that establish commitments to create or enforce competition laws and agencies and PTAs that focus on cooperation and coordination between the parties, on notifications, and on the behavior of state enterprises and state monopolies. There are notable exceptions to these broad models; for example, the Canada–Costa Rica PTA is more comprehensive and more procedurally demanding than other Canadian PTAs.

Consumer Policy

Most of the competition regimes in the PTAs surveyed focus on the supply-side behavior of firms and aim to identify and remove barriers (such as cartels, monopolies, and other restrictive business practices) to a firm's entry into a market. Such provisions can help protect both consumers and firms, but they do not directly address demand-side market imperfections stemming from lack of consumer information or inability to switch suppliers. Although this supply-side type of regulation traditionally falls within the scope of consumer law, there are PTAs that mainstream their consumer law provisions within or alongside the competition regimes to address the legislative and enforcement gaps in cross-border trade relating to consumer protection. Enhanced notification, information sharing, and investigative assistance among member states can work to protect foreign consumers from domestic anticompetitive business practices and to shield domestic consumers from parallel foreign practices.

Australian regional competition agreements are notable in their inclusion of consumer protection provisions. In the Australia–U.S. agreement, Article 14.6 of the chapter on competition-related issues is dedicated to cross-border consumer protection.[9] The parties, under this article, are to further strengthen cooperation and coordination among their respective agencies, including the U.S. Federal Trade Commission (FTC) and the Australian Competition and Consumer Commission (ACCC), in areas of mutual concern. Such areas include (a) assistance with enforcement and investigations and (b) consultation and coordination on enforcement actions against violations of consumer protection law that have a significant cross-border dimension. Unlike the Australia–Papua New Guinea and Australia–Republic of Korea PTAs, Australia's agreement with the United States includes separate agency-to-agency agreements in the fields of competition and consumer protection. Another difference is that the notification provisions are stronger, in that notifications are to take place without the necessity of requests by the other country. The Australia–U.S. PTA also contains a reciprocal agreement to provide relevant evidence in cases where national consumer protection laws have been violated (Article II.C).

The Australia–Korea PTA contains provisions on the application of the parties' competition and consumer protection laws; the notification provisions are weaker than in the PTA with the United States. The agreement with Papua New Guinea has an objective of promoting cooperation and coordination in the application of the countries' competition and consumer protection laws. In these cases, the parties have, at the national level, joint competition and consumer protection agencies.

An example of a South-South PTA that addresses the consumer welfare aspect of regional competition frameworks is the COMESA treaty. The COMESA Competition

Commission has powers and duties to enforce the consumer protection provisions of the competition regulations and to provide support to member states in promoting and protecting consumer welfare (Articles 6 and 7).

Hard versus Soft Law

Little evidence is available for making strong recommendations regarding the design of appropriate dispute settlement mechanisms covering competition provisions. It can be noted, however, that when PTAs contain few binding competition provisions, there is less reason for a binding dispute settlement system. There is not much to be gained by arbitrating "best endeavor" principles that merely encourage the application of effective domestic competition laws or cooperation principles.

A halfway house toward incorporating a dispute settlement mechanism is a PTA that allows parties to subject disputes arising from the application of the competition provisions to specific consultation procedures, short of dispute settlement procedures. This is the case in the Canada–Costa Rica PTA, discussed above.

Under a partially centralized competition regime such as CARICOM's, an intergovernmental committee, rather than a specially created independent authority, implements the agreement. It is not clear whether such bodies can exert enough influence to ensure that a member state complies with certain treaty obligations relating to competition law. In the absence of a central authority, treaty objectives can easily be undermined by differences in domestic laws and judgments.

There are further challenges to overcome where regional competition provisions include binding commitments to set up domestic competition laws or to provide for domestic procedures such as positive comity, which implies that each country will consider the other's national interest when enforcing its own competition laws.[10] Not only may individual members be inexperienced in implementing competition law, but there may also be political reasons, related to preservation of sovereignty, for deciding to exclude these obligations from the general dispute settlement mechanism. The parties may want to avoid having rulings or decisions of national competition authorities and courts overturned by supranational dispute settlement proceedings. It may be that the negotiators were only able to agree to language that ultimately was too vague to be subject to formal legalistic dispute settlement proceedings. There are also unwanted consequences attached to enforcing another party's competition obligations, as it may lead to tit-for-tat retaliation whereby a party seeks to ensure that the complaining party enforces all its obligations, as well.

Where dispute settlement mechanisms are made available for the competition provisions, the complaints tend to be limited to those between states. A private party wishing to bring a complaint must first persuade a government to submit a claim on its behalf. Governments tend to bring claims only after a cost-benefit analysis has been conducted, in view of the political and economic resources required. Clearly, a country complainant needs to believe that it has some chance of winning the dispute. Furthermore, it must have determined that winning will not set a precedent which will not be in its longer-term self-interest.

In the competition provisions found in regimes such as COMESA, the EU, and NAFTA, this area of private action is seen as an effective setting for addressing, for example, exclusionary practices and abuses of dominance in supply chains. It is there that private complainants can more easily identify the contractual practice that is affecting their commerce and bring that practice before a court or authority for legal assessment and action. A system of private rights is arguably more effective at catching minor actions that may go undetected by competition authorities. Private rights of action can promote the competition rules and principles that aim to create a level playing field and harness the beneficial economic effects of liberalization.

Nevertheless, private rights of action are not in themselves sufficient to effectively address cross-border competition issues relating to implementation and enforcement. Individual consumers or firms cannot obtain the necessary information to assess anticompetitive practices or do not have the expertise to determine their full effect. This is particularly the case for such restrictive business practices as cross-border hard-core cartels and vertical restraints. Collusive activity is generally conducted with great secrecy. Information relating to cartel activities tends to be obtained through investigations, from whistle-blowers who seek formal amnesty in exchange for incriminating information, or through other actions that require resources and powers not available to individual actors. Without this information, it is rare for a cartel to face charges and for remedies to be identified and imposed. In supply chains where anticompetitive behavior leads to high prices, costs can be passed to the end user without being identified along the way. Consequently, the likelihood that a private actor will be able to bring complaints about such practices before a national court is not great. Although private rights of action are important as rights and serve as an effective monitoring and enforcement mechanism, there are cases where they are neither sufficient nor appropriate and therefore require support through active governmental intervention.

Implementation Issues

It is difficult to assess the implementation of competition provisions. Some regional regimes commit the parties to establish national competition laws and policies that, in fact, were already in place prior to the agreement and therefore cannot be attributed to the PTA—although the PTA may have a reinforcing effect. If regional competition provisions are excluded from dispute settlement provisions, there will not be any disputes or case law to indicate nonimplementation. Finally, it is difficult to attribute evidence of interagency cooperation solely to the provisions of a PTA, rather than to interagency contacts through, for example, the International Competition Network.

Where assessment is possible, most existing research suggests that the level of implementation of regional competition provisions tends to be low, particularly in developing countries. This has led to questioning of the value of incorporating such provisions into PTAs, in view of the burdens of negotiating them and building institutions. But the research has also generated analyses that seek to identify and solve implementation challenges in order to harness the regional public goods that such provisions can potentially provide.

To some extent, domestic implementation is hampered because, in most regions, competition policy is a relatively new area of regulation. Time is required to build the necessary expertise and competition culture to establish the law and enforce it effectively on the domestic level, before an agency is able to take advantage of the benefits of interagency cooperation. It is apparent that in some cases competition culture is lacking at the national level, and consequently there is not sufficient political will to provide the necessary resources, and not enough institutional authority to push competition reform measures through.

In South-South arrangements, implementation tends to be particularly poor in countries in which national competition laws and authorities were underdeveloped prior to signature of the agreement. In the absence of the requisite laws, institutions, and expertise, the country cannot absorb or take advantage of the benefits offered by the provisions. Indeed, if there is no national competition regime, it is clear that the fundamental economic benefits of prohibiting restrictive business practices within the national economy have not in fact been realized. Without national institutional structures, implementation of regional laws to address cross-border anticompetitive practices will be seen to create more costs than benefits. Even where regional regimes establish measures such as cooperation, notification, consultations, and so on, they are of no use without the human resources and expertise to request information

or utilize it properly, or to engage in case coordination. Where national laws and agencies already existed prior to the regional agreement, there is more likelihood that the provisions will be implemented and that benefits will be realized.

Poor implementation performance based on lack of structural preconditions on the domestic front can to some extent be addressed through the negotiation of more appropriate competition provisions in the PTA. These regional laws can prioritize the development of competition regimes at the national level and, in so doing, address behavioral issues by offering the legislative impetus and policy lock-in necessary for sustained reform. Regional policy can be used as an exogenous force to overcome domestic inertia or vested interests that are obstacles to implementation. A regional law can compensate for an absence of national laws, and this has been an important feature of COMESA-type centralized arrangements.

In a fully centralized competition regime such as COMESA, the competition laws are underpinned by institutions and dispute settlement mechanisms that have been empowered to investigate, prosecute, and remedy anticompetitive practices. Where the agreement is between southern parties, some without any national competition regimes, the acknowledged first challenge is to harmonize national competition laws and regional competition. This dynamic is seriously constrained by the differing capacities of individual national competition authorities, which limit the usefulness of regional law and reduce political support for the competition authority among members. The structural and behavioral factors reinforce each other because implementing such a fully centralized model of regional competition policy requires ongoing advocacy and capacity building, in addition to legislative development to ensure that the regional law is appropriate for national conditions and needs. The focus on both structural and behavioral variables involved in implementing the EU competition regime evolved over the course of 50 years, with several modernizing phases to increase efficiency, reduce the costs of implementation, and foster buy-in by member states.

Reliance on bottom-up implementation initiatives will be less successful where a competition culture and buttressing regional laws and institutions are lacking. Mercosur is a South-South PTA that differs from COMESA in having only a loose intergovernmental framework, with little supranational power to promote competition at the national level. In the absence of national competition regimes, there is no regional authority with the mandate to promote and advocate implementation. The competition regime under Mercosur is often described as moribund.

In North-South agreements, the implementation record is clearly better, although the motivation to include competition law in PTAs is usually driven by the more developed party. The effectiveness of implementation is partly a function of the ability of the northern party to push its interest in ensuring a competitive playing field for its firms in the less developed parties, through national laws and authorities. Although this transfer of competition law does not bode well for implementation, particularly if the provisions negotiated are based on a model exported from a developed region, there are also positive factors. To counterbalance the challenges that arise from transplanting a competition regime, the more developed party can offer technical assistance, capacity building, and information, increasing the chances that the less developed regional partner will achieve a positive implementation record.

If the southern parties to a North-South agreement do not possess the characteristics necessary to absorb the benefits from exchange of information, the full potential of the benefits to be gained from the northern party's experiences and know-how cannot be realized. If, however, the agreement prioritizes the provision of technical assistance and capacity building, the parties will be more likely to cooperate effectively in the long run, to the benefit of both the northern and the southern parties. It is then that positive results emerge from the avoidance of duplication of research and other activities, and of conflicts in judgments and legal interpretations. When the advantages of regional competition provisions are tangible and significant, as manifested in lower prices, better quality, and more efficient regional markets, the economic and political costs of implementation are more likely to be perceived as justified in light of the economic and consumer welfare gains.

The Brazil–U.S., NAFTA, Canada–Costa Rica, EU–Jordan, and EU–South Africa competition regimes have had some success in advocating a competition culture and in promoting cooperation between competition authorities through learning by doing.[11] In these decentralized North-South regional competition regimes, the commitments are confined to national implementation and cooperation buttressed by technical assistance. Although there is no explicit reference to special and differential treatment for the southern party, flexibility in implementation can be built into the competition provisions. For example, the EU–Jordan treaty states that Jordan is to have five years to implement the provisions regulating unfair competition, and further flexibility is offered with respect to the removal of competition-distorting state aid (Article 53.3).

In North-North PTAs with fully centralized competition regimes, the implementation record is better. The EU, for example, is regularly ranked by the *Global Competition Review* as having one of the world's three best competition authorities. In the EU treaty, which establishes an independent law and competition authority with the resources and independence to implement the competition commitments, there have been notable successes in tackling cartels and other restrictive cross-border business practices. The binding nature of the provisions, with supporting monitoring and enforcement agencies, is clearly much more likely to meet with success than when agreements have loose, nonbinding clauses that are not subject to dispute settlement. Furthermore, the regime has had several decades to create the structural and behavioral qualities needed for success in investigating, prosecuting, and remedying regional anticompetitive practices.

By contrast, the Australia–New Zealand deep integration PTA does not include a regional competition agency and is not subject to a binding formal dispute settlement mechanism. Both countries' courts do, however, have jurisdiction throughout the region, and the PTA has a good implementation record. Here, as with the EU, the countries have the added advantage of a close geographic, historical, and cultural relationship. Although their national competition laws were initially based on different models, they were at relatively similar stages of institutional development, which promoted harmonization. In situations such as this, and where competition agencies already exist, the main focus of the provisions is on enhancing cooperation and coherence among the parties on the basis of comity rules—positive, negative, or both. A well-designed regime of cooperation mechanisms can facilitate the implementation of measures to tackle hard-core cartels, just as legislative shortcomings inhibit cooperation (Alvarez and Wilse-Samson 2007).

It is evident and significant that the implementation of competition provisions at a regional level depends on adequate enforcement of competition polices at the national level (Alvarez and Wilse-Samson 2007; Alvarez and Horna 2008). Enforcement will be improved if, in addition to focusing on the necessary structural changes, behavioral changes are effected. Where competition is a new phenomenon, the inclusion of competition provisions in regional agreements will merely signal the importance of regulating the restrictive practices of businesses, rather than provide substantive means of regulating anticompetitive practices. That is, regional competition provisions will be a first step in the long process of competition advocacy aimed at creating a competition culture.

To increase the advocacy of competition, PTAs should emphasize cooperation on competition provisions. Some areas for cooperation are case investigations, legal treaties, exchange of staff, exchange of experience, and peer reviews, in addition to compliance with regional competition rules. Strengthening of implementation capacity in developing PTA members must be accompanied by a reinforced commitment on the part of developed countries to effectively address the main competition policy concerns of their trading partners. This is particularly important where regional competition provisions were negotiated as a small part of a much broader trade agreement and were pushed by more developed parties with an interest in opening up developing-country markets to foreign trade and business activity.

Implementation will be more successful where the provisions reflect the diversity of social policy objectives within the regional framework. A PTA can explicitly promote the existing domestic policy priorities of the parties, such as support for small and medium-size enterprises or for disadvantaged groups. The domestic policy space for fostering marginalized communities, consumer welfare, or small businesses through exclusions from competition regulations, as well as for promoting market efficiency and market access, will make the agreement more appropriate to local needs and increase the chances of successful implementation. If the regional competition provisions are viewed in the light of the existing trade policies operating in the parties to the PTA, they are more likely to be implemented.

Levels of implementation will also relate to the ability of the parties to enforce the competition provisions effectively. Because most of the provisions are excluded from the dispute settlement mechanism covering the general trade provisions, only consultation mechanisms are available for discussing issues related to implementation. These, however, are unlikely to provide the same incentives to implement as would binding provisions covered by binding dispute settlement mechanisms that provide legal certainty and remedies.

Although competition provisions are generally not subject to dispute settlement processes and procedures, enforcement mechanisms can nevertheless be incorporated within the provisions themselves. For example, the inclusion of private rights of action will enable individuals harmed by anticompetitive practices to seek redress and damages in local courts.

Finally, implementation will be facilitated if regional authorities are endowed with strong investigative powers, adequate resources and expertise, and the ability to issue cease-and-desist orders and collect fines. The greater the independent powers, budgets, and resources of the competition agencies, the greater the chances of satisfactory implementation will be. Such powers will only be bestowed on competition agencies where there exists a competition culture to demand them and to allow the competition authority to implement its decisions without undue interference from lobbying groups.

Conclusions

Despite limited evidence about the impact of the regional competition regimes, it is clear that lack of regional competition can undermine the benefits from liberalization of regional markets. Implementation of effective regional competition law and policy can help address cross-border restrictions or regional market failures and generate positive spillovers, such as more efficient markets that offer better-quality goods for lower prices, further encouraging investment. Additional benefits may be derived by mainstreaming consumer policy into regional competition laws, given that the option of cooperation in dealing with cross-border consumer protection issues complements both economic and social development objectives.

Although the number and variety of North-South and South-South PTAs with some element of competition law is increasing, implementation records have been poor. This is particularly the case for PTA members that did not possess a national competition law prior to accepting regional commitments and for PTAs whose members are at very different stages of competition regime development. A regional competition regime in which effective national laws are lacking offers no legal basis for a member to take action against anticompetitive practices organized in another member state on the basis of the effects on its own territory. Even where regional regimes establish measures such as cooperation, notification, and consultations to generate regional benefits, these are of no use nationally without the human resources and expertise to absorb or respond to the information.

Implementation is more successful in North-South agreements, partly because of the ability of the northern party to push its interests in ensuring that the less developed parties provide a competitive playing field for its firms through national law and authority. The more developed party will be able to offer technical assistance, capacity building, and information that can increase the less developed regional partner's potential to achieve a positive implementation record.

By crafting appropriate regional competition provisions, PTAs can serve as vehicles for addressing both the structural and the behavioral challenges obstructing successful implementation. In countries with little or no experience with competition policy, regional laws can act, even if temporarily, as an alternative to the expense of establishing and implementing domestic competition laws. For members with nascent or nonexistent competition regimes, technical assistance should be designed to impart the requisite expertise and experience over the long term. This will also assist in promoting the necessary behavioral reforms.

Although PTA competition provisions can offer the legislative impetus and the policy lock-in necessary for sustained reform, a more appropriate first objective may be to focus on establishing at the national or subregional level a culture that values competition. In PTAs involving members with no or little experience with competition, the provisions could initially be restricted to information exchange, technical assistance, and capacity building. More general commitments could be implemented after the necessary expertise and cooperation mechanisms have been developed. Provisions could also be included that oblige members, over a specified period of time, to adopt competition laws that can address the full range of private and state-created anticompetitive practices and outcomes. In such a scenario, soft law may offer advantages if governments are uncertain of the underlying technical issues or the judicial consequences of the provisions. If competition regimes are at an early stage of implementation, nonjudicial mechanisms such as voluntary peer review, consultations on implementation issues, and informal diplomatic methods may be more appropriate. These can subsequently be complemented by a nonbinding mechanism for review of competition policy and by nonbinding consultations, promotion of voluntary implementation of competition policy obligations, and, ultimately, convergence or harmonization.

If highly centralized regimes are to function adequately, the regional monitoring and enforcement body must be endowed with strong investigative powers, adequate resources and expertise, and the ability to issue cease-and-desist orders and collect fines. When the advantages of regional competition provisions are tangible and significant, the resource requirements and political costs of implementation will be perceived as being justified by the economic and consumer welfare gains alone. Identification of these gains will require further empirical research and cost-benefit analyses, along with the necessary advocacy and legislative revisions at the national and international levels to build an economic and social environment that is better able both to demand competitive markets and to supply them.

Notes

1. Some provisions of U.S. law may allow litigation in the United States. These were unsuccessfully invoked in the *Empagran* case concerning alleged price fixing for vitamins; see Popofsky (2005).

2. This prohibition can be reversed in specific cases, for example, when authorized by the U.S. International Antitrust Enforcement Assistance Act of 1994.

3. According to the effects doctrine, domestic competition laws are applicable to foreign firms, but also to domestic firms located outside the state's territory, when their behavior or transactions produce an "effect" within the domestic territory. The "nationality" of firms is irrelevant for the purposes of antitrust enforcement, and the effects doctrine covers all firms irrespective of their nationality (Institute of Competition Law database, http://www.concurrences.com/article.php3?id_article=12374&lang=en).

4. Some authors believe all competition and antitrust policy is captured by "losers"—that is, inefficient firms that lose market share when faced with competition from stronger firms (see McChesney and Shughart 1995)—but there is no convincing evidence for this view.

5. A billion is a thousand million.

6. For a description of Indian interest in this area, see Shroff (2005).

7. For example, *Internationale Handelsgesellschaft mbH v. Einfuhr-undVorratsstelle für Getreide und Futtermittel*, ECJ case 11/70, 1970 ECR 1125.

8. Exceptions to this rule must meet four requirements. The two positive requirements are that the agreement, decision, or concerted practice contribute to the improvement of the production or distribution of goods or the promotion of technical or economic progress and that it allow consumers a fair share of the resulting benefit. The two negative requirements are that the agreement not impose restrictions unnecessary to the attainment of the positive objectives stated and that it not afford the firms concerned the possibility of eliminating competition in a substantial part of the market in question.

9. The text is available at Office of the U.S. Trade Representative, "Free Trade Agreements Australia," http://www.ustr.gov/trade-agreements/free-trade-agreements/australian-fta.

10. For example, the European Commission's report on the application of the EU–U.S. agreement states,

> In all cases of mutual interest it has become the norm to establish contacts at the outset in order to exchange views and, when appropriate, to coordinate enforcement activities. The two sides, where appropriate, seek to coordinate their respective approaches on the definition of relevant markets, on possible remedies in order to ensure that they do not conflict, as well as on points of foreign law relevant to the interpretation of an agreement or to the effectiveness of a remedy. Cooperation under this heading has involved the synchronization of investigations and searches. This is designed to make fact-finding action more effective and helps prevent companies suspected of cartel activity from destroying evidence located in the territory of the agency investigating the same conduct after its counterpart on the other side of the Atlantic has acted. (European Commission 1999, 313)

11. Brazil and the United States have a competition cooperation agreement (rather than an free trade agreement).

Selected Bibliography

Alvarez, Ana María, and Pierre Horna. 2008. "Implementing Competition Law and Policy in Latin America: The Role of Technical Assistance." *Chicago-Kent Law Review* 83 (1): 91–128. http://www.cklawreview.com/wp-content/uploads/vol83no1/Alvarez.pdf.

Alvarez, Ana María, and Laurence Wilse-Samson, eds. 2007. "Implementing Competition-Related Provisions in Regional Trade Agreements: Is It Possible to Obtain Development Gains?" UNCTAD/DITC/CLP/2006/4, United Nations Conference on Trade and Development (UNCTAD), New York and Geneva. http://www.unctad.org/en/docs/ditcclp20064_en.pdf.

Anderson, Robert, and Frédéric Jenny. 2005. "Competition Policy, Economic Development and the Role of a Possible Multilateral Framework on Competition Policy: Insights from the WTO Working Group on Trade and Competition Policy." In *Competition Policy in East Asia,* ed. Erlinda Medalla. Abingdon, U.K.: Routledge.

Baldwin, Richard, Simon Evenett, and Patrick Low. 2009. "Beyond Tariffs: Multilateralising Deeper PTA Commitments." In *Multilateralising Regionalism: Challenges for the Global Trading System*, ed. Richard Baldwin and Patrick Low. Cambridge, U.K.: Cambridge University Press.

Belderbos, Rene, and Peter Holmes. 1995. "The Economics of Matsushita Revisited." *Antitrust Bulletin* 20 (Winter): 825–57.

Bhagwati, Jagdish N., and Arvind Panagariya. 1996. *The Economics of Preferential Trade Agreements*. Washington, DC: American Enterprise Institute Press.

Botta, Marco. 2009. "The Cooperation between the Competition Authorities of the Developing Countries: Why Does It Not Work? Case Study on Argentina and Brazil." *Competition Law Review* 5 (2): 153–78.

Bourgeois, Jacques H. J., and Patrick A. Messerlin. 1999. "The European Community's Experience." In *Brookings Trade Forum: 1998 Trade, Competitiveness, Global Economics, Antidumping*, ed. Robert Z. Lawrence. Washington, DC: Brookings Institution Press.

Bourgeois, Jacques, Kamala Dawar, and Simon J. Evenett. 2007. "A Comparative Analysis of Selected Provisions in Free Trade Agreements." Prepared for the Directorate General for Trade, European Commission, Brussels.

Brusick, Philippe, Ana María Alvarez, and Lucian Cernat, eds. 2005. *Competition Provisions in Regional Trade Agreements: How to Assure Development Gains*. Geneva: United Nations Conference on Trade and Development (UNCTAD).

Brusick, Philippe, Lucian Cernat, Ana María Alvarez, and Peter Holmes, eds. 2004. "Competition, Competitiveness and Development: Lessons from Developing Countries." United Nations Conference on Trade and Development (UNCTAD), Geneva. http://www.unctad.org/en/docs/ditcclp20051_en.pdf.

Connor, John M. 2004. "Price-Fixing Overcharges: Legal and Economic Evidence." American Antitrust Institute Working Paper 04-05, American Antitrust Institute, Washington, DC. SSRN: http://papers.ssrn.com/sol3/papers.cfm? abstract_id=1103516##.

CUTS (Consumer Unity and Trust Society). 2003. *Pulling Up Our Socks*. Report based on the 7-Up Project. Jaipur, India: Consumer Unity and Trust Society.

Dawar, Kamala, and Simon J. Evenett. 2008. "The CARIFORUM-EC EPA: An Analysis of Its Competition and Government Procurement Provisions." Working Paper, German Agency for Technical Cooperation (GTZ), Eschborn, Germany. http://www.gtz.de/en/dokumente/en-epa-cariforum-and-beyond-procurement-and-competition-2008.pdf.

de Araújo, José Tavares, Jr. 2001. "Toward a Common Competition Policy in Mercosur." Presented at the conference on "Competition Policy in Infrastructure Services: Second Generation Issues in the Reform of Public Services," Inter-American Development Bank, Washington, DC, April 23–24. Organization of American States (OAS), Washington, DC. http://www.sedi.oas.org/DTTC/TRADE/PUB/STAFF_ARTICLE/tav01_merc_e.asp.

Dutz, Mark, and Aydin Hayri. 1999. "Does More Intense Competition Lead to Higher Growth?" Policy Research Working Paper 2320, World Bank, Washington, DC. http://www-wds.worldbank.org/external/default/WDSContentServer/IW3P/IB/2000/05/25/000094946_000504 05325137/Rendered/PDF/multi_page.pdf.

Dutz, Mark A., and Maria Vagliasindi. 2002. "Competition Policy Implementation in Transition Economies: An Empirical Assessment." OECD CCNM/GF/COMP/WD(2002)13, Organisation for Economic Co-operation and Development (OECD), Paris.

European Commission. 1999. *XXVIII Report on Competition Policy 1998*. Luxembourg: European Communities. http://ec.europa.eu/competition/publications/annual_report/1998/en.pdf.

———. 2007. *Report on Competition Policy 2006*. Luxembourg: Office for Official Publications of the European Communities. http://ec.europa.eu/competition/publications/annual_report/2006/en.pdf.

Evenett, Simon J. 2004. "Cost-Benefit Analyses of Implementing Competition Law and Policy." Presented at a seminar on "Strengthening and Capacity Building in the Area of Competition and Consumer Policy for Latin American Countries," United Nations Conference on Trade and Development (UNCTAD), Lima, March 22–24. http://www .evenett.com/publicpolicy/presentations .html.

Evenett, Simon J., Margaret C. Levenstein, and Valerie Y. Suslow. 2001. "International Cartel Enforcement: Lessons from the 1990s." *World Economy* 24 (9, September): 1221–45. Also issued as Policy Research Working Paper 2680, World Bank, Washington, DC, 2002.

Heimler, Alberto, and Robert D. Anderson. 2007. "What Has Competition Done for Europe? An Inter-Disciplinary Answer." *Aussenwirtschaft* 4. SSRN: http://ssrn.com/ abstract=1081563.

Hoekman, Bernard. 1999. "Free Trade and Deep Integration: Antidumping and Antitrust in Regional Agreements." Policy Research Working Paper 1950, World Bank, Washington, DC. http://www-wds.worldbank.org/external/default/WDSContentServer/WDSP/IB/1998/07/01/000009265 _3980928162543/Rendered/PDF/multi0page.pdf.

Hoekman, Bernard, and Peter Holmes. 1999. "Competition Policy, Developing Countries and the WTO." *World Economy* 22 (August): 875–93.

Hoekman, Bernard, and Kamal Saggi. 2004. "Trading Market Access for Competition Policy Enforcement." Policy Research Working Paper Series 3188, World Bank, Washington, DC. http://www-wds.worldbank.org/external/default/WDSContentServer/WDSP/IB/2004/02/10/00001 2009_20040210145554/Rendered/PDF/325550wps3188.pdf.

Holmes, Peter, Anna Sydorak, Anestis Papadopoulos, and Bahri Özgür Kayali. 2005. "Trade and Competition in RTAs: A Missed Opportunity?" In *Competition Provisions in Regional Trade Agreements: How to Assure Development Gains*, ed. Philippe Brusick, Ana María Alvarez, and Lucian Cernat. Geneva: United Nations Conference on Trade and Development (UNCTAD). www.unctad.org/en/docs/ditcclp20051_en.pdf.

Hughes, Timothy T. 2004. "Designing Competition Institutions for Different Stages of Institution Building." Presented at the Asia-Pacific Economic Cooperation (APEC) Fourth Training Program on Competition Policy, Ho Chi Minh City, August 3–6. http://www.jftc.go.jp/eacpf/05/APECTrainingProgramAugust2004/usa.hughes.pdf

Kulaksizoglu, Tamer. 2004. "Measuring the Effectiveness of Competition: Evidence from the Turkish Cement Industry." Munich Personal RePEc Archive (MPRA) Paper 357, Munich University Library, Munich, Germany. http://mpra.ub.uni-muenchen.de/357/1/MPRA _paper_357.pdf.

Levenstein, Margaret, and Valerie Suslow. 2001. "Private International Cartels and Their Effect on Developing Countries." Background paper for *World Development Report 2001*, World Bank, Washington, DC. http://www-unix.oit.umass.edu/~maggiel /WDR2001.pdf.

McChesney, Fred S., and William F. Shughart II, eds. 1995. *The Causes and Consequences of Antitrust: The Public-Choice Perspective*. Chicago, IL: University of Chicago Press.

Phlips, Louis. 1998. "On the Detection of Collusion and Predation." In *Applied Industrial Economics*, ed. Louis Phlips, 269–83. Cambridge, U.K: Cambridge University Press.

Popofsky, Mark S. 2005. "Extraterritoriality and the Empagran Case." ABAnet, American Bar Association, Washington, DC. http://www .abanet.org/antitrust/at-committees/at-ic/pdf/spring/05/popofsky.pdf.

Qaqaya, Hassan, and George Lipimile, eds. 2008. "The Effects of Anti-Competitive Business Practices on Developing Countries and Their Development Prospects." United Nations Conference on Trade and Development (UNCTAD), New York and Geneva. http://www.unctad .org/en/docs/ditcclp20082_en.pdf.

Rosenberg, Barbara, and Mariana Tavares de Araújo. 2005. In *Competition Provisions in Regional Trade Agreements: How to Assure Development Gains*, ed. Philippe Brusick, Ana María Alvarez, and Lucian Cernat, 189–212. Geneva: United Nations Conference on Trade and Development (UNCTAD). http://www.unctad.org/en/docs/ditcclp20051_en .pdf.

Shroff, Natashaa. 2005. "Bilateral Antitrust Cooperation Agreements." Research Report, Competition Commission of India, New Delhi. http://www.cci.gov.in/images/media/ResearchReports/BilateralAntitrust Natashashroff09022007_20080411101524.pdf.

Solano, Oliver, and Andreas Sennekamp. 2006. "Competition Provisions in Regional Trade Agreements." OECD Trade Policy Working Paper 31, Organisation for Economic Co-operation and Development (OECD), Paris. doi:10.1787/344843480185. http://www.oecd.org/officialdocuments/displaydocumentpdf/?cote=com/daf/td%282005%293/final&doclanguage=en.

Sykes, A. O. 1999. "Antidumping and Antitrust: What Problems Does Each Address?" In *Brookings Trade Forum: 1998 Trade, Competitiveness, Global Economics, Antidumping,* ed. Robert Z. Lawrence. Washington, DC: Brookings Institution Press.

UNCTAD (United Nations Conference on Trade and Development). 2000. "The Set of Multilaterally Agreed Equitable Principles and Rules for the Control of Restrictive Business Practices." United Nations, New York. http://www.unctad.org/en/docs/tdrbpconf10r2.en.pdf.

Utton, Michael A. 2008. *International Competition Policy.* Cheltenham, U.K.: Edward Elgar.

Vedder, Christoph. 1990. "A Survey of Principal Decisions of the European Court of Justice Pertaining to International Law: I. Wood Pulp." *European Journal of European Law* 1 (1–2): 365–77. http://207.57.19.226/journal/Vol1/No1/sr2.html.

17

GOVERNMENT PROCUREMENT

Kamala Dawar and Simon J. Evenett

Theoretical and empirical knowledge on issues related to government procurement in preferential trade agreements (PTAs) is sparse. It consists mainly of taxonomies of legal provisions on government procurement and economic models of across-the-board (i.e., nondiscriminatory or nonpreferential) reductions in discrimination against foreign bidders for state contracts. To the best of our knowledge, no ex post empirical assessments have been conducted on the impact of PTA provisions dealing with government procurement on trade flows or on the effectiveness of national procurement institutions, nor are there evaluations of the extent to which these PTA provisions have been implemented or of whether national procurement authorities have changed their practices as a result of PTA provisions. The analysis of government procurement in PTAs is a nascent discipline, and readers are cautioned accordingly.

The purpose of this chapter is to describe what is known concerning public procurement provisions in PTAs and what factors ought to be taken into account by policy makers and analysts as they evaluate policy options in this area. Although an effort is made to draw appropriate policy implications, the findings are largely tentative and will need to be revised in the light of new evidence and changes in thinking as to what constitutes effective public procurement policy.

The section that follows examines the developmental aspects of government procurement and associated reforms in the context of trade agreements. The second section surveys the major types of PTA provisions on government procurement found in selected agreements, with particular attention to dispute settlement provisions. The third section then assesses the government procurement provisions found in PTAs in a multilateral context, focusing on the important matter of discrimination. Some lessons for policy making are set forth in the concluding section.

Economic and Developmental Dimensions of Government Procurement

At the outset, it is critical to understand the development context in which discussions of government procurement policy in trade agreements take place. Proposals for public procurement provisions should be informed by circumstances in developing countries. As with many "trade and . . ." matters, it would be unwise to design or assess proposals for trade disciplines related to public procurement without a clear understanding of existing state purchasing practices and their potential developmental significance. In particular, it is important to examine the potential scope of government procurement, the relevant factors affecting national procurement regimes, the objectives of these regimes, and the underlying principles of good procurement policy before drawing inferences about trade negotiations and obligations bearing on public procurement.

Procurement Spending as a Share of Total Government Spending

A distinction must be made between all government spending and what is typically referred to as state spending on goods and services. (Spending on wages, salaries, and pensions is part of the former, but not the latter.) The significance of this difference for development is that wage rates are much lower in developing countries than elsewhere, and so the cost-effective way of supplying a given level of public service is to use more labor-intensive methods. Consequently, the share of spending on capital and intermediate goods will, other things being equal, be lower in developing countries, and this—setting aside the level of national income—accounts for the relatively small size of these countries' public procurement expenditures.[1]

However small public procurement expenditures are in relation to the size of the economy, the manner in which such monies are spent has an important developmental effect. Many public goods and services have a direct or indirect effect on economic performance and living standards—in particular, the living standards of the poor, who tend not to be able to afford private alternatives. Effective national procurement policies can help improve the execution of state infrastructure projects, yielding export and growth benefits. A government that is pursuing recognized development goals should, consequently, strive to limit waste and corruption in its public procurement regime.

Factors Affecting National Procurement Regimes in Developing Countries

Procurement regimes do not necessarily affect all levels of government in the same way. Total state spending on goods and services is distributed across various levels of government within a nation. Constitutional arrangements—in particular, federalist structures—affect which levels of government do the spending, how much they spend, and for what purposes. It is unwarranted to assume that just because one level—say, the central government—engages in public procurement reform (perhaps unilaterally, perhaps in the context of a trade agreement), other levels will follow suit. Constitutional niceties matter when evaluating the likely significance and impact of public procurement reform.

Government procurement in developing countries could also conflict with other—at times, externally imposed—constraints on the composition and implementation of public spending. Externally funded budget support programs, tied aid from donors, and debt relief initiatives all affect the level of government spending on goods and services and the extent to which the associated contracts are open to national and international competition. A distinct implication of these schemes is that their existence may limit the scope of national or regional public procurement reform initiatives, unless particular care is taken to reconcile the latter initiatives with bilateral or other international obligations.

In addition, many developing-country governments experience institutional and administrative capacity constraints, including a paucity of trained procurement staff. As the discussion below illustrates, there are many methods of public procurement, and the state officials responsible need to be well versed in their design and execution. Performance evaluation of contractees is required, and contract management, reporting, and accountability are important tasks, especially in an era in which a premium

is placed on transparency and good governance. A number of jurisdictions recognize that the management of procurement systems is a distinct, highly valued profession, and that, as in many cases involving talented personnel, staff retention and motivation are important challenges.[2]

Objectives of National Procurement Regimes

A common feature of public procurement policies that almost always colors debates about reform in both developing and industrial countries is the multiplicity of objectives assigned to these policies. A review of national public procurement legislation and implementing regulations shows that the following objectives are commonly targets of public procurement policy:

- Value for money, typically taken to mean minimizing procurement costs
- Macroeconomic management
- National security
- Redistribution to the poor
- Industrial and regional development
- Promotion of small and medium-size enterprises (SMEs)
- Support for state-owned enterprises and their employees
- Pursuit of governance-related targets.

In practice, pursuit of any but the first target amounts to designing procurement systems that sacrifice the value-for-money goal, in whole or in part, for some other objective. Advocates for giving preference to a particular regime typically appeal to some apparently inviolable principle such as transparency or defense of small business, but the risk of wasting scarce state resources is high if governments are swayed by abstract principles.

The alternative for governments is to use other state instruments, when available, to attain a particular target.[3] It is, to be sure, possible to use a national procurement regime to support local industrial development, and a government policy of imposing high costs on foreign enterprises attempting to establish and do business in the country will indeed stimulate incumbent firms. But if those existing firms are particularly confident, they may simply raise the prices charged the state buyer. In such a case, not only is the policy misguided, but it might exacerbate the exercise of market power and the distortion of resources within the economy. Much is at stake in the design of public procurement policy—not just the capacity to do some good, but also the danger of doing further harm!

When pursuing an objective other than value for money, policy makers and analysts need to ask under what circumstances government demand would directly and least expensively meet the targeted objective. To this line of argument, some will respond that the "real" world is imperfect and often requires second- or third-best solutions. Experience indicates that this objection would be stronger if it were made after alternative government policy instruments had been evaluated and rejected as potential means to a stated end.

Four Broad Principles of Good Procurement Policy

Despite, or because of, the variety of government objectives for public procurement policy, most jurisdictions, international accords, and pronouncements of international organizations on public procurement tend to refer to a core set of "principles" for the implementation of national policy in this area. Governments desire to retain the freedom to use procurement policy to pursue policy objectives that may be different from their neighbors' objectives. In this context, the core principles may be seen either as a limited approach to liberalization or as an agreement on higher-level disciplines that guarantee good policy making and governance. For governments negotiating a common approach to procurement reform—perhaps through a PTA—these similarities in principles may make it easier to reach consensus despite differences in overall objectives for public procurement policies.

Over time, the following four principles appear to have gained considerable common support: (a) efficiency (value for money); (b) equality of opportunity to compete for state contracts (nondiscrimination); (c) transparency (control of corruption; accountability); and (d) encouragement of investments and partnerships (public-private partnerships).[4] The principles may be codified in national constitutions, national and subnational laws, implementing regulations, and binding and nonbinding international accords. Associated with the principles are particular steps that the government can take to attain them.

Efficiency. It is widely accepted that the value-for-money objective is best achieved by encouraging (through the design of an easy-to-understand, easy-to-participate-in, and fair procurement regime) the maximum number of bidders for a state contract. Simulation evidence strongly suggests that the expected cost to the government of a contract falls as the number of bidders increases, and especially as the number rises toward five or six (McAfee and McMillan 1989; Deltas and Evenett 1997).

For many developing countries, the inefficiency and opportunity cost of suboptimal levels of competition in national procurement regimes can be substantial. For an average developing country that spends about 15 percent of its national income on goods and services, a 10 percent saving on procurement contracts is equivalent to 1.5 percent of gross domestic product (GDP)—an amount that may exceed the total amount of aid received by many developing countries.

Equality of opportunity. Entrenching equality of opportunity to compete for state contracts involves eschewing provisions that limit, bar, or discourage firms from bidding, on the basis of location, sourcing decisions, and employment practices.[5] Bans on foreign bidders, as seen in certain "buy-national" legislation passed during the 2008–09 global economic downturn, involve violations of equality of opportunity (see box 17.1). The matter here is not simply a case of domestic versus foreign firms but also of discrimination between foreign firms, as discussed in the next section.

The adverse welfare effect from discriminating against foreign bidders is, however, not straightforward to establish theoretically. Baldwin (1970) and Baldwin and Richardson (1972) show that when the quantity of a good that the government seeks to buy is smaller than the total quantity supplied by domestic firms, prohibiting foreign firms from bidding on state contracts merely reshuffles

---

Box 17.1. Persistence of Discrimination: Procurement Practices and the Global Economic Crisis

The 2008–09 global economic downturn has created doubts about the effectiveness of the rules and disciplines governing government procurement contained in trade agreements. The widespread use of fiscal stimulus packages has added a further layer of factors and potential complexity. Some governments have included "buy-national" provisions in fiscal stimulus packages to coerce state agencies into buying "domestic products." Defining what exactly a domestic product is often proves elusive, and so the laws underpinned by such notions can be confusing.

This being said, buy-national provisions have the potential to affect the international outsourcing decisions of firms and the operation of their supply chains. A developing country may find that both its intermediate and final goods producers lose sales abroad when a trading partner implements restrictive buy-national policies. These policies introduce a form of cross-border discrimination against foreign commercial interests in an area of corporate strategy making (international supply chains) that has benefited significantly from open borders over the past two decades. Moreover, for developing countries in which participation in international supply chains is viewed as a way of encouraging the upgrading of exporters, the consequences of being barred from certain commercial opportunities through buy-national provisions may not be confined to lost sales.

purchases from foreign producers from state buyers to local private sector buyers, without any impact on local prices and local production levels. In other words, the existence of discrimination and its subsequent removal may have no effect on resource allocation.

The same analyses showed that only when the total amount demanded by a government exceeds the total quantity supplied by domestic firms does banning foreign bidders increase domestic output and prices and limit imports. If the good in question is one that is supplied in small quantities in a developing country—perhaps because the legal and governance environment is less than ideal for business—such a ban on foreign procurement can indeed lead to expansion of domestic output.[6] For this reason, nationalistic procurement policies are regarded in some quarters as part of the industrial policy toolkit.

In brief, the economics of discrimination in public procurement is different from that of tariffs, precisely because the former applies only to a subset of buyers.

More recent analyses focus on cases in which discrimination did limit market access (see, e.g., Evenett and Hoekman 2005). The increase in prices paid by state buyers following a ban on foreign procurement tends to encourage the entry of domestic firms willing to supply the government, and so the longer-term effects of procurement discrimination depend on the magnitude of local barriers to entry. With no such barriers (whether administrative or in the shape of anticompetitive practices by incumbent firms), the procurement discrimination could, in the long term, lead to an expansion of domestic output. In a competitive market, moreover, prices would fall in the longer term to the lowest level of average costs of the most efficient local firm, which may or may not be equal to those of the most efficient foreign rival. If it turns out that in the longer run the most efficient local firm has costs equal to or less than those of its most competitive foreign rival, the government will end up paying prices at or below world prices; implying that under these circumstances there is no adverse price impact from discrimination in the long run. The policy implication of this argument is as follows: the longer-term impact of procurement discrimination on resource allocation and state budgets is contingent on national competition law and its enforcement and on policies toward the entry of new business.

In some cases, such as the provision of health care and other professional services, the principle of equality of opportunity is tempered by the realization that it should only apply to qualified or sufficiently expert or experienced bidders. Without challenging the contention that expertise is needed to fulfill certain government contracts, the question arises as to whether the qualifications to bid can be

made as nondiscriminatory as possible. For instance, if a particular skill is absolutely needed, the qualification requirement should be based on that skill—on nothing else, and certainly not on how that skill was acquired. In many instances, however, governments are adamant in asserting that only the graduates of specified national institutions have the skill in question.

Transparency. The importance of transparency in government procurement is generally well accepted. It is often argued (Anderson et al. 2009) that transparency helps improve governance and limit corruption and discrimination; the latter consideration points to a potential complementarity across principles. However, not every aspect of the procurement process can be made mechanical and transparent (the evaluation of intangible attributes of bidders is an example), and the pursuit of more transparent procurement policies will not completely eliminate opportunities to engage in discrimination. Furthermore, achieving transparency is costly. Although transparency can encourage more firms to bid for state contracts, thereby intensifying competition and lowering procurement costs, it also entails costs, such as delays in awarding procedures. The optimal degree of transparency is therefore unlikely to be infinite, and reasonable people can disagree over that degree. Still, the general principle that the procurement process should be known, understandable, and inexpensive to monitor remains key.

The relationship between transparency and market access can be ambiguous (Evenett and Hoekman 2005). Making procurement regulations easier to understand and more accessible will encourage foreign bidders for state contracts but will also attract domestic ones. Whether the share of state contracts awarded to foreign firms goes up or down will depend on the relative responsiveness of both types of firm to improvements in transparency. It is quite possible that a foreign trading partner could argue for the inclusion of transparency-related provisions in a PTA and subsequently discover that the implementation of those provisions actually benefits the domestic contractors of the partner country.

Improved transparency is one of the few areas in which there is some empirical evidence of the impact of procurement reform.[7] Information on contracts entered into by member states of the European Union (EU) between 1995 and 2002 and on the number and "nationality" of firms bidding for those contracts shows that during the period, the average number of bidders increased by 30 percent, the number of foreign subsidiary bidders rose to 30 percent of the total, and the dispersion of prices paid for comparable products by state buyers fell by 30 percent. Interestingly, it was found that during the same period, 78 percent of all state contracts examined went to small and medium-size enterprises, suggesting that transparency reform has not eliminated the capacity of SMEs to compete for these contracts.

Encouraging investment and public-private partnerships. Since the early 2000s, the principle of encouraging public-private partnerships in government procurement has gained momentum. In recognition of both tight budget constraints and the growth of private sector capital markets, governments have sought to fund investment (or capital) projects with contributions from the private sector. Although the contractual circumstances are hardly uniform, a private sector partner typically puts up the capital for a state project in return for the right to operate the related state facilities and charge users of those facilities. Many such partnerships are effectively off the government's balance sheet, precisely because the private sector advanced all the financing, but the associated transactions are still part of government procurement and ought to be treated as such.

Implications for Negotiation of Trade Obligations Concerning Public Procurement

The motives for negotiating and agreeing on public procurement provisions in PTAs are not limited to market access. Provisions of trade agreements fall broadly into three categories, delineated by their specific objectives: entrenching rules, limiting cross-border discrimination (thereby opening markets), and promoting state-state cooperation and the orderly settlement of disputes. Government procurement, like other behind-the-border issues, falls into a fourth category, as the provisions on this subject also deal with the establishment, funding, operations, and review of the public institutions associated with the national procurement regime. A government might strategically accept binding rules on its national procurement regime because, in the government's assessment, these rules are the most effective way of reforming national practices. Consequently, it is misleading to think in terms of the gains of these provisions solely in terms of what additional sales can be made in a trading partner. Market access is not the only possible benefit, and PTAs can contribute toward institutional improvements that have significant development payoffs.

The possibility that trade obligations can be used to improve a national procurement regime immediately raises the question of whether there are other, potentially more effective, vehicles available to governments for attaining the stated ends. In principle, changes in national legislation or in a nation's constitution are alternatives, and the

question arises as to why provisions in a trade agreement present a more credible, more effective, or more feasible option. Much depends on the legislative and constitutional history of the developing country in question—reneging on national legislative and constitutional commitments may involve less risk for some governments than breaking their pledges to a powerful trading partner. The key point is that alternative reform vehicles exist for public procurement regimes, and the case needs to be made that, given its history and other relevant circumstances, a developing country's interests are best served by signing public procurement provisions. Put this way, it may be the case that no generalizations about the desirability of public procurement provisions in trade agreements are possible. And just because not every developing nation will benefit from such provisions does not imply that no developing country will.

As is shown in figure 17.1, two-thirds of the PTAs notified to the World Trade Organization (WTO) since 2000 include provisions related to government procurement, and about 28 percent of extant PTAs treat government procurement in a comprehensive way. (See the annex to this chapter for a list of PTAs with government procurement provisions.) But PTAs are not the only instruments that regulate government procurement on an international scale (see box 17.2) Nonbinding guidelines, such as the

Figure 17.1. PTAs Containing Government Procurement Provisions, 2009

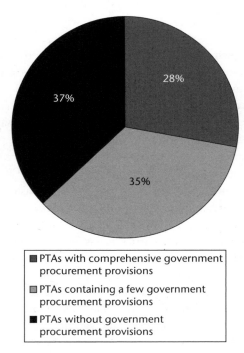

- ■ PTAs with comprehensive government procurement provisions
- ■ PTAs containing a few government procurement provisions
- ■ PTAs without government procurement provisions

Source: Anderson et al. 2009.

Box 17.2.   Three International Government Procurement Instruments

The three basic types of international instruments on government procurement, and the principal examples or actors, are as follows:

Model procurement codes, guidelines, and statements of principles or best practices

- United Nations Commission on International Trade Law (UNCITRAL) Model Law on Procurement of Goods, Construction and Services
- United Nations Convention against Corruption
- Asia-Pacific Economic Cooperation (APEC) Nonbinding Principles

Procurement guidelines imposed by central financial institutions

- World Bank
- Regional development banks

Binding agreements or directives

- World Trade Organization (WTO) Government Procurement Agreement (plurilateral)
- Preferential trade agreements (PTAs): European Union (EU) directives; Common Market for Eastern and Southern Africa (COMESA); West African Economic and Monetary Union/Union Économique et Monétaire Ouest-Africaine (WAEMU/ UEMOA)

United Nations Commission on International Trade Law (UNCITRAL) Model Law and the Asia-Pacific Economic Cooperation (APEC) Nonbinding Principles, as well as guidelines of lending agencies, play important roles in setting out international norms for reforming domestic procurement frameworks.[8]

The APEC principles, as stated in the 1994 Bogor Declaration, include a transparency standard, value for money, open and effective competition, accountability and due process, fair dealing, and nondiscrimination. These principles are similar to the objectives, whether binding or nonbinding, enunciated in other international instruments, including the WTO's Government Procurement Agreement (GPA). All international frameworks stress the importance of transparency and an optimal use of resources and acknowledge the need for nondiscrimination and competition in procurement markets, within a rules-based procurement system. The nonbinding principles cannot, however, provide any significant degree of legislative push or legislative certainty.

PTAs with government procurement provisions have similar general objectives, but PTA negotiations, particularly among similar countries, can allow for the provisions to be better tailored to parties' needs. Parties to a PTA may share cultural interpretations of principles such as fairness, accountability, and integrity, and the consequent ability of a PTA to promote the harmonization of procurement rules may enable bidders to better predict methods of tendering, selection, and adjudication, thereby increasing the efficiency and competitiveness of the system. There is, however, a risk of creating a patchwork of different procurement processes internationally, reducing transparency and competition.

A government procurement provision may be explicitly discriminatory, but this does not imply that the implementation of the provision is necessarily harmful to the commercial interests of third parties. Indeed, many provisions in PTAs require changes in national procurement regimes that, as a legal matter, need only be shared with signatories. If, however, operating dual administrative systems is very costly, a signatory may decide that it is cheaper to share all the PTA-induced improvements with all of its trading partners. In that case, the agreement may allow de jure discrimination with respect to a particular provision, but, de facto, no discrimination occurs. This observation does not imply that there is no discrimination in the public procurement provisions in PTAs but, rather, that it is possible for a discriminatory provision to generate most favored nation (MFN) benefits. Put simply, criticism of PTAs on the basis of the effects of discriminatory tariff reforms need not carry over to public procurement provisions. Again, straightforward generalizations may not be possible.

Just because a PTA contains potentially discriminatory provisions does not imply that its implementation will cause harm to nonsignatories; a PTA may trigger MFN improvements in public procurement institutions. It would also be wrong to infer that because a national procurement regime could be improved, PTA provisions are the best vehicle for doing so. Open-minded, case-by-case assessments of the merits of such provisions are probably the best counsel for policy makers and those that advise them.

Finally, reverting to the earlier discussion, individual governments' preferences as to the objectives of procurement vary. Procurement provisions negotiated in a PTA should reflect both agreement on policy-neutral ways to achieve better regulation (such as transparency) and some degree of acceptable exceptionality that can be accommodated through specific exceptions or exemptions, as discussed in the next section.

An Overview of Government Procurement Provisions in PTAs

Surveys of government procurement provisions in PTAs worldwide indicate that these regimes exhibit a wide variety and may overlap (Bourgeois, Dawar, and Evenett 2007; Dawar and Evenett 2008). The most comprehensive regimes—for example, the PTA between the EU and Chile, the North American Free Trade Agreement (NAFTA), and the Dominican Republic–Central America Free Trade Agreement (CAFTA–DR) PTA—contain detailed provisions on government procurement and related issues, such as dispute settlement. At the other end of the spectrum, some PTAs omit procurement altogether; examples are the East African Community (EAC) and the Association of Southeast Asian Nations (ASEAN). Other agreements set out minimal provisions covering only transparency, cooperation, or the gradual liberalization of procurement markets.

The variety of regimes largely stems from the fact that government spending is the preserve of sovereign decision making, providing a readily available (but not necessarily effective) tool for favoring particular domestic policies, sectors, or communities. Consequently, the willingness of governments to use PTAs to reform, or to codify the reform of, public purchasing practices depends on national circumstances and international opportunities. Policy makers have many options available to them as they consider their country's strategy toward government procurement provisions in PTAs. Where governments have been proactive, significant provisions have been developed, as discussed next.

Examples of Government Procurement Provisions in PTAs

The most comprehensive government procurement agreement to date is the Australia and New Zealand Government Procurement Agreement (ANZGPA). The general principle behind this agreement is to form a single government procurement market "to maximise opportunities for competitive [Australia and New Zealand] suppliers and reduce costs of doing business for both government and industry." The procurement provisions are designed to ensure that both parties' suppliers are given equal access to each others' government procurement markets.

EU and U.S. PTAs with industrial economies such as Chile and Australia, although regarded as relatively comprehensive, are less ambitious regarding market access, containing instead general principles of nondiscrimination, reciprocity and transparency.[9] The economic partnership agreement (EPA) between the EU and the Caribbean Forum of African, Caribbean, and Pacific (ACP) States (CARIFORUM) is unique in including only transparency as a general principle, without any binding commitments regarding market access.

The U.S.–Jordan PTA contains a single commitment on government procurement, to the effect that the parties support Jordan's accession to the WTO Government Procurement Agreement. This clause could promote the market access interests of both parties and of all existing members of the GPA. So far, PTAs entered into by the EU have not included clauses committing a party to accede to the GPA. Instead, their negotiated texts tend to set reciprocal and gradual liberalization of procurement markets as a goal without specifying the scope or coverage of the agreement. This is the case with the EU–Morocco association agreement, which states that the council set up by the agreement must implement the mutual opening of procurement markets.[10]

To make the picture even more varied, not all industrial countries have chosen to include government procurement provisions in their agreements, as illustrated by the Canada–Costa Rica and New Zealand–China PTAs. South-South PTA provisions also vary widely. In ASEAN, the EAC, and the Southern Cone Common Market (Mercosur, Mercado Común del Sur), for instance, no government procurement provisions have been negotiated, whereas in the CAFTA–DR agreement, the general principles accord national treatment and nondiscrimination to all parties to the PTA. In the Common Market for Eastern and Southern Africa (COMESA), the guiding principle is to promote regional procurement integration through cooperation and information exchange rather than through binding procurement laws.

Defining the Scope of Government Procurement Provisions in PTAs

Most PTAs that include government procurement provisions tend to follow the WTO GPA positive-list approach. This means that the scope of the provisions is defined during the negotiations, and the obligations apply only to procurements by the entities listed in the annexes to the text. (In the GPA, the relevant provisions are Annexes 1–3 to Appendix I.) The positive-list system allows for greater national flexibility and a more incremental approach to procurement reform for the included entities. For example, NAFTA only regulates federal or central government enterprises and certain parastatals.[11] State and provincial government entities are excluded, although the governments "encourage" voluntary and reciprocal participation by their respective subnational units. The PTA between the EU and Chile includes a positive list for the European federal entities covered for each EU member state. Although most member states also follow a positive-list approach at the subnational level, some EU members, such as Finland, have chosen to employ a negative-list approach, which means that, except as explicitly specified, all public or publicly controlled entities or undertakings that do not have an industrial or commercial character are subject to the government procurement provisions. Chile, by contrast, follows a strict positive list for both central and municipal levels.

The negative-list approach is used most notably in the deep integration PTA between Australia and New Zealand: all government entities are subject to the procurement obligations except those that are explicitly listed as exempt. This broad approach complements the objectives of the Australia–New Zealand Closer Economic Relations Trade Agreement (ANZCERTA), of creating a single market between the two parties and achieving the maximum benefits from bilateral trade. The choice of a negative-list approach to negotiations on the entities covered by government procurement provisions is typically taken to signal greater liberalizing ambition. The total amount of commercial opportunities created depends, however, on a wider range of factors.

Following the WTO GPA approach, and mirroring its text, the EU–Chile obligations apply to "any law, regulation, procedure or practice regarding any procurement, by the entities of the Parties, of goods and services including works, subject to the conditions specified in the relevant Annexes."[12] As with the WTO GPA and most PTAs, the EU–Chile obligations do not apply to some kinds of contracts, including international agreements; contracts pertaining to land acquisition, broadcasting, arbitration, employment, and financial services; and certain research and development (R&D) contracts. U.S. PTAs, the ANZGPA, and the WTO GPA include both goods and services and, most notably, big-ticket items such as construction services.

Thresholds

The coverage of government procurement provisions in a PTA applies only if the value of the procurement is at or above the thresholds negotiated by the parties. To the extent that other PTA provisions limit or condition discrimination, the thresholds agreed in a PTA have an important effect on the extent to which domestic firms will face additional competition from foreign rivals after the PTA comes into effect.

Thresholds may differ according to the type of procurement and the level of government making the purchase. In effect, these thresholds allow for a partial opening up of the covered sectors, offering governments flexibility to promote other policy objectives through certain excluded sectors of the procurement market. Using thresholds to promote an incremental approach to reform extends shelter from these obligations to sectors and entities operating below the threshold. The provisions of the EPA between the EU and CARIFORUM, for example, apply only to central government contracts in excess of one of the highest thresholds yet negotiated, US$200,000.

Notwithstanding the need to tailor procurement provisions to the domestic circumstances of a country, a cost-benefit analysis of high thresholds and preferential policies is essential. Such analyses, however, are scarce. As was noted above, using discriminatory procurement as a development tool detracts from the beneficial effects of applying value-for-money criteria to the expenditure of public funds. These benefits are usually sought in the most integrated PTAs, such as the ANZGPA, which, consequently, do not set any thresholds.

Countries that are parties to PTAs and are also members of the WTO GPA cannot set higher thresholds in bilateral and regional agreements involving other GPA members than those stated in the GPA. That agreement's thresholds vary according to level of government (central government, subcentral government entities, and government-owned enterprises) and are expressed as special drawing rights (SDRs), an accounting unit used by the International Monetary Fund (IMF).[13] In order to capture further benefits from liberalizing procurement markets, the more recent U.S. agreements (except those with Bahrain and Morocco) have negotiated thresholds lower than those agreed to in the GPA.

Incorporating Development or Domestic Policy Objectives

To afford further flexibility in implementing government procurement provisions, parties to PTAs with government procurement regimes may negotiate specific exceptions in the scope or coverage of the agreement (see box 17.3). Most of the more comprehensive agreements explicitly prohibit government entities from imposing measures aimed using requirements regarding domestic content,

---

Box 17.3. Examples of Flexible Provisions in Government Procurement PTAs

Scope: Level of entities covered by the provisions

- Central or federal level only: U.S. preferential trade agreements (PTAs); set to commitments in the World Trade Organization (WTO) Government Procurement Agreement (GPA)
- Subcentral entities: European Union (EU) PTAs; set to WTO GPA commitments
- All entities: Australia and New Zealand Government Procurement Agreement (ANZGPA); New Zealand–Singapore PTA

Thresholds: Minimum value at which procurement is covered by provisions

- WTO GPA thresholds or lower: GPA parties
- Transitionally higher than WTO GPA thresholds: PTAs between the United States and Bahrain, the United States and the Dominican Republic–Central America Free Trade Agreement (CAFTA–DR), and the United States and Oman
- Higher than WTO GPA thresholds: economic partnership agreement (EPA) between the EU and the Caribbean Forum of African, Caribbean, and Pacific (ACP) States (CARIFORUM)
- No thresholds: ANZGPA; New Zealand–Singapore PTA; Chile–Costa Rica PTA

Exclusions

- Defense procurement
- Transport: U.S. PTAs
- Financial services: Chile PTAs (e.g., U.S.–Chile; Mexico–Chile)
- Health, education, and welfare: New Zealand (e.g., Trans-Pacific Strategic Economic Partnership)

Set-asides

- Preferential opportunities for indigenous persons: Australian agreements (e.g., Singapore–Australia PTA, Article 15)
- Small and minority businesses: U.S. general note to annexes

Offsets

- Prohibited: U.S.–Singapore, Japan–Switzerland, EU–Chile, and other PTAs
- Not prohibited: EU–CARIFORUM EPA, European Free Trade Association (EFTA), Singapore–Australia PTA, EU–Jordan PTA, and others

---

licensing of technology, investment, and the like to encourage local development or improve balance of payments accounts. These measures are known as offsets and are defined in Article XVI of the WTO GPA. There are, however, other measures that give the parties flexibility to promote domestic policy objectives. For example, under NAFTA's joint programs for small business, a committee is established to report on the efforts being made to promote government procurement opportunities for members' small enterprises. NAFTA also initially allowed Mexico's national oil and electric companies to set aside one-half of their procurement each year for domestic suppliers. (This provision was entirely phased out by 2003.) Unlike the United States and Canada, Mexico is not a member of the WTO GPA, and its procurement is therefore subject only to the obligations negotiated in PTAs. Another NAFTA exception allowed Mexico to impose local-content requirements for turnkey construction projects. For capital-intensive projects, Mexico negotiated set-asides for as much as 25 percent for local inputs, and for up to 40 percent Mexican content for labor-intensive projects.

In the free trade agreement (FTA) between Mexico and Nicaragua, in addition to set-asides, both parties negotiated rules allowing minimum local-content rules for awardees of state contracts. Such provisions are not confined to South-South arrangements. Promotion of the development of local industry and local employment is included in the Australia–Singapore FTA, which explicitly allows the Australian government to promote employment for significant indigenous communities.

In addition to provisions allowing for set-asides and other exceptions, cooperation and technical assistance can also be specified in the agreement. For instance, the EU–Chile government procurement provisions state that the parties will seek to provide technical assistance on issues connected with public procurement, paying special attention to the municipal level. The North-South EU–CARIFORUM agreement includes provisions on cooperation and technical assistance, with commitments of financial resources. There are also asymmetrical requirements that the EU show "due restraint" in resolving disputes in favor of CARIFORUM parties. This is ambiguous, but it could result in the EU's resolving disputes by giving the CARIFORUM partners the benefit of the doubt, or demanding less retaliation. The agreement also allows a significant implementation period to give CARIFORUM countries ample time to prepare for implementation and provides for development support.

In addition to exceptions in individual schedules, procurement obligations in U.S. PTAs (like those of the WTO GPA) are subject to national security and general exceptions, to exclude sensitive sectors from the overall rules. These exceptions vary in their scope and details. The U.S. PTAs with Chile and Singapore include "essential security" provisions specifically applicable to government procurement obligations, but this type of national security exception is not present in the U.S.–Morocco and U.S.–Australia agreements. In general, the government procurement exceptions in the EU's PTAs broadly follow the template contained in Article XX of the General Agreement on Tariffs and Trade (GATT); Article 161 in the EU–Chile PTA is an example. U.S. PTAs are different in that they include additional specific measures, such as those necessary to protect human, animal, or plant life or health (e.g., U.S.–Chile PTA, Article 9.16).[14]

Settling Disputes over Government Procurement in PTAs

An effective dispute resolution mechanism is critical to the effectiveness of government procurement disciplines in PTAs. It also has broader application because government procurement dispute settlement provisions include a number of features that might usefully be employed in other behind-the-border policies (see Porges, ch. 22 in this volume).

Within a comprehensive PTA government procurement regime, there can be two or possibly three levels of dispute settlement. The first level consists of the procedures and institutions governing disputes between the procuring entity and a disappointed bidder (the disputes being those relating to the procurement procedure itself). The second level is the system governing disputes between the parties to the agreement—that is, state-state disputes regarding compliance or the implementation of the government procurement provisions within the agreement. At the third level, there may be a clause governing disputes between state parties that are simultaneously members of other relevant international agreements with overlapping jurisdictions that also include dispute settlement mechanisms.

Complaints about the procurement process. The availability of dispute settlement of complaints matters because it means there is a self-policing and self-enforcing mechanism for the procedural provisions set out in an agreement.[15] A dispute settlement mechanism provides an essential forum for airing complaints and obtaining relief, and it offers the parties due process rights while enhancing

the accountability of the officials and the procuring agencies. The existence of the mechanism improves the system's reputation, reducing barriers to entry caused by a poor perception of the integrity or due process of procurement markets. An important point is that complaints do not concern the performance of the contract, once it has been initiated. (That type of performance complaint is covered in the contract itself.)

Domestic review mechanisms can be located within a contracting agency, a dedicated independent entity, or the general court system. Each option has advantages and disadvantages relating to issues such as perceived independence, expertise, efficiency, and authority. A common model used in the more comprehensive PTAs is to house the bid challenge mechanism in a designated body or agency. A deep integration model such as the ANZGPA typically embeds the monitoring procedures in an annex to the agreement. The annex then commits the parties to identify a designated body as the responsible authority and point of contact for complaints. Monitoring is triggered by the examination of alleged breaches of the agreement by the other party. The designated body investigates the complaint, and if the matter cannot be resolved, it has the power to refer the case to the ministerial level for further investigation, if necessary. This is a very streamlined model that is able to balance the lack of formal procedures with speed and efficiency and is mainly suitable for more highly integrated markets.

The NAFTA bid challenge system is much more procedurally extensive. It obligates the parties to adopt and maintain bid challenge procedures that allow suppliers to submit challenges concerning any aspect of the procurement process. It seeks to ensure that the contracting entities accord fair and timely consideration to any complaint and sets out minimum time limits for the submission of complaints. Independent reviewing authorities must be identified, and the "entities normally shall follow the recommendations of the reviewing authority" for bringing the actions into conformity with their obligations.

A similar template obligating the parties to provide procedures that are transparent, timely, impartial, and effective can be found in the CAFTA–DR, EU–Chile, U.S.–Chile, and EU–CARIFORUM agreements. Most of these agreements do not specify the measures available for remedy of breaches or the amount of compensation. The EU–Chile agreement, for example, states that the challenge procedures shall provide for correction of breach of the provisions or for compensation for damages, which is limited to the costs of tender preparation and protest. The government procurement provisions in the EU–Mexico FTA concerning the gradual and reciprocal liberalization of signatory procurement markets are less ambitious, and the challenge procedures are correspondingly less well developed. The agreement simply states that the PTA's joint council should decide on the construction of "clear" challenge procedures.

As a model for some of the more comprehensive PTA provisions, Article XX of the WTO GPA, on challenge procedures, includes similar language concerning first-instance consultation procedures, transparency and good governance of the review proceedings, and time limits. The article further states that the review body should be a court or impartial entity subject to judicial review or similar procedures. The challenge provisions include the option of taking rapid interim measures to correct breaches of the agreement and limitation of compensation for damages suffered to the costs of tender preparation or protest.

Those PTAs that have soft cooperation provisions covering government procurement or best-endeavor clauses do not include bid challenge mechanisms because these are to be developed within domestic legislation. Where review mechanisms are included in such agreements, they necessarily apply only to procurement that lies within the scope and coverage negotiated by the parties.

Existing approaches in state-state disputes. Where neither party to a PTA is a member of the WTO GPA, disputes about nonimplementation of the government procurement provisions are governed only by the PTA itself. This is the case, for instance, with ANZCERTA, the deep integration PTA between Australia and New Zealand. No specific procedure is established to govern disputes related to noncompliance of government procurement provisions; instead, the agreement states that "the close and long-standing political relationship between Australia and New Zealand means that any issues of grievance or concern are addressed through discussion between the two Governments."

NAFTA's dispute resolution provisions are applicable to all disputes regarding the interpretation of application of NAFTA and are "intended to resolve disputes by agreement, if at all possible." Because the process encourages the use of arbitration for settlement of disputes between parties, it begins with government-to-government consultations. When these general disputes are not resolved through consultation within a specified period of time, either party can request that the dispute be referred initially to the "good offices" of NAFTA's Free Trade Commission. If the dispute is not resolved within a fixed time period, the matter can be referred to a panel for ad hoc arbitration. Each party selects two panel members, and the chair is chosen by consensus. The panel's recommenda-

tions are binding. Thus, in comparison with integrated systems such as those of the EU, EFTA, or COMESA, which have permanent international courts to settle disputes between member states, individuals, and the organization's institutions, NAFTA is less institutionalized and relies mostly on ad hoc arbitration and diplomacy.

The state-state dispute settlement provisions in the U.S.–Chile and CAFTA–DR agreements have a similar framework, typically reflecting the multimember nature of the PTAs. Both sequence dispute settlement procedures in the same manner, although the CAFTA–DR PTA has an additional provision allowing for multiple complainants and third-party participation in dispute proceedings and setting out different procedures. Under this agreement, a party that considers it has a substantial trade interest in a dispute between other parties to the agreement may participate after sending a written notice explaining its interest in the matter to the other parties within seven days of delivery of the initial request for consultations (Article 20.4, on consultations). That party automatically becomes one of the consulting parties and may request a meeting of the agreement's commission if the matter is not resolved within a specified time.

Overlapping jurisdictions and dispute settlement mechanism "shopping." Article XXII of the WTO GPA, on consultations and dispute settlement, provides that the WTO Dispute Settlement Understanding (DSU) applies if a GPA party considers that an objective of the agreement or a benefit accruing to the party from the agreement is being nullified or impaired because another member has failed to carry out its obligations. The Dispute Settlement Body (DSB) has the sole authority to establish panels of experts to consider the case and to accept or reject the panels' findings or the results of an appeal. It monitors the implementation of the rulings and recommendations and can authorize retaliation when a country does not comply with a ruling. The DSB's recommendations are to be implemented, and the relevant party must state its intention of doing so at a DSB meeting held within 30 days of the report's adoption. If it does not, the complaining side may ask the DSB for permission to impose limited trade sanctions against the noncompliant party; these sanctions are ideally restricted to the same sector as the nullification or impairment.

Because of its legalistic and binding framework, the DSB is one of the strongest trade arbitration forums. Its strength makes it attractive to weaker states that are unable to exert diplomatic pressure on a noncompliant party. But a lack of coherence in international trade law can result when governments are faced with multiple and overlapping obligations and jurisdictions to choose from when trying to settle a dispute.

To offer more predictability and transparency, some PTAs include rules that dictate the choice and sequencing of dispute settlement systems. In some PTAs, a request for the establishment of a WTO panel excludes the jurisdiction of the regional forum, or the use of one mechanism excludes the use of another (to prevent "forum hopping"). A PTA cannot take away the jurisdiction of the WTO GPA: if a party to both a PTA and the GPA appeals to the WTO Dispute Settlement Body, the panel will not refuse it because of PTA rules. (The panel will, however, refuse the dispute if it does not concern the application of the GPA or another WTO agreement.)

The U.S.–Chile and CAFTA–DR PTAs have clauses clarifying the forum to be used in a dispute. A complaining party may select the forum, which may be either the PTA concerned, another PTA to which the parties are party, or the WTO DSM, as appropriate. Once the party requests a panel under the jurisdiction of one agreement, the forum selected is to be used to the exclusion of others.

The arrangement in the EU–Chile agreement is more elaborate: it provides that unless the parties agree otherwise, when a party seeks redress for a violation of an obligation under the forum exclusion clause (which is equivalent in substance to an obligation under the WTO), it shall have recourse to the relevant rules and procedures of the WTO Agreement, which apply notwithstanding the provisions of the PTA. Once dispute settlement procedures have been initiated in a selected forum, that forum is to be used to the exclusion of any other

NAFTA's members are the United States and Canada, which are parties to the WTO GPA, and Mexico, which is not. In the case of a dispute relating to procurement between the United States and Canada, those countries can choose whether to use the PTA or the WTO forum. Mexico's procurement is exclusively governed by NAFTA, and so it must adhere to the procedures specified in that agreement.

The NAFTA dispute settlement procedures are oriented toward diplomatic or negotiated solutions. They provide that disputes regarding any matter that arises under both NAFTA and the General Agreement on Tariffs and Trade (GATT), or under any agreement negotiated under these arrangements, or under any successor agreement, may be settled in either forum at the discretion of the complaining party. A party is to notify any third party of its intention to bring a dispute, with a view to agreement on a single forum. If the parties cannot agree, the dispute is normally to be settled under the NAFTA procedure. This has led in the past to some danger of legal fragmentation, as can be seen in the U.S.–Mexico soft drinks dispute, when Mexico tried to bring a NAFTA dispute to the WTO on the

grounds that the United States refused to form a panel to settle the dispute under NAFTA. The WTO Dispute Settlement Body declined jurisdiction because the dispute did not fall within the scope of the WTO agreements.

Clearly, parties tend to choose the recourse most likely to generate a favorable outcome for themselves. The variables considered will include the scope and legal status of the measure in dispute; the applicable law; the procedures, structure, and time frame of each mechanism; the remedies available; and the inherent characteristics of each dispute settlement process. That is, consideration of the political circumstances of the dispute can also influence its resolution, as is seen in the dispute between Mexico and the United States over soft drink sweeteners (for background, see Davey and Sapir 2009).

Costs of Implementing Government Procurement Provisions

Information on the costs of implementing government procurement provisions in PTAs is scarce.[16] Still, enough is known about the content of potential PTA provisions that some tentative observations can be made about the nature and extent of these costs.

Setting up an effective government procurement regime requires specialized institutional frameworks and expertise. Although the economic and welfare benefits to be gained from fair and transparent procurement markets are likely to be sizable as a share of the total amount spent on goods and services by the government, the procedures and challenge mechanisms which enable bidders to feel confident that procurement processes are fair and transparent will require resources. The implementation of a PTA, however, does not necessarily entail new costs, as the government may have borne some or all of these costs beforehand. What share of additional implementation costs is PTA-specific is an open, factual question, the answer to which is likely to differ according to the country and the preexisting procurement regime.

Implementation costs are likely to vary across government procurement provisions. For example, transparency provisions that require signatories to publish all relevant procurement regulations in a foreign language will require translators with legal expertise, and retaining the specialized legal talent to adjudicate complaints on procurement matters and present appeals before tribunals is a distinct resource challenge. The nature and timing of implementation costs will thus differ among classes of government procurement provisions and capacity-building needs.

The costs associated with setting up an effective national procurement system are usually borne by the jurisdiction concerned. The review of PTAs in this section indicates that no regional institutions had to be created to implement any of the agreements. Even in the PTAs with the most comprehensive government procurement commitments, the institutional implications are all at the national level. This contrasts with regional competition regimes that have established a regional competition law and a competition authority to monitor the implementation of the provisions (see Dawar and Holmes, ch. 16 in this volume). Although setting up an effective and transparent government procurement system is costly, there are no further costs for establishing and running the regional procurement institutions provided for in these PTAs. This is so even in the case of the deepest government procurement integration framework, the ANZGPA between Australia and New Zealand. The implementation of the agreement relies on existing national bodies, and no supranational institutions need to be established. The agreement contains the monitoring requirement that each jurisdiction must have at least one designated body to be the point of contact for complaints, with the authority, responsibility, and expertise to handle and investigate complaints across government and public sector agencies covered by the agreement. If the complaint is multijurisdictional, all the relevant designated bodies and, where necessary, ministers are included in the procedure.

Similarly, the CAFTA–DR procurement regime includes commitments to establish or designate at least one impartial administrative or judicial authority, independent of procuring entities, to receive and review challenges by suppliers relating to the obligations of the party. Again, this bid challenge mechanism is to be established at the national level and does not entail any institutional buildup, assuming that there is already a domestic institution for reviewing domestic complaints. The same is true of those PTAs with provisions that are restricted to ensuring transparency in government procurement, such as the EU–CARIFORUM agreement. Each party must identify or designate at least one impartial administrative or judicial authority that is independent of its procuring entities to receive and review challenges by suppliers arising in the context of covered procurement.

In the case of the U.S.–Jordan agreement, the institutional implications are broader than a commitment to establish national procurement institutions to implement the obligations of the PTA. Article 9 of the agreement states that, pursuant to Jordan's application for accession to the WTO GPA in 2000, the parties shall enter into negotiations with regard to Jordan's accession to the WTO GPA. The GPA requires that a committee on government procurement, composed of representatives from each the party, be established. This committee is to meet as necessary, but not less than once a year. It may establish working parties to carry out specific functions. Jordan's decision to accede to the GPA, however, was made independently and before the agreement with the United States.

In sum, much of any burden of implementation of PTA obligations is borne at the national (and, potentially, subnational) levels. But there is another significant opportunity cost that some governments may perceive from signing government procurement provisions: constraints on the use of state spending as an "industrial policy" tool for promoting targeted industries.[17] This is not the place for a full exposition on industrial policy; suffice it to say that assertions about the implications of government procurement reforms for such policies have been made in both developing and industrial countries. An important question is whether public procurement policies optimally target whatever market failure is holding back the industries in question.

Technical Assistance

Technical assistance requirements related to government procurement in PTAs may be quite substantial. For example, NAFTA requires the parties to provide, on a cost-recovery basis, information concerning training and orientation programs relevant to their government procurement systems and to grant nondiscriminatory access to any programs they conduct. Such activities include training of government personnel directly involved in government procurement procedures; training of suppliers interested in pursuing government procurement opportunities; an explanation and description of specific elements of the party's government procurement system, such as its bid challenge mechanism; and information about government procurement market opportunities. NAFTA parties are also required to establish at least one contact point to provide information on the training and orientation programs. These NAFTA provisions are much more extensive than the analogous obligations in other PTAs. For instance, the EU–Chile PTA states only that the parties will seek to provide technical assistance on issues connected with public procurement, with special attention to the municipal level.

For PTA developing-country members that are also signatories of the WTO GPA, the technical assistance provisions are more substantive than at the regional level. Article V of the GPA, on special and differential treatment for developing countries, states that each developed-country party shall, on request, provide all the technical assistance which it may deem appropriate to developing-country parties to help resolve their problems in the field of government procurement and that this assistance must be provided in a nondiscriminatory way. Assistance is to be directed toward the solution of particular technical problems relating to the award of a specific contract and is to include translations into an official WTO language of qualification documentation and of tenders made by suppliers of developing-country parties. Developed-country members are required to establish, individually or jointly, information centers to respond to reasonable requests from developing-country parties for a variety of specified procurement information.

Government Procurement Provisions in PTAs in a Multilateral World

In assessing the trade-negotiating options facing a government in the area of government procurement practices, it is commonplace to compare nondiscriminatory PTA options with multilateral reform conducted on an MFN basis. Such assumptions, however, should not always guide policy advice in the government procurement arena, precisely because the GPA is a plurilateral accord that extends "concessions" only to other signatories to that accord. As far as market access is concerned, there is no nondiscriminatory multilateral benchmark to rely on, and as long as the national institutions associated with implementing public procurement are exempted from the WTO's national treatment provisions, there is no multilateral benchmark there, either.

The absence of benchmarks does not imply that pursuit of nondiscriminatory reform through a trade agreement is impossible. At present, such reform can take place unilaterally or, somewhat paradoxically, in the context of a preferential PTA. In the future, however, should WTO members extend traditional nondiscriminatory disciplines on a multilateral scale, another means of liberalizing public purchases on an MFN basis will become available. With these remarks, it should be clear that any analogies between tariff reform strategies and public procurement reform strategies in the context of trade agreements have to be drawn very carefully. Blanket application of the logic of the former to the latter is likely to be misleading.

Theoretical versus Actual Costs of Discrimination

There are theoretical reasons why provisions on government procurement in PTAs could be discriminatory. First, as in any situation in which a buyer has market power—as some state buyers with large budgets might—discrimination against certain suppliers can, in principle, reduce the costs to the purchaser. In the context of government procure-

ment, as in other situations of less-than-perfect competition (see Baldwin, ch. 3 in this volume), deviations from free trade could theoretically be welfare improving. For instance, imposing price preferences on foreign suppliers (i.e., raising their bids by a certain percentage) will induce them to lower their bids for state contracts. If enough of those foreign suppliers enjoy a cost advantage over their domestic rivals, the probability that a foreign supplier could still win the contract may be high enough that the expected cost of the government procurement will fall. In these circumstances, promoting a level playing field may not necessarily be welfare maximizing. Yet, the lack of capacity to collect and analyze the necessary information to discriminate optimally between suppliers calls into question whether a state purchaser could in practice tap the gains from exploiting its buying clout. Moreover, as Deltas and Evenett (1997) show in a series of simulations of procurement bidding situations, the gains from discrimination may be small (when expressed as a percentage of the purchase price), and even tiny mistakes in setting the optimal degree of discrimination could result in increased, not reduced, procurement costs. All in all, a rule of thumb of open competition is recommended to policy makers. This implies opening up state procurement contracts to the maximum number of appropriately qualified bidders.

Second, traditional concerns related to PTAs about the risk and cost of trade diversion could also apply to the preferential liberalization of government procurement in these agreements. Whether trade is diverted from efficient to less-efficient foreign suppliers will depend on the treatment of foreign bids before the PTA was concluded. If bids from foreigners were allowed and price preferences were applied on an MFN basis before the PTA was enacted, the traditional concerns about trade creation and trade diversion arise.[18] By contrast, if no bids from foreign firms were allowed before the PTA was signed, the additional competition for state contracts is likely to push down the price paid by the public buyer, and there was no trade to divert in the first place. Overall, this suggests that if a PTA generates, for the first time, significant foreign competition for state contracts, there are likely to be economic benefits in the form of lower procurement costs. For procurement regimes that already benefit from considerable foreign competition, the benefits of preferential reform through PTAs may be ambiguous and even adverse.

A third consideration is that there are various forms of discrimination in government procurement systems against foreign bidders. Simulations have been conducted of the increases in procurement costs created by price preferences, by measures that raise the costs of foreign bidders, and by outright limitations on the number of foreign bidders.

Although these simulations do not claim to have covered every single case or procurement setting, price preferences were found to inflict the least harm, and cost-raising measures were the next least harmful. Given these findings, it is paradoxical that discrimination though price preferences is most often singled out for banning in PTAs. A perhaps preferable alternative might be to eliminate or limit the other forms of discrimination, even if it comes at the expense of higher price preferences, at least initially.[19]

Transparency and Third-Party MFN

The implementation of PTA provisions that improve the transparency of government procurement procedures (on the plausible assumption that the entry of both domestic and foreign firms is encouraged by such improvements) may lead to either reductions or increases in the share of state contracts awarded to foreign firms (Evenett and Hoekman 2005). There is some evidence that small and medium-size enterprises are more sensitive to the transparency of national procurement regimes, in which case PTA-induced improvements in transparency may increase the proportion of state contracts awarded to a class of firms that governments, for other reasons, typically wish to favor.

The example of implementation of improvements in transparency on an MFN basis carries over to other PTA-induced improvements in public procurement regimes that are implemented on a nondiscriminatory basis. One might ask why a government would voluntarily extend benefits to non-PTA signatories.[20] The answer is that the implementation costs of operating two or more procurement regimes for different trading partners may exceed the cost of operating a single reformed regime. Indeed, consistent with the literature on multilateralizing regionalism (e.g., Baldwin and Low 2009), it is possible that a PTA can induce in a signatory an institutional innovation or improvement that is willingly shared with all trading partners. Again, concerns about the inherently discriminatory nature of PTAs must be tempered. The fact that certain PTA provisions on public procurement are written in a discriminatory manner does not mean that they are so implemented or that the net effect of all the PTAs provisions is to limit the commercial opportunities of nonsignatories.

There may, however, be more subtle intertemporal relationships between PTA provisions on government procurement and nondiscrimination. The use of third-party MFN clauses is a case in point. Under such a clause, should A, a party to a PTA with B, subsequently sign another PTA with a third party, C, and in so doing offer C better access to A's government procurement market than B, then B is entitled to the same access as C.[21] (The better market access

here could relate to more contracts, lower price preferences, lower thresholds, and so on) The use of such a provision would ratchet up the degree of competition over time in government procurement markets while simultaneously ensuring that all beneficiaries of this clause fight for contracts on the same terms (limiting discrimination between PTA signatories.) Third-party MFN provisions do not, of course, limit discrimination against exporters from countries that have not signed a PTA, so it would be wrong to conclude that they eliminate all forms of discrimination across trading partners.

Because of the potential confusion regarding third-party obligations in future PTAs, it is becoming more common to clarify these issues of overlapping PTA membership and jurisdictions within the agreement itself. Government procurement provisions in the more comprehensive PTAs aim to open public procurement to foreign competition on a preferential basis. In order to protect these preferences, some procurement provisions require third-party MFN guarantees so as to limit the extent to which preferential procurement is undermined by subsequent PTAs.[22]

Third-party MFN clauses that extend preferential access automatically reduce the geographic discrimination implied by proliferating PTAs. They also allow a government to free ride on the negotiating clout of their PTA partners in future agreements: countries with relatively small procurement outlays can choose to negotiate for the inclusion of these provisions if it seems that the other party may subsequently negotiate an agreement with a larger country. Albania, the former Yugoslav Republic of Macedonia, and Turkey have in the past included third-party MFN provisions and have followed this strategy.

It should be noted that the arguments reviewed above are based on economic principles and evidence from simulations of procurement auctions. We do not know of a single econometric analysis that seeks to estimate the effect of implementing the government procurement provisions of a PTA.[23] Policy makers and readers should bear this in mind when assessing the above arguments.

Relationship to Open Regionalism

Some experts, recognizing the pervasive nature of PTAs, have argued that their discriminatory impact might be limited if terms could be defined ex ante under which nonsignatories could enter a trade bloc. Clarity of terms of entry and the desire to limit the loss of commercial opportunities from being outside a bloc are said to encourage entry and, ultimately, to expand the amount of trade conducted under freer, if preferential, terms. In principle, the key ingredients for such open regionalism to work are present in the context of PTA provisions on government procurement, as long as these provisions are implemented on a nondiscriminatory basis.

Yet, it could be that the preferential trade-related government procurement accord most likely to induce entry is the WTO's plurilateral GPA, which now has 40 members. Existing GPA members are unlikely to offer more market access to a new member (so, the terms of entry are clear), and the scope of public procurement covered in the GPA is greater than under any existing PTA. This is not to say that open regionalism could not happen anywhere else but only that it would be strange to see such developments happening outside the WTO when the WTO accord provides the greatest incentives to join. If that logic is to be taken seriously, the best hope for open regionalism is probably open plurilateralism. Then, the provision of the U.S.–Jordan PTA that supports Jordan's accession to the WTO GPA could be seen to promote open regionalism and open plurilateralism most directly.

Implications for Trade Negotiating Strategy and for Evaluation of Policy Options

In recent years, more and more PTAs have included provisions on government procurement, ranging from transparency-only clauses to the creation of a single regional procurement market. These provisions affect an important area of state behavior—public purchasing—and there is, no doubt, interest in their potential development impact. The word "potential" is used deliberately because policy makers, officials, and analysts would be wise to differentiate between what has been done and what could be done. Arguably, this is an area of trade policy making in which, at present, the former is far from approaching the latter.

For many countries, government procurement outlays are a sensitive matter, at least in terms of interest groups and politics. The desire for value for money in public purchasing has often been tempered by support for favored industries and groups. This has complicated but has not precluded the negotiation of government procurement provisions in PTAs, often with the full range of exceptions and other devices used to limit the impact of such provisions. Procedures to review the cost of those exceptions and to suggest alternative measures of helping favored industries should be given greater consideration in the future.

More generally, many of the rules of thumb that trade economists have developed concerning the relative efficacy of different tariff reform strategies do not carry over to public procurement reforms. Evaluations of public policy

options should not be approached dogmatically. Rather, a case-by-case evaluation is appropriate, taking due account of the state of national purchasing practices before any reform was launched. For example, PTA provisions that call for improvements in transparency should be treated differently from those relating to market access. Moreover, pointing to WTO obligations as a nondiscriminatory benchmark is not an accurate reflection of the existing state of that organization's plurilateral accord. Even more confusingly, the tension between discrimination and liberalization in PTAs may not be as relevant for public procurement as it is for tariffs.

Policy analysts would do best to understand, first, national procurement regimes and, second, the potential sources and magnitudes of benefits from reform. Then, consideration should be given to which reform vehicle (unilateral, bilateral, regional, or multilateral) offers the greatest promise over the time frame contemplated. The ability to motivate and sustain a constituency in favor of procurement reform is an important consideration and is likely to vary across reform options, time spans, and jurisdictions. To date, there is insufficient evidence to confidently recommend one reform vehicle over another.

For analysts, much remains to be done in analyzing compliance with, and the effect of, government procurement provisions in PTAs. It is unsatisfactory that the evidential base, whether in terms of legal compliance or of economic effects, that is needed to guide policy making is so thin. The hard and, some might say, tedious work of tracking what has happened after governments have taken on obligations on procurement in PTAs is still to be done. For example, in many PTAs the emphasis has been on trying to eliminate the more transparent forms of discrimination (such as price preferences), and this may have had the unintended consequence of driving discrimination into nontransparent forms.

Annex. PTAs with Government Procurement Provisions

The following PTAs containing government procurement provisions had been notified to the WTO as of December 2009.

Australia–Chile
Canada–Costa Rica
Canada–European Free Trade Association (EFTA)
Canada–Peru
Caribbean Community (CARICOM) (services)
Central European Free Trade Agreement (CEFTA)
Chile–China
Chile–Colombia

Chile–Costa Rica
Chile–El Salvador
Dominican Republic–Central America–United States Free Trade Agreement (CAFTA–DR)
EFTA (services)
EFTA–Chile
EFTA–Croatia
EFTA–Egypt, Arab Rep.
EFTA–Jordan
EFTA–Korea, Rep.
EFTA–Lebanon
EFTA–Macedonia, FYR
EFTA–Mexico
EFTA–Morocco
EFTA–Singapore
EFTA–South African Customs Union (SACU)
EFTA–Tunisia
European Union (EU)–Albania
EU–Algeria
EU–Cameroon
EU–Caribbean Forum of African, Caribbean, and Pacific (ACP) States (CARIFORUM) economic partnership agreement (EPA)
EU–Chile
EU–Egypt, Arab Rep.
EU–Israel
EU–Jordan
EU–Mexico
EU–Montenegro
EU–Morocco
EU–South Africa
Iceland–Faroe Islands
Israel–Mexico
Japan–Brunei Darussalam
Japan–Chile
Japan–Indonesia
Japan–Mexico
Japan–Philippines
Japan–Singapore
Japan–Switzerland
Japan–Thailand
Japan–Vietnam
Jordan–Singapore
Jordan–United States
Korea, Rep.–Chile
Korea, Rep.–Singapore
Mexico–Chile
Mexico–Costa Rica
Mexico–El Salvador
Mexico–Guatemala
Mexico–Honduras (goods)

Mexico–Honduras (services)
Mexico–Nicaragua
Pacific Island Countries Trade Agreement (PICTA)
Panama–Costa Rica
Panama–El Salvador
Singapore–Australia
Singapore–New Zealand
Singapore–Panama
Singapore–Peru
Thailand–Australia
Thailand–New Zealand
Trans-Pacific Strategic Economic Partnership
Turkey–Albania
Turkey–Bosnia and Herzegovina
Turkey–Croatia
Turkey–Egypt, Arab Rep.
Turkey–Georgia
Turkey–Macedonia, FYR
Turkey–Morocco
Turkey–Palestinian Authority
Turkey–Syrian Arab Republic
Turkey–Tunisia
Ukraine–Macedonia, FYR
Ukraine–Moldova
United States–Australia
United States–Bahrain
United States–Chile
United States–Morocco
United States–Oman
United States–Peru
United States–Singapore

Source: WTO data.

Notes

1. A feature of the literature on government procurement is the paucity of comparable cross-country estimates of the total amounts spent on goods and services. OECD (2001) is the most recent study to have assembled information for many industrial and developing countries, and it used 1998 United Nations data. The study shows that in 1998 the level of government spending on goods and services worldwide was, on average, 14.5 percent of gross domestic product (GDP); in industrial countries it was 17.1 percent.

2. Although the functions listed in this paragraph may be less intensively executed in developing countries, the experiences of certain industrial countries would suggest that it is unwise to assume that resource constraints are confined to poorer countries.

3. This argument is developed at greater length and with specific reference to the imprecise notion "policy space" in Dawar and Evenett (2008).

4. Strictly speaking there is a wrinkle in the value-for-money principle. To the extent that a government buyer has market (monopsony) power, the pursuit of this objective may result in prices at which market outcomes are inefficient—that is, the prices do not equal the marginal costs of production or the societal costs of producing the last unit of the

good or service in question. Given the size of many government purchasers relative to total demand in the market for a given good or service, this logical possibility has received remarkably little consideration.

5. Prevalent forms of discrimination against foreign firms in national procurement regimes include price preferences (which raise foreign bids by a certain percentage before they are compared with the bids of domestic firms), outright bans on foreign bidders, local content-related restrictions, and standards adopted in the procurement process that raise the costs of foreign firms.

6. Observant readers will have noted that any such procurement ban does not remedy the ultimate cause of the small size of the private sector.

7. There is some evidence in the corruption literature that improvements in the transparency of government procurement processes result in a shift of government spending toward more homogeneous goods and away from goods that are so heterogeneous that bids cannot be easily compared (which increases the potential for graft to affect the allocation of state contracts). For a summary of such evidence, see Evenett and Hoekman (2005). Bourgeois, Dawar, and Evenett (2007) summarize the little empirical evidence, mostly from the European Union, on the impact of procurement reforms and PTA procurement provisions. The principal findings are summarized in this chapter.

8. United Nations Commission on International Trade Law, "1994—UNCITRAL Model Law on Procurement of Goods, Construction and Services, with Guide to Enactment," http://www.uncitral.org/uncitral/en/uncitral_texts/procurement_infrastructure/1994Model.html.

9. The type of discrimination referred to in the general principles is sometimes referred to as conditional MFN, in that each party offers MFN treatment to every other party to the accord. Nonsignatories are not offered MFN.

10. This clause is also seen in the EU agreements with Mexico and Jordan. The Trade, Development, and Cooperation Agreement (TDCA) between the EU and South Africa directs the Cooperation Council established under the agreement to review progress made in opening fair, equitable, and transparent procurement markets.

11. The parastatals referred to are government-controlled enterprises; they include the U.S. Tennessee Valley Authority (TVA), Canada's St. Lawrence Seaway Authority, and Mexico's national oil company Petroleos Mexicanos (PEMEX) and national electric company, the Comisión Federal de Electricidad (CFE).

12. The WTO GPA obligations apply to the goods and services listed in Annexes 4 and 5 of the agreement, again typically following a negotiated positive-list approach.

13. The thresholds are, for central government entities, 130,000 SDRs for procurement of goods and services and 5 million SDRs for procurement of construction services; for subcentral government entities, 200,000 SDRs for goods and services (except for the United States and Canada, which apply a 355,000 SDR threshold) and 5 million SDRs for construction services (except for Japan and the Republic of Korea, which apply a 15 million SDR threshold); for government-owned enterprises, 400,000 SDRs for goods and services (except for the United States, which sets a US$250,000 threshold for federally owned utilities) and 5 million SDRs for construction services (except for Japan and Korea, which apply a threshold of 15 million SDRs).

14. By contrast, the exceptions to Article XXIII of the WTO GPA are more streamlined in that they cover security interests and social and philanthropic protection within one article.

15. A variety of terminology, depending on the country or organization, exists to describe the mechanisms for resolving a complaint by a would-be contractor on the conduct of the procurement process prior to the decision on selection: domestic review mechanisms; protests by disappointed bidders; complaints; or, simply, appeals. The WTO GPA refers to "bid challenges," and the UNCITRAL Model Law, to "bid review."

16. This paucity of information should not be surprising, given that, unlike the tariff provisions of PTAs, the behind-the-border provisions of such accords are a much more recent policy innovation.

17. Government procurement policies may be used to favor outright a certain group in society or, indeed, specific individuals. Leaving aside whether such favoritism is legal, it has long been suspected that resistance to reform of public purchasing practices in some jurisdictions has been influenced by the desire to preserve such practices. It is unclear why there would be less resistance to reform induced by a trade agreement than to unilateral reform.

18. Formally, the case of price preferences is different from that of tariffs in that the PTA leads to a loss of government revenues (the lost tariff revenues on the favored trade).

19. The replacement of other forms of discrimination by a transparent price-based instrument of discrimination is, of course, not new, as attempts at "tariffication" of nontariff measures can attest. The same logic applies in the procurement case.

20. Indeed, it is frequently contended by European Commission officials that many government procurement contracts in the EU can be contested by parties from all its trading partners.

21. One feature of these provisions is that a "weak" negotiating partner can benefit from a subsequent "tougher" negotiator's ability to extract more market access concessions from trading partners with which both the weak and stronger parties ultimately sign a PTA. These tactical considerations may add to the attraction of third-party MFN clauses for weaker negotiating parties, which may number among them many developing countries.

22. For example, according to Article 67, on further negotiations, of the EFTA–Mexico PTA, "In the case that the EFTA States or Mexico offer, after the entry into force of this Agreement, a GPA or NAFTA Party, respectively, additional advantages with regard to the access to their respective procurement markets beyond what has been agreed under this Chapter, they shall agree to enter into negotiations with the other Party with a view to extending these advantages to the other Party on a reciprocal basis." Article 18, on review of commitments, of the South Asian Free Trade Area (SAFTA), states, "If, after this Agreement enters into force, a Party enters into any agreement on government procurement with a non-Party, it shall give positive consideration to a request by the other Party for incorporation herein of treatment no less favourable than under the aforesaid agreement. Any such incorporation should maintain the overall balance of commitments undertaken by each Party under this Agreement." Article 160, on further negotiations, of the EU–Chile agreement specifies, "If either Party should offer in the future a third party additional advantages with regard to access to their respective procurement markets beyond what has been agreed under this Title, it shall agree to enter into negotiations with the other Party with a view to extending these advantages to it on a reciprocal basis by means of a decision of the Association Committee." Article 9, on further negotiations, of the U.S.–Chile PTA states, "On request of either Party, the Parties shall enter into negotiations with a view to extending coverage under this Chapter on a reciprocal basis, if a Party provides, through an international agreement entered into after entry into force of this Agreement, access to its procurement market for suppliers of a non-Party beyond what it provides under this Agreement to suppliers of the other Party."

23. There are studies that seek to forecast the increase in trade if government procurement policies were liberalized. These forecasts, however, are not the same as an estimate of the impact of the implementation of an actual PTA with government procurement provisions.

Bibliography

Anderson, Robert D., and Christopher R. Yukins. 2007. "Policy & Legal Frameworks for Opening the Chinese Procurement Markets." GWU Law School Public Law Research Paper 407, George Washington University Law School, Washington, DC.

———. 2008. "International Public Procurement Developments in 2008: Public Procurement in a World Economic Crisis." GWU Law School Public Law Research Paper 458, George Washington University Law School, Washington, DC.

Anderson, Robert D., Anna Caroline Müller, Kodjo Osei-Lah, Josefita Pardo De Leon, and Philippe Pelletier. 2009. "Government Procurement Provisions in Recent Regional Trade Agreements: Characterization, Analysis, and Implications vis-à-vis The WTO Agreement on Government Procurement." World Trade Organization, Geneva.

Arrowsmith, Sue, and Arwel Davies, eds. 1998. *Public Procurement: Global Revolution.* The Hague: Kluwer Law International.

Arrowsmith, Sue, and Martin Trybus, eds. 2003. *Public Procurement: The Continuing Revolution.* The Hague: Kluwer Law International.

Arrowsmith, Sue, John Linarelli, and Don Wallace, Jr. 2000. *Regulating Public Procurement: National and International Perspectives.* The Hague: Kluwer Law International.

Baldwin, Richard, and Patrick Low, eds. 2009. *Multilateralizing Regionalism: Challenges for the Global Trading System.* Cambridge, U.K.: Cambridge University Press.

Baldwin, Robert E. 1970. *Nontariff Distortions of International Trade.* Washington, DC: Brookings Institution.

Baldwin, Robert E., and J. David Richardson. 1972. "Government Purchasing Policies, Other NTBs, and the International Monetary Crisis." In *Obstacles to Trade in the Pacific Area: Proceedings of the Fourth Pacific Trade and Development Conference,* ed. H. Edward English and Keith A. J. Hay, Ottawa: Carleton School of International Affairs.

Bourgeois, Jacques, Kamala Dawar, and Simon J. Evenett. 2007. "A Comparative Analysis of Selected Provisions in Free Trade Agreements." Prepared for the Directorate General for Trade, European Commission, Brussels.

Campos, J. Edgardo, and Jose Luis Syquia. 2006. *Managing the Politics of Reform: Overhauling the Legal Infrastructure of Public Procurement in the Philippines.* World Bank Working Paper 70. Washington, DC: World Bank. http://www-wds.worldbank.org/external/default/WDS ContentServer/WDSP/IB/2005/10/31/000090341_20051031141413/ Rendered/PDF/340440Man0Politic0Reform.pdf.

Davey, William J., and André Sapir. 2009. "The Soft Drinks Case: The WTO and Regional Agreements." *World Trade Review* 8 (1): 5–23. http://journals.cambridge.org/action/displayFulltext?type=1&fid= 4591316&jid=WTR&volumeId=8&issueId=01&aid=4591308.

Dawar, Kamala, and Simon J. Evenett. 2008. "Cariforum EPA and Beyond. The Cariforum–EC EPA: An Analysis of Its Government Procurement and Competition Law–Related Provisions." Working Paper, Deutsche Gesellschaft für Technische Zusammenarbeit (GTZ), Eschborn, Germany.

Deltas, George, and Simon J. Evenett. 1997. "Quantitative Estimates of the Effects of Preference Policies." In *Law and Policy in Public Purchasing:*

The WTO Agreement on Government Procurement, ed. Bernard M. Hoekman and Petros C. Mavroidis. Ann Arbor, MI: University of Michigan Press.

Dimitri, Nicola, Gustavo Piga, and Giancarlo Spagnolo, eds. 2006. *Handbook of Procurement.* Cambridge, U.K.: Cambridge University Press.

Evenett, Simon J., and Bernard M. Hoekman. 2005. "Government Procurement: Market Access, Transparency, and Multilateral Trade Rules." *European Journal of Political Economy* 21 (1, March): 163–83.

Hunja, Robert R. 2003. "Obstacles to Public Procurement Reform in Developing Countries." In *Public Procurement: The Continuing Revolution,* ed. Sue Arrowsmith and Martin Trybus, 13–22. The Hague: Kluwer Law International.

Jones, D. S. 2007. "Public Procurement in South East Asia: Challenge and Reform." *Journal of Public Procurement* 7 (1): 3–33.

McAfee, R. Preston, and John McMillan. 1989. "Government Procurement and International Trade." *Journal of International Economics* 26 (3–4): 291–308.

OECD (Organisation for Economic Co-operation and Development). 2001. *The Size of Government Procurement Markets.* Paris: OECD.

Schooner, Steven L. 2002. "Desiderata: Objectives for a System of Government Contract Law." Public Law and Legal Theory Working Paper 37, George Washington University Law School, Washington, DC.

Schooner, Steven L., and Christopher R. Yukins. 2003. "Model Behaviour? Anecdotal Evidence of Tension between Evolving Commercial Public Procurement Practices and Trade Policy." *International Trade Law and Regulation 9.* SSRN: http://papers.ssrn.com/sol3/papers.cfm?abstract _id=346000.

Schooner, Steven L., Daniel I. Gordon, and Jessica L. Clark. "Public Procurement Systems: Unpacking Stakeholder Aspirations and Expectations." George Washington University Law School, Washington, DC. SSRN: http://ssrn.com/abstract=1133234.

Thai, Khi V., and Gustavo Piga, eds. 2007. *Advancing Public Procurement: Practices, Innovation and Knowledge Sharing.* Boca Raton. FL: PRAcademics Press.

WTO (World Trade Organization). 2000. "Synopsis of 'Systemic' Issues Related to Regional Trade Agreements Committee on Regional Trade Agreements." WT/REG/W/37, March 2, WTO, Geneva.

Yukins, Christopher R. 2006. "A Case Study in Comparative Procurement Law: Assessing UNCITRAL's Lessons for U.S. Procurement." *Public Contract Law Journal* 35 (3, Spring).

Yukins, Christopher R., and Steven L. Schooner. 2007. "Incrementalism: Eroding the Impediments to a Global Public Procurement Market." *Georgetown Journal of International Law* 38 (529).

18

INTELLECTUAL PROPERTY RIGHTS

Carsten Fink

Rules for the protection of intellectual property rights (IPRs) have become a common feature of preferential trade agreements (PTAs). Historically, the North American Free Trade Agreement (NAFTA), which came into force in 1994, was the first major trade agreement to include specific obligations on protection of patents, trademarks, copyright, and other forms of IPRs. As PTAs have proliferated over the past two decades, so has the number of bilateral or regional IPR rulebooks. Many PTAs, however, contain no obligations for IPR protection.

On the multilateral level, 1994 also saw the signing of the Agreement on Trade-Related Aspects of Intellectual Property Rights (TRIPS), at the close of the Uruguay Round of trade negotiations. The TRIPS Agreement is now about 15 years old, and the intellectual property field has undergone many changes. Governments have accordingly felt a need to update and clarify certain IPR standards in their international commercial relations, leading to the introduction of IPR provisions in many PTAs.

Another reason to embed IPR rules in a PTA is that these rules typically represent an important element in the overall package of quid pro quos necessary to strike a trade deal. For developed countries that host substantial IPR-producing industries, stronger protection of IPRs in foreign countries is usually an important market access concern. In exchange for preferential access to their markets for manufactured or agricultural goods, developed countries therefore press their trading partners to commit to strong standards of IPR protection. From this point of view, it is not surprising to find IPR chapters more frequently in North-North and North-South PTAs than in South-South PTAs.

Just as the TRIPS Agreement is probably the most controversial agreement among the multilateral trading rules of the World Trade Organization (WTO), the negotiation of new IPR standards at the bilateral and regional level is often a divisive topic. Developed-country industry groups typically advocate the inclusion of a comprehensive IPR chapter in the PTAs signed by their governments. For example, the U.S. Chamber of Commerce states on its Web site, "We strongly advocate legislative and enforcement actions by our top trading partners to bar the theft of intellectual property created and owned by U.S. artists, researchers, and companies. The U.S. government should push our trading partners to uphold intellectual property rights, and countries that fail to do so should be subject to sanction under existing multilateral trade rules and *bilateral accords*" (emphasis added).[1] In some developing countries, by contrast, PTA negotiations have been accompanied by street protests alleging harmful consequences if the government were to sign on to higher levels of IPR protections.

This chapter presents an introduction to the treatment of IPRs in PTAs. It begins with a brief discussion of the context in which negotiations on IPRs take place, emphasizing the difference between traditional trade negotiations on tariff liberalization and negotiations on IPR standards. Subsequent sections summarize the main IPR provisions found in PTAs, with a focus on the extent to which PTA obligations go beyond the WTO's TRIPS Agreement ("TRIPS+" provisions). The PTAs of the two main trading blocs are surveyed first. U.S. agreements contain TRIPS+ obligations for most forms of IPRs; agreements concluded by the European Union (EU) are not equally comprehensive but do introduce new rules in certain areas. The treatment of IPRs in other PTAs is then briefly described.

In addition to self-standing IPR chapters in PTAs, intellectual property obligations are also found in bilateral or regional investment accords. Sometimes these investment agreements take the form of another PTA chapter, and sometimes they are separate treaties. Regardless of their form, these accords are part of the legal framework governing bilateral or regional commercial relations and are therefore briefly reviewed. Finally, the last section summarizes the main messages emerging from the discussion.

Before proceeding, it is worth pointing out what this chapter does not cover: it offers neither a thorough introduction to the economics of different forms of IPRs nor a comprehensive review of the TRIPS Agreement. The annex to the chapter contains additional resources on these topics.

Negotiating Considerations

It is instructive to compare trade negotiations that involve the adoption of new IPR standards with more traditional trade negotiations focused on the exchange of tariff reduction commitments. In the latter case, country A promises to lower its tariffs faced by exporters in B, and country B promises to lower its tariffs faced by exporters in A. Although this type of proposition seems only "fair," it is not grounded in pure economic logic. Economic theory mostly makes a case for unilateral trade liberalization: countries are always better off if they eliminate import protection, regardless of what other countries do.[2] Nonetheless, economists go along with the concept of reciprocity because governments may find it politically easier to make a case for own-market opening if other countries also open their markets. Protectionist lobbies that may expect to lose from greater foreign competition may be less powerful if they are pitted against export-oriented constituents that stand to gain from enhanced market access abroad.

At first sight, the logic for negotiating IPR rules in trade agreements seems similar. For example, a developing country with weak IPR protection may not find it politically feasible to strengthen its level of protection without the support of exporters that benefit from enhanced commercial opportunities in a large developed-country market. Similarly, the developed-country government may find it difficult to overcome protectionist agricultural or industrial lobbies that fear competition from lower-wage developing-country producers without the support of IPR-producing industries seeking stronger protection of their intellectual assets abroad. More generally, policy makers may perceive the "inadequate" protection of domestically generated IPRs in foreign countries as inherently "unfair," undermining support for market opening at home.

Notwithstanding these parallels, there are two important differences between traditional negotiations on tariffs and negotiations on IPRs. First, whereas most trade theories predict economic welfare gains as a result of reciprocal

tariff liberalization, the same cannot be said about the adoption of ever-higher protection standards for IPRs. Patents, copyright, and related intellectual property rights seek to give incentives for inventive and creative activities. Owners of these forms of intellectual property benefit from temporary market exclusivity, which allows them to generate rents above competitive returns and so recoup the initial knowledge-generating investments. Governments, however, need to strike a proper balance between the interests of intellectual property holders and the public at large, which experiences market exclusivity as a barrier to the free dissemination of new knowledge. In practice, this balance is reflected in, for example, the limited duration of and the exceptions to the market exclusivity conferred by IPRs.[3]

"Optimizing" the degree of intellectual property protection is a challenging task. It is difficult to predict the future productivity of firms' research and development activities and the societal value of new technologies. In the absence of reliable empirical guidance, existing patent and copyright regimes are typically an outcome of history, rules of thumb, and the influence of vested interests. There is thus no guarantee that the adoption of IPR rules in trade agreements will necessarily improve economic welfare. At some high level of protection, further strengthening is bound to be welfare reducing. In addition, although the argument for free trade applies to all PTA partners, a case can be made for differential levels of IPR protection. For example, poorer developing countries often host few IPR-producing industries, and consumers and governments face tighter budgets than in developed countries, suggesting that a stronger emphasis on the free dissemination of technologies than on strong incentives for innovation may be appropriate.

The second major difference between negotiations on tariffs and on IPR rules pertains to the preferential character of trade commitments. In the case of tariffs, it is the parties to a PTA that benefit from liberalization commitments, whereas goods imported by a PTA member from a nonmember continue to face the higher tariff prevailing prior to the conclusion of the PTA (unless the nonmember has its own preferential agreement with the member). In theory, the same could be done with the adoption of new intellectual property standards: the beneficiaries of these standards could be confined to nationals of one of the PTA parties. For example, country A could say that only intellectual property owners from its PTA partner B may benefit from the PTA's intellectual property rules, whereas intellectual property owners from nonmember country C are treated according to the previously prevailing standards. Implementing such a discriminatory approach would not be straightforward, as what constitutes nationality in the case of intellectual property ownership would have to be determined.[4] Still, just as PTAs incorporate elaborate rules on the origin of traded goods, it would be possible to specify detailed nationality criteria for intellectual property titles.

Nevertheless, IPR rules in PTAs are almost always nondiscriminatory in character.[5] The reason is that most PTA parties are also WTO members and are therefore bound by the rules of the TRIPS Agreement. Article 4 of TRIPS applies one of the WTO's cornerstone principles—most favored nation (MFN) treatment—to the protection of intellectual property. Specifically, this article states, "With regard to the protection of intellectual property, any advantage, favour, privilege or immunity granted by a Member to the nationals of any other country shall be accorded immediately and unconditionally to the nationals of all other Members. . . ." Unlike the WTO's agreements on trade in goods and in services, the TRIPS Agreement does not provide for an exception to the MFN principle that permits preferential treatment emanating from a PTA. In other words, if a country were to extend superior treatment to intellectual property holders in its PTA partners, other WTO members could invoke the WTO's dispute settlement mechanism to request the extension of the special benefits to its own nationals.

The fact that PTA concessions on IPRs are typically not granted preferentially has important bargaining implications. Suppose that country A is negotiating separate bilateral PTAs with countries B and C. In the case of goods trade, it is possible to "sell" the same liberalization concession twice. For example, country A could offer a lower import tariff for sugar to country B in exchange for country B's reducing its import tariff on T-shirts. Simultaneously, country A could offer the same reduction of its import tariff for sugar to country C in exchange for country C's reducing its import tariff on toys. Compare this with a commitment to protect IPRs more stringently. If country A subscribes to stronger IPR rules in its PTA with country B, country C automatically benefits without needing to offer any tariff concession to country A. From a bargaining perspective, the MFN requirement in the TRIPS Agreement therefore provides incentives to negotiate IPRs at the multilateral level, where broader bargains involving the whole WTO membership can be struck.

The above considerations raise a basic question: why do developing countries still find it beneficial to sign PTAs that entail a substantial strengthening of the IPR regime? Since most intellectual property titles in poorer nations are held by foreign residents, it is not clear that higher standards of protection will necessarily be welfare enhancing. In addition, in the typical grand bargain under a North-South PTA, the developing country makes a nonpreferential commitment on IPRs in exchange for preferential market access to northern markets for agricultural or manufactured goods. The latter, however, may be temporary because the value of trade preferences diminishes if the northern PTA partner signs additional PTAs with third countries or reduces tariffs on an MFN basis in the context of a multilateral trading round.

These considerations are important and explain why developing countries typically adopt a "defensive" negotiating stance in PTA negotiations on IPRs. Nevertheless, there are several reasons why developing countries, in the end, are willing to go along with a comprehensive PTA that entails new IPR rules.

To begin with, governments may expect certain economic benefits from stronger IPRs. Domestic IPR owners stand to benefit, even if they are still small in number. The possibility of attracting foreign direct investment (FDI) through stronger IPRs is also often considered an important benefit—although the empirical evidence on the importance of IPRs in FDI decisions is mixed.[6]

Even if the net welfare effect of signing on to a PTA intellectual property chapter is negative, the economic benefits from the full package of PTA commitments may be sufficiently large to lead to a positive overall welfare effect. For example, it is conceivable that for a small developing country, the (discounted) welfare gains from obtaining preferential market access to a large developed-country market such as the United States or the EU will outweigh any negative welfare effects in the IPR domain, even if preferential market access is temporary.[7] At the same time, it is important to recognize that certain segments of society would still be worse off with a PTA in such a scenario. Although the presence of positive nationwide welfare effects suggests that losers from the PTA could be compensated, the establishment of compensation mechanisms (e.g., tax reforms) is entirely a matter of domestic policy and may face its own political-economy constraints—a dilemma well-recognized in the literature on the distributional implications of trade reform.

The above considerations suggest that governments are well advised to study carefully the potential economic benefits and costs associated with a new trade agreement. Although it is an obvious step, carrying out a cost-benefit analysis of the effects of a PTA with a diverse set of liberalization commitments and legal undertakings—including the adoption of new IPR standards—is a challenging task. Typically, the government agency conducting the trade negotiations (e.g., the ministry of trade or of foreign affairs) has only partial responsibility for—and only partial expertise in—the trade-related topics negotiated in a PTA. In particular, the adoption of new intellectual property standards affects multiple sectors and requires cooperation from other ministries, ranging from health and education to agriculture and industry. Internal coordination of prior analysis and the development of negotiating positions often face bureaucratic obstacles, especially in resource-constrained environments.

Methodology and data availability pose special challenges for assessing the economic effects of new IPR standards. The first need is for an understanding of the likely legislative changes that will be required as a consequence of the conclusion of the PTA. For example, many developing countries already have IPR laws that exceed the requirements of the TRIPS Agreement, and a PTA may just lock in these existing standards. To be sure, such lock-ins have economic ramifications, because they reduce the freedom of governments to change their minds and amend laws at some future time, but the economic effects of a lock-in are different from those of an actual legislative change.

Once the legislative landscape has been mapped, the next step is to model the potential impact of the stronger IPR rules. When assessing the trade effects of tariff reductions, economists can draw on large datasets that provide information on actual and bound tariff rates, as well as current and past trade flows. Partial and general equilibrium models for assessing policy changes are readily available from different sources. By contrast, data on the economic variables relevant for assessing the effects of IPR policy changes—for instance, prices, research and development (R&D) investments, or license fees—are much harder to come by, and economists cannot draw on ready-made

assessment models.[8] Notwithstanding these challenges, some analysis should be possible in most countries and can usefully inform policy making before, during, and after the negotiation of a PTA.

TRIPS+ Provisions in U.S. PTAs

Having considered the context in which PTA negotiations on IPRs take place, it is only natural to ask, where is the beef? What is the content of the "new" IPRs rules most commonly found in PTAs? We start with a review of U.S. PTAs (generally called free trade agreements, or FTAs, in U.S. official usage) because the IPR chapters negotiated by the United States are arguably the most comprehensive and far-reaching among the bilateral and regional IPRs rulebooks found worldwide.

Having concluded only two PTAs before the mid-1990s—the agreement with Israel, and NAFTA—the U.S. government embarked on a series of bilateral and regional negotiations in the late 1990s. These "new generation" negotiations have so far led to the conclusion of 14 agreements, encompassing 20 trading partners; negotiations with additional trading partners are pending. Table 18.1 offers an overview of the current U.S. PTA landscape.[9]

The negotiation of strong IPR standards is a central objective in the U.S. agreements. Indeed, the U.S. Trade Promotion Authority Act of 2002, under which most agreements have been negotiated, expressly states as a negotiating objective the promotion of intellectual property rules that "reflect a standard of protection similar to that found in United States law."[10] The negotiating mandate of the executive branch of the U.S. government was refined in 2007, following the congressional elections in

Table 18.1. U.S. Free Trade Agreement (FTA) Landscape

FTAs ratified by U.S. Congress	FTAs signed but not yet ratified	Negotiations launched, but no agreement concluded
Israel, 1985	Colombia	Malaysia
North American Free Trade Agreement (NAFTA), 1994 (Canada, Mexico)	Korea, Rep.	Thailand
Jordan, 2001	Panama	Southern African Customs Union (SACU)
Chile, 2003		United Arab Emirates
Singapore, 2003		Trans-Pacific Strategic Economic Partnership (Brunei Darussalam, Chile, New Zealand, Singapore)
Australia, 2004		
Morocco, 2004		Free Trade Area of the Americas (FTAA)
Dominican Republic–Central America Free Trade Agreement (CAFTA–DR), 2005 (Costa Rica, Dominican Republic, El Salvador, Guatemala, Honduras, Nicaragua)		
Bahrain, 2006		
Oman, 2006		
Peru, 2007		

Source: Office of the U.S. Trade Representative, www.ustr.gov.

November 2006. In what follows, we first discuss the main provisions of U.S. PTAs that were signed between 2001 and 2006.[11] We then describe the change in the negotiating mandate and outline how it was reflected in the free trade agreement between the United States and Peru—the only agreement to have been ratified by the U.S. Congress since the revisions of 2007.

Agreements Ratified between 2001 and 2006

IPR chapters of U.S. PTAs include provisions on all types of intellectual property instruments and specify the mechanisms available for enforcing exclusive rights. (This discussion draws on Fink and Reichenmiller 2005.) A detailed review of all these provisions is beyond the scope of this chapter. Instead, we focus on some key obligations in which these agreements go beyond the protection standards found in the TRIPS Agreement. We do not analyze the extent to which these TRIPS+ obligations required (or will require) domestic legislative changes. As noted above, U.S. PTA partners may have already protected IPRs more stringently than required by TRIPS, leaving the agreement to bind only existing policies under international law.

Table 18.2 outlines the key TRIPS+ provisions in U.S. PTAs ratified between 2001 and 2006. The details vary from agreement to agreement, but there are certain common elements, as described next.

Protection of patents and pharmaceutical test data. As in TRIPS, all the agreements provide for a patent term of 20 years. All except the agreement between the United States and Jordan require, in addition, the extension of the patent term to compensate for delays caused by regulatory approval processes, such as approval for marketing a new drug. Some agreements call for patent term extensions when delays in the granting of the patent itself occur.

Four U.S. agreements (those with Australia, Bahrain, Morocco, and Oman) extend the scope of patentability by mandating that patents be available for new uses of known products. All agreements go beyond TRIPS in enhancing patent protection for plants and animals. The strongest agreement in this regard is the one with Morocco, which explicitly mandates the provision of patent protection for life forms. Others do not exempt plants or animals from patentability, which is a flexibility provided for under TRIPS. The weakest agreement is the one with the six countries of the Central America Free Trade Agreement and the Dominican Republic (CAFTA–DR), which only calls for "reasonable efforts" to provide for patentability of plants.[12]

Much controversy has surrounded the provisions in U.S. FTAs that strengthen the market exclusivity of

pharmaceutical producers. The TRIPS Agreement strikes a balance by requiring the protection of pharmaceutical patents and processes but allowing WTO member states to override the market exclusivity of patents by issuing what are termed compulsory licenses. These are government authorizations that allow generic pharmaceutical companies to produce a particular drug and sell it in competition with the patent holder, on payment of a license fee. Over the past decade, more than 10 developing countries have resorted to compulsory licensing—primarily, but not exclusively, for HIV/AIDS drugs—with the aim of making medicines available at affordable prices to patients in need (see Fink 2008).

U.S. PTAs contain a number of provisions that limit the ability of governments to introduce competition from generic producers. First, three agreements (those with Australia, Jordan, and Singapore) limit the use of compulsory licensing to emergency situations, antitrust remedies, and cases of public, noncommercial use. The TRIPS Agreement does not contain any such limitation, merely requiring that compulsory licenses be considered on their individual merits.[13] Thus, under TRIPS, a government may, for example, invoke the protection of public health as a reason for issuing a compulsory license, without the need to declare a national emergency.

Second, to effectively make use of compulsory licenses, generic drug manufacturers need to be able to obtain regulatory permission to enter the market. Provisions in U.S. PTAs impose an obstacle in this respect. Except for the agreement with Jordan, all agreements require that regulatory agencies prevent marketing approval of a generic drug during the patent term without the consent of the patent holder; this is sometimes referred to as "patent-registration linkage." (The TRIPS Agreement does not impose any obligation of this kind.) In other words, even if a government is able to issue a compulsory license, generic producers may not be able to market their drugs, rendering the compulsory licensing instrument ineffective.

Third, obtaining marketing approval for drugs requires the submission to regulatory authorities of test data on a drug's safety and efficacy. Such data are protected by separate legal instruments that differ from country to country. The TRIPS Agreement only requires that test data be protected against "unfair commercial use." By contrast, most U.S. PTAs explicitly mandate test data exclusivity, as provided for under U.S. law. Once a company has submitted original test data, no competing manufacturer is allowed to draw on these data for a period of five years to request marketing approval for its own drug.[14] The new compilation of comparable test data by competing manufacturers may take several years and may be prohibitively

Table 18.2. Principal TRIPS+ Provisions in U.S. Free Trade Agreements (FTAs) Ratified between 2001 and 2006

Provision	U.S.–Jordan	U.S.–Singapore	U.S.–Chile	U.S.–Morocco	U.S.–Australia	CAFTA–DR	U.S.–Bahrain	U.S.–Oman
Protection of patents and pharmaceutical test data								
Patent term	Extension given for delays caused by regulatory approval process.	Extension given for delays caused by regulatory approval process. In addition, extension given when a delay in the granting of the patent exceeds four years from the filing of the application (five years for U.S.–Chile) or two years after a request for examination (three years for U.S.–Chile).						
Second-use patents	No specific provision.			Obligation to provide patents for new uses of known products.		No specific provision.	Same as U.S.–Australia.	
Patenting of life forms	No general exclusion of plants and animals from patentability.[a]			Explicit obligation to provide patent protection for plants and animals.	Exclusions allowed only for moral, health, and safety reasons.	"Reasonable efforts" have to be undertaken to provide for patentability of plants.	Explicit obligation to provide patent protection for plants, but animals can be excluded.	General patentability exclusion for animals, but not for plants.
Compulsory licenses	Compulsory licenses limited to national emergencies, as antitrust remedy, and for public noncommercial use.	TRIPS standards apply.			Same as U.S.–Singapore.	TRIPS standards apply.		
Linkage between patent status and drug marketing approval	Patent owner must be notified when marketing approval is sought during the patent term.	Marketing approval of a generic drug is prohibited during the patent term, unless authorized by the patent owner. In addition, the patent holder must be notified of the identity of the generic company requesting marketing approval.						
Test data protection for pharmaceutical products	TRIPS standards apply. In addition, length of protection should be the same as in the originator's country.	Data exclusivity for five years. In addition, where drug regulators rely on foreign marketing approvals, data exclusivity applies automatically at home.	Data exclusivity for five years.	Data exclusivity for five years. Additional three-year data exclusivity triggered by "new clinical information."	Data exclusivity for five years. In addition, data exclusivity applies in all PTA member countries, once first obtained in another territory. In the case of the U.S.–Bahrain and U.S.–Oman agreements, additional three-year data exclusivity is triggered by "new clinical information" (with equivalent provisions on cross-border application).			
Parallel imports of patented products	TRIPS standards apply.	Patent holders may limit parallel imports of pharmaceutical products through licensing contracts.	TRIPS standards apply.	Patent holders may limit parallel imports through licensing contracts.		TRIPS standards apply.		
Side letters on public health?	No.			Yes.	No.	Yes.		

392

Copyright protection

Membership in WIPO conventions	Only certain provisions apply.	Yes.	No.	Yes.		
Term of copyright protection	Same as TRIPS.	Life of author plus 70 years. If decided on a basis other than the life of the author, the term is 70 years (95 years in the U.S.–Oman agreement) from the publication or creation of the work.				
Technological protection measures	"Adequate" protection and "effective" remedies against acts of circumvention. Ban on circumvention devices.	"Adequate" protection against acts of circumvention. Ban on circumvention devices. Civil liability in case of willful infringement. Criminal liability in case of willful infringement for commercial purposes. Exempted are nonprofit libraries, archives, and educational institutions, as well as acts related to reverse engineering, troubleshooting, protection of minors, computer or network security, and lawfully authorized government activities.				
Liability of Internet service providers	No specific provision.	Limited liability of Internet service providers on the condition that they block infringing content upon notification by the copyright holder.[b]				
Burden of proof in case of copyright infringement		Burden of proof placed on the defending party to show that works are in the public domain, but copyright owners still have to prove infringement.				
Parallel importation of copyrighted works	Copyright holder has right to block parallel imports.	TRIPS standards apply.	Copyright holder has right to block parallel imports.	TRIPS standards apply.		

Enforcement of intellectual property rights

Institutional flexibility in IPR enforcement	No specific provision.	Resource constraints cannot be invoked as an excuse for not complying with specific enforcement obligations.	No specific provision.	Same as U.S.–Chile.	Same as U.S.–Singapore,	
Border measures	Scope of border measures not specifically defined.	Apply to imported, exported, and transiting goods.	Apply only to imported goods (similar to TRIPS).	Same as U.S.–Chile.		
Civil and administrative procedures		Obligation to fine infringers of copyright and trademark rights irrespective of the injury suffered by rights holders.				
Criminal procedures and remedies	Scope of criminal procedures and remedies not specifically defined.	Similar to TRIPS. In addition, criminal procedures apply in case of willful infringements, not only for a financial gain.	Similar to TRIPS. In addition, criminal procedures apply in cases of willful infringements, not only for financial gain, and specifically for knowingly trafficking in counterfeit labels affixed to certain copyrighted works (e.g., CDs, software).			

Source: Adapted and updated from Fink and Reichenmiller 2005.

Note: CAFTA–DR, Dominican Republic–Central America Free Trade Agreement; IPR, intellectual property right; TRIPS, Trade-Related Aspects of Intellectual Property Rights; WIPO, World Intellectual Property Organization.

a. The U.S.–Chile agreement does not explicitly oblige protection of life forms under the patent system but mandates "reasonable efforts" to develop legislation related to patent protection for plants within four years from entry into force of the agreement.

b. A side letter to the U.S.–Morocco agreement specifies the form in which notifications in case of alleged copyright infringement must be made.

expensive, and it raises ethical concerns. U.S. FTAs do not expressly provide for exceptions to test data exclusivity, especially when a government grants a compulsory license. Exceptions may be justified through other provisions in the IPR chapter (e.g., on anticompetitive practices), although such an interpretation remains legally uncertain (see box 18.1). Thus, test data exclusivity may pose another obstacle to governments' effective use of compulsory licensing.

Several U.S. FTAs go further on data exclusivity. When pharmaceutical companies seek marketing approval for previously unapproved uses of already registered drugs, regulatory authorities typically require the submission of "new" clinical information. The agreements with Bahrain, Morocco, and Oman provide for an additional three-year data exclusivity period triggered by such new clinical information. Drugs benefiting from this type of marketing exclusivity include not only new patented products but also older generic products for which the patents have expired, although generic competition for previously approved uses of such drugs would remain unaffected.

Sometimes drug regulatory authorities recognize the marketing approval decisions of foreign regulators in granting marketing approval for the same product at home. The intellectual property chapter of the U.S.–Singapore agreement mandates, in this case, that foreign data exclusivity also applies domestically. In other words, no competing manufacturer is allowed to rely on the test data submitted to a foreign regulator in seeking marketing approval in a PTA member.

The agreements with Australia, Bahrain, CAFTA–DR, and Oman are even more far-reaching with respect to the

---

Box 18.1. Patent-Registration Linkage and Test Data Protection: The Case of Chile

The free trade agreement (FTA) between the United States and Chile mandates patent-registration linkage and exclusive rights to pharmaceutical test data (see the summary in table 18.2). Chile has implemented these obligations in a way that has sought to protect public health, promote coherence with patent rules, prevent anticompetitive behavior, and avoid imposing an undue burden on Chile's public health authority, the Institute of Public Health (Instituto de Salud Pública de Chile). Specifically, Articles 89–91 of Chile's Industrial Property Law provide for the five-year exclusivity period for pharmaceutical test data stipulated in the FTA but also create several exceptions to the acquisition and maintenance of exclusive rights, as follows:

- If the owner of the test data has engaged in conduct deemed contrary to free competition
- For reasons of public health, national security, public noncommercial use, national emergency, or other circumstances of extreme urgency
- If the pharmaceutical product is the subject of a compulsory license
- If the pharmaceutical product has not been marketed in Chilean territory within 12 months from the registration or health authorization issued in Chile
- If the application for registration or health authorization of the pharmaceutical product is filed in Chile 12 months or more after the same product was first registered or authorized abroad.

With respect to the patent-registration requirement, Resolution 5572 obligates the Institute of Public Health to publish on its website all applications for health registration. In addition, companies that already possess a health registration can request that all new applications submitted to the institute be sent to them by electronic mail. Patent holders can thus monitor incoming applications and, if they believe that a pharmaceutical product for which health registration is sought infringes on a patent, can request an injunction from a Chilean court to prevent the institute from issuing the registration.

The U.S. government has not been satisfied with Chile's implementation of its obligations under the agreement. In 2006 it launched an "out-of-cycle" review of the protection of IPRs in Chile that was sparked by complaints by the Pharmaceutical Research and Manufacturers of America (PhRMA), a U.S. pharmaceutical industry association. Specifically, PhRMA contends that exceptions to test data exclusivity are not allowed under the terms of the FTA and that Chile has not instituted a mechanism whereby the Chilean authorities by themselves prevent the granting of marketing approval of a patent-infringing pharmaceutical product. As a result, PhRMA claims, several copies of drugs protected by patents have obtained health registration from the Institute of Public Health. The Office of the U.S. Trade Representative placed Chile on the U.S. priority watch list in 2007 and 2008 and has raised its concerns in bilateral discussions with the Chilean government, but it has not explicitly accused Chile of violating its FTA obligations, nor has it invoked the FTA's formal dispute resolution mechanism.

It is uncertain how a dispute panel would rule on Chile's compliance with its FTA obligations. A likely key question would be whether the exceptions to test data rules can be justified by the FTA articles on anticompetitive behavior, by the references in the FTA to the Doha Declaration on Trade-Related Aspects of Intellectual Property Rights (TRIPS) and Public Health, or by other provisions. Another question would probably be whether the issuance of a health authorization by the Institute of Public Health constitutes an act of "marketing approval," as conceptualized in the FTA's patent-registration linkage requirement.

Sources: Chile, Industrial Property Law (Law 19.039); Resolution 5572 of the Chilean Institute of Public Health; various articles published by *Inside U.S. Trade;* "Special 301" submission by PhRMA, available at http://members.phrma.org/international/PhRMA_2005_Special_301.pdf; "Special 301" reports, Office of the U.S. Trade Representative, http://www.ustr.gov.

cross-border application of data exclusivity. Even if regulatory authorities do not recognize foreign marketing approvals, competing manufacturers are prevented from using test data submitted to a drug regulatory agency in another territory for five years, starting from the date of submission in the foreign country. That is, test data exclusivity applies automatically in all PTA jurisdictions, once a company submits test data to a drug regulator in one territory—even outside the PTA area. Furthermore, pharmaceutical companies can wait for up to five years to seek marketing approval in a PTA member and still benefit from the full five-year exclusivity term in that member.

The provisions on test data exclusivity are especially important for small countries. Pharmaceutical companies may not seek out patents in every jurisdiction for every initially promising pharmaceutical compound. The registration of patents can be costly and at the stage of patenting, it is uncertain whether the pharmaceutical compound in question will turn into a commercial product or how successful it will be. The incentive to seek out patents in small countries is therefore less. However, even in the absence of patent exclusivity, pharmaceutical companies can still benefit from five years of market exclusivity when they introduce a new product because of the rights these companies hold to the product's clinical test data.

Finally, whether the parallel importation of pharmaceutical products that have been placed on the market in foreign jurisdictions is permitted is another issue covered by PTA rule books on IPRs. Parallel importation can be a means of exerting downward pressure on pharmaceutical prices, if products are sold more cheaply abroad. The TRIPS Agreement affords WTO members flexibility in determining whether to permit parallel importation of patented drugs.[15] By contrast, the U.S. agreements with Australia, Morocco, and Singapore allow patent holders to prevent parallel importation of goods.[16]

The TRIPS+ provisions in U.S. PTAs have attracted much criticism from nongovernmental organizations (NGOs) concerned with affordable access to medicines. They argue that stronger market exclusivity would curtail competition from generic producers and would ultimately lead to high drug prices that are out of reach for poor population segments (MSF 2004; Oxfam 2006). They also allege that IPR provisions in PTAs are at odds with efforts at the WTO to ensure that IPR rules are consistent with public health objectives. At their 2001 ministerial meeting in Doha, WTO members issued a declaration recognizing the gravity of the public health problems afflicting many developing and least-developing countries. Among other things, the declaration reaffirmed the right of WTO members to use the flexibilities of TRIPS in the area of

compulsory licensing and parallel importation to "promote access to medicines for all."[17] In August 2003, WTO members created a special mechanism under the TRIPS Agreement that allows countries with insufficient manufacturing capacity to effectively use compulsory licenses by importing generic drugs (see Fink 2005).

Technically, the Doha Declaration and the August 2003 decision by WTO members do not address questions of marketing approval during the patent term or of test data exclusivity. However, the provisions of U.S. PTAs on these matters can still be seen as being at odds with the spirit of the multilateral accords, to the extent that they preclude the effective use of compulsory licenses.

In side letters to the U.S. agreements with Bahrain, CAFTA–DR, Morocco, and Oman, the respective governments shared understandings that the intellectual property chapters "do not affect" their ability to "take necessary measures to protect public health by promoting medicines for all. . . ."[18] The U.S. government, however, does not view the side letters as creating any kind of exemption that would allow parties to the FTAs to ignore obligations in the agreements' intellectual property chapters (Fink and Reichenmiller 2005). In the U.S. view, the side letters merely signal the parties' belief that the intellectual property rules of the PTAs will not interfere with the protection of public health.[19]

Copyright protection. Most U.S. PTAs require accession to the World Intellectual Property Organization (WIPO) Copyright Treaty and the WIPO Performances and Phonograms Treaty. These treaties were concluded in 1996 after the end of the Uruguay Round and are therefore not incorporated in the TRIPS Agreement. They were negotiated to adapt copyright protection to advances in information and communication technologies that greatly facilitated the distribution of literary or artistic works in digital form. The provisions of the two WIPO treaties go beyond TRIPS in several ways—for example, by making it clear that storage of protected works in digital form is a reproduction that can be controlled by copyright owners and by conferring certain moral rights on performers. (See Abbott, Cottier, and Gurry 2007 for a detailed discussion of the treaties.)

In addition to incorporating the two WIPO treaties, U.S. PTAs set new substantive protection standards. First, except for the agreement with Jordan, they extend the TRIPS copyright term of life of author plus 50 years by an additional 20 years, reflecting U.S. practice.

Second, most U.S. bilateral PTAs include obligations to prevent circumvention of technological protection measures—devices and software developed to prevent unauthorized copying of digital works. This issue is not covered under TRIPS, and the provisions on the subject in the two WIPO treaties are fairly general. The U.S. Digital Millennium Copyright Act of 1998 set more far-reaching standards on circumventing technologies that are designed to prevent unauthorized copying of digital content. Those standards have found their way, to varying degrees, into seven of the bilateral agreements. Related provisions in six of the PTAs define the liability of Internet service providers when infringing content is distributed through their servers and networks. Again, these provisions are based on standards found in the U.S. Digital Millennium Copyright Act.

Third, all of the bilateral PTAs place the burden of proof in copyright infringement cases—that is, of showing that works are in the public domain—on the defending party. TRIPS does not impose any such obligation. The FTAs thus strengthen the position of copyright holders, as artistic and literary works are generally considered protected unless they obviously belong in the public domain.

Finally, as in the case of pharmaceutical products, TRIPS does not mandate any rule on the permissibility of parallel imports of copyrighted works, such as books or musical CDs, that have been lawfully sold in foreign markets. Some countries, such as New Zealand, permit parallel importation of certain copyrighted products as a way of stimulating price competition. By contrast, the U.S. bilateral agreements with Jordan and Morocco give copyright holders the right to block parallel importation.

From an economic perspective, the welfare consequences of new and stronger copyright protection standards are ambiguous. Most countries have industries that rely on copyright protection and that may benefit from strengthened protection. Furthermore, new technologies that make copying of digital works much easier pose challenges which policy makers must address. At the same time, copyright laws have historically sought to strike a balance between the interests of copyright producers and those of the general public; for example, so-called fair use exemptions allow the copying of protected works for educational or research purposes. There are concerns that new rules with respect to the term of protection, technological protection measures, the liability of Internet services providers, and the burden of proof in case of copyright infringement could diminish the rights of consumers and the general public (CIPR 2002).

Such concerns have also been voiced in the United States itself, not only by consumer rights advocates and academic institutions but also by computer manufacturers and communications service providers that distribute copyrighted works. For example, specific amendments to the Digital Millennium Copyright Act have been proposed

that would permit the circumvention of technological protection measures if such action does not result in an infringement of a copyrighted work.[20] Ensuring fair use of copyrighted material seems particularly important for accessing educational material. The opportunities and gains from the use of digital libraries, Internet-based distance learning programs, and online databases would be limited if access to such tools were unaffordable or otherwise restricted by copyright law.

Enforcement of IPRs. The TRIPS Agreement—for the first time in an international agreement on intellectual property—introduced detailed obligations on the enforcement of IPRs. Certainly, without judicial enforcement of intellectual property laws, rules on patents, copyright, and other forms of protection could be seriously undermined. However, the agreement, recognizing the institutional limitations in many developing countries, does not create any obligation "with respect to the distribution of resources as between enforcement of intellectual property rights and the enforcement of law in general."[21] Such a caveat may be important. The enforcement of intellectual property rights can be a costly exercise in terms of both budgetary outlays and the employment of skilled personnel. For developing countries that face many institutional deficiencies, there is a risk that stronger enforcement of IPRs would draw away financial and human resources from other development priorities.

The U.S. agreements with Australia and Jordan do not explicitly allow for the same institutional flexibility. In these cases, it may be difficult to defend derogations from the specific enforcement provisions of the agreements' IPR chapters on the grounds of inherent institutional constraints, such as limited budgetary or human resources. The agreements with Bahrain, CAFTA–DR, Chile, Morocco, Oman, and Singapore go further, spelling out that resource constraints cannot be invoked as an excuse for failure to comply with the agreements' specific enforcement obligations.[22] Indeed, some of these obligations seem to create additional institutional requirements. For example, as in the case of TRIPS, the PTAs require customs authorities to block trade in counterfeit and pirated goods. But TRIPS requires such measures only for imported goods, whereas most PTAs mandate the application of border measures to imported goods, goods destined for export, and even, in some cases, transiting goods.

Finally, the enforcement rules of the bilateral agreements mandate a stronger deterrent against IPR infringement. For example, TRIPS requires only the imposition of fines adequate to compensate IPR holders for the monetary damages they suffered. In the case of copyright piracy and trademark counterfeiting, all the PTAs require the imposition of fines irrespective of the injury suffered by IPR holders. TRIPS mandates criminal procedures only in cases of willful trademark counterfeiting or copyright piracy on a commercial scale. Many PTAs go beyond this broad standard and define more explicitly the scope of acts of infringement subject to criminal procedures—including, for example, copyright piracy with a significant aggregate monetary value that is not necessarily undertaken for financial gain. Thus, certain forms of end-user piracy may be considered a criminal offense.

The May 2007 Bipartisan Agreement and the U.S.–Peru FTA

As pointed out above, the adoption of TRIPS+ standards in U.S. PTAs has received much criticism from NGOs, particularly in the area of pharmaceuticals. Over time, these standards have become controversial within the United States, as well as abroad. The U.S. Congress has for many years considered legislation that would authorize the parallel importation of medicines from Canada and other countries. Concerned that such legislation would violate obligations under PTAs, the Congress inserted language in a 2005 appropriations bill that effectively prohibits the Office of the U.S. Trade Representative (USTR) from negotiating PTA provisions that would block parallel imports of patented pharmaceuticals (see Abbott 2006).

More fundamentally, with Democrats winning both houses of Congress in the November 2006 elections, the Bush administration and the congressional leadership started to negotiate a new trade framework. The resulting May 2007 Bipartisan Agreement led to a de facto revision of the USTR's negotiating mandate. In the area of IPRs, the agreement sets out flexibilities that roll back some of the TRIPS+ provisions outlined above.[23] Specifically, it turns the obligation to grant patent term extension for delays in obtaining marketing authorization into a voluntary option that governments "may" choose to adopt. Similarly, drug regulators would no longer be required to deny marketing approval on the basis of a drug's patent status. Governments would only be required to make available certain mechanisms to allow patent holders to effectively enforce their rights.[24] Crucially, the agreement creates an express exception to the test data exclusivity rules for measures to protect public health "in accordance with the Doha Declaration and subsequent protocols for its implementation." In other words, it removes any legal uncertainty about countries' ability to make effective use of compulsory licensing.

The Bipartisan Agreement applied only to those U.S. PTAs that had been signed by the administration but not yet ratified by Congress. In May 2007, these were the free trade agreements with Colombia, the Republic of Korea, Panama, and Peru. In the case of Korea, continued disagreement between the Congress and the administration on automotive trade led to the exclusion of this FTA from the Bipartisan Agreement.[25] In the case of the other three agreements, USTR initiated the renegotiation of the FTA texts with the concerned governments. Only the revised U.S.–Peru FTA has so far gained congressional approval.

Examination of the revised U.S.–Peru text reveals that the elements of the Bipartisan Agreement outlined above have found their way into the final IPR chapter: patent term extension is mentioned as a voluntary option, as is patent-registration linkage, and only certain enforcement mechanisms need to be made available to the patent holder. Whereas the FTA provides for five years of pharmaceutical test data exclusivity, a special exception to exclusive rights is created for measures to protect public health in accordance with WTO rules.[26]

Other TRIPS+ elements of the FTA with Peru were not affected by the Bipartisan Agreement. These follow closely the provisions found in the CAFTA–DR agreement (see table 18.2). An important exception is that the U.S.–Peru FTA does not feature the provisions on the cross-border application of test data exclusivity described above.

As a final note, although the immediate impact of the bipartisan trade deal has been limited to the FTAs negotiated with Colombia, Panama, and Peru (with the former two still awaiting congressional approval), the deal marks an important shift in U.S. trade policy toward more sensitivity to public health concerns in global IPR rules.

TRIPS+ Provisions in EU PTAs

The European Union's drive toward concluding PTAs is more recent than that of the United States. In the second half of the 1990s, the EU launched PTA negotiations with a variety of trading partners, which led to the conclusion of agreements with Chile, Mexico, and South Africa. Starting in 1999, however, the EU practiced a de facto moratorium on new negotiations. This moratorium was not a formal policy, but it reflected the consensus of the EU member states and the European Commission that priority should be given to the conclusion of a comprehensive multilateral trading round. The one exception to the moratorium was the negotiation of economic partnership agreements (EPAs) with countries belonging to the Africa-Caribbean-Pacific (ACP) group of former European colonies. In this case, the negotiation of reciprocal trade agreements was driven by the expiry of trade preferences granted by the EU under the Cotonou Agreement and deemed incompatible with WTO rules. So far, the EU has concluded a full EPA with the Caribbean Forum of ACP States (CARIFORUM) and several interim EPAs with other ACP partners.

Despite the early setbacks in the negotiations under the Doha Development Agenda (DDA), the EU maintained its moratorium until about 2006, when it announced the negotiation of a PTA with Central America. Since then, negotiations with a considerable number of additional trading partners have been launched. Among other factors, this shift in the EU's trade policy strategy was driven by two developments. First, the prospects of an ambitious and comprehensive Doha agreement became increasingly remote, especially with respect to some of the EU's priority trade concerns—trade facilitation, competition policy, investment rules, and geographical indications (GIs). Second, PTAs involving major economies were proliferating rapidly in all regions, putting increased pressure on the EU to not lose out on commercial opportunities abroad and to negotiate its own set of preferential treaties. (For a more in-depth discussion of the shift in EU trade policy, see Woolcock 2007.) Table 18.3 offers an overview of the current EU PTA landscape.[27]

Turning to the IPR dimension of EU agreements, the "early generation" PTAs with Chile, Mexico, and South Africa focused primarily on establishing strong and comprehensive rules for GI protection. For the "new generation" PTAs that are currently being negotiated, the EU's

agenda has become substantially more ambitious. In 2004 the European Commission issued a Strategy for the Enforcement of Intellectual Property Rights in Third Countries that calls for "a long-term line of action" to strengthen the protection of IPRs outside EU territory. The strategy expressly calls for revisiting the approach to the IPR chapters of bilateral agreements.[28]

"Early Generation" Agreements with Chile, Mexico, and South Africa

The IPR sections in the EU agreements with Chile, Mexico, and South Africa are short, hardly taking up the space of a single page. In the case of the Mexico and South Africa agreements, the provisions are nonbinding and general. They emphasize the importance of adequate intellectual property protection and call for the establishment of consultation mechanisms should "difficulties" arise in the protection of intellectual property. In the Chile agreement, the IPR provisions are more ambitious. The agreements incorporate several WIPO conventions, including the WIPO Copyright Treaty and the WIPO Performances and Phonograms Treaty. As explained in the previous section, these conventions go beyond the copyright rules of the TRIPS Agreement, and their incorporation into a PTA therefore constitutes a TRIPS+ element. (Interestingly, the two WIPO Conventions are not incorporated into the U.S.–Chile FTA, as is shown in table 18.2.)

The most far-reaching TRIPS+ provisions are found in separate agreements on wines and spirits that strengthen

Table 18.3. European Union (EU) Preferential Trade Agreements (PTAs) and Economic Partnership Agreements (EPAs)

Concluded PTAs and EPAs	Provisional EPAs	PTAs and EPAs under negotiation
Mexico, 2000	West Africa, 2007 (Côte d'Ivoire, Ghana)	Southern Cone Common Market (Mercosur, Mercado Común del Sur) (Argentina, Brazil, Paraguay, Uruguay)
South Africa, 2000	Central Africa, 2007 (Cameroon)	
Chile, 2003	Eastern African Community (EAC), 2007 (Burundi, Kenya, Rwanda, Tanzania, Uganda)	Central America (Costa Rica, El Salvador, Guatemala, Honduras, Nicaragua)
Caribbean Forum of African, Caribbean, and Pacific (ACP) States (CARIFORUM), 2008 (Antigua and Barbuda, Bahamas, Barbados, Belize, Dominica, Dominican Republic, Grenada, Guyana, Haiti, Jamaica, St. Christopher and Nevis, St. Lucia, St. Vincent and the Grenadines, Suriname, Trinidad and Tobago)	Eastern and Southern Africa, 2007 (Comoros, Madagascar, Mauritius, Seychelles, Zimbabwe)	India
	Southern African Development Community (SADC), 2007 (Botswana, Lesotho, Mozambique, Namibia, Swaziland)	Association of Southeast Asian Nations (ASEAN) (Brunei Darussalam, Cambodia, Indonesia, Lao PDR, Malaysia, Myanmar, Philippines, Singapore, Thailand, Vietnam)
	Pacific, 2007 (Fiji, Papua New Guinea)	Andean Community (Bolivia, Colombia, Ecuador, Peru)
Korea, Rep., 2010		Pending EPA negotiations with countries in West Africa, Central Africa, EAC, Eastern and Southern Africa, SADC, and the Pacific

Source: Woolcock 2007; European Commission data, http://ec.europa.eu/trade/.
Note: This table does not include the EU's association agreements with Eastern European countries and Euro-Mediterranean partners.

GI protection. In the case of the PTA with Chile, the provisions on wines and spirits are separate annexes. The EU negotiated self-standing agreements on wines (with South Africa only) and on spirits (with Mexico and South Africa), outside the formal PTA framework. These special agreements were, however, negotiated in parallel with the broader trade agreements and may have formed part of the overall package of legal obligations undertaken by the parties. It is worth pointing out that the EU has negotiated agreements on wines or spirits (or both) with three developed countries—Australia, Canada, and the United States—with which it has not entered into bilateral PTAs.

The key substantive element of the EU agreements on wines and spirits is the establishment of lists of geographic names to which signatories must apply the "highest" level of GI protection. This means that nonoriginal producers in the PTA parties are not allowed to use a listed name even if they display the true origin of the good and even if use of the name is accompanied by expressions such as "kind," "type," or "style" (e.g., "Champagne-style sparkling wine"). The lists of geographic names are often extensive; the EU–South Africa agreement on wine alone is 120 pages long. Several of the European GIs listed in the agreements, especially for spirits, were being used by producers in EU PTA partner countries, and this use had to be (or will have to be) phased out. In most cases, use of the relevant GIs would likely have been among the exceptions in the TRIPS Agreement.[29] The phase-out of these generic names may have affected exports of third countries to EU partner countries, raising the possibility that the adoption of a GI list leads to a de facto trade preference.

In principle, GIs, like trademarks, are important for reducing information asymmetries in markets for "experience goods"—goods whose quality cannot be easily observed by simple inspection at the time of purchase. From the perspective of consumers, these indications can lower search costs, particularly for heterogeneous products such as wines or cheeses. For producers, GIs offer a means of attaching a reputation for quality to a place name that may then be marketed and used on labels. A number of empirical studies have quantified substantial price premiums associated with certain products labeled with protected GIs (see Fink and Maskus 2005 for a review).

More controversial is the precise scope of exclusive rights that should be conferred on rights holders. In the United States, Mexico, Chile, and other "New World" countries, nonoriginal producers have traditionally been allowed to use GIs for certain products as long as the true geographic origin of the products is made clear. This has given rise to "semigeneric" expressions such as "American-made Pecorino cheese." The EU, with its long tradition of

regional heterogeneity in agricultural production, affords GI owners stronger exclusive rights than in the United States. In addition, EU laws protect "traditional" expressions that describe certain methods of production, such as "ruby" for port from Portugal.

Unfortunately, little systematic evidence exists to assess whether the more lenient approach toward GIs in the Americas has led to confusion on the part of consumers. What also complicates an economic assessment of different protection regimes is that certain products known by GIs are likely to have significant status value. Economists define "status goods" as products for which the mere display of a particular label confers prestige on their buyers, regardless of the product's quality. Champagne, Beluga caviar, and Kobe beef may fall into this category. Since use of these GIs by nonoriginal producers may undermine the status value attached to the original varieties, the price premiums of the original producers may suffer, even if consumers are not confused about the true origin of their purchases.

Although the EU's agreements on wines and spirits are clearly driven by the interests of EU producers of specialty foods, certain producers in EU partner countries may also benefit. For example, the EU–Mexico agreement on spirits establishes GI protection for the Tequila and Mezcal designations. In addition, the disuse of semigeneric expressions may lead only to a temporary adjustment; evidence from Australia's wine industry suggests that the rebranding of the affected products and associated marketing efforts provided a boost for local producers.[30]

"New Generation" EU Agreements

A first impression of the EU's revised approach to the treatment of IPRs in its trade agreements can be gained by looking at the EPA with CARIFORUM.[31] The intellectual property chapter of the agreement is comprehensive, covering most forms of IPRs, as well as measures for their enforcement. As in the EU–Chile PTA, the EU–CARIFORUM agreement incorporates the WIPO Copyright Treaty and the WIPO Performances and Phonograms Treaty.[32] The EPA also establishes TRIPS+ standards for GIs, requiring CARIFORUM members to establish a dedicated system for their protection. This obligation is TRIPS+ in the sense that the TRIPS Agreement allows the implementation of its GI standards through the trademark system. More substantially, the EPA requires a high level of GI protection for all products, preventing nonoriginal producers from using a GI even if the true origin of the good is indicated or the name is accompanied by expressions such as "kind," "style," or "imitation." In the TRIPS Agreement, this high-level protection standard is limited to wines and spirits. The EU has been among the leading proponents at the WTO for extending strong protection to all products but has encountered resistance from other WTO members, notably producer countries in the Americas. Discussions on this topic in the Doha Development Agenda have to date not led to any outcome.[33]

Extensive new IPR obligations are found in the enforcement part of the IPR chapter, reflecting the emphasis on strengthened enforcement outlined in the 2004 strategy document described above. Interestingly, the EPA enforcement obligations are rooted in the EU's internal approach toward upholding IPRs, notably Directive 2004/48, on the enforcement of intellectual property rights, and two regulations dealing with border measures.[34] In fact, certain enforcement provisions of the EU–CARIFORUM EPA have been copied word for word from the 2004 Enforcement Directive.[35]

To summarize, the EPA clarifies and expands the TRIPS provisions on measures for the preservation of evidence, the collection of information on the origin and destination of IPR-infringing products, injunctions, and several other matters. Probably the most significant TRIPS+ element is the extension of border measures to the importation, exportation, reexportation, and other border movements of goods. In addition, border measures are to apply not only to counterfeit trademark goods and pirated copyright goods (as in the TRIPS Agreement) but also to goods infringing on a design right or a GI. Like many of the U.S. FTAs, the EU–CARIFORUM EPA does not recognize the institutional limitations of developing countries, as the TRIPS Agreement does. Thus, CARIFORUM members may not be able to invoke resource constraints as a reason for not complying with the agreements' specific enforcement obligations. As pointed out above, this lack of institutional flexibility may be a concern, as it is not clear that increased government spending on the enforcement of IPRs is warranted in environments in which many public goods are underprovided.[36]

The EU–CARIFORUM EPA provides a window into the EU's revised approach to the treatment of IPRs. Future PTA chapters on IPRs may well be more ambitious, not least because some of the EU's prospective PTA partners are more developed than the Caribbean countries. Early indications point in this direction. The leaked EU proposal for the IPR chapter in the PTA between the EU and the Association of Southeast Asian Nations (ASEAN) shows more far-reaching TRIPS+ obligations, including an extension of the copyright term, pharmaceutical test data exclusivity, rules on the liability of Internet service providers, and an extension of border measures to all forms of IPRs.[37]

Similarly, leaked information on the EU's proposal for the PTA with the Andean Community suggests the inclusion on the EU's wish list of test data protection, as well as a broadening of criminal sanctions and border measures to infringements of all types of IPRs (see Hernández 2009). Of course, it is uncertain how far the EU's proposals will be reflected in the final PTA texts. A definite assessment of the treatment of IPRs in the "new generation" PTAs will have to await the conclusion of the latest set of negotiations.

TRIPS+ Provisions in Other PTAs

In addition to the agreements negotiated by the United States and the EU, numerous PTAs contain provisions on the protection of intellectual property. For the most part, these are of a general nature, merely calling for the adequate and effective protection of IPRs. Sometimes they incorporate certain provisions of the TRIPS Agreement into the PTA. Although such incorporation may not be seen as TRIPS+, it is still significant, as it may subject TRIPS disciplines to the dispute settlement mechanisms of bilateral PTAs.[38]

Several FTAs that do not involve the United States or the EU set TRIPS+ protection standards. Most prominently, the European Free Trade Association (EFTA), with Iceland, Liechtenstein, Norway, and Switzerland as members, has negotiated a considerable number of PTAs that feature certain TRIPS+ elements. Specifically, the EFTA agreements with Chile, Colombia, Korea, Lebanon, and Singapore incorporate the WIPO Copyright Treaty and the WIPO Performances and Phonograms Treaty. The agreements with Chile, Korea, and Singapore also provide for an extension of the patent term as compensation for unreasonable delays in regulatory approval processes, along the lines of some of the U.S. agreements.

The EFTA's agreements with Chile, Korea, Singapore, and Tunisia require pharmaceutical test data exclusivity, again following the U.S. approach. In the Korean case, the relevant provision also allows for an alternative to exclusive test data rights, whereby any company would be allowed to rely on test data submitted to a regulatory agency if the company first submitting these data is adequately compensated. Such a compensatory liability approach has been advocated by academic scholars as a superior way of protecting test data because it allows research-based companies to recoup investments in clinical trials without inhibiting market competition (Reichman 2004). Interestingly, the EFTA–Colombia agreement, signed in 2008, incorporates an exception to exclusive test data rights to protect public health in accordance with WTO rules. The language used in this PTA is identical to that in the revised U.S.–Colombia agreement, illustrating how the U.S. policy shift described above influenced norms in a treaty that does not involve the United States.

A second remarkable feature of the EFTA–Colombia PTA is its incorporation of a mandatory disclosure requirement in patent applications of the origin or source of genetic material. Several developing-country WTO members have argued that the TRIPS Agreement affords inadequate safeguards against "biopiracy"—the acquisition of patent rights for biological materials (and related traditional knowledge) that are simply taken from one country's biological resources, without inventive effort. These members have long advocated the inclusion of a disclosure requirement in the TRIPS Agreement, but such a move has been resisted by other WTO members, and discussions on the topic in the context of the Doha negotiations have not yet led to any compromise.[39] It is interesting that Colombia, as one of the leading proponents of a disclosure requirement, persuaded EFTA countries to insert such a clause in their PTA, showing that the negotiation of IPR chapters can advance the interests of developing countries.

In February 2009, Switzerland signed a comprehensive economic partnership agreement with Japan that incorporates the TRIPS+ protection standards found in the EFTA agreements described above: incorporation of WIPO treaties, patent term extension, and exclusive test data rights. As an agreement between two developed countries, it introduces a number of additional obligations. In particular, it mandates the highest-level GI protection for all goods, along the lines of the EU–CARIFORUM agreement.[40] In the area of rights enforcement, it broadens the application of border measures and criminal sanctions to a wider range of IPR infringements, similar to what the EU has negotiated or is reportedly seeking in its "new generation" PTAs.[41]

Finally, it is worth pointing out that Chile and Mexico have signed a considerable number of PTAs that include lists of specific GIs related to wines and spirits which receive protection either as set out in the terms of the respective agreements or according to TRIPS standards. In the case of Chile, these lists include the names of Chile's many wine regions, as well as the Pisco (or Pisco Chileno) liquor distilled from grapes. Agreements that have incorporated at least some of these GIs are the Trans-Pacific Strategic Economic Partnership, with Brunei Darussalam, Chile, New Zealand, and Singapore, and Chile's bilateral PTAs with Canada, Japan, Korea, and Mexico. Mexico's interests are confined to the Tequila and Mezcal names, and their protection is expressly mandated in Mexico's PTAs with Nicaragua and Uruguay and in the Northern Triangle PTA involving El Salvador, Guatemala, and Honduras.

IPRs and Bilateral Investment Rules

In addition to the rules contained in the intellectual property chapters of PTAs, IPRs are subject to separate bilateral investment disciplines. Many PTAs contain separate investment chapters in which IPRs are expressly listed in the definition of what constitutes an investment. This is the case in the U.S. agreements with Australia, CAFTA–DR, Chile, Morocco, Oman, and Singapore. Moreover, parties to some PTAs that do not feature a separate investment chapter have concluded self-standing bilateral investment treaties (BITs) that include IPRs in the definition of investment; examples are the U.S. agreements with Bahrain and with Jordan. There are also numerous BITs between countries that have not entered into a PTA. Since no multilateral agreement on investment exists at the WTO or elsewhere, these bilateral investment rules break new ground.

A broad definition of investment that encompasses IPRs makes government measures affecting the intellectual property portfolios of foreign investors subject to the investment disciplines of PTAs or BITs. This raises such questions as whether granting a compulsory license is considered an act of expropriation. Many PTA investment chapters expressly remove compulsory licenses from the scope of expropriation, as long as such licenses comply with the obligations of the TRIPS Agreement and the intellectual property chapter of the respective PTA. This, however, is not always the case; the U.S. BITs with Bahrain and Jordan do not feature such a safeguard. Thus, if, say, Jordan were to issue a compulsory license in case of a national emergency, there is a question as to whether the patent holder could challenge such a decision as an act of investment expropriation.

Questions like this may be important because many investment agreements provide for direct investor-to-state dispute settlement, going beyond the more traditional state-state dispute settlement procedures included in trade agreements.[42] Investor-state dispute settlement may be more attractive to foreign investors, who can seek arbitration awards for uncompensated expropriation. By contrast, state-state dispute settlement can typically authorize only the imposition of punitive trade sanctions.

How widespread are investment treaties that have the potential to discipline government measures relating to the protection of IPRs? Given the rapid proliferation of PTAs and BITs, it is difficult to answer this question precisely. Some 421 trade agreements had been notified to the WTO up to December 2008 and there are estimated to be more than 2,500 BITs in force.[43] Not all trade agreements feature investment disciplines, and some only establish limited disciplines on foreign direct investment or commercial presence, which does not encompass IPRs.[44] Where PTAs adopt fully fledged investment chapters, intellectual property rights are typically included in the definition of investment. The same is true for BITs, including most treaties concluded between developing countries. There is more variation on the specifics of investor-state arbitration mechanisms; for example, in some agreements, the initiation of arbitration proceedings is subject to the consent of the affected governments.

As a final note, it is important to point out that the reach of investment agreements into the intellectual property domain remains in many ways legally uncertain (Correa 2004). So far, no arbitration claim related to government measures in the IPR field has been made. At the same time, given the proliferation of investment disciplines over the past decade, private investors may well initiate claims if they feel their IPRs have been unduly "expropriated." In this context, it is worth pointing out that some arbitral decisions have been criticized for their expansive interpretation of BIT provisions, creating more burdensome obligations than those originally intended by the signatories.[45] It is therefore important for governments to carefully consider all the implications of signing onto investment disciplines that cover measures affecting IPRs.

Annex. Further Information

The IPRs module of the World Bank Institute (WBI)–Columbia University Executive Training Course (Fink 2007) offers a basic introduction to the economics of IPRs and discusses the main obligations of the TRIPS Agreement. For an in-depth legal analysis of the TRIPS agreement and the multilateral IPR treaties administered by the WIPO, interested readers are referred to UNCTAD–ICTSD (2005) and Abbott, Cottier, and Gurry (2007). Maskus (2000) provides a comprehensive economic analysis of the IPR system, including the perspective of developing countries. Abbott (2006) and Roffe (2004) analyze U.S. FTA chapters in light of U.S. and Chilean law, respectively; Santa Cruz (2007) and Vivas Eugui and Spennemann (2005) review the treatment of IPRs, especially GIs, in EU agreements.

A number of NGOs have campaigned against the inclusion of TRIPS+ provisions in PTAs. Some of their policy

papers and positions can be found on the following Web sites:

- Knowledge Ecology International, http://www.cptech .org/ip/health/trade/
- Oxfam, http://www.oxfam.org.uk/resources/policy/ health/bp102_trips.html
- Médecins Sans Frontières, http://www.doctorswithout-borders.org/news/issue.cfm?id=2379

The following Web sites contain some industry positions on the inclusion of IPR provision in trade agreements:

- International Intellectual Property Alliance, http:// www.iipa.com/fta_issues.html
- Pharmaceutical Research and Manufacturers of America (PhRMA), http://www.phrma.org

International agreements referred to in this chapter can be accessed at the following Web sites:

- WTO Secretariat, http://www.wto.org/english/tratop_e/ TRIPS_e/TRIPS_e.htm
- World Intellectual Property Organization, http://www .wipo.int
- U.S. Trade Representative, http://www.ustr.gov
- European Commission, Directorate General for Trade, http://ec.europa.eu/trade/issues/index_en.htm
- European Free Trade Association, http://www.efta.int

Notes

The views expressed are the author's own and were written during his tenure as Professor of International Economics at the University of St. Gallen, Switzerland. They do not necessarily reflect the views of the World Intellectual Property Organization or its member states.

1. U.S. Chamber of Commerce, http://www.uschamber.com/issues/ index/international/ipr.htm.

2. An important caveat is that when trade opening takes the form of preferential tariff liberalization, the welfare consequences from increased trade are more ambiguous. In fact, it is possible that preferential tariffs will lead to the displacement of imports from nonmember countries to such an extent that overall welfare may fall. See Panagariya (2000) for a review of the standard economics of preferential trade agreements.

3. The rationale for the protection of trademarks and geographical indications is different. These two forms of IPRs seek to promote an orderly functioning of markets by reducing information asymmetries between buyers and sellers of goods and services. Fink (2007) provides more detailed treatment of the various economic arguments for protecting IPRs.

4. For example, would a patent owner in the form of a juridical person qualify if that person were established in the territory of one of the PTA parties but 50 percent of its equity were owned by another juridical person in a nonmember state?

5. A possible exception is the inclusion in PTAs of lists of protected geographical indications, which may lead to a de facto trade preference. See the section "TRIPS+ Provisions in EU PTAs," in this chapter.

6. Fink and Maskus (2004) review studies that assess econometrically the link between the strength of intellectual property protection and the extent of inward FDI. They conclude that countries which strengthen their IPR regimes are unlikely to experience a dramatic boost in FDI inflows; other factors account for most of the variation across countries in the activity of multinational enterprises. At the same time, the empirical evidence does point to a positive role of IPRs in stimulating cross-border licensing activity and so affecting the nature of formal technology transfers.

7. In many recently concluded North-South PTAs, the willingness of developing-country governments to enter into the arrangements was arguably not the lure of preferential market access to a large market but the threat of losing previously existing unilateral trade preferences. For example, Colombia and Peru faced the expiry of the so-called Andean trade preferences extended by the United States, and countries belonging to the Africa-Caribbean-Pacific (ACP) group (former European colonies) faced the expiry of trade preferences granted by the EU under the Cotonou Agreement.

8. A notable exception is a project by the International Center for Trade and Sustainable Development (ICTSD), the World Bank Institute (WBI), and the World Health Organization (WHO) that focuses on the pharmaceutical sector. The aim of the project is to develop a partial equilibrium model to assist researchers in assessing the price and expenditure effects of prolonged market exclusivity for pharmaceutical products. For further information, see the website on intellectual property rights sponsored by the ICTSD and the United Nations Conference on Trade and Development, http://www.iprsonline.org/ictsd/Dialogues/2007-05-27/2007-05-27_desc.htm.

9. In addition to FTAs, the United States has negotiated several bilateral trade agreements (BTAs) with countries that are not yet members of the WTO and therefore do not enjoy full MFN treatment by the U.S. government. Some of these BTAs, notably that with Vietnam, provide for obligations on IPRs; for reasons of space, these are not discussed here. For further details, see Fink and Reichenmiller (2005).

10. U.S. Trade Promotion Authority Act of 2002, http://frwebgate.access.gpo.gov/cgi-bin/getdoc.cgi?dbname=107_cong_public_laws&docid=f:publ210.107.

11. Given their older vintage, we do not review the IPR provisions of the U.S.–Israel FTA or of NAFTA.

12. The CAFTA–DR agreement requires countries that already provide patent protection for plants to maintain such protection.

13. In addition, the TRIPS provisions on compulsory licensing require a government to first make efforts to obtain a voluntary license from the patent holder, although this requirement can be waived in emergency situations or for public, noncommercial use. The obligations of bilateral agreements are similar or identical in this respect.

14. In the case of agrochemical products, most of the bilateral agreements require data exclusivity for 10 years.

15. The permissibility of parallel importation is governed by rules on the exhaustion of patents. A system of international exhaustion is associated with free parallel trade, whereas patent holders can restrict parallel importation if patent rights exhaust only nationally. TRIPS Article 6 does not mandate a particular exhaustion regime, only nondiscriminatory application.

16. Governments may, however, limit the right to prevent parallel importation to cases in which the patent holder includes territorial restraints in contractual agreements with wholesalers or retailers.

17. Paragraph 4, Doha Declaration on TRIPS and Public Health, http://www.wto.org/english/thewto_e/minist_e/min01_e/mindecl_trips_e.htm.

18. The side letters also clarify that the intellectual property chapters of the FTAs "do not prevent the effective utilization" of the August 2003 decision by WTO members, described in the text.

19. The agreements with Australia, CAFTA–DR, Chile, and Jordan contain provisions affirming the rights and obligations of member countries under the TRIPS agreement. To some extent, these provisions may be interpreted as preserving the flexibilities of the TRIPS agreement.

However, the value of these nonderogation clauses in bilateral disputes is legally uncertain (Abbott 2004).

20. See the proposed Digital Media Consumers' Rights Act, introduced in the U.S. House of Representatives, http://en.wikipedia.org/wiki/Digital_Media_Consumers'_Rights_Act.

21. Article 41.5, TRIPS Agreement, http://www.wto.org.

22. The U.S.–Chile and CAFTA–DR agreements contain language similar to that of the TRIPS Agreement, acknowledging that no obligation is created regarding the distribution of law enforcement resources. However, the proviso that resource constraints may not be invoked as an excuse for not meeting the agreements' specific enforcement obligations appears to significantly weaken this flexibility.

23. The Bipartisan Agreement covers not only IPRs but also a number of other trade-related topics: basic labor standards, environment and global warming, government procurement, port security, investment, and worker assistance and training. The text of the agreement is available at http://www.cpath.org/sitebuildercontent/sitebuilderfiles/2007_new_trade_policy_details5-10-07.pdf. Roffe and Vivas-Eugui (2007) offer a commentary on the agreement.

24. For instance, drug regulators need to give general notice of submissions of applications for marketing approval so that patent holders have the opportunity to discover products that may infringe on their patents.

25. In the case of the U.S.–Colombia FTA, the Bipartisan Agreement identified additional concerns about violence against trade unionists and demanded that this issue be addressed in a satisfactory way—along with the other proposed revisions set out in the agreement—before the revised FTA is submitted for congressional approval.

26. The same changes have been introduced into the texts of the U.S. FTAs with Colombia and Panama.

27. Table 18.2 does not include the EU's association agreements with countries in Eastern Europe and the Euro-Mediterranean partners. Some of these agreements incorporate soft-law provisions that generally call for the protection of IPRs in conformity with the highest international standards or at a level similar to that existing in the EU. They also make reference to existing multilateral treaties, in particular the TRIPS Agreement and selected WIPO conventions, sometimes including the WIPO Copyright Treaty and the WIPO Performances and Phonograms Treaty. For the most part, accession to these treaties is voluntary. See Santa Cruz (2007) for further discussion.

28. *Official Journal of the European Union,* document 2005/C 129/03.

29. For a more detailed discussion of GI obligations in EU bilateral agreements, see Vivas Eugui and Spennemann (2005); Santa Cruz (2007).

30. See Battaglene (2005). In addition, Schamel and Anderson (2003) find that regional origin has become a major determinant of prices in the Australian wine industry, with price premiums averaging about 31 percent for wines carrying Australian GIs.

31. Although the interim EPAs that have been negotiated so far with other ACP partners do not yet contain a full IPR chapter, they do call for the negotiation of such a chapter in the final agreement.

32. The EU–CARIFORUM EPA foresees full implementation of the IPR chapter by 2014. Least-developed CARIFORUM members are granted a special transition period until 2021.

33. In fact, there is no consensus among WTO members as to whether the Doha Ministerial Declaration of 2001 provides a negotiating mandate for extension of GI protection; see Fink and Maskus (2005).

34. See Council Regulation (EC) 1383/2003, concerning customs action against goods suspected of infringing certain intellectual property rights and the measures to be taken against goods found to have infringed such rights, and Commission Regulation (EC) 1891/2004, which lays down provisions for the implementation of Council Regulation (EC) 1383/2003.

35. See, for example, Article 154 of the EPA, on measures for preserving evidence, and Article 155 on the right of information.

36. The EU–CARIFORUM EPA foresees the provision of technical assistance by the EU for implementing the IPR obligations undertaken by CARIFORUM members. Although aid of this type may alleviate the

budgetary pressure associated with strengthened IPR enforcement, a similar caveat still applies: are the EU's scarce aid resources best spent in the IPR field as opposed to, say, education or health?

37. The EU's draft IPR chapter is available at http://www.bilaterals .org/article.php3?id_article=14281.

38. For example, Japan's PTAs with Indonesia, Malaysia, Mexico, Singapore, Thailand, and Vietnam fall into this category. The same is true for the Japan–Philippines economic partnership agreement, except for one notable TRIPS+ obligation: the expansion of criminal sanctions beyond trademark counterfeiting and copyright piracy to include, as well, infringements of patents, utility models, layout designs for integrated circuits, and plant variety rights.

39. See Fink (2005) for additional background on this topic. The EFTA–Colombia PTA also contains strong language on the fair and equitable sharing of benefits arising from the use of genetic resources and traditional knowledge, although it does not make an agreement on benefit sharing a precondition for the grant of a patent. General language on the use of biological resources and traditional knowledge and the equitable sharing of benefits is also found in the agreements between the United States and Peru, the EU and the Caribbean Community (CARICOM), and Guatemala and Taiwan, China.

40. The GI provisions of the Japan–Switzerland agreement have two other noteworthy features. First, they introduce the concepts of indications of services and country names, which equally benefit from protection against misleading use. Second, the parties exchanged lists of geographic names that serve as a source of information about GIs protected under domestic laws in the parties' respective territories. These lists are not limited to wines and spirits but include cheeses, meat-based products, bread, pastry, cakes, watches, textile products, pharmaceutical products, and other goods.

41. The Japan–Switzerland EPA extends border measures to goods destined for export, as well as transiting goods.

42. An exception is the investment chapter of the U.S.–Australia FTA, which only allows for the possibility of investor-state dispute settlement procedures being negotiated in the future.

43. See WTO, http://rtais.wto.org/UI/PublicMaintainRTAHome.aspx; Dolzer and Scheuer (2008).

44. The EU–CARIFORUM, EU–Chile, Australia–Thailand, Chile–EFTA, and Mexico–EFTA agreements are examples of the latter.

45. For example, certain interpretations of obligations relating to "fair and equitable treatment" and measures "tantamount to expropriation" have been considered to go beyond parties' original intentions. In response to some of these arbitral decisions, the United States and Canada have included interpretive notes in their BITs and their FTA investment chapters clarifying the scope of the fair and equitable treatment and expropriation provisions. See Sornarajah (2004).

References

Abbott, Frederick. 2004. "The Doha Declaration on the TRIPS Agreement and Public Health and the Contradictory Trend in Bilateral and Regional Free Trade Agreements." Occasional Paper 14, Quaker United Nations Office, New York.

———. 2006. "Intellectual Property Provisions of Bilateral and Regional Trade Agreements in Light of U.S. Federal Law." International Center for Trade and Sustainable Development (ICTSD)–United Nations Conference on Trade and Development (UNCTAD) Project on IPRs and Sustainable Development, Issue Paper 12, UNCTAD, Geneva.

Abbott Frederick, Thomas Cottier, and Francis Gurry. 2007. "International Intellectual Property in an Integrated World Economy." New York: Aspen Publishers.

Battaglene, Tony. 2005. "The Australian Wine Industry Position on Geographical Indications." Paper presented at the Worldwide Symposium on Geographical Indications, Parma, Italy, June 27–29.

CIPR (Commission on Intellectual Property Rights). 2002. "Integrating Intellectual Property Rights and Development Policy." Report of the Commission on Intellectual Property Rights established by the U.K. Secretary of State for International Development, London.

Correa, Carlos M. 2004. "Bilateral Investment Agreements: Agents of a New Global Standard for the Protection of Intellectual Property Rights?" Briefing paper, GRAIN, Barcelona, Spain, and Los Banos, the Philippines. http://www.grain.org/briefings/?id=186.

Dolzer, Rudolf, and Christoph Scheuer. 2008. *Principles of International Investment Law.* New York: Oxford University Press.

Fink, Carsten. 2005. "Shifting Tides: TRIPS in the Doha Round." *World Trade Brief.* London: Haymarket Management.

———. 2007. "Intellectual Property Rights: Economic Principles and Trade Rules." Training module prepared for the World Bank Institute–Columbia University Executive Course on Trade Policy for Development, World Bank, Washington, DC.

———. 2008. "Intellectual Property and Public Health: An Overview of the Debate with a Focus on U.S. Policy." Working Paper 146, Center for Global Development, Washington, DC.

Fink, Carsten, and Keith E. Maskus. 2004. *Intellectual Property and Development: Lessons from Recent Economic Research.* Washington, DC: World Bank; New York: Oxford University Press.

———. 2005. "The Debate on Geographical Indications in the WTO." In *Trade, Doha, and Development: Window into the Issues,* ed. Richard Newfarmer. Washington, DC: World Bank.

Fink, Carsten, and Patrick Reichenmiller. 2005. "Tightening TRIPS: The Intellectual Property Provisions of Recent US Free Trade Agreements." Trade Note 20, World Bank, Washington, DC.

Hernández, Xavier Seuba. 2009. "Health Protection in the European and Andean Association Agreement." Health Action International, Amsterdam. http://www.haiweb.org/23032009/18%20Mar%202009%20Policy%20Paper%20EU-CAN%20Association%20Agreement%20FINAL.pdf.

Maskus, Keith E. 2000. *Intellectual Property Rights in the Global Economy.* Washington, DC: Institute for International Economics.

MSF (Médecins Sans Frontières). 2004. "Access to Medicines at Risk across the Globe: What to Watch Out for in Free Trade Agreements with the United States." MSF Briefing Note, MSF. Geneva.

Oxfam. 2006. "Patents versus Patients: Five Years after the Doha Declaration." Oxfam Briefing Paper 95, Oxfam, Oxford, U.K. http://www.oxfam.org/sites/www.oxfam.org/files/Patents%20vs.%20Patients.pdf.

Panagariya, Arvind. 2000. "Preferential Trade Liberalization: The Traditional Theory and New Developments." *Journal of Economic Literature* 32 (2): 287–331.

Reichman, Jerome H. 2004. "Undisclosed Clinical Trial Data under the TRIPS Agreement and Its Progeny: A Broader Perspective." Presented at the United Nations Conference on Trade and Development (UNCTAD)–International Centre for Trade and Sustainable Development (ICTSD) Dialogue, "Moving the Pro-Development IP Agenda Forward: Preserving Public Goods in Health, Education and Learning," Bellagio, Italy, November 29–December 3. http://www.iprsonline.org/unctadictsd/bellagio/docs/Reichman_Bellagio4.pdf.

Roffe, Pedro. 2004. "Bilateral Agreements and a TRIPS-Plus World: The Chile–USA Free Trade Agreement." TRIPS Issues Paper 4, Quaker International Affairs Programme, Ottawa.

Roffe, Pedro, and David Vivas-Eugui. 2007. "A Shift in Intellectual Property Policy in US FTAs?" *Bridges* (International Center for Trade and Sustainable Development) 11 (5): 15–16. http://ictsd.org/i/news/bridges/4128/.

Santa Cruz, Maximiliano S. 2007. "Intellectual Property Provisions in European Union Free Trade Agreements: Implications for Developing Countries." Issue Paper 20, ICTSD Programme on Intellectual Property Rights (IPRs) and Sustainable Development, International Center for Trade and Sustainable Development, Geneva.

Schamel, Günter, and Kym Anderson. 2003. "Wine Quality and Varietal, Regional and Winery Reputations: Hedonic Prices for Australia and New Zealand." *Economic Record* 79 (246): 357–69.

Sornarajah, Muthucumaraswamy. 2004. *The International Law on Foreign Investment.* 2nd ed. Cambridge, U.K.: Cambridge University Press.

UNCTAD-ICTSD (United Nations Conference on Trade and Development–International Center for Trade and Sustainable Development). 2005. *Resource Book on TRIPS and Development.* Cambridge, U.K.: Cambridge University Press. http://www.iprsonline.org/unctadictsd/ResourceBookIndex.htm.

Vivas Eugui, David, and Christoph Spennemann. 2005. "The Treatment of Geographical Indications in Recent Regional and Bilateral Free Trade Agreements." In *The Intellectual Property Debate: Perspectives from Law, Economics, and Political Economy,* ed. Meir Perez Pugatch, 305–44. Cheltenham, U.K.: Edward Elgar.

Woolcock, Stephen. 2007. "European Union Policy towards Free Trade Agreements." ECIPE Working Paper 03/2007, European Centre for International Political Economy, Brussels.

19

ENVIRONMENT

Anuradha R. V.

The linkage between trade and environment is a sensitive and controversial issue for many countries. Trade, like any other economic activity, has environmental implications, but whether trade as a policy instrument should address environmental concerns is a question to which there are no unanimous answers. Although practically all countries recognize the critical importance of the environment, a number of developing countries do not believe that addressing environmental issues as part of trade agreements is necessarily the best approach. Accordingly, a few developing countries have entered into regional agreements on environmental issues that are distinct from preferential trade agreements (PTAs). Developed countries have been the primary drivers for PTAs comprising environmental provisions. Neither approach has been proved more effective than the other.

This chapter does not seek to build a rationale for the trade-environment linkage or to determine whether environmental issues should be addressed in trade agreements or in stand-alone environmental agreements. The focus, instead, is on the main contours of the trade and environment debate at the multilateral level and on the increasing incorporation of environmental provisions into PTAs, especially those involving major developed economies. The chapter addresses issues relating to (a) the nature of the legal obligations emerging from provisions dealing with the environment in PTAs; (b) the potential economic costs of particular environmental requirements, including obligations to maintain specific environmental regulatory standards and to adhere to particular environmental sanitary and phytosanitary measures or technical regulations; (c) the need for technical assistance and capacity building to ensure compliance with environmental obligations; (d) the nature and extent of financial assistance required for implementing such provisions; and (e) the dispute settlement and enforcement mechanisms for such provisions. It analyzes the extent to which PTAs can be a vehicle for

countries to address regional environmental concerns, including concerns relating to shared natural resources, and it concludes by discussing practical steps for developing countries to consider when negotiating PTAs.

The analysis relies on a review of those PTAs that incorporate environmental provisions and on secondary literature on the subject. Inclusion of environmental provisions in PTAs is of fairly recent date, and the literature analyzing the impact of the linkage is also at a nascent stage. The most comprehensive study on environmental provisions in PTAs was conducted by the Organisation for Economic Co-operation and Development (OECD 2007). That study identifies the United States, the European Union (EU), Canada, and New Zealand as the principal proponents of environmental provisions in PTAs. The study underscores the paucity of experience with actual implementation of environmental provisions and the ongoing learning process. It emphasizes the need for preparation and coordination in dealing with environmental issues in PTAs and stresses that developing countries often require financial support and capacity-building assistance to this end.

Asia-Pacific Economic Cooperation (APEC) and the Organization of American States (OAS) maintain databases that summarize environmental provisions in PTAs.[1] Studies by research institutions and think tanks have also been consulted for this chapter.

The only PTA to have been analyzed in substantive detail is the North American Free Trade Agreement (NAFTA), which was concluded by the United States, Canada, and Mexico in 1994. Studies have been conducted to evaluate NAFTA's implications for the environment in Mexico, its economic costs, and the effectiveness of using a PTA to address environmental issues (see Gallagher 2004; Tiemann 2004; Hufbauer and Schott 2005; Environment Canada 2007). The findings have been mixed, with some analysts hailing NAFTA's achievements and others highlighting its limitations and unresolved issues, including the inadequacy of financial resources for combating environmental problems.

Trade and Environment Linkages

This section looks at the economic and political-economy dimensions of PTAs and discusses WTO policies that affect environmental provisions in trade agreements.

Economic Perspectives

Initial discussions on the subject of trade and environmental linkages revealed two distinct schools of thought, one arguing for the integration of adequate environmental safeguards within trade agreements and the other maintaining that free trade should not be subject to any restrictions. According to the first school, free trade does not necessarily lead to efficiencies, and it can bring about a deterioration of environmental standards. Firms whose main concern is to maximize profits may be inclined to move their operations to developing countries, where pollution control is inexpensive and lax—this scenario has been termed the "pollution haven" hypothesis (Daly 1993a, 1993b). Porter (1991), drawing on experience in northern Europe and Japan, concludes that stronger environmental regulation is not only necessary but could also make firms more competitive.

On the other side of the spectrum is the argument that there should be no environmental or other restrictions on free trade, on the grounds that free trade will eventually lead to economic growth, increased income levels, and, as a consequence, investment in higher environmental standards (Bhagwati 1993). The argument of this group is not that free trade has no environmental implications; it is, rather, that trade should not be used as a tool to impose environmental standards because the welfare implications of free trade are independent of those standards (Bhagwati and Srinivasan 1996; Bhagwati 2004).

More recent literature explores the subject from other angles and leads to findings somewhere between the first two schools. Empirical evidence on the pollution haven hypothesis has been mixed. Studies have demonstrated that lower environmental regulations do not necessarily lead to a race to the bottom and that environmental regulations are not the only factors that guide investment decisions (see, for example, Friedman, Gerlowski, and Silberman 1992; Mani, Pargal, and Huq 1997). At the same time, empirical research demonstrates that although trade liberalization can promote economic growth, it may have adverse environmental consequences, which it would be necessary to address simultaneously by strengthening environmental regulation (see Mani and Jha 2006).[2] A study of PTAs in Latin America similarly

found that although trade-led growth resulted in a shift toward cleaner production by a number of industries, industrial pollution increased overall because nations in the hemisphere "lack the proper policies to stem the environmental consequences of trade-led growth."[3]

The only literature to examine whether, as a policy matter, trade agreements are an appropriate forum for addressing environmental issues is a World Trade Organization (WTO) background note (WTO Secretariat 1997). It observes that trade instruments are not the first-best policy for addressing environmental problems and finds a positive correlation between removal of trade restrictions and increased availability of environmental goods and services and of cleaner technologies.

Political-Economy Considerations

Turning to the political-economy dimension of the trade-environment debate, the divide between developed and developing countries is distinct. Developed economies such as the United States, Canada, New Zealand, and the EU have been among the strongest proponents of environmental measures in trade agreements, both at the multilateral level and in PTAs. In fact, the domestic policies of these countries require that environmental assessments of PTAs be carried out and that adequate provisions on the environment be included in the agreements. U.S. Public Law 107-210, the Trade Promotion Act (TPA) of 2002, requires, among other things, that countries signing trade agreements with the United States ensure that their environmental laws are enforced. The EU mandates sustainability impact assessments (SIAs) of PTAs (European Commission 2006). New Zealand's Framework for Integrating Environment Issues into Free Trade Agreements emphasizes the harmonization of the "objectives for trade and for the environment, with both serving the overarching objective of promoting sustainable development."[4]

Developing countries, by contrast, have been skeptical about the trade-environment linkage, their concern being that environmental issues might become a means of imposing protectionist measures (see, for example, Khan et al. 2004; Rodriguez 2009). India, among other countries, has emphasized that harmonization may be easier for developed countries and that among developing countries, with their widely differing environmental standards in accordance with their national priorities, harmonization would be both difficult and inadvisable (India 2000). However, countries such as Chile, China, and Mexico have been incorporating environmental provisions into their PTAs, although the scope and depth of such provisions are not as elaborate as those proposed by developed countries.

Trade and Environment at the WTO

Any discussion of trade and environment is perhaps best appreciated when set in the context of the multilateral discussions at the WTO. Countries entering into PTAs typically focus on the rights and obligations under a PTA that are additional to or different from those under the WTO's multilateral system. As noted above, not all WTO members agree on whether and to what extent environmental provisions should be reflected in trade agreements. The WTO agreements, however, do confirm the right of WTO members to protect the environment, provided that certain conditions are met. Environmental provisions find a place within the preamble of the Agreement Establishing the WTO, in general exceptions to trade obligations, and in agreements on technical barriers to trade (TBTs) and sanitary and phytosanitary measures (SPS).[5] At the Doha ministerial conference, WTO members reaffirmed their commitment to environmental protection and agreed to embark on a new round of trade talks, including negotiations on certain aspects of the linkage between trade and environment.

There have been several prominent disputes at the WTO concerning the trade and environment interface.[6] Some basic propositions emerge from the jurisprudence that has been developed so far:

- WTO law does not exist in clinical isolation from international law and international developments, including environmental concerns. However, environmental measures to restrict trade can be adopted only under certain strict conditions.
- Multilateral solutions to environmental issues are preferred, and WTO members should therefore make serious efforts to negotiate such solutions. If, despite such efforts, an agreement cannot be concluded, unilateral measures for protection of the environment may be taken, even outside the country's jurisdiction.
- Adequate scientific evidence and risk assessment must underlie any action under the WTO's SPS Agreement, which allows for measures to protect human, animal, and plant life and health.
- Tests of necessity and of the availability of less trade restrictive measures are to be applied prior to application of any trade restriction on environmental grounds.

Overview of Approaches to Environmental Concerns in PTAs

As has been noted, the primary proponents of environmental provisions in PTAs have been the United States, the EU, Canada, and New Zealand. Developing countries have increasingly agreed to environmental obligations in PTAs with these countries. With the exceptions of perhaps Chile and Mexico and, more recently, China, developing countries have not themselves initiated environmental provisions in PTAs.

Proponents of environmental provisions in PTAs either incorporate such provisions into the main text of the PTA or place them in separate side agreements. Such provisions typically pertain to any or all of the following matters: obligations relating to "high standards" in domestic environmental laws; mechanisms for resolving disputes involving environmental provisions; principles of cooperation on environmental issues; and provisions on technical assistance and capacity building. These obligations are a blend of legally binding and nonbinding provisions. (The annexes to this chapter summarize environmental provisions in U.S. and EU PTAs.)

Since the conclusion, in 1994, of NAFTA and a side agreement, the North American Agreement on Environmental Cooperation (NAAEC), all PTAs negotiated by the United States have included environmental considerations both in environmental chapters and in separate instruments that focus mainly on environmental cooperation. Examples include the agreements with Singapore, Chile, Australia, Bahrain, and Morocco and the PTA with the five countries of the Central America Free Trade Agreement, plus the Dominican Republic (CAFTA–DR).[7] These agreements explicitly establish an obligation by the parties to effectively enforce their environmental laws, and they include provisions to ensure enforcement of this commitment through mechanisms for dispute settlement and public submissions. They provide for environmental cooperation between the parties and are accompanied by an environmental cooperation agreement or memorandum of understanding that establishes a framework for such cooperation. Canada's PTAs also contain comprehensive provisions on the environment, similar to those in U.S. PTAs.

The EU's early PTAs, such as those with Mexico, Chile, and the Mediterranean countries, contain fewer and more broadly worded provisions on the environment.[8] It is only in the recently concluded economic partnership agreement (EPA) between the EU and the Caribbean Forum of African, Caribbean, and Pacific (ACP) States (CARIFORUM) that the EU has devoted a separate chapter to environmental provisions.

The most significant difference between U.S. and EU PTAs lies in the dispute settlement mechanism. All U.S. PTAs except the one with Jordan prescribe remedies in the form of monetary compensation for noncompliance with environmental provisions. In the event that such compensation is not paid by a party, then—as a last resort—tariff concessions may be suspended. EU PTAs leave the issue of "compliance measures" to the judicial mechanism hearing the dispute. Remedies may include monetary compensation, but not suspension of concessions. Several U.S. PTAs also provide for public submission of complaints to the institutional authority responsible for implementing the PTA; this provision is absent in EU PTAs.

New Zealand has so far addressed environmental concerns in side agreements on environmental cooperation, using the softer language of "intent" and "endeavour" to achieve environmental objectives and ensure environmental cooperation. Japan's approach, like New Zealand's, seems to be focused on principles of cooperation to achieve specified environmental goals. More recently, Japan has been introducing environmental provisions, primarily worded as principles of cooperation, into its PTAs. Australia, so far, is the only major developed country to maintain a stand that environmental issues need to be addressed separately from trade agreements. In its PTA with the United States, however, Australia has agreed to environmental provisions that are similar to those in other U.S. PTAs.

A number of regional economic groups of developing countries recognize environmental issues as an important matter for regional cooperation. They include the Southern Cone Common Market (Mercosur, Mercado Común del Sur); the Andean Community; the Association of Southeast Asian Nations (ASEAN) Free Trade Area (AFTA); the South Asian Association for Regional Cooperation (SAARC); the Caribbean Community (CARICOM); the East African Community (EAC); and the Southern African Development Community (SADC).[9] These groups deal with environmental issues in separate agreements or understandings, not as part of a PTA. Their agreements contain no provisions on linkages between trade and environment. Although economic cooperation is one of the pillars of these groups, environmental issues are not regarded as part of the economic relationship. Environment and economics are treated as distinct and separate elements of the regional interrelationships between the countries.

Among the major developing economies, Brazil, the Russian Federation, India, and China have supported and participated in all major multilateral environmental agreements. Their PTAs typically contain references to the environment as part of the preamble or the general objectives. These are worded as statements of intent, rather than as binding legal obligations. Recent PTAs entered into by China contain environmental provisions of a more elaborate nature. These are primarily couched as "soft" obligations in its agreements with ASEAN, New Zealand, and Singapore.

Regional Public Goods

What motivates countries in a region to address a common environmental concern? Agreements between neighboring countries, whether PTAs or stand-alone regional environmental agreements, often provide a platform for addressing environmental concerns with transboundary implications. The OECD study on regional trade agreements observes that when partners share ecosystems, there is risk of "environmental blowback" from unmanaged growth across the border (OECD 2007, 83). For instance, concern in U.S. border states about the growth of polluting industries in Mexico is perceived to have provided a strong impetus for building environmental elements into the NAFTA relationship (ibid). Another example is the ASEAN–China PTA, which, in Article 7.1(3), emphasizes Mekong River Basin development as a priority area for cooperation.[10] Environment, fisheries, forestry, and forestry products are among the many policy areas in which the parties commit to cooperate (Article 7.2).

PTAs are not the only vehicle for addressing regional environmental issues (and in any case, PTA partners are not necessarily geographically proximate). As was seen in the preceding section, several regional groups of developing countries have addressed environmental concerns in stand-alone environmental agreements rather than in PTAs. For example,

- ASEAN countries have concluded an agreement that provides for work on transboundary haze, nature conservation and biodiversity, the coastal and marine environment, global environmental issues, and cross-cutting environmental initiatives.
- The SAARC Plan of Action on Environment sets the parameters for enhanced action at the regional level and has led to the establishment of two Regional Centers of Excellence in the field of environment.[11]
- The SADC Wildlife Programme of Action promotes coordinated action by member states for protection of wildlife in the region.
- The Caribbean Environment Program focuses on environmental management, training, and awareness programs in relation to regional issues such as coastal zone management, biodiversity, coral reef management, protected areas, and wildlife protection.

Experience so far indicates that countries in a region are most likely to address a problem that is transboundary in nature and affects all of them. The framework of a trade agreement such as a PTA is not a necessary precondition.

It is also important to note that such agreements emphasize principles of cooperation, rather than legally binding obligations.

PTAs, and other regional agreements between countries that are geographically proximate, are more likely to successfully address regional environmental concerns than global issues—for which multilateral cooperation would be necessary. PTAs are probably less likely to tackle global environmental problems such as climate change, declining biodiversity, depletion of ocean fisheries, and overexploitation of shared resources. There are, however, a few PTAs that seek to address environmental issues that are not purely regional. An example is the Japan–Mexico PTA, which contains provisions on environmental cooperation on activities to implement the Clean Development Mechanism and the Kyoto Protocol. The U.S.–Peru PTA includes detailed annexes on biodiversity protection and conservation and on forestry governance, and U.S. PTAs with Colombia and Costa Rica also address biodiversity protection. These PTAs exhibit a mix of legally binding and non-binding approaches that seek to complement multilateral efforts on similar issues.

Benefits of the Alternative Approaches for Economic Development and the Environment

The above discussions reveal three broad approaches:

- Environmental provisions worded as binding commitments and obligations and incorporated in PTAs
- Environmental provisions included in PTAs as non-binding soft obligations, in the form of arrangements for cooperation and statements of intent
- Environmental agreements or understandings, mostly worded as soft obligations, outside the purview of PTAs.

No study has been carried out on the relative effectiveness, from the perspective of promoting sustainable development, of these alternatives.

The effectiveness of any approach will hinge on the nature of commitments by member countries to a specific agreement and on the political and financial resources for implementing such commitments. Technology sharing and transfer, technical assistance and capacity building, and financing of environmental initiatives are critical determinants of the economic development benefits of these approaches. This is borne out by experience with implementation of environmental provisions, as discussed below. These experiences underscore that environmental provisions in PTAs need to be accompanied by sustained support for regulatory and institutional building to promote

higher environmental standards. Box 19.1 lists a number of considerations for developing countries in negotiating environmental issues in PTAs.

The United States, Canada, and New Zealand have undertaken pre-PTA environment impact assessments (EIAs) of the environmental impacts of PTAs in their own countries. The EU approach is slightly different; sustainability impact assessments (SIAs) are carried out for both EU member states and the trading partners with which the PTA is being negotiated. No study has yet been done on the extent to which the findings from these assessments are reflected in the drafting of PTA provisions, but such assessments are likely to be valuable tools for designing effective environmental provisions that can have developmental benefits. It would stand to reason that the broader scope of an EU-type SIA inquiry into environmental and sustainable development impacts in all the trading partners to a PTA is a conceptually superior method of addressing economic development in the trading parties.

Regional Environmental Policy in a Multilateral World

One of the main criticisms of PTAs is that they lead to proliferation of diverse rules and to increased complexity in trade relations between countries. Several visually descriptive phrases have emerged in trade linguistics to describe this effect of PTAs, such as "spaghetti bowl," "noodle bowl," and more recently, "termites in the trading system" (Bhagwati 2008).[12] The essential point, as summarized in a recent WTO publication, is that the proliferation of PTAs has created an array of criss-crossing arrangements, with little attention to coherence among agreements or to the implications of so many regimes for trade costs and efficiency (Baldwin and Low 2009).

Against the above argument, it is sometimes asserted that multiplication of PTAs need not necessarily be viewed as enhancing complexities and that liberalization through PTAs may in fact lead to greater multilateral liberalization over time. It is still early for a definitive assessment on this issue. The discussion here asks whether environmental provisions offer potential for the extension of open regionalism and whether they discriminate against nonparties.

Open Regionalism

One of the main issues concerning the use of PTAs as against a multilateral approach to trade negotiations is whether PTAs can eventually lead to open regionalism—that is, to external liberalization by regional trading blocs.

Box 19.1. Considerations for Developing Countries in Negotiating PTAs

In view of the growing tendency to include environmental provisions in PTAs, it is important for developing countries to (a) assess the likelihood that a trading partner will raise environmental issues as part of the PTA agenda, (b) analyze the potential implications of such provisions, and (c) develop a proactive agenda of their own concerns and desired positions. Some specific considerations and recommendations follow.

1. *Preparedness.* Examine the potential partner's existing PTAs to assess beforehand what environmental provisions the other party is likely to suggest. Flexibilities offered in other PTAs entered into by the other country should be explored to the fullest.
2. *Assistance for pre-PTA impact assessments.* If sustainable impact assessment (SIA) in both parties to the PTA is to be part of the negotiating process, seek technical, financial assistance, and capacity-building assistance from the party that has more experience with such assessments.
3. *Key substantive issues.* Keep in mind the following issues in negotiating environmental provisions: (a) the legal obligations emerging from the provisions; (b) the potential economic costs of environmental requirements, including obligations to maintain specific environment regulatory standards and requirements relating to adherence to any environmental SPS measures or technical regulations; (c) the need for technical assistance and capacity building to ensure compliance with environmental obligations; (d) the financial assistance required; and (e) dispute settlement and enforcement mechanisms.
4. *Implications for domestic law and institutions.* Evaluate the nature, extent, and feasibility of regulatory and legal changes that may be required at the domestic level to ensure compliance with the proposed environmental provisions in the PTA.
5. *Economic costs.* Carefully assess the economic costs of implementing environmental provisions, including the cost of new regulations and new institutional mechanisms for enforcement and the effects of more stringent environmental standards on export competitiveness. Capacity-building and technical assistance may be needed to ensure adherence to such requirements, and adequate and sustained support for such purposes should be built into the PTAs. Pre-PTA assessments would be valuable tools for understanding the costs.
6. *Provisions for resolving conflicting norms.* Determine whether the PTA contains provisions for resolving conflicts between different aspects of the PTA—for example, between trade and investment priorities and environmental priorities. Adequate mechanisms for dialogue between the institutional frameworks responsible for these norms are necessary.
7. *Specific environmental concerns.* Developing countries' environmental agendas when negotiating PTAs need not always be reactive; identify and raise specific environmental matters of concern. Examples may include SPS measures or technical regulations faced by exporters, or exporters' need for access to environmentally friendly technology. Cooperation and technical assistance may be required under the PTA to facilitate market access to the developed country's market.
8. *Preferential market access.* Identify provisions that could be built into the PTA concerning preferential access to clean technologies and to renewable and energy-efficient goods and services. Requirements for technical assistance and capacity building to enhance domestic capacity for developing environmental goods and services and clean technologies could also be considered.
9. *Technical, financial, and capacity-building assistance.* Determine whether proposed provisions on environmental obligations are binding. Legally binding obligations would need to be accompanied by binding commitments from developed-country partners to provide technical, financial, and capacity-building assistance to the developing partner to support the enactment and enforcement of environmental regulations. Specific obligations by a developing country to enact and maintain environmental regulations should be made conditional on actual development assistance and capacity-building support from the developed-country partner. Clear benchmarks for monitoring implementation of such provisions are necessary. Specific areas in which cooperation and assistance are required should be prioritized, and the associated work programs need to be monitored.
10. *Dispute settlement provisions.* Consider negotiating dispute settlement mechanisms that emphasize consultation and cooperation. Binding dispute resolution mechanisms may be theoretically superior for ensuring the effectiveness of a law, but the implementation of environmental provisions depends on other factors, such as the availability of technical and financial resources. In view of this, it may be advisable to opt for binding dispute resolution only if all the elements for securing effective implementation of the provisions, including the technical and financial assistance required for implementing any new environmental laws and standards, are built into the PTA.

Several working definitions of the phrase have been proposed, differing from each other as to the extent of openness necessary if the trade policy of a regional bloc is to qualify as open regionalism.[13]

The concept of open regionalism in the context of environmental provisions in PTAs is interpreted here as an assessment of whether countries adhering to environmental obligations in one PTA are replicating similar provisions in other PTAs. In other words, is there a possibility that common environmental standards will be applied through replication of regional approaches?

Countries have taken disparate approaches toward incorporating environmental provisions into their PTAs.

Broadly, as described above, developed actors such as the United States, the EU, Canada, and New Zealand are the primary drivers of stronger environmental provisions in PTAs, exerting pressure that a developing country partner may find difficult to resist during the trade negotiations. PTAs entered into by these countries are likely to replicate similar provisions, which may create a certain degree of harmonization between agreements over time.

A developing country may agree to environmental provisions in a PTA with a developed country but may not choose to replicate such provisions in its PTAs with other countries, whether developed or developing. Even when it does, the environmental provisions are likely to be milder (i.e., couched as softer obligations) than those negotiated with developed-country partners. An illustration is the approach adopted by Chile and Mexico, both of which adhered to comprehensive environmental obligations for the first time in their PTAs with the United States and Canada. Subsequent PTAs concluded by Chile and Mexico with other countries incorporate environmental provisions, but these are not as elaborate as the provisions in their PTAs with the United States and Canada. Chile has signed a memorandum of environmental cooperation with China, and it has also concluded PTAs with Japan, Mexico, Peru, and the Republic of Korea that contain some provisions on the environment.[14] Apart from NAFTA, Mexico's only significant PTA to incorporate environmental provisions is the one with Japan. Consistent with Japan's approach so far, the agreement emphasizes soft principles of environmental cooperation.

The overall picture of environmental provisions in PTAs, as it stands today, thus seems to be one of disparate provisions that depend on the parties involved and their inter-se relationships. The OECD study of regional trade agreements highlights the diversity of environmental commitments in PTAs as a matter of potential concern. It notes that countries are likely to be faced with an increasingly complex problem of managing various levels of environmental commitments, and different types of environmental cooperation programs, under a variety of PTAs to which they are parties and that this situation may require closer attention in the near future (OECD 2007, 35).

To sum up, although open regionalism is a theoretically desirable goal of PTAs, experience to date with these provisions does not permit conclusions as to whether the goal is achievable through PTAs in general or, more specifically, in the context of environmental provisions in PTAs.

Discrimination under Environmental Provisions in PTAs

Do environmental provisions under PTAs discriminate against nonparties? At the outset, it needs to be emphasized that a PTA, by its very nature, gives preferential market access to the parties to it, as opposed to nonparties. Environmental provisions in a PTA are structured as obligations to adhere to certain standards, but such adherence is not directly linked to preferential market access (except in a few U.S. PTAs that provide for suspension of concessions as a consequence of nonadherence to environmental provisions). Environmental provisions in PTAs are by themselves unlikely to result in discrimination against third parties in terms of preferential market access. Concerns about preferential access for parties and discriminatory treatment of nonparties could arise in the context of PTA provisions dealing with environmental

goods and services if liberalization is confined to parties to the PTA and is not undertaken on a most favored nation (MFN) basis.

Liberalization of trade in environmental goods and services (EGS) was made part of the WTO's agenda under the Doha Round negotiations.[15] It remains a contentious issue.[16] To the extent that countries agree on preferential treatment of EGS at the bilateral level, discrimination against third parties could result. However, the provisions on EGS in PTAs have so far only been in the form of broad commitments to cooperate, rather than of concrete obligations to liberalize trade.

Some examples of provisions in PTAs dealing with EGS will illustrate the point:

- The agreement between the EU and CARIFORUM includes specific provisions dealing with the commitment of the parties "to make efforts to facilitate trade in goods and services which the Parties consider to be beneficial to the environment. Such products may include environmental technologies, renewable and energy-efficient goods and services and eco-labelled goods."[17]
- The CAFTA–DR agreement contains provisions for cooperative action for developing and promoting environmentally beneficial goods and services.[18]
- The Japan–Mexico PTA refers to cooperation in the field of "encouragement of trade and dissemination of environmentally sound goods and services."[19]
- The U.S.–Morocco PTA states, "Parties recognize that strengthening their co-operative relationship on environmental matters can encourage increased bilateral trade in environmental goods and services."[20]

Whether implementation of these provisions could result in discrimination against third parties has not yet been tested.

Experiences with Implementation of Environmental Provisions

Since most PTAs are very recent, there are not many empirical studies examining the implementation of their provisions. The OECD study reports that in some countries, the negotiation of a PTA which included environmental commitments was a driver of reform or led to the acceleration of internal reform processes. In Morocco and Chile, the conclusion of PTAs with the United States accelerated the adoption of several environmental laws, as well as the overhaul and codification of environmental legislation (OECD 2007, 48). There is, furthermore, anecdotal evidence that the commitments in the U.S.–Singapore PTA influenced Singapore to more effectively enforce its domestic laws regarding illegal wildlife transshipment and to enact a new endangered species act that brought transshipment under the country's enforcement mandate and increased penalties tenfold. The study observes, however, that the causality for Singapore's law is difficult to determine and that the country's environmental efforts may also be related to the ASEAN-wide push to cooperate on stronger implementation and enforcement of measures against illegal wildlife trade (OECD 2007, 125).

The effectiveness of PTAs in promoting the enforcement of environmental laws has not been definitively studied. Domestic enforcement of environmental laws is often influenced by such factors as availability of adequate resources and the presence or absence of effective institutional mechanisms. Although several PTAs entered into by the United States and the EU specify that the developed-country partner would provide assistance through financial resources and technical capacity-building support, effective enforcement of environmental laws has not necessarily resulted. A recent report by the U.S. General Accountability Office (U.S. GAO 2009) studies U.S. PTAs with Chile, Singapore, Morocco, and Jordan and concludes that although the trading partners have improved their environmental laws, enforcement has been a challenge and that U.S. assistance has been limited in this regard. The report cites lack of reliable funding as one of the main reasons for lack of progress on environmental provisions, and it identifies the absence of effective elements for monitoring and managing environmental projects as a shortcoming.

NAFTA and the NAAEC

Some of the significant studies and analyses of the effectiveness of the implementation of environmental provisions under a PTA have looked at the NAAEC, the environmental side agreement to NAFTA. These studies highlight some advantages and practical limitations of implementing environmental provisions under a PTA. A recent paper from the Office of the U.S. Trade Representative (USTR) emphasizes the contribution of NAFTA and the NAAEC in providing a clean and healthy environment for residents along the U.S.–Mexican border.[21] Independent studies (for example, Markell and Knox 2003) have commended the technical cooperation efforts of the North American Commission for Environment Cooperation (NACEC) that was established under the agreement and have identified a number of achievements:

- The commission's role in establishing a pollution release and transfer registry (PRTR) in Mexico

- Its support for research and symposiums dedicated to understanding the effects of trade on the environment in North America
- The establishment of public submission mechanisms whereby civil society organizations and citizens can petition the commission on issues relating to compliance with the agreement's environmental obligations (Articles 14 and 15 of the NAAEC)
- The initiation of pilot funding programs to build the environmental capacity of small and medium-size enterprises and civil society organizations.

Other studies have highlighted some limitations in implementing environmental provisions under the NAAEC. Inadequate resources are blamed for the shortcomings. For instance, Gallagher (2004, 74–76) reasons, using persuasive data and analysis, that environmental conditions worsened in Mexico in the post-NAFTA period and that Mexico failed to steer the benefits of economic integration toward increased environmental protection. Gallagher points out that the NACEC was not "designed to significantly reverse environmental consequences of economic growth in Mexico" and argues that the NACEC, with its annual budget of US$9 million, was "insufficient" to make a dent in the problems that cost the Mexican economy US$40 million annually. Similarly, Hufbauer and Schott (2005, 159–60) find that the budgetary allocation for the NAAEC was inadequate for its mandate and represents an "insignificant fraction of resources dedicated to the environment in North America." Audley and Ulmer (2003, 3) evaluate U.S. trade policy and capacity-building initiatives in the context of PTAs and conclude that it is "challenging to translate good intentions into effective policy."

Technical and Financial Assistance

Technical and financial assistance is intrinsically linked to the issue of implementation of environmental provisions. The financial costs of implementation, and the costs of framing new legal and institutional frameworks, could be especially high for small and medium-size enterprises in developing countries (India 2000).

Two studies for the World Bank emphasize that to ensure implementation of the environmental provisions of a PTA, it would be more rational to address costs and capacity-building requirements than to resort to trade sanctions in the event of noncompliance. Wheeler (2000) shows that there is a cost-benefit rationale for requiring stricter environmental controls while fostering economic relationships between countries but that sustained support for building regulatory and institutional capacity is necessary. Wilson, Otsuki, and Sewadeb (2002) conclude that imposing higher environmental regulatory standards as part of trade agreements would mean higher costs for non-OECD countries than for OECD countries and would affect the former's export competitiveness; adequate policy instruments are needed to offset that effect. More important, both studies conclude that use of trade sanctions is not an effective method of enforcing environmental provisions. They recommend, instead, sustained support for environmental provisions and a coordinated approach by the parties involved.

Despite such findings, few PTAs deal with the issues of financial assistance, technical assistance, and capacity building, and any such provisions are typically worded in a nonbinding and open-ended manner (see OECD 2007, 86–87). This is true of both U.S. and EU PTAs. (See the annexes to this chapter for an overview of relevant provisions.) The scope and depth of the provisions vary, from general statements on cooperation, to support for capacity building. Although important initiatives for assistance and capacity building have been undertaken under most of the U.S. and EU PTAs, the agreements themselves do not incorporate any language on linkages between assistance and capacity building, on the one hand, and legally binding obligations for maintenance of environmental standards under the PTA, on the other hand. Inadequate funding and lack of effective structures for monitoring and managing environmental projects are seen as the main reasons for ineffective implementation of environmental provisions (U.S. GAO 2009).

The EU–CARIFORUM EPA refers to "development cooperation" as an imperative; cooperation can take both financial and nonfinancial forms (Article 7.1). The provisions on cooperation on environment in Article 28.2(a) of the EU–Chile agreement refer to the recognition of the relationship between poverty and environment. No studies have assessed the actions taken as a consequence of such generic statements.

Parties to a PTA need to give greater consideration to the construction of adequate linkages between commitments by a lower-income trading partner to adhere to certain environmental standards and the obligation of the higher-income trading partner to commit to capacity-building and resource assistance to ensure compliance with such obligations. An important precedent is the 2004 U.S. PTA with CAFTA–DR, which sought to benchmark and monitor provisions relating to environmental cooperation. During the negotiations, each Central American country submitted a capacity-building report identifying its priorities. The current EU negotiations of EPAs with African, Caribbean, and Pacific (ACP) countries follow a similar pattern. Translating these provisions into an assessment of the economic costs of implementation, and benchmarking the implementation of the provisions, are steps that would need to be built into PTA negotiations.

Another area with implications for economic costs and capacity-building requirements in developing countries is adherence to developed countries' product standards and regulatory requirements, which may be justified on "environmental" grounds. Several of the EU's SIAs include a finding on training and capacity-building requirements in this respect. Funding for such activities is sometimes addressed as part of the preparatory process or during the implementation of the PTA, but this is not specified as an obligation under the PTA. An example is the Trade Investment Development Program between the EU and India, which includes a component on capacity-building initiatives aimed at equipping Indian laboratories to meet EU requirements for product testing and certification.[22] There has, however, been no comprehensive exercise to assess the costs of implementation of such requirements and the monitoring and evaluation thereof, although these elements would be necessary for any effective compliance with such requirements under the framework of the PTA.

Conflicting Priorities

A curious and interesting issue in relation to implementation of environmental standards under PTAs is that of conflicting norms within a PTA, when some provisions promote and others restrict the space for environmental policy. Studies have indicated that provisions dealing with investment under PTAs tend to constrict countries' policy space for channeling foreign investment into their territories and also carry high environmental costs (Working Group 2008). PTAs that deal with investment often incorporate provisions on investor-state disputes in the investment chapters. In several such disputes, regulatory measures enacted for environmental purposes have been interpreted as resulting in "expropriation," leading to awards for compensation for private investors.[23] Some of these disputes challenging environmental regulations as infringing on investors' rights have arisen under NAFTA, even though that agreement has, in the NAAEC, perhaps the strongest side agreement on environmental issues. The Council for Environmental Cooperation (CEC), which is the main institution charged with the task of implementing the NAAEC, is required to assist NAFTA's Free Trade Commission (FTC) in environment-related matters. Implementation of this provision has, however, been limited, and in reality, the

CEC and the FTC have been reported to have little contact (Hufbauer and Schott 2005, 158). The result has been the treatment of environmental issues as subsidiary to investor-related concerns.

The prospect of investor-state arbitration regarding environmental measures (often referred to as "regulatory takings" in investment literature) could be a potential hurdle in the implementation of environmental provisions under a PTA. A study by the United Nations Commission on Trade and Development (UNCTAD) finds that it could result in a "regulatory chill" because concern about liability exposure might lead host countries to restrict the ambit of or soften a necessary regulation (UNCTAD 2005; see also Cosbey et al. 2004).

Some recent PTAs, such as the U.S.–Singapore agreement, have attempted to address this concern through side letters dealing with the interpretation of "expropriation" and specifying that, except in "rare" circumstances, nondiscriminatory regulatory measures undertaken for "public welfare benefits," including "environment," will not constitute expropriation. How such "rare" circumstances would be interpreted in an actual dispute has yet to be tested.

Hard- and Soft-Law Approaches to Environmental Provisions

Although it is perhaps too early to assess the implementation of environmental provisions and their effect on multilateral relations, it is useful to examine in greater detail the nature of environmental provisions in PTAs and the basis for their enforcement. In this section, we examine both legally binding ("hard-law") and nonbinding ("soft-law") provisions in PTAs; various approaches to resolution of disputes concerning environmental provisions; and the effect of the chosen approach on environmental policy in members of the PTA.

Theoretically, legally binding provisions could be expected to be more effective than provisions that are expressed in nonbinding language. In the context of international relations, legally binding language in an agreement also provides insights into the political will and intent of parties to be bound by such obligations. At the same time, nonbinding provisions do not necessarily indicate a lack of legal intent to implement the provisions, and they often create significant pathways for dialogue and assessment to enable implementation. Moreover, the implementation and impact of such provisions do not solely depend on the legally binding or nonbinding language in which the provisions are formulated; preexisting conditions and the availability of adequate financial and technical assistance are also important factors.

The Dynamics of Binding and Nonbinding Provisions on Environment

The U.S., Canadian, and EU approaches to environmental provisions in PTAs represent a blend of binding obligations and nonbinding principles of intent and cooperation. A key area covered by these provisions is domestic environmental policy in the trading partners. This is a sensitive subject for most countries because international agreements rarely make incursions into domestic policy space. U.S. and EU PTAs refer to the obligation of a party to ensure adherence to "high levels of environment protection" in its domestic law and policy, but this obligation is often accompanied by an explicit recognition of the right of parties to establish their "own levels of environmental protection and environment development policies."[24] This language seems to create a tenuous balance between "high standards" and sovereign rights. The approach using binding legal obligations appears to create some flexibility for parties while holding them to "high" standards, by allowing them to determine their "own level of protection."

Because the environmental obligations are broadly worded, scrutiny of specific environmental measures in a country under these provisions would have to be very case specific. None of the provisions has as yet led to any dispute resolution situation. Hence, to date, there is no jurisprudence on, for instance, the exact nature of standards that would be identified as "high," or on whether a particular environmental measure seeks to encourage trade by "lowering levels" of environmental protection, or on whether the resulting trade in goods and services is supportive of the environment.

U.S. PTAs contain provisions referring to the "right of each party to retain discretion with respect to investigatory, prosecutorial, regulatory, and compliance matters and to make decisions regarding the allocation of resources to enforcement with respect to other environmental matters determined to have higher priorities."[25] How this provision is interpreted will need to be examined through the development of case law. It is significant that this discretion is not unfettered; it is circumscribed by statements that the exercise of discretion is to be "reasonable" or that the exercise of discretion is to be based on "a bona fide decision regarding allocation of resources." The standards for determining "reasonable," and the factors in considering whether a decision is "bona fide," have yet to evolve through jurisprudence.

U.S. PTAs also typically oblige a party to ensure the availability of judicial, quasi-judicial, or administrative proceedings that are fair, equitable, and transparent and to provide for appropriate administrative and procedural protections in accordance with its law, for the enforcement of the party's environmental laws. What is "fair, equitable and transparent," and what would qualify as "appropriate," are not defined in the PTAs.

Each of the approaches discussed above affords a trading partner the possibility of examining the domestic content and implementation of environmental laws in another trading partner, whether or not there is any effect on trade between the countries because of such laws. The exact parameters of such scrutiny, and how the balance between sovereign discretion and obligations will play out in the event of a dispute, are yet to be tested.

Japan's agreement with Mexico on environment cooperation (a side agreement to the Japan–Mexico PTA) represents a variation in that it mandates parties to cooperate. Article 147 of the agreement states, "The Parties, recognizing the need for environmental preservation and improvement to promote sound and sustainable development, *shall* cooperate in the field of environment" (italics added). The description of cooperative activities is, however, drafted in nonbinding, inclusive language, allowing scope for the parties to develop further agreements on implementation in the future.

An example of a purely nonbinding approach is the New Zealand–Thailand Environmental Cooperation Agreement. Section 4.1 states, "The Arrangement . . . represents a political commitment between New Zealand and Thailand but does not legally bind either country."

Approaches to Dispute Resolution

The remedies available, and the mechanisms for resolution of disputes in the event of contravention of environmental obligations, are fundamental indicators of the nature of hard- and soft-law approaches in a PTA. The approaches to dispute resolution for environmental provisions can be categorized as follows:

- Binding dispute resolution with remedies in the form of compensation and possible suspensions of concessions (found in U.S. PTAs)
- Binding dispute resolution with remedies in the form of compensation (typical of EU agreements)
- Dispute resolution with an emphasis on principles of cooperation and adoption of a nonbinding approach (in PTAs involving New Zealand and Japan).

These approaches are discussed in detail below.

U.S. PTAs. PTAs entered into by the United States provide for two means of addressing disputes on environmental provisions: state-state procedures, and public consultations. With regard to state-state mechanisms, the PTA provides for consultations, appointment of experts, formal dispute resolution, and enforcement.

Most U.S. PTAs provide that the panel constituted for dispute resolution can recommend appropriate remedies for noncompliance with environmental obligations under the PTA. These remedies can include monetary compensation, to be deposited into a fund for environmental initiatives.[26] If the losing party does not provide such compensation, then, as a matter of last resort, the other party can suspend tariff concessions. PTAs with differing provisions include the U.S. agreements with Korea and Israel. The PTA with Korea provides that the amount of compensation is to be determined through consultations between the parties rather than by the panel (Article 22.13). The U.S.–Israel PTA states that the recommendations of the panel on settlement of a dispute is nonbinding; the winning party has the right to take "appropriate measures" (Article 19).

Several U.S. PTAs also provide for a public submission process. NAFTA and NAAEC and the CAFTA–DR, U.S.–Panama, and U.S.–Peru agreements contain detailed provisions allowing for members of the public to submit complaints of noncompliance with environmental obligations to an environmental commission or secretariat or another institutional mechanism constituted for the purpose.[27] This is not a uniform feature and is not found in the U.S. PTAs with Chile and Singapore.[28] Under PTAs that do provide for this process, the commission or secretariat is required to prepare a factual record and forward it to the environment affairs council, which can make recommendations. The recommendations are not binding on the state parties to the PTA; the parties would need to trigger formal state-state consultations and go through the dispute resolution process under the PTA to secure any enforceable remedies.

The OECD study on regional trade agreements (OECD 2007) analyzed the extent to which public submission procedures under U.S. PTAs have been exercised and concludes that these procedures have been used to a greater extent than have the state-state mechanisms. The greatest usage of the public submission process has been under the NAAEC, which has received 68 submissions since 1995.[29] The study finds some evidence that in at least two cases, one against Mexico and the other against Canada, the process has brought about improved environmental protection, although the exact nature of such improvements was not discussed (OECD 2007, 127; see also Kirton 2004). Other studies (for example, Hufbauer et al. 2000) have criticized these public submission processes for not being effective enough. The costs and time expended in the NAAEC submission process, and the absence of monitoring of enforcement of the recommendations, are regarded as shortcomings.

EU PTAs. Like U.S. PTAs, PTAs entered into by the EU emphasize consultation and cooperation in environmental matters. Under the EPA with CARIFORUM, if consultations fail, the matter can be referred to a committee of experts formed under the EPA. The committee's findings are provided to the consultative committee responsible for implementing the EPA. If there is no resolution within nine months from the initiation of consultations, an arbitration panel for dispute resolution can be requested by the complaining party. Measures for compliance may include compensation, but unlike the case of U.S. PTAs, remedies for violation of the environmental provisions of the PTA cannot include suspension of concessions.

New Zealand. The New Zealand–Thailand arrangement on environmental cooperation provides that if any differences about the arrangement arise between the parties, the environment committee set up under the agreement will attempt to resolve them through consultation (Section 3). The Trans-Pacific Strategic Economic Partnership (TPSEP), of which New Zealand is a member, goes a step further, providing that if consultations between the parties fail, any interested party may refer the issue to the TPSEP Commission for discussion and that the report emerging from such discussions would need to be implemented (Article 15.6).

Japan. Japan's PTA with Mexico, which contains principles of environmental cooperation, specifically states that the provisions for dispute resolution under the PTA do not apply to the chapter containing those principles (Articles 147 and 148).

Devising a Suitable Dispute Resolution Mechanism

None of the provisions on state-state dispute resolution described above have ever been resorted to in practice, and so their effectiveness, in terms of remedies and consequences, has not been tested. The OECD study notes that "countries may simply hesitate to incur the costs—financial, political, and other—of initiating a dispute leading to imposing penalties on another country, even if the letter of the agreement would entitle them to do so" (OECD 2007, 124).

From a developing-country perspective, any specific approach to dispute settlement under a PTA will need to be determined in light of the overall framework of the PTA, the nature of the legally binding obligations it imposes, and the resources required to implement those obligations. As discussed earlier, studies have shown that the use of trade sanctions to enforce environmental obligations in a poorer country would have unjust consequences because such

sanctions fail to discriminate between clean and dirty firms in the affected countries and because they would inevitably penalize workers in such countries by reducing opportunities for jobs and higher wages (Wheeler 2000). Such instruments would also not be effective in achieving the desired environmental goals.

As a theoretical principle, the availability and enforceability of binding dispute resolution mechanisms are critical for ensuring the effectiveness of any law. In the case of environmental provisions, effective implementation of the provisions depends on several other factors, such as the technical and financial resources committed for implementation. This issue is particularly significant for developing countries, which need to take into account the financial and technical costs of implementing environmental provisions. Accordingly, it may be advisable to opt for binding dispute resolution as an enforcement measure only when all the elements for securing effective implementation of the provisions are built into the PTA, including the technical and financial assistance required for implementing new environmental laws and standards (Wheeler 2000).

Dispute settlement mechanisms emphasizing consultation and cooperation may therefore be a better option for dealing with noncompliance with environmental regulations than binding dispute settlement and sanctions. A phased approach may be desirable: in the first few years, disputes would be handled through a cooperative approach, and then, after experience with environmental provisions under the PTA has been gained, stronger remedies, such as monetary compensation or trade sanctions, could be considered.

Conclusions

The findings that have emerged from this analysis of key PTAs that incorporate environmental provisions are summarized here.

1. *Approaches to environmental concerns in international agreements.* Certain developed economies (the United States, Canada, the EU, New Zealand, and, more recently, Japan) have pushed for the incorporation of environmental provisions into PTAs. Regional economic groups of developing countries, as well as Australia, have tended to address environmental issues in separate agreements or understandings rather than within PTAs. In addition, environmental provisions are sometimes addressed in separate side agreements. No one approach has proved superior in delivering environmental and economic benefits. The choice of side agreements does not necessarily

imply that environment is only an incidental issue; some of the strongest environmental provisions are contained in the NAAEC, a side agreement to NAFTA.

2. *Increasing use of environmental provisions in PTAs.* Environmental provisions are increasingly being incorporated into PTAs. Developing countries should plan for negotiations accordingly, as described in "Considerations for Developing Countries in Negotiating PTAs," below.

3. *Pre-PTA environmental impact assessments.* The United States, Canada, and New Zealand regularly conduct assessments of the potential environmental impacts of PTAs within their own countries. (A few recent U.S. PTAs have considered the trading partner as well.) The EU's approach is to conduct sustainability impact assessments that focus on the potential economic, social, and environmental effects of the agreement on both the EU and the trading partner. Conceptually, the EU's approach offers a better framework for addressing environmental and sustainable development concerns in both parties to the PTA, but no studies have as yet monitored to what degree the findings of such assessments are translated into the provisions of the PTA or their effectiveness in furthering intended environmental and development goals.

4. *Binding and nonbinding provisions.* Both legally binding and nonbinding environmental provisions appear in U.S., Canadian, and EU PTAs. PTAs entered into by New Zealand and Japan have so far contained mainly nonbinding language on environmental matters. There has been to date insufficient experience for making an assessment as to the relative effectiveness of binding and nonbinding principles. Some countries have implemented environmental provisions even under a nonbinding legal obligation.

5. *Regional public goods.* Countries within a region are likely to address problems that are transboundary in nature and affect them all. PTAs, or any other regional agreements between countries that are geographically proximate, are more likely to successfully address regional environmental concerns than global issues, for which multilateral cooperation between many countries would be necessary. Nevertheless, some PTAs between geographically distant countries do seek to address environmental issues that are not purely regional, such as climate change and protection of biodiversity. Agreements of this kind can complement the multilateral framework addressing similar issues.

6. *Economic costs.* Enactment of new laws, establishment of new institutions, or changes in manufacturing practices undertaken to ensure adherence to environmental standards have cost implications. Environmental standards also affect the export competitiveness of countries that are required to raise their environmental standards. Yet the costs of compliance are not typically taken into account in the PTAs in the form of financial assistance. A fair amount of literature exists on the economic implications for Mexico of implementing the trade and environmental provisions arising from NAFTA. Concrete studies and assessments have not yet been carried out for other PTAs.

7. *Implementation of environmental provisions.* Since environmental provisions in PTAs are of fairly recent date, their implementation has not been studied in detail. In a few instances, stronger environmental laws have been enacted and implemented after the countries entered PTAs. Such developments are also influenced by other internal and external factors, and it may therefore not always be possible to state definitively that the environmental measures were taken solely or primarily because of the PTA.

Implementation of environmental provisions may sometimes conflict with other provisions of the PTA, such as those relating to investment. Not all PTAs have adequate linkages for addressing these conflicts.

8. *Technical assistance, capacity building, and financial assistance.* Technology sharing and transfer, technical assistance and capacity building, and financing of environmental initiatives are critical determinants of how effectively environmental provisions can be implemented. Some PTAs have incorporated provisions relating to technical and capacity-building assistance; fewer contain provisions on financial assistance. Provisions on these forms of support are not worded in legally binding terms. While several important initiatives for such support have been undertaken under both U.S. and EU PTAs, further studies are required to evaluate their adequacy.

9. *Dispute settlement and remedies.* Dispute settlement provisions in PTAs typically consist of consultations followed by recourse to formal dispute settlement mechanisms. Most U.S. PTAs prescribe remedies in the form of monetary compensation for noncompliance with environmental provisions, with suspension of tariff concessions as a last resort. EU PTAs leave the issue of compliance measures to the judicial mechanism hearing the dispute; remedies may include monetary compensation but not suspension of concessions. A few U.S. PTAs contain provisions allowing public submissions to the environmental committee constituted under the PTA. Such submissions result in fact-finding reports but do not lead to any binding rulings. Examples of nonbinding

approaches to dispute resolution are found in PTAs entered into by Japan and New Zealand, which emphasize consultations and a noncontentious approach to resolving environmental concerns.

None of the provisions on dispute resolution has been resorted to in practice, and so their effectiveness, in terms of remedies and consequences, has yet to be tested. Studies have, however, pointed out that trade sanctions against a poorer country to enforce environmental compliance do not offer real solutions for environmental issues and would only exacerbate problems for workers in such countries by limiting employment opportunities and the prospect of higher wages.

10. *Overall conclusions.* Environmental provisions in PTAs could potentially be useful in addressing specific environmental concerns of either party, but only insofar as they are preceded by assessment of the specific environmental and developmental concerns, are couched in clear language, and are backed by adequate technical and financial support for implementation.

Annex A. Provisions on Environment in U.S. PTAs

The provisions cited here have been extracted mainly from NAFTA and the NAAEC, the CAFTA–DR agreement, and U.S. PTAs with Australia, Bahrain, Chile, Colombia, Morocco, Oman, Panama, and Peru. Provisions found in only some U.S. PTAs are also described.

General Principles

- Obligation of both parties to cooperate in the field of environment
- Obligation to ensure that trade and environmental policies are mutually supportive

Right to Establish Levels of Environmental Protection

- Right of each party to establish its own levels of environmental protection and environmental development policies

Provisions with Respect to Domestic Environmental Laws

- Obligation of each party to strive to ensure that its laws and policies provide for and encourage high levels of environmental protection.
- Right of each party to retain discretion with respect to investigatory, prosecutorial, regulatory, and compli-

ance matters and to make decisions regarding the allocation of resources to enforcement or to other environmental matters determined to have higher priorities. This discretion is not unfettered; it is circumscribed by language stating that a party is in compliance with this provision provided that the exercise of discretion is "reasonable" or that the exercise of discretion results from "a bona fide decision regarding allocation of resources."
- Commitment by each party to strive to ensure that, in the process of encouraging trade and investment, it does not waive or derogate from its environmental laws in a manner that weakens or reduces the protections afforded in those laws.
- Obligation of each party to ensure that judicial, quasi-judicial, or administrative proceedings for the enforcement of its environmental laws are fair, equitable, and transparent and to provide for appropriate administrative and procedural protections in accordance with its law.

The PTAs with Chile and Korea clarify that the chapter on environment shall not be construed to empower a party's authorities to undertake environmental law enforcement activities in the territory of the other party. The PTA with Peru allows for such enforcement only in the context of the annex on forest governance.

Environmental Cooperation, Technical Assistance, and Capacity Building

U.S. PTAs differ in the scope and content of provisions dealing with environmental cooperation. Environmental cooperation typically pertains to provisions for technical assistance and capacity building in relation to environmental standards. Provisions on environmental cooperation in NAFTA's side agreement on environment, the NAAEC, for instance, focus on environmental impacts on trade, as well as labeling, financing, purchase of environmentally friendly products, and so on. The provisions on environmental cooperation in the U.S.–Peru PTA pertain to protection of biological diversity and indigenous knowledge.

The provisions on environmental cooperation in the U.S.–Chile PTA highlight the following areas in which the United States is committed to cooperate with Chile:

- Development in Chile of a pollutant release and transfer register (PRTR)—a publicly available database of chemicals that have been released to air, water, or land or transferred offsite for further waste management
- Reduction of mining pollution in Chile

- Improvement of environmental enforcement and compliance through training and exchange of information
- Training to help reduce pollution from agricultural practices in Chile
- Cooperation to reduce methyl bromide emissions
- Improvement of wildlife protection and management in Chile.

TBTs and SPS Product Standards

Most U.S. PTAs contain provisions relating to formation of a specific committee to oversee implementation of SPS and TBT standards and to assist in trade facilitation. The CAFTA–DR agreement and the U.S. PTAs with Panama and Peru include provisions on the responsibility of this committee to make recommendations for capacity building in trade and for the design of programs of technical assistance to support adherence to SPS and TBT standards. These provisions contain no references to financial assistance. The U.S.–Korea PTA has a separate provision on automotive standards and regulations that may be adopted for environmental or other reasons.

Public Participation

Most U.S. PTAs contain fairly detailed language, ranging from binding obligations to best-efforts provisions, on public participation. The CAFTA–DR agreement *mandates* that each party provide for the receipt and consideration of public communications on matters related to the chapter on environment. Each party is also required to convene a national consultative or advisory committee, made up of members of its public, to provide views on matters related to implementation. The U.S. PTAs with Morocco and Singapore contain a less onerous obligation to put in place "procedures" for dialogue with the public and to make "best efforts" to respond to requests by members of the public with regard to implementation of environmental provisions.

Institutional Arrangements

All U.S. PTAs provide for a separate body, termed a joint committee or environmental affairs council, that is responsible for overseeing implementation of the provisions of the agreement and providing recommendations for implementation.

Dispute Resolution

State-state consultations. All U.S. PTAs except that with Jordan specify a separate dispute resolution mechanism for enforcement of provisions regarding domestic environmental laws in each party to the PTA. If consultations between the parties fail, the PTAs provide for engagement of experts to advise on the matter. If this step does not lead to resolution of the dispute, formal dispute settlement proceedings under the PTA can be commenced. Remedies for noncompliance with domestic environmental obligations can include monetary compensation, to be deposited in a fund for environmental initiatives. If the losing party does not provide such compensation, then, as a matter of last resort, the other party can suspend tariff concessions. Such provisions have not been appealed to under any of the U.S. PTAs, and so there has been no experience with possible outcomes.

Public submission process. NAFTA, the CAFTA–DR agreement, and the U.S.–Panama and U.S.–Peru PTAs include detailed provisions allowing members of the public to submit complaints of noncompliance with environmental obligations to the environmental commission or secretariat set up under the agreement. That body is required to prepare a factual record and provide it to the environmental affairs council (EAC) constituted under the PTA, which can make recommendations. The recommendations are not binding on the parties to the PTA.

Annex B. Environmental Provisions in EU PTAs

The outline below draws on key provisions of the EU EPA with CARIFORUM and on the EU agreements with Chile and Mexico.

General Principles

- Emphasis on the objectives of sustainable development and protection of the environment.

Provisions with Respect to Domestic Environmental Laws

- Right of the parties to regulate in order to achieve their own levels of domestic environmental and public health protection and their own sustainable development priorities and to adopt or modify their environmental laws and policies accordingly
- Obligation of parties to seek to ensure that their own environmental and public health laws and policies provide for and encourage high levels of environmental and public health protection and to strive to continue to improve those laws and policies
- Recognition that "special needs and requirements of CARIFORUM States shall be taken into account in the

design and implementation of measures aimed at protecting environment and public health that affect trade between the parties"

- Obligation not to encourage trade or foreign direct investment or to enhance or maintain a competitive advantage by lowering the level of protection provided by domestic environmental and public health legislation or by derogating from or failing to apply such legislation.

Obligations for Technical Assistance and Capacity Building

The EU–CARIFORUM EPA and the EU's agreements with Chile and Mexico contain provisions on "facilitating support" to ensure technical assistance for implementation of the provisions of the agreement, including the provisions relating to environmental obligations. The EU–Chile agreement also emphasizes cooperation on projects to reinforce Chile's environmental structures and policies.

Article 190 of the EU–CARIFORUM agreement contains the most detailed provisions. Examples include the parties' obligations to ensure cooperation for "facilitating support" with respect to

- Capacity building for environmental management in tourism areas at the regional and local levels
- Technical assistance to help producers meet relevant product and other standards in EU markets
- Technical assistance and capacity building, in particular for the public sector, for the implementation and enforcement of multilateral environmental agreements
- Facilitation of trade between the parties in natural resources (including timber and wood products) from legal and sustainable sources
- Assistance to producers to develop or improve production of goods and services that the parties consider to be beneficial to the environment
- Promotion and facilitation of public awareness and education programs related to environmental goods and services in order to foster trade in such products between the parties.

TBT and SPS Product Standards

The EU's PTAs with Chile and Mexico, and the EPA recently negotiated with the CARIFORUM countries, include provisions for technical assistance to help producers meet relevant product and other standards.

The EU–CARIFORUM agreement sets forth detailed provisions with specific relevance for environmental standards:

- Technical assistance to help producers meet relevant product and other standards applicable in EU markets
- Promotion and facilitation of private and public voluntary and market-based programs, including relevant labeling and accreditation schemes.

Dispute Resolution

EU PTAs emphasize consultation and cooperation in environmental matters. The EPA with CARIFORUM provides for consultations. If consultations fail, the matter can be referred to a committee of experts formed under the EPA, and the committee's findings are then provided to the consultative committee responsible for implementing the EPA. If no resolution is achieved within nine months of the initiation of consultations, an arbitration panel for dispute resolution can be requested by the complaining party. Measures to enforce compliance may include compensation, but not suspension of concessions.

Notes

The author thanks Jean-Pierre Chauffour and Muthukumara Mani of the World Bank for their invaluable comments and guidance. The author also expresses her sincere thanks to John Strand, Charles Di Leva, and Sachiko Morita for their comments, which were very helpful in refining the contents and focus of the study. Thanks are also due to Sumiti Yadava and Deepak Raju for their research assistance. The findings, interpretations, and conclusions expressed in this paper do not necessarily reflect the views of the reviewers or the World Bank. Any errors or oversights are attributable only to the author.

1. A pilot database that enables a comparison of the provisions of the 30 PTAs analyzed in the APEC study is available at www.mincetur.gob.pe/apec_fta. The OAS database is at http://www.oas.org/dsd/EnvironmentLaw/EnvlawDB/Default.htm. Thirty-five countries in the Americas are OAS members.

2. Mani and Jha (2006) explore the impact of trade liberalization in Vietnam and the nature of regulatory interventions that would be required to address environmental harm.

3. Working Group (2004). The trade policy context covered in the report includes NAFTA, the Free Trade Area of the Americas (FTAA), the Central America Free Trade Agreement (CAFTA), the U.S.–Chile Free Trade Agreement, and negotiations toward a pact between the United States and the Andean nations.

4. New Zealand Ministry of Foreign Affairs and Trade, "Framework for Integrating Environment Issues into Free Trade Agreements," http://www.mfat.govt.nz/Trade-and-Economic-Relations/0—Trade-archive/WTO/0-environment-framework.php#tradepolicies (accessed May 5, 2009).

5. The general exceptions are embodied in Article XX of the General Agreement on Tariffs and Trade (GATT) and Article XIV of the General Agreement on Trade in Services (GATS).

6. United States–Standards for Reformulated and Conventional Gasoline, WT/DS/1 (May 20, 1996); United States–Import of Certain Shrimp and Shrimp Products, WT/DS/58 (November 6, 1998); United States–Import of Certain Shrimp and Shrimp Products–Recourse to Article 21.5 of the Dispute Settlement Understanding, WT/DS/58 (November 21, 2001).

7. The documents, respectively, are the U.S.–Singapore Free Trade Agreement (FTA) (May 6, 2003), http://www.ustr.gov/Trade_Agreements/ Bilateral/Singapore_FTA/Final_Texts/Section_Index.html (accessed May 5, 2009); the U.S.–Chile FTA (June 6, 2003), http://www.ustr.gov/ Trade_Agreements/Bilateral/Chile_FTA/Final_Texts/Section_Index.html (accessed May 5, 2009); the U.S.–Australia FTA (May 18, 2004), http://www.ustr.gov/Trade_Agreements/Bilateral/Australia_FTA/Final_Text/ Section_Index.html (accessed May 5, 2009); the U.S.–Bahrain FTA (September 14, 2004), http://www.ustr.gov/Trade_Agreements/Bilateral/ Bahrain_FTA/final_texts/Section_Index.html (accessed May 5, 2009); the U.S.–Morocco FTA, http://www.moroccousafta.com/studies.htm; and the CAFTA–DR FTA, http://www.ustr.gov/trade-agreements/free-trade-agreements/cafta-dr-dominican-republic-central-america-fta. The members of CAFTA are Costa Rica, El Salvador, Guatemala, Honduras, and Nicaragua.

8. EU–Mexico Economic Partnership, Political Coordination and Cooperation Agreement (December 8, 1997), http://www.fco.gov .uk/resources/en/pdf/pdf13/fco_ref_ts13-01a_coop_eco (accessed May 5, 2009); EU–Chile Association Agreement (November 18, 2002), http:// trade.ec.europa.eu/doclib/html/111620.htm (accessed May 5, 2009); Euro-Mediterranean Agreement Establishing an Association between the European Communities and their Member States, of the One Part, and the State of Israel, of the Other Part (November 20, 1995), http:// europa.eu/eur-lex/pri/en/oj/dat/2000/l_147/l_14720000621en00030156.pdf, (accessed May 5, 2009); Euro-Mediterranean Interim Association Agreement on Trade and Cooperation between the European Community, of the One Part, and the Palestine Liberation Organization for the Benefit of the Palestinian Authority of the West Bank and the Gaza Strip, of the Other Part (1997), http://eur-lex.europa.eu/LexUriServ/LexUriServ .do?uri=CELEX:21997A0716(01):EN:HTML (accessed May 5, 2009); Euro-Mediterranean Agreement Establishing an Association between the European Communities and their Member States, of the One Part, and the Arab Republic of Egypt, of the Other Part (June 25, 2001), http://ec.europa.eu/external_relations/egypt/aa/06_aaa_en.pdf (accessed May 5, 2009).

9. The following are the members of the organizations named: Mercosur—Argentina, Brazil, Paraguay, and Uruguay; Andean Community—Bolivia, Colombia, Ecuador, and Peru; AFTA—Brunei Darussalam, Cambodia, Indonesia, Lao People's Democratic Republic, Malaysia, the Philippines, Singapore, Thailand, and Vietnam; SAARC—Bangladesh, Bhutan, India, the Maldives, Nepal, Pakistan, and Sri Lanka; CARICOM—Antigua and Barbuda, Bahamas, Barbados, Belize, Dominica, Grenada, Guyana, Haiti, Jamaica, Montserrat, St. Kitts and Nevis, St. Lucia, St. Vincent and the Grenadines, Suriname, and Trinidad and Tobago; EAC—Kenya, Tanzania, and Uganda; SADC—Angola, Botswana, Lesotho, Malawi, Mozambique, Swaziland, Tanzania, Zambia, and Zimbabwe.

10. The Mekong River runs 4,800 kilometers, from the Tibetan plateau through China's Yunnan Province and on through Myanmar, Thailand, Cambodia, the Lao PDR, and Vietnam. Development of the basin presents a variety of transboundary environmental issues for the riparian states.

11. These centers are the Coastal Zone Management Center in the Maldives and the SAARC Forestry Center in Bhutan. See the SAARC website, http://www.saarc-sec.org/?t=2.5.

12. Bhagwati popularized the term "spaghetti bowl" in his earlier writings.

13. For instance, an International Monetary Fund working paper (Frankel and Wei 1998) proposes that the degree of liberalization for imports from nonmembers to a PTA need not be as high as that for

member countries. A stricter view (Bhagwati 2006) is that open regionalism would require members of a regional group to undertake trade liberalization in concert and to extend it worldwide on a most favored nation basis. The concept of open regionalism has been discussed to a large extent in the context of the APEC; see for example, Bergsten (1997).

14. For the Chile–China agreement (Chile y China Firmaron Acuerdo Ambiental), see http://www.sice.oas.org/TPD/CHL_CHN/CHL_CHN _e.ASP (accessed May 5, 2009). The joint statement by Chile and Japan, March 27, 2007, is available at http://www.direcon.cl/documentos/ japon/joint.pdf (accessed May 5, 2009). The other agreements are, respectively, the Chile–Mexico Free Trade Agreement (April 17, 1998), http://www .sice.oas.org/trade/chmefta/indice.asp (accessed May 5, 2009); Acuerdo de Libre Comercio Chile–Perú (August 22, 2009), http://www.sice .oas.org/Trade/CHL_PER_FTA/Index_s.asp (accessed May 5, 2009); Chile–Korea Free Trade Agreement, (February 15, 2003), http://www.sice. oas.org/Trade/Chi-SKorea_e/ChiKoreaind_e.asp (accessed May 5, 2009).

15. Paragraph 31(iii) of the Doha Declaration is focused on the reduction or, as appropriate, the elimination of tariff and nontariff barriers to environmental goods and services.

16. For a good overview on the EGS negotiations at the WTO, see World Bank (2008, ch. 4).

17. Article 183(5), EU–CARIFORUM EPA. Article 190 refers to promotion and facilitation of public awareness and education programs with respect to environmental goods and services to foster trade in such products between the parties.

18. Article 17.9(3), CAFTA–DR FTA (August 5, 2004), http://www .ustr.gov/trade-agreements/free-trade-agreements/cafta-dr-dominican-republic-central-america-fta.

19. Article 147(1)(c), Agreement between Japan and the United Mexican States for the Strengthening of the Economic Partnership (September 17, 2004), http://www.mexicotradeandinvestment.com/ agreement.html (accessed May 5, 2009).

20. Article 17.3(7), U.S.–Morocco Free Trade Agreement (June 15, 2004), http://www.ustr.gov/Trade_Agreements/Bilateral/Morocco_FTA/ FInal_Text/Section_Index.html (accessed May 5, 2009).

21. Office of the United States Trade Representative, "NAFTA Facts," March 19, 2008, http://www.ustr.gov (accessed April 21, 2009). According to the note, as of March 2008, nearly US$1 billion had been provided for 135 environmental infrastructure projects, with an estimated cost of US$2.89 billion, and US$33.5 million in assistance and US$21.6 million in grants had been allocated to more than 450 other border environmental projects. The note also emphasizes that the Mexican government has made substantial new investments in environmental protection, increasing its federal budget for the environmental sector by 81 percent between 2003 and 2008. The USTR refers to two funds set up for this purpose: the NACEC Fund for Pollution Prevention Projects in Mexican Small and Medium Enterprises (FIRPEV), and the North American Fund for Environmental Cooperation (NAFEC).

22. See "Delegation of the European Union to India," http:// www.delind.ec.europa.eu/en/eco/tidp.htm#WHAT%20DOES%20TIDP% 20AIM%20TO%20ACHIEVE (accessed May 29, 2009).

23. See, for example, *Metalclad Corporation v. United Mexican States,* International Centre for Settlement of Investment Disputes (ICSID) Tribunal Decision, August 30, 2000. The case concerned the alleged expropriation caused by an ecological decree of Mexico that interfered with the operation of a hazardous waste landfill constructed by a subsidiary of the complainant. The tribunal found that indirect expropriation had occurred and awarded compensation under NAFTA, Chapter 11. See also Higgins (1982); OECD (2004).

24. For example, Article 3, NAAEC; Article 17.1, U.S.–Panama PTA; Article 17.1, U.S.–Australia PTA; Article 17.1, U.S.-Morocco PTA; Article 184.1, EU–CARIFORUM EPA.

25. For example, Article 17.3, U.S.–Panama PTA; Article 18.2, U.S.–CAFTA–DR PTA; Article 19.2, U.S.–Australia PTA.

26. For example, Article 20.17, in the CAFTA–DR, U.S.– Panama, and U.S.–Colombia agreements.

27. Articles 14 and 15, NAAEC; Article 17.7, CAFTA–DR PTA; Article 14, Canada–Chile PTA.

28. In the case of the Chile–U.S. PTA, each party is required to make best efforts to accommodate requests for consultations by persons or organizations (Article 19.4.2).

29. See the Commission for Environmental Cooperation website, http://www.cec.org/citizen/status/index.cfm?varlan=english (accessed April 21, 2009).

Bibliography

Anríquez, Gustavo. 2002. "Trade and Environment: An Economic Literature Survey." Working Paper 02-16, Department of Agricultural and Resource Economics, University of Maryland, College Park, MD. http://ageconsearch.umn.edu/bitstream/28598/1/wp02-16.pdf.

APEC (Asia-Pacific Economic Cooperation). 2008. "Identifying Convergences and Divergences in APEC RTAs/FTAs." Report 2008/AMM/010, presented at the 20th APEC Ministerial Meeting, Lima, Peru, November 19–20.

ASEAN (Association of Southeast Asian Nations). 1997. "ASEAN Vision 2020." ASEAN Secretariat, Jakarta. http://www.aseansec.org/1814.htm. Accessed April 21, 2009.

———. 2007. "Combating Haze in ASEAN: Frequently Asked Questions." ASEAN Secretariat, Jakarta. http://www.aseansec.org/Fact%20Sheet/ASCC/2007-ASCC-001.pdf.

———. 2009. "Minerals and Energy." ASEAN Secretariat, Jakarta. http://www.aseansec.org/4948.htm.

Audley, John, and Vanessa Ulmer. 2003. "Strengthening Linkages between U.S. Trade Policy and Environmental Capacity Building." Carnegie Paper 40, Carnegie Endowment for International Peace, Washington, DC.

Baldwin, Richard, and Patrick Low. 2009. "Introduction." In Multilateralizing Regionalism: Challenges for the Global Trading System, ed. Richard Baldwin and Patrick Low. Cambridge, U.K.: Cambridge University Press.

Bergsten, C. Fred, ed. 1997. Whither APEC? The Progress to Date and Agenda for the Future. Washington, DC: Institute for International Economics.

Bhagwati, Jagdish. 1993. "The Case for Free Trade." Scientific American 269 (5, November): 41–57.

———. 2004. In Defense of Globalization. New York: Oxford University Press.

———. 2006. "Why Asia Must Opt for Open Regionalism on Trade," Financial Times (Asian edition), November 3: 12.

———. 2008. Termites in the Trading System: How Preferential Agreements Undermine Free Trade. Oxford, U.K.: Oxford University Press.

Bhagwati, Jagdish N., and T. N. Srinivasan. 1996. "Trade and Environment: Does Environmental Diversity Detract from the Case for Free Trade?" In Fair Trade and Harmonization: Economic Analysis, ed. Jagdish N. Bhagwati and Robert E. Hudec. Cambridge, MA: MIT Press.

Colyer, Dale. 2008. "Green Trade Agreements: Comparison of Canada, U.S. and WTO." Presented at Joint Annual Meeting of the Canadian Agricultural Economics Society and Northeastern Agricultural and Resource Economic Association, Quebec City, June 30–July 1. http://ageconsearch.umn.edu/bitstream/37329/2/NAREA%20Paper%202008%20revised.pdf.

Cosbey, Aaron. 2007. "Regional Arrangements." In Trade and Development: A Resource Book, ed. Adil Najam, Mark Halle, and Ricardo Meléndez-Ortiz, 169–78. International Institute for Sustainable Development (IISD), International Centre for Trade and Sustainable Development (ICTSD) and the Regional and International Networking Group (The Ring). http://www.iisd.org/pdf/2007/trade_and_env.pdf.

Cosbey, Aaron, Howard Mann, Luke Eric Peterson, and Konrad von Moltke. 2004. Investment and Sustainable Development: A Guide to the Use and Potential of International Investment Agreements. Winnipeg, Manitoba, Canada: International Institute for Sustainable Development.

Daly, Herman. 1993a. "The Perils of Free Trade." Scientific American 269 (5, November): 24–29.

———. 1993b. "Problems with Free Trade: Neoclassical and Steady State Perspectives." In Trade and the Environment: Law, Economics, and Policy, ed. Durwood Zaelke, Paul Orbuch, and Robert F. Housman. Washington, DC: Island Press.

Environment Canada. 2007. "Evaluation of Canada's Participation in the Commission for Environmental Cooperation (CEC)." Environment Canada, Gatineau, Quebec, Canada. http://www.ec.gc.ca/doc/ae-ve/CEC-CCE/toc_eng.htm.

European Commission. 2006. "Handbook for Trade Sustainability Impact Assessment." European Commission, External Trade, Brussels.

Frankel, Jeffrey, and Shang-Jin Wei. 1998. "Open Regionalism in a World of Continental Trade Blocs." IMF Working Paper WP/98/10, International Monetary Fund, Washington, DC.

Fredriksson, Per G., ed. 1999. Trade, Global Policy, and the Environment. World Bank Discussion Paper 402. Washington, DC: World Bank.

Friedman, Joseph, Daniel A. Gerlowski, and Johnathan Silberman. 1992. "What Attracts Foreign Multinational Corporations? Evidence from Branch Plant Location in the United States." Journal of Regional Science 32 (4, November): 403–18.

Gallagher, Kevin P. 2004. Free Trade and the Environment: Mexico, NAFTA and Beyond. Stanford, CA: Stanford University Press.

Harrison, Glenn W., Thomas F. Rutherford, and David G. Tarr. 2001. "Chile's Regional Arrangements and the Free Trade Agreement of the Americas: The Importance of Market Access." Policy Research Working Paper 2634, World Bank, Washington, DC.

Heal, Geoffrey. 1998. "New Strategies for the Provision of Global Public Goods: Learning from International Environmental Challenges." Columbia Graduate School of Business Working Paper, Columbia University, New York.

Higgins, R. 1982. "The Taking of Property by the State: Recent Developments in International Law." Recueil des Cours (Académie de Droit International) 176: 276–77.

Hufbauer, Gary Clyde, Daniel C. Esty, Diana Orejas, Luis Rubio, and Jeffrey J. Schott. 2000. NAFTA and the Environment: Seven Years Later. Policy Analyses in International Economics 61. Washington, DC: Peterson Institute for International Economics.

Hufbauer, Gary Clyde, and Jeffrey J. Schott, assisted by Paul L. E. Grieco and Yee Wong. 2005. NAFTA Revisited: Achievements and Challenges. Washington, DC: Peterson Institute for International Economics.

Hufbauer, Gary, and Yee Wong. 2005. "Prospects for Regional Free Trade in Asia." Working Paper Series WP 05-12, Peterson Institute for International Economics, Washington, DC.

IISD (International Institute for Sustainable Development) and UNEP (United Nations Environment Programme). 2005. Environment and Trade: A Handbook. 2nd ed. Winnepeg, Manitoba, Canada: IISD.

India. 2000. "The Study of the Effects of Environmental Measures on Market Access." WT/CTE/W/177, submission to the Doha Ministerial Conference, World Trade Organization, Geneva, October 27.

———. n.d. "India and the World Trade Organization." Ministry of Commerce and Industry, New Delhi. http://commerce.nic.in/trade/international_trade_enviro_te.asp.

Khan, S. R., et al., 2004. "Southern Agenda for Trade and Environment." Background paper prepared for ICTSD/IISD/RING Southern Agenda Phase II Project, Regional Consultation for South/Southeast Asia, Kandalama, Sri Lanka, January.

Kirton, John. 2004. "NAFTA Dispute Settlement Mechanisms: An Overview." Prepared for Experts' Workshop on "NAFTA and Its Implications for ASEAN's Free Trade Area," Asian Institute, Munk Centre for International Studies, Toronto, May 27.

Krugman, Paul. 1997. "What Should Trade Negotiators Negotiate About?" *Journal of Economic Literature* 35 (March): 113–20.

Langton, Danielle. 2008. "United States–Southern African Customs Union (SACU) Free Trade Agreement Negotiations: Background and Potential Issues." CRS Report for Congress, RS21387, Congressional Research Service, Library of Congress, Washington, DC.

Less, Cristina Tébar, and Joy Aeree Kim. 2008. "Checklist for Negotiators of Environmental Provisions in Regional Trade Agreements." OECD Trade and Environment Working Paper 2008-2, Organisation for Economic Co-operation and Development, Paris. http://fiordiliji.sourceoecd.org/vl=27461473/cl=19/nw=1/rpsv/cgi-bin/wppdf?file=5kzc06k3c823.pdf.

Low, Patrick, ed. 1992. *International Trade and the Environment*. World Bank Discussion Paper 159. Washington, DC: World Bank.

Mani, Muthukumara, and Shreyasi Jha. 2006. "Trade Liberalization and the Environment in Vietnam." Policy Research Working Paper 3879, World Bank, Washington, DC.

Mani, Muthukumara, Sheoli Pargal, and Mainul Huq. 1997. "Does Environmental Regulation Matter? Determinants of the Location of New Manufacturing Plants in India in 1994." Policy Research Working Paper 1718, World Bank, Washington, DC.

Markell, David L., and John H. Knox, eds. 2003. *Greening NAFTA: The North American Commission for Environmental Cooperation*. Stanford, CA: Stanford University Press.

Maskus, Keith E., Tsunehiro Otsuki, and John S. Wilson. 2005. "The Cost of Compliance with Product Standards for Firms in Developing Countries: An Econometric Study." Policy Research Working Paper 3590, World Bank, Washington, DC.

Morici, Peter. 2002. *Reconciling Trade and the Environment in the World Trade Organization*. Washington, DC: Economic Strategy Institute. http://www.econstrat.org/images/ESI_Research_Reports_PDF/reconciling%20trade%20and%20the%20environment%20in%20the%20world%20trade%20organization%20%28peter%20morici%29.pdf.

Najam, Adil, Mark Halle, and Ricardo Meléndez-Ortiz, eds. 2007. *Trade and Development: A Resource Book*. International Institute for Sustainable Development (IISD), International Centre for Trade and Sustainable Development (ICTSD) and the Regional and International Networking Group (The Ring). http://www.iisd.org/pdf/2007/trade_and_env.pdf.

OECD (Organisation for Economic Co-operation and Development). 2004. "'Indirect Expropriation' and the 'Right to Regulate' in International Investment Law." Working Papers on International Investment 2004/4, Directorate for Financial and Enterprise Affairs, OECD, Paris.

———. 2007. *Environment and Regional Trade Agreements*. Paris: OECD.

Porter, Michael E. 1991. "America's Green Strategy." *Scientific American* 264 (4, April): 168.

PricewaterhouseCoopers. 2007. "Sustainability Impact Assessment of the EU–ACP Economic Partnership Agreements: Key Findings, Recommendations and Lessons Learned." Prepared for the European Commission, PricewaterhouseCoopers, Paris.

Rodríguez, Enrique Valerdi. 2009. "The European Union Free Trade Agreements: Implications for Developing Countries." Working Paper 8/2009, Real Instituto Elcano, Madrid.

SAARC (South Asian Association for Regional Cooperation). "Areas of Cooperation." SAARC Secretariat, Kathmandu. http://www.saarc-sec.org/?t=2#.

———. "Regional Centres." SAARC Secretariat, Kathmandu. http://www.saarc-sec.org/Regional-Centers/12/.

Tiemann, Mary. 2004. "NAFTA: Related Environmental Issues and Initiatives." CRS Report for Congress, Congressional Research Services, Library of Congress, Washington, DC. http://assets.opencrs.com/rpts/97-291_20040323.pdf.

UNCTAD (United Nations Conference on Trade and Development). 2005. *Investor-State Disputes Arising from Investment Treaties: A Review*. UNCTAD Series on International Investment Policies for Development. New York: United Nations.

U.S. GAO (General Accountability Office). 2009. "Four Free Trade Agreements GAO Reviewed Have Resultved in Commercial Benefits, but Challenges on Labor and Environment Remain." Highlights of GAO-09-439 (July), GAO, Washington, DC.

USTR (Office of the U.S. Trade Representative). 2008. "NAFTA—Myth vs. Facts." March, USTR, Washington, DC. http://www.ustr.gov/sites/default/files/NAFTA-Myth-versus-Fact.pdf.

———. 2009. "The President's Trade Policy Agenda." USTR, Washington, DC. http://www.ustr.gov/sites/default/files/uploads/reports/2009/asset_upload_file810_15401.pdf.

Wheeler, David. 2000. "Racing to the Bottom? Foreign Investment and Air Pollution in Developing Countries." Policy Research Working Paper 2524, World Bank, Washington, DC.

Wilson, John S., Tsunehiro Otsuki, and Mirvat Sewadeb. 2002. "Dirty Exports and Environmental Regulation: Do Standards Matter to Trade?" Policy Research Working Paper 2806, World Bank, Washington, DC.

Working Group (Working Group on Development and the Environment in the Americas). 2004. *Globalization and the Environment: Lessons from the Americas*. Washington, DC: Heinrich Böll Foundation North America.

———. 2008. *Foreign Investment and Sustainable Development: Lessons from the Americas*. Washington, DC: Heinrich Böll Foundation North America.

World Bank. 2008. *International Trade and Climate Change: Economic, Legal, and Institutional Perspectives*. Washington, DC: World Bank.

WTO (World Trade Organization) Secretariat. 1997. "Environmental Benefits of Removing Trade Restrictions and Distortions." WT/CTE/W/67, WTO, Geneva.

———. 2004. "Trade and Environment at the WTO: Background Document." WTO, Geneva.

Zaelke, Durwood, Paul Orbuch, and Robert F. Housman, eds. 1993. *Trade and the Environment: Law, Economics, and Policy*. Washington, DC: Island Press.

LABOR RIGHTS

Kimberly Ann Elliott

Within international trade rules, the only reference to labor rights is not a positive obligation, but an exception that permits member countries to ban imports produced with prison labor. Despite increased attention to the issue with the spread of globalization, member countries have not agreed to any new provisions on labor rights in the World Trade Organization (WTO), primarily because of the collective opposition of developing countries. By contrast, such provisions are becoming increasingly common in bilateral negotiations, particularly those between large, powerful developed countries and smaller, poorer developing countries.

Demands to include labor rights in trade agreements began with the United States and the negotiation of the North American Free Trade Agreement (NAFTA) with Mexico and Canada in the early 1990s. NAFTA represented a departure from past U.S. practice in two respects. It was the first U.S. preferential trade agreement (PTA) with a developing country (and only the third U.S. PTA of any kind), and, to ensure legislative approval, it included side agreements to protect worker rights, as well as the environment. Every U.S. PTA since then has incorporated legally binding and enforceable provisions on labor rights in the text of the agreement. These provisions, in U.S. PTAs and in those of other countries taking similar approaches, are generally based on the Declaration on Fundamental Principles and Rights at Work that was issued by the International Labour Organization (ILO) in 1998. (U.S. and Canadian agreements refer, in addition, to "acceptable conditions of work" relating to wages, hours, and health and safety.)

The ILO document lists four core labor standards as deserving of universal application. They are, in brief,

- Freedom of association and "effective recognition" of the right to collective bargaining
- Elimination of forced labor

- Effective abolition of child labor
- Elimination of discrimination in employment.[1]

About the same time as NAFTA was signed, U.S. negotiators began pushing for discussion of labor rights at the WTO. Developing countries, however, have successfully opposed creation of a study group or the inclusion of labor rights issue in the Doha Round of multilateral trade negotiations.

Except for Chile, developing countries generally do not include labor provisions in their agreements with one another, either. With one recent exception, enforceable labor rights provisions are absent from agreements that involve Asian countries and do not include the United States.

Traditionally, agreements to which the European Union (EU) is a party often have language addressing human rights, not worker rights specifically, but that may be changing. Canada is the only country besides the United States that includes labor provisions in its agreements with developing countries, but this is always done in side agreements, and with institutional mechanisms that emphasize cooperation rather than sanctions.

Labor standards language, where it exists outside U.S. trade agreements, is usually either hortatory or only nominally binding, with no or only weak enforcement measures. Nor do most agreements, including those that involve the United States, provide much in the way of meaningful cooperation or technical assistance for improving labor standards. Moreover, those U.S. PTAs that contain enforceable labor provisions and binding dispute settlement mechanisms generate few formal complaints, and no PTA has yet come close to the use of trade or other sanctions to enforce the labor provisions. The potential for exerting leverage is, in fact, greatest during the negotiation phase, when American trade negotiators sometimes condition the conclusion of an agreement on changes in labor laws to bring them closer to international norms (Hornbeck 2009).

This chapter begins with a review of the debate over the economics of linking trade and labor standards. It then examines actual practice with respect to labor rights in PTAs and surveys how those provisions have been implemented and enforced. The discussion concludes with lessons from this experience for developing countries that are considering such agreements.

The Economics of Labor Rights in PTAs

The policy debate and the accompanying literature on whether trade and labor standards should be linked, and if so, how, is extensive.[2] One strand of the literature focuses on the relationship, if any, between labor laws and regulations, on the one hand, and international trade and investment flows, on the other. Alongside the discussion of the economics of trade and labor markets, there is a political-economy debate about the appropriate role for the WTO in enforcing international labor standards. The central issue in this debate, which is relevant to the inclusion of labor provisions in PTAs, is whether labor standards should be enforced through trade sanctions or whether that possibility would lead to protectionist abuse (see, e.g., CITEE 2004).

In broad terms, free trade advocates argue that trade encourages growth, which, in turn, will bring about higher wages and better working conditions. In this view, no special attention to labor standards in trade agreements is needed. Some argue that pushing developing countries to adopt higher standards would make them uncompetitive in export markets and lead to fewer jobs and worse conditions. On the other side, labor standards advocates, led by unions and many human rights groups, maintain that competition to attract foreign investment or to capture a larger export market share causes countries to suppress labor standards, or at least not to raise them, leading to a "race to the bottom."

Many of those who assert a negative link between trade and labor rights also view the ILO with skepticism, regarding it as toothless and ineffective. The 1995 launch of the WTO, with a legally binding dispute settlement system and sanctions for noncompliance, seemed an attractive alternative to those concerned that globalization would lead to a race to the bottom. Most developing-country governments and free traders viewed more forceful international enforcement of labor standards as anathema, convinced that it would hinder developing countries' development and poverty reduction prospects and would be used by developed countries for protectionist purposes.

There is, however, little compelling evidence in the empirical literature either of a race to the bottom in labor standards or of protectionist abuse of trade-labor linkages where they exist. The effect of higher standards on competitiveness is more complicated than is usually assumed, and any higher costs of compliance that do materialize are often offset by higher productivity (Freeman and Medoff 1984). A meta-survey of the literature published by the World Bank in 2002 found "little systematic difference in performance between countries that enforce [union rights] and countries that do not" (Aidt and Tzannatos 2002, 4). Nor does the experience of nearly two decades offer support for the concern that trade sanctions to enforce labor standards are simply protectionism in disguise. A 2003 review of trade-labor standards linkages, particularly under the generalized system of preferences (GSP) program, found little evidence that labor rights have been introduced or used for protectionist purposes (Elliott and Freeman 2003, ch. 4). Since that review, several new PTAs have been implemented, and several more years of experience with the NAFTA agreement have been amassed, and no trade or other sanction has yet been imposed because of violations of labor standards embedded in trade agreements.

An alternative analysis suggests that labor standards and globalization are complements, with each compensating for weaknesses in the other.[3] Globalization can contribute to growth, and the jobs it creates are generally better than those in agriculture or the informal sector, but it is also associated in some cases with increased income inequality. Those arguing that no special attention to labor standards is needed also tend to ignore the disproportionate influence that multinational corporations have on trade negotiations and the possibilities that exist for improving conditions for workers in developing countries at low cost and without jeopardizing economic growth. Promoting global labor standards simultaneously with trade could spread the benefits of globalization more broadly, discourage the worst abuses of workers, and increase public support for trade agreements.

One key to realizing the complementarities and avoiding potential negative effects is to distinguish "core" labor standards from others. Some labor standards—for example, wages and health and safety regulations—will clearly have to vary with the countries' level of development and the local standards of living. However, the four core labor standards set forth in the 1998 ILO Declaration are meant to be upheld by all countries, regardless of their level of development. As noted at the beginning of this chapter, the core standards are freedom of association and the right to organize and bargain collectively; freedom from forced labor; the effective abolition of child labor, beginning with the "worst forms"; and nondiscrimination.[4]

These standards are part of the framework rules that govern labor market transactions; they do not specify particular outcomes, such as wages. They are comparable to the rules that protect property rights and freedom of transactions in product markets, which most economists view as necessary if market economies are to operate efficiently. The core labor standards are also fundamental elements of well-functioning democracies. And, just as the universality of property rights and freedom of market transactions does not imply identical laws or institutions among countries, universality of these core labor standards does not imply uniformity in the details of protection or in the institutions that implement it.

Even if improved implementation of core labor standards in developing countries can contribute to economic, political, and social development, there is still a question as to the appropriate scope and treatment of those standards in trade agreements. Extensive research into these questions finds no systematic evidence that globalization is leading generally to a race to the bottom, or—the flip side of this argument—that higher labor standards negatively affect comparative advantage. There is also little question that the worst conditions in most developing countries are in the nontraded agricultural and services sectors.

The results of this research into the alleged race to the bottom have been used to argue that there is no need to incorporate minimum labor standards into trade agreements. But repression of those standards could give a short-run competitive edge to particular firms or sectors, and there certainly is evidence that many firms and a few governments perceive competitive disadvantages associated with higher labor standards. Thus, while there is no evidence of a race to the bottom driving down standards in rich countries, there could be a race to the bottom *from the bottom* among low-wage countries—especially those

with export sectors that are highly price competitive, require few skills, and are geographically mobile, such as clothing and footwear.

This scenario suggests a role for international promotion of core labor standards to overcome potential collective action problems among poor countries competing against one another in similar markets. The incorporation in trade agreements of measures against trade-related violations of labor standards could help build support for such agreements in rich countries. Poor countries could also point to such provisions to reassure consumers (and international buyers serving them) that imported goods are produced under decent conditions (box 20.1).

The Practice of Labor Rights in PTAs

The formal treatment of labor standards in PTAs has evolved significantly over the past two decades, both within countries and among them, but implementation generally remains weak. Language on labor standards in PTAs entered into by the United States—the leading proponent of the linkage—has become more intrusive and nominally more enforceable, but neither vigorous enforcement nor significant capacity building is consistently part of the process. A few other countries or regions are increasingly including labor standards in trade agreements, but legal approaches vary greatly, and, again, little attention is accorded to implementation or capacity building.

Labor Rights Provisions in PTAs

Unlike other parts of PTAs, labor provisions do not in themselves raise questions about the compatibility of the obligations with multilateral trade rules. The reason is that the WTO says virtually nothing about labor standards (box 20.2). The General Agreements on Tariffs and Trade (GATT), now incorporated into the WTO, contains only

---

Box 20.1. Sweatshop Scandal Insurance for Brand-Name Buyers

Better Work, a joint project of the International Labour Organization (ILO) and the International Finance Corporation (IFC), is designed to improve workers' conditions and firms' productivity, build government capacity to enforce labor standards, and reassure brand-name firms that sweatshop scandals in their supply chains are less likely to occur if factories participate in the program. The program is based on Better Factories Cambodia, a program that stemmed from an agreement in which the United States offered additional market access for Cambodian apparel exports under the Multifibre Arrangement (MFA) if factories were in "substantial compliance" with local labor laws and the ILO core standards and if ILO monitors were put in place to verify compliance. (See Elliott and Freeman 2003; Polaski 2006.) When the MFA was phased out at the beginning of 2005, Cambodia negotiated an extension of the ILO program as part of its strategy for attracting brand-name buyers and maintaining competitiveness in the post-quota situation. A Better Work project, the successor to Better Factories, was recently launched in Jordan, and one may begin soon in Vietnam.

Source: ILO website, http://www.ilo.org/wow/Articles/lang—en/WCMS_094381/index.htm.

Box 20.2. Labor Rights and the WTO

The issue of trade and labor standards has been with the WTO since its birth. At the ministerial conference of the General Agreement on Tariffs and Trade (GATT), held in Marrakesh in April 1994 to sign the treaty that formed the World Trade Organization (WTO), nearly all ministers expressed a view on the subject. The chairman of the conference concluded that there was no consensus among member governments at the time and thus no basis for agreement on the issue. At the 1996 Singapore ministerial conference, the United States again pushed for the WTO to address the issue and suggested formation of a working group to study the linkages between trade and core labor standards. Most other members rejected that proposal, however, and defined the WTO's role on this question, as follows:

We renew our commitment to the observance of internationally recognized core labour standards. The . . . ILO is the competent body to set and deal with these standards, and we affirm our support for its work in promoting them. We believe that economic growth and development fostered by increased trade and further trade liberalization contribute to the promotion of these standards. We reject the use of labour standards for protectionist purposes, and agree that the comparative advantage of countries, particularly low-wage developing countries, must in no way be put into question. In this regard, we note that the WTO and ILO Secretariats will continue their existing collaboration.

At the time, there was no collaboration between the institutions, but the secretariats of the WTO and the ILO subsequently began to work together on technical issues under the banner of "coherence" in global economic policy making. No work on this subject is currently being undertaken in the WTO's councils and committees, and labor standards are not subject to WTO rules and disciplines.

Source: WTO.

one article on the subject—Article XX(e), which permits import bans for products made with prison labor. Still, a violation of international rules could arise if trade sanctions were used to enforce labor provisions under a PTA. If a sanctions-related tariff increase should lead to an applied tariff rate higher than what is bound in a country's WTO schedule, that would be a violation which could be challenged at the WTO.

Labor standards in PTAs also raise no issues of discrimination against third parties because the focus is on ensuring that a country's labor laws are consistent with international standards and are adequately enforced. There could even be positive spillovers for other, nonmember countries in a region if conditions for their own migrant workers in the PTA member country improve as a result of better compliance with labor standards under the PTA. There is some evidence of this happening in Jordan under its PTA with the United States.

Evolution of Worker Rights Provisions in U.S. PTAs

Starting with NAFTA in the mid-1990s, and continuing until the conclusion in May 2007 of a bipartisan agreement intended to resolve intra-U.S. political differences, U.S. PTAs focused on requiring that countries effectively enforce their labor laws, while "striving to ensure" that those laws were consistent with international standards. The agreement reached between President George W. Bush and the leaders of both parties in the U.S. Congress broadened the scope of labor standards enforceable in U.S. PTAs, put more emphasis on international norms, and expanded

enforcement measures from monetary fines to include the possibility of trade sanctions. Since then, only the agreement with Peru has been implemented, but, after renegotiation of some issues related to auto trade, the PTA with the Republic of Korea is expected to be approved by Congress by the summer of 2011. PTAs with Colombia and Panama remain in limbo, in part because of concerns by some in Congress that the labor provisions are still not strong enough.

Although respect for workers' rights has been a condition of U.S. unilateral trade preference programs since 1984, it became an issue in reciprocal trade negotiations only with the decision to pursue a deep integration agreement with Mexico in the early 1990s (see Mayer 1998 for a thorough discussion). Since then, U.S. negotiators have routinely failed to persuade developing countries to discuss labor standards in regional or multilateral negotiations. In bilateral bargaining, however, they have insisted that trade agreements include labor standards.

The inclusion of labor provisions in U.S. PTAs is primarily the result of the need to gain congressional approval for these agreements.[5] Trade agreements with small, distant countries with relatively high standards, good working conditions, and few sensitive exports, such as Australia, Chile, and Singapore, or agreements driven by foreign policy (e.g., Jordan), have received relatively strong congressional support. But gaining congressional approval of agreements with countries where labor standards are perceived to be inadequate has proved more difficult, especially if the countries also export import-sensitive products such as apparel, sugar, or certain other agricultural products.

Over the years, the approach to worker rights in U.S. PTAs has fluctuated with the distribution of political power in Washington, and the debate has become increasingly partisan and rancorous. Four distinct periods in the treatment of labor rights in U.S. PTAs can be identified: the period leading to the NAFTA agreement, with its side agreements on labor (and the environment); the 2000 "Jordan standard" agreement; the PTAs negotiated and ratified during 2002–06; and the period following the conclusion of the May 2007 Bipartisan Agreement.

Despite differences in the specific standards addressed and in dispute resolution mechanisms (see also Porges, ch. 22 in this volume, for a discussion), all the agreements in the first three periods share a common approach that requires the parties to enforce their own labor laws, without a clear, legally binding commitment to ensure that those laws are consistent with internationally agreed labor standards. The "enforce-your-own-laws" standard reflects, in part, the fact that the U.S. government has ratified only two of the eight fundamental ILO conventions—those on forced labor and on the worst forms of child labor. Some American constituencies are concerned that a legally binding reference to ILO standards in a U.S. trade agreement might be used to challenge the United States' own labor laws and practices.

A key implication of the "enforce-your-own-laws" approach for potential U.S. partner countries has become that their labor laws may not diverge very far from international standards; otherwise, this approach in the PTAs could have the perverse effect of encouraging enforcement of laws that undermine worker rights. Thus, during negotiations, or even before they are formally launched, U.S. negotiators often identify changes to a partner country's labor laws that need to be made before the agreement can be concluded. Countries such as Bahrain, Chile, Guatemala, and Morocco undertook major labor law reforms, at least in part in anticipation of negotiations on PTAs with the United States. Oman had a labor law like others in Middle East that prohibited or tightly restricted labor organizing; it had to make major changes in its law as a condition for completing PTA negotiations.

In sum, having labor laws that are largely in compliance with the ILO fundamental principles is now a de facto condition for negotiating a PTA with the United States. Moreover, if recent pressure on Panama and Peru to make extensive changes to their labor laws is an indication of things to come, the emerging condition for concluding a PTA with the United States may be full compliance with the technical details of core ILO conventions—despite the United States' own gaps in compliance.[6]

The careful political balancing act required for congressional approval sharply constrains U.S. negotiators'

flexibility. Consequently, the content of the labor chapters (indeed, of most chapters) of the PTAs is remarkably similar, regardless of the level of development in the partner country. The labor chapter in the U.S. PTA with Australia, for example, is virtually identical to those in all the other PTAs negotiated between 2002 and 2006, except that it does not contain an annex on cooperation and technical assistance. And, despite concerns over violations of worker rights in Colombia, U.S. negotiators were constrained when Colombian negotiators suggested strengthening the labor chapter by adding the ILO core standard on nondiscrimination. U.S. negotiators at the time concluded that adding this standard to the labor chapter would result in the loss of more votes from labor standards opponents in the Congress than there would be gains from supporters. Overall, to the extent that there is variation in the template used, as is discussed next, it has been largely driven by changing political balances in the United States, not conditions in or preferences of the partner-country government.

NAFTA side agreement on labor. NAFTA, negotiated by Canada, Mexico, and the United States in the early 1990s, was the first U.S. PTA with a low-wage developing country. The agreement was signed by President George H. W. Bush but had not been ratified by Congress by the time he left office. In an attempt to assuage the concerns of workers and unions about the agreement, President Bill Clinton opted to negotiate a side deal on labor (and another on the environment) before submitting the agreement to the Congress for approval (Mayer 1998).

The resulting North American Agreement on Labor Cooperation (NAALC) is 44 pages long and is unique in several respects. First, it was negotiated before the ILO had agreed on the Declaration on Fundamental Principles and Rights at Work, which created a consensus on core labor standards. The NAFTA negotiators developed their own list of labor standards, based on the worker rights conditions in the U.S. GSP program. Second, the NAALC has the most elaborate institutional arrangements of any PTA, including a Labor Cooperation Commission, a governing Labor Council, and a secretariat to manage daily operations. There is also a mechanism for ministerial consultations, to deal with accusations that one of the parties has not adequately enforced its labor laws.

The full range of dispute settlement mechanisms is available in cases relating to alleged violations of technical labor regulations on minimum wages or occupational health and safety, or involving child labor. In these cases, if neither consultations nor an expert evaluation resolves the problem, the parties can appoint an arbitral panel, and the panel may ultimately impose a monetary fine if the situation is not rectified.[7] Allegations of forced labor and discrimination are subject to evaluation by a panel of independent experts, but no monetary or other penalties may be imposed if the issues are not resolved. Finally, complaints involving violations of union rights are limited to ministerial consultations. In addition, disputes are referred for consultation or further dispute settlement only if there is a "persistent pattern" of failure to enforce relevant labor laws and if the violations are in trade-related sectors.

The "Jordan standard." The U.S.–Jordan PTA, negotiated in late 2000, established a new precedent by including a (far less elaborate) section on labor in the main text of the agreement and by making it subject to the same dispute settlement procedures and remedies as the rest of the agreement. Thus, if consultations, a dispute settlement panel, and the joint committee created to implement the agreement as a whole do not resolve a dispute, the complaining party is authorized "to take *any* appropriate and commensurate measure" (emphasis added).

The U.S.–Jordan labor text is also the first to reference the 1998 ILO declaration defining core labor standards—although achieving compliance with the ILO standards is stated as an aspiration rather than an obligation. Whereas the ILO core labor rights include nondiscrimination, as well as freedom of association and prohibitions on forced labor and child labor, the agreement with Jordan, like those that followed up to 2007, continues to use the previous U.S. definition of "internationally recognized labor rights," which excludes nondiscrimination and includes "acceptable conditions of work" with respect to minimum wages, hours of work, and occupational safety and health.

In addition to calling on parties to "strive to ensure" that domestic laws are consistent with "internationally recognized labor rights," as the United States defined them, the agreement also discourages the parties from "waiv[ing] or otherwise derogat[ing] from . . . [labor] laws as an encouragement for trade." As in NAFTA, the only binding obligation is that a party "shall not fail to effectively enforce its laws" on a sustained basis in a way that affects trade. Other paragraphs preserve the discretion of governments to adopt, modify, and enforce labor laws and regulations. Thus, according to Article 6, Section 4(b), of the agreement, a party will be in compliance with its labor obligations under the agreement if "a course of action or inaction [in enforcing labor laws] reflects a reasonable exercise of such discretion, or results from a *bona fide* decision regarding the allocation of resources."

The standard for determining that a violation has occurred is thus set rather high. The language calling on parties to "strive to ensure" that labor laws are consistent with ILO core principles and that those laws are not weakened for competitive reasons is not explicitly excluded

from enforcement, as it is in later agreements. But "striving to ensure" something is a vague standard and would be difficult to enforce in practice.

U.S. PTAs negotiated between 2002 and 2006. Although there are minor differences from one text to the next, the PTA labor chapters negotiated during the period 2002–06 retain the core approach from the Jordan agreement and differ mainly in their enforcement provisions. In addition, they add more detailed provisions for cooperation on labor matters, and they pay greater attention to transparency and due process. Several of them add articles encouraging efforts within countries to promote public awareness of labor laws and enforce procedural fairness in their implementation. None of these provisions, however, are subject to dispute settlement.

In these agreements, the parties' reaffirm their commitment to the ILO Declaration. As in other agreements, they also make a commitment to "strive to ensure" that their laws are consistent with internationally recognized labor rights and not to lower or weaken labor laws to encourage trade or investment involving the other party. But these provisions are hortatory and are explicitly excluded from dispute settlement. Each of the seven PTAs negotiated during the period—those with Australia, Bahrain, Chile, Morocco, Oman, Singapore, and the five countries of Central America plus the Dominican Republic (CAFTA–DR)—includes an article providing that the "enforce-your-own-laws" provision is the only provision subject to dispute settlement.

These agreements did retain the Jordan practices of incorporating the labor chapter into the main text and using the same general dispute settlement process for labor as for other parts of the agreement. But, as in the NAFTA side agreement, the agreements limit the potential penalty for violations of the labor chapter to imposition of a "monetary assessment," and this "fine" can be no higher than US$15 million (to be adjusted for inflation), regardless of the income level or size of the partner. If the party charged with the violation does not pay the assessment as ordered by an arbitral panel, the complaining party can collect it by suspending trade benefits as a last resort, as in NAFTA. Violations of provisions in other chapters of these agreements can lead to trade sanctions that are generally commensurate with the injury suffered.

These agreements, although they contain more detailed provisions on institutional mechanisms and cooperation than does the Jordan PTA, do not have as elaborate or complex a structure as NAFTA (and few have any funding attached). Indeed, dissatisfaction with the perceived lack of enforcement under the NAFTA labor side agreement led then-candidate for president Barack Obama to call for reopening NAFTA, perhaps by incorporating the side agreements into the main text. During the presidential primary campaign, Obama even threatened to "use the hammer of a potential opt-out as leverage to ensure that we actually get labor and environmental standards that are enforced."[8] As is discussed below, however, the enforcement provisions in agreements in which labor provisions are contained in the main text are untested, and so there is no basis on which to conclude that one model is better than the other. Ultimately, the impact of these agreements depends on the desire of the parties to see them effectively enforced, not the details of the formal procedures.

Bipartisan agreement on labor rights in PTAs. U.S. PTA negotiations with Colombia, Korea, and Panama, which were at various stages, came to a standstill after the 2006 midterm elections. Many in the newly elected Democratic majority in Congress opposed all three negotiations for various reasons, including, in the case of Colombia, concern over violations of the human rights of union organizers and members. More generally, the new congressional majority regarded the "enforce-your-own-laws" approach as too weak and insisted on changes to the PTA template, as well as in the three pending agreements (Elliott 2007).

In May 2007, President Bush and the leaders of both parties in Congress reached an agreement on how to address labor issues, as well as environmental, intellectual property, and other matters, in U.S. PTAs. The compromise on labor standards requires parties "to adopt and maintain in its statutes and regulations, and practices thereunder," the labor rights, "as stated" in the 1998 ILO Declaration. A footnote specifies that these obligations refer "only to the ILO Declaration," since some in the U.S. Congress did not want the United States to refer in reciprocally binding trade agreements to ILO conventions it had not ratified. The agreement also revises the definition of the standards covered to include nondiscrimination, as in the ILO Declaration, but it retains the "acceptable conditions of work" standard from U.S. practice.

The May 2007 compromise also makes the nonderogation article, which prohibits parties from lowering labor standards for competitive advantage, legally binding and enforceable, and it appears to reduce countries' flexibility in choosing how to allocate resources to enforcement and prosecution of labor law violations. Although the new template states that decisions regarding the "distribution of enforcement resources shall not be a reason for not complying with the provisions of this Chapter," it retains the language about parties having "the right to the reasonable exercise of discretion and to *bona fide* decisions with regard to the allocation of resources." Finally, the new framework makes the labor chapter subject to the same

dispute settlement procedures—and potential penalties—as other PTA chapters.

Whether President Obama will follow or amend the May 2007 template for labor chapters in PTAs, or what the template means for negotiations at the WTO, remains to be seen. As of early 2011, none of the three pending PTAs had been submitted to Congress for approval, although submission of the Korean agreement appeared imminent at the time of writing. What is clear is that the issue will not disappear, as President Obama's first trade policy agenda report in 2009 emphasized the role of worker rights in making "support for global markets sustainable," and the policy's second priority, after support for a rules-based system, is to "advance social accountability" in U.S. trade policy (USTR 2009).

Worker Rights Provisions in Non-U.S. PTAs

Recent studies examining the array of provisions in various trade agreements found few non-U.S. PTAs that include language on labor rights.[9] Canada is the exception, as it typically includes side agreements on labor in its PTAs with developing countries. Chile often, but not systematically, incorporates references to labor issues either in its PTAs or in associated memoranda of understanding. Traditionally, the European Union had some language on human rights in its PTAs, but that may be changing to include specific references to worker rights, as well. The recently concluded economic partnership agreement (EPA) between the EU and the Caribbean region contains provisions on worker rights, but it remains to be seen whether this will become a consistent template for these agreements in other regions. An additional review by the author of PTAs involving these countries, as well as Australia, New Zealand, Japan, and China, found very few additional examples of agreements that contain language promoting improvements in worker rights.[10]

Canada. After the United States, Canada most consistently includes legally binding labor provisions in its trade agreements. One difference from U.S. practice is that Canada only insists on labor provisions in PTAs with developing countries, whereas they are part of the U.S. template regardless of the level of development of the partner country. Thus, U.S. agreements with Australia and Singapore include labor chapters, but Canada's agreements with Israel and the European Free Trade Association (EFTA) contain no specific provisions on labor issues. As of mid-2010, Canada had implemented three additional PTAs with developing countries (with Chile, Costa Rica, and Peru), in addition to NAFTA, and it had signed three more, with Colombia, Jordan, and Panama.[11] These agreements appear to be modeled broadly on the NAFTA precedent, incorporating provisions on labor and environmental cooperation in side agreements, along with separate consultation and dispute resolution mechanisms that do not include trade sanctions.

Canada's PTA with Chile was explicitly and closely modeled on the NAFTA side agreement in order to facilitate Chile's accession to that agreement at a later date. (Instead, the United States subsequently negotiated a separate agreement with Chile, as described above.) Subsequent Canadian PTAs retained the model employing a labor side agreement because, under Canada's federal system, national policy makers cannot negotiate international treaties that limit provincial jurisdiction over labor law without the provinces' explicit acquiescence.

Canada's agreement with Chile, like the later ones with Colombia and Peru, follows the NAFTA precedent in providing for fines for noncompliance with the labor side agreement. The agreement with Costa Rica, by contrast, provides no penalties for violations, other than "the modification of cooperative activities." All the agreements that followed the one with Chile incorporate references to the ILO core standards, as defined in the 1998 Declaration, and the agreements with Peru and Colombia hew closely to the language used in the U.S. agreements with those countries. These agreements also restrict reviews of compliance to the ILO core standards only, not implementation of other labor laws. Canadian agreements do retain language calling for attention to improvement of other working conditions, similar to the U.S. definition of "acceptable conditions of work."

Perhaps because of the nature of the parties to the two agreements that have been implemented long enough to be analyzed—those with Chile and Costa Rica, both of them democratic countries with relatively good labor practices—there has been little activity under Canada's labor cooperation agreements. There have been no public communications under either agreement, and the website where public communications and information about cooperative activities under particular agreements is posted has not been updated since 2005.[12] Several technical workshops, public conferences, and seminars were held in the early years of implementation of the Chile PTA, but none has occurred in several years. The only cooperative activity specified under the agreement with Costa Rica is a technical assistance program to be carried out by the ILO to strengthen labor administration, to which Canada contributed US$1 million. As for the agreement with Colombia, the Canadian Trade Ministry website says only that Canada "has offered to provide Colombia with labour-related technical assistance which will allow Colombia to better

meet its obligations under the [labor cooperation agreement]."[13] The website for the International Trade and Labour Grants and Contributions Program, which "is designed to help the Government of Canada meet its commitment to address the labor dimensions of international trade and economic integration," has not been updated for more than a year, and a notice at the top of the page declares that the program is not currently accepting applications for grants.[14]

In sum, Canada has followed a path regarding labor standards in trade agreements with developing countries that is adapted to its constitutional structure and political needs, but with language on labor standards that is similar to that in U.S. PTAs. The key differences are not so much in the legal obligations that each country seeks to promote as in the enforcement measures and the relative role of cooperation in promoting worker rights. The similarities could facilitate coordination of approaches toward linking trade and labor rights, if the two countries so chose.

Chile. Chile is unusual among developing countries in that it frequently seeks to include labor provisions in its agreements with other developing countries—although these provisions are often general and aspirational in nature, rather than legally binding. For example, Chile's PTA with China includes a memorandum of understanding calling for both parties to "enhance their communication and cooperation on labor, social security and the environment." The Trans-Pacific Strategic Economic Partnership, which includes (in addition to Chile) Brunei Darussalam, New Zealand, and Singapore, also includes a memorandum of understanding that affirms the parties' commitment to the ILO core standards and calls on them to promote better understanding of one another's labor systems and practices, provide a forum for discussion of labor issues, and, if questions over the interpretation of the memorandum of understanding arise, to consult and perhaps discuss them in joint meetings. The agreement between Chile and the EU includes an article on social cooperation stating that the parties "shall give priority to domestic measures aimed at developing and modernising labour relations, working conditions, social welfare and employment security." But there are no further details or stipulations on how to promote or monitor these activities (Bourgeois, Dawar, and Evenett 2007, 27).

The most far-reaching agreement is Chile's PTA with Colombia, signed in 2006, which is the only PTA found that involves only developing countries and includes a separate chapter in the main text addressing labor standards. The language is similar to that contained in PTAs involving the United States, with which Colombia was negotiating at the time, but it contains no enforcement provisions beyond consultation and cooperation, and both labor and the environment are excluded from the dispute settlement chapter that applies to the rest of the agreement.

European Union. The EU has not traditionally included labor rights in its PTAs, but it may be moving in that direction, at least in the economic partnership agreements that it is negotiating with former African, Caribbean, and Pacific (ACP) beneficiaries of unilateral preferences under the Cotonou Agreement. Horn, Mavroidis, and Sapir (2010) examined 14 EU trade agreements going back decades and found that only the recently concluded EPA with the Caribbean Forum of African, Caribbean, and Pacific States (CARIFORUM) included an article on labor rights. Prior to that, EU agreements focused on broad human rights and did not single out worker rights for special attention.

The relevant section in the CARIFORUM agreement reaffirms the parties' commitment to internationally recognized labor standards, as defined in the ILO Declaration, but it also recognizes the right of the parties to "establish their own social regulations and labor standards in line with their own social development priorities." The parties then agree that they should not "encourage trade or foreign direct investment to enhance or maintain a competitive advantage" by weakening labor laws. Complaints related to this chapter are to be investigated under the normal dispute settlement procedures of the agreement, but "compensation or trade remedies [may not] be invoked against a Party's wishes" (EU 2008). In other words, although the provision is nominally enforceable, it carries no penalties for violations, other than scrutiny. As this agreement is quite recent, it is not yet known how it will be implemented or whether technical assistance will be provided to improve labor standards.

Whether the labor standards language used in the CARIFORUM agreement will be repeated in other EPAs is unclear; no other agreements have been finalized. Interim agreements have been initialed with a number of countries, but they are mostly limited to addressing market access for goods. For example, the interim agreement with Cameroon, which is intended to lead eventually to a full EPA with Central Africa, says only that the parties "agree to ensure that sustainability considerations are reflected in all titles of the EPA and to draft specific chapters covering environmental and social issues." Thus, large questions loom as to whether the EU will now place greater attention on worker rights in its trade agreements and, if so, how much effort it will put into implementing those provisions.

Japan. Finally, the only other obligation to protect labor rights in a PTA seen thus far is in the Japan–Philippines agreement, which contains a provision stating that domestic labor laws should not be weakened as a means of attracting investment. Article 103 is similar to the language on labor rights in U.S. PTAs in affirming the parties' recognition that it is "inappropriate" to weaken labor laws in order to encourage investment and that each "shall strive to ensure" that this does not happen "in a manner that weakens or reduces adherence to the internationally recognized labor rights." Not only is this language strikingly similar to that included in the labor chapters of U.S. PTAs, but the list of "internationally recognized rights" included in the agreement also mimics the list contained in U.S. agreements rather than the core labor standards reflected in the ILO Declaration of 1998. Under the Japan–Philippines agreement, if neither consultation nor arbitration resolves a dispute arising under Article 103, the complaining party can temporarily suspend its obligations under the agreement, preferably in the same sector—that is, foreign direct investment—affected by the violation. None of Japan's other PTAs that have been notified to the WTO includes such language, including subsequent agreements with Brunei Darussalam and Indonesia.

To sum up, developing countries negotiating PTAs with the United States, Canada, Chile, and, perhaps, the EU can expect to confront demands for inclusion of labor standards in some form. At this stage, only U.S. negotiators insist on trade sanctions as a potential enforcement measure—a key concern for developing countries. But whatever the model followed, and whether the emphasis is on sanctions or on cooperation and capacity building, implementation of labor provisions does not seem to be a high priority in these PTAs.

Implementation and Enforcement of Labor Rights Provisions in PTAs

To the extent that worker rights have been incorporated in PTAs, most countries have used a "soft-law" approach. The language is usually hortatory or, if it is nominally binding, many agreements explicitly exclude the labor provisions from sanctions for noncompliance. The U.S. approach, however, has been quite different. Although specific commitments and procedures differ from agreement to agreement, every U.S.-negotiated PTA since NAFTA has incorporated into the main text legally binding provisions protecting worker rights that are subject to dispute settlement and that include some form of sanction for noncompliance. But despite the striking differences in attention to enforcement issues, implementation across countries has not been as different as the legal templates imply.

U.S. negotiators are constrained in how they treat labor issues in PTAs by the need to obtain congressional approval. The role of dispute settlement procedures and, especially, trade sanctions in enforcing labor provisions has been a key source of disagreement between the United States and its trading partners, but the partner countries have little influence over labor language because the approach is settled in negotiations among various U.S.-based constituencies, the two major political parties, and the executive and legislative branches. Although these internal political battles have brought about changes in the language of the labor provisions, depending on the distribution of political power among the various interests, enforcement of the labor provisions in U.S. PTAs has varied surprisingly little.

Between 1994 and 2008, two U.S. presidents, each from a different political party, presided over the implementation of PTAs. Both were restrained in their approaches to enforcement, with neither coming close to invoking sanctions of any sort. The big unknown today is how aggressive President Obama will be on this issue, given the statements in his official trade agenda on the crucial role that worker rights should play in trade policy (USTR 2009), and the decision on July 30, 2010, to formally request consultations with Guatemala over alleged violations of the CAFTA–DR labor chapter.[15]

On the other side, technical and financial assistance to partner governments to strengthen their capacity to implement and enforce labor standards has also been neglected. Other than the agreement between the United States and CAFTA–DR, there has been no dedicated program of capacity-building assistance related to the signing and implementation of PTAs. The U.S. Agency for International Development (USAID) is providing technical and financial assistance to address labor rights violations in special export zones in Jordan that export clothing to the

United States. That program, however, was developed in response to a report on exploitative conditions involving migrant workers, not as part of a strategy for implementing the PTA or as a result of systematic monitoring. A key problem is that the congressional committees that oversee trade agreements are not the same as those that appropriate funds for capacity building, and close collaboration is often lacking.

Although the details differ, the dispute settlement process for labor violations under U.S. PTAs is generally as follows. The agreements do not provide for a private right of action, but they do require parties to designate a national contact point to accept submissions from citizens or groups requesting consultations over potential problems under the agreement. It is then up to the receiving government to decide whether to request consultations with the other government. If consultations do not resolve the problem, the government alleging a violation can request appointment of a dispute settlement panel to investigate. If the panel agrees that a violation exists, the responding country will have a certain amount of time to bring its practices into compliance and if it does not, penalties—either fines or trade sanctions, depending on when the agreement was negotiated—may be authorized (see table 20.1).

Thus far, only three of the nine U.S. PTAs in force have seen any enforcement activity, and most of that has been under NAFTA. There have been only two other requests for consultations regarding labor rights violations, involving Jordan in 2006 and Guatemala in 2008.

In the Guatemala case, first filed in 2008, the U.S. Department of Labor (U.S. DOL 2009) investigated the issues raised in the submission from the AFL-CIO trade union, affirmed that problems existed, and recommended actions the government of Guatemala could take to address them. In early 2009, the Department of Labor opted not to recommend formal consultations under the

Table 20.1. Sanctions Authorized for Labor Violations in U.S. Preferential Trade Agreements

Agreement partners, and year approved	Enforcement mechanisms permitted
Canada, Mexico, 1993	In Canada, fines only; for Mexico and the United States, monetary assessments that may be collected by suspending tariff concessions if not paid
Jordan, 2002	"Any appropriate and commensurate measure"—the same as in other parts of the agreement
Chile, 2003; Singapore, 2003; Australia, 2004; Morocco, 2004; Bahrain, 2005; Oman, 2005; CAFTA–DR, 2005; Korea, Rep., pending	Monetary assessments, capped at US$15 million (adjusted for inflation)
Peru, 2007; Panama, pending; Colombia, pending	Compensation, fines, or trade sanctions—the same as for other parts of the agreement

Source: Office of the U.S. Trade Representative, http://www.ustr.gov.
Note: CAFTA–DR, Dominican Republic–Central America Free Trade Agreement.

PTA but promised to reassess the situation within six months and "determine whether further action is warranted. . . ."[16] The review was extended again when that deadline passed with little movement. Finally, on July 30, 2010, the U.S. trade representative and the secretary of labor jointly sent a letter requesting formal consultations under the trade agreement to their counterparts in Guatemala, "the first labor case the United States has ever brought against a trade agreement partner."[17] If those consultations do not resolve U.S. concerns, a dispute settlement panel that might lead to sanctions could be appointed in coming months.

A recent U.S. General Accountability Office investigation of the implementation of four U.S. PTAs, with Chile, Jordan, Morocco, and Singapore, concluded that

> [free trade agreement] negotiations spurred some labor reforms in each of the selected partners, according to U.S. and partner officials, but progress has been uneven and U.S. engagement minimal. An example cited was Morocco's enactment of a long-stalled overhaul of its labor code. However, partners reported that enforcement of labor laws continues to be a challenge, and some significant labor abuses have emerged. In the [free trade agreements] we examined, [the U.S. Department of] Labor provided minimal oversight and did not use information it had on partner weaknesses to establish remedial plans or work with partners on improvement. (U.S. GAO 2009, ii)

An escalation in the Guatemala case could send important signals about whether there will be a change in the aggressiveness with which labor standards are enforced and effective implementation pursued in U.S. PTAs.

NAFTA and "Enforcement" of Labor Standards

As of mid-2010, 37 submissions had been made under the NAALC, of which 6 were filed in Canada, 9 in Mexico (all against the United States and mostly involving complaints about mistreatment of migrant Mexican workers), and 22 in the United States (all but two against Mexico).[18] Roughly two-thirds of the submissions alleged violations of freedom of association or of the right to organize and bargain collectively. According to a detailed analysis by Hufbauer and Schott (2005), only 14 cases resulted in reports, and 13 of these recommended ministerial consultations. Most of the consultations led to public outreach seminars, studies or consultants' reports, or government-to-government discussions. Most others were rejected for review (11 cases), and a handful was withdrawn or settled before the review was completed.[19]

Hufbauer and Schott (2005, 128) conclude that "the NAALC has had practically no impact on North American labor-market conditions." Another view, however, is that the NAALC and activity under it has been helpful in social mobilization, as "part of larger strategies involving public education on the issues, media, legislative lobbying and mobilization" across borders (Buchanan and Chapparo 2008, 33). For example, although problems remain, pressures on Mexico to improve respect for freedom of association have led to important changes requiring that secret ballots be used in union-organizing elections (ibid.).

The submissions made in the United States against Mexico have generally been of two types. One common pattern involves complaints by U.S. unions against U.S. multinational companies with operations in Mexico, alleging violations of the right to organize. The other common type involves complaints by human rights groups and worker rights activists against Mexican federal or state governments, alleging a failure to adequately enforce labor laws, or to provide fair and impartial procedures for the consideration of labor disputes under Mexican law. In addition to problems with union rights, these complaints also often involve occupational safety and health issues and gender discrimination.

It is difficult to separate out the impact of the NAFTA dispute settlement process on any improvements that occurred in these cases because so many other factors that could have had an effect were operating at the same time. Perhaps most important, the tradition of single-party control in Mexican politics ended in this period, opening space for independent unions to more effectively challenge the traditional corporatist union structure in Mexico. Interestingly, some of the most tangible benefits of implementation of the NAALC accrued not to Mexican workers in Mexico, but to migrant Mexican workers in the United States. Several of these cases appear to have resulted in at least temporary improvements in conditions for the workers directly involved. More broadly, they highlighted the fact that U.S. federal laws protect the rights of workers, regardless of their legal status in the United States. One case in particular, described in box 20.3, contributed to changing the practices of U.S. agencies with respect to protecting migrant rights in the workplace.

U.S.–Jordan PTA: Capacity Building as Enforcement

In contrast to NAFTA, protection of labor rights in the U.S.–Jordan agreement was included in the main text of the agreement, and enforcement was the same as for all other parts of the agreement. But in order to gain sufficient political support among labor standards skeptics in the U.S. Congress, the United States and Jordanian

---

Box 20.3. NAFTA as a Tool for Promoting Rights of Mexican Migrants in the United States

In 1998 the Yale Law School Workers Rights Project, along with roughly 20 other nongovernmental organizations concerned with immigration and worker rights, filed a submission under the labor agreement with Mexico alleging that a 1992 memorandum of understanding between the U.S. Department of Labor and the U.S. Immigration and Naturalization Service (INS) had led to a failure to enforce U.S. labor laws with respect to migrant workers. Under the memorandum of understanding, the Labor Department was expected to inspect employment eligibility verification forms when investigating complaints regarding violations of wage laws and to report any discrepancies that might indicate the presence of illegal immigrants to the INS.

The petition alleged that this practice had a chilling effect on migrant workers, who would fear being deported if they reported underpayment of wages in violation of U.S. labor laws. Shortly after the submission was accepted for review, the U.S. agencies concerned signed a new memorandum of understanding stating that the Labor Department would no longer inspect employment eligibility forms when investigating complaints under its jurisdiction. This revision, in effect, restored the migrant workers' rights under U.S. federal law to be protected from illegal behavior on the part of employers, regardless of the workers' legal status in the country. After additional consultations between the U.S. and Mexican ministries of labor, the parties agreed that the U.S. Labor Department would produce and disseminate materials in Spanish and English explaining the rights of migrant workers.

Source: U.S. Department of Labor website, http://www.dol.gov/ilab/programs/nao/status.htm#iib5; National Immigration Law Center, "Law Students File Petition under North American Free Trade Agreement (NAFTA) Challenging Collaboration between Department of Labor and INS," *Immigrants' Rights Update* 21 (8), December 21, 1998.

---

authorities exchanged letters stating that they did not anticipate using the dispute resolution mechanism for labor issues.[20]

Then, in September 2006, the AFL-CIO filed a complaint with the Office of the U.S. Trade Representative claiming that Jordan's labor law was inadequate in several areas regarding freedom of association and that Jordan was not adequately enforcing its labor laws. The AFL-CIO asked that the administration formally request consultations on the matter, as called for under the PTA's dispute settlement provisions, but the administration declined to do so. Instead, the U.S. trade representative turned to the joint committee created to implement the trade agreement to "address these issues as a matter of priority," and the committee, in turn, created a Working Group on Labor Affairs. The formal dispute settlement procedures under the PTA were never invoked, but the two governments collaborated with the ILO and the International Finance Corporation to create a Better Work program to monitor labor standards in the clothing sector and to beef up the capacity of Jordan's Labor Ministry to enforce its laws (box 20.4).

CAFTA–DR: Capacity Building and Coalition Building

The agreement signed in August 2004 between the United States and CAFTA–DR (the five Central American countries of Costa Rica, El Salvador, Guatemala, Honduras, and Nicaragua, plus the Dominican Republic) was the most politically controversial PTA since NAFTA. When finally approved by Congress in 2005, it passed the House

of Representatives by only a slim margin, mainly because of concerns about the adequacy of labor standards in the region. In order to build support for the agreement in the United States, a package of technical and financial assistance to support capacity building for improved implementation and enforcement of labor standards in the region was negotiated. The initial appropriation for the program was US$57 million for fiscal years 2005–07; an additional US$15 million was appropriated for fiscal 2008 (U.S. DOL 2009).

In April 2005 the labor ministries from the six partner countries, with support from the Inter-American Development Bank, issued a white paper, "Building on Progress: Strengthening Compliance and Enhancing Capacity." The ILO, as part of a verification project funded by USAID, issued a baseline report for assessing implementation of the white paper recommendations in 2007. In January 2009 the International Affairs Bureau of the U.S. Department of Labor issued its first report to Congress on progress in implementing the capacity-building provisions under the labor chapter of the PTA, concluding that results had been mixed (U.S. DOL 2009). It is difficult to assess the degree to which working conditions have really changed because the progress report mainly cites measures of inputs—budget increases, inspectors hired or trained, workshops held, and radio advertisements aired. It seems likely that economic conditions in Central America—increased competition from China and the rest of Asia after expiration of the Multifibre Arrangement quotas on textiles and clothing, and a global economic recession—have had greater, and negative, effects on jobs, wages, and working conditions.

Box 20.4. Responding to a Sweatshop Scandal through Capacity Building and Monitoring

In early 2006, the National Labor Committee (NLC), a New York-based nongovernmental organization that investigates labor abuses around the world, released a report alleging serious violations of worker rights in Jordanian garment factories employing mainly migrant workers from South Asia and China and exporting to the United States. The AFL-CIO, the main U.S. union federation, took up the case, filing a petition under the U.S. preferential trade agreement (PTA) with Jordan and pointing out a major gap in Jordanian labor laws, which require workers to be citizens in order to be eligible to join unions.

The Jordanian government responded immediately and, in coordination with the U.S. Agency for International Development (USAID), ordered an independent investigation, which confirmed many of the NLC's allegations. The government also took a number of immediate steps between May 2006 and the end of the year, which included raising the minimum wage, increasing the Ministry of Labor budget by 80 percent, beefing up inspections and closing some factories, creating a multilingual hotline for worker complaints, launching a review of its labor laws with the aim of bringing them closer to international standards, and reaching agreement with the ILO on developing a Decent Work country program.

In February 2008, Jordan, the ILO, and the International Finance Corporation (IFC) launched the Better Work Jordan Project, to be jointly funded by the Jordanian government and USAID. In addition to independent monitoring and transparent reporting on factory conditions to encourage improvements in labor standards compliance, the project also has an explicit objective of improving "enterprise performance in global supply chains in developing countries." The factory assessments will be entered in a database that can be made available to buyers or others as desired by participating factories. Public reports will be issued containing aggregated data on trends and the key issues uncovered, as well as documents naming individual factories and providing indicators of performance in key areas. It is hoped that the system will be credible enough that international buyers will forgo their own factory audits, as Wal-Mart and Sears/Kmart have agreed to do, thereby lowering costs for both factory and buyer.

Source: ILO and IFC 2007; Jordan 2008; NLC 2006.

Conclusions

In recent years, there appears to have developed, at least among a few major rich countries, a degree of convergence that worker rights should be addressed in trade agreements and that they should be based on the principles in the 1998 ILO Declaration. Beyond that, four main conclusions emerge from this review of experience with labor provisions in PTAs.

First, enforceable provisions for labor standards are a condition for negotiating a PTA with the United States and are likely to remain so. Moreover, recent experience suggests that developing countries contemplating negotiation of a PTA with the United States should be prepared to undertake reforms to bring their laws into broad conformity with the eight ILO conventions associated with the four core labor standards.

Second, labor provisions in PTAs not involving the United States or Canada are unusual and are almost always hortatory, rather than legally binding or enforceable. In the Canadian case, the provisions are in side agreements, with a separate dispute settlement process and a focus on cooperation, rather than negative sanctions—although the latter are not always ruled out.

Third, the EU also appears to be joining the trend, if the model used in its economic partnership agreement with the Caribbean is replicated in other similar agreements. However, the language on labor, although nominally binding, includes no sanctions for noncompliance.

Fourth, whatever the details of the language on labor standards in trade agreements, there has been little attention to implementation in most cases, and therefore little impact on the developing countries that sign these agreements. Even under U.S. PTAs, which contain the strongest language on paper, enforcement is rare, and sanctions have never been applied. Unfortunately, financial and technical capacity-building assistance to improve labor standard implementation is also rare.

The experience analyzed here suggests that developing-country governments need not fear the inclusion of labor standards in PTAs, although the evolution of the U.S. trade policy approach bears careful watching. Indeed, governments seeking to strengthen their economies and societies by, among other things, spreading the benefits of globalization and growth more broadly, may welcome rather than resist pressures concerning labor standards. Moreover, if the issue remains important to the United States, developing countries should bargain for something they want—perhaps assistance in creating or strengthening safety nets or other adjustment programs to address the costs borne by workers or firms negatively affected by the PTA.

Notes

1. For the text of the declaration, along with the follow-up reports, see http://www.ilo.org/declaration/ (accessed June 17, 2010).

2. This section draws heavily on Elliott and Freeman (2003, ch. 1) and the references cited therein.

3. The evidence and analysis are presented in detail in Elliott and Freeman (2003); Elliott (2004) applies the analysis to the U.S. PTA with Central America.

4. The declaration applies to all ILO members, whether or not they have ratified the associated conventions. Thus, all members are expected to promote those broad principles, but those that have not ratified a convention, with the exception of Conventions 87 and 98, dealing with freedom of association and the right to collective bargaining, cannot be challenged for failing to implement all of the detailed obligations contained in the conventions. Freedom of association is considered so fundamental that there is a special review and complaints mechanism for those conventions. The other conventions are Conventions 29 and 105, concerning prohibition of forced labor; Conventions 138 and 182, calling for the eradication of harmful child labor; and Conventions 100 and 111, covering nondiscrimination and equal remuneration in wages.

5. Hafner-Burton (2009) compellingly analyzes the political versus the moral and other motivations for including human rights provisions in trade agreements.

6. See, for example, the issues of *Inside U.S. Trade* for January 19, 2009, on Peru, and April 10, 2009, on Panama. Information on all these trade agreements, including, in many cases, fact sheets on the labor provisions and on how countries have responded to demands for labor law reform, can be found on the Office of the U.S. Trade Representative website, http://www.ustr.gov/trade-agreements/free-trade-agreements. See also Rogowsky and Chyn (2007).

7. In the case of a bilateral dispute between the United States and Mexico, bilateral tariff concessions can be withdrawn to the extent necessary to collect the value of the fine, but this provision is not regarded as authorizing trade *sanctions*. Elliott (2001) analyzes the fine mechanism and how it might work if implemented.

8. "Clinton, Obama Pledge to Withdraw from NAFTA unless Renegotiated," *Inside U.S. Trade*, February 29, 2008.

9. Horn, Mavroidis, and Sapir (2010) examine 14 U.S. and 14 EU PTAs. Bourgeois, Dawar, and Evenett (2007), in a study for the European Commission, examine 27 PTAs involving Western Hemisphere, Asian, and European Free Trade Association (EFTA) countries.

10. The discussion that follows is based on an examination of agreement texts identified on national government websites; the WTO database on regional trade agreements, http://rtais.wto.org/UI/PublicMaintainRTAHome.aspx; and the Organization of American States database, http://www.sice.oas.org/agreements_e.asp.

11. This discussion draws on the agreement texts and related information posted on the website of the Canadian Department of Foreign Affairs and International Trade, http://www.international.gc.ca/trade-agreements-accords-commerciaux/index.aspx?lang=eng.

12. See the links to the individual agreements at the Human Resources and Skills Development Canada website, "International Labour Affairs," http://www.hrsdc.gc.ca/eng/labour/labour_globalization/ila/index.shtml (accessed June 22, 2010).

13. Human Resources and Skills Development Canada website, "Canada–Colombia Agreement on Labour Cooperation," http://www.hrsdc.gc.ca/eng/labour/labour_agreements/ccalc/index.shtml.

14. Human Resources and Skills Development Canada website, "Overview: The International Trade and Labour Grants and Contribution Programme," http://www.hrsdc.gc.ca/eng/lp/ila/Overview.shtml (accessed June 25, 2010).

15. The letter to Guatemala requesting consultations may be found at the USTR website, http://www.ustr.gov/trade-agreements/free-trade-agreements/cafta-dr-dominican-republic-central-america-fta/kirk-solis-le.

16. Office of Trade and Labor Affairs, Bureau of International Labor Affairs, U.S. Department of Labor, Public Report of Review under the Dominican Republic–Central America–United States Free Trade Agreement, Chapter 16: "Labor," January 16, 2009.

17. U.S. Trade Representative Ron Kirk, "Remarks on Enforcement at Allegheny Technologies, Washington, Pennsylvania," July 30, 2010, http://www.ustr.gov/about-us/press-office/speeches/transcripts/2010/july/remarks-ambassador-ron-kirk-enforcement-alleghn.

18. See the website of the U.S. contact point, http://www.dol.gov/ilab/programs/nao/naalc.htm.

19. An updated list of submissions and their status may be found at the NAALC website, http://www.naalc.org/userfiles/file/NAALC-Public-Communications-and-Results-1994-2008.pdf.

20. Bolle (2001, 6); this report also provides a useful summary of the debate over labor standards in trade agreements as of the early 2000s.

References

Aidt, Toke, and Zafiris Tzannatos. 2002. *Unions and Collective Bargaining: Economic Effects in a Global Environment*. Washington, DC: World Bank.

Bolle, Mary Jane. 2001. "Jordan–U.S. Free Trade Agreement: Labor Issues." Report RS20968, Congressional Research Service, Library of Congress, Washington, DC.

Bourgeois, Jacques, Kamala Dawar, and Simon J. Evenett. 2007. "A Comparative Analysis of Selected Provisions in Free Trade Agreements." Prepared for the Directorate General for Trade, European Union, Brussels.

Buchanan, Ruth, and Rusby Chaparro. 2008. "International Institutions and Transnational Advocacy: The Case of the North American Agreement on Labor Cooperation." *UCLA Journal of International Law and Foreign Affairs* 13(1): 129–60.

CITEE (Centre for International Trade, Economics and Environment). 2004. "Trade-Labour Debate: The State of Affairs." Research Report, CUTS (Consumer Unity & Trust Society) International, Jaipur.

Destler, I. M. 2005. *American Trade Politics*. 4th ed. Washington, DC: Peterson Institute for International Economics.

Elliott, Kimberly Ann. 2001. "Fin(d)ing Our Way on Trade and Labor Standards?" International Economics Policy Brief PB01-5, Peterson Institute for International Economics, Washington, DC. http://www.piie.com/publications/pb/pb.cfm?ResearchID=73.

———. 2004. "Labor Standards, Development, and CAFTA." International Economics Policy Brief PB04-2, Peterson Institute for International Economics, Washington, DC. http://www.piie.com/publications/pb/pb04-2.pdf. Also published as "Trading Up: Labor Standards, Development, and CAFTA," *CDG Brief* 3 (2, May) (Washington, DC: Center for Global Development).

———. 2007. "Appendix A. Treatment of Labor Issues in US Bilateral Trade Agreements." In "American Trade Politics 2007: Building Bipartisan Consensus," ed. I. M. (Mac) Destler, Policy Brief PB07-5, Peterson Institute for International Economics, Washington, DC.

Elliott, Kimberly Ann, and Richard B. Freeman. 2003. *Can Labor Standards Improve under Globalization?* Washington, DC: Peterson Institute for International Economics.

EU (European Union), Directorate General for Trade. 2008. "CARIFORUM–EU Economic Partnership Agreement." Information Paper, EU, Brussels.

Freeman, Richard B., and James L. Medoff. 1984. *What Do Unions Do?* New York: Basic Books.

Hafner-Burton, Emilie M. 2009. *Forced to Be Good: Why Trade Agreements Boost Human Rights*. Cornell, NY: Cornell University Press.

Horn, Henrik, Petros C. Mavroidis, and Andre Sapir. 2010. "Beyond the WTO? An Anatomy of EU and US Preferential Trade Agreements." *World Economy* 33 (11): 1565–88.

Hornbeck, J. F. 2009. "Free Trade Agreements: U.S. Promotion and Oversight of Latin American Implementation." Inter-American Development Bank Policy Brief, Inter-American Development Bank, Washington, DC.

Hufbauer, Gary Clyde, and Jeffrey J. Schott, assisted by Paul L. E. Grieco and Yee Wong. 2005. *NAFTA Revisited: Achievements and Challenges*. Washington, DC: Peterson Institute for International Economics.

ILO (International Labour Office) and IFC (International Finance Corporation). 2007. "Better Work Jordan: Project Document." Prepared for Ministry of Labour, Amman, Jordan, and U.S. Agency for International Development, Washington, DC.

Jordan, Ministry of Labour. 2008. "Labour Administration and Compliance in Jordan: A Multi-Stakeholder Collaboration."Ministry of Labour, Amman.

Mayer, Frederick W. 1998. *Interpreting NAFTA: The Science and Art of Political Analysis.* New York: Columbia University Press.

NLC (National Labor Committee). 2006. "Campaigns: Jordan." National Labor Committee, Pittsburgh, PA. http://www.nlcnet.org/campaigns?id =0017.

Polaski, Sandra. 2006. "Combining Global and Local Forces: The Case of Labor Rights in Cambodia." *World Development* 34 (5, May): 919–32.

Rogowsky, Robert A., and Eric Chyn. 2007. "U.S. Trade Law and FTAs: A Survey of Labor Requirements." *Journal of International Commerce and Economics* (July). United States International Trade Commission, Washington, DC. http://www.usitc.gov/publications/332/journals/ trade_law_ftas.pdf.

U.S. DOL (Department of Labor), Bureau of International Labor Affairs. 2009. "Progress in Implementing Capacity-Building Provisions under the Labor Chapter of the Dominican Republic–Central America–United States Free Trade Agreement. First Biennial Report Submitted to Congress Pursuant to Section 403(a)(3) of the Dominican Republic–Central America–United States Free Trade Agreement Implementation Act." January 14, U.S. DOL, Washington, DC.

U.S. GAO (General Accountability Office). 2009. "Four Free Trade Agreements GAO Reviewed Have Resulted in Commercial Benefits, but Challenges on Labor and Environment Remain." Highlights of GAO-09-439 (July), GAO, Washington, DC.

USTR (Office of the U.S. Trade Representative). 2009. "The President's Trade Policy Agenda." USTR, Washington, DC. http://www.ustr.gov/assets/ Document_Library/Reports_Publications/2009/2009_Trade_Policy_ Agenda/asset_upload_file810_15401.pdf (accessed March 12, 2009).

21

HUMAN RIGHTS

Susan Ariel Aaronson

Many of the world's most important trading economies have introduced human rights language into their preferential trade agreements (PTAs). As a result, more than 70 percent of the world's governments now participate in PTAs with human rights requirements. The growing number and scope of these trade agreements reflects a new reality: policy makers understand that economic integration will not be successful without a stronger focus on improving governance among trade partners. If human rights provisions are designed carefully, they can work both to improve governance and to empower people to claim their rights. Yet policy makers, scholars, and activists still know very little about the effects of including human rights provisions in trade agreements.

As long as men and women have traded, they have wrestled with how to advance human rights while expanding trade. In some instances, policy makers have used the incentive of trade expansion; at other times they have used trade sanctions—the disincentive of lost trade—to punish officials from other countries that have undermined human rights. For example, after the United Kingdom and the United States outlawed the slave trade in 1807, the United Kingdom signed treaties with Denmark, Portugal, and Sweden to reinforce its own ban. After the United States banned goods manufactured by convict labor, Australia, Canada, and the United Kingdom adopted similar measures. These efforts stimulated international cooperation, and in 1919 the signatories of the Treaty of Versailles formed the International Labour Organization (ILO) to establish fair and humane rules regarding the treatment of labor (Bidwell 1939).

The United States and the European Union (EU) were the first trade entities to include human rights language in trade agreements. In the 1980s and 1990s, U.S. and EU officials began to include human rights conditionality clauses in their preference programs (Charnovitz 2005, 29, n. 103–05). The 1993 North American Free Trade Agreement (NAFTA),

signed by Canada, Mexico, and the United States, was the first PTA to include explicit human rights provisions. Trade policy makers agreed to include labor rights in a side agreement. They also included additional chapters and language focused on encouraging transparency (access to information) and public participation. These obligations went beyond the provisions of the General Agreement on Tariffs and Trade (GATT) and its successor organization, the World Trade Organization (WTO); scholars call this WTO+.

Some analysts see these provisions as "legal inflation" and assert that governments are using trade agreements to globalize their social policies or regulatory approaches. They argue that trade agreements are not the right place to address human rights issues, and they point out that trade agreements in themselves, even without special provisions, may have positive human rights spillovers. Whatever the arguments, the proliferation of human rights provisions signals the new reality for trade liberalization. Many PTAs go far beyond commercial policy; they are really governance agreements that contain thousands of pages of obligations related to topics ranging from corporate governance to environmental policy to human rights. Still, the association of trade and human rights in PTAs is a relatively new phenomenon. In a sense it is a shotgun wedding; and it is too early to tell whether this marriage will be effective and enduring. This chapter examines the who, what, when, where, how, and why of the trade–human rights linkage and why we should care about it.

Who? The demandeurs for the link include both industrial and developing countries, and at least 131 countries have accepted such links.[1]

What? Human rights are rights and freedoms to which all humans are entitled. Our discussion is limited to only those human rights set forth in the Universal Declaration of Human Rights (UDHR).[2] This study finds that only some of the human rights contained in the declaration have been incorporated into trade agreements.

When? Policy makers first made an explicit link between human rights and trade in the U.S. generalized system of preferences (GSP) program in 1984. NAFTA, signed in 1993, was the first preferential trade agreement to include specific human rights language.

Where? The provisions may be found in the preamble, in side agreements, or in the body of the agreement.

How? Some countries condition the agreement on the partner's changing its laws to meet international standards (the U.S. approach); others commit governments "not to reduce" high standards in the interests of attracting investment or trade. Examples of the latter approach are the agreement between the European Free Trade Association (EFTA) and the South African Customs Union (SACU), and the PTA between the United States and Colombia (Bartels 2009a). The "how" can also relate to whether the demandeur and the target government adopt monitoring or enforcement strategies in concert with the agreement; whether they link the agreement to capacity building designed to build governance expertise and will; and whether one signatory can challenge human rights violations of the trade agreement or suspend it.

Why? We discuss below the reasons why nations might include human rights provisions and why states accept them.

So what? We also discuss the outcomes of efforts to link trade and human rights. Some governments have changed their attitudes and behavior toward particular human rights. We don't know if this change in attitudes and behavior toward human rights is temporary or permanent. This chapter does not cover all the human rights provisions in all PTAs. The discussion is limited to PTAs with explicit human rights objectives, language, or policies, no matter whether the language occurs in the preamble, in the provisions of the agreement, or in a side agreement.[3] We also explore human rights spillovers from provisions related to access to information (transparency), political participation, and due process, according to which foreign and domestic producers can comment on policies or regulations affecting trade. Although property rights are important human rights, we do not focus on them except when trade agreements mention the intersection of property rights with other important human rights such as access to medicines (Drahos and Mayne 2002; WHO 2006).

The chapter is organized in three sections. The first section is foundational; it defines human rights, examines the history of the global trading system and the role of human rights, and reviews the literature in this area. The second section describes how and why the United States, the EU, EFTA, and Canada became the main demandeurs of provisions for human rights governance. Next, we examine human rights language in PTAs negotiated by emerging economies. Finally, the third section explores some of the problems and questions raised by the union of trade and human rights. I then offer a conclusion about why governments are increasingly wedding trade and human rights and whether this policy union will thrive.

Definitions and Background on Human Rights

This section discusses the international law of human rights and the role of human rights in trade agreements, including the International Trade Organization (ITO), the GATT, and the WTO. We then briefly review the findings of scholars active in human rights and trade issues.

Human Rights Obligations of Trading Nations

States are obligated to act in certain ways in order to protect, respect, and advance human rights. These obligations are delineated in the Universal Declaration on Human Rights (UDHR), which was approved by the members of the United Nations in 1948 and which spells out more than 30 rights that member states are supposed to promote and protect. But the declaration does not legally bind member states (Petersmann 2000). To ensure that human rights would be binding obligations, policy makers developed two covenants that included all the UDHR rights: the International Covenant on Civil and Political Rights (ICCPR), and the International Covenant on Economic, Social and Cultural Rights (ICESCR).[4] The ICCPR enumerates the rights that a state may not take away from its citizens, such as freedom of speech and freedom of movement. In contrast, the ICESCR generally defines rights (often, necessities) that a state should provide for its citizens, such as basic education or health care. The signatories of the ICESCR recognize that governments need expertise and funds to provide all their citizens with rights such as access to education, jobs, and health care. But it is difficult for governments to advance, respect, and realize human rights; it takes considerable governance expertise, funds, and will. Accordingly, a government is only obligated to provide these cultural, economic, and social rights as far as "it is able."[5]

The declaration and the covenants have different standings in international law. The Universal Declaration of Human Rights is universal in scope; it applies to everyone, whether or not individual governments have formally accepted its principles or ratified the covenants. The covenants, by their nature as multilateral conventions, are legally binding only on those states that have accepted them by ratification or accession. They did not go into force until 1976, when 35 member states of the United Nations ratified them. However, many nations have not ratified both covenants.[6] In addition, the Universal Declaration does not include all the human rights found in national constitutions, nor does it include many new human rights, such as the right to a healthy environment. Since these newer rights are not embodied in the covenants, they are, thus far, not binding on states, and so they are not discussed in this chapter.

Of the 38 human rights set forth in the UDHR, some rights are not affected by or are not relevant to trade, but others, such as labor rights, have been explicitly mentioned in trade agreements (see table 21.1). Table 21.2 summarizes some of the human rights embedded in trade agreements, as of 2010. Some human rights provisions are in the preamble; others are in the body; and still others are expressed in side agreements. Some provisions are binding on the signatories of the agreement, and others are rhetorical.

Under international law, states are supposed to do everything in their power to respect, promote, and fulfill human rights. But advancing human rights is not easy. As noted above, many states are unable to meet all of their "international" human rights responsibilities. Moreover, few officials win or maintain office on the basis of their efforts to promote the human rights of noncitizens.

However, many people are not comfortable knowing that other human beings lack basic rights in other countries, or live in countries where government officials undermine human rights. These individuals may demand that policy makers take action to protect human rights in other countries. Trade policy is not the only or the best means of extending such protection, but policy makers

have few options short of force for changing the behavior of leaders of other countries. Market access can be an important instrument of leverage because it can affect the economic and political health of targeted countries. Furthermore, in recent years policy makers have come to understand that failure to protect human rights (such as labor rights) can affect market access conditions for their own producers.[7]

Although policy makers may respond to public pressure to use trade to advance human rights, most policy makers do not make human rights a top priority for trade policy making. In most countries, policy makers develop trade policies as though they were strictly commercial instruments. They weigh the interests of their producers and consumers, and although they may consider national security or political concerns, they rarely introduce the interests of the global community into such deliberations. Although policy makers are well aware of the human rights consequences of some of their trade decisions, they have few incentives to ensure that trade policies advance the human rights outlined under the UDHR. Moreover, trade policy makers are generally not charged with ensuring that trade policies or trade flows do not undermine specific human rights at home or abroad. In trade negotiations, governments are charged with pursuing national commercial interests, not global interests (Commission on Human Rights 2004; 3D 2005; Aaronson and Zimmerman 2007).

ITO, GATT, and WTO Provisions on Human Rights

During World War II, the postwar planners devised several international institutions to govern the global economy. They envisioned an International Trade Organization (ITO)

Table 21.1. Examples of Human Rights Embedded in PTAs: Demandeurs and Position of Provisions in Agreement

Labor rights	Democratic rights	Access to affordable medicines	Right to cultural participation	Freedom of movement	Indigenous minority rights	Political participation and due process	Privacy
Canada Preamble and side agreement	*Mercosur* Linked protocol	*Costa Rica*	*Canada*	*EFTA/EEA* Body	*Canada* Preamble and side agreements	*Canada* Body and side agreements	*Canada* Body
Chile Side agreement		*United States* Side letters	*New Zealand*	*CARICOM* Body	*New Zealand*		*EU* Body
Mercosur Body					*Australia*	*United States* Body	
United States Body							
New Zealand							

Source: Susan Ariel Aaronson.
Note: CARICOM, Caribbean Community; EEA, European Economic Area; EFTA, European Free Trade Association; EU, European Union; Mercosur, Southern Cone Common Market (Mercado Común del Sur); PTA, preferential trade agreement.

Table 21.2. The Universal Declaration on Human Rights and Its Two Covenants

International Covenant on Civil and Political Rights	International Covenant on Economic, Social and Cultural Rights
Right to life (Art. 3)	Right to marriage and found a family (Art. 16)
Right to liberty (Art. 3)	Right to social security (Art. 22)
Right to security (Art. 3)	*Right to work, free choice of employment, just and favorable conditions of work, and protection against unemployment (Art. 23.1)*
Right to the abolition of slavery and slave trade (Art. 4)	*Right to equal pay for equal work (Art. 23.2)*
Right to the prevention of torture or cruel, inhuman, or degrading treatment or punishment (Art. 5)	Right to just and favorable remuneration (Art. 23.3)
Right to recognition before the law (Art. 6)	*Right to form and join a trade union (Art. 23.4)*
Right to equality before the law and to equal protection of the law (Art. 7)	Right to rest and leisure, including reasonable limitation of working hours and periodic holidays with pay (Art. 24)
Right to effective judicial remedy (Art. 8)	*Right to a sustainable standard of living (including food, clothing, housing, medical care, and necessary social services); right to security in the event of unemployment, sickness, disability, widowhood, old age, or other lack of livelihood in circumstances beyond his control (Art. 25.1)*
Right to the prevention of arbitrary arrest, detention, or exile (Art. 9)	Right to special care and assistance for motherhood and childhood (Art. 25.2)
Right to fair and public hearing by a neutral tribunal (Art. 10)	Right to education (Art. 26)
Right to presumption of innocence (Art. 11.1)	*Right to cultural participation (Art. 27.1)*
Right to nonretroactive penal code (Art. 11.2)	*Right to the protection of intellectual property (Art. 27.2)*
Right to privacy (Art. 12)	
Right to freedom of movement and residence in the country (Art. 13.1)	
Right to leave the country and return (Art. 13.2)	
Right to seek and enjoy asylum from prosecution (Art. 14)	
Right to a nationality (Art. 15)	
Right to freedom of thought, conscience, and religion (Art. 18)	
Right to freedom of opinion and expression (Art. 19)	
Right to freedom of peaceful assembly and association (Art. 20)	
Right to governmental participation, directly or through freely chosen representatives (Art. 21.1)	
Right of equal access to public services (Art. 21.2)	
Right to periodic and fair elections (Art. 21.3)	

Source: Prepared by Philip Van der Celen; in Aaronson and Zimmerman 2007.
Note: Italics indicate that the right is included in one or more preferential trade agreements (PTAs).

to reduce barriers to trade. The draft treaty for the ITO was the first trade agreement to include explicit human rights language (related to labor rights). The ITO was designed to ensure that signatories to the agreement did not "export their unemployment" and thereby undermine the ability of workers to provide for their families. In addition, the draft ITO allowed signatories to breach its rules through an "exception" for domestic policies "necessary to protect public morals" or to protect human or plant life and health. (It also included a national security exception.) But the ITO was abandoned after the U.S. Congress failed to vote on implementing legislation (Wilcox 1949; Diebold 1952; Charnovitz 1987).

The end of the ITO was not the death knell of efforts to link trade and human rights. In 1995 the members of the GATT agreed to join a new international organization, the World Trade Organization (WTO). The WTO contains the GATT agreement, and it has a stronger system of dispute settlement. GATT and WTO signatories must adhere to two key principles to reduce trade distortions: the most favored nation principle and the national treatment principle. The most favored nation principle (MFN) requires that the best trading conditions extended to one member by a nation must be extended automatically to every other nation. The national treatment principle provides that once a product is imported, the importing state may not subject that product to regulations less favorable than those that apply to like products produced domestically. The WTO does not explicitly prohibit countries from protecting human rights at home or abroad, but its rules do constrain the behavior of governments in providing that when member states seek to promote human rights, at home or abroad, they must not unnecessarily or unduly distort trade. It is hard to use trade to promote human rights when nations can't use trade to distinguish among those nations that may undermine the human rights of their citizens and those that strive to advance these rights.

The GATT and the WTO do not directly address how governments relate to their own citizens, and they say very little about human rights.[8] But human rights are seeping into the workings of the WTO (Aaronson 2007). Some WTO members have used the GATT/WTO exceptions to advance human rights abroad or to protect human rights at home. Under Article XX, nations can restrict trade when necessary to "protect human, animal, or plant life or health" or to conserve exhaustible natural resources. This article also states that governments may restrict imports relating to the products of prison labor. Although it does not refer explicitly to human rights, the public morals clause of Article XX is widely seen as allowing WTO members to put in place trade bans in the interest of promoting human rights (WTO 2001; Howse 2002; Charnovitz 2005). Brazil used the Article XX exception to ban imports of retreaded tires, which could not easily be disposed of.

The national security exception, Article XXI, states that WTO rules should not prevent nations from protecting their own security. Members are not permitted to take trade action to protect another member's security or to protect the citizens of another member. If, however, the United Nations Security Council authorizes trade sanctions, WTO rules allow countries to use such measures to promote human rights, as when sanctions were instituted against South Africa's apartheid regime in the 1980s (Aaronson and Zimmerman 2007, 19).

Members of the GATT/WTO can use other avenues to protect human rights at home and within other member states (table 21.3). In recent years, member states have used temporary waivers of GATT rules to promote human rights. For example, after the UN called for a ban in trade in conflict diamonds, WTO member states agreed to temporarily waive WTO rules to allow trade in only those diamonds certified by the Kimberley process to be free of

conflict (Aaronson and Zimmerman 2007, 43). In addition, some members bring up human rights during accessions, when new members are asked to make their trade and other public policies transparent, accountable, and responsive. They have also discussed human rights issues at trade policy reviews, when member states review the trade and governance performance of other member states. Finally, members have discussed some human rights issues during recent trade negotiations: examples include food security, intellectual property rights (IPRs), and public health (Aaronson 2007).

Although the GATT/WTO contains no explicit human rights provisions, it does refer to human rights implicitly. Some of these provisions relate to economic rights such as the right to property, and others, to democratic and political rights. For example, under GATT/WTO rules, member states give economic actors "an entitlement to substantive rights in domestic law including the right to seek relief; the right to submit comments to a national agency or the right to appeal adjudicatory rulings" (Charnovitz 2001). Member states must also ensure that "Members and other persons affected, or likely to be affected, by governmental measures imposing restraints, requirements and other burdens, should have a reasonable opportunity to acquire authentic information about such measures and accordingly to protect and adjust their activities or alternatively to seek modification of such measures."[9] These can be termed due process, information, and political participation rights (Powell 2005); see box 21.1.[10]

A Brief Review of the Literature on Trade and Human Rights

In recent years, scholars from many disciplines have examined the relationship between trade and human rights. Many economists argue that human rights is not a trade issue, but trade can have positive human rights spillovers. As trade expands, individuals exchange ideas, technologies, processes, and cultural norms and goods. With more trade, people in countries with fewer rights and freedoms become aware of conditions elsewhere, and with such knowledge, they may demand greater rights. Isolated

Table 21.3. Examples of Avenues and Actions at the WTO Related to Human Rights, 2005–10

Avenue	Human right affected
Accessions	Labor rights, access to information, due process (Vietnam, Saudi Arabia, Cambodia)
Trade policy reviews	Members discussed labor rights, women's rights, access to medicines
Disputes	Right to health (Brazil tires)
Negotiations	Access to safe, affordable food

Source: Susan Ariel Aaronson.

Box 21.1. Transparency, Due Process, and Democracy Spillovers from the WTO

From 1948 to 1964, contracting parties to the General Agreement on Tariffs and Trade (GATT) were required to promptly publish laws, regulations, and judicial decisions affecting imports and exports (GATT Article X). In this way, exporting interests could learn about legal developments affecting trade and respond to them. GATT contracting parties gradually strengthened these notification requirements, and members were required to administer trade-related laws, regulations, rulings, and agreements in a uniform, impartial, and reasonable manner. Today, the World Trade Organization (WTO) has strong rules for transparency and due process. It requires governments to make their trade laws and regulations transparent and public and to allow citizens to comment on and challenge these laws and regulations. However, neither the GATT nor the WTO *requires* that members involve their publics in trade policy making. Moreover, many countries do not have a free press, adequate funds, informational infrastructure, or the political will to effectively involve their citizenry in public policy making.

The GATT/WTO may also have some unintended human rights spillovers. Member states must provide the same rules and privileges to domestic and foreign actors. These provisions may prod policymakers to provide access to information and enforce rights to public comment in countries where governance is not transparent and participatory. In repressive states, WTO rules may empower domestic market actors (consumers and taxpayers, as well as producers) who may not have been able to use existing domestic remedies to obtain information, influence policies, or challenge their leaders (Aaronson and Abouharb forthcoming). In WTO countries without a strong democratic tradition, member states may make these changes because they want to signal investors that they can be trusted to enforce property rights, uphold the rule of law, and act in an evenhanded, impartial manner (Dobbin, Simmons, and Garrett 2007; Büthe and Milner 2008; Mansfield and Pevehouse 2008, 273).

societies, by contrast, may be more prone to human rights abuses (van Hees 2004). Thus, many of these economists conclude that policy makers need not include human rights provisions in trade agreements (Bhagwati 1996, 1; Sykes 2003, 2–4). Other analysts disagree; they believe that human rights are trade issues, and they cite history and the increasing number of human rights provisions in PTAs as evidence for their perspective. Some legal scholars have proposed ways of finding common ground between WTO trade law and international human rights law (Charnovitz 1994; Dunoff 1999; Garcia 1999; Mehra 1999; Petersmann 2001). Some believe that the best strategy is to enhance the international human rights system and make it more like the WTO, with stronger dispute settlement and enforcement mechanisms. Others believe that the WTO should have explicit human rights provisions (Lim 2001). Some academics have used case studies to discuss the relationship between trade agreements and specific human rights, such as the right to food (Cottier, Pauwelyn, and Bürgi 2005). Others have suggested bridging mechanisms to ensure better dialogue and coordination between trade and human rights officials (Petersmann 2002). Finally, some scholars have examined how the WTO's dispute settlement system might address a trade dispute involving human rights (Bal 2001; Marceau 2001). However, as policy makers began to refocus their trade liberalization efforts on new PTAs, the debate over how best to reach trade and human rights goals has moved to examining the record of these PTAs.

Most of the scholars who have examined human rights provisions focus on labor and environmental language—what some call "trade and" provisions. Dawar (2008) finds that labor and environmental provisions "constitute an unnecessary, inefficient and inappropriate use of a trade agreement." Bourgeois, Dawar, and Evenett (2007) argue that the current approach to mainstreaming labor rights in PTAs is ineffective because the provisions commit parties to enforce domestic labor law only. Horn, Mavroidis, and Sapir (2010) conclude that U.S. and EU environmental and labor standards in PTAs are groundbreaking "means for the two hubs to export their own regulatory approaches to their PTA partners." In short, some scholars see the link as ineffective; others as a means of exporting governance. But these scholars did not examine the panoply of trade–human rights links; they have focused only on labor rights

Scholars who have examined human rights provisions in PTAs agree that these provisions are intended to improve governance and advance human rights. Petersmann (2006), a legal scholar, has argued that governments use their PTAs to achieve extraterritorial political reform. As evidence, he cites the growing number of governments that explicitly refer to human rights as an objective or as a fundamental principle of economic integration. Damro (2006) argues that governments include extensive human rights and rule of law provisions in their PTAs because they recognize they must develop coordinated policies in order to address regional threats to security, such as environmental damage, illegal migration, drug smuggling, and international terrorism.

In a number of studies, Bartels examines how governments incorporate human rights into their trade agreements (Bartels 2005b, 2008, 2009a, 2009b, and, for an analysis of the objectives of the agreements, Bartels 2005a). He concludes that provisions linking trade and human rights are useful because they set up mechanisms for dialogue, allow civil society in multiple countries to monitor compliance with international norms, and make human rights part of the trade relationship. Hafner-Burton (2009, 22) compares EU and U.S. approaches toward linking human rights and trade in their GSP and free trade agreements. She notes that although policy makers may be motivated by "protectionist intent," the agreements appear to be having a positive impact on the realization of human rights in many countries. Aaronson and Zimmerman (2007, 207) compare how the United States, the EU, South Africa, and Brazil make trade policy and find that governments are increasing the scope of human rights, as well as the number of agreements with human rights provisions. They conclude that if people are the "wealth of nations," policy makers that weigh human rights as they make trade policy are more likely to ensure that their citizens thrive at the intersection of trade and human rights.

Few scholars have examined the PTA–human rights nexus empirically. Hafner-Burton (2009, 160–64) focuses on physical integrity rights such as freedom from arbitrary imprisonment and finds that about 82 percent of the countries that have a PTA with the EU improve their human rights protection, as against 75 percent for countries without a trade agreement. However, she relies on personal integrity rights (for example, freedom from arbitrary imprisonment) to make a generic case about human rights, which is not fully convincing. PTAs may have different effects on different human rights. Finally, some scholars have examined whether PTAs serve as an anchor or lock-in mechanism for domestic reforms, including laws advancing human rights. U.S. International Trade Commission (USITC) economist Michael Ferrantino (2006) examined negotiations on PTAs with the United States. He argues that these agreements may improve governance but warns that it is difficult to ascertain whether a particular reform is stimulated by negotiations or by the

domestic reform process. Clearly, to better understand the impact of the PTAs, we need both more empirical work and country-specific case studies.

Case Studies: PTAs and Human Rights

This section examines how Canada, the EU, EFTA, and the United States incorporate human rights provision into their PTAs: table 21.4 summarizes their approaches.[11] Table 21.5 examines these provisions according to specific human rights and shows that industrialized countries are not the only countries to link human rights and trade in PTAs. We begin our analysis with Canada, which has become an enthusiastic negotiator of PTAs.

Canada

Canada is a trade-dependent nation; trade represents more than 70 percent of its gross domestic product (GDP). In recent years the Canadian government has embraced PTAs, on the grounds that this strategy will ensure trade-related economic growth and international competitiveness.[12] Canadian policy makers assert that these agreements can help Canada foster a commitment to human rights, freedom, democracy, and the rule of law.[13] In Canada the executive branch makes trade policy, which is then approved by the parliament. Although there is no explicit mandate regarding the relationship between trade and human rights, the Canadian government has included several types of human rights in its recent trade agreements: labor rights, cultural rights, indigenous rights, and rights to political participation and due process.[14]

Table 21.4. Human Rights in Preferential Trade Agreements: Comparing EFTA, the EU, the United States, and Canada

	EFTA	EU	United States	Canada
Strategy	Universal human rights	Universal human rights and specific rights	Specific human rights	Specific human rights
Which rights?		Labor rights, transparency, due process, political participation, and privacy rights	Transparency, due process, political participation, access to affordable medicines, and labor rights	Transparency, due process, political participation, labor rights, privacy rights, cultural and indigenous rights
How enforced?	No enforcement	Human rights violations lead to dialogue and possible suspension, depending on nature of violation.	In newest agreements, labor rights can be disputed under a dispute settlement body affiliated with the agreement; process begins with bilateral dialogue to resolve issues	Only labor rights (monetary penalties); use dialogue first
Any challenge?			First challenge: Guatemala	

Source: Susan Ariel Aaronson.
Note: EFTA, European Free Trade Agreement; EU, European Union.

Table 21.5. Examples of Human Rights Embedded in Preferential Trade Agreements

Labor rights	Democratic rights	Access to affordable medicines	Right to cultural participation	Freedom of movement	Indigenous rights	Political participation	Privacy
Canada	Mercosur	Costa Rica	Canada	EFTA	Canada	Canada	Canada
Chile		United States	New Zealand	EEA	New Zealand	United States	EU
Mercosur				CARICOM	Australia		
United States							
New Zealand							

Source: Susan Ariel Aaronson.
Note: CARICOM, Caribbean Community; EEA, European Economic Area; EFTA, European Free Trade Agreement; EU, European Union; Mercosur, Southern Cone Common Market (Mercado Común del Sur).

As of March 2011, Canada has negotiated eight PTAs: the Canadian–U.S. Free Trade Agreement (CUSFTA, now part of NAFTA), and agreements with Peru, EFTA, Costa Rica, Chile, Israel, Jordan, Panama, and Colombia, of which seven are in force. The Canadian government is soliciting public comment on negotiations with about 12 other countries or trading entities. It is engaged in active negotiations with many of these countries or entities.[15]

Canadian officials clearly see these trade agreements as governance agreements, although they do not call them that. The government asserts that "Canadians recognize that their interests are best served by a stable, rules-based international system. Countries which respect the rule of law tend to respect the rights of their citizens, [and] are more likely to benefit from development."[16] The Department of Foreign Affairs and International Trade (DFAIT) also notes that "The UN Charter and customary international law impose on all countries the responsibility to promote and protect human rights. This is not merely a question of values but a mutual obligation of all members of the international community."[17]

Overview of Canada's human rights–trade strategy. Canada's approach toward embedding human rights is both broad and specific. The preambles of recent agreements with EFTA, Jordan, Peru, and Colombia refer to human rights objectives, citing the UDHR, labor rights, cultural participation, and protection of human rights and freedoms.[18] These agreements include chapters with language on labor rights, transparency, and the environment. The agreements also contain a chapter on exceptions (akin to those in the WTO) and a provision safeguarding the right to regulate and to maintain high standards. The exceptions chapter notes that nothing in the agreement is to apply to cultural sectors and mentions the need to be supportive of trade waivers.[19]

Labor rights. Because of the division of powers in the areas of environmental and labor regulation under the Canadian constitution, Canadian policy makers believe that labor and environmental provisions cannot be included in the body of a trade agreement but must be in side agreements, termed labor cooperation agreements.[20] According to Human Development and Skills Resources Canada, which negotiates and monitors labor rights internationally, Canada has ratified six labor cooperation agreements in its PTAs with Chile, Costa Rica, Colombia, Jordan. Peru, and NAFTA. (Interestingly, Canada has also negotiated memoranda of understanding on labor cooperation outside its PTAs.)[21] The labor side agreements state that signatories must ensure that their labor laws comply with ILO standards and must establish offices to evaluate complaints related to labor rights. In this way, the side agreements are clearly governance agreements, since they attempt to build labor rights governance capacity.

The recent agreements also include a nonderogation clause stating that neither party shall waive or otherwise derogate from, or offer to waive or otherwise derogate from, its labor laws in order to encourage trade or investment (Article 2). Both parties commit not only to core standards but also to acceptable occupational health and safety protection and acceptable minimum employment standards. They also agree to provide migrant workers with the same legal protections as nationals with respect to working conditions.

These provisions go beyond ILO core labor standards because they also focus on both the demand (public) and supply (policy maker) sides of good labor governance. Signatories are required to educate and involve their publics regarding their rights under labor law. Article 4 articulates a right to private action: "Each party shall ensure that a person with a legally-recognized interest . . . has appropriate access . . . to administrative or tribunal proceedings . . ."[22] Article 5 contains procedural guarantees designed to ensure that proceedings "are fair, equitable, and transparent and respect due process of law." Canadian policy makers seem to agree that by educating foreign workers as to their rights, these workers are more likely to use these rights.

Due process provisions. Canada has expanded on the WTO's due process provisions for trade-related policy making. Chapter 19 (transparency) in recent Canadian PTAs requires each party to "ensure that in its administrative proceedings . . . persons of the other Party that are directly affected by a proceeding are provided reasonable notice . . . and reasonable opportunity to present facts and arguments in support of their positions."[23] The environmental side agreement also contains due process requirements.[24] Here again, Canada uses human rights language to prod its PTA partners to make trade-related policies in a transparent and accountable manner.

Political participation provisions. The Canadian government has incorporated several references to political participation into its recent trade agreements. This language is included in Chapter 19 on transparency, as well as in the labor and environmental side agreements. The transparency chapter obligates signatories to include regulations guaranteeing public participation, public comment, and the ability to challenge relevant regulations. The environmental chapter commits the parties "to promote public awareness of environmental laws and policies by ensuring that information regarding environmental laws and policies, as well as compliance and enforcement is available to the public." These provisions also commit the countries to ensure that the public is able to participate in environmental assessment procedures. In addition, they include a provision allowing any person residing in or established in the territory of either country to submit a written question to either country obliging the country to make the questions and responses available to the public. Although the language is binding, it is also relatively weak: the signatories are asked to *strive to cooperate* in these areas, *endeavor to engage the public,* or as the Colombia labor side agreement says, "*encourage[e]* education of the public regarding its labor laws" (emphasis added).

Cultural reservations and exemptions. Canada includes provisions in all its PTAs to ensure that these trade agreements do not affect Canada's ability to maintain the cultural heritage of the Canadian people or to determine Canadian cultural policies. These provisions are contained in the agreements' chapters on exceptions. The agreements define Canada's cultural industries as persons engaged in the publication, distribution, or sale of books, magazines, periodicals, newspapers, music, films and videos, and so on.[25]

Indigenous rights. The Canada–Colombia (as well as Canada–Peru) side agreement on the environment states, "The Parties also reiterate their commitment, as established by the Convention on Biological Diversity, to respect, preserve and maintain traditional knowledge, innovations and practices of indigenous and local communities that contribute to the conservation and sustainable use of biological diversity, subject to national legislation."[26] Because the provision is aspirational, nonbinding, and not disputable, some Canadian nongovernmental organizations (NGOs) see it as inadequate.

Response of Canadian NGOs to these human rights provisions. Canadian NGOs working on development, human rights, and labor rights remain critical of the country's approach. They demanded that Canada perform human rights impact assessments before it initials trade agreements with countries, such as Colombia, where the rule of law is inadequate.[27] They argue that such assessments must be conducted by international human rights bodies rather than by the two governments (CCIC 2009). This debate has influenced Canada's parliament, which seems increasingly interested in the relationship between trade agreement provisions and human rights and in whether Canada's approach to dealing with these rights is effective.[28] In 2010 Canada and Colombia agreed to perform yearly human rights impact assessments of their PTA.[29] Canada became the first nation to require such assessments with future trade agreements. However, as of March 2011, Canada has yet to do such a human rights impact assessment or to provide the public with information as to how it will evaluate human rights at home and abroad.

Canada's PTAs and human rights: A summary. The Canadian government has incorporated a wide range of human rights into its PTAs. Canada sees its human rights and trade work as complementary. Its approach is both hortatory and pragmatic, making use of language that sets forth explicit obligations and delineates objectives that the signatories will strive or endeavor to meet.

Some of this language, such as obligations focused on transparency and political participation, reflects longstanding Canadian norms on how to govern. Some of the provisions are designed to encourage some of Canada's trade partners to comply with international human rights norms such as labor rights. But Canadian policy makers recognize that it is not sufficient for outsiders to demand good governance. The public, both in Canada and in Canada's trade partners, must be informed about and involved in the development of rules if these rules are to be perceived as evenhanded and effective. Yet the Canadian public has not been very supportive of Canada's approach. Many Canadian NGOs see Canada's PTAs as opaque, ineffective at improving governance, and undemocratic (CCIC 2009).

Canada does not require all of its trade partners to adopt these human rights obligations. For example, it has not embedded many of these provisions in its PTA with EFTA, but, as the next section shows, neither EFTA nor

Canada "requires" such obligations in its PTAs. It will be interesting to see how Canada negotiates with the EU on labor and other human rights in preparation for a transatlantic free trade agreement. Negotiators working on scoping documents for these negotiations agreed that "it would be appropriate to address sustainable development issues through provisions on the environment and labor rights, including the core labor standards embodied in the 1998 ILO Declaration . . . Such provisions could include, inter alia: the right to regulate while aiming for high levels of protection; effective enforcement of environment and labor laws; a commitment to refrain from waiving such laws in a manner that affects trade or investment; a framework for cooperation; public involvement; and mechanisms to monitor and address disputes."[30]

European Free Trade Association (EFTA)

EFTA began in 1960 as a framework for liberalizing trade and promoting economic cooperation among several European nations. At that time, some EFTA member states were unwilling or unable (for reasons of sovereignty or neutrality) to join the EU. The membership of EFTA has changed over time; Austria, Denmark, Finland, Portugal, Sweden, and the United Kingdom left to join the EU. Iceland, Liechtenstein, Norway, and Switzerland are the members of EFTA as of March 2011.

In recent years, EFTA has become an active PTA negotiator. EFTA has 22 free trade agreements, covering 31 countries.[31] It is now negotiating with Algeria; Bosnia and Herzegovina; Hong Kong SAR, China; India; Indonesia; Montenegro; the Russian Federation, Belarus, and Kazakhstan; and Thailand. EFTA's PTAs do not include explicit human rights provisions, although trade policy makers have included references to human rights in both the preamble and the investment chapters of several agreements (Bartels 2009a). The preamble typically mentions the desire to create new employment opportunities, improve working conditions and living standards, and promote sustainable development, and it reaffirms the parties' "commitment to the principles and objectives set out in the UN Charter and Universal Declaration." But the agreements do not aim to improve human rights or strive toward sustainable development; they do not go beyond WTO exceptions regarding public morals, public health, and trade in goods made with prison labor.[32] For FTAs with African states, EFTA includes language in its investment chapter noting that "the parties recognize that it is inappropriate to encourage investment by relaxing health, safety, or environmental standards."[33] The agreements also note that the EFTA states are to provide technical assistance to implement the objectives of the agreement and support partner countries' efforts to achieve sustainable economic and social development.[34] Some recent PTAs, such as those with Canada, Colombia, and the Gulf Cooperation Council (GCC), refer to ILO principles, but contracting parties have no obligations in the agreement regarding the ILO.

Since late 2008, EFTA has been exploring whether to include environmental and labor and social standards in its PTAs. The Committee of Members of Parliament of the EFTA countries has commissioned a study on environmental policies and labor standards in PTAs but is not looking at human rights per se as an issue to be included in trade agreements.[35] Regarding the addition of labor and environmental provisions, the study notes that although a growing number of nations have such provisions, they may "breach" the regulatory framework of any of the parties to a PTA. The authors stress that much of the evidence regarding the quality of these provisions is qualitative rather than quantitative, and they conclude that it is difficult to assess the effectiveness of their inclusion.[36] EFTA has set up working groups to examine whether or how to embed such provisions, but as of the time of writing (March 2011), they had not reached a decision. Thus, EFTA does not seem to be enthusiastic or to see an urgency about including further provisions in its PTAs.

Human rights in the EEA treaty. Although EFTA has not played a leading role in linking trade and human rights, the European Economic Area (EEA) treaty—EFTA's main agreement with the EU—does use the language of human rights. This agreement, however, is much more than a trade agreement. It is designed to ensure "four freedoms"—free movement of goods, services, persons, and capital—throughout the 30 EEA states. The agreement guarantees equal rights and obligations within the internal market for citizens and economic operators in the EEA. The provisions on social security are meant to coordinate the respective national systems of the EEA states and thus to ensure social protection in case of, among other contingencies, sickness, maternity, invalidity, death, or unemployment. EFTA also has language to safeguard the pension rights of persons who exercise their fundamental right to move and reside freely within the EEA.

The preamble of the EEA agreement discusses "the contribution that a European Economic Area will bring to the construction of a Europe based on peace, democracy and human rights." The preamble also notes the importance of "equal treatment of men and women" and cites the signatories' desire "to ensure economic and social progress and to promote conditions for full employment, an improved standard of living and improved working conditions."[37] Part III, Article 28, of the agreement refers to free movement of persons. It seeks to secure freedom of movement for workers through "the abolition of any discrimination based on nationality between [European Community] member states and EFTA states."[38] Taken in sum, the EEA agreement is very much a human rights document.

EFTA's PTAs and human rights: A summary. Although EFTA includes some human rights language in its PTAs, it is just beginning to examine whether it should go further, by making human rights provisions actionable and/or disputable. EFTA policy makers might seek inspiration in their most important agreement, the treaty that set up the EEA. We can best understand this trade agreement as a governance agreement that harmonizes a wide range of laws and regulations that could distort trade but does so in ways that enhance human rights.

European Union (EU)

The EU is the behemoth of world trade; it is the world's largest trade bloc.[39] It is also the most enthusiastic proponent of the inclusion of human rights provisions in PTAs. With nearly 500 million citizens, the EU possesses approximately a quarter of the world's economic wealth. Given its size and political influence, its policies move markets.

The EU is an active participant in and negotiator of bilateral and regional PTAs. Since 1995, the European Commission Directorate General for Trade, which makes trade policy for the members of the EU, has included social and labor clauses in all its free trade agreements.[40] EU policy makers have incorporated social and labor clauses into more than 50 trade agreements involving more than 120 countries. The EU includes human rights in many of its agreements with other countries, including its partnership and cooperation agreements[41] and its generalized system of preferences (GSP) program with developing countries. However, in this chapter we focus only on the economic partnership agreements, such as that with the Caribbean Forum of African, Caribbean, and Pacific (ACP) States (CARIFORUM) and recent free trade agreements.

The EU and its member states have a long history of using trade agreements to promote human rights. In 1992 the European Commission included "an essential elements clause" in trade agreements with developing countries. The clause states that respect for human rights is an essential element of the agreement. The signatories to such agreements agree that either party may suspend the agreement without notice if these "essential elements" are violated. In 1995 the EU decided to include the human rights clause in all future international trade agreements, whether with developing or with industrial countries (Bartels 2005a).[42]

This human rights clause is given operative effect through a "nonexecution" clause stating that a failure to fulfill an obligation under the agreement, including human rights obligations, entitles the other party to take appropriate measures, subject to a consultative procedure (Bartels 2009a).

As of October 2009, the EU also included human rights clauses in nine regional trade agreements (association agreements), with Algeria, the Arab Republic of Egypt, Israel, Jordan, Lebanon, Morocco, the Palestinian Authority, the Syrian Arab Republic, and Tunisia. Similar human rights clauses were also incorporated into stabilization and accession trade agreements with Croatia and the former Yugoslav Republic of Macedonia; in pending agreements with Albania, Bosnia and Herzegovina, and Montenegro; and in regional trade agreements with Chile, Mexico, and South Africa.[43] The EU is currently negotiating a PTA with Canada. As noted above, it will be interesting to see how the two reconcile their unique human rights and trade strategies.

Economic partnership agreements (EPAs). The nations of the EU have long-standing trade relationships with their former colonies. Not surprisingly, the EU is determined to maintain these relationships, but also to use them to foster development and economic growth and to improve governance. In 1975, the members of the EU and their 79 former colonies signed a treaty, the Lomé Convention, which set out standards for development cooperation. In 2000 the EU and its Lomé partners adopted the Cotonou Agreement.[44] The Cotonou Agreement was based on four principles: equality of partners; political participation; dialogue and mutual obligations, including human rights obligations; and differentiation, based on the idea that each country is unique. Under the Cotonou Agreement, the EU and its development partners agreed to develop regional trade agreements (called economic partnership agreements) with regionally specific rights and obligations. The EU is currently negotiating with, or has completed negotiations with, six regional groupings of countries: West Africa (Ghana); the Southern African Development Community (SADC), with Botswana, Lesotho, Namibia, Mozambique, and Swaziland as members; Pacific (Fiji and Papua New Guinea); Eastern and Southern Africa (ESA), encompassing the Comoros, Madagascar, Mauritius, the Seychelles, Zambia, and Zimbabwe; and the East African Community (EAC), composed of Burundi, Kenya, Rwanda, Tanzania, and Uganda.[45] The EU and the CARIFORUM countries concluded negotiations on their EPA in October 2008.[46] The EU uses the CARIFORUM EPA agreement as a model for delineating human rights obligations in other EPAs. Although several countries have signed these regional agreements, the European Commission is waiting on other countries to approve these agreements, which are quite controversial both in Europe and in the developing world.[47]

The CARIFORUM agreement refers to human rights, democratic principles, and the rule of law as essential elements of the Cotonou Agreement and cites "good governance" as a fundamental element.[48] The signatories agree to respect basic labor rights in line with their ILO commitments. Article 3 of the agreement states that the parties agree to work cooperatively toward the realization of "sustainable development centered on the human person." Article 5 continues with that focus on human beings, noting that the parties will continuously monitor the agreement to ensure that benefits for people are maximized. Article 32 calls for transparent rules and for public explanation of legislation. Labor issues are delineated in Chapter 5; the EU refers to labor provisions as the "social aspects" of the agreement. In Article 191 the parties reaffirm their commitment to labor standards and decent work; in addition, the parties recognize the benefits of fair and ethical trade products. Finally, Article 193 is the non-derogation clause, which requires the parties not to try to gain competitive advantage by lowering standards or ignoring their laws. Article 195 sets out a process for consultation and monitoring and creates a committee of experts to examine compliance with the agreement. The committee can be called on to examine concerns among the members regarding "obstacles that may prevent the effective implementation of core labor standards."[49] Chapter 6 of the agreement refers to trade in data. Articles 196 and 197 continue the focus on individuals; here the parties recognize their "common interest in protecting fundamental rights and freedoms of natural persons, and in particular, their right to privacy, with respect to the processing of personal data."[50]

Although these agreements contain considerable human rights language, most of it is aspirational and non-binding. Only the sustainable development chapters of the EPAs, on the environment and on social issues, employ public scrutiny, expert panels, and consultations as means of resolving disputes (Bartels 2005a, iv–vi). The agreements have no dispute settlement mechanism. The only way to hold governments to account is for citizens to monitor human rights violations and press policy makers to discuss any such violations bilaterally. In short, the EU relies on negotiations to monitor human rights linked to trade in these EPAs.

Free trade agreements (FTAs). In 2006 EU member states agreed to negotiate what it calls FTAs with several rapidly growing Asian nations. The EU made it clear that these trade agreements would include a wide range of issues not typically covered in the WTO, such as investment, the environment, and social and labor clauses.[51] As of March 2011, the EU was actively negotiating FTAs with Colombia, Peru, Central America, Canada, India, Malaysia, Singapore, the Southern Cone Common Market (Mercosur, Mercado Común del Sur), and Ukraine, as well as regional and bilateral Euro-Mediterranean agreements.[52] The European Commission completed its first FTA, with the Republic of Korea, in 2009. In February 2011, the European Parliament approved by agreement.[53]

The Korean agreement illuminates the EU's new approach toward linking sustainable development (social and environmental) clauses to trade. The preamble reaffirms both parties' commitment to the Universal Declaration of Human Rights and to sustainable development. It also notes the parties' desire to "strengthen the development and enforcement of labor and environmental laws and policies, promote basic workers' rights and sustainable development and implement this agreement in a manner consistent with these objectives."[54] Like the CARIFORUM agreement, this FTA contains language protecting the right to privacy. Article 7.43, in the services chapter, states that each party should reaffirm its commitment to protecting the fundamental rights and freedoms of individuals and should adopt adequate safeguards for the protection of privacy.

The agreement with Korea includes a separate chapter on trade and sustainable development. Article 13.4 commits the two parties to respect, promote, and realize core labor rights. The parties also reaffirm their commitment to effectively implement the ILO conventions that both states have ratified. Article 13.6 states that the parties "shall strive to facilitate and promote trade in goods that contribute to sustainable development, including goods that are the subject of schemes such as fair and ethical trade." Article 13.7 contains the nonderogation clause, in which the parties agree to effectively enforce environmental and labor laws and not to weaken, waive, or derogate from those laws in a manner affecting trade or investment. Finally, Article 13.9 commits the parties to "introduce and implement any measures aimed at protecting the environment and labor . . . in a transparent manner with due notice and public consultation." To achieve that goal, the agreement creates a unique domestic advisory group on sustainable development, as well as a civil society forum on these issues (Annex 13). Thus, the agreement sets up a citizen monitoring process.

The new paradigm includes a strategy for government consultations on social issues, as well as a panel of experts to examine issues that cannot be settled through governmental consultations. In contrast with the U.S. model, the EU has designed no formal mechanism for trade disputes related to these issues; instead, civil society will monitor commitments (Articles 13.14 and 13.15).

The new model PTA also has a transparency chapter (Chapter 12) requiring that information be made available to all interested persons, as well as rules for public comment (Article 12.3) and due process (Article 12.5, on administrative proceedings). This new chapter is very similar to the U.S. and Canadian transparency chapters, but it also includes a nondiscrimination section that provides, in part, "Each party shall apply to interested persons of the other Party transparency standards no less favourable than those accorded to its own interested persons, to the interested persons of any third country, . . . whichever are the best." Finally, Protocol 3 provides for cultural cooperation and recognizes cultural diversity and cultural heritage.[55]

The new FTA model, as embodied by the FTA with Korea, contains a wide range of human rights provisions, some of which are binding on the signatories. But, as with the EPAs, neither policy makers nor citizens can challenge another state's nonperformance. Thus, this model is unlikely to satisfy the many NGOs that are critical of how the EU links trade and human rights.[56] Moreover, the EU does not examine the broad impact of its trade policies on human rights, but it does hire independent consultants to carry out sustainability impact assessments. These consultants look at income, poverty, and biodiversity; except in the area of gender inequality, they do not attempt to assess how the provisions of a free trade agreement might affect human rights conditions in trading-partner nations.[57]

Given their concerns about the EU model, some NGOs have asked EU policy makers not to conclude or ratify trade or partnership agreements with countries that have questionable human rights records. They fear that such agreements could strengthen or reward repressive regimes.[58] EU policy makers, however, are not eager to cut off trade in the interest of promoting human rights, and they believe it is important to use trade as a tool for shaping relations with emerging markets.

The EU's PTAs and human rights: A summary. At first glance, the EU's approach is supportive of the human rights set forth in the UDHR. The EU takes the position that human rights are universal and indivisible and that these rights are key aspects of the rule of law. Although the trade agreements include considerable human rights language, much of it is rhetorical, nonbinding, and not disputable. In its new FTAs and EPAs, the EU not only refers to the UDHR; it also emphasizes sustainable development (social and environmental issues). This approach creates new advisory roles for experts and civil society, but neither states nor individuals can use these provisions to challenge human rights violations.

In considering a potential agreement, the EU hires consultants to assess the impact of its trade agreements on sustainable development. It seems strange that these assessments do not focus on the bulk of human rights delineated in the UDHR (Aaronson and Zimmerman 2007, 138–43; Bartels 2009a). EU policy makers believe that dialogue and capacity building are the best means of changing the behavior of other countries.[59] EU policies focus on the supply side of governance but seem to be less focused on empowering citizens in other countries. Moreover, the EU rarely cuts trade or adopts trade sanctions toward trade agreement partners that may violate human rights. Thus, despite the EU's professed belief in the universality and indivisibility of international human rights, policy makers are sending a message that some rights are more important than others and that only some countries can be prodded with trade policy tools to change their behavior.[60]

United States

The United States bears much of the responsibility for the world's recent renewed focus on PTAs. In 2001 U.S. Trade Representative Robert Zoellick proposed that the U.S. government reorient trade liberalization toward bilateral and regional PTAs in the hope of encouraging "competitive trade liberalization." He theorized that if countries saw significant progress in bilateral PTAs, they might accept deeper market access concessions at the WTO. But instead of stimulating a renewed commitment to multilateral trade talks, the U.S. focus on PTAs prodded other countries to negotiate their own PTAs, which in turn has stimulated ever more PTAs.[61]

U.S. policy makers don't describe American PTAs as governance agreements, but the United States does use the lure of its huge market to encourage other countries to make significant policy changes. The United States has pushed for governance improvements that protect foreign investors. Recent research has found that these provisions have human rights spillovers—they seem to empower domestic as well as foreign actors who gain benefits from increased transparency, greater evenhandedness, and the due process rules promoted in these agreements. But the United States promotes only some human rights in its trade agreements. At the behest of labor unions and their congressional allies, the United States is most concerned about using these agreements to advance labor rights among U.S. PTA partners. U.S. trade policy is complicated, confusing, and often inconsistent, vacillating between market-opening strategies and protectionist measures. To some degree, this is because no one individual is in charge of trade policy making; authority is shared between the legislative and executive branches. The 535 members of

Congress and the president have divergent views about trade and about the linkage between trade and human rights (Smith 2006). Members of Congress "think local" and, in times of recession, are focused on local economic growth. Without a great understanding of what trade agreements do, many members have little enthusiasm for negotiating them. As a result, Congress has not provided authority to negotiate new trade agreements at the bilateral or multilateral level since 2002. Yet, during the eight years of the George W. Bush administration, the U.S. Trade Representative (USTR) negotiated trade agreements with Australia, Bahrain, CAFTA–DR (Central America Free Trade Agreement—Costa Rica, El Salvador, Guatemala, Honduras, Nicaragua—and the Dominican Republic), Chile, Colombia, Jordan, Morocco, Oman, Panama, Peru, and Singapore (U.S. GAO 2009). As of March 2011, Congress had approved all but the agreements with Colombia, Korea, and Panama. The Obama administration has agreed to move these agreements forward, but it has also asked Korea, Panama, and Colombia to make additional changes in order to win congressional approval. As of March 2011, the Korean government had agreed to several changes, but the Obama administration continues to work with Panamanian and Colombian officials.[62] With two wars and a burgeoning budget deficit, these agreements do not seem to be a top priority for either the administration or the Republican-dominated house. Congress sets the objectives for trade policy making, but it has not made the advancement of human rights through trade agreements a top priority. In the Trade Promotion Act of 2002 (hereafter, TPA), which grants the president "fast-track" authority to negotiate trade agreements, the words "human rights" never appear.[63] Congress has directed negotiators to focus on the following specific human rights: labor rights, access to information, public participation, and due process. In recent years, negotiators have also been directed to balance the rights of U.S. intellectual property rights (IPR) holders with U.S. obligations in the Doha Declaration on Public Health. Almost all recent PTAs contain language related to these human rights.

Negative spillovers of the focus on labor rights rather than on broader human rights. Activists and legislators have focused most of their attention on provisions addressing labor rights (see Elliott, ch. 20 in this volume). This is partly attributable to the clout of trade unions, but also to the failure of many U.S. trade partners to enforce the labor laws on their books. These partners' difficulties regarding labor rights may be a symptom of a larger governance problem, and the focus on labor rights may make it more difficult to use the agreements to promote good governance and human rights. The dilemma is most visible in the case of Colombia.

The U.S.–Colombia FTA has been pending since 2006. Many Democratic members of Congress have signaled that they cannot vote for the agreement because of Colombia's problems with labor rights. They note the high rate of violence (murders, arbitrary detentions, and kidnappings of trade unionists), as well as weak enforcement of labor laws. Colombia's labor rights problems are part of a greater problem of impunity, inadequate governance, and corruption (Bolle 2009). The pending PTA is not designed to address these issues per se, yet its fate rests on the public's and policy makers' perception of these problems as mainly labor rights issues. In this way, the PTA illuminates the inadequacies of the U.S. focus on labor rights, rather than good governance per se.[64]

Moreover, the United States seems to be moving from using these PTAs as an incentive to improve human rights to using them to hold nations accountable for specific human rights performance. In July 2009 the Obama administration announced that it would make important changes in trade policy making to advance "the social accountability and political transparency of trade policy" (USTR 2009). On July 16, 2009, U.S. Trade Representative Ron Kirk made it clear that the U.S. government was less interested in delineating labor rights provisions or providing incentives for international labor rights through its trade agreements than in establishing "a level playing field for American workers." He added that the "USTR will, proactively monitor and identify labor violations and enforce labor provisions . . . When efforts to resolve violations have been expired, USTR will not hesitate . . . to invoke formal dispute settlement."[65] However, as of March 2011, the United States has filed only one such case, against Guatemala, under the CAFTA-DR agreement, for alleged violations of obligations on labor rights.[66] Nonetheless, the United States has signaled that labor rights violations under FTAs will be investigated, and if violations are not remedied, the United States could bring the issue to a trade dispute. This new policy has clearly elevated labor rights.

Public participation, transparency, and due process. As noted above, the U.S. Congress requires its trade agreement partners to agree to PTA provisions related to transparency, due process, and political participation.[67] These provisions are embedded in the transparency, anticorruption, and regulatory practices sections of the TPA. The Congress declared that the United States aims to "obtain wider and broader application of the principles of transparency" through "increased transparency and opportunity for the participation of affected parties in the development of regulations." The legislation also states that trade negotiators should "establish consultative mechanisms among parties to trade agreements to promote increased transparency in developing guidelines, rules, regulations and laws."[68] Finally, the act notes that to avoid corruption, the United States intends "to obtain high standards and appropriate domestic enforcement mechanisms applicable to persons from all countries participating in the applicable trade agreement."[69]

The United States has been promoting transparency and due process rights in multilateral trade agreements since the end of World War II (Aaronson and Zimmerman 2007). U.S. policy makers have long argued that "transparency is the starting point for ensuring the efficiency, and ultimately the stability of a rules-based environment for goods crossing the border."[70] All U.S. PTAs approved since 2002 contain a chapter on transparency, and they thus go beyond the WTO rules—they are "WTO+." (There are also transparency provisions in other chapters of the PTA.) Although the language in these chapters varies from agreement to agreement, in general, the passages are framed in the language of human rights. They require governments to publish, in advance, laws, rules, procedures, and regulations affecting trade, thereby giving "persons of the other party that are directly affected by an agency's process . . . a reasonable opportunity to present facts and arguments in support of their positions prior to any final administrative action." These agreements also contain a section on review and appeal, designed to give the parties a reasonable opportunity to support or defend their respective positions.[71] Such provisions are not intended to promote human rights as such, but they may have human rights spillovers.

In contrast, U.S. efforts to foster public participation are relatively new, dating from 1992. The United States and its partners first experimented with public participation provisions in the environmental side agreements to NAFTA. As part of that agreement, Mexico, Canada, and the United States set up a mechanism, the Citizen Submissions on Enforcement Matters, to enable members of the public from any of the three countries to submit a claim when a government is allegedly not enforcing its environmental laws.[72] The commission investigates the allegation and issues nonbinding resolutions. These investigations have occasionally led governments to change course. For example, the Mexican government has become more responsive to the environmental side effects from trade. Based on public pressure from citizen submissions, the Mexican government promised remediation in the case of toxic pollutants abandoned at a lead smelter in Tijuana, and Mexico's president declared the Cozumel Coral Reef a protected area (Silvan 2004).

The George W. Bush administration (2001–09) decided to enhance public participation provisions. Administration officials believed that trade agreements could act as an incentive for democracy in the Middle East and might also cement democracy in Latin American nations such as Colombia and El Salvador that had experienced conflict.[73] These officials recognized that democracy could not simply be exported; they understood that some countries need help in strengthening democratic institutions, processes, and accountability.[74] They hoped that if the United States helped such countries to become more democratic and accountable to their publics, they (and the United States) would gain greater legitimacy, and over time these allies would become more stable. They also believed that trade agreements with the United States would gain public support if citizens in partner countries could comment on various versions of the agreement and in so doing shape key public policies.

Under pressure from several members of Congress, trade policy makers developed three models for public participation, which were incorporated first in the environmental chapters of PTAs and later in the labor chapters, as well. The first model was for developed democratic countries such as Australia, and it thus contained minimal public participation provisions in the environmental chapter. The second model was designed for countries with relatively weak systems of environmental regulation and accountability, or countries relatively new to democracy; it was used for Bahrain, Chile, Morocco, Oman, and Singapore.[75] Under this second model, the bilateral trade partners set up an advisory committee, an Environmental Affairs Council, that would meet regularly and engage the public in discussion on the environment.[76] Policy makers also agreed to provide capacity-building assistance to support public participation (USTR 2005).

Senator Max Baucus, a Democrat from Montana, played an important role in developing a third, more extensive, approach. In 2004 he called on the USTR to put the public participation provisions directly in the trade agreement, to develop benchmarks and "ways to measure progress over time," and to find ways to encourage objective monitoring and scrutiny by the public (Aaronson and Zimmerman 2007, 174–76). The CAFTA–DR agreement was the USTR's first test of the third model. In February 2005 the United States and its six partners in CAFTA–DR agreed to establish a mechanism and secretariat allowing the general public to submit petitions regarding the operation of the agreement's labor or environmental provisions. If members of the public from any party to CAFTA–DR believe that any party is not effectively enforcing its labor or environmental laws, they can make a new submission to this subbody, which reports to the Environmental Affairs Council. The agreement states that each party should review and respond to such communications in accordance with its own domestic procedures.[77] CAFTA–DR also authorizes the tribunal "to accept and consider amicus curiae submissions from a person or entity that is not a disputing party." To develop a workable system, the United States agreed to fund the first year of the secretariat's work.[78] The USTR has replicated this model in more recent PTAs, such as those with Colombia, Korea, Panama, and Peru.[79] The labor chapter of these PTAs, Article 19.4, notes, "Each party shall ensure that persons with a recognized interest under its law in a particular matter have appropriate access to tribunals for the enforcement of the Party's labor laws." In addition, "Each party shall promote public awareness of its labor laws including by (a) ensuring that information related to its labor laws and enforcement and compliance procedures is publicly available; and (b) encouraging education of the public regarding its labor laws."[80] The United States and its trade partners have also established Labor Affairs Councils with other PTA partners.[81]

As readers might imagine, the placement of participation provisions in trade agreements cannot magically stimulate democracy. Such an approach may not work in countries lacking a tradition of political participation or free speech, and it may appear to violate another country's sovereignty or cultural mores. However, these provisions might push partner governments to allow more public participation and could gradually teach citizens how to engage and challenge policy makers. Since signing a free trade agreement with the United States, PTA partners Chile, the Dominican Republic, Jordan, Kuwait, Mexico, and Morocco have established channels through which organized civil society can comment on trade policies (Cherfane 2006: Aaronson and Zimmerman 2007).

Access to affordable medicines. Congress has long viewed protecting intellectual property rights (IPR) holders as a top priority. The United States is by far the most assertive country in defending intellectual property rights within the context of trade policies and agreements, even when trade partners and human rights activists argue that U.S. policies undermine the ability of policy makers or citizens to obtain access to affordable medicine or to protect indigenous knowledge. U.S. assertiveness stems from a long-standing belief among policy makers that the country's economic future is rooted in America's global economic dominance of creative industries such as software, biotechnology, and entertainment.[82] These intellectual property–based industries represent the largest single sector of the U.S. economy.[83] To protect that future, U.S. policy makers work with their overseas counterparts to enforce intellectual property rights, seize counterfeit goods, pursue criminal enterprises involved in piracy and counterfeiting, and "aggressively engage our trading partners to join our efforts" (CEA 2005, 226).

U.S. policy makers are increasingly sensitive to public concerns that there are costs to elevating IPR protection. Drugs and vaccines are increasingly expensive, and the policy does not encourage the development of generic brands. Moreover, some argue that the policy does not adequately protect indigenous knowledge—knowledge passed down through familiar and cultural ties, but not protected under domestic law. In the 2002 TPA, Congress required the Bush administration to rethink its approach, and "secure fair, equitable, and nondiscriminatory market access opportunities for United States persons that rely upon intellectual property protection; and to respect the Declaration on the [Trade-Related Aspects of Intellectual Property Rights (TRIPS)] Agreement and Public Health."[84] The executive branch, however, was not given a mandate to ensure access to affordable medicines.

Beginning in April 2004, all PTAs include a letter entitled "Understandings Regarding Certain Public Health Measures" that is signed by representatives of both governments. The letter, found in the Bahrain, CAFTA–DR, Colombia, Morocco, Oman, and Peru PTAs, says that the IPR provisions of the agreement "do not affect a Party's ability to take necessary measures to protect public health."[85] But the letter does not make it clear that governments can breach IPR obligations in order to ensure that their citizens have access to affordable medicines. These side letters do not assuage critics, including the World Bank (Mercurio 2006, 234–35). Interestingly, this policy may not change dramatically under the Obama administration. There is no mention of public health in the President's Trade Policy Agenda, and the Trade Agreements Report, like others before it, simply stresses that strong intellectual property protection is essential for protecting public health (USTR 2011).

U.S. PTAs and human rights: A summary. The U.S. approach to linking PTAs and human rights is contradictory. On the one hand, it ignores the internationally accepted notion that human rights are universal and indivisible, yet on the other hand, the United States works hard to promote specific human rights and now makes some of these rights binding. The United States is essentially saying to its partner nations: make the rights we value top priorities. In this way, the U.S. strategy toward linking human rights is insensitive toward other cultures, which may have different human rights priorities. This strategy may inspire U.S. trade partners to do more to advance some human rights, but it is unlikely to inspire these governments to devote more resources to human rights in general.

The United States (like Canada) uses its trade agreements to improve governance and, in so doing, to empower citizens to demand their rights. However, the United States uses the leverage of trade agreements to induce other nations to invest in the governance priorities valued by U.S. policy makers instead of in human rights as delineated in international law.

South-South Agreements

Although developed countries are the main demandeurs of human rights provisions in PTAs, a number of emerging economies include such links in their trade agreements. Policy makers have incorporated language dealing with access to affordable medicines, indigenous or minority rights, due process, cultural rights, and labor rights. These provisions are usually located in the preamble of the agreement, with a few in the body of the text.

Some developing countries link trade and human rights by building on the exceptions in GATT/WTO Article XX described earlier. For example, Article 8 of the agreement between Egypt and Jordan allows measures "for *religious*, hygienic, security or environmental reasons as long as they are in conformity with the applicable laws and regulations in both countries." (This is the only provision that we have found that associates trade and freedom of religion.) Other countries target different human rights. For example, the Caribbean Community (CARICOM) allows for the free movement of university graduates and those in listed occupations. Some countries have more restricted provisions regarding free movement of people. (See Stephenson and Hufbauer, ch. 13 in this volume, on labor mobility.) For example, NAFTA and the Canada–Chile and U.S.–Chile PTAs contain chapters on temporary entry of business persons.[86] Article 6 of the treaty establishing the Common Market of Eastern and Southern Africa (COMESA) commits members to promote democracy and human rights.[87] Several human rights are embedded in the Mercosur agreement between Argentina, Brazil, Paraguay, and Uruguay.[88] If any party to Mercosur fails to protect ILO core labor standards, a supranational Commission on Social and Labor Matters can review allegations at the behest of another member state, although it cannot impose trade sanctions or other penalties in the event of such a violation.[89]

Like the EU, Mercosur is built on the recognition that if the members want to jointly expand trade, they must collaborate on a wide range of issues. Thus, it is more of a governance agreement than simply a trade agreement. In 1998 Mercosur members adopted the Ushuaia Protocol on democratic commitment, which prohibits the entry of undemocratic states into the common market. Although the protocol text itself makes no explicit mention of human rights, Mercosur members invoked the protocol as a joint response to a 1996 coup d'état in Paraguay, and the Brazilian delegation cited numerous human rights motivations when it presented the protocol to the United Nations in 2000. For instance, when explaining the rationale for a democracy clause, Brazilian policy makers argued that "democracy, development, and respect for human rights and fundamental freedoms are interdependent and mutually reinforcing."[90] Thus, although the Mercosur trade agreement contains no binding human rights commitments, Brazil and its Mercosur partners see the protection of human rights and democracy as a rationale for, and a side effect of, the agreement (Anderson and Zimmerman 2007, 106). Nevertheless, Mercosur refused to investigate allegations of human rights abuses by member state Argentina (Garcia 2003).

Chile has incorporated labor rights language into several of its more recent bilateral PTAs. For example, as noted by Elliott (ch. 20 in this volume), the trade agreement between Chile and China includes two labor and environmental side agreements. Article 108 commits both parties "to carry out cooperation activities in the fields of employment and labor policies and social dialogue." Although Chile's language is aspirational, this language does underscore the importance of labor rights.[91] In addition, Chile's agreements with Costa Rica, Colombia, and Korea, as well as the CARICOM–Costa Rica PTA, refer to social protection (Bartels 2009a).

Summary

These South-South trade and human rights provisions, as well as those in the U.S., European, and other agreements, reflect a changing attitude about what trade agreements should include and what they are about. According to Bartels, "the idea that these links are valid seems to be gaining its own dynamic" (Bartels 2009a, 365). Moreover although many of these provisions are aspirational and not binding, such provisions may not remain rhetorical. Bartels concludes that as the number of agreements containing preambular references to human rights grows in number and scope, "this may well lead to operative provisions at a later stage," as happened with EU human rights provisions (365).

The Effects of the Marriage of PTAs and Human Rights

Although the wedding of trade and human rights is new, this marriage is leading to important changes in the way policy makers make trade policy. The sheer number and dispersion of PTAs with human rights links seem to be changing some policy makers' opinions about human rights. These provisions have thus contributed to the recognition and internationalization of human rights norms. Second, these provisions are changing the behavior of government officials in a wide variety of countries, as described below.

Mauritania. The European Commission used consultations to warn the new government of Mauritania that the government's behavior breached that country's commitments under the Cotonou Agreement. Soon thereafter, the new Mauritanian regime pledged to hold free and fair elections and initiated a process to establish an independent National Commission for Human Rights. In 2007 the government held free and fair elections. While one can't say that the PTA's human rights provisions pushed the military government to protect human rights, political scientist Hafner-Burton concludes that these provisions gave the EU leverage over the government's progress toward reforms (Hafner-Burton 2009, 151–60).

Thailand. In 2003 Thailand entered into PTA negotiations with the United States. In 2005 the Thailand National Human Rights Commission drafted a report on the human rights implications of the proposed trade agreement, expressing concern about traditional knowledge and intellectual property rights. The report concluded that Thailand would have to adopt U.S. laws if it agreed to the trade agreement.[92] The Thai public began to oppose the agreement. The Thai prime minister pledged to ensure greater public involvement in the negotiating process to shape the agreement.[93] However, the negotiations ended after a military coup.

El Salvador and Guatemala. The USTR asserted that El Salvador and Guatemala held their first public hearings on trade as they negotiated CAFTA. These governments continue to engage their citizens in trade. during the negotiations of CAFTA. With such hearings, individuals and NGOs learn how to influence trade policy. Trade policy makers in these countries may have acted under U.S. pressure, but they may also have recognized that they must involve their publics if they don't want to engender significant opposition to such agreements (Aaronson and Zimmerman 2007, 176). As noted earlier, other nations with little tradition of civil society or even business involvement in trade, such as Bahrain, Jordan, and Oman, also created public advisory bodies (Cherfane 2006; Lombardt 2008).

Mexico. Since joining NAFTA, Mexican trade policy has become more responsive to public concerns. For example, the Mexican government revamped its agricultural policies. It has also begun to work internationally to protect its citizens' labor rights. For example, in September 2009, Mexican consulates attempted to educate Mexican guest workers in the United States regarding their labor rights. NAFTA leaders meet regularly, and human rights and the rule of law have become important parts of their discussions.

Thus, at their meeting in August 2009, the leaders of the three NAFTA countries discussed public health, border controls, and public safety—all issues relating to human rights.[94]

Linkages and Knowledge Gaps: Some Problems Presented by Current PTAs

The many variants of PTAs raise questions about the linkage of trade and human rights and what it means for both the international human rights regime and the status of human rights.

1. Countries Have a Wide Range of Views about Using Trade to Advance Human Rights Abroad.
The United States, the EU, and Canada are quite comfortable using their trade agreements to advance human rights in other countries. While some developing and middle-income countries have included some human rights provisions in their PTAs, policy makers in these countries may not believe it is appropriate to intervene in the affairs of other nations, even in the most extreme cases of human rights abuse.

2. Countries Have a Wide Range of Views as to Whether They Should Accept Human Rights Provisions in Trade Agreements.
Some nations, such as Australia, have actually refused to negotiate trade agreements with human rights provisions. Yet China has accepted human rights provisions in its PTAs with Chile and New Zealand. How do we explain these differences? Some countries are comfortable using their economic power to promote political change; some countries are neutral and noninterventionist; and others may be using their acceptance of these provisions to signal investors and funders. Perhaps China sees adopting these provisions as a way to signal foreign investors that it is evenhanded and is attempting to promote the rule of law.

3. Incentives Work Better Than Disincentives to Change Behavior.
Some countries have decided to use disincentives as a means of advancing the human rights embedded in particular trade agreements. However, sanctions or fines can do little to build demand for human rights or to train governments or factory managers in how to respect human rights. Isolating a government or punishing it will do little to increase the targeted country's commitment to human rights over time. Other countries rely on dialogue to prod changes, but dialogue may do little to encourage a country to change its behavior. Still others rely on incentives. We

need to understand whether these incentives are really effective and, if so, when these incentives should be offered.

4. There Is a Lot Scholars Don't Know about This Relationship.

Scholars are just beginning to examine the relationship between human rights and trade performance.[95] Aaronson and Zimmerman did a simple correlation and found that states that protect human rights signal investors that they are evenhanded and promote the rule of law (Aaronson and Zimmerman 2007, 193–95). Scholars also don't know if human rights provisions in trade agreements lead to greater trade distortions.

5. These Provisions Have Costs as Well as Benefits.

The world and its people benefit when more governments protect, respect, and realize human rights. Yet some human rights provisions are expensive for developing countries to implement. These governments often have few resources, and yet under many recent trade agreements, they must choose to protect intellectual property, provide access to affordable medicines, and/or invest in education. Trade agreements may prod policy makers to make the human rights priorities of their trade partners their human rights priorities. We don't know if this strategy ultimately increases the demand for and supply of human rights. To gain better understanding of the costs and benefits of the association of trade and human rights, scholars, policy makers, and activists could use qualitative studies, empirical studies, or human rights impact assessments. Scholars have several global datasets they can use to do empirical research (for example, the Cingranelli-Richards [CIRI] Human Rights Dataset or the now open World Bank datasets).[96] Human rights impact assessments are relatively new; they are designed to measure the potential impact of a trade agreement on internationally accepted human rights standards. Trade and human rights policy makers should collaborate with scholars, NGOs, and others to develop a clear and consistent methodology for evaluating such impact (3D 2009; Walker 2009).

Conclusions

More countries are marrying trade and human rights. If this marriage is to endure, we need greater understanding as to whether this union is effective and whether it can and should endure. We can begin by doing a comprehensive study of which PTA strategies encourage policy makers to do a better job of advancing human rights and if particular trade agreements help people realize their human rights under law.

Notes

1. The United States has included human rights language in all its PTAs (17 in force and 3 pending), except that with Israel, as well as in its generalized system of preferences (GSP) program with 131 countries. The EU has PTAs with 14 countries, and 13 of these agreements include human rights provisions; about 120 countries are subject to human rights provisions in the EU's GSP program.

2. United Nations High Commissioner for Human Rights website, http://www.unhchr.ch/Huridocda/Huridoca.nsf/0/c462b62cf8a07b13c12 569700046704e?Opendocument.

3. See the databases at the World Trade Law website, http://www.world tradelaw.net/fta/ftadatabase/PTAs.asp; WTO, Regional Trade Agreements Information Service, http://rtais.wto.org/UI/PublicMaintainRTAHome .aspx; and, for the latest news, Bilaterals.org, http://www.bilaterals.org.

4. The two covenants and the UDHR together form the International Bill of Rights.

5. United Nations High Commissioner for Human Rights, "Fact Sheet," http://www.unhchr.ch/html/menu6/2/fs2.htm (accessed February 12, 2006).

6. Ibid.

7. For example, if a government ignores its own labor laws, it is effectively allowing its labor-intensive firms to become more cost-competitive with imports (see GATT 1989; Bagwell and Staiger 1998; Brown 2001, 29–31).

8. *Some* WTO agreements require governments to accord due process rights (such as the right to recognition before the law) to importers as well as exporters. For example, under the WTO's Safeguards Agreement, when workers or industries petition their government for import relief, the responding government must give public notice and hold hearings in which interested parties can respond to a safeguard investigation (Interpretation and Application of Article 1 of the WTO Agreement on Safeguards, http://www.wto.org/english/res_e/booksp_e/analytic_index_e/safeguards _02_e.htm#). The Agreement on Safeguards envisages that the interested parties will play a central role in the investigation and that they will be a primary source of information for the competent authorities. The Agreement on Technical Barriers to Trade requires governments to publish standards and technical regulations and allow interested parties (whether foreign or domestic) to become acquainted and respond to the regulation (http://www.wto.org/english/res_e/booksp_e/analytic_index_e/tbt_01_e. htm#p). The Customs Valuation Agreement requires governments to establish in law the right of the importer to appeal a determination of customs value. Appeal may first be to a higher level in the customs administration, but the importer shall have the right in the final instance to appeal to the judiciary (Text of Interpretive Note to Article XI, http:// www.wto.org/english/res_e/booksp_e/analytic_index_e/cusval_02_e.htm #article11A).

9. Paragraph 2(a) General 319, GATT Analytical Index, http://www .wto.org/english/res_e/booksp_e/analytic_index_e/gatt1994_04_e.htm# articleXA.

10. Powell (2005) notes, as an example, that provisions to implement transparency are embedded in NAFTA Articles 510, 909, 1036, and 1411.

11. See World Trade Law database, http://www.worldtradelaw.net/fta/ ftadatabase/PTAs.asp; WTO Regional Trade Agreements Information System database, http://rtais.wto.org.

12. See discussion in House of Commons Committee, "Government Response to the Seventh Report of the Standing Committee on International Trade," March 2007, 39th Parliament, 1st Session, 1–3.

13. "Speaking Notes for Honorable Jean-Pierre Blackburn, Minister of Labor and Minister of the Economic Development Agency of Canada at Montreal Council on Foreign Relations, Montreal, Quebec, February 29, 2008," http://www.hrsdc.gc.ca/eng/corporate/newsroom/speeches/ blackburnjp/2008/080229.shtml.

14. Foreign Affairs and International Trade Canada (DFAIT), "Negotiations and Agreements," http://www.international.gc.ca/trade-agreements- accords-commerciaux/agr-acc/index.aspx. Canada's four most recent PTAs

are with Peru (in force as of August 1, 2009); Jordan (signed June 28, 2009, but not yet approved by Parliament); Colombia (signed November 28, 2008, but not yet approved); and EFTA (in force as of January 28, 2009).

15. DFAIT, "Negotiations and Agreements."

16. United Nations Association in Canada (UNAC), "Canada and Human Rights," http://www.unac.org/rights/actguide/canada.html.

17. DFAIT, "Canada's International Human Rights Policy," http://www.international.gc.ca/rights-droits/policy-politique.aspx.

18. The Peru, Colombia, and Jordan agreements share the same basic preamble.

19. DFAIT, "Canada-Peru Free Trade Agreement," http://www.international.gc.ca/trade-agreements-accords-commerciaux/agr-acc/andean-andin/can-peru-perou.aspx?lang=en; DFAIT, "Canada-Jordan Free Trade Agreement," http://www .international.gc.ca/trade-agreements-accords-commerciaux/agr-acc/jordan-jordanie/chapter15-chapitre15.aspx?lang=eng.

20. Canada's approach to labor rights is discussed by Elliott, in chapter 20 of this volume; the present chapter focuses on how the labor rights side agreement addresses other important human rights. Canadian officials state that labor and environmental provisions need to be embedded in side agreements rather than in chapters because the provinces, which regulate labor, could challenge the right of the federal government to force them to adhere to a treaty in their areas of jurisdiction. The side agreements allow for voluntary adherence by the provinces. This arrangement respects provincial jurisdiction on labor matters but gives Canada the ability to immediately access the dispute resolution process, regardless of the level of provincial participation in the labor cooperation agreement.

21. Human Resources and Skill Development Canada, "International Labour Affairs," http://www.hrsdc.gc.ca/eng/lp/ila/index.shtml/.

22. See the 32-page "Agreement on Labour Cooperation" between Canada and Colombia, http://www.hrsdc.gc.ca/eng/labour/labour_agreements/ccalc/Canada-Colombia_LCA.pdf.

23. DFAIT, "Canada-Peru Free Trade Agreement, Chapter 19, Transparency," http://www.international.gc.ca/trade-agreements-accords-commerciaux/agr-acc/peru-perou/peru-toc-perou-tdm.aspx?lang=eng.

24. DFAIT, "Canada-Colombia Free Trade Agreement, Chapter 19, Transparency," http://www.international.gc.ca/trade-agreements-accords-commerciaux/assets/pdfs/EN%2019%20Colombia%20FTA%20-%20Transparency.pdf.

25. Media Awareness Network, "Canada's Cultural Policies," http://www.media-awareness.ca/english/issues/cultural_policies/canada_cultural_policies.cfm; DFAIT, "Culture," http://www.international.gc.ca/trade-agreements-accords-commerciaux/fo/index.aspx?lang=en.

26. For Colombia, http://www.ec.gc.ca/caraib-carib/default.asp?lang=En&n=F24F07DD-1; for Peru, http://www.ec.gc.ca/caraib-carib/default.asp?lang=En&xml=5CBDDB77-6054-4FD3-A348-125840CEDF29.

27. Human Rights Impact Resource Center, http://www.humanrightsimpact.org/news/newsitem/article/roundtable-on-human-rights-impact-assessments-in-canada-on-16-november-178/?tx_ttnews[backPid]=769&cHash=0a3f7f441d60fbea25cc641a768a1a1c; Canadian Labour Congress, http://www.canadianlabour.ca/news-room/publications/canada-colombia-free-trade-agreement-round-two-0.

28. Hearing on Canada–South America Trade Relations, 40th Parliament, 2nd session, Standing Committee on International Trade, June 16, 2009, http://www2.parl.gc.ca/HousePublications/Publication.aspx?DocId=4000400&Language=E&Mode=1&Parl=40&Ses=2.

29. International Centre for Trade and Sustainable Development (ICTSD), "Canada–Colombia FTA Gets Human Rights Amendment," http://ictsd.org/i/news/bridgesweekly/73372/.

30. DFAIT, "Canada–European Union Joint Report: Towards a Comprehensive Economic Agreement," http://www.international.gc.ca/trade-agreements-accords-commerciaux/agr-acc/eu-ue/can-eu-report-can-ue-rapport.aspx?lang=eng.

31. EFTA, "Free Trade Agreements," http://www.efta.int/free-trade/free-trade-agreements.aspx.

32. See, for example, EFTA–Colombia, http://www.efta.int/free-trade/free-trade-agreements/colombia/fta-en.aspx; for Chile, http://www.efta.int/free-trade/free-trade-agreements/chile/fta.aspx, Article XXI.

33. World Trade Law, "Free Trade Agreement between the EFTA States and the SACU States," http://www.worldtradelaw.net/fta/agreements/SACU_EFTA_FTA.pdf.

34. Ibid., Article 30.

35. Committee of Members of Parliament of the EFTA Countries, "Environmental Policies and Labor Standards in PTAs," August 24, 2009, Brussels.

36. Committee of Members of Parliament of the EFTA Countries, "Environmental Policies and Labor Standards in PTAs," Ref. 1090382, March 18, 2009, Brussels, 3–4.

37. EFTA, http://www.efta.int/eea/eea-agreement.aspx, 5–6.

38. European Commission, Employment, Social Affairs, and Inclusion, "Free Movement of Workers," http://ec.europa.eu/social/main.jsp?catId=458&langId=en; "Equal Treatment," http://ec.europa.eu/social/main.jsp?catId=462&langId=en.

39. The European Community was founded as the European Economic Community on March 25, 1957; in 1993 it was renamed the European Union.

40. European Commission, Trade, "FTA Negotiations," http://trade.ec.europa.eu/doclib/docs/2006/december/tradoc_118238.pdf; Aaronson and Zimmerman (2007, 139).

41. European Union, "Partnership and Cooperation Agreements (PCAs)," http://europa.eu/legislation_summaries/external_relations/relations_with_third_countries/eastern_europe_and_central_asia/r17002_en.htm.

42. Bartels and other analysts have noted that Australia refused to accept a human rights clause in its trade agreement, and thus, the EU and Australia were unable to negotiate a PTA.

43. European Union, "EC Regional Trade Agreements," http://trade.ec.europa.eu/doclib/docs/2006/december/tradoc_111588.pdf.

44. European Commission, "The Cotonou Agreement," http://ec.europa.eu/development/geographical/cotonouintro_en.cfm; European Commission, Trade, "Economic Partnerships," http://ec.europa.eu/trade/wider-agenda/development/economic-partnerships/.

45. EU, "Economic Partnerships."

46. European Commission, "An Overview of the Interim Agreements," http://trade.ec.europa.eu/doclib/docs/2009/january/tradoc_142188.pdf; and, according to http://www.bilaterals.org, as of 2009:

EU–ACP subgroup	Status of agreement
Caribbean	• Full EPA initialed in December 2007 and signed in October 2008 (but not by Haiti) and approved by the European Parliament (March 2009).
Central Africa	• Interim EPA initialed (December 2007) and signed by Cameroon only (January 2009). • Seven countries have not initialed anything yet.
West Africa	• Interim EPA initialed (December 2007) and signed by Côte d'Ivoire (November 2008) and approved by the European Parliament (March 2009). • Interim EPA initialed by Ghana (December 2007). • Fourteen countries have not initialed anything yet.
East Africa	• Interim EPA initialed by Zimbabwe, the Seychelles, Mauritius, the Comoros, Madagascar, and Zambia (November–December 2007) and signed by Zimbabwe, the Seychelles, Mauritius, and Madagascar only (August 2009). • Interim EPA initialed by East African Community members Burundi, Kenya, Rwanda, Tanzania, and Uganda (November 2007). • Five countries have not initialed anything yet.

Southern Africa
- Interim EPA initialed by Botswana, Lesotho, Namibia, Swaziland, and Mozambique (November–December 2007) and signed by Botswana, Lesotho, Swaziland, and Mozambique only (June 2009).
- Angola has not initialed anything yet.

Pacific
- Interim EPA initialed by Papua New Guinea and Fiji (November 2007) and signed by Papua New Guinea only (July 2009).
- Thirteen countries have not initialed anything yet.

47. TradeMark Southern Africa, http://www.trademarksa.org/node/485; http://ictsd.org/i/news/tni/57509/; Forbes.com, "Africa–E.U. Economic Agreement Stalls," http://www.forbes.com/2010/08/11/eu-africa-epa-business-oxford-analytica.html.

48. European Commission, *Official Journal of the European Community*, "Economic Partnership Agreement between the CARIFORUM States, of the One Part, and the European Community and Its Member States, of the Other Part," http://trade.ec.europa.eu/doclib/docs/2008/february/tradoc_137971.pdf.

49. The EPAs can be examined at http://www.bilaterals.org/spip.php?rubrique17.

50. Ibid. Canada has similar provisions.

51. European Commission, Trade, "European Competitiveness," http://ec.europa.eu/trade/creating-opportunities/trade-topics/european-competitiveness/index_en.htm; European Commission, "Global Europe: Competing in the World," http://ec.europa.eu/trade/creating-opportunities/trade-topics/european-competitiveness/global-europe/.

52. European Commission, Trade, "Overview of FTA and Other Trade Negotiations," updated March 3, 2011, http://trade.ec.europa.eu/doclib/docs/2006/december/tradoc_118238.pdf.

53. European Commission, Trade, "Overview of FTA and Other Trade Negotiations."

54. European Commission, "Free Trade Agreement between the European Community and Its Member States, of the One Part, and the Republic of Korea, of the Other Part," http://trade.ec.europa.eu/doclib/docs/2009/october/tradoc_145139.pdf.

55. On transparency, European Commission, Trade, http://trade.ec.europa.eu/doclib/docs/2009/october/tradoc_145184.pdf; on the cultural protocol, http://trade.ec.europa.eu/doclib/docs/2009/october/tradoc_145194.pdf.

56. Much of the text that follows is from Aaronson and Zimmerman (2007, 139–47).

57. European Commission, Trade, "Sustainability Impact Assessments," http://ec.europa.eu/trade/analysis/sustainability-impact-assessments/.

58. Human Rights Watch, Christian Solidarity Worldwide, and International Crisis Group, "No Trade Agreement for Turkmenistan-Joint Letter," March 20, 2006, http://hrw.org/english/docs/2006/03/20/turkme13040.htm (accessed April 24, 2006).

59. EU, "Human Rights and Democracy in the World: Report on EU Action July 2008 to December 2009," 2010, http://www.eeas.europa.eu/_human_rights/docs/2010_hr_report_en.pdf.

60. European Commission, Communication from the European Commission to the Council and the European Parliament, "The European Union's Role in Promoting Human Rights and Democratisation in Third Countries," COM(2001)252 final, May 8, 2001, Brussels.

61. For two views of "competitive liberalization," see Evenett and Meier (2008) and Aaronson (2002).

62. USTR (2011); for Colombia, http://www.ustr.gov/trade-agreements/free-trade-agreements/colombia-fta; for Korea, http://www.ustr.gov/trade-agreements/free-trade-agreements/korus-fta; for Panama, http://www.ustr.gov/trade-agreements/free-trade-agreements/panama-tpa.

63. Public Law 107-210, August 6, 2002, Section 2102 (a) Trade Negotiating Objectives of the Bipartisan Trade Promotion Authority Act of 2002; USTR 2009.

64. "The President's 2011 Trade Policy Agenda," http://www.ustr.gov/webfm_send/2587.

65. USTR, "Trade Policy: A Level Playing Field for America's Workers," July 16, 2009, http://www.ustr.gov/about-us/press-office/fact-sheets/2009/july/trade-policy-level-playing-field-american-workers.

66. USTR, "Guatemala Submission under CAFTA-DR," http://www.ustr.gov/trade-topics/labor/bilateral-and-regional-trade-agreements/guatemala-submission-under-cafta-dr; USTR, "USTR Kirk Addresses Workers in Pennsylvania on Obama Administration Enforcement of U.S. Trade Agreements," http://www.ustr.gov/node/6046, 4; USTR, "The 2010 National Trade Estimate Report: Key Elements," http://www.ustr.gov/about-us/press-office/fact-sheets/2010/march/-2010-national-trade-estimate-report-key-elements.

67. Transparent, accountable governance can foster democracy, capitalism, and political stability. Thus, by promoting transparency, the rule of law, and political participation, policy makers can promote many human rights. See UNDP (2002), 2–4.

68. Bipartisan Trade Promotion Authority Act, Section 2102 (b) (5), (8).

69. Ibid., Section 2102 (b) 6 (A).

70. U.S. communication on Article X of GATT 1994, G/C/W/384, June 7, 2002; Robert B. Zoellick, "Free Trade and the Hemispheric Hope," Council of the Americas meeting, May 7, 2001, http://ctrc.sice.oas.org/geograph/westernh/zoellick_3.pdf.

71. For example, Chapter 20 of the Australia–U.S. FTA, http://www.dfat.gov.au/trade/negotiations/us_fta/final-text/chapter_20.html; Chapter 17 of the U.S.–Bahrain FTA; Section 19 of the Peru FTA, www.ustr.gov/Trade_Agreements/Bilateral.

72. Commission for Economic Cooperation of North America, "A Guide to Articles 14 and 15," http://www.cec.org/Page.asp?PageID=122&ContentID=1388&SiteNodeID=210.

73. According to President Bush, "open trade . . . spurs the process of economic and legal reform. And open trade reinforces the habits of liberty that sustain democracy over the long term." Quoted in testimony by USTR Robert Zoellick to the Senate Finance Committee, "America's Trade Policy Agenda," March 5, 2003.

74. Robert B. Zoellick, "Global Trade and the Middle East: Reawakening a Vibrant Past," World Economic Forum, Jordan, June 23, 2003; statement by Peter F. Algeier, Acting U.S. Trade Representative, before the Senate Finance Committee, April 13, 2005, 6–8. On Central America, see Robert B. Zoellick, "A Free Trade Boost for Our Hemisphere," *Wall Street Journal*, November 17, 2003; Zoellick, "The Route From Miami to Economic Freedom," *Financial Times*, December 9, 2003.

75. Interview with Mark Linscott, Assistant USTR for the Environment, and Jennifer Prescott, Deputy Assistant USTR for the Environment, August 1, 2006.

76. See Article 19.3 and 19.4 of the U.S.–Chile FTA, http://www.ustr.gov/Trade_Agreements/Bilateral/Chile_FTA/Final_Texts/Section_Index.html.

77. Part of the agreement's work program is to build capacity to promote public participation in environmental decision making. The agreement was negotiated by the Department of State; see Environmental Cooperation Agreement, February 1, 2005, http://www.state.gov/g/oes/env/trade/caftacooperation/142688.htm. Also see "U.S., Central America, Dominican Republic Sign Environment Pacts," U.S. Department of State, http://www.america.gov/st/washfile-english/2005/February/20050218133452GLnesnoM0.3828546.html. The Environmental Affairs Council met for the first time on May 24, 2006.

78. On dispute settlement, see CAFTA-DR, Article 10.20. 3; "Communiqué of the Environmental Affairs Council of the Dominican Republic–Central America–United States Free Trade Agreement," May 24, 2006, http://www.worldtradelaw.net/fta/agreements/CAFTADR_RelDoc_CommEnvAff.pdf .

79. Interview with Mark Linscott and Jennifer Prescott, Office of the USTR, August 2, 2006. For the Peru agreement, see http://www.ustr.gov/trade_agreements/bilateral/; for the draft Colombia FTA, see

http://www.ustr.gov/Trade_Agreements/Bilateral/Colombia_FTA/Draft
_Text/Section_Index.html.

80. Chapter 19, Labor, in the Korea, Panama, Peru, and Colombia
FTAs. See, for example, Chapter 19 in the U.S.–Korea FTA, http://www
.ustr.gov/sites/default/files/uploads/agreements/fta/korus/asset_upload_
file934_12718.pdf; Article 20, http://www.ustr.gov/sites/default/files/
uploads/agreements/fta/korus/asset_upload_file852_12719.pdf.

81. USTR (2011, 149–51). "As part of increased engagement in 2010,
Labor Affairs Council and labor subcommittee meetings, as provided for
under the FTAs, were held with several FTA partners, including first-time
meetings with Peru, Morocco, and Bahrain. (*For additional information,
see Chapter III.A*)."

82. "House Chairmen Warn USTR against Patent Changes in Doha
Round," *Inside U.S. Trade* (April 14, 2006), 7.

83. Press release, "Commerce Secretary Carlos Gutierrez Unveils Initiatives to Fight Intellectual Property Theft," September 21, 2005,
http://www.commerce.gov/opa/press/Secretary_Gutierrez/2005_Releases
/September/09-21-05%20IPR%20initiatives.htm. Keyder (2005) has an
interesting scholarly take on this issue.

84. Trade Promotion Authority Act of 2002, Section 2102, (4) (A) (B) (C).

85. See, for example, "Understandings Regarding Certain Public
Health Measures," Colombia, http://www.ustr.gov/Trade_Agreements/
Bilateral/Colombia_FTA/Draft_Text/Section_Index.html (accessed August
7, 2006).

86. Basically, free movement of skills entails the right to seek employment in any member state and the elimination of the need for work permits and permits of stay. See CARICOM, http://www.caricom.org/jsp/sin
gle_market/skill.jsp?menu=csme.

87. COMESA's Integration Agenda also rests on the belief that the
consolidation of democracy and the rule of law are the foundation stones
for regional socioeconomic development and political stability.

88. Mercosur is incorporated into the Latin America Integration
Association/Asociación Latinoamericana de Integración (LAIA/ALADI)
legal regime, as Economic Complementarity Agreement 18. These agreements are open to accession by any LAIA/ALADI country.

89. See "Treaty Establishing a Common Market," March 26, 1991, UN
Doc. A/46/155 (1991), reprinted in 30 I.L.M. 1041 (1991).

90. For the full text of the Brazilian delegation's speech, see
http://www.un.int/brazil/speech/00d-mercosul-human-rights-2610.htm.

91. Memorandum of Understanding, http://www.sice.oas.org/Trade/
CHL_CHN/CHL_CHN_e/Labor_e.asp.

92. The English version of the draft report is available at http://www
.measwatch.org/autopage/show_page.php?t=5&s_id=3&d_id=7.

93. MCOT News, "PM Calls for More Public Participation in
FTA Deals," http://www.bilaterals.org/article.php3?id_article=953&var_
recherche=public+information (accessed August 3, 2006). Meanwhile, the
EPA is reviewing its public participation efforts.

94. USTR, "Joint Statement of the 2009 NAFTA Commission Meeting," http://www.ustr.gov/about-us/press-office/press-releases/2009/
october/joint-statement-2009-nafta-commission-meeting.

95. In a widely cited, albeit out-of-date, study, the Organisation for
Economic Co-operation and Development (OECD) examined the relationship between freedom of association and trade and investment patterns and found that, the more successful is trade reform, the greater is
respect for association rights. The authors concluded that freer trade does
not lead industrialized countries to lower their standards, and higher
standards do not jeopardize trade reforms (OECD 1996, 9, 105).

96. http://ciri.binghamton.edu/; http://econ.worldbank.org/WBSITE/
EXTERNAL/EXTDEC/EXTRESEARCH/0,,contentMDK:20388241~menuPK:
665266~pagePK:64165401~piPK:64165026~theSitePK:469382,00.html.

Selected Bibliography

Aaronson, Susan Ariel. 2002. "George W. Bush: Protectionist." *International Economy* 16: 54–56.

———. 2007. "Seeping in Slowly: How Human Rights Concerns Are Penetrating the WTO." *World Trade Review* 6 (3): 413–49.

Aaronson, Susan Ariel, and Rod Abouharb. Forthcoming. "Strange Bed-
fellows: The WTO and Democratic Rights." *International Studies
Quarterly.*

Aaronson, Susan Ariel, and Jamie M. Zimmerman. 2007. *Trade Imbalance:
The Struggle to Weigh Human Rights in Trade Policymaking.* New York:
Cambridge University Press.

Bagwell, Kyle, and Robert W. Staiger. 1998. "The Simple Economics of
Labor Standards and the GATT." NBER Working Paper 6604, National
Bureau of Economic Research, Cambridge, MA. http://www.nber.org/
papers/w6604.

Bal, Salman. 2001. "International Free Trade Agreements and Human
Rights: Reinterpreting Article XX of the GATT." *Minnesota Journal of
International Trade* 10 (62): 62–108.

Bartels, Lorand. 2005a. "Human Rights and Democracy Clauses in the
EU's International Agreements." Prepared for the Subcommittee on
Human Rights, Committee on Foreign Affairs, European Parliament,
EP/EXPOL/B/2005/, Brussels.

———. 2005b. *Human Rights Conditionality in the EU's International
Agreements.* Oxford, U.K.: Oxford University Press.

———. 2008. "The Application of Human Rights Conditionality in the
EU's Bilateral Trade Agreements and Other Trade Arrangements with
Third Countries." Report for the European Parliament, Brussels.

———. 2009a. "Social Issues: Labour, Environment and Human Rights."
In *Bilateral and Regional Trade Agreements: Commentary and Analysis,*
ed. Simon Lester and Bryan Mercurio, 340–66. Cambridge, U.K.:
Cambridge University Press.

———. 2009b. "Trade and Human Rights." In *Oxford Handbook of International Trade Law,* ed. D. Bethlehem et al., 571–96. Oxford, U.K.:
Oxford University Press.

Bartels, Lorand, and Federico Ortino. 2006. *Regional Trade Agreements
and the WTO Legal System.* Oxford, U.K.: Oxford University Press.

Barton, John H. 2006. The *Evolution of the Trade Regime: Politics, Law, and
Economics of the GATT and the WTO.* Princeton, NJ: Princeton University Press.

Bhagwati, Jagdish. 1996. "Introduction." In *Economic Analysis.* Vol. 1 of
Fair Trade and Harmonization: Prerequisites for Free Trade? ed. Jagdish
Bhagwati and Robert Hudec. Cambridge, MA: MIT Press.

Bidwell, Percy. 1939. *The Invisible Tariff: A Study of the Control of Imports
into the United States.* New York: Council on Foreign Relations.

Bolle, Mary Jane. 2009. "Proposed Colombia Free Trade Agreement:
Labor Issues." Report RL34759, Congressional Research Service,
Library of Congress, Washington, DC. http://88.80.13.160/leak/crs/
RL34759.pdf.

Bourgeois, Jacques, Kamala Dawar, and Simon J. Evenett. 2007. "A Comparative Analysis of Selected Provisions in Free Trade Agreements." Prepared for the Directorate General for Trade, European Union, Brussels.

Brown, Drusilla K. 2001. "Labor Standards: Where Do They Belong on the
International Trade Agenda?" Working Paper, Department of Economics, Tufts University, Medford, MA. http://ase.tufts.edu/econ/
papers/200113.pdf.

Büthe, Tim, and Helen V. Milner. 2008. "The Politics of Foreign Direct
Investment into Developing Countries: Increasing FDI through International Trade Agreements?" *American Journal of Political Science* 52
(4, October): 741–62.

CCIC (Canadian Council for International Co-operation), Americas Policy Group. 2009. "What Role for Canada in the Americas?" CCIC,
Ottawa. http://www.ccic.ca/_files/en/working_groups/003_apg_2009-
04-15_statement_what_role_for_cda_in_americas.pdf.

CEA (Council of Economic Advisors). 2005. *Economic Report of the President, 2005.* Washington, DC: CEA.

Charnovitz, Steve. 1987. "The Influence of International Labor Standards
on the World Trading Regime: A Historical Overview." *International
Labour Review* 126 (5): 565–84.

———. 1994. "The World Trade Organization and Social Issues." *Journal of World Trade* 28 (5, October): 17–33.

———. 1998. "The Moral Exception in Trade Policy." *Virginia Journal of International Law* 38 (4, Summer): 689–745. http://www.world-tradelaw.net/articles/charnovitzmoral.pdf.

———. 2001. "The WTO and the Rights of the Individual." *Intereconomics* 36 (2, March): 98–108. SSRN: http://ssrn.com/abstract=282021.

———. 2005. "The Labor Dimension of the Emerging Free Trade Area of the Americas." GWU Law School Public Law and Legal Theory Paper 140, George Washington University, Washington, DC. SSRN: http://ssrn.com/abstract=705301.

Cherfane, Carol Couchani. 2006. "Trade and Environment Decision-Making in the Arab Region." United National Economic and Social Commission for Western Asia, Muscat, Oman. http://css.escwa.org.lb/25mar06/14.pdf.

Commission on Human Rights. 2004. "Economic, Social and Cultural Rights: On Human Rights Resolution 2003/25." E/CN.4/2004/10, United Nations, New York.

Compa, Lance A., and Stephen F. Diamond, eds. 1996. *Human Rights, Labor Rights, and International Trade.* Philadelphia, PA: University of Pennsylvania Press.

Cottier, Thomas, Joost Pauwelyn, and Elizabeth Bürgi, eds. 2005. *Human Rights and International Trade.* Oxford, U.K.: Oxford University Press.

Cox, Phyllida, Peter Newell, Tracy Tuplin, and Diana Tussie. 2006. "Civil Society Participation in Trade Policy-Making in Latin America: Reflections and Lessons." IDS Working Paper 267, Institute of Development Studies, University of Sussex, Brighton, U.K. http://www.iadb.org/intal/intalcdi/PE/2009/02463.pdf.

Damro, Chad. 2006. "The Political Economy of Regional Trade Agreements." In *Regional Trade Agreements and the WTO Legal System,* ed. Lorand Bartels and Federico Ortino. Oxford, U.K.: Oxford University Press.

Dawar, Kamala. 2008. "Assessing Labour and Environmental Regimes in Regional Trading Arrangements." University of Amsterdam Law School, Amsterdam, Netherlands.

Diebold, William. 1952. "The End of the I.T.O." *Essays in International Finance* 16: 1–37.

Dobbin, Frank, Beth Simmons, and Geoffrey Garrett. 2007. "The Global Diffusion of Public Policies: Social Construction, Coercion, Competition, or Learning?" *Annual Review of Sociology* 33: 449–72.

Dommen, Caroline. 2002. "Raising Human Rights Concerns in the World Trade Organization: Actors, Processes and Possible Strategies." *Human Rights Quarterly* 24 (1, February): 1–50.

Drahos, Peter, and Ruth Mayne. 2002. *Global Intellectual Property Rights: Knowledge, Access and Development.* London: Macmillan.

Dunoff, Jeffrey L. 1999. "Does Globalization Advance Human Rights?" *Brooklyn Journal of International Law* 25 (1).

Evenett, Simon J., and Michael Meier. 2008. "An Interim Assessment of U.S. Trade Policy of Competitive Liberalization." *World Economy* 31 (1): 31–66,

Ferrantino, Michael. 2006. "Policy Anchors: Do Free Trade Agreements and WTO Accessions Serve as Vehicles for Developing-Country Policy Reform?" U.S. International Trade Commission, Washington, DC. SSRN: http://papers.ssrn.com/sol3/papers.cfm?abstract_id=895272.

Florentine, Robert V., Luis Verdeja, and Christelle Toqueboeuf. 2007. "The Changing Landscape of Regional Trade Agreements: 2006 Update." WTO Discussion Paper 12, World Trade Organization, Geneva.

Garcia, Frank. 1999. "The Global Market and Human Rights: Trading Away the Human Rights Principle." *Brooklyn Journal of International Law* 25: 51–97.

———. 2003. "Integrating Trade and Human Rights in the Americas." Research Paper 26, Boston College of Law, Boston, MA. SSRN: http://papers.ssrn.com/sol3/papers.cfm?abstract_id=470201.

GATT (General Agreement on Tariffs and Trade), Negotiating Group on Dispute Settlement. 1989. "Non-Violation Complaints under GATT Article XXIII: 2." Note by the Secretariat, MTN.GNG/NG13/W/31, GATT, Geneva. http://www.worldtradelaw.net/history/urdsu/w31.pdf.

Hafner-Burton, Emilie M. 2009. *Forced to Be Good: Why Trade Agreements Boost Human Rights.* Ithaca, NY: Cornell University Press.

Hamilton, Carl B. 2002. "Globalization and Democracy." CEPR Discussion Paper 3653, Centre for Economic Policy Research, London.

Harrison, James. 2009. "Conducting a Human Rights Impact Assessment of the Canada–Colombia Free Trade Agreement, Key Issues." Americas Policy Group, Canadian Council for International Co-operation, Ottawa. http://www.ccic.ca/_files/en/working_groups/003_apg_2009-02_hr_assess_of_cfta.pdf.

Horn, Henrik, Petros C. Mavroidis, and André Sapir. 2010. "Beyond the WTO? An Anatomy of EU and US Preferential Trade Agreements." *World Economy* 33 (11): 1565–88.

Howse, Robert. 2002. "Human Rights in the WTO: Whose Rights, What Humanity? Comment on Petersmann." *European Journal of International Law* 13 (3): 651–59.

Keyder, Virginia Brown. 2005. "From Information to Property and Back Again." *Information and Communications Technology Law* 14 (3, October): 299–312.

Lester, Simon, and Bryan Mercurio. 2009. *Bilateral and Regional Trade Agreements: Commentary and Analysis.* Cambridge, U.K.: Cambridge University Press.

Lim, Hoe. 2001. "Trade and Human Rights: What's at Issue?" E/C 12/2001/WP.2, United Nations Economic and Social Council, New York. http://www.unhchr.ch/tbs/doc.nsf/0/907f88e4d28e4cb9c1256a63003069fd?Opendocument.

Lombardt, Ivin. 2008. "Role and Influence of Civil Society in Malawi's Trade Policy Making Process: The Case of the Malawi Economic Justice Network." One World Action, London. http://www.oneworldaction.org/OneStopCMS/Core/CrawlerResourceServer.aspx?resource=2BAA53AE-4BEF-44CD-9CD0-B5679F7411C4&mode=link&guid=bd9097b13c2f433e891e779111c14bc3.

Mansfield, Edward D., and Jon C. Pevehouse. 2008. "Democratization and the Varieties of International Organizations." *Journal of Conflict Resolution* 52 (2, April): 269–94.

Marceau, Gabrielle. 2001. "WTO Dispute Settlement and Human Rights." Prepared for the joint meeting of the American Society of International Law and the World Trade Forum on "International Economic Law and Human Rights."

Mehra, Malini, ed. 1999. *Human Rights and Economic Globalisation: Directions for the WTO.* London: Global Publications Foundation and International NGO Committee on Human Rights in Trade and Investment.

Mercurio, Bryan. 2006. "TRIPS-Plus Provisions in RTAs: Recent Trends." In *Regional Trade Agreements and the WTO Legal System.* ed. Lorand Bartels and Federico Ortino. Oxford, U.K.: Oxford University Press.

Morales-Moreno, Isidro. 2005. "Mexico's Agricultural Trade Policies: International Commitments and Domestic Pressure." In *Managing the Challenges of WTO Participation: 45 Case Studies,* ed. Peter Gallagher, Patrick Low, and Andrew L. Stoler. Cambridge, U.K.: Cambridge University Press. http://www.wto.org/english/res_e/booksp_e/casestudies_e/case28_e.htm.

Nickel, James. 2006. "Human Rights." In Stanford Encyclopedia of Philosophy: Fall 2006 Edition, Stanford University, Stanford, CA. http://plato.stanford.edu/archives/fall2006/entries/rights-human/.

OECD (Organisation for Economic Cooperation and Development), 1996. "Trade Employment and Labor Standards: A Study of Core Workers' Rights and International Trade." OECD, Paris.

Petersmann, Ernest-Ulrich. 2000. "The WTO Constitution and Human Rights." *Journal of International Economic Law* 3 (1): 19–25.

———. 2001. "Human Rights and International Economic Law in the 21st Century: The Need to Clarify Their Interrelationship." *Journal of International Economic Law* 4 (1, March): 3–39.

————. 2002. "Time for a United Nations 'Global Compact' for Integrating Human Rights into the Law of Worldwide Organizations: Lessons from European Integration." *European Journal of International Law* 13 (3): 621–50.

————. 2006. "The WTO and Regional Trade Agreements as Competing Fora for Constitutional Reforms: Trade and Human Rights." In *Regional Trade Agreements and the WTO Legal System,* ed. Lorand Bartels and Federico Ortino, 281–312. Oxford, U.K.: Oxford University Press.

Powell, Stephen J. 2005. "Regional Economic Arrangements and the Rule of Law in the Americas: The Human Rights Face of Free Trade Agreements." *Florida Journal of International Law* 17 (1): 59–100. SSRN: http://papers.ssrn.com/sol3/papers.cfm?abstract_id=1115298.

Silvan, Laura. 2004. "10 Years of NAFTA's Commission on Environmental Cooperation in Mexico: Resolving Environmental Problems and Fostering Citizen Participation." IRC Strategic Dialogue 1, International Relations Center, Silver City, NM.

Smith, Carolyn C. 2006. "Trade Promotion Authority and Fast-Track Negotiating Authority for Trade Agreements: Major Votes." Report RS21004, Congressional Research Service, Library of Congress, Washington, DC. http://fpc.state.gov/documents/organization/73937.pdf.

Sykes, Alan O'Neil. 2003. "International Trade and Human Rights: An Economic Perspective." John M. Olin Law and Economics Working Paper 188, Law School, University of Chicago, Chicago, IL. SSRN: http://papers.ssrn.com/sol3/papers.cfm?abstract_id=415802.

Thomas, Melissa. n.d. "The Rule of Law in Western Thought." World Bank Rule of Law and Development website, World Bank, Washington, DC. http://web.worldbank.org/WBSITE/EXTERNAL/TOPICS/EXTLAWJUSTINST/0,,contentMDK:20763590~menuPK:1989584~pagePK:210058~piPK:210062~theSitePK:1974062,00.html.

3D. 2005. "Planting the Rights Seed: A Human Rights Perspective on Agriculture Trade and the WTO." Backgrounder 1, 3/2005, 4, 3D, Geneva.

————. 2009. "Insights on Human Rights Impact Assessments of Trade Policies and Agreements." 3D, Geneva. http://www.3dthree.org/pdf_3D/HRIAsbackgroundinformation.pdf.

Trebilcock, Michael J. 2001. "Trade Policy and Labour Standards: Objectives, Instruments and Institutions." Law and Economics Research Paper 02-01, University of Toronto Faculty of Law, Toronto, Canada. SSRN: http://ssrn.com/abstract_id=307219.

UNDP (United Nations Development Programme). 2002. *Human Development Report: Deepening Democracy in a Fragmented World.* New York: UNDP. http://hdr.undp.org/reports/global/2002/en/.

U.S. Congress. 2002. *Bipartisan Trade Promotion Authority Act of 2002.* Washington, DC: Government Printing Office. http://www.law.cornell.edu/uscode/html/uscode19/usc_sup_01_19_10_24.html.

U.S. GAO (General Accountability Office). 2009. "Four Free Trade Agreements GAO Reviewed Have Resulted in Commercial Benefits, but Challenges on Labor and Environment Remain." Highlights of GAO-09-439 (July), GAO, Washington, DC.

USTR (Office of the U.S. Trade Representative). 2005. "Participation, Empowerment, Partnership: Seeking Sustainable Results through US Trade Capacity Building." USTR, Washington, DC.

————. 2009. "The President's Trade Policy Agenda and 2008 Trade Agreements Report." USTR, Washington, DC. http://www.ustr.gov/about-us/press-office/reports-and-publications/2009/2009-trade-policy-agenda-and-2008-annual-report.

————. 2011. "2011 Trade Policy Agenda and 2010 Annual Report of the President of the United States on the Trade Agreements Program." USTR, Washington, DC. http://www.ustr.gov/webfm_send/2597.

van Hees, Floris. 2004. "Protection v. Protectionism: The Use of Human Rights Arguments in the Debate for and against the Liberalization of Trade." Åbo Akademi University, Turku, Finland. http://web.abo.fi/instut/imr/norfa/floris.pdf.

Walker, Simon. 2009. *The Future of Human Rights Impacts Assessments of Trade Agreements.* Mortsel, Belgium: Intersentia.

WHO (World Health Organization). 2006. "Public Health, Innovation and Intellectual Property." Commission on Intellectual Property Rights, Innovation and Public Health, WHO, Geneva. http://www.who.int/intellectualproperty/report/en/.

Wilcox, C. 1949. *A Charter for World Trade.* New York: Macmillan.

WTO (World Trade Organization). 2001. "Trade and Labour Standards: A Difficult Issue for Many WTO Member Governments." DOHA Ministerial 2001, Briefing Notes, WTO, Geneva. http://www.wto.org/english/thewto_e/minist_e/min01_e/brief_e/brief16_e.htm.

22

DISPUTE SETTLEMENT

Amelia Porges

The past 15 or so years have seen the emergence and elaboration of ever more complex preferential trade agreements (PTAs), forming multiple and rapidly proliferating networks. Almost all of these PTAs include a dispute settlement clause of some sort. Indeed, dispute settlement provisions have become a sine qua non for PTA negotiators, even though the number of actual government-government disputes within PTAs is only a fraction of the hundreds of existing agreements.

Governments enter into PTAs expecting to secure economic benefits. In particular, estimates of the welfare benefits of PTAs normally assume that the parties will faithfully implement their market access commitments. If private investors doubt that the partners to a PTA will actually keep their commitments, they will not engage in the type of risk-taking investment that the PTA could otherwise generate. If a PTA is to be fully implemented and to yield the expected benefits, the agreement should, at a minimum, be equipped with institutions that facilitate information exchange among the parties, help the parties monitor implementation, and provide an incentive structure that meaningfully supports compliance.

A dispute settlement arrangement is part of this necessary structure because there will inevitably be disagreements in a PTA concerning the scope and nature of the commitments that the parties have made. The PTA must provide an orderly way for its members to settle disputes and move on, or else the disputes will poison bilateral relations, reduce the PTA's benefit, and perhaps even lead to the demise of the agreement.

Dispute settlement mechanisms are also needed to ensure that the promises in a PTA are kept. Economic studies on PTAs teach that where the parties' tariffs are low ex ante, a PTA between them will only produce gains if it involves deep integration provisions. Those provisions need to be backed up by enforcement. Every economic projection of the gains from a PTA is based on the assumption

of 100 percent compliance with the PTA's obligations. Ensuring compliance through enforcement is essential if the gains are to materialize. PTAs therefore typically include some mechanism incorporating elements of both compliance enforcement and dispute settlement.

By participating in a PTA with strong dispute settlement provisions, a government signals its level of commitment to private and public interests at home and abroad. Each PTA competes with other PTAs for investment, jobs, and economic growth, in a field that becomes more crowded every year. Even if no disputes are anticipated, enforcement provisions in a PTA reinforce the precommitment of the governments, make their promises more credible, and signal that the PTA is a solid platform for investment that will create jobs and economic growth.

Solid dispute settlement is even more important in North-South (or South-South) PTAs with asymmetrical power relations. Recently concluded PTAs in Latin America, Europe, and Asia demonstrate to a striking extent that as PTA obligations deepen, become more complex, and provide more value, PTA partners seek more certainty than purely diplomatic dispute settlement can provide.

In theory, the parties to a PTA are the masters of their own treaty and could design an original dispute settlement mechanism from the ground up, or have no dispute settlement mechanism at all. In practice, almost all PTAs rely on one of the three general types of dispute settlement mechanisms: diplomatic settlement by negotiation; judgments by standing tribunals; or the World Trade Organization (WTO) model, in which an ad hoc panel is convened to hear the dispute. Many recent PTAs have adopted the third system, based on the WTO's Dispute Settlement Understanding (DSU). The WTO model has provided a useful focal point for bargaining; its familiarity means that negotiators and stakeholders understand how it works and what trade-offs can be made.

This chapter, the last in the volume, discusses the options available for dispute settlement and enforcement provisions in PTAs. Following a brief literature review, we outline the three models of dispute settlement in PTAs, discuss their scope and exclusions, and compare them from the standpoint of development, infrastructure cost, and open regionalism. We then examine how PTAs define the scope of disputes that they will deal with, their handling of overlap and forum choice between the PTA and WTO dispute settlement systems, and various procedural and institutional issues. Subsequent sections describe alternative dispute resolution procedures and examine compliance procedures and enforcement issues and decisions. The final sections explore the reasons for the limited use of PTA dispute settlement procedures to date and present the conclusions and recommendations that emerge from the study.

Literature on PTA Dispute Settlement

The surge in the number of PTAs is a rather recent phenomenon. As yet, few cross-regional comparative surveys of PTA dispute settlement have been published, and those that do exist focus on the dispute settlement mechanisms in particular PTA agreements, regions, or networks rather than on the application of the mechanisms. The reason is that the number of cases of government-to-government PTA disputes that can be examined is still small.

General Surveys

The most significant recent general survey, by Donaldson and Lester (2009), concentrates on a sample of 20 recently concluded PTAs, primarily in the Asia-Pacific area, and almost all with dispute settlement systems based on the WTO model. The authors provide a detailed comparison of the various stages of handling disputes in these PTAs and in the DSU and include a useful discussion of the institutions that administer dispute settlement. An older study (Smith 2000) evaluates legalism in PTA disputes by analyzing a coded dataset of 60 pre-1996 PTAs. Smith finds that legalism improves compliance by increasing the costs of opportunism and the probability of detection. He argues that negotiators, in drafting PTAs, weigh the benefits of improved treaty compliance against the costs of limited policy discretion for their own countries. PTA parties with high relative economic power accordingly favor less legalistic dispute settlement, and so standing tribunals such as the European Court of Justice (ECJ) exist only in those PTAs in which asymmetry of power is low. Deeper integration also favors legalism because it generates more economic gains and because the trade barriers involved are more complex.

Kwak and Marceau (2006) present an updated cross-regional summary of PTA dispute settlement provisions and conclude that there is a real possibility of overlaps or conflicts of jurisdiction between the WTO and PTA dispute settlement mechanisms. They outline in tabular form the dispute settlement provisions of the main PTAs in all regions, with attention to issues that affect such overlaps or conflicts. Morgan (2008) confirms the trend toward greater legalism in PTA dispute settlement but argues that the absence of effective enforcement mechanisms forces the parties to find negotiated solutions. He points out that even within the North American Free Trade Agreement (NAFTA), Canada opted for a negotiated settlement to its long-running softwood lumber dispute with the United States, after a series of rulings in NAFTA and the WTO.

European Union (EU) PTAs

Garcia Bercero (2006), a negotiator for the European Commission, surveys the development of the Commission's thinking on dispute settlement in trade agreements, starting with the traditional diplomatic approach seen in the EU's association agreements and other agreements before 2000, and discusses why the Commission's preferences have shifted toward ad hoc arbitration procedures in the free trade agreements (FTAs) with Mexico and Chile. In studies of earlier EU PTAs, Ramirez Robles (2006) finds that the political model of dispute settlement has been the dominant model for EU association agreements, and Broude (2007) surveys the disputes brought under these earlier PTAs. Broude argues that the dispute settlement provisions of most EU PTAs contribute to EU regional hegemony by encouraging and perpetuating nonjudicialized bilateral dispute settlement, where the EU has advantages. He points out that EU PTA partners do not even use the WTO system for settlement of their own disputes and do not have the real option of recourse to judicial dispute settlement procedures in their relations with the EU.

U.S. PTAs

EU association agreements have opted for political settlement of bilateral disputes. Thus, the first PTAs to incorporate formal panel procedures of the type used in the WTO and its predecessor, the General Agreement on Tariffs and Trade (GATT), were the Canada–U.S. FTA (CUSFTA) and NAFTA. U.S. PTAs still largely follow the CUSFTA/NAFTA model, although post-2001 PTAs have departed from it in some respects, as discussed below. Annex A gives an account of the dispute settlement choices made in negotiating these agreements—choices that influenced the design of the WTO

Dispute Settlement Understanding (DSU). Hart, Dymond, and Robertson (1994); Kreinin (2000); and Cameron and Tomlin (2002) provide detailed accounts of the negotiations. Among the abundant literature on these agreements, Loungnarath and Stehly (2000) analyze CUSFTA and NAFTA disputes and argue that political pressure has impaired outcomes for Canada, as the weaker partner. Davey (1996) presents a detailed retrospective on every CUSFTA dispute. He concludes that binational review of trade remedy decisions under CUSFTA Chapter 19 has been generally reasonable but could be improved, and he makes suggestions for minor changes to that end. He also finds that the general trade dispute procedures of Chapter 18 were not an improvement on GATT procedure; in practice, the parties largely preferred GATT for their bilateral disputes, and he predicts that the NAFTA governments will continue to prefer WTO procedures wherever possible. Gantz (2006) surveys experience under the three NAFTA dispute settlement mechanisms (state-to-state trade disputes, antidumping and countervailing duty binational reviews, and investor-state arbitration), reviews U.S. attitudes toward NAFTA dispute settlement, and discusses the decline in U.S. government support for NAFTA since 1994. He rates Chapter 19 review of antidumping and countervailing duty decisions as a success—although it enjoys little support in the U.S. government, which has not included such a provision in any post-NAFTA PTA.[1]

East Asian PTAs

As Baldwin (2008) points out, East Asia's regional integration into "Factory Asia" took place initially not through PTAs but through unilateral cuts in most favored nation (MFN) tariffs. Baldwin notes the potential insecurity of such liberalization, which is not backed by any enforceable legal obligations. He characterizes the Association of Southeast Asian Nations (ASEAN)–China FTA initiative in 2000 as the trigger for similar moves by Japan, the Republic of Korea, and others, resulting in the current "noodle bowl" of East Asian PTAs. Wang (2009) describes the Dispute Settlement Mechanism Agreement of the ASEAN–China FTA as a "landmark agreement," since it is China's first PTA to provide for settlement of bilateral or regional disputes through formal procedures, even to the extent of authorizing trade retaliation. Snyder (2009) analyzes China's PTAs and finds that almost all have used WTO dispute settlement as a template, with the exception of China's Closer Economic Partnership Agreements (CEPAs) with Hong Kong SAR, China, and Macao SAR, China. Disputes under the CEPA agreements are settled diplomatically, by consultation and agreement between the parties.

Choi (2004) analyzes the dispute settlement provisions of a selection of East Asian PTAs and makes a number of specific suggestions for PTA dispute settlement procedures. Choi suggests that opening panel hearings in such disputes would be undesirable because it would increase pressure on panelists by domestic interest groups. Luo (2005) discusses the "Asian way" of dispute settlement under ASEAN and points out that, following the establishment of the ASEAN Dispute Settlement Mechanism (DSM) in 1996, there were many actual disputes among ASEAN members concerning implementation of the ASEAN Free Trade Area, but none were brought to the DSM. Luo suggests the use of an independent enforcement body, or access for private parties, to counteract governments' reluctance to engage in open conflict. Nakagawa (2007) analyzes the use of dispute settlement by East Asian governments in the WTO and in PTAs. He argues that most trade disputes between Asian PTA parties will be brought to the WTO and that settlement of disputes through negotiated deals will continue to be the trend in East Asia because of underlying economic factors and the limits on what dispute settlement mechanisms can accomplish. Kawai and Wignaraja (2009) present the results of a survey of firms in East Asia. They find that most of the firms surveyed do not use PTA preferences because of lack of information, costs related to rules of origin, and low margins of preference. Obviously, if firms are not using PTAs, there will be fewer PTA-related disputes.

Latin American PTAs

A wealth of data is available on dispute settlement in PTAs in Latin America and the Caribbean.[2] Sáez (2007) finds that countries in the region have been very active in dispute settlement, that they use the WTO even when PTA dispute settlement mechanisms exist, and that in Latin American PTAs, disputes on tariff application, drawback, and excise tax discrimination have tended to peak during an agreement's initial period, when tariffs are being phased out.

There is a substantial scholarly literature in Spanish examining the Andean Community institutions, the dispute settlement mechanism of the Southern Cone Common Market (Mercosur, Mercado Común del Sur), the Latin American Integration Association/Asociación Latinoamericana de Integración (LAIA/ALADI), and other regional institutions in the light of Latin American domestic and international legal doctrine. English-language sources consulted for this chapter include the valuable recent empirical studies on the Andean Community by Helfer and Alter (2009) and Alter and Helfer (2011), as well as a collection edited by Lacarte and

Granados (2004), which covers dispute settlement under LAIA/ALADI (Rojas Penso 2004), Mercosur (Opertti 2004; Whitelaw 2004), the Andean Community (Vigil Toledo 2004), and various Central American trade agreements (Echandi 2004).

African PTAs

World Bank and International Monetary Fund (IMF) studies on African regionalism (Foroutan 1992; Yang and Gupta 2005), as well as discussions in World Bank (2000), Schiff and Winters (2003), Gathii (2010), and Thorp (2010), note the dense web of PTAs in Africa. These studies generally find that, although most African PTAs have a high level of ambition for integration, they have not been effective in eliminating intraregional trade and investment barriers and have struggled with (or succumbed to) economic conflict resulting from an asymmetric distribution of gains from liberalization. Implementation of PTAs has been beset with obstacles, including linguistic differences, intra-PTA differences between common law and civil law systems, and a pervasive shortage of resources for PTA institutions, including those involved in dispute settlement. As noted by Essien (2006), general information on the status of PTA courts in Africa is difficult to find. Gathii (2010) presents a broader portrait of African PTAs, arguing that they must be understood as flexible regimes that incorporate variable geometry, asymmetric obligations, mechanisms for redistributing benefits, and commitments that are perhaps not meant to be enforced. If enforcement is not intended, a scarcity of formal trade agreement disputes should be no surprise.

Dispute Settlement and Enforcement: The Basic Options

In theory, the negotiators of a PTA start with a blank slate and can choose any form or type of dispute settlement they wish. In practice, dispute settlement mechanisms in PTAs fall into three broad groups: political or diplomatic dispute settlement; systems based on a standing tribunal; and referral to an ad hoc arbitral panel, as in the WTO. In a negotiating situation, the choice of system depends, first, on whether the governments wish to have a third-party dispute settlement procedure, rather than rely solely on negotiation to settle disputes. If they opt for a third-party decision maker, they can go down the path of establishing a standing tribunal, or they can follow the currently dominant approach of using a WTO-type ad hoc panel procedure. The pros and cons of each approach are discussed next.

Political or Diplomatic Dispute Settlement

Political or diplomatic dispute settlement consists of settling disputes by negotiation and agreement. It gives the parties to a PTA maximum flexibility. The agreement may have no dispute settlement provisions at all; it may provide only for consultations; it may provide for consultations and refer disputes to a political body for resolution; or it may provide for referral to a third-party adjudicator but allow a party or parties to block the referral.

The choice of a political dispute settlement model often reflects asymmetric power relations between the PTA parties. For instance, China's Closer Economic Partnership Agreements with Hong Kong SAR, China, and with Macao SAR, China, state that the parties "shall resolve any problems arising from the interpretation or implementation of the 'CEPA' through consultation in the spirit of friendship and cooperation." In pre-2000 European Union PTAs and in the 1969 Southern African Customs Union (SACU), disputes were settled exclusively through political processes. The use of political dispute settlement may also reflect a low level of ambition for implementation of intra-PTA liberalization, as in the case of partial-scope agreements in LAIA/ALADI, in ASEAN trade liberalization in the 1990s, and in the Economic Cooperation Organization Trade Agreement entered into by Central Asian countries.

The choice of political dispute settlement method may also reflect a level of deep integration that gives both sides in a PTA real leverage, even without third-party adjudication, as in the Australia–New Zealand Closer Economic Relations Trade Agreement (ANZCERTA) and in the relations between Australia and New Zealand under the recently signed ASEAN–Australia–New Zealand agreement.

The diplomatic model of dispute settlement was the dominant model in all the EU's pre-2000 association agreements and PTAs. These include the Europe Agreements with Eastern European accession candidate countries; the Euro-Mediterranean Agreements with the Arab Republic of Egypt, Israel, Jordan, Morocco, and Tunisia; and the Stabilization and Association Agreements with Balkan countries (Ramirez Robles 2006). A party to one of these agreements may refer to the agreement's Association Council any dispute concerning the application or interpretation of the agreement, and the Association Council may, by consensus, adopt a binding decision to resolve the dispute. Broude (2009) describes this concept as "a case of *faux* institutionalization—the Association Council is a ministerial-level body, designed to meet but once a year." He notes that, in practice, disputes are officially delegated to an Association Committee that reports to the Council and are handled by diplomatic negotiation. In theory, these agreements permit any party to have recourse to arbitration if negotiations fail to settle a dispute, but the appointment of arbitrators can be blocked, and there are no deadlines or procedures. The agreements provide no organized procedures for ensuring compliance with arbitral awards except for a "nonexecution clause" that permits a party to take "appropriate measures," even without going through a dispute settlement procedure, if it considers that the other party has failed to fulfill an obligation under the agreement.

Garcia Bercero (2006) states that this diplomatic approach has been an effective means of settling "low profile trade irritants" but that some disputes linger unresolved for years, if one party is stubborn and the other is unwilling to blow up the relationship by taking retaliatory action. He reports that the arbitration procedure has seldom been used, that the nonexecution clause has been invoked very sparingly, and that most of these invocations have involved EU disputes with the Russian Federation.

The standard dispute settlement procedure in LAIA/ALADI is set forth in Resolution 114 of the association's Committee of Representatives. The resolution, adopted in 1990, provides for consultations between the parties, after which a member country may request the Committee of Representatives to propose a nonbinding solution. The association's secretary-general has characterized this system as "virtually useless" and ineffective in resolving disputes (Rojas Penso 2004). As a result, parties to the partial-scope agreements within LAIA/ALADI have adopted specific dispute settlement procedures. Some agreements simply rely on direct negotiations, and some recent ones provide for third-party panels.

The 1992 ASEAN Framework Agreement and the Agreement on the Common Effective Preferential Tariff Scheme for the ASEAN Free Trade Area both provided for settlement of disputes by agreement between the parties, with referral of nonsettled disputes to a ministerial-level body. (This scheme has since been replaced by a panel mechanism, as discussed below.)

To a notable extent, PTAs that started with diplomatic or political dispute settlement have moved toward rule-oriented third-party dispute settlement modeled on the DSU. Examples include ASEAN, which replaced earlier arrangements with the 2004 ASEAN Protocol on Enhanced Dispute Settlement Mechanism; SACU, which implemented a DSU-type scheme in the 2002 SACU Agreement; and Mercosur, an agreement formally within the LAIA/ALADI framework, which provides an elaborate third-party dispute settlement system, including appellate review. The FTAs and economic partnership agreements (EPAs) negotiated by the EU since 2007 have shifted to panel-based third-party dispute settlement.

Standing Tribunals

The standing tribunals of the European Union represent the oldest system of this kind. Its example has been highly influential worldwide, but especially in countries with historical ties to Europe.

The EU system. The European Court of Justice (ECJ) is the original PTA standing tribunal. Established in 1952 as the Court of Justice of the European Coal and Steel Community, it later became the Court of Justice of the European Communities and is now known formally as the Court of Justice of the European Union. It now consists of the 27-judge Court of Justice itself; a 27-judge court of first instance, the General Court; and the Civil Service Tribunal, for EU civil service employment disputes. In 2009 the ECJ received 562 new cases, completed 588 cases, and had 742 cases pending at the end of the year. The 562 new cases comprised 302 requests from EU member state courts for preliminary rulings on issues of EU law, 143 direct actions, 105 appeals, and a few other cases (ECJ 2010a).

Direct actions include enforcement actions brought by the European Commission against a member state for failure to fulfill an obligation under Article 258 of the Treaty on the Functioning of the European Union and (very rarely) cases brought by one member state against another regarding nonfulfillment of EU Treaty obligations (Article 259). In enforcement actions, the Commission sends a letter of formal notice to a member state—the most recent official figures show that about 68 percent of complaints are settled before this point (European Commission 2009). After giving the member state an opportunity to reply, the Commission delivers a "reasoned opinion"; about 84 percent of infringement procedures based on a complaint are settled before this stage. If the member state does not comply with the reasoned opinion by a deadline set by the Commission, the Commission may bring a case before the ECJ; around 94 percent of these infringement procedures are settled before an ECJ ruling. Thus, only 6 percent of all procedures are resolved by the court. Judgments under Article 259 or its predecessor provisions have been extremely rare (fewer than five since 1951). In practice, if an EU government or stakeholder has a problem with another member state's compliance with EU Treaty rules, it lobbies the Commission to negotiate with the noncomplying government and possibly bring an action under Article 258. The Commission then takes on the resource and reputational costs of negotiation and litigation and is also free to pursue its own institutional agenda.

The ECJ and the European Commission enforcement infrastructure represent the maximum in treaty enforcement, as measured by activity and resources. At the end of 2008, the Commission was handling 1,557 complaints and infringement files. Complaints accounted for two-thirds of all cases other than those regarding late implementation of EU directives. In 2008 the Commission opened 2,223 infringement procedures, sent 512 reasoned opinions, and referred 209 cases to the ECJ (European Commission 2009).

The ECJ also provides guidance to the courts in all member states, through preliminary rulings on EU law requested by national courts. These preliminary references ensure uniform application of EU law, and the principles they establish affect the entire EU legal order. They have given the ECJ a platform for establishing fundamental principles of EU law, such as its direct effect in national law, and legal doctrines safeguarding freedom of movement of goods and services. Private actors can bring domestic court cases in order to obtain an ECJ preliminary ruling.

The ECJ and the judicial structure under it represent a very large commitment of resources. Its 27 judges, one for each member state, are assisted by a registrar; 8 Advocates-General who provide impartial advisory opinions on the cases before the Court; and a large staff, including many translators, housed in a new building in Luxembourg. The ECJ also acts as an appellate court for cases brought before the 27-judge General Court or the Civil Service Tribunal. The 2011 draft budget for the Court of Justice of the European Union, comprising all these courts, is projected at 345,293,000 euros (about US$450 million), not including the Commission's enforcement expenses. Of the total, 75 percent goes for personnel and 25 percent for buildings and other costs (EU 2010).

Other standing tribunals. The obligations of the European Free Trade Area (EFTA) and the European Economic Area (EEA) are enforced by the EFTA Surveillance Authority and the EFTA Court. The most recent figures, for 2008, show an actual cost for both of 3,606,035 euros (EFTA Court 2009).

A number of South-South PTAs have patterned their dispute settlement institutions on the ECJ and the European Commission: they include the Andean Community, the Economic Community of West African States (ECOWAS), the West African Economic and Monetary Union/Union Économique et Monétaire Ouest-Africaine (WAEMU/UEMOA), the Economic and Monetary Community of Central Africa (CEMAC, Communauté Économique et Monétaire de l'Afrique Centrale), the East African Community (EAC), and the Common Market for Eastern and Southern Africa (COMESA).The reasons for following the EU model are partly historical and (in the case of African PTAs) partly attributable to the influence of the EU as the regional hegemon. At the time many of these PTAs were negotiated, the GATT dispute settlement mechanism was in disuse or did not otherwise provide a positive model for enforcement of obligations. The project of building the European Community and then the European Union provided a stronger model for PTA ambitions.

The most judicialized South-South PTA dispute settlement institutions, the Andean Tribunal of Justice (ATJ) and the Andean Community General Secretariat, were established in 1979 as part of the Andean Pact. Treaty amendments in 1996 created a new Andean Community, strengthened the ATJ, gave the General Secretariat a stronger role, and reduced diplomatic elements in the procedures. The General Secretariat may now initiate a noncompliance investigation on its own and must initiate an investigation in response to a complaint by a government or private party. There have been up to 30 such cases per year.[3] The General Secretariat sends a notice to the government concerned, which must respond. The General Secretariat then issues a reasoned opinion, which is published and with which the government concerned is obligated to comply. If the government does not comply, then the General Secretariat, a complaining member state, or a private party whose rights have been affected may bring a noncompliance case (*acción de incumplimiento*) against the noncomplying country to the ATJ, which sits in Quito. There have been up to 20 such cases per year.[4] If the ATJ makes a finding of noncompliance and the losing government fails to comply by the deadline set by the ATJ, the ATJ may initiate a summary procedure (*procedimiento-sumario*) in response to a request by the General Secretariat, a member state, or an affected private party and may authorize sanctions against the noncomplying government by other member states (Vigil Toledo 2004; CAN 2008a). Alter and Helfer (2011) observe that, compared to the ECJ, the ATJ has been deferential to Andean states and unwilling to push for compliance with Andean law and that the ATJ has "refused to serve as the engine of Andean legal integration"—which they characterize as a politically prudent path in the face of Andean states' "tepid" commitments to Andean integration.

The ATJ also can issue rulings in response to references from national courts; such rulings account for 90 percent of ATJ case law. Ninety-six percent of preliminary references through 2007 involved intellectual property disputes, for three reasons: first, private litigants have rarely used Andean rules to challenge other policies; second, intellectual property agencies in the Andean countries actively encouraged such references and incorporated them into their domestic decision making; third, national courts rarely send novel questions to the ATJ; fourth, there is no infrastructure of scholars and practitioners proselytizing for Andean law; and, fifth, these conditions have continued the same no matter what the level of political support for the Andean Community project (Helfer and Alter 2009; Alter and Helfer 2011). The fiscal 2008 budget for the Andean Tribunal was US$1,170,667.[5]

As part of an overall initiative to strengthen Central American regional integration, governments in the region established the Central American Court of Justice (CACJ), or Corte de Justicia Centroamericana, in 1994. The CACJ has almost never been used for trade disputes. In the late 1990s, the countries established a Central American Trade Dispute Resolution Mechanism, modeled on the WTO, which, since 2003, has applied to all countries in the region (Echandi 2004).

The Caribbean Court of Justice was created in 2001 with a dual role: to serve as a final court of appeal in civil and criminal cases for its member states, and to interpret the Treaty of Chaguaramas, which established the Caribbean Community (CARICOM). The extent of regional support for this court is unclear, and it lacks the institutional support of a secretariat to monitor compliance (INTAL 2005). In 2007 the CCJ's administrative expenses amounted to US$32.2 million (CCJ 2008).

A number of African PTAs have also established courts on the ECJ model; these include ECOWAS, WAEMU/ UEMOA, CEMAC, the EAC, and COMESA. As the following examples illustrate, a regional tribunal created to enforce trade law may also become involved in other issues, and vice versa:

- The ECOWAS Community Court of Justice was created in 1991, but its members were only appointed in 2000. The court sits in Abuja and has a modest budget for handling both enforcement of ECOWAS norms and human rights issues. Originally, only states could bring disputes, but since 2005, individuals have been able to bring cases, including complaints based on human rights instruments. The court has been active recently, but mostly on cases with a human rights dimension (Banjo 2007; Hessbruegge 2011; *Daily Independent* 2011).
- The UEMOA court has a permanent building at its seat in Ouagadougou, and a modest budget.[6] CEMAC's Court of Justice sits in Ndjamena. Each court issues fewer than 10 decisions per year.
- The Court of Justice of the East African Community, which meets in Arusha, Tanzania, was dormant from 1999 until receiving its first case in December 2005. It hears both disputes between member states and preliminary references by courts in member states. Its fiscal 2010/11 budget was US$2,841,777, out of a total EAC

budget of US$60 million, half of which is financed by aid donors (see EAC 2010).
- The COMESA Court of Justice was established in 1994 and appointed in 1998, but since moving to Khartoum in 2006, it has reportedly faced problems with inadequate funds and staff, lack of a physical location, and the need to adapt to *shari'a* law. It has been unable to meet even twice a year. Its 2001 budget was US$595,538 (COMESA 2000, 2009; *East African* 2006; AICT data).[7]
- The SADC Tribunal of 10 part-time members was formally established in 1992 and was inaugurated in 2005. It meets, as required, in Windhoek. It has a registrar and 16 employees. The SADC budget is largely funded by donor countries. The tribunal's cases have included appeals by SADC employees and three cases in which the court condemned Zimbabwe's land reform program as racially discriminatory and illegal under the SADC Treaty. Faced with noncompliance, the complainants have used South African courts to seize property of the Zimbabwe government, and the tribunal has asked the SADC heads of state to consider a request by one of the complainants that the SADC expel Zimbabwe (Nyaungwa 2010; Reuters 2010).

Dispute Settlement by Referral to Ad Hoc Panel (WTO Model)

The third, currently dominant, model for PTA dispute settlement is based on the WTO's dispute settlement system (originally developed in the GATT). A panel is convened for one dispute (thus, it is "ad hoc"), with terms of reference limited to that dispute. The panel hears the written and oral arguments of disputing parties, issues a written ruling applying the trade agreement's law to the dispute, and then disbands. The WTO's dispute settlement procedures have shaped expectations of governments and stakeholders regarding credible dispute settlement and enforcement within trade agreements. As a result, PTA negotiators have converged on the WTO-like model. Dispute settlement procedures of this type are very widespread and appear in virtually all new PTAs, such as the following list, which includes some PTAs that have been signed but not yet ratified:

- Australia: FTAs with Chile, Singapore, and Thailand
- ASEAN Enhanced Dispute Settlement Mechanism, which covers disputes under at least 46 ASEAN agreements on tariff preferences, tariff nomenclature, investment, services, mutual recognition of standards or certification, customs, and the like; ASEAN FTAs with China and Korea; the ASEAN–Australia–New Zealand FTA

- Canada: FTAs with Chile, Colombia, Costa Rica, Israel, Jordan, Panama, and Peru
- Chile: FTAs with Central America, China, Colombia, EFTA, Japan, Korea, Mexico, Panama, and Peru
- China: FTAs with Costa Rica, New Zealand, Pakistan, Peru, and Singapore
- EFTA: FTAs with Canada, Colombia, Croatia, Egypt, Israel, Jordan, Korea, Lebanon, the former Yugoslav Republic of Macedonia, Morocco, and the Palestinian Authority
- EU: FTAs with Chile, Korea, and Mexico and the recent EPA with the Caribbean Forum of African, Caribbean, and Pacific (ACP) States (CARIFORUM)
- India: FTAs with Chile and Mercosur
- Japan: EPAs with Brunei Darussalam, Chile, Indonesia, Malaysia, Mexico, the Philippines, Singapore, Switzerland, Thailand, and Vietnam
- Mercosur: Protocol of Olivos, with Argentina, Brazil, Paraguay, and Uruguay
- Mexico: FTAs with Bolivia, Colombia, EFTA, Israel, Nicaragua, the Northern Triangle countries (El Salvador, Guatemala, and Honduras) and Uruguay
- New Zealand: FTAs with Thailand and Singapore
- Singapore: FTAs with the Gulf Cooperation Council (GCC), India, Jordan, Korea, Panama, and Peru; Trans-Pacific Strategic Economic Partnership (Trans-Pacific SEP).
- United States: NAFTA; U.S. FTAs with Australia, Bahrain, Dominican Republic–Central America Free Trade Agreement (CAFTA–DR), Chile, Colombia, Israel, Jordan, Korea, Morocco, Oman, Panama, Peru, and Singapore

The cost of an ad hoc panel system depends on how many panels exist. If there are none, the cost of dispute settlement approaches zero, as the disputes that do not reach the panel stage will be supervised by existing PTA institutions. The out-of-pocket system costs of panels—panelist compensation and expenses; hearing venue; and clerical, translation, and interpretation services—depend on the parties' procedural choices and the number of disputes. The WTO's annual budget for dispute settlement panels (excluding the organization's first three years) has ranged from a high of 1,195,300 Swiss francs (Sw F) in 1999 to a low of Sw F 655,592 in 2006. For 2011, it was estimated at Sw F 987,000 for panels and Sw F 50,000 for arbitrations (WTO 2009, 52). The WTO's costs for panel proceedings are low in relation to the number of disputes handled because WTO members whose delegates serve as panelists contribute their services without compensation. The estimated 2011 budget for the WTO Appellate Body is

Sw F 5,691,000, of which personnel costs account for 69 percent, or Sw F 3,909,500 (WTO 2009, 52).

These system costs exclude the costs of participation for the parties. Some governments maintain an internal legal staff or otherwise represent themselves in trade disputes. Others hire counsel or expect stakeholders to pay for counsel engaged by the government. The standard ceiling fees for legal assistance (without further subsidy) set by the Advisory Centre for WTO Law provide a lower-bound estimate for legal costs in the WTO: Sw F 47,628 for consultations and Sw F 143,856 for panel proceedings, or Sw F 191,484 together (ACWL 2007).

Choosing among the Options

In considering dispute settlement, the first choice is whether to rely exclusively on diplomatic or political dispute settlement or to provide for third-party dispute settlement of some sort. The key difference between the two is that in the former, a complaining party that has tried and failed to negotiate a mutually satisfactory solution does not have the option of obtaining a determination by a neutral third party. In a tribunal or ad hoc panel system, if there is no agreement, the complaining party can refer the dispute to a neutral decision maker who rules on the dispute. Settlement by negotiation is possible in any system; indeed, the classic WTO model requires that the complaining party give the responding party an opportunity to settle the problem through bilateral consultations, and the preliminary stages in a tribunal system may also result in compliance or a compromise settlement.

Negotiators may choose to rely solely on diplomatic or political dispute settlement if the PTA is unambitious or represents only a low sunk investment in integration. They may also feel that government-government dispute settlement is not necessary if the PTA partners have a transparent commercial and legal environment with stable trade relations and a high degree of economic integration, as in ANZCERTA. And there may be no place for third-party dispute settlement in a PTA with strongly asymmetric relations, such as the CEPAs that China has negotiated with Hong Kong SAR, China, and with Macao SAR, China. Political or diplomatic means of dispute settlement are unlikely, however, to provide a sufficient incentive structure to keep markets open in times of economic stress.

Most recent PTAs have opted for third-party dispute settlement because of significant factors that distinguish the new and enhanced PTAs negotiated since 1994 from their predecessors of the GATT era, as described by Schiff and Winters (2003).

First, many of these agreements have embraced *deep integration*, going well beyond border measures to cover subjects such as investment, services, and domestic regulation. Where a partner has relatively low border barriers, expansion of the scope of the PTA to behind-the-border measures may be necessary if the PTA is to offer substantial economic benefits—as Francois and Manchin (2009) find for a possible PTA between the EU and the Commonwealth of Independent States (CIS). The increased level of ambition involved in a deep integration agreement requires the parties to make a greater resource investment in implementing the agreement. Accordingly, negotiators typically choose legalized, formal dispute settlement, following some widely understood model—currently, that of the WTO. In North-South PTAs with asymmetrical power relations, binding third-party dispute settlement becomes even more important (World Bank 2000, 69–70). Recently concluded PTAs in Latin America, Europe, and Asia demonstrate to a striking degree that as PTA obligations deepen, become more complex, and provide more value, PTA partners seek more certainty than can be had through purely diplomatic dispute settlement.

Second, the dominant paradigm has shifted to integration into the globalized economy through *open regionalism*. "Open regionalism" implies that PTA parties actively seek inclusion in global supply networks under transparent, rule-of-law conditions by using the PTA to secure market access rights, and by turning away from import-substituting industrialization or administrative protectionism. Open regionalism can also lead to coexistence of PTA networks, docking (legal connection) of PTA networks, and even multilateralization of PTA networks. Dispute settlement can reinforce open regionalism in the first sense by ensuring full PTA implementation and reinforcing the PTA's lock-in effect. Systems based on a regional court can be an important focus of region building, as seen in the case of the European Court of Justice. However, if the goal is to connect PTAs into larger networks, ad hoc panel systems are easier to merge than court-based systems of dispute settlement.

Structuring a PTA Dispute Settlement System: More Decisions

Some threshold decisions are required in order to set the system's parameters. The agreement will need to define the range of possible complaints, or "causes of action," as well as their potential subject scope. Since practically all PTAs overlap with the WTO (and may overlap with other PTAs), PTA negotiators must also decide what will happen in the event that a party brings claims under the WTO concerning a measure disputed in the PTA.

Defining the Grounds for Complaint

Breach of obligations. Many PTAs simply state that dispute settlement will be available in cases of violation of the PTA obligations or of failure to implement the PTA; some also allow for the use of the mechanism to settle disputes regarding interpretation of the PTA. For instance, in CUSFTA and later U.S. FTAs, the dispute settlement provisions apply with respect to avoidance or settlement of disputes regarding the interpretation or application of the agreement, or regarding measures considered to be inconsistent with the obligations of the agreement. Some PTAs (e.g., the Japan–Chile and ASEAN–Australia–New Zealand agreements) draw instead on the formulation in GATT Article XXIII:1(a), which permits invocation of the dispute settlement mechanism when a "benefit accruing . . . directly or indirectly under this Agreement is being nullified or impaired . . . or the attainment of any objective of this Agreement is being impeded as the result of the failure of another [party] to carry out its obligations under this Agreement."

Nonviolation nullification or impairment of concessions or obligations. Some PTAs give their parties not just a remedy against violation or noncompliance by another party, but also a remedy against measures of other parties that are PTA-consistent but still take away the benefit of bargained-for PTA market access. These "nonviolation nullification or impairment" remedies are modeled on GATT Article XXIII:1(b).[8] GATT and WTO panels have interpreted Article XXIII:1(b) as providing for recourse when (a) benefits that could reasonably have been expected at the time of a negotiated market access concession (b) are nullified or impaired by (c) a later (GATT-consistent) government measure that upsets the conditions of competition between domestic and imported products. Under the GATT and now the DSU, remedies in such "nonviolation" cases are limited to compensatory tariff reduction on other products; the WTO cannot require a member to alter measures that are WTO-consistent. Almost all GATT nonviolation disputes concerned subsidies that were GATT-consistent but distorted trade.

PTAs with panel-based dispute settlement show continued interest in nonviolation remedies as a means of protecting the market access and other benefits that these agreements provide. However, the PTAs that provide such remedies tend to explicitly identify which benefits are thus protected, typically by citing specific PTA chapters. For instance, all U.S. FTAs explicitly permit disputes regarding nonviolation impairment of benefits accruing under specific identified chapters, usually those concerning market access and national treatment for trade in goods (including rules of origin), cross-border services trade, procurement, intellectual property rights (IPRs), and, sometimes, technical barriers to trade (TBTs). Some PTAs provide nonviolation remedies only for certain chapters— for example, only for goods, or for goods and services, or for goods, services, and various other categories that may include TBTs, sanitary and phytosanitary (SPS) measures, aviation, procurement, and IPRs.[9] A few PTAs make provision for disputes regarding nullification or impairment of PTA benefits generally (e.g., Japan–Switzerland and Canada–Israel). Other PTAs only provide for settlement of disputes regarding noncompliance with obligations under the agreement (the Australia–Singapore, Chile–China, Chile–EU, Japan–Indonesia, and Japan–Mexico PTAs, and many others) or explicitly exclude any possibility of nonviolation complaints (the ASEAN–Australia–New Zealand agreement).

The Target of a Complaint

Measures by a government. It goes without saying that PTA dispute settlement deals with *government* measures—that is, existing laws, regulations, or other official actions or failures to act that engage state responsibility, as opposed to actions of private parties. Although there is at least one case of a dispute (in Mercosur) concerning trade-obstructing actions by private parties (see annex B), the actionable measure was a PTA party's failure to ensure free circulation of goods as required by the PTA.

Proposed measures. Some PTAs permit disputes concerning proposed measures, such as pending legislation. The first modern example of such a provision appears in CUSFTA Chapter 18. Both CUSFTA and NAFTA provide for consultations and for requests for a panel decision regarding whether pending legislation in a partner is consistent with the PTA. Since 2001, U.S. PTAs have permitted consultations, but not arbitral panel proceedings, on pending legislation.

As Donaldson and Lester (2009) note, dispute settlement about proposed measures raises significant policy issues. It can be a waste of resources for panels to consider measures that may never be enacted, but early consultations can help limit or prevent trade damage by persuading governments not to enact measures that would violate their PTA obligations.

Subject matter exclusions. PTA dispute settlement procedures generally apply only with respect to the rights and obligations provided in that PTA. Some subject areas are often excluded from dispute settlement even when they are included in a PTA.

If a PTA contains "soft-law" obligations that urge but do not mandate economic or other cooperation, those obligations are often excluded from formal dispute settlement. Such an exclusion makes sure that no dispute settlement panel will ever read "should" as "shall."[10] As a corollary, when obligations regarding a subject area are limited to soft law, that area is likely to be excluded from formal dispute settlement.[11]

PTAs may also exclude areas from dispute settlement in order to ensure policy space for domestic regulation or to avoid PTA challenges to determinations by domestic regulators in particular cases. For instance, some PTAs exclude from dispute settlement any complaint regarding denial of rights to temporary entry and stay by business visitors unless the complaint concerns a pattern of practice and the nationals involved have exhausted local administrative remedies.[12] The objective is clearly to prevent the agreement's being used for immigration litigation. Some PTAs exclude TBT or SPS issues, or both, for similar reasons. The Japan–Switzerland FTA limits possible complaints regarding the effect of taxation on the PTA while subordinating the PTA to tax treaty obligations, following the example of Article XXII:2 of the WTO General Agreement on Trade in Services (GATS). In PTAs with competition chapters, the relevant chapter is often excluded from dispute settlement because competition authorities see panel review of their decisions as unwelcome and inappropriate.

PTAs may exclude areas from PTA dispute settlement when the PTA's obligations merely reaffirm WTO obligations. For instance, if a PTA simply confirms TBT or SPS obligations that are derived from the WTO Agreement, it may exclude TBT or SPS issues from PTA dispute settlement.

Finally, PTAs may exclude panel interpretation of subjects that are reserved to specific bodies in one of the parties. For instance, all New Zealand PTAs that have formal dispute settlement mechanisms provide that the interpretation of the 1840 Treaty of Waitangi between the British Crown and Maori tribes shall not be subject to dispute settlement under the PTA. Under New Zealand law, matters concerning this treaty are reserved to a special tribunal.

Overlap between the PTA and Another Forum

Overlap in obligations between two legal regimes occurs when the same parties take part in two separate regimes and both regimes regulate the matter in dispute at the same time. Almost all PTAs overlap with the WTO Agreement, as PTAs and the WTO both require national treatment and ban quantitative restrictions in trade. Indeed, many PTAs simply incorporate GATT Articles III and XI by reference. Some PTA members are also members of another overlapping PTA, as happens with CAFTA–DR and the Central American Common Market (CACM), SACU and the

Southern African Development Community (SADC), and ANZCERTA and the ASEAN–Australia–New Zealand FTA (Pauwelyn 2004).

When both legal regimes have independent dispute settlement regimes, overlap affords opportunities for a complaining party to choose the most advantageous forum or to relitigate a case in one forum (usually, the WTO) after an unsatisfactory outcome in another (the PTA). For example, Brazil brought a Mercosur challenge to an Argentine antidumping measure on poultry; the Mercosur arbitral tribunal found that the measure was not regulated by Mercosur law and was therefore not inconsistent with Argentina's Mercosur obligations. Brazil then went to the WTO, and the WTO panel found that the antidumping measure violated the WTO Agreement on Antidumping (Piérola and Horlick 2007). In another case, Brazil prevailed in a Mercosur challenge to an Argentine textiles safeguard, but Argentina did not remove its quotas, and Brazil obtained a settlement only after bringing the dispute to the WTO (Kwak and Marceau 2006). Similarly, Argentina brought a complaint against Chile's price band tariffs to the WTO after Chile failed to comply with a nonbinding PTA panel decision (Tussie and Delich 2005).

For any government, and particularly for developing countries, relitigation poses a resource burden, particularly if a developing country must mount multiple defenses of the same measure in different forums. Overlap also presents the possibility of conflicting rulings, as in the Argentina poultry case (Pauwelyn 2006). A WTO panel does not have jurisdiction to rule on whether a measure violates a PTA, and vice versa. Domestic law doctrines that curb duplicate litigation, such as *lis alibi pendens* and *res judicata*, are not a solution because the obligations are not the same.[13] Even if GATT Article III is incorporated by reference into a PTA, in the PTA context it is part of PTA law and is subject to exceptions and dispute settlement procedures that may not be the same as in the WTO (Kwak and Marceau 2006).

Resolving Overlap

There are three options for dealing with forum shopping in dispute settlement: give precedence to the PTA proceeding; give precedence to the WTO or other proceeding; or allow the parties to choose but prohibit relitigation.

Preference for PTA rules. A PTA may require that all disputes between PTA parties involving PTA provisions be settled exclusively within the PTA. The EU Treaty has such a requirement, and in the MOX Plant Case, the ECJ interpreted the relevant EU Treaty article as barring Ireland from bringing a dispute against the United Kingdom under

the UN Convention on the Law of the Sea or any other treaty concluded by the European Community (MOX Plant Case 2006).

PTA negotiators have also required parties to give precedence to PTA rules that provide more policy space than WTO rules (or otherwise are "WTO-minus") by specifying the forum for particular disputes. For instance, NAFTA's Article 104 provides that in the event that obligations under certain listed environmental agreements are inconsistent with NAFTA obligations, the environmental agreements prevail, and under Article 2005(3), if a defending party claims that Article 104 would apply, the complaining party can only bring the dispute under NAFTA. Article 2005(4) similarly gives the responding party the right to have an SPS or TBT dispute heard only under NAFTA, which was considered to afford more policy space. The Chile–Mexico and Canada–Chile FTAs have similar clauses.

NAFTA also gives a third NAFTA party the right to force a preference for PTA dispute settlement. Under NAFTA Article 2005(2), before a NAFTA party initiates WTO dispute settlement against another party on grounds that are "substantively equivalent" to those available under NAFTA, it must notify the third NAFTA party. If the third party wishes to litigate regarding the matter under NAFTA, it must inform the complaining party and consult; if the parties fail to agree on the forum, the dispute is normally to be settled in NAFTA.

Preference for the WTO. The other extreme is represented by the EU–Chile PTA, which provides that if a dispute concerns a breach of a PTA obligation that is equivalent in substance to a WTO obligation, it must be brought in the WTO. Once a forum is selected, it is to be used to the exclusion of any other, and all arguments regarding forum choice must be resolved within the first 30 days (Garcia Bercero 2006).

Binding election of forum. Most recent PTAs use some variant of the approach adopted first in CUSFTA. That model allows disputes arising under both the PTA and the WTO to be settled in either forum at the discretion of the complaining party but provides that, after the "initiation" of dispute settlement, the procedure employed must be used to the exclusion of any other. (The "initiation" point can be defined as the parties wish; CUSFTA pegs it at the point of referral to a panel, so that the complaining party can make its choice after consultations.) The complaining party thus has the option to choose the strongest substantive and procedural rules, while duplicative proceedings are excluded. Provisions of this type appear, for instance, in CUSFTA and all later U.S. FTAs; in Mexican PTAs; and in the China–New Zealand, Japan–Indonesia, Japan–Switzerland, Australia–Thailand, and SACU–EFTA PTAs. Under Mercosur's Protocol of

Olivos, which was signed in 2002 in the wake of the poultry case discussed above, if a dispute may be brought in more than one forum, the complaining party may select the forum, or the parties may agree on a forum, but once the dispute is initiated, none of the disputing parties may go to another forum. Variations on this formula permit a dispute to be brought again in another forum if the parties have so agreed (as in the China–ASEAN and ASEAN–Australia–New Zealand PTAs), or if substantially separate and distinct rights and obligations under different international agreements are in dispute (e.g., under the ASEAN–Japan and Australia–Chile PTAs).

Given a choice between bringing a dispute under the WTO or under a PTA, most complainants now choose the WTO, which is one reason there are so few PTA disputes. Before the establishment of the WTO, two Canada–U.S. disputes that could have been brought under GATT Articles XI and III were brought under CUSFTA instead, because at the time, CUSFTA offered the quickest and most binding dispute settlement mechanism.[14] The choice would be different today.

Complainants prefer the WTO for several reasons: the large body of cases (with appellate review), which offers greater clarity and certainty about WTO obligations, and greater predictability about the likely outcome of a dispute; the fact that the WTO panel process cannot be blocked; the stabilizing effect of WTO institutions; and the availability of postjudgment compliance obligations and remedies. WTO proceedings may also provide a unique opportunity to mobilize third-party support and exert political pressure on the respondent party (Piérola and Horlick 2007). Furthermore, WTO panels are composed of neutrals, whereas PTA panels often include representatives of the parties. Gantz (2006) suggests that this is a factor in the U.S. preference for the WTO forum over NAFTA.

Options for Procedures

In constructing a dispute settlement mechanism, negotiators need to consider what procedures to make available, what financial and infrastructural support will be necessary, and what complaints the panels or tribunals may handle.

Consultations

Whether a diplomatic or political dispute settlement scheme or an ad hoc panel procedure is employed, a formal dispute officially starts with a request for bilateral consultations. The consultation clause may require that the request be in writing and that it state the legal grounds for the complaint. It typically also requires the respondent party to consult promptly, and it may obligate the respondent to bring relevant officials to consultations and to provide sufficient information to facilitate settlement of the dispute.

The consultation clause must define the scope of issues on which the parties are obligated to consult upon request. Some agreements define this broadly: the consultation clause in the ASEAN Enhanced DSM includes "any matter affecting the implementation, interpretation or application of the Agreement or any covered agreement." The consultation clause will also determine whether a consultation request can include both existing and proposed measures and whether it can include both breaches of the rules and nonviolation nullification or impairment of trade benefits. As already noted, the consultation or pre-panel phase of a dispute may also extend to mediation, conciliation or good offices, or other forms of alternative dispute resolution.

A consultation clause is important because it gives any PTA party a right to get another party to have a focused talk about market access barriers in relation to the PTA's rights and obligations. The consultations provide a cost-effective opportunity for the parties to settle their dispute with maximum control over the outcome, by negotiation and agreement. The consultation request is the first visible formal document, but it usually only comes after extensive contact between stakeholders and the complaining government, or between the governments concerned.

Consultations are also important because they provide a key opportunity to clarify the facts. Governments normally do not know the details of a PTA partner's trade or regulatory regime; they do not know foreign law; and they do not know what aspects of government regulation will have the most impact on trade flows or the interests of stakeholders. Before the consultations, the government may not have collected the facts that it needs to determine its PTA rights and prove a violation of PTA law. The government may also not have a sense of the range of options for PTA-consistent implementation. Consultations provide an opportunity for a government to gather information to help evaluate a case before committing to it and to orient its litigation strategy and settlement negotiations to maximize commercial benefit. For the respondent government, consultations may offer an opportunity to reduce litigation costs by persuading the other side that certain claims are not worth litigating.

Both functions of consultations—settlement and fact-gathering—can also be fulfilled through discussions in the framework of a specialized PTA committee. Some PTAs provide that committee consultations can take the place of dispute settlement consultations procedurally, as discussed below.

Cases of urgency or perishable products. Some PTAs (e.g., the Chile–U.S., Canada–Peru, and ASEAN–Japan agreements and the Trans-Pacific SEP) provide accelerated consultation timetables for cases of urgency, including those involving perishable products, following the example of Article 4.8 of the DSU. Most agreements do not define "perishable," but some do define it as including perishable agricultural or fish products. The 2009 Canada–Colombia and Canada–Peru PTAs provide accelerated consultations for "cases of urgency, including those concerning perishable goods or otherwise involving goods or services that rapidly lose their trade value, such as seasonal goods or services." This clause recognizes that if the harvest period for a crop is limited and the crop is perishable, delay can make dispute settlement worthless except as a deterrent to repetition.

Requirement to have consulted. The GATT, the WTO, and all PTAs reviewed for this chapter require that before a party can use the agreement's common resources for third-party arbitration of a dispute, it must give the responding party an opportunity to settle the dispute through consultations. In the WTO, written consultation requests serve as evidence that such an opportunity was provided. PTAs generally require a written consultation request, and plurilateral PTAs require that the request be circulated to all PTA parties so that they will have an opportunity to participate in consultations as third parties. The consultation procedures may also afford a minimum consultation period by stipulating that the next step can be taken only after a certain number of days have elapsed after the consultation request.

The Formal Phase of a Dispute

During or after the consultations, the complaining party may decide that a beneficial settlement by negotiation is not possible. At that point, it begins to draw on the collective resources of the PTA and to seek a formal determination—by submitting a request to a political body (in PTAs with political dispute settlement, such as the EU association agreements), or by submitting legal documents as required by the rules in a tribunal system, or by submitting a formal request for establishment of an ad hoc panel. Dispute settlement rules that use ad hoc panels generally require that the request be in writing and that it identify the measure or measures at issue and the legal and factual basis for the complaint.

PTAs based on ad hoc panel arbitration use two approaches toward invocation of the panel process. In the first, delivery of a panel request to the other party or to the PTA's central institutional body (or both) directly triggers

the obligation to start the panel appointment process; the Korea–Singapore, China–Singapore, and Australia–Chile PTAs are in this category. Under the other approach, after consultations are exhausted, the complaining party refers the dispute to a political body for conciliation, and after a specified period of time, or if conciliation otherwise fails, the complaining party delivers a written request for a panel to the other party, triggering the panel selection process. This is the approach taken in NAFTA, in later U.S. PTAs, and in some later Mexican and Canadian agreements, under which the political body is a commission or joint committee, nominally at the ministerial level. Where there is potential for settlement, the conciliation phase provides another chance to negotiate, but in practice, the required meeting of the political body can consist of a brief conference call.

Infrastructure and Support for Dispute Settlement

Institutions. PTA negotiators will need to decide how the PTA's institutions will be used to support formal PTA dispute settlement. Dispute settlement requires management of document exchanges and hearings; coordination of any roster; secretarial, translation, and interpretation services; provision or rental of a place to hold hearings; research and drafting assistance to panelists; payment of panelist fees and expenses; information services; and capacity building. Negotiators may decide to have an existing secretariat take on these functions. For instance, the ASEAN Secretariat provides support to the ASEAN Enhanced Dispute Settlement Mechanism; the Mercosur Administrative Secretariat supports Mercosur dispute settlement; and each national section of the NAFTA Secretariat provides support for dispute settlement under NAFTA Chapters 19 and 20. This approach can foster consistency of approach and build common knowledge. PTAs can also have each panelist arrange his or her own support services on a reimbursable basis in the event of a dispute; this approach is more economical in the short run but can lead to uneven or legally inconsistent results from case to case.

Expenses. Where dispute settlement is conducted through a political body, each side supports its own diplomatic efforts. Where dispute settlement is conducted by a standing tribunal, the tribunal and its associated secretariat will have a standing budget process that involves substantial contributions by the parties. The expenses and payment for an ad hoc panel process typically depend on whether the process is supported by a secretariat. The parties can set a standard scale for panelists' fees and expenses, eliminating fee competition between them and making costs more predictable.

A PTA that provides for an ad hoc panel process without drawing on existing institutional support typically calls on the disputing parties to split the expenses. For instance, where a panel is selected by each party choosing an arbitrator, with a third or presiding arbitrator chosen by agreement, each party usually pays its own expenses and the fees and expenses for its arbitrator, and the parties divide equally the tribunal expenses (including the costs of the venue and the interpretation and secretarial services for the hearing) and the fees and expenses of the presiding arbitrator. A few agreements—for example, the Colombia–EFTA and Canada–EFTA PTAs, and the Mercosur Protocol of Olivos—permit the arbitrators to apportion costs or expenses among the parties as part of their award. In 2006, when the Mercosur Permanent Review Tribunal rejected as inadmissible an interlocutory appeal by Argentina against the designation of a panel chairman in a case, it assessed all costs and expenses against Argentina (Mercosur 2006).

An existing secretariat, where there is one, may provide dispute settlement support from its budget. This support affords extra benefits to those who make more frequent use of dispute settlement (but also provides public goods for other PTA parties). PTAs can also budget and pay for dispute settlement separately or case by case. The ASEAN Enhanced DSM provides for ASEAN member states to initially contribute equally to a separate revolving ASEAN DSM Fund, to pay for the expenses of ASEAN panels, the ASEAN Appellate Body, and related administrative costs of the secretariat. The parties to a dispute otherwise bear their own legal and other expenses and can be assessed for system expenses to replenish the DSM Fund.

Languages. Negotiators may also wish to consider the working language for dispute settlement submissions, hearings, and decisions. They may need to preserve the option to conduct disputes in their own language or languages, or they may wish to choose a single common language in order to economize on costs, as translation of submissions and interpretation at hearings can substantially increase the expense and time for dispute settlement. On the one hand, NAFTA provides meticulously for the use of up to three languages in dispute settlement, as do the Canada–Peru PTA and other Canadian PTAs with Latin American countries. On the other hand, some PTAs opt for disputes to be conducted in English (Japan–Switzerland, Korea–Singapore, Chile–China, Chile–Korea, ASEAN–Australia–New Zealand). The EU–CARIFORUM EPA states that the parties are to negotiate a common working language but that if they cannot agree, the defending party chooses the language, and each disputing party pays its own costs of translating submissions into that language.

Whatever the language actually used in the dispute, it may be politically necessary for texts of the decision to be made available in all the official languages of the disputing parties, to ensure public acceptance.

Panel Procedures

Predictability and consistency yield major benefits for any litigation process, and PTA dispute settlement is no exception. In a PTA that settles disputes through a standing tribunal, the tribunal has standard rules of procedure that establish expectations regarding requirements for submission of pleadings, evidence and arguments, deadlines, conduct of hearings, and other issues relevant for an orderly and predictable proceeding. In those PTAs that settle disputes diplomatically, procedure is less important, but if a PTA relies on ad hoc panels to settle disputes, the negotiators may wish to lay down agreed rules of procedure to ensure that the panels make consistent procedural decisions.

Many PTAs require the establishment of model rules of procedure.[15] Typically, the PTA text requires the establishment of model rules and specifies key issues that these rules must cover, leaving details to be negotiated later.

Model rules may deal with issues such as how to commence a proceeding; the number and spacing of submissions to the panel; responsibility for administering dispute settlement proceedings; who may attend hearings; deadlines and places for filing documents; languages, translation, and interpretation; protection of business confidential information; how the panel makes decisions (consensus or vote); whether there can be separate arbitrators' opinions; and whether such separate views must be anonymous. The rules can also provide for transparency.

Panel requests for information; handling of business confidential information. Some PTA disputes may concern product bans, SPS measures, or other measures, and in such cases the parties may base their arguments on assertions of scientific or environmental fact. Examples are the disputes on SPS measures and on Argentina's ban on retreaded tires that were adjudicated by Mercosur tribunals and the SPS measure on milk imports that went before a CUSFTA panel.

A panel faced with evaluating such issues and arguments may wish to seek help. The DSU permits a panel, without limitation, to seek information from any relevant source, and so do some PTA provisions or model rules of procedure. Some PTAs, such as the Trans-Pacific SEP, require that any information obtained must be submitted to the disputing parties for comment. Under some agreements (e.g., the ASEAN–Australia–New-Zealand PTA), the panel has to ask the disputants before seeking outside information; the parties have a veto over such a request; and any information obtained has to be submitted to the parties for comment. Some PTAs, such as the China–New Zealand agreement, further require that if a panel takes information or technical advice into account in its report, it must also take into account any comments on that information by the parties.

Claims regarding a breach of PTA rules may involve reliance on proprietary or business confidential factual data. Even information on government programs can be business confidential in nature; for example, information about Canadian government subsidies to the dairy industry was excluded from a WTO panel report (WTO 1999). Some WTO disputes (e.g., the dispute about the EU's banana import regime and the aircraft subsidies disputes) have involved information extremely sensitive to the companies providing it. If PTAs are to be able to handle such disputes, negotiators may wish to consider requiring panelists and panels to respect the confidentiality of the data.

Formalized expert groups. NAFTA, in Article 2015, authorizes panels to request a written report from a scientific review board on factual issues concerning environmental, health, safety, or other scientific matters raised by a disputing party; the Canada–Chile and Chile–Mexico PTAs contain similar provisions. These provisions have never been used. Parallel provisions in the WTO (DSU Article 13.2 and Appendix 4) also have never been used; WTO panels in cases involving health or safety issues have consulted individual experts, who did not draw up any group report.

Duration of Panel Process

The governments that have negotiated PTAs have shown a strong preference for speed in the panel process. For panel-based dispute settlement procedures that call for initial and final panel reports, PTAs' notional deadlines for a panel to produce its initial report vary widely: 30 days in SACU–Mercosur; 60 days in Mercosur and the ASEAN Enhanced DSM; 90 days in NAFTA and the Canada–Peru PTA; 120 days in the Chile–U.S. PTA; and 180 days in the U.S.–Korea and Chile–Australia agreements. These PTAs typically allow two weeks for comments from the parties and then ask the panel to finalize its report within 30 to 45 days after the initial report.

Stakeholders favor short deadlines. The consultations and other preliminary phases of a dispute, including panel selection, can take considerable time, and business stakeholders are almost never compensated for damage caused them by the breach of trade obligations. In practice, these deadlines may be more aspirational than real. So far,

NAFTA panel proceedings have taken well in excess of the prescribed time. Defending parties are often motivated to delay, and even complaining parties may prefer to take time to prepare. If the panelists cannot coordinate their timetables to schedule a hearing, or do not meet deadlines, there is little that the parties can do.

Appeal, Correction, and Remand

Where a trade agreement relies on ad hoc panels to settle disputes, the PTA parties may seek greater assurance that the decisions of successive panels will be consistent and legally sound. Such assurance may be essential to secure domestic acceptance of panel rulings. Tribunal systems such as the ECJ respond to the same concerns with appellate review, or provisions for revision or interpretation of past judgments. An appellate body involves incremental cost to the parties, but it generates public goods in the form of enhanced certainty and uniformity in the application of international trade law.

The WTO and some PTAs now use two methods to prevent and correct panel error. The first method is to give the parties to a dispute an opportunity to comment on a panel's report in draft form before the report is finalized; this innovation in CUSFTA was incorporated into the WTO DSU and has been adopted in many PTA ad hoc panel processes. The second method is appeal. The DSU includes an Appellate Body, which the EU required as a quid pro quo for accepting binding dispute settlement in the WTO. The EU has instituted a two-level process, with the General Court as a court of first instance for certain types of disputes, with appeal to the ECJ. Mercosur's 2003 Protocol of Olivos created the Tribunal Permanente de Revisión (TPR), an appellate tribunal (box 22.1). The Olivos Protocol reacted to a number of difficult disputes and responded in part to smaller states' concerns about compliance with Mercosur law (Whitelaw 2004). The TPR reflects a high level of institution-building ambition and helps enforce and build not only treaty law but also the decisional law being created by Mercosur institutions (Opertti 2004).

The ASEAN Protocol on Enhanced Dispute Settlement Mechanism of 2004 calls for the ASEAN Economic Ministers to establish a seven-person Appellate Body patterned on the WTO Appellate Body. As of early 2011, this had not yet taken place.

Labor, Environment, Financial Services, and Other Special Sectors

As noted in earlier chapters of this volume, many PTAs provide special dispute settlement procedures for particular

---

Box 22.1. The Protocol of Olivos

The Mercosur Protocol of Olivos established a new five-person Permanent Appeals Tribunal (Tribunal Permanente de Revisión, TPR). It consists of one arbitrator (with an alternate) appointed for a renewable two-year term by each of the four Mercosur members, plus a fifth arbitrator appointed for one three-year term by agreement between the members. The TPR's permanent headquarters is in Asunción.

Disputes between Mercosur members are normally first heard by an ad hoc arbitral tribunal, which provides its award within 60 days (extendable to a total of 90 days). Within 15 days after the award, any party to the dispute may bring a motion for review to the TPR. The TPR may consider only the legal issues dealt with in the dispute and the legal interpretations in the award, not issues of fact. It renders its decision within 30 days. If the dispute involves two members, it is heard by three judges, and if more, by five judges. (Whitelaw 2004). The TPR has heard two appeals. In one, it reversed the panel decision, and in the other, it ruled the request inadmissible.

Under the Protocol of Olivos, parties to a dispute may also, by agreement, submit their dispute directly and in a single instance to the TPR; in that case, the TPR acts like a panel and issues a nonappealable award in 60 days, which may be extended by 30 days. The TPR also may rule on appeals by disputants regarding failure to comply with tribunal awards, or regarding the extent of suspension of concessions after a failure to comply, and it may provide opinions to the Mercosur Common Market Group on request.

---

subject matter. Special procedures may refer particular disputes to a political process for settlement, but even in the context of binding third-party dispute settlement, the parties may wish to bring to bear special expertise, to provide special opportunities to participate, to provide particular forms of redress, or to limit the possible scope of sanctions by a prevailing party. The key examples are labor, environment, and financial services.

Labor and environment. Chapters 19 and 20 of this volume describe the substantive obligations, including dispute settlement, in those PTAs that deal with environment and labor issues. Such obligations exist in all U.S. PTAs concluded since NAFTA, in some Canadian PTAs, in New Zealand's PTA with Thailand, in the Trans-Pacific SEP, in the EU–CARIFORUM EPA, and in the chapter on trade and sustainable development of the EU–Korea agreement.

As Bartels (2009) observes, the treatment of these issues in North American PTAs has changed over time. These dispute settlement provisions can be grouped into four categories.

1. The side agreements to NAFTA—the North American Agreement on Labor Cooperation (NAALC) and the North American Agreement on Environmental Cooperation (NAAEC)—represent one model. They establish institutional frameworks for cooperation, require that domestic legislation adhere to high standards, and obligate each party to enforce and strive to improve its own legislation. Panel proceedings require a two-thirds vote of the three NAFTA parties. They are to be preceded by consultations and a report by a committee of experts, and they are only available in cases of persistent, trade-related patterns of failure to effectively enforce worker

safety, child labor, or minimum wage standards that are covered by mutually recognized labor laws (a failure that violates the NAALC), or to effectively enforce domestic environmental law relating to production of traded goods or services (a breach of the NAAEC). The panelists must be from a specialized labor or environment roster. If the panel agrees that such an enforcement failure exists, and if no remedial action is taken, the panel may ultimately set a monetary assessment, to be paid by the losing party into a fund to promote (depending on the sector) labor law enforcement or improvement of the environment or of environmental enforcement in the party complained against. The Canada–Chile PTA contains similar provisions (Bartels 2009). The side agreements also provide for citizen submissions claiming that a party is not enforcing its own laws. The NAFTA governments received 37 submissions on labor issues in 1994–2010, of which 24 concerned conditions in Mexico, 13 pertained to the United States, and 2 were against Canada (U.S. DOL 2010). The NAFTA Commission on Environmental Cooperation received 77 citizen submissions from 1995 through early 2011; of these, 39 focused on Mexico, 9 on the United States, 27 on Canada, and 1 on a cross-border Canada–U.S. issue (CEC 2011). The Canada–Costa Rica FTA also provides for citizen submissions, as well as government-government dispute settlement without fines or trade measures (Bartels 2009).

2. Under the Jordan–U.S. agreement, parties must not fail, through a sustained or recurring course of action or inaction, to effectively enforce domestic environmental or labor laws in a manner affecting trade between the parties. These labor and environmental obligations are

enforceable through the same procedures as the rest of the agreement, but a side letter provides that they will not be enforced so as to block trade (Bartels 2009).

3. Seven other U.S. PTAs negotiated in 2000–07, with Australia, Bahrain, CAFTA–DR, Chile, Morocco, Oman, and Singapore, adopt the same standard as in the Jordan agreement. They also provide that parties may not weaken, reduce, or waive environmental or labor protections to encourage trade or investment. These obligations are enforceable through the same dispute settlement procedures as the rest of the agreement, but no trade retaliation is possible—only fines capped at US$15 million (adjusted for inflation). Fines are collected through suspension of concessions, if necessary, and are spent on labor or environmental initiatives in the territory of the party complained against. These agreements also create cooperative institutions and provide for receipt of input from the public.

4. In May 2007 the Bush administration agreed with the leadership of Congress (then controlled by Democrats) on elements that future free trade agreements must have in order to be considered by Congress. These elements include increased substantive standards for labor rights provisions and an enforcement standard like that in the Jordan agreement. The provisions are subject to the same dispute settlement mechanisms and penalties as in other provisions, but dispute settlement must be preceded by consultations in a specialized labor or environment council. The Peru–U.S. FTA and pending FTAs with Colombia, Korea, and Panama all follow this pattern (Bolle 2009).

On July 30, 2010, the United States initiated the first formal PTA labor complaint, under the labor chapter of CAFTA–DR. In a letter signed by U.S. Trade Representative Ron Kirk and Secretary of Labor Hilda Solis, the United States formally requested consultations with the Guatemalan government regarding (a) failure by the Guatemalan Ministry of Labor to investigate alleged labor law violations or to take enforcement action when the ministry had identified a violation, and (b) failure by the Guatemalan courts to enforce Labor Court orders in cases involving labor law violations. The complaint expressed concerns about the Guatemalan government's alleged failure to protect those attempting to exercise labor rights against violence and threats. It followed a submission by U.S. and Guatemalan unions and informal consultations that had been going on since January 2009 (Kirk and Solis 2010; USTR 2010).

New Zealand has negotiated labor and environment side agreements to the Thailand–New Zealand FTA and the Trans-Pacific SEP. In both, the labor obligations are only enforced through consultations. Dispute settlement provisions in the environment agreements provide for referring a dispute to the interested parties for a report. Those affected are obligated to implement the report's recommendations (Bartels 2009).

Historically, most EU PTAs have treated labor and environment as "matters for cooperation" (Bartels 2009). However, the EU's Global Europe policy, announced in late 2006, calls for environment and labor to be part of the trade agreement negotiations. For instance, the chapter on trade and sustainable development in the EU–Korea FTA calls for high levels of protection in both areas and obligates both parties not to fail to effectively enforce environmental and labor laws "through a sustained or recurring course of action or inaction" and not to waive or derogate from its environmental or labor laws, regulations, or standards in a manner affecting trade or investment between the parties. Enforcement, however, consists exclusively of bilateral consultations and an advisory report by a group of experts.

In the EU–CARIFORUM EPA, the labor and environment obligations in Chapters 4 and 5 of Title IV are enforceable through the agreement's regular dispute settlement procedures, but only after separate procedures in the labor or environment chapters are pursued for at least nine months. These procedures call for bilateral consultations, possibly including advice from relevant international environmental bodies or the International Labour Organization (ILO), and may also include a report by a three-member committee of experts. In any ensuing dispute, at least two of the three arbitrators must have specific expertise on the subject matter and must be drawn from a special roster. The panel report must recommend how to ensure compliance with the EPA's trade or environment obligations, and measures taken in case of noncompliance may not include suspension of EPA trade concessions. Separately, the agreement's investment chapter (Article 72) obligates the parties to ensure that investors act in accordance with core labor standards and do not behave in a manner that circumvents international environmental or labor obligations in agreements to which the EU and the CARIFORUM states are parties. This obligation is subject to the agreement's regular dispute settlement procedures.

Financial services. As Stephanou (2009) observes, PTA parties have been particularly cautious about covering financial services because of regulatory sensitivities and strategic considerations. Countries that follow the GATS approach for services in their PTAs have used it for financial services as well, with special adaptations or a separate chapter expanding on the GATS Annex on Financial

Services. Others follow the NAFTA model, in which investment to provide services is treated like any other type of investment and has access to investor-state dispute settlement. Stephanou (2009) points out that an increasing number of countries prefer a dedicated chapter on financial services because it facilitates customizing the application of services disciplines in this area and allows financial sector policy makers to control negotiation and implementation of the obligations.

Governments have demonstrated in their PTAs that they want special procedures for settling financial services disputes. As in the WTO, PTA provisions often require that panels for such disputes have specific regulatory or other financial sector expertise, and they prohibit trade retaliation against financial services in any dispute in any other sector. In NAFTA-model PTAs that have a separate financial services chapter, that chapter limits the scope of investor-state dispute settlement to claims regarding expropriation or transfer of payments. National treatment claims, for instance, are only subject to state-state dispute settlement, giving a host state additional flexibility to discriminate in favor of domestic financial services providers if its PTA partners agree (Sauvé and Molinuevo 2008). NAFTA-model financial services chapters also refer claims regarding prudential or monetary or exchange-rate measures for a consensus decision by a financial services committee composed of financial services regulators; if the committee agrees, its decision binds the tribunal.

Other sectors. PTA negotiators can provide specialized dispute settlement for any subject they wish, or they can require that arbitrators for disputes on technical subjects have specialized expertise. For instance, the EU–Chile FTA contains a chapter on trade in wine that includes provisions on regulation of labeling and oenological practices. The chapter requires the parties to establish a roster of arbitrators with oenological expertise for disputes regarding obligations under the agreement.

Participation in PTA Dispute Settlement and Enforcement

This section reviews participation in PTA dispute settlement, including qualification and selection of decision makers, third-party participation, use of experts, and participation by civil society in the dispute settlement process.

Qualifications and Selection of Decision Makers

Selection of decision makers is a key issue for international dispute settlement; if governments are to give a third-party decision maker (a standing tribunal or an ad hoc panel)

power to make binding decisions that matter, the tribunal must be composed of people who are perceived as trustworthy, impartial, and confidence-inspiring. Negotiators solve this problem by specifying criteria for decision makers such as neutrality, geographic distribution, and professional expertise. They may also try to expedite panel formation by agreeing in advance on a roster of persons who meet the criteria.

Standing tribunals. In a standing tribunal, judges are selected on the basis of certain criteria and some form of geographic distribution. The governments bound will need to agree on the judges' terms of service, their payment, and the funding of the necessary infrastructure. The original model, the International Court of Justice (ICJ), consists of 15 judges elected to nine-year terms by the United Nations (UN) General Assembly and the UN Security Council. The Statute of the International Court of Justice requires that its judges be persons of high moral character who possess the qualifications required in their countries for appointment to the highest judicial office or who are lawyers of recognized competence in international law. Each judge participates in all cases. The Statute also requires that in the ICJ as a whole "the representation of the main forms of civilization and of the principal legal systems of the world should be assured." If a state party to an ICJ case does not have a judge of its nationality on the Court, it may appoint an ad hoc judge for that case only.

The European Court of Justice has one judge for each of the 27 member states and normally hears cases in panels of 3, 5, or 13. The judges must have the qualifications or competence needed for appointment to the highest judicial positions in their home countries. Both the ICJ and the ECJ are backed by an elaborate and expensive infrastructure of buildings, legal and support staff, libraries, and translators. The four judges of the Andean Tribunal (one per member state) also serve full time. Other standing tribunals, for ECOWAS, COMESA, and the EAC, are composed of member-state judges who serve part-time (Banjo 2007).

The WTO Appellate Body consists of seven part-time members, appointed by consensus for a renewable term of four years, who must be "persons of recognized authority, with demonstrated expertise in law, international trade and the subject matter of the covered agreements generally" (DSU Article 17.3). They are geographically balanced through informal agreement. Members have included public international lawyers, trade lawyers, and diplomats with no formal legal training. A division of three members, determined randomly, considers each case. The Appellate Body has a small staff and shares in the infrastructure provided by the WTO.

Ad hoc panels. The DSU requires that WTO dispute settlement panels be composed of impartial, "well-qualified governmental and/or non-governmental individuals" and lists types of acceptable experience (WTO litigation; service as a delegate, or in the WTO Secretariat, or as a senior trade policy official; teaching or publishing on trade law or policy). Many PTA dispute settlement mechanisms modeled on the DSU specify similar characteristics of impartiality and expertise. Some, such as the China–New Zealand PTA, also require that the panelists comply with the WTO DSU's rules of conduct for panelists. NAFTA and other U.S. FTAs require compliance with a code of conduct to be established by the parties.

Another issue is citizenship or nationality. In the WTO, citizens of parties or third parties to a dispute cannot serve on the panel, unless the parties agree otherwise. The most common model in PTAs is for each party in a bilateral dispute to select an arbitrator, who can be (and usually is) a national of that party. The parties to the dispute then select a neutral chair by agreement, with a fallback to selection by lot or by an appointing authority, as discussed below.

Ad Hoc Panels and the Blockage Problem

Ad hoc panels, as bodies created to settle a particular dispute, present particular moral hazard problems that the text of a PTA can and should anticipate and prevent. The central problem arises when a defending party refuses to cooperate with the process by declining to name its arbitrators or to cooperate with the panel selection process.

The WTO's DSU procedures have successfully overcome this problem. The WTO Secretariat takes the initiative to nominate panelists to the parties. If a panel has not been completed by agreement within 20 days from the decision by the Dispute Settlement Body (DSB) to establish the panel, then, if either party so requests, the WTO Director-General can and will select the missing panelists, in consultation with the WTO's political leadership.

Some PTAs deal with the failure-to-appoint situation by designating an appointing authority, such as the WTO Director-General, the Secretary-General of the Permanent Court of Arbitration in the Hague, or a regional secretariat.[16] Other PTAs provide for the missing arbitrator or neutral to be selected by lot; this is the method chosen by the Japan–Mexico, Japan–Chile, and Japan–Thailand PTAs and by NAFTA and other U.S. FTAs. If negotiators choose selection by lot, the selection should be conducted by a body that is not controlled by the defending party.

In practice, governments may wish a PTA panel, and its decision, to have the legitimacy that flows from consent. They may therefore be reluctant to actually use these fallback mechanisms. But the existence of a fallback mechanism does provide an incentive to reach agreement.

Panel selection can take considerable time. The panel selection process has been a significant obstacle for NAFTA disputes, according to Gantz (2006), who observes that the NAFTA dispute on cross-border trucking services was delayed for 15 months by panel formation and that in the NAFTA sugar dispute, the U.S. authorities declined for more than four years to appoint panelists.

Rosters

A roster can speed panel selection by providing a preapproved list of persons who are qualified and willing to serve. Since 1907, arbitral institutions, which now include the International Centre for Settlement of Investment Disputes (ICSID), the Permanent Court of Arbitration, and many others, have maintained rosters of arbitrators to facilitate dispute resolution (Schreuer 2001). In the WTO, DSU Article 8.4 provides for the maintenance of a roster of governmental and nongovernmental individuals qualified to serve on panels (WTO 1996b, 724). For special obligations in agreements (on labor, environment, financial services, or other designated topics), PTAs may require specialized rosters to ensure that the decision makers in a dispute have the necessary expertise.

A roster of panelists can be open or closed. The WTO has an open roster; disputing parties may choose any panelists they wish. The WTO's DSB accepts practically all names nominated by members. At the other extreme is a closed roster, like that provided for in the EU–Chile FTA. As required by that agreement, the EU–Chile Association Committee has established a list of 15 persons. Of these, five are Chilean, five are from the EU, and five, of neither nationality, are identified as possible chairpersons (European Commission 2007). The FTA provides that within three days of any panel request, the chair of the Association Committee must select by lot two arbitrators, one each from the EU and Chilean sublists, as well as a chair from the list of individuals identified as potential chairs. Panel selection takes days instead of months. (The initial list was not finalized until two years after the FTA entered into force, however.) Similarly, panelists for ad hoc tribunals for Mercosur disputes are selected from sections of a Mercosur roster; if a disputant fails to appoint its arbitrator, or if there is no agreement on the presiding arbitrator, the arbitrator in question is appointed by Mercosur's Administrative Secretariat from the roster.

The PTA rules can also favor panel selection from the roster—for instance, by barring any veto of panelists selected from the list—without excluding nonroster candidates. If a roster is used, it is advisable that it remain valid until it is replaced. NAFTA provides for each party to select panelists from the roster who are not its citizens ("cross-selection") but this innovation has not been picked up in any other PTA, including later U.S. FTAs.

Some other PTAs, such as the ASEAN Enhanced DSM, provide for indicative lists modeled on that of the WTO. Many do not use a roster for panel selection at all, however, permitting governments to select the candidates that they prefer when the dispute arises.

Panelist Ethics

PTA provisions on the qualifications of panelists often include qualitative requirements designed to ensure impartiality. In December 1996 the WTO's DSB adopted a code of conduct for panelists (WTO 1996b) that is also applied by the WTO Appellate Body. This code requires that panelists be independent and impartial, avoid direct and indirect conflicts of interest, and respect the confidentiality of WTO proceedings. The disclosures required by this code have become a routine aspect of panel disputes in the WTO.

Influenced by the WTO example and by the requirement for a code of conduct in NAFTA, a number of PTAs call for panelists to adhere to a code of conduct to be agreed by the parties. These PTAs include the Singapore–GCC, Mexico–Northern Triangle, Chile–Colombia, Chile–Australia, Canada–Peru, and Chile–EU agreements; NAFTA; and all later U.S. PTAs. In addition, following the example of Article 18.1 of the DSU, PTA model rules of procedure or codes of conduct may prohibit ex parte contact with panelists, as do the ASEAN Enhanced DSM and the Singapore–GCC PTA.

Plurilateral PTAs and Multiparty Disputes, Joinder and Consolidation, and Other Third-Party Participation

When a dispute arises in a plurilateral PTA, another party to the PTA may wish to join the complaint or merely to observe and submit views. The reasons for wanting to do so may include commercial competition in the markets concerned, a desire to prevent discriminatory settlements, an interest in the interpretation of common PTA rules such as rules on market access or rules of origin, and concern for endeavors such as regional public goods. Third-party participation can also be a useful way for developing countries to build capacity in dispute settlement. Similar motives have built a rich practice of joinder and consolidation of disputes, multiparty cases (as in the EU banana import regime dispute), and third-party participation, under the

GATT (WTO 1996a) and the WTO. Rules for multiparty disputes also exist in, for example, NAFTA, CAFTA–DR, the Trans-Pacific SEP, and PTAs involving EFTA.

NAFTA permits a third party to join as a complaining party as of right, if it delivers a timely notice to the disputing parties and the NAFTA Secretariat. The third party can then participate in the consultations, but if it fails to join the dispute, it is "normally" precluded from initiating or continuing a NAFTA or WTO dispute on the same matter, in the absence of a significant change in circumstances. The NAFTA Commission must consolidate two or more pending NAFTA disputes regarding the same measure and may consolidate other cases that are appropriately considered jointly. Similar provisions exist in the CAFTA–DR and Chile–Central America PTAs. The Trans-Pacific SEP Agreement requires consolidation of disputes on the same measure, and the Colombia–EFTA, China–ASEAN, and ASEAN–Australia–New Zealand PTAs express preference for consolidation or use of common arbitrators. Where there are multiple complaining parties, the panel selection procedure may be adjusted accordingly, as is done in NAFTA and the CAFTA–DR, Chile–Central America, and Mercosur agreements.

Most plurilateral PTAs permit another PTA member to participate in dispute settlement consultations as of right; some make such participation conditional on consent by the disputing parties. Many also permit another PTA member to attend panel hearings, to make written and oral submissions to the panel, and to receive some or all written submissions of the disputing parties (as in WTO panel proceedings).[17] Broader participation is not cost-free, of course. It involves costs for the third party or extra complainant and for the defending party, and it decreases the likelihood of early settlement (Busch and Reinhardt 2003).

Transparency and Civil Society Participation

One of the parties to a PTA negotiation may seek to have the PTA dispute settlement provisions incorporate elements of procedural transparency. WTO practice has been evolving since 1995 in the direction of increased transparency in dispute settlement, but views are still divided within the WTO as to whether to mandate such transparency. PTA practice varies widely, but it too has evolved substantially in recent years. Some U.S. PTAs now mandate considerably more dispute settlement transparency than the WTO.

The WTO's dispute settlement rules largely codify the informal, diplomatic, nontransparent practice under the GATT, which treated dispute settlement as a private negotiating process between the parties. The DSU provided that disputing parties could make their submissions and non-confidential summaries public but made no other changes. Since 1998, the United States has advocated that all panel submissions be available to the public; that panel hearings be open to public observation, except where there is a need to protect confidential business information; and that panels accept amicus curiae submissions from the public or from nongovernmental organizations (NGOs). These proposals have gained at least partial support from the EU, Canada, and others, to help strengthen public support for trade liberalization. The United States has made all of its dispute settlement submissions since 1995 public; other members have made some of their submissions public; amicus briefs have been submitted and even considered; and in a number of WTO disputes, at the request of the parties, the panel or Appellate Body hearing has been open for public observation via closed-circuit television.

Not all governments agree. As described by Mercurio and LaForgia (2005), some WTO delegations have argued that openness would undermine the character of the WTO as a forum for confidential discussion between governments, that it would burden members' ability to participate effectively in disputes, and that allowing observers at hearings would lead to trials by media. Although almost all WTO members strongly criticized the Appellate Body for accepting amicus submissions in the asbestos dispute in 2000, later panels and the Appellate Body have continued to accept such submissions. Many developing countries continue to oppose amicus submissions as a resource burden.

Direct participation by stakeholders and civil society. No government opposes all participation by civil society in dispute settlement. On the contrary, governments usually welcome stakeholder input and guidance on facts, commercial data, and negotiating priorities. WTO studies (Tussie and Delich 2005; Xuto 2005) illustrate the critical role played by developing-country stakeholders in disputes. Governments also have put in place organized structures for receiving stakeholder complaints.[18] Moreover, PTA provisions on labor and environment have provided for receipt of public submissions on these issues; the first PTA labor dispute ever, initiated by the United States against Guatemala in July 2010, followed an April 2008 public submission by the AFL-CIO labor group in the United States and by Guatemalan unions, under the labor chapter of the CAFTA–DR PTA (USTR 2010).

Practically all governments involved in trade disputes now expect stakeholders to hire or pay for legal counsel to assist the government. A few PTAs (Canada–Israel, EU–Chile, Canada–Chile, Chile–Central America) explicitly guarantee the right of parties to be assisted by counsel and impose conditions regarding the counsel's conduct.

Complaints by stakeholders against governments. Articles 39–44 of the Mercosur Protocol of Olivos permit individuals or juridical persons to bring complaints against any Mercosur party for applying legal or administrative measures that have a restrictive, discriminatory, or unfairly competitive effect, in violation of the Treaty of Asunción or the associated agreements and legal instruments. Such complaints must be filed with the national section of the Common Market Group of the country in which the claimant resides or has its headquarters. If the national section supports the complaint, it must negotiate directly for 15 days to resolve the matter with the defending country's national section. If the complaint is not resolved, it must be brought to the Common Market Group. Unless the Common Market Group rejects the complaint summarily by consensus, it must convene a group of three neutral experts, who are to report in 30 days. If the panel unanimously agrees with the complaint, any Mercosur party can demand that corrective measures be adopted, or that the dispute measure be annulled, and can then proceed to Mercosur state-state dispute settlement if the defending state does not comply within 15 days. If the panel's report is not unanimous, the claim terminates. Any Mercosur party can bring the same complaint.

Amicus curiae submissions. Civil society groups have argued that panels should consider not just the arguments presented by governments but also facts and arguments presented by others, even those who may be at odds with the governments participating in dispute settlement. If dispute settlement provisions are neutral regarding amicus submissions, presumably a panel could consider them.

Some PTAs go further and explicitly favor consideration of amicus submissions. U.S. FTAs after NAFTA have required that panels consider requests from nongovernmental entities in the parties' territories to provide written views that may assist the panel in evaluating the submissions and arguments of the parties. A number of other recent PTAs explicitly authorize the panel to accept and consider amicus submissions under certain conditions. For instance, the Trans-Pacific SEP and the EU–Chile, EU–Korea, Chile–Panama, Canada–Colombia, and Canada–Peru PTAs all permit amicus submissions, but only if timely (submitted within 10 days of panel composition), concise (not over 15 typed pages, including annexes), and directly relevant to the factual and legal issues before the panel. The submission must also describe the submitter, its activities, its source of funding, and the nature of its interest in the proceeding. The Canada–Peru PTA adds more requirements: in deciding whether to permit an NGO to make a submission, a panel must consider, among other matters, whether there is a public interest in the proceeding, whether the NGO has a substantial interest in the proceeding, and whether the written submission would add a perspective, particular knowledge, or insight that is different from that of the parties. (A footnote clarifies that an interest in jurisprudence, in the interpretation of the PTA, or in the subject matter of the dispute is not enough to establish an NGO's substantial interest.) An NGO submission may not introduce new issues to the dispute, must stay within the dispute's terms of reference, and must avoid disrupting the proceeding. It must preserve the equality of the disputing parties, who must have an opportunity to respond.

Transparency in the dispute settlement process. All U.S. PTAs after NAFTA have required that any dispute settlement submission (including written submissions, texts of oral statements, and other documents) must be made public within 10 days. Other PTAs authorize, but do not require, their parties to make their own submissions public; these include the Canada–Colombia, Canada–Peru, ASEAN–Australia–New Zealand, and Japan–ASEAN agreements.

All U.S. PTAs after NAFTA have required that hearings in disputes are to be open to the public; the recent Canada–Colombia, Canada–Peru, and EU–Korea PTAs also require open hearings. The 2009 Japan–Switzerland PTA provides for open hearings unless either disputing party objects. In some other PTAs (the Trans-Pacific SEP and the EU–Chile agreement), hearings are closed unless the disputing parties agree otherwise.

Alternative Enforcement and Dispute Settlement Methods

Formal disputes take place only in exceptional cases; the universe of large and small trade disputes in a PTA is much larger. Statistics on dispute settlement, which record formal disputes, systematically understate the total number of disputes and the proportion of disputes that is settled.

Most PTAs set up an institution or institutions to maintain the PTA, to address practical problems of PTA implementation and market access, and to provide a framework for further negotiations. These institutions may include joint committees or councils at the ministerial or senior official level to oversee the operation of the PTA. As Donaldson and Lester (2009) note, most such committees meet annually (and more often, as required), and a few meet biennially. They may be ad hoc or standing committees at the working level, or even joint public-private working groups. Maintaining these institutions requires a commitment of resources and personnel but can be economical and effective in resolving problems.

PTA institutions can provide a cost-effective channel for gathering information. Governments, and particularly those of resource-poor developing countries, normally do not know the details of a PTA partner's trade or regulatory regime and may not have access to foreign legislation. Institutional contacts provide a way to obtain those facts. Cooperation within PTA institutions, and the regular contact that it implies, offer a means of building mutual confidence at the personal level, resolving routine trade irritants and minor issues, and negotiating further trade liberalization. Asia-Pacific Economic Cooperation (APEC), for instance, has provided useful settings for dialogue and regulatory harmonization on customs and trade facilitation, chemical regulation, SPS measures, and automotive standards.

Specialized Institutions

PTA institutions can be particularly helpful for regional integration in complex issue areas or regulated industries. PTAs may establish specialized committees composed of regulators from each country. Contacts between regulators build trust in each other's judgments, facilitating market access for regulated products or services. Some agreements provide an incentive to consult about issues in these technical committees by providing that such discussions will satisfy the usual requirement for consultations before recourse to a dispute settlement panel. The CAFTA–DR agreement, for instance, establishes committees on agricultural trade (Article 3.19), market access for goods, rules of origin, and customs issues (Article 3.30), SPS measures (Article 6.3), TBTs (Article 7.8), and financial services (Article 12.16). Each committee is able to consider routine market access issues. Consultations that have taken place in the TBT Committee may substitute for the first step in the dispute settlement process. The Chile–EU FTA establishes special committees on rules of origin (Article 81); standards, technical regulations, and conformity assessment (Article 88); and financial services (Article 128), as well as special consultation processes on SPS requirements, trade in wine, and trade in spirits; these can substitute for the consultation stage of dispute settlement proceedings (Articles 89, 129, Annex 5).

Collective Enforcement Procedures

The adversary process used in panel-based dispute settlement procedures, and triggered only if one PTA party brings a formal complaint against another, is not the only possible structure for enforcement of PTA obligations. In the EU, for instance, the predominant method of enforcement is through action by the supranational European

Commission, which actively monitors member states' actions and can bring enforcement actions before the EU's courts even in the absence of any stakeholder or member state complaint. The secretary-general of the Andean Community has similar enforcement powers, as do the secretaries-general of COMESA and the EAC. Enforcement of this type is typically coupled with a standing tribunal empowered to adjudicate cases and impose sanctions. Where PTA members have pooled their sovereignty, as in the EU, such enforcement is strong, but where the members are less ambitious, it is not (Alter and Helfer 2011).

As another example, ASEAN formally agreed in 2004 to establish an ASEAN Compliance Body (ACB), modeled on the WTO Textiles Monitoring Body. The optional compliance procedures (Yoshimatsu 2006) provide for group peer review of measures on a 90-day timeline. The ACB's findings, drawn up by countries not party to the dispute, would not be binding but could serve as inputs for formal dispute settlement. However, the ACB does not appear to be operational at present.

True multilateral sanctioning mechanisms (such as the UN Security Council) are quite rare, but collective persuasion mechanisms exist, including the specialized institutions described in the preceding subsection. The Montreal Protocol on the Protection of the Ozone Layer has such a mechanism in its Implementation Committee of 10 treaty parties, which regularly examines the treaty parties' compliance reports, can receive other parties' submissions, and can investigate and provide reports and recommendations to the Meeting of the Parties. But accounts indicate that it is ineffective at stopping even intentional and continuing violations (Yang 2007).

Alternative Dispute Resolution: Good Offices, Mediation, and Conciliation

Good offices, mediation, and conciliation all are traditional, widely recognized means of dispute settlement in public international law, as well as means of alternative dispute resolution (ADR) used in commercial situations. In each case, the parties cooperate voluntarily with a neutral, uninvolved third party. The third party, which, in a public international law context, could be an individual, an international organization, or a state, offers to assist the parties in settling their differences by negotiation and agreement, without arbitrating the merits of the legal claims concerned. The three types of ADR overlap but are distinguished by the extent and nature of the neutral party's involvement.

Article 5 of the WTO DSU provides for the possibility of good offices, mediation, or conciliation, if agreed to by the "parties to a dispute." The implication is that a dispute exists, but Article 5 has never been used *during* a dispute. The only known WTO mediation, in 2002 on European Community tariff preferences for canned tuna, was used in place of dispute settlement proceedings.

Good offices may include using shuttle diplomacy, restoring contact between the parties, inviting them to meetings, or offering suggestions for settlement. In public international law, good offices can also include supervision of plebiscites or armistices. The UN Secretary-General, the Swiss government, and the Holy See have provided good offices in international conflicts. When an organization is called on to provide good offices, a senior official is often appointed to take charge of the issue. The Director-General of the GATT, through a designated representative, provided good offices in a number of instances, notably in the GATT dispute between Latin American countries and the EU regarding banana trade (WTO 1996a, 765–67). Gathii (2010) reports a recent dispute in COMESA over the Kenya Sugar Board's nontransparent auctioning of import licenses for sugar, which affected import trade from COMESA members. In September 2009 COMESA sent to Kenya a Sugar Sector Safeguard Assessment Mission, which recommended elimination of auctioning as a nontariff barrier but apparently did not characterize the auctioning as a treaty violation. The intervention successfully persuaded Kenya to eliminate the auctioning.

In *mediation,* the neutral party actively proposes options for settlement. The success of mediation depends very much on the mediator and on the willingness of the parties to make concessions (Merrills 1991, 29, 39–41). There are few widely reported cases of such mediation within a PTA. An example involving the EU is the 2002 WTO tuna mediation. Its success is attributable to a number of factors: the complainants' ability to use leverage (a threat to block an EU waiver and indirectly prevent the launch of the Doha Round) as a means of obtaining the EU's political commitment to the process; skilled mediation by a veteran, neutral dealmaker who suggested a practical solution; EU goodwill in promptly implementing a solution that increased the complainants' market access; and the fact that the problem was framed not in terms of legal rights but as a question of impairment of interests (Porges 2003).

In *conciliation,* the parties set up a permanent or ad hoc commission, or refer a dispute to a conciliator that is to impartially examine the dispute and suggest an acceptable settlement. Historically, conciliation has worked best when the main issues in a dispute are legal but the parties wish to settle (Merrills 1991, 77). For instance, conciliation was used to wind up the defunct original East African Community in the 1980s. In response to a request by Kenya, Tanzania, and Uganda, a Swiss diplomat, Victor Umbricht, acted as conciliator to locate and value the EAC's assets and liabilities, propose a formula for dividing them among the member states, and assist in an agreement winding up the organization (Merrills 1991, 65–72).

A number of WTO-model dispute settlement systems in PTAs provide for these alternative dispute resolution mechanisms—because of a preference for consensual settlements, because negotiators view ADR as potentially fruitful and as free or low cost, or as a reaction against the time the WTO takes to determine rights and obtain compliance.[19] For instance, Annex 14-A of the EU–Korea FTA sets out a mediation procedure for nontariff measures affecting industrial products. The parties can appoint a single mediator who is a subject matter expert and who would use an informal, confidential process to help the parties clarify the problem and its trade effects and reach a mutually agreed solution. The process is agnostic regarding rule violations. The mediation process, and the positions taken in the process, are confidential and would not be admissible in dispute settlement. The EU–CARIFORUM EPA similarly provides for nonbinding, confidential mediation by agreement between the parties to a dispute and for keeping a roster of mediators.

As the COMESA example discussed above illustrates, ADR can serve as a useful channel through which the other members of a PTA can focus efforts in a practical, time-effective way on removing a PTA member's illegal trade barriers; the benefits of providing for ADR in a PTA are speculative but are very likely to exceed any cost. Formal ADR mechanisms may also offer a pathway for less formal diplomatic settlement. Further empirical research would be useful to determine the extent to which the parties to existing PTAs use ADR in practice, the disputes they use it for, the solutions produced by ADR, and factors leading to the success or failure of ADR. The use of ADR may well be underreported in the existing literature because it may not be characterized as dispute settlement and because the internal records of ADR proceedings are usually not publicly available.

Implementation, Compliance, and Sanctions in PTA Dispute Settlement

When an ad hoc panel, arbitral tribunal, or other third party produces its decision, the process of rights determination may be complete, but trade agreement enforcement is far from done. The WTO DSU procedures recognize this by outlining an organized compliance process.

WTO compliance procedures begin by requiring the party found in breach of the agreement to set a deadline for compliance, through negotiations or an arbitration process, with a 15-month benchmark for the compliance deadline. During the period before the deadline, the complying party must report on its actions, and after the deadline elapses, if compliance has not occurred, the Dispute Settlement Body will authorize the complainant to suspend concessions or other obligations under the WTO, in an amount equivalent to the nullification or impairment (trade damage) caused by the breach of the rules. If there is a dispute regarding compliance, it must be settled under the DSU by recourse (whenever possible) to the original panel; a dispute regarding the amount of the suspension of concessions must be arbitrated (whenever possible) by the original panel.

PTAs' approaches toward compliance vary. PTAs based on diplomatic or political settlement of disputes rely on settlement by agreement, not sanctions, and a failure to comply with an agreement settling a case simply means the start of another negotiation. In PTAs with standing tribunals, the tribunal remains available to enforce its judgments on a continuing basis, and a strong tribunal may have the power to impose sanctions on a noncomplying government. When the European Commission considers that an EU member state has not complied with a judgment by the ECJ, under Article 260 of the Treaty on the Functioning of the EU, the Commission may issue a reasoned opinion and then bring the case before the ECJ, specifying an appropriate fine; the Court may impose a fine on the member state as a lump sum or on a continuing basis during the period of noncompliance. In the Andean Community, Article 27 of the 1996 treaty establishing the Andean Tribunal requires a member state to comply within 90 days with any tribunal judgment of noncompliance with its Andean Community obligations, and authorizes the tribunal to determine suspension of benefits against a noncomplying state by the claimant state or any other member; the tribunal may decree other measures if such a suspension would be ineffective or would make the situation worse. Under Article 30 of the same treaty, private persons may use the tribunal's verdict as sufficient basis for claiming compensation in domestic courts for damage caused to them by the noncompliance. Because member states have often responded with changes that did not bring them into compliance, the tribunal often mandates that a member state comply and refrain from employing any measure that is contrary to the tribunal's judgment (SIEL 2010).

A PTA ad hoc panel is convened for the limited purpose of deciding a dispute, or making recommendations and rulings to the parties. For this reason, it generally is not given the power to enforce its own decisions; either the PTA itself or the parties to the PTA authorize enforcement-related actions such as suspension of concessions. U.S. FTAs currently take the following approach, exemplified by the Peru–U.S. FTA. After the panel report, the parties are to agree on the resolution of the dispute. If they cannot agree on elimination of the noncompliance, they must negotiate on compensation. If they cannot agree on compensation, or if the complaining party considers that the defending party has failed to carry out a settlement agreement, the complaining party may notify the defending party that it will suspend concessions, and at what level, and may suspend concessions 30 days later. The defending party can then ask the panel to reconvene to rule on whether it has actually complied or whether the suspension is manifestly excessive. The same approach to compliance and suspension appears in a number of other PTAs—for instance, the Canada–Colombia, Canada–Peru, Canada–Israel, and Thailand–Australia agreements.

Since 2001, U.S. FTAs have provided that concessions may not be suspended if the defending party provides timely notice that it will pay an annual monetary assessment to the complaining party. The assessment amount is set by agreement between the parties, with a fallback to 50 percent of the trade damage determined by the panel or by the complaining party. When the circumstances warrant, the PTA's supervisory body can direct that the assessment be paid into a fund to be spent on initiatives to facilitate trade between the parties. This provision responds to criticism that trade retaliation damages the economies of both parties and harms innocent exporters in the other party, without achieving compliance.

Some countries are unable to accept the U.S. approach to compliance and suspension of concessions because that approach affords very little flexibility regarding the period for compliance and relies in the first instance on the complaining party's unilateral determination regarding compliance. These countries have adopted a different approach patterned on the DSU and on proposals tabled for DSU reform. The ASEAN–Australia–New Zealand agreement, for instance, provides for a DSU-like process for determining the postpanel compliance period by negotiation or by arbitration by the panel. Any disagreement about compliance must be resolved by the original panel, reconvened for this purpose, which hands down a quick ruling. If the defending party states that it will not comply, or if the panel has found a failure to comply, the defending party must negotiate on compensation, and if there is no agreement, the complaining party has the right to suspend concessions equivalent to the nullification or impairment. The defending party can ask the panel to reconvene again if it believes it has complied or that the level of the suspension is excessive (in some agreements, "manifestly excessive"). This pattern

is followed in, for example, the Chile–Japan, EU–Korea, India–Korea, Japan–Indonesia, Japan–Switzerland, and China–New Zealand agreements. In another variation, the original panel determines the level of the suspension when it rules on compliance (e.g., the ASEAN–India Framework Agreement on Dispute Settlement and the Australia–Singapore and China–Singapore PTAs).

Some recent PTAs also provide explicitly for arbitration by the original panel if the defending party believes it has complied with the panel decision after concessions were suspended; examples are the China–New Zealand, EU–Korea, Korea–U.S., and Peru–U.S. agreements. The WTO DSU does not make explicit provision for this situation.

PTA Disputes: The Experience

We now examine disputes brought using PTA dispute settlement procedures and the written decisions that have resulted from them. A survey of PTA dispute settlement experience presents a mixed picture, complicated by a shortage of organized information and by a definitional question: at what point does a bilateral trade irritant ripen into the status of being a dispute? It is difficult to know the full extent of dispute settlement activity under any PTA, particularly those featuring settlement of disputes by negotiation or by ad hoc panels. Comparison with the WTO is useful and demonstrates that to some extent, disputes are being brought not in PTAs, but in the WTO.

For PTAs with *diplomatic or political dispute settlement,* the true level of dispute activity is unknown and perhaps unknowable. Disputes do exist: for instance, the long-running, legally focused dispute in the EC–Israel Association Agreement regarding the status of products made in the West Bank, East Jerusalem, the Golan Heights, and the Gaza Strip (see Harpaz 2004; Broude 2007). Because these agreements treat dispute settlement as a diplomatic issue, they do not systematically require that panel decisions (if any) or dispute outcomes be public. As Broude (2007) observes, the EU has no official list of disputes under its association agreements, and (at least at the time of that article) there is no group within the European Commission whose job is PTA dispute settlement.

The true level of formal disputes in these agreements may also be low. In the EU's association agreements, either party can block a panel proceeding. Moreover, the lack of detail in the agreements means that the disputing parties must agree on procedures before they can convene a panel, further increasing the burden on a would-be disputant. A dispute may simmer for years as a diplomatic issue without going through any formal process. Garcia Bercero (2006) mentions a long-standing dispute between Turkey and the

EU over nonadoption of the EU *acquis* on pharmaceuticals, and a dispute between the EU and Ukraine was blocked because of disagreement on how to split the costs of the arbitration. In a PTA with no third-party dispute settlement procedures at all—for instance, the Closer Economic Partnership Agreement between China and Hong Kong SAR, China—no dispute can even be considered unless both parties recognize it exists.

There are also selection effects at work; as Broude (2007) observes, the EU's partners in its association agreements have not even litigated much in the WTO. Thus, PTAs with diplomatic or political dispute settlement arrangements may attract governments that do not place a high value on enforcement. And in the EU context, some issues that might have been litigated in bilateral dispute settlement, such as the application to PTA members of rules of origin or border trade measures, have instead been litigated in the EU courts (see, e.g., ECJ 2010b).

Tribunal-based PTA dispute settlement has an extremely broad range. The ECJ and its related supranational court system, benefiting from abundant resources at the EU level and linking to the domestic court systems in EU member states, have handled thousands of cases since 1952. By contrast, some African PTA tribunals, struggling with lack of infrastructure or resources, have little or no reported activity. The Andean Tribunal falls somewhere in the middle; 85 tribunal cases against members for noncompliance were initiated during the period 1987–2006, although much of the Andean Tribunal's work focuses on relatively narrow intellectual property issues (Helfer and Alter 2009). The República Bolivariana de Venezuela's 2006 withdrawal from the Andean Community eliminated a significant number of pending disputes about Venezuelan trade measures.[20]

Panel-based dispute settlement has also been quite variable, but there have been relatively few panel decisions or arbitral awards. There have been 25 known decisions in PTA formal proceedings, relating to 16 disputes, as listed in annex B. By comparison, in the WTO (1995 through March 3, 2011) there have been 423 WTO complaints; 136 panel reports; 78 Appellate Body reports; 28 panel reports and 18 Appellate Body reports in compliance proceedings; and 45 arbitration awards of various types.[21] As in the WTO, the disputes formally raised under PTAs may substantially exceed the number of panel reports. Information available on dispute settlement under Chapter 20 of NAFTA indicates that whereas there have been only 3 reports of Chapter 20 panels from 1994 through March 1, 2011, at least 11 disputes in this period were settled or were abandoned after formal consultations.

Why are PTA dispute levels so low? The first, and primary, reason is that so many PTAs are very new, and bene-

fits are still being phased in. It is natural for a PTA to postpone implementation for difficult sectors to the latest point possible (as for sugar and Mexican corn in NAFTA, for instance). If implementation is postponed, so are disputes about failure to implement. The implication is that an upsurge can be expected in the future. Second, PTA institutions, and the repeated contacts they involve, provide opportunities to avoid or proactively resolve disputes, diminishing the amount of trade conflict. Third, where a market access dispute can be brought either in the WTO or in a PTA, the WTO may be a more attractive forum for complainants for several reasons: the WTO's familiar institutions and unblockable dispute settlement; the desire to be able to mobilize greater pressure against illegal denial of market access by suspending MFN tariffs and other WTO obligations (particularly where the PTA's margin of preference is low); the larger pool of neutral panelists in the WTO; the broader issue scope of the WTO compared with some PTAs; the possibility of forming alliances; access to technical assistance such as the Advisory Centre for WTO Law; and the price tag. (The system cost of WTO dispute settlement is included in a member's annual assessment, but in most PTAs the parties pay the panelists or pay for the cost of the tribunal.)

The list of disputes in annex B, however, shows that some real issues can only be dealt with through PTA dispute settlement. Among them is denial of rights that are only created by the PTA agreement, such as preferential market access, or application of preferential rules of origin. Because Mercosur creates a right of free circulation, Uruguay brought and won a dispute in Mercosur against Argentina's toleration of blockades on international bridges. Moreover, where the MFN tariff rate is high (35 percent for all the Mercosur countries), the PTA, and the enforcement of PTA rights, may be essential for obtaining real market access, as is shown by the high number of Mercosur panel proceedings listed in annex B. The Mercosur partners have fully litigated 12 disputes in the Mercosur forum, but they have only litigated three disputes against each other in the WTO, and two of those concerned antidumping measures not covered by Mercosur.

Conclusions

Since the beginning of the world economic crisis in 2008, protectionist measures have increased. PTA negotiation has increased as well, both as an economic life raft and in reaction to the lack of progress in multilateral trade liberalization. Reports on Mercosur, for instance, indicate an increase in pure border protection measures such as nonautomatic import licensing by Argentina, sectoral private voluntary restraints on exports to Argentina precipitated by import licensing, and up-valuation of imports using reference prices, which have affected almost 11 percent of Argentina's imports from Brazil and 22 percent of its imports from China (INTAL 2010). And Mercosur is not the only jurisdiction involved: elsewhere there are also tariff increases, valuation issues, new preshipment inspection requirements, buy-local or bi-national requirements, export restrictions on strategic materials, and other restrictions on trade in goods and services (Evenett 2010). All these measures have been put in place with no great apparent upsurge in PTA dispute settlement.

Periods of sustained unemployment are a difficult time to push back against protection, but a rollback will be needed when recovery occurs—and in order for recovery to occur. Both WTO and PTA dispute settlements and institutions will have a part to play, and it will be a considerable challenge. Only time will tell whether these institutions will do their job in helping move governments away from crisis protectionism.

Some practical conclusions of use to negotiators emerge from the discussion in this chapter.

- Every PTA has to have a way of settling disputes, and a PTA that promotes growth needs enforcement provisions. Economic projections of the gains from a PTA are based on the assumption of 100 percent compliance with the PTA's obligations. Ensuring compliance through enforcement is essential if the projected gains are to materialize. Even if no disputes are anticipated, enforcement provisions in a PTA reinforce the precommitment of the governments, make their promises more credible, and signal that the PTA is a solid platform for investment that will create jobs and economic growth.
- PTAs create public goods, in the form of economic growth, transparency, and stability in the trading regime and an environment for trading goods and services based on the rule of law. They also promote open regionalism by strengthening institutions to make trade liberalization more transparent, less exclusionary to traders outside the PTA, and more accessible to firms investing in the PTA area.
- The best time to reach agreement on fair rules to settle disputes is during the PTA negotiation, and in advance of any known dispute.
- Even if the parties start with low ambitions, experience demonstrates that stronger, more ambitious rules can evolve later.
- Most PTA dispute settlement procedures are now based on those in the WTO, but negotiators remain free to add

to, subtract from, or vary those procedures. There is no reason not to borrow from other PTAs' creative and constructive ideas for addressing dispute settlement.

Annex A. Dispute Settlement in CUSFTA and NAFTA

Since the early 1990s, almost all dispute settlement procedures in preferential trade agreements have been based on referral of disputes for decision by ad hoc panels. This "NAFTA model" started with the Canada–U.S. Free Trade Agreement (CUSFTA) in 1988 and underwent minor revisions in NAFTA. The choices made in 1988 and 1993 remain influential today, and so it is useful to examine some key decisions and the rationales described by negotiators.

The CUSFTA negotiations took place against a background of increasing trade conflict, particularly over U.S. trade remedies. According to Canada's dispute settlement negotiator, Canada's overarching goal for the negotiation was to obtain secure access to the U.S. market, which meant obtaining agreement to binding dispute settlement (von Finckenstein 2000). Canada sought a permanent tribunal that could bind both parties and issue remedial orders. The United States preferred ad hoc panels; it wanted to avoid creating a new bureaucracy or a tribunal that might see itself as an independent player in bilateral relations and might be perceived as telling the U.S. government what to do, and it wished to preserve a right to retaliate for noncompliance (Hart, Dymond, and Robertson 1994, 302). The FTA eventually included two dispute settlement procedures: binational review (Chapter 19) for antidumping and countervailing duty decisions, and government-government procedures for other disputes (Chapter 18). Chapter 18 was designed to address both sides' objections about GATT dispute settlement procedures: the GATT process was too lengthy and could be delayed; it involved panelists from other countries who might not have the required expertise; and it provided no certainty regarding adoption or implementation of panel reports (von Finckenstein 2000).

Chapter 18 provided a specific timetable, a standing roster of panelist candidates, and procedures designed to prevent most ways of blocking dispute settlement. It established a ministerial-level commission to oversee the functioning of the agreement and to administer disputes. In a provision sought by Canada, disputes could address not just actual measures but also proposed measures such as pending legislation. The dispute process included consultations, referral to the commission, and then referral to a panel for arbitration. Arbitration would be binding only if the parties agreed (or if the disputes concerned safeguards). In CUSFTA disputes, as it turned out, the parties never chose nonbinding arbitration (von Finckenstein 2000).

As for panel composition, CUSFTA called for five-person panels composed of two citizens from each side, chosen wherever possible from a standing roster. If a party failed to appoint its panelists, they would be selected from the roster by lot. The fifth panelist would be selected jointly and, in the absence of agreement, would be chosen by the four already selected panelists, or by lot. In practice, the two sides initially decided by lot (by coin flip) which party would choose the panel chair, and they then discussed candidates (Winham 1993). The panel then provided an initial report and a final report responding to any objections by the parties.

If, after receipt of a final panel report, the commission was not able to reach agreement on a settlement within 30 days, and a party considered that its fundamental rights or benefits under CUSFTA would be impaired by implementation or maintenance of the measure at issue, that party would be free to suspend CUSFTA benefits of equivalent effect. At the time, the GATT did not automatically authorize suspension of concessions.

Because CUSFTA incorporated by reference the GATT provisions on national treatment and quantitative trade restrictions, the negotiators also included a choice of forum provision. Article 1801(2) provided that disputes arising under both CUSFTA and the GATT could be settled in either forum, at the discretion of the complaining party, but that once an election of forum had been made by initiation of dispute settlement, the procedure initiated would be used to the exclusion of any other. This provision gave the complaining party the option to choose the strongest substantive and procedural rules, while duplicative proceedings were ruled out.

NAFTA's Chapter 20 continues the framework of CUSFTA Chapter 18, with a few changes.

- Because NAFTA is trilateral, Chapter 20 gives intervention rights to a NAFTA party not involved in a dispute, including rights to attend hearings and to receive and make submissions; the procedures also allow for two-complainant cases.
- Chapter 20 makes provision for a consensus roster of 30 individuals experienced in law, international trade, and dispute settlement. Each party selects two panelists who are citizens of the other disputing country. The selection cannot be blocked if a panelist is on the agreed roster.
- Because panels under Chapter 18 had visibly split on national lines, views in Chapter 20 panel reports are anonymous.

- The provision on choice of forum remains, and before a NAFTA party initiates a WTO dispute against another party on grounds substantially equivalent to those available to it under NAFTA, it must consult with the third party. If the three cannot agree, the dispute must normally be settled under NAFTA.

A few changes responded to environmental concerns. NAFTA's Article 103 gives precedence to obligations under five environmental treaties. In a WTO dispute between NAFTA parties, if the responding party claims that its measures are subject to Article 103, the complaining party can only bring a NAFTA dispute. Similarly, if a dispute between NAFTA parties concerns sanitary and phytosanitary (SPS) measures or environmental standards, the responding party can insist that the dispute be pursued only under NAFTA. A panel or a party can request a scientific review board on factual issues concerning environmental, health, safety, or other scientific matters. All of these changes responded to criticism that GATT panels and GATT rules were hostile to environmental regulation.

Annex B. PTA Dispute Settlement: Ad Hoc Panel Decisions

In comparison with experience in the GATT and the WTO, ad hoc panel proceedings under preferential trade agreements (PTAs) have yielded relatively few completed decisions. The known panel decisions are listed and briefly described here. The sources for this annex are Davey (1996); Reich (1996; Grebler (2003); Tussie and Delich (2005); Gantz (2006); Barral (2007); SIEL (2010); Mercosur arbitral awards on the Organization of American States (OAS) website at http://www.sice.oas.org/Dispute/mercosur/ind_s.asp; and newspaper reports.

Canada–U.S. FTA (1988–93), Chapter 18

1. *Canada's landing requirement for Pacific Coast salmon and herring,* final report, October 16, 1989. At issue was a Canadian landing requirement that replaced GATT-inconsistent export restrictions on certain fish.
2. *Lobsters from Canada,* final report, May 21, 1990. The case involved a U.S. ban on interstate transport or sale of whole live lobsters smaller than a minimum size.
3. *Article 304 and the definition of direct cost of processing or direct cost of assembling,* final report, June 8, 1992. The complaint concerned a U.S. rule that did not allow certain nonmortgage interest payments to count toward meeting CUSFTA rules of origin.

4. *The interpretation of and Canada's compliance with Article 701.3 with respect to durum wheat sales,* final report, February 8, 1993. The United States claimed that sales of durum wheat by the Canadian Wheat Board for export to the United States violated a CUSFTA ban on a government entity's selling products for export at a loss (that is, at a price below the acquisition price of the goods, plus storage, handling, and other costs incurred with respect to those goods).

5. *Puerto Rico regulations on the import, distribution and sale of ultra-high-temperature (UHT) processed milk from Quebec,* final report, June 3, 1993. The case concerned milk standards in Puerto Rico.

Israel–U.S. FTA

Machine tools from Israel, settled informally after the panel report. The dispute concerned the U.S. decision to count imports of machine tools assembled by Sharnoa Ltd., in Israel, from parts from Taiwan, China, against the U.S. import quota for machine tools from Taiwan, China.

NAFTA (Since 1994)

1. *Tariffs applied by Canada to certain U.S.-origin agricultural products,* final report, December 2, 1996. The dispute was brought by the United States against Canada's maintenance of tariff-rate quotas on certain dairy and poultry products after full tariff elimination. Examining the relationship between the CUSFTA chapter on agricultural trade, the Uruguay Round tariffication of agricultural import quotas, and NAFTA, the panel found no breach by Canada.

2. *U.S. safeguard action taken on broom-corn brooms from Mexico,* final report, January 30, 1998. The dispute brought by Mexico concerned the application of global safeguard action on broom-corn brooms to imports of such brooms from Mexico. The panel found the measure in breach.

3. *Cross-border trucking services,* final report, February 6, 2001. In a dispute brought by Mexico, the panel found a U.S. breach of the NAFTA commitment to permit operation of Mexican trucking firms in four U.S. border states. After U.S. congressional action terminating the pilot program for Mexican trucking, Mexico, on March 19, 2009, announced suspension of NAFTA concessions (i.e., an increase in tariffs to most favored nation, or MFN, levels) on imports of 90 products from the United States.

Other matters settled or abandoned after consultations but before panel proceedings concerned uranium exports

(United States v. Canada, 1994); import restrictions on sugar (Canada v. United States, 1995); restrictions on small-package delivery (United States v. Mexico, 1995); restrictions on tomato imports (Mexico v. United States, 1996); the Helms-Burton Act (Mexico and Canada v. United States, 1996); Mexican rebalancing for U.S. safeguards on broom-corn brooms (United States v. Mexico, 1996); restrictions on sugar imports (Mexico v. United States, 1998); farm products blockade (Canada v. United States, 1998), bus service (Mexico v. United States, 1998); sport fishing laws (United States v. Canada, 1999); and restrictions on potatoes (Canada v. United States, 2001).

Mercosur (Since 1998)

1. *Application by Brazil of restrictive measures to trade with Argentina,* award, April 28, 1999. The panel found that Brazilian import-licensing requirements on imports from Argentina breached the Mercosur treaty and recommended compliance by December 31, 1999.

2. *Subsidies on production and export by Brazil of pork to Argentina,* award, September 27, 1999. The panel rejected claims by Argentina regarding a system for corn stocking and Brazil's advances on exchange contracts. It found that use of the PROEX export-financing program by Brazil was only acceptable for capital goods.

3. *Application by Argentina of safeguard measures on textiles from Brazil,* award, March 10, 2000. The panel found that Argentina's application of safeguards to textiles was incompatible with the Mercosur legal regime and ordered revocation of the safeguard measure within 15 days. Brazil brought a complaint about the same textile safeguard to the WTO Textiles Monitoring Body and requested a WTO panel (WT/DS190), which was established on March 20, 2000. The parties notified a settlement to the WTO in June 2000.

4. *Application of antidumping measures on imports of whole chickens from Brazil,* award, May 21, 2001. The panel found that Mercosur law did not regulate the application of antidumping measures and rejected the claim by Brazil. Brazil then took the same dispute to the WTO (WT/DS241) and prevailed there.

5. *Market access restrictions in Argentina on bicycles imported from Uruguay,* award, September 23, 2001. Argentina treated Uruguayan bicycles made by one company as non-Mercosur in origin and therefore subject to the common external tariff. The panel ruled that this measure violated Argentina's Mercosur obligations and ordered its revocation and the restoration of market access.

6. *Brazilian import ban on remolded tires from Uruguay,* award, January 9, 2001. The panel found that Brazil's ban on imports of remolded tires was incompatible with the Mercosur standstill on new trade restrictions. Brazil later defended related measures in the WTO, raising environmental defenses not mentioned in the Mercosur proceedings.

7. *Barriers to entrance of Argentine phytosanitary products into the Brazilian market,* award, April 9, 2002. The panel found that Brazil had failed to implement in its domestic law five Mercosur Common Market Group resolutions designed to create a streamlined phytosanitary system for evaluating and registering food. It found that Brazil was obligated to implement these measures within a reasonable period of time and that six years was not reasonable; the panel ordered enactment within 120 days.

8. *Application of Uruguay's specific internal taxes on the sale of cigarettes,* award, May 21, 2002. The panel found that Uruguay's method of calculating taxes on imported cigarettes discriminated against Paraguayan cigarettes, denying national treatment. It ordered Uruguay to cease discrimination within six months.

9. *Uruguayan subsidies for processing of wool,* award. April 3, 2003. The panel found that Uruguayan export subsidies for processed wool products exported to Mercosur were inconsistent with Mercosur law and had to be eliminated within 15 days.

10. *Discriminatory and restrictive measures by Brazil on trade in tobacco and tobacco products,* award, August 5, 2005. Uruguay brought a complaint concerning a Brazilian decree raising tariffs on tobacco and tobacco products to 150 percent. Brazil repealed the decree during the proceedings.

11. *Argentine ban on imports of remolded tires,* award, October 25, 2005. In the first case under the Protocol of Olivos, the panel found that the Argentine ban was consistent with Mercosur law.

12. *Appeal by Uruguay of award on Argentine ban on imports of remolded tires,* award, December 20, 2005. The appellate tribunal reversed the award, finding that the Argentine measure was incompatible with Mercosur laws.

13. *Request for ruling regarding excess in compensatory measures in the dispute between Uruguay and Argentina on the prohibition of imports of remolded tires from Uruguay,* award, June 8, 2007. The appellate tribunal found that the Uruguayan compensatory measure was proportional and lawful.

14. *Review of tribunal decision regarding Argentine compliance with the tribunal award on remolded tires,* award, April 26, 2008. The tribunal found that Argentina had not brought itself into compliance and that until it did, Uruguay had the right to maintain compensatory measures.

15. *Failure by the Argentine state to adopt appropriate measures to prevent and/or cease impediments to free circulation caused by blockages in Argentine territory of access roads to the international bridges General San Martín and General Artigas, which connect Argentina and Uruguay,* award, September 6, 2006. Uruguay challenged Argentina's failure to act against environmental groups that blocked international bridges between Uruguay and Argentina from December 2005 to May 2006 to protest the construction of pulp mills in Uruguay. Uruguay argued that the blockage injured imports, tourism, and transport, in violation of Mercosur guarantees of free circulation of goods, services, and factors of production via the elimination of quantitative restrictions and measures of equivalent effect. The panel largely agreed. The underlying dispute concerned Argentina's objections to the construction of pulp mills in Uruguay, which Argentina separately appealed to the International Court of Justice.

16. *Interlocutory appeal by Argentina objecting to selection of the panel chairman in the free circulation dispute,* award, July 6, 2006. The tribunal rejected Argentina's appeal as inadmissible under Mercosur rules and assessed all costs and expenses of the proceeding against Argentina.

Other

Chilean price bands (application of price-band tariffs on imports of vegetable oils). (a) Bolivia brought a dispute against Chile in 2000 under Chapter XIII of the Bolivia–Chile (LAIA/ALADI) Economic Complementation Agreement 22, which provides that a dispute settlement panel decision is fully binding on the parties. Chile then reimbursed the safeguard duties collected. (b) Argentina brought a complaint in 2000 under the Administrative Commission of the Mercosur–Chile (LAIA/ALADI) Economic Complementation Agreement 35, which provides that a panel decision is nonbinding. After Argentina prevailed but Chile failed to comply, in October 2000 Argentina brought a dispute in the WTO (WT/DS207, *Chile–Price Band System and Safeguard Measures Relating to Certain Agricultural Products*), and prevailed in 2002. Argentina later prevailed in WTO compliance proceedings in 2007 but has not suspended concessions.

Notes

The views expressed herein do not represent those of any present or past client or employer.

1. CUSFTA and NAFTA panel decisions are available from many sources, including the NAFTA Secretariat website, http://www.nafta-sec-alena.org/. Panel decisions of CUSFTA, NAFTA, and Mercosur, as well as the texts of PTAs involving Western Hemisphere countries, are available at the website of the Organization of American States (OAS) Foreign Trade Information System, http://www.sice.oas.org/.

2. During the period 1996–2000, the OAS Trade Unit prepared an inventory of dispute settlement in the Western Hemisphere (FTAA 2000), as an input for the Free Trade Area of the Americas (FTAA) Negotiating Group on Dispute Settlement. The FTAA negotiations have been stalled since 2003, but the inventory remains a useful snapshot of these provisions as they stood in 2000. Considerable information on dispute settlement and institutions in Latin America and the Caribbean is available at the websites of Mercosur, the Andean Community (CAN), the Central American Court of Justice, the Caribbean Court of Justice, and regional institutions, including the OAS, the Inter-American Development Bank (IADB), the secretariat of the Latin American Integration Association/ Asociación Latinoamericana de Integración (LAIA/ALADI), and the United Nations Economic Commission for Latin America and the Caribbean/Comisión Económica para América Latina (ECLAC/CEPAL). The last-named organization maintains a database on trade agreement dispute settlement, "Base de Datos Integrada de Controversias Comerciales de América Latina y el Caribe/Integrated Database of Trade Disputes for Latin America and the Caribbean," http://badicc.eclac.cl/.

3. CAN, "Procesos del Tribunal de Justicia: Acciones de Incumplimiento" (updated list of all Andean Tribunal noncompliance proceedings), http://www.comunidadandina.org/canprocedimientosinternet/ListaEx pedientes11.aspx?CodProc=7&TipoProc=%27S%27.

4. Ibid.

5. Andean Community Decision 680 of 2007 (authorizing ATJ budget for fiscal year 2008), http://www.comunidadandina.org/norma tiva/dec/D680.htm.

6. Investir en Zone Franc (IZF) website, http://www.izf.net/pages/ institutions-afrique---zone-uemoa-et-cemac/2199. The site contains information on trade and investment in the Central and West African franc zones, including the legislation and jurisprudence of WAEMU/ UEMOA and CEMAC. Information on legal systems in francophone Africa is also found at http://www.archive.org.

7. African International Courts and Tribunals (AICT), http://www .aict-ctia.org/.

8. The term "nonviolation nullification or impairment" comes from the pioneering work by Robert E. Hudec, *The GATT Legal System and World Trade Diplomacy* (Hudec 1975).

9. Nonviolation remedies apply as follows in the PTAs studied: Chile–Japan, only for the chapters on trade in goods; India–Korea, Korea–Singapore, Panama–Singapore, Canada–Costa Rica, Canada–Chile, Canada–Colombia, and Chile–Peru, goods and services; Panama–Taiwan, China, goods, services, and TBTs; El Salvador–Honduras–Taiwan, China, goods, services, SPS measures, and TBTs; Chile–Central America, goods, services, TBTs, and aviation; Chile–Colombia and the Trans–Pacific SEP, goods, services, TBTs, and procurement; Nicaragua–Taiwan, China, goods, services, TBTs, SPS measures, and IPRs; and Chile–Australia, goods, services, TBTs, procurement, and IPRs.

10. Examples include the general cooperation chapters in the following PTAs: China–New Zealand, Japan–Mexico, Japan–Malaysia, Japan–Philippines, Japan–ASEAN, ASEAN–Australia–New Zealand, Australia–Thailand, and Korea–Singapore.

11. Examples include intellectual property cooperation provisions in the Japan–Philippines and Japan–Thailand PTAs and the competition policy cooperation obligations of the Australia–Chile, Australia–Thailand, ASEAN–Australia–New Zealand, Australia–U.S., Peru–U.S., and SACU–EFTA PTAs.

12. This is the case for the Japan–Mexico, Japan–Chile, Australia–Chile, ASEAN–Australia–New Zealand, Chile–U.S., and Singapore–U.S. agreements.

13. *Res judicata* is the legal doctrine that once a case has been determined, neither party can bring the same claims regarding the same subject matter against the other in another court. *Lis alibi pendens* is the legal doctrine that proceedings regarding the same facts cannot be commenced in a second court if the *lis* (i.e., action) is already *pendens* (pending) in another court.

14. The two disputes brought under CUSFTA rather than the GATT were those on Canada's landing requirement for Pacific Coast salmon and herring (final report October 16, 1989) and on lobsters from Canada (final report May 21, 1990).

15. PTAs that require model rules of procedure include NAFTA and all later U.S. PTAs; the Mercosur Protocol of Olivos; the Singapore–GCC, Chile–EU, Chile–Australia, Chile–Colombia, Chile–Central America, ASEAN–China, and Korea–Singapore PTAs; the ASEAN Enhanced DSM; and the Trans–Pacific SEP.

16. Appointing authorities named in PTAs include the WTO Director-General (e.g., the China–New Zealand, ASEAN–Japan, Japan–Malaysia, Japan–Vietnam, and New Zealand–Singapore PTAs and the Trans-Pacific SEP), the Secretary-General of the Permanent Court of Arbitration in the Hague (e.g., the Japan–Switzerland and Canada–EFTA PTAs), or a regional secretariat (the Mercosur Administrative Secretariat for disputes under the Mercosur Protocol of Olivos, and the ASEAN Secretary-General for the ASEAN Enhanced DSM).

17. Participation by another PTA member is permitted by NAFTA, the ASEAN Enhanced DSM, the Trans-Pacific SEP, and the ASEAN–Australia–New Zealand, Canada–EFTA, Colombia–EFTA, Japan–ASEAN, China–ASEAN, Chile–Central America, and CAFTA–DR agreements.

18. Examples of provisions for stakeholder input are the EU Trade Barriers Regulation, U.S. Section 301, and China's analogous legislation.

19. Examples of PTAs with provisions for alternative dispute resolution include China–New Zealand (Article 187), Thailand–Australia (Article 1803), Singapore–Australia (Article 16.3), the Trans-Pacific SEP (Article 15.5), NAFTA (Article 2007) and later U.S. FTAs, and the ASEAN Enhanced DSM, which authorizes good offices, mediation, or conciliation by the ASEAN secretary-general (Article 4).

20. CAN, "Procesos del Tribunal de Justicia: Acciones de Incumplimiento."

21. "Facts and Figures on WTO Dispute Settlement," http://www .worldtradelaw.net.

Bibliography

ACWL (Advisory Centre on WTO Law). 2007. "Decision 2007/7 Adopted by the Management Board on 19 November 2007: Billing Policy and Time Budget." ACWL/MB/D/2007/7, ACWL, Geneva. http://www .acwl.ch/e/documents/ACWL-MB-D-2007-7.pdf.

Alter, Karen J., and Laurence R. Helfer. 2011. "Legal Integration in the Andes: Law-Making by the Andean Tribunal of Justice." SSRN: http://ssrn.com/ abstract=1757772. Forthcoming in *European Law Journal* 17 (5).

Apaza, Pamela. 2006. "The Interaction between the Dispute Settlement Mechanisms of the American Regional Trade Agreements and the WTO." Master's thesis, World Trade Institute, Bern.

APEC (Asia-Pacific Economic Cooperation). 2004. "Best Practices for RTAs/FTAs in APEC." 2004/AMM/003, 16th APEC Ministerial Meeting, Santiago, Chile, November 17–18.

———. 2008. "Managing the Noodle Bowl: The Fragility of East Asian Regionalism." *Singapore Economic Review* 53 (3): 449–78.

Banjo, Adewale. 2007. "The ECOWAS Court and the Politics of Access to Justice in West Africa." *Africa Development* 32 (1): 69–87.

Barral, Welber. 2007. "The Brazilian Experience in Dispute Settlement." ECLAC Project Documents Collection, UN Economic Commission for Latin America and the Caribbean, Santiago.

Bartels, Lorand. 2009. "Social Issues: Labour, Environment and Human Rights." In *Bilateral and Regional Trade Agreements: Commentary and Analysis*, ed. Simon Lester and Brian Mercurio. Cambridge, U.K.: Cambridge University Press.

Blackwood, Robin. 2008. "Report on International Organizations: Mercado Comúndel Sur/Southern Common Market." Report on Mercosur PTR Decision of April 2008 on Argentina Remolded Tires Dispute, American Society of International Law, Washington, DC. http://www.asil.org/rio/mercosur.html.

Bolle, Mary Jane. 2009. "Overview of Labor Enforcement Issues in Free Trade Agreements." Report Rs22823, Congressional Research Service, Library of Congress, Washington, DC.

Bolle, Mary Jane, and M. Angeles Villarreal. 2009. "Peru Trade Promotion Agreement: Labor Issues." Report Rs22521, Congressional Research Service, Library of Congress, Washington, DC.

Bown, Chad, and Bernard Hoekman. 2007. "Developing Countries and Enforcement of Trade Agreements: Why Dispute Settlement Is Not Enough." CEPR Discussion Paper 6459. Centre for Economic Policy Research, London. http://www.cepr.org/pubs/dps/DP6459.asp.

Broude, Tomer. 2007. "From *Pax Mercatoria* to *Pax Europea*: How Trade Dispute Procedures Serve the EC's Regional Hegemony." In *Economics of European Union Law*, ed. Paul B. Stephan, 319–34. Cheltenham, U.K.: Edward Elgar. Also available as bepress Legal Series Working Paper 650, http://law.bepress.com/expresso/eps/650.

———. 2009. "Regional Economic Integration in the Middle East and North Africa: A Primer." Research Paper 12–09, Hebrew University of Jerusalem. SSRN: http://ssrn.com/abstract=1333292.

Busch, Marc, and Eric Reinhardt. 2003. "The Evolution of Dispute Settlement." In *Trade Policy Research 2003*, ed. John M. Curtis and Dan Ciuriak. Ottawa: Department of Foreign Affairs and International Trade.

Cameron, Maxwell, and Brian Tomlin. 2002. *The Making of NAFTA: How the Deal Was Done*. Ithaca, NY: Cornell University Press.

CAN (Comunidad Andina/Andean Community). 2008a. "Manual de Procedimientos del Sistema Andino de Solución de Controversias." Secretaría General de la Comunidad Andina, Lima. http://www.comunidadandina.org/public/libro_Manual.pdf.

———. 2008b. "Decision 680: Presupuesto del Tribunal de Justicia de la Comunidad Andina para el año 2008." CAN Commission, Lima. http://www.comunidadandina.org/normativa/dec/dectema_inst_pres.htm.

Cárdenas, Emilio J., and Guillermo Tempesta. 2001. "Arbitral Awards under Mercosur's Dispute Settlement Mechanism." *Journal of International Economic Law* 4 (2, March): 337–66.

CCJ (Caribbean Court of Justice). 2008. "Annual Report 2007–2008. Appendix: Financial Statements of the Caribbean Court of Justice." CCJ, Port of Spain. http://www.caribbeancourtofjustice.org/annualreport0708.html.

CEC (Commission on Environmental Cooperation). 2011. "Registry of Citizen Submissions." NAFTA Commission on Environmental Cooperation, Montreal, Quebec. http://www.cec.org. Accessed February 7, 2011.

CEPAL/ECLAC (Comisión Económica para América Latina/Economic Commission for Latin America and the Caribbean). 2006. "Reducir la Incertidumbre Juridica, Un Desafio de la Integración Subregional en America Latina y el Caribe." *Boletin FAL* (Facilitatión del Comercio y el Transporte en America Latina y el Caribe)" 235 (March 2006). Santiago: CEPAL/ECLAC.

Choi, Won Mog. 2004. "Making a Better Dispute Settlement Mechanism for Regional Trade Agreements: Lessons of Integration Efforts in East Asia." In *WTO and East Asia: New Perspectives*, ed. Mitsuo Matsushita and Dukgeun Ahn. London: Cameron May.

———. 2007. "Legal Analysis of Korea: ASEAN Regional Trade Integration." *Journal of World Trade* 41 (3): 581–603.

COMESA (Common Market for Eastern and Southern Africa). 2000. "Official Gazette of COMESA." COMESA, Lusaka. http://about.comesa.int/attachments/062_2000%20Gazette%20Vol.%206%20No5.pdf.

———. 2009. "COMESA Court of Justice." COMESA, Lusaka. http://about.comesa.int/lang-en/institutions/court-of-justice.

Daily Independent (Lagos). 2011. "Ecowas Court Rules on Oil Pollution: Says FG, NNPC Can Be Sued." January 19.

Damro, Chad. 2006. "The Political Economy of Regional Trade Agreements." In *Regional Trade Agreements and the WTO Legal System*, ed. Lorand Bartels and Federico Ortino. New York: Oxford University Press.

Davey, William. 1996. *Pine & Swine: Canada–United States Trade Dispute Settlement. The FTA Experience and NAFTA Prospects*. Ottawa: Centre for Trade Policy and Law.

Donaldson, Victoria, and Simon Lester. 2009. "Dispute Settlement." In *Bilateral and Regional Trade Agreements: Commentary and Analysis*, ed. Simon Lester and Brian Mercurio. Cambridge, U.K.: Cambridge University Press.

EAC (East African Community). 2009. "East African Court of Justice: Information, Documentation, Rulings, Judgments and Advisory Opinions." EAC, Arusha, Tanzania. http://www.eac.int/eacj.html.

———. 2010. "EALA Passes Budget Estimates for FY 2010/2011." Press release, May 3, EAC, Arusha, Tanzania. http://www.eac.int/component/content/article/1-latest-news/449-press-release-eala-passes-eac-budget-estimates-of-us-59963040-for-financial-year-20102011.html.

East African (Nairobi). 2006. "COMESA Court Faces Legal, Funding Woes." March 29.

Echandi, Roberto. 2004. "Settlement of Trade Disputes between States: The Experience of Central American Countries." In *Inter-Governmental Trade Dispute Settlement: Multilateral and Regional Approaches*, ed. Julio Lacarte and Jaime Granados. London: Cameron May.

ECJ (European Court of Justice). 2010a. *Annual Report 2009 of the Court of Justice of the European Communities*. Luxembourg: ECJ. http://curia.europa.eu/jcms/jcms/Jo2_7000/.

———. 2010b. *Brita GmbH v. Hauptzollamt Hamburg-Hafen, Case C-386/08*, OJ C 100/4, April 17, Luxembourg.

EFTA (European Free Trade Association) Court. 2009. "Financial Statements for 2008." EFTA Court, Luxembourg. http://www.eftacourt.int/index.php/court/mission/financial_statement/.

Essien, Victor. 2006. "Regional Trade Agreements in Africa: A Historical and Bibliographic Account of ECOWAS and CEMAC." Hauser Global Law School Program, New York University, New York. http://www.nyulawglobal.org/globalex/CEMAC_ECOWAS.htm.

EU (European Union). 2010. "Budget on Line." EU, Brussels. http://eur-lex.europa.eu/budget/www/index-en.htm: Draft 2011 Budget, Section 4 on Court of Justice, at http://eur-lex.europa.eu/budget/data/DB_2011/EN/SEC04.pdf.

European Commission. 2007. "Proposal for a Council Decision on a Community Position within the EU–Chile Association Committee on the Establishment of a List of Arbitrators as Required by Article 185 Paragraph 2 of the Agreement Establishing an Association between the European Community and its Member States, of the One Part, and the Republic of Chile, of the Other Part." COM(2007)47, February 7, OJ C 138/9, June 22, 2007, Brussels.

———. 2009. "26th Annual Report on the Monitoring and Application of Community Law." COM(2009) 675, European Commission, Brussels. http://ec.europa.eu/community_law/infringements/infringements_annual_report_26_en.htm.

Evenett, Simon J., ed. 2010. "Will Stabilisation Limit Protectionism? The 4th GTA Report. A Focus on the Gulf Region." Global Trade Alert, Centre for Economic Policy Research, London.

Fiorentino, Roberto V., Luis Verdeja, and Christelle Toqueboeuf. 2006. "The Changing Landscape of Regional Trade Agreements: 2006 Update." Discussion Paper 12, World Trade Organization, Geneva.

Foroutan, Faezeh. 1992. "Regional Integration in Sub-Saharan Africa: Experience and Prospects." Policy Research Working Paper 992, World Bank, Washington, DC.

Francois, Joseph, and Miriam Manchin. 2009. "Economic Impact of a Potential Free Trade Agreement (FTA) between the European Union and the Commonwealth of Independent States." CASE (Center for

Social and Economic Research), Warsaw. SSRN: http://ssrn.com/abstract=1393697.

FTAA (Free Trade Area of the Americas). 2000. "Inventory of Dispute Settlement Mechanisms, Procedures and Legal Texts Established in Existing Trade and Integration Agreements, Treaties and Arrangements in the Hemisphere and in the WTO." FTAA ngds/w/08/Rev.4, February 7. http://www.ftaa-alca.org/ngroups/NGDS/publications/dsw8r4_e.asp.

Gama Sá Cabral, Jeanine, and Gabriella Giovanna Lucarelli de Salvio. 2008. "Considerations on the Mercosur Dispute Settlement System and the Impact of Its Decisions on the WTO Dispute Settlement System." *Journal of World Trade* 42 (6): 1013–40.

Gantz, David. 2006. "The United States and NAFTA Dispute Settlement: Ambivalence, Frustration and Occasional Defiance." Arizona Legal Studies Discussion Paper 06-16, University of Arizona, Tucson, AZ. SSRN: http://ssrn.com/abstract=918542.

Garcia Bercero, Ignacio. 2006. "Dispute Settlement in European Union Free Trade Agreements: Lessons Learned?" In *Regional Trade Agreements and the WTO Legal System*, ed. Lorand Bartels and Federico Ortino. New York: Oxford University Press.

Gathii, James Thuo. 2010. "African Regional Trade Agreements as Flexible Legal Regimes." *North Carolina Journal of International Law and Commercial Regulation* 35 (3, Spring). SSRN: http://ssrn.com/abstract=1622274.

Gómez, R., Hernando Jose, and Javier Gamboa.2007. "Cambios institucionales para la negociación del TLC de Colombia con los EEUU y derivados de su implementación." Colección de documentos de proyecto, LC/W.146, Comisión Económica para América Latina/Economic Commission for Latin America and the Caribbean (CEPAL/ECLAC), Santiago.

Gonzalez, Anabel. 2006. "La solución de controversias en los acuerdos regionales de America Latina con paises desarrollados." Serie Comercio Internacional 68, Division de Comercio Internacional y Integracion, LC/L.2525-P, Comisión Económica para América Latina/Economic Commission for Latin America and the Caribbean (CEPAL/ECLAC), Santiago.

Goode, Walter. 2005. *Negotiating Free-Trade Agreements: A Guide*. Canberra: Department of Foreign Affairs and Trade, Australia. http://www.dfat.gov.au/publications/negotiating_ftas/index.html.

Granados, Jaime, and Ann Casanova. 2004. "Treatment of Asymmetries in Size and Development in Trade Agreements: Some Suggestions for Regional North-South Dispute Settlement Negotiations." In *Inter-Governmental Trade Dispute Settlement: Multilateral and Regional Approaches*, ed. Julio Lacarte and Jaime Granados. London: Cameron May.

Grebler, Eduard. 2003. "Dispute Settlement: Regional Approaches, 6.2 Mercosur." Module for the United Nations Conference on Trade and Development (UNCTAD) Course on Dispute Settlement in International Trade, Investment, and Intellectual Property, UNCTAD/EDM/Misc.232/Add.28, United Nations, New York and Geneva.

Guira, Jorge. 2000. "Mercosur: The Emergence of a Working System of Dispute Resolution." *NAFTA Law and Business Review Americas* 6: 255–75.

Harpaz, Guy. 2004. "The Dispute over the Treatment of Products Exported to the European Union from the Golan Heights, East Jerusalem, the West Bank and the Gaza Strip: The Limits of Power and the Limits of the Law." *Journal of World Trade* 38 (6): 1049–58.

Hart, Michael, Bill Dymond, and Colin Robertson. 1994. *Decision at Midnight: Inside the Canada–US Free Trade Negotiations*. Vancouver, Canada: UBC Press.

Helfer, Laurence R., and Karen J. Alter. 2009. "The Andean Tribunal of Justice and Its Interlocutors: Understanding Preliminary Reference Patterns in the Andean Community." Vanderbilt University Law School Law and Economics Research Paper 09-01, Vanderbilt University Law School, Nashville, TN. SSRN: http://ssrn.com/abstract=1334733.

Hessbruegge, Jan Arno. 2011. "ECOWAS Court Judgment in Habré v. Senegal Complicates Prosecution in the Name of Africa." American Society of International Law, *Insights* (February 3). http://www.asil.org/insights110203.cfm.

Hicks, Raymond, and Soo Yeon Kim. 2009. "Credible Commitment through PTAs and Their Effects on Trade: A Study of Asia's Reciprocal Trade Agreements." Prepared for the Annual Meeting of the American Political Science Association, September. SSRN: http://ssrn.com/abstract=1449204.

Horn, Henrik, Petros C. Mavroidis, and André Sapir. 2010. "Beyond the WTO? An Anatomy of EU and US Preferential Trade Agreements." *World Economy* 33 (11): 1565–88.

House Committee on Ways and Means. 2007. "Congressional-Administration Agreement on a New Trade Policy for America." U.S. House of Representatives, Washington, DC. http://waysandmeans.house.gov/News.asp?FormMode=release&ID=513.

Hudec, Robert E. 1975. *The GATT Legal System and World Trade Diplomacy*. New York: Praeger.

ICJ (International Court of Justice). 1950. *Interpretation of Peace Treaties with Bulgaria, Hungary and Rumania*, Advisory Opinion, *First Phase* [1950] ICJ Rep., 65; *Second Phase* [1950] ICJ Rep. 221. Luxembourg, ICJ.

Inama, Stefano. 2005. "The Association of South East Asian Nations–People's Republic of China Free Trade Area: Negotiating beyond Eternity with Little Trade Liberalization?" *Journal of World Trade* 39 (3): 559–79.

INTAL (Institute for the Integration of Latin America and the Caribbean). 2005. "CARICOM Report No. 2." INTAL, Inter-American Development Bank, Buenos Aires.

_____. 2006. "MERCOSUR: The Permanent Review Tribunal Issued Its First Award." *INTAL Monthly Newsletter* 114 (January).

———. 2009. "MERCOSUR Report No. 13, 2007 (Second Semester)–2008 (First Semester)." INTAL, Inter-American Development Bank, Buenos Aires.

———. 2010. "MERCOSUR Report No. 14, 2008 (Second Semester)–2009 (First Semester)." INTAL, Inter-American Development Bank, Buenos Aires.

Karli, Mehmet. 2008. "Assessing the Development Friendliness of Dispute Settlement Mechanisms in the Economic Partnership Agreements and an Analytical and Comparative Guide to the Dispute Settlement Provisions in the EU's FTAs." European Studies Centre, Occasional Paper, University of Oxford, Oxford, U.K. SSRN: http://ssrn.com/abstract=1270111.

Kawai, Masahiro, and Ganeshan Wignaraja. 2009. "The Asian Noodle Bowl: Is It Serious for Business?" ADBI Working Paper 136, Asian Development Bank Institute, Manila.

Keck, Alexander, and Roberta Piermartini. 2005. "The Economic Impact of EPAs in SADC Countries." Staff Working Paper ERSD-2005-04, World Trade Organization, Geneva.

Keck, Alexander, and Simon Schropp. 2007. "Indisputably Essential: The Economics of Dispute Settlement Institutions in Trade Agreements." Staff Working Paper ERSD-2007-02, World Trade Organization, Geneva.

Kirk, Ron, and Hilda Solis. 2010. Consultation request addressed to Minister of Economy and Minister of Labor and Social Protection of Guatemala, July 30, USTR, Washington, DC.

Kreinin, Mordechai, ed. 2000. *Building a Partnership: The Canada–United States Free Trade Agreement*. Lansing, MI: Michigan State University.

Kwak, Kyung, and Gabrielle Marceau. 2006. "Overlaps and Conflicts of Jurisdiction between the WTO and Regional Trade Agreements." In *Regional Trade Agreements and the WTO Legal System*, ed. Lorand Bartels and Federico Ortino. New York: Oxford University Press.

Lacarte, Julio, and Jaime Granados, eds. 2004. *Inter-Governmental Trade Dispute Settlement: Multilateral and Regional Approaches*. London: Cameron May.

Loungnarath, Vilaysoun, and Céline Stehly. 2000. "The General Dispute Settlement Mechanism in the North American Free Trade Agreement and the World Trade Organization System: Is North American Regionalism Really Preferable to Multilateralism?" *Journal of World Trade* 34 (1): 39–71.

Luo, Yan. 2005. "Dispute Settlement in the Proposed East Asian Free Trade Agreement: What We Can Learn from the EU and the NAFTA."

Presented at ILA British Branch Spring 2005 Conference, Edinburgh, Scotland, May. http://www.hss.ed.ac.uk/ila/Day2.htm.

Mercosur (Southern Cone Common Market, Mercado Común del Sur), Tribunal Permanente de Revisión. 2006. "Laudo del Tribunal Permanente de Revisión Constituido en Plenario para Entender en el Recurso de Revisión Presentado por la República Argentina contra la Decisión del Tribunal Arbitral AD HOC de Fecha 21 de junio de 2006, Constituido para Entender en la Controversia Promovida por la República Oriental del Uruguay contra la República Argentina sobre: 'Impedimientos a la Libre Circulación derivado de los Cortes en Territorio Argentino de Vías de Acceso a los Puentes Internacionales Gral. San Martín y Gral.Artigas.'" Award of July 6, 2006. http://www.sice.oas.org/Dispute/mercosur/Laudo002_006_p.pdf.

Mercurio, Bryan, and Rebecca LaForgia. 2005. "Expanding Democracy: Why Australia Should Negotiate for Open and Transparent Dispute Settlement in Its Free Trade Agreements." *Melbourne Journal of International Law* 6: 485–514.

Merrills, J. G. 1991. *International Dispute Settlement*. 2nd ed. Cambridge, U.K.: Grotius Publications.

Morgan, David. 2008. "Dispute Settlement under PTAs: Political or Legal?" In *Challenges to Multilateral Trade: The Impact of Bilateral, Preferential and Regional Agreements*, ed. Ross Buckley, Vai Io Lai, and Laurence Boulle. Alphen aan den Rijn, Netherlands: Kluwer Law International. Also available as University of Melbourne Legal Studies Research Paper 341, SSRN: http://ssrn.com/abstract=1203022.

MOX Plant Case. 2006. *Commission v. Ireland*, Case No. C-459/03, Judgment in OJ C 165, July 15. http://eur-lex.europa.eu/LexUriServ/LexUriServ.do?uri=OJ:C:2006:165:0002:0003:EN:PDF.

Nakagawa, Junji. 2007. "No More Negotiated Deals? Settlement of Trade and Investment Disputes in East Asia." *Journal of International Economic Law* 10 (4): 837–67.

Nyaungwa, Nyasha. 2010. "Zimbabwean Government Could Lose More Assets in SADC." *Namibia Economist* (April 23). http://allafrica.com/stories/201004230689.html.

Opertti, Didier. 2004. "The New MERCOSUR Dispute Settlement Mechanism." In *Inter-Governmental Trade Dispute Settlement: Multilateral and Regional Approaches*, ed. Julio Lacarte and Jaime Granados. London: Cameron May.

Pauwelyn, Joost. 2004. "Going Global, Regional, or Both? Dispute Settlement in the Southern African Development Community (SADC) and Overlaps with the WTO and Other Jurisdictions." *Minnesota Journal of World Trade* 13: 231–304.

———. 2006. "Adding Sweeteners to Softwood Lumber: The WTO-NAFTA 'Spaghetti Bowl' Is Cooking." *Journal of International Economic Law* 9: 1–10.

Peña, Felix. 2004. "Overview of New Trends in Dispute Settlement Mechanisms under Preferential Trade Agreements." In *Inter-Governmental Trade Dispute Settlement: Multilateral and Regional Approaches*, ed. Julio Lacarte and Jaime Granados. London: Cameron May.

Piérola, Fernando, and Gary Horlick. 2007. "WTO Dispute Settlement and Dispute Settlement in the 'North-South' Agreements of the Americas: Considerations for Choice of Forum." *Journal of World Trade* 41 (5): 885–908.

Porges, Amelia. 2003. "Settling WTO Disputes: What Do Litigation Models Tell Us?" *Ohio State Journal on Dispute Resolution* 19 (1): 141–84.

Ramirez Robles, Edna. 2006. "Political and Quasi-Adjudicative Dispute Settlement Models in European Union Free Trade Agreements: Is the Quasi-Adjudicative Model a Trend or Is It Just Another Model?" Staff Working Paper ERSD-2006-09, WTO Economic Research and Statistics Division, Geneva. http://www.wto.org/english/res_e/reser_e/ersd200609_e.pdf.

Reich, Arie. 1996. "From Diplomacy to Law: The Juridicization of International Trade Relations." *Northwestern Journal of International Law & Business* 17 (2/3): 775–849.

Reuters. 2010. "Tribunal Wants SADC to Suspend Harare over Land Case." July 17. http://www.polity.org.za/article/tribunal-wants-sadc-to-suspend-harare-over-land-case-2010-07-17.

Rojas Penso, Juan. 2004. "New Dispute Settlement Perspectives in the Latin American Integration Association (ALADI)." In *Inter-Governmental Trade Dispute Settlement: Multilateral and Regional Approaches*, ed. Julio Lacarte and Jaime Granados. London: Cameron May.

Sáez, Sebastian. 2007. "The Countries of Latin America and the Caribbean and Trade Disputes: An Analysis." *Boletin FAL* (Facilitation del Comercio y el Transporte en America Latina y el Caribe) 249 (May). Also published in Spanish by Comisión Económica para América Latina/Economic Commission for Latin America and the Caribbean (CEPAL/ECLAC) as "América Latina y el Caribe en las Controversias Comerciales: Un Análisis Aplicando BADICC," CEPAL/ECLAC, Santiago.

Sauvé, Pierre, and Martin Molinuevo. 2008. "Does Architecture Matter? The Treatment of Trade and Investment in Financial Services in Selected Preferential Trade Agreements." NCCR Trade Regulation Working Paper 2008/9, Swiss National Centre of Competence in Research, Bern. http://www.nccr-trade.org/nccr-publications/8.html.

Schiff, Maurice, and L. Alan Winters. 2003. *Regional Integration and Development*. New York: Oxford University Press.

Schreuer, Christoph. 2001. *The ICSID Convention: A Commentary*. Cambridge, U.K.: Cambridge University Press.

SIEL (Society of International Economic Law). 2010. "Mercosur Award No. 1/2005." SIEL Translation Project. http://www.sielnet.org/siel-translationproject.

Smith, James McCall. 2000. "The Politics of Dispute Settlement Design: Explaining Legalism in Regional Trade Pacts." *International Organization* 54: 137–80.

Snyder, Francis. 2009. "China, Regional Trade Agreements and WTO Law." *Journal of World Trade* 43 (1): 1–57.

Stephanou, Constantinos. 2009. "Including Financial Services in Preferential Trade Agreements: Lessons of International Experience for China." Policy Research Working Paper 4898, World Bank, Washington, DC.

Sucharitkul, Sompong. 2003. "Dispute Settlement: Regional Approaches, 6.3 ASEAN." Module for the United Nations Conference on Trade and Development (UNCTAD) Course on Dispute Settlement in International Trade, Investment, and Intellectual Property, UNCTAD/EDM/Misc.232/Add.29, United Nations, New York and Geneva.

Szepesi, Stephen. 2004. "Comparing EU Free Trade Agreements: Dispute Settlement." *In Brief* 6G (July). Maastricht, Netherlands: European Centre for Development Policy Management. http://www.ecdpm.org/inbrief6g.

Thorp, Teresa. 2010. "Challenges of Incorporating the Economic Acquis Communautaire of the East African Community in a New Common Market." Society of International Economic Law (SIEL), Second Biennial Global Conference, University of Barcelona, July 8–10. SSRN: http://ssrn.com/abstract=1632439.

Tussie, Diana, and Valentina Delich. 2005. "Dispute Settlement between Developing Countries: Argentina and Chilean Price Bands." In *Managing the Challenges of WTO Participation: 45 Case Studies*, ed. Peter Gallagher, Patrick Low, and Andrew L. Stoler. Cambridge, U.K.: Cambridge University Press.

Unzurrunzaga Valle, Maria Ester. 2005. "Trade Disputes Settlement in the European Union Agreements with Mexico and Chile." Inter-American Development Bank (IADB), Washington, DC. http://www.iadb.org/intal/aplicaciones/uploads/ponencias/Foro_ELSNIT_2005_02_Unzurrunzaga.pdf.

U.S. DOL (U.S. Department of Labor). 2007. "Status of Submissions under the North American Agreement on Labor Cooperation (NAALC)." List updated to September 2007, U.S. DOL, Washington, DC. http://www.dol.gov/ilab/programs/nao/status.htm.

———. 2010. "Status of Submissions under the NAALC." Division of Trade Agreement Administration and Technical Cooperation, U.S. Department of Labor, Washington, DC. http://www.dol.gov/ilab/programs/nao/status.htm.

USTR (Office of the U.S. Trade Representative). 2010. "USTR Kirk Announces Labor Rights Trade Enforcement Case Against Guatemala." Press release, July 30, USTR, Washington, DC.

Victor, David G. 1998. "The Operation and Effectiveness of the Montreal Protocol's Non-Compliance Procedure." In *The Implementation and Effectiveness of International Environmental Commitments,* ed. David G. Victor, Kal Raustiala, and Eugene B. Skolnikoff. Cambridge, MA: MIT Press.

Vigil Toledo, Ricardo. 2004. "Dispute Settlement in Andean Community Law." In *Inter-Governmental Trade Dispute Settlement: Multilateral and Regional Approaches,* ed. Julio Lacarte and Jaime Granados. London: Cameron May.

Vinuesa, Raul Emilio. 2005. "Enforcement of Mercosur Arbitration Awards within the Domestic Legal Orders of Member States." *Texas International Law Journal* 40: 425–42.

von Finckenstein, Konrad W. 2000. "Dispute Settlement under the Free Trade Agreement." In *Building a Partnership: The Canada–United States Free Trade Agreement,* ed. Mordechai Kreinin. Lansing, MI: Michigan State University.

Wang, Jiangyu. 2009. "ASEAN–China Free Trade Agreement." In *Bilateral and Regional Trade Agreements: Commentary and Analysis,* ed. Simon Lester and Brian Mercurio. Cambridge, U.K.: Cambridge University Press.

Whitelaw, James. 2004. "The MERCOSUR Dispute Settlement System." In *Inter-Governmental Trade Dispute Settlement: Multilateral and Regional Approaches*, ed. Julio Lacarte and Jaime Granados. London: Cameron May.

Winham, Gilbert. 1993. "Dispute Settlement in NAFTA and the FTA." In *Assessing NAFTA: A Trinational Analysis,* ed. Steven Globerman and Michael Walker. Vancouver, Canada: Fraser Institute. http://oldfraser .lexi.net/publications/books/assess_nafta/dispute.html.

Woolcock, Stephen. 2007. "European Union Policy towards Free Trade Agreements." ECIPE Working Paper 03/2007, European Centre for International Political Economy, Brussels.

World Bank. 2000. *Trade Blocs.* World Bank Policy Research Report. New York: Oxford University Press.

WTO (World Trade Organization). 1996a. *Analytical Index/Guide to GATT Law and Practice.* 6th ed. Geneva: World Trade Organization.

———. 1996b. "Rules of Conduct for the Understanding on Rules and Procedures Governing the Settlement of Disputes." WT/DSB/RC/1, WTO, Geneva.

———. 1999. "Canada–Measures Affecting the Importation of Milk and the Exportation of Dairy Products." Panel Report, WTO, Geneva.

———. 2009. "2010–2011 Budget Proposals." WT/BFA/W/189, WTO, Geneva.

Xuto, Nilaratna. 2005. "Thailand: Conciliating a Dispute on Tuna Exports to the EC." In *Managing the Challenges of WTO Participation: 45 Case Studies,* ed. Peter Gallagher, Patrick Low, and Andrew Stoler. Cambridge, U.K.: Cambridge University Press.

Yang, Tseming. 2007. "International Treaty Enforcement as a Public Good: Institutional Deterrent Sanctions in International Environmental Agreements." *Michigan Journal of International Law* 27: 1131–84.

Yang, Yongzheng, and Sanjeev Gupta. 2005. "Regional Trade Arrangements in Africa: Past Performance and the Way Forward." IMF Working Paper WP/05/36, International Monetary Fund, Washington, DC.

Yoshimatsu, Hidetaka. 2006. "Collective Action Problems and Regional Integration in ASEAN." *Contemporary Southeast Asia: A Journal of International and Strategic Affairs* 28: 115–40.

INDEX

Notes are indicated with *n* following the page number.

A

Absorption principle, 168
Abuja Treaty of 1991, 113
ACCC. *See* Australian Competition and Consumer Commission
ACP. *See* African, Caribbean, and Pacific states
Ad hoc panels, 485, 494–96
ADR. *See* Alternative dispute resolution
Africa
    African Common Market, 113
    African Economic Community, 113
    African Growth and Opportunity Act, 149, 173–74
    Common Market for Eastern and Southern Africa, 24, 155, 169, 328, 361
    dispute settlement, 470
    European Union-South Africa Trade and Development Cooperation Agreement, 222–24
    preferential trade agreement participation, 56–57
    Southern African Customs Union, 223, 330, 358
    Southern African Development Community, 155, 174–75, 223, 330
    West African Economic and Monetary Union, 154–55
African, Caribbean, and Pacific states, 52
African Common Market, 113
African Economic Community, 113
African Growth and Opportunity Act, 149, 173–74
AFTA. *See* ASEAN Free Trade Agreement
Agency for International Development, 436, 439
Agglomeration forces, 78–80
Agreement on Agriculture, 145–46
Agreement on Rules of Origin, 163
Agreement on Safeguards, 461*n*
Agreement on the Application of Sanitary and Phytosanitary Measures, 210–13, 218
Agreement on the Technical Barriers to Trade, 210–13, 218
Agricultural trade
    bilateral preferential trade agreements, 153–75
    domestic subsidies, 152–53
    economic integration, 146–47
    economics of, 144–47
    European Union agreements, 154–55
    evaluating trade preferences, 149–51
    export subsidies, 152–53
    institutions, 153
    multilateral commitments, 144–46
    preferential commitments, 144–46
    public goods, 153
    regional preferential trade agreements, 151–53
    regional trade flows, 148
    safeguards, 152

    tariff cuts, 151–52
    trade flows and preferences, 148–49
    U.S. agreements, 155–57
    World Trade Organization agreement, 146
AIA. *See* ASEAN Investment Agreement
Aid for trade, 263
Alternative dispute resolution, 489
American National Standards Institute, 199
AMU. *See* Arab Maghreb Union
Andean Community
    services trade, 270*n*
Andean Tribunal of Justice, 472
ANSI. *See* American National Standards Institute
Antidumping rules, 182–86, 194
ANZCERTA. *See* Australia-New Zealand Closer Economic Relations Trade Agreement
ANZGPA. *See* Australia and New Zealand Government Procurement Agreement
APEC. *See* Asia-Pacific Economic Cooperation
Arab Maghreb Union, 56
ASEAN. *See* Association of Southeast Asian Nations
ASEAN Free Trade Agreement, 343
ASEAN Investment Agreement, 320
ASEAN Trade in Goods Agreement, 228–29
Asia. *See also* Association of Southeast Asian Nations
    Asia-Pacific Economic Cooperation, 23, 205–206, 328, 343, 372
    dispute settlement, 469
    preferential trade agreement participation, 50–56
    services trade, 262
Asia-Pacific Economic Cooperation, 23, 205–206, 328, 343, 372
Association of Southeast Asian Nations
    certification and accreditation services, 109
    liberalization strategy, 84
    preferential trade agreements, 42, 55–56
    Trade in Goods Agreement, 228–29
At-the-border policies, 18–19
ATIGA. *See* ASEAN Trade in Goods Agreement
ATJ. *See* Andean Tribunal of Justice
AUSFTA. *See* Australia-United States Free Trade Agreement
Australia
    Australia and New Zealand Government Procurement Agreement, 373
    Australia-New Zealand Closer Economic Relations Trade Agreement, 152, 357
    Australia-United States Free Trade Agreement, 219–20
    Australian Competition and Consumer Commission, 359
    labor agreements with developing countries, 297–99, 303
    labor mobility in preferential trade agreements, 283–84
Australia and New Zealand Government Procurement Agreement, 373

ECO-AUDIT
Environmental Benefits Statement

The World Bank is committed to preserving endangered forests and natural resources. The Office of the Publisher has chosen to print *Preferential Trade Agreement Policies for Development: A Handbook* on recycled paper with 50 percent postconsumer fiber in accordance with the recommended standards for paper usage set by the Green Press Initiative, a nonprofit program supporting publishers in using fiber that is not sourced from endangered forests. For more information, visit www.greenpressinitiative.org.

Saved:
• **24 trees**
• **10 million BTUs of** total energy
• **2,430 pounds of** net greenhouse gases
• **10,959 gallons of** waste water
• **694 pounds of** solid waste